Advance Praise for
Sounds of Innate Freedom

"*Sounds of Innate Freedom* is destined to become a classic in the field of tantric Buddhist literature. Karl Brunnhölzl's translations of Saraha's poetry capture the concise wisdom and embodied elegance of the original Sanskrit and Tibetan. He is both authoritative and lyrical, bringing us into the heart of the mahāsiddha's vision of a layperson's path to awakening. This critical collection provides an enlightened template for our place and time, essentialized practice and unmediated access to embodied wisdom that leads to radical awakening in this life."

—Willa Blythe Baker, PhD, founder and spiritual director of Natural Dharma Fellowship and author of *The Wakeful Body*

"As clearly emerges from the collection of texts so excellently presented by Mitra Karl, this is a lineage of kindness and wisdom, here delivered with the precision and detail of extensive scholarly research that is equally a matter of the heart, quite beyond words, and a treasury of insight rising from devotion and dedication to the lineage of masters who have realized the nature of mind and who so kindly, often unexpectedly, and even sometimes in a way that might seem over the top, share with us the methods for accomplishing this. The rest is up to us."

—Jim Scott, long-time translator and dharma teacher in the lineage of Khenpo Tsultrim Gyamtso Rinpoche

Sounds of Innate Freedom: The Indian Texts of Mahāmudrā

Sounds of Innate Freedom: The Indian Texts of Mahāmudrā are historic volumes containing many of the first English translations of classic mahāmudrā literature. The texts and songs in these volumes constitute the large compendium called *The Indian Texts of the Mahāmudrā of Definitive Meaning*, compiled by the Seventh Karmapa Chötra Gyatso (1456–1539). The collection offers a brilliant window into the richness of the vast ocean of Indian mahāmudrā texts cherished in all Tibetan lineages, particularly in the Kagyü tradition, giving us a clear view of the sources of one of the world's great contemplative traditions. In its modern Tibetan edition, there are six volumes containing seven kinds of texts: the *Anāvilatantra* (as a tantric source of mahāmudrā attributed to the Buddha himself) and its commentary, songs of realization, commentaries on songs of realization and other texts, independent tantric treatises, nontantric treatises, edifying stories, and doxographies (presenting hierarchies of different Buddhist and non-Buddhist philosophical systems). This volume 2 contains two long-established sets of mahāmudrā works: "The Sixfold Pith Cycle" and Maitrīpa's "Twenty-Five Dharmas of Mental Nonengagement," as well as two commentaries by Maitrīpa's students.

Sounds *of* Innate Freedom

The Indian Texts of Mahāmudrā

Volume Two

Translated and Introduced
by Karl Brunnhölzl

Wisdom

Wisdom Publications
132 Perry Street
New York, NY 10014 USA
wisdomexperience.org

Library of Congress Cataloging-in-Publication Data
Names: Chos-grags-rgya-mtsho, Karma-pa VII, 1454–1506, author. | Brunnhölzl, Karl, translator.
Title: The sounds of innate freedom: the Indian texts of Mahāmudrā / translated and introduced by Karl Brunnhölzl.
Other titles: Nges don phyag rgya chen po'i rgya gzhung. English
Description: Somerville, MA, USA: Wisdom Publications, 2021– | Includes bibliographical references.
Identifiers: LCCN 2020021301 (print) | LCCN 2020021302 (ebook) | ISBN 9781614296355 (v. 5; hardcover) | ISBN 9781614296362 (v. 5; ebook)
Subjects: LCSH: Mahāmudrā (Tantric rite) | Tantric Buddhism—Rituals.
Classification: LCC BQ8921.M35 C47713 2021 (print) | LCC BQ8921.M35 (ebook) | DDC 294.3/85—dc23
LC record available at https://lccn.loc.gov/2020021301
LC ebook record available at https://lccn.loc.gov/2020021302

ISBN 978-1-61429-709-3 ebook ISBN 978-1-61429-714-7

28 27 26 25 24
5 4 3 2 1

Cover design by Gopa & Ted 2.
Interior design by Tony Lulek, typeset by Gopa & Ted 2.

Printed on acid-free paper that meets the guidelines for permanence and durability of the Production Guidelines for Book Longevity of the Council on Library Resources.

Printed in the United States of America.

Publisher's Acknowledgment

The publisher gratefully acknowledges the generous help of the Hershey Family Foundation and the Tsadra Foundation in sponsoring the production of this book.

Contents

Foreword by Dzogchen Ponlop Rinpoche xi

Preface xiii

Abbreviations xix

Introduction 1

(12) The Accomplishment of Glorious True Reality 85

(13) A Dohā Treasure Song 93

(14) The Succession of the Four Mudrās 113

(15) A Discussion of the Purification of the Mind 119

(16) An Illumination of Prajñā Wisdom 139

(17) A Synopsis of Positions 171

(18) Pith Instructions on the Tradition of Inconceivable Nonduality 197

(19) Eradicating Bad Views 215

(20) A Commentary on the [Initial] Passage of "Eradicating Bad Views" 229

(21) An Illumination of Unity 233

(22) Pith Instructions on True Reality Called "A Dohā Treasure" 235

(23) Five Stanzas on the Love between Means and Prajñā 239

(24) An Illumination of Utter Nonabiding 241

(25) Six Stanzas on the Connate 245

(26) Six Stanzas on the Middle 247

(27) In Support of Mental Nonengagement 249

(28) Five Stanzas on Penetrating Insight 255

(29) Five Stanzas on Love 257

(30) A Discourse on Illusion 259

(31) A Discourse on Dream 263

(32) Ten Stanzas on True Reality 265

(33) The Illumination of Great Bliss 267

(34) A Jewel Garland of True Reality 271

(35) An Illumination of True Reality 287

(36) A Commentary on the Five Seals of the Tathāgatas 291

(37) A Compendium of the Purport of Empowerment 299

(38) A Compendium of the Procedures of Empowerment 305

(39) The Five Aspects (of Vajrasattva) 335

(40) Twenty Stanzas on the Mahāyāna 341

(41) Twenty Stanzas on True Reality 345

(42) Instructions on Empowerment 349

(43) A Pith Instruction on Letting Cognizance Be without Projecting and Withdrawing, "The True Secret" 357

(44) A Commentary on the Four Mudrās, Called "Jewel Heart" 359

(45) A Critical Commentary on "Instructions on Empowerment" 473

Appendix 1: *A Compendium of Beginner Activity* 525

Appendix 2: *Taking the Pith Instructions of the Philosophical Systems as the Path* 531

Appendix 3: Tipi Bumlabar's Outline of Divākaracandra's *An Illumination of Prajñā Wisdom* 539

Appendix 4: Tipi Bumlabar's Outline of Sahajavajra's *A Synopsis of Positions* 543

Appendix 5: Outline of *A Commentary on the Four Mudrās* 547

Appendix 6: Tipi Bumlabar's Outline of Rāmapāla's *A Critical Commentary on "Instructions on Empowerment"* 553

Appendix 7: The Fivefold Classification of the Creation and Completion Processes in the Texts of Maitrīpa and His Students 559

Notes 567

Bibliography 1059

About the Translator 1085

Foreword

A greatly renowned South Indian Buddhist scholar-monk by the name of Rāhulabhadra was once passing through a town. As he maneuvered through the fair, he became mesmerized by a young woman who was straightening a piece of bamboo with three segments. Noticing her exceptional powers of concentration, he asked: "Young lady, what are you doing? Are you an arrow-maker?" Moving in closer, he saw that she had one eye closed and the other looking directly at the piece of bamboo. She was one-pointedly focused on her task, not distracted or disturbed by all the hustle and bustle of the marketplace.

Nevertheless, she answered Rāhulabhadra, saying: "The intention of the Buddha can only be known through signs and skillful means, not through words and concepts." In that moment, the three-kāya nature of buddha-mind became apparent to him through the signs and symbols the young woman, secretly a wisdom ḍākinī, had displayed.[1] A classical text relates the insights that arose in his mind:

> Her one eye closed and the other open is the symbol of closing the eyes of consciousness and opening the eyes of wisdom; the bamboo is the symbol of the nature of mind; the three segments symbolize the three-kāya nature; straightening is the direct path; cutting the bamboo from the root is cutting the root of samsara; cutting the top of the bamboo is cutting ego-clinging; making four slots [for feathers] is the four unborn seals of mindfulness; adding the arrowhead at the end is the need for sharp prajñā; . . . [2]

Sudden awakening took place in his heart and he fully realized mahāmudrā. Recognizing that a wisdom ḍākinī was in front of him, he proclaimed, "You are not an arrow-maker but a symbol-maker!" From that time onward he followed her, abandoning scholarship and adopting the tantric path. He became known as Saraha or Sarahapāda, the "arrow shooter," referring metaphorically to "he who has shot the arrow of nonduality into the heart of duality." Saraha became the foremost mahāsiddha of the tantric tradition of Buddhism.

The dohā lineage in tantric Buddhism began when Saraha, also known as "the Great Brahmin," started singing spontaneous songs of realization to his disciples: the king, the queen, and the people of the kingdom. Since then, the great siddhas of the Mahāmudrā lineage have continued to express their realization and instructions to their disciples in pithy and spontaneous songs known as *dohās*. The most renowned of these many songs of realization is Milarepa's *Ocean of Songs*, commonly known as the *Hundred Thousand Songs*. The dohā tradition continues today with numerous songs from my own guru, Dechen Rangdrol, a contemporary mahāsiddha.

I am genuinely excited to have this opportunity to work with Mitra Karl Brunnhölzl to translate the large compendium of texts called *The Indian Texts of the Mahāmudrā of Definitive Meaning*, compiled by the Seventh Karmapa Chötra Gyatso (1456–1539). Making this classic mahāmudrā literature available in English for the first time is a historic and noteworthy project.

As many readers may already be aware, Mitra Karl is not only well versed in Buddhist philosophy and the Tibetan and Sanskrit languages but has also practiced these teachings for many years under the guidance of my guru, Dechen Rangdrol. Mitra Karl has also been studying with me, and I have full confidence and trust that his translation work here will be true to the original.

I want to thank Wisdom Publications for their openness and support in bringing these treasures of the East to the West.

May this book help all to discover the treasure within our ordinary mind of neurosis.

Dzogchen Ponlop Rinpoche
Nalanda West, Seattle, WA

PREFACE

The large anthology that is called *The Indian Texts of the Mahāmudrā of Definitive Meaning*[3] was compiled by the Seventh Karmapa Chötra Gyatso.[4] The vast majority of the 217 works that are included in the anthology stem from the Tengyur,[5] and they range from a single sentence to almost two hundred pages. Roughly categorized, they fall under seven genres:

1. the *Anāvilatantra* (selected as a tantric source of mahāmudrā attributed to the Buddha himself) and its commentary[6]
2. songs of realization (dohā, caryāgīti, and vajragīti)
3. commentaries on songs of realization and other texts
4. independent tantric treatises
5. nontantric treatises
6. edifying stories
7. doxographies (presenting hierarchies of different Buddhist and non-Buddhist tenet systems)

In its modern Tibetan book edition, the anthology consists of six volumes (with the modest number of 2,600 pages). Volume 1 opens with the catalogue of the collection by Karma Dashi Chöpel Lodrö Gyatsö Drayang[7] (a student of Jamgön Kongtrul Lodrö Tayé).[8] The eleven Indian mahāmudrā texts in this volume consist of the *Anavilatantra* and its commentary, followed by "The Seven Siddhi Texts,"[9] tantric treatises based on the *Guhyasamājatantra*: (1) Padmavajra's *Guhyasiddhi*, (2) Anaṅgavajra's *Prajñopāyaviniścayasiddhi*, (3) Indrabhūti's *Jñānasiddhi*, (4) Lakṣmīṃkarā's *Advayasiddhi*, (5) Dārikapa's *Mahāguhyatattvopadeśa*, (6) Vilāsavajrā's *Vyaktabhāvānugatatattvasiddhi*, and (7) Ḍombi Heruka's

Śrīsahajasiddhi. The final two texts are Indrabhūti's *Sahajasiddhi* and his sister Lakṣmīṃkarā's commentary *Sahajasiddhipaddhati*.[10]

Volume 2 (thirty-four texts) begins with Kerali's *Tattvasiddhi*, followed by "The Sixfold Pith Cycle:"[11] (1) Saraha's *Dohakoṣa* (popularly known as the "People Dohā"), (2) Nāgārjuna's *Caturmudrānvaya*, (3) Āryadeva's *Cittaviśuddhiprakaraṇa*, (4) Divākaracandra's *Prajñājñānaprakāśa*, (5) Sahajavajra's *Sthitisamāsa*, and (6) Kuddālī's *Acintyādvayakramopadeśa*.[12] Next are the mostly short texts of Maitrīpa's "Cycle of Twenty-Five Dharmas of Mental Nonengagement,"[13] which present a blend of Madhyamaka, Mahāmudrā, and certain tantric principles. This volume concludes with two commentaries by students of Maitrīpa: *Kāropa's *Caturmudrāṭīkāratnahṛdaya* on the *Caturmudrānvaya* and Rāmapāla's *Sekanirdeśapañjikā* on Maitrīpa's *Sekanirdeśa*.

Volume 3 (twenty-four texts) starts with Sahajavajra's *Tattvadaśakaṭīkā* (a commentary on Maitrīpa's *Tattvadaśaka*), followed by a number of brief instructional works by Maitrīpa's student Vajrapāṇi, and by Nāropa and Śākyaśrībhadra. The bulk of the volume consists of dohās by Saraha, one autocommentary on them, two commentaries on his "People Dohā" by Advayavajra and Mokṣākaragupta, and an anonymous commentary on his *Twelve Stanzas*.[14] Also included is Kṛṣṇapāda's *Dohakoṣa* and its commentary by Paṇḍita Amṛtavajra. This volume ends with the *Karṇatantravajrapāda*, transmitted by Tilopa and Nāropa.

The first text in volume 4 (twenty-one texts) is Advayavajra's extensive commentary on Saraha's "People Dohā." This is followed by a number of dohās and instructional texts by Virūpa, Tilopa, Nāropa, Maitrīpa, Saraha, Kṛṣṇa, and others. The volume ends with a famous collection of fifty songs by twenty different authors (originally in Eastern Apabhraṃśa), including a commentary by Munidatta called *Caryāgītikoṣavṛtti* (half of the songs in this collection are by the three mahāsiddhas Kṛṣṇa, Bhusuku, and Saraha).

Volume 5 contains by far the most texts (112). With only five prose works, the bulk consists of versified songs of realization. The opening *Commentary on "Four and a Half Stanzas"* consists of edifying stories, including summarizing songs. Next, Advayavajra's *Caturmudropadeśa* discusses the four mudrās (karmamudrā, dharmamudrā, samayamudrā, and mahāmudrā). Almost all remaining texts in this volume consist of usually brief tantric songs composed by various mahāsiddhas and others, many of them by Atiśa, the mahāsiddha Jaganmitrānanda,[15] Saraha, Kṛṣṇa, Kambala, Ḍombipa, Nāgārjuna, Lūhipa, and Maitrīpa. There are also seven anthologies of tantric songs by a wide variety of male and female siddhas, yogīs, yoginīs, and ḍākinīs, the longest one among them containing almost four hundred songs. In addition, this volume contains two autocommentaries by Atiśa on two of his songs as well as Āryadeva's *The Hidden Path of the Five Poisons* on how to work with our main mental afflictions.

Volume 6 (fifteen texts) consists mainly of tantric treatises. Virūpa's *Suniṣprapañcatattvopadeśanāma*, Āryadeva's *Pratipattisāraśataka*, and Lūhipa's *Buddhodaya* are related to the perfection processes of the *Raktayamāritantra*, *Hevajratantra*, and *Cakrasaṃvaratantra*, respectively. Vajrapāṇi's *Guruparamparākramopadeśa* (a commentary on Maitrīpa's *Tattvaratnāvalī*), Jñānakīrti's *Tattvāvatāra*, and Śāntarakṣita's *Tattvasiddhi* (as well as the *Bodhicittavivaraṇa*) are all considered important general source texts of mahāmudrā in the Kagyü school of Tibetan Buddhism. Furthermore, there are Trivikrama's often-quoted *Nayatrayapradīpa*, Dharmendra's **Tattvasārasaṃgraha*, Udbhaṭa *Coyaga's *Mantranayāloka*, and Jñānavajra's **Cittamārgaśodha*, all on general Vajrayāna principles. In addition, this volume contains two short songs by Mahāśabara, Nāgārjuna's *Cittavajrastava*, and the *Bodhicittavivaraṇa* (also attributed to Nāgārjuna).

As this series overview shows, most of the authors of these works are well-known figures among the eighty-four male and female mahāsiddhas or otherwise highly accomplished tantric adepts. That the greatest number of texts is attributed to Maitrīpa and Saraha[16] highlights their being considered as the most significant forebears of the Mahāmudrā lineage in the Kagyü school. In sum, it is no overstatement to consider this collection as "the corpus of Indian Buddhist mahāsiddha literature."

These practitioners were a very mixed crowd, and many lived and taught outside the framework of institutionalized Buddhism in their time. We find kings and queens, princes and princesses, top-notch Buddhist scholars, dropouts, philosophers, housewives, shoemakers, courtesans, monks, male and female lovers, farmers, weavers, prostitutes, cowherds, fishermen, gamblers, musicians, thieves, hermits, hunters, alchemists, rich merchants, barmaids, outcastes, brahmans, gluttons, fools, pearl divers, and many more varieties of practitioners.[17] Besides the officially recognized mahāsiddhas, there were many other male and female yogic practitioners, as well as ḍākinīs, who composed texts and uttered songs of realization. This shows that the teachings and the path of mahāmudrā are accessible to and can be practiced by anyone from any walk of life—whether a king, a servant in a brothel, or a housewife—often even without having to renounce their day jobs.

As for the language of the texts and the songs in this collection, it is the specific context that dictates the meaning of certain expressions. Also, many terms and phrases can have a range of different meanings (in both the common Mahāyāna context and the uncommon contexts of tantra and mahāmudrā). Several layers of meaning often exist simultaneously, some of them only understandable through additional comments, instructions, or certain experiences, many of them restricted to the initiated. Another notable feature is that the antinomian tantric approach often labels the highest and purest spiritual principles with the most despicable and impure names possible in the context of ancient Indian society.

For example, the term "Caṇḍāla" ordinarily refers to a class of people in India who are generally considered to be untouchable outcastes.[18] Figuratively speaking, Caṇḍāla also refers to any vile, filthy, loathsome, criminal, ferocious, or lascivious persons or deeds; the same goes for other outcaste names, such as Ḍombi (wandering troubadours and dancers). On the other hand, in both Hindu and Buddhist tantric practices, outcaste Caṇḍāla or Ḍomba women play a significant role in the worship of the female sexual organ and the subsequent production of a fluid, powerful substance through sexual intercourse with them. The related term "Cāṇḍālī" either designates a woman in the first day of her menses, the female subtle energy located in the lower abdomen, or the tantric practices related to that energy. In the latter context, "Caṇḍālī" sometimes also serves as a name for the central channel (*avadhūtī*). In addition, among the "divine herbs" that are said to grow in places where Śiva and his wife once made love, the *cāṇḍālī* plant is obviously named for those outcaste women whose menstrual blood has perennially been prized by tantric practitioners for its transformative powers, and the root of this plant exudes a red milk that is used for the alchemistic fixing of mercury.

For reasons of space, it is beyond the purview of this six-volume publication to give detailed explanations for all such terms or provide commentaries on its songs and texts. Another reason for this is that traditionally the practices behind certain texts and terms with multilayered meanings are not explained publicly but only within an established teacher-student relationship after certain prerequisites have been fulfilled.[19]

I would like to offer my heartfelt gratitude and appreciation to Khenchen Tsültrim Gyamtso Rinpoche and Dzogchen Ponlop Rinpoche for having introduced me to the tradition of Indian and Tibetan Buddhist songs of realization. Both of these masters also inspired me as accomplished composers of their own spontaneous poems and songs of insight and realization, in both Tibetan and English. Furthermore, Dzogchen Ponlop Rinpoche is to be thanked for starting me on the project of translating the collection of Indian mahāmudrā texts compiled by the Seventh Karmapa, as well as for his ongoing support during this project in many ways. Without these two masters of both ancient and contemporary expressions of realization, this volume would never have been possible, and on a personal note, I probably would never have started to enjoy singing Buddhist songs.

On the practical side of things, I am deeply grateful for the funding received from *Causa* that enables me to work on this collection of mahāmudrā songs. Heartfelt thanks go to Daniel Aitken at Wisdom Publications for his willingness to publish these texts and for all his ongoing support. I also thank Mary Petrusewicz as my skillful, friendly, and enthusiastic editor at Wisdom Publications. Last but not least, a big thanks to Stephanie Johnston for being my sounding board (both literally and metaphorically) for these songs and her willingness to listen to, participate in, and improve both their words and musical arrangements as these were evolving over time.

Whatever in this volume sounds good, makes sense, inspires, and serves as an antidote to ignorance, confusion, and suffering may be relished as originating from realized masters and scholars truly vast in learning. Everything else, including all mistakes, can safely be said to be mine.

Sarva maṅgalam

Abbreviations

AIBS	The Buddhist Canons Research Database (http://databases.aibs.columbia.edu/)
Apa	Apabhraṃśa
BA	Gö Lotsāwa's *Blue Annals* ('Gos lo tsā ba gzhon nu dpal 1996)
BDRC	Buddhist Digital Research Center (tbrc.org)
BGTC	*Bod rgya tshig mdzod chen mo* (Krang dbyi sun et al. 1985)
BKC	*'Bri gung bka' brgyud chos mdzod chen mo* (A mgon rin po che 2004)
C	Cone Tibetan Tripiṭaka
D	Derge Tibetan Tripiṭaka
DKPA	Apabhraṃśa of Saraha's *Dohakoṣa* ("People Dohā") in DKPS
DKPS	Advayavajra's *Dohakoṣapañjikā* (Bagchi 1938)
GZ	"The Indian Mahāmudrā Texts" (*Phyag chen rgya gzhung*)
GZ1	Dpal spung edition of GZ (Phun tshogs rgyal mtshan n.d.)
GZ3	Ludrub Gyatso's edition of GZ (Khro ru klu sgrub rgya mtsho 2009)
H	Lhasa Tibetan Tripiṭaka
IaS	Isaacson and Sferra 2014
Kg	Kangyur (Tib. *bka' 'gyur*)
KTP	Karma Trinlépa's commentary on the "People Dohā" (Karma phrin las pa phyogs las rnam rgyal 2009, 1–118)
N	Narthang Tibetan Tripiṭaka
NG	Catalogue of GZ (Bkra shis chos 'phel 2009)
P	Peking Tibetan Tripiṭaka

PDMT	*Dpe bsdur ma* edition of Tengyur (Dpe bsdur ma 1994–2008)
PTMC	Tipi Bumlabar's commentary on *A Commentary on the Five Seals of the Tathāgatas* (Ti pi 'bum la 'bar 2004b)
Tg	Tengyur (Tib. *bstan 'gyur*)
TOK	Jamgön Kongtrul Lodrö Tayé's *Treasury of Knowledge* (Kong sprul blo gros mtha' yas 1982)
TRVC	Tipi Bumlabar's commentary on *A Jewel Garland of True Reality* (Ti pi 'bum la 'bar 2004a)

Introduction

The bulk of volume 2 of the Seventh Karmapa's compilation of Indian texts on mahāmudrā consists of two long-established sets of mahāmudrā works: "The Sixfold Pith Cycle" and Maitrīpa's "Cycle of Twenty-Five Dharmas of Mental Nonengagement." Among the thirty-four texts in this volume, only Kerali's *Accomplishment of Glorious True Reality* (text 12), *Kāropa's *Commentary on the Four Mudrās* (text 44), and Rāmapāla's *Critical Commentary on "Instructions on Empowerment"* (text 45) do not belong to these two cycles. However, the latter two works are commentaries on two of Maitrīpa's texts attributed to two of his Indian students. Among the works in "The Sixfold Pith Cycle," Divākaracandra's *Illumination of Prajñā Wisdom* (text 16) and Sahajavajra's *Synopsis of Positions* (text 17) are composed by two other Maitrīpa disciples.[20] In addition, *The Succession of the Four Mudrās* (text 14) is found in the Sanskrit collection of Maitrīpa's works (**Advayavajrasaṃgraha*)[21] and is indeed attributed by some to Maitrīpa (though he is clearly not its author).[22] Thus, given that the overwhelming majority of the texts in this volume are either by Maitrīpa himself[23] or his students, it could justifiably be called "the Maitrīpa volume" within the Karmapa's mahāmudrā collection.[24]

The first work in this volume, Keralipa's *Accomplishment of Glorious True Reality* (text 12), is considered by GZ and NG as being related to "The Seven Siddhi Texts" (just like Indrabhūti's *Sahajasiddhi* and Lakṣmīṃkarā's commentary on it in volume 1).[25] According to Padma Karpo, the "true reality" (*tattva*) in the title of this text is expressed by its first line, "the vajra of the awakening of a buddha," and "accomplishment" (*siddhi*) is expressed by the following line, "is accomplished in this life, not in others." The text ascertains mahāmudrā by primarily emphasizing the practice of "the lower gate" (karmamudrā).[26] In his initial stanzas, Kerali declares that true reality will not be accomplished without the continuous enjoyment of desire. Illustrated by a number of "homeopathic" examples ("treat like with like"), such as poison serving as the remedy for poison, desire is said to be the medicine for those who are tormented by desire. By contrast, austerities should be avoided because they dry out the elements of the body, which leads to suffering and distraction, thus preventing the attainment of siddhis (stanzas 1–12). This is followed by the actual instructions on karmamudrā by way of the pertinent techniques based on nāḍīs, vāyus, and bindus,[27] and their related templates of the four ecstasies,[28] four moments, four empties, and four illuminations, including the fruition (13–44).

According to NG, "The Sixfold Pith Cycle" consists of (1) Saraha's *Dohā Treasure Song* ("People Dohā"), (2) Nāgārjuna's *Succession of the Four Mudrās*, (3) an Āryadeva's *Discussion of the Purification of the Mind*, (4) Divākaracandra's *Illumination of Prajñā Wisdom*, (5) Sahajavajra's *Synopsis of Positions*, and (6) Kuddālapāda's *Pith Instructions on the Tradition of Inconceivable Nonduality* (texts 13–18).[29]

In its initial short overview of this cycle, BKC[30] says that it bears this name because at the time of Saraha, Nāgārjuna and his followers, as well as Śavaripa and his followers, the conventional expression "essential reality"[31] had spread for mahāmudrā. However, apart from this very generic statement, the rationale or criteria as to why these six texts with their mostly heterogenous contents and styles—including poetic, systematic, and speculative works based or not based on the tantras—were grouped together as a set remains unclear.

Two of these six texts—Saraha's "People Dohā" and Āryadeva's *Purification of the Mind*—do not even mention the term "mahāmudrā," and Kuddālapāda's *Pith Instructions* uses it just once. Saraha's famous dohā in Apabhraṃśa, with its sprawling and informal style, is a classical mahāsiddha song of realization. Among the remaining texts of these six that are in Sanskrit, the gist of Kuddālapāda's equally meandering *Pith Instructions* is the immediate realization of the self-arising wisdom of inconceivable nonduality in a nongradual manner (the text also exhibits strong inclusivist tendencies, using a number of Hinduist terminologies). Āryadeva's idiosyncratic *Purification of the Mind* has a clear underpinning of Yogācāra and tathāgatagarbha themes and, similar to Keralipa's *Accomplishment of Glorious True Reality*, abounds with "homeopathic examples" for revealing mind's natural purity. By contrast, Nāgārjuna's *Succession of the Four Mudrās* (karmamudrā, dharmamudrā, mahāmudrā, and samayamudrā) and Divākaracandra's *Illumination of Prajñā Wisdom* (an extensive defense of the superiority of the Vajrayāna in general and the practice of karmamudrā in particular) are formal Vajrayāna treatises. Sahajavajra's versified *Synopsis of Positions* is an equally formal doxographical work on the four sūtra-based Buddhist schools of the Vaibhāṣikas, Sautrāntikas, Yogācāras, and Mādhyamikas, concluding with an extensive presentation of the Vajrayāna in accordance with Nāgārjuna's *Succession of the Four Mudrās* that abounds with citations from tantric literature.

The first text of "The Sixfold Pith Cycle" is Saraha's *Dohā Treasure Song* (text 13), popularly known as the "People Dohā," which is undoubtedly his most famous work.[32] According to Saraha's life story among the biographies of the eighty-four mahāsiddhas, he sang the "King Dohā," the "Queen Dohā," and the "People Dohā" in order to instruct the king, the queens, and their subjects after he had passed all kinds of tests of his realization, such as drinking a bowl of molten copper without being harmed, in front of them.[33] According to Karma Trinlépa's commentary, some say that what is now known as these three texts was originally sung by Saraha as a single song. Later, this song was written down by Nāgārjuna, and then, by virtue of different ways of expressing it, it was turned into three distinct texts. Others say that Nāgārjuna passed on Saraha's words only orally, while it was Śavaripa who wrote them down for the sake of Maitrīpa.[34] Jomden Rigpé Raltri's[35] commentary reports that upon a request by the mahāsiddha Padmavajra, Saraha taught the "People Dohā" to Padmavajra, Nāgārjuna, and Śavarīpa.[36] According to Padma Karpo, in the manner of an arrow-smith straightening an arrow, Saraha straightened out all the crookedness in his mind. Then, seeing that this straight arrow of the mind had directly hit the target that is basic nature's actuality, he put this triad of dohās for the king, the queens, and the assembly of subjects to song and then proceeded to the buddhabhūmi.[37]

The most commonly known and used Apabhraṃśa version of the "People Dohā" (DKPA) has been extracted from the later Sanskrit commentary *Dohakoṣapañjikā* by an Advayavajra.[38] The first edition of this text appeared in Śāstrī 1916, based on a single incomplete manuscript discovered by him in Nepal in 1907. Another edition based on that manuscript was published by Shahidullah in 1928. In 1929, Bagchi found two further manuscripts in Nepal and published editions based on all those manuscripts in 1935 and 1938. In 1934, Sāṃkṛtyāyana discovered a further Apabhraṃśa version at Sakya Monastery in Tibet and published it in 1957 (Bhāyāṇī's edition of 1997 is primarily based on Sāṃkṛtyāyana's, as well as Bagchi's). More recently, a number of further independent Apabhraṃśa manuscripts of the "People Dohā" have come to light.[39]

Thus, apart from DKPA (112 stanzas),[40] Saraha's "People Dohā" is preserved in several other independent Apabhraṃśa versions of different lengths and sometimes contents,[41] the canonical Tibetan translation (541 lines),[42] text 13 (555 lines; 138 stanzas),[43] text 68 (a greatly expanded and reworked Tibetan version based on the canonical one; 799 lines),[44] the different versions quoted and commented on in texts 66 and 67, the *Dohakoṣahṛdayārthagītāṭīkā* (appendix 4 in volume 3), the versions in various Tibetan commentaries, a version in Jamgön Kongtrul's *Treasury of Precious Instructions*,[45] and one in a collection of Kagyü texts.[46] Thus Saraha's text exists in a plethora of versions, all of which show more or less substantial differences in terms of length or content.

That there were already various versions of the "People Dohā" by the very beginning of the twelfth century (and in all probability much earlier) is shown by the fragmentary manuscript of the text found by Bagchi in the Darbar Library of Kathmandu in 1929. This manuscript is dated 221 Nepal Saṃvat (corresponding to 1101 CE), and thus is the oldest available manuscript of any dohā that we know. Its stanza 12 and the colophon explicitly say that it was compiled from different texts:

> These verses, which were lost or destroyed, on the heart-meaning . . .
> were collected here from three dohās composed by Saraha[47]
> . . .
> This *Dohākoṣa* "as found" is finished. It was compiled by paṇḍita

> Śrī Divākaracandra out of the desire to benefit others in Samvat 221, during the bright fortnight of Śrāvaṇa's full moon.[48]

This statement and the dating of the text make it clear that by that time, there already existed different manuscripts from which the stanzas of this fragment were compiled. In addition, none of the stanzas in this fragmentary manuscript are found in any other versions of the "People Dohā" that are currently preserved.

Given this early evidence and the many Apabhraṃśa and Tibetan versions of Saraha's dohā that still exist, it is impossible to identify any kind of single "urtext." Rather, the "People Dohā" is a classic example of the fluid approach of dohās being edited, rearranged, and compiled from different sources. It is clear that Saraha's text underwent such a process of being constantly reworked, probably already in India, but definitely in Nepal and obviously even in Tibet. Thus, especially in a tradition that is transmitted in oral form from teacher to student, it soon became impossible to determine which of these stanzas had been sung by Saraha himself.[49]

Interestingly, the Tibetan of text 13 largely agrees with the version of the "People Dohā" found in the translation of Mokṣākaragupta's commentary (text 67).[50] However, since not all of the lines of text 13 are cited in text 67, text 13 cannot simply be an extract from text 67, and it is unclear where its lines that are not found in text 67 come from. It is not impossible that at some point there was an independent Apabhraṃśa version that text 67 used and that was translated as text 13, but given the above evidence that Saraha's text had been edited and reworked from early on, that is not very likely.[51]

Not only are there issues with many different versions of the "People Dohā," but it is also unclear who actually translated the canonical Tibetan version, because its colophon does not indicate any translator. By contrast, the colophon of text 13 says that it was translated by Vajrapāṇi[52] and Mapen Chöbar,[53] and edited and finalized by Drogmi José Yeshé Dorje[54] and Nagtso Lotsāwa.[55] Schaeffer[56] quotes the Sakya scholar Tragpa Dorje,[57] saying that there were three translations of the "People Dohā": one by Atiśa and Nagtso Lotsāwa, one by Mapen Chöbar, and one by Balpo Asu.[58] According to the colophon of Rigpé

Raltri's commentary, Nagtso Lotsāwa, Mapen Chöbar, and Balpo Asu were Vajrapāṇi's translators, but the "People Dohā" was also translated by Nyal Dengpa Lotsāwa[59] and others.[60] Karma Trinlépa's commentary says that the versions of the "People Dohā," "Queen Dohā," and "King Dohā" that he comments on (which do not always correspond to the canonical translation) were translated by Balpo Asu on his own from a manuscript he received from Vajrapāṇi.[61] The colophons of Jamyang Shébé Dorje's[62] commentary on the "People Dohā" and the version in Rin chen rnam rgyal say exactly the same.[63]

In my translation of Saraha's *Dohakoṣa* from the Tibetan in GZ, I note significant differences between it and the canonical Tibetan translation, occasionally also referring to the Apabhraṃśa.[64] However, it is definitely beyond the scope of this book to conduct an analysis of which lines or stanzas in text 13 and the canonical translation are or are not found in which Apabhraṃśa version, or to compare the different versions in different commentaries.[65] Interested readers can compare text 13, the canonical Tibetan translation, the available translations from the Apabhraṃśa versions, and the versions quoted and commented on in texts 66, 67, 70, and the *Dohakoṣahṛdayārthagītāṭīkā* (appendix 4 in volume 3).

As for the contents of Saraha's *Dohakoṣa*, similar to the beginning of his *Kāyakoṣāmṛtavajragītā* (text 53) and Kṛṣṇa's *Dohakoṣa* (text 63), its initial stanzas contain a sweeping dismissal of Buddhist and non-Buddhist approaches in India.[66] Thereafter, Saraha outlines his own approach of mahāmudrā (though the text never uses that term) in a meandering series of stanzas that keeps returning to the same vital point: any kind of spiritual approach that involves contrivance, such as using certain meditation techniques, visualizations, or recitations, is mistaken. Instead, the genuine awakening of buddhahood is found only within our own mind through the pith instructions of a true guru, allowing the mind to simply rest in its own natural state without ever becoming distracted from just that.

The Succession of the Four Mudrās[67] (text 14) was in all likelihood authored by (a) Nāgārjuna.[68] However, the text is also included in the Sanskrit **Advayavajrasaṃgraha*, the collection of texts on mental nonengagement by Maitrīpa (though the text's colophon does not mention any author). As Isaacson, Sferra, Mathes, and Almogi[69] have pointed out, the attribution of *The Succession of the Four Mudrās* was already controversial in eleventh-century India. Its attribution to Nāgārjuna is explicitly contested in Raviśrījñāna's *Amṛtakaṇikā* and Abhayākaragupta's *Āmnāyamañjarī*,[70] as well as later in Vibhūticandra's (twelfth/thirteenth century) *Amṛtakaṇikoddyotanibandha*.[71] Several Tibetan authors also voiced doubts about Nāgārjuna's authorship.[72] Furthermore, Tipi Bumlabar's outlines of Maitrīpa's texts on mental nonengagement also include *The Succession of the Four Mudrās*.[73]

In any case, the strongest argument for Nāgārjuna's (and not Maitrīpa's) authorship of *The Succession of the Four Mudrās* is that Rāmapāla's *Critical Commentary on "Instructions on Empowerment"* (text 45) explicitly attributes it to Nāgārjuna twice and also says twice that Maitrīpa's *Instructions on Empowerment* (text 42) follows this text.[74] If *The Succession of the Four Mudrās* had indeed been authored by Maitrīpa, it would have been impossible for Rāmapāla, one of his direct disciples, not to properly credit his master with it, let alone ascribe it to someone else. Also, it would not be very illuminating to say that Maitrīpa just follows another one of his own texts. Further significant evidence for Nāgārjuna's authorship is that Maitrīpa's own *Pith Instructions on the Four Mudrās*[75] and Divākaracandra's *Illumination of Prajñā Wisdom*[76] refer to Nāgārjuna as explaining karmamudrā as a result of concordant outflow, which is a position explicitly held in *The Succession of the Four Mudrās*. Nāgārjuna's authorship is also corroborated by the colophons of the text's Tibetan translations in GZ and CDNP, as well as in *Butön's Record of Teachings Received*.[77]

The text begins with the remarkable statement that the reason for beings drifting about in the ocean of saṃsāra is their delusion about the succession of the four mudrās. Therefore the correct explanation of these four is presented. (1) The karmamudrā is discussed through the proper sequence of the four ecstasies—ecstasy, supreme ecstasy, connate ecstasy, and cessational ecstasy—and the corresponding four moments (to list connate ecstasy as the third ecstasy is a distinctive feature of this text).[78] However, all of this is merely a reflection of the ultimate connate, and the wisdom based on a karmamudrā is just a result that is a concordant outflow of the actual connate. Thus, without understanding the dharmamudrā, the uncontrived connate will not manifest through the contrived practice of karmamudrā alone. (2) The dharmamudrā is the dharmadhātu's nonconceptual and uncontrived nature free from discursiveness, which is the inseparability of emptiness and compassion. Thus the path should be understood as the proximate cause that has the form of suchness. Through familiarizing with that path, the nature of the connate will be directly perceived. By virtue of not being different from mahāmudrā, the dharmamudrā serves as its cause. (3) Mahāmudrā, appearing like the stainless midday sky, is free of any nature and any obscurations, and is the single nature of saṃsāra and nirvāṇa, nonreferential compassion, and great bliss. Through this inconceivable mahāmudrā that is the result of stainlessness, the result that is the samayamudrā arises. (4) The samayamudrā consists of the clear appearance of the sambhogakāyas and nirmāṇakāyas for the welfare of sentient beings. The deity maṇḍala is meditated on as the five wisdoms by way of the five yogas.[79] However, through the contrived merit of this alone, the result of the uncontrived dharmamudrā will not be attained. Rather, it is through being penetrated by accomplishing the connate that all imaginary entities of ordinary beings turn into the causes of perfect awakening.

A Discussion[80] *of the Purification of the Mind* (text 15) is available in a single Sanskrit manuscript (discovered in Nepal and first edited by Śāstrī in 1898, later reedited in Patel 1949, Varghese 2008, and Jadusingh 2017), as well as three Tibetan translations.[81] The Tibetan tradition usually considers the author of this text to be the same Āryadeva (third century) who was Nāgārjuna's main Mādhyamika student and the author of the *Catuḥśataka*, supposedly also identical with mahāsiddha no. 18 (a.k.a. Karṇaripa, Kaṇheri, and Vairāginath). However, according to most modern scholars, its author was another ("tantric") Āryadeva, possibly living during some time in the ninth or tenth century, or someone else altogether.[82]

Though many Tibetan scholars associate this text with the *Guhyasamājatantra*, particularly the stage of "mind isolation" or "mind purification" among the five stages in the *Pañcakrama*,[83] BKC reports diverging positions:

> Bu[tön] Rinpoche [said] that *The Purification of the Obscurations of the Mind* written by master Āryadeva was composed as a text that teaches the mental focus of the *Guhyasamāja[tantra]*, while Jé Rinpoche stated that though it is a text of the sphere of mind, it is not a text on the intention[84] of the *Guhyasamāja[tantra]*. It is well to take it as one [text] among "The Sixfold Pith Cycle," as the earlier gurus did. Therefore the story of this master is explained below.[85]

Wedemeyer provides evidence that the author of *A Discussion of The Purification of the Mind* (abbr. CVP) cannot be the same as the (tantric) Āryadeva who wrote the important *Caryāmelāpakapradīpa*[86] (abbr. CMP) in the ārya commentarial tradition of the *Guhyasamājatantra*:

> The CVP is an interesting case, as this work—the first published esoteric work attributed to Āryadeva—has accordingly since been taken as definitive of "Tantric Āryadeva." This work is cited again and again in works on Buddhist Tantrism—A. L. Basham having gone so far as to have it stand as an exemplar not merely of Āryadeva, but of Buddhist Tantrism as a whole. The CVP is, however, a highly idiosyncratic text, more in the nature of a compendium than a deliberate work on esoteric practice. It does not treat of the mind isolation stage as presented in the CMP, but a wide range of general esoteric themes, chiefly the nature of the mind and the general tantric theme of forbidden acts as vehicles for liberation. Its polyvocality was noted early on by Louis de La Vallee Poussin, who commented on his surprise in finding sloppy and unprofessional verses rubbing elbows with some that are quite elegant. This inchoate and inconsistent quality contrasts sharply with the composition of the CMP and the S[K]P.[87] These latter are coherent, well-written, and deliberately-argued. Hence, though it is attributed to Āryadeva by several traditional authorities, I do not think it can be rightly taken as sharing the same author as the CMP.[88]

Thus, Wedemeyer agrees with Tsongkhapa's assessment about the contents of the text:

> The . . . *Cittaviśuddhiprakaraṇa* is commonly considered to be a work detailing the Guhyasamāja Perfection stage practice of Mind Isolation. Tsong Khapa states, however, that the CVP, while it is a "Tantric text teaching chiefly about the mind, it is not a special Esoteric Communion text." My reading of this text would seem to concur with that of Tsong Khapa. Nowhere in the CVP does Āryadeva lay out any teaching which is exclusive to or distinctive of the Guhyasamāja. In fact, I cannot but entertain serious doubts about whether this text was deliberately authored by one person, as it jumps around from one topic to another without any discernible internal logic.[89]

Interestingly, Padma Karpo[90] does not associate the text with the *Guhyasamājatantra* at all but declares that it is the best scriptural source of the long tradition of the Tagpo Kagyü, taking one's own mind as the basis of ascertaining mahāmudrā, because its lines 4cd say:

> I shall discuss just a little bit here
> in order to realize my own mind

Furthermore, Padma Karpo says, the text is a detailed explanation of the meaning of the famous stanza in Saraha's "People Dohā":

> Mind as such alone is the seed of everything:
> existence and nirvāṇa spring forth from it
> To the mind that is like a wish-fulfilling jewel
> bestowing the desired results, I pay homage[91]

Thus, Padma Karpo holds, master Āryadeva is the one who establishes the entirety of ground, path, and fruition as mind.[92]

The Purification of the Mind has a clear underpinning of Yogācāra, as evidenced in stanzas 5 (Yogācāra as what is to be studied and practiced), 7–8 (*cittamātra*), and 10 (the preeminence of the mind).[93] Furthermore, the theme of mind's intrinsic purity along the lines of the teachings on tathāgatagarbha (though that term is not explicitly used) is found throughout. Stanzas 27–28, 74, 91–92, 117, and 131 speak about the natural purity of the jewel of the mind needing to be purified from its temporary obscurations of ignorance and thoughts through prajñā and means. Stanzas 96–97, 115–116, and 118–120 contain a number of further metaphors that are well known from the teachings on buddha nature being unaffected by any adventitious stains, such as butter extracted from milk, a lotus unstained by mud, a clear crystal not tinted by colors, a reflection of the moon untainted by water, the sun freed from clouds, the cocoon of ignorance cut down by the sword of prajñā, and a lamp within a vase shining forth once the vase is broken (some of these examples are also found in the *Uttaratantra* and in Nāgārjuna's *Dharmadhātustava*).[94]

To give a brief overview of our text, it begins with four stanzas of homage to Padmanarteśvara, the Lotus Lord of Dance,[95] and the commitment to compose the text. Stanzas 5–9 highlight that the basis of what is to be studied and practiced consists of Yogācāra and the notion of "mere mind" (*cittamātra*) in its connection to twofold identitylessness (personal and phenomenal identitylessness).[96] Stanzas 10–16 further underscore the primacy of the mind (echoing the first two stanzas of the *Dhammapada*) and declare that the results of actions depend on the intention with which they were done, not on the actions themselves.

This sets the stage for the radical view and skillful means of Vajrayāna yogīs who overcome the great demon of thinking, realize thought-free wisdom, recognize all phenomena to be like illusions and dreams, and thus turn any problem into its solution. As repeated with many "homeopathic" examples throughout the text, this resembles expertly using poison as the antidote for poison (stanzas 17–26). Like a pure crystal that reflects all other colors but does not have any of these colors, the jewel of the mind is naturally stainless and never tainted by the plethora of thoughts. Thus yogīs, with the motivation of bodhicitta, as the means to purify the mind, must do everything that ordinary people dislike. Just as poison is detoxified by poison, passion is liberated by passion. Ultimately, however, since the world's true state is pure from the beginning, unborn, and without any nature, the mind of a yogī is actually neither bound nor liberated. Further examples here include removing water from the ear with more water, removing a thorn with another thorn, making clothes stainless by staining, turning an iron ball into a vessel that does not sink in water, or a goose extracting milk from a mixture of milk and water. Likewise, the wise should eradicate flaws by means of flaws. Thus, thanks to enjoying passion, the mind made into a vessel through prajñā and means is liberated and likewise liberates others. Even things that are dangerous become assets when handled with the proper know-how: just as copper rubbed with mercury turns into gold, when purified by wisdom, the afflictions turn into virtue (27–51).

This is followed by a praise of the great compassion, prajñā, and means of bodhisattvas, which enable them to endure all kinds of suffering for the benefit of others (52–57). As also found in other dohās, the text then launches an extensive critique of other spiritual practices perceived as purifications, such as austerities, fasting, ritual bathing, and various forms of "village dharma." However, since the body is impure by its very nature, it cannot be purified by such outer physical methods. If bathing in the Ganges had a purificatory effect, all the fish and fishermen (considered to be impure by brahmans) who spend their time in its waters should be completely purified. But the fundamental flaws are the mind's afflictions, which arise from ignorance and clinging to a self, and none of these can be removed by outer means. Similar to the error of seeing mother-of-pearl as silver, or a rope as a snake, which disappear when seen for what they are, through the vajra wisdom of seeing the lack of a self and real phenomena, a self, afflictions, and truly existing phenomena dissolve for good. Nevertheless, childish beings do not see the body's stainless nature but are tormented by taking it to be suffering (58–70).

Disregarding ordinary conventions imputed by thoughts, yogīs should enjoy themselves without any thoughts, motives, and fears, doing everything as they please. All parts of the body and the mind are to be experienced as consisting of buddhas. By virtue of their special intention, their awakening conduct, and the purification of their minds, the great bodhisattvas who know true reality will thus attain the special fruition of buddhahood in this life through merit and wisdom. Just as forms appear clearly in a stainless mirror, wisdom appears in the mirror of stainless prajñā for those yogīs whose pure minds are freed from the web of thoughts. Just as a fire ignited by rubbing two sticks together illuminates everything, yogic wisdom blazes thanks to uniting prajñā and means. Similar to extracting ghee from milk, by expertly churning the milk of prajñā with great means, the pure dharmadhātu manifests as the true bliss that overcomes all suffering (71–101). There follows an argument about the notion of caste being untenable and an exhortation to worship women, irrespective of caste, appearance, and familial relationship (102–6).

In conjunction with the yoga of their own deity, yogīs should use everything they do as the practice of mind being absorbed in bliss, including singing, playing music, and dancing, without the slightest clinging to anything. In this way, there are no misdeeds. Just as a lotus growing from mud is not stained by that mud, yogīs are not stained by the flaws of thoughts' imprints. Just as the moon reflected in water is not tainted by that water, yogīs are not tainted by seeing all kinds of phenomena that are like reflections. Freed from the clouds of bad views, the sun of the mind shines forth. By cutting through the cocoon of ignorance with the sword of prajñā, the dharmadhātu radiates. Once the hammer of prajñā breaks the vase of thoughts, the lamp of wisdom within it illuminates everything (107–22).

After three stanzas of admonishment to not abandon the Three Jewels, bodhicitta, and the guru, to avoid killing, to keep samaya, and to bless certain substances, yogīs are again encouraged to deal with everything without any doubts. The wise should deliver a good fight or make a good run for it, but any state in between is pointless. The qualities of the guru—Vajradhara in person—should be regarded as supreme, while any perceived flaws are to be disregarded—devotion purifies the jewel of the mind. Nevertheless, to avoid delusion, even those with devotion must develop the prajñā of scripture and realization. The concluding dedication aspires for all beings to become happy through the bliss that is attained by taking up the purification of the mind (123–34).

An Illumination of Prajñā Wisdom (text 16) was written by Divākaracandra.[97] According to BA,[98] he was born as an only son to a noble family in the big city Yamgal[99] in the southern Kathmandu valley. At age eight, he refused to be married, and instead wanted to practice the dharma and go to India. Residing in Vikramaśīla, he studied the *Sampuṭatantra* and *Hevajratantra* under the Nepalese guru Ratnaśrī and became a great scholar. When he was twenty, he returned home and subsequently became very wealthy. From his guru Paiṇḍapātika Jinadatta (an Indian who had moved to the Kathmandu valley), he received the empowerment of Vajravārāhī together with Jinadatta's other main students Mahe Bhāro,[100] Puṇyākarabhadra,[101] and Buddhadatta. During this empowerment, Jinadatta blessed a cup of alcohol, and it remained full, no matter how much they drank. During another empowerment, he made five young women invisible so that only the cups they held were seen as if floating in midair. Later, Jinadatta and his four main students traveled to Bodhgayā. On the way, they met a gang of robbers, but through Jinadatta's blessing, the robbers were compelled to dance and the travelers managed to escape. Upon his return, Divākaracandra practiced meditation for six years and attained special siddhis. However, because he had written two texts on Vajravārāhī against the will of his guru earlier, his worldly possessions dwindled. Still, eventually, he became a major author and propagator of the lineage of "The Six Texts of Vajravārāhī."[102] Divākaracandra also became one of the "four special disciples" of Maitrīpa (the other three being Vajrapāṇi, Sahajavajra, and Rāmapāla).[103]

The title *An Illumination of Prajñā Wisdom* suggests that the text's topic is the third empowerment (prajñā-jñāna empowerment) and its related practice of karmamudrā. However, the work has three parts: (1) a discussion of the necessity of karmamudrā and the succession of the four mudrās, (2) an extensive defense of the superiority of the Vajrayāna compared to the Pāramitāyāna in the form of a commentary on an often-cited stanza from the *Nayatrayapradīpa*, and (3) a short overview of Maitrīpa's fivefold classification of the creation and perfection processes.[104]

(1) Divākaracandra defines prajñā wisdom as "self-aware great bliss," "nonreferential great compassion," "the emptiness endowed with all supreme aspects," and "the Bhagavatī Prajñāpāramitā."[105] He repeatedly emphasizes that this prajñā wisdom—the great bliss arising in the practice of karmamudrā—is the indispensable means to accomplish fully perfect awakening. Though karmamudrā in itself is contrived, when joined with the proper understanding of the uncontrived dharmamudrā, it will result in the realization of uncontrived mahāmudrā.

(2) The second part of the text begins with the quotation of this well-known stanza from the *Nayatrayapradīpa*:

> Though the goal is the same, since it lacks ignorance,
> since it is abundant in means, since it lacks difficulty,
> and since it is the prerogative of those of sharp faculties,
> it is the mantra teaching that is more distinguished[106]

Though the following lengthy objection of an opponent accepts the same goal of the Pāramitāyāna and the Mantrayāna, it denies the stanza's four reasons for the superiority of the Mantrayāna (lacking ignorance, abundant in means, lacking difficulty, and for those of sharp faculties). In answer, after a general explanation of the Pāramitāyāna and the Mantrayāna sharing the same goal in principle but still being taught separately, Divākaracandra rebuts the objections to those four reasons in detail. In that context, he also says that great bliss is accomplished only through the Mantrayāna, that the complete buddhahood that is endowed with the seven constituents of union[107] is superior to the buddhahood attained in the Pāramitāyāna, that the Mantrayāna's pride of being the deity is an essential means to attain that superior buddhahood, that the Pāramitāyāna and the Mantrayāna differ in that the latter fearlessly enjoys the sense pleasures, that the Mantrayāna and not the Pāramitāyāna is the definitive meaning of the Buddha's teachings, and that only the Mantrayāna has the means to accomplish buddhahood in a single lifetime.

(3) The fivefold classification of the creation and completion processes that consists of "the outer creation process," "the profound (inner) creation process," "the perfection process," "the full-perfection process," and "the essence process" is a unique template found only in a number of texts by Maitrīpa and his disciples.[108]

Divākaracandra first typically divides the creation process into "the outer creation process" and "the profound creation process," and the perfection process into "the perfection process," "the full-perfection process," and "the essence process." For the description of the outer and profound creation processes as subdivisions of the creation process, he merely refers to the above two passages in Maitrīpa's *Nairātmyāprakāśa*. Then, within the overall category of the perfection process, he speaks again of the outer and profound creation processes, followed by the perfection process, the full-perfection process, and the essence process. That is, for Divākaracandra, "the outer creation process" within the perfection process appears to consist of the preliminaries of karmamudrā and "the tathāgata relief," while he matches "the profound creation process," "the perfection process," "the full-perfection process," and "the essence process," respectively, with the karmamudrā (and "the Vajradhara relief"), the dharmamudrā, the samayamudrā (both in relation to the four ecstasies), and mahāmudrā.[109]

The author of *A Synopsis of Positions*[110] (text 17) is Sahajavajra, another one of Maitrīpa's main students, on whom there is not much information. According to BA[111] and Maitrīpa's biographies, before he became a Buddhist, his name was Natekara. As a great Hindu master, he engaged in debate with Maitrīpa and, after having lost, became his student, together with his own two thousand students.[112] Sahajavajra's *Synopsis* is available in a single incomplete Sanskrit manuscript and two Tibetan translations.[113] Its outline is as follows:

Introductory stanza
Vaibhāṣika I.1–8 (ms. fols. 1b.2–2a.4)
Sautrāntika II.1–22 (fols. 2a.4–4b.1)
Nonaspectarian Yogācāra III.1–12 (fols. 4b.1–6a.2)
Aspectarian Yogācāra IV.1–8 (fols. 6a.2–7a.1)
Mādhyamika V.1–43 (fols. 7a.1–11a.3)
Mantra tradition VI.1–41 (fols. 11a.3–19)

The text shows commonalities with Maitrīpa's doxographical approach as found in his **Dohānidhināmatattvopadeśa*, *Tattvaratnāvalī*, and *Taking the Pith Instructions of the Philosophical Systems as the Path*,[114] but also exhibits significant differences on a number of points.[115] In terms of philosophical positions, the sections on the Vaibhāṣikas and Sautrāntikas are pretty standard. However, the *Synopsis* includes the pratyekabuddhas at the end of the discussion of the Vaibhāṣika position, while in Maitrīpa's doxographical writings they are discussed as a category separate from the Vaibhāṣikas and Sautrāntikas. Also, while Maitrīpa explicitly (and uncommonly) includes the Sautrāntikas in the Mahāyāna, the *Synopsis* says that belonging to the Hīnayāna or Mahāyāna is not determined by one's philosophical position but by the presence or absence of compassion as the root of buddha awakening. Thus even people whose views accord with the positions of Vaibhāṣikas and Sautrāntikas can be followers of the Mahāyāna in terms of their intention and practice, if they develop compassion and bodhicitta.

Usually, in Maitrīpa's texts and other Indian and Tibetan doxographies, the presentation of Aspectarian Yogācāra precedes the one of Nonaspectarian Yogācāra (considered as the higher Yogācāra view), while the *Synopsis* is unique in switching its presentations of these two.[116] The section on Nonaspectarian Yogācāra centers around incorporating four famous stanzas from the *Laṅkāvatārasūtra*, and unsurprisingly declares that objects other than mind do not exist, because subject and object are merely the delusional split of nondual mind under the sway of latent tendencies. This section concludes by matching the four realities of the noble ones with the three natures: the reality of suffering consists of the imaginary nature (the diversity of appearances of perceiver and perceived), the reality of the origination of suffering consists of the dependent nature (the latent tendencies in the ālaya-consciousness), and the two realities of the path and cessation consist of the perfect nature (aspect-free mere cognizance). The brief section on Aspectarian Yogācāra says that all appearances have the nature of consciousness. Its last half is dedicated to discussing the fruition—the cessation of all suffering that consists of "nondual diversity."[117] This is said to be the dharmakāya of self-experienced nonconceptual wisdom—the emptiness of perceiver and perceived endowed with all supreme aspects[118] and free of the four extremes of existence, nonexistence, and so on. From this dharmakāya, the sambhogakāya and nirmāṇakāya radiate. It seems that this more detailed description of the ultimate fruition is meant to apply to both Nonaspectarian and Aspectarian Yogācāra: while the section on Nonaspectarian Yogācāra refers only briefly to the reality of cessation as aspect-free mere cognizance, the description at the end of Aspectarian Yogācāra appears to be an apt portrayal of buddhahood in both systems. This has a clear parallel in what Maitrīpa's **Dohānidhināmatattvopadeśa* says on buddhahood at the end of its stanzas on Yogācāra that do not explicitly differentiate between Aspectarians and Nonaspectarians:

> The nonduality that is equal to space, inconceivable, and pure,
> that has compassion's nature and no aspect is perfect
> buddhahood
> The two kāyas with form are those that issue forth from this
> root[119]

Within Madhyamaka, though Maitrīpa's default distinction consists of the position of illusion-like nonduality (Māyopamādvayavāda) and the position of the utter nonabiding of all phenomena (Sarvadharmāpratiṣṭhānavāda), the *Synopsis* does not mention these two at all.[120] A lot of the text's Madhyamaka section treads familiar ground, saying things such as: Madhyamaka is what relinquishes all positions; all phenomena (including the mind) do not arise from themselves, something other, existence, or nonexistence; and they are without nature, free of being one or many, and like reflections, illusions, and dreams.

However, unexpectedly, the Madhyamaka section of the *Synopsis* silently incorporates thirteen stanzas from the *Laṅkāvatārasūtra*. Beginning with *Laṅkāvatārasūtra* X.568, as *Synopsis* V.21 (mind seeing itself being unlike a sword unable to cut itself and a fingertip unable to touch itself), Sahajavajra advocates self-aware mind even in a Madhyamaka context, as long as this self-awareness is qualified by being unborn,[121] nondual, without any aspects, and equivalent to emptiness, suchness, the dharmadhātu, and prajñāpāramitā. Moreover, in the *Synopsis* the first two stanzas of the section on the mantra tradition summarize the pāramitā approach by saying that true reality, which is free of the four extremes and without arising, abiding, ceasing, and characteristics but is dependent origination, is to be experienced through self-awareness.[122] This seems to be in accord with Maitrīpa's stance on ultimate unborn awareness in his Madhyamaka of utter nonabiding, and is also what Sahajavajra's *Tattvadaśakaṭīkā* says on this topic.[123]

Having already said before in the Yogācāra sections that mind is unborn, lacks the duality of subject and object, and is free of the three spheres and the four extremes, the Madhyamaka section further states that mind is equivalent to emptiness, the dharmadhātu, and so on. It also declares that the world without real entities is to be realized as mere mind—that is, nondual mind without a distinct perceiver and perceived. In worldly beings, this mere mind may turn into duality, but mind's essential characteristic is nonduality (there are no referents apart from mind), and this mind is neither existent nor nonexistent. Upon analysis, ultimately, the ālaya as well as the three natures—the imaginary, dependent, and perfect natures—do not exist. Nevertheless, bodhisattvas should never relinquish unborn seeming reality, but realize the unity of the two realities.[124] This kind of Madhyamaka represents the supreme Mahāyāna among the sūtras of definitive meaning—the Madhyamaka that is the unity of emptiness and compassion.

The opening of the section on the Mantra tradition says that it follows Nāgārjuna's *Succession of the Four Mudrās* (text 14) and that, without analysis and doubt, the great bliss of prajñā and means needs to be self-experienced through special experiences of emptiness thanks to the guru (VI.1–3). The text continues by citing and briefly explaining the famous stanza from the *Nayatrayapradīpa* on the superiority of the Vajrayāna versus the Pāramitāyāna (lacking ignorance and difficulty, abundant in means, and for those with sharp faculties), which is also quoted in Maitrīpa's *Tattvaratnāvalī* (VI.4–12). The brief announcement of the succession of the four mudrās (karmamudrā, dharmamudrā, mahāmudrā, and samayamudrā) as the topics of the Mantrayāna is followed by a more detailed discussion in accordance with *The Succession of the Four Mudrās*.[125] The karmamudrā is presented in terms of those with lower faculties (VI.14–24ab), the dharmamudrā in terms of those with medium faculties (VI.24cd–25), and mahāmudrā in terms of those with highest faculties (VI.26–37).[126] Each one is in turn classified as lower, medium, and highest. Finally, Sahajavajra proclaims that (in terms of the instantaneous or simultaneous approach) he does not have any stages of meditation, since cause and result are inseparable.[127] Mahāmudrā means to fully awaken to great bliss, and buddhahood consists of the attainment of the five kāyas (the fifth one being the inseparability of the first four; VI.39–40).[128]

As Isaacson, Sferra, and Mathes have remarked, the presence of quotations from the *Sekoddeśa* as a text related to the *Kālacakratantra* in the

Synopsis is an element that is not found in any works by Maitrīpa and his other students.[129] Moreover, while Sahajavajra's own stanzas VI.16–18 follow the sequence of the four ecstasies as given in *The Succession of the Four Mudrās* and throughout Maitrīpa's works (ecstasy, supreme ecstasy, connate ecstasy, and cessational ecstasy), in the first stanzas quoted from the *Sekoddeśa* following VI.19, the order of the last two ecstasies is reversed. Though Sahajavajra does not comment on or explicitly resolve this apparent contradiction, as already pointed out by Mathes, one can assume that he had Maitrīpa's own explanation of this in mind in his *Caturmudropadeśa*:

> "However, [most other] scriptures have connate ecstasy as the last one." That is certainly true, but such is explained by mixing up [the order of the ecstasies] for the sake of persons who fail to rely on a guru and [just] become learned through tomes of scriptures. In such [scriptures], [connate ecstasy] is the fourth in number, but in terms of the meaning it corresponds to the third [moment].[130]

Given this, the solution of the apparent contradiction seems rather simple. Since the stanzas from the *Sekoddeśa* follow immediately after Sahajavajra's critique of the forceful empowerment, they are no doubt simply intended as a scriptural example of that kind of empowerment.[131] Thus there is no conflict within the *Synopsis*, or with Nāgārjuna's *Succession of the Four Mudrās*, or with Sahajavajra's guru Maitrīpa.

Furthermore, as Isaacson and Sferra themselves say, the Kālacakra "influence manifests itself primarily in the quotation of numerous verses from the *Sekoddeśa*." In fact, Sahajavajra nowhere comments on or even endorses these stanzas but adduces them as an example of the forceful empowerment that he rejects. Beyond that, there is no other detectable influence of Kālacakra material in the *Synopsis*. Thus, to say that this text shows a strong Kālacakra influence, as Isaacson, Sferra, and Mathes do, is definitely an overstatement. If anything, given said position of these stanzas in Sahajavajra's text, it is more probable to regard their citation as a rejection of the Kālacakra tradition (at least as far as the forceful empowerment and the related practice goes). In that vein, the inclusion of the stanzas from the *Sekoddeśa* is certainly not sufficient to doubt Sahajavajra's authorship of the *Synopsis* or to think that he may have adapted his Vajrayāna presentation to a growing Kālacakra influence during his time.[132]

Kuddālapāda's *Pith Instructions on the Tradition of Inconceivable Nonduality* (text 18) is available in four Sanskrit manuscripts (edited in Samdhong and Dvivedī 1987) and in two Tibetan translations.[133]

In BKC,[134] the work is introduced with the following story. One day in Uḍḍiyāna, when a monk asked a farmer for alms, the farmer did not want to give him anything, saying that he had many daughters to feed and did not believe in the positive karmic effects of almsgiving. The monk narrated many great examples of the karmic fruitions of almsgiving and finally pledged to be consciously reborn as the farmer's son so as to alleviate his hardships. The monk stopped eating and breathing, remaining in meditation until he passed away in a charnel ground.

Nine months later, the farmer's wife gave birth to a son, and the farmer found many precious treasures. His son did not weep during the day but wept a lot during the night. A brahman skilled in reading signs said that the son wept because he saw the causes of both saṃsāra and nirvāṇa. When he had become a grownup, a siddha told him to practice dharma for twelve years. One of his masters, who also went to do farm work, accidentally struck the son's leg with a hoe. Later, that master went to look after him and asked: "Don't you experience physical suffering?" The son replied by proclaiming his realization:

> Ordinary mind wakes up in the center of the heart
> If the six collections are pure,[135] bliss is uninterrupted
> All that is done is meaningless, the cause of suffering
> With nothing to meditate, let be in the native state[136]

The master replied, "You have finished your hoe work for all times!" and left. From then on, the son was known as Kuddālapāda ("the hoe man").

However, the wound caused his entire leg and lower body to become putrefied and infested with maggots. He was staying in the center of town as a beggar when a physician came by, giving him medicine and asking about his state. Not feeling any suffering, he sang a song of realization:

Bhavata bhavata kanaka kanaka bhiruna bhiruna citoha citoha
The inconceivable, the inconceivable is perfected in me
The entirety of suffering, the entirety of suffering,
if it is realized to be equal, will come to be at peace

The entirety of distraction, the entirety of distraction
is contained within the root that consists of bodhicitta
Where might solitude be, where might solitude be?
If mind as such is realized, solitude is in any place

The physician asked him: "Without a nurse, aren't you afflicted? Without sustenance, doesn't your body deteriorate? Eaten by flesh flies, aren't you in pain? Tormented by disease, don't you faint?" Kuddālapāda said, "I am not sick!" and repeated his song. Having returned to his village, the physician also sang Kuddālapāda's song. Meeting a wood seller, who asked him whose song he was singing, the physician replied: "In town there is a sick man, and I'm his physician. Usually physicians are there for sick people, but this sick man *is* a physician." The physician escorted the wood seller to Kuddālapāda, who asked him: "Who are you?" "I am Bhadra." "And I am Kuddāla." Since Bhadrapāda was Kuddālapāda's guru from his previous life, when Bhadrapāda merely licked Kuddālapāda's wound, it healed on its own without a physician. Later, Kuddālapāda passed on his instructions on the inconceivable to Kambala, who transmitted it to Tilopa, and so on.

As for Kuddālapāda's identity and his lineage, stanzas 88–89 of his text provide the following names: Paramāśva, Vīṇapāda, Indrabhūti, Lakṣmī, Vilāsavajra, Guṇḍerī, Padmācārya, Dharmapāda, and Bhadrapāda.[137] All in all, Kuddālapāda mentions his guru Bhadrapāda nineteen times (Dharmapāda two times). Given this lineage and the comments by Tragpa Gyaltsen, Padma Karpo, Jamgön Kongtrul, and BKC, it is clear that this Kuddālapāda is not the mahāsiddha of the same name who is included among the eighty-four mahāsiddhas (no. 44) and whose guru was Śāntipa (no. 12).[138] Rather, the lineage of this Kuddālapāda is obviously connected to several well-known masters from Uḍḍiyāna, such as Indrabhūti, Lakṣmī, Vilāsavajra, and most probably Padmavajra, who are among the authors of "The Seven Siddhi Texts" and are listed in the lineages in Indrabhūti's *Sahajasiddhi* (text 10) and Lakṣmī's *Sahajasiddhipaddhati* (text 11). Furthermore, in the life stories of the eighty-four mahāsiddhas, the mahāsiddhas named Bhadrapāda and Dharmapāda (nos. 24, 36, and 48) do not have any connection with each other, with the mahāsiddha Kuddālapāda (no. 44), or with any of the above-mentioned authors of some of the "Siddhi Texts," nor are those mahāsiddhas Bhadrapāda, Dharmapāda, and Kuddālapāda said to have been from Uḍḍiyāna. Thus it seems very clear that the Bhadrapāda and Dharmapāda mentioned in Kuddālapāda's lineage here are not the mahāsiddhas of the same names; rather, they are closely related to the lineage of the Uḍḍiyāna authors of "The Seven Siddhi Texts."[139]

Furthermore, Padma Karpo[140] says that four transmission lineages came together in our Kuddālapāda, which he passed on to Kambala, who then handed them down to Tilopa. Subsequently, the entirety of "The Seven Siddhi Texts" and "The Sixfold Pith Cycle" was transmitted by Tilopa and Nāropa. There is also another lineage from Kuddālapāda to Śavaripa and Maitrīpa.

As for the contents of Kuddālapāda's text, just like the works of many other mahāsiddhas, it is not a systematic or linear teaching manual, but has a rather sprawling nature. In addition, the work shows strong inclusivist tendencies in that it uses a significant number of Hinduist terminologies and concepts while reinterpreting them in a Buddhist sense.[141]

The poem's opening stanzas describe "inconceivable nonduality" as "the wisdom that arises on its own," which is reiterated several times throughout. This inconceivable nonduality is the source of all phenomena of saṃsāra and nirvāṇa, including all the elements of the creation and perfection processes and all non-Buddhist systems. It is further described as having the form of equal taste, nonthought, natural luminosity, and mahāmudrā. In being beyond all distinctions and limitations—such as being and nonbeing, permanence and extinction, perceiver and perceived, meditator and something to meditate on, creation and perfection, arising, abiding, and ceasing, a nature, or even emptiness—it is free from all extremes and reference points, including a middle. Though this nonduality is free from any thinking, as manifestations of this nonduality, thoughts are regarded as utterly beautiful by the buddhas, and all sentient beings' conceptions are naturally cradled within the womb of prajñā. Thus the target of great bliss should be pierced with the arrow of awakening compassion. A series of stanzas contrasts the five ordinary sense objects with blissful nonduality as the supreme form, sound, taste, smell, and touch. The five skandhas are the five wisdoms and the five buddhas families, with the sixth one being great bliss as their unity. Likewise, the five elements are nothing other than self-arising nonduality's awakening. The one to point out the plethora of appearances as nothing but expressions of this single nonduality is the guru, the embodiment of all buddhas and the supreme ocean of wisdom. Stanzas 98–120 offer an oblique instruction on the practice of karmamudrā. Finally, Kuddālapāda concludes with his aspiration to always serve true gurus throughout his rebirths, and that, by virtue of this motivation, even the hells turn into Sukhāvatī, no matter whether he himself becomes a buddha or ends up in hell.[142]

According to Padma Karpo,[143] "inconceivable" in the text's title means "beyond mind," which refers to the first two lines of its second stanza: "The great secret of prajñā and means, characterized by inconceivable compassion." He continues, saying that the Drugpa Kagyü gurus have included the text in "The Cycle of Fusion,"[144] explaining it as just the eight perfections of the path.[145] However, in the text itself, the inconceivable consists of five points: (1) the inconceivability of the nature (stanzas 2–35), (2) the inconceivability of the manner of subsuming all phenomena (36–59ab), (3) the inconceivability of the means (59cd–88), (4) the inconceivability of the conduct (89–97ab), and (5) the inconceivability of the bhūmis, paths, and fruition (97cd–120).[146]

An instruction manual on Kuddālapāda's text by Jamgön Kongtrul[147] also speaks about five kinds of inconceivability, though they are named and described very differently, initially saying that the wisdom ḍākinī bestowed "empowerment and instructions on the fivefold inconceivable" or "instructions on the five inconceivable empowerments"[148] upon Paramāśva. In more detail,[149] Jamgön Kongtrul states that when ascertaining the mind, though there are no divisions in terms of its essence, in terms of conceptual isolates, the inconceivable is of five kinds.

(1) The inconceivability of the characteristic refers to its being unmixed and fully complete. Since everything is the single experiential awareness of the mind, there is only this single type, but by virtue of different ways

of realizing this essence, there appear the path of tīrthika outsiders[150] and the path of Buddhist insiders, as well as all kinds of philosophical systems imputed by their distinct assertions.

(2) The inconceivability of qualities resembles the example of a wish-fulfilling jewel: due to its single essence encountering the conditions of means, it arises as whatever is needed for whomever. As with the orb of the sun, due to its single essence encountering certain place conditions, many different appearances arise. Without moving from dharmatā's own essence, all kinds of paths and philosophical systems appear in accordance with the distinct constitutions and faculties of those to be guided, just as the sun shines nowhere but in the sky yet is individually seen in different places as rising and setting only over the peaks of mountains.

(3) The inconceivability of power refers to being neither bound nor free. It is not bound, because the power to generate virtue exists in the mind by virtue of its essence. It is not free, because freedom will not occur without meeting the proper conditions. For example, when sesame seeds meet the condition of being pressed, oil appears, but if they do not meet that condition, oil will not appear. Since this very single mind appears as all causes, paths, and results, there is no room for conceiving this. Therefore it is inconceivable, which represents the side of means.

(4) The inconceivability of nature refers to all three inconceivabilities of characteristics, qualities, and power being ultimately empty of the triad of cause, own essence, and result. For example, by thinking of any cause, result, and so on, something like empty space is not found. Therefore it is inconceivable, which represents the side of prajñā.

(5) The inconceivability of essence refers to not being disassociated and not being possessed. Since two seemingly contradictory phenomena do not abide within a single phenomenon, there is no disassociation. When analyzed thoroughly with reasoning, since that phenomenon is not found as being established as anything whatsoever, there is no possession. Since it is not asserted as conceivable, it is inconceivable, which represents unity. "Unity" is neither like blending both existence and nonexistence, nor like meditating on one as two, nor like one side existing and the other side not existing [or existing on one hand and not

existing on the other hand], nor like combining two into one. In brief, if one searches by thinking in terms of means, everything is existent. If one searches by thinking in terms of prajñā, everything is nonexistent. In short, the mere fact that it cannot be made dual is called "nondual unity," which is said to be beyond any object of all cognitions and expressions.[151]

As for the main cycle of texts in this volume, "The Twenty-Five Dharmas of Mental Nonengagement" by Maitrīpa (a.k.a. Maitrīgupta, Advayavajra, Avadhūt(ip)a, and Maitreyanātha),[152] different sources show variations in both the titles and the numbers of texts in this collection. Compared with the twenty-four texts contained in the Sanskrit collection of Maitrīpa's works (**Advayavajrasaṃgraha*),[153] GZ omits the *Mūlāpattaya*, the *Sthūlāpattaya* (both not contained in Tg either), and *The Succession of the Four Mudrās* (*Caturmudrānvaya*; text 14), which is attributed to Nāgārjuna and included in "The Sixfold Pith Cycle." Instead, GZ includes *Pith Instructions on True Reality Called "A Dohā Treasure"* (text 22), *Five Stanzas on Love* (text 29), and *A Compendium of the Procedures of Empowerment* (text 38). In addition, NG as well as the position of the anonymous *Pith Instruction on Letting Cognizance Be without Projecting and Withdrawing* (text 43) in GZ suggest that this text is also included in that cycle.[154]

Thus, depending on the counting, GZ and NG list twenty-three, twenty-four, or twenty-five texts in this cycle of Maitrīpa's texts. If, as GZ and NG do, the virtually identical *Five Stanzas on the Love between Means and Prajñā* (text 23) and *Five Stanzas on Love* (text 29) are counted separately, there is a total of twenty-four texts. If text 43 is also included in this cycle, that makes a total of twenty-five works. In fact, GZ appears to be the only collection of mahāmudrā texts that includes text 43 as one of Maitrīpa's works (or at least as being related to him in some way): besides not being found in the **Advayavajrasaṃgraha*, the text is not listed in *Butön's Record of Teachings Received*,[155] BKC,[156] and Padma Karpo's list[157] either, and Tg considers it to be anonymous.

As Maitrīpa's biographies tell us, after he had spent some time with his guru Śabara (or Śavaripa), Śabara told Maitrīpa to return to his former academic environment as his representative and teach the ācāryas how things really are, taking care of suitable disciples. By combining his prior scholarly training in sophisticated terminology and instructions with his advanced realization of mahāmudrā thanks to Śabara, the hallmark of many of Maitrīpa's works is his unique way of blending the mainstream sūtra teachings of the Mahāyāna—specifically his Madhyamaka of utter nonabiding, but also Yogācāra notions such as "self-awareness," "nonduality," and "luminosity"—with tantric elements, mahāmudrā, and the oral instructions of the mahāsiddhas.[158] The mahāmudrā approach of the mahāsiddhas, which had so far been transmitted within their communities outside of monastic and academic institutions, thus found entrance into mainstream Indian Buddhism and became accessible to many more people.[159] Though this did not happen without some controversies, Maitrīpa was able to spread mahāmudrā in his former world of the Buddhist monastic and scholarly establishment.[160] In this context, he is said to have won many debates with rival scholars, such as his former teacher Ratnākaraśānti (who held the position of Nonaspectarian Yogācāra)[161] and the Hindu master Natekara, who then became one of his main disciples, henceforth known as Sahajavajra. Later, Maitrīpa spent much time in retreat in several charnel grounds and hermitages, such as Cool Grove and Mount Blazing Fire. During that time, he also met his consort, the princess of Malabar, who became known as the wisdom ḍākinī Gaṅgādharā.[162]

As for Maitrīpa's typical blend of sūtric and tantric terminologies, there is no room here to undertake a thorough analysis of the usage of all the key terms in his writings. Hence a brief surview of three of his trademark terms—(1) "mental nonengagement" (Skt. *amanasikāra*),[163] (2) "utter nonabiding" (*apratiṣṭhāna*),[164] and (3) "unity" (*yuganaddha*)[165]—shall suffice. In the course of this, Maitrīpa's use of the notion of "(self-) awareness" will also be clarified. (1) The term "mental nonengagement" (or "mental disengagement") that gave the cycle of Maitrīpa's works its name—in its mahāmudrā meaning of not only being the process of letting go of dualistic conceptualization but also being a direct nonanalytical approach to realizing mind's natural luminosity—is also known from several texts by Saraha, Tilopa, Nāropa, and others.[166] Somewhat surprising, though, there are only three texts among Maitrīpa's "Cycle of Twenty-Five Dharmas of Mental Nonengagement" in GZ that mention this term. As its name says, *In Support of Mental Nonengagement* (text 27) is Maitrīpa's only work that provides a substantial discussion of the term. *A Pith Instruction on Letting Cognizance Be without Projecting and*

Withdrawing (text 43) mentions the term once, and it is also found once in *A Commentary on the Five Seals of the Tathāgatas* (text 36), but only in a quote from the *Jñānālokālaṃkārasūtra* that is also cited in *In Support of Mental Nonengagement*.[167]

In Support of Mental Nonengagement is a detailed defense against criticisms of the expression "mental nonengagement" that justifies its use in the Buddhist teachings and clearly explains its meanings, combining a broad range of Indian scholarly approaches with the Vajrayāna language of meditative experience, which is so typical of many of Maitrīpa's works. It seems that this detailed defense of "mental nonengagement" was the reason why Maitrīpa's entire approach later came to be identified with this term.

After presenting some grammatical considerations and then tracing the term back to both the sūtras and tantras, Maitrīpa's text says that mental nonengagement is not a nonimplicative negation, since it refers to negating all mental engagement that exists in terms of perceiver and perceived and so on but does not negate mind as such. What that term teaches is the complete transcending of all conceptions. Nevertheless, to regard it as an implicative negation is without flaw—referring to an awareness that lacks any nature is the understanding of those Mādhyamikas who speak of illusion-like nonduality. When one calls that awareness "illusion-like" or "not truly established," this is not a wholesale negation of its existence.

Then, Maitrīpa gives two special etymologies of *amanasikāra*. (a) He says that the (correct) mental engagement (*manasikāra*) in the letter *a* as the main element is mental nonengagement (*a-manasikāra*). That kind of mental engagement means to realize that everything is *a*—primordially unborn—since *a* is the seed syllable of identitylessness. Hence all such mental engagement refers to the lack of nature.[168] (b) Alternatively, the meaning of *amanasikāra* is that *a* stands for luminosity and "mental engagement" (*manasikāra*) stands for self-blessing. In this way, the state of *amanasikāra* means to bring forth the pure awareness that is the continuous flow of the nondual inseparable unity of emptiness and compassion, which has the character of self-blessing with or within inconceivable luminosity.[169]

Thus, in other words, Maitrīpa's key notion of "mental nonengagement" is just the subjective side of emptiness, or what is called "freedom from discursiveness or reference points." The only way in which the mind can engage in the "object" that is the absence of discursiveness is precisely by not engaging in or fueling any reference points, but rather letting it naturally settle of its own accord. In other words, the absence of reference points can be realized only by a nonreferential mind, since that is the only cognitive mode that exactly corresponds to it. At the same time, when the mind rests in its own natural state, free from all discursiveness and reference points, it is not like a coma or being spaced out, but is vivid and luminous intrinsic awareness. This is precisely how TOK explains "sūtra mahāmudrā":

> Within the object—luminosity free from discursiveness that accords with the sūtra approach—the subject rests in meditative equipoise through the instructions of mental nonengagement.[170]

Maitrīpa's above two etymologies of "mental nonengagement" highlight the two crucial features of his mahāmudrā approach that is explicitly spelled out by his student Sahajavajra, and by others later. Maitrīpa's linking mental nonengagement with the syllable *a* is an indication that his mahāmudrā corresponds to prajñāpāramitā (in the prajñāpāramitā sūtras, the letter *a* stands for emptiness, or that everything is primordially unborn). To connect mental nonengagement with the three highest levels of the perfection process of the *Guhyasamājatantra* ("self-blessing" or "illusory body," "luminosity," and "unity") is a clear sign that this mahāmudrā also entails Vajrayāna elements—not necessarily in terms of tantric rituals or techniques but in terms of inner experiences that represent the essence of the former and can also be cultivated in Maitrīpa's sūtra-based approach with the help of the pith instructions of a guru.[171]

In brief, as per Maitrīpa, mental nonengagement can generally be understood as either (1) no engagement in the mind (locative *tatpuruṣa* compound), (2) no engagement of or by the mind (genitive *tatpuruṣa* compound), or (3) proper mental engagement, in the sense of prajñāpāramitā (being unborn or the lack of any nature; *karmadhāraya* compound in the sense of "a B that is A").

(1) In a specifically tantric context, as per the *Guhyasamājatantra*

literature, mental nonengagement refers to the unity of self-blessing and luminosity (or the inseparability of prajñā and compassion) as the final stage of perfection-process practices.[172]

(2) Besides this discussion of the notion of "mental nonengagement," Maitrīpa repeatedly advocates the Madhyamaka view of utter nonabiding (*apratiṣṭhāṇa*) that he considers to be supreme. BKC[173] provides a stanza that summarizes Maitrīpa's view as utter nonabiding and his meditation as mental nonengagement:

> Because nonabiding constitutes the view,
> it gets rid of all superimposition and denial
> As mental nonengagement is the meditation,
> the native basic nature is realized through it

However, this Madhyamaka of utter nonabiding refers not just to sheer emptiness but to mind's intrinsic wisdom nature that is utterly ungraspable, yet at the same time self-aware, luminous, and blissful.

Thus Maitrīpa's *Discourse on Dream* (text 31), *Five Stanzas on Penetrating Insight* (text 28), and *Illumination of Utter Nonabiding* (text 24) agree that mind's utter nonabiding is the greatest wealth of Buddhists. *An Illumination of Utter Nonabiding* adds that this is only so if nonabiding is coupled with promoting the welfare of beings in an effortless way. Furthermore, with all reference points of negation, affirmation, arising, extinction, and so on abandoned, even mind's self-awareness cannot be reified as existent, be it within meditation or outside of it—mind is without any findable nature of its own. The dependent origination of phenomena by way of native self-awareness is inconceivable—this is what is referred to as "emptiness," which is, however, not some kind of extinction. The seed and the fruition of nonabiding stand in direct opposition to those of contrivance. *Five Stanzas on Penetrating Insight* states that our inexpressible and nonabiding inner wealth consists of the primordial buddhahood that is innate in all beings, which has effortless compassion's character, arises in dependence, and is the blissful connate.

A Commentary on the Five Seals of the Tathāgatas explains that nonabiding awareness's dependent arising actually means that it is without any arising by way of a nature of its own:

> Once the thorn that this kind [of consciousness] exists ultimately is removed, the Mādhyamika tenet that consists of the establishment of the awareness that has the nature of not abiding anywhere at all and is the continuous flow of effortless nondual unity is superior. This is realized through the kindness of the venerable true guru. You may wonder, thinking: "If awareness is established here, by virtue of the undesired consequence of this [thus] being the proposition of illusion-like nonduality, it is not utter nonabiding in every respect." This is not the case:
>
> > That which has arisen in dependence
> > has not arisen through its own nature
> > What has not arisen by its own nature,
> > how could that be designated "arisen?"[174]
>
> Awareness too is something that has arisen in dependence. Therefore this very awareness does not at all abide [as anything in any respect, but] constitutes the state of being unarisen.[175]

Maitrīpa's *Instructions on Empowerment* (text 42) equates "utter nonabiding in anything at all" with mahāmudrā. According to Rāmapāla's commentary[176] on stanzas 29–30, "utter nonabiding" refers to mental nonengagement and being without any superimpositions. "In anything at all" refers to the dependently arisen skandhas, dhātus, āyatanas, and so on. Since mahāmudrā—self-awareness—is stainless, the three stained moments of variety and so on, as well as the corresponding first three among the four ecstasies, do not arise in it. This utter nonabiding is the effortless inconceivable wisdom that does not come from analysis but occurs in its own natural flow.[177]

Similarly, Maitrīpa's *Six Stanzas on the Middle* (text 26, 4–6) speaks of "awareness empty of being an entity, without aspect, unborn, and unsullied" as representing utter nonabiding, and also links this to the Vajrayāna by saying that "lucidity free of the four extremes possesses the character of the deity, has the nature of nondual bliss, and is sheer dependent origination."[178]

Several of Maitrīpa's works also speak of "the yoga of nonabiding." *A*

Discourse on Illusion 7cd says that yogīs adopt the appropriate conduct by properly abiding through the yoga of nonabiding. *The Illumination of Great Bliss* (text 33, 12–13) declares that what is to be accomplished through the yoga of nonabiding is the union of bliss and emptiness (means and prajñā), symbolized by the tantric deity couple:

> The blissful mind has the form of the deity
> The cakra of totality[179] serves as the means
> The prajñā [consort] is called "emptiness"
> Their identity is taken as what's to be gained
>
> True reality has the character of prajñā and means,
> because it consists of external and internal purity
> Once realized by their union, mantra practitioners
> are delighted by way of the yoga of nonabiding

Outside of Maitrīpa's "Cycle of Twenty-Five Dharmas of Mental Nonengagement," his *Taking the Pith Instructions of the Philosophical Systems as the Path*[180] explains the yoga of nonabiding in more detail along the lines of mahāmudrā-type pith instructions. It says that the dhyāna of utter nonabiding of the Mādhyamikas of utter nonabiding consists of putting an end to delusive clinging, which consists of calm abiding and superior insight. Calm abiding refers to methods for doing meditation. Gaze directly at an object in front of you and focus on it. Similar to putting an end to clinging to a reflection, through examining the very mind of having put an end to clinging to that entity you gaze at in terms of whether this mind is one or many, this entity does not even abide as a mere illusion free from clinging but appears as a mere imputation: rest in that empty unceasing appearance. Familiarize with lucid experience as being empty. Thus, looking nakedly at the mind that appears as what is immobile, and at your own body, familiarize with this as above. Having become familiar with the mind, and having trained with other appearances in this way, familiarize with any appearing object just as before. If mind is able to look at that empty appearance, then train with the mind that appears as afflictions such as desire. Having looked at mind like that, then again, familiarize as before by mind nakedly looking at space. To thus realize that all appearances are empty is superior insight. To focus in accord with the emptiness of emptiness is to gaze directly, and thus all entities are destroyed. This is utterly nonabiding emptiness. You may wonder at the need for this view of emptiness with regard to phenomena being illusions. It is the means to subdue and be free from clinging to their being illusion-like. The realization of the actuality of utter nonabiding moisturizes the mind stream. Within the mind streams of the persons who have such an experience, the experience of equality arises.[181]

In this vein, Maitrīpa's[182] *Commentary on Half a Stanza on True Reality Teaching That All Phenomena Are Utterly Nonabiding* says that "the unknowing and nonabiding expanse of equality is the mind without hope or fear that knows all times."[183] As the text's name indicates, Maitrīpa explains the Madhyamaka of utter nonabiding, which is his most detailed and systematic discussion of this approach (in the contexts of both sūtras and tantras). At the end, Maitrīpa explicitly identifies his guru Śabara as the source of these instructions:

> I obtained the approach of teaching that ultimately all phenomena do not abide as anything whatsoever from the mouth of the glorious lord Śabara in the jungles of the south.[184]

In classical scholarly fashion, Maitrīpa begins by explaining the Madhyamaka of utter nonabiding by way of scripture and reasonings. First, he provides a passage from the *Dharmatāsvabhāvaśūnyatācalapratisarvālokasūtra* as being a fully sufficient scriptural source of this kind of Madhyamaka:

> All these five means for examining phenomena are taken to be correct. (1) I think some teach the dharma that all phenomena exist in just the way they appear. Why is that? Because the four elements and what is produced by them exist conventionally just like illusions.
>
> (2) I think some teach the dharma that all phenomena exist as nothing other than mere mind. Why is that? Because through the power of the latent tendencies of imagining them to be permanent and immutable that are input into the mind, [the appearances] that are labeled as all kinds of phenomena

> appear at all times as a self and phenomena. Though they thus appear to be different, they ultimately lack any nature; there is nothing but mere mind.
>
> (3) I think some teach us the dharma that mind itself is unborn as well. Why is that? Because it does not have any shape, color, three times, fringe, or middle.
>
> (4) I think some teach the dharma that all phenomena appear like illusions and, just like illusions, are not established. Why is that? Because all phenomena arise and originate from causes and conditions.
>
> (5) I think some teach the dharma that all phenomena are naturally unborn, naturally nonabiding, free of all extremes of object and activity, beyond being any object of thought and nonthought, and pure of discursiveness since beginningless time. Why is that? Because this is all phenomena's own unmistaken nature.[185]

Especially the last three "means" here properly characterize Maitrīpa's Madhyamaka tenets of illusion-like nonduality and utter nonabiding, which also emphasize that mind is unborn. Thus this excerpt is indeed a suitable scriptural support for his sūtra-based Madhyamaka.

Next, Maitrīpa presents the reasonings of this approach as consisting of the two main arguments that Mādhyamikas use: the reasoning of dependent origination and the vajra sliver reasoning (phenomena do not arise from themselves, something other, both, or without any cause). By means of these two reasonings, all phenomena are established as being utterly nonabiding and unarisen. Therefore there is nothing to mentally engage in and nothing whatsoever to aspire for, which, Maitrīpa says, is "this approach of mine."

In the following step, he equates this utter nonabiding with the highest among the four ecstasies in the context of properly practicing karmamudrā in the Vajrayāna:

> In the texts of secret mantra, it is exactly this true actuality that is asserted as the connate ecstasy that is accomplished by virtue of a karmamudrā as its cause.[186]

Having differentiated the correct practice of karmamudrā versus the wrong approaches to it, Maitrīpa concludes that those who see karmamudrā as the true path but do not know the actuality of mahāmudrā are mistaken.[187] By contrast, the definitive meaning (the lion of Maitrīpa's own approach) is what allows merging with mahāmudrā—the fourth empowerment, the vajra-like bodhicitta that is seen thanks to the lineage of perfect gurus and is beyond scriptures and reasonings.[188] Thus Maitrīpa lists the following three criteria that make those who follow the lion of his own approach perfect yogīs:

> Perfect yogīs are as follows: by realizing the final point of all phenomena being dependent origination, they make a thorough distinction between the path and what is not the path; by comprehending the teaching that the yānas are divided into three but are not contradictory in meaning, they respectfully trust [all] the teachings of the guides; by determining through threefold valid cognition[189] that phenomena are identityless, they understand that ultimately [all] is equality and are in natural harmony with that. Thus it is said, "The lion who defeats it is this approach of mine."[190]

As for using a lion to represent perfect yogīs who follow this approach, Maitrīpa explains:

> Bodhicitta is endowed with natural power even at the time of saṃsāra when it is not realized. Immediately upon the [initial] realization of bodhicitta arising, it is endowed with the power of outshining others. At the time of consummate familiarity with bodhicitta, it is endowed with the power of vanquishing [everything] antagonistic at its root. The genuineness of being endowed with such [power] is rare, and it is courageous. It dwells on the mountain and the stronghold of emptiness. It utters the roar of no-self. It is well-settled in its own way of being . . . Lions cannot be defeated by any other [creatures] who are herbivores, and they eventually die by virtue of their own conditions. Their corpses cannot be destroyed by others either,

> but will perish on their own without any remainder of their skandhas. Likewise, yogīs who propound that all phenomena are utterly nonabiding should be understood in the same way.[191]

This is immediately followed by Maitrīpa linking the practice of utter nonabiding with the relinquishment of the four conceptions to be relinquished, as per the *Avikalpapraveśadhāraṇī*'s discussion of how bodhisattvas enter the expanse of nonconceptuality by letting go of all coarse and subtle characteristics of conceptions:

> By virtue of the conditions of having become familiar for a long time with the yogas of fire-like discriminating wisdom, the path-like samādhi of the web of illusory manifestations, the water-like samādhi of suchness, and space-like connate bodhicitta in the manner of abiding [in these yogas] in a nonabiding way, the conceptions about antagonistic factors, the conceptions about remedial factors, the conceptions about true reality, and the conceptions about a fruition are relinquished in their entirety.[192] Having attained the state of the equality of the three times, there will not be any abiding in anything whatsoever at all.[193]

In sum, for Maitrīpa, the approach of utter nonabiding is the supreme one in both the Pāramitāyāna and the Vajrayāna, being nothing other than the direct realization of mind's ultimate true nature: the nondual and luminous great bliss of mahāmudrā without any clinging and reification.[194]

(3) As a technical term, "unity" (*yuganaddha*) is usually a tantric expression, referring to the fifth and final stage of perfection-process practices in the *Guhyasamājatantra* literature according to its commentarial tradition in Nāgārjuna and Āryadeva. In this specific context, unity stands for the inseparable union of the third and fourth stages—illusory body and luminosity. In more general terms, unity refers to the unity of the emptiness endowed with all supreme aspects (object) and immutable great bliss (subject), the unity of connate bliss (means) and the emptiness of luminosity (prajñā), or the unity of emptiness (prajñā) and great

compassion (means).[195] However, in his typical fashion of freely employing sūtric and tantric terminologies in both contexts, Maitrīpa discusses the notion of "unity" from both a tantric and a nontantric Madhyamaka point of view (in the sense of the unity of dependent origination and emptiness).[196]

In Maitrīpa's *Illumination of Unity*—his text that is specifically dedicated to the term "unity"—dependent origination is first equated with nonarising and the lack of any nature, adding that whatever appears is thus changeless purity, and that yogīs who realize this are not separated from supreme bliss. Thus, without any arising or ceasing, being or nonbeing, the unity of nonarising and dependent origination keeps manifesting.[197] The nonconceptual unity of emptiness and compassion is the natural unity of emptiness and lucidity (Skt. *prakāśa*). This is the direct realization of the native emptiness that is endowed with all supreme aspects. Thus, in a nontantric context, Maitrīpa here identifies three ways to speak of unity, which can be matched with ground, path, and fruition: the unity of emptiness (nonarising) and dependent origination (the basic ground or view), the unity of emptiness and compassion that cannot be created by thoughts (the practice of bodhisattvas), and the natural unity of emptiness and lucidity, which is the fruition that consists of the realization of native emptiness endowed with all supreme aspects.

The last stanza of *An Illumination of True Reality* identifies its purpose as all beings coming to realize unity, which is discussed in the text as follows. Ordinary beings' perceptions are said to be like what people with blurred vision see,[198] while yogīs with pure vision see only the sky of true reality without removal or creation. If the purport of the middle in Madhyamaka were superior to other tenets such as Yogācāra only by virtue of its relinquishment of the four extremes, the same would go for Yogācāras because they know a cognition that is free from the four extremes. Thus the nature of true reality, as well as the three kāyas, is to be utterly unborn yet inseparable from dependent origination, and Maitrīpa explicitly refers to the Buddha and Nāgārjuna as the authorities on that. After briefly referring to the tantric notions of "self-blessing" and "luminosity" as the means to avoid the view of the extreme of extinction, he says that buddhahood is accomplished through the effortless path without any attachment to the fruition, true reality, or remedies, thus linking his Madhyamaka here with the relinquishment of conceptions in the sūtric *Avikalpapraveśadhāraṇī*.[199]

Though *Twenty Stanzas on the Mahāyāna* is a mostly tantric text, it also explains unity as the unconditioned, characteristic-free, native kāya endowed with all supreme aspects, the true reality that is free from the four extremes, and emptiness and compassion inseparable. In that vein, stanza 17 says that emptiness is simply another name of compassion, emphasizing that these two are a natural unity, not two different things that are somehow joined:

> We don't speak of them as something put together
> If we are speaking about them, it is as a unity

A Compendium of the Purport of Empowerment says on the meaning of the fourth empowerment that, according to some, it is the prajñā-jñāna [empowerment] itself, which has the form of the natural state, the form of any modulations of the natural state, the character of natural arising, and the nature of the pure continuous flow of nondual unity.[200] As the last explanation of "mental nonengagement" in *In Support of Mental Nonengagement* says, "the continuous flow of nondual unity" refers to "the inconceivable state of luminosity and self-blessing—the awareness that is the continuous flow of the nondual unity of emptiness and compassion inseparable."[201] As mentioned before, *A Commentary on the Five Seals of the Tathāgatas* also speaks about "the continuous flow of nondual unity" and explicitly identifies this as the supreme Madhyamaka: "The Mādhyamika tenet . . . of the awareness that has the nature of not abiding anywhere at all and is the continuous flow of effortless nondual unity is superior."[202]

The Illumination of Great Bliss says that the nonduality of the two realities—emptiness and the seeming reality of yogīs—is to be established. Once yogīs, through tantric yoga and submerged in bliss, have reached the state of unity, beings' welfare is their prime concern. This true reality has the character of prajñā and means, and once mantra practitioners have gained realization through their union, they are delighted by way of the yoga of nonabiding. Since great bliss is sheer dependent origination, it is neither an existent nor emptiness, and its manifestation in the form of deities is naturally without any nature of its own.

Similarly, in terms of beings' welfare being linked to the attainment of the state of unity, *Eradicating Bad Views* says that in nonlearners, such as Buddha Śākyamuni, who have cast off any thoughts about remedies, true reality, and the fruition (as per the *Avikalpapraveśadhāraṇī*), their uninterrupted accomplishment of the welfare of sentient beings unfolds naturally through the impetus of their former aspiration prayers and the effortless yoga of unity.[203]

Maitrīpa's *Pith Instructions on the Four Mudrās* says that the fourth empowerment is the unity as the essence of dependent origination that is not different from the three ecstasies whose nature is the prajñā-jñāna empowerment. Mahāmudrā is the unity that is unborn, free of perceiver and perceived, of all afflictive and cognitive obscurations, as well as of all extremes and even a middle. Being all-pervading, immutable, and omnipresent, it is perfect buddhahood in a single instant, which lacks any division into the four moments or the four ecstasies.[204]

Though *Five Stanzas on the Love between Means and Prajñā* does not explicitly mention the term "unity," its theme is clearly the inseparable union of emptiness and dependent origination, which is symbolized by the bride and bridegroom couple.[205]

Given Maitrīpa's above explanations of unity that link them with Madhyamaka, it is no surprise that among his disciples, Sahajavajra, in his commentary on Maitrīpa's *Ten Stanzas on True Reality*, explicitly and repeatedly speaks of "the suchness of unity" and "the Madhyamaka of unity," declaring that both are realized through the pith instructions of pāramitā adorned with the pith instructions of the true guru. He also repeatedly defines true reality as the unity of the two realities or of dependent origination and emptiness, adding that true reality is the unity of arising and nonarising, not just nonarising.

Sahajavajra's *Synopsis of Positions*, in stanzas V.35–43 of its Madhyamaka section, similarly explains "unity" as the unity of the two realities and of dependent origination and being unborn. He also equates this unity with many terms that are usually (though not exclusively) given as synonyms of emptiness in texts such as the *Madhyāntavibhāga*, including suchness, dharmadhātu, the true end, nirvāṇa, signlessness, and prajñāpāramitā. In stanzas VI.29–35 of the mantra section, Sahajavajra glosses "the unity that is completely without effort" as the lack of self, suchness, the world's diversity, means, compassion, thought-free, the supreme of all aspects, without any aspect, beyond the senses, the character of being and nonbeing yet devoid of any being and nonbeing, pure of the four extremes yet based on the four extremes,[206] and great bliss without any attachment and superimpositions. Since it is not matter, it is to be self-experienced, but without any knower or anything to be viewed. It is formless, immutable, and without any kind of extinction because it is the source of the arising of seeming reality. Furthermore, it constitutes the indestructible connate of all phenomena, native ecstasy, and self-arising self-blessing.

Vajrapāṇi's *Guruparamparākramopadeśa* frequently uses the term "unity," but only in its section on the Vajrayāna.[207] There, Vajrapāṇi speaks of "the unity of luminosity and emptiness," "the unity of thought and nonthought," and "the unity of experience and emptiness (the nonduality of emptiness and compassion and of means and prajñā—not abiding in the two extremes)," and equates unity with nondual wisdom, connate ecstasy, and the wisdom of effortless mahāmudrā. Vajrapāṇi's commentary on the *Heart Sūtra* explains a large part of this sūtra through a number of interlinked templates of sets of four, including Saraha's tetrad of symbolic terms (minding, nonminding, being unborn, and being beyond mind) and four kinds of nonabiding: the nonabiding of unity, the nonabiding of emptiness, the nonabiding of equanimity, and the nonabiding of discontinuation.[208]

Two commentaries on two of Saraha's major dohās by *Ajamahāsukha, a student of Vajrapāṇi, explicitly link all three of Maitrīpa's key terms—"mental nonengagement," "nonabiding," and "unity"—and also speak of the four types of nonabiding. *Ajamahāsukha's *Dohakoṣahṛdayārthagītāṭīkā* on stanza 18 of Saraha's "People Dohā" says this:

> The highest yogīs say that medium yogīs [just] label wisdom with names. The inseparability of illusion-like minding and mental nonengagement is the sheer nonabiding of unity. That which is nonminding and not to be engaged mentally is the nonabiding of emptiness. That which is unborn and unceasing is the nonabiding of equanimity. Due to not being touched by mind and being inconceivable, it is the nonabiding of discontinuation.

> These [kinds of] nonabiding are inseparable from mental nonengagement. Therefore, [Saraha speaks of] those who are capable of uniting those two. The three forms of saṃsāra and the three [kinds of] nirvāṇa[209] are miraculous creations of mind and wisdom, respectively.[210]

On stanza 27 of Saraha's "King Dohā," *Ajamahāsukha's *Dohakoṣanāmacaryāgītiṭīkārthapradīpa* comments that the correct view consists of understanding the nonabiding of unity—the inseparability of bliss and emptiness, which is also the unity of appearance and emptiness:

> By being thus united, bliss and emptiness are identified. The nonappearance [of real entities] in this state of bliss is sealed with the emptiness of not mentally engaging in its characteristics: this inseparability of appearance and emptiness is the nonabiding of unity, and to understand this is the view.[211]

In sum, as this overview has made clear, Maitrīpa's key terms "mental nonengagement," "utter nonabiding," and "unity" do not refer to sheer emptiness alone but to mind's intrinsic nature that is utterly ungraspable as anything yet at the same time self-aware, luminous, and blissful. This is also beautifully expressed in Maitrīpa's *A Discourse on Dream*:

> While awakening removes the imaginary,
> it does not do away with the experience
> The character of the lucidity of real mind's diversity,
> which exists, is a magnificent experience[212]

In this vein, further key terms in Maitrīpa's works include "(great) bliss,"[213] "true reality" (*tattva*),[214] "(self-)awareness,"[215] "the inseparability of emptiness and compassion,"[216] "illumination" (*prakāśa*),[217] "mahāmudrā,"[218] and "the connate" (*sahaja*).[219]

In sum, given that only three texts in Maitrīpa's cycle on mental nonengagement mention the term "mental nonengagement" and only a single one explains it, while many of his works both within and outside of this cycle use and discuss the terms "utter nonabiding" and "unity" (often side by side), one could argue that a more encompassing label for this cycle (and his works as a whole) could be "The Cycle of Texts on Utter Nonabiding" or even "The Cycle of Texts on the Utter Nonabiding of Unity."[220]

To give a brief overview of the contents of Maitrīpa's texts, with a few exceptions (such as *Five Stanzas on the Love between Means and Prajñā* and *A Pith Instruction on Letting Cognizance Be without Projecting and Withdrawing*), they usually do not have the typical flavor and style of songs of realization. Rather, most of them are "mini-treatises" that spice up philosophical or technical discussions with more experiential statements. Often, Maitrīpa combines scholarly approaches, the radical view of the Madhyamaka of utter nonabiding and mental nonengagement, Vajrayāna doctrines (including emphasizing the importance of the guru), and the experiential language of mahāmudrā, thus arriving at blending the strata of the sūtras and the tantras.

Maitrīpa's works cover a wide range of topics. There are ten texts whose titles indicate their elucidating specific terms or topics: *An Illumination of Unity, An Illumination of Utter Nonabiding, The Illumination of Great Bliss, An Illumination of True Reality, A Discourse on Illusion, A Discourse on Dream, Six Stanzas on the Connate, Six Stanzas on the Middle, Five Stanzas on the Love between Means and Prajñā* (dependent origination and emptiness), and *In Support of Mental Nonengagement*. Three are doxographical works, ranging from the Śrāvakayāna to the Vajrayāna: *A Jewel Garland of True Reality, Pith Instructions on True Reality Called "A Dohā Treasure,"* and *Taking the Pith Instructions of the Philosophical Systems as the Path* (elements of doxography are also found in a number of other texts).[221] Three works are about conventional practices in the Mahāyāna and Vajrayāna: *Eradicating Bad Views*, its commentary, and *A Compendium of Beginner Activity*. Another three texts discuss the details of tantric empowerments: *A Compendium of the Purport of Empowerment, A Compendium of the Procedures of Empowerment*, and *Instructions on Empowerment*. Two works explain the five tathāgatas and the seals of Akṣobhya and Vajrasattva: *A Commentary on the Five Seals of the Tathāgatas* and *The Five Aspects (of Vajrasattva)*. Two texts teach on all four mudrās (*Twenty Stanzas on True Reality* and *Instructions on Empowerment*) and two on mahāmudrā alone (*Ten Stanzas on True Reality* and *A Pith Instruction on Letting*

Cognizance Be without Projecting and Withdrawing). *Twenty Stanzas on the Mahāyāna* centers around the four kāyas (with the "native kāya" being foremost), and *Five Stanzas on Penetrating Insight* discusses "the buddha within."[222]

A number of Tibetan sources identify the topics of the texts in Maitrīpa's cycle in various ways. According to *Butön's Record of Teachings Received*,[223] *In Support of Mental Nonengagement* eliminates flaws with regard to the term "mental nonengagement." *Eradicating Bad Views* teaches the activities of beginners. *A Jewel Garland of True Reality* presents the common view, *Six Stanzas on the Middle* the view of mantra, *Six Stanzas on the Connate* the conduct, *A Discourse on Dream* the view by way of example, and *A Discourse on Illusion* the conduct by way of example. *An Illumination of Utter Nonabiding* ascertains the meaning of the view, and *Ten Stanzas on True Reality* the meaning of the conduct. *An Illumination of Unity* teaches the inseparability of prajñā and means, *Five Stanzas on the Love between Means and Prajñā* the inseparability of appearance and emptiness, *Five Stanzas on Penetrating Insight* the inseparability of buddhas and sentient beings, and *The Illumination of Great Bliss* that creation and perfection are not different. *An Illumination of True Reality* explains the means of realization of the three kinds of persons, and *Twenty Stanzas on the Mahāyāna* the means of meditation of the three kinds of persons. *Twenty Stanzas on True Reality* discusses the three kāyas, *A Commentary on the Five Seals of the Tathāgatas* considers deity yoga and so on, *Pith Instructions on True Reality Called "A Dohā Treasure"* discusses the common views and the mantra view, and *The Five Aspects (of Vajrasattva)* examines the meaning of all phenomena being pure. *A Compendium of the Purport of Empowerment* explains the purpose of empowerment, *A Compendium of the Procedures of Empowerment* presents the practice of empowerment, and *Instructions on Empowerment* distinguishes good and bad empowerments.

According to Padma Karpo,[224] *A Jewel Garland of True Reality* teaches the common philosophical system, *Pith Instructions on True Reality Called "A Dohā Treasure"* applies its meaning to mantra, and *In Support of Mental Nonengagement* or *An Illumination of Nairātmyā* rebuts disputes.[225] *Eradicating Bad Views*, its commentary, and *A Compendium of Beginner Activity* were composed in order to counteract contempt for the means.

Instructions on Empowerment, A Compendium of the Purport of Empowerment, A Compendium of the Procedures of Empowerment, and *The Purity of Empowerment* teach that the path of mantra is connected to empowerment. *A Commentary on the Five Seals of the Tathāgatas, Five Stanzas on the Love between Means and Prajñā*, and *Five Stanzas on Penetrating Insight* were composed for the sake of sealing. *Six Stanzas on the Middle* and *Six Stanzas on the Connate* were taught to differentiate the view of unity, and *Twenty Stanzas on the Mahāyāna* and *Twenty Stanzas on True Reality* to explain the unity that involves that view. *The Illumination of Great Bliss* and *An Illumination of Unity* teach utter nonabiding. *A Discourse on Dream* and *A Discourse on Illusion* join the progressive stages of the view with examples. *Ten Stanzas on True Reality* and *An Illumination of True Reality* summarize profound actuality, and *An Illumination of Utter Nonabiding* teaches the subtle distinctive features of the profound. Furthermore, the texts that make the unrealized realized[226] are *A Commentary on Half a Stanza on True Reality* (text 73; Maitrīpa's own two lines as root text and his autocommentary), Sahajavajra's *A Synopsis of Positions* (text 17), and Sahajavajra's *A Commentary on "Ten Stanzas on True Reality"* (text 46).[227]

To briefly introduce these texts individually, according to Padma Karpo and BKC,[228] Maitrīpa composed the triad of *Eradicating Bad Views* (text 19), its commentary (text 20), and *A Compendium of Beginner Activity* (appendix 1) in order to counteract contempt for the means and to teach the existence of conventional conduct. BKC also provides the following report on the background for the composition of these texts:

> The mighty adept [Maitrīpa] had exclusively requested nothing but Śrī Śavaripa's pith instructions and only taught the view of utter nonabiding. At that time, some denigrated him, saying: "Though it is said that Maitrīpa's view is high, he does not teach any dharma conduct based on the scriptures. Therefore he seems to disregard [the aspect of] means. Given that, his is the view of extinction and hence a bad view." At that time, the former tīrthika *Śāntakāryanivāraṇa[229] was reborn as the brahman paṇḍita called Gaganagarbha[230] in Bodhgayā. He was learned in Madhyamaka and resided at *Vimalaśrī.[231] He approached the mighty adept [Maitrīpa] and said: "My friend,

> [some] keep saying that your view is bad. In order to dispel such denigration, I request you to compose a treatise that is a compendium of initial activity." Faced with this [request, Maitrīpa] composed *Eradicating Bad Views*, its autocommentary *A Recollection*,[232] and *A Compendium of Beginner Activity*.[233]

In this vein, Mathes says that *Eradicating Bad Views* "deals with one of the greatest dangers of mahāmudrā practice; the possible cultivation of bad views such as that one does not need to engage in generosity and the other first five perfections, which in this text go under the name of 'initial activity' . . . From the extensive biography of Atiśa we know that Maitrīpa composed the *Kudṛṣṭinirghātana* together with the *Svapnanirukti* and the *Māyānirukti* in the monastery of Vikramaśīla in order to atone for a transgression he was accused of by Śāntipa, Maitrīpa having been seen secretly carrying alcohol for a yoginī practice."[234]

As mentioned before, Maitrīpa's works feature his unique way of blending the mainstream sūtra teachings of the Mahāyāna with tantric elements and the oral instructions of the mahāsiddhas, prominently among them the notion of "mental nonengagement." Naturally, such an approach raised some controversies. Wallis elaborates on the tensions between the conventions of more institutionalized forms of Buddhism and Maitrīpa's unconventional mahāsiddha background by referring to a statement by Tāranātha that some people did not believe in Maitrīpa's teachings on mental nonengagement:

> This statement suggests that it is not only the non-controversial nature of the *ādikarma* that is at stake in the *Kudṛṣṭinirghātana*, but the acceptability of Advayavajra's teachings as a whole. The concept of "non-attentiveness" (*amanasikāra*) mentioned here, for example, constitutes a principal doctrine of Advayavajra. Because of the outright contradiction of *amanasikāra* to the term *manasikāra*, a concept of utmost importance and unquestioned exactitude in the earliest Buddhist literature, Advayavajra's teaching sounds, to the conventionally trained ear, scandalous, not to mention controversial, as a Buddhist doctrine. But by refuting this view of his central teaching's problematic nature

> "in accordance with the prescriptions for the *ādikarma*," Advayavajra is practicing an ancient prerogative of Buddhist teachers: establishing an innovation on the foundation of tradition. As we will see, the *ādikarma* consists largely of the cultivation of the six perfections as known from the *Prajñāparāmitā*, by means of a daily practice known from the *tantras*, i.e., involving rituals employing *mantras, mudrās, maṇḍalas*, and so on. In its blending of ideas and rituals stemming from mainstream Mahāyāna and Vajrayāna, Advayavajra's *ādikarma* thus conforms easily to the *mantrayāna* form of Buddhism that was being taught in the educational-monastic institutions of late medieval India. The less transparently Buddhist notions of *amanasikāra, mahāmudrā, sahaja*, and *yuganaddha*, founded as they are on the *ādikarma*, are thus rendered more acceptable as Buddhist doctrines.
>
> The audience being addressed by Advayavajra in the *Kudṛṣṭinirghātana*, following this interpretation, is the skeptical ones referred to by Tāranātha as those who "did not believe him." The very fact that Advayavajra recorded his teachings in written form at all is a significant clue in this regard. A shared feature of the assorted group of teachers classed as *mahāsiddhas* is the insistence on direct, extra-linguistic, preconceptual realization, and doubts concerning the value of the "analytical-inferential" approach informing the writing, reading, and debate of texts. An additional divergence from the spirit of the *mahāsiddhas'* teachings, is the fact that Advayavajra wrote the *Kudṛṣṭinirghātana* in scholarly Sanskrit rather than the Apabhraṃśa of the *dohās*. All of this, in brief, points to the *ācaryā*-s of the monastic-educational institutions as the targeted readers of the text. As a former *ācārya* himself, with its concomitant mastery of all the marks of learning, Advayavajra served as an ideal link between the "mountain man" and the "professor."[235]

Thus Wallis summarizes the general and specific purposes of Maitrīpa's *Eradicating Bad Views* as follows:

> Advayavajra, in prescribing the *ādikarma* in the rhetorical manner that he does, is aiming to accomplish several aims. These

> can be grouped under two broad concerns. The first is institutional in nature, the second, ritual. First, Advayavajra seems to be creating a bridge between the antinomian, extra-monastic forms of Buddhist practice that were gaining influence in his day, and the established institutional structures that had, for centuries already, represented the norm for Buddhist learning and practice. This reconciliatory project required him to argue for the legitimization of certain ritual and doctrinal innovations that were, in fact, divergent from established practices and views. Second, in his prescriptions for the *ādikarma* itself, Advayavajra aims to establish a clear relationship between preliminary training and expert accomplishment. He connects this concern with the first by founding unconventional expertise on conventional training. The strategy employed by Advayavajra in this regard is to prescribe the *ādikarma* not merely as "preliminary," as is generally the case, but as "primary," in the sense of a continuously constituted foundation. In so doing, Advayavajra presents what he holds to be the necessary conditions for ritual efficacy. Finally, in the *Kudṛṣṭinirghātana*, Advayavajra shares the basic twofold concern of all liturgicists: to define a world, and to create a blueprint for the formation of a specific type of practitioner, the person who inhabits that world. The *ādikarma*, as both text and practice, is the place where world and person become mutually constituted.[236]

In stanza 5 of his *Eradicating Bad Views*, Maitrīpa defines "initial activity" (*ādikarma*) as the first five pāramitās, with the sixth, the chief pāramitā of prajñā representing their nature. Maitrīpa uses this term "initial activity" frequently (sixteen times) in this text and, in its concluding stanzas, explicitly refers to the entire work as "initial activity" and "the procedure of initial activity." By contrast, the expression "eradicating bad views" is mentioned only once—in the opening stanza—when Maitrīpa brings these two expressions together by saying that the way in which bad views are eliminated is exactly by performing this initial activity.

The first part of the text discusses the reasons for and the purpose of the initial activity of bodhisattvas on the path (even those who engage in the advanced Vajrayāna discipline of the conduct of a lunatic) in order to avoid the trap of nihilism (obviously the chief "bad view" addressed here). In that vein, even buddhas are said to perform what is called "initial activity." In their case, however, this refers to their promotion of the welfare of sentient beings that unfolds naturally through the ongoing impetus of their former aspiration prayers and their effortless yoga of unity.[237]

The second part describes the practical details of the specific activities that are to be performed by bodhisattvas throughout the day, beginning with the preliminary practices of taking refuge, vows for monastics and lay bodhisattvas, avoiding the ten nonvirtuous actions while engaging in the ten virtuous ones, and cultivating the four immeasurables. This is followed by instructions on how to prepare for and visualize a maṇḍala with the buddhas of the five families; worship paintings, volumes, statues, and such; make sacred clay images; build caityas (stūpas); and dedicate and rejoice in merit; as well as other daily activities related to eating, reciting, reading, and going to sleep. Finally, Maitrīpa explains the meaning of the word *upāsaka* through the meanings of its four syllables.

As its title says, *A Commentary on the [Initial] Passage of "Eradicating Bad Views"* (text 20) is not a full commentary on text 19 but provides only brief glosses on Buddhist path learners and the nonlearners (buddhas) who are mentioned at the beginning of *Eradicating Bad Views*. Learners are said to dwell in the causal state, while nonlearners remain in the fruitional state and the state of promoting the welfare of sentient beings. The text mainly discusses the causal state, which is divided into the states of intention, application, and having attained power.

BKC reports the following story about the origin of *An Illumination of Unity* (text 21).[238] A householder who had killed his father and brothers was seeking redemption by asking a number of Buddhist monks how to remedy his misdeed. Finally, he met Maitrīpa, who prescribed eating human corpses, enjoying waste products, staying alone in charnel grounds, roaming the cities of hungry ghosts, begging for alms, transgressing proper behavior, and doing what he does not like to do. Then, Maitrīpa blessed him and composed this text. After three years of following Maitrīpa's guidance, that householder attained siddhi.

As one of the typical examples of Maitrīpa's blend of sūtra and tantra, this text discusses the originally tantric notion of "unity" (*yuganaddha*) from a Madhyamaka point of view.[239] In this vein, a brief commentary on this text in BKC adds that one needs to know the two ways in which unity appears: either connected or not connected to empowerment.[240] Maitrīpa first establishes his view in the first four-and-a-half stanzas, equating dependent origination with nonarising and the lack of any nature, in the sense that whatever appears is thus changeless purity. The remaining stanzas begin by saying that yogīs who realize this are not separated from supreme bliss. Though there is nothing to adopt or to relinquish, conventional reality remains functional. Without any arising or ceasing, being or nonbeing, the unity of nonarising and dependent origination keeps manifesting. The nonconceptual unity of emptiness and compassion is the natural unity of emptiness and lucidity. This is the direct realization of the native emptiness that is endowed with all supreme aspects, serving as the worship of all buddhas. No matter what they do, the conduct of those immersed in this realization is enhanced by it.

Pith Instructions on True Reality Called "A Dohā Treasure" (text 22) is neither contained in the **Advayavajrasamgraha* nor available in Sanskrit. The text represents a brief versified summary of Maitrīpa's *Jewel Garland of True Reality* (text 34), likewise discussing the three yānas, the four Buddhist schools, and their subdivisons, with the Madhyamaka of utter nonabiding as the supreme one.[241] However, while the *Jewel Garland* only briefly refers to the Mantrayāna without commenting on it, the last three stanzas of this text also contain brief tantric teachings, primarily based on the practice of karmamudrā, using bliss as a skillful means.

The context in which Maitrīpa composed his *Five Stanzas on the Love between Means and Prajñā* (text 23), which discusses the natural union of dependent origination and emptiness, is described in BKC as follows:

> The brother and the sister of the connate that is primordial,
> abandoning the shame of perceiver and perceived, united
> By that, the son of self-arising wisdom arose on his own
> Therefore this is an entirely unprecedented wonder indeed
>
> The great venerable Maitrīpa saw the following. Worldly couples do not give up loving each other as long as they are not

> separated, the satisfying bliss of loving each other arises, and finally, a son is born in dependence on both. Likewise, the ground consists of the impossibility [of the two components] of connate unity [dependent origination and emptiness] giving up each other. At the time of the path, the two play with each other as the two lovers of uniting bliss and emptiness. The fruition is characterized by their unity having been accomplished. [Having seen this,] he composed the *Premapañcaka*.[242]

BKC[243] introduces *An Illumination of Utter Nonabiding* (text 24) with a short summary of the view and the meditation:

> Because nonabiding constitutes the view,
> it gets rid of all superimposition and denial
> As mental nonengagement is the meditation,
> the native basic nature is realized through it

Following this, the circumstances of Maitrīpa teaching this text are described as follows. While he was meditating, two yoginīs arrived and sat down without bowing. Maitrīpa said: "Ladies, it is the way of noble people to bow down." The yoginīs replied:

> Oh intelligent one, if you have such arrogant pride
> because you are the renowned brahman Maitrīpa
> who is learned in the five fields of knowledge,
> since scholars seized by the evil spirit of tenets
> always engage in commenting in prideful ways,
> you no doubt suffer for a long time in saṃsāra

Then, Maitrīpa ate from a decomposed and rotten human corpse, full of maggots and flies, threw up, and transformed the vomit into food. Next, he stripped down naked, went to town and other places, and returned to the two yoginīs, who said:

> He is one who enters the blessings
> of the ḍākinīs as well as the yakṣas[244]

The bodies of yoginīs do not abide
If cognition is nonabiding, it's the best yoga

Maitrīpa answered:

Within a cloudless sky, it is impossible to rain
To a mother without father, a child is not born
A fruit that lacks any seed will not come forth
If freedom from the two extremes is not known through
realization,
conduct without destruction and harm will not occur
Creating differences, why do you think so inanely?

The two yoginīs declared:

Hey, you vīra who has mastered the dharmakāya,
as all appearances and sounds are the dharmakāya,
you have mastery over enjoying whatever appears
Unborn lord, glorious mighty adept of great bliss,
nonabiding protector of beings, please explain it![245]

Thereupon, in the local Khasarpaṇa[246] temple Maitrīpa composed *An Illumination of Utter Nonabiding* for the two yoginīs, the king, bhikṣus, dharma kings, and so on.

This text says that mind's utter nonabiding is the greatest wealth of Buddhists, but only if it is coupled with promoting the welfare of beings in an effortless way. Any notions of negation, affirmation, arising, and extinction represent the ideas of stupid people. With all reference points abandoned, even mind's self-awareness cannot be reified as existent, be it in meditative equipoise or thereafter—mind is without any findable nature of its own. The dependent origination of phenomena by way of native self-awareness is inconceivable—this is what is referred to as "emptiness," which is, however, not some kind of extinction. The seed and fruition of nonabiding are genuine, while those of contrivance are not. As for phenomena arising dependently through self-awareness, mind as such, its emptiness, and its diversity[247] represent the sambhogakāya, the dharmakāya, and the nirmāṇakāya, respectively.

Six Stanzas on the Connate (text 25) is introduced by BKC with the following stanza:

> The connate that constitutes the primordial unity,
> ascertained through reasoning, represents a tenet
> Made a living experience by means, it is great bliss
> Maitrīpa's text, few in words, clear in meaning, is a delight[248]

In the text, true reality—the connate—is taught to be free from permanence and extinction, affirmation and exclusion, existence and nonexistence. Yogīs of true reality overcome all superimpositions in their mind, no matter how they may appear. The uncontrived connate is the realization of bliss without attachment, in which saṃsāra's diverse phenomena appear as gurus.

Six Stanzas on the Middle (text 26) is introduced by BKC by saying that Maitrīpa's intention to compose it was the following:

> All phenomena abide primordially as the middle—
> thus the Victor taught in just the way he saw this,
> discriminating based on various beings to be guided
> It is my delight to explain his approach a little bit
>
> Thus it was for the proponents of philosophical systems, who each maintain that their own philosophical system represents the middle, that this treatise teaching their differences was composed.[249]

Accordingly, the text explains how the "middle" as the proper view is understood by the two Yogācāra approaches of Aspectarians and Nonaspectarians and the two Madhyamaka approaches of illusion-like nonduality and the utter nonabiding of all phenomena, with the latter—as Maitrīpa's own standard approach—presented as the supreme one. The last stanza describes this approach by combining it with the Vajrayāna notions of "having the character of the deity" and "great bliss."

According to Tipi Bumlabar, *In Support of Mental Nonengagement* (text 27) was composed in order to refute various objections. Probably the same author concretizes these objections in the introduction to the text in BKC,[250] saying that there were disputes about this hard-to-fathom expression "mental nonengagement" in terms of it supposedly exhibiting linguistic flaws, flaws in meaning, and even discord with the Buddhists' own texts. Therefore, he says, Maitrīpa justifies the term by means of linguistics, scriptures, reasonings, examples, and pith instructions. Indeed, as explained in more detail before, Maitrīpa establishes the flawlessness of "mental nonengagement" and its various meanings by combining a range of Indian scholarly approaches, the via negativa of Madhyamaka, and the positive descriptions of immediate meditative experience couched in the language of mahāmudrā and the Vajrayāna, which is so typical of many of his works. Maitrīpa initially presents some grammatical considerations of the term *amanasikāra* and then traces it back to both the sūtras and tantras. He rejects the idea that mental nonengagement is a nonimplicative negation but supports it being considered as an implicative negation. The text ends with two special etymologies of *amanasikāra*. (1) *A-manasikāra* is the (correct) mental engagement (*manasikāra*) in the letter *a* (engaging in all phenomena being primordially unborn and lacking any nature). (2) Since *a* stands for luminosity and *manasikāra* for self-blessing, *amanasikāra* is the pure awareness that is characterized by their nondual inseparable unity (or the unity of prajñā and compassion).

According to the introduction of *Five Stanzas on Penetrating Insight* (text 28) in BKC, Maitrīpa composed this text out of the wish to explain mahāmudrā (the experience of the actuality of the fourth empowerment), it being indivisible by thoughts of perceiver and perceived, and the experience of the suchness of unity. This is followed by an additional stanza:

> After the yogī who is referred to as "Advayavajra"
> withdrew all thoughts of dualistic clinging into the expanse
> and proceeded to see the state of nondual wisdom,
> he uttered the five stanzas on not creating duality
> that eradicate even mere dualistic appearance's stains[251]

The text consists of both stanzas and brief prose explanations on them. Beginning with the fruition of realizing the primordial buddhahood that is innate in all sentient beings, the text then describes buddha wisdom as having effortless compassion's character and arising in dependence, being the blissful connate that is our inexpressible and nonabiding inner wealth. The last stanza considers the bodhisattvas' compassionate heart of actively taking care of all suffering sentient beings.

As mentioned before, *Five Stanzas on Love* (text 29) and *Five Stanzas on the Love between Means and Prajñā* (text 23) are two variant translations of the same text, the *Prajñopāyapremapañcaka*.

As Padma Karpo says, both *A Discourse on Illusion* (text 30) and *A Discourse on Dream* (text 31) elucidate the progressive stages of the view through examples. BKC[252] describes the specific context in which Maitrīpa composed *A Discourse on Illusion*. Performing a show for a king, an illusionist had manifested a three-storied palace made of various jewels and then burned it down, which caused the queen to weep and the crowd of people to be amazed. The brahman Kambala commented on this with two stanzas:

> Those who are mistaken like the king
> fixate upon illusion-like appearances
> Those minds that are like the queen
> are beset by emptiness's blazing fire
>
> The wise, like the illusionist, are beyond misery
> People of the mahāyāna disposition are amazed
> Not tormenting yourself with nonexistent objects,
> let go of any activity of fixating on hollow jewels![253]

The king said: "Since your reasoning will be understood by a wise person, invite the paṇḍita Ratnākaraśānti and ask him about it!" Another brahman's son was sent with the invitation, but on the road he met Maitrīpa, who then uttered *A Discourse on Illusion* in accordance with this event.[254]

Maitrīpa's work highlights the need to realize the illusion-like nature of all phenomena, which neither arise nor cease but appear from emptiness. This is also the reason why a buddha's omniscience effortlessly turns the wheel of dharma, and why buddhahood is only attained by way of properly abiding through the yoga of nonabiding (the practice of awareness). Then, all phenomena appear as sustenance, and the dharmatā of nonarising is the flow of effortless compassion. In this way, what is detrimental for worldly beings is mastered through the conduct of yogīṣ, reaching the nondual state beyond the world.

According to BKC,[255] Maitrīpa composed *A Discourse on Dream* in answer to a man dreaming of being repeatedly born and dying as different persons. Finally, in that dream, while looking at the sun and moon, the man heard a voice in the sky that said: "Let go[256] of your activities! Let go of your activities!" Upon that, the sun and moon disappeared, and his body became pure as the element of space. Maitrīpa's text briefly presents the positions of Vaibhāṣikas, Sautrāntikas, Aspectarian and Nonaspectarian Yogācāras, and Mādhyamikas propounding illusion-like nonduality and phenomena's utter nonabiding with regard to the Buddha's statement that all phenomena are dream-like. Among these, the Vaibhāṣikas and Sautrāntikas are refuted, while Yogācāra and Madhyamaka are accepted as being suitable foundations for buddha awakening. However, as usual in Maitrīpa's works, the Madhyamaka position of phenomena's utter nonabiding is considered to be supreme.

As for Maitrīpa's famous *Ten Stanzas on True Reality* (text 32), BKC[257] presents the following story of its origin. Among many mountain birds, there once lived a ruddy shelduck[258] who remembered his previous life as a god and whose mere sight had the power to cure others' illnesses. One day, a man named Āryadeva, who was learned in reasoning and had a certain disease, saw that shelduck and was healed. Then, the bird reported his previous life: "As a god, I worshipped a throne in a grove where the Buddha had taught prajñāpāramitā. As a result, a goddess bestowed the siddhi of total recall upon me and I became very learned in the five fields of knowledge.[259] Teaching treatises to the other gods, I was revered by them but then became attached to sense pleasures, stopped meditating, and lacked proper discipline. When the gods thus withheld the sense pleasures from me, I became angry and eventually was reborn as a shelduck. Therefore you should meditate!" Then, the shelduck, Āryadeva, and another paṇḍita meditated and debated together in the forest. When doubts about their individual philosophical positions arose in them, they requested Maitrīpa to settle these doubts, and so he composed this text.

Ten Stanzas on True Reality, together with its commentary by Maitrīpa's student Sahajavajra (text 46) , is regarded as one of the major Indian sources of what later became called "sūtra mahāmudrā" in Tibet.[260] The text says that the suchness that is free of existence and nonexistence, when becoming stainless due to being realized for what it is, manifests as buddhahood (stanza 1). However, it cannot be realized by any Aspectarians or Nonaspectarians (be they Mādhyamikas or otherwise), but only by the supreme Mādhyamikas who are adorned with the pith instructions of a true guru (2). The character of this Madhyamaka is awakening's own nature, once all clinging has been let go of. The cause of clinging is delusion, but this delusion has no ground at all (3). This true reality, which has no form, manifests at the same time as form. It is both the ultimate cause and fruition (4). All phenomena have this true reality's one taste, which is unobstructed yet has no ground. Their being natural luminosity is realized through the samādhi of reality as it is (the unity of calm abiding and superior insight) (5). This samādhi comes from the special engaging bodhicitta (unlike the general Mahāyāna's engaging bodhicitta), which is a nonanalytical mind. Being aware of true reality's ground, it dawns ceaselessly in every moment (6). Free of the duality of perceiver and perceived, the entire world is nondual. Even the very presumptuousness of being free of duality, in its very nature, is nothing other than natural luminosity (7). Yogīs who realize this true reality wander through the world with wide-open eyes (full awareness), not rejecting or adopting anything, as fearless as lions (8). Going beyond any worldly phenomena, such yogīs engage in "the conduct of a lunatic," acting spontaneously without any deliberate thinking and reference points while being adorned with the self-blessing of realizing mind's luminous nature (9). Thus the wise, who have insight, realize untainted and nondual true reality by letting go of any sameness and difference (clinging to nirvāṇa and saṃsāra) (10).

Presenting the context of the composition of *The Illumination of Great Bliss* (text 33), BKC[261] initially refers back to Maitrīpa's *Twenty Stanzas on True Reality* (text 41):[262]

It was the glorious Advaya Avadhūtipa,
risen from the *Tattvaviṃśikā*'s samādhi,
who entered the "Mahāsukhaprakāśa"
samādhi and proclaimed this approach

BKC continues that once a prostitute dreamt of two bhikṣus from Nālandā passing away and being reborn as her two sons, who would become great yogīs if they trained in the Mantrayāna. After nine months, she gave birth to two sons who remembered their past lives and eventually announced that they would enter monastic life. Their mother told them about her dream and encouraged them to adopt the Mantrayāna. Thus she sent them to Paṇḍita *Kalyāṇākara, who introduced them to the creation and perfection processes of the *Mahāmāyātantra*. Once they had practiced these for thirteen years, upon the request of this paṇḍita, Maitrīpa composed *The Illumination of Great Bliss* for the sake of these two yogīs.

In his text, Maitrīpa describes great bliss as the nonduality that is the true nature of entities. He speaks about the union of the creation and perfection processes, with the bliss that arises in dependence on these methods needing to be realized as the natural bliss of primordial peace, which cannot be determined as either existent or nonexistent. Maitrīpa then distinguishes the two realities[263] as "the nonarising of all phenomena" (ultimate reality) and "the delusive display of pleasure" (pure seeming reality), but says that they are really nondual. By means of practicing the creation and perfection processes, yogīs become submerged in bliss and thus see the diversity of appearances as illusion-like and nondual. The blissful mind assumes the form of the deity, while one's consort (prajñā) is called "emptiness." The union of bliss and emptiness (means and prajñā), symbolized by the tantric deity couple, is what is to be accomplished through the yoga of nonabiding. No matter how bliss may manifest, it has the character of emptiness. Yogīs with the pride of Heruka[264] take all phenomena as their gurus and fearlessly roam the earth like lions.

The basic structure of *A Jewel Garland of True Reality* (text 34) presents a detailed explanation of Maitrīpa's unique template of the three yānas, the four Buddhist schools, and the nine approaches.[265] These approaches are those of the lower, medium, and highest śrāvakas (lower and medium Vaibhāṣikas from the west and highest Vaibhāṣikas from Kashmir), the pratyekabuddhas, and the three kinds of followers of the Mahāyāna with their subdivisons: the lower (Sautrāntikas), the two medium (Aspectarian and Nonaspectarian Yogācāras), and the two highest (Mādhyamikas who are proponents of illusion-like nonduality and proponents of the utter nonabiding of all phenomena). The text extensively discusses those nine approaches through four subtopics each: (1) explanation (or analysis), (2) dhyāna, (3) stains of samādhi, and (4) view.[266]

Quite unusual, Maitrīpa says that both the Śrāvakayāna and the Pratyekabuddhayāna are explained according to the position of the Vaibhāṣikas, while the Sautrāntikas, together with the Yogācāras and Mādhyamikas, make up the Pāramitāyāna as one of the two approaches of the Mahāyāna. The other part of the Mahāyāna is the mantra approach, which can only be practiced on the basis of the Yogācāra and Mādhyamika views. However, Maitrīpa does not discuss this approach here for the following reasons: it is very profound, it is only for persons who have faith in this profound approach, and the presentation of its methods, such as the four mudrās, is extensive. For details, Maitrīpa refers the reader to his *Instructions on Empowerment* (text 42).[267]

Maitrīpa's template of the three yānas, the four Buddhist schools, and the nine approaches is also found in his **Dohānidhināmatattvopadeśa* (text 22) and *Taking the Pith Instructions of the Philosophical Systems as the Path* (appendix 2), at the beginnings of his *Caturmudropadeśa* (text 92) and his student Vajrapāṇi's *Guruparamparākramopadeśa* (text 213), in *Ajamahāsukha's *Dohakoṣahṛdayārthagītāṭīkā* (appendix 4 in volume 3), and in a Jñānavajra's **Tattvadarśanamārga* (D3715).[268] As the colophon of *Taking the Pith Instructions of the Philosophical Systems as the Path* explicitly says, the template of the three yānas, four positions, and nine approaches comes from both Śabara (Śavaripa) and Maitrīpa. However, in this text, the four positions are not presented as the standard four of Vaibhāṣikas, Sautrāntikas, Yogācāras, and Mādhyamikas (as in the *Tattvaratnāvali* and so on) but as śrāvakas, pratyekabuddhas, Yogācāras, and Mādhyamikas. Thus, this must have been Śavaripa's original template of these four, which was then adapted by Maitrīpa later. That this template originated with a practice-oriented mahāsiddha like Śavaripa is also supported by the fact that *Taking the Pith Instructions of the Philosophical Systems as the Path* is not so much a philosophical text but mainly focuses on the actual meditation instructions of the schools by blending mahāmudrā-style pith instructions with more formal analytical meditations.[269]

When comparing Maitrīpa's approaches to this template in the four texts in which he uses it, in the *Tattvaratnāvalī*, he employs it only to explain the Sūtrayāna approach. In the **Dohānidhināmatattvopadeśa* and *Taking the Pith Instructions of the Philosophical Systems as the Path*, he summarizes it and adds a bit of Vajrayāna at the end. Finally, in the *Caturmudropadeśa*, he presents it briefly at the beginning, while the bulk of the text consists of a discussion of the Vajrayāna by way of the four mudrās (karmamudrā, dharmamudrā, mahāmudrā, and samayamudrā). In its portion that is an extensive commentary on the *Tattvaratnāvalī*, Vajrapāṇi's *Guruparamparākramopadeśa* further elaborates on this template, but the bulk of the text focuses on the Vajrayāna.[270]

BKC[271] begins its introduction to *An Illumination of True Reality* (text 35) with a stanza:

> Seeing that the two final Madhyamaka approaches
> of illusion-like [nonduality] and utter nonabiding
> have a subtle difference in terms of what is negated,
> [Maitrīpa] composed the *Tattvaprakāśa* for that sake

This is followed by a short account of how the text came to be written. Once, a learned man named Prakāra from Kashmir heard the following in a dream: "In Bengal in the east, there is a jewel called 'Salu.' Not even a thousand powerful wrestlers have laid eyes on it. This jewel also pacifies any poisons in all directions. You should go there and you will find a hundred jewels. Your needs will also be accomplished according to your hopes." When he woke up, he asked a yoginī about this and she answered:

> The precious gem that is named "Maitreya"
> is adorned with the jewel Salu of Śavaripa
> It is what bestows the wishes of great bliss
> The wrestlers who are scholars have not seen this bliss

> To the glorious one vanquishing all poisons of thoughts,
> direct your prayers and extract the essence of true reality!

When he arrived in Bengal, he asked around for Maitrīpa and received the following answer: "There is someone called Maitrīpa who was at first very learned in the pure fields of knowledge. But then he went to Śrī Parvata, met the yakṣa Śavaripa, and became blessed by the māras. [Now] he is crazy." When Maitrīpa heard about this, he said:

> As for such dreams in which doubts come up,
> in these persons who entertain wrong views,
> even wrong ideas about the perfect Buddha arose
> I shall make efforts so that doubts do not arise
> in these thought-ridden childish beings' character

With great effort Maitrīpa searched and found [a solution] while on the charnel ground Rinata. Making a prayer, he composed *An Illumination of True Reality* there.

The text's opening stanza of homage to the three kāyas, whose character is prajñā and means, says that both saṃsāra and nirvāṇa arise from them. Ordinary beings' perception of the world is compared to some people seeing apparitions in the sky caused by blurred vision, while yogīs with pure vision see nothing but the sky of true reality that is without removal or creation. This is also how the welfare of beings is accomplished through the form kāyas emerging within the sky of the dharmakāya yet not being different from it. If the purport of the middle in Madhyamaka were superior to other tenets such as Yogācāra only by virtue of its relinquishment of the four extremes, the same would go for the Yogācāras because they know a cognition that is free from the four extremes. Thus the nature of true reality, as well as the three kāyas, is to be utterly unborn yet inseparable from dependent origination, and Maitrīpa explicitly refers to Nāgārjuna and the Buddha as the authorities on that. Through the path without any effort and any attachment to the fruition, true reality, or remedies, the state of buddhahood is accomplished.

In *A Commentary on the Five Seals of the Tathāgatas* (text 36), Maitrīpa discusses the well-known Vajrayāna position that the true nature of the five skandhas consists of the five tathāgatas. In other words, all sentient beings have the nature of the five tathāgatas. The first four skandhas (whose nature consists of Vairocana, Ratnasambhava, Amitābha, and Amoghasiddhi) are sealed with Akṣobhya to make it clear that they are nothing but mind. In this way, the seal of Akṣobhya represents the realization of Yogācāra emptiness: awareness without any duality of perceiver and perceived. Maitrīpa refutes that this nondual awareness (in both its Aspectarian and Nonaspectarian forms), as well as the Madhyamaka view of illusion-like nonduality, constitute the subsequent and higher seal of Vajrasattva.[272] In Maitrīpa's own approach, the seal of Vajrasattva—the true realization of emptiness as awareness's ultimate nature—refers to seeing that this awareness also lacks any pinpointable nature of its own, even being illusion-like. This emptiness of the Madhyamaka of utter nonabiding is symbolized by sealing the seal of Akṣobhya with the seal of Vajrasattva, which also includes the realization that mind's nature constitutes the inseparability of emptiness and compassion. Thus, though Maitrīpa emphasizes the notion of nondual (self-)awareness even in his supreme Madhyamaka system of utter nonabiding, he is equally adamant that this awareness lacks any findable essence and arises in dependence, just like other phenomena.

A Commentary on the Five Seals of the Tathāgatas and *The Five Aspects (of Vajrasattva)* (text 39) complement each other. Despite its name, text 36 does not describe the seals of the five tathāgatas. Its main topic consists of the specific function of the seal of Akṣobhya sealing the first four tathāgatas and the seal of Vajrasattva in turn sealing Akṣobhya, with the proper understanding and difference of these two seals being defended extensively against Aspectarians, Nonaspectarians, and the view of illusion-like nonduality. By contrast, text 39 describes the five tathāgatas as well as their female counterparts in detail, and then briefly adds that the first four tathāgatas are to be sealed with Akṣobhya (indicating their being mere consciousness), while Akṣobhya must be further sealed with Vajrasattva (indicating that consciousness has no nature of its own).[273]

In GZ, Maitrīpa's cycle of texts on mental nonengagement contains three works on empowerment: *A Compendium of the Purport of Empowerment* (text 37), *A Compendium of the Procedures of Empowerment* (text 38), and *Instructions on Empowerment* (text 42). A short appendix to the latter in BKC[274] presents the reasons why Maitrīpa composed these three texts plus two more related to empowerment:

> Since his disciples asked master [Maitrīpa] what empowerment is like by being connected with the pith instructions, he composed *A Compendium of the Procedures of Empowerment*. Since they [also] asked about the intention of empowerment, he composed *A Compendium of the Intention*[275] *[of Empowerment]*. Since they asked [further] about the practice of empowerment, he composed *A Manual for the Practice [of Empowerment]*. By distinguishing between the excellent and the poor [prajñā-jñāna] empowerment, he composed *An Ascertainment of Empowerment*.[276] Since they [moreover] asked about the purity of empowerment, he composed *The Purity of Empowerment*. [However,] manuscripts of the other [three] texts have not been found. Since *An Ascertainment of Empowerment* is a commentary on the meaning of *[The Succession of] the Four Mudrās* in "The Sixfold Pith Cycle," it came first [in this collection], and *A Compendium of the Intention [of Empowerment]* is as follows.[277]

Thus, according to this record, Maitrīpa originally wrote five texts on empowerment in response to five questions by his students. However, the **Advayavajrasaṃgraha* contains only two—*A Compendium of the Purport of Empowerment* (*Sekatātparyasaṃgraha*) and *Instructions on Empowerment* (*Sekanirdeśa*)—while GZ and CDNP also include *A Compendium of the Procedures of Empowerment*.[278]

When thus comparing Maitrīpa's three available texts on empowerment, text 37 mainly focuses on the meanings and the purposes of the four empowerments of the *niruttarayoga* tantras, while text 38 greatly elaborates on the details of the actual performance of these empowerments. Text 42 is limited to elucidating the proper way of performing and receiving the third empowerment—the prajñā-jñāna empowerment[279]—and a brief discussion of the four mudrās.

In more detail, *A Compendium of the Purport of Empowerment* (text 37) presents an overview of the entire progression of the four main empowerments in the *niruttarayoga* tantras. It mainly consists of a more extensive discussion of the first empowerment—the vase empowerment—in its six parts (the water, crown, vajra, bell, name, and master empowerments), which is followed by very brief descriptions of the three remaining empowerments: the secret empowerment, the prajñā-jñāna empowerment, and the fourth or word empowerment. The text also provides etymological derivations of these four empowerments, as well as some intriguing explanations of the symbolism of vajra and bell as ritual implements.[280]

A Compendium of the Procedures of Empowerment (text 38) follows the exact same outline of the four empowerments as text 37. However, text 38 provides the many practical details of the things that are to be done and to be recited during all those empowerments. Thus, to see the complete picture of the process of those empowerments, it is helpful to read these two texts in conjunction. Similar to text 37, the bulk of text 38 is a detailed discussion of the six parts of the vase empowerment (with the water and master empowerments taking up about 90 percent of this explanation). The secret empowerment is dealt with only briefly, while the prajñā-jñāna empowerment and the fourth one receive comparatively more attention.[281] Note also that, with some variants, the format of text 38 and many of its lines of verse to be uttered by the vajra master and the disciples during the empowerments are also found in several similar works on empowerment and maṇḍala arrangement.[282]

The Five Aspects (of Vajrasattva) (text 39) first describes the five male tathāgatas—Akṣobhya, Vairocana, Ratnasambhava, Amitābha, and Amoghasiddhi (as well as Vajrasattva)—as objects of worship and offering, located in the center and the four cardinal directions of the maṇḍala of the five buddha families. In typical Vajrayāna fashion, each tathāgata is matched with his specific hand-held sign, mudrā, skandha, affliction, buddha family, wisdom, bodily substance, season, taste, time of day, class of Sanskrit letters, and mantra. Next, Maitrīpa says that the first four tathāgatas are to be sealed with Akṣobhya in order to realize that they are nothing but consciousness. Akṣobhya must in turn be sealed with Vajrasattva so as to realize consciousness's lack of nature and the inseparability of emptiness and compassion. The text concludes with a description of the female counterparts of the five tathāgatas—Vajradhātvīśvarī, Locanā, Māmakī, Pāṇḍaravāsinī, and Tārā—located in the center and the four intermediate directions of the maṇḍala.

In *Twenty Stanzas on the Mahāyāna* (text 40), seeing the native kāya, which is the three kāyas' own nature, is taken as the appropriate practice to attain awakening: it consists of superior insight without any superimpositions. The text states several times that this kāya—true reality—and its appearances are free from the four extremes. Once the world's single taste of stainless luminosity is realized, without being afraid of thoughts, yogīs may live as they please. Afflictions are not different from awakening, but they do not arise within it. They arise from delusion, yet delusion is naturally stainless. If illusory appearances are recognized as delusion, those who realize true reality succeed. Emptiness is not realized by virtue of analysis, but through the guru. For the wise in whom thoughts have vanished, everything is bliss, but this bliss cannot be pinpointed as anything, be it emptiness, nonduality, awakening, or even bliss. Nevertheless, it is the source of all forms of the yogīs' appropriate conduct. Emptiness and compassion inseparable constitute the wisdom of awakening—they are not put together in any way but are a natural unity. By continuously meditating in that sense even when perceiving all kinds of sense objects, yogīs will become great buddhas. Unconditioned mind is the dharmakāya, realization the sambhogakāya, and variety the nirmāṇakāya.[283]

In his *Twenty Stanzas on True Reality* (text 41), Maitrīpa uses the term "prajñā" both in the sense of "consort" and "wisdom" or "realization." In the first five stanzas, he describes the prajñā that is endowed with all supreme aspects as being equivalent to the three kāyas and as the unsurpassable "mind once consciousness is gone" that is free from focal objects, peaceful, pure, and without appearance. Among the four mudrās, practitioners of lower faculties are said to rely on the karmamudrā and samayamudrā (stanza 7), those of medium faculties on the jñānamudrā (8–10), and those of highest faculties on mahāmudrā (11–19). The latter realize that all appearances are merely mind, yet mind is said to be "no-mind," and this "no-mind" is the self-awareness that is recognized by virtue of the guru. Thus unawareness becoming pure by means of suchness turns into awareness. The yogīs whose character is inconceivable embody mahāmudrā and the three kāyas. Having accomplished everything and being free from all attachment, they are always buddhas, no matter what they do.

The main topic of *Instructions on Empowerment*[284] (text 42) is the correct understanding and practice of karmamudrā based on properly receiving the prajñā-jñāna empowerment. This is followed by a brief presentation of all four mudrās, primarily discussing mahāmudrā. As the introduction in Rāmapāla's commentary on this text correctly states, it is based on Nāgārjuna's *Succession of the Four Mudrās* (text 14).[285]

After the initial stanza of homage to EVAṂ as the cause of the four ecstasies in the four moments, Maitrīpa puts forward his position that connate ecstasy is the third one in the sequence of the four ecstasies, rejecting "the forceful empowerment" (Skt. *haṭhaseka*) and "the poor empowerment" (Skt. *duḥseka*), which, from a Buddhist point of view, refer to the mistaken practices of karmamudrā (stanzas 2–6). This is followed by an interesting series of citations from a wide range of non-Buddhist texts, from Śaiva tantras to the *Mahābhārata*. Their purpose is to demonstrate how close the mistaken approaches of "the forceful empowerment" and "the poor empowerment" are to certain non-Buddhist teachings (7–18). Another argument against these approaches is that nondual mind ("the seal of Akṣobhya") is not the ultimate—that is, connate ecstasy—because it must be sealed with emptiness and compassion ("the seal of Vajrasattva") (19–20), which starts the discussion of the proper way of empowerment ("the excellent empowerment"; Skt. *suśeka*). This connate ecstasy is not truly experienced while the bindu abides in certain locations, but is experienced within fundamental awareness (21–22). Correctly understood through the true guru's instructions, different passages in the *Hevajratantra* and other scriptures accord with all this (23–24). Stanza 25 then recapitulates the approach of the "excellent empowerment."

The following presentation of the four seals begins with presenting their sequence as karmamudrā, dharmamudrā, mahāmudrā, and samayamudrā (26).[286] The four ecstasies—ecstasy, supreme ecstasy, connate ecstasy, and cessational ecstasy—are related to each mudrā (except mahāmudrā), and they individually match the four moments of variety, maturation, lack of characteristics, and consummation, respectively (27–28).

Stanzas 29–36 discuss mahāmudrā as the state of mind of not nonabiding in anything whatsoever, which is not only the very middle free from any superimpositions (that is, the Madhyamaka of utter nonabiding) but also stainless, inconceivable, and effortless self-aware wisdom. Thus, for those who realize the world to be unborn, everything is the native state, and thoughts are nothing other than nirvāṇa. Those who do not even cling to any remedies, true reality, or the fruition will realize mahāmudrā.

This portrayal of mahāmudrā is followed by a stanza about the four ecstasies in the context of the samayamudrā, in which they are arrayed in just the way as they are in the karmamudrā (37). The next stanza matches the four moments with the four mudrās (38).[287] In conclusion, Maitrīpa repeats his warning against the mistake of solely relying on a karmamudrā without understanding mahāmudrā (39). Finally, he highlights the importance of his guru Śavaripa's instructions, which are essential for correctly understanding the four mudrās and the four moments, and dedicates his merit of having presented the correct empowerment devoid of the forceful and poor empowerments (40–41).

Since *Sekanirdeśa* 29–36 not only presents mahāmudrā in the tantric context of the four mudrās but also equates it with the Madhyamaka view of utter nonabiding, it represents a prime example of Maitrīpa's approach of discussing mahāmudrā in union with the Madhyamaka view that he considers supreme, as well as his notion of "mental nonengagement." Here, it is important to understand that, as made clear in his *Amanasikārādhāra* (text 27), Maitrīpa understands "mental nonengagement" not only as mind's sheer freedom from any discursiveness and reference points but also in the sense of "self-blessing" and "luminosity" (the third and fourth among the five stages of perfection-process practices discussed in the literature related to the *Guhyasamājatantra*). In other words, in Maitrīpa's mahāmudrā approach, "mental nonengagement" stands for a direct realization of the blissful unity of luminosity and emptiness.[288] In that vein, *Sekanirdeśa* 29 opens this discussion with Maitrīpa's basic view of mahāmudrā:

Utter nonabiding in anything at all
is proclaimed to be "mahāmudrā"
Since self-awareness is stainless,
variety and so forth do not arise[289]

In terms of the practice of mahāmudrā, *Sekanirdeśa* 35 refers to its well-known approach that the recognition of the essence of any thought is mind's ultimate awakened state (mahāmudrā). Thoughts whose intrinsic connection with their true nature has not been discovered manifest as dependent originating experiences and appearances. By contrast, the direct realization of a thought's very nature is nothing other than nirvāṇa,[290] and Maitrīpa encourages our mind not to cover up its own innate nirvāṇa with futile dualistic delusion.

Finally, *Sekanirdeśa* 36 concludes with the standard mahāmudrā notion that not only do mahāmudrā meditation and realization not rely on any remedies for any thoughts and mental afflictions but the contrivances of any such remedies represent nothing but obscurations of mind's uncontrived nature. Furthermore, mahāmudrā meditation involves letting go of any ideas about what true reality is, as well as any expectation of "getting it" and trepidation of "not getting it." By virtue of that, the fruition of mahāmudrā is indeed completely free of any hope and fear:

Those who do not abide in the remedies,
who even lack attachment to true reality,
and who have no desire for the fruition,
it is they who will discover mahāmudrā[291]

A Pith Instruction on Letting Cognizance Be without Projecting and Withdrawing, "The True Secret"[292] (text 43) advocates an instantaneous "path" of nondual mahāmudrā without any stages. Mindfulness without any grasping or nongrasping allows for all appearances to dawn as the experience of great bliss. By experiencing the taste of emptiness, meditation as well as unfavorable conditions represents the realization of relaxed and inconceivable mahāmudrā. Any sense of duality arises from that and dissolves back into it, without any hope, fear, or mental engagement. Thus there is no distinction between meditation and aftermath in this direct, fresh, and pellucid experience. Within the state of unborn mind as such, what could be withdrawn and what projected?

A Commentary on the Four Mudrās, Called "Jewel Heart"[293] (text 44), an extensive explanation of Nāgārjuna's *Succession of the Four Mudrās* (text 14), is traditionally ascribed in its colophon and in NG, BA, and AIBS to Bhitakarma (a.k.a. *Kāropa), another close student of Maitrīpa.[294] According to BA,[295] *Kāropa was born as Maṇigarbha, the middle son of a king in Sahor in East India.[296] At age seven he received a prophecy from a ḍākinī, upon which he studied grammar and Vijñaptivāda with a number of teachers. At age thirty-four he was ordained as a monk at Vikramaśīla by the great Sarvāstivāda master Mitratāra. Thereafter, he studied Vinaya, valid cognition, prajñāpāramitā, Abhidharma, and all kinds of tantras with a number of great paṇḍitas. Having practiced a sādhana at Bodhgayā until he was sixty-four, he looked only sixteen when he was seventy-two. Still wishing to explain the sources of learnedness, he met the yoginī Padminī, who was meditating on prajñāpāramitā. She said this to him:

> Though buddhahood exists within them for sure,
> sentient beings who don't realize this are pitiable!
> Though they may become learned in conventions,
> if they do not realize the true reality of the mind,
> being similar to paupers who are threshing chaff,
> it is impossible for a fruition to emerge from such
>
> They may find the vidyādhara state of longevity,[297]
> but if they become attached to worldly activities,
> as they sink into the swamp of desire and hatred,
> they will not be happy but suffering will emerge
>
> Hey, son, realize your own mind and make its not being
> anything at all a living experience!
> Rely on a supreme guru and engage in efforts in the
> instructions!

Leave the eight worldly dharmas behind and set great bliss
ablaze!
Stamp this saṃsāra here with the seal of its being unborn!

Relying on this prophecy of the yoginī and two emanated boys, with a lot of riches from his father, *Kāropa went to meet the yogī Nāgapuri in the outer ocean at a distance of forty-two yojanas.[298] Nāgapuri blessed him with a gaṇacakra, and *Kāropa then studied and practiced an abundance of tantras for seventeen years. Having returned to Bodhgayā, Natekara,[299] who had been a fellow student of grammar, told him: "If you wish to meditate, go to the mighty adept Maitrīpa who has the pith instructions on mahāmudrā that cannot be meditated on!" Having received the instructions, *Kāropa went to a hermitage for seven years, training in essential reality, and later meditated in a charnel ground[300] for five years. Thereafter, he performed all kinds of conducts in the country Malla, the city Kambala, Kashmir, and elsewhere. *Kāṛopa held the instructions of nine lineages and had attained supernatural knowledges. Among his many disciples, the foremost was the yogī Nirūpa, whom *Kāropa encouraged several times to go to Tibet to benefit beings. Later, *Kāropa and his consort also traveled to Tibet and met Nirūpa there in his new body.

This brings up the role of Prajñāśrījñānakīrti/Kor Nirūpa[301] as the "translator," or rather the redactor/(re)writer, of *A Commentary on The Four Mudrās*, just as with *A Commentary Elucidating Native True Reality on "A Song That Is a Completely Filled Dohā Treasure Store"* (text 70), since the modus operandi of these two texts is clearly the same in many respects.[302]

Kor Nirūpa's complex persona is described in detail in Gö Lotsāwa's *Blue Annals*.[303] As a young boy, the Tibetan Tampa Kor[304] was initially a student of Vairocanarakṣita during the latter's sojourn in Tibet. At the age of thirteen, Kor traveled to Nepal and studied and practiced many tantric texts, such as the *Cakrasaṃvaratantra*, "The Seven Siddhi Texts," "The Sixfold Pith Cycle," and further works by Saraha (during an empowerment, he also received the name Prajñāśrījñānakīrti). When he suddenly passed away in Nepal at age nineteen, the seventy-three-year-old yogī Nirūpa, who was staying in the same house, performed the practice of his consciousness entering Tampa Kor's corpse, thus reviving it. Nirūpa's old body was cremated, and he went to Tibet with his new one, wearing Indian clothes and henceforth bearing the double name Kor Nirūpa. Once he had arrived in Tibet, he wore only Tibetan clothes and taught many tantras, dohās, and mahāmudrā there for twenty-one years, also translating numerous tantric texts on his own (thus, it could have been during that time that Nirūpa also translated or composed text 44). Gö Lotsāwa concludes his account by saying that he presented Kor Nirūpa's life story in detail because he was a great siddha but is—wrongly—not considered important by Tibetan teachers of Gö Lotsāwa's time.

In the same vein, it is noteworthy that the Eighth Karmapa Mikyö Dorje explicitly identifies Kor Nirūpa as an authentic transmitter of the dohā lineage in the tradition of Maitrīpa. As mentioned previously in the notes, he says that in Tibet there were three distinct ways of fulfilling the intended meaning of Maitrīpa's "Madhyamaka of mental nonengagement": (1) the practice that emphasizes the profound and luminous Madhyamaka of mantra, (2) the practice that emphasizes the profound Madhyamaka of the sūtras, and (3) the practice that emphasizes "the Madhyamaka of False Aspectarian Mere Mentalism."[305] The latter explains that the actual meaning of the dohās of the siddhas lies in the ultimately established, self-aware, and self-luminous cognition that is empty of perceiver and perceived. This view was represented by many in India and Tibet, such as Vajrapāṇi, Balpo Asu, and Kor Nirūpa.[306]

By contrast, some Tibetan masters as well as contemporary academic scholars accuse Prajñāśrījñānakīrti/Kor Nirūpa of being a forger of Indic commentarial literature. It is obvious that the stanzas found in *A Commentary Elucidating Native True Reality on "A Song That Is a Completely Filled Dohā Treasure Store"* (text 70; attributed to an Advayavajra) represent a version of Saraha's "People Dohā" that differs in many ways from the known Apabhraṃśa versions, the Tibetan canonical versions, and the version in text 13. Therefore, said Tibetans and academic scholars suggest that the commentary in text 70, as well as those lines in it that differ from the above versions and those that were added, was actually written by Kor Nirūpa in Tibetan rather than translated by him.[307]

While it is quite obvious that text 70 was written in Tibetan, it is not possible to decide whether it was actually composed by Kor Nirūpa, though that seems to be very likely. If he is indeed the author of the comments in text 70 as well as the phrases and stanzas not found in the canonical versions of Saraha's "People Dohā," and if the above story of his life is true, though text 70 was written in Tibetan, it can at least be said that it was an Indian master in the lineage of Maitrīpa (one of the main transmissions of Saraha's dohās) who reworked Saraha's "People Dohā" and wrote a commentary on it. However, given the lack of clear evidence one way or another, it is not possible to determine the author(s) or reviser(s) of this text or its precise textual history with certainty.

Still, it should also be noted that the mere fact that the stanzas in text 70 differ greatly from both the known Apabhraṃśa versions and the Tibetan canonical versions of the "People Dohā" does not discredit them per se, because it is well known that there are a significant number of versions of this dohā with very different lengths and contents, in both Apabhraṃśa and Tibetan, and it is impossible to identify any one of them as "the original."[308]

In any case, no matter whether one wants to consider the author of text 70 as a "forger" or not, Schaeffer rightly points out that he can also be regarded as the most creative among those who brought the "People Dohā" to Tibet, its version in text 70 often being the most evocative of the many versions of this dohā.[309] After all, in line with the fluid approach of the dohā tradition, whoever the author or redactor of text 70 may have been, he just did in a very extensive fashion what many others did as well, which is explicitly sanctioned in the opening stanzas of another commentary on Saraha's "People Dohā," *Ajamahāsukha's *Dohakoṣahṛdayārthagītāṭīkā*. *Ajamahāsukha declares that his own tradition "writes the root [text] in accordance with the explanation" and "relies solely on the awakened mind of Śrīmat Śabarapāda." In this vein, the author of text 70 seems to have relied on and conveyed the message that comes directly from an accomplished master's realization, as this was deemed appropriate for a certain audience in a certain situation.[310]

All of these considerations with regard to text 70 are equally pertinent to *A Commentary on the Four Mudrās*,[311] making it more than questionable that *Karopa was its actual author.[312] This commentary is a typical "gray text": there are many clear signs that it is not a straight translation from Sanskrit but was at least heavily redacted if not entirely written in Tibetan.[313] The passages in it that are presented as citations from *The Succession of the Four Mudrās* frequently vary from that text's Sanskrit and often also from its canonical Tibetan translations, though they are generally closer to the latter. Some passages are cited in a different order than in *The Succession of the Four Mudrās*, and, just as in the significantly expanded "root text" in text 70, there is a significant number of additional or greatly reworked passages that are not found in either the Sanskrit or the canonical translations. Thus, there are often comments on words that are only found in the canonical translations or only in the particular Tibetan version of *The Succession of the Four Mudrās* in this commentary. Generally, the text comments in the order of the words of that Tibetan version of *The Succession of the Four Mudrās* that is embedded in it.[314]

Further evidence that this commentary was composed in Tibetan includes the fact that it twice speaks of "father tantras" and "mother tantras," a typical Tibetan distinction not attested in any known Indic works. The text also contains a lengthy insertion (almost one-third of its length) that, unlike its actual commentarial sections, uses the unique Tibetan system of a multileveled outline.[315] Furthermore, there are a number of glosses and hermeneutical etymologies of technical terms that are either not possible in Sanskrit or are based on the Tibetan. Just as in text 70, there is a plethora of unidentified quotations adduced to support certain comments, many of which give the impression of being deliberately tailored to match those comments.

There are further specific terms or passages, most of which do not have any known Sanskrit equivalents, that are only found in texts 44 and 70 but nowhere else in Kg and Tg. These constitute definitive evidence that both texts are (at least for the most part) by the same author. Examples include the etymology of Tib. *'jig rten* (for Skt. *loka*, "world") by splitting it into its two components (*'jig cing rten*), and the expressions "connate appearance," "connate mind as such," "natural mind,"[316] "appearing and resounding phenomena,"[317] and "that isn't anything whatsoever"[318] as a qualifier of terms such as great bliss, emptiness, nonconceptual wisdom, nondual wisdom, dharmakāya, ordinary mind, and nonduality.[319] Finally, three in a series of quotes from Saraha's "People Dohā" in text 44 are found nowhere else but in the unique enlarged version of the "People Dohā" in text 70.[320]

To give a brief overview of the contents of *A Commentary on the Four Mudrās*, its introduction begins with the common meaning of empowerment and the mudrās in four points, followed by another five points on the dharmamudrā[321] and short general presentations of the karmamudrā and samayamudrā. It concludes with a brief explanation of the famous stanza from the *Nayatrayapradīpa* on the Mantrayāna being more distinguished than the Pāramitāyāna.

As mentioned above, the actual comments on *The Succession of the Four Mudrās* follow the unique Tibetan version of this text that is found only in this commentary, expanding numerous passages and adding further ones.[322] The commentary gives a rather detailed presentation of the sixfold vase empowerment and a much shorter one of the secret empowerment, dividing it into an outer one and an inner one. Following the order of the four mudrās in *The Succession of the Four Mudrās*, they are explained as karmamudrā, dharmamudrā, mahāmudrā, and samayamudrā. The comments on the karmamudrā are by far the longest, mainly because of extensively differentiating the correct empowerment from the forceful and poor empowerments that are to be rejected.

Toward the end of its comments on the samayamudrā, the text contains the lengthy insertion that can be considered as a greatly expanded version of its introduction (or even a text on its own), giving a general presentation of the four mudrās. Though this insertion repeats some materials from the introduction, some of them are matched in ways that differ from the introduction.[323] The location of this insertion is awkward (and probably misplaced), because it interrupts the last part of the comments on the samayamudrā as per *The Succession of the Four Mudrās*. In addition, its format is rather jumbled in that it does not have a single consistent outline throughout but contains several sections with their own separate outlines.[324]

Nevertheless, this insertion provides valuable additional details on the four mudrās. It begins with some general points on the four mudrās, followed by presentations of just the karmamudrā and mahāmudrā. Its main part starts with instructions on the reasons for positing four mudrās, followed by the bulk of more detailed presentations of the karmamudrā, dharmamudrā, mahāmudrā, and samayamudrā. Finally, there are three shorter sections on the special means (the four moments, four ecstasies, four locations, and four dharmas), the pith instructions on making the four mudrās a living experience (in the order of causal samayamudrā, dharmamudrā, karmamudrā, mahāmudrā, and samayamudrā as the welfare of others), and the way in which certainty about the instructions on the four mudrās arises.

After this insertion, the text returns to its remaining comments on the samayamudrā in *The Succession of the Four Mudrās* and ends with brief concluding remarks on all four mudrās.

A Critical Commentary on "Instructions on Empowerment"[325] (text 45) was composed by Rāmapāla, about whom not much is known. BA[326] says only that he was one of Maitrīpa's four main disciples, that he composed this commentary on Maitrīpa's *Sekanirdeśa*,[327] and that at one point he was active at Nālandā University, where he and his consort Ratnadevī were among the teachers of the founder of the Shangpa Kagyü school, Kyungpo Naljor.[328] Tāranātha's *Seven Instruction Lineages*[329] adds that Rāmapāla was born in Karṇāṭaka in a kṣatriya family, and was very learned from a young age. He studied for twelve years with Maitrīpa, and after the latter's death, spent three years in silent mourning at the stūpa *Śriguṇavān,[330] practicing one-pointedly. Once he had directly perceived essential reality in its entirety, he lived in the south promoting the welfare of sentient beings. Having received the siddhi of the sword from Mahākāla, he went to the subterranean regions through a miraculous gateway without leaving his physical from, and he was even seen in the asura realm. Among those whom he taught mahāmudrā were the younger master Kuśalabhadra, *Asitaghana, and especially Jñānamitra. Tāranātha explicitly says that among Maitrīpa's four main disciples, Sahajavajra, Divākaracandra, and Vajrapāṇi did not attain the state of a vidyādhara in their body, thus implying that Rāmapāla did attain such a state.[331] Tāranātha also states that Rāmapāla's powerful awareness consort Ratnadevī was well-known for her realization being equal to that of the mighty adept Maitrīpa himself, while Rāmapāla was known to have attained half of the status of Maitrīpa's own consort Gaṅgādharā.[332]

Following the main themes of Maitrīpa's *Instructions on Empowerment*, Rāmapāla extensively explains the correct understanding and practice of karmamudrā based on properly receiving the prajñā-jñāna empowerment while rejecting the forceful and the poor empowerments. This is followed by a presentation of all four mudrās, primarily discussing mahāmudrā.[333]

Appendix 1 is a translation of *A Compendium of Beginner Activity*, another text attributed to Advayavajra (Maitrīpa), besides *Eradicating Bad Views* (text 19), about beginner conduct or initial activity. This work is found only in BKC, and not in the **Advayavajrasaṃgraha* or Tg. As mentioned before, while *Eradicating Bad Views* is from a more general Mahāyāna point of view, *A Compendium of Beginner Activity* is written specifically from the perspective of Vajrayāna practitioners.[334]

Appendix 2 consists of a summarized paraphrase of Maitrīpa's *Taking the Pith Instructions of the Philosophical Systems as the Path*, which seems to be entirely unknown among Tibetan and other scholars. According to the text's colophon, the instructions on the three yānas, four positions, and nine approaches came from both Śavaripa and Maitrīpa, and then Maitrīpa's student Vajrapāṇi passed them on to *Ajamahāsukha.[335] The work is clearly based on Maitrīpa's *Tattvaratnāvalī* (text 34) and *Dohānidhināmatattvopadeśa* (text 22), following their template of the three yānas, four positions, and nine approaches. Different from these two texts, however, in that it does not present much philosophical discussion in terms of the four positions and their nine approaches but mainly focuses on the actual meditation instructions of each of these approaches by blending direct pith instructions familiar from a mahāmudrā context with more formal teachings on analytical meditation. Thus the text is a compendium of Śavaripa's and Maitrīpa's version of the progressive stages of meditation on emptiness (or the two kinds of identitylessness) that are well-known in different Buddhist schools.

Appendices 3, 4, and 6 present Tipi Bumlabar's extensive outlines of Divākaracandra's *An Illumination of Prajñā Wisdom* (text 16), Sahajavajra's *A Synopsis of Positions* (text 17), and Rāmapāla's *A Critical Commentary on "Instructions on Empowerment"* (text 45), respectively. Appendix 5 consists of a partial outline of *A Commentary on the Four Mudrās*.[336]

Appendix 7 offers a comparative overview of the unique fivefold classification of the creation and completion processes in a number of texts by Maitrīpa and his students.

A Note on Dohā, Vajragīti, and Caryāgīti

Nowadays, both Indian and Tibetan Buddhist songs of realization are often popularly called *dohās* or "vajra songs." However, not all songs of realization are dohās. In fact, there are three genres of Indian songs of realization: (1) dohā ("couplet"), (2) vajragīti ("vajra song"), and (3) caryāgīti ("conduct song"). The Tibetan word *mgur* (often loosely rendered as "dohā" or "vajra song") simply means "song," but over time came to refer specifically to spiritual songs of realization.

The Sanskrit word *dohā* (Apabhraṃśa *doha*, lit. "two-say") has two meanings. Originally, it indicated a distinct poetic meter of four feet in which the second and fourth feet rhyme, similar to couplets in Western poetry. Since many poems of realization were composed in that meter, *dohā* also came to be a general designation for a genre of rhapsodies, emotionally charged stanzas, and spiritual aphorisms. Such stanzas could also contain or be entirely composed in other meters but would still generically be referred to as dohāṣ. As with our songs here, such poems were often spontaneous expressions of spiritual experiences and realizations. However, it is not certain that all dohās were actually sung, at least not from the outset; they could simply have been recited as poetry. As will be shown below, the transmission of these poems of realization was very fluid and involved constant adaptation, so sometimes melodies for certain stanzas may have been composed or changed by people other than the original composer.

In his commentary on Saraha's famous *Dohakoṣagīti* (popularly known as "People Dohā"), the Kagyü master Karma Trinlépa provides a detailed explanation of the meaning of the common title *Dohakoṣagīti* (*Dohā Treasure Song*), being a profound description of mind's native state—mahāmudrā—and how it is revealed through the path.[337]

First, *doha* (or *dvaha*) means the lack of the two extremes, nonduality, and union; thus it refers to overcoming dualistic thoughts by letting them dissolve within nonduality. At the time of the ground, mind's native state is not recognized and thus falsely appears as the duality of perceiver and perceived. This duality and the clinging to it are overcome by making path mahāmudrā a living experience, which leads to the fruition (the unity of the two *kāyas*) promoting the welfare of beings.

Second, since Sanskrit *dohā* means "being filled up" or "milking," it is similar to a container being filled by milking. Thus, since the masters are filled with the wisdom of the ultimate nature, they sing songs of such wisdom. Or being filled through milking refers to being inexhaustible. Or *dohā* indicates the overflowing of meditative experiences. In addition, the word *dohā* refers to being natural, uncontrived, and loose, the ultimate, true reality, freshness, and so on.

Just as a "treasure" (*koṣa*) is a place where many precious items are stored so that they do not disappear, mind's native state is the locus of all awakened qualities such as connate wisdom. "Song" (*gīti*) means that the instantaneous revelation of this wisdom is spontaneously set to melody from within one's experience, without hiding anything. For the sake of being easily understood by all people high and low, such songs are not constrained by prosody but sung in an ad hoc manner. Hence, they are songs that point out the treasure of the inexhaustible qualities of connate wisdom.

Vajra songs (*vajragīti*), the second genre of songs of realization, are recognizable either by the fact that their titles contain the word *vajragīti* or by being identified as sung in the context of a *gaṇacakra* (originally, vajragītis were only recited or sung at such tantric ritual feasts). Vajra songs often exhibit more ornate poetic refinement than dohās, are usually short (most of them consist of just a single stanza), and are rich in metaphors. They often evoke particular feelings, experiences, or realizations rather than just giving certain instructions.

Finally, conduct songs (*caryāgīti*) speak about the way of life ("conduct") of tantric yogic practitioners.[338] Originally, such songs were probably sung spontaneously at different occasions, but eventually they came to be standalone performance songs (often with music and dance). Usually these songs are rather short, many consisting of about five stanzas. However, they are often incorporated in a collection of such songs and accompanied by musical instruments as well as one or more dancers in richly adorned attire, symbolizing Buddhist tantric deities. Thus a tantric performance of such a cycle can last several hours or even an entire day. In this way, following their ad hoc origins, over time these songs tended to become more elaborate through such musical arrangements and choreographies.[339] The best-known historical example of this genre is a collection of fifty songs called *Caryāgītikoṣa*, which also contains the names of the *rāgas* (melodies) in which each song is to be sung. These kinds of songs are still regularly performed to this day during certain ceremonies in the Newar Vajrayāna Buddhist community in Nepal.

However, just as the songs themselves do not follow any strict pattern, the distinctions between these three genres are far from being hard and fast. For example, dohās can be sung at a gaṇacakra, and vajragītis outside of a gaṇacakra. Also, any of them can be in the dohā meter or other meters, can include more sophisticated prosodic elements, and may or may not be accompanied by music and dancing.

Who Composed These Texts and How?

It can be quite safely assumed that all the treatises and commentaries in this collection were written in Buddhist Sanskrit. However, when it comes to the songs, matters are more complicated. A few of them were probably composed in Sanskrit, such as those by Atiśa, but for most we do not know in which languages they were uttered originally. The majority of songs were definitely not composed in Sanskrit, since many of the authors did not even know Sanskrit, which was the language of the educated elite in India. For the same reason, Sanskrit would not have been a suitable medium to reach a general audience. Thus they were usually presented in local middle-Indic languages or dialects, which are generically referred to as Apabhraṃśas. Used from approximately 300 to 1200 CE, these tongues are distant predecessors of modern North Indian languages such as Bihari and Bengali, and to some extent also Assamese, Oriya, Maithili, and certain forms of Hindi. However, the fact that some dohās, caryāgītis, and vajragītis exist in old Apabhraṃśa manuscripts does not mean that Apabhraṃśa is their actual original language, close as it may be, because Apabhraṃśa refers to literary languages and not vernaculars. At present, apart from the songs in the Newar Vajrayāna tradition (which according to this tradition have always been in Newari), the vast majority of ancient Indian Buddhist dohās, caryāgītis, and vajragītis are only extant in Tibetan translations.

As for the authorship of our texts, while there seems to be greater certainty for most of the treatises and commentaries, when it comes to the songs, it is hard to say who actually composed them. First, these songs were originally spontaneous expressions of spiritual experiences and realizations as a part of the enlightened activity of great masters and, in virtually all cases, were written down only later by others. Thus it is not surprising that for many of them, especially some of Saraha's songs, there exist several versions in different languages (such as Sanskrit, Apabhraṃśa, and Tibetan) that greatly differ in content, stanza order, and overall length of the text—it can be somewhat difficult to even consider them as different versions of one and the same text. This is mainly due to many rounds of later editing and rearranging, either by commentators or in popular usage. It seems safe to assume that some of the songs as they are preserved now may not be by a single author, let alone the one to whom they are attributed at present. All of this is further evidenced by some of the anthologies of such songs in the Tengyur in that many of the songs that these collections share show more or less significant variant readings and are attributed to completely different persons.

Thus the transmission and shaping of these songs always has been fluid, similar to the way in which the songs of the medieval troubadours in Europe were passed on. That is, single lines of a stanza, entire stanzas, or blocks of stanzas may be shifted around in a given text, exchanged between different works (some songs attributed to different authors share common lines or stanzas), or removed from or inserted into preexisting songs. It is clear that almost all these songs have been rewritten and resung many times. Therefore there often seems to be no fixed wording, as the wording primarily depends on the meaning to be conveyed and thus may be shifted in different contexts and for different audiences. This is nothing unusual in an Indian context; the same approach is shown with medieval and contemporary non-Buddhist devotional songs. They can be sung with different rāgas, stanzas moved around, vocabulary changed, and dialects transposed. As Roger Jackson says,

> Indeed, we only can assert with confidence that when we examine the *Treasury* of Saraha, Kāṇha, or Tilopa, what we have before us is a later compilation by an editor who, for purposes of his own, brought together dohās or groups of dohās that had come to be associated with one or another of those names, names that might or might not once have denoted an

> actual person. In this sense, there is probably a considerable arbitrariness built in to the compilation of any single *Treasury*, and though commentators on the texts find order and meaning in their arrangement (sometimes, in fact, it is they who have arranged them!), it is quite imaginable that the texts could have been ordered in many different ways and still been found meaningful by readers.[340]

This fluid approach is also explicitly acknowledged by *Ajamahāsukha in the introduction to his commentary on Saraha's *People Dohā*:

> Others give explanations by commenting in accordance with the root of a text
> The tradition of people like me writes the root in accordance with the explanation
> This also entails not to quote the words of the scriptures of any of the piṭakas:
> there is no end to writing down the words of the scriptures of mantras and tantras
>
> Relying solely on the awakened mind of Śrīmat Śabarapāda,
> I shall write this memorandum that is a nectar drop of his speech
> for the welfare of myself and those with faith just like myself
> by summarizing nothing but the instructions on true actuality[341]

Kurtis Schaeffer says this about Saraha's *Dohakoṣa* and Avadhūtīpa's approach, which applies equally to all other songs of realization:

> The reader must know the words of Saraha despite the fact that his subject is ineffable. In an ironic twist, the power of Saraha's words is precisely their message of ineffability. This seems ultimately to debase the power of the word, and yet the final lines suggest something more; it is not the written word of the tantras that holds the power to express the inexpressible, but song itself. Much as the tales of his life tell us, the realization of the enlightened state encourages Saraha not to write another

> treatise, another commentary, but to inspire others through the medium of song, which stands above the ordinary language of treatises and tantras.
>
> It is perhaps this claim that gave the commentators on the *Treasury of Dohā Verses* license to write according to the meaning of the dohās as taught by the masters and not according to the letter. . . . This gives Advaya Avadhūti himself, and other commentators after him, the license to change, rearrange, and transform Saraha's words. In short, Advaya Avadhūti gives himself permission to "author" the words of Saraha by claiming that the real message of Saraha is not in any text of the *Treasury of the Dohā Verses* but rather in the meaning that lives in the hearts of the masters who have realized the message of the dohā.[342]

Thus this tradition explicitly permits changing and rearranging the words of Saraha and other masters, since what they convey is not found in words but only in the awakened minds of those who have already realized the nature of this mind. How this realization is conveyed to others must always depend on the unique circumstances of a living interactive situation—a teacher guiding a particular student in a particular way in accordance with the individual propensities, capacities, and obstacles of that student. Thus it can never be exactly the same for any two people and must be adapted to the situation at hand. This is clearly shown in the greatly differing stories of how certain mahāsiddhas gained realization through the verbal and nonverbal instructions of their gurus. For example, Nāropa awakened by being smacked on the forehead with Tilopa's sandal, Vīṇāpa by playing music, Tantipa by weaving, Lūhipa by eating the entrails of fish, and Kaṅkaripa by being taught to visualize his deceased wife as a ḍākinī, with the nature of bliss and emptiness being inseparable, without any substance or self.

From an ordinary or literary point of view, all this may sound like an arbitrary copy-and-paste approach of plagiarism where anything goes and things are just made up. But from the point of view of the mahāsiddhas and their commentators and editors, this approach is a clear example of what Buddhists call "skillful means." These masters obviously had a different sense of authorship and copyright; they simply used the words of the songs of realization as tools to make the points that they deemed meaningful in a given context, for a given audience, and at a given time. Thus the singing of these songs should not be understood as just a poetry reading or a musical performance but as always situated within an interactive mind-to-mind transmission between teacher and student (or an exchange between realized persons), where the songs are the vehicles through which that transmission takes place.

In that way, these songs of realization (and to some extent the other texts in this collection too) were considered more like a huge, common pool of awakened wisdom, as well as the methods to realize this wisdom, from which the entire community of commentators, editors, and practitioners felt free to pick and choose to suit their particular settings, audiences, and purposes. Thus the transmission of dohās, caryāgītis, and vajragītis is more about using individually adapted tools and methods to convey certain messages and not about preserving original literary documents. In that way, transmission is always fresh and immediate, in tune with real-life interactions between teachers and students. This means that mahāsiddhas such as Saraha are not just historical persons to be emulated; working with and singing their songs can evoke the essence of the realization of such masters—the unmediated presence of the awakened state itself—within ourselves.

The concept of transmission or lineage here is like teaching someone to bake fresh bread. It is not about preserving the specific loaf of bread that someone like Saraha baked many hundreds of years ago by handing it down wrapped up in ornate brocades through the generations, because after a few days nobody could eat such bread. Rather, it is like a hands-on transmission of Saraha's recipe that enables us to bake our own fresh bread with our own ingredients today. Just as there are different kinds of bread (and even the same kinds of bread taste differently in different bakeries), the basic recipe can and needs to be adapted to different circumstances, resources, and tastes. In this way, the fluid transmission of the songs of realization is also a vehicle for creative innovation in Buddhism, which is otherwise officially deemed inappropriate or frowned upon in the traditional framework of strictly adhering to the words of the lineage and one's own guru.

In brief, in the end it is our own true heart—our buddha nature—that expresses itself through these songs and with which we connect through singing. Besides contemplating their meaning, the purpose of singing songs of realization is to gain inspiration, receive blessings, and evoke experiences and realizations from within. Thus we go beyond a merely rational or intellectual approach, activate the element of devotion, and allow our inspiration and openness to become a vehicle for transcending our dualistic mindset.

May this book be considered a small and humble contribution to the living tradition of Mahāmudrā in general and Buddhist songs of realization in particular. May the texts here inspire and be of benefit to countless beings. May these beings realize what those songs sing about—mind's true nature of great bliss beyond any clinging and suffering.

Sarva maṅgalaṃ—May everything be auspicious!

(12) The Accomplishment of Glorious True Reality

In the language of India: *Śrītattvasiddhi*[343]
In the language of Tibet: *Dpal de kho na nyid grub pa*

I pay homage to Śrī Vajrasattva

The vajra of the awakening of a buddha
is accomplished in this life, not in others
Without body, speech, and mind being in
good condition, it won't be accomplished [1]

Without the continuous enjoyment of desire,
true reality will not come to be accomplished
The reliance upon whatever may be desired[344]
is thanks to the nondual wisdom that is pure [2]

If such is not the case, you fall into wrongness
From that, suffering arises as a matter of course
Therefore the wise ones who are blessed by
mantra engage in the preliminary for purity[345] [3]

Just as water drops become salty
if they are falling into the ocean,
if salt has entered the Milk Ocean,
it will in turn become nectar[346] [4]

Just as those who know venomous snakes'
nature are able[347] to take away their power,
in the mind streams of others, true reality
does not go beyond the state of the five[348] [5]

Furthermore, if oppressed by desire,
this very desire constitutes medicine,
just as for those tormented by poison,
that very poison is great as medicine [6] {2}

Just like fire for those burned by fire
and thorns for those pained by thorns,
so for those disturbed by the afflictions,
these very afflictions are great as nectar [7]

For example, those who know poison's nature
will not be harmed even if they ingest poison[349]
Likewise, those who know the nature of objects
will not be harmed by the enjoyment of desire [8]

Similar to the case of a lotus in the mud[350]
dwelling in mud but not being tainted by it,
those who know true reality should always
engage in desire by means of relishing it [9]

Hence, without fearing anything,
this will be enjoyed in particular
If relying on the five desirables,
siddhis will be attained swiftly [10]

Through austerities, yogic disciplines,
and fasting,[351] the elements will dry out
By having dried out, there is suffering,
and by suffering, the mind is distracted
By distraction, siddhi[352] becomes altered[353] [11]

Therefore those who strive for[354] the supreme siddhi
shouldn't engage in austerities and yogic disciplines!
In just the way there is bliss, thus receive it!
If bliss is relinquished, there exists no siddhi [12]

Therefore, in a pleasant location,
with the twelve lovely young ladies
who are endowed with large eyes,
are striking in their form and youth, [13]

and have stable, unwavering samaya
as well as noses that resemble lotuses,[355]
they frolic with great passion's taste—
supremely skillful as well as charming, [14]

these impassioned yogīs unite with them,
thus abiding in the cakra's center themselves[356]
Those who possess samaya should gather {3}
in a pure continuous stream day and night [15]

Hairs aquiver, shivering and trembling,
smiling, giggling, as well as laughing,[357]
and reaching the state of intoxication
are called "the seven that cause descent" [16]

Swooning, becoming intoxicated, shifting,
frolicking, irrigating, and greatly increasing,
thrusting out the legs, moving around the arms,
with mudrās, signs, and physical expressions, [17]

and shouting out KILI KILI and PHAṬ[358]
in fearful,[359] excited, fierce ways and such,
the frolicking vīras are churning away,
biting,[360] indulging in all kinds of chatter, [18]

wailing while fainting, and reversing[361]—
within the ocean of love and ecstasy,
the light born from the signs of bliss
is the mind that is lucid by nature [19]

It possesses nondual and lucid miraculous
powers as well as supernatural knowledges
It is thus beautified by the twelve distinct
features of the utter peace of true actuality [20]

The divine syllable E, which is
adorned with VAṂ at its center,[362]
represents all bliss's repository,
the jewel casket of buddhahood [21]

From that, the ecstasies will arise,
distinguished by different moments[363]
Due to the progression of the number
of ecstasies, they are to be manifested [22]

Through the three emptinesses' union,
the all-emptiness becomes luminosity[364]
Through pure true reality manifesting,
the supreme state will clearly manifest [23]

Hence the intelligent should perceive
the subtle mind that is without motion
As long as it does not clearly manifest,
they should engage in familiarization [24] {4}

When luminosity's state is attained,
it arises in its own way as it pleases[365]
It is there that the four moments
and likewise the four ecstasies lie [25]

This should be understood by the wise ones
as the distinctions that are designated as

"the moment of variety," "maturation,"
"consummation," and "characteristics' lack" [26]

Variety consists of a lot of aspects,
such as embracing as well as kissing
Maturation constitutes its reversal—
thinking, "I am experiencing bliss" [27]

Consummation has the character of experience
"That I am experiencing bliss is beautiful"
Characteristics' lack is other than those—
free of characteristics of passion and dispassion[366] [28]

More supreme than ecstasy, supreme ecstasy,
and cessational ecstasy is the connate one[367]
The bliss of ecstasy is merely a slight one[368]
Supreme ecstasy is superior compared to it [29]

Cessational ecstasy is dispassion—
the connate one is devoid of those,
being the three moments of "swoon,"
"about half a mātrā," and "a mātrā"[369] [30]

By differentiating the native taste[370]
of true bliss, the connate is known
Fainting lacks wisdom completely
Cognizing it a bit is half a mātrā [31]

The wisdom endowed with the supreme
of all aspects is what constitutes a mātrā
For that reason, the wisdom of true reality
is nondual wisdom's lucid manifestation [32]

It lacks passion and dispassion
It is not both, nor is it emptiness
It is none of all, nor is it not all
In other words, all is dissolved [33]

As all kinds of rain streaming down
have many different tastes and forms, {5}
but once they enter a single vessel,
merge and become of a single taste, [34]

likewise, the great bliss of wisdom,
in its form, is lucid by its essence
Through nondual equality's[371] yoga,
phenomena's entirety is overcome [35]

With a mind of letting wisdom's stream flow,
the wise ones are perceiving exactly this
Having the form of a motionless, subtle,
and unobscured bindu, it is free of thought [36]

True reality without beginning or end
is unarisen, uncreated, and supreme
The ground of all the phenomena
of living creatures is this suchness[372] [37]

Since the buddhas, bodhisattvas,
and yogīs who view true reality
do not see this true reality at all,
what could those outside of it think?[373] [38]

Therefore, what is the point of outsiders
engaging in made-up[374] worship and such?
Giving up all, familiarize with true reality!
Everything will be accomplished by this [39]

At the time when the jewel is entered
by virtue of the union of āli and kāli,[375]
the vāyu is seized by pith instructions
Then, wisdom is achieved by seeing[376]
Throughout the infinity of eons,
it is there that passion remains[377] [40]

Attaining the state of luminosity,
the yogīs of ordinary appearance[378]
who are venerated by all beings
are to rely on the fourth's reality
Yogīs who cultivated this before
will swiftly gain accomplishment [41]

The cause is sealed with the result and
the result is also sealed with the cause[379]
Due to sealing cause and result as one, {6}
it is mahāmudrā that will spring forth [42]

Night (the dimension of illumination), lucid sun rays radiating (the increase of illumination),
and their boundary (the culmination of illumination), by their own natures, move not together[380]
That which is neither night,[381] nor day, nor their boundary, and is free from any of these natures
constitutes what the supreme guru has declared to be awakening—it is the sphere of yogīs [43]

Just like outside, so inside
Just like inside, so outside
It is apt to be accomplished
by this yoga that is nondual [44]

This concludes "The Accomplishment of Glorious True Reality" composed by the great master Keralipa. It was translated, edited, and finalized by the Indian upādhyāya Vajrapāṇi and the Tibetan lotsāwa Mapen Chöbar.[382] {7}

(13) A Dohā Treasure Song

In the language of India: *Dohakoṣagīti*[383]
In the language of Tibet: *Do ha mdzod kyi glu*

I pay homage to youthful Mañjuśrī[384]

As the unfortunate, like venomous snakes,
are most definitely tainting[385] wise beings
with the stains that consist of their flaws,
be terrified by merely glimpsing them! [1]

Brahmans who do not know true reality
are reciting their four miserable Vedas[386] [2]

They purify with earth, water, and kuśa,
dwell in their homes, and burn in a fire
Their making meaningless fire offerings
just amounts to smoke hurting their eyes [3]

With single staff or triple staff,[387] in a saintly lord's attire,[388]
they pose as sages through goose instructions[389]
Equal[390] in not knowing dharma and nondharma,
they are leading beings astray into deception [4]

Airis[391] keep smearing[392] ashes onto their bodies
and carry a load of dreadlocks on their heads

Lighting[393] lamps, they dwell in their homes
Seated in a corner, they are dinging their bell [5]

Assuming the cross-legged posture, they close their eyes
By whispering in their ears, they are deceiving people
Teaching widows, shaven-headed women,[394] and other such,
they bestow empowerments and take guru donations [6]

With long nails {8} and their bodies covered with dirt,
they are without any garments and pull out their hair
With their mind of space,[395] they embody the path of harm
For the sake of liberation, they deceive themselves and beings
Possessing endurance, they are the yānas' laughingstock[396] [7]

If anyone who is naked were to become free,
why would dogs, foxes, and so on not be free?
If you became free through shaving your hairs,
women who shave their hairs would be free[397] [8]

If you became free through flashing a tail,
peacocks, yaks, and so on would be free[398]
If you became free by eating while standing,
why then would horses and elephants not be? [9]

This is what Saraha says: for those who have
a mind of space, there is never any liberation,
as they are divorced from bliss's true reality
and possess solely the austerities of the body [10]

The so-called śrāmaṇeras, bhikṣus, and sthaviras,[399]
those bandhes who thus went forth into homelessness,
some sit[400] there while expounding the sūtra collections,
some are seen to adopt the approach of one-taste mind,
and some are of one taste within mere mind as such[401] [11]

Some are busy running around[402] within the Mahāyāna
with its textual traditions and epistemological treatises

Others meditate on the maṇḍala circles in their entirety
Some engage in explaining the meaning of the fourth [12]

Some seem to ponder the element of space
Yet others keep looking[403] at emptiness
Most of them engage in what is discordant [13]

Others divorced from the connate
meditate on that which is nirvāṇa {9}
but none of them will accomplish
even a single bit[404] of the ultimate [14]

Is it the case that those who possess faith in this
will attain liberation by resting in dhyāna, or what?
What need for lamps, what need for deity oblations?
What does relying on secret mantra do for them?[405] [15]

No need for going to bathing places and austerities
Is liberation attained by a dunk in the water, or what? [16]

Those engaging in emptiness devoid of compassion
will not come to discover the path that is supreme
However, even if compassion alone is cultivated,
stuck in this saṃsāra, liberation will not be attained [17]

Those who are capable of uniting those two
neither abide in saṃsāra nor abide in nirvāṇa [18]

Hey, discard those false lies that are uttered![406]
Let go of anything to which you may cling!
If that has been realized, everything is it
Nobody will know anything other than that [19]

Reading is it, memorization and meditation are it
What is explained in treatises and Purāṇas is it too[407]
There exists no view that is not pointed out by it,
and yet it is solely reliant upon the guru's mouth [20]

What is uttered by the guru and has entered your heart
is like seeing a treasure sitting in the palm of your hand[408]
While childish beings[409] are not seeing the native nature,
childish beings are deceived by delusion,[410] Saraha says [21]

Without any dhyāna or going into homelessness,
if you remain at home together with your wives
and won't become free of bondage by liking objects, {10}
I,[411] Saraha, say that you do not[412] know true reality [22]

If it is manifest, why bother with dhyānas?
If it is hidden, you are gauging darkness
This very nature that is the connate
is neither any being nor any nonbeing—
thus Saraha always shouts out loudly [23]

"Seizing it, there will be birth, death, as well as living;
seizing the very same, supreme great bliss is achieved"
Saraha proclaims this with his secret and grand[413] speech,
but the world of animals doesn't get it—what can you do? [24]

As it is free of dhyāna, what is there to be contemplated?
In what manner could you discuss what is inexpressible?
All beings are deceived by the mudrā of saṃsāric existence
There is nobody who has embraced their native nature [25]

No tantra, no[414] mantra, nothing to contemplate, no dhyāna
All of these are causes that make your own mind[415] deluded
Without this mind as such that is pure by its own nature
ever becoming blemished by means of any dhyānas,[416]
remain in your own bliss[417] and don't torment yourself! [26]

Eating and drinking, ecstatic by uniting the two,[418]
filling up the cakras again and again at all times,
this dharma accomplishes what's beyond the world
I am trampling on the head[419] of the world of fools [27]

Where[420] neither the breath[421] nor the mind roam
and neither the sun nor the moon are active,
fool, let your mind find relief in that state![422]
Saraha is teaching the entire pith instructions [28] {11}

You should not make it into two but make it single![423]
Not making any distinctions within the disposition,
all these three realms here without any exception
will assume the color of this single great passion[424] [29]

Neither beginning, nor middle, nor end,
neither saṃsāric existence nor nirvāṇa:[425]
within this great bliss that is so supreme,
there exists neither any self nor any other[426] [30]

In the front, in the back, in the ten directions,
whatever may be seen constitutes true reality
Today, delusion has now been cut through[427]
Now there is no need to ask[428] anybody! [31]

When the sense faculties have vanished there,[429]
an essence of its own will disintegrate as well
Oh you friend, this constitutes the connate[430]
Ask the guru's mouth for it in a clear manner! [32]

Where mind is bound and where the breath fades,[431]
it is based on this ground that the branches rest[432]
Oh fool, fully realize this to be the borderline![433]
Nescience's ocean is cut off upon its realization[434] [33]

This is the great bliss so supreme
Having conveyed it, Saraha goes [34]

Hey! This is what constitutes self-awareness—
refrain from creating any delusion within it!
Being and nonbeing are the sugata's bondage

Not making existence and equality different,
focus[435] solely on this native mind, oh yogī!
Know this to be like water poured into water![436] [35]

Liberation is not found through delusive dhyānas
How can you clasp onto illusion's web in your lap?
If you trust in reality through the true guru's words,[437]
there is nothing for me to say, Saraha proclaims [36]

The nature of the sky is pure from the beginning
Looking and looking at it, {12} seeing will cease[438]
At exactly this point in time, cessation will happen
The childish are deceived about native mind by flaws[439] [37]

All people without exception completely ruin themselves
and cannot perceive true reality due to the flaw of pride
The entire world will be ignorant on account of dhyānas
The native nature is not perceived[440] by anybody at all [38]

Not perceiving the nature of mind's root,[441]
through the three aspects of the connate,[442]
it's not clearly known where it arises from,
where it vanishes, and where it abides [39]

For those who contemplate true reality free of a root,
it is sufficient to obtain[443] the guru's pith instructions
Fool, you must calmly[444] understand what Saraha says:
It is saṃsāra's[445] nature to have mind as its essence! [40]

Although the native nature is not expressed by any words,
it will be seen with the eye of the master's pith instructions
Through gladly consuming dharma as well as nondharma,
there does not even exist a speck of any flaw in this [41]

It is at the time of having purified native mind
that the qualities of the guru will enter the heart

Once it's realized like that, Saraha sings a song
I do not even see it through mantras or tantras[446] [42]

Beings are bound individually by virtue of their karmas
If it is free from karma,[447] it is the mind that is liberation
If your own mind[448] is free, there is definitely nothing else:
what will be attained is the very nirvāṇa that is supreme [43]

Mind as such alone is the seed of everything:
existence {13} and nirvāṇa spring forth from it
To the mind that is like a wish-fulfilling jewel
bestowing the desired results, I pay homage [44]

By mind being bound, you will be bound
If it becomes free, you are free, no doubt[449]
By whatever it may be that fools are bound,
through that, the wise become free swiftly[450] [45]

The mind is to be grasped as being like space
Regard all phenomena as being equal to space![451]
If this mind is contemplated as inconceivable,[452]
unsurpassable awakening will thereby be gained [46]

If it is rendered space-like,[453] the breath is bound
By means of fully perceiving equality, it dissolves
This is what Saraha says: if you possess such power,
you'll swiftly be rid of the impermanent and moving [47]

When wind, fire, and the great mighty one[454] have ceased,
at the time of the nectar's flow, the breath enters the mind
At the point of the four yogas having entered a single spot,
supreme great bliss does not fit into the realm of space [48]

Tales of this may be told in house after house,
but the state of great bliss is not fully fathomed
Saraha says all beings are trounced by thinking,
but none of them accomplishes the unthinkable[455] [49]

In the entirety of all creatures that are alive,
true reality is present, but it is not realized
As everything has the nature of equal taste,
this is inconceivable unsurpassed wisdom[456] [50]

Yesterday, today, likewise tomorrow, and thereon,
people keep wishing for things[457] that are excellent
Hey, you good people, just as with water seeping
through your cupped hands, {14} you do not feel the loss [51]

If doing things as well as not doing things[458]
are realized, there's no bondage, no letting go[459]
Engaging in what is letterless as explainable,[460]
which among a hundred yogīs will reveal it? [52]

If this mind wound up into twisted knots
is loosened up, there's no doubt it is free[461]
By whichever things fools may be bound,
through just those, the wise become free [53]

Bound, it toils,[462] roaming the ten directions
If it is let go,[463] it rests still and motionless
I have realized this camel-like paradox
Son, look by searching thus in yourself![464] [54]

Hey, look with the sense faculties![465]
I haven't realized[466] anything but this
Before a person done[467] with their deeds,
you need to resolve your mind![468] [55]

Do not think of yourself in binding the breath, hey![469]
Do not dwell in wooden yogas at your nose's tip![470]
AHO! Undistracted,[471] be passionate about the supreme connate!
Give up being bound to the nose tip of existence! [56]

This is surging, since mind and breath move,
being like very unruly horses—let them go!

If the nature of the connate has been realized,
the mind will thereby become unwavering[472] [57]

At the time of mentation having ceased,
the bondage of the body will be severed
Where there's the connate's equal taste,
there are neither śūdras nor brahmans[473] [58]

Here we have the Ocean of the Moon
Here is the Yamunā, the Ganges Ocean,
as well as Vārānasī {15} and Prayāga
Here are the moon and the illuminator[474] [59]

To all the fields, sites, secondary sites, and so forth
I have gone and looked—I declare I fathomed them
In the lake of the pilgrimage site of body and minding,[475]
I truly see virtue in a manner that is definitive[476]
There is no way for me to see even in my dreams
Dwelling in mountain retreat, generate heedfulness![477] [60]

In the middle of the anthers of a lotus stalk with petals,
there is a very subtle filament with its scent and color[478]
Cast away distinctions, oh you fool! Do not let being
tormented[479] by such misery annihilate the fruition! [61]

Where Brahmā, Viṣṇu, as well as Trilocana[480]
serve as the foundation of the entire world,[481]
if you worship the one who has no family,
the host of actions' outcomes fully vanishes[482] [62]

Hey, listen, son! Knowing the true state by delighting in the taste of
debate,[483]
you are not able to know this through beings' explanations, recitations,
and such[484] [63]

Hey, listen, son! This wonderful taste of true
reality is not anything that could be taught[485]

The supreme state of bliss lacks any thoughts:
this bears a resemblance to beings arising[486] [64]

Where mind has ceased, mentation has subsided,[487]
and haughtiness has been split asunder as well,
this is realized as the supreme nature of illusion,
so what could the bondage of dhyāna do to it? [65]

If the arising of entities, just like space, has subsided,[488]
given the absence of entities, what could arise later on?
Within what is the nature of being primordially unborn, {16}
today, rest in the complete removal of any distinctions
in the teachings of the protector who is the glorious guru![489] [66]

Within seeing, hearing, thinking, and touching,
eating, being thirsty, standing, walking, sitting,[490]
idle conversations, as well as giving answers,
solely engage in[491] the single trait "It is mind!" [67]

Those who do not drink to their satisfaction the cooling nectar
water of the pith instructions of the guru that dispels torment
will end up with nothing but being tormented by their thirst
in the desert of the misery of treatises' many meanings, and die[492] [68]

If the gurus do not express the teachings,
the disciples don't have any understanding
The taste of the nectar that is the connate—
how could anybody possibly teach it?[493] [69]

Those fools who[494] are under the sway of clinging
to valid cognition keep finding their distinctions
At that point, having fun in the hut of an outcaste,
you will still not become tainted by any stains [70]

If you are begging, you may use a clay bowl in an alley;
if you are a king, of what further use would it be to you? [71]

Having relinquished distinctions, to rest in true reality
is naturally immovable, equanimous, innately present[495]
Remaining in nirvāṇa, saṃsāric existence is beautified
Do not treat one disease with the medicine for another! [72]

Having abandoned thinking and what is thought,
you should rest in just the way a small child does
If you strive with firm respect[496] for the guru's words,
there is no doubt that the connate will emerge [73]

Devoid of colors, letters, qualities,[497] and examples,
it cannot be articulated yet I point it out just roughly
Like a young woman grasping at bliss in her heart, {17}
to whom could this All-Powerful One[498] be taught? [74]

In those who[499] have severed being as well as nonbeing,
the world, without exception, will dissolve completely
When mind is made motionless, fully resting, and steady,[500]
it will be free on its own from saṃsāra's state of being [75]

When you yourself do not perceive that other one,
will the unsurpassable body then be accomplished?[501]
Being undeluded for sure about what I[502] taught thus,
realize it by yourself showing it well to yourself![503] [76]

It lacks particles, is not particle-free, nor is it mind
There is no clinging to these entities from the start
Saraha declares that this is really all it boils down to
Hey, realize the ultimate that's the stainlessness of all! [77]

Going outside, they search for the one who is[504] in the house[505]
Seeing the head of the household, they still ask the neighbors
This is what Saraha has to declare: you need to know yourself!
It's not a fool's dhyānas, contemplative objects, or recitations [78]

Even if the guru has taught it and you understand all of it to be true,
it's not realized by your own analysis—you find liberation, or what?[506]

Even if you travel the lands and are in danger of being tormented,
you will not find the connate but be in the grip of wrongdoing [79]

Not being tainted by any objects through relying on objects
is like plucking an utpala while not being touched by water[507]
They have taken their refuge in the root in this kind of manner[508]
How could those with a poison mantra be affected by poison? [80]

Even if you have worshipped the gods tens of thousands of times, {18}
you yourself will still be in bondage, so what's the point of that?[509]
Through that kind of approach, this saṃsāra will not be severed
Except by becoming familiar with this, its entirety is not traversed[510] [81]

When the eyes are not closed and the mind has stopped,[511]
the breath's standstill is realized thanks to the glorious guru
When the continual flow[512] of the breath is not in motion,
what would there be to do for yogīs at the time of dying?[513] [82]

As long as you fall into the sense objects' village,
for that long your own bad karma[514] is flourishing
Think what you do now and where you go, hey![515]
This is entered by way of a very difficult mindset
That which is present within somebody
is not caught sight of in that somebody [83]

By expounding the treatises, all those erudite
do not realize buddhahood exists in the body
Just as mind is placid once an elephant is trained,[516]
having stopped coming and going, it is at ease[517]
If it is realized like this, there is nobody to ask
Thus I state shamelessly, "The erudite is me!"[518] [84]

Someone who is alive and does not change,
could they possibly be aging or die, or what?
The stainless insight that is taught by the guru
is true reality's treasure—never mind any others! [85]

The purity of objects isn't anything to rely on[519]
Practice by means of nothing but emptiness!
This resembles a crow flying off from a ship—
it keeps circling and then lands right back on it[520] [86]

As with a venomous snake that's a black rope,
you will be terrified through merely seeing it
Oh friend, even those persons who are wise
may be bound by the flaws of the two objects [87] {19}

Do not bind yourself by clinging to objects!
Hey, you fool, this is what Saraha declares
You should regard[521] this as in the case of fish,
butterflies, elephants, bees, as well as deer [88]

Whatever may proliferate from the mind
likewise[522] has the nature of the protector
Are water and its waves anything other?[523]
The equality of existence and peace has space's nature[524] [89]

Who would be taught? Who would hear it?[525]
With the ultimate intention being reached,[526]
the noxious hideout is ruined just like dust[527]
It will settle right within this very heart [90]

Just as when water is poured into water
and all has the same taste as that water,[528]
mind, with its equal flaws and qualities,
is the protector, not made out[529] by anybody [91]

For fools, there is no remedy whatsoever
Like a raging fire[530] spreading in a forest,
so are all appearances before your eyes [92]

Bring the root of mind[531] together with emptiness!
Given this mind that is so pleasurable or equal,

being that which you cherish deep in your heart,[532]
even a pain that is merely a sesame husk's worth
always amounts to causing nothing but suffering [93]

Oh you friend, take a look at pigs and elephants!
It is similar to that. It does not constitute that[533]
It resembles the purposes of a wish-fulfilling jewel
The erudite in whom delusion has collapsed[534] are amazing—
the propensity form of great bliss self-aware of itself[535] [94]

At that point, all will be rendered equal to space
It is not at all appropriate to speak about kālakūṭa[536]
The nature {20} equal to space is seized by the mind
If the mind becomes rendered what is not mind,
the connate's nature[537] is extraordinarily beautiful[538] [95]

That is what is proclaimed[539] in house after house,
but the state of great bliss is not fully fathomed
Saraha says all beings carry their mental burden[540]
That, the unthinkable, is not realized by anyone [96]

AHO! Oh you yogīs, please ask your familiarization!
Rid of head, heart, navel, secret, legs, and arms, I see it
By means of contemplation, objects are perceived
By contemplating what's other, the breath will cease[541] [97]

If the mind comes to be revealed through the mind,
breath and mentation[542] do not stir and rest steady
Similar to the case of salt dissolving in water,[543]
thus mind will dissolve within its own nature [98]

At that time, self and other are seen as equal
What could practicing dhyāna with effort do? [99]

The single deity is seen as a multitude of scriptures[544]
Many individual claims appear distinctly and clearly [100]

I alone am the protector, in opposition to others
In house after house, this doctrine is established
Through eating one, all others will be satisfied[545]
Going outside, you search for the household's head [101]

It is neither seen coming,[546] nor is there going
Though it sits right here, it is not recognized
This is the All-Powerful One that is waveless,[547]
constituting the dhyāna that is unblemished [102]

Let clear water and a self-luminous lamp be!
I neither adopt nor reject any coming or going
Upon meeting the unprecedented charming lady, {21}
the mind sleeping with her relies on groundlessness [103]

Don't regard it to be different from your own mind![548]
This[549] is buddhahood being placed into your hand
When body, speech, and mind become inseparable,
at that time, the nature of the connate is beautiful[550] [104]

The husband and the mistress are having fun[551]
Objects seen by persons should be enjoyed
Within me, being engaged in playing games,
childish beings become completely exhausted[552] [105]

Leaving the mother behind, no child is born[553]
Fire burns its very fuel by way of conditions
AHO! There is nothing else that is existent[554]
Well, is it then present elsewhere, or what?[555]
The conduct of yoga is free of any example[556] [106]

The husband is devoured and the nature is beautiful
This very mind that is filled with objects of desire,[557]
rid of desire and desire's lack, entered naturalness[558]
By virtue of mind being messed up, I see the yoginī[559] [107]

While eating and drinking, there is no thinking
Friend, thinking what appears here in the mind
is external means being in the grip of suffering[560]
The illusory yoginī[561] is indeed without compare [108]

Thinking of activities as being merely this,
the mind made inseparable from any effort[562]
is stainless anywhere on the three planes
Gems cannot help but dripping moon water
Means grant power over the entire kingdom[563] [109]

The mind as such is the yoginī of accomplishment
It is to be understood as the magic of the connate [110]

The world without exception is letters[564]
There isn't even a single letterless one
For as long as there aren't any letters,
for that long letters are understood {22}
This represents the letterless letter[565] [111]

Through rubbing the ink, there isn't anything to read
Through reciting Vedas without effort, you are ruined[566]
Good people, think![567] If the other one is not known,
from where is there arising, and where is disappearing? [112]

Just like the outside, thus is the inside,
constantly abiding on the fourteenth bhūmi[568]
The bodiless is hidden within the body[569]
Those who realize it will become free [113]

I recited the syllables of accomplishment first[570]
But thanks to drinking the elixir, I will forget
Those who have knowledge of the single letter
do not know anything at all about its name [114]

Within the three groves, there is the single letter
In the middle of the three letters, there is the deity

That which keeps descending from those three
indeed represents the four Vedas of an outcaste[571] [115]

Those[572] who do not realize everything as this nature,
yet accomplish great bliss in kunduru's opportunity,[573]
like thirsty people who are chasing after a mirage,[574]
will die from thirst—can they find water in the sky? [116]

Since what is generated by means of the bliss
present in the midst of the vajra and lotus pair
is powerless to demonstrate what this is like,
where's hope for fulfillment on the three planes?[575] [117]

It is either the momentary bliss of the means
or, alternatively, exactly that in its being two
Thanks to the kindness of the guru, yet again,
just a few among hundreds will realize this[576] [118]

Oh friend! That which is profound and vast
is without any other and it is not a self either
At the time of the connate ecstasy, the fourth,
the natural state is known through experience[577] [119]

Similar to the case of some moonstone
that illuminates a great black darkness, {23}
in the instant[578] of supreme great bliss,
all wrongdoing will become defeated[579] [120]

At the time when the illuminator of suffering sets,
the lord of the stars[580] rises together with the planets
Through abiding thus, emanations are emanated,
and that constitutes the ultimate maṇḍala circle [121]

Hey! The mind of a fool that realizes mind
means to become free from all bad views[581]
If resting within that through the power of
supreme great bliss, it is the highest siddhi [122]

Let mind's elephant go free![582]
Let it question itself![583]
Don't ask it by thinking![584]
Let it drink the sky mountain's water!
Let it settle at its banks as it pleases! [123]

Once the master's hand seizes the objects' elephant,
this may appear like having the license to kill
In those yogīs who are like elephant herders,
it will be returning from precisely that[585] [124]

It is certain that what is saṃsāra represents nirvāṇa
Don't think of them as other by distinguishing objects![586]
Being devoid of any distinctions of[587] a single nature,
I have fully realized them to be without any stains [125]

Mentation's true reality has a focus
The lack of any focus is emptiness[588]
There exist flaws in both of them
Yogīs do not meditate with either [126]

What is to be meditated[589] on has a focus or lacks a focus,
lacking any conventions of meditation and nonmeditation
It constitutes the nature that manifests in the form of bliss
That which is supremely unsurpassable and self-arising
is realized by relying on the timely means of the guru[590] [127] {24}

Neither go into the forest nor remain[591] at home!
If the mind fully realizes this wherever you are,[592]
all is constantly present as awakening's realization,[593]
so what is saṃsāra and what would nirvāṇa be? [128]

Mind is stainless—the state of the connate
Then, the classes of beings are not entered
To be resting in just that with certainty
represents the victor, without distinctions[594] [129]

Awakening[595] does not dwell in the forest or at home
If this kind of distinction[596] has been fully realized,
it is by virtue of the nature of the stainless mind
that all needs to be relied on[597] as being thought-free! [130]

Just that is the self, and the other too is just that[598]
What is meditated on and what is meditation?
It should be freed from distinctions' bondage
Despite all that, I'm the one who is utterly free [131]

Just as in the case of reflections in the ocean,[599]
do not create delusion about self and other!
All are buddhas who were present previously:[600]
this is the state that is stainless and supreme,
when the mind is pure by its very own essence[601] [132]

The supreme tree of the mind that is nondual,
pervading all three planes[602] without exception,
bears compassion's flowers and fruits of others' welfare[603]
This is what is named "the benefit of others"[604] [133]

On emptiness's supreme tree, flowers blossom,
endowed with a great variety of compassion
Effortlessness[605] is what constitutes its final fruit,
but this bliss is not a mind that is something else [134]

Emptiness's supreme tree lacks compassion[606]
It does not have any root, leaves, or petals {25}
Through turning this into a point of reference
and plunging into that, the branches will break[607] [135]

From a single seed, there are two trees
The fruit from that cause is a single one
Those considering it as being indivisible
are free from saṃsāra as well as nirvāṇa [136]

At the time when a person who has a wish arrives,
if they were to leave with their hopes all dashed,
you're better off picking up a clay bowl tossed out
the door, leaving your home, and living like that [137]

Not promoting the welfare of benefiting others
and not giving a gift to those who wish for it,
what saṃsāric result is there supposed to be?
You are better off leaving behind yourself[608] [138]

This concludes the "Dohakoṣa," the ultimate letters that naturally point out true reality, composed by the great mighty lord of yogīs, Śrī Saraha.[609] *It was translated by the Indian upādhyāya Vajrapāṇi and lotsāwa Mapen Chöbar. It was subsequently edited and finalized by Drogmi José and bhikṣu Tsültrim Gyalwa.*[610] {26}

(14) The Succession of the Four Mudrās

In the language of India: *Caturmudrānvaya*[611]
In the language of Tibet: *Phyag rgya bzhi rjes su bstan pa*[612]

I pay homage to Vajrasattva[613]

EVAṂ[614]

Having first paid homage to Vajrasattva,
whose nature consists of pure wisdom,
I compose *The Succession of the Mudrās*
in a brief way for my own understanding[615]

Here, it is by being deluded about the succession of the mudrās that those with the minds of fools drift about miserably in the ocean of saṃsāric existence. In order that they may easily realize the meanings of the four mudrās, the means to accomplish great bliss is presented by following the tantras.[616] "The four mudrās" are (1) the karmamudrā, (2) the dharmamudrā, (3) mahāmudrā, and (4) the samayamudrā.

(1) Here, the karmamudrā's own nature is examined. "Karma" refers to the consideration related to body, speech, and mind, which is primary. "Mudrā" refers to its own nature being imagination.[617]

> It is in her that the ecstasies will originate,
> distinguished by the moments' distinction[618] {27}
> Due to knowing the moments, the wisdom
> that is bliss is based in the syllables EVAṂ[619]

The ecstasies are four: ecstasy, supreme ecstasy, connate ecstasy, and cessational ecstasy. Otherwise, the following statement would not be suitable:

> Seeing what is to be marked in the middle
> of the supreme and cessational, stabilize it![620]

The moments are [also] four: variety, maturation, lack of characteristics, and consummation. That the lack of characteristics is placed[621] in the middle [between maturation and consummation] is to be understood in the [correct] empowerment. It should be understood, however, that in the forceful yoga, the pair of connate [ecstasy] and the lack of characteristics is positioned at the end. The Bhagavān has pointed this out in the [correct] empowerment and in the forceful yoga.[622]

All that is the connate [in essence]; it is called "the connate" because it mimics it in being [merely] a resemblance of the [actual] connate.[623] This resemblance of the connate leads to realizing the wisdom that is similar to the connate. Thus, [in this limited sense,] the connate [here] refers to the wisdom [that is based on a] prajñā. Hence there is no arising of the [actual] connate in the wisdom [that is based on a] prajñā. [However,] inasmuch as what is called "the connate" is all phenomena's own nature, whose very own characteristic it is to be uncontrived, therefore, by having obtained a karmamudrā, {28} the result that is a concordant outflow [of the actual connate] arises.[624]

"Outflow" refers to a flow that is similar. A reflection of a face contingent on a mirror is similar [to that face but is] not the [actual] face—it was neither established before, nor is it established at present; this [mirror] produces a face's reflection that is a mere likeness. Accordingly, by being deluded, [thinking] they have seen their own face [rather than merely its reflection], worldly people are satisfied. Similarly, having accomplished the wisdom [that is based on a] prajñā, masters of weak intelligence, thinking they have experienced the [actual] connate, give rise to satisfaction. Being satisfied [with that], they do not even understand a basic account of the dharmamudrā.

Solely through the contrived [practice with a] karmamudrā, how could what is called "the connate that is uncontrived" arise in those who do not understand the dharmamudrā? It is [only] from a cause of its own type that a result of this same type arises, not from a different type. Just as the sprout of black cumin, and not [one] of Kodo millet, grows from a black cumin seed,[625] the uncontrived connate arises from the presence of the uncontrived dharmamudrā. Therefore, by figuratively making a distinction [between cause and result] in what is [in fact] without [such] a distinction, it is only the dharmamudrā that is the cause of mahāmudrā.[626]

Why then did the Bhagavān teach the following?

> The divine syllable E, which is {29}
> adorned with VAṂ at its center,
> represents all bliss's repository,
> the jewel casket of buddhahood[627]

As for "the jewel casket of buddhahood," it is a casket, a basis, and a foundation because it mimics the reflection of buddhahood. Therefore it is the lotus that is the source of the jewel of abundant ecstasy thanks to a shapely woman who is a karma[mudrā]. Here, when the conventional bodhicitta has entered from the avadhūtī in the interior of the jewel through the union of the fluids of the bola and the kakkola[628] (the churner and the churned),[629] then the wisdom that is designated as "the lower[630] connate"—[also] called "the momentary [connate]"—arises. [However,] this is not the [actual] connate; it is only its concordant outflow. By its own nature, it is the wisdom [that is based on a] prajñā and associated with the [first] three ecstasies and the set of the four moments. In [the context of] empowerment and the forceful yoga, it is called "the karmamudrā's result of concordant outflow."

This is the instruction on the karmamudrā as the result of concordant outflow, which is the first one.[631]

(2) OṂ The dharmamudrā has the dharmadhātu's own nature, is free from discursiveness, is nonconceptual, uncontrived, and unborn, has the nature of compassion, and constitutes the unique beautiful means for supreme ecstasy.[632] By virtue of the nature of the connate that is a permanent continuous flow, {30} thanks to the arising of the connate, it is not different from the prajñā.[633] This is what is called "dharmamudrā."[634]

Another characteristic of the [dharmamudrā] should be understood as follows. Being like sunrays in the darkness of dense ignorance, thanks to the guru's pith instructions, it is free from the torments[635] of delusion that are mere straw chaff. It is to be understood as the threefold world's single nature associated with the great elements (the entirety of earth, water, wind, and fire) that is waveless, the inseparability of emptiness and compassion.[636] Moreover, the Bhagavān said this:

> The lalanā abides as having prajñā's
> nature and the rasanā as the means
> The avadhūtī in the middle region
> is free from perceiver and perceived[637]

By being an expert in this, the path should be understood as the proximate cause that has the form of suchness. When the path is understood, by training in that path in an attentive and uninterrupted manner, the cessation that has the nature of the connate will be directly perceived.[638] Thus the following is said:

> There is nothing to be removed from this
> and not the slightest that is to be added
> Actual reality is to be seen as it really is—
> whoever sees actual reality is liberated[639]

The avadhūtī is the one that dwells in the middle region of the pair that consists of the lalanā and the rasanā. This is realized {31} through cultivating the mindset of singularly focusing on all things having the nature of the connate and thanks to the pith instructions of a true guru. By not being different from mahāmudrā, the dharmamudrā serves as its cause.[640]

This is the instruction on the dharmamudrā as the result of maturation, which is the second one.[641]

(3) ĀḤ "Mahāmudrā" is both "great" (*mahatī*) and a "seal" (*mudrā*), thus being the great seal. It lacks any nature of its own, is free from the cognitive obscurations and so forth, has the appearance of the stainless midday sky in autumn, serves as the foundation of all accomplishment, is saṃsāric existence's and nirvāṇa's single own nature, embodies nonreferential compassion, and has the single form of great bliss.[642] Accordingly, [this is said]:

> The dharmas of mental nonengagement are proper
> The dharmas of mental engagement are not proper[643]

In the Buddha's words, [the following is declared]:

> To you who are without any imaginary thinking,
> whose mind is in the state of utter nonabiding,
> who lack any minding and mental engagement,
> and who are without focus, let there be homage![644]

This is what is called "mahāmudrā."[645] Through this mahāmudrā, whose nature is inconceivable, the result that is called "samayamudrā" arises.[646]

This is the instruction on mahāmudrā as the result of stainlessness, {32} which is the third one.[647]

(4) HŪṂ The "samayamudrā" is Vajradhara's manifestation in the form of Heruka, having the nature of the forms of sambhoga[kāyas] and nirmāṇakāyas and being of clear appearance, for the welfare of sentient beings. This is what is designated "samayamudrā." Once they have taken up this samayamudrā,[648] imagining the five kinds of wisdom as the fivefold ritual[649] in the form of a [maṇḍala] circle, the masters meditate on this circle of the samayamudrā as mirror-like [wisdom], [the wisdom of] equality, discriminating [wisdom], all-accomplishing [wisdom], and [the wisdom of] the pure dharmadhātu by way of the initial yoga, the supreme king of the maṇḍala, the supreme king of activity, the yoga of the bindu, and the yoga of the subtle.[650] Through that, they will generate merit. However, by virtue of that [alone], they will not attain the result of the dharmamudrā, because it is said: "From a cause that is a specific thing, a specific result arises."[651]

Therefore, through being penetrated by the taste of the accomplishment of the connate, [all] things such as the mobile and the immobile that are imagined by childish beings turn into the causes of perfect awakening. Through this, the threefold world will be contemplated well as the [maṇḍala] circle.[652] {33} Accordingly, the Bhagavān declared this:

> There are no mantra recitations, no austerities, no fire
> offerings,
> no inhabitants of any maṇḍalas, nor the maṇḍalas themselves

> This is mantra recitation, this is austerities, this is fire offering,
> this is the inhabitants of maṇḍalas and the maṇḍalas
> themselves
> In brief, those are mind, which has the nature of communion[653]

"In brief" means "in terms of the single form of all phenomena," that is to say, "in terms of the form of great bliss." "Mind" refers to bodhicitta. "Has the nature of communion" refers to the wisdom whose nature consists of the empowerment of dharmamudrā and mahāmudrā, which is called "communion."[654]

This concludes the instruction on the samayamudrā as the result produced by persons, which is the fourth one.[655]

This concludes "The Succession of the Four Mudrās," an expedient[656] *in four stages, composed by master Nāgārjuna.*[657] {34}

(15) A Discussion of the Purification of the Mind

In the language of India: *Cittaviśuddhināmaprakaraṇa*[658]
In the language of Tibet: *Sems kyi sgrib pa rnam par sbyong ba zhes bya ba'i rab tu byed pa*[659]

I pay homage at the feet of the true guru
I pay homage to youthful Mañjuśrī[660]

Without beginning or end, peaceful,[661]
devoid of any being and nonbeing,
free from thought, without support,[662]
utterly nonabiding,[663] and nondual, [1]

inconceivable, without example,
inexpressible, indemonstrable,
abodeless, without residence,[664]
without change, unconditioned, [2]

the abode of every single buddha,
the body with compassion's nature,
is the one teaching beings of various
aspirations through various means[665] [3]

I pay homage to the way of great passion,[666]
the master who is the Lotus Lord of Dance[667]

I shall discuss just a little bit here
in order to realize my own mind[668] [4]

Through the general Yogācāra approach,
this is completely certain in all respects
What is to be discussed is exactly this
Hence this is what should be practiced[669] [5]

Whichever the awful actions may be {35}
through which people are in bondage,
by having the means, the very same
liberate from the bonds of existence[670] [6]

As mere mind alone is utterly pure,
the fruition will also be utterly pure[671]
In the Mahāyāna, this is declared
very clearly and very extensively [7]

As phenomena and persons lack identity,
the Sage has proclaimed mere mind
Hence the fact that everything is arising
is convincing and exceptionally clear[672] [8]

It is those who find themselves in the grip
of the demon of clinging to [real] existence
that he of compassionate character clearly
and extensively urged on in the scriptures[673] [9]

Phenomena are preceded by mind
The mind is foremost, mind is swift
It is due to mind being preeminent
that we are speaking or acting[674] [10]

Once a bhikṣu had urged on[675] his own
elderly[676] father to walk[677] more quickly
and he died from a fall,[678] but this qualifies
not as an act of immediate consequence[679] [11]

If an arhat who is severely ill[680]
tells his disciple, an attendant
bhikṣu,[681] to wring his neck[682] and
he dies, there is no flaw in it[683] [12]

Killing others with another
intention, no[684] flaw accrues
This is clearly stated in the Vinaya—
no flaw in those without a bad mind[685] [13]

When a stupa is excavated[686] with the mindset
of renovating it, this does not represent a flaw
So,[687] by committing secondary acts of immediate
consequence,[688] there's nothing but a host of merit[689] [14]

With a good intention, one placing
a pair of shoes on the Sage's head {36}
and likewise another removing them—
both attain the result of kingship[690] [15]

Therefore the determination of merit[691]
and wrongdoing is rooted in intention[692]
As it is declared thus in the scriptures,
no flaw exists in those of virtuous mind [16]

Those yogīs[693] who embody the yoga
of their own supreme deity,[694] strive
to promote the welfare of the world, and
enjoy objects are liberated, not tainted[695] [17]

This is like those knowing poison's reality,
understanding[696] the poison, consuming it—
they alone will not become unconscious[697]
but end up being relieved from sickness[698] [18]

Regarding the entirety of the world
as being like an illusion, a mirage,

a city of gandharvas, and a dream,[699]
who would enjoy what and how? [19]

It is childish beings who delight[700] in forms
The medium ones go for freedom of desire
Those with the highest insight who know
the nature of forms[701] become liberated[702] [20]

Keeping in mind the entirety of samaya
and the ritual of worshipping the deity,
regarding them as pure, what is enjoined
by mantra is to be enjoyed without doubt[703] [21]

By means of uniting with the three syllables,[704]
you should purify, realize, and also illuminate[705]
It is the tathāgatas whom you should please[706]
with the tips[707] of the thumb and the ring finger[708] [22]

What is "real" for childish beings
is of course delusive for the yogīs
Those who thereby reach the end[709]
are neither bound nor liberated[710] [23]

Those who do not see true reality
think[711] about saṃsāra and nirvāṇa
Those who see true reality think
about neither saṃsāra nor nirvāṇa[712] [24] {37}

It is the great demon of thinking that
plunges[713] us into the ocean of saṃsāra
The great ones without any thinking
are freed from the bonds of existence [25]

Through doubt's poison, ordinary beings
are troubled[714] as if it were by [real] poison[715]
Eradicating[716] exactly this at its very root,
those with compassionate nature act[717] [26]

In the same way as a[718] pure and clear
crystal becomes tinted by other colors,[719]
so the jewel of the mind becomes
colored by the hues of thoughts [27]

The jewel of mind that is devoid
of the colors of ordinary thoughts[720]
is pure from the beginning, unborn,
and its own nature is without taint[721] [28]

Whatever it is that childish beings[722] detest,
just that is to be performed with exertion
by means of the yoga of your own deity,
as it is the cause[723] of mind's stainlessness[724] [29]

Passionate women tortured by[725] the poison
of passion's fire, when loved passionately
by way of the yogīs' mindset that is pure,
truly yield the result of liberation by passion[726] [30]

It is like meditating on yourself as a garuḍa
and, in that garuḍa's form, drinking poison—[727]
effecting its nontoxicity to be accomplished,
you will not be overpowered by that poison[728] [31]

A wheel twelve yojanas across[729]
is revolving on top of the head
Once bodhicitta is generated,[730]
it is removed,[731] so we have heard[732] [32]

Once[733] you have given rise to bodhicitta
with a mind set on complete awakening,
with the intention of setting[734] the world free,
there isn't anything that is not to be done[735] [33] {38}

Pure from the beginning, unborn,
without any nature, and taintless—

seeing this as the world's true state,[736]
you are neither bound nor liberated[737] [34]

Yogīs who, with their apt know-how,
contemplate the deity's vast qualities
are delighted[738] by the mind of passion
and are liberated by enjoying passion[739] [35]

What do we do? Where[740] to get
all kinds of powers of things?
It is like someone in poison's grip[741]
detoxifying it with that very poison[742] [36]

Like water from the ear with water
and a thorn by means of a thorn,
so the wise ones should remove
passion through that very passion [37]

Similar to a launderer making
clothes stainless through stains,
the wise are to make themselves
stainless through the very stains[743] [38]

Just as a mirror becomes clean
by means of rubbing it with dust,
likewise the wise should attend to
eradicating flaws[744] through flaws[745] [39]

All that an iron ball that is thrown
into the water does is sinking down
Once it has been made into a vessel,
it floats and carries others across[746] [40]

Just so, the mind that is made a vessel
by the expedient of prajñā and means,
thanks to[747] enjoying desire, is liberated
and likewise liberates others as well [41]

The passion that the unwise attend to
is the passion that becomes bondage
The same as attended to by the wise
is the passion that bestows liberation[748] [42] {39}

It is well known in all the world[749]
that poison is eradicated by milk
The same when drunk by snakes
boosts their poison tremendously[750] [43]

Just like a goose being an expert
on drinking milk mixed with water,[751]
so, enjoying poisonous objects,
the wise ones become liberated[752] [44]

Just as, when consumed with the proper
know-how, even poison becomes nectar,
for children, ghee cakes[753] and so forth
become poison when eaten improperly[754] [45]

This very mind that is purified
by means of wholesome causes
appears thought-free, unsupported,
and stainless by its very nature[755] [46]

This is similar to even a small flame,
put together with oil, a wick, and so on,
becoming a stainless, unwavering lamp
that eliminates any enduring darkness[756] [47]

It is like a banyan tree's tiny seed,
joined with cooperative conditions,
becoming the founder of a large tree
that has roots, branches, and fruits[757] [48]

Due to joining turmeric and quicklime,
there will be another color, so it is said[758]

Due to the joining of prajñā and means,
they likewise perceive the dharmadhātu[759] [49]

Ghee that is mixed with honey
in equal parts[760] turns into poison[761]
The same, enjoyed with proper
know-how, is the supreme elixir[762] [50]

Just as copper rubbed[763] with mercury
turns into[764] gold that is without flaw, {40}
thus, by being purified by wisdom,
the afflictions truly produce virtue[765] [51]

Those who entered[766] the Hīnayāna
are terrified of death at every step[767]
The mind set on victory in battle[768]
thus remains at a far distance [52]

But those who have entered the Mahāyāna,
armored with the dharma[769] of compassion,
having a bow and arrow with prajñā's string[770]
and the intention of setting the world free,[771] [53]

those mahāsattvas with great means,
of unyielding mind and undaunted,[772]
having won the battle difficult to win,[773]
are then liberating others as well [54]

Solely devoted to their own welfare,
animals are those who are afflicted
Those caring for the world's welfare
are indeed rare and fortunate people[774] [55]

Those hankering after their own welfare
endure sufferings such as cold and wind,
so how would those who are dedicated
to the world's welfare not endure them?[775] [56]

The compassionate are to endure
even the sufferings of the hells,
so who would even think about
hardships such as cold and wind?[776] [57]

Do not perform any practice of hardships[777]
and do not engage in any ritual of fasting,[778]
any bathing, and any ritual cleansing here
The village dharma should be abandoned[779] [58]

Nails, teeth, bone, and marrow arise
as the fatherly semen's modifications,[780]
while flesh, blood, hair, and so forth
emerge from the blood of the mother [59]

In such a way, the body that is born
from the impure is full of[781] the impure
How could such a body[782] be purified
by means of a bath in the Ganges?[783] [60] {41}

An unclean jar, even if washed with water
again and again, will not [become purified]
Likewise, this body as well, being filled
with impurity, will not become purified[784] [61]

Even if a dog were to cross the Ganges,
it is certainly not able of becoming pure
Thus,[785] bathing at sacred places is fruitless
for men whose mind is set on the dharma[786] [62]

If the dharma came from bathing,[787]
fishermen would arrive at that goal
What need to mention fish and such
who stay in the water night and day?[788] [63]

It is for sure that wrongdoing
is not terminated[789] by bathing,

for[790] desire and so on are seen
to be rampant[791] in ritual bathers [64]

Desire, hatred, and ignorance,
jealousy, and greed are always[792]
declared[793] as wrongdoing's roots—
these are not purified by bathing [65]

Due to grasping at me and mine,
these arise in living beings here[794]
Its cause[795] is ignorance, and this
ignorance is held to be delusion[796] [66]

As the perception[797] of silver in mother-of-pearl
disappears once it is seen as mother-of-pearl,
it is by virtue of beholding the lack of identity
that this likewise perishes[798] from its very root [67]

As the perception[799] of a snake in a rope
disappears once it is seen to be a rope,
there will never again be any perception
of a snake there in this person here[800] [68]

Just so, the perception of what is real[801]
here disappears through vajra wisdom
Existence[802] will not [re-]emerge there,
just as with a sprout from a burned seed [69] {42}

The body as a blend of identitylessness
and impurity[803] is stainless by its nature
In the torments of that [body], childish
beings imagine the dharma as hardship[804] [70]

Based on[805] the moon's rising and setting,
we entertain the concept of a lunar day
Through the rising and setting of the sun,
we distinguish between day and night[806] [71]

Conventional terms such as "east"[807] too[808]
are created in reference to conceptions[809]
Planetary, lunar, solar positions,[810] and such,
are conceived of by all worldly people[811] [72]

In the same manner, it is based on[812] cold, heat,
and rain that the seasons are conceived of[813]
The experiences of the results of our own karma
are indicated by good and bad planetary positions[814] [73]

A wise man, having set out to cleanse
this wish-fulfilling jewel of the mind
besmeared with the mud of ignorance,
what could increase ignorance again?[815] [74]

Disregarding planetary positions, lunar days,
lunar positions, locations, time, and so forth,
enjoy yourself[816] without having any thoughts,
without any motive, and without any fear[817] [75]

By virtue of whatever it is that becomes
the path of the senses having this nature,
all, through the yoga of superb absorption,
is to be experienced as made of buddhas[818] [76]

The eye is the Buddha[819] Vairocana[820]
The ear represents Vajrasūryaka[821]
The nose is indeed[822] Paramāśva
The mouth is Padmanarteśvara [77]

The body is Śrī Heruka, the king
The mind represents Vajrasattva[823]
Yogīs with compassion's character
should always[824] perfectly practice thus[825] [78]

Those with this tenet,[826] free from thought,
with stable resolve,[827] and rich in insight, {43}

are skylarking[828] in just the way they like,
thus consuming all and doing everything[829] [79]

They do everything they desire,
behaving in the way they please,[830]
be it standing up, sitting down,
walking around, or sleeping[831] [80]

Even the ones who have not entered the maṇḍala[832]
or those who are endowed with all the obscurations,
embodying the yoga of their own supreme deity,[833]
will be accomplished, even if they are of little merit[834] [81]

By this, those knowing true reality,
in this life here, attain total courage[835]
and buddhahood in its completeness—
there isn't any doubt at all about this[836] [82]

In the same way as the world of yogīs
is not overruled by the ordinary world,
through differences in insight, yogīs too
are overruled by higher and higher ones[837] [83]

What is pointed out in the Mahāyāna
by way of aspiring for great prajñā,
great means, and great compassion
represents the sphere of mahāsattvas[838] [84]

The buddhahood desired by many
and not attained for incalculable[839] eons
is attained in this very life here—
there isn't any doubt about this[840] [85]

The greatness[841] of the Mahāyāna,
contained[842] in merit and wisdom,
is that omniscience's pleasant state
is attained immediately in this life[843] [86]

The contemplation of Āgama and of Śruti[844]
is not[845] something adopted in the Mahāyāna
The distinction of the yānas[846] is illuminated
by distinctions in intention and disposition[847] [87] {44}

Here, this is another aspiration,[848]
also another[849] awakening conduct,
another purification of the mind,
and another fruition we speak of[850] [88]

As in a nearby[851] stainless mirror,
for stainless eyes, forms appear
in a very clear, pellucid, and
naturally stainless manner,[852] [89]

so does wisdom through the mirror
of stainless prajñā for those yogīs
whose very clear and pure minds
are freed from the web of thoughts[853] [90]

Similar to fire blazing up suddenly
within a jewel that is a sunstone[854]
while struck by the light[855] of the sun,
enabling you to accomplish your own goal, [91]

the mind that resembles a sunstone
and has cast off the web of thoughts,
while fused with prajñā's sun rays,
is blazing in the same way in yogīs[856] [92]

Similar to a fire that is blazing up
by means of[857] rubbing two sticks,
pure at the start, middle, and end,
and shedding light on all things,[858]
so they realize that yogic wisdom
is due to uniting prajñā and means[859] [93]

This is similar to a single lamp,
in dependence upon other wicks,
matching your own goal and setting,
bestowing powerful illumination[860] [94]

The manifestations of limitless bodies,
through cultivating prajñā and means,
should carry out activities according
to the diverse aspirations[861] of beings[862] [95]

It is like one with the know-how[863]
extracting ambrosia from milk,
which is flawless, cool, pleasant,
and overcomes all the diseases[864] [96] {45}

Having arisen from expertly churning
the milk of prajñā with great means,[865]
the utterly pure dharmadhātu consists
of the true bliss that overcomes pain[866] [97]

Similar to a creeper that grows
endowed with fruits and flowers,
perfect awakening in a single moment
is joined with the two accumulations[867] [98]

Subjugating, aversion, expelling, paralyzing,[868]
the summoning of rainfall,[869] and so forth—
yogīs who are indulging in wine and meat
perform those but do not become defiled[870] [99]

Why would you look in a mirror
for the bracelets on your wrists?[871]
Thus, in the Mahāyāna, even today,[872]
the power of mantras is shown[873] [100]

The relationship of mother and daughter
is [merely] an imputation, not true reality

Resembling well-arranged iron pellets,
the Tathāgata declared the world to be[874] [101]

Semen has the five elements'[875] character,
and blood is exactly like that as well
This body is indeed composed of them,
so who's a brahman, who a lowest-born?[876] [102]

Oh bhikṣus, it is for sure that all bodies
have the character of the five skandhas[877]
Being impermanent, suffering, and empty,
they aren't any caste, nor belong to a caste[878] [103]

Someone who is born from a fisherwoman's
womb belongs to the caste of the caṇḍālas[879]
Through austerity, he is born as a brahman
For this reason, caste is without any cause[880] [104]

Be they mother, sister, daughter,[881]
the mother-in-law, or the niece,
brahman, kṣatriya, vaiśya, śūdra[882]
women, by having the know-how,[883] [105] {46}

whether missing a limb, being inferior,
reviled, or belonging to the lowest caste,
women are always to be worshipped
by the wisdom vajra's manifestations[884] [106]

By means of always having a smiling face
and with their eyes wide open, the mantrīs,
setting their mind upon perfect awakening
and meditating on their own supreme deity,[885] [107]

should look at what is seen in that moment,
should likewise listen to whatever is heard,
should be free from what is true and untrue,
and dauntlessly say what needs to be said[886] [108]

By way of making efforts in bathing, anointing,
clothing, and so on, food, drink, and so forth,
these are to be regarded as the ritual of worship
through the yoga of your own supreme deity[887] [109]

It is in songs, music, and likewise dance that
those of yogic discipline engage with the means
They should not entertain the slightest clinging
toward any among the entire range of entities[888] [110]

They should not torment themselves with austerity
through relinquishing their very own character
In accordance with being absorbed in mind as bliss,
this constitutes the future perfect buddhahood[889] [111]

Due to the enjoyments[890] of all desires,
there is joy, as liberation is not feared
Don't be afraid! There is no misdeed!
The samaya is very hard to transgress[891] [112]

Wood and so on treated with mantra
will attain the state of being divine,
so what about the body possessing wisdom?
Yet conduct based on nescience is difficult[892] [113]

Having relinquished the self-centeredness
of being ordinary, in meditative absorption
and by the expedient of prajñā and means,
it is these actions that are to be performed[893] [114] {47}

Just as a lotus that is born from mud
is not stained by any flaws of mud,
so the yogīs do not become stained
by the flaws of thoughts' imprints[894] [115]

Just as the moon [reflected] in water
does not become stained by any water,

by seeing various reflection-like [things],
you will not be stained by any flaws[895] [116]

The jewel of mind that is stained
by muds of beginningless imprints,
if washed with the water of prajñā
and means, will be shining brightly[896] [117]

For the intelligent with stable minds
and their own supreme deity's yoga,
freed from the clouds of bad views,
the sun of the mind is shining forth[897] [118]

Having ascertained the ultimate
by cutting[898] with prajñā's weapon,
the dharmadhātu shall shine forth
from its cover of ignorance's cocoon[899] [119]

Once the hammer of prajñā breaks
the vase of thoughts instantaneously,
the lamp of wisdom, being naturally
stainless and clear, illuminates [all][900] [120]

The well-known[901] elements—
earth, water, fire, and wind—
are transformed[902] by the wise
with mantra-power's yoga[903] [121]

Having relinquished all talking,
mantra talk should be practiced[904]
Thanks to the power of mantra,
The state of bliss[905] is achieved too[906] [122]

The Three Jewels[907] are not to be abandoned,
and the same goes for bodhicitta and the guru[908]
Not even a single living being should be killed[909]
and the samayas[910] should also be blessed[911] [123] {48}

Wine, blood,[912] and camphor,
combined with red sandalwood,
and the vajra water of a sage[913]—
these five should also be blessed[914] [124]

Through other divine samayas[915]
that serve to elevate the mind,
to still the turbulence of wind,
please the mind-vajra's bearer![916] [125]

Doubt-free about [actions of] immediate consequence,[917]
it is by making efforts in thought-free yoga
and with a readily embracing[918] frame of mind
that mantrīs should engage in everything[919] [126]

[If not,] they are overcome by poison
that consists of a mere mosquito's leg
Just an atom of aversion and doubt
will entail hardships equal to death[920] [127]

The wise should fight a good battle[921]
or they should make a good run for it,[922]
but any state in between is pointless—
it will simply become their downfall[923] [128]

The commands, the seals, and the shadow
of the guru should not be stepped over[924]
Their qualities are to be held as supreme[925]
but never ever a single one of their faults[926] [129]

The master is the supreme deity
to be worshipped with great vigor
He himself is King Vajradhara,
residing in a form before your eyes[927] [130]

Similar to a pure[928] water-gem
purifying[929] water that is turbid,[930]

likewise, the gem of devotion[931]
is said to purify mind's jewel[932] [131]

When they miss out on the eye of prajñā,
some who possess devotion[933] get deluded[934]
Hence they should give rise to the prajñā
characterized by scripture and realization[935] [132]

Those with prajñā, devotion, and erudition
have the character of compassion by nature {49}
It is in order to remove the world's suffering
that they are discovering the means of bliss[936] [133]

Through the bliss that I attained
taking up the purification of mind,
taking up the purification of mind,
may [all] people come to be happy[937] [134]

This concludes "A Discussion Called 'The Purification of Mind's Obscurations'" composed by master Āryadeva.[938] {50}

(16) An Illumination of Prajñā Wisdom

In the language of India: *Prajñājñānaprakāśa*[939]
In the language of Tibet: *Shes rab ye shes gsal ba*

I pay homage to the true gurus[940]

Being similar to the light rays of the shining sun opening the groves of closed lotuses,
the state beautified by incorporating all the bliss of omniscience, in just a single instant,
severs the fetters that connect with rebirth and dispels the flaws of beings' cloudy vision
Thanks to the victory of the victor's speech coming from spiritual friends, may beings always be at peace![941]

In whom is it that the path of the children of the victors,
such as Mañjuvajra, realizing consummate wisdom exists?
The way it is expressed as mere recollection[942] in the insight
of low ordinary beings such as me deserves forbearance

This path coming from what the teacher Śrīmat Śabareśvara found on Mount Bālārka[943]
has been demonstrated to me in a most direct manner by the victorious illuminating guru[944]
I shall discuss it here with a mindset that is stainless {51}—you people, muster some faith!

Whatever is not tenable here through scripture and reasoning is to be rid by the learned!

The skandhas, the dhātus, and the āyatanas,
empty of imputations of being and nonbeing,
are precisely like this prajñā wisdom itself
Therefore I shall discuss this prajñā wisdom

This refers to the lack of nature that bears the other name "the unsurpassable suchness that consists of the Bhagavān's marvelous and nonreferential great compassion and is endowed with all supreme aspects."[945] Nevertheless, though the Bhagavān, through the power of his former aspiration prayers, taught [this] profound and vast yoga of great bliss by effortlessly and excellently taking on the kāya of unity that solely benefits all sentient beings,[946] with the intention of benefiting infinite sentient beings who wander in saṃsāric existence due to their delusion, through all kinds of statements endowed with all kinds of means to liberate many sentient beings, he provided the progressive stages[947] of the Śrāvaka[yāna], the Pratyekabuddha[yāna], and the Mahāyāna.

Yet for the sake of disciples with the mindset of the pure conduct of paying service and respect to the gurus, the buddhas, and the bodhisattvas out of utter devotion, who possess the prajñā of utterly pure insight, who have well-prepared insight by virtue of understanding the sūtra collection, the Abhidharma, the Vinaya, and the Jātaka [tales], {52} who, thanks to being trained and guided [well], have the mindset of relinquishing nonvirtuous actions, dwelling in virtuous actions, and engaging with compassion, and who have turned their backs on any clinging to saṃsāra, in order to make them swiftly attain unsurpassable completely perfect awakening thanks to their nature of relying on true spiritual friends, preceded by them entering the maṇḍala and [receiving] the water and crown empowerments and so on, he taught the prajñā wisdom that is supreme.

"But why did he teach this? Passion and so on are the causes for wandering through the lower realms in saṃsāra for a long time. Having clung to that [passion and so on], sentient beings are ignorant about thus ending up in terrifying rebirths. Being attached, they [likewise] give rise to hatred, thereby committing evil nonvirtuous actions and then experiencing great sufferings as animals, hungry ghosts, and hell beings [as a result]. Don't you see that in those who cling to this kind of poison, joining them with passion and so on [only] increases this poison, just like pouring milk [onto this poison]?"[948]

This is true, [but only for] those without spiritual friends who, by entertaining attachment due to passion and such, solely suffer. For that reason, a lot has been taught [about dispassion] in the Śrāvaka[yāna] and Pratyekabuddhayāna. Furthermore, since those who are greatly dispassionate hate passion, {53} they give rise to very much suffering, but passion has not been taught for their sake. The following is stated:

> Those who are without any passion[949]
> will come to entertain doubts again
> In order that they relinquish passion,
> dispassion is not to be made suitable[950]

The Bhagavān said this:

> In the three realms, there's no other
> evil that is like being dispassionate
> It is for that reason that you should
> never make yourself dispassionate[951]

For those who have passion and are not dispassionate, great passion is taught. As it is stated:

> Objects that some[952] enjoy in passion,
> some relinquish thanks to dispassion
> Those yogīs who have stainless minds
> don't deal in adopting or relinquishing

Śrī Saraha declared this:

> There are some who abandon objects
> and some who are fettered by objects

Some, the best among humans, attain
awakening through these very objects[953]

Therefore, sentient beings with passion [are made to enter] dispassion, and those who are dispassionate are made to enter moderate passion. Those with moderate passion are established in great passion.[954] Hence this unsurpassable and very profound prajñā wisdom is taught with regard to those sentient beings who are supreme. Here, the Bhagavān declared this: {54}

It is through the very bit of poison
through which all people will die
that those knowing poison's nature
destroy that poison through poison[955]

Elsewhere, we find: "Passion is a branch of awakening. Hatred is a branch of awakening," and so forth. The *Jñānasiddhi* declares the following:

As in the example of copper pierced
by mercury becoming beautiful gold,
by way of being pierced by wisdom,
the afflictions do produce virtue[956]

Therefore the five skandhas are called "form," "feeling," "discrimination," formations," and "consciousness," but [actually] they are pure Vairocana, Ratnasambhava, Amitābha, Amoghasiddhi, and Akṣobhya, respectively. The twelve āyatanas are the six sense faculties and the six objects. The twelve dhātus are to be known as the eye dhātu, the form dhātu, the eye-consciousness dhātu, and likewise the ear-consciousness dhātu and so on. The four great elements consist of the earth element, the water element, the fire element, and the wind element; since they hold their own specific characteristics, they are the dhātus. Since they are empty of thoughts about existence and nonexistence, they are free from the four extremes: the knowledge that they are unborn, unperishing,[957] and without any nature is {55} what is called "prajñā." The following is stated:

That which is born from conditions is unborn
It does not possess any nature of being born
That which depends on conditions is empty
Those who understand emptiness are heedful[958]

In the *Tattvāvatāra*, this is said:

What is not any discursiveness's object,
that is not the object of speech either
The true reality known by Vajradhara
is greatly renowned as being "prajñā"[959]

Therefore the diverse states of mind that originate in dependence are sheer self-aware great bliss—that is, the prajñā wisdom that bears the other name "nonreferential great compassion."[960] [We speak of] the compound ["prajñā wisdom"] because it is both prajñā and wisdom. The mouth of the true guru declares this:

For the wise in whom thoughts vanished,
all aspects are the true reality that is bliss
[But] this blissful reality is not emptiness
Bliss is neither inconceivable nor bliss[961]

And:

Aspects constitute direct awakening—
the great insight that is thinking-free
If it were other, it would be blindness
If it were not other, it would be matter[962]

The Bhagavān said the following:

Hence, bliss is not declared to be true reality
because bliss consists of the great elements[963]

He furthermore stated this and more in detail:

Bliss is black, bliss is yellow,
bliss is red, bliss is white,
bliss is green, bliss is blue,
bliss is all mobile and immobile

Bliss is prajñā, bliss is method,
bliss also arises from kunduru,
bliss is being, bliss is nonbeing,
and Vajrasattva is known as bliss[964] {56}

This is the emptiness endowed with all supreme aspects, the Bhagavatī Prajñāpāramitā, who abides everywhere in the form of shapely women who are karma[mudrās].[965] As it is said:

Those fully desiring liberation
should rely[966] on prajñāpāramitā
who abides in the pure ultimate
and yet assumes seeming bodies

And:

The divine syllable E, which is
adorned with VAṂ at its center,
represents all bliss's repository,
the jewel casket of buddhahood[967]

Since the Bhagavān declared such, this is to be taken as the prime true means to accomplish fully perfect awakening. Hence, with a mind free of doubts,[968] the intention of pulling out all beings [from saṃsāra], the taste of great compassion, and the empowerment and permission[969] for the perfect bliss of passion, in accordance with the pith instructions, you should rely on[970] a prajñā who possesses samaya as described [above].[971] As it is said:

No buddhahood through other means—
the three worlds consist of that purity

It is for that reason that you should
never separate yourself from this[972]

And:

This is all the buddhas' unsurpassable
yogic discipline of an awareness consort
If some fools choose to go beyond this,
they will be without the supreme siddhi

"But how could this {57} be tenable? For the following is said:

"The karmamudrā is devious, wrathful,
evil, and cunning, as well as terrifying—
you should stay very far away from her[973]

"Furthermore, the *Ārali[tantra]* declares this:

"The way of being of human females[974] is to perish[975]
The wisdom from them certainly perishes [too][976]

"The *Jñānasiddhi* states this:

"Some wretched people say the pleasure
born from the two organs is true reality
However, the greatly excellent victors
do not proclaim that that is great bliss[977]

"Since this and more is stated, karmamudrā does not have the nature of the connate and is therefore to be relinquished."

This is true because karmamudrā is contrived. Thus, "karma" refers to actions, which have the characteristics of the body, speech, and mind's intentions. The mudrā that illustrates this and has the essence of imagination[978] is what is expressed as "karmamudrā." Since the dharmamudrā is not contrived, its characteristic is to be nondifferent, and therefore it is without difference. Mahāmudrā has the characteristic of realizing this as the lack of any nature of its own—it is uncontrived. Merely through contrived prajñā wisdom, the essence of great bliss that is uninterrupted, like the stream of a river—the omniscient wisdom that is the indestructible true reality of suchness, unsurpassable in all respects—will definitely not arise. Therefore Nāgārjuna taught it as a result of concordant outflow {58} because even its being taught as the connate is just like a resemblance of the connate.[979] Thus my guru declared this:

> Those yogīs who do not know mahāmudrā,
> with the karmamudrā as their single device,
> fall away from sacred tradition's[980] true reality
> and will then take their journey to Raurava[981]

"But then how does [the above line] 'No buddhahood through other means' teach that the jewel casket of buddhahood is without any doubt thanks to this very karmamudrā?" This is not untenable either. What is called "great passion" is the great passion that consists of mahāmudrā, whose nature is infinite bliss, and which is the essence of all entities. This is the passion that has the essence of the unity of the pair of emptiness and compassion—being blissful and passionate within the highest culmination of the illumination of this passion. Since this is not experienced except through a karmamudrā, it cannot be demonstrated directly; rather, it will be attained through becoming familiar with the highest culmination of great [passion] and through the pith instructions of the guru. Therefore there is no contradiction in teaching karmamudrā first. In the pith instructions of the true guru, we find this:

> Once you obtained[982] the karmamudrā,
> you should cultivate the dharmamudrā
> What is higher than this is mahāmudrā,
> from which the samayamudrā arises[983]

In the *Caturmudrā[nvaya]*, master [Nāgārjuna] thus stated that the mere ecstasy [thanks to a karmamudrā] is a result of concordant outflow, {59} and [the three remaining mudrās] in their succession are like[984] results of maturation and stainlessness, and then [the result] that is produced by persons.[985] The true guru declares this:

Variety constitutes the karmamudrā
The dharmamudrā arises in maturation
Lack of characteristics is mahāmudrā
Consummation is the samaya[mudrā][986]

Here, since the four ecstasies arise in each mudrā, except for mahāmudrā, they are to be realized through the pith instructions in accordance with shapely women who are karma[mudrās] and the enumerations of the four ecstasies and the four moments. The following is stated:

Due to being variegated, variety is up to friction
Due to being bliss, maturation is before the jewel
True reality needs to be understood from the guru
Due to consummation, cessation is in dispassion[987]

In the Buddha's words, this is declared:

Variety is known as various kinds:
embracing and kissing and so forth
Maturation constitutes its opposite:
the blissful experience of wisdom

Consummation is proclaimed to be the
consideration "I have partaken of bliss"[988]

Therefore the connate that consists of the inseparability of emptiness and compassion, which is situated in the middle between supreme ecstasy and cessational ecstasy, rid of the forceful empowerment and the wrong empowerment, and devoid of passion and dispassion, is to be realized by experiencing it from the mouth of the true guru. Nobody at all is able to realize this anywhere else than in such a [setting]: {60} what is to be accomplished [here] is that all phenomena in this way lack any nature of their own. This [accords with] scriptural passages such as "Form is empty. Emptiness also is form. Likewise, feeling . . ." and

> That which has arisen in dependence
> has not arisen through its own nature
> What has not arisen by its own nature,
> how could that be designated "arisen?"[989]

This is what authoritative statements declare: whichever cognitions may arise in whichever ways, they are without any nature of their own. Hence all phenomena are completely pure by nature, not just the karmamudrā. This is the teaching on the wisdom thanks to a shapely woman who is a prajñā, which is preceded by the purity of the tathāgatas. This shall be enough elaboration on a lot of procedures.[990]

Then, the final tenet of those who follow the Pāramitāyāna is this: one becomes a perfect buddha through [practicing for] incalculable eons. Those who realize that through the mantra approach they will become a buddha or Vajrasattva in this very lifetime assert [buddhahood] as the goal to be accomplished that is endowed with the seven constituents. The following is declared:

> Here, what I hold to be endowed with the seven constituents
> of complete enjoyment, union, great bliss, the lack of nature,
> being filled with compassion, uninterrupted, and unceasing
> is the goal praised by those whose minds valid cognition
> penetrated[991] {61}

"Isn't one able to know this experience without a shapely woman[992] who is a karmamudrā?" This [question] is not nice: an outer [karma]mudrā is said to be a result of concordant outflow, but this is [of course] not true reality. It is tenable for what is endowed with these seven constituents to be the wisdom of emptiness and compassion inseparable. (1) Since it is completely enjoyed in such a way, complete enjoyment refers to experience: thanks to dependent origination, it appears as all aspects.[993] (2) It is union because emptiness and compassion are completely unified in an inseparable manner. (3) It is great bliss because all thoughts of existence, nonexistence, and so on have been relinquished. (4) It lacks a nature [because] it is unborn. (5) It is filled with compassion because it has the character of compassion. (6) It is uninterrupted because it is permanent in terms of its continuum. (7) It is unceasing because it is not discontinued.[994] Those special features do not exist in the wisdom, thanks to a shapely woman who is a karma[mudrā].

"The statement 'I will be a buddha or great[995] Vajradhara in this very lifetime' seems to be like the words of small children. Saying 'I am Vajrasattva' due to being inflated like that, why do those who are involved in thinking about themselves deride[996] themselves? For example, this is like wood gatherers[997] {62} saying 'I am a king.' Not only are they not kings at all, but isn't [such talk] also well known as[998] [a sign of] suffering from wind disease? Therefore, compared to the Pāramitāyāna, we do not see any difference with regard to the Mantra[yāna]."[999]

It is not like in such a statement for the following reasons. This is stated [in the mantra treatises]:

> Though the goal is the same, since it lacks ignorance,
> since it is abundant in means, since it lacks difficulty,
> and since it is the prerogative of those of sharp faculties,
> it is the mantra teaching[1000] that is more distinguished[1001]

The following is declared in the Mantrayāna:

> The purity of all phenomena
> is maintained to be suchness[1002]

"(1) That the goal is the same because both [the Pāramitāyāna and the Mantrayāna] practice alike is definitely true.

"(2) However, since the reason of lacking ignorance applies equally to the Pāramitā[yāna], what would be the difference? Does this [ignorance] here refer to the flaws of ignorant people or to the flaws of this [Pāramitā]yāna? First, in a yāna that is characterized by dealing with the lack of nature, there is no ignorance because [otherwise] the same [flaw of ignorance] would equally follow for both [yānas]. You may say that [ignorance must then] refer to the ignorant minds of the persons who aspire for the goal. Though that seems to be the case, [this cannot be a criterion for distinguishing these two yānas] because the ignorance of persons also appears in the Mantrayāna.

"(3) Being abundant in means [cannot be a criterion of distinction] either because through becoming familiar with the means (such as the pāramitā of generosity in which the three spheres are unobservable) and the three natures (the imaginary, the dependent, and the perfect [natures]), {63} suchness—the lack of nature—will be seen. It is not reasonable [for this to happen] merely through engaging in passion just because there are the special means of ecstasy and so on. For it is declared that 'bodhisattva mahāsattvas who are embraced by the skill in the means of prajñāpāramitā will swiftly and fully perfectly awaken into unsurpassable and completely perfect awakening.'[1003]

"(4) To lack difficulty also applies equally to both [the Pāramitāyāna and the Mantrayāna]: since all entities, such as blue and yellow, are realized to be pure by nature, what could there be in them that could be called a 'difficulty'?

"(5) That it is the prerogative of those with sharp faculties are entitled to it also applies equally [to both the Pāramitāyāna and the Mantrayāna]: since all phenomena that arise from conditions do not arise and do not cease through any nature of their own, it is those of sharp faculties who aspire for this, but not those of lower [faculties].

"Furthermore, if their individual own natures are analyzed, since it is only the pāramitā treatises that are of definitive meaning, they are supreme, while others are of expedient meaning. For example, [in the Mantrayāna,] just like a fire arising from a fire-kindling stick, a fireboard, and so on, or sounds arising from a vīṇā, form represents Vairocana, {64} and that is sealed with consciousness bearing the name Akṣobhya, and that [in turn] has the nature of being sealed with Vajrasattva.[1004] Therefore this is mere discursiveness. In actuality, sheer diverse experiences are to be accomplished as primordial luminosity. What is stated[1005] here by those who delight in great discursiveness is [actually] sufficient[1006] in its condensed form, whereas the karmamudrā, which is [like] needing to wash what has already been washed, is unnecessary. This corresponds to the following statement:

> "Who has been teaching that the protector
> is the expresser or support of this here?
> Did he teach by his head's crown curling
> to the right and his hands being crooked?[1007]

"Furthermore, those who assert that the bliss of karmamudrā is the [ultimate] reality[1008] [refer to] a limited purity: what has the nature of the skandhas, dhātus, and āyatanas needs to be purified through prajñā.[1009] So why not familiarize with the purity of all entities in a direct manner? Yet in this yāna of great passion, it is said that the perfect buddhahood that has the form of uncontaminated bliss will be accomplished through enjoying the five sense pleasures:

> "By virtue of bringing about great bliss
> through the joining of the two organs,
> the supreme state of buddha awakening—
> unsurpassable true reality—is achieved[1010]

"However, [this is not appropriate,] because in the pāramitā teachings it is declared that 'you should enjoy the five sense pleasures in the manner of being very frightened [of them].' {65} [But] through some bliss that involves fear and anxiety, awakening will not be attained."

(1) This [objection] is not nice for the following reasons. Sentient beings are of three kinds by being classified as lower, medium, and highest. It is for the lower and medium ones that these [Pāramitāyāna teachings] are taught, but the highest ones who course in nonreferentiality relish the five sense pleasures without any fear, just as the noble Dharmodgata did in the company of 68,000 women.[1011] Thus, by enjoying the five sense pleasures, they do not relinquish them.

Moreover, it is taught that the kāyas of a tathāgata arise from the dharmadhātu, and that that [dharmadhātu] is not dispassionate. What are called "happiness" and "suffering" are what those whose minds are impaired by ignorance cling to. Thus, [their] activities swiftly perish in a single instant or in a very short time. Those who are afraid of[1012] the illuminating moon will even be tormented by a shooting star. Unlike them, we have neither fears nor likes. Therefore, since both are equal,[1013] there is neither cold nor heat because ultimately there is no imagination [of any of this].

"But what[1014] is the nature of the goal?"[1015] {66} The Bhagavān taught joining the two organs for the sake of those to be guided who are guided through passion.[1016] Hence [the goal in] the Pāramitāyāna is to be taken as the definitive meaning [here too].[1017] The following is said:

> If the karmamudrā is missing,
> then mahāmudrā does not exist
> If the karmamudrā and so forth
> aren't there, it is not mahāmudrā
> Those who savor their own words
> deserve no respect by the realized[1018]

Therefore the cultivation of the karmamudrā and so on is also primordially pure. This is stated:

> The specifics of causes and their results
> are described so as to introduce beings[1019]
> It is through the specifics of mahāmudrā
> that the karmamudrā and so forth abide
> Apart from mahāmudrā, a karmamudrā
> and so on has never ever any existence

The *Tattvāvatāra* teaches the following:

> Karmamudrā meditation and so on
> are what is more and more supreme
> Thus the previous are to be given up
> Such is what our guru has explained[1020]

"How is this explanation of true reality not [some form of] extinction?"[1021] This is not reasonable: the dependent origination of arising from conditions means being unborn. The following is declared:

Just what is dependent origination
is what you hold to be emptiness
Of like kind is the genuine dharma
and the Tathāgata is the same as it[1022]

Furthermore this is said:

Those who see dependent origination {67} see the dharma, and those who see the dharma will see the unsurpassable buddhakāya.[1023]

The *Brahmaviśeṣacintiparipṛcchāmahāyānasūtra* states the following:

Those who understand dependence
are those who understand dharmatā
Those who understand dharmatā
are those understanding emptiness
Those who understand emptiness
are the ones who see the guides[1024]

This dependent origination constitutes experience:

This is the character of the great bliss
that has the nature of boundless bliss

Anaṅgavajra declares this:

Since it has the nature of infinite bliss,
it is designated as "glorious great bliss"[1025]

The diversity of all aspects, such as blue and yellow, surely appears like a dream and like the city of the gandharvas, but it is not permanent, because it is without any being. As it is said:

By virtue of having arisen in dependence,
they manifest like the gandharvas' city

Diversity is not established as any nature,
nor is it comparable to a lotus in the sky[1026]

Therefore dependent origination is the continuum[1027] of effortless nondual unity, and its diversity refers to the experience of great bliss, which is to be accomplished as the primordial lack of any nature. Hence, this is stated: {68}

Whatever may originate in dependence
is the mind that is diverse and nondual
The division into emptiness, mind, and diversity
is the dharma-, sambhoga-, and nirmāṇa[kāyas][1028]

Those whose meditation consists of sheer emptiness, has the nature of extinction, is the nondifference of dependent origination and emptiness, is without aspects, is with aspects, or has the form of equanimity will never accomplish the essence of great bliss because [the unity] that has the form of great bliss is not realized without the union of the two organs. Without that, the sambhogakāya that has the essence of great bliss will not be accomplished. Thus what is to be cultivated is the realization that, just like waves on the ocean, the distinct instances of the skandhas, dhātus, and āyatanas [actually] are the wisdom of thought-free bliss that has the character of means and prajñā. If that cultivation has reached its highest culmination, it becomes the great bliss that is the essence of all entities, but such is not the case by way of cultivating any remedies. Therefore it is by cultivating the wisdom that is [based on] a karmamudrā and so on that the completely perfect buddhahood whose nature is great bliss is accomplished, but not even the slightest bliss will be experienced by [simply] abandoning all thoughts. {69} For thereby the result is seen in accordance with its cause.

Furthermore, being thought-free has the essence of great bliss, but how could [being thought-free] be accomplished from thoughts about the characteristics[1029] of remedies, true reality, and the fruition due to being afraid of the five sense pleasures? The following is stated:

Those who do not abide in the remedies,
who even lack attachment to true reality,

and who have no desire[1030] for the fruition,
it is they who will discover mahāmudrā[1031]

Without any doubt, whether the mind is stable or agitated, it should rely on the five sense pleasures without any anxiety. Therefore,[1032] by keeping in mind that even the afflictions are naturally pure, there is no fear of being bound by the afflictions. Thus, this is declared:

Afflictions are not different from awakening,
nor do afflictions arise within awakening
Thoughts of afflictions are due to delusion,
yet delusion is naturally without any stain[1033]

Therefore, within this the afflictions don't stand a chance, because the seeming [reality] of yogīs invalidates the seeming [reality] of ordinary beings.[1034] Through generating bodhicitta for the sake of sentient beings by always cultivating virtue, just like a wish-fulfilling jewel,[1035] they engage in the welfare that is desired by all sentient beings and therefore will never[1036] regress.

Moreover, it is important to aspire for the lack of nature:[1037] {70} if fear and anxiety arise, at that time, the way things truly are is not realized. The following is stated:

The śrāvaka yogīs are those tormented by thirst
The pratyekabuddhas[1038] are cautious about the body
In the mahāyāna, there exists dread and anxiety
The five afflictions' purity is the mantra approach

Therefore, even if such [fear of the sense pleasures] may be discussed in the pāramitā approach, without karmamudrā and so on, this kind of buddhahood that is free of thoughts and endowed with the seven constituents is not directly perceived.

Furthermore, AHO, since these people are overcome by mistakenness, they do not realize their own character as being the nature of the deity whose essence is nirvāṇa and entertain [their own wrong] pride that is like blurred vision. It is unreasonable for those who have the pride of the deity as it should be to quarrel with [people who are like] wood gatherers; rather, [the latter] are worthy of being treated with great[1039] compassion. Therefore, by looking at sentient beings who are overcome by the blurred vision of great nescience, the mindset of great compassion arises in bodhisattvas.

> Through these diverse forms of emptiness,
> the welfare of sentient beings is promoted
> Your own body is what represents deities,
> so why not wish for something like that?
>
> Do beings not have the character of victors?
> By its own nature, self-awareness is stainless—
> still, they have a very childish way of being

Here, {71} since lion cubs have little fear, even though they do not know their own strength, they have the power of defeating others who are their opponents. Likewise, ordinary beings do not become exhausted by their ways of being people with one face, two hands, and so on, but they are also not two-handed vajra holders. There is not the slightest to adopt or to reject—seeing your own nature[1040] well is awakening.[1041] Thus, without being in contradiction to the creation process, by cultivating self-blessing, the connate is accomplished through the maṇḍala circle of diversity having the character of deities.[1042] As Nāgārjuna says:

> This is the palace, not the three realms, nor objects, faculties, elements, and such,
> neither form and so forth, nor living creatures, nor humans—these are the victors
> The cakra lord has the character of dharmatā, thus they are the maṇḍala's inhabitants
> If these three realms' diversity is known as the cakra, why, oh mind, create delusion?[1043]

In the *Śrīhevajratantra*, this is declared:

> There are no mantra recitations, no austerities, no fire offerings,
> no inhabitants of any maṇḍalas, nor the maṇḍalas themselves

This is mantra recitation, this is austerities, this is fire offering,
this is the inhabitants of maṇḍalas and the maṇḍalas
themselves
In brief, those are mind, which has the nature of communion[1044]

Elsewhere, {72} this is said:

Beyond cultivating the body's entirety,
being free from thoughts and thinking,
transcending minute portions and bindus—
that constitutes the supreme maṇḍala[1045]

By cultivating this true reality, you need to effortlessly cultivate dependent origination: the very pure approach, thanks to rising from[1046] both meditative equipoise and not being in meditative equipoise, is the unmistaken view. Anaṅgavajra says this:

Where there isn't any meditator,
there isn't any meditation either
There is nothing to meditate upon
It's named "true reality meditation"[1047]

The Bhagavān stated the following in the *Laṅkāvatāra[sūtra]*:

Those in dhyāna, dhyānas, dhyāna objects,
relinquishment, and the seeing of reality—
[all] these constitute nothing but thoughts
Those ones who understand this are free[1048]

The *Śrīguhyasamājatantra* declares this:

With no being, there's no meditation
Meditation indeed is not meditation
Given that being is not being,
meditation is not observable[1049]

Hence, this is stated:

Conduct without purpose constitutes dhyāna
"Existence" or "nonexistence" are not voiced,
because, similar to a flavor[1050] that always arises,
this is what constitutes dependent origination

Due to true reality being searched,[1051] having
the notion that it exists is called "dhyāna"
Other than familiarity, there is no buddha[1052]
Hence you should make efforts in dhyāna {73}

Therefore, except with karmamudrā, the direct perception of being unborn cannot be demonstrated[1053] because then its concordant cause cannot be demonstrated. Though this [being unborn] is expressed through the Pāramitāyāna instructions, the thoughts [behind it] are not complete.

Though there exists no difference between
directly seeing this in such a manner and
the way of seeing, hearing, and talking too,
the former represents desire's termination

For the mighty Victor has taught true reality through scriptures and reasonings in the pāramitā approach. However, as far as the true reality that is the means of accomplishing self-awareness goes, doesn't its direct perception exist [only] in the mantra approach? Hence, though the goal is the same,[1054] the Bhagavān taught the Prajñāpāramitāyāna that is called "the causal teaching" separately. This Vajrayāna is the fruitional teaching because it demonstrates the fruition.

(2) Those who are experts in talking say: "Ignorance occurs in both [the Pāramitāyāna and the Mantrayāna]." This is [not correct,] because [the Mantrayāna] is similar to some who, by virtue of knowing the true reality of poison, eat food mixed with poison and make snakes into adornments without being harmed by the poisons. To have the mindset of thinking "there is nothing other than realizing this ultimate [reality]" does not become ignorance. Likewise, though by virtue of scriptures and reasonings, this so-called poison [of ignorance] does not exist at all, {74}

since there are doubts about what is not the ultimate,[1055] [ultimate true reality] will not be entered. Though there is no[1056] remedy that includes a mantra that pacifies the poison of ignorance, once a speck of that poison has been tasted, one cannot say that it is not overcome as something other than that.

(3) To say that, in [the context of] cultivating the pāramitās, the means that consists of meditating on the three natures (the imaginary, dependent, and perfect [natures]) equals the abundance of means [in the Mantrayāna] is a bad approach when examined. For example, wishing to show something beneficial to a blind person who lacks any experience of perceiving forms, with that mindset, someone with eyesight may tell[1057] them: "The nature of forms is such and such." Then, [that blind person] may meditate by aspiring for [what forms are like] by way of having heard about them and so on, but they will not quickly perceive [forms] in a direct manner. Likewise, since those in the Pāramitā[yāna] have never experienced the four ecstasies associated with the four moments, such as variety, they do not realize the essence of the connate because they do not directly perceive the moment of the lack of characteristics; without that, they are not able to directly perceive the great full awakening.

By contrast, the Mantrayāna [is different] for the following two reasons. By virtue of consisting of the purity of the five[1058] tathāgatas, it lacks any latent tendencies of ordinary beings. Directly perceiving equal taste by engaging in all samayas through the yoga that is endowed with the pride of the deity, {75} through the means of accomplishment such as the four mudrās, the completely perfect buddhahood that is endowed with the seven constituents is directly perceived in the form of self-aware perception in this very lifetime. [Consequently,] the abundance of means refers to the self-blessing that consists of karmamudrā and so on. The Bhagavān declared this:

> No buddhahood through other means[1059]

The **Guhyakoṣasūtra* says the following:

> Listen, Vajrasattva! You are able to attain buddhahood through this great secret empowerment[1060] of the supreme yāna of secret

> mantra, but buddhahood will not be attained through any other yānas even in ten million incalculable eons.[1061]

The *Sarvabuddhasamāyogatantra* says this:

> In millions of incalculable eons,
> all the buddhas are not attained
> Through the ritual of this mudrā,
> they will be attained in this life[1062]

The intention behind this is as follows. Through any other means, apart from mere buddhahood, the buddhahood that is completely perfect is not attained, because mahāmudrā—the union whose essence is bliss—is lacking; for [even] for great bodhisattvas such as Mañjuśrī, the sambhogakāya does not arise through enjoying the taste of wisdom.[1063] For the joining of emptiness and compassion {76} is not said [specific] union; rather, it is through the mere creation process or through becoming familiar[1064] with this kind [of union] that the wisdom that has the form of bliss as self-awareness and emptiness arises from uniting the two organs—it will not be experienced in such a way through anything [else] at all. Therefore, by lacking [this kind] of familiarity, the state of Vajrasattva that has the character of the great bliss of true reality[1065] is not attained. Hence, in this approach of great passion here, [this kind of] union is taught in order to accomplish Vajrasattva. Consequently, since there is a difference in buddhahood here, it is referred to as "Vajradhara."

"But in the pāramitā approach as well, the sambhogakāya is accomplished. The noble protector Maitreya says this:

> "As this [kāya] of the Sage, whose character lies in
> the thirty-two major marks and eighty minor marks,
> is the one that enjoys the Mahāyāna,
> it is held to be the sāmbhogikakāya[1066]

"So why should there be any flaw[1067] in this [sambhogakāya] existing [in the Pāramitāyāna]?" I do not refute the sambhogakāya in those [statements], nor is it that there is no completely perfect buddhahood [in the Pāramitāyāna]. For the following is declared:

These beings in their entirety[1068] will become buddhas[1069]
There is no sentient being here at all who is not a vessel[1070]

Furthermore, through cultivating the pāramitā of generosity and so on by not observing the three spheres, {77} [those in the Pāramitāyāna] attain the [first] bhūmi and then accomplish [the remaining ones] up through the tenth bhūmi during three incalculable eons, upon which they directly perceive the lack of nature: having gathered the accumulations of merit and wisdom, it is as a mere play[1071] that they display the essence of buddhahood, and they will be able to attain completely perfect buddhahood before long. Seeing directly that all tathāgatas arrive and take care of them, they obtain instructions by means of the mantra approach,[1072] and thus directly perceive completely perfect buddhahood in the time of a finger snap.[1073]

In the Mantrayāna, even those who committed the five actions of immediate consequence, if they have the [proper] conditions, such as the disposition, accomplish the way things truly are thanks to relying on a true spiritual friend and through the means of karmamudrā. Thus, through the pith instructions on how things are,[1074] they engage in virtue while relinquishing evil nonvirtuous actions, and through the distinctive feature of being skilled in means, in just a finger snap complete the unsurpassable accumulation of merit that consists of generosity and such, thus attaining buddhahood or[1075] [the state of] Vajradhara in this very lifetime. This is the difference [between the Pāramitāyāna and the Mantrayāna]. As it is stated in the *Hevajratantra*:

Those committing the five actions of immediate consequence,
those who take delight in taking the lives of living beings,
even the ones who have assumed births that are inferior,
those who are fools, those who perform deeds of cruelty,

those who are deformed, and also those who miss limbs {78}
will gain accomplishment by virtue of [proper] thinking[1076]

The *Vajrāralli[tantra]* declares this:

> Desire, hatred, and nescience
> are enjoyed in the Mahāyāna[1077]

The same [text] says the following:

> This Mahāyāna is as follows: it teaches two—the Pāramitāyāna and the Mantrayāna that have the nature[1078] of being of cause and result, respectively.[1079]

The intention behind this is that both yānas engage in true reality.[1080]

"Since it is taught that [bodhisattvas] abide on the first bhūmi, Supreme Joy, by virtue of generosity and so on, having attained such and such [bhūmis] through cultivating the six pāramitās, they will attain irreversibility[1081] and then swiftly accomplish unsurpassable and completely perfect buddhahood. Since the statement 'The first bhūmi is accomplished supremely' teaches the Pāramitāyāna, why would the Pāramitāmahāyāna[1082] not accomplish [completely perfect buddhahood]?"

It is not like that. Though [completely perfect buddhahood] can be [accomplished through the Pāramitāyāna], it will take a long time by such [means]. It is also possible that this will not happen[1083] because [the Pāramitāyāna] lacks the means to accomplish great bliss (such as karmamudrā), wherefore it is still possible to fall down into some lower yānas even if the bhūmis have been attained through such and such [pāramitās]. Thus[1084] the Bhagavān stated this:

> The bhūmis of the victors' children are attained,
> but it is not the case that their insight is stable
> For as long as up to the eighth bhūmi, {79}
> they will be afraid of the inferior yānas
>
> Those with the character of the victors
> who reside[1085] in this great secret maṇḍala,[1086]
> being immersed within the Mahāyāna,
> are those who will come to find relief[1087]

Therefore, merely by virtue of [the Pāramitāyāna's] small amount of means that do not [even] represent the primary ones, while lacking the special means such as karmamudrā, the abundance of means is not the same in both [the Pāramitāyāna and the Mantrayāna].

(4) True reality lacks difficulty because the great fruition whose essence is Vajradhara will be attained before long by means of enjoying the five sense pleasures. For the following is declared:

> Relying on[1088] austerities and yogic disciplines,
> the body will come to suffer and thus dry out
> By virtue of suffering, the mind is distracted
> By distraction, awakening becomes altered[1089]

Elsewhere this is said:

> Through relying on fierce austerities as well as
> yogic disciplines, no accomplishment will come
> Through enjoying and relying on the five sense
> pleasures, there will be swift accomplishment[1090]

This is also taught:

> In the pāramitā approach, the fruition matures through long-term difficulties
> In the mantra approach lacking difficulty, awakening will be attained swiftly[1091]

To think that all phenomena are pure by nature exists nowhere outside of self-awareness, this self-awareness is called "great bliss," {80} and except for in the instructions in the mantra teachings, it is never aspired that this [great bliss] may arise. This extensive elaboration shall suffice.

(5) As for those with sharp faculties, in this Mantrayāna, even ordinary beings are able to realize the true reality of mantra because by dwelling in the pride of deities[1092] such as Hevajra and Mañjuśrīvajra, it will be possible to rely on this [true reality of mantra] even during the phase of being in training. Having brought causes and results together,

irreversibility will be attained. For those who follow the Pāramitāyāna [only] become irreversible on the eighth bhūmi. As it is said:

> Later, on the eighth bhūmi,
> there is no reversal by doubt[1093]

[Some] say that this kind [of irreversibility of ordinary beings] occurs in the Pāramitāyāna. However, since there is no experience of such [irreversibility] [in the Pāramitāyāna,] ordinary beings cannot be called "irreversible" because it is taught that for as long as the end of the eighth bhūmi has not been reached, this is not the bhūmi of relief.[1094]

Friends, listen, even when enjoying objects,
those in the Mahāyāna are instantly afraid
AHO, as far as all these saṃsāric things go,
by way of realizing the essence of objects,
they are utterly pure by virtue of suchness
Though they may be wondering, "Is it so?"[1095]
like monkeys touching a bunch of bunja,[1096] {81}
they are in the grip of fear and intoxicated[1097]

"[In the Pāramitāyāna,] there are those of sharp faculties who aspire for all phenomena being unborn and unceasing." This is not the case, because such is not possible without the pith instructions of the Vajrayāna. These many details shall suffice.

To speak about the noble Dharmodgata, who had attained the tenth bhūmi and was fearless in enjoying the five[1098] sense pleasures, is definitely reasonable [to support my argument]: in his case, there is the concordant distinctive feature of him training through the power of having special means. Furthermore, as far as learners go, in the context of their engaging in the path in a powerful way or without power, it is definitely not reasonable to take a mighty bodhisattva on the tenth bhūmi as an example.

Moreover, to say, merely based on suchness, that the Mahāyāna is of definitive[1099] meaning is not reasonable, because that [definitive meaning] is not directly perceived except when realizing the true reality of mantra. Who is there [in the Mahāyāna] who does not assert that all entities are emptiness? The following is stated:

> This nature of the entirety of entities
> is difficult to be experienced personally[1100]

To speak of this as "being free of thoughts of happiness and suffering" is true. For us, in what is accomplished through self-awareness[1101] in the middle between supreme and cessational ecstasy, it is not that there is the realization of the path of suffering as happiness.[1102] {82} The Bhagavān declared this:

> Neither passion nor dispassion,
> nor a middle are to be observed
> Thanks to being free of the three,
> the connate is called "awakening"[1103]

To say "But since there is no imaginary thinking, self-awareness[1104] is not established as dependent origination"[1105] is directly contradictory because it would follow that [the extreme of] extinction is put forth. As it is said:

> If thought-free self-aware
> wisdom is being engaged,
> buddha wisdom is not pure
> The wise are to abandon it

Śrī Saraha declares the following:

> The mind in which thoughts perish will also perish—
> this is what some with inferior intelligence proclaim
> By adopting this excellent mindset, anything is fine
> So why would the wise ones not be more superior?
>
> This mind in which all thoughts are overcome
> is lucidly manifest as the bliss that is genuine

It is the wise having done what was to be done,
but others are simply cattle who have two legs[1106]

Others say: "This [karmamudrā and so on] was taught for the sake of those who are tormented[1107] by passion, but it is not true reality." [Clearly,] these are not the words of any Buddhists. "It is not reasonable to teach great passion for the sake of guiding those who have passion. Isn't it repulsiveness that is taught in order to pacify their passion?" {83}

To pacify the passion of the passionate,[1108]
they are primarily made to settle evenly
Dispassion as well as moderate passion
are overpowered through great passion

The yāna of this is a single one,
which consists of the Mahāyāna
The teaching is also a single one,
being the teaching of great passion[1109]

As the Bhagavān said:

What has been taught as the three yānas
represents the way of my skill in means
The yāna is one, the approach too is one,
and thus the teaching of the guides is one[1110]

Furthermore, he declared this:

For as long as the mind operates,
there is no upper limit for yānas
But once mind has changed state,
there is no yāna and none to travel[1111]

Moreover, the power of [this wish-fulfilling] jewel, mantra, and medicine is inconceivable: once they obtain it, even those who committed the five actions of immediate consequence will attain the supreme siddhi in this very lifetime and become like blissful gods.

Having traveled this path so long,
the winged birds of dry dialectics
went to the infinite other shore of
mind's ocean, saw it,[1112] and returned

The true reality that is not mind's object
is the unborn, being born from conditions
This diversity constitutes self-awareness,
but it does not without the genuine guru

It is in this yāna of secret mantra
that the true guru has taken birth
In that manner, I see that people {84}
cross the ocean of the afflictions

Now, the teachings of the Mahāyāna of secret mantra are twofold: the creation process and the perfection process. The creation process is also of two kinds: the outer creation process and the [inner] profound creation process. The perfection process is threefold: the perfection [process], the full-perfection [process], and the essence process. These five elements are individually matched with those two processes.

Here, the outer creation process is taught in the *Nairātmyāprakāśa*, and the meditation on the [maṇḍala] circle of Nairātmyā as it is described [there][1113] is to be understood thanks to the kindness coming from the mouth of the true guru. I do not write it down here for fear of prolixity.[1114]

"What is the perfection process?" In order to guide the gods in the desire realm,[1115] the Bhagavān declared this:

The master's is by the purity of smiling
The secret is just so in terms of looking
The prajñā is with regard to embracing
Then that again for the pair in its union [1116]

Elsewhere, it is stated that the six empowerments are "the tathāgata relief." Therefore this is the outer creation process.

The profound creation[1117] process consists of the wisdom that is [based on] a woman who is a karmamudrā, consisting of the tathāgata relief and the Vajradhara relief.[1118]

The perfection process is described as having the character of the dharmamudrā. {85} Since it is said that this is the attainment of natural bliss, it is the cognition of[1119] seeing. Since [this bliss] is directly perceived by nonreferential great compassion in an instant, perceiver and perceived fall away, and thus this is expressed as "the dharmamudrā," which has the character of supreme ecstasy. This mudrā of all phenomena that have the forms of blue and so on is what ties [them all] together—that is, their one taste. [Thus,] since what is not this essence [still] has the nature of this essence, it is described as "the dharmamudrā." The presentation of ecstasy and so on should be understood here by relying on a true spiritual friend. The true guru taught that "variety constitutes the karmamudrā . . ."[1120]

The full-perfection process constitutes the samayamudrā. The samayamudrā consists of the sambhogakāyas and nirmāṇakāyas; in order to promote the welfare of sentient beings, which have the character of prajñā and means, they assume the forms of Hevajra, Mañjuvajra, and so on endowed with all qualities such as the thirty-two major marks, and are clearly manifest as the nature of the maṇḍala circles. As with the karmamudrā, ecstasy and so on should be understood from the pith instructions of a true guru. This is declared: "Just as ecstasy and such are arrayed . . ."[1121] {86}

The essence process is where [everything] is ever-excellent. Thanks to the distinctive feature of the accumulations of[1122] merit and wisdom that are inconceivable, this is the knowledge of all aspects of effortless full awakening in a single instant by means of the pith instructions of the true guru. This is expressed as "mahāmudrā": it is great, and it is a seal because it seals everything. Therefore, by being sealed with this mudrā, all obtains the state of mahāmudrā. The Bhagavān stated this:

> The third—the connate—is inexpressible[1123]

Since this mahāmudrā has the essence of being incomprehensible,[1124] yet is not easy to expound[1125] [either], it shall not be analyzed here.

Even victors don't analyze with the prajñā,
saying, "If analyzed with insight, it is this"
Nonetheless, the thought manifests clearly
that its character consists of this true reality

As it is empty of adopting and rejecting,
due to people like us having no stability,
even if we ponder it for billions of eons,
we don't realize it, no matter how we think

Awakening is close, but becomes distant
The essence that is without any analysis—
dharmatā, suchness—represents diversity

Being endowed with all supreme aspects,
it does not lack[1126] compassion's character
It is emptiness and compassion inseparable,
by virtue of relying upon the genuine guru[1127]

Therefore, by arduously[1128] relying upon {87}
the two lotus feet of the genuine guru,
the darkness of delusion about entities
is cleared as if by a hundred suns' light

Having obtained the kindness of the dust
on the genuine spiritual friend's lotus feet,
in sync with arriving on perception's path,
this is the remaining on attainment's path[1129]

I bow to awareness-emptiness[1130] as the equal taste of existence and peace[1131]
For the sake of myself attaining the state of a tathāgata during future times,
with absolute respect, only for a moment, I take upon the crown of my head

the two lotus feet of the one with a body of virtue who is to be relied
upon
and whose mind as such illuminates in the same way as a flash
of lightning

May the entirety of all these worlds come to behold
this suchness adorned with all aspects in which the
blazing jewel light from the dust on the guru's feet
dispels the mind's darkness in just a single instant

Through the virtue that I have accumulated by teaching
my experience, thanks to the instruction of the true guru
that is linked with the Mahāyāna's entire secret mantra,
may all beings come to attain the supreme victor's state!

This *Illumination of Prajñā Wisdom*
was crafted by paṇḍita Padmavajra
in order to attain the genuine path
for the sake of benefiting all beings[1132]

This concludes "An Illumination of Prajñā Wisdom" composed by mahāpaṇḍita Devacandra.[1133] *It was translated by paṇḍita Vajrapāṇi and lotsāwa Dharmakīrti.*[1134] {88}

(17) A Synopsis of Positions

In the language of India: *Sthitisamāsa*[1135]
In the language of Tibet: *Gnas pa bsdus pa*

OṂ I pay homage to Mañjuśrī[1136]

Having bowed to the identitylessness
of phenomena and persons, it is taught
clearly as per the sequence of Vaibhāṣā,
Sūtra, Vijñāna[vāda], and the very middle[1137]

Space and the two cessations constitute the
three permanent unconditioned phenomena[1138]
Some talk about the person as being
neither permanent nor impermanent[1139] [I.1]

Everything conditioned is impermanent
Beings have the five skandhas' character
They are to be understood as the state of
the reality of suffering that is the result[1140] [I.2]

The cause—origination—is to be abandoned[1141]
It has the character of afflictions and karma
Both of these realities are contaminated[1142]
The following two are uncontaminated [I.3]

Due to afflictions and karma being ended,
this cessation is henceforth everlasting[1143]—
the wise ones' directly realized[1144] liberation,
which is the supreme peace of suffering[1145] [I.4]

The eightfold path of the noble ones[1146] to that
is to be cultivated as deliverance's best means[1147]
This eightfold path, consisting of the correct
view and so forth, {89} was declared by the Sage[1148] [I.5]

This represents the nirvāṇa of the śrāvakas
The pratyeka[buddhas] perform meditation
without any instructions, and on their own,
by virtue of their former aspiration prayers[1149] [I.6]

Once they have directly realized their goal
as they wish and demonstrated the nirvāṇa
with remainder in their body, they are then
passing into parinirvāṇa similar to a lamp[1150] [I.7]

By the ability for their own and others' welfare,
this represents their magnificence in all regards
Thereby, such is middling buddhahood for them
This constitutes the position of the Vaibhāṣikas[1151] [I.8]

[This is the synopsis of the position of the Vaibhāṣikas.][1152]

Everything conditioned—the skandhas,
āyatanas, and dhātus[1153]—is momentary
It is as the absence of any self[1154] that they
are taken as objects by perfect wisdom [II.1]

It is direct perception and inference that are
asserted[1155] as the two kinds of perfect wisdom
Being imperceptible, objects are still visible
as specifically characterized phenomena[1156] [II.2]

Time as well as location are universals[1157]
Hence minutest particles are momentary
As they are able to perform functions,[1158]
just they constitute the ultimate reality[1159] [II.3]

By disregarding space and so forth,[1160]
it is those that are scrutinized[1161] here
as being the objects of valid cognition
by all who wish to perform functions[1162] [II.4]

The forms of jars and such thus always
executing the performance of functions,
it is by virtue of their own nature that
they are made distinct in every moment[1163] [II.5]

It is not the case that such a function is executed
once a single performance of it has been executed
By virtue of not linking the execution of that which
has been executed, this executes[1164] yet another one[1165] [II.6]

In every respect, any previous form[1166]
does not continue in other moments[1167] {90}
As the continuum of moments is similar,
supernatural knowledges and such abide [II.7]

In accordance with the positive determination
of referents that are directly perceived like that,
the negative determination of just that [follows]:
it is meditation arising from direct perception[1168] [II.8]

For the disappearance of appearances,
there is no need for any other causes[1169]
By virtue of another arising perishing,[1170]
they disappear through their own cause[1171] [II.9]

The body, wood, earth, and so forth
that represent aggregations of minute
particles being seen as coarse forms
are not coarse in the slightest degree [II.10]

Just so, happiness, suffering,
jars, and so forth are distinct
By moving or reddening one,
all will be moved or reddened [II.11]

Likewise, by shifting a single one,
this will pervade the whole body
"But by moving a part and so on,
it is not so for the part-possessor" [II.12]

If the part-possessor were not moved,
how would other objects be obtained?
The momentary external appearances
thanks to the aggregation of particles [II.13]

emerge as cognition's own aspects,
by which objects will be obtained
By the perceptual range of just that,
omniscience will not be attained [II.14]

As an aggregation is contingent on a single one,
causes are equal to[1172] the faculties of the senses
Through examining partition and nonpartition,[1173]
there is no referent arising as cognition's instance [II.15]

By scrutinizing matter and nonmatter,[1174]
there exists no arising in any respect
The insightful here also meditate on
the four realities of the noble ones [II.16] {91}

The mindset toward completely perfect awakening
does not exist without completing the accumulations
You should not stand in opposition to that—
if you do, this will turn into the Hīnayāna[1175] [II.17]

By cultivating the progressive stages of the profound,
it is compassion that constitutes the root of awakening
By virtue of joining with the root that is compassion,
the very same thing even applies to the Vaibhāṣikas [II.18]

By cultivating the progressive stages of the Mahāyāna,
through what should perfect awakening be prevented?
Otherwise, how could this[1176] represent the Mahāyāna
for those ones who realize the wisdom of the sūtras?[1177] [II.19]

Because of that, without such impartiality,[1178]
there is no buddhahood[1179] for them either
Hence, merely by way of the positions,
the distinction of the yānas is uncertain[1180] [II.20]

Arhathood by virtue of nothing but prajñā[1181]
is not something that is seen in impartiality[1182]
But by joining it with Mahāyāna compassion,
the path[1183] is superior due to generosity and such[1184] [II.21]

By means of the distinctions of the positions,
the realities such as suffering are also otherwise[1185]
When the distinctions are intended in terms of
the distinctions of lesser, medium, and so on,
with yānas and positions[1186] thus distinguished,
then each one of them becomes of nine kinds[1187] [II.22]

This is the synopsis of the position of Sūtrānta.[1188]

Since minutest particles lack any parts,[1189]
they are not connected with each other

If they were joined[1190] with all their being,
there would never be anything coarse[1191] [III.1]

An aggregation of independent ones[1192]
beyond the senses too is just like that[1193]
How could a phenomenon for cognition
exist if there exist no coarse referents?[1194] [III.2]

Nor is there[1195] a phenomenon that is a referent
due to thoughts of partition and nonpartition
Given the subtle is partitioned and the coarse {92}
is partitioned, how could this be a substance?[1196] [III.3]

In one, there is no partition and nonpartition,
because being and nonbeing are contradictory[1197]
A single one does not exist as a part-possessor
due to the flaw of motion, nonmotion, and such[1198] [III.4]

By distinguishing locations, aspects, and so on,
there is no certainty about accomplishing a goal
For this is so even when there are no referents
in dreams, in reflections, and similar cases[1199] [III.5]

Thus there are no referents[1200] such as blue,
yet consciousness does not oppress[1201] them
Nor is it single by any means,[1202] because it
appears as diverse aspects such as blue[1203] [III.6]

But consciousness is not in this diversity,
as they are not associated with each other[1204]
Thus, by latent tendencies' power, it looks
as if it is split into perceiver and perceived[1205] [III.7]

Due to delusion, what is real[1206] without aspects
appears as the distinctions of blue and so on[1207]
It is just as the Bhagavān has proclaimed:
this world consists of mere cognizance[1208] [III.8]

External[1209] referents, as imagined
by childish beings, are not existent[1210]
It is mind[1211] agitated by latent tendencies
that operates as appearing as referents[1212] [III.9]

By virtue of the triad being unobservable
by aspiring for the nonexistence of aspects,
generosity, discipline, patience, and vigor
are to be cultivated as being threefold each[1213] [III.10]

Once the prajñā that consists of hearing,
reflection, and meditation has emerged,
through the yoga of dhyāna, you should
rely on calm abiding and superior insight[1214] [III.11]

The Bhagavān declared the following:

> When relying upon mere mind,
> outer[1215] objects are not to be imagined {93}
> When resting in suchness's support,
> mere mind[1216] should be transcended[1217]
>
> When transcending this mere mind,[1218]
> nonappearance should be transcended
> The yogīs who rest in nonappearance
> will come to behold the Mahāyāna[1219]
>
> The state of effortlessness is peaceful
> and purified through aspiration prayers[1220]
> The supreme wisdom that is identityless[1221]
> beholds by means of appearances' lack[1222]

This diverse imagination that shines forth constitutes suffering
The origination of its latent tendencies is the dependent nature[1223]
Due to perfecting the path of generosity and so forth, cessation
is perfect liberation[1224]—mere cognizance that is without aspects[1225]
[III.12]

This is the synopsis[1226] of the position of Nonaspectarian Yogācāra.[1227]

Anything that may appear
is very clear as cognition,[1228]
just as it[1229] appears as forms
and so forth within dreams[1230] [IV.1]

How indeed could appearances
be in the state of noncognition?[1231]
If they were not consciousness,[1232]
how to otherwise perceive blue etc.?[1233] [IV.2]

The appearance of referents in the world represents
a case of mistaken identity due to facing outwardly
Hence the Sage spoke[1234] about the lack of appearance[1235]
that is empty of a perceiver as well as a perceived[1236] [IV.3]

Therefore there are no referents such as blue,
since they are appearances of consciousness[1237]
For that reason, to contemplate all the aspects
constitutes thought-free great compassion[1238] [IV.4]

The arising[1239] of what is called "latent tendencies" {94}
is destroyed by the path of generosity and so on
What is attained[1240] is the cessation of the entirety
of suffering, which constitutes nondual diversity[1241] [IV.5]

Once the emptiness of perceiver and perceived
that is endowed with all the supreme aspects[1242]—
the dharmakāya—has been made manifest,
the sambhoga[kāya] and emanations radiate[1243] [IV.6]

It is due to appearances' power that it is not nonexistent
By being the state of perceived and such, it is not existent[1244]
In this manner, it is not both either, nor is it the absence
of any form, as in the case of there being no perception[1245] [IV.7]

In this way, it is free of the four extremes[1246]
because it does not lack a nature of its own,
and since, by its own nature, nonconceptual[1247]
wisdom is self-experienced within itself[1248] [IV.8]

This is the synopsis of the position of Aspectarian Yogācāra.[1249]

It's nonexistence that is torn to pieces[1250] by the
three wretched tīrthikas[1251] who are Buddhists[1252]
Such adornment is good,[1253] yet superimposing
some existence of phenomena is still their evil[1254] [V.1]

Having paid homage to the ascertainment
of the middle[1255] free of all superimpositions,
it is in order to annihilate superimposition
that reasoning and scripture are discussed[1256] [V.2]

The ones that are established as the dhātus
arise from conditions, as they are momentary
These are indeed without a nature of their own
because they lack singularity and multiplicity[1257] [V.3]

Through the body being partitioned into
hands, feet, eyes, head, back, and such,
not even a single hand and so on exists,
for they arise by individual partitioning[1258] [V.4]

By way of dividing them into their parts,
they are probed down to minutest particles
By virtue of this very body, mountains,
the earth, and so forth are well known[1259] [V.5] {95}

By a single one having the nature of many,
multiplicity therefore does not exist either[1260]
This is not an annulment of the former one,
given that they are present as if in a dream[1261] [V.6]

As cognition's own nature does not exist,
any objection [to that] is not reasonable
For it is the stance of the wise to apply
the forms of reason in a general manner[1262] [V.7]

This diversity that is the progression of
performing select functions lacks a nature
It is the duality of cognition and cognized—
what would be the point of us investigating?[1263] [V.8]

As it is nothing but this consciousness that
keeps appearing here as forms and so forth,
it is thus reasonable for the wise not to draw
conclusions not warranted by that premise[1264] [V.9]

What is born as the seeming,
that is unborn in actual fact[1265]
Hence, as the mind is unborn,
by nature, it is without nature[1266] [V.10]

There is no birth of an existent, as it is [already] established,
and [also none] of a nonexistent, nor is there any from itself
Neither exists there any birth from the absence of any causes
or from something other, as far as a nature of its own goes[1267] [V.11]

Just as some forms that are reflections
are neither real nor delusive for people,
in the exact same way, all phenomena's
own nature is asserted by the wise ones[1268] [V.12]

By virtue of being collections, designations of houses,
garments, and so forth constitute entities of the seeming
Likewise, as the [designations] of collections and so on
are without birth, this is what constitutes peacefulness[1269] [V.13]

Hence, the Bhagavān has spoken thus:
The universe consists of mere names[1270]

Thus I have indeed also illustrated the
statements of others in their entirety[1271] [V.14]

But as for those theses uttered first,
their opinions are done away with[1272] {96}
Once their opinions are eliminated,
I then demonstrate my own thesis[1273] [V.15]

It is not seen that the nature of entities
exists right there within these entities,[1274]
similar to all kinds of things in mirrors
being devoid of oneness and difference[1275] [V.16]

The world is like illusions and dreams,
being devoid of causes and conditions
About what is always without a cause,[1276]
no thoughts will ever be set in motion [V.17]

Where entities are not existent,
it is mere mind that does exist[1277]
How could mind without entities
not be reasonable as mere mind?[1278] [V.18]

Once mind operates with the distinction
of a perceiver and something perceived,
it is indeed this worldly mind[1279] that then
becomes unreasonable as mere mind [V.19]

If the appearance of enjoyments thriving
within the body arises similar to a dream,
what ensues is the state of mind of duality,
but mind lacks the characteristic of duality[1280] [V.20]

In the same way that a sword does not
cut its own blade, and in the same way
that a finger does not touch its own tip,
so it is with mind in [its] seeing itself[1281] [V.21]

It is the mind whose origin is without any
beginning that is seen similar to an image
It has an object's form, but there is no object
It should be perceived in just the way it is[1282] [V.22]

The person, the continuum, the skandhas,
likewise conditions and minutest particles,
the primal substance,[1283] Īśvara, and a creator
are [all] conceived as being mere mind[1284] [V.23]

Seeing external referents is mistakenness
Referents do not exist—they are just mind
For those with insight in the proper way, {97}
perceiver and perceived come to a stop[1285] [V.24]

For those examining with insight,
any nature cannot be ascertained
Therefore they are inexpressible
and taught as the lack of a nature[1286] [V.25]

If they are scrutinized through insight,
there is no dependent and no imaginary,
nor is there an entity that is the perfect
How could they be examined by insight?[1287] [V.26]

There is no nature, no cognizance,
neither any entity, nor any ālaya,
but corpse-like childish beings who
are bad dialecticians discern these[1288] [V.27]

Characteristics, entities, cognizance—
these are the mistakenness of the mind
Having gone beyond it, these, my sons,
are coursing within nonconceptuality[1289] [V.28]

Suchness, emptiness, [true] end,[1290]
nirvāṇa, plus the dharmadhātu

and phenomena's being unborn,
are the nature that is the ultimate[1291] [V.29]

There's no outer entity, nor a nonentity,
nor is there any grasping of the mind
That which relinquishes all the views
is the characteristic of being unborn[1292] [V.30]

It is a collection of conditions
that arises and comes to an end
Once that collection is undone,
there is neither birth nor ceasing[1293] [V.31]

Entities are not existent, being without birth,
not nonexistent, nor existent and nonexistent
The only exception, though, is that collection,
which does indeed arise and come to an end[1294] [V.32]

At the time of this entire world
being beheld as a concatenation,
then just this mere concatenation
is contemplated as being mind[1295] [V.33] {98}

That of which nothing is born at all
and of which nothing ceases at all[1296]
is neither existent nor nonexistent,
so the world is visible as being void[1297] [V.34]

Thanks to[1298] fully understanding unity,[1299]
bodhisattvas have great compassion
The wise ones should practice while
not relinquishing this very seeming [V.35]

For, by parting with the seeming,
there isn't any true reality at all
Just what is born as the seeming
precisely that is actually unborn[1300] [V.36]

This true reality[1301] is what represents unity
characterized by dependent origination[1302]
It represents suchness, the dharmadhātu,
the pāramitā of prajñā that is supreme, [V.37]

the true end, being unborn,
unobservability, nirvāṇa,
emptiness, signlessness,
wishlessness, and nonformation[1303] [V.38]

Through the examples of dreams, illusions, and so on,
exactly this has been established[1304] by the victorious[1305]
This Mahāyāna here constitutes what is most excellent
within the collection of the sūtras of definitive meaning[1306] [V.39]

Having reviewed and listened to the sūtras,
they are thus to be contemplated with effort
Generating compassion for sentient beings
is what constitutes bodhicitta's precursor[1307] [V.40]

Those who have great vigor and abide by the vow
should familiarize themselves with nature's lack[1308]
They abide on the eightfold path of the noble ones
and are devoted to generosity, discipline, and such[1309] [V.41]

It is indeed this nonduality of the two realities that the fortunate ones,
in accordance with being similar to extinction in terms of true reality,[1310]
are observing[1311] as the arising and ceasing that is perceptually
determined
If birth did exist in actuality,[1312] the flaw of annihilation would accrue[1313]
[V.42] {99}

Indeed, in the manner in which an image is seen in the middle
of a mirror,
by the power of examining with reasoning, it does not exist and
is not seen[1314]

There are no referents on the outside, nor is there a mind of diversity here
Still, this is clear insight, as supreme nonexamination is not contradictory[1315] [V.43]

This is the synopsis of the position of the very middle.[1316]

Thus has been analyzed and confirmed
the true reality in the pāramitā approach,[1317]
which is free from the four extremes,
neither abides, nor arises,[1318] nor ceases,
lacks characteristics, arises dependently,
and is something to be self-experienced[1319] [VI.1]

Then, while resorting to the tradition of mantra[1320]
as per the text *Succession of the Four Mudrās*,
without analysis and doubt, through the special
experiences of emptiness thanks to the guru,[1321] [VI.2]

it is this emptiness that should be self-experienced
in the form of the great bliss of prajñā and means
As if[1322] abiding in the fruition and being nondual,
it is this bodhicitta[1323] that needs to be cultivated[1324] [VI.3]

Those who know the mantra tradition[1325] declared
that the mantra tradition[1326] is more distinguished:[1327]
though the goal is the same, since it lacks ignorance,
since it is abundant in means, since it lacks difficulty,[1328]
and since it is the prerogative of those of sharp faculties,
it is the mantra teaching that is more distinguished[1329] [VI.4]

The certainty that the skandhas represent
the tathāgatas or Vajrasattva is far better
than the certainty that they are momentary,
have the nature of cognition, or are empty[1330] [VI.5]

Through the power of analysis, the realization[1331]
of the goal is determined to be free of analysis[1332]
[But] how could it be [realized], without any {100}
deliberation,[1333] without the mantra approach?[1334] [VI.6]

How could there be undefiled great bliss,
which is incomparable in every respect[1335]
and fully grown through the deity's pride,
[merely] due to the experience of emptiness?[1336] [VI.7]

Once the karmamudrā has been achieved,[1337]
through the dharmamudrā's distinctions,
without any mutual desire, how could the
fruition called "samaya[mudrā]" be [won]?[1338] [VI.8]

The extraordinary abundance[1339] of means,
or that of experiences which are special,[1340]
is due to the specifities of karma-, dharma-,
and mahāmudrā—how could it be otherwise?[1341] [VI.9]

By virtue of the experience of suchness
due to having extremely sharp faculties,[1342]
the fully perfect awakening to great bliss[1343]
is thanks to enjoying all objects of desire[1344] [VI.10]

By virtue of the overwhelming pleasure right there,
and due to that very [pleasure] serving as the means,
this takes place at the time of the initial cultivation—
otherwise, how could this be without any difficulty?[1345] [VI.11]

[Vowing] "By the power of meditation,
I shall complete the pāramitās' entirety[1346]
and accomplish the awakening to bliss,"
where [else] would the sharp faculties lie?[1347] [VI.12]

Paying homage to [the syllable] EVAṂ—
the means of realizing connate ecstasy—

it is the succession of the mudrās in brief
that is communicated in the Mantrayāna[1348] [VI.13]

Prajñā in its beautiful emanated form[1349]
is the karmamudrā who is without self,
the prime actress of body, speech, and
mind, the means to accomplish wisdom[1350] [VI.14]

The cognition that[1351] arises as the progression of
ecstasy and such within her and thanks to her—
the consciousness that enters into the middle—[1352]
is that which is expressed as "prajñā-jñāna"[1353] [VI.15]

This is the aspectarian or[1354] the nonaspectarian,
and likewise {101} the path that is the middle
The wisdom thanks to the according aspiration
is attained by means of the pith instructions[1355] [VI.16]

The connate should be known as the third one
In the forceful empowerment, it is the fourth[1356]
This is due to the working of wind, the yoga
of changelessness by being placed at the nose[1357] [VI.17]

In just the ways that blissful wisdom[1358]
is flourishing by virtue of the means,
in the very same ways, thoughts are
ceasing—this is the supreme connate[1359] [VI.18]

In the forceful empowerment, it is asserted
that what resembles the result is the connate
For this reason, the cakra being uncontrived
for a long period is indeed quite pointless[1360] [VI.19]

The following is declared:[1361]

> Ecstasy is the descent of the semen
> from the uṣṇīṣa to the ūrṇā's lotus,[1362]

supreme ecstasy from throat to heart,
and cessational ecstasy[1363] from there,

with all kinds of love play, when arrived
at the navel's and the secret place's lotus,
for as long as it is in the secret's jewel of
the vajra, it is unemitted connate ecstasy[1364]

This represents the nonabiding nirvāṇa,
the lord who is immutable great passion
The bliss that is emitted due to dispassion
constitutes the one of abiding in nirvāṇa[1365]

There is no greater evil than dispassion,
and there is no greater merit than bliss
For that reason, oh king, let your mind
always enter the bliss that is immutable![1366]

Due to emission, dispassion is born
Due to dispassion, suffering is born
Due to suffering, men's dhātu wanes
Due to its waning, we speak of death[1367]

Due to death, another existence of theirs
Due to existence, again emission—death {102}
For that reason, it is with all your efforts
that you should avoid emitting passion[1368]

With dispassion, you aren't even a lover,
nor do you strive after erotic instructions[1369]
So why should yogīs yet again strive after
suffering in the tantra that I proclaimed?[1370]

By virtue of the nature of immutable semen,[1371]
the supreme immutable is to be accomplished
Having entered into emission in the support,
this is [also] the dispassion of the supported[1372]

The bindus that prajñā's passion
melted gradually from the head
and that entered fullness's abode
are bound in the ultimate sense[1373]

Just as the risen[1374] moon becomes
gradually full through the times,
just so the risen wisdom becomes
gradually full through the bhūmis[1375]

Having sprung forth from the ūṣṇīṣa,
it becomes full in the jewel of the vajra
Through dispassion, the digits are lost
By loss from the vajra, there is fullness[1376]

Its nature of great bliss is designated[1377]
by means of the sound of fullness
In fullness, fully complete buddhahood
in a single instant becomes motionless[1378]

Just as the water in rivers that has entered[1379]
the ocean becomes the same as its water,
in the immutable,[1380] the totality of saṃsāric
existence becomes just as immutable as it[1381]

Similar to the totality of the elements
that is consumed turning into chyle,
the totality of entities also has been
consumed as the supreme immutable

Having become the supreme immutable,
it is the bearer of the nature of all aspects[1382] {103}
The cause is reflections born from emptiness[1383]
The result is the bliss born from the immutable

The cause is sealed with the result[1384] and
the result is also sealed with the cause[1385]

The cause is the emptiness that bears reflections
The result is compassion bearing the immutable[1386]

The bodhicitta that has not been emitted[1387]
is emptiness and compassion inseparable[1388]
The elements will neither come to perish
nor arise by virtue of a nature of their own

This diversity is without any nature of its own—
the single characteristic of being and nonbeing[1389]
Someone who has been bitten does not notice
any pain at the snakebite, nor anywhere else,

nor any objects through the gates of the senses,
once the venom arrived at the state of saturation[1390]
This is like the mercury that has been placed
upon just a single area of a piece of iron

is fully penetrating that iron everywhere,
once it has been heated red-hot with a fire[1391]
In the exact same way, the immutable bliss
that has been placed within just a single area

should fully pervade the mind everywhere,
once it has been heated with passion's fire[1392]
Just as pieces of iron thus penetrated
do not become stained anywhere at all,

likewise the minds thus penetrated do not
turn into latent tendencies anywhere at all[1393]
A piece of iron that has turned into gold
through fire has indeed become stainless

In the same way, more and more, mind
becomes stainless by the fire of passion[1394]
What point is there to be verbose here
in terms of the world's seeming reality

about iron not penetrating the true state
of mercury that cannot be pondered?[1395] {104}
Why should you again ponder in terms
of the ultimate about the mind that is

blemished through adventitious stains
not penetrating wisdom's true state?[1396]
Just as iron penetrated by mercury
does not reassume the state of iron,

likewise the mind penetrated by bliss
does not reassume suffering's state[1397]

Furthermore, the following is declared:

It is the nāḍī of Vajradhātvīśvarī that
resides within the center of the bhaga
It is obtained through making efforts
by being familiar with the guru's words[1398]

By being stimulated a bit with the index,
the outer and inner tongue, and the vajra,
this nāḍī will flourish, and through that
the bliss that is supreme will descend[1399]

The ten pāramitās, powers,
and masteries are perfected
Gone beyond the ten bhūmis,
the marks are stable thereby[1400]

Additionally, this is stated:

At the time when wisdom is seen
by the yogīs, they rest within bliss
Changeless, from a session to a day,
half of a month, a month, or a year,

> a single eon, or thousands of eons,
> they rest by persevering in wisdom[1401]

Moreover, the following is said:

> For as long as yogīs refrain[1402]
> from emitting the bodhicitta,
> they continuously attain any
> bliss that arises from ecstasy
>
> Once the bodhicitta—the treasury of
> all the siddhis—has descended and the
> skandha of consciousness has fainted,
> where would irreproachable[1403] siddhi be?[1404]

Within the context of the dharmamudrā,
the connate {105} is realized as the fourth one[1405]
The connate of the two—the dharmamudrā
and mahāmudrā—constitutes the supreme[1406] [VI.20]

Being without bodhicitta,
bliss will never be attained
Without great bliss, there
is never any Mantrayāna[1407] [VI.21]

Having thereby obtained that prajñā-jñāna,
by way of the dharmamudrā that is connate,
its nature is to be contemplated as a maṇḍala
by being classed as lower, medium, and such[1408] [VI.22]

By means of the union with a karmamudrā,
the samaya maṇḍala is to be contemplated[1409]
The lower are to contemplate with creation,
and the medium ones without the ritual parts [VI.23]

But what the superior should contemplate
consists of the maṇḍala that's instantaneous[1410]

Moreover, the lower are to contemplate the
dharmamudrā[1411] with nāḍīs and syllable[1412] rows, [VI.24]

the medium ones caṇḍālī with its specifics,
and the highest ones what is indestructible[1413]
The yogīs realize subtle bindus and so on
in a global manner in the way they desire[1414] [VI.25]

The lowest of the highest are to contemplate
that the three realms constitute the palace,
sentient beings are the maṇḍala inhabitants,
and the yogī is the maṇḍala's supreme lord[1415] [VI.26]

The following is declared:

> This is the mansion at its top, not the threefold world; these are not beings, but victors
> I am the cakra lord, not a human; these are not objects, not eyes, nor the earth and so on,
> nor form and such; as they have dharmatā's character, they are the maṇḍala inhabitants
> Observing that this diversity is the maṇḍala circle, oh mind, how can you be deluded?[1416] {106}

It is the four elements[1417] and the skandhas,
the wisdom of Heruka and of the goddess,[1418]
the cakra that is sealed with suchness, space—
so the medium of the highest [contemplate][1419] [VI.27]

The world's diversity[1420] is Nairātmyā and suchness
[Heruka] is the means, the power of compassion
[Their] unity that is completely without any effort
is the maṇḍala because it incorporates the essence[1421] [VI.28]

Though it is linked to conception and thought,[1422]
that [unity] is inconceivable and thought-free[1423]
It is the supreme of all aspects, it is everything,

without aspect, and utterly beyond the senses[1424] [VI.29]

It is the character of being and nonbeing,
yet is devoid of any being and nonbeing[1425]
It is pure[1426] of the four extremes,
yet based on the four extremes[1427] [VI.30]

Not superimposing all kinds of superimpositions,[1428]
it is the great bliss that is without any attachment[1429]
It is the examination of the fruition, true reality,
and the remedies that constitutes nonexamination[1430] [VI.31]

Once this has been attained, it is born
by virtue of its nature of being unborn[1431]
As it is not matter, it is to be self-experienced,
without being a knower, without being a seer [VI.32]

Since it is without any form, it is not uniform
It is permanent by virtue of being immutable[1432]
It is not nonbeing,[1433] because it is not extinction,
and since it is the source of the seeming's arising[1434] [VI.33]

It constitutes the connate of all phenomena,
as its own nature consists of native ecstasy[1435]
It is self-blessing because it is self-arising
It is indestructible because it is not ruined[1436] [VI.34]

[Thus it is] for the yogīs of supreme faculties,
who represent the highest among the highest
and are the ones who speak of realizing[1437] the
nonduality of dharmamudrā and mahāmudrā[1438] [VI.35] {107}

Because cause and result are not different,
there exist no stages of meditation for me
There is no mindfulness or nonmindfulness,
because it is experienced as it actually is[1439] [VI.36]

By perceiving[1440] the taste of being unborn,
meditation as well is of exactly this kind[1441]
It is[1442] indeed just this prajñā that is dhyāna,
being the one that penetrates emptiness[1443] [VI.37]

The Bhagavān declared this clearly
in the tantras, such as Śrī Hevajra: [VI.38][1444]

> As all phenomena's full knowledge,
> meditation is indeed not meditation[1445]
>
> It is indeed this stage of the self-blessing
> that equally represents the stage of unity
> The fully perfect awakening to great bliss
> likewise constitutes supreme mahāmudrā[1446]
>
> Those who realize phenomena's true reality
> do not become exhausted by what they do[1447]
> So that phenomena's true reality is entered,
> the distinctions have been taught for them[1448]
>
> This is clear thanks to the true guru's
> pith instructions, but not otherwise[1449]
> That which is proclaimed by others[1450]
> therefore does not teach the meaning[1451]
>
> It is the wisdom born from the dharmodaya[1452]
> that is accordingly declared to be "wisdom"[1453]
> The meaning of words due to your own aspiration
> is not something real that is to be adopted[1454]
>
> Likewise, it is the entirety of all four
> that is proclaimed here and so forth
> Just as they are, all the four[1455] kāyas are
> clear thanks to the true guru's means[1456]

The true state of the bliss of emptiness
is asserted as the bliss that is great bliss
The bliss that is the bliss of equal taste[1457]
constitutes the connate, the dharmakāya[1458]

By performing the function of true reality's {108}
bliss, the sambhoga[kāya] and nirmāṇa[kāya]
constitute the true reality of fivefold taste[1459]
Within the native state, all are not different[1460]

"Buddhahood with the five kāyas' character"—[1461]
such and further things have been declared
It is the attainment of the five kāyas that is
the mode of being of true reality's one taste [VI.39]

As the distinctions of the four kāyas
are inseparable, this is the fifth kind[1462]
It is this oneness as sheer true reality
that is thus also asserted as a kāya[1463] [VI.40]

It is in just the way my insight experiences this
that it thus rests within meditative equipoise
Through having discussed this a little bit here
in accordance with how it is attained by insight
through prajñā about the object of true dharma,
may living beings come to realize this actuality
in just the way it is[1464] and become vessels for it [VI.41]

This concludes "A Synopsis of Positions" composed by the great master Śrī Sahajavajra. It was translated by guru Dhiriśrījñāna and the Tibetan lotsāwa Mapen Chöbar, who is endowed with respect. Subsequently, upon being requested by Pardön,[1465] it was finalized by the Indian guru and Tsur Lotsāwa by consulting the original manuscript.[1466] {109}

(18) Pith Instructions on the Tradition of Inconceivable Nonduality

In the language of India: *Acintyādvayakramopadeśanāma*[1467]
In the language of Tibet: *Bsam gyis mi khyab pa'i rim pa'i man ngag ces bya ba*

I pay homage to Śrī Vajrasattva
I pay homage to the bhagavān Lokeśvara

Having paid homage to the lord[1468]—inconceivable
nonduality born from supreme prajñā's womb—
I have written it down [here] in a proper manner
as it has come down from Bhadrapāda's tradition[1469] [1]

The great secret of prajñā and means,
characterized by inconceivable compassion,
is the wisdom that arises on its own,
the sphere beyond the path of speech[1470] [2]

Bodhisattvas who are vajra-bearers
do not see this supreme nonduality,
which is self-arising, as having a
nature of being, nor as nonbeing[1471] [3]

Distinctions of permanence and extinction
are not declared to be ultimate nonduality

Familiarization is not in terms of a nature,
nor in terms of observation or emptiness[1472] [4]

Through analyzing the two,
nondual wisdom is blazing
All is nonduality's aspects,
but duality does not exist[1473] [5] {110}

Equal, the manifestation of equal taste,
this inconceivable wisdom is supreme
Supreme nonduality is not to be cultivated
through the yoga of conceptual wisdom[1474] [6]

The thought-free inconceivable is not
attained by bearers of the vajra of bliss
Creation represents the cause of thought,
and just the same goes for noncreation[1475] [7]

Being devoid of both of these aspects,
being free of impressed and impresser,
and being rid of impressed tendencies,
wisdom came as Bhadrapāda's tradition[1476] [8]

It is indeed self-arising, waveless,
free from the entirety of thinking,
and being's and nonbeing's nature,
yet bound by impressions' duality[1477] [9]

Due to its nature of nonthought,
the inconceivable is not sundered
It is the web of thoughts' stains
that tarnishes the mind's jewel[1478] [10]

Thanks to the stains' departure, nonduality
is buddhahood, which is called "wisdom"
Yogīs should always regard everything
as having the character of nonthought[1479] [11]

As for this samādhi cultivation
that was taught by Bhadrapāda,
its own nature exists neither as
any arising nor as any perishing[1480] [12]

Its wisdom is called "nonduality,"
which is free from all thinking
The buddhas, such as Vajradhara,
say thoughts are utterly beautiful[1481] [13]

Those giving rise to the actuality of nonthought
are the bearers of the vajra of glorious great bliss[1482]
All the worlds are supported through the thoughts
that have the character of the inner and the outer[1483] [14] {111}

Nonduality is free from any duality
and arises as wisdom all on its own[1484]
It is not familiarization with being,
nor familiarization with nonbeing [15]

Unattainable is the blissful cognition
that is inconceivable nonduality's state
In all sentient beings, their conceptions
are cradled within the womb of prajñā[1485] [16]

With the arrow of compassion waking up,
the target of great bliss should be pierced
Being free from any fear[1486] in its entirety,
duality's lack is supreme and auspicious[1487] [17]

That which, similar to space, is free
from thoughts is called "nonduality"
With the inconceivable state's yoga,
all entities are to be familiarized with [18]

The tradition coming from Dharmapāda
that has been discussed by Bhadrapāda

is that the aspects of the world manifest
through this nature that is a single one [19]

Those who are deceived in terms of
the protector of glorious great bliss[1488]
through the distinctions of nonduality's aspects
by false talk, speaking of observing emptiness, [20]

by being bound by the dullness of thoughts,
do not realize this kind of glorious bliss
The thoughts that consist of bad thinking
lie outside[1489] the purity of prajñā and means[1490] [21]

The nondual wisdom of mahāyoga
is nothing but this single great bliss
The entirety of mobile and immobile
entities is present as nonduality[1491] [22]

In the peaceful space that is originally
pure by nature, they are truly stainless
Nonduality is indeed a mere name, {112}
and it does not exist as any name[1492] [23]

Not perceptible as known and knower,
nonduality indeed represents great bliss
Buddhahood is not an object of mind
It is inconceivable by its very nature[1493] [24]

Everything is indeed of its nature,
beyond conception and self-arising
All living beings on earth perish
through the web of thoughts [25]

Nondual wisdom is indeed single,[1494]
devoid of the entirety of thinking
The whole duality of the hosts of
permanence and extinction isn't there [26]

Even a middle is not observable[1495]
Nondual wisdom is marvelous
Free from all reference points,
similar to space, it is stainless [27]

With the web of thoughts cut through,
inconceivable nonduality is supreme
Penetrated by the elixir of nonduality,
what is made of wood, stone, and earth [28] {113}

turns into manifestations of the deity
This is what Bhadrapāda has taught,
as the manifestation of the equal taste
of prajñā, means, and great compassion is one[1496] [29]

Then and there, the wisdom that is
nondual—great bliss—springs forth,[1497]
being beyond form, sound, and taste,
and free from smell, touch, and such [30]

What consists of the dharmadhātu
is pure, nondual, supreme wisdom,[1498]
which is free from all thinking[1499] and
devoid of perceiver and perceived [31]

The abode that is naturally pure,
the nonduality that is ultimate,[1500]
does not perish, does not arise,
doesn't change, and doesn't stay [32]

This mahāmudrā is the nonduality
that is infinite—supreme wisdom
The mind is said to be the substrate
of flaws as well as qualities[1501] [33]

Here, supreme all-pervasive wisdom
is without any waves by its nature

This wisdom arises all on its own
You shouldn't meditate on anything[1502] [34]

For this dharma that is inconceivable
is the state of the buddhas' nonduality[1503]
It is utterly stainless and greatly pure,
rid of anything to meditate and meditator [35]

By virtue of being free of thought, all
is seen as the source of glorious bliss:[1504]
the abundance of forms of the deities,
the bodies of Vajrasattva and so on, [36]

the entirety of images of the buddhas,
the maṇḍala of the host of yoginīs,
the assemblies of the wrathful kings,[1505]
and likewise awareness goddesses, [37] {114}

the maṇḍala circle that is divine,
a stainless manifestation of light,
the sūtra collection plus the Vinaya,
as well as the pāramitā approach[1506] [38]

The same goes for mantras and mudrās,
awareness consorts invited into the heart,[1507]
the entirety of the doctrine of mantra,
maṇḍalas, the activities of fire offerings, [39]

and the rituals of recitation and worship—
all arise on their own in their due order[1508]
The same goes for the doctrines: the Śaivas,
the Sauras, the Arhantas,[1509] the Vaiṣṇavas, [40]

and those proclaiming the Vedas' authority
Those others as well arise all on their own
This union with the state of omniscience
is inconceivable and free of any thoughts [41]

The divine state called Samantabhadra,
like a wish-fulfilling jewel, is nondual
The underground, the sword, the pill,
the yakṣiṇī, [swift] feet, the perfect vase,[1510] [42]

alchemy, the eye lotion, and the celestial[1511]
are accomplished on their own, not otherwise
By virtue of having faith in nonthought,
everything keeps arising all on its own[1512] [43]

Mantrīs should not meditate on being,
nor should they meditate on own-being[1513]
What to say about this? The Buddha
is not Śiva and is free of being Viṣṇu[1514] [44]

In it, there are no names and forms,
nor are there characteristics of color[1515]
The holder of illusory manifestations,
the divine skandha, is naturally stainless[1516] [45]

The manifestation of natural luminosity,
the source of the bliss of eternal ecstasy,
being free from body, speech, and mind,
is [like] a mirror and a wealth of magic[1517] [46]

This manifestation of ultimate rapture's bliss[1518] {115}
is the great bliss that springs forth perpetually
Through connecting the words of the teaching,
there are explanations of names and syllables[1519] [47]

Moreover, being beyond speech's path,
there is no way this could be described
By your play with its nature of guidance,[1520]
the goals of activities that are desired, [48]

at the time of the worship that is secret,
have been demonstrated by Bhadrapāda

with the wisdom consisting of nonduality
by the nature of the one's manifestations[1521] [49]

Latent tendencies will be terminated
and buddhahood is attained for good
through the diversity of various kinds[1522]
and due to the yogas of various views[1523] [50]

Due to impregnating[1524] latencies' stains,
this very nonduality will not be realized
It is free of beginning, middle, and end
and devoid of perfection and creation [51]

With mind and spirit[1525] left behind,
this is the supreme nondual wisdom
Bhadrapāda taught what is named
"the nonduality of buddhahood"[1526] [52]

Thanks to realizing this as buddhahood,
supreme practitioners become buddhas
By connecting the words of the teaching,
buddhahood is conceived as nonduality[1527] [53]

In the form of distinguishing the ultimate,
there is no buddhahood, nor nonduality
When the true state of wisdom arises,
the stains of thoughts are far away[1528] [54]

It is by virtue of true reality that the entirety
of thinking about entities[1529] turns imperceptible
by means of the yoga of constantly practicing[1530]
what was heard due to Bhadrapāda's kindness [55]

I take hold of what is named "nonduality"
The yogīs should have patience with me[1531] {116}
With effort, the wise should bring about
the termination of the latent tendencies [56]

Otherwise, there is no buddhahood
in tens of millions of incalculable eons
Wisdom, the protector of nonduality,
is what terminates latent tendencies [57]

Due to the termination of latencies occurring,
nonduality is indeed designated "buddhahood"
In the state of being free of latent tendencies,
[even] the persons who are low or mediocre [58]

are referred to as being buddhas
In that, there are no sides anywhere
By its own nature of naturelessness,
the sphere of prajñā indeed remains[1532] [59]

Due to being those two's foundation, it is single[1533]
thanks to the yoga of equal taste's manifestation
This constitutes the supreme nonduality
that was demonstrated by Bhadrapāda [60]

She whose beautiful form is ultimate rapture
is neither talk, nor meditation, nor conception
Bhadra has described that which is excellent,
which is the cause of attaining buddhahood[1534] [61]

One is not able to provide any
example among all phenomena
The eyes up to mental cognition
fail to serve as any illustration[1535] [62]

It is strictly singular and beginningless,
being present as infinite[1536] manifestation
It is known as the single supreme one
thanks to the revered guru's kindness[1537] [63]

Yoga is designated as "person"
Anuyoga is the conventional {117}

Mahāyoga is nondual wisdom[1538]
Yogīs proceed to buddhahood[1539] [64]

In the eclipses of the moon and sun,
thanks to joining prajñā and vajra,
when immersed in nondual wisdom,
there is buddhahood in this life here[1540] [65]

The yoga of rapture for others' welfare
is free from perceiver and perceived
The nature of a siddha is without doubt—
it is the supreme nondual compassion[1541] [66]

The phenomena that are forms
seen with the eyes are mediocre
Supreme nonduality is to be seen
as the form of ultimate rapture[1542] [67]

Whatever is heard with the ears
is so in proportion to the sounds
Ultimate wisdom beyond sound
is to hear supreme nonduality[1543] [68]

The bad tastes which are tasted
by the tongue are to be realized
as the best taste, supreme nonduality,
through the six tastes' oneness[1544] [69]

When the nose is cognizing smells,
foul sensations of deer musk and such
are realized as supreme nonduality
through the nature of their oneness[1545] [70]

By way of the nature of bodily touch
in proportion to proper and improper,[1546]
the supreme nonduality is completed[1547]
through the yoga that is powerful[1548] [71]

Through the radiance[1549] of wisdom's light,
it is without end and pervades everything
This nonduality that is the spontaneous
ultimate rapture is a buddha's true bliss[1550] [72]

Formation, feeling, discrimination,
and form, as well as consciousness, {118}
are the kāya made of the five wisdoms,
the five buddhas' supreme nonduality[1551] [73]

Eternally, this is thus Akṣobhya,
Ratna, Āyur, and Amogha indeed
The unit of these five being one
is the sixth, which is great bliss[1552] [74]

Earth, water, likewise fire,
wind, and space as well—
the five elements' great creation—
are the nonduality of awakening[1553] [75]

Through the mirror-like, equality, all-accomplishing,
and discriminating [wisdoms] and the dharmadhātu,
thoughts, having the nature of conceptual constructs,[1554]
are the nonduality that is self-arising and single [76]

Yet through the examinations of the doctrines and so on,
and by the power of the dispositions[1555] of sentient beings,
this single nonduality becomes the Śaivas and so forth,
as well as the Vaiṣṇavas, Brahmā, and also Sarvajña[1556] [77]

The deficiencies of the eyes and so on
represent the sphere beyond the mind
named "the nonduality that is ultimate,"
but verbal discursiveness is conventional[1557] [78]

By discriminating the state of the ultimate,
there is no buddha, nor is there nonduality,

yet speech's discursiveness is expressed
through the union of thoughts and space[1558] [79]

This is by way of following all treatises
and discerning the expositions' words—
otherwise, one is not able to discuss
this nonduality that is buddhahood[1559] [80]

What are called the sixteen emptinesses,[1560]
what are thought of as the ten prajñās,
what are enumerated as the five buddhas
and the six rebirths[1561] are also nonduality [81]

Similar to everything being observed
in the reflections appearing in a mirror, {119}
likewise, the awakening of the buddhas
is inconceivable within nondual wisdom[1562] [82]

Within the entirety of all three realms,
due to the causes of arising and abiding,
all of that, as well as all living beings,
keeps emerging as nondual wisdom[1563] [83]

Oceans, mountains, trees,
grass, bushes, and vines
spring from nondual wisdom—
there exists no doubt here [84]

Mother and father are in this single spot[1564]
There does not exist any duality here
It is within nondual wisdom's true state[1565]
that everything else keeps originating [85]

Through the union with means,
thanks to prajñā's nondual nature,
buddhahood is attained instantly
by yogis in this very lifetime [86]

This has been taught by Bhadrapāda
from ear to ear and mouth to mouth
by virtue of Bhadrapāda employing
numerous means out of his kindness [87]

Through inconceivable meditation's yoga,
buddhahood is attained in a lasting way[1566]
It is thanks to Paramāśva, Vīṇāpāda,
Indrabhūti, including Lakṣmī[ṃkarā], [88]

Vilāsavajra, as well as Guṇḍerī,
Padmācārya of great compassion,
and Dharmapāda that, in due order,
their tradition came to Bhadrapāda[1567] [89]

The single intention[1568] of everything
is the nondual wisdom that is supreme
So it is for the whole mantra discourse[1569]
as well as the approach of the pāramitās [90]

In the sūtra collection's piṭaka and such, {120}
it is this single, nondual great bliss here
The Arhantas, Sauras, Śaivas, and such,
as well as the Somasiddhānta,[1570] [91]

Vaiṣṇavas, and the *Mānavadharma*[1571]
are indeed being taught as nonduality
But there is no speech for nonduality,
so gods, asuras, and humans are base[1572] [92]

But everything is seen as nondual
wisdom due to being its semblance
Nonduality's fusion with compassion
is the possession of prajñā and means [93]

The one to distinguish emptiness's distinctions
is the guru, the embodiment of all buddhas,

According to the assertion of Bhadrapāda,
that one is the supreme ocean of wisdom[1573] [94]

All that's supreme arises as manifestations
of the churning of the ocean of milk[1574]
They are celebrated as Brahmā, Viṣṇu,
Maheśvara, the Buddha, and so on [95]

The moon, the sun, and the stars
arise from the ocean of wisdom
Just so do Lakṣmī and Sarasvatī,
as well as nectar, the best elixir[1575] [96]

Everything comes forth from this nectar,
including gods, asuras, and human beings,
as does the bhūmi called "the thirteenth,"
which is the most charming Vajradharī[1576] [97]

The source of triangular form
is designated as "dharmodaya,"
filled with moon and sun water,
prajñā's form, blazing greatly[1577] [98]

From bliss [comes] the great bliss in all[1578]
She allows for attaining buddhahood
A great lotus with millions of petals
is situated right there in the center [99]

Always, within its anthers and so on,
it remains endowed with āli and kāli,
is swathed in moon and sun garments, {121}
and is associated with the nine prajñās[1579] [100]

Flowing and with a blazing form,
the bindu moon's supreme dawn
is what gives rise to ecstasy and
grants all divine goals' fruition[1580] [101]

Being completely filled[1581] with clear nectar
and being endowed with precious jewels,
the foundation of infinite qualities is the state
of the holder of the vajra of glorious bliss [102]

She is the one to refresh[1582] everything,
being the one who creates and dissolves
That which has the form of many deities
emerges from this ocean-like nonduality[1583] [103]

The dharma and the sambhoga forms,
and likewise the nirmāṇakāya as well,
are the turners of the wheel of dharma
for the welfare of all numerous beings [104]

everywhere within the worldly realms,
extending infinitely in the ten directions
Endowed with the ten wisdoms' powers,[1584]
this is the supreme preeminent prajñā [105]

The crooked path being firm and the sky's sphere[1585]
being reached came down as Bhadra's tradition:
the lotus in the heart,[1586] the lotus in the navel,
likewise the lotus that is found in the throat, [106]

and the lotus that is an array of sixty,
being situated at the crooked door,
are seen as a continuous flow[1587] and
remain firm through sensations[1588] [107]

Coursing through the nine doors
that emit feces, urine, and semen,[1589]
having a form like a lotus filament,
she abides below as well as above[1590] [108]

Called "she with the name prajñā"
by all buddhas, she is their mother

The deity residing in the middle there
is the supreme lord who is nonduality[1591] [109]

In the three lotuses, there plays {122}
the omniscient one, great bliss,
being greatly adorned by fire,
water, earth, and also wind [110]

Gently[1592] circling, through union,
it is guided to the three lotuses[1593]
via the small-bell orifice's path
by joining it with the nostrils[1594] [111]

Within the dark-blue vajra aperture,
it is nonduality that is being realized[1595]
Resting the portion deprived of parts
by the cakras at the small bell's tip,[1596] [112]

the drink of nectar is imbibed
by joining with the vajra tongue
Thereby, the body becomes pure
and is naturally without stains [113]

The lady of prajñā so divine[1597]
has destroyed aging and death
This yoga was conveyed to me
by Bhadrapāda through his play[1598] [114]

What is called "the nectar of samādhi"
is true—there's no doubt that it is true[1599]
By way of different inhalations through
the nose, the syllable HA is unstruck[1600] [115]

In the paths of the small-bell orifice,[1601]
there are thirty-two nāḍīs, it is held
The instruction given on thirty-two
is that no digits and digits are nondual[1602] [116]

By way of different inhalations through
the nose, the syllable KA is unstruck
Guided via the path of the small-bell
opening, the passageway is steady[1603] [117]

Resting at ease there at the door,
luminosity manifests in a pure way
Called "beginningless nonduality,"
it abides in the form of glorious bliss[1604] [118]

Then, vāyu is set in motion
and Mahendra is guided {123}
The steady path flourishes
Parameśvara is unstruck[1605] [119]

The thirteenth bhūmi becomes attained
The kāya of bliss is indeed unrivaled
Form accomplished[1606] without beginning
is that which turns the wheel of dharma[1607] [120]

It is this sacred tradition[1608] of Bhadrapāda
that has thus become a bit of a literary work
That which has been heard and ascertained
is familiarized with by hearing and reflecting[1609] [121]

Through the yoga of repeatedly cultivating
what I heard due to Bhadrapāda's kindness,
this is what has been strung together here[1610]
by the virtuous one[1611] who is named Kuddāla [122]

May I become a servant of Bhadrapāda
and other masters and yogīs, as well as
all sentient beings without exception,
throughout the succession of my births[1612] [123]

By way of this motivation,
when I become a buddha,

or else [even] if I go to hell,
hell itself shall be Sukhāvatī[1613] [124]

This is the final yoga, thanks to the stainless guru tradition, which is held to be the true state of mantra with all its vast qualities, the yoga of the perfection process that arose as a fraction of inconceivable nonduality, the sacred tradition that has the nature of the deity as the heart of guidance. For the sake of remembering it, I wrote it down for dull people with little intelligence like myself.[1614]

*This concludes "Pith Instructions on the Tradition of the Inconceivable" composed by the mahāmudrā siddha Śrī Kuddālapa. It was translated and finalized by paṇḍita *Sukhāṅkura and the great editor-lotsāwa Gö Lhedsé.*[1615] {124}

(19) Eradicating Bad Views

In the language of India: *Kudṛṣṭinirghātananāma*[1616]
In the language of Tibet: *Lta ba ngan pa sel ba zhes bya ba*

I pay homage to youthful Mañjuśrī[1617]
I pay homage to the Buddha

I shall discuss the elimination of bad views
thanks to the performance of initial activity
By means of spending your time[1618] with such
efforts, the state [of buddhahood] is attained[1619] [1]

[Initial activity in learners and nonlearners][1620]
Here, there are two types of sentient beings: learners and nonlearners. From the [superior] intention,[1621] the engagement through aspiration,[1622] and the engagement when having arrived on the bhūmis, all the way up through the attainment of power,[1623] learners, who are in the causal state, gather the two accumulations by performing utterly pure initial activity and then attain completely perfect awakening. In nonlearners, who have cast off any thoughts about remedies, true reality, and the fruition,[1624] just as in the case of [Buddha] Śākyamuni, their uninterrupted initial activity, which is characterized by promoting the welfare of sentient beings, unfolds [naturally] through the power of the impetus of their [former] aspiration prayers and through the effortless yoga of unity. {125} This is what is generally accepted.[1625] Accordingly, [the following is said]:

Protector, there is neither conceit,[1626]
nor thought, nor wavering in you
Without any effort, your buddha
activity is unfolding in the world[1627]

The consummate welfare of others is held
to be the principal fruition of the buddha
What is other than buddhahood and so on
is held to be a fruition by virtue of that sake[1628]

Like a wish-fulfilling jewel, he cannot
be shaken by all the winds of volitions[1629]
Still, without any exception, he fulfills
the wishes of the entirety of beings[1630] [2]

Due to relinquishing affirmation and exclusion
in terms of fruition, true reality, and antagonists,
the wise ones awaken to complete awakening
but [still perform] initial activities thereafter[1631] [3]

"The performance of initial activity is indeed suitable for learners, but how could there be any exertion in initial activity for nonlearners who manifest[1632] the lack of nature? This [initial activity] too is simply being fettered by a golden chain." This is true because it is devoid of the realization of prajñāpāramitā. The pāramitā of prajñā, however, is the nature of the five pāramitās. Therefore "the emptiness that is endowed with all supreme aspects" is spoken of. Moreover, the Bhagavān said that the five pāramitās devoid of the pāramitā of prajñā {126} do not [even] receive the nominal designation "pāramitā." This is also stated in the *Āryavimalakīrtinirdeśa[sūtra]*:[1633]

Means divorced from prajñā is bondage
Prajñā divorced from means is bondage
Means joined with prajñā is liberation
Prajñā joined with means is liberation[1634]

Thanks to the pith instruction of the true guru, the identity of these two is understood to be established as what is connate, similar to a lamp and its light. Therefore [the following is said]:

All yogīs need to perform the initial
activity in the way it was described
Emptiness and compassion inseparable
is held to be the wisdom in awakening[1635] [4]

Initial activity [is described thus]:[1636]

The five pāramitās that were discussed
[are known] by the name "initial activity"
The pāramitā that is prajñā is asserted
as the nature and the sovereign[1637] of these[1638] [5]

Likewise, [this is said] here:

To generosity, discipline, patience,
vigor, dhyāna, and prajñā, always
and attentively, the intelligent tend
They will become happy and wise[1639] [6]

The causes of the sambhoga- and nirmita[kāyas]
are the three of generosity, discipline, and patience
Dhyāna and prajñā are those of the dharma[kāya]
Vigor is what is asserted as the [cause] of both [7]

Therefore it is necessary for bodhisattvas to rely on very pure initial activity. In the opposite case, there would be the undesired consequence of nihilism.[1640] {127} This is stated [as follows]:

Even though virtue and nonvirtue lack any nature,
still, virtue and not nonvirtue should be performed
In the worldly seeming, like a water-moon's reflection,
happiness is pleasant and suffering ever unpleasant[1641] [8]

"Among learners, how then should initial activity be carried out by those who abide in the yogic discipline of a lunatic and aspire for nonconceptuality?" It is said they engage in [such yogic] conduct after having given away their body:[1642]

> Having given the gift of the body,
> later, conduct is to be undertaken[1643]

Since this is declared, generosity is [accomplished through] gifts up to and including [one's own] body; discipline through restraining body, speech, and mind for the sake of all sentient beings; patience through [even] enduring being killed by extreme heat, saws, and so on; vigor through enduring harm by the eight worldly dharmas; dhyāna through the effortless flow of its own essence in accord with the nature of everything; and prajñā through the realization that is characterized by the nonobservability of all phenomena.[1644]

In those for whom the effortless taste's breakthrough always unfolds,
it is in them that all supreme pāramitās in their entirety unfold[1645] [9]

Therefore initial activity definitely unfolds even in those with the yogic discipline of a lunatic. The bestial Cārvākas' statement about the absence of any next world {128} is not endorsed [by us], because it is unreasonable in every respect. For, in this regard, the following is said in the *Hevajra[tantra]* about the learners among bodhisattvas:[1646]

> First, poṣadha should be bestowed
> Then, instruct on the precept points[1647]

[Preliminary procedures]
As for first bestowing the poṣadha, [monastics should say] the following twice or thrice: "Please consider me, venerable master! I, the upāsaka with such and such a name take refuge in the Buddha, the dharma, and the saṃgha until I reach the heart of awakening."[1648] Having gone for the triple refuge in this way, [there follows] the poṣadha formula:[1649] "Vener-

able one, may you take care of me! Master, please consider me! From this time of day onward until sunrise tomorrow in this place here, I, the upāsaka so-and-so, refrain from harming any living creatures, stealing from others, impure conduct, and likewise divisive speech, lying, drinking crafted beverages that are intoxicating, eating food in the afternoon [and thereafter], garlands, fragrant ointments, dancing, singing, entertainment, and raised beds and seats. For that long, I [remain in] this [practice of poṣadha] with its eight qualities."[1650] {129}

Following taking refuge in the Three Jewels, householder bodhisattvas refrain from these five: destroying life, taking what is not given, sexual misconduct out of desire, and false speech (which are unacceptable by nature), as well as drinking intoxicating beverages.[1651] Householder bodhisattvas, who are endowed with discerning knowledge [derived from] hearing [the dharma], abandon the ten nonvirtues, restrain themselves so as to not commit them again, and [instead] perform the [ten] virtuous actions, clean their face and so on during the morning watch after rising, and then recollect the Three Jewels. Having protected themselves and their own yoga with OṂ ĀḤ HŪṂ, they should undertake dhyānas, recitations, praises, and so on in accord with [their own] realization. They should also recite the *Nāmasaṃgīti* three times [a day].[1652]

Thereafter, reciting OṂ JAMBHALAJALENDRĀYA SVĀHĀ [one hundred and eight times], they should offer one hundred and eight handfuls of water to Jambhala.[1653] Then, they recite the mantra NAMAḤ SAMANTABUDDHĀNĀṂ SARVATATHĀGATĀVALOKITE OṂ SAMBHARA SAMBHARA HŪṂ PHAṬ SVĀHĀ seven times. With five streams of nectar dripping from the five extended fingers of their right hand, they should visualize that balls of boiled rice with water and oblation food placed at the doorstep {130} are multiplied and turn into a Magadha droṇa [each].[1654] Having offered these to satisfy all hungry ghosts and piśācas[1655] while snapping their fingers three times, they should offer the bodhisattva oblation.[1656]

Now, they should cultivate the love that has the form of cherishing all sentient beings as if they were their only son, the compassion whose nature consists of the wish to pull them out of the ocean of saṃsāra that consists of suffering and the causes of suffering,[1657] the joy that consists of the splendor of mind being exhilarated due to having taken refuge in the Three Jewels, and the equanimity that has the characteristic of being completely unattached.[1658]

[Visualizing and worshipping the maṇḍala]
With the mindset of being zealous about the welfare of all sentient beings, on a portion of the ground to set up a maṇḍala with pure cow dung and clean water, [blessing it with] "OṂ ĀḤ VAJRAREKHE HŪṂ," they craft any four-sided maṇḍala (such as a square one) as they desire and meditate as follows.[1659] In its middle, on a sun disk on the anthers[1660] of a multicolored eight-petaled lotus, arising in his complete form from a blue syllable HŪṂ, there is Akṣobhya, dark-blue in color, forming the earth-touching mudrā. Thereafter, on the eastern petal, arising from a white syllable OṂ, there is Vairocana, white in color, forming the mudrā of supreme awakening. Then, on the southern petal, born from a yellow syllable TRĀṂ, there is Ratnasambhava, yellow in color, forming the mudrā of supreme generosity. {131} Then, on the western petal, originating from a red syllable HRĪḤ, there is Amitābha, red in color, forming the mudrā of samādhi. Then, on the northern petal, born from a green[1661] syllable KHAṂ, there is Amoghasiddhi, green in color, forming the mudrā of fearlessness.[1662]

Consecrating it with OM ĀḤ VAJRAPUṢPE HŪṂ and so on, they should offer everything that is highly desirable. These five tathāgatas wear saffron-colored robes and have uṣṇīṣas, their heads and faces are shaven, and they sit on sun disks, while Vairocana [sits] on a moon disk. Among them, the four [other buddhas on the petals] face Akṣobhya [in the middle], while Akṣobhya faces the practitioner. In front of these [buddhas], making them clearly visible, in accordance with [the practitioner's] understanding, [the practitioner] should recite the stanzas of the triple refuge. Here, the stanzas of the triple refuge are as follows:[1663]

I pay homage to the Buddha, the guru
I pay homage to the dharma, the protector
I pay homage to the saṃgha that is great
To these three, I pay homage at all times

To the Three Jewels that are my refuge,
I confess the entirety of my wrongdoings
By rejoicing in the merits of the world,
my mind is set on buddha awakening

Until [attaining] awakening, I go for refuge
to the Buddha, dharma, and supreme assembly, {132}
I give rise to this mindset for awakening[1664]
to accomplish my own and others' welfare

I give rise to supreme awakening's mindset
I call upon and invite every sentient being
I shall engage in the desirable conduct for supreme awakening[1665]
I shall become a buddha to benefit the world

Having revealed all wrongdoings
and having rejoiced in [all] merits,
I will be performing the upavāsa,
the noble poṣadha's eight branches[1666]

Then, they recite the following:

Limbs anointed with discipline's sandalwood,
you are swathed in the garments of dhyāna
and covered in awakening's branches' flowers—
spend your time in just the way you please![1667]

They should utter "OṂ VAJRAMAṆḌALA MUḤ." In this way, they should also worship Mañjuśrī in accordance with the pith instructions.[1668] This is the procedure of worshipping the maṇḍala.[1669]

[The benefit of the maṇḍala]
Cow dung with water is generosity
and discipline represents cleansing
Patience means to remove tiny ants
Vigor is to perform the ritual activity [10]

Dhyāna makes mind one-pointed in that instant
Prajñā means the beauty of drawing fine lines
Having constructed the maṇḍala of the sages,
they attain these six pāramitās in such a way [11]

They will come to have a golden hue, become liberated from all diseases,
be distinguished among gods and humans, shine brightly like the moon,
and be born into a royal family, possessing an abundance of gold and wealth, {133}
having performed such bodily activities for the sugatas' supreme mansion[1670] [12]

These are the stanzas on the benefit of the maṇḍala.[1671]

Having crafted the maṇḍala on a daily basis
with cow dung and water, as well as flowers,
offering something to the guru at the three times,
they should pay their homage with devotion [13]

Being delighted by their mindset for others,
they should turn away from egocentric mind
Being happy, full of kindness, and fortunate,
they will come to take a rebirth in Sukhāvatī [14]

They shall perfect the six pāramitās,
being blessed by buddhas and so on
Those who are crafting the maṇḍala
will be replete with infinite qualities [15]

[This further describes the maṇḍala's] benefits.[1672]

[Worshipping scriptures, paintings, statues, and so on]
They should always recite and worship
prajñāpāramitā correctly according to
the procedure of the maṇḍala and so on,
immersing themselves in her meaning [16]

[Likewise,] the *Ekagāthā*, the *Caturgāthā*,
the *Gāthādvitayadhāraṇī*, the *Ṣaṇmukhī*,
as well as the *Bhadracarī[praṇidhāna]*,[1673]
three times during the day's three periods [17]

In meditative absorption from one syllable
all the way up to one hundred thousand,[1674]
the wise whose determination is unbroken
should recite according to what they find [18]

[That is,] they should also worship paintings, books, statues, and so on of buddhas and bodhisattvas. This is the procedure of worshipping paintings and books.[1675]

[Making stamped clay images]
Now, {134} by following the *Mahāmaṇḍalavyūhatantra*, the procedure of forming stamped clay images is discussed.[1676]

NAMAḤ SAMANTABUDDHANĀṂ
OṂ VAJRAPUṢPE SVĀHĀ is the mantra when picking up the clay.
OṂ VAJRODBHAVĀYA SVĀHĀ is the mantra for making the rough version of the image.
OṂ ARAJE VIRAJE SVĀHĀ is the mantra for protecting it with oil.
OṂ DHARMADHĀTUGARBHE SVĀHĀ is the mantra for casting it into the mold.
OṂ VAJRAMUDGARĀKOṬANA SVĀHĀ is the mantra for smoothing it out.
OṂ DHARMARATE SVĀHĀ is the mantra for attracting [the deity into the image].
OṂ SUPRATIṢṬHITAVAJRE SVĀHĀ is the mantra for erecting [the image].
OṂ SARVATATHĀGATAMAṆIŚATADĪPTE JVALA JVALA DHARMADHĀTUGARBHE SVĀHĀ is the mantra for consecrating [the image].
OṂ SVABHĀVAVIŚUDDHE ĀHARA ĀHARA ĀGACCHA ĀGACCHA DHARMADHĀTUGARBHE SVĀHĀ is the mantra for delivering [the image].[1677]

OṂ ĀKĀŚADHĀTUGARBHE SVĀHĀ is the mantra for begging pardon.[1678]
This is the procedure of forming stamped clay images.[1679]

[Building caityas]

OṂ NAMO BHAGAVATE VAIROCANAPRABHĀRĀJĀYA TATHĀGATĀYĀRHATE SAMYAKSAṂBUDDHĀYA / TADYATHĀ OṂ SŪKṢME SŪKṢME SAME SAMAYE ŚĀNTE DĀNTE SAMĀROPE ANĀLAMBE TARAMBE YAŚOVATI MAHĀTEJE NIRĀKULA-NIRVĀṆE SARVABUDDHĀDHIṢṬHĀNĀDHIṢṬHITE SVĀHĀ[1680]

Reciting this dhāraṇī[1681] twenty-one times over lumps of clay or lumps of sand, they should build a caitya [with them]. [Thereby,] as many infinitesimal particles as there are in this [lump], that many tens of millions of caityas become created. They attain merits as numerous as the number of those infinitesimal particles, {135} become mighty lords of the ten bhūmis, and will swiftly awaken to unsurpassable, completely perfect awakening. That is what the bhagavān and tathāgata Vairocana declared. This is the dhāraṇī of great benefit.[1682]

> As for the phenomena arisen from a cause,
> the Tathāgata has spoken about their cause
> and also about that which is their cessation
> In this way the great Śramaṇa has taught[1683]

Having consecrated [the caitya] with this stanza, they should pay homage to the caitya with the [dhāraṇī] "OṂ NAMO BHAGAVATE RATNAKETURĀJĀYA TATHĀGATĀYĀRHATE SAMYAKSAMBUDDHĀYA / TADYATHĀ OṂ RATNE RATNE MAHĀRATNE RATNAVIJAYE SVĀHĀ."[1684] Through paying homage to a single caitya with this dhāraṇī, they will pay homage to tens of millions of caityas. This is the procedure of building caityas out of clay, sand, and so on.[1685]

[Dedicating and rejoicing in merit]
Through the great dedication that is mentioned in the prajñāpāramitā [sūtras]—a distinguished fruition that is of the extent of what is dedicated will be invoked by dedicating all this in a distinguished manner—

they should dedicate [all this merit] as follows: "Just as the tathāgata arhats, the completely perfect buddhas, know by means of their buddha wisdom and see by means of their buddha eye the roots of virtue in terms of their types, their categories, their characteristics, their natures, and through which dharmatā they exist, so {136} these roots of virtue [exist] in me rejoicing [in them]. Just as the tathāgata arhats, the completely perfect buddhas, approve these roots of virtue as the extent of what is dedicated, so I dedicate them to unsurpassable, completely perfect awakening." Furthermore, [they should say this]:[1686]

By means of these virtuous actions, may I
become a buddha in the world before long,
teach the dharma for the world's benefit,
and free beings troubled by many sufferings[1687]

This is the procedure of rejoicing in and dedicating merit.

[Other daily activities
The practitioners should say the following:]

Whichever livelihood of whomever it may be,
it is a pure livelihood that should be acquired
You should consider this to be like medicine
for the sake of patience and pacifying disease[1688]

Then, with [reciting] "OṂ AKĀRO MUKHAṂ SARVADHARMĀṆĀṂ ĀDYANUTPANNATVĀT OṂ ĀḤ HŪṂ PHAṬ SVĀHĀ" over [their food,] however it may be prepared, they should offer an oblation [from it]. With "OṂ ĀḤ SARVABUDDHABODHISATTVEBHYO VAJRANAIVEDYE HŪṂ," they should give the food offering. Reciting "OṂ HĀRĪTI MAHĀYAKṢIṆI HARA HARA SARVAPĀPĀN KṢĪṂ SVĀHĀ," they should offer two rice balls to Hārītī.[1689] [Saying] "OṂ AGRAPIṆḌĀŚIBHYAḤ SVĀHĀ," they offer the choice rice ball. Thereafter, while blessing the food in their own bowl with "OṂ AH HŪṂ," they first touch it with their thumb and ring finger so that any defects such as poison become alleviated, and then enjoy it. After that, {137} once they have eaten to their content, [reciting] "OṂ

UTSṚṢṬAPIṆḌĀŚANEBHYAH SVĀHĀ," they should offer [some of] the food that is left over as the leftover ball. The food that still remains should be discarded without any interest in it. Accordingly, [this is said]:[1690]

They should offer the oblation, the food offering,
the one for Hārītī, including the choice rice balls,
and present the leftover, which is the fifth one,
in order that the great fruition will be enjoyed[1691] [19]

Thereafter, having sipped water and so on, with a completely pure mind endowed with special bliss, they should recite the following three times for the benefit and happiness of all sentient beings:[1692]

May the kings, the benefactors,
and others, the hosts of beings,
always come to obtain happiness,
long lives, good health, and wealth![1693]

Afterward, they should spend their time with pure activities of body, speech, and mind as they like. Once they have settled down later, either for half a day or at midday,[1694] they should pass their time by discussing [episodes from] the Jātaka [tales], Nidānas, and Avadānas together with their spiritual friends.[1695] Then, at the evening's twilight, they should cultivate a mind free of weariness in accordance with their realization, [engaging in] dhyānas, recitations, praises, and so on. With the mantra that begins with "AKĀRA,"[1696] they should offer an oblation and sleep with the sleep of yoga.[1697] {138}

[Hermeneutical etymology of *upāsaka*]
How is the term upāsaka to be understood?[1698]

[*u* signifies this:]
They are to strive to revere buddhas,
show a predilection for tranquility,
and be endowed with the methods
to bring benefit to sentient beings [20]

pā signifies this:
They should always abandon wrongdoing
and any companionship with wrongdoers,
hold people back from their wrongdoings,
and point out wrongdoings everywhere[1699] [21]

sa signifies this:
The wise free from superimpositions,
who are perfectly absorbed in samādhi
and always endowed with supreme joy,
should accomplish perfect awakening[1700] [22]

ka signifies this:
At all times, they are making efforts and
should completely maintain compassion
Even if facing hardships, they do nothing
undesirable but perform utmost benefit[1701] [23]

Since such is stated, the upāsakas who are endowed with [the qualities signified by] these four syllables have abandoned nonvirtuous actions, gathered the accumulation of merit, and, thanks to the power of their continuous practice, perform virtues even when they are asleep, just as if they were in the waking state.[1702]

Seeing it as being just like a reflection,
the world is pure and without any taint
Like a person of illusion, they should do
everything without observing anything[1703] [24]

Therefore they are declared to be irreversible. Always acquiring the accumulation of merit in such a way continuously by day and by night, they should remain for the sake of the benefit of sentient beings until reaching the heart of awakening.[1704]

The one whose name is Gaganagarbha,
fully devoted to Madhyamaka's actuality {139}

and well-absorbed in this initial activity,
is the one who makes such a firm resolve [25]

Having come from Vajrapīṭha,
he is a noble-minded brahman[1705]
Upon being requested by him,
I composed this *Initial Activity* [26]

Through what I have discussed here, due to the request of
Gaganagarbha,
in the form of a reference work on initial activity with just a few words,
discarding wrongdoing's blurred vision, may the afflictions' eradication
swiftly happen for those with stainless insight by training for
awakening! [27]

Through the virtue of this performance
of initial activity that I have obtained,
may the world attain this performance
of initial activity that is so excellent![1706] [28]

This concludes "Eradicating Bad Views" composed by the well-learned master and Mahāpaṇḍita Śrī Advayavajra. It was translated, edited, and finalized by the Indian upādhyāya and guru Vajrapāṇi and the Tibetan lotsāwa Tsurdön Yeshé Jungné.[1707] {140}

(20) A Commentary on the [Initial] Passage of "Eradicating Bad Views"

In the language of India: *Kudṛṣṭinirghātavākyaṭippinikā*[1708]
In the language of Tibet: *Lta ba ngan pa sel ba'i dka' 'grel*

I pay homage to Vajradhara[1709]

There are three states: the causal state, the fruitional state, and the state of promoting the welfare of sentient beings. Here, the [state] of learners is the causal state. Those of tathāgatas are the fruitional state and the state of promoting the welfare of sentient beings.

What is called "the causal state"[1710] begins with the [generation of] bodhicitta and extends up through sitting on the seat of awakening.[1711] What is called "the fruitional state" is the state in which the wisdom of completely perfect awakening has arisen, all afflictions have been abandoned, and [all] qualities have been attained. What is called "the state of promoting the welfare of sentient beings" begins with the first turning of the wheel of dharma and lasts until the teaching disappears.

The causal state here is threefold: (1) the state of intention, {141} (2) the state of application, and (3) the state of [having attained] power.

(1) The state of intention consists of the aspiration that all[1712] sentient beings will be liberated. Its four pillars[1713] are as follows: the consideration of removing the suffering of others, the consideration of the necessity, the consideration of the aids, and the consideration of enjoyment. Through these becoming the means, [bodhisattvas] aspire for [all

sentient beings to attain] awakening.[1714] For the four causes[1715] of this are stated as follows:

> The causes: the disposition, a true friend,
> compassion, and fearlessness of suffering
> It is by means of these four conditions
> that bodhicitta becomes generated[1716] [1]

The state of intention [is also presented] through ten points.[1717]

(2) [The state of] application here is twofold: the ten pāramitās on the path of preparation by way of engagement through aspiration and[1718] the seven pāramitās when having attained the bhūmis. Here, the ten pāramitās of engagement through aspiration are as follows:

> Generosity, discipline, patience,
> vigor, dhyāna, prajñā, means,
> aspirations, power, and wisdom—
> these are the ten pāramitās[1719]

The generosity when having attained the bhūmis is accomplished through four accomplishments: the accomplishments of intention, application, recipient, and what is to be given.[1720] The seven pāramitās [here] are generosity, {142} discipline, patience, vigor, dhyāna, prajñā, and means. These are more distinguished than the pāramitās practiced during the engagement through aspiration. These constitute the twofold state of application.

(3) Here, the five powers [in the state of having attained power] are as follows: [the powers over] afflictions, birth, karma, means, and the state of[1721] maturing sentient beings.

The entirety of initial activity is to be performed by those dwelling in the causal state. For those dwelling in the fruitional state and the state of promoting the welfare of sentient beings, just as in the case of [Buddha] Śākyamuni, this initial activity unfolds without any effort.[1722] This is to be understood in detail [as it is explained] in "Eradicating Bad Views."

This concludes "A Commentary on the Difficult Points—or A Recollection—of 'Eradicating Bad Views'" composed by Śrīmat Advayavajra, who was well-trained. It was translated, edited, and finalized by the Indian upādhyāya Vajrapāṇi and the Tibetan lotsāwa Tsurdön Jñānākara.[1723] {143}

(21) An Illumination of Unity

In the language of India: *Yuganaddhaprakāśanāma*[1724]
In the language of Tibet: *Zung du 'jug pa ta rab tu gsal ba bstan pa zhes bya ba*

I pay homage to youthful Mañjuśrī[1725]

Once it has been realized that whatever
appears is pure, there is no more change
Change refers to having arisen through conditions
These too [arise] through such[1726]—that's nonarising [1]

Form is not found in form,
nor is it found in the eyes,
nor in the consciousness arising with it,
as in talking about a stick and fire[1727] [2]

Whether it is in a kindling stick,
a fireboard, or a person's hands,
at first, fire is not established—
it arises as a dependent thing[1728] [3]

Is it that ignorance is born before
its own son or once he was born?[1729]
If the son were not [born] before,
then it has no real substance[1730] [4]

As they are thus nothing but conditions,
phenomena lack any nature of their own
The yogīs who abide within that [view]
do not part from the bliss that is supreme [5]

There is never anything to rid or to adopt,
and yet the conventional is taking its course {144}
Like an illusion, it has no nature of its own
because dependent origination is realized[1731] [6]

Due to lacking a nature, there is no arising
By virtue of conditions, there is no ceasing
Therefore neither being nor nonbeing stand,
but unity keeps manifesting nevertheless[1732] [7]

The oneness of emptiness and compassion
is not bestowed by your own thoughts
It consists of the natural unity
of emptiness and lucidity[1733] [8]

Understanding how to directly realize
the native emptiness that is profound
and endowed with all supreme aspects,
may those with superb yoga venerate the buddhas[1734] [9]

The wise,[1735] always immersed [in this]
with their body, speech, and mind,
whether engaging or not engaging in conduct,
are called "observers of conduct" [10]

This concludes "An Illumination of Unity" composed by master Avadhūtipa Advayavajra. It was translated and edited by the Indian upādhyāya Vajrapāṇi and the Tibetan lotsāwa Tsültrim Gyalwa.[1736] {145}

(22) Pith Instructions on True Reality Called "A Dohā Treasure"

In the language of India: **Dohānidhināmatattvopadeśa*[1737]
In the language of Tibet: *Do ha ti zhes bya ba de kho na nyid kyi man ngag*

I pay homage to Śrī Heruka

The three yānas are explained as the four positions[1738]
The Vaibhāṣikas are to be understood as twofold:[1739]
the lower and medium śrāvakas are from the west,
the highest and the pratyekabuddhas from Kashmir [1]

The five skandhas constitute the tenet of them all
The two from the west assert an inexpressible person
All take refuge in the Three [Jewels] as long as they live
The compassion of disciplining themselves arises vividly [2]

Those in the lower [Śrāvaka]yāna meditate on repulsiveness—[1740]
the mindset of the body being pure is to be understood as a stain
Exhaling and inhaling are the meditation of the medium ones—
The stain of that [meditation] is to unite them within the vase [3]

The highest ones' meditation consists of the four realities—
the eightfold[1741] path as well as the emptiness of the person
Saṃsāra represents suffering, attachment is its origination,
nirvāṇa is cessation, and what is uncontaminated is the path[1742] [4]

To focus on permanent[1743] peace is understood as being their stain
Pratyekabuddhas meditate by themselves on the inconceivable {146}
The stains of this meditative equipoise are understood as two:
they are to be understood as intoxication and states without mind[1744] [5]

Aggregations of minutest [particles] represent the Sautrāntika system
Meditating on the inconceivable, their stains are like the previous ones
Their view consists of nothing but the six pāramitās themselves
Through the power of compassion, they engage in dedications[1745] [6]

The world is mere mind[1746]—there are no minutest particles
The Yogācāras[1747] [assert that it] is similar to a dream
The diverse appearances of blue, yellow, and so forth—
everything that may be asserted—has this nature [7]

Everything represents the dhyāna of self-awareness
The view of permanence is known as their meditation's stain
Moreover, they assert saṃsāric existence's latent tendencies
The entirety of aspects is present as adverse factors[1748] [8]

The nonduality that is equal to space,[1749] inconceivable, and pure,
has compassion's nature, and has no aspect is perfect buddhahood
The two kāyas with form[1750] are those that issue forth from this root
The stains of dhyāna and view have the nature of the previous ones [9]

Mere self-awareness once the four extremes are relinquished
is what resembles a water-moon, an illusion, and a dream
This is what is proclaimed to be the dhyāna of that view
The abandoning of self-awareness is their stain of extinction[1751] [10]

Beings attain something other from various others
[However,] the entirety of aspects[1752] is naturally pure—
this constitutes the utter nonabiding that is unmatched[1753]
The stains of dhyāna and view are known as extremes[1754] [11]

This aspect constitutes the Pāramitāyāna that is external
Experiencing the nature of bliss is the great secret mantra
The state of mind of joining the vajra and the lotus {147}
is the union of the moon and the sun of supreme passion [12]

By the power of compassion's means, all beings
[are able to] rest in that desire as being suchness[1755]
That which has the nature[1756] of the bodhicitta of
equal taste constitutes the bliss that is connate [13]

At that point, two have actually fallen down there[1757]
Moreover, emptiness and compassion became equal there
The entire world is realized as aspects of the connate,
in sync with the teachings given by[1758] the supreme guru [14]

This concludes "Pith Instructions on True Reality Called 'A Dohā Treasure'" composed by the great master Avadhūtipa Śrī Advayavajra. It was translated by venerable Dhiriśrījñāna.[1759] {148}

(23) Five Stanzas on the Love between Means and Prajñā

In the language of India: *Prajñopāyadayāpañcaka*[1760]
In the language of Tibet: *Thabs dang shes rab rtse ba lnga pa*

I pay homage to Śrī Vajrasattva[1761]

Were it not for the adorable bridegroom
of appearance as mere dependent origination,
the impassioned bride of emptiness
would be no better than dead[1762] [1]

Emptiness is the most lovely bride,
a ravishing beauty beyond compare
If he ever became separated from her,
that handsome bridegroom would be crushed[1763] [2]

Therefore trembling with anxiety,
bride and bridegroom approach the guru
It is through their inborn pleasure
that he turns it into connate love [3]

AHO! The sagacity of the true guru
and his great skill are so wonderful—
the two are indivisible from the native state,
nonreferential, and unsurpassable [4]

With all characteristics complete
and free from the two[1764] extremes,
this couple is the nature of all that is
but always manifests[1765] without a nature [5]

This concludes "Five Stanzas on the Love between Means and Prajñā" composed by master Maitrīpa. It was translated, edited, and finalized by the Indian upādhyāya {149} *Vajrapāṇi and the Tibetan lotsāwa Tsurdön Jñānākara.*[1766] {150}

(24) An Illumination of Utter Nonabiding

In the language of India: *Apratiṣṭhānaprakāśanāma*[1767]
In the language of Tibet: *Rab tu mi gnas pa gsal bar ston pa zhes bya ba*

I pay homage to the Buddha[1768]

It is the utter nonabiding of cognition that
is held to be the Buddhists' entire wealth,[1769]
but only when it promotes the welfare of
beings by way of effortless application [1]

Once exclusion and affirmation have arisen,
there are positions of extinction and creation
But nonarising and nonceasing are perpetual,
so arising and extinction is the talk of cattle[1770] [2]

Assuming that self-awareness is valid cognition,
the existence of awareness [could be] asserted
But since all delineation has been abandoned,
such existence is not agreeable there[1771] [3]

If existence is asserted subsequently,
then existence is for sure not a substance
The meaning of propositions extinguished
and nullified then refers to "nondelineation"[1772] [4]

In actual [practice], awareness is found
because it manifests [so] subsequently
At the beginning, it is free of thought
Thereafter, this wisdom is the perceiver[1773] [5]

As any remaining of minds of the past,
the future, and so forth is not possible,
they therefore are without any nature {151}
This is what the lord of the worlds taught[1774] [6]

The very arising of phenomena by way
of native self-awareness is inconceivable[1775]
Exactly this is what is called "emptiness,"
but it does not veer off into extinction [7]

From the seed that is nonabiding
comes the fruition that is nonabiding,
the protectors' supreme true reality,
just as contrivance does from contrivance [8]

Thus, we don't say "Dhyāna does not exist"
to those whose conduct is nonattachment
For by virtue of dependent origination,
it always arises in sync with its natural flow[1776] [9]

Whatever may originate in dependence
is the mind that is diverse and nondual
The division into emptiness, mind, and diversity
is the dharma-, sambhoga-, and nirmāṇa[kāyas][1777] [10]

Through whatever virtue I obtained
that consists of showing nonabiding,
may beings arrive at nonabiding's state
by way of everything they experience[1778] [11]

This concludes "An Illumination of Utter Nonabiding" composed by master Advayavajra. It was translated by the Indian upādhyāya Vajrapāṇi and the Tibetan lotsāwa bhikṣu Tsültrim Gyalwa.[1779] {152}

(25) Six Stanzas on the Connate

In the language of India: *Sahajaṣaṭka*[1780]
In the language of Tibet: *Lhan cig skyes pa drug pa*

I pay homage to Vajradhara[1781]

The followers of the Sugata hold true reality
to be free from permanence and extinction
As for phenomena born through that nature,
affirmation and exclusion are the talk of cattle [1]

For those who propound existence, we declare
that, when analyzed, everything is nonexistent
To those who propound nonexistence, we say
that, when not[1782] analyzed, everything is existent [2]

In whatever manner superimpositions
may emerge in the yogīs of true reality,
it is in like manner that superimpositions
are vanquished by the yogīs of true reality [3]

Since the connate is without contrivance,
thus the connate lacks any attachment
Bliss is nothing other than the connate—
bliss is characterized by nonattachment [4]

Once its character free of attachment is realized,[1783]
it is the genuine bliss[1784] associated with realization
Once diversity has been turned into self-realization,
it is immersed within the ocean of the connate [5]

Yogīs who abide in the true reality of mantra
stand firmly in the actuality of nonattachment
Once they turn saṃsāric existence into gurus,
the sphere of nonattachment should be theirs[1785] [6] {153}

This concludes "Six Stanzas on the Connate" composed by guru Maitrīpa. It was translated by the Indian upādhyāya Vajrapāṇi and the Tibetan lotsāwa Tsur bhikṣu Jñānākara.[1786] {154}

(26) Six Stanzas on the Middle

In the language of India: *Madhyamaṣaṭka*[1787]
In the language of Tibet: *Dbu ma drug pa*

I pay homage to the Buddha[1788]

The nondual wisdom that is really existent,[1789]
completely free from the four extremes,
empty of thoughts, and without focal objects
is what the proponents of aspects understand[1790] [1]

Since self-awareness is not extinguished,
since blue and so forth do not appear,[1791]
and since characteristics do not arise,[1792]
it is asserted as being the middle path[1793] [2]

The lucidity free of the four extremes
has the characteristic of being delusive
This[1794] constitutes illusion-like nonduality
and represents a tenet that has validity[1795] [3]

But awareness empty of being an entity,
which is without aspect and unsullied,
precisely that represents the middle path
In the aftermath, it is the pure seeming [4]

Whether [awareness] is lucid or not lucid,
neither is observable as far as true reality goes
Since it has the nature of being entirely unborn,
it is understood[1796] as the middle by the superior [5]

Lucidity free of the four extremes
possesses the character of the deity
It has the nature of nondual bliss[1797]
and is sheer dependent origination[1798] [6]

This concludes "Six Stanzas on the Middle" {155} *composed by the learned master Maitrīpa. It was translated by guru Vajrapāṇi and Nagtso [Lotsāwa].*[1799] {156}

(27) In Support of Mental Nonengagement

In the language of India: *Amanasikārādhāra*[1800]
In the language of Tibet: *Yid la mi byed pa ston pa zhes bya ba*

I pay homage to the Buddha[1801]

Many are mistaken about [the term] "mental nonengagement (*amanasikāra*)" here.

[1. Objection] Some say about this that [*amanasikāra*] is an ungrammatical term: in a compound [the proper form] should be *amanaskāra*. With regard to that, [Pāṇini] says: "In a *tatpuruṣa* [compound], when there is a [noun with a] *kṛt* [suffix, the locative ending] is often [preserved]." Since [Pāṇini] says "often" here, [this means that the ending of] the seventh case has not been elided. When compounds are formed without the elision [of this case ending], the forms *amanasikāra* [instead of] *amanaskāra*, *tvacisāra* (lit. "firmness in the skin"—that is, "fine skin") [instead of] *tvaksāra* ("skin firmness"), and *yudhiṣṭhira* ("resolute in battle") are obtained. Therefore the [term *amanasikāra*] is not ungrammatical.[1802]

[2. Objection] Some others say the following: "Well then, this [term] is proven to have [accurate grammatical] characteristics, but it is in no way established as the words [of the Buddha]." That is not the case, because it is seen in various sūtras and tantras.[1803] In the *Āryasarvabuddhaviśayāvatārajñānālokālaṃkāramahāyānasūtra* {157} [it is stated]:

> The dharmas of mental nonengagement are proper
> The dharmas of mental engagement are not proper[1804]

In the same [sūtra, the following is said]:

> To you who are without any imaginary thinking,
> whose mind is in the state of utter nonabiding,
> who lack any minding and mental engagement,
> and who are without focus, let there be homage![1805]

Likewise, in the *Avikalpapraveśadhāraṇī* [we find this]:

> Once bodhisattva mahāsattvas have relinquished all aspects of the characteristics of conceptions through not mentally engaging [in them] . . .[1806]

Various other [similar passages] are not written down [here] for fear of [citing] too extensive scriptural passages.[1807]

[3. Objection] Now, others may say: "This [term] is a word [of the Buddha] that belongs to the sūtra collection but not to the mantra [approach] because it is seen [only] in the sūtra collection."[1808] That is not the case—it is used in the chapter on true reality in the *Hevajra[tantra]*:

> In terms of a nature of their own . . . there are neither mind nor mental factors[1809]

Likewise:

> The world's entirety is meditated on
> in a way of mind not meditating on it[1810]

In terms of the meaning, it is understood that [such meditation occurs] through mental nonengagement.[1811]

[4. Objection] Some others may say: "[Granted, the term 'mental nonengagement'] exists in the tantras too, but what it refers to does not exist, because it is the object of the privative in a nonimplicative negation."[1812] That is not the case. [A nonimplicative negation] is a negation of the point in question. [The characteristic of] a nonimplicative negation is not to negate what is not applicable, {158} as in [the phrase] "the wives of the king who do not see the sun." The meaning of this is as follows. The wives of the king are called "hidden" [that is, protected from other men], so that they do not even see the sun.[1813] [The negation] here [obviously] does not refer to the nonexistence of the sun. What does it refer to? [It refers to] what is applicable: that the wives of the king see the sun—this is what is refuted [here]. In the case of mental nonengagement as well, what is negated by the privative is what is applicable—mental engagement (*manasikāraṇa*), which consists of perceiver, perceived, and so on—not the mind (*manaḥ*) [itself]. Therefore there is no flaw.[1814]

[5. Objection] When some say that the Bhagavān asserted a mental engagement that has the characteristics of permanence and extinction, we say the following. Are permanence, extinction, and so on mental engagement or mental nonengagement? This term "mental nonengagement" refers to the relinquishment of all clinging.[1815] Accordingly, the Bhagavān declared this in the *Avikalpapraveśadhāraṇī*:

> Sons of good family, for what reason is the dhātu of nonconceptuality called "mental nonengagement"? [This is said] in terms of being beyond all characteristics of conceptions. This term "mental nonengagement" indicates being beyond all characteristics of conceptions.[1816]

[6. *Amanasikāra* being suitable as an implicative negation] There is no flaw in the position that ["mental nonengagement"] is an implicative [negation] either. When [someone] says: "Bring a non-brahman!" [what is intended] is to bring somebody such as a kṣatriya who is similar to a brahman, {159} not a low-born person such as a wagoner.[1817] In this case [of "mental nonengagement" as an implicative negation] as well, the awareness of the lack of any nature remains. Thereby, [such an implicative negation] serves as the stance that is the [Madhyamaka] proposition of illusion-like nonduality. [Thus,] from what would the undesired consequence of propounding extinction follow?[1818]

[7. *Amanasikāra* as a compound in which the middle word is elided and the letter *a* is the main element] Or, alternatively, the privative [*a*] is used here[1819] only in a conventional sense. This word [this privative] has two [meanings], which shall be discussed. (a) Since [everything] is [like] an illusion or not truly established, [the privative *a*] is not a negation of either existence or nonexistence. Through this rationale, it is ruled out [that the privative *a*] has the meaning of negating the world. To explain the etymological formation [of the compound] in this case, *amanasikāra* refers to the *manasikāra* in which the letter *a* is the main component. It is a compound in which the middle word is dropped, just as in the case of "vegetable king." Thereby, as much mental engagement (*manasikāra*) as there may be, all of it represents the letter *a*, which means having the character of being unborn.[1820]

"Where did the Bhagavān teach that the letter *a* stands for being unborn?" This is as it is stated in the chapter on mantras in the *Hevajra[tantra]*:[1821]

> [OṂ] The letter *a* is the source of all phenomena because they are unborn from the beginning . . .[1822]

The meaning of this is that since all phenomena are unborn from the beginning, the letter *a* as [their] source is the main thing. The letter *a* is related to the characteristic of being unborn. Accordingly, in the *[Mañjuśrī]nāmasaṃgīti*, this is said:

> The letter *a* is the highest one of all characters
> of great significance, and the supreme syllable {160}
>
> It is of great power,[1823] unborn,
> free from speech and analogy[1824]

Or, alternatively, the letter *a* here represents the seed [syllable] of Nairātmyā. Accordingly, this is declared in the *Hevajra[tantra]*:

> The first of the vowels is Nairātmyā[1825]

Therefore all mental engagement is declared to lack a self and to lack a nature.[1826] Moreover, [the following is stated]:

> She has the first vowel's nature
> Buddhas[1827] think of her as "insight"

She's indeed the Bhagavatī Prajñā
in the yoga of the perfection process[1828]

(b) Or, alternatively, *a* refers to the word "luminous" and *manasikāra* to the word "self-blessing." It is both *a* and *manasikāra*, so it is *amanasikāra*.[1829] Due to that, the words *a*, *manasikāra*, and so on refer to the inconceivable state of luminosity and self-blessing—the awareness that is the continuous flow of the nondual unity of emptiness and compassion inseparable.[1830]

This concludes "In Support of Mental Nonengagement, An Illumination of Nairātmyā"[1831] *composed by the great master Śrī Advayavajra. It was translated by the Indian upādhyāya Vajrapāṇi and the Tibetan lotsāwa Mapen Chöbar. It was corrected by Nyenchung.*[1832] {161}

(28) Five Stanzas on Penetrating Insight

In the language of India: *Nirvedhapañcaka*[1833]
In the language of Tibet: *Mi phyed pa lnga pa*[1834]

I pay homage to the omniscient one[1835]

Realizing the buddha, the world becomes pure,
through realizing the friend who is the buddha
The great buddha is pure in a primordial way[1836]
How is the teaching of the buddha realized? [1]

This is a statement about the nature of those in whom the thoughts about remedies, true reality, and the fruition are terminated and who partake of penetrating insight into the connate.[1837]

Wisdom is without any taints and empty,
having effortless compassion's character
It is something that arises in dependence,
free from any own-being and nonbeing[1838] [2]

This describes the model for penetrating insight.[1839]

Phenomena's emptiness—amazing!
Compassion—even more amazing!
Amazing, the power of bliss![1840]
Amazing, the pure seeming! [3]

This utters the roar of the profound connate.[1841]

Alas, what to say, how to express it?
Even if told, where are the people?
For those in whom buddhahood occurs,
this is full of wealth without any effort[1842] [4]

This proclaims[1843] that people who, by virtue of compassion, {162} have faith in the approach of the profound dharma of utter nonabiding are difficult to find.[1844]

Cutting to the vitals of the seeds of the threads
of one's own karma is indeed my fruition
I do not harm [even] those who are violent
Even those kinds of persons, alas, I endure![1845] [5]

This considers the bodhisattvas' [compassionate] heart of actively taking care of all sentient beings whose minds are fettered and afflicted by the threads of their own karma.[1846]

This concludes "Five Stanzas on Penetrating Insight" composed by master Maitrīpa. It was translated by the Indian upādhyāya Vajrapāṇi and the Tibetan lotsāwa Mapen [Chöbar].[1847] {163}

(29) Five Stanzas on Love

In the language of India: *Prīṇapañcaka*[1848]
In the language of Tibet: *Dga' gcugs lnga pa*

I pay homage to the Buddha

If the supreme darling of appearance,
who is mere dependent origination,
did not exist, the truly impassioned
paramour of emptiness would be fettered [1]

The utterly cherished lover of emptiness
is endowed with a body beyond compare
If he ever became separated from her,
the chief of ecstatic bliss[1849] would be crushed [2]

Hence, anxious, both husband and wife
dwell before the eyes of the true guru
Through their pleasure, just as before,
he is turning this into connate love [3]

AHO! That the supreme skillful guru
has this kind of expertise is wonderful—
both arise as the nondual native state,[1850]
nonreferential, and unsurpassable [4]

With all characteristics complete
and free from the two extremes,
it represents the nature of all entities,
which always dawns without a nature [5]

This concludes "Five Stanzas on Love" composed by master Avadhūtipa[1851] *Śrī Advayavajra. It was translated by the Indian upādhyāya Vajrapāṇi and the Tibetan lotsāwa Tsur [Jñānākara].*[1852] {164}

(30) A Discourse on Illusion

In the language of India: *Māyānirukti*[1853]
In the language of Tibet: *Sgyu ma nges par bstan pa zhes bya ba*

I pay homage to the Buddha[1854]

Given that it is realized through observation
that the world, like an illusion, lacks a nature,
why are those intent on happiness deluded
here[1855] despite such an understanding?[1856] [1]

An illusionist may create the illusion
of the radiance of a burning house,
which may appear to be real for some—
to those knowing it, illusion is just illusion[1857] [2]

Seeing it as illusion, what is desired
comes without effort, all on its own
When you enjoy this as an illusion,
you encounter everything as illusion[1858] [3]

Alas, without [realizing them] to be delusive,
you must declare illusions to be permanent
[But] since the dharmadhātu lacks arising,
their extinction does not follow either [4]

As phenomena neither arise nor cease,
they do not turn into materiality[1859]
Phenomena arise from being empty
Dharmatā is not different from them[1860] [5]

It is for that reason that the omniscience
of buddhahood does not operate in vain
By the power of lacking superimposition,
the entire wheel of the dharma is turned[1861] [6]

While refraining from stretching their legs, {165}
and abandoning thoughts of pride and such,
yogīs are adopting the [appropriate] conduct,
properly abiding through the yoga of nonabiding[1862] [7]

Those obtaining the flavor of food and drink[1863]
and verbally proclaiming that which is pure,
[but] failing to adopt the [appropriate] conduct,
do not represent vessels of perfect awakening [8]

People keep talking about true reality
and also approve of [proper] conduct,
but people accomplished in fulfilling
the practice of awareness are hard to find [9]

The earth is the bed, the directions the garment,
and the portion of going for alms is the food
Poised readiness for the dharmatā of nonarising
constitutes the flow of effortless compassion[1864] [10]

The phenomena that defeat people
are also defeated through conduct
Its fruition is observable in this life—
the unsurpassable is so just as much[1865] [11]

Through the excellently obtained merit of
having explained illusion with good intent,
may worldly people reach the nondual state,
being established in what's beyond the world![1866] [12]

This concludes "A Discourse on Illusion" composed by master Advayavajra. It was translated, edited, and finalized by the Indian upādhyāya Vajrapāṇi and the Tibetan lotsāwa bhikṣu Tsültrim Gyalwa.[1867] {166}

(31) A Discourse on Dream

In the language of India: *Svapnanirukti*[1868]
In the language of Tibet: *Rmi lam nges par bstan pa*

I pay homage to the omniscient one[1869]

In the Vinaya, Abhidharma, and the sūtras,
the victor as well as the eminent masters
declare that phenomena resemble dreams
This is proclaimed in a clear manner [1]

Are dreams something real or unreal,
the mind's diversity or mind itself,[1870]
or are they illusions or nonabiding?
What is the opinion of the wise here? [2]

"By virtue of not being realized, dreams are real;
once they are realized, they turn into falsities"
In the first case, they'd be permanent cognitions[1871]
In the second case, they would be nonexistent [3]

While awakening removes the imaginary,
it does not do away with the experience
The character of the lucidity of real mind's diversity,
which exists, is a magnificent experience[1872] [4]

Instantaneous perishing is by virtue of the ālaya,
diversity by virtue of the active ones from this root
Here, they possess the aspects of such [diversity]
It is asserted that this [diversity] is just the mind[1873] [5]

When there is a dream after a dream,
then the diversity of the mind is falsity
It is not real, as it perceives the unreal,
nor is it extinct, because it is lucidity[1874] [6] {167}

Why would the nameless be given a name?
Or is it that a name is called "illusion"?
But a name for a name is not appropriate,
and there is no abiding [of it] in the nameless[1875] [7]

Among the six here, two are to be abandoned[1876]
Four are asserted for the sake of awakening[1877]
The entire universe[1878] is similar to a dream—
thus it is declared by the supreme buddhas [8]

Moreover, know thus that nonabiding
is the Buddhists' entire supreme wealth[1879]
In particular, do so through awareness,
the true guru's efforts, and the conduct[1880] [9]

This concludes "A Discourse on Dream" composed by master Avadhūtipa Advayavajra. It was translated and edited by the Indian upādhyāya Vajrapāṇi and the Tibetan lotsāwa Tsültrim Gyalwa.[1881] {168}

(32) Ten Stanzas on True Reality

In the language of India: *Tattvadaśaka*[1882]
In the language of Tibet: *De kho na nyid bcu pa zhes bya ba*

I pay homage to Vajrasattva[1883]

I pay homage to and salute this suchness,
disjoined from existence and nonexistence,
since this very [suchness], in being stainless,
has awakening's nature thanks to realization[1884] [1]

Those who have the desire to realize suchness
won't in Aspectarianism or Nonaspectarianism[1885]
Not being adorned with the words of the guru,
even the very middle is nothing but middling[1886] [2]

This entity constitutes awakening indeed
It is so by nature once rid of attachment[1887]
Attachment is what's born from delusion,[1888]
and delusion is without basis, it is held [3]

What is true reality? It is entities' form,
while form is that which has no form,
because what has no form is also form,
given its very nature of result and cause[1889] [4]

Thus phenomena are of single taste,
unobstructed,[1890] and without abiding
They are luminosity in their entirety
through the samādhi of reality as it is [5]

This samādhi of true reality as it is
comes from the mind of engagement,[1891]
because true reality dawns ceaselessly
in those who are aware of its ground[1892] [6] {169}

Free of cognition and what is cognized,
this very world is asserted to be nondual
Even the conceit of being free of duality,
in like manner, constitutes luminosity[1893] [7]

By having realized this true reality,
by any means and in any manner,[1894]
the yogīs whose eyes are wide open
roam[1895] everywhere, just like lions[1896] [8]

Those who abandoned the worldly dharma
and rely upon the yogic conduct of a lunatic
do everything without any reference point,
while being adorned with their self-blessing[1897] [9]

What has been taught as untainted true reality
and is proclaimed as consisting of nonduality—
those with insight are worthy of realizing it,
having rid from it sameness and difference [10]

This concludes "Ten Stanzas on True Reality" composed by the great master Avadhūtipa Advayavajra. It was translated by the Indian upādhyāya Vajrapāṇi and the Tibetan lotsāwa bhikṣu Tsültrim Gyalwa.[1898] {170}

(33) The Illumination of Great Bliss

In the language of India: *Māhasukhaprakāśa*[1899]
In the language of Tibet: *Bde ba chen po gsal ba*

I pay homage to the Buddha[1900]

Having paid my homage to Vajrasattva,
whose own nature is prajñā and means,
in brief, I shall explain the nonduality
of great bliss, the true reality of entities[1901] [1]

The meditation of creation constitutes the one,
and the meditation of the created[1902] is the second
Therefore the meditation of both together
is here described as their identical nature[1903] [2]

It is certain that there is no such thing as
phenomena not arising in dependence
Since dependent arising is their nature,
why would what arises from HŪṂ and MAṂ not be so? [3]

From awakening in emptiness, the seed
comes forth, and from the seed an image
This image has placement and dissolution[1904]
Therefore everything arises in dependence [4]

That which was taught by the Sage
as the external union of the couple
is to be known clearly in the tantras
in order to realize the in-between[1905] [5]

If bliss did not exist, there would be no awakening,
which is asserted to possess the nature of bliss[1906]
But if it did exist, it would be great attachment,
which constitutes the cause of saṃsāra's arising [6]

Realize the bliss that arises in dependence {171}
as being the bliss that is primordial peace!
Since it does not constitute an entity, we say
that bliss is neither existent nor nonexistent[1907] [7]

True reality is, first of all, the nonarising
of phenomena on the level of the ultimate
But the pure seeming is to be understood
as being the delusive display of pleasure[1908] [8]

These two realities are what is pure—[1909]
emptiness and the seeming of yogīs
This pair's nonduality is to be established,[1910]
once what is meaningless has been cast off[1911] [9]

With their character of the yoga of mantra and form,
those gifted with insight become submerged in bliss[1912]
Then, it is in such a fashion that they see diversity
as being like an illusion and without any duality[1913] [10]

Then, they arrived at the true end
and have reached the state of unity
For those yogīs who dwell in unity,
beings' welfare is of prime concern[1914] [11]

The blissful mind has the form of the deity
The cakra of totality[1915] serves as the means

The prajñā [consort] is called "emptiness"
Their identity is taken as what's to be gained[1916] [12]

True reality has the character of prajñā and means
because it consists of external and internal purity
Once realized by their union, mantra practitioners
are delighted by way of the yoga of nonabiding[1917] [13]

Because it is sheer dependent origination,
[bliss] is neither an existent nor emptiness,
and its manifestation in the form of deities
is naturally without any nature of its own[1918] [14]

No matter in which ways [such bliss] may manifest,
it is in those ways that it has emptiness's character
Whether it is perceived as duality or as nonduality,
in this context, it is the fruition of mental imprints[1919] [15]

Yogīs take pride in being the Heruka,
resting in the actuality of the Heruka[1920] {172}
Having made [all] entities into gurus,
they roam the earth just like lions[1921] [16]

Thanks to its purity, always and everywhere, the world's diversity
appears to be pure for the victors
Neither arisen nor ceasing, throughout millions of eons, it lacks any
deliberations in terms of self and other
Yet it is indeed the delusive display of pleasure, whose nature is the
nonduality that is the equality of existence and peace
Within this cakra, the cakra lord who is the repository of the qualities
of the victors is the vajraḍāka and the mighty Sage[1922] [17]

This concludes "The Illumination of Great Bliss" composed by master Avadhūtipa Śrī Advayavajra. It was translated by guru Vajrapāṇi and Mapen.[1923] {173}

(34) A Jewel Garland of True Reality

In the language of India: *Tattvaratnāvalī*[1924]
In the language of Tibet: *De kho na nyid rin po che'i phreng ba zhes bya ba*

I pay homage to Śrī Vajrasattva
I pay homage to youthful Mañjuśrī[1925]

Having bowed at the pair of lotuses
that make up the feet of Vajrasattva,
as bright as the spotless autumn moon,
we shall proclaim the *Tattvaratnāvalī* [1]

For those people who have fallen from
true tradition and whose sight is veiled,
this *Tattvaratnāvalī* will perfectly serve
as the means to illuminate true reality[1926] [2]

There are three yānas: the Śrāvakayāna, the Pratyekabuddhayāna, and the Mahāyāna. There are four positions by way of the division into Vaibhāṣikas, Sautrāntikas, Yogācāras, and Mādhyamikas. Here, the Śrāvakayāna and the Pratyekabuddhayāna are explained in terms of the position of the Vaibhāṣikas. The Mahāyāna is of two kinds: the pāramitā approach and the mantra approach. Here, the pāramitā approach {174} is explained in terms of the positions of the Sautrāntikas, Yogācāras, and Mādhyamikas, but the mantra approach is explained in terms of the positions of the Yogācāras and Mādhyamikas [alone].[1927] The Yogācāras are of two kinds by way of the division into Aspectarians and Nonaspectarians. Likewise, the Mādhyamikas are of two kinds twofold by way of the division into the proponents of illusion-like nonduality and the proponents of the utter nonabiding of all phenomena.[1928]

[Śrāvakayāna]

Now, the śrāvakas are of three kinds by way of the division into lower, medium, and highest. The lower and medium are the Vaibhāṣikas from the west,[1929] while the highest are the Vaibhāṣikas from Kashmir.[1930]

[1. Lower śrāvakas]

(a) Here is the analysis[1931] of the lower śrāvakas. Preceded by the agreement that there are outer referents such as blue or yellow, they speak of a person that is free from being permanent and impermanent. This is their explanation, which is stated as follows:

> "[Objects] indeed exist" and "the world consists
> of blue and such"—thus it is for the most stupid,
> who are possessed by the demon of the clinging
> to entities and fear the approach that is profound[1932] [3]

[The Buddha said:] "The person who is the bearer of the burden exists. I neither call them permanent, nor do I call them impermanent" and "The person who has desire roams [saṃsāra]."[1933]

(b) In order to relinquish desire, their dhyāna consists of the meditation on the repulsiveness [of the body]. This meditation on repulsiveness {175} consists of examining the body as having the nature of a collection of feces, urine, semen, blood, phlegm, mucus, intestines, joints, lungs, liquids, kidneys, spleen, liver, and so forth.[1934] This is expressed [as follows]:

> To begin, with your own mind,
> pull apart this wrapping of skin
> With the blade of prajñā, separate
> the flesh from the cage of bones

Having cracked open the bones,
look at the marrow that is inside[1935]
In this way, examine for yourself
what kind of pith there could be[1936]

(c) The stain of their samādhi is desire,[1937] which is preceded by the view of the permanence of the person.

(d) Their view is as follows: "As long as I live, I go for refuge in the Buddha, the dharma, and the saṃgha. I venerate the two Elders[1938] and the Sugata.[1939] Through however many roots of virtue there may be, I will discipline myself alone, will calm myself alone, and will make myself alone enter parinirvāṇa!"[1940]

[2. Medium śrāvakas]

The view (d) and explanation (a) of the medium [śrāvakas] are just like [those of] the previous [śrāvakas]. They like working for the welfare of others to a certain extent.

(b) By means of the samādhi of exhaling and inhaling, their dhyāna is [to meditate on] the view of a person that is free from being permanent and impermanent.

(c) The stain of their samādhi is that [their mind] becomes motionless through vase breathing because [this technique] invites [mental] numbness.[1941]

[3. Highest śrāvakas]

(a) The explanation of the highest śrāvakas {176} is to assert external referents and to determine the body's lack of a self.

(b) Thoroughly knowing the four realities of the noble ones, their dhyāna is [to meditate on] the view of the emptiness of the person. In this regard, suffering is the five skandhas' own nature, which is what is to be understood. The origin [of suffering] is thinking, which is what is to be relinquished. Cessation is superior insight, which is what is to be directly perceived. The path is emptiness, which is what is to be meditated on.

(c) The stain of their dhyāna is to wrongly superimpose a nature of continuous peace onto emptiness.

(d) With regard to their view though, [compared to the other śrāvakas,] they excel in performing the welfare of others.[1942]

Here, some [claim] that the lower śrāvakas [attain only] the awakening of śrāvakas because their disposition is definite and they lack compassion. Others, however, say this:

Everybody will become a buddha
On earth, no one lacks that fortune
Hence you shall not be disheartened
about accomplishing perfect awakening

[Thus,] they think that among sentient beings, even the lower śrāvakas will become completely perfect buddhas. For those whose disposition is definite [as the one of a lower śrāvaka], this depends a little bit on a buddha. The medium [śrāvakas] are future pratyekabuddhas, and the highest [śrāvakas] will accomplish buddhahood after four incalculable eons.[1943]

[4. Pratyekabuddhayāna]

(a) The explanation of the Pratyekabuddhayāna is precisely that of the highest śrāvakas.

(b) They have realized {177} the characteristic of the inconceivability of the person being empty, the self-arising wisdom without having a master, superior insight, and calm abiding. Here, superior insight consists of the cessation of [the operation of] the sense faculties [on account of] a person not being observable. Calm abiding consists of the control of body, speech, and mind. This is their dhyāna.

(c) The stains of their samādhi here consist of the dhyāna that is the blissful state of mind being close to being asleep and the dhyāna of mind's state of being fast asleep.[1944] In the former case, this means following[1945] the claim of Bhāskara.[1946] This is expressed as follows:

One should cultivate with effort
the state of mind that manifests
when, being on the verge of sleep,
external objects have disappeared[1947]

In the latter case, this means following the claim of the Vaiśeṣikas.[1948] This is what venerable Nāgārjuna says:

> Noncognizant wisdom is established
> by means of the example of sleep,
> just as the cognition with blocked
> senses claimed by the Vaiśeṣikas

Furthermore, the Bhagavān declares this:

> I'm better off roaming as a jackal
> in the delightful Jetavana Grove,
> but it's not acceptable to arrive at
> the Vaiśeṣikas' cow-like liberation[1949]

(d) The view [of the pratyekabuddhas] also resembles the previous one [of the highest śrāvakas].[1950] They also accomplish the state of buddhahood after four incalculable eons. {178} The compassion of both śrāvakas and pratyekabuddhas is focused on sentient beings. Focusing on sentient beings in terms of their suffering of suffering and their suffering of change day after day, the compassion that they give rise to [in this way] is focused on sentient beings. The teachings of the śrāvakas are related to speech, and those of the pratyekabuddhas are related to the body.[1951] This is stated as follows:

When perfect buddhas do not appear
and śrāvakas, for their part, are gone,
the wisdom of the pratyekabuddhas
emerges without encountering those[1952]

[The Mahāyāna: the pāramitā approach]
[5. Sautrāntikas]
Now, the yogīs in the pāramitā approach are discussed. Here, the lower ones are the Sautrāntikas.

(a) Their [understanding of an external] referent is that it has the nature of being an aggregation of infinitesimal particles that produces a cognition that has a [mental] aspect [of that referent]. This is their examination, which is referred to as "that which produces a cognition that has a [mental] aspect [of that referent]."[1953] This is what [Dharmakīrti] declares:

> How could it be perceived when being at a
> different time? The wise [say] it's perceptible
> For those who know reasoning, it is a cause
> capable of imposing an aspect upon cognition[1954]

This is their explanation.

(b) The inconceivability of the sense faculties being turned away from the village of their objects is their dhyāna.[1955] This is stated [in the following]:

> This refers to the time of repeated familiarization, not the time of direct perception. Therefore frequent repetition is to be practiced.

Such frequent repetition [is described like this]:[1956]

> When familiarizing with mind through
> the realization of having ascertained it, {179}
> at that time, I do not see the mind—
> where did it go and where does it stay?[1957]
>
> Even householders should meditate
> every moment by way of resting in
> the vajra posture and having placed
> their unsteady mind on the nose tip[1958]

(c) The stains of their samādhi are like [those of] the previous ones.[1959]

(d) By way of the nature of the pāramitā of prajñā (not observing the triad [of agent, action, and object]), their conduct of the [first] five pāramitās is to bring the welfare of sentient beings to its maturation while turning their face away from the fruition. This is their view.[1960]

[6. Aspectarian Yogācāra]
The medium [practitioners of the pāramitā approach] are the Yogācāras.
(a) Here, the proponents of consciousness with aspects [say this]:

> By virtue of six being joined together,
> a minutest particle would have six parts[1961]

By means of reasonings [such as this], even infinitesimal particles fail to be provable. Hence this [entire world] is mere mind. [The mind] bears mental aspects, is free from the state of perceiver and perceived, and clearly displays [everything]. That is the realization that they possess.[1962] This is stated [as follows]:

> Oh sons of the victor! This [saṃsāra] with its three realms is mere mind.[1963]

Likewise, [Dharma]kīrti says this:

> If the mind has the form of something blue and such,
> what foundation does an external referent have then?
> If mind doesn't have the form of something blue etc.,
> what foundation does an external referent have then?[1964]

This is also stated elsewhere:

> The sense faculties' referents do not exist
> outside the mind by a nature of their own
> It is rather this very mind that appears {180}
> as the semblances of form and so forth[1965]

Therefore the mind itself, which has the aspects of diverse [appearances] yet does not depend on anything other [than itself], clearly displays [all these appearances]. This is the explanation[1966] of the Yogācāras who are proponents of consciousness with aspects.[1967]

[7. Nonaspectarian Yogācāras]

The Yogācāras who are Nonaspectarians also think that this [entire world] is nothing but mind, whose nature is self-awareness without any [really existing] aspects.[1968]

(a) Their explanation is discussed in the following:

> External referents, as imagined
> by childish beings, are not found
>
> It is mind agitated by latent tendencies
> that arises as what seem to be referents[1969]

As long as something is appearing,
it appears as nothing but an illusion
In reality, [mind] lacks appearances,
just like the pure and infinite sky[1970] [3]

Nondiscursive and without appearance
is the dharmakāya of the great Sage
The two form kāyas emerge from it
and subsequently abide like illusions[1971] [4]

(b) The dhyāna of the Aspectarians is to directly perceive [mind's] nonduality [of perceiver and perceived] together with its diversity, in which all thoughts have been shaken off. The following is said:

> Wherever it may go, just there,
> the mind bonds with knowables
> Once stirred up, where it will go,
> all of that is of its nature indeed[1972]

(b) The dhyāna of the Nonaspectarians is to directly perceive mind without appearances, which is nondual inconceivable bliss free from discursiveness.[1973] {181} Accordingly, [the following is declared]:

Its nature is held to be pellucid,
without aspect, and spotless
The ones who are simply fools
will never be able to realize it[1974]

But even [thinking,] "This is mere cognizance"
[is a case in point] because it involves focusing
With anything placed before [the mind],
there is no dwelling in merely that[1975]

When cognition as such does not
observe any object of focus, then
it rests in mere consciousness's very being (*vijñānamātratā*)
For without a perceived, there is no perceiver of it[1976]

(c) With regard to the samādhi of [clinging to] an ultimately real, permanent consciousness with aspects, [the Aspectarians] follow what is claimed by the proponents of Vedānta, namely in the *Bhagavatsiddhānta*.[1977] They assert that the world has the nature of being a modulation [of the Brahman] that is not different from the Brahman, whose nature is one's own ultimately real and permanent mind.[1978] Accordingly, the following is said:

Whatever is seen, as tiny as it may be,
is conceived of as being "the Brahman"
Therefore the mind is not anything else
It is present within the Brahman alone[1979]

This is the stain of the samādhi of the Aspectarians.

(c) Likewise, with regard to the Nonaspectarians' familiarization with a permanent, self-aware consciousness without appearances and free of discursiveness, there is the undesired consequence of following [another] claim by the proponents of Vedānta, namely the position asserted by Bhāskara. He maintains that [such a permanent consciousness] is the Brahman, which is entirely free from all names and forms, pure of the disturbance of discursiveness, {182} lucid, infinite, uninterrupted, and permanent.[1980] Thus [the following is declared]:

> The empty water bubbles of diversity are
> so clear for me in the ocean of realization
> No matter whether they arise or dissolve,
> there is nothing conceived by thinking[1981]

This is the stain of the samādhi of the Nonaspectarians.

(d) The view of both [Aspectarians and Nonaspectarians] is like the previous one.[1982]

[8. The Madhyamaka proponents of illusion-like nonduality]
The highest [practitioners of the pāramitā approach] are the Mādhyamikas.

(a) Here is the explanation[1983] of the proponents of illusion-like nonduality:

> Neither existent, nor nonexistent, nor existent and nonexistent,
> nor of a character that is neither of the two—
> the true reality[1984] free of the four extremes
> is what is understood by the Mādhyamikas[1985]

The meaning of this is as follows. [True reality] is not existent, because this is impossible due to being invalidated [by reasoning]. Nor does it not exist, which is because of the power of appearances. Likewise, because of these two flaws, it is not both [existent and nonexistent] either. Similarly, it is not neither of the two, because that would be incomprehensible. Furthermore, by means of a consideration [of the extreme of existence] that is other than the previous one, there would be the undesired consequence that the diversity [of the world], in just the way it manifests, in the same way constitutes the power of [real] entities. This is the explanation of the proponents of illusion-like nonduality.[1986]

(b) The familiarization with this illusion-like nonduality is their dhyāna.[1987]

(c) The stain of their dhyāna here is the clinging to [the extreme of] extinction.

(d) To perfect the six pāramitās by way of being confident about illusion-like nonduality {183} is their view.[1988]

[9. The Madhyamaka proponents of utter nonabiding]
(a) The following is the analysis of the proponents of the utter nonabiding of all phenomena:

Diversity is not asserted as permanent,
nor is it held to be extinct [altogether]
Not a pair of permanence and extinction,
it is not both either, nor without both[1989] [5]

The wise realize the true reality of entities
as being the utter nonabiding in anything
Now, this is not just some kind of thinking—
the mind does not perceive mind as such[1990] [6]

All superimpositions, however many there are,
in their entirety are not present in any respect
The middle's actuality is superimposition's lack—
where could there be removal or accomplishing?[1991] [7]

That which is effortless wisdom
is proclaimed to be inconceivable
But a conceived inconceivable
cannot truly be inconceivable[1992] [8]

In those who realize the world to be unborn,
the mind is pure by virtue of this realization
For those intelligent ones, without any effort,
the world is the reality that is the native state[1993] [9]

This is [also] stated in the following:

When free of all superimpositions,
true reality shines all on its own
Designations such as emptiness
remove superimpositions from it[1994] [10]

(b) Their dhyāna is to directly perceive, by resting in it without any clinging, this actuality that has been analyzed [here] and whose nature is to be free from any superimpositions.

(c) The extinction of all referents or [mental] numbness [in a state of dull nothingness] are the stains of their samādhi.

(d) To perfect the six pāramitās by being without any superimpositions is their view.[1995]

Here [in the pāramitā approach], {184} the compassion of those who are lower and medium [Sautrāntikas and Yogācāras] is the one that focuses on dharma. [This compassion] that focuses on dharma is to be understood as the one that arises by focusing on all dharmas encountering the wind of impermanence. The compassion of those who are the highest [Mādhyamikas] is the one that is without focus [or nonreferential]—the realization of phenomena by mentally engaging in the lack of nature of any focus.[1996]

Their presentation of the three kāyas is given by Maitreyanātha. Accordingly, [he says this]:

> The perpetual nairmāṇikakāya of the Sage
> is the one through which various benefits
> for the world are promoted in an equal way
> until the end of saṃsāric existence
>
> As this [kāya] of the Sage, whose character lies in
> the thirty-two major marks and eighty minor marks,
> is the one that enjoys the Mahāyāna,
> it is held to be the sāmbhogikakāya
>
> Those who attained purity in every respect,
> as well as the uncontaminated dharmas,
> theirs is the svābhāvikakāya of the Sage,
> having the characteristic of the nature of these[1997]

[Mantra approach]

We do not explain the mantra approach here, because it is very profound, because it is an object [only] for persons who have faith in this profound approach, and because the presentation of the means of accomplishment—the four mudrās and so on—is extensive. Accordingly, this is declared as follows:

> Though the goal is the same, since it lacks ignorance,
> since it is abundant in means, since it lacks difficulty,
> since it is the prerogative of those of sharp faculties
> it is the mantra teaching that is more distinguished[1998]

In this regard, we have composed a text titled *Sekanirṇaya*.[1999] {185}

[Mahāyāna Hermeneutics]

"Well, if this reality that is ascertained only in the Mahāyāna is the ultimate,[2000] for what purpose did the Bhagavān then teach the two yānas of śrāvakas and pratyekabuddhas?" This is not [a valid objection] because the two staircases of the Śrāvaka[yāna] and Pratyekabuddhayāna were provided only for the sake of attaining what is to be attained by the Mahāyāna.[2001] The following is stated:

> To introduce those sentient beings
> who are beginners to the ultimate,
> the perfect buddhas have provided
> these means just like a staircase[2002]

In the *Saddharmapuṇḍarīka* too, this is stated:

> The yāna is single, the approach is single,
> and the teaching of the guides is single
> It is the nature of my skill in methods
> that I put on the show of the three yānas[2003]

Venerable Nāgārjuna also says the following:

> Since the dharmadhātu is without difference,
> there is no difference between the yānas, lord
> You have discoursed on the three yānas
> for the sake of introducing sentient beings[2004]

Elsewhere, this is declared:

> Liberation is by virtue of the view of emptiness
> The remaining meditations are for that purpose[2005]

This illumination of the three yānas is the emptiness that is being investigated [here]. It is to be understood by virtue of the Bhagavān.[2006] Accordingly, the following is said:

> You have not taught anything, {186}
> not even a single word, oh lord
> Yet all the people to be guided
> are satisfied by this dharma rain[2007]

Like a wish-fulfilling jewel, he cannot
be shaken by all the winds of volitions[2008]
Still, without any exception, he fulfills
the wishes of the entirety of beings[2009] [11]

It is with the momentum of a turning wheel
that the protector's teaching is set in motion
despite not thinking, due to their capacities
based on their differences in accumulation [12]

> For as long as the mind operates,
> there is no termination of yānas
> But once mind's state has changed,
> there is neither a yāna nor traveling[2010]

The[2011] speech here indeed represents a garland
strung up with jewels made of true dharma
O steadfast ones, keep this *Tattvaratnāvalī*
in your hearts for the sake of your delight! [13]

I, who am fond of concise summaries
and have a dislike for verbose treatises,

did not discuss this in an extensive way—
you who like verbosity, bear with me![2012] [14]

Upon requests by fortunate ones, I delivered
this text of unsurpassable meaning with effort
By the merit I laid a hand on, may the world
attain the tathāgata state that is unattainable![2013] [15]

This concludes "A Jewel Garland of True Reality" composed by the master and paṇḍita Avadhūtipa Advayavajra. It was translated, edited, and finalized by the Indian upādhyāya Vajrapāṇi and the Tibetan lotsāwa bhikṣu Tsültrim Gyalwa.[2014] {187}

(35) An Illumination of True Reality

In the language of India: *Tattvaprakāśanāma*[2015]
In the language of Tibet: *De kho na nyid rab tu bstan pa zhes bya ba*

I pay homage to the Buddha[2016]

I salute the three buddhakāyas' embodiment,[2017]
which has the character of prajñā and means
Through its power, the saṃsāric existence
and the nirvāṇa that are supreme are born[2018] [1]

Just as persons with blurred vision may think
there are hairnet-like apparitions in the sky,
so do extremely childish beings, obscured
by the darkness of ignorance, [see] the world[2019] [2]

Just as those with pure vision recognize those hairs
[arising] from delusion as being [nothing but] the sky,
for those yogīs who are endowed with pure vision,
all states of existence appear in the same manner[2020] [3]

"I see hairnet-like apparitions,
oh my, look up into the sky!"
Then, one with pure vision says:
"Not so, your mind is muddled"[2021] [4]

In order to dispel the delusion of blurred vision,
that one says it will not be there at a later time
As this display is empty of being anything else,
in true reality, there is no removal or creation[2022] [5]

Likewise, the welfare of sentient beings unfolds
from the dharma[kāya] that is uncontaminated
through the [sam]bhoga- and nirmāṇakāyas {188}
by way of aspiration prayers in dependence[2023] [6]

Those two are not different from it,
since the two have it as their nature
Their identity is established as the native [kāya]—
the distinction is to dispel mind's attachment[2024] [7]

If their nonarising were not asserted,
they would be different by exclusion
How would the meaning of the middle
then be other than the Yogācāra stance? [8]

If the meaning of the middle were more distinguished
[only] due to its relinquishment of the four extremes,
then the same would follow for the Vijñāna[vādins][2025]
because those [four] are relinquished there as well [9]

A cognition free from the four extremes,
which is real as an entity and nondual,
empty of thought, and has no focal object,
is known by the followers of Vijñānavāda[2026] [10]

It is from the true end that this diversity
keeps springing forth in dependence
It is empty of entity,[2027] without arising,
standing on its own, and a sheer name [11]

The omniscient one spoke of a distinction
between self-blessing and luminosity
If either one of these two is proclaimed,[2028]
[the view of][2029] extinction is thereby rid [12]

In those in whom there is no attachment
to the fruition, true reality, or remedies,[2030]
the state of a buddha becomes perfected
through the yoga that is without effort [13]

As was maintained by the noble Nāgārjuna,
who has been prophesied by the tathāgatas,
and in conformity with the buddhadharma,
the true reality of phenomena is nonarising [14]

Through the merit I have gathered[2031]
by composing the *Tattvaprakāśa*,
may it come to pass that the entire {189}
world becomes a vessel for unity! [15]

This concludes "An Illumination of True Reality" composed by the master and paṇḍita Avadhūtipa Advayavajra. It was translated and edited by the Indian upādhyāya Vajrapāṇi and the Tibetan lotsāwa bhikṣu Tsültrim Gyalwa.[2032] {190}

(36) A Commentary on the Five Seals of the Tathāgatas

In the language of India: *Pañcatathāgatamudrāvivaraṇa*[2033]
In the language of Tibet: *De bzhin gshegs pa lnga'i phyag rgya rnam par bshad pa*

I pay homage to Śrī Vajrasattva

They arose in dependence, are empty of the imaginary,[2034]
empty of a nature of their own, and don't exist as entities
Not extinct, their nature is the one mind in its diversity—
form and all the rest are victorious as the five victors[2035] [1]

The five skandhas are the five tathāgatas. Here, the [first] four of them are sealed with Akṣobhya in order to establish that they are mere consciousness. Since outer appearances are thus mere mind, given that something [outer] that is perceived does not exist, the emptiness of the perceiver [is established as well]. By virtue of that, [it is said that] this very consciousness remains as an ultimately existing sheer awareness that is free from perceiver and perceived. Exactly this is what is to be accomplished by the Nonaspectarians—the actual[2036] cognition that is like the stainless stretch of the midday sky in autumn.[2037] Thus the following is declared:[2038]

What is empty of the imaginary nature
is without appearance and has no form {191}

It is the sheer bliss that is real awareness,
yet [also] the confusion of the subsequent hosts of forms[2039] [2]

[The *Uttaratantra*] says this:

> and the latter two are the two form kāyas[2040]

Furthermore, [the following is declared]:

Nondiscursive and without appearance
is the dharmakāya of the great Sage
The two form kāyas emerge from it
and subsequently abide like illusions[2041] [3]

"Since this is [already] established through the seal of Akṣobhya, what is the point of the scriptural passage: 'Akṣobhya is sealed with Vajrasattva?' As far as this goes, [the seal of Vajrasattva] is for the [same] purpose of setting forth the emptiness of imaginary forms."[2042]

That is not the case, because [the emptiness of the imaginary] is established by just the former seal [of Akṣobhya]. Therefore, by virtue of the seal of Akṣobhya, there is the actual cognition, and the other one [consciousness] is what is subsequent; likewise, by virtue of the seal of Vajrasattva, consciousness is again the subsequent one, while the vajra [of emptiness] is the actual one.[2043] This is also stated in the *Vajraśekhara[tantra]*:

> Having a steadfast essence, not being hollow,
> marked by being unbreakable and indivisible,
> being incombustible as well as indestructible,[2044]
> emptiness is what is designated as a "vajra"[2045]

If there subsequently is form and so forth due to
the actual cognition by means of Akṣobhya's seal,
hey, why would this not be asserted as the sattva
subsequently by means of the seal of the vajra?[2046] [4]

"But if the sattva were what is subsequent, there would be the undesired consequence of proclaiming extinction because the [sattva's] compassion would not exist [during the meditation on the vajra of emptiness]." [The inseparability of emptiness (vajra) and compassion (sattva)] is asserted in detail as follows:[2047]

Through vajra, emptiness is declared {192}
Through sattva, mere cognition's state
The identity of both is established
through the nature of Vajrasattva [5]

The difference of emptiness and compassion
is similar to that of a lamp and its light
The oneness of emptiness and compassion
is similar to that of a lamp and its light [6]

> Emptiness is not any other than entities,
> nor is there any entity that is without it,
> due to invariably not existing without each other,
> just as being produced and impermanent[2048]

Just as the seeming is not extinguished
when true reality, just as it is, is spoken,
so true reality does not become observed
through the exclusion of the seeming[2049] [7]

"Thus Akṣobhya and Vajrasattva would be one. If they were, then the position of nondual diversity[2050] would be superior because consciousness, form, and so on are not abandoned." This is what is declared [next]:

Indeed, for me, the assertion of Aspectarianism is held
to be mere mind with its diversity, empty of all thought
This is similar to touching the grass while walking
Others pronounce it to be the meaning of the middle[2051] [8]

However, for those who propound nondual diversity, [consciousness] is ultimately existent, [but to claim the ultimate existence of] consciousness is not clever. For through the seal of Vajrasattva, it is ruled out that a cognition whose nature is that of Akṣobhya—the nondual [consciousness] with its diversity, which is empty of perceiver and perceived—could be a really existent entity.[2052] {193} This is declared in the following:

If cognition is empty of thoughts of form
and such by virtue of Akṣobhya's seal,
it is by virtue of the seal of Vajrasattva
that it being real as an entity is ruled out [9]

It is not that mere cognizance's
emptiness of imaginary aspects
is created through Vajrasattva,
for it did not [ever] abide before[2053] [10]

Once the thorn that this kind [of consciousness] exists ultimately is removed, the Mādhyamika tenet that consists of the establishment of the awareness that has the nature of not abiding anywhere at all and is the continuous flow of effortless nondual unity is superior. This is realized through the kindness of the venerable true guru.[2054]

You may wonder: "If awareness is established here, by virtue of the undesired consequence of this [thus] being the proposition of illusion-like nonduality, it is not utter nonabiding in every respect."[2055] This is not the case:

> That which has arisen in dependence
> has not arisen through its own nature
> What has not arisen by its own nature,
> how could that be designated "arisen?"[2056]

Awareness too is something that has arisen in dependence. Therefore this very awareness does not at all abide [as anything in any respect, but] constitutes the state of being unarisen.[2057] Accordingly, [the following is declared]:

Indeed, awareness[2058] is unarisen,
and so is the existence of entities
The Sage declared this very world
is of Vajrasattva's own nature[2059] [11]

[Mañjuśrī] has this to say:

> Moreover, the Tathāgata asked Mañjuśrī: {194} "What is this inconceivable dhātu like?" Mañjuśrī replied: "This dhātu that is inconceivable, not to be understood by the mind, not to be fathomed by the mind, and not to be realized through any perception of the mind is called 'the inconceivable dhātu.' But again, Bhagavān, the inconceivable dhātu is the very mind. What is the reason for this? Mind is not found in no-mind, but in mind. [The dhātu] that is without mind is mind because [through it] mind is realized in just the way it really is. Again, all aspects, Bhagavān, are the inconceivable dhātu."[2060]

[The same] is also said elsewhere:

> To you who are without any imaginary thinking,
> whose mind is in the state of utter nonabiding,
> who lack any minding and mental engagement,
> and who are without focus, let there be homage![2061]

In the *Candrapradīpa[sūtra*, this is stated]:

> That which is born from conditions is unborn
> It does not possess any being born by a nature
> What depends on conditions is said to be empty
> Those who understand emptiness are not heedless[2062]

In the *Āryalaṅkāvatāra[sūtra*, it is further declared]:

> Should characteristics still arise
> after all delusion is abandoned,

that itself is delusion about this
The impure is like blurred vision[2063]

Likewise, [the following is said]:

"Let there not be any abiding in cognizance"—[2064]
since he was afraid of exactly that, the Sage {195}
has differentiated the dharma of his teachings,
repeatedly stating it has emptiness's character[2065]

In the *Hevajra[tantra]*, this is stated:

What is originally unborn by nature
is neither real nor is it delusive[2066]

Furthermore, [we find this]:

When analyzed with the powerful intelligence
of keenest insight, the doctrine is all the same,
if the one thing—emptiness—that distinguishes
Buddhists and outsiders were not indicated here [2067]

In order to remove [any notion of] an emptiness that constitutes extinction, the following is said:[2068]

Those who set their eyes on suchness[2069]
according to the middle's meaning
are the fortunate realizing true reality
If directly known, it is by awareness[2070] [12]

In the *Ḍākinīvajrapañjara[tantra]*, this is stated:

Wherever the mind of emptiness and
compassion inseparable is cultivated,
this indeed constitutes the teaching of
the Buddha, the dharma, and the saṃgha[2071]

Therefore, since the five skandhas[2072] that arise in dependence have the nature of the five tathāgatas, and since this nature in turn is the inseparability of emptiness and compassion, it is established that beings are the inseparability of emptiness and compassion. Exactly this represents the uninterrupted dhyāna, thanks to the pith instructions of the true guru.[2073]

> Like the continuous flow of a river
> and like the steady light of a lamp,
> uninterrupted dhyāna is attained[2074] {196}
> by following mantra's true reality[2075]

Likewise, venerable Nāgārjuna[2076] says this:

> This is the mansion at its top, not the threefold world; these are not beings but victors
> I am the cakra lord, not a human; these are not objects, not eyes, nor the earth and so on,
> nor form and such; as they have dharmatā's character, they are the maṇḍala inhabitants
> Observing that this diversity is the maṇḍala circle, oh mind, how can you be deluded?[2077]

By virtue of having arisen in dependence,
they manifest like the gandharvas' city
Diversity is not established as any nature,
nor is it comparable to a lotus in the sky[2078] [13]

The *Hevajra[tantra]* declares this:

> These phenomena, however, constitute nirvāṇa
> Due to nescience, they assume saṃsāric forms[2079]

This concludes "A Commentary on the Five Seals of the Tathāgatas" composed by the great master Śrī Advayavajra. It was translated, edited, and finalized by the Indian upādhyāya Vajrapāṇi and the Tibetan lotsāwa Mapen Chöbar.[2080] {197}

(37) A Compendium of the Purport of Empowerment

In the language of India: *Sekatātparyasaṃgraha*[2081]
In the language of Tibet: *Dbang gi dgos pa mdor bsdus pa*

I pay homage to the Buddha[2082]

Any kind of speech of the spiritual friend
that has greatness excels—it bestows the
unfathomable true reality that isn't speech's
object as if it were in the palm of our hand[2083] [1]

Having known the supreme vajra master's wisdom,
we are composing *A Compendium of the Purport of Empowerment*, [drawn] from an abundance of texts
on empowerment and in accordance with scripture[2084] [2]

> First is the vase empowerment,
> second the supreme secret one,
> third is indeed the prajñā-jñāna,
> and the fourth is again like that[2085]

[The six vase empowerments]
The meaning of this is as follows. "First is the vase empowerment" refers to the six vase empowerments, which have the characteristics of water, crown, vajra, bell, name, and master. Empowerment refers to

being besprinkled in order to wash away the stains of ignorance, just as external stains [are washed away] by external water.[2086] Because all these [empowerments] are performed with a vase, they are called "vase empowerment." {198} They are also referred to as irreversible empowerments because they have the nature of the six tathāgatas. Accordingly, the water empowerment has the nature of Akṣobhya, who has the character of mirror-like wisdom. The crown empowerment has the nature of Ratnasambhava, who has the character of the wisdom of equality. The vajra empowerment has the nature of Amitābha, who has the character of discriminating wisdom. The lord empowerment[2087] has the nature of Amoghasiddhi, who has the essence of all-accomplishing wisdom. The name empowerment has the nature of Vairocana, who has the character of the wisdom of the utterly pure dharmadhātu, conforming to the awareness[2088] [that manifests] by virtue of having put an end to unawareness. The master empowerment has the nature of Vajrasattva. Here, the [first] five empowerments are the empowerments of the awareness consorts because they are the activities of Locanā and the other awareness consorts during those five.[2089]

[The water empowerment]

Here, in order to wash away the stains of ignorance, the vajra master, who has the form of Akṣobhya, should bestow the water empowerment upon the disciple, who is visualized as the form of Vairocana. Such is the [vajra] pride {199} at all times.[2090]

[The crown empowerment]

The crown empowerment represents the seed of the uṣṇīṣa that is appropriate for becoming a future buddha.[2091]

[The vajra empowerment]

[One uses] a vajra [here] in terms of its twelve finger-widths size [representing] the purity of the twelve links of dependent origination. In its middle part there is a syllable HŪṂ, which indicates unsurpassable dharmatā. Its meaning is as follows: "HA" refers to being free of causes, "Ū" to being free of deliberation,[2092] and "AṂ"[2093] to all phenomena being utterly nonabiding.[2094]

Where the sages, having the forms of five spokes,
emerge from the aperture of the lotus of existence,
it is by virtue of the purity of the five skandhas
that they come forth as the bodies of existence[2095] [3]

What this indicates here is that, through the spokes at the sides facing the spoke in the middle, everything such as form [the skandhas] has the character of consciousness [the seal of Akṣobhya]. In order to signify that everything has the character of everything, [the spokes] are quadrangular everywhere.[2096]

Now, those who realized the dharma,
its own nature signified by HŪṂ's roar,
also constitute the five vimuktikāyas,
springing forth at their different sides[2097] [4]

The three flowers in all of them are for the sake of teaching emptiness, signlessness, and wishlessness. {200} Through the pith instructions of the guru, they should be understood to have the character of the five wisdoms that have the characteristics of [likeness to] a mirror, equality, discrimination, all-accomplishing, and the pure dharmadhātu. The specification of indivisible wisdom is the meaning they have in common.[2098]

> Having a steadfast essence, not being hollow,
> marked by being unbreakable and indivisible,
> being incombustible as well as indestructible,[2099]
> emptiness is what is designated as a "vajra"[2100]

In the *Hevajra[tantra]* too, this is said: "The vajra is indivisible."[2101] The performance of the vajra empowerment is to provide what resembles the receptacle for the seed for the arising of indivisible wisdom.

[The bell empowerment]
Likewise, by virtue of its connection with the previous one [the vajra], the vajra bell has the size of twelve finger-widths, represents an upside-down lotus, and is in union with the vajra, so as to illustrate[2102] the nature

of all phenomena as the lack of any nature. In order to realize that the dharmodaya is the foundation of indivisible wisdom, it is surrounded by a pair of vajra garlands, [one] on its upper and [one] on its lower part. In order to make it known that it is the mansion at the top that is the nature of [saṃsāra] with its three realms, it shows the forms of loops and pendants [in between]. Therefore it is also marked with the [seed syllables of the] five tathāgatas. In order to point to it as being the cause of the wisdom of inseparable emptiness and compassion, {201} the face of prajñā is displayed [on the lower part of the vajra] on top of the [bell's body]. In order to declare that the wisdom whose own nature is the dharmadhātu has the character of the five tathāgatas such as Vairocana, is the nature of the five skandhas such as form, and is also the nature of the five elements such as earth, its top is embellished by five spokes. Here too, the connection of [the four outer spokes] facing the spoke that is located in the middle and so forth is as above. The empowerment by way of this resounding vajra bell should serve as an introduction to the unsurpassable awakening toward all phenomena without exception. Here, in order to demonstrate its preeminence and to indicate its being the [main] cause, the vajra empowerment is given first, while the empowerment of the vajra bell is set aside [temporarily] despite it being the instrumental cause.[2103]

[The name empowerment]
In order to illustrate the namelessness of all phenomena and in order to acquire the foundation of a worthy name when [attaining] the state of a mighty sage in the future, the name empowerment [is given] by removing one's previous name and by [bestowing a new name] in accordance with the disposition of the family of one's own deity.[2104]

[The master empowerment]
The master empowerment has the characteristics of the vajra samaya, the bell samaya, the mudrā samaya, suitability, permission, [vajra] discipline, {202} and prophecy and reassurance. The vajra samaya is to make [the disciple] realize: "From now on, you have the samaya to realize the continuous flow of unconditioned indivisible unity." The bell samaya is for the sake of teaching [the disciple] this: "[Now] you are a holder of the eighty-four-thousand dharma collections." The mudrā samaya makes

the following known [to the disciple]: "You have the nature of your own chosen deity."[2105] Suitability consists of the true reality of the maṇḍala, the characteristic of the maṇḍala's purity, the true reality of the deity, the characteristic of the deity's purity, the activity[2106] of the master, the wisdom of the means of accomplishing the maṇḍala, and the food of the five lamps and the five nectars.[2107] True reality [here] refers to the lack of nature of these in terms of the domain of the perfection process. Permission [is given] in order to turn the wheel of dharma. The vajra discipline is given in order to abandon external spiritual disciplines. A prophecy [is made] in order to indicate that one will have the nature of earth and so on [when attaining awakening]. Accordingly, this is the meaning of [the mantra] *bhūr bhuvaḥ svar*: *bhuvaḥ* means "of earth and so on," *svaḥ* means "nature," and *bhūr* means "may you be."[2108] "From now on, you are free from all obscurations and equal to all buddhas and bodhisattvas" {203} is the reassurance [that is given] for the sake of realization.[2109]

[The secret empowerment]

The secret empowerment is the conferring of the bodhicitta that is brought forth by both [the guru and his consort] at the same time in order to render [the disciple] a [fertile] field of prajñā and faith and in order to protect samaya. Being bestowed by means of this dual secret of prajñā and means is the etymological derivation [of "secret" here].[2110]

[The prajñā-jñāna empowerment]

[The compound] "prajñā-jñāna" admits two etymological derivations here: "the wisdom of prajñā" and "the wisdom that is prajñā itself." Now, the former etymological derivation is as follows. Prajñā refers to the mental state that [still] bears the [two] aspects of perceiver and perceived and is the nature of a well-shaped woman consisting of the four elements, the five skandhas, and the six objects such as forms. The bodhicitta that has this [form of prajñā] as its cause is wisdom. The latter etymological derivation is that wisdom[2111] refers to this very [prajñā] in its being empty of said two aspects [of perceiver and perceived].[2112]

[The fourth empowerment]

Some say that the meaning of the fourth [empowerment] refers to what is to be accomplished, which is characterized by prajñā-jñāna and endowed with the seven constituents.[2113] Others say that the meaning of the fourth [empowerment] is the appearance [of mind] that is like the stainless autumn sky while becoming [further] familiar with this very prajñā-jñāna [empowerment]. Yet others say that {204} the meaning of the fourth [empowerment] is the prajñā-jñāna [empowerment] itself, which has the form of the natural state, the form of any modulations of the natural state,[2114] the character of natural arising, and the nature of the pure continuous flow of nondual unity.[2115] Other positions are not mentioned [here] for fear of prolixity.[2116]

By virtue of the stanzas and the related merit that came about
by creating this compendium of the very secret empowerment,
may the entire world come to be endowed with poised readiness
for the stainless and clear words so well spoken by the Sugata[2117] [5]

This concludes "A Compendium of the Purport of Empowerment" composed by the mahāpaṇḍita and renunciate Advayavajra. It was translated, edited, and finalized by the Indian upādhyāya Vajrapāṇi and the Tibetan lotsāwa Tsültrim Gyalwa.[2118] {205}

(38) A Compendium of the Procedures of Empowerment

In the language of India: *Saṃkṣiptasekaprakriyā*[2119]
In the language of Tibet: *Dbang gi bya ba mdor bsdus pa*

I pay homage to Śrī Vajrasattva

The kāya of the Sage constitutes great bliss,
the connate ecstasy that is always glowing
without beginning—having paid homage to it,
I clearly explain empowerment's procedure

Yogīs who have obtained empowerments and permissions in the appropriate order, are proficient in the three samādhis,[2120] know[2121] recitation, and wish to take care of their own well-examined disciples, in a maṇḍala house and such, in a place free from any harm by kings, robbers, and so on, should offer the five kinds of offerings to a colored sand maṇḍala, a scroll-painting maṇḍala, and so forth that are crafted in accordance with procedure and make [the deities] reside in a vase in the evening. On nineteen, nine, five, or one [deities], in due order, they should draw the marks[2122] of the sages—Vajrasattva and [the buddhas of] the [vajra,] tathāgata, ratna, padma, and karma families; {206} Moha[rati], Dveṣa[rati], Rāga[rati], and Vajrarati; Rūpa[vajrī]; Śabda[vajrī], Gandha[vajrī], Rasa[vajrī], Sparśa[vajrī], and Dharmavajrī; and Yamāntaka, Prajñāntaka, Padmāntaka, and Vighnāntaka.[2123] [Further to be procured] are a viśvavajra, a blue vajra with five prongs [like] expanded snake hoods, a white wheel with eight spokes, an emerald gem with nine facets, a red lotus, a blue sword, a pair of white eyes with blue pupils, a black five-pronged vajra, a lotus with branches, a blue utpala [flower], a white mirror, a blue vīṇā of the gandharvas, a yellow conch shell, a red begging bowl of a corpse, various garments, a white dharmodaya, a black vajra hammer, a white staff, a red lotus, and a blue vajra with [prongs like] expanded snake hoods. Vajrasattva, Vairocana, and the ten female deities [sit] on multicolored lotuses[2124] and moon [disks]. The remaining [deities] dwell on seats consisting of multicolored lotuses and sun [disks]. On the sarvakarmikas,[2125] Vajrasattva or Amṛtakuṇḍalī should be painted.

[The water empowerment]
There, the all-victorious vase[2126] has no crooked beak, no black base, a bulging body, a long neck, {207} well-drawn marks, its neck is wrapped in a clean cloth, and its opening is adorned with a bodhivṛkṣa[2127] and so on. Gold, silver, lapis lazuli,[2128] pearls, and corals; barley, wheat, wild rice, sesame, and beans; and bṛhati,[2129] kaṇḍakara, śvetāparajitā, daṇḍotpala, and sahadevā[2130]—the five precious substances, the five field fruits, and the five medicinal substances—are poured into that vase; it is filled with scented water and thought of as the maṇḍala. Having offered drinking water, water for the feet, and so on, they enter it in the form of having melted into wisdom nectar. Thereafter, it is placed on top of a vajra embellished with flower garlands and consecrated with one hundred and eight mantras of the deity of one's own family[2131] or the mantra of Amṛtakuṇḍalī. The other vases are [consecrated] with the concordant yogas and the mantras of the deities who inhabit the maṇḍala. Having offered flowers, incense, and such and presented oblations, they are praised with "Akṣobhya, great vajra . . ."[2132] Preceded by scent, bells are to be rung. This is the procedure of making [the deities] reside in a vase.

After that, the vajra disciples construct a maṇḍala and, while holding flower garlands, place their kneecaps on the ground[, saying]:

Those with the fortune for the Mantrayāna,
who are striving for the siddhis of mantra,
should enter into this maṇḍala here {208}

Those who desire merit, striving for what is
other than this, elsewhere, beyond the world,
keep focusing on what is beyond the world
By thus becoming endowed with faith anew,
these intelligent ones are to enter the maṇḍala

Through this [life], the fruition is not found,
nor will what's beyond the world be achieved
Accordingly, if for the sake of what's beyond,
you are striving for what is beyond the world,
the fruition is accomplished without effort

Following this, the faithful disciples should mentally enter the [master's] own body, exit through the vajra, and dwell in the lotus of his own secret awareness consort. There, by requesting the tathāgatas, they should observe the empowerment, settling into abiding at the eastern gate of the maṇḍala. One among the chief disciples should say this:

You who teach me great ecstasy,
being in your union with Māmakī,
oh great protector, I beseech you!

Bestow upon me this very samaya
that shows great awakening's way!
Bestow bodhicitta upon me as well!
Bestow on me the triple refuge too,
the Buddha, dharma, and saṃgha!
Protector, please allow me to enter
the supreme city of great liberation!

[The master] answers thus:

Oh sons, over here, in the Mahāyāna,
I'll teach you the procedural approach
of the conduct of the secret mantra
You are vessels of the great approach

By the power of the vajra empowerment
of the buddhas coming in the three times,
with their vajras of body, speech, and mind,
the equality of wisdom {209} is attained

By the unequaled yoga of secret mantra,
the supreme Śākya lion, as well as others,
after having vanquished the formidable
great power[2133] of the greatly fierce māras,

approached in accordance with the world,
turned the wheel, and passed into nirvāṇa
Therefore, in order to attain omniscience,
oh you sons, bring forth this insight here!

The disciples should read this stanza of taking refuge in the Three [Jewels]:

I take refuge in the Three Jewels,
confess all of my wrongdoings,
rejoice in the virtues of beings,
and set my mind on buddha awakening

They are protected with Amṛtakuṇḍalī's mantra OṂ ĀḤ VIGHNĀNTAKṚT HŪṂ PHAṬ. They should imagine HŪṂ, ĀḤ,[2134] and OṂ, respectively, in the centers of a vajra, lotus, and wheel standing on a moon [disk] in their heart, throat, and forehead.[2135] Seizing the vajra with the fist of his right hand, the master rises, touches the heart, throat, and head of the disciples, utters HŪṂ, ĀḤ, and OṂ, respectively, and offers flowers to their head, incense in front, and likewise scents and lamps to their heart.

Thereafter, [the master] should give the disciples a toothpick that is twelve finger-widths in length [and made] of madar, an aśvattha tree[2136] not eaten by bugs, and so on, over which the mantra of Amṛtakuṇḍalī has been recited and whose tip is bound with a flower garland. {210} Looking to the east or north, the [disciples] should hold its tip in the mouth and then cast it into a place the size of an ox hide that is sprinkled [with perfume]. There, the activities of pacifying and so on are demonstrated:

Wherever it may point when it falls down,
the siddhis of that are known as supreme
The tip being in the direction of the east
is known as representing middling siddhis

Looking to the north and outside too
are held to represent worldly siddhis
If it is pointing to the south, then,
they become very fierce thereby

By virtue of facing to the west,
subtle siddhis will exist in them
Likewise, if the toothpick is cast
and faces downward, there will be
the siddhi of [moving] underground
This cannot be analyzed definitively

Thereafter, drinking three handfuls of scented sipping water from the palms of their hands, they should rinse their mouths with the mantra OṂ HRĪḤ VIŚUDDHĀḤ SARVADHARMĀḤ SARVAPĀPAṂ NIŚCAYASYA[2137] SAṂŚODHAYA VIKALPĀPANAYA HŪṂ.[2138] Being oriented like that, kuśa [grass] should be consecrated with the mantra of Amṛtakuṇḍalī and given to them as mats and cushions. They need to make three knots into a consecrated [string of] three intertwined threads and tie it around their right upper arm for protection. [Then, the master] teaches the dharma:

In the world, the omniscient ones,
similar to the uḍumbara flower,[2139]
are just occasional and very rare,
maybe not even arising in the future {211}

The emergence of the approach of secret
mantra's conduct is even rarer that that—
who is able to promote the unequaled,
unsurpassable welfare of sentient beings?[2140]

Immediately upon seeing this maṇḍala,
the previously committed wrongdoings
throughout scores of millions of eons
will then come to be extinguished

Those whose insight is very stainless
with regard to this supreme conduct
will cut off these miserable realms
in which all sufferings spring forth

It is you, the magnanimous ones, who
will find the unsurpassable find today
Thereby, you all will come to possess
the character of holding the teachings
of all the victorious ones, as well as
their children, in every single respect

Therefore you will proceed toward
excellency within this Mahāyāna
Glorious is this supreme path arising
as the greatest one in the Mahāyāna

Through traveling on it, it is you
with the great self-arising fortune
who will become those tathāgatas
who know the world in its entirety

[The disciples] should listen to these dharma teachings. Being thus properly protected by the mantra of Amṛtakuṇḍalī, they need to adopt the specific vow [here]:

Protector, bestow the empowerments
of the cakra that's irreversible upon me!
The true reality of this cakra's deities,
the activities of the master, as well as
the samayas of the entirety of buddhas
represent the supreme and secret vow
Great master, at all times you shall
promote all sentient beings' welfare {212}

Then, the disciples need to sleep on the spread-out kuśa [grass]. [The master] says: "Whatever little thing you see in your dreams, tell me in the morning!" This is the procedure of making [the deities] reside in the disciples.

Entering the empowerment house again [the next morning], the master should recite the mantra of Amṛtakuṇḍalī for the sake of protection. He [also] offers oblations. At dawn, he summons the disciples and looks at their virtuous and nonvirtuous dreams. If the disciples have seen nonvirtuous dreams, they need to be protected with the mantra of Amṛtakuṇḍalī. Thereafter, they make offerings to this vast painted maṇḍala. Preceded by [the master's] own deity yoga, his own disciples perform their own engagement in accord with procedure. Engagement [here] refers to what will be obtained mentally from the Bhagavān, the lord [of the maṇḍala], until arriving at the permission and the [actual] empowerment that will be explained [below].

Then, in order to make the disciples enter [the maṇḍala], [the master] needs to proclaim reality as follows:

Phenomena are like reflections:
pure, clear, without any sullies,
ungraspable and inexpressible,
arising in accord with causes

Similarly, true reality transpires
Due to this reality,[2141] in the maṇḍala
that is a clear reflection, may the
disciples attain all that is stainless!

While [the master] proclaims such and more, the disciples make offerings outside the curtain. {213} [The master] visualizes these disciples who have the fortune for this empowerment as having the form of Vairocana. For them, he utters the mantra Ā KHAṂ VĪRĀ HŪṂ, ties flower garlands [around their necks,] and blindfolds them. Cleansing them with the water in the vase, he needs to ask them the following so that they can enter the maṇḍala: "Son, what do you like?" They should answer the following: "I have the fortune for great bliss." Properly placing a vajra at the heart of the disciples, saying "OṂ VAJRAYOGACITTA UTPADAYĀMI OM SURATE SAMAYAS TVAṂ BODHICITTAVAJRA YATHĀ SUKHAṂ," they should give rise to bodhicitta. [The master says:] "Today, all tathāgatas will bless you. But you should not divulge this supreme secret of all tathāgatas to those who have not entered the maṇḍala, nor to those without faith. OṂ AH JAḤ HŪṂ." With this, [the disciples] are summoned and brought inside the curtain. Being properly placed at the eastern gate of the maṇḍala, [the master] should declare the following: "Today, you have entered the family of all tathāgatas. Through their wisdom, you will also attain the siddhis of all tathāgatas, so what need to mention any other siddhis? I will give rise to such wisdom in you, but you should not divulge this in front of those who have not seen the maṇḍala. {214} [Otherwise,] you will indeed impair samaya." Furthermore, properly placing the vajra on their head, he should proclaim this:

My dear, if you speak about this,
through this vajra of the samaya,
your head will be shattered and
instantly torn asunder—you die!

Properly placing the vajra, together with flowers, at their heart, he should declare the following:[2142]

OṂ It is today that Vajrasattva
has properly entered your heart
If you speak of this state of being,
you're instantly torn apart and die!

Thereby, [the disciples] should take this oath. Properly placing the five nectars into the lotus vessel, they are blessed with the three syllables and the [mantra] OṂ VAJRĀMṚTA UDAKATHAḤ[2143] is recited up to seven times. Reading the following constitutes the samaya:

This represents the water of your hell
If you ruin the samaya, it burns you
If you keep samaya, you get siddhis
Drink this vajra-nectar water down!

Then, [the master] should declare the following: "From today on, I'm your Vajrapāṇi. Whatever I command you to do, you must do it! Don't entertain any contempt for me either! If you do, when the time of death comes without having abandoned fear, you will indeed plunge into hell." With this, he gives them the samaya water. Then, the disciples say the following: "Through the blessings of all tathāgatas and Vajrasattva, {215} let bodhicitta descend upon me!"

Next, [the master] imagines the following. In the heart of the disciples, standing on a four-cornered earth maṇḍala that has arisen from a yellow LAṂ and is marked with a three-pronged vajra, there is a syllable HŪṂ. At the crown of the head, standing on a round water maṇḍala that has arisen from a BAṂ and is marked with a vase, there is a syllable HA. At the throat, standing on a wind maṇḍala with the shape of a bow that has arisen from a YAṂ and is marked with a fluttering banner, there is a syllable ĀḤ. Underneath [each] foot, on a wind maṇḍala, standing on a triangular fire maṇḍala that radiates light rays, which has arisen from a blazing syllable RAṂ and is marked with a red-colored vajra, there is a syllable JHAIḤ with light rays. With an air of pride, [the master] should then brandish the vajra and[2144] ring the bell. Uttering "ĀVEŚĀYA STAMBHAYA RARA CĀLAYA CĀLAYA HŪṂ HA ĀḤ RAṂ JHAIḤ," he should meditate on a red syllable ĀḤ on the tongue as being the form of Amitābha. Having arrived [there], he should say: "Oh sons, tell us about virtue and nonvirtue!" By saying "TIṢṬHA VAJRA," this should be stabilized, and he should ask: "What appears to your eyes?" Then the [disciples] say: "What appears is white, yellow, red,[2145] and black." [The master] states: "You will become a vessel for accomplishing pacifying, enriching, subjugating, and wrathful [activities]."[2146]

[Next,] he should bless them with reality: {216}

Into this, "the perfect maṇḍala,"
I shall make you disciples enter
In accord with the deity families
and in accord with merit, come!

You will achieve the siddhis
Accomplishing your family
and following your merit here,
come like that to this maṇḍala!

Then, with the [mantra] PRATĪCCHA VAJRA HOḤ [the disciples] toss flower garlands into the maṇḍala. [The place where] the flowers fall shall illustrate [the attainment of] lower, medium, or highest siddhis. If they fall onto a buddha's head, ūrṇā hair,[2147] or uṣṇīṣa, this grants the siddhi of mahāmudrā. By virtue of [falling onto] the higher limbs, the higher [siddhis are granted]. By virtue of [falling onto] the middling limbs, the middling [siddhis are granted]. By virtue of [falling onto] the lower limbs, the lower [siddhis are granted]. By virtue of [falling] far away from a [buddha] image, [siddhis are granted] after a very long time. By virtue of [falling] close [to a buddha image], the siddhis will be swift. The deities' respective own locations[2148] are to be known from analyzing the diagram [of the maṇḍala] and so on. If [the flowers] fall between two deities, one belongs to the family of the one to whom [the flowers] are closer. If falling outside of the maṇḍala, lower siddhis [are attained]. If falling onto the outline[2149] [of the drawn maṇḍala], [the flowers need to be] tossed again. If falling onto this [outline] three times, there will not be any siddhis. If falling outside of the vajra fence, there will not be any siddhis [either]. If falling onto the platform,[2150] things will be very difficult. This is the procedure of tossing flowers. {217}

Now, as for seizing the garland and tying it onto the head, [the master] says:

You powerful beings
must seize this firmly!

Looking at a syllable OṂ [each] in the two eyes, he says:

OṂ Today, Vajrasattva makes
the effort to open your eyes!
Opening them, all will be seen
The vajra eye is unsurpassable

[Upon this, the disciples] should remove their blindfolds. Then, the maṇḍala should be shown. The skandha of consciousness in the middle is Akṣobhya. In the directions of the east and so on, form is Vairocana, feeling Ratnasambhava, discrimination Amitābha, and formation Amoghasiddhi. In the intermediate directions of the southeast and so on, the earth element is Buddhalocanā, the water element Māmakī, the fire element Pāṇḍaravāsinī, and the wind element Tārā. In the intermediate directions of the southeast and so on outside of the maṇḍala, in the two southern sides, there are Rūpavajrī, Śabdavajrī, Gandhavajrī, Rasavajrī, Sparśavajrī, and Dharmadhātuvajrī. Yamāntaka, Prajñāntaka, Padmāntaka, and Vighnāntaka dwell at the [four] gates that are in the east and so on. This is the procedure of entering the maṇḍala.

[Now, the disciples] should speak about the empowerment in which they put their trust:

Just as Bodhicittavajra and the buddhas
are providing such a festive occasion, {218}
for the sake of giving me your guidance,
Ākāśavajra, provide this for me today!

[The master] should visualize the disciples who pray like this as having the form of Akṣobhya and pour the water of the vase of all forms into the water that is endowed with the awareness persons. Looking at a vajra [arising] from a HŪṂ, with the power of Vajrasattva, he pours the water of the vase with his fist holding the vajra:

The empowerment is the great vajra,
to which the three realms pay homage
It arises from the three vajras' abodes
All the buddhas should bequeath it

OṂ VAJRĀBHIṢIÑCĀMI TVAṂ

By saying this, he should bestow the empowerment onto the disciples, who are like cakravartins. This is the procedure of the water empowerment. It represents mirror-like wisdom.

[The crown empowerment]
Through the gradual steps right after having shown it, [the master] gives a crown made of gold or silk and so on to the disciples. This is the yoga of Ratnasambhava—that is, the maṇḍala of all buddhas is venerated: "MAHĀMUKUṬAṂ PRATICCHA VAJRA HO." By saying this, [all] think of the crowns belonging to the individual families of all tathāgatas who have arrived in the maṇḍala in space. This is the procedure of the crown empowerment. It represents the wisdom of equality.

[The vajra empowerment]
Next, with his [right] hand, [the master] should place a big five-pronged vajra at his heart and then confer it to the right hand[2151] of the disciples, whom he takes to be Lokeśvara: {219}

It is today that I shall bestow upon you
the vajra empowerment of all buddhas
This represents the one of all buddhas
So as to accomplish it, seize this vajra!

By saying this, touching the heart and so on with the vajra, [the master] should give the vajra into the right hand [of the disciples]. This is the procedure of the vajra empowerment. It represents discriminating wisdom.[2152]

[The bell empowerment]
Next, visualizing the disciples in the form of Amoghasiddhi, [the master] gives a bell into their left hand. He gives the vajra and the bell together into their hands, in such a manner that the hands of the disciples are in an embrace, saying: "OṂ VAJRĀDHIPATIS TVAṂ ABHIṢIÑCĀMI TIṢṬHA VAJRASAMAYAS TVAṂ." This is the procedure of the bell empowerment. It represents all-accomplishing wisdom.

[The name empowerment]
Next, viewing [the disciples] as Vairocana, [the master] should bestow the name empowerment. Placing the vajra and the bell together on their head, he should [say] "OṂ VAJRASATTVAS TVAṂ ABHIṢĪÑCĀMI VAJRANĀMĀBHIṢEKATA" and give them names in accordance with their [buddha] families, such as "Hey, Śrī Mohavajra," "Hey, Śrī Rāgavajra," "Hey, Śrī Īrṣyāvajra," "Hey, Śrī Dveṣavajra," and "Hey, Śrī Mātsaryavajra."[2153] This is the procedure of the name empowerment. It represents the wisdom of the pure dharmadhātu.

Through these empowerments, [the disciples] become [suitable] vessels for explaining and listening to the tantras and for practicing the mantras. These five empowerments are designated as "the empowerments of the awareness consorts" because the activities of Locanā and so on operate in all of them.[2154]{220}

[The master empowerment]
Next, [the disciples say this:]

I ask to bestow upon me today
the vajra-master empowerment
for the sake of myself and others
out of compassionate kindness

[The master] visualizes the disciples praying in this way, who are adorned with a parasol and a canopy, on top of [already] being embellished with all the ornaments [from the previous empowerments], and dwell at the eastern gate on a lion throne in the form of Vajrasattva on an eight-petaled multicolored lotus. Looking at a vajra [arising] from a syllable HŪṂ, [he says]:

The sattva with no beginning or end
is Vajrasattva, who is great ecstasy,
Samantabhadra, the character of all,
the lord of lords with vajra pride's air,
Bhagavān, glorious, supreme primal being[2155]

With this being said, [the disciples] receive this [empowerment].
Next, [looking at] a bell [arising] from a syllable AḤ,[2156] [the master says]:

This is the one of all of the buddhas,
said to accord with prajñā's expanse
You too have to retain it at all times!
The victors hold it is utmost awakening

Saṃsāric existence, pure by nature,
becomes rendered naturally nondual
It is the naturally pure mind[2157] that will
make saṃsāric existence into reality

With this being said, the disciples should ring [their bells].
Next, [the master says]:

As the mental body is stable,
it is called the "mudrā samaya"
As the mental body is stable,[2158]
it is well known as the seal

With this being said, [the master] visualizes himself as his own chosen deity, {221} blesses himself as being mahāmudrā, and embraces[2159] [the disciples].

Next, the master imagines for a short while that a host of female deities sprung forth from the seed [syllable] in his own heart dwell in the sky and that thereby the empowerment is bestowed, [saying]:

The empowerment is the great vajra,
to which the three realms pay homage
It arises from the three vajras' abodes
All the buddhas should bequeath it

With this being said, the empowerment is bestowed. As it is said:

> Embracing a sixteen-year-old
> prajñā with your pair of arms,
> due to bell's and vajra's union,
> the master empowerment is held[2160]

Thereafter, [the master] should explain the true reality of the maṇḍala and the purity of the maṇḍala in brief with the following and other words:

The lotus maṇḍala is the stable maṇḍala[2161]
It is the supreme maṇḍala that is mental
The storied house represents the wisdom
The mind is the palace's true condition
Evenly relying upon the five skandhas
is well known as being the five buddhas

Next, [the master] gives the disciples, who are visualized as Vairocana and so on, the permission [to turn the wheel of dharma]:

In order to benefit all sentient beings,
within the entirety of worldly realms,
set the wheel of the dharma in motion
in accord with all kinds to be guided!

Through this, the terms of the vajra, jewel, lotus, and karma [families] are instilled into the abode of dharma [in the mind stream] and thus the permission is given through a succession of stanzas.

Next, {222} visualizing [the disciples] in the form of Akṣobhya, [the master] bestows the vajra discipline.

This is the one of all of the buddhas
It abides in the hands of Vajrasattva
You too have to retain it at all times!
The discipline of Vajrapāṇi is steady

With this, [the master] gives them a vajra arisen from a syllable HŪṂ, saying: "OṂ SARVATATHĀGATA SIDDHI VAJRASAMAYA TIṢṬHA EŚA TVAṂ DHARAYĀMI VAJRASATTVA[2162] HI HI HI HI HŪṂ." The disciples seize the vajra. This is the giving of vajra discipline.

Next, visualizing himself in the form of the Buddha, [the master] displays the way of seizing his dharma robes at the heart with his left hand while holding the right one in the mudrā of fearlessness. The disciples are to be visualized in the forms of whatever their [buddha] families are and should be given the prophecy:

OṂ Today I will give you the prophesy:
it is the tathāgata Vajrasattva who pulls
you out of existence and lower realms,
because saṃsāric existence is utterly pure

HE MAHĀMUKANĀMA TATHĀGATA SIDDHI SAMAYAS TVAṂ BHŪR BHUVAḤ SVAḤ

Thus [the master] should make the prophecy through this above stanza of prediction and these mudrās: with a single voice, all tathāgatas, all bodhisattvas with their retinues, and the inhabitants of the maṇḍala make this prophecy about [the disciples'] unsurpassable and completely perfect awakening. [Then,] he says this to the disciples:

Through the strong power of these mudrās
and the force of this mantra, develop faith! {223}

This is the prophecy.

Next, [the master] says: "MAHĀSAMAYA HŪṂ HANA HANA HŪṂ PHAṬ PHAṬ." With this, he should provide reassurance as follows:

Through being admitted into and seeing
the maṇḍala of the supreme great secret,
you become free from all wrongdoings
It is today that you dwell within bliss

Within this yāna of great bliss,
from now on there is no death
Thus, as existence is utterly pure,
existence's suffering is expelled

The mudrā that is called "vajra"
and bodhicitta are not to be rid
Merely by virtue of their arising,
there's no doubt about buddhahood

Don't give up the true dharma—
you should never abandon it![2163]
You should not be teaching this
to the ignorant or nescient ones

You should never abandon
the vajra, bell, and mudrā
Because of being equal to all buddhas,
you should never disparage the master

Don't torment yourself with asceticism
by fully abandoning your own character!
Seize bliss in any way it is pleasurable!
This is perfect buddhahood in the future

Today you became the maṇḍala's master
That you hold the mantras and the tantras
is what is maintained by the buddhas
and bodhisattvas, as well as the deities

In order to take care of sentient beings,
in accord with the maṇḍala procedure,

you draw it up in a perseverant manner,
connecting practitioners with the tantras

This is to provide reassurance.

Now, the permission is given: {224} It should be given after the five empowerments of the awareness consorts and following the master empowerment. The master empowerment is [also] called "the irreversible empowerment." [All six are called "the vase empowerment,"] because the activities of the vase are performed in all of them. These empowerments do not contradict any of all the tantras. These [empowerments that culminate in] the master empowerment represent the purification of the vajra of the body.

[The secret empowerment]
Next, in a location that has been made free from obscurations and so on, for the sake of [the master] bestowing the secret empowerment [upon them], the disciples should offer their own prajñā—possessing a pleasing form and youthfulness and being endowed with samaya and vows—to the guru and make this prayer for the state of liberation:[2164]

Just as Bodhicittavajra[2165] and the buddhas
are providing such a festive occasion,
for the sake of giving me your guidance,
Ākāśavajra, provide this for me today!

The guru should manifest the three samādhis and cultivate self-awareness. Taking from the lotus of the prajñā expanding from the element of space, [he says]:

The face of the prajñā is bound,
and so is the face of the means
The elderly without any names
are to drop into the student's mouth

AHO MAHĀSUKHA HO

With this, [the master] should rest in the place of enjoyment. This has the character of Vairocana. Once risen from it, he gives to the [disciples]. The secret empowerment represents the purification of the vajra of speech. This is the procedure of the secret empowerment.

[The prajñā-jñāna empowerment]
Next, {225} in order to realize the personally experienced dharmakāya based on a single mudrā or in others who are different from her, [the master] joins her hand with the hand of the disciple, who has prayed with the stanza as taught above. Together with that,[2166] the vajra of the body of the tathāgatas is placed, and guru Vajradhara says the following:

All the buddhas praise that this consort
who is so delightful is to be relied upon
Through the cakras' progressive yogas,
the genuine bliss will be experienced

Through that, the threefold world is pure
There's no awakening due to other means
For that reason, you should never allow
yourself to become separated from her

This is all buddhas' unsurpassable
discipline of the awareness consort
Some foolish people abandon her—
for them, there is no supreme siddhi

With these words, he gives [her to the disciple]. Anointing her with saffron and sandalwood, the [disciple] beautifies her with fragrant scents and flower garlands. By taking off her clothes, she clearly displays her excellent lotus and says the following:

Foods such as excrement and urine,
blood, semen, and likewise flesh,
boy, do you enjoy them as you like?
Just so, devoted to the best woman,

do you kiss the lotus of the bhaga?
Oh boy, tell me how you like this!

The [disciples] say:

Goddess, why wouldn't I be delighted?
I feed on semen, blood, and all the rest
and am devoted to women all the time {226}
I place my kisses right onto your bhaga!

Then, with amorous thoughts and loving gazes, the [disciple] looks at her like a husband does.[2167] Exposing her excellent lotus, she says the following:

AHO! This lotus here of mine
is endowed with all the bliss
I remain right in front of those
who rely on me, as per the rite

Do the lotus deeds as they should be,
the best service to the perfect buddhas!
It is the self-arising king of great bliss
who perfectly resides right within here

BHAJA HŪṂ MOKṢA HOḤ[2168]

Having the character of [cultivating] their own deity yoga, in due order, they array the five families by way of OṂ, HŪṂ, SVĀ, ĀḤ, and HA at the head, the heart, the navel, the secret place, and the feet. Thereafter, they meditate on a syllable PHAṬ within the anthers of the syllables ĀḤ and OṂ [in] a lotus and a vajra [arising] from a syllable HŪṂ. The nāḍī of Vajradhātvīśvarī that resides on the left side is stimulated a bit with a finger, which is known from the pith instructions of the guru.[2169]

Thereafter, saying "OṂ SARVATATHĀGATĀNURĀGAṆA VAJRASVABHĀVĀTMAKO 'HAM," they should undertake [the activities of] ecstasy. Then, [the master says this]:

Placing the vajra into the lotus,
you should not lose bodhicitta
You should meditate by being filled
with a mind excited through ecstasy

For as long as yogīs do not ask
for the bodhicitta to approach, {227}
this one that arises from ecstasy
is attained in a continuous way

Through bodhicitta plunging down,
the skandha of consciousness[2170] faints
For that long, any siddhi is inferior[2171]

Great is the marvel due to the touch
of space expanse and vajra uniting
This bliss that thus springs forth
constitutes true supreme ecstasy
Right within cessational ecstasy,
perceive, look, and stabilize this![2172]

In the spot of the vajra posture restraining
the anthers of the vajra in the lotus's space,
mind should look at entering into the jewel
Wisdom forms adorn the wisdom that arises

Neither passion, nor dispassion,
nor a middle is to be observed[2173]
The yogīs who behold wisdom
rest in bliss, without emission

For half of a session or a single one,
a day, a month, half a month, a year,
an eon, or during thousands of eons,
yogīs rest [in this] through wisdom

The disciples keep looking at union,
while the four of Moharati and so on,
who spring from the heart of the guru,
are arrayed by them in mind as such

Cultivate the marks of a disciple well!
Make them emerge within the lotus!
As the mind that extracts the essence
from this precedes awakening, seize it!

This is the procedure of the prajñā-jñāna empowerment. It represents the purification of the vajra of mind.

[The fourth empowerment]
For those who have embraced the prajñā-jñāna empowerment through the process as it was explained in the procedure of the prajñā-jñāna empowerment, {228} likewise, the word [empowerment]—the precious empowerment that represents the fruition and is the fourth one—is to be proclaimed. Otherwise, it is said, samaya and so on will deteriorate:[2174]

> Otherwise, not bestowing empowerment,
> who could be asserted as being a yogī?
> This is like striking space with your fists
> or [trying to] drink the water of a mirage[2175]

Therefore, in bestowing this empowerment of true reality according to the [proper] procedure, [the master] looks at the faithful mind of the disciples: if they have faith in the vast and profound, the precious word empowerment is granted. Otherwise, it is not. "But how does he know whether they have faith in the vast nature?" As it is said:

> Just as recognizing fire due to smoke
> and water on account of waterfowl,
> an intelligent bodhisattva's disposition
> is recognized on account of its signs[2176]

You display a very radiant face,
your body flourishes like a lotus,
and you see the vast true reality
The masters who are proficient
take good care of such disciples[2177]

As the Bhagavān declared:

Empowerments are well known
as three kinds in this tantra here:
the master's, the secret, the prajñā,
and the fourth is again like that[2178]

And:

Smiling, looking, and holding hands,
and thereafter the two in sexual union:
ecstasy as well as the supreme ecstasy,
the cessational one, and the connate one

Variety as well as maturation, {229}
consummation, characteristics' lack—
the empowerment's entire sequence
springs from the body of the prajñā[2179]

Furthermore, he states this:

The divine syllable E, which is
adorned with VAṂ at its center,
represents all bliss's repository,
the jewel casket of buddhahood[2180]

There, [he also said the following]:

The master's is by the purity of smiling
The secret is just so in terms of looking

The prajñā is with regard to embracing
Then that again for the pair in its union [2181]

By virtue of ecstasy, there is slight bliss
Supreme ecstasy is more intense than it
With the cessational, there is dispassion
Connate ecstasy [exists] as the remainder[2182]

The first one is thanks to expecting touch,
the second one due to the desire for bliss,
the third due to the extinction of passion,
and the fourth is experienced through that[2183]

During variety, there is the first ecstasy,
during maturation, it is supreme ecstasy,
during consummation, cessational ecstasy,
during characteristics' lack, connate ecstasy

Variety is known as various kinds:
embracing and kissing and so forth
Maturation constitutes its opposite:
the blissful experience of wisdom

Consummation is proclaimed to be the
consideration "I have partaken of bliss"
Characteristics' lack is other than the three,
being free from passion and dispassion[2184]

He [likewise] stated this:

Neither passion, nor dispassion,
nor a middle is to be observed
What's free of the three ecstasies
is designated as "the connate"[2185] {230}

The Bhagavān also taught this very meaning in the *Guhyasamāja[tantra]*:

The union of accomplished and accomplishment
is that which is designated as "the approach"
It is the union of the vajra and the lotus that
is explained as being "close accomplishment"

Accompanied by the syllables HŪṂ and PHAṬ,
the motion is explained to be "accomplishment"
The nature, its own bliss, as well as peacefulness
are explicated as being "great accomplishment"[2186]

Ecstasy constitutes the final activity of the
vajra of accomplished and accomplishment
Supreme ecstasy represents the final
bodhicitta that is vigorously moving

Due to emission, it is cessational ecstasy
Through resting within these [ecstasies],
that which is stated to be the fourth bliss
constitutes the one that is connate[2187]

This is the meaning of understanding accomplishment. [He also] said the following and more:

There is no beginning, end, or middle,
neither saṃsāric existence nor nirvāṇa
This constitutes the supreme great bliss
There exists neither any self nor other

Supreme ecstasy is said to be existence
Nirvāṇa occurs by virtue of dispassion
Mere ecstasy is the state in the middle
However, the connate is free of these

When the supreme ecstasy is attained
in the moment that is free of diversity,

the teacher should say: "Oh mahāsattva,
you should hold the bliss that is great!

As long as awakening is not attained, {231}
promote beings' welfare, vajra holder!"[2188]

"How is that?"

Since in what is taught as three divisions
there exists no other result than the cause
The three divisions are well-known before
Within the cessational one and ecstasy,
what is clearly manifest is the fourth one[2189]

"Well, how is it clearly manifest within the mind?" [This is answered by] passages such as the following one:

At the supreme's end and cessation's start,
this is empty yet nonempty, being Heruka[2190]

"How it is empty yet nonempty?"

The inexhaustible lord of being and nonbeing
is without any beginning or end, yet peaceful
Emptiness and compassion being inseparable
is that which is expressed as "bodhicitta"[2191]

This is the tenet [asserted here]. "Through which means is it generated?"

Through means such as the maṇḍala circle
and the progressive stages of self-blessing[2192]

In detail, [these and other passages] apply here. [However,] I do not explain them [here]. "Why is that?" Because this wisdom of self-awareness is beyond the path of the sphere of speech.

This represents the stages of blessings,
identical with the omniscient's wisdom[2193]

Furthermore, this is stated:

The connate is not uttered by anyone else,
and it is not obtained anywhere either
It is realized by yourself thanks to merit
and by attending to the guru's observances[2194]

Due to the venerable guru's kindness,
your own merit will become so great
The wisdom of instantaneous realization {232}
is beyond the path of speech's sphere[2195]

[Also,] the following is declared:

It is the king of great bliss alone that they know
They always know it in beings' mind streams,
but at the times when they are teaching about it,
even the omniscient will be deprived of words[2196]

Saraha proclaims this:

Through the gurus not teaching its words,
the disciples don't have any understanding
Oh friends, all this is the taste of the nectar
that is the connate—who could teach what?

It is not the sphere of mind, there is no movement of speech
The guru's expressions engage in talk far from the true state
Gradually,[2197] the qualities of compassion and so forth increase
In the abode of the heart of those with devotion, it grants itself[2198]

"But what is the characteristic of bodhicitta?" He declares the following:

Looking as if the senses fell asleep,
as if mentation has entered inside,
and as if the mind has disintegrated,
the body faints due to genuine bliss

The hosts of the sense faculties have vanished,
thoughts disintegrated, saṃsāra's seed is gone
Through this appearance of ecstasy, there is
the amazing cool experience that is like space

The sense faculties will have vanished and
an essence of its own will disintegrate too
About this connate ecstasy that is supreme,
ask the guru's mouth in a clear manner![2199]

He [also] said this:

To what dawns at the time of falling apart, I prostrate
The objects and sense faculties have vanished equally
It's the sole body that's beautified by fainting in ecstasy {233}
Swiftly rising in the heart, so is an irreversible wise one

The mind in which all thoughts are relinquished
will have the power of the bliss that is genuine
This is a wise one who did what had to be done
Others, however, are simply cattle with two legs[2200]

Therefore true disciples should pay their services and respect to the perfect guru. It is by themselves that they need to gain the awareness of the essence of the great bliss that is in accord with the three kāyas. Once the activities of obtaining empowerment have been done, they should declare the following:

It is today that my birth has become fruitful
and my efforts have become fruitful as well
Today, I'm born in the family of the buddhas
Now, I have become a child of the buddhas

Then:

I heap my offerings onto the genuine guru
With various ornaments, garments, and such,
whose characteristic is the tathāgata's speech,
my own body has become very distinguished

Thereafter, they should perform fire offerings, offer oblations, and then teach the dharma to the saṃgha of those persons who possess the Vinaya.[2201] They should also satisfy those who are without protection and suffer.

Through the immeasurable merit that has arisen
from writing *A Compendium of Empowerment's Procedures*,[2202]
may it be so that the character of the great bliss
which is nondual and inconceivable is attained!
May people be fulfilled on Vajradhara's bhūmi![2203]

This concludes "A Compendium of the Procedures of Empowerment" composed by Śrī Advayavajra.[2204] {234}

(39) The Five Aspects (of Vajrasattva)

In the language of India: *Pañcākāra*[2205]
In the language of Tibet: *Rang bzhin lnga pa*

I pay homage to the Buddha[2206]

Having paid my homage to Vajrasattva,
free of discursiveness and unsurpassable,
I will explain [his] five aspects in a brief[2207]
manner for the sake of understanding [1]

Once you have protected the abode, yourself, and the yoga by OṂ ĀḤ HŪṂ, you should venerate the five tathāgatas and the five yoginīs in the middle of a quadrangular or other maṇḍala in a place suffused with fragrant scents and so forth.

[Akṣobhya]
In its center is the multicolored syllable PAṂ, which transforms into a multi[colored], eight-petaled, blossoming lotus. On its anthers is the red letter RAṂ,[2208] which transforms into a sun disk. From a blue syllable HŪṂ[2209] standing on it springs, [Akṣobhya],[2210] with one face and two arms. He displays the earth-touching mudrā and [sits in] the cross-legged vajra posture. His body is adorned with the thirty-two major marks and the eighty minor marks [of a buddha]. He is the single repository of a host of qualities, such as the ten powers and the [four] fearlessnesses. {235} He is without porosity,[2211] flesh, and bones, a mere

appearance like a reflection in a mirror, neither real nor delusive. Since he has the character of loving-kindness, he is of dark-blue color, and his [hand-held] sign is a dark-blue vajra. He is the nature of the skandha of consciousness, which is the completely pure dharmadhātu. His head and face are shaven, and his body is covered with ochre robes.[2212] The [crown of his] head is marked with Vajrasattva, which means he has the nature of Vajrasattva, the inseparability of emptiness and compassion.

Therefore he has the character of cause and result and the characteristic of the emptiness that is endowed with all supreme aspects. Since he has the character of being unconditioned and of suchness, he constitutes the dharmakāya. Since he is a mere reflection, he is the sambhogakāya. Since he has the character of imaginative consciousness, he is the nirmāṇakāya. Since he is the single taste of all three kāyas, he is the svābhāvikakāya.[2213] This is what is said:

> Unconditioned mind represents the dharma[kāya]
> Realization[2214] is the sambhoga[kāya]'s characteristic
> Just that constitutes the diversity that is emanated[2215]
> The native [kāya] is the nature of all of them[2216]

Since he is untouchable by thoughts and such, he belongs to the vajra family. This vajra family is not touched[2217] by worldly people. Anger, vajra water, the cool season, noon, a pungent taste, hearing, space, sound, and the *ca*-series[2218]—their purities that represent Akṣobhya {236} are a presentation of his outer and inner [features]. The presentation of the four kāyas here is as before. His mantra to recite is OṂ ĀḤ VAJRADHṚK HŪṂ.[2219]

[Vajrasattva]

Now, Vajrasattva [on Akṣobhya's crown] is born from a syllable HUṂ.[2220] White, with one face and two arms, he holds a vajra and a vajra bell. Being the nature of mentation [or consciousness],[2221] he embodies astringent taste and represents the purity of the autumn season. He is the character of [the letters] *ya, ra, la, va,* and so on. [His time of day is] from midnight until the time of dawn.[2222] Another name [for him] is "dharmadhātu."

[Vairocana]

Then, on the eastern petal [of the lotus], white-colored Vairocana is born on a moon disk from a syllable OṂ.[2223] His [hand-held] sign is a white wheel, and he displays the mudrā of supreme awakening. He is the character of the skandha of form and the nature of nescience. He is the purity of excrement, belongs to the tathāgata family, and abides as mirror-like [wisdom].[2224] He is the purity of the winter season and embodies sweet taste. He is [related to] the *ka*-series, is the character of the morning period, and has the nature of the body. His mantra to recite[2225] is OṂ ĀḤ JINAJIK HŪṂ.[2226]

[Ratnasambhava]

On the southern petal [of the lotus], yellow-colored Ratnasambhava is born on a sun disk from a syllable TRĀṂ.[2227] His [hand-held] sign is a jewel and he displays the mudrā of granting wishes. {237} He is the nature of the skandha of feeling, embodies slander,[2228] is the nature of blood, belongs to the ratna family, and has the wisdom of equality.[2229] He is the character[2230] of the spring season and embodies salty [taste]. He is [related to] the *ṭa*-series and is the character of the third and fourth watches of the day.[2231] His mantra to recite[2232] is OṂ ĀḤ RATNADHṚK HŪṂ.

[Amitābha]

Then, on the western petal [of the lotus], red-colored Amitābha is born on a sun disk from a red syllable HRĪḤ.[2233] His [hand-held] sign is a lotus and he displays the mudrā of samādhi. He is the nature of the skandha of discrimination and embodies desire. He is the nature of semen, belongs to the padma family, and has the characteristic of discriminating wisdom. He is the nature of the season of summer and embodies sour taste. He is [related to] the *ta*-series and represents the first part of the night. His mantra to recite is OṂ ĀḤ ĀROLIK HŪṂ.[2234]

[Amoghasiddhi]

Next, on the northern petal [of the lotus], green-colored Amoghasiddhi[2235] is born on a sun disk from a green syllable KHAṂ.[2236] He is the nature of flesh. His [hand-held] sign is a sword and he displays the mudrā of fearlessness. He is the nature of the skandha of formations and belongs to the karma family. He embodies envy and has the characteristic of all-accomplishing wisdom. He is the nature of the rainy season[2237] and the character of bitter taste. He is the purity of the *pa*-series and the nature of midnight. His mantra to recite[2238] {238} is OṂ ĀḤ PRAJÑĀDHṚK HŪṂ.

They [all sit in] the cross-legged vajra posture and have one face, two arms, and an uṣṇīṣa. Their heads and faces are shaven. They wear ochre robes, are adorned with the thirty-two major marks and the eighty minor marks, and are the single repository of a host of qualities, such as the ten powers and the [four] fearlessnesses. They are without porosity, flesh, and bones, like a reflection in a mirror. They are sambhogakāya forms, which are mere stainless appearances, with all thoughts of being real, unreal, and so on having been relinquished. Grounded in the svābhāvikakāya, which is the state of the single taste of the three kāyas, they are not different from the dharmakāya, which has the character of unconditioned suchness, and the kāya of imaginative consciousness [the nirmāṇakāya].[2239]

Their heads are adorned with Akṣobhya—that is, they are sealed with Akṣobhya in order to realize that Vairocana, Ratnasambhava, Amitābha, and Amoghasiddhi, who are the nature of the skandhas of form, feeling, discrimination, and formation, respectively, are mere consciousness. In order to realize consciousness's lack of any nature, as well as the identical nature of emptiness and compassion, Akṣobhya is in turn sealed with Vajrasattva. Through this, it is realized that the world has the character of cause and result and is the sheer single taste of saṃsāric existence and nirvāṇa.[2240] Accordingly, [the following is said]: {239}

Wherever the mind of emptiness and
compassion inseparable is cultivated,
this indeed constitutes the teaching of
the Buddha, the dharma, and the saṃgha[2241]

Just as sweetness is the nature
of sugar, and hotness that of fire,
so the nature of all phenomena
is asserted to be emptiness[2242]

Likewise, [this is declared]:

> Full knowledge of saṃsāric existence
> itself is what is designated as "nirvāṇa"[2243]

[Locanā]
On the petal in the southeastern intermediate direction, white-colored Locanā is born on a moon disk from a white syllable LĀṂ.[2244] Her [hand-held] sign is an eye. She is the earth element's own nature, springs from the tathāgata family, and delights in nescience. Her seed [syllable] and mantra[2245] are OṂ ĀḤ LĀṂ HŪṂ SVĀHĀ.

[Māmakī]
In the southwest, dark-blue-colored Māmakī is born on a moon disk from the dark-blue seed syllable MĀṂ. Her [hand-held] sign is a dark-blue vajra. She is the nature of the water element, belongs to the vajra family, and delights in hatred. Her seed [syllable] and mantra are OṂ ĀḤ MĀṂ HŪṂ SVĀHĀ.

[Pāṇḍaravāsinī]
In the northwest, red-colored Pāṇḍaravāsinī[2246] is born on a moon disk from the seed syllable PĀṂ. Her [hand-held] sign is a red lotus. She is the fire element's own nature, belongs to the padma family, and delights in desire. Her seed [syllable] and mantra are OṂ ĀḤ PĀṂ HŪṂ SVĀHĀ.

[Tārā]
In the northeast, {240} green-colored Tāriṇī is a transformation of the gold-green syllable TĀṂ[2247] on a moon disk. Her [hand-held] sign is a blue-green utpala [flower]. She is the wind element's own nature, belongs to the karma family, and delights in envy. Her seed [syllable] and mantra are OṂ ĀḤ TĀṂ HŪṂ SVĀHĀ.

These four [female deities] are sixteen years old, extraordinarily well-shaped, and full of youthfulness,[2248] as if being the epitomes of beauty itself. They have the character of the four kāyas, just as [explained] above. They enrapture the mind, serve as the foundations[2249] of all the qualities of the victors, and are the five tathāgatas' own nature.

[Vajradhātvīśvarī]
In their middle is [their] mistress, Vajradhātvīśvarī, who is the nature of the *a*-series[2250] and Vajrasattva's own nature. She is designated as Bhagavatī, suchness, emptiness, prajñāpāramitā, the true end, and Nairātmyā.[2251]

My effort [here] is not to procure
any dexterity in composing texts
What is it then? To put it briefly,
I shall make disciples understand [2]

Having duly expressed, for the sake of sentient beings,
what accords with all victors' scriptures and reasonings,
may [all] those people become Vajrasattva by means of
the entirety of the virtue that I have accumulated here![2252] [3]

This concludes "The Five Natures of Vajrasattva" composed by Śrī Advayavajra.[2253] {241}

(40) Twenty Stanzas on the Mahāyāna

In the language of India: *Mahāyānaviṃśikā*[2254]
In the language of Tibet: *Theg pa chen po nyi shu pa*

I pay homage to the essence kāya[2255]

I pay homage to the native kāya,
unconditioned, characteristic-free,
endowed with all supreme aspects,
and united with the state of unity[2256] [1]

As their own nature, the native [kāya] is within
the dharma-, sambhoga-, and nirmāṇa[kāyas]
Seeing it in them is what is appropriate for
accomplishing completely perfect awakening[2257] [2]

To see this is superior insight,
as there is no superimposition
It shall be explained right now
in accord with the Mantrayāna [3]

Diversity is not asserted as permanent,
nor is it held to be extinct altogether[2258]
Not a pair of permanence and extinction,
it is not both either, nor without both[2259] [4]

Those in the know of true reality know
the true reality free of the four extremes
Though it is pure of the four extremes,
it is still based on the four extremes[2260] [5]

It is similar to space, without equal,[2261]
peaceful, free of origin, middle, end,
inconceivable yet this mind as such,[2262] {242}
and the very nature of all entities [6]

Once the single taste of the world,
luminous and unsullied, is realized,
if you aren't afraid of any thoughts,
you may live in any way you please[2263] [7]

Afflictions are not different from awakening,
nor do afflictions arise within awakening
Thoughts of afflictions are due to delusion,
yet delusion is naturally without any stain[2264] [8]

For the insightful ones free from thoughts,
the body's actions are the mendicant's way,[2265]
those of speech are the dharma teachings,
and mental action consists of firm resolve[2266] [9]

As for the illusion that the world is an illusion,
do not take an illusion to be [just] an illusion!
[Rather,] illusion is nescience, great delusion
The wise assert delusion is [simply] delusion[2267] [10]

In short, the buddhas and so on
perceive this in just the way it is
Experiencing all fully [like that],
true reality's knowers succeed[2268] [11]

In the thousands of collections of the dharma,
what is named "emptiness" may be realized,

[but] it is not realized by virtue of analysis
Annihilation's meaning comes from the guru[2269] [12]

For the wise in whom thoughts vanished,
all aspects are the true reality that is bliss
[But] this blissful reality is not emptiness
Bliss is neither inconceivable nor bliss[2270] [13]

As for those who, ultimately speaking, do not
see awakening as the lack of superimposition,
if they do not see [it that way], it is suitable
for them to engage in a concordant way later[2271] [14]

Those for whom there is no duality or nonduality
and awakening is not different from existence,
such great yogīs are free from any expectations
and have arrived at the condition of all aspects[2272] [15] {243}

All yogīs need to perform the initial
activity in the way it was described
Emptiness and compassion inseparable
is held to be the wisdom in awakening[2273] [16]

Emptiness is nothing other than loving-kindness—[2274]
it [simply] represents another name of compassion
We don't speak of them as something put together
If we are speaking about them, it is as a unity [17]

Through applying continuous dhyāna
[even] when perceiving a vase and such,[2275]
they will turn into those great buddhas
whose single kāya possesses all aspects[2276] [18]

Unconditioned mind represents the dharma[kāya]
Realization is the sambhoga[kāya]'s characteristic
Just that constitutes the diversity that is emanated[2277]
The native [kāya] is the nature of all of them[2278] [19]

Through the merit I, the fortunate one,
have accumulated and so forth by this,
may the entire world become devoted
to the awakening that is buddhahood![2279] [20]

This concludes "Twenty Stanzas on the Mahāyāna" composed by paṇḍita Advayavajra. It was translated by the upādhyāya Vajrapāṇi and the Tibetan lotsāwa bhikṣu Tsur Jñānākara.[2280] {244}

(41) Twenty Stanzas on True Reality

In the language of India: *Tattvaviṃśikā*[2281]
In the language of Tibet: *De kho na nyid theg pa chen po nyi shu pa*

I pay homage to the omniscient one[2282]

Prajñā is [related to] variety, maturation,
consummation, and characteristics' lack[2283]
Therefore realize true reality from her,
which makes you the world's sovereign[2284] [1]

Prajñā is[2285] the same as saṃsāric existence
She is the three kāyas and the three yānas
She represents the cakra, the means of bliss,
and the yoginī—this is me and the other [2]

As Mañjuvajra,[2286] Mahāmāyā,
vajraḍāka, and others as well,
prajñā itself appears distinctly[2287]
She is liberation, having the victors' makeup [3]

She is inconceivable yet conceived,
nonduality and nevertheless duality,
endowed with all supreme aspects,
being yet nonbeing, perception yet nonperception[2288] [4]

The mind once consciousness is gone,
free from focal objects, unsurpassable,
peaceful, pure, and without appearance,
is the awareness known as "prajñā"[2289] [5]

The entry into that [prajñā] is clearly
in accord with the mantra teachings[2290]
For there are manifold means in it {245}
for the low, middling, and highest[2291] [6]

Meditating in a perfect way on the cakra
by way of the karma- and samayamudrās,
the lower ones contemplate awakening,
facing pure true reality on the outside[2292] [7]

To be in union with the jñānamudrā,
with Mañjuvajra and so on as chief,[2293]
neither real nor a false appearance,[2294]
refers to middling yogīs' character [8]

For those who are incapable of comprehending
the state of self-blessing in terms of true reality,
this path is taught in a progressive manner
for the sake of accomplishing awakening[2295] [9]

If there exists affection for the deity,[2296]
how could there not be mental imprints?
Though these mental imprints are pure,
they will still be like in all other cases [10]

But yogīs who have seen true reality
and are fully devoted to mahāmudrā,
their faculties being unsurpassable,
should rest within all entities' nature[2297] [11]

The bliss that is naturally attained
is free of the entirety of thinking

As this is exactly what the world is,
therefore everything is unsullied[2298] [12]

The outer entities that are perceived by mind
do not appear as delusion, and for that reason
such clear forms are like a woman in a dream—
merely mind, yet still performing functions[2299] [13]

For awakening, there is merely mind,
and mind is asserted as being no-mind
This no-mind in turn is self-awareness,[2300]
and such awareness depends on the guru[2301] [14]

The emptiness of the entirety of entities
is not held to be the name of anything[2302]
This nature of the entirety of entities {246}
is difficult to be experienced personally[2303] [15]

Just as rice becomes boiled rice in this world
through being associated with fire and so on,
likewise, the unawareness that becomes pure
by means of suchness turns into awareness[2304] [16]

For those for whom thinking is meditation,
there isn't anything that is inconceivable
What the buddhas proclaimed to the world
is that yogīs have an inconceivable character[2305] [17]

These yogīs constitute the cakra
They themselves are mahāmudrā
The dharma-, sambhoga-, and nirmāṇa[kāyas],
and all manifestations they are[2306] [18]

Those who did what had to be done and are wishless
have turned away from any and all attachments
Thriving by means of the four ways of conduct,
they are buddhas, and are asserted to be buddhas[2307] [19]

Having presented nonduality as nonduality,
through the merit that I have accumulated,
on this very day, may the world turn into
nonduality as well as great bliss[2308] [20]

This concludes ["Twenty Stanzas on True Reality"] composed by Avadhūtipa Śrī Advayavajra. It was translated by the venerable Dhiriśrījñāna and lotsāwa Sengkar Śākya Ö.[2309] {247}

(42) Instructions on Empowerment

In the language of India: *Sekanirdeśanāma*[2310]
In the language of Tibet: *Dbang bskur ba nges par btsan pa zhes bya ba*

OṂ I pay homage to the Buddha[2311]

I pay homage to the syllables EVAṂ,
being the causes of the four moments
in which the ecstasies arise distinctly,
for the sake of realizing awakening[2312] [1]

That there is variety, then maturation,
thirdly, the lack of any characteristics,
and then consummation is to be known
because of rejecting the forceful yoga[2313] [2]

If consideration is consummation,
how could it be held to be the third?
For there, there is no consideration—
awareness is to be characteristics' lack[2314] [3]

Therefore, look! It is proper to understand
the lack of characteristics as the third one
This is established through self-awareness,
and the scriptures' meaning also agrees[2315] [4]

For whom variety is in kissing and embracing,
what is called "maturation" lies within friction,
and the lack of characteristics is in the jewel—
they are those knowing the poor empowerment[2316] [5]

But if it were the case that this very awareness
that is on the jewel's inside were true reality, {248}
it would be the Śaivist and Vedic true reality
However, this is not asserted by the Buddhists[2317] [6]

Thus, in the *Devīparipṛcchāśivanirnādatantra*, [this is said]:[2318]

It is this very jewel city,[2319] oh you goddess,
that turns into water within the filament
Rudra in the pair is Śiva, the excellent one
This is Śakti, more supreme than supreme[2320] [7]

Free of characteristic and characterized,
and devoid of any utterances of speech,
thanks to the union of Śiva with Śakti,
the bliss that is marvelous springs forth[2321] [8]

Entities do not exist in true reality
They are manifested in Śakti's form
But Śakti is the view of emptiness,
the destroyer of all superimpositions[2322] [9]

In the *Ucchuṣmatantra* too, [the following is declared]:[2323]

The true bliss, supremely nondual,
thanks to Śiva's and Śakti's union,
being neither Śiva, nor being Śakti,
abides in the interior[2324] of the jewel [10]

In the *Yogādhyāya* as well, [this is taught]:[2325]

For yogīs satiated with wisdom's nectar
who have done what needs to be done,
there isn't anything that should be done
If there is, they don't know true reality[2326] [11]

Also, the proponents of Vedānta state this:[2327]

Bhāskara asserts that wisdom is beyond
the sense faculties and without awareness
Those who follow the Bhagavān assert
that awareness consists of sheer ecstasy[2328] [12]

The bliss that is the true reality of the Brahman
due to being excited in the union with the Śakti,
which is at the end of the passion with[2329] the Śakti,
that bliss is proclaimed to be your very own one[2330] [13]

There exists no coming of suffering
There, bliss is a continuous stream
Ecstasy is the nature of the Brahman {249}
This becomes manifest in liberation[2331] [14]

No matter what it is that may be seen,
it is to be conceived as "the Brahman"
Hence mind does not go elsewhere—
it remains within the Brahman alone[2332] [15]

The beloved woman alone is the only sight
What is the point of different other sights?
[The sight] by which nirvāṇa is attained
is even with a mind that is full of passion[2333] [16]

Abandon dharma as well as nondharma
Abandon both, the truth as well as fiction
Having abandoned both, truth and fiction,
abandon that by which you abandon them[2334] [17]

In the *Bhagavadgītā* too, [this is proclaimed]:

There's no nonexistent's being,
nor any nonbeing of an existent
The end of both of these is seen
by those who see the true reality[2335] [18]

Moreover, if this were said to be Akṣobhya—
the mind, empty of the perceived and so on—
this is invalidated through our own scriptures,
because it would lack the seal of Vajrasattva[2336] [19]

What then is the reason that this is
invariably taught by the teachers?
This is illuminated first by way of
having the tathāgata relief in mind [20]

Being inside the bola is to be with aspect
Being at its tip means to be without aspect
Some claim this as being the very middle
The guru's view is that this is not the case[2337] [21]

Neither inside the vajra, nor at its tip,
nor as having dropped into the kapāla,
nor in between is true reality asserted
As per the guru's mouth, it's in awareness[2338] [22]

"How then could 'variety is known
as various kinds' and so forth and {250}
'within the jewel' and so on be fine?"
Based on a true guru, it's fully coherent[2339] [23]

The master [empowerment] and such are held
by virtue of the purity of smiling and so forth
This is to be established according to creation
and not according to the nature of perfection[2340] [24]

Due to being variegated, variety is up to friction
Due to being bliss, maturation is before the jewel
True reality needs to be understood from the guru
Due to consummation, cessation is in dispassion[2341] [25]

Once you obtained[2342] the karmamudrā,
you should cultivate the dharmamudrā
What is higher than this is mahāmudrā,
from which the samayamudrā arises[2343] [26]

The ecstasies are related to each mudrā,
with the exception of mahāmudrā though,
thanks to the scriptures, self-awareness,
and the pith instructions of the true guru [27]

Variety, [arising] from the karmamudrā,
and maturation are the world's own being[2344]
Characteristics' lack is the stability[2345] in that
Consummation is the looking at the world [28]

Utter nonabiding in anything at all
is proclaimed to be "mahāmudrā"
Since self-awareness is stainless,[2346]
variety and so forth do not arise [29]

Effortless indeed is that which
is called "inconceivable wisdom"
But what is inconceivable, once
conceived, is not inconceivable[2347] [30]

Those who set their eyes on suchness
in line with the very middle's actuality
are the fortunate realizing true reality
If directly known, it is by awareness[2348] [31]

All superimpositions, however many there are,
are not present in any respect in their entirety
The middle's actuality is superimposition's lack—
where could there be removal or accomplishing?[2349] [32] {251}

In that [state] in which there are no superimpositions
of cognition and cognizable, thinking is not otherwise
Everything is just the same way as it had been before,
[but] cognition is certainly not the same as it had been[2350] [33]

As for those who realize the world as unborn,
their mind is simply pure by this realization
For those insightful ones, in an effortless way,
the world is the native state, which is reality[2351] [34]

The thought whose connection has not
yet been perceived arises in dependence
That is, exactly this represents nirvāṇa,
so do not create any delusion, oh mind![2352] [35]

Those who do not abide in the remedies,
who even lack attachment to true reality,
and who have no desire for the fruition,
it is they who will discover[2353] mahāmudrā[2354] [36]

Just as ecstasy and such are arrayed
distinctly within the karmamudrā,
it is the same in the samayamudrā
due to the vajra master's kindness[2355] [37]

Variety constitutes the karmamudrā
The dharmamudrā arises in maturation
Lack of characteristics is mahāmudrā
Consummation is the samaya[mudrā] [38]

Those yogīs who do not know mahāmudrā,
with the karmamudrā as their single device,

fall away from sacred tradition's[2356] true reality
and will then take their journey to Raurava[2357] [39]

For as long as the dust on the feet
of Śabareśa[2358] has not been touched,
for that long the four mudrās and
the four moments are not known[2359] [40]

Having laid out the correct empowerment,
devoid of forceful and poor empowerments,
through the merit that I have accomplished, {252}
may the world come to experience bliss![2360] [41]

This concludes "Instructions on Empowerment" composed by the master and victor Maitrīpa. It was translated, edited, and finalized by the Indian upādhyāya Kṛṣṇa Paṇḍita and the Tibetan lotsāwa Tsültrim Gyalwa.[2361] {253}

(43) A Pith Instruction on Letting Cognizance Be without Projecting and Withdrawing, "The True Secret"[2362]

I pay homage to the true gurus

It is the yogīs who are inconceivable who
suddenly awaken compassion's own mind,
being sealed with the prajñā that is unborn,
characterized by inconceivable nonduality [1]

Through appearances,[2363] they are mindful of the unborn
The nature of mindfulness lacks anything to be grasped
It is through the nature of the entities of form and so on
that the taste of great bliss becomes an experience
It is thereby that the inconceivable yoga is realized [2]

Thanks to the kindness of the guru, once again,
this has the nature of penetrating awakening[2364]
Because it is arising just as it is experienced,
there's nothing for mindfulness to grasp or not grasp[2365] [3]

Because cause and result are inseparable,
there exist no stages of meditation for me
By experiencing the taste of emptiness,
meditation as well represents realization[2366] [4]

For it's by means of cultivating prajñā[2367]
that everything represents mahāmudrā[2368]
Anything among what is unfavorable,
exactly that represents mahāmudrā [too] [5]

Its nature is to be relaxed and inconceivable
As long as the duality of distinctions arises,
it arises from it and[2369] dissolves back into it [6]

Those with completely blissful wisdom[2370]
do not entertain any hope for[2371] a fruition {254}
For yogīs who lack mental engagement—
nothing to think about emptiness's pith [7]

Within this nondual prajñā's own place,
equipoise and aftermath are unsuitable[2372]
The yogīs of the inconceivable stream
don't make it dual, [leaving it in] its own seat [8]

It is what is unborn that awakens as entities,
and entities[2373] dissolve back into the unborn
In fact, it accords with the vajra of nonduality
Being under flaws' sway and such is fleeting [9]

Thus this is straightforward, direct, and fresh—
experience[2374] it and its true reality directly!
Oh yogīs, you who behold what is unborn,
don't grasp cognition, let its own lucidity be![2375] [10]

Within the state of unborn mind as such,
what could be withdrawn, what projected? [11]

This concludes the *Upadeśaparamopāya*,[2376] "*The True Secret*."[2377] {255}

(44) A Commentary on the Four Mudrās, Called "Jewel Heart"

In the language of India: *Caturmudrāṭīkāratnahṛdaya*[2378]
In the language of Tibet: *Phyag rgya bzhi'i rgya cher 'grel pa rin po che'i snying po*

I pay homage to the Bhagavān, the supreme being of speech, Mañjuśrīghoṣa

Dharmadhātu wisdom, difficult to realize, the nature of the five elements,
the wisdom that is the vajra essence's essence, the lotus within the heart,
the principal one within this genuine maṇḍala of blessing that is supreme—
the true guru is the ground from which to extract the essence, so I bow well

By uniting in a nondual way with karma[mudrā], dharma[mudrā], mahāmudrā,[2379] and samaya[mudrā],
which have the character of EVAṂ MAYĀ, the welfares of oneself and others are superbly complete
It is for people who are similar to the master *Sumati that I shall explain this in an excellent manner
This is known to be equal[2380] to having a good family lineage, resembling a garland of kumuda [flowers][2381]

By virtue of being endowed with the flaws
of desire, hatred, nescience, pride, and envy,
I am just a fool who doesn't know anything,
unsuitable to unite[2382] with penetrating insight[2383]

Nevertheless, since the true guru has ordered it {256}
and so that the five realizations of the five arise,
I shall write down the meaning that I have seen
thanks to the tantras' king and the venerable one[2384]

However many deluded flaws this may have,
it is deserving of the supreme venerable one,
the assemblies of vīras, and the yoginīs who
gave me their blessings to be greatly patient

The Bhagavān and Tathāgata Heruka in nondual union, who is endowed with the wisdoms of the inexhaustible secrets of awakened body, speech, and mind, has taught the primordially present siddhi of mahāmudrā (the result) [that arises] from the means for maturation (the cause). In terms of the causal tantra, the instructions that pertain in due order to the practitioners—the persons representing the [psychophysical] supports—who have the highest of highest, highest, medium, and lower fortunes consist of the kriyātantras, caryātantras, yogatantras, yogottara[tantras], and [yoga]niruttaratantras.[2385] By training well in these, the result—the inseparable four kāyas—will emerge. For the following is stated:

> The process that consists of creation
> as well as the process of perfection—
> the vajra holder's dharma instruction
> is based upon these two processes[2386]

The creation process consists of the outer creation process and the inner creation process. The perfection process consists of the perfection process, the full-perfection process, and the essence process. These {257} are to be understood as illusion-like [body], mind focus, vajra recitation, luminosity, and unity, respectively.[2387] By way of karmamudrā, dharmamudrā, mahāmudrā, and samayamudrā, which have the characteristics of EVAṂ MAYĀ, one's own welfare and the welfare of others are to be made consummate.

Thus those who possess understanding should understand the common meaning. This is to be adorned with [the following four] expressions:

(1) subject matter
(2) essence
(3) defining characteristics
(4) the pertinent word

(1) Here, the subject matter is empowerment because the words of the Buddha say the following:

First is the vase empowerment,
second the secret empowerment,
third is indeed the prajñā-jñāna,
and the fourth is again like that[2388]

The main point of empowerment is the connate because [this is declared]:

It is the union[2389] of all buddhas that
is based in the syllables EVAṂ[2390]

For example, the supreme one among all gems is the precious wish-fulfilling jewel that is hard, firm, and blazing, and the connate is just like that. For thus the words of the Buddha say the following:

I am the nature of connate ecstasy,
at supreme's end and cessation's start
In this way, my son, have confidence—
it is similar to a lamp in the darkness[2391]

(2) The essence consists of means and prajñā. The words of the Buddha declare this: {258}

It is experience and the lack of nature
that are mutually sealing each other
Means and prajñā not abiding in two
constitutes the essence of the Heruka

Therefore prajñā lacking means entails the extreme of extinction. Means lacking prajñā entails the extreme of permanence. Their unity refers to their being inseparable—that is, the terms vīra and vīrā, lotus and vajra, cause and result, Akṣobhya and Vajradhara,[2392] experience and lack of nature, creation and perfection, saṃsāra and nirvāṇa, entity and emptiness, E and VAṂ, ĀḤ and HŪṂ, sun and moon, the *a*-series and the *ka*-series, and seeming and ultimate are to be matched with means and prajñā, respectively. For the *Mañjuśrīmāyājāla[tantra]* also states this:

By virtue of prajñā, it is not saṃsāra
Due to compassion, no abiding in nirvāṇa
Having abandoned the two extremes,
this constitutes the nonabiding unity[2393]

(3) The defining characteristics are appearance and emptiness. Appearance occurs as the defining characteristic of realizing emptiness and emptiness occurs as the defining characteristic of appearance dawning. Therefore it is to be understood that the three appearances are eminent in that they are empty.[2394] The words of the Buddha say this:

Appearance is superior due to being empty
Being empty is superior due to appearance {259}
Since being superior consists of emptiness,
empty appearance is said to be the Bhagavān

Furthermore, as for the realization of emptiness that is the weightiest one among what arises, the guru[2395] that makes one realize that diversity—these knowable objects that appear as all kinds of things—is of a single taste is emptiness. Therefore it should be understood that appearance-emptiness represents the master. For the words of the Buddha state this:

Yogīs should not be searching for[2396] the guru
Knower and knowable are the supreme guru—
the true one, as they teach[2397] twofold realization
There is no other guru more supreme than this

Furthermore, at the time when there are appearances, they are experienced, and at the time when they are experienced, they are unborn. Therefore these diverse appearances are not actually established: if analyzed in terms of being one or many, they lack any nature. [However,] they are not as absolutely nonexistent as the horns of a rabbit [either] because there are reasonings to establish appearances as emptiness, while a reasoning to establish emptiness as emptiness[2398] is absent. Appearances [occur] from that emptiness: hence, at the time when there are appearances, they are experienced, and this very experience is unborn because it is born from conditions. The *Āryacandrapradīpasūtra* says this:

That which is born from conditions is unborn
It does not possess any nature of being born
That which is born from conditions is empty
Those who understand emptiness are heedful[2399]

Therefore experience does not go beyond experiencing bliss, experiencing emptiness, and experiencing [their] nonduality. {260} For the following is stated by[2400] the Mādhyamika Avalokitavrata:

That which is experienced
you are not able to negate[2401]

Therefore, since appearance-emptiness gives rise to experience, this is to be understood as the instruction.

With regard to that, others think: "[But then] there would be no need for the five kinds of tantra collections that are the means, relying on a guru who is endowed with a lineage would be pointless, and there would be no need for searching for the inexhaustible vajra-chain casket."[2402] This is not the case. This [instruction on appearance-emptiness] is [given] with regard to persons who possess the realization of the path of the dharmamudrā. Therefore the words of the Buddha state this:

> Bathing and cleansing are not needed here,
> nor are austerities and hardships needed here
> There will be accomplishment by always
> uniting with the buddhas and mahāsattvas

Otherwise, beginners rely on true gurus through the approaches that are found in the tantras of the Tathāgata: [their mind streams] need to be moistened by the nectar from his mouth.

(4) The pertinent word [here] consists of [the syllables] E and VAṂ. Through the succession of the four mudrās, in terms of the differences of lotus and vajra, term generality and object generality,[2403] bliss and emptiness, and subject and object, and by virtue of being classified as shapes, sonic phonemes, meanings, and what illustrates, the [two syllables] are to be adopted as the basic ground.[2404] The words of the Buddha declare the following:

> Through resting in union[2405] on the vajra seat,
> the essence of bodhicitta is to be realized {261}

Hence the following—a fully qualified awareness consort, appearances, mind, and aspiration prayers endowed with compassion—constitute the seat. As for the specific meaning, [this is said]:

> The karmamudrā is related to body,
> dharmamudrā is related to speech,
> mahāmudrā is related to the mind,
> and samayamudrā is omnipresent[2406]

Consequently, the Secret Mantrayānas[2407] are where the two kinds of siddhis arise from being preceded by the guru. Hence, since the guru is chief, [these siddhis] must be preceded by speech, and therefore it is reasonable to ascertain the dharmamudrā. Through this, one is able to find the fruition in both [the dharmamudrā] and the karmamudrā.[2408]

Here, the [dharmamudrā] should be understood in terms of

(1) subject matter
(2) pertinent word
(3) essence
(4) defining characteristics
(5) benefit

(1) The subject matter consists of the instructions of the guru that have the nature of sonic phonemes. This is said:

> What is in accord with applying the meaning
> of that which is not contradictory to their own[2409]
> words, to valid cognition, and to the scriptures
> is proclaimed to be the instructions of the guru[2410]

Hence it should be realized that all phenomena are born from conditions other [than themselves], that the essence of true reality[2411] is to be unborn, and that [these two] are not different.

(2) The pertinent word consists of [the syllables] E and VAṂ. The Bhagavān stated this in the *Devendraparipṛcchā[tantra]*:[2412]

> Of all the items of the eighty-four-
> thousand collections of the dharma,
> the two syllables are conveyed as
> the basis of all, father and mother[2413]

{262} Hence this very [word EVAṂ] constitutes the introductory word of the discourses of the Bhagavān or their summarized meaning.

(3) The essence consists of appearance and emptiness, which refers to their nondual union, as stated in the same [text]:

> The syllable E represents the mother,
> and VA[2414] is known to be "the father"
> The bindu represents the two's union
> This union is supremely wonderful[2415]

The union in which there is no notion of duality is connate wisdom.

(4) The defining characteristics consist of what is to be expressed and the means to express it: E, as the essence of emptiness, is what is to be expressed, while VAṂ, as the essence of bliss, is the means to express it. [Furthermore,] the instructions of the guru, in their form of term generalities, should be understood as the means to express, while the bliss-emptiness that is the realization taught by those [instructions], in its form of an object generality, should be known as what is to be expressed.

(5) "Do the means to accomplish awakening exist in those [syllables]?" First, from the EVAṂ that consists of sonic phonemes and their meanings, the four moments arise in a successive manner and, through the arising of the four ecstasies in[2416] those [moments], [all] afflictions including their latent tendencies are relinquished, and thus the fruition—mahāmudrā—dawns all on its own, which is the great significance [of this]. From that [fruition], through the power of aspiration prayers and compassion, the two kinds of form kāyas arise within the appearances of sentient beings, which is the great benefit. This [is said in the *Devendraparipṛcchātantra*]:

> The knowers of true reality who know
> those two syllables, the dharmamudrā,
> will become those who turn the wheel
> of dharma for sentient beings' entirety {263}

Those persons[2417] who lack the ability to engage in this kind of dharmamudrā should engage in the karmamudrā. The [karmamudrā] is suitable[2418] as the exemplifying wisdom and suitable as the dharmodaya, the forceful yoga is rejected while the correct empowerment is established as the exemplifying [wisdom], and [connate ecstasy] is made a living experience by way of connecting with what boosts it.

Here, just as the four moments and the four ecstasies exist[2419] in the dharmamudrā, so they exist in the karmamudrā. Therefore, and because [the connate experienced with a karmamudrā is only] a facsimile [of the actual connate], it is not the actual one: for it is able to illustrate [the actual connate] that is to be illustrated, but what is experienced [with a karmamudrā] is [just] what illustrates [the actual connate]. Also, if [the practice of karmamudrā] is not embraced by [skillful] means, saṃsāra occurs, but if it is embraced by such means, nirvāṇa occurs. For passages such as the following are taught:

> The syllable E is said to be the lotus
> The syllable VA is simply the vajra
> The bindu there represents the seed
> From it, the three worlds come forth[2420]

And:

> The divine syllable E, which is
> adorned with VAṂ at its center,
> [represents all bliss's repository,
> the jewel casket of buddhahood][2421]

[Further] reasons [for this] are that the forceful empowerment is deluded about both the realization[2422] and the sequence [of the four ecstasies], the poor empowerment is deluded about the realization, and the correct empowerment is not deluded about the realization and the sequence.[2423] [Yet another] reason is as follows. By virtue of the union of lotus and vajra [as symbolized by] EVAṂ in its [written] shape[2424] and the distinctions of the moments, the afflictions, including their latent tendencies, are gradually relinquished. What is experienced in that [process] is what illustrates [the actual connate], {264} and this is able to illustrate [the connate] that is to be illustrated.

Those persons who are not able to follow this kind of karmamudrā should engage in the samayamudrā. The three kinds of training, the modes of the four [ways of] being born, the four kinds of yoga, and, in accordance with the faculties of the practitioner, the completion through a single recollection, the threefold ritual, and the arising through five [steps][2425] represent the purification by mind—the dependent [nature]—cleansing the imaginary [nature].

As for the connate [in the context] of the samayamudrā, in the middle of the union of the sun and moon of means and prajñā, there abide the two bindus that have the essence of bliss and emptiness—though they are established as color and shape, what is to be demonstrated in the experience of the specifically characterized [connate] is prajñā-jñāna. Thereby, though it is [only] the exemplifying [wisdom of the connate] that is experienced [here], its being free from thoughts about object generalities and not being experienced [as such thoughts] is to be demonstrated as being born and being unborn, not being different. If becoming familiar with exactly that, it will become the specifically characterized actual [connate]. Those [statements] teach the common meaning [of the tantras] in brief.

Thus those who are endowed with this common meaning [of the tantras] are more distinguished than [those in] the Mahāyāna of the pāramitās, because the *Nayatrayapradīpa* says this:

> Though the goal is the same, since it lacks ignorance,
> since it is abundant in means, since it lacks difficulty,
> and since it is the prerogative of those of sharp faculties,
> it is the Mantrayāna that is more distinguished[2426] {265}

Since the goal—the basic nature of the Madhyamaka of utter nonabiding and the basic nature of mahāmudrā—is free from creating and blocking [or affirmation and negation],[2427] [the goal] is the same, but there is a difference with regard to the path of persons at the time of accomplishing [that goal]. Madhyamaka is ascertained through scriptures and reasonings, so it [still] represents ignorance, whereas this [Mantrayāna] is not ignorant, because it is more distinguished by virtue of the [special] instructions. For the words of the Buddha say the following:

> Because of having a lineage with great blessings,
> possessing the pith instructions of empowerment,
> being made comprehended by means of symbols,
> and experiencing the marks, there is no ignorance

[In] the Pāramitāyāna, what serve as the means are generosity, discipline, patience, vigor, dhyāna, and prajñā, which have the nature of the two accumulations. [In] this [Mantrayāna], what serve as the means are the paths of sealing the imaginary [nature] with the samayamudrā, taking afflictions as the path through the karmamudrā, and thoughts blazing as wisdom through the dharmamudrā.

The pāramitās entail difficulties: wishing to relinquish the afflictions that are the factors to be relinquished, one wishes to rely[2428] on the remedies that are the means to relinquish them; hence this is the path of relinquishing the basis,[2429] and it is declared that one will awaken after three incalculable eons. Here, by dealing with those of highest faculties, what is relinquished is the character of mental states involving clinging: {266} since there is awakening through realizing that nondual wisdom isn't anything whatsoever, there is no difficulty.

Even those of medium and lower faculties are able to enter the Pāramitāyāna, but this [Mantrayāna] here is different because it is the experiential sphere of those with highest faculties alone, whereas it is not the experiential [sphere] of others.[2430] Hence, those [statements] express the uncommon meaning [of the tantras].

Now, the meaning of the words [of the *Caturmudrānvaya*] shall be explained. First, in order to make himself be in accord with the way of noble people, to create auspiciousness, and for the sake of pacifying hindrances to himself putting this text together, before engaging in the [actual] task at hand, venerable [Nāgārjuna] utters an homage to the object that is his own chosen deity:

> **Having first paid homage to Vajrasattva,**
> **whose nature consists of pure wisdom**[2431]

First, I shall elucidate the expression of **homage** to the ultimate nature and then the meaning of its words. As for the [first one], it is the dharmakāya that is **pure wisdom**. It is beyond the extremes of existence, nonexistence, both, and neither. It is the domain of stainlessness, devoid of superimposition and denial, beyond any objects of knowing and expression, and not made into an object by the mind: this is mahāmudrā. Its[2432] appearance as the sambhoga[kāya] and the nirmāṇakāya is established by the minds of sentient beings, but since [all three kāyas] consist of the native state, they are inseparable; hence they have the **nature** of the svābhāvikakāya. This is {267} the great bliss of inseparable bliss-emptiness, which is **Vajrasattva**. It should be understood that

["Vajrasattva"] teaches the bliss that entails "vajra"[2433] illustrating emptiness and "sattva" illustrating compassion. For the words of the Buddha declare the following:

> Having a steadfast essence, not being hollow,
> marked by being unbreakable and indivisible,
> being incombustible as well as indestructible,
> emptiness is what is designated as a "vajra"[2434]

Furthermore:

> Blissful mind experiences emptiness—
> sattvas are of altruistic mind thereby
> Bliss and compassion inseparable—
> this represents the sattva of the heart

To pay homage to these in a nondual manner is the most excellent one among all homages because we find this:

> As water is poured into water
> and just as ghee is into ghee,
> Wisdom sees itself on its own,
> which represents homage here[2435]

To elucidate the meaning of the words [of Nāgārjuna's homage], he says "**pure**," and the presentation of the defining characteristics of that is as follows. Since the five skandhas are pure, they are regarded as having the character of the five [buddha] families; since these are pure, they should be seen as Akṣobhya, the essence of consciousness; this in turn should be viewed as self-aware **wisdom**, and all aspects are known to have the nature of that. In those who [know that], from the **vajra** of emptiness that consists of the [three] doors to liberation that are emptiness, signlessness, and wishlessness, the **sattva** of great nonreferential compassion—{268} the assemblies of the sambhoga[kāyas], nirmāṇa[kāyas], and the glorious protectors who are the venerable gurus—[arises]. To them, **homage** is **paid** for the sake of obtaining the common and supreme siddhis. To say this is the purport in dependence on future activity, meaning that once antagonistic factors have been eliminated through the blessings of the special field [of merit] by virtue of the strength of merit, this is the commitment to explain [the text] through the power of vigor.

Purification through the character of sealing is contingent on empowerment. In the approach of gradually entering [the four empowerments], the vase empowerment precedes [the others]. Hence the samayamudrā that represents its cause shall be explained first. Here, empowerment is based on a maṇḍala. Since a vase is the experiential object of persons with coarse thoughts, they should imagine a colored sand maṇḍala.

This has two aspects: approach and accomplishment.[2436] Approach should be understood in terms of time, number, and characteristics. Accomplishment consists of the master's activity ritual and the disciple's ritual of entering [the maṇḍala].

[The master's activity ritual] consists of the ritual of the earth, the preparatory ritual, drawing the line patterns, drawing [the maṇḍala with] colored [sand], blessing the maṇḍala, arranging the vases, the day ritual of the maṇḍala, and the master himself entering [the maṇḍala].

The other one [the disciple's ritual of entering the maṇḍala] consists of [first] entering [the maṇḍala] and [then] the bestowal of the [actual] empowerment [in it].

The first one consists of supplicating, not supplicating, {269} asking about the special point, making an offering, entering inside [the maṇḍala], proclaiming the samaya, taking the oath and pouring the oath water, the command being given, letting wisdom descend, tossing a flower, asking what is seen, removing the blindfold, being empowered as the deity of one's own family, and showing the deity's face.

Second, the bestowal of the [actual] empowerment consists of [bestowing the empowerment of] the vajra disciple and bestowing the empowerment of the [vajra] master. As for the [first one], the water, crown, vajra, lord,[2437] and name empowerments, overcoming the [fivefold] affliction of unawareness (the mental consciousness, the consciousnesses of the five [sense] gates, the afflicted mind, the ālaya-consciousness, and [the duality of] perceiver and perceived), [allow one to] realize the wisdom of awareness (mirror-like [wisdom], [the wisdom of] equality, discriminating [wisdom], all-accomplishing [wisdom], and dharmadhātu wisdom). Since these [wisdoms] arise as the crown ornaments of the five [buddha] families, one is connected to these families as awareness[2438] and the crown ornaments. Therefore, since this is not explained as anything other than the vase empowerment and accomplishment, it is also suitable as the empowerment of the disciple.

Now, it shall be explained [how] thoughts are changed through those [empowerments]. This is stated in the words of the Buddha:

> It is by virtue of pouring and purification that
> it is said to be empowerment with realization

Therefore, [first, during the water empowerment,] by uniting with the maṇḍala of one's own supreme deity in a nondual manner, {270} merely by virtue of pouring the nectar water of the wisdom of melting onto the crown of one's head, the stains of the two kinds of obscurations are washed away through the power of blessing, samādhi, and mantra.

Second, [during the crown empowerment,] until the siddhi of mahāmudrā is attained, the promotion of the welfare of others like a wish-fulfilling tree, and the appearance of qualities of greatness like a precious gem are obtained in an invisible manner, like the uṣṇīṣa on [a buddha's] head.

Third, [the vajra empowerment] is to be understood through symbols—the actuality that is illustrated by those symbols is to be realized. Here, the hub [of the vajra] represents the dharmadhātu free from all extremes. As the symbol for being without a cause, being free from the hosts of thoughts, and not abiding in any extremes of permanence and extinction whatsoever, [the hub] is marked with the syllable HŪṂ.[2439] As for this to be realized, just as a [lotus] fruit comes forth from a lotus, the fruit of the five kinds of skandhas comes forth from the lotus of saṃsāra. Since [the five skandhas] are sealed with the five [buddha] families, [the vajra] has five spokes. Since the [five buddha families] are sealed with Akṣobhya (the essence of consciousness), the four [outer] spokes bend toward the middle. Since the [essence of consciousness, Akṣobhya] is sealed with Vajradhara, the tips of the spokes are each marked with three opened flowers that have the character of the three doors to liberation.

Fourth, [during the lord or bell empowerment,] since they are born from the letter A, all phenomena are unborn. That [the bell] is twelve finger-widths in size [symbolizes that,] through realizing this [being unborn], the twelve [links of] dependent origination, such as ignorance, are terminated. Its being hollow inside {271} [illustrates] not being clearly manifest because its essence is emptiness. Being surrounded by vajras on its [lower] rim means that for as long as saṃsāra exists, it bears the seal of the dharmakāya. Being covered by a lotus on the top [of its body] means that if suchness is realized, one is not tainted by the flaws of saṃsāra even if one relies on the sense pleasures. This means that [the bell] is adorned by the neck of experience, the body of doubtlessness, the lotus of the lack of superimposition,[2440] and the spokes of the five kinds of wisdoms. That sound arises [from it] means that the practitioners who are endowed with said realization are never at any time separated from the sound of emptiness.

Through the fifth [the name empowerment], in casting off one's status, fortune, and previous name, there are three realizations, which means casting off any inferior focus, torments of conduct, and denigrations of the fruition. Being given a [new] name subsequently means not being separated from having faith in [one's own buddha] family at all times.

These [five] constitute the explanation of the empowerment of the vajra disciple.

The [sixth] empowerment of the [vajra] master consists of (1) the three samayas, (2) suitability,[2441] (3) permission, (4) vajra discipline, (5) prophecy, and (6) encouragement and reassurance.

(1) The samaya of mind consists of blessing [the vajra] as the vajra of mind, and the samaya of speech consists of blessing the bell as the vajra of speech, handing them over into the right and left [hands, respectively, of the disciple]. The samaya of body consists of giving the permission to cultivate the pride of the deity of one's own [buddha] family. {272} (2) [As for suitability,] the true reality of the maṇḍala and the true reality of the deity consist of joining with the thirty-seven dharmas concordant with awakening and so on. The means of accomplishment of the maṇḍala[2442] are approach and accomplishment. The activity of the master consists of bestowing empowerment, consecration, fire offering, and so on. As for relying on the five kinds of nectar, one needs to be skilled in

their order and the means to enjoy them. (3) Through the permission, others who have not matured and are not free are matured and freed. (4) Through vajra discipline, one should never be separated from bodhicitta. (5) Through prophecy, irreversibility should be understood. (6) Encouragement and reassurance mean showing that this Mantrayāna is more distinguished than other [yānas] or that one has the status and fortune [for it]. All these [empowerments] are to be performed by using water because the words of the Buddha declare this:

> For the sake[2443] of sentient beings' siddhis,
> empowerment is declared to be fourfold
> The empowerment is designated thus
> because one is besprinkled and abluted[2444]

The [desired] realizations through those [empowerments] are that one should never at any time be separated from experiencing the lack of nature; should explain the eighty[-four]-thousand collections of the dharma and so on; should not be separated from the pride of the deity; should put an end to clinging to what is stable and what is moving; {273} should accomplish the welfare of others from the very beginning by bringing the result onto the path, sealing the imaginary [nature] with the dependent [nature]; should increase nonthought and pacify thoughts; and should be able to pacify wrongdoing, enrich merit, subjugate others, and annihilate antagonistic factors through pacifying, enriching, subjugating, and wrathful activities. These represent the welfare of others. Given that empowerment brings out the special power in those activities,[2445] this is said:

> This is the entirety of all buddhas
> It rests in the hand of Vajrasattva
> You too, always take hold of it!
> Vajrapāṇi's yogic discipline is firm[2446]

In other [approaches], one should [not] cling to saṃsāra,[2447] not fall into levels that are not that, and [rather] turn them into the definitive meaning.[2448] "Other" means "those to be practiced with assiduousness."

Since oneself possesses the pride [of the deity], this is [called] "the empowerment of Vajrasattva"; since it has power, it is [called] "the master empowerment"; since there is connection, it is [called] "the vase empowerment"; since it is special, it is [called] "the unmistaken empowerment"; and since one engages in all kinds of activities, it is called "the cakravartin empowerment." The cause of that is called[2449] "the samayamudrā." This was a brief introduction to the vase empowerment.[2450]

Now, [Nāgārjuna] teaches the commitment to discuss the true reality of yogic discipline:

> **I explain the progression of the four mudrās**
> **briefly for the sake of my own understanding**[2451] {274}

"**Mudrā**" has the meaning of "sealing" and the meaning of "not going beyond" [the dictum of the seal]. The triad of body, speech, and mind is sealed with the connate, [all] appearing and resounding phenomena are sealed with being unborn, experience is sealed with mental nonengagement, and the welfare of others is sealed with the power of aspiration prayers and compassion. Bliss, emptiness, and appearing do not go beyond nonduality. "**Four**" posits a definite number. For by being bestowed as four states by way of being known from four persons and relying on the four empowerments and the four maṇḍalas, the four [kinds of] antagonistic factors become pure and one possesses the four instructions, through which the fruition—the four kāyas—dawns all on its own. "**The progression**" refers to progressive engagement. "**The sake**" refers to the meaning of the five kinds of tantra collections.[2452] This is contained in the path of a person. Since others have very weak faculties and do not possess the fortune [for this], it is not suitable [for them], and hence realization will not arise. Nevertheless, [the composition of this text] is **for the sake of my own**—venerable [Nāgārjuna's]—**understanding**. This is not to dismiss others who have the fortune [for this]—**I** also **explain** this so that it becomes something that is for their sake. This is said:

> One should explain by having a subject matter
> that is not meaningless, does not lack a purpose,
> and possesses a special purpose and connection[2453]

The gist of this consists of the subject matter, the purpose, the purpose of the purpose, and the connection. Here, {275} the first one consists of what is to be expressed and the means to express it. That is, the cause, the path, and the result of secret mantra are [expressed] through aspects that are term generalities, aspects that are object generalities, specifically characterized sounds, and specifically characterized referents. By virtue of the certainty that is uncommon, the experience of the generality aspect of bliss-emptiness,[2454] and this becoming a specifically characterized phenomenon, the welfare of others arises and one is able to demonstrate the connection, the acquaintance [with this], and the special meaning—this is the meaning of mere indispensability. For this is said:

Since one is not incapable of practicing it,
it is not meaningless, not inferior, and so on,
it is indeed appropriate to endeavor in this
dharma here that is endowed with meaning[2455]

Now, the synopsis of the text is taught. Others may think: "There is no special purpose in teaching this dharma." [In answer, Nāgārjuna] teaches the following:

> **Here, in order that the fools who are deluded and ignorant about the succession of the four mudrās, are very ignorant about it, are associated with hardships, suffer very much in the ocean of saṃsāric existence, and roam in it may realize and understand the meanings of the four mudrās as bliss . . .**[2456]

Here—on this special path—**the fools** are those who are nescient and [have] the [other features] following below. **The four mudrās** have already been explained. [These fools] **are deluded** about **the succession of** the four moments **and ignorant about** realization—{276} since they are thus not different from the outsiders [in that regard], this refers to the forceful empowerment. "**Very ignorant**" refers to the poor empowerments, because after not being deluded about the succession, they are [still] not suitable.[2457] "**Associated with hardships**" refers to the

Yogācāras and Mādhyamikas, because it is declared that they will be buddhas [only] after three incalculable eons. "**Suffer very much in the ocean of saṃsāric existence**" refers to the western and the Kashmiri Vaibhāṣikas: through the disease of views about a self, they suffer very much in the difficult-to-cross ocean of saṃsāric existence with its three realms and are devoid of happiness. "**Roam**" refers to outsiders and ordinary beings, because [all they do] is meaningless. What arises from the connate (the cause), being unborn (the path), and great bliss (the result) for such people is [in fact] not different—it arises **as bliss**. "**Realize the meanings of the four mudrās**" means that the karmamudrā is [realized] at the time of empowerment, the dharmamudrā [is realized] at the time of dawning as the aspect that is an object generality,[2458] mahāmudrā at the time of the specifically characterized actuality, just as it is, and the samayamudrā at the time of manifestation and maturation. "**In order that they may understand**" means that the first [mudrā] makes bliss understood. The second one makes emptiness understood.[2459] The third one makes their inseparability understood. "**In order that**" {277} refers to the purpose,[2460] which means making fools into people who possess prajñā.

[Objection:] "This contradicts [the Vajrayāna] 'being the sphere of those of highest faculties alone.'" Not so:

The child-like ones who have little insight,
once trained with the instructions' elixir[2461]
by the guru who is similar to their mother,
become a support of the unsurpassed yāna[2462]

Therefore this refers to dependent origination, which pertains to those whose minds have been trained but not to those whose minds have not been trained.

This is not something that [Nāgārjuna] made up by himself: so that it is endowed with authoritativeness, [Nāgārjuna] teaches the phrase "**by following excellent tantras**." Here, "tantra" refers to continuum, which is threefold: having the characteristics of the two processes [of creation and perfection], being inalienable, and cutting through what is other [than it]. "Excellent" means that [Nāgārjuna] composed [this text] by following the father tantra *Guhyasamāja*, the mother tantra *Cakrasaṃvara*, and the [*Hevajratantra* in] Thirty-Two Chapters.[2463]

[Some] may think: "Though [this text] is associated with those tantras, is it not the case that it teaches the uncommon meaning?" [In answer] to that, the unsurpassable specialness shall be taught, saying "**the means to accomplish the siddhi of great bliss**." "Great bliss" is free from superimposition and denial—the uncontrived wisdom that does not depend on anything else and isn't anything whatsoever. For [this is said]:

> Due to the nature being uncontrived,
> how could it depend on anything else?[2464]

[Objection:] "If entities are without any nature, why do they appear in all kinds of ways?" There is no flaw, {278} because the eyes of ordinary beings are impaired by the blurred vision of ignorance. This comes down to nothing but entities that are without any nature being conceived[2465] as all kinds of natures, whereas such is not the case for yogīs with the eyes of insight free from the stains of ignorance. The words of the Buddha declare this:

> AHO—Samantabhadra's possessing
> the vajras of body, speech, and mind
> is what is proclaimed here[2466] to be birth
> in the manner of being without birth[2467]

Therefore, as for what is unborn appearing as all kinds of things, persons who see just this life do nothing but engage in it merely by way of what appears clearly[2468] in front of them, whereas those who are experts in true actuality [realize its] being unborn. Having realized that, to not [even] cling to just that is great bliss. "Siddhi" refers to the supreme siddhi, the fourteenth bhūmi.[2469]

"**That is swiftly accomplished in this way**" refers to the means of being endowed with the fifth.[2470] To those who think, "Though the true reality of the tantras and instructions exists, [the author] does not possess the qualification to compose [this text]," the following is to be explained.

"It is composed by being associated with the supreme actuality" means that seeing the true reality of all phenomena—the highest actuality that was not seen before—constitutes the path of seeing, which is the wisdom of emptiness. The words of the Buddha state this:

> Being free of the entirety of all being
> and being devoid of skandhas, dhātus,
> āyatanas, and perceiver and perceived,
> due to phenomenal selflessness's equality,
> your own mind, unborn from the origin, {279}
> in its own nature consists of emptiness[2471]

Thus [Nāgārjuna] composed [this text] by being associated with that [true reality]—these [words] by venerable [Nāgārjuna] do not represent a treatise that is meaningless.

"Which[2472] persons should practice that [treatise]?"

> **In order to obtain [this], those with supreme faculties should practice intensely by being in accord with a true [guru].**

This is established through the power of what preceded it. That is, those who have [previously] relied on spiritual friends, gathered the two accumulations, trained in the native state, and made great aspiration prayers then have respect for the guru, are certain about the teachings, experience [what is said in] the instructions, and are not afraid of what is profound: they are **those with supreme faculties**—they practice **in order to obtain** what is to be accomplished. [But] if they do not have a guru, they will not obtain any siddhis—so they **should practice intensely by being in accord with a true** guru who has a lineage, whose blessings are like medicine, and who is skilled and taintless.[2473] These [passages] teach the purpose [of the text], including its authoritativeness.

Now, in order to facilitate realization,[2474] the following brief introduction shall be given:

> **Here, "the four mudrās" are the karmamudrā, dharmamudrā, mahāmudrā, and samayamudrā.**

"**Karma**" refers to bliss and "**mudrā**" to gauging [this bliss] at the crucial point in time.[2475] "**Dharma**" refers to realizing the skandhas and so on to be unborn, and "**mudrā**" to gauging this through the instructions of the guru. "**Mahā**" refers to nondual bliss-emptiness, and "**mudrā**" {280} to gauging the view through mental nonengagement. "**Samaya**" has the meaning of excellence, and "**mudrā**" refers to gauging the welfare of others through the two kinds of form kāyas.

Now, this is explained in detail:

> **Here, the karmamudrā's own essence is to be examined. "Karma" refers to [what occurs] equally in the triad of body, speech, and mind, with intention being primary. "Mudrā" refers to its own essence being examined through the guru's instructions.**

"**The karmamudrā's own essence**" is the connate: it **is to be examined** through yogas other [than it]. "Yoga" is to be understood as **karma** ("action"). [The actions of] the **body** consist of the eyes gazing, the tongue sucking, the teeth biting the lower lip, kissing, embracing, caressing the breasts, tickling, and the friction of the bola in the kakkola. [The actions of] **speech** consist of passionate talk and the vajra recitation. [The actions of] **mind** consist of blessing vajra and lotus and having the mindset of being perfect buddhas.

These should also be known in the context of the inner secret empowerment. "In dependence on the inner one, is there an outer one?" There are also those who have not been matured[2476] in dependence on the outer one. The words of the Buddha say this:

> From that, the maṇḍala is to be constructed
> three cubits and three thumb-widths in size
>
> A divine awareness consort born from the
> five families should be introduced into it[2477]

This refers to the vase empowerment explained above. [However,] it is not that those who are not matured {281} do not also receive the secret empowerment. This is to be understood from the same [text]:

Or else, the same goes for any
available girl of sixteen years
As long as she possesses śukra,
that long the mudrā is served[2478]

[In] the outer secret empowerment, the bodhicitta that is the transformation of EVAṂ MAYĀ in the union of the male and female masters is to be taken from the lotus and the vajra with the tip of the tongue.[2479] By applying this three times, it will become the cause for the arising of uncontaminated wisdom. In the words of the Buddha, [this happens] in the following manner:

The face of the mudrā is covered,
and just so is the face of the means
What emerged through service there
is to be ejected in the student's mouth[2480]

Those fortunate students should understand this in the following way:

It should not be taken in the hand,
nor in mother-of-pearl or conches
The tongue should take the nectar
with the aim of boosting strength[2481]

They should not deviate from this point.

[In] the inner secret empowerment, the moment of maturation—supreme ecstasy—is experienced in the lotus, and then this one taste [of supreme ecstasy] that is associated with self-aware wisdom should be reversed with force. The words of the Buddha state this:

Exactly there, equal taste is to be made
the experiential sphere of the disciple[2482]

Therefore this should be realized. "**With intention being primary**" means that the [first] three ecstasies are rendered the essence of the connate, and since the connate {282} is not different from cognition, it is intention; hence it is primary. The words of the Buddha declare this:

It is from self-awareness that wisdom comes,
being free from awareness of self and other,
similar to space, free from stains, and empty,
the supreme character of being and nonbeing
It represents the blending of prajñā and means,
as well as the fusion of passion and dispassion

This is the life force of those with a life force,
and it is the imperishable one that is supreme
It constitutes that which pervades everything
and resides within all bodies in their entirety

Both being and nonbeing originate from it[2483]

Thus this is to be realized in [or as] what bears the name of the syllable HŪṂ.

"**Mudrā**" **refers to** the awareness of body, speech, and mind. "**Through the pith instructions**" means that the yoga of great passion, which is the opposite of [ordinary] passion,[2484] is embraced **through the guru's instructions**. Through those, the connate's **own essence is examined**.

For those who wonder in what kind of succession the connate arises, the following shall be taught:

From that karmamudrā, the four ecstasies that arise by being distinguished by the distinctions of the moments will arise.[2485]

The distinctions of the moments are four. Since these arise without being mixed with one another, the wisdoms of **the four ecstasies that** are **distinguished by** those times **will arise**. [Some] may wonder from what they arise. For them, this is to be taught:

As for the mudrā[2486] **being concordant, we find this in the words of the Buddha:**

A sixteen-year-old of lovely shape,
once the connate becomes mature[2487]

"**Sixteen**" refers to her **years**—that is, she has the power for the arising of emptiness.[2488] {283} "**Lovely**" means ravishing—that is, she has the power for the arising of bliss. "**Shape**" means that blessings will arise through a **mudrā** who bears the signs of being peaceful, gentle, good-natured, and holding the instructions—that is, she is declared to be the support for becoming nondual with **connate** wisdom.[2489]

[Some] may wonder what the distinctions in terms of time[2490] are like. For them, the four moments are to be taught:

> **The moments are [also] four: variety, maturation, lack of characteristics, and consummation.**

[The four moments of] "**variety**" [and so on, in due order,] consist of clinging to the six forms of existence as different, the aspects of perceiver and perceived being **matured** as emptiness, the **lack of characteristics** of the duo of bliss and emptiness in it being experienced as nonduality, and not being different from mundane cognition, because it does not have any aspect of its own but engages in anything that [seems to] exist.[2491] Since thoughts involve arising and ceasing, they are posited as **moments**. Since they are dissimilar by way of relinquishing afflictions,[2492] it is suitable for them to be distinct.

[Some] may wonder how the wisdom that consists of those times arises. For them, this is to be taught:

> **The ecstasies are four: ecstasy, supreme ecstasy, connate ecstasy, and cessational ecstasy.**

Ecstasy is empty of the perceived. **Supreme ecstasy** is more intense than ecstasy—that is, being empty of perceiver and perceived. **Connate** {284} **ecstasy** is the reversal of the extremes of permanence and extinction—that is, being connate with all phenomena. From its own side, **cessational ecstasy** lacks ecstasy, but it has the mindset of identifying[2493] the higher wisdoms.

These [ecstasies] arise from lotus and vajra, but [some] may think that they will not arise from lotus and vajra. For them, this is stated:

Momentary wisdom, great bliss
is what is based within EVAṂ[2494]

Therefore this should be ascertained.

That the moment of consummation[2495] is posited as the third one in the tantras but posited as the fourth one here means that, thanks to the nectar from the mouth of the true guru, the forceful yoga is rejected. It is the supreme [approach] **that** the moment of **the lack of characteristics is taught in the middle** [between maturation and consummation]. Therefore this **is to be understood as the** correct **empowerment**. This is reasonable because [Maitrīpa] states the following:

That there is variety, then maturation,
thirdly, the lack of any characteristics,
and then consummation is to be known
because of rejecting the forceful yoga[2496]

If that were not the case, the following statement would not be tenable:

Knowing what is to be marked[2497] **in the middle**
of the supreme and cessational, stabilize it!

[Objection:] "[But usually] consummation is asserted as the third one." This is clarified by the following words:

If consideration is consummation,
how could it be held to be the third?[2498]

Therefore the forceful yoga lacks reasonings and contradicts the scriptures.

[Objection:] "This [above compound] is in the sixth case [used] in a partitive sense.[2499] {285} This refers to the middle of supreme ecstasy and cessational ecstasy,[2500] in dependence on ecstasy and connate [ecstasy]: since the main one among those [two—supreme ecstasy and cessational ecstasy—] is the third one, it is reasonable to be cessational ecstasy."[2501] This is clarified by the words of the Buddha declaring the following:

> [At] the cessational's start and the supreme's end,
> this is empty yet nonempty, being the Heruka[2502]

[Objection:] "Here, the third one is cessational ecstasy, which, in relation to connate [ecstasy], is the start—that is, the end of supreme [ecstasy]." This is not so—it is clarified by the following statement:

> It is to be marked at the cessational one's
> beginning, free from the three ecstasies[2503]

[Objection:] "This is just as [what we said] above." It is not—this is clarified by the following declaration:

> Consummation is proclaimed to be the
> consideration "I have partaken of bliss"[2504]

Therefore, how could thought be nonthought?[2505] It is not. Hence this is even invalidated by common worldly consensus, and it also contradicts ascertainment[2506] [through scripture and reasonings]. Furthermore, this is declared:

> During variety, there is the first ecstasy;
> during maturation, it is supreme ecstasy;
> during consummation, cessational ecstasy;
> during characteristics' lack, connate ecstasy[2507]

Therefore cessational ecstasy is [the moment of] consummation. Moreover, the following is stated:

> The first ecstasy has a worldly nature
> Likewise, supreme ecstasy is worldly
> Cessational ecstasy is worldly as well
> The connate is not found in these three[2508]

Hence cessational ecstasy is taught to be saṃsāric.

Now, if cessational ecstasy were the third one, this would contradict the tantras that teach connate [ecstasy] to be thought-free, {286} and thus the following statement would not be tenable:

> I have the nature of connate ecstasy,
> at supreme's end and cessation's start[2509]

Therefore [Maitrīpa] says this:

> For there, there is no consideration—
> awareness is to be characteristics' lack
>
> Therefore, look! It is proper to understand
> the lack of characteristics as the third one
> This is established through self-awareness,
> and the scriptures' meaning also agrees[2510]

Therefore it should be understood that connate [ecstasy] is the third one. [Nāgārjuna] continues as follows:

> **Hence, the inferior [empowerment] does not entail realization: though the [correct] sequence [of the four ecstasies] abides, it is [therefore] not the correct [empowerment]. In the forceful empowerment, the lack of characteristics and connate [ecstasy] are asserted to be at the end.**

"**The inferior** [empowerment]" refers to the poor [empowerment]. Because of not being sealed [by emptiness], apart from mere experience, [the forceful empowerment] **does not entail** the **realization** of nonduality. Therefore, **though** it **abides** by way of **the** [correct] **sequence**[2511] of the moments and the ecstasies, it does not entail [the correct] meaning [of realization]: **it is not the correct** [empowerment], just like saying that an outcaste is a king.

"**Forceful**" means to be performed by force. **In the** [forceful] **empowerment**, the moment of **the lack of characteristics and connate** ecstasy **are asserted to be at the end**. Hence it is also deluded about the sequence, and the realization is [as deficient] as above [in the poor empowerment]—it is definitely not the excellent [empowerment]. Any assertions that are other than this are to be refuted by us. This is clarified by [Maitrīpa] saying this:

Being inside the bola is to be with aspect
Being at its tip means to be without aspect
Some claim this as being the very middle {287}
The guru's view is that this is not the case[2512]

"Why is that?" Because for them nothing but clinging[2513] is the main thing, and because going beyond that means to fall into the extreme of extinction. [Maitrīpa] states this:

Neither inside the vajra, nor at its tip,
nor as having dropped into the kapāla,
nor in between is true reality asserted
As per the guru's mouth, it's in awareness[2514]

This refers to the Bhagavān who is the holder of sixteen bindus twice halved.[2515] This is to be realized from the mouth of the guru:

Once two have passed, two are even
Falling from the vajra, they touch the lotus

Falling from the vajra is Akṣobhya
Touching the lotus is Vajra[sattva]
The cause is sealed with the result and
the result is also sealed with the cause—
this represents the king of great bliss[2516]

Therefore it should be understood that the actuality that is like a gem is found.

[Objection:] "The tantras represent the definitive meaning, but here they become of expedient meaning. Or, endeavoring [in this] is meaningless, being deluded." It is not so: this is the meaning that is to be understood from the [guru's] mouth because the Mantrayāna depends on the guru's mouth and because others' engagement in it with a mind proud of [its own] prajñā is to be relinquished.

[Objection:] "It is not reasonable to formulate [the above as] the forceful empowerment, because it is established in actuality."[2517] No—since certainty is established in dependence, venerable [Nāgārjuna] taught just as [the Buddha] has taught through true statements:[2518]

> **Just as the Bhagavān taught certainty about empowerment and what is concordant with it,** {288} **I explain these here in detail.**

This is easy to understand.

Now, it is to be taught[2519] that [the connate experienced with a karmamudrā] is [just] a resemblance[2520] of the [actual] connate:

> **Having understood the practice from the mouth of the guru, the meaning of realization is to be explained. In their entirety, the two theses of the opponents and [our own] assertion [of the correct empowerment] are a resemblance [of the actual connate] because connate wisdom is not found [through them].**

[The karmamudrā is called] "the connate" because what is to be pointed out can be pointed out by way of experiencing what points it out. However, since it is merely similar [to the actual connate], it is not the actual [connate], and therefore [connate] **wisdom is not found** [through it]; thus it **is a resemblance** of the dharmamudrā. [Some] may think that it cannot be pointed out through mere similarity. [But this is possible] because the connate that is a resemblance, by virtue of being **similar to the** [actual] **connate, leads to realizing** [connate] **wisdom**. For through realizing the exemplifying connate that is a resemblance, like [a reflection of] the moon in water, the actual connate can be pointed out like the moon in the sky.

"What is the reason for positing the exemplifying wisdom of karmamudrā as a resemblance?" Therefore [Nāgārjuna] teaches this:

> **To speak of the connate as a resemblance refers to prajñā.**

Prajñā[2521] refers to karmamudrā: this is reasonable because[2522] the wisdom that arises from her arises from conditions that are other [than the connate], is [dangerously] close to the razor of passion, is deliberately contrived, and arises from a woman who is an [actual] human. Therefore this is taught by the following:

> **The wisdom that is based on a prajñā {289} is prajñā wisdom.**[2523]

"Can the actual wisdom be pointed out by that?[2524] How can the actual wisdom—the dharmamudrā—be pointed out? What is the actual wisdom like?" Therefore this is to be taught:

> **The connate wisdom that is demonstrated by prajñā wisdom is unborn.**

"Why is the dharmamudrā taught to be the connate?" [Nāgārjuna] says this:

> **For, given that it is the connate, it is all phenomena's own nature: since it is uncontrived, inasmuch as that, its own characteristic is pure.**

"**For**" means that it is reasonable [for the dharmamudrā] to be posited [as the connate], in that this has a reason. Since being unborn and free from discursiveness[2525] is **connate** with the skandhas and so on, **it is all phenomena's own nature**: at the time of it appearing as all kinds of things, it consists of phenomena, but by analyzing them, they are unborn. Therefore they are the connate. "How is it made a living experience?" "**Since it is uncontrived**"—that is, cognitions by virtue of any efforts of the triad of body, speech, and mind cannot express it as something other, cannot express it by something other, cannot express something other,[2526] and cannot express it to others. **Inasmuch as that** is concerned, the dharmamudrā is the connate: because of being inseparable, **its own characteristic is pure**. The words of the Buddha declare this:

> The connate is not uttered by anyone else,
> and it is not obtained anywhere either {290}
> It is realized by yourself thanks to merit
> and by attending to the guru's observances[2527]

Therefore this is the actual wisdom.

> **Hence, the karmamudrā is able to illustrate what is to be illustrated. Therefore, by having obtained a karmamudrā, the result that is a concordant outflow [of the actual connate] is produced.**

"How is that understood?" "**Because it arises in a way that is similar to its concordant outflow.**" This is easy to understand. [Some] may wonder how it arises. To them, [Nāgārjuna] says this:

> **Because we find this statement:**
>
> **The divine syllable E, which is**
> **adorned with VAṂ at its center,**
> **represents all bliss's repository,**
> **the jewel casket of buddhahood**[2528]

"**E**" refers to E dharmadhātu: phenomena—saṃsāra and nirvāṇa—[arise] within the three doors to liberation[2529] because this is the expanse in which they all originate. "**The attire**" refers to being in accord with the yogic disciplines and the requisite number of years that derive from the five [buddha] families. "**Excellent**" means fully qualified, which refers to the following statement:

> Whitish, light-blue, blond-bronze hair,
> with firm breasts and a slender waist,
> the bhaga in the manner of a vast coil,
> a beautiful face, a skilled disposition,
>
> devoted, compassionate, gathering accumulations,
> vigorous,
> a gentle mind stream, knowing bodhicitta,
> being neither overly long nor overly short,
> having rid the flaws of anger and afflictions,

youthful, being endowed with samādhi,
displaying her respect toward the vīras,
detached from passion, altruistic mind— {291}
she represents the supreme companion[2530]

"**Center**" refers to the **repository** of the bindu of great bliss maturing into the bliss that has the character of emptiness filled with bliss[2531]—the kakkola that has the character of E. What will experience that is the bola that has the character of **VAṂ**. From the nondual union of those two,[2532] instantaneously, what **is adorned with** the wisdom of ecstasy arises. "**Bliss**" refers to the result. "**All**" means without exception, which refers to [this bliss] having the character[2533] that is the essence of the four kāyas and the five kinds of wisdom. [Thus] the cause and the result are very similar. This is said:

Ecstasy is nirmāṇa, supreme is sambhoga,
the connate constitutes the dharmakāya,
and cessational ecstasy is the svābhāvika

And:

Neither passion, nor dispassion,
nor a middle are to be observed
Thanks to being free of the three,
the connate is called "awakening"[2534]

Therefore it is to be taken as the five wisdoms. "**Buddhahood**" has the sense of what sentient beings arise as. "**Jewel**"[2535] is [said] by virtue of being able to illustrate the actual [connate].[2536] "**Casket**" has the sense of experience arising. This is so because all sentient beings are alike in that mahāmudrā inherently exists in them and since this is what is to be revealed.

If [some people] cling to this as being supreme because it has such benefits, they are to be refuted, as taught by the following:

Similarly, having accomplished the wisdom [that is based on

> **a] prajñā, masters of weak intelligence {292} will not obtain the fruition because they do not possess realization. Nevertheless, saying they have experienced the [actual] connate, satisfaction will arise [in them]. This is similar to the example of the arising of a reflection of a face contingent on a mirror not becoming the [actual] face. For it was neither established before, nor is it established at present.**

As for "**weak intelligence**," intelligence refers to prajñā:[2537] in its sense of penetrating insight into all phenomena, it renders them unborn. To not possess that means "weak." **Having accomplished** the path of learning[2538] by possessing the pith instructions of the vase [empowerment], the secret [empowerment], [the empowerment of] **the wisdom** [that is based on a] **prajñā**, and the fourth [empowerment], such **masters, because they do not possess realization** (the dharmamudrā), lack the [actual] four empowerments and thus **will not obtain the fruition** (mahāmudrā). **Nevertheless**, because they have [a sense of] reassurance and sealing by virtue of **having experienced the** exemplifying connate wisdom at the crucial point in time, **saying** "This is supreme," the pride of having reached the culmination [of actual connate wisdom] **will arise** [in them]. For **example, the arising of an** alike **reflection of a face contingent on** a face, **a mirror**, the space in between, and bright light is nothing but an appearance through the power of dependence on conditions, but it will **not become the** [actual] **face**. Likewise, the exemplifying wisdom **is similar to this** in that it is nothing but an experience by virtue of a collection of conditions, but just that [experience] {293} will not become the actual wisdom that is unborn.[2539] **For it was neither established** [as such] by the buddhas of the past, present, and future in the tantras taught by them or at the time of the third empowerment, **nor is it established** as the actual wisdom by the wise through scriptures, reasonings, the gurus' instructions, and experiences **at** the **present** time.

[Objection:] "[But then] such [wisdom based on a karmamudrā] is not even suitable as an example."[2540] [The answer to that] is taught by this:

> **Thus a face's reflection is to be understood as a mere likeness.**

For though **a face's reflection** that is present in a mirror is contrived, its ability of [assisting in] removing stains from the uncontrived face[2541] is its being present **as a mere likeness**. Likewise, the karmamudrā at the contrived crucial time is able to show the essence of the dharmamudrā—it is to be realized through exactly this likeness.

> **Therefore this is what ascertains[2542] true reality. By being deluded about seeing merely a face's reflection that is a natural outflow [of their actual face], [thinking] they have seen[2543] their own face, worldly people will be satisfied.**

True reality refers to the dharma[mudrā] and mahā[mudrā]—generally [characterized] and specifically characterized bliss-emptiness, respectively. **What ascertains** that actuality **is** the karmamudrā: since it arises from conditions that are other, it is [the connate that comes] from something other. Since it is not the actual [connate], it is a reflection. Since it is what illustrates [the actual connate], it is its natural outflow. Hence, {294} **by being deluded about merely** an example **that is an outflow** [of their actual face], [thinking] **they have seen their own face, worldly people will be satisfied**—they are ignorant. It is solely those who see just this life that are called "worldly people"; since they mostly have little fortune, they are ignorant.[2544] Those who will be satisfied with contaminated bliss by being deluded about the basic nature of things—"the mahāmudrā that exists within us, seeing its own nature by itself"—are fools.

> **Being satisfied and happy with that, they are not even acquainted with a basic account of the dharmamudrā. If the dharmamudrā is not understood, how could uncontrived connate wisdom arise by clinging to nothing but the contrived [practice with a] karmamudrā? It will not.**

"**With that**" refers to the karmamudrā. "**Being satisfied**" means to be immersed in passion. **Happy** by virtue of bliss[2545] means that they do not take relying on the guru and the guru's instructions as the main thing—**they are not even acquainted with a basic account**[2546] **of the**

dharmamudrā. Hence they do not possess realization: since they are not able to experience what is to be known, **the dharmamudrā is not understood**. Consequently, since it is produced by **karmamudrā**, [the resultant experience of bliss] is impermanent; since it is born from conditions, it is [in fact] unborn; and since it is mere bliss, it has an end. Thus, **by** lacking said kind of realization [of the actual connate] and **clinging to nothing but the contrived** cause [of it], **how could uncontrived connate wisdom**—mahāmudrā—{295} **arise** [in such people], since they lack the [proper] path [to realize it]**? It will not.**

Now, it is taught by way of examples that [this connate wisdom] is tenable because it is uncontrived.[2547] "Why is that?" [Nāgārjuna] says this:

> **A result of this same type arises [only] from a cause of its own type, but not from a different one. Rice arises from rice seeds, but not from Kodo millet.**[2548]

This is easy to understand. Therefore [Nāgārjuna] continues:

> **Uncontrived connate wisdom arises from the uncontrived dharmamudrā.**

[Objection:] "Since both the dharma[mudrā] and mahā[mudrā] are uncontrived, they are not suitable as the duo of path and fruition—they are one." This is not so. What is examined [here] is whether they are one as the actual wisdom or in experience. It is true that they are the same ultimately: by virtue of appearance-emptiness being inseparable, bliss-emptiness is inseparable. As for experience, it is reasonable to posit a distinction in terms of generally [characterized] and specifically characterized [bliss-emptiness]. "What is the reason for positing it as such?" Therefore **the uncontrived dharmamudrā** is uncontrived in that it involves being of equal taste [with the actual bliss-emptiness]: it is the generally characterized [bliss-emptiness]. The **uncontrived connate wisdom**—mahāmudrā—that **arises from** that [dharmamudrā] is the specifically characterized [and directly realized bliss-emptiness] that is free from being of [such] equal taste.[2549]

[Some] may think that mahāmudrā will not dawn no matter how one may have trained in the dharmamudrā. For them, this is to be taught:

> **Therefore, if engaging in the dharmamudrā without making a distinction [between cause and result], the result—mahāmudrā—will dawn.** {296}

As for "**engaging in the dharmamudrā without making a distinction,**" [if] no distinction is made between bliss and emptiness thanks to the equal taste of their being nondual, because this [inseparable bliss-emptiness] is experienced through the pith instructions on the fourth ecstasy, and **if** this [inseparable bliss-emptiness] is engaged in without any distraction, **the result—mahāmudrā—will dawn** and emerge all on its own.

[Objection:] "But that contradicts what was explained before." You do not realize[2550] the difference between those: [the stanza] beginning with "The divine syllable E" teaches the qualities of the exemplifying [wisdom]. The meaning of not contradicting this [statement] here has already been explained by [the line] "the jewel casket of buddhahood."

Now, it is taught that if the karmamudrā is associated with the dharmamudrā, it is suitable as the exemplifying [wisdom] that illustrates [the actual wisdom]:

> **The mudrā is a resemblance of buddhahood: it is the basis and the foundation of the jewel of wisdom.**

"**The mudrā**" refers to the awareness consort.[2551] "**Buddhahood**" is the goal. "**Resemblance**" refers to supramundane wisdom. "**The jewel of wisdom**" refers to what is illustrated, which is illustrated by that [supramundane wisdom]. Therefore **it is the basis** for seeing it **and the foundation** for experiencing it.

> **Therefore, since it mimics it, it is its resemblance.**

This means that **since** it lacks the dharmamudrā, **it is** [still] saṃsāric.

Since that exemplifying wisdom is the cause of the arising of supreme wisdom, it is from the lotus of the karmamudrā—the precious source of all buddhas—{297} **that the hosts of ecstasy will arise.**

"**Lotus**" means being stainless—it is that which seizes bliss. For this is said:

OṂ PADMA SUKHĀDHĀRA MAHĀRĀGASUKHAṂDADA CATURĀNANDASVABHAGA VIŚVA HŪṂ HŪṂ HŪṂ KĀRYAṂ KURUṢVA ME[2552]

And:

Seizing the bliss of the five wisdoms,
bestowing bliss through great passion,
the sovereignty over the four ecstasies
is the fruition included within the lotus

"**Of all buddhas**" refers to the buddhahood that is essential reality. "**The source**" labels the source of sentient beings [the lotus] because [buddhahood] is contingent on sheer realization. "**Precious**" means that what is desired[2553] emerges. "**The hosts of ecstasy**" refers to the four [ecstasies]. "**Will arise**" means that they are experienced in a progressive manner. This is also to be understood by the following statement:

Where the tathāgatas have stood,
have wandered around, have sat,
and have slept their lion-like sleep,[2554]
to those locations, I pay homage[2555]

Now, the four ecstasies of the karmamudrā are to be taught:

Here, thanks to the mudrā of EVAṂ (the union of the bola and the kakkola—the churner and[2556] **the churned), by the conventional bodhicitta, which is nondual with the ulti-**

mate that pervades it by not being different [from it], having arrived from the avadhūtī in the interior of the jewel, connate wisdom, which bears the names of the ecstasies that consist of the times of the moments, will arise.

"**E**" refers to prajñā, {298} the locus of the arising of emptiness. "**VAṂ**" refers to means, the locus of bliss. "**The mudrā**" refers to shape. "**The bola and the kakkola**" is a symbolic statement. "**Thanks to the union of the churner and the churned**" refers to friction and special friction.[2557] "**A**" refers to being unborn, "**va**" to bliss, "**dhūtī**" to nonduality empty of duality, and "**conventional**" to being like kunda.[2558] It is **bodhicitta** because it has the power to give rise to wisdom.[2559] As for "**pervades it by not being different [from it]**," wherever they are located in the body, the nāḍīs are pervaded by the bindu, the [bindu] by prajñā, and the [prajñā] by wisdom, and thus they are nondual. That the essence of the four awarenesses as the nature of what arises from the four cakras abides as the four ecstasies concordant with the features of the four mudrās means that the conventional [bodhicitta] **is nondual with the ultimate**. This is declared:

The syllable E is to be known as
earth, karmamudrā, and Locanā,
located within the nirmāṇacakra,
with sixty-four petals in the navel

The syllable VAṂ is to be known as
water, the dharmamudrā, and Māmakī,
being located within the dharmacakra,
in a lotus with eight petals in the heart

The syllable MA is taught to be
fire, mahāmudrā, and Pāṇḍarā,
located in the sambhogacakra,
in a sixteen-petaled lotus in the throat

The syllable YĀ is proclaimed to be
wind, the samayamudrā, and Tārinī,

being located in the mahāsukhacakra,
within a lotus with thirty-two petals[2560]

Therefore this is what is to be realized. "**By having arrived in the interior of the jewel**" refers to two ecstasies: {299} it is the second and the third [ecstasies] that are to be understood implicitly [here].[2561] As for "**consist of the times of the moments**," the moments are four: variety, maturation, lack of characteristics, and consummation. As for the times [of these four moments], [the first one] begins with outer [activities such as] kissing and [lasts] until [the bindu reaches] the neck of the jewel. [The second moment is when the bindu] pervades the interior of the jewel and reaches its end. [The third moment is when every last] scent[2562] of [ordinary] passion has disappeared through the emission of two [bindus] and the unity [of bliss and emptiness is experienced] by virtue of two [bindus] remaining. [The fourth moment is when all bindus] have been fully emitted without any remainder. When what consists of these times and **bears the names ecstasy**, supreme ecstasy, connate ecstasy, and cessational ecstasy[2563] is embraced by the pith instructions on the fourth [ecstasy],[2564] it is the **connate wisdom** that accords with all phenomena.

"Does the forceful yoga (the opponents' thesis) not serve as the concordant outflow that is the exemplifying wisdom?" It is to be taught that it does serve [as such]. As for it serving as **the concordant outflow of the connate, the** four **ecstasies and the four moments,** when being deluded about **prajñā** and ecstasy, also exist in the inferior and **forceful yogas**. Therefore even when one relies on[2565] **a karmamudrā** in the manner of the opponents' thesis, a mere concordant outflow in the form of bodhicitta cannot be dismissed. Hence it is declared that **the connate** arises from something that is similar[2566] to the fully matured **result of concordant outflow**, which is established in dependence [on a karmamudrā]. Consequently, it is reasonable to refute[2567] the authoritativeness[2568] [of the inferior and forceful yogas]. {300} [The fully matured result of concordant outflow] is not something that arises automatically. [Rather,] it is declared that it is by relying on a karmamudrā[2569] [in a proper manner] that the [actual] result of concordant outflow arises.

"Does connate wisdom arise later [than] the experience at the crucial point in time?" [Connate wisdom] is not anything other than what is the main thing at that very time. Therefore [to say] "It simply follows after cessational ecstasy because it is sheer wisdom" means that [such wisdom] becomes an entity. The ascertainment[2570] of this is stated in the words of the Buddha:

> By being stirred by latent tendencies,
> emptiness-wisdom becomes an entity,
> which is similar to water turned into[2571]
> ice by virtue of the force of the wind

"**Latent tendencies**" refers to thinking about distinctions. Since these [latent tendencies] draw in[2572] nondual wisdom, even when the wisdom of emptiness and mindfulness are experienced, at the end, they become entities. This is just as in the example of the water of a stream having turned into chunks of ice through the force of the wind. Therefore one should make efforts in being associated with the path of the dharmamudrā.

As for "**the result of concordant outflow of karmamudrā**," through the power of dependently originating causes, the Bhagavatī who is the ultimate prajñā is experienced. This is like a [result] of concordant outflow that is similar [to its cause].[2573] "**This is the instruction**" because it refutes the forceful yoga. {301} For this is stated:

> The Bhagavatī Prajñā who is propelled
> through the karmic vāyus is experienced
> In just the way this is done, she is seen
> This is known as "concordant outflow"

"**The first one**" refers to the first [mudrā] that serves as one's own welfare by virtue of gradual engagement.

"Through which means should one familiarize with this bodhicitta?" [The means] consists of one's own body that is associated with the means and the body of another that is fully qualified—thus, the karmamudrā is connected with the samaya[mudrā][2574] and also connected with the mahāmudrā of wisdom.[2575] The words of the Buddha say the following:

By the means such as maṇḍala circles
and through the stages of self-blessing,
one should give rise to the bodhicitta
that has uncovered and covered forms[2576]

"What is the specialness of this?"

The covered one has the look of kunda
The uncovered has the nature of bliss[2577]

"As what is the body of another meditated on?"

In the kakkola of a woman, Sukhāvatī,
which has the syllable EVAṂ's form[2578]

"Does bliss arise in that?"

It is by virtue of guarding bliss[2579]
that it is designated "Sukhāvatī"[2580]

"Why is it associated with bliss?"

It is the abode of the buddhas,
bodhisattvas, and vajra holders[2581]

"Nirvāṇa will not arise[2582] in this place of being born into saṃsāra."

Indeed this is what saṃsāra is like
Indeed this is what nirvāṇa is like
Apart from saṃsāra, there isn't a
nirvāṇa that is other, it is declared[2583]

"Saṃsāra {302} will not arise as nirvāṇa."[2584]

Saṃsāra is forms, sounds, and so on
Saṃsāra consists of feelings and such

Saṃsāra is made up by the faculties
Saṃsāra consists of hatred and so on

These phenomena, however, represent nirvāṇa
Due to nescience, they assume saṃsāra's form
Those who are not ignorant keep circling in it
but release saṃsāra by means of purification[2585]

"How is it experienced?"

This release is indeed the bodhicitta
with its uncovered and covered forms[2586]

"By relying on whom is bliss blazing?"

She features a beautiful face and wide eyes,
is adorned with a handsome form and youth,
is dark[2587] complexioned, steadfast, of good family,
and springs from frankincense and camphor[2588]

She has been self-empowered into Hevajra,
has lovely hair, and affection for the sādhaka[2589]

"What is the substance that nurtures bliss like?"

[The yogī] should make her drink alcohol
and then he should likewise drink himself[2590]

"For what purpose should one meditate?"

Thereafter, he should arouse[2591] the mudrā
to accomplish his own and others' good[2592]

"How is this made a living experience?"

Thrusting the bolaka into the kakkola,

they with yogic discipline enact kunduru
The wise ones should not dispose of the
camphor that springs forth in this yoga[2593]

"How is it not disposed of?"

It should not be taken in the hand,
nor in mother-of-pearl or conches
The tongue should take the nectar
with the aim of boosting strength[2594]

"Is it not released all the time?"

When not fivefold equal taste's time, {303}
the bodhicitta should not be released
In the yoga of the perfection process,
however it may be engaged, this is true

Therefore, if this is familiarized with in an attentive and uninterrupted manner,[2595] the supreme siddhi of great bliss will be revealed.

Through the union of the pair of means and prajñā,
the two thumbs are crossed, the fingers evenly raised
The thumbs and ring fingers that rest upon the tongue
block in an equal way—this is what the wise are to do

EVAṂ BOLA KAKKOLA HEḌAṂ IDAṂ[2596] A AṂ

These [passages] constitute the explanation of the karmamudrā.

Having taught the exemplifying connate that illustrates [the actual one] through those [passages], now, the dharma wisdom[2597] that is the path is to be taught. As for "**OṂ The dharmamudrā**," "OṂ" refers to the five kinds of wisdom.

The terminological specifications (1) "mind," (2) "appearance," and (3) "nonduality" are to be taken as having a single essence. (1) Since self-aware and experiencing mind is born by virtue of dependent origination, it is unborn. Not being contingent on anything else, self-awareness is lucid, free from the four extremes, and not tainted by the flaws of perceiver and perceived, and the realization of that is the perfect [nature]. This is its nonaspectarian character. What is other than that is also unborn, aspects and mind are lucidly experienced as being nondual, the mind that is nondual with all kinds of appearances appears as diversity, and appearances are able to perform functions on the level of correct seeming [reality]. This is its aspectarian character. {304}

(2) Appearances that are born by virtue of dependent origination are unborn. Apart from diversity, there is no need for [any other kind of] being unborn; the two of being born and being unborn are not different, the unborn itself dawns as diversity, and one applies oneself assiduously to certain characteristics through certain instructions. This is the second one.

(3) Nonduality is free from superimposition and denial, naturally clear, free from partiality, lucid, empty, blissful, and, if realized by being revealed, constitutes buddhahood. This is the third one.[2598]

In order to teach that [the dharmamudrā] is not other than that, "dharma" refers to the skandhas, dhātus, āyatanas, what originates dependently, and the four elements. The mudrā that seals these consists of the connate wisdom that is realized from the mouth of the guru. Its defining characteristic is taught by the phrase "**it has the dharmadhātu's nature**." The dharmadhātu is the nonduality of bliss and emptiness, which has the defining characteristic of being omnipresent. [The following is said] in the words of the Buddha:

> [All] phenomena are luminous by nature,
> pure from the beginning, similar to space
> There is no awakening or clear realization—
> this is the steadfast approach to awakening[2599]

"Nature" refers to the general aspect of bliss and emptiness. "Through what is this to be realized?" It is to be realized through the four ecstasies, which [Nāgārjuna] states as follows:

> **It is free from discursiveness, nonconceptual, uncontrived, {305} has the nature of compassion, is realized to be supreme[, and is unborn].**[2600]

"**Discursiveness**" means that the connate dawning as diversity represents the moment of variety, which is ecstasy. "**Free from**" means being free from dualistic thoughts—what dawns as diversity is [nothing but] the connate. To realize it as being **nonconceptual** is the moment of maturation, which is supreme ecstasy. "**Uncontrived**" means that by virtue of dualistic appearances having ceased, [the connate] is experienced as nonduality. To not even cling to this as sheer experience represents the moment of the lack of characteristics, which is connate ecstasy. The object of **compassion** consists of all three realms because though the connate is naturally present in those [three realms], [the beings in them] are deluded about it appearing as diversity; thus, it is due to [their] delusion in terms of not realizing this that they are pitiable. "**The nature**" means that what appears as diversity during subsequent attainment [simply] appears as the connate. This is the moment of consummation, which is cessational ecstasy. "**Realized to be supreme**" means to realize through the pith instructions on the fourth [ecstasy] that connate ecstasy as the supreme one is not different from the [other] three [ecstasies in essence]. Thereby, thanks to the cause that consists of compassion for saṃsāric sentient beings,[2601] delusion is realized as supreme [connate ecstasy].

"How does one train in the path of those [ecstasies]?" This is taught by the phrase "**is unborn**," which refers to not being separated from the experience of [everything] being unborn in all respects at all times. For the words of the Buddha state this:

> In phenomena that are without birth,
> there is no being and no[2602] meditation {306}
> Due to union with the state of space,
> they are then proclaimed as "being"[2603]

"What is the fruition of this path of being unborn?" [Nāgārjuna] says "**the unique beauty**." "The unique" refers to nondual wisdom, mahāmudrā. "Beauty" refers to being beautified by the sambhoga[kāya] and nirmāṇakāya. Therefore [the dharmamudrā] constitutes the **means** [for that].

"With how many [characteristics] is this kind of realization endowed?" It is endowed with seven characteristics. (1) Appearances dissolving into being unborn is the constituent of complete enjoyment. (2) Appearance and emptiness not being different is the constituent of union. (3) Their being experienced as not being different is the constituent of bliss. (4) [This bliss] existing in yourself, arising as what is desired, and arising when it is desired is the constituent of being filled with compassion. (5) Bliss-emptiness not being contingent on anything other but existing as being perfect on its own is the constituent of entity.[2604] (6) Never being separated from experience is the constituent of being uninterrupted. (7) Appearances not ceasing at the time of experience is the constituent of being unceasing. The experience through this kind of realization and not being distracted [from it] is called "**being permanent in terms of its continuum**."[2605]

"Through what is this connate that is the dharmamudrā illustrated, and at which time[2606] should it be experienced through what?" This is taught through the following passage:

> **The nature of the connate is what is not different from what arises from the union with the prajñā—that is the dharma-mudrā.** {307}

"**The nature of the connate**" is simply nothing but what has [already] been explained above. As for "**what arises from the union with the prajñā**," "the prajñā" refers to the karmamudrā. "Union" refers to [the union of] bola and kakkola. "What arises from it" means that what is to be illustrated is illustrated by what illustrates it. The means to teach that [the dharmamudrā] **is not different from** this point consist of the aspects that are the term generalities of the guru's instructions teaching bliss-emptiness. The realization by virtue of that[2607]—the aspects that are the object generalities of bliss-emptiness—**is the dharmamudrā**.

[Some] may think that the guru's instructions are not able to dispel delusion. For them, this is to be taught:

> **As for [its characteristic] other than that, similar to the example of sunrays for those who are disturbed by darkness, for those who are disturbed by the delusion of ignorance and who are enmeshed in the infinite web of thoughts, even the**

> **pain of just a speck of delusion is cut through by virtue of the teachings on training connected with the guru's instructions: it is realized by relinquishing the character of the mind.**

"**Other than that**" means that this teaches the power[2608] [of the dharmamudrā], which is other than its essence. As for "**the example . . . for those who are disturbed by darkness**," darkness arises as a matter of course when the light fades away, and to not even see one's hand flexing and extending means to be disturbed. At the time of the essence of darkness becoming pure and utterly lucid[2609] through **sunrays** shining, {308} there is nothing that makes the darkness be dispelled[2610] and nothing that accomplishes the light. **Similar to** that, since beginningless [time], [beings] are oppressed **by the delusion** of thinking about distinctions under the sway **of ignorance**, do not even see a fraction of nondual wisdom, **are disturbed** by all kinds of thoughts, **and are enmeshed**[2611] **in** the [karmic] maturations of **the infinite** afflictions that arise from the **web of thoughts**. **For those, the teachings on training—the** pith **instructions** associated with a lineage that represents the mother who gives birth to unsurpassable and completely perfect awakening, their being **connected with** terms, and the blessings through the body—are like the sun. **By virtue of** their power, **even the pain of just a speck of delusion is cut through**: appearance and emptiness **are realized** to be inseparable **by relinquishing the character of the mind** that makes appearance and emptiness into [distinct] objects.

"How could mentally set-up being become nonbeing?" The words of the Buddha declare this:

> Due to the change of state of the three realms,
> perceiver and perceived are fully relinquished
> Or, the means is the realization that the being
> of everything has the characteristic of nonbeing

Therefore, all this is about is [that kind of] realization. "If all being is primordially nonbeing, what is it that is called 'being'?" This is to be taught: "**By [the entirety of] earth, water, fire, and wind being one**." Earth is hard, {309} making [things] solid. Water is moistening, making [things] grow. Fire is hot, ripening [things]. Wind is moving, making [things] light and stir. Though the entirety of those is not established by[2612] any nature of their own, there is delusion [about them] through the power of latent tendencies. This is what is called "being." "Being one" refers to being sealed by being unborn.

[Objection:] "If the thoughts[2613] of [such] sealing are thoughts by virtue of being, this is like not being able to eliminate poison through poison. If [being] is eliminated through nonbeing,[2614] since this is thought-free, any sealing is not suitable either." That is not so. Being is eliminated through being, just as in the example of washing away stains with stains. For the words of the Buddha say this:

> They are liberated through being itself,
> oh Vajragarbha with great compassion[2615]

Therefore, it is by examining being through being that being is eliminated.

[Objection:] "[Then] it would be reasonable for all [sentient beings in] the three realms to be buddhas because they [already] enjoy being." That is not so either. Those [sentient beings] do not fully understand being—because they conceive [of being], they will not be liberated. Rather, it is those who fully understand [being] that will be liberated. For the words of the Buddha state this:

> They are bound by the bondage of being
> and are liberated by fully understanding it[2616]

"How is there realization through fully understanding this?" This is to be taught: {310}

> **All three worlds' nature of inseparability is connate wisdom [that is waveless].**[2617]

"**World**" refers to the mobile's and immobile's character of being destroyed and supporting.[2618] "**All three**" refers to the desire [realm], form [realm], and formless [realm]. The thoughts of those [realms] consist of the afflictions, including their latent tendencies. Their relinquishment consists of the four moments, including the four ecstasies that come from the guru. What makes them inseparable consists of the pith instructions on the fourth [ecstasy]: **the nature of** the **inseparability** of bliss and emptiness **is connate wisdom**.

"Does such happen merely though teaching the fourth?" No, and the reasons are as follows: [empowerment] is taught as "pouring and washing away," it is beyond the sphere of speech, and those to whom true reality cannot be taught, even if they are taught through the instructions of a guru, are not able to reveal [this true reality] through [just] hearing [about it]. Therefore the words of the Buddha declare the following:

> What is experienced by the speaker is true reality,
> The listener does not see that in a direct manner
> Rather, that which comes forth from terminology
> constitutes nothing but a reflection of thinking[2619]

By having analyzed those [words], possessing the confidence of understanding them, and having gained experience through the pith instructions, one will be endowed with effortless samādhi. There will not be[2620] any contrived thoughts and the **waves** of fabrication will **not** surge—that is, there are none.

"What is the character of that like?" This is to be taught:

> **The character of that does not change into anything other—**
> {311} **it is the inseparability of emptiness and compassion.**

"**Of that**" refers to the connate. "**The character**" refers to the means of resting. "**Anything other**" refers to being made into an object. "**Does not change**" means that it will not be under the sway of permanence and extinction. "**Emptiness**" refers to the realization that all phenomena are unborn. "**Compassion**" refers to the gate that is the cause: the cause of sentient beings' delusion and the cause for one's own experience. "**Inseparability**" means uncontrivedness—that is, nonduality. This is to be elucidated [further]:

The Bhagavān said this in his supreme words:

> **The lalanā abides as having prajñā's**
> **nature and the rasanā as the means**
> **The evil-shaker in the very middle**
> **is free from perceiver and perceived**
>
> **Because this is not dual and the duo is the same,**
> **it is mahāmudrā, which isn't through verbal clues,**
> **the cause and path that brings accomplishment**[2621]

"**Destroy**" refers to the four māras. "**Endowed**" means having six qualities. "**Transcend**" refers to being perceived as the suchness of realization.[2622] "**Words**" means speech. "**Supreme**" means speaking the truth—that is, being without deceit.[2623] "**In**" means that [these statements] are established as the meaning of authoritative[2624] instruction in scriptural and result reasons.[2625] "**The lalanā**" is a nāḍī—the one that conveys blood. The activity of that nāḍī, whose character consists of differentiating prajñā, is performed[2626] by sharp vāyus. The power of the sixteenfold āli[2627] dwells [in it], it is located on the left side, and {312} it experiences the blissful wisdom thanks to an awareness consort. Since these are its main [features], it represents **prajñā**. "**Nature**" refers to [its nature], including its power. "**The rasanā**" is the [nāḍī] that conveys semen. "**The means**" refers to experiencing in the manner of moving and being aware. The power of the fortyfold kāli[2628] dwells [in it], it is located[2629] on the right side, and it experiences the bliss of the conventional kunda-like [bodhicitta]. This means that these are its main [features] and it is contingent on the vīra. "**Abides**" refers to it functioning as the support of bliss-emptiness. "**Evil**" (*sdig*) means "extreme." "**Shaker**" (*spangs pa*) refers to being free from extremes. Being feminine (*ma*) refers to being the source of all qualities.[2630] "**The middle**" refers to the avadhūtī. "**Very**" refers to the vāyu that is inseparable [from the avadhūtī].[2631] "**Perceived**" refers to what is external. "**Perceiver**" refers to what is internal. "**Is free**"[2632] means being released from those two.

This being released **is not dual** as bliss and emptiness [separately]. Nor is it devoid of **that duo**: since [bliss and emptiness] are inseparable, they **are the same**. **Because** of not [even] clinging to just that, it is free from superimposition and denial. Therefore **it is mahāmudrā, which** can**not** be ascertained **through verbal clues**: this is **the cause and path** of maturation [through which mahāmudrā] is **accomplished** as the ultimate.[2633]

"How should one make efforts in that?" [Nāgārjuna] says this:

> **By making efforts in such a way, this serves as the cause for finding the fruition close by. Therefore it should be understood as the path.**

"**In such a way**" means in the way that has been taught above.[2634] "**By making efforts**" means possessing undistracted certainty. "**The fruition**" is mahāmudrā. "**Close by**" refers to this life. "**Finding**" refers to being undeceiving. {313} "**As the cause**" refers to being uncontrived. "**Serves**" refers to being a cause of concordant type. The gist of needing to become familiar with this is expressed as "**it should be understood as the path**."

"What is that path like?" This is to be taught:

> **By being an expert in the path, realization will occur: by having familiarized with it, the inseparability of cessation with the nature of the connate will be directly perceived.**

"**Being an expert in the path**" refers to the means being sealed with prajñā and prajñā being sealed with the means—this is the sealing with nonduality. Here, [first,] the [three] characteristics of encountering appearance, many being of a single taste, and diversity being equivalent are free in their own place, become familiar, and are realized.[2635] Second, the bodily nose tip is incited, self-blessing is incited, and the mental nose tip is incited. Third, bliss and emptiness are of equal taste as nonduality. Since that yields the fruition, [Nāgārjuna] says "**realization will occur: by having familiarized with it**." "**Cessation**" refers to [the cessation of] phenomena that are seen and resound. "**The inseparability with the nature of the connate**" refers to the ultimate dharmamudrā, which **will be directly perceived** by natural mind.

In order to ascertain that,[2636] [Nāgārjuna] says this:

Furthermore, the following is said:

> **There is nothing to be removed in this**
> **and not the slightest that is to be added**
> **Actual reality is to be seen as it really is—**
> **whoever sees actual reality** {314} **is liberated**

"**In this**" refers to the dharmamudrā. As for "**removed**," appearances are the dharmakāya, the guru, the instructions, and the volumes [and thus not to be removed]. If something is a nonexistent, there is no need to remove it, and even if [one tries to] remove an existent, it [can]not be removed. Therefore it is declared that "**there is nothing to be removed**." For the words of the Buddha state this:

> Form lacks a nature of its own, and there is no seer either. There is no sound, nor is there a hearer. There is no smell, nor is there a smeller. There is no taste, nor is there a taster. There is nothing tangible, nor is there a toucher. There is no mind, nor is there anything to mind.

"**Added**" means to meditate—if there are two, it is therefore reasonable [for the one] to meditate [on the other], but since there are no two [here], **there is not the slightest to be** meditated on. For the words of the Buddha declare this:

> There is no meditator and no meditation
> Nor exists there any mantra[2637] or any deity
> It is as the nature of nondiscursiveness
> that mantras and deities take their forms[2638]

Hence, there is not the slightest to be observed [or to be focused on]. Therefore, unborn appearances and unborn mind[2639] not being divided into two is "**actual reality**." Seeing this in the manner of not being anything whatsoever is called "**seen as it really is**." This being revealed is "**seeing actual reality**." Immediately upon that, one will **be liberated** in an instant.[2640] Therefore [Nāgārjuna] {315} continues:

The middle of the pair that consists of the lalanā and the rasanā is the evil-shaker—this is connate wisdom.

This is easy to understand.

"Since this liberation arises from familiarizing, what is this familiarizing like?" [Nāgārjuna] says this:

Always familiarizing with this is similar to Canaracava.

Since **Canaracava**, the king of the country Ramala, had a disease, a seer skilled in [the fields of] knowledge examined him, and the king's minister, his royal brahman priest, gave Canaracava a bowl full of sesame oil and sent the king to the southern region *Prakampa.[2641] Two strong princes brandished very sharp swords and [said to the king]: "If you spill [any oil] while carrying this [bowl] for a yojana,[2642] we will cut your body into a hundred pieces and then, oh father king, you will pass away." Therefore, with his two feet very steady and his two hands very steady, [the king] held [the bowl firmly] on its left and right sides. Holding his mind steady and firm, he did not let his eyes become distracted from the oil toward anything else and thereby reached his destination [without spilling any oil]. Thus the king's illness was cleared away, and then the king[2643] [again] received his sovereign rule over the kingdom from the minister.[2644]

Similar to this example, the dharmakāya king who is in the grip of the disease of thoughts is examined by the guru's knowledge, the minister of ordinary mind looks in the direction of having the realization of equality in the region of great bliss, and [the dharmakāya king] makes his feet of prajñā and means steady through certainty {316} and seizes[2645] the bowl of nonduality with his right and left hands of bliss and emptiness. Holding it firmly without spilling[2646] the oil of experience, he looks [at it] with the two eyes of nondistraction and mental nonengagement, thinking: "Well, if I become separated from the experience of being unborn, the princes of clinging will use their weapons of permanence and extinction and kill me in the two extremes." If the dharmakāya king **familiarizes** by [thinking thus], he will be free from the disease of thoughts and regain his sovereignty over the kingdom of the inseparable three kāyas.

"From where do the means for this arise?" [Nāgārjuna] says this:

The realization of that and all referents constitute the non-dual nature of the connate: engaging in a one-pointed mind is thanks to the instructions of the true guru.

The **realization** and experience **of that** which was taught above will dawn in the following way. **All** outer **referents** such as blue **constitute the nondual nature of the connate**: they become inconceivable. Here, first, there is becoming familiar with the connate, resting in a way of this not being different from thoughts,[2647] thoughts dissolving within experience, and letting be without anything to engage mentally. Once realization has arisen from that, letting be occurs in a way of not being different from the previous mental nonengagement. Such **engaging in a one-pointed mind** will **be** made manifest **thanks to** requesting **the instructions of the true guru** {317} given to the disciple—the actuality of nondiscursiveness—many times, [this actuality] emerging at the time of gaṇacakras, and it emerging without deliberate focusing at the time of conduct through the power of experience blazing.

Therefore the dharmamudrā serves as the cause of inconceivable mahāmudrā.

This is easy to understand.

[Objection:] "Though this is experienced as nonduality when resting in meditative equipoise, since it appears as diversity during subsequent attainment, one is separated from that experience." The following is to be taught:

For the Buddha's words declare this:

Forms, sounds, and so forth are unborn indeed
Should someone become aware of the connate,
when their mind experiences forms and so on,
isn't this an experience entailing[2648] being unborn?

Just as some who have experienced bladder dock,[2649]
even when they just catch sight of something sour,
experience it as entailing the taste of bladder dock,
nondual appearance-emptiness has one taste as bliss

First, by analyzing the meaning one heard from the mouth of the guru with one's own mind, all phenomena (**forms, sounds, and so forth**) are realized to **be unborn**. To experience this meaning as nonduality means that **someone becomes aware of the connate**. By becoming familiar with this, even in the dream state, **when their mind experiences forms and so on, isn't this** the very **experience entailing being unborn?** This is **just as** in the example of **some** men and women {318} **who**, for the reason of **having** previously **experienced bladder dock**, **even when they just catch sight of something** other that is **sour** later, **experience it as entailing**—that is, not being different from—**the taste** they experienced through **bladder dock**. Therefore [the experience of the connate] will not be harmed[2650] by the subsequent attainment during which it dawns as diverse **appearances**, but this will rather serve as an aid for realizing [appearances] to be **nondual** with **emptiness**.

That [Nāgārjuna] speaks of "**the dharmamudrā as the result of maturation**" is due to its suitability for the arising of mahāmudrā, the maturation of gathering the accumulations, the maturation of the instructions taught by the guru, and a great result [arising] from a small action. For the words of the Buddha state this:

> Maturation is the opposite of that—
> a great result despite small action[2651]

"**This is the instruction**" refers to the instruction on the uncontrived general aspect of bliss-emptiness. It **is the second one** because it is contingent on the first one. Through these [passages], the dharmamudrā is explained in a summarized way.

The breasts are two, the palms are two,
the palms are folded and evenly aligned

ARTARTA DUDAE A AṂ SAR[2652]

Now, the fruition—mahāmudrā—is to be taught:

ĀḤ Since "mahāmudrā" is both "great" and a "seal," it is the great seal.

"**ĀḤ**" means *akāmatas*[2653] ĀḤ: being unborn throughout the triad of cause, path, and fruition. Being born from dependent origination and being unborn are not different. "**Seal**" has the meaning of not going beyond—{319} one cannot go beyond it by way of example, pervasion, existence (*yod pa*), or being something (*yin pa*). It is like space, the jewel of the wrestler,[2654] and poison inactivated by a mantra.[2655] It is "**great**" because it is supreme compared to the three great functions[2656] of karma[mudrā], dharma[mudrā], and samaya[mudrā]. **Since both is** the case, **it is the great seal.**

"What are the reasons to posit mahāmudrā as the fruition?" This is to be taught:

It has the essence of lacking any nature of its own and is devoid of superimposition and denial.[2657]

It is suitable as mahāmudrā, and **it lacks any nature of its own**. The moments of variety involving clinging, maturation involving examination and analysis,[2658] and consummation involving perceiver and perceived [still] represent stains, but the state of mind of this [mahāmudrā], which lacks any nature of its own, is suitable to be free from stains. Its essence **is** to be free **of superimposition and denial**. For example, by lighting a fire with all kinds of firewood, they turn into a single flame, and the fire does not remain once the firewood has been consumed. Likewise, all kinds of phenomena turn into the single flame of being unborn[2659] [that arises] from them. Once this being unborn has been realized, it is not even clung to as mere being unborn: it is not clung to as anything whatsoever. Those who realize this have become buddhas, which is contingent on just this realization. Therefore since [the tantras] speak of "perfect buddhahood in a single instant,"[2660] {320} it is reasonable for [mahāmudrā] to be free from any creating and blocking [or affirmation and negation]. "**Devoid**" means "empty."

"What is this mahāmudrā like?" It consists of cutting through any hope—that is, it "**is free from the cognitive obscurations and so forth**."

The cognitive obscurations consist of the very subtle afflictions and secondary afflictions that are difficult to relinquish. "And so forth" refers to the very coarse afflictions and secondary afflictions. "Free" means there is no desire to free oneself from what one should free oneself from—avarice, corrupt discipline, a malicious mind, laziness, distraction, and corrupt prajñā—through [the pāramitās of] generosity and so on: there is no hope for a remedy. There is [also] no thinking that the fruition will be attained by having trained well through these two paths of creation and perfection: there is no hope for true reality. There is [likewise] no thinking that some perfect buddhahood as the fruition will be attained from somewhere outside: there is no hope for a fruition.[2661] This is because the afflictions are taken as the path,[2662] the suchness of all phenomena cannot be meditated on, and great bliss exists inherently.

This [mahāmudrā] is endowed with five features. That it "**is as stainless as the midday sky in autumn**" means that the midday sky at the time of autumn that is unperturbed by clouds, rainbows, mist, fog, and wind (1) is unborn, (2) lacks[2663] a nature of its own, {321} (3) pervades [all] past, present, and future times, (4) is primordially changeless, and (5) pervades all of saṃsāra and nirvāṇa. Likewise, mahāmudrā (1) is not born through any essence. (2) It lacks a nature of its own in terms of existence, nonexistence, both, and neither. (3) It is mahāmudrā throughout [all] times—its time of being in saṃsāra, training [in it on the path], training in a special manner, being unsurpassable, and being revealed. (4) Though diversity appears from this very [mahāmudrā], it lacks even the slightest change, just as in the examples of space never changing from being space despite clouds, rainbows, and so on appearing in it and water never changing from being water [despite] waves, silt, bubbles, ripples, and so on. (5) Just as [mustard] oil pervades white mustard seeds, [mahāmudrā] pervades the [entire] character of saṃsāra. Mahāmudrā simply appears [as saṃsāra's essence], but it is not in the way of a pervader and something pervaded. Therefore this is to be understood from the words of the Buddha:

> I am the expounder, I am the dharma,
> I'm the listener with good assemblies
> I'm the goal, I'm the cosmos' teacher
> I am the world as well as the worldly

I have the nature of connate ecstasy,
at supreme's end and cessation's start
In this way, my son, have confidence—
it is similar to a lamp in the darkness[2664]

"How are the differences of the kāyas posited in that [mahāmudrā]?" This is to be taught: in the phrase "**is the source of all qualities**," {322} "qualities" refers to the dharma[kāya], sambhoga[kāya], nirmāṇa[kāya], and svābhāvika[kāya], which are posited [to be present] in[2665] one's own experience: respectively, they are the freedom from superimposition and denial, experience, appearance as diversity, and the single essence of the natural state. This means being fresh, natural, and relaxed.[2666] [First,] venerable [Saraha] declares this:

Hey, you friends! This connate here
isn't found anywhere else—ask the guru's mouth!

If the ultimate is realized by their mouth's essence,
mind lacks bondage and the breath lacks extinction[2667]

Therefore, this is what the essence of the unborn and unceasing moment is like. Second, venerable [Saraha] says this:

This resembles a crow flying off from a ship—
it keeps circling and then lands right back on it[2668]

Therefore it is inconceivable. Third, venerable [Saraha] states this:

When mind is placid once an elephant is trained,
having stopped coming and going, it is at ease
It is realized like that, so what need for dharma?[2669]

Thus, it is continually blissful and at ease. This [mahāmudrā] is the source of everything because [Saraha] says this:

I, the erudite one, speak without any shame like that[2670]

[Nāgārjuna] continues:

> **The wisdom of this kind of path serves as the foundation of all excellence.**

"**Excellence**" refers to the host of bliss just as desired. "**Of all**" refers to [all] happiness of saṃsāra and the great bliss of nirvāṇa. {323} "**Serves as the foundation**" means being like a gem, which serves as the foundation of the arising [of wealth and happiness]. "How does it serve [as such a foundation]?"[2671] [Nāgārjuna] continues:

> **It is pure, genuine, and inconceivable, the nondual nature of saṃsāra and nirvāṇa.**

"**It is pure**" means being effortless—that is, primordial buddhahood. "**Genuine**" refers to the unity of bliss and emptiness that is free from the extremes of permanence and extinction. "**Inconceivable**" means lacking any extremes of distraction. The words of the Buddha say this:

> The wisdom of all the buddhas
> is without the slightest activity
> Free of distraction's extremes,
> it is the time of inconceivability

For, by virtue of that essence, the character of **saṃsāra** and of thoughts blazes as unborn wisdom; therefore, if **the nature of** [saṃsāra] **and nirvāṇa** being **nondual** is realized, this is the fourteenth bhūmi, and if it is not realized, it is saṃsāra. This is also [declared] by the venerable one from the eastern charnel ground:[2672]

> **Since it is without cause, it is primordial buddhahood—that is, pure. Since it exists inherently in all sentient beings, it is genuine. "Not" refers to [not] being suitable as belonging to the sphere of speech. Since it has discriminating prajñā, it is free from all extremes—that is, inconceivable. Since this very experience is experienced at all times like a river stream, it is**

not divided by duality—it is the nondual nature of saṃsāra and nirvāṇa. {324}

"Does the welfare of others arise from this?" This is to be taught: "**It embodies nonreferential great compassion**." Through the power of nonreferential great compassion and extraordinary aspiration prayers, its embodiments—the two rūpakāyas—respectively arise from the very pure and pure appearances [of those to be guided].

"Is this embodiment something other than true reality?" This is to be taught: "**It is the essence that is the nature of great bliss**." Great bliss constitutes the kāya of not mentally engaging in the freedom from superimposition and denial. That which is its nature consists of the form kāyas—that is, it is their essence.

"What is the point of such arrogant opposition to mental engagement?" This is to be taught:

The words of the Buddha declare this:

The dharmas of mental nonengagement are virtuous
The dharmas of mental engagement are nonvirtuous

Amanasi[2673] is to be understood through its distinct designations and terms. In that regard, *a* means being unborn. *Mana* means mentation—that is, thoughts. *Si* means engagement [in that]. Therefore, since thoughts and engagement obstruct *a*, they are negated as being true reality, and hence this constitutes **mental nonengagement**. Therefore, since nonengagement refers to being without[2674] engagement and engagement is not engaged in, this **is virtuous**. The antagonistic factors that are other are called *manasi*[2675]—that is, engagement in thoughts.[2676] These are **the dharmas of mental engagement**: since they arise as **nonvirtuous** [dharmas], {325} they should be regarded[2677] as saṃsāra.

"This cannot [actually] be put into practice, similar to [fetching] the jewel on the crown of the head of [the nāga king] Takṣaka."[2678] This is not so. It is through the kindness of the venerable true guru that [mahāmudrā,] which is characterized[2679] by being endowed with all supreme aspects, can be experienced.

[Objection:] "Why is mahāmudrā then not posited as [all] four moments?" Because it is stainless and self-awareness.[2680]

[Objection:] "But then it is improper to conceive [of anything,] because if one conceives [of anything], [this conceiving] arises as a stain." [Mahāmudrā] is the inconceivable wisdom that is nonabiding and free from effort: it is familiarized with in the way of it not arising from analysis. [Objection:] "After what is conceivable has been analyzed, it is [only] at the [subsequent] time of no conception that conceiving does not occur." This effortless wisdom is described as being nonconceptual.[2681] Therefore there is no cause for anything to be conceived.

[Objection:] "It is not that there is nothing to be conceived because there is no cause [of it]—there is [a cause]. [But your position] will be an extinction." This is not so. Since suchness—the true end—is experienced by directly perceiving it, this will not be an [extinction].

[Objection:] "But then this is no different than [the doctrine of mere] cognizance." Here, even being illusion-like is a superimposition—there is no clinging to any superimpositions in Madhyamaka.

"So what difference is there between Yogācāra and Madhyamaka?" [The doctrine of mere] cognizance [claims] that the actually existent cognition that is [not] imagined by thoughts represents self-awareness,[2682] that the existence of entities by virtue of the latent tendencies of ignorance represents the subsequent attainment, {326} and that the experience of a compound of aspects and nonduality is lucidity, but that is nonrealization.

Madhyamaka uses conventional terms on the level of the seeming for the welfare of sentient beings. In order for childish beings to see "the ultimate," everything, for as long as it is made into an object by the mind, is labeled as "the seeming." Since [all] this appears in [the context of] a mere collection of favorable conditions and the continuum of appearances is something that bears the feature of being deceiving, it is to be seen as an illusion. Contingent on itself, it is posited as being momentary, and since it has parts, it lacks any nature of its own. It is beyond permanence, extinction, both, and neither:[2683] it is nonnominal ultimate reality, and its dimension of stainlessness that [can]not be made into an object by the mind is free from superimposition and denial.

For example, at the time of having the notion that a mirage is water, there is no water: these two—the notion of it being water and the nonexistence of water—are not different. There isn't any mirage to be removed or even the slightest water to be accomplished. Likewise, there isn't any saṃsāra to be removed or any nirvāṇa to be accomplished. This constitutes unity: that in which there isn't any notion of duality.

As for this final actuality, [Nāgārjuna] says this:

In the Buddha's words, [the following is declared]:

To what is without imaginary thinking,
the kāya consisting of utter nonabiding,
mentally engaging by lacking minding
and being without focus, I pay homage![2684]

These [lines] should be understood as view, meditation, {327} and conduct being three inseparable [aspects]. The analysis free from duality **that is without any imaginary thinking** represents conduct. The **utter nonabiding** in bliss or emptiness and passion being free of sleep constitute **the kāya** of great bliss, which is the view. **Mentally engaging by lacking** any **minding** of the sequential order of preparation, main part, and conclusion constitutes meditation. Not separating [these three] through imagining them as three [distinct things] means to be **without focus**. To familiarize[2685] with that means to **pay homage**. **This** passage **should be understood as mahāmudrā**.

From this mahāmudrā—the great bliss that isn't anything whatsoever—the result that is the supreme samayamudrā will arise.

This is easy to understand.

[Objection:] "It is not suitable for the samayamudrā (cessational ecstasy) to arise from mahāmudrā (the connate)." [Nāgārjuna continues:]

The words of the Buddha [say this]:

If someone wishing for a nyagrodha

> **then plants elephant-head amaranth,**[2686]
> **it will just be elephant-head amaranth:**
> **causes and results cannot be separated**
>
> **Just so, to those wishing to be filled**
> **with bliss, once they have attained**
> **mahāmudrā, without accomplishing,**
> **forms will appear just like a dream**

If some king, aspiring for coolness, out of **the wish for a nyagrodha** tree **plants elephant-head amaranth,**[2687] a nyagrodha [tree] will not[2688] grow: from the cause that is elephant-head amaranth, the result that is a nyagrodha [tree] does not arise. A nyagrodha [tree] {328} will only grow naturally on its own,[2689] but what grows from elephant-head amaranth **will just be elephant-head amaranth: causes and results cannot be separated. Likewise, to those wishing** for [both] the state of great renown[2690] and for sentient beings who are other than those [in that state] **to be filled with bliss, once they have attained** supreme **mahāmudrā, without** [needing to] **accomplish** the sambhoga[kāya] and the nirmāṇakāya, **forms** that are **just like a dream will appear** naturally on their own.

ĀḤ This is the instruction on mahāmudrā as the result of stainlessness, which is the third one because it is contingent on the second one.

Having thus taught one's own welfare in a fully complete manner, now, the consummate welfare of others is to be [taught]: "**HŪṂ The samayamudrā**." "HŪṂ" is the syllable of the nondual mind of all tathāgatas. "HA" means causeless because the wisdom of all tathāgatas does not arise from existence, nonexistence, both, or neither. "U" means being free from the hosts of thoughts about permanence, extinction, matter, awareness, saṃsāra, and nirvāṇa. "AṂ"[2691] means being free from all extremes[2692]—great bliss.[2693] This is also to be understood as the way of being of the five kinds of wisdom. Therefore, since it serves as the mother, it gives birth; since it appears as diversity, it emanates; since it is not other[2694] than true reality, it reabsorbs [its emanations]; and since it is specifically characterized, it is the fruitional {329} samayamudrā.

"Samaya" refers to this: with an intention that is motivated by great compassion, to commit[2695] to the welfare of others in front of the master or the Three Jewels, to aspire[2696] for the welfare of others on the worldly plane, and to engage in the welfare of others[2697] after having experienced the dharmamudrā. [Here,] "mudrā" means the following: through the power of such aspiration prayers, to teach the dharma to bodhisattvas on the ten bhūmis through [sambhoga]kāyas that [manifest as] palaces (the support) and circles of deities adorned with the major and minor marks (the supported) and are experiential objects of the sense faculties; to teach the dharma to practitioners by being present[2698] in the forms of their own supreme deities; and to appear as someone like the lion of the Śākyas to those whose appearances are concordant [with him] and as all kinds of things for the [world in] common. These constitute the fruition that is the consummate welfare of others. That is, from the dharmakāya of completely pure mahāmudrā as the chief one, for those with very pure appearances, those with pure appearances, and those with common appearances, respectively, [various] **forms of sambhoga**[kāyas] **and nirmāṇakāyas** will come forth. Therefore master Dharmakīrti says this:

> Hence whatever is intensely meditated on,
> no matter whether it may be real or unreal,
> once the power of meditation is perfected,
> results in a clear mind free from thoughts[2699]

Therefore this is what is to be realized. [Nāgārjuna] continues:

> **Since this is an appearance of mahāmudrā itself, it has its nature.**

This {330} **is** not like some subsequent attainment without any aspects—it is like the precious [wish-fulfilling] jewel, the wish-fulfilling tree, and the excellent [wish-fulfilling] vase. Therefore the result should be understood as the samayamudrā. [Nāgārjuna] continues:

> **By seizing the past continuum for the welfare of sentient beings, this consists of Vajradhara Heruka and so on.**

"**The welfare of sentient beings**" is what is to be accomplished by the followers of the Mahāyāna. **For** that sake, because of compassion and [former] aspiration prayers, **seizing the past**—the chain of these [aspiration prayers and compassion] being uninterrupted as a **continuum**—is the means to accomplish [the welfare of others]. **By** [doing so], what is to be accomplished[2700] **consists of Vajradhara Heruka**, the assemblies of the deities of the four tantra classes, **and so on.**[2701] To emanate in accordance with the realizations[2702] of others represents the samayamudrā of emanation.

"How should one train [in this] at the time of the cause?" This is to be taught:

> **The samayamudrā refers to taking the vajra master empowerment.**

This has already been explained. "What is the path of this like?"

> **Imagining the circles of the deities, the forms of the deities, and the natures of the five wisdoms as the fivefold ritual refers to this becoming mirror-like [wisdom], [the wisdom of] equality, discriminating [wisdom], all-accomplishing [wisdom], and [the wisdom of] the pure dharmadhātu and meditating [on them] in the manner of aspiring.[2703] This consists of the initial yoga, the supreme king of the maṇḍala, and the supreme king of activity. What is imagined in the perfection process consists of the yoga of the bindu and the yoga of the subtle. The masters who familiarize with the samayamudrā {331} will generate great merit.**

Through the vase empowerment, the body is purified. Since this represents the samayamudrā, it involves all kinds of discursive elaborations, and hence is to be practiced by those of lower and medium[2704] fortunes. In taking the vajra master empowerment, one makes the commitment[2705] that oneself will become free and that one frees others. First, in order for this to become mahāmudrā [eventually], one washes and anoints oneself, since these are signs of compassion and becoming a buddha. Since one has the [proper] fortune, [one gives rise to] the pride of the deity. In order to make this auspicious, one gathers the accumulations. In order to make this meaningful, [one cultivates] the four immeasurables. In order to demonstrate the essence of all phenomena, [one familiarizes with] emptiness. In order to pacify obstacles, [one visualizes] the protection circle. Since all phenomena arise from the dharmadhātu whose character consists of the three doors to liberation, one blesses space.

In order to counteract clinging to the support, [one visualizes] the palace. In order to counteract clinging to abodes, [one visualizes] the lotus seat. In order to counteract clinging to mounts, [one visualizes] the sun and moon seats. In order to counteract clinging to clothing, [one visualizes or wears] elephant and tiger hides. In order to counteract clinging to ornaments, [one visualizes or wears] the ornaments of charnel grounds. In order to counteract clinging to anointments, [one visualizes or applies] the anointment with ashes. In order to counteract clinging to fear of being seen [naked], [one visualizes or adopts] the manifestation of nakedness. {332} In order to counteract clinging to retinues, [one visualizes] assemblies of deities. In order to counteract clinging to body, speech, and mind, [one familiarizes with] the three [kinds of] true reality. In order to counteract clinging to the āyatanas, [one visualizes] the six bodhisattvas. In order to counteract clinging to the elements, [one visualizes] the four female deities. In order to counteract clinging to the body, one regards it as a maṇḍala.

For the sake of purifying desire, [one engages in] the yoga of great bliss. For the sake of purifying hatred, [one engages in] the yoga of the Heruka. For the sake of purifying nescience, [one familiarizes with] the true reality of ignorance. For the sake of purifying pride, [one familiarizes with] the experience of being unborn. For the sake of purifying envy, [one familiarizes with] the wisdom of not being distracted from equality.

For the sake of purifying the flaws of killing, [one familiarizes with] the nāḍīcakras. For the sake of purifying taking what was not given, one is mindful of the locations where the vāyus enter and exit. For the sake of purifying impure [sexual] conduct, [one familiarizes with] the subtle bindu. For the sake of purifying lying, [one practices] the vajra recitation. For the sake of purifying slander, one praises the guru. For the sake of purifying idle chatter, [one recites] Vajrasattva's hundred-syllable [mantra]. For the sake of purifying harsh words, [one practices] recitation. For the sake of purifying a covetous mind, one looks at the mind. For the sake of purifying a malicious mind, one looks at the object. For the sake of purifying wrong views, [one familiarizes with] the emptiness that has a heart of compassion.

For the sake of purifying avarice, [one familiarizes with] nonattachment. For the sake of purifying corrupt [discipline], [one familiarizes with] not being separate from a vast mindset. For the sake of purifying anger, {333} one regards everybody as one's own deity. For the sake of purifying laziness, one looks at [the precious human body] that is difficult to attain and will die quickly. For the sake of purifying distraction, one relies on hermitages.[2706] For the sake of purifying thoughts about characteristics, one should analyze whatever may arise.

In order to counteract clinging to food, one should rely on the five kinds of nectars and also make them into gaṇa[cakra offerings]. For the sake of purifying adversities, one should be an expert in the distinctions of symbols.

As for the purposes that are more special than those [mentioned so far], in order to attain the siddhi of mahāmudrā, [one cultivates] the creation process. In order to attain the supreme siddhi, [one cultivates] the creation process.[2707] In order to bring the deity close by, one should perform recitations. In order to accomplish activity, [one offers] oblations. In order to gather[2708] the special accumulation of merit and so on, [one performs] gaṇacakras. In order to swiftly attain siddhis, [one performs] fire offerings. In order to please the guru, [one offers] maṇḍalas. In order to make [everything] auspicious, [one makes] offerings. In order to counteract obstacles, one should perform[2709] the activities related to stūpas. In order to make cognition pellucid,[2710] one reads scriptures. For the sake of attracting disciples, [one performs] the maṇḍala rituals of empowerments. For the sake of becoming an expert in the aspect of activity, one consults the tantras and so on.

By being contingent on oneself, all these {334} are to make other things clearly manifest. On the other hand, to purify oneself,[2711] the five skandhas that are **the forms of the deities** in **the circles of the deities**[2712] are to be sealed with [the buddhas of] the five families: form is Vairocana, feeling is Ratnasambhava, discrimination is Amitābha, formation is Amoghasiddhi, and consciousness is Akṣobhya. These have **the natures of the five wisdoms**: appearing as diversity [is realized as] **mirror-like** [wisdom]; their own essence [is realized as the wisdom of] **equality**; by appearing as the five families, [they are realized] as **discriminating** [wisdom]; by way of enlightened activity, [they are realized as] **all-accomplishing** [wisdom]; and by way of being free from superimposition and denial, they are realized as **the dharmadhātu**. Here, nothing but the explanations of Akṣobhya and Vajradhara are given.

"**Imagining as the fivefold ritual**" refers to fivefold full awakening. This consists of (1) sun and moon adorned with the *a*-series and the *ka*-series,[2713] (2) the globe of their being of equal taste, (3) the mind syllable, (4) the five-pronged vajra, and (5) the fully complete physical form, to be matched respectively with mirror-like [wisdom], [the wisdom of] equality, discriminating [wisdom], all-accomplishing [wisdom], and dharmadhātu wisdom, which have the characters of the following awakenings: generating the mindset for supreme awakening, discriminating the mind, pure awakened speech, awakened mind being utterly inexhaustible, and the supreme [maṇḍala] circle of the awakened body. Their becoming completely pure is similar to a fruit growing from a flower. The way of the sharp {335} is to be one-pointed[2714]—this is the assertion of the masters. It is suitable to familiarize with such because the following is said:

> Put in brief, the five skandhas are
> proclaimed to be the five buddhas
> The vajra āyatanas themselves are
> the supreme bodhisattva maṇḍala[2715]

"**The initial yoga**" consists of yoga and anuyoga.[2716] "**The supreme king of the maṇḍala**" refers to atiyoga. "**The supreme king of activity**" refers to mahātiyoga. Those kinds of paths are to be understood as follows:

> Friends, the moon in water
> is neither real nor delusive
> The maṇḍala circle as well
> is a lucid natureless body

This is declared in the words of the Buddha. Since these [stages] are imaginary, they constitute the creation process.

Now, clearly manifesting what exists is to be taught. "**Perfection**" is within oneself. "**Process**" refers to the succession of the four cakras. What is conceived is EVAṂ MAYĀ. "**The bindu**" is the semen of bodhicitta, which has color and shape. "**The yoga**" [here] is to render bliss and mind not different. "**The subtle**" refers to the vāyus and nāḍīs. The nāḍīs consist of the four kinds of cakras. "**The yoga**" [here] is to unite the mind with these. Since this is free from the extremes of discursiveness, it is **the samayamudrā**. "**Familiarize**" refers to focusing [or visualizing]. "**The masters**" refers to the welfare of others that is disclosed through empowerment. Since these practitioners overcome the afflictions, {336} they **will generate great merit**.

"Is this not the supreme result?" [Nāgārjuna] continues:

> **Though it is like that, [by virtue of that alone], they will not realize the character of the dharmamudrā and the result. This is said: "From a cause that is a specific thing, a specific result will arise."**

Though it is like that—that merit purifies the afflictive obscurations—[by virtue of that alone,] **they will not realize the character of the dharmamudrā** (the general aspect of bliss-emptiness) **and the result** (mahāmudrā, specifically characterized bliss-emptiness). "Why is that?" The samayamudrā involves all kinds of discursiveness, is the experiential object of thoughts, involves clinging, and is a cause of saṃsāra: thus, it is contrived. Therefore **this is said: "From a cause that is a specific** uncontrived **thing, a specific** [uncontrived] **result will** be realized.**"**

[Objection:] "Since it is contrived, it is not even suitable as just the path." [This is not so.] For this is declared:

> In order that childish beings with little insight
> come to understand identitylessness and such,
> by relying on supreme true spiritual friends,
> they should rely on gradual stages accordingly

And in the words of the Buddha we find the following:

> The Sage has made his statements
> that all these constitute mere mind
> in order to remove childish beings'
> fear but not in terms of suchness

Therefore this is the samayamudrā that gives rise to the ultimate lack of nature. This teaches the true reality of entities.

"How are entities {337} included in true reality?" This is to be taught:

> **Therefore, through the nondual taste of the realization of the path[2717] of experiencing the connate, yogīs penetrate [all] mobile and immobile things imagined by childish beings as being true reality—it is exactly this not being different that turns into the gold[2718] of unsurpassable awakening. Through this, the circle[2719] of the threefold world will be contemplated well. Connate ecstasy, the realization of the path of experiencing exactly this, and what is free[2720] from superimposition and denial have the character of being inconceivable. This is attained by having cultivated the supreme siddhi that is directly found.**

"**Childish beings**" are those who are ignorant about true reality. These kinds of people, under the sway of thoughts due to the very dense latent tendencies of ignorance[2721] **imagining** conventions, suffer by viewing all **mobile and immobile things** with clinging. When they **experience** the karmamudrā[2722] that is the exemplifying connate, **through the nondual taste of the connate** that is the dharmamudrā, they **penetrate** everything that is imaginary[2723] as **being true reality**. If what is to be relinquished and what is to be adopted **are not different**, just as in the example of a gold-making elixir turning iron into gold, **exactly this** true state **turns into the gold**[2724] **of unsurpassable awakening. Through this path,**[2725] **the worlds** of desire, form, and formlessness {338} **will be contemplated well** as **the** inseparable **circle** of the **threefold** [kāyas]—the dharma[kāya], sambhoga[kāya], and nirmāṇa[kāya]. At the very time of this **realization**, the exemplifying **connate ecstasy, the realization**[2726] **of the path** of the actuality **of experiencing exactly this** [actual connate] wisdom that is illustrated by that [connate ecstasy], **and** the fruition[2727] of mahāmudrā **that is free from superimposition and denial have the character of being inconceivable**. Those who realize this have [always] been the buddhahood of essential reality before, will be so in the future, and **attain** it at present **by having cultivated the supreme siddhi that is directly found**.

"Is one able to definitely accomplish this?" This is to be taught as follows.

> **Therefore the words of the Buddha [declare this]:**
>
> > **This is the palace, not the body,**[2728] **nor the sense faculties, nor the elements or such,**
> > **nor form and so on, nor living creatures, nor humans or others, but perfect buddhas**
> > **I,**[2729] **the cakra lord, am the dharmakāya; it is not the diversity of all these maṇḍala inhabitants,**
> > **deities, and three realms—if the cakra is realized, how could delusion be created?**[2730]

This—[all] that is imagined—**is the palace**: since it is great bliss itself that appears as the palace, by realizing what the palace is, [yogīs] should be aware of it as being mahāmudrā; however, [when realizing this,] there isn't any palace to be removed[2731] or any great bliss to be accomplished. {339} One's own **body** and those of others are likewise **not** [anything other] either. **Nor** are **the sense faculties** (the eyes, ears, nose, tongue, body, and mind) anything other, just as above. **Nor** are **the elements** (earth, water, fire, and wind) **or such** (the twelvefold dependent origination) anything other. **Nor** are **forms and so on** (sounds, smells, tastes, and tangible objects) anything other. Those who have the life-force prāṇa, happiness and suffering, and birth and death are called "**living creatures**," and they are **not** anything other either. **Nor** are **humans or** those who are **other** than them (gods, asuras, animals, hungry ghosts, and hell beings) anything other. Since [all of them] are free from being other than this very [great bliss] or uniting with it, they are primordially **perfect buddhas**. **The lord** of the deity **cakra** and the maṇḍala, **I**, the yogī, **am the dharmakāya**. Therefore what appears as **the diversity of all these maṇḍalas** (the supports), practitioners, **deities, and three realms**[2732] **is not** anything other. **If realized** as **the cakra** of nonduality, since there is nothing other in any way whatsoever, there is neither anything that **creates delusion**[2733] nor will delusion occur. Given that, [great bliss] is neither anything other than delusion nor does it become delusion.

[Insertion][2734]
Mahāmudrā is pursued above and karmamudrā is pursued below. "How are they pursued?" {340} Since the dharmamudrā is also just as uncontrived as mahāmudrā is uncontrived, [mahāmudrā] is pursued above. Since the four ecstasies exist in the dharmamudrā in just the way they exist in the karmamudrā, [karmamudrā] is pursued below.[2735] Furthermore, since this is preceded by the instructions[2736] of the gurus of the tradition[2737] of secret mantra, two kinds of siddhis arise. Hence, since this must be preceded by the guru's instructions, it is suitable for the dharmamudrā to be ascertained. This should also be understood through the following:

> The karmamudrā is related to body,
> dharmamudrā is related to speech,
> mahāmudrā is related to the mind,
> and samayamudrā is omnipresent[2738]

[The presentation of the four mudrās] consists of the following [five parts]:

1. subject matter
2. the pertinent word
3. essence
4. defining characteristics
5. benefit

1. Here, the subject matter is the general aspect of bliss-emptiness. Since this is contingent on mahāmudrā, the greatness of this general aspect is [the great bliss] that is specifically characterized.

2. The pertinent word is EVAṂ, representing the vowels and the consonants. In utter nonabiding, [this is said]:

> The guru's great speech with blessing
> is the root of the eighty-four-thousand
> collections of the dharma resounding[2739]
> It is the two father and mother syllables,
> which serve as the basis of everything[2740]

Hence everything that exists in the five tantra classes[2741] and so on is included in the pair of the vowels and the consonants, and these are in turn included in the two [syllables] E and VAṂ.

3. As for the essence, by virtue of the guru's instructions being expressed as the nature of sonic phonemes, in the minds of the disciples, {341} what is to be expressed—the aspect of an object generality—dawns as bliss-emptiness.

4. The defining characteristics consist of appearance and emptiness being nondual: emptiness occurs as the defining characteristic of appearance dawning, while appearance arises as the defining characteristic of realizing emptiness. For this [is stated as follows]:

> Empty appearance is said to be the Bhagavān[2742]

Furthermore:

> It is within those phenomena that keep appearing
> as diversity that the state of being unborn is present
> Emptiness and appearance are the same characteristic

5. The benefit is twofold:

a. the great significance
b. the great benefit

5a. As for the great significance, realization dawning in the minds of the disciples through the power of the sonic phonemes of the guru's instructions means that the four ecstasies that consist of the [four] moments arise: dawning as various appearances is ecstasy, thinking that dawning in this way is the connate is supreme ecstasy, being confident about [these appearances] being the connate is connate ecstasy, and dawning as pure appearances[2743] thereafter is cessational ecstasy. The attainment of the dharmakāya—mahāmudrā—as one's own welfare through having familiarized with it while sealing all phenomena with the connate in such a way is the great significance.

5b. Then, through the power of the [former] aspiration prayers for the welfare of sentient beings, the two form kāyas appear as the sambhogakāya and the nirmāṇakāya by virtue of the distinctions of the pure and impure appearances of sentient beings. This is the great benefit.

For those who are not able to engage in this kind of [dharmamudrā], **the karmamudrā is taught, which has four points:**

1. the reason to posit [the karmamudrā] as the dharmodaya
2. this very [karmamudrā] {342} being suitable as the exemplifying wisdom
3. while excluding the two inferior and forceful [empowerments], the wisdom of the correct [empowerment] is suitable as the exemplifying wisdom
4. making [connate ecstasy] a living experience by way of connecting with what boosts it

1. As for positing the [karmamudrā] as the dharmodaya, if one has realization and is embraced by the guru's instructions, nirvāṇa will arise, because the following is said:

> The divine syllable E, which is
> adorned with VAṂ at its center,
> represents all bliss's repository,
> the jewel casket of buddhahood[2744]

If one has no realization and is not embraced by the guru's instructions, saṃsāra will arise. This is stated as follows:

> The syllable E represents the mother
> VAṂ is known as being "the father"

The bindu constitutes the bodhicitta
From it, all of existence comes forth[2745]

Therefore [the karmamudrā] is suitable as the dharmodaya.

2. This very [karmamudrā] is suitable as the exemplifying wisdom because just as the four ecstasies exist in the dharmamudrā, the four ecstasies also exist[2746] in the karmamudrā. For example, just as the [reflection of] the moon in water is able to illustrate the moon in the sky, in the experience of the exemplifying connate [ecstasy] (what illustrates), one is able to illustrate the ultimate connate [ecstasy] (what is illustrated), but this is not the actual [connate ecstasy]. Yet since it is similar, it is suitable as the exemplifying [wisdom]. For [this is said]:

What is similar to the actual
will be based upon examples

3. What is to be posited as the exemplifying [wisdom] is the wisdom of the correct [empowerment] that excludes the two inferior and forceful [empowerments]. The forceful empowerment {343} is deluded about the sequence, the location, and the realization. Being deluded about the sequence means that the moment of the lack of characteristics and connate ecstasy are asserted to be the last, while the moment of consummation and the wisdom of cessational ecstasy are asserted to be the third. Being deluded about the location means being deluded by identifying bodhicitta pervading the jewel of the vajra as connate [ecstasy]. As for being deluded about the realization, bodhicitta pervading the jewel of the vajra is supreme ecstasy, which is realized as sheer self-awareness,[2747] but [here] there is delusion by saying that this is the fundamental state of entities.

Though the poor[2748] empowerment is not deluded about the sequence, it is deluded about the location and the realization. As for the realization, it is asserted that bodhicitta pervading the interior of the jewel is realized as the fundamental state of entities. The location is identified as [bodhicitta] pervading the glans[2749] of the vajra. Therefore those two [empowerments] are not suitable as the exemplifying [wisdom].

The correct empowerment being posited as exemplifying wisdom refers to being without error about [the location of] bodhicitta [and the accompanying realization]. First, [everything] beginning with kissing and embracing until [bodhicitta] pervades up to the neck of the vajra is ecstasy. [Bodhicitta] pervading the interior of the jewel is supreme ecstasy. [The phase when] two [bindus] have been emitted while two remain is connate ecstasy. By two [bindus] having been emitted, any whiff of [ordinary] passion disappears. As for two remaining, the one that remains at the aperture of the lord of the family is the bindu of Akṣobhya {344}—that is, bliss. The one that remains at the crown of the beauty's head[2750] is Vajradhara—that is, emptiness. Taking these two as cause and result, respectively, by the bindu of Vajradhara rendering [the experience of bliss] lacking a nature, the extreme of permanence is eliminated. By the bindu of Akṣobhya sealing the bindu of Vajradhara, its very lacking a nature is to be rendered experience; thus the extreme of extinction is eliminated. This is beyond both permanence and extinction—that is, connate [ecstasy].[2751] For [this is said]:

> The cause is sealed with the result and
> the result is also sealed with the cause—
> this represents the king of great bliss[2752]

Furthermore, utter nonabiding declares the following:

> I have the nature of connate ecstasy,
> at supreme's end and cessation's start,[2753]
> which will be cognized in the middle[2754]
>
> Akṣobhya represents falling from the vajra
> and great Vajradhara is touching the lotus
> By the cause being sealed with the result,
> it is the assertion of Vedānta that is refuted
> By the result being sealed with the cause too,
> the Upaniṣad proponents'[2755] assertion is refuted
> Through duality being sealed with nonduality,
> it is the assertion of Kambala that is refuted[2756]

4. As for making [connate ecstasy] a living experience by way of connecting with what boosts it, by experiencing connate [ecstasy even] through cessational ecstasy, [all] three ecstasies are integrated into or will become connate [ecstasy].[2757] For this is said:

The essence of the entirety of phenomena
should be familiarized with as the connate

Those persons who are not able to engage in such [a practice of karmamudrā] {345} should train in the samayamudrā. Here too, the four ecstasies are counted as follows. First, beginning with gathering the accumulations, the creation of the deity through the fivefold awakening represents ecstasy. Having invited the maṇḍala, it enters through the mouth, and the semen of the deity, having dissolved, fills up the body, which represents supreme ecstasy. To remain as two bindus once oneself [as the deity] has also dissolved represents connate ecstasy. Rearising as the physical form [of the deity] after having been supplicated by the four goddesses represents cessational ecstasy. To integrate the four ecstasies as not being different is the pith instruction on the fourth [ecstasy]. For utter nonabiding [states this]:

The fivefold awakening of mahāmudrā
is nothing but the wisdom of ecstasy
After the buddhas have been assembled
through the light rays of great passion,
the form representing semen's essence
is what constitutes the special ecstasy

[Then] the union of means and prajñā—
red and white bindus at start and end—
has the character of the three syllables
The diversity of the circles of deities
is to be known as cessational ecstasy

Though this is experienced as the shape and color of these kinds of two bindus of the dharmamudrā, doubt about whether the defining characteristics of the two bindus are experienced may arise. Then, in order to experience their defining characteristics, one needs to rely on a karmamudrā and thus experience connate [ecstasy fully]. Though it is the exemplifying wisdom that is experienced through the [karmamudrā], {346} the experience of actual bliss-emptiness free from generic thoughts [about it] is to be demonstrated as the dharmamudrā. That is, the dharmamudrā is the experience [of this] as nondual bliss-emptiness by virtue of demonstrating that it is not different from all arising phenomena. Here too, this is brought onto the path through the four ecstasies, just as it has been taught above that what dawns as diversity represents ecstasy and so on.[2758]

The ascertainment of mahāmudrā has two parts:

1. the persons who are the [psychophysical] supports
2. the instructions for them

1. The persons who are the [psychophysical] supports are those who have made special aspiration prayers before, have gathered the special accumulations, have trained in the native state for a long time, are skilled in relying on the guru's timely means, and are able to engage in the conduct of being victorious in all directions.[2759] For the following is declared:

> The connate is not uttered by anyone else,
> and it is not obtained anywhere either
> It is realized by yourself thanks to merit
> and by attending to the guru's observances[2760]

2. As for the instructions for those [persons], mahāmudrā is to be demonstrated through symbols. This has three parts:

a. the symbol for all phenomena being born
b. the symbol for their being unborn
c. the symbol for experiencing being born and being unborn as nondual

2a. That all phenomena dawn as all kinds of displays is the symbol for their being born.

2b. The realization that these very [phenomena] lack any nature of their own is the symbol for their being unborn.

2c. The experience that unceasing displays and their lack of any nature are nondual is the symbol for [being born and being unborn] not being different.

[Main part:] The pith instructions on bringing these [four mudrās] onto the path have five parts:

1. the pith instructions on the reasons [for positing four mudrās] {347}
2. the pith instructions on pursuing true reality[2761]
3. the pith instructions on the special means[2762]
4. the pith instructions on making [these mudrās] a living experience[2763]
5. the pith instructions on certainty about the instructions arising

1. As for the pith instructions on the reasons, the reasons for positing the mudrās as only four consist of having four [kinds of] persons in mind: persons of inferior fortune aspire for the creation process; those of medium fortune aspire for the nāḍīs, vāyus, and bindus; those of highest fortune give rise to certainty about the guru's pith instructions; and those of very highest fortune are able to make the basic nature a living experience. [In due order,] those [persons] have the ability to make the four mudrās a living experience.[2764]

Here, the four mudrās are taught as follows. The samayamudrā means that all kinds of means serve as the objects of the conceptual [mind]. The karmamudrā means that the experience of bliss serves as an object of thoughts. The dharmamudrā means that the experience of emptiness serves as an object without any cognition of clinging. Mahāmudrā means that the experience of the native state is an object that isn't anything whatsoever. [This is how these four] are to be taught. For the tantras say this:

> Once you obtained the karmamudrā,
> you should cultivate the dharmamudrā
> What is higher than this is mahāmudrā,
> from which the samayamudrā arises[2765]

This is connected to the four empowerments, the four being the vase, secret, and prajñā-jñāna empowerments and the empowerment of pith instructions as the ultimate one. For this [is said]:

As it is linked to water, it is the vase empowerment {348}
Springing from what is secret, it is the secret one
Because of wisdom being born from the shapely
form of a prajñā, exactly this is an empowerment
The one that is present[2766] as the very essence of all
and is the ultimate one is the fourth empowerment

The four empowerments are also connected to the four maṇḍalas: the maṇḍala of colored sand, the maṇḍala of the secret space, the maṇḍala of bodhicitta, and the maṇḍala of inseparable bliss-emptiness.[2767] This [is said]:

The excellent maṇḍala that is secret, as well as
the maṇḍalas of ultimate bindu and inseparability,
are the abodes of granting heart wisdom to oneself

The locations upon which those empowerments are bestowed are four: the vase empowerment is bestowed upon the crown of the head, bodhicitta is offered onto the tongue, the third one is bestowed upon the mind, and the fourth one is bestowed upon the inseparable triad of body, speech, and mind. This [is said]:

Water is poured on the tip of the body
and the inconceivable on speech's tip

Those [empowerments] also purify the four obscurations: they cut through the obscurations of the body, the obscurations of speech, the obscurations of mind, and all superimpositions and denials. This [is said]:

Taking life, taking what is not given,
impure [sexual] conduct, telling lies,
slandering, idle chatter, harsh words,

desire, hatred, malice, wrong views,
extremes of perceiver, perceived, superimposition, and denial—
this is the supreme power of cutting through them all

[Objection:] "But the fourth empowerment alone is surely sufficient—there is no need for those up through the third one." {349} It is taught that they are needed [because] they are the ecstasies of the simultaneist persons in whose mind stream the fourth one arises and because they are the means for the fourth one to arise in the mind stream.

Here, four instructions are taught: the outer creation process (the [actual] creation process), the profound creation process (familiarizing with nāḍīs and vāyus), the full-perfection process (realizing [all] that appears and resounds to be emptiness), and the essence perfection process (being effortless without being contingent on causes and conditions). For this [is said]:

The two of the creation process
and the process of perfection
having outer and inner aspects
and full-perfection and essence

From those [empowerments], four results arise: the nirmāṇakāya, the sambhogakāya, the dharmakāya, and the svābhāvikakāya. For this [is said]:

Diversity arises from diversity
Sukhāvatī is others' aspirations
Qualities arise from the infinite
Inseparability is the sole essence

2. The pith instructions on pursuing true reality have four parts:

a. the pith instructions on pursuing the true reality of the karmamudrā
b. [the pith instructions on pursuing the true reality of] the dharmamudrā

c. [the pith instructions on pursuing the true reality of] mahāmudrā
d. the pith instructions on pursuing the true reality of the samayamudrā

2a. The pith instructions on pursuing the true reality of the karmamudrā have seven parts:

1. action (karma)
2. sealing with which mudrā
3. through what it is accomplished
4. what is accomplished
5. through what it is ascertained
6. what its name is
7. which result is attained[2768]

2a1. As for action, {350} since intention is chief in the triad of body, speech, and mind, the actions of the body consist of [the expressions of] passion: the six yogas of arousal and the union of the churner and the churned. The former one has six parts: scratching with the fingernails, caressing the breasts, embracing, tongue-sucking, biting the lower lip with the teeth, and tickling. [The actions of] speech are two: one should utter common passionate talk and especially do the vajra recitation. [The actions of] the mind are three: identifying the four ecstasies and blessing the lotus and the vajra. With [all] those, intention is chief.

2a2. The mudrā [here] refers to being sealed with the guru's instructions, which are twofold: the genuine union of the two and the special means. The former one has five parts: the equality of body, speech, and mind, the equality of desire, the equality of blessing, the pure mudrā, and being embraced by the guru's instructions. The first consists of equality in that the body is the deity, speech is the vajra recitation, and the mind thinks of identifying the connate. The second is the equality of the desire of thinking: "I shall attain the siddhi of mahāmudrā in this life." The third is equality in that the vajra is blessed by a HŪṂ and the lotus by an ĀḤ. The pure mudrā is a woman with the sixteen [attributes] of the body, the twenty of speech, and the twenty-five of the mind. To be embraced by the guru's instructions means not indulging in the afflictions and not [doing] something like engaging in a self-styled manner. For the tantras say this: {351}

Body, speech, and mind are equal as the victor
The power of intention is to be made excellent
It is from the aspects of prajñā and the means
that the vīra and the vīrā receive the blessings
Body type, speech type, as well as mind type,[2769]
empty, a transitory collection, number of years,
and on top the number of months[2770] are supreme
In whatever conferral of empowerment it may be,
to hold the guru in the highest esteem is supreme

{352}[2771] 2a3. "Through what is [this practice of karmamudrā] accomplished?" It is accomplished through a fully qualified awareness consort. As for "awareness consort," awareness[2772] refers to being aware of the five wisdoms. Since momentary wisdom is free from all superimposition and denial, it is dharmadhātu wisdom. Since it is self-lucid by itself, it is mirror-like [wisdom]. Since it has no bias, it is the wisdom of equality. Since it appears as anything whatsoever, it is discriminating wisdom. Since it accomplishes all goals by realizing true reality, it is all-accomplishing wisdom. Since this momentary wisdom endowed with those five wisdoms arises by relying on a fully qualified[2773] [female] body, it is called "consort."

"By virtue of which causes is this fully qualified awareness consort established?" She is endowed with the three causes of initial abiding. She has made special aspiration prayers before, is [thus] known at present by virtue of her respect for the guru, her lineage extends from one excellent family {353} to other excellent ones, and she has a guru and is embraced by the guru's instructions. She is [further] known by virtue of a beautiful face and by not being afraid of what is profound.[2774] This applies in due order.[2775] By virtue of that, she is endowed with the seven causes of abiding at present: a beautiful face, blond-bronze hair, the scent of an utpala [flower] exuding from her mouth, large breasts, a slender waist, a tight bhaga, and a character filled with bodhicitta. It is through these kinds [of causes] that [the awareness consort] is established. This [is said]:

It is the wisdom without abiding that is
accomplished by relying upon a mudrā

2a4. "What is accomplished?" It is the momentary connate wisdom that is accomplished. The connate is what is connate with all appearing and resounding phenomena. Here, connate appearance is inseparable appearance-emptiness. Connate mind as such is inseparable bliss-emptiness. Those [two] being nondual is connate wisdom.[2776] This [is said]:

> When the mind experiences form and such,
> isn't that equality[2777] entailing being unborn?

2a5. "Through what is it ascertained?" It is ascertained through the tantric texts because [it is stated there] that "[the Bhagavān] was dwelling in the bhagas of the vajra ladies, being the body, speech, and mind of all tathāgatas."[2778] That the bodies [of the tathāgatas] dwell [in those bhagas] means that all deities arise from there. That their speech dwells [there] means that all tantra classes are included there. That their minds dwell [there] means that connate wisdom is realized there.

2a6. Its name refers to the EVAṂ that has a shape. E refers to the kakkola, {354} which illustrates emptiness having the character of prajñā. VAṂ refers to the bola, which illustrates great bliss having the nature of means. What has the nature of empty bliss refers to means and prajñā being inseparable—that is, their not being different.

2a7. The result [here] is the result of concordant outflow. The four ecstasies are a concordant outflow in terms of the bindu—they are concordant in terms of the bodhicitta [that is] the bindu.[2779] The four mudrās are a concordant outflow in terms of the moments—they are concordant in terms of the moment of the lack of characteristics. There is also concordance in terms of the pair of sentient beings and buddhas: these two—the mind streams[2780] of sentient beings (the cause) and[2781] the awakened minds of buddhas—are not different.

2b. The pith instructions on pursuing the true reality of the dharmamudrā have seven parts:

1. dharma
2. sealing with which mudrā
3. through what it is accomplished
4. what is accomplished

5. through what it is ascertained
6. what its name is
7. what its result is

2b1. Here, dharma is twofold: knowing and what is to be known. What is to be known is conceptual and nonconceptual. What is nonconceptual is twofold: the suchness of what is pure and the suchness of what is impure.

2b2. As for mudrā, there is sealing with the connate, which has three parts:

a. sealing the means with emptiness
b. sealing emptiness with the means
c. sealing difference with nonduality

2b2a. Sealing the means with emptiness has three parts.

2b2a1. Appearances to be encountered means that whichever appearances may be encountered, they are sealed with the connate.

2b2a2. Diversity {355} to be made equivalent means that no matter what things may appear as and what they may be possible as, they are the same in that they are unborn.

2b2a3. Many to be made of a single taste means that everything, no matter what it may appear as, is to be pervaded by the taste of the connate.

These are to be understood as being like meeting a king, like the moon appearing in many water containers, and like different forms of brown-sugar candy—the examples are matched in due order.

2b2b. Sealing emptiness with the means has four parts:

1. familiarizing with all phenomena as the connate
2. letting go of clinging to the experience of that
3. embracing upcoming sensations with mindfulness
4. the signs of familiarity

2b2b1. As for familiarizing with [all phenomena] as the connate, at the time of familiarizing with the connate, one clearly brings to mind that all phenomena of saṃsāra and nirvāṇa are the connate and familiarizes with that. For this [is said]:

The essence of the entirety of phenomena
should be familiarized with as the connate

2b2b2. As for letting go of clinging to the experience of that, by familiarizing in this way, all phenomena dissolve into the connate and are experienced as the connate[, but] the clinging of grasping at that [experience] should be let go—that is, nothing is to be engaged mentally. For this [is said]:

Whichever experience it may be,
it should not be engaged mentally[2782]

2b2b3. As for embracing upcoming sensations with mindfulness, it is possible for adventitious thoughts to arise again from within the natural state of such mental nonengagement. In that case, these two—the previous mental nonengagement and the adventitious thoughts—are let be as not being different: the experience of the connate {356} should be embraced with mindfulness. For this is declared:

Whichever adventitious thoughts may arise,
all should be familiarized with as its essence

2b2b4. The signs of familiarity are threefold:

a. the common signs
b. the uncommon sign
c. the special sign

2b2b4a. The common signs are fourfold: [a mindset of] equality with regard to food by having no bias toward it, [a mindset of] equality with regard to clothing by having no bias toward it, [a mindset of] equality with regard to places by having no bias toward them, and [a mindset of] equality with regard to friends by having no bias toward them. This [is said]:

To be traveled, not to be traveled,
what is food and what is not food,

likewise drink, clothing, and such—
everything [abides] within equality

2b2b4b. The uncommon sign is that meditative equipoise and subsequent attainment are equal in being clearly aware, like having woken up from sleep. For this [is said]:

No equipoise or subsequent attainment—
in this stream, there is no interruption
Great yogīs who familiarized with this
will not come to be broken into pieces

2b2b4c. The special sign is that yogīs with such realization have no hope or fear: they have no hope to attain buddhahood through gathering the accumulations, nor are they afraid of going to the miserable realms through committing wrongdoing.

2b2c. Sealing [difference] with nonduality means that there is no difference between the four ways of conduct—there is no distraction from the native state. For this [is said]:

Walking, standing, lying, sitting, and all the rest—
one is to think of them with excellent recollection!

2b3. "Through what is [this dharmamudrā] accomplished?" {357} It is accomplished through the instructions, which have three parts:

a. in terms of what is to be explained
b. [in terms of] the instructions' own essence
c. in terms of the way of explaining

2b3a. What is to be explained is threefold: what is explained for a [general] assembly, what is explained for one's disciples, and [the instructions] given to one's [spiritual] children. Among these, [the dharmamudrā] is accomplished through [the instructions] given to one's [spiritual] children.

2b3b. In terms of the instructions' own essence, they are threefold: with elaborations, without elaborations, and utterly elaboration-free.

Among these, [the dharmamudrā] is accomplished through [the instructions that are] utterly elaboration-free.

2b3c. In terms of time, they are fourfold: [the time of] being supplicated again and again, the time of a gaṇacakra, the time of paying service and respect, and the time of conduct. Among these, [the dharmamudrā] is accomplished through the [instructional] conduct at the time of conduct.

2b4. "What is accomplished?" Appearances are accomplished as being unborn. Even at the time of dreams of being unborn,[2783] they are realized as being unborn.

2b5. "Through what is it ascertained?" Appearances are ascertained through equal taste. This is twofold: equal taste as bliss and equal taste as emptiness. The former one is twofold: equal taste as outer bliss and equal taste as inner bliss. There is no clinging by imputing anything onto outer appearances, and there is mindfulness of the experience of the inner third empowerment. Equal taste as emptiness is twofold: equal in the manner of being equal and equal in the manner of sealing. The former one is so because in the basic nature—the natural state of mind not being anything whatsoever—all is equal. Appearances are equal in the way of sealing them with that. {358}

2b6. The term that is its name is EVAṂ, which is fourfold: connecting it with the lineage as the lineage, connecting it with the lineage as terms, connecting it with terms as the body, and connecting it with the body as blessing.

2b7. The result [here] is the result of maturation, which has three parts:

a. maturation of the past
b. maturation in the present
c. maturation in the future

2b7a. Maturation of the past means that, thanks to having gathered the accumulations before, one has the fortune for cultivating the dharmamudrā in the present.

2b7b. Maturation in the present means that, thanks to relying on a guru in the present, the instructions are given to oneself[2784] in the present and then made a living experience.

2b7c. Maturation in the future means that, thanks to bringing the dharmamudrā onto the path, the fruition—mahāmudrā—will be accomplished.

2c. The pith instructions on pursuing the true reality of mahāmudrā have seven parts:

1. mudrā
2. being great
3. through what it is accomplished
4. what is accomplished
5. through what it is ascertained
6. what its name is
7. which result is accomplished

2c1. As for mudrā, mudrā is meant in the sense of not going beyond, which is fourfold:

a. not going beyond the actual unity
b. not going beyond the exemplifying unity
c. not going beyond the unity of abiding
d. not going beyond the unity of being

2c1a. [Mahāmudrā as] the actual unity refers to luminosity and emptiness being a unity in that they are nondual. Luminosity refers to dualistic experience. Emptiness {359} refers to the realization of this very [experience] lacking a nature of its own. [Objection:] "But then this has become absolutely nonexistent." [No,] true reality is experienced. "But since this is experience, it is not true reality." It is experienced as not being anything whatsoever. Therefore luminosity and emptiness are a unity in that they are inseparable. Others declare this to be a unity, because any clinging to dualistic appearance is negated. In its own basic nature, [however,] it does not even abide as just unity or nonduality. Hence [it does not have any] name, [cannot] be identified, and cannot be demonstrated as being "this."

2c1b. [Mahāmudrā] is the exemplifying unity: for since it is the actuality of inseparable bliss-emptiness that is illustrated by the exemplifying karmamudrā, nothing goes beyond it.

2c1c. [Mahāmudrā as] the unity of abiding refers to connate wisdom because nothing goes beyond its abiding in the mind streams of all sentient beings by pervading them.

2c1d. [Mahāmudrā] is the unity of being: for since it is the great bliss of the entirety of saṃsāra and nirvāṇa being nondual, nothing goes beyond it.

2c2. As for being great, [mahāmudrā] is great because it is visibly endowed with the causes [of being great]. It is great because it is more supreme than the [other] three [mudrās]. It is great because mahāmudrā is contingent on mere realization. It is great because mahāmudrā does not hold on to any support whatsoever.

2c3. "Through what is it accomplished?" It is accomplished through fresh, uncontrived[2785] cognition, which is twofold:

a. freshness through examination
b. freshness in meditation

2c3a. Freshness through examination [occurs] by virtue of examining all phenomena {360} as being born from other conditions, examining what was born from other conditions as being unborn, and examining this being unborn as not being anything whatsoever. This [is said]:

All states of mind are born from conditions
Thus they should be known as being unborn
Inseparability is the union of all the buddhas[2786]

2c3b. Freshness in meditation is threefold: first, free of any effort and accomplishing, relaxing body and mind from within, like spinning cotton into yarn;[2787] in the middle, free of doubt, letting mind be in an uncontrived manner; in the end, by virtue of certainty, letting all upcoming sensations dissolve as being unborn. For this [is said]:

Resting in the means of being similar to cotton,
without any accomplishing through any efforts,
you are to cast out activities of the double mind,
cultivate the glorious, supreme, original person,
and, by being certain, understand this as the root
of all kinds of miraculous displays of experience

2c4. "What is accomplished?" What is accomplished is being free of blocking and creating.[2788] The view is not blocked, because all tenets are this true reality.[2789] Meditation is not blocked, because everything conceived is this true reality. Conduct is not blocked, because all contrivances are this true reality. The view is not created, because effortlessness exists on its own accord.[2790] Meditation is not created, because freshness exists on its own accord. Conduct is not created, because self-arising exists on its own accord.[2791] For this [is said]:

Great nonduality free of blocking and creating
constitutes the mahāmudrā that is the fruition {361}

2c5. "Through what is it ascertained?" It is ascertained by virtue of experience not being anything whatsoever, which is threefold. The view, not being anything whatsoever, is free from the two assertions. Meditation, not being anything whatsoever, is free from the three progressive stages. Conduct, not being anything whatsoever, is free from the two analyses. For this [is said]:

The wisdom that isn't anything whatsoever
is the mahāmudrā of mental nonengagement

2c6. "What is its name?" Its meaning is EVAṂ, which is threefold:

a. cutting through three [kinds of] hopes
b. being endowed with five features
c. the four kāyas being naturally perfect

2c6a. Cutting through three [kinds of] hopes refers to any hope for remedies, any hope for true reality, and any hope for a fruition.[2792] For this [is said]:

It does not even represent a remedial factor,
is free of true reality,[2793] and is not born as other

2c6b. Being endowed with five features has five parts:

1. not being born through any essence
2. not having any nature of its own
3. being all-pervasive
4. being changeless
5. being omnitemporal

2c6b1. Not being born through any essence has three reasons: all phenomena are not born from any other conditions, an essence of being born cannot be demonstrated as being "this," and [phenomena] are not contingent on other causes and conditions. For this [is said]:

> The very first one with no beginning or end
> is the ever-excellent vajra of being unborn

2c6b2. Not having any nature of its own means not having any nature of existence, nonexistence, both, or neither. For this [is said]:

> Not conceiving as self, not conceiving as other,
> neither should you conceive of it as both

And: {362}

> Not at all existing as self or other anywhere,
> it originates from itself and pervades itself

2c6b3. As for being all-pervasive, since there is none among all appearing and possible phenomena that is not pervaded by mahāmudrā, it is all-pervasive. For this [is said]:

> It is all-pervasive, similar to space
> All is fully perfect in its continuum
> Nothing ever becomes other than it

2c6b4. Being changeless means that there is no change from mahāmudrā at the time of being in saṃsāra, training [on the path], training in a special manner, and being revealed.[2794] For this [is said]:

It is during all times that true reality occurs—
supreme wisdom without change or alteration

2c6c. As for the four kāyas being naturally perfect, the dharmakāya consists of this basic nature being free from all superimposition and denial, the sambhoga[kāya] of the experience of this true reality, and the nirmāṇakāya of appearing as diversity despite not being other[2795] than true reality, thus being designated accordingly as [all kinds of] conventions. Since all these are ultimately uncontrivedness, this is the svābhāvika[kāya]. For this [is said]:

Through lacking duality, it is nonduality
The great experience is the second kāya
By virtue of diversity, it is the third kāya
The svābhāvika[kāya] possesses oneness

2c7. The result [here] is the result of stainlessness.[2796] This is eightfold. (1) For, not coming from analysis,[2797] the wisdom of suchness's own essence is unborn. (2) Since it is associated with the accomplishment of the wisdom of the path, it is uninterrupted. (3) It lacks a nature of its own. {363} (4) It is the relinquishment of [all] obscurations such as the cognitive ones. (5) It serves as the basis of all excellencies. (6) It is the oneness of saṃsāra and nirvāṇa. (7) It embodies great nonreferential compassion. (8) It is the sole mahāsukhakāya. Thus, through these eight, it is suitable to be free from stains.[2798] Furthermore, it is free from the stains of the three ecstasies by virtue of the three moments because mahāmudrā is the actual connate.

2d. The pith instructions on pursuing the true reality of the samayamudrā teach primarily the welfare of others. The *Candrapradīpa[sūtra]* says:

Buddhahood, which is the perfection of the welfare
of others, is taught to represent the primary fruition
For, relinquishing the welfare of sentient beings,
there is nothing other that is of great significance[2799]

This has seven parts:

1. samaya
2. mudrā
3. through what it is accomplished
4. what is accomplished
5. through what it is ascertained
6. what its name is
7. which result is attained

2d1. Samaya refers to the causal samayamudrā. The samayamudrā of making a pledge for the consummate welfare of others is the first generation of [bodhi]citta. The samayamudrā of maturing as[2800] the consummate welfare of others is to wish for the virtues of the gathered two accumulations to be for the welfare of others. As for the samayamudrā of engaging in the consummate welfare of others, in terms of the Pāramitā[yāna], this refers to [the time of engagement] from the path of preparation up through the tenth bhūmi. In terms of the secret mantra, {364} this refers to the time of familiarizing with the dharmamudrā [up through] mahāmudrā.

2d2. "With which mudrā is there sealing?" There is sealing with the two kinds of form kāyas. As for what appears for those with very pure appearances, for the bodhisattvas on the ten bhūmis, in the palace (the support), the way in which the principal deity and the retinue (the supported) appear is that they have a wrathful or peaceful character. Thus the appearances that are distinguished by greater or lesser numbers of deities with elaborations or without elaborations are what appear to those who are very pure. As for those with pure appearances, for those on the path of preparation, nirmāṇakāyas appear as [someone like Buddha] Śākyamuni and so on. For those with common appearances, [nirmāṇakāyas] promote their welfare by appearing in the ways of medicines and physicians or in the ways of upādhyāyas and ācāryas.

2d3. "Through what is it accomplished?" This has two parts. In terms of what is common, it is accomplished by the three who have highest, medium, [and lower] faculties.[2801] In terms of what is special, it is accomplished by the four who have the very highest, highest,[2802] medium, and lower fortunes: they accomplish mahāmudrā, dharmamudrā, karmamudrā, and samayamudrā, respectively.

2d4. "What is accomplished?" In terms of what is common, the individual views, meditations, conducts, and fruitions are accomplished. In terms of what is special, all four mudrās are accomplished by the [very] highest among the four of [very highest,] highest, medium, [and lower fortunes].

2d5. "Through what is it ascertained?" In terms of the Pāramitā[yāna], it is ascertained through the buddha words or treatises of the three yānas. In terms of the Mantra[yāna], it is ascertained through the five tantra classes or the pith instructions that are based on them.

2d6. The name {365} through which it is illustrated is EVAṂ: it is illustrated as cause and result, means and prajñā, ultimate and seeming, or creation process and perfection process, and so on.

2d7. The result [here] consists of the further and further increase of the progressive stages or the result produced by persons. The increase of the progressive stages refers to [gradually engaging in] the four mudrās or gradually engaging in what is ancillary through the nine approaches.[2803] The result produced by persons is threefold:

a. the result that has been produced by persons
b. the result of persons
c. the result produced by persons

2d7a. [The result] that has been produced by persons refers to someone like Prince Sarvasiddhārtha: having gathered the accumulations for three incalculable eons in the past, his two[2804] kinds of form kāyas appeared[2805] for the welfare of sentient beings and then were enjoyed [by beings].

2d7b. The result of persons refers to having accomplished a special [psychophysical] support at present by having gathered the accumulations before, thus possessing the fortune of [being able to] cultivate the causal[2806] samayamudrā.

2d7c. The result produced by persons refers to the later arising of the samayamudrā's appearance for the welfare of others by virtue of having engaged in the progressive stages of the path [in the past]. Furthermore, at the time of the result of having cultivated the cause that consists of the creation process, the two kinds of form kāyas arise for the welfare of others. Thus it is declared.

{351}[2807] 3. [The pith instructions on] the special means are four:

a. the four moments in order to ascertain the time
b. the four ecstasies in order to ascertain the wisdom
c. the four locations in order to ascertain the realization
d. the four dharmas in order to ascertain the defining characteristics

3a. Here, the four moments are the moment of variety, the moment of maturation, the moment of the lack of characteristics, and the moment of consummation. For [this is said]:

Variety, maturation, consummation, and lack of characteristics[2808]

3b. The four ecstasies are ecstasy, supreme ecstasy, connate ecstasy, and cessational ecstasy. For [this is stated]:

Ecstasy, supreme ecstasy, cessational ecstasy, and connate
ecstasy[2809]

3c. The four locations are the neck of the vajra, the tip of the vajra, two having been emitted and two being [distributed] evenly, and all having been emitted. For [this is declared]:

It is by virtue of the sexual union of great passion
that, thanks to close union as well as the churning,
the neck and tip of the vajra come to be pervaded {352}
After two have passed beyond, two [remain] even
Once the rest has passed,[2810] this is cessational ecstasy[2811]

3d. The four dharmas are as follows. In ecstasy, the thoughts of the entirety of perceiver and perceived exist. In supreme ecstasy, [the thoughts of] the perceived exist but [those of] the perceiver do not exist. In connate ecstasy, [ecstasy] is beyond all extremes of perceiver, perceived, permanence, and extinction. Cessational ecstasy involves all kinds of thoughts of coarse appearances. Again [this is said]:

Ecstasy is what is endowed with clinging
Supreme ecstasy is more excessive than it
Consummation has thoughts of perceiver and perceived
Connate [ecstasy] is not observed in the three[2812]

{365} 4. [The pith instructions on] making [these mudrās] a living experience have five parts:

a. the samayamudrā that appears as cause
b. the karmamudrā that is the example
c. the dharmamudrā that is the path
d. the mahāmudrā that is the result
e. the samayamudrā that is the welfare of others[2813]

4a. The samayamudrā that is the cause refers to cultivating the creation process {366}. This should be understood in other [sources].

4b. Making the karmamudrā a living experience has five parts:

1. what is to be realized
2. self-blessing
3. training in bliss
4. the yoga of the syllables
5. [the bliss] that is to be made to abide

4b1. What is to be realized is twofold: when it is to be realized and what is to be realized. "When [is it to be realized]?" It is to be realized at the time that consists of the moment of the lack of characteristics. "What is [to be] realized?" It is connate wisdom— inseparable bliss-emptiness—that is to be realized.

4b2. As for self-blessing,[2814] one constructs the maṇḍala of the five nectars, invites the guru couple, and offers it to them. Then one invites them onto the crown of one's head on top of a sun disk and a moon disk that have five holes the size of a grain.[2815] By supplicating them, one meditates that bodhicitta descends from the place of the union of the couple and enters one's own brahmarandhra, thereby completely filling up the body.[2816] By clearly bringing the experience of the third empowerment to mind, one should cultivate special bliss.

4b3. Training in bliss is twofold: eliciting wisdom through appearances and sealing appearances with wisdom. Eliciting wisdom through appearances means that by eliciting experiences through the power of the eyes seeing forms, the ears hearing sounds,[2817] the nose sensing smells, and so on, as well as the entire range of any thoughts arising[2818] in the mind, one should familiarize with all discursive thinking as being inseparable bliss-emptiness. {367} Sealing appearances with wisdom means that though the eyes see forms, this is sealed with bliss-emptiness. Likewise, sounds, smells, tastes, and so on, as well as any arising thoughts,[2819] are sealed with bliss-emptiness.

4b4. The yoga of the syllables is as follows. In the place where the experience of the empowerment arises, one should meditate on a red E the size of one's hand lines whose middle is adorned with VAṂ. Bliss arises there, and then one meditates on this in the navel. Bliss arises there, and then one meditates on this in the heart. Bliss arises there, and then one meditates on this in the throat. Bliss arises there, and then one meditates on this in the crown of the head. When one is filled up with bliss, the nāda should be made to abide. This has three parts:

a. the conditions for emission
b. the means for guarding it
c. the means for abiding[2820]

4b4a. The conditions [for emission] are eight: emission due to being filled with bliss, emission due to encountering [certain] conditions, emission due to illness, emission due to conduct, emission due to nonhumans, emission due to disagreeable food, emission due to samaya breaches, and emission due to the blessings fading.

4b4b. The means for guarding it are eight. (1) For emission due to being filled [with bliss], having wound the fret string of a vīṇā[2821] around the neck of the bola and tied it around the waist, one [should] strike out with the legs, direct one's cognition to the navel, pull it upward with the sound "hri," and moderate [the intercourse, making it] less intense. (2) For emission due to encountering [certain] conditions, one [should] strike out with the legs, close the lower gate, and counteract the six changes. {368} (3) For emission due to illness, having assumed the cross-legged position, one should apply twenty-five moxibustions each at the places where the left and right ankles come to rest, bind the smell of carnivorous beasts, eat fresh nutritious food, consume ground powders of the three hot spices[2822] on an empty stomach, wear[2823] warm clothes, and eat myrobalan cooked with milk. (4) For emission due to conduct, one's demeanor should be at ease and one should sit upright blocking one's lower gate with some cotton cloth, thus not falling asleep during the day, while lying down at night without preventing sleep.[2824] (5) For emission due to nonhumans, one should anoint oneself with a fivefold mix of human fat, frankincense, the ashes of white mustard seeds, human brains, and padmarakta,[2825] wrap a blue string over which one has recited Vajrayoginī's mantra around one's waist, and anoint the vajra's head with calcite over which one has recited the mantra of any oath deity. (6) If there is emission due to disagreeable food, one should ward off māras with the five[2826] nectars and drink the milk of nettles with garlic that have been smoked.[2827] (7) If there is emission due to the blessings fading, one [should] gather the accumulations, arrange gaṇacakras, and ask the guru for blessings. (8) If there is emission due to samaya breaches, one should request the four empowerments from the guru and make confessions.

4b5. The bliss that is to be made to abide has ten parts. (1) In order to make the bliss of experience abide, one should not be separated from the crucial point in time. (2) In order to make the lower bliss abide, one should allow one's conduct to be at ease. {369} (3) In order to make the upper bliss abide, one should abide by the yogic discipline of a dumb person.[2828] (4) In order to make the pervasive bliss abide, one should perform prāṇāyāma. (5) In order to make the bliss of subsequent attainment abide, one should make appearances of equal taste as bliss. (6) In order to make nonconceptual bliss abide, one should partake of the five kinds of nectar. (7) In order to make the bliss of blessings abide, one should arrange gaṇacakras. (8) In order to make contaminated bliss abide, one should rely on a karmamudrā. (9) In order to make the bliss of realization abide, one should pay homage and service to the guru and request instructions from the guru. (10) In order to make the bliss that is the fruition abide, one should assiduously apply oneself to the pith instructions.

4c. Making the dharmamudrā a living experience has five parts:

1. what is to be realized

2. the familiarization
3. the aids
4. the defining characteristics
5. equal taste

4c1. What is to be realized is inseparable bliss-emptiness. This means to bring the four ecstasies onto the path. That is, what appears as all kinds of appearing and resounding [phenomena] constitutes ecstasy. Thinking there is [even] more bliss and more emptiness than that [ecstasy] constitutes supreme ecstasy. Being free from all thoughts constitutes connate ecstasy. Though it is this way in meditative equipoise, subsequent attainment appears as all kinds of things, which constitutes cessational ecstasy.

4c2. About familiarizing with the dharmamudrā, you may wonder: "Having realized such, what should one familiarize with?" First, one should familiarize with all phenomena as being the connate. {370} [Then,] one familiarizes with thoughts, thereby dissolving within the connate and not even mentally engaging in this as the mere connate. [Finally,] one familiarizes with any thoughts that arise from such mental nonengagement as not being different from that previous mental nonengagement.

4c3. The aids are four:[2829]

a. if water is predominant, it is [made] of equal taste with wind
b. if wind is predominant, it is [made] of equal taste with earth
c. if earth is predominant, it is [made] of equal taste with fire
d. if fire is predominant, it is [made] of equal taste with space

4c3a. If water is predominant, that is, if cognition is heavy and quivering, it is [made] of equal taste with wind: appearances are analyzed and let be as being unborn. By cognition being mounted on wind, cognition is made to ascend.

4c3b. If wind is predominant, it is [made] of equal taste with earth: the connate is let be in a stable manner without coming and going—it is let be in a relaxed way[2830] as inseparable bliss-emptiness.

4c3c. If earth is predominant, that is, if body and mind are greatly obstructive, it is [made] of equal taste with fire: one should be mindful of the crucial point in time and, without any inside or outside, make [body and mind] of equal taste as bliss.

4c3d. If fire is predominant, that is, if cognition is mainly joyful and blissful, it is [made] of equal taste with space: it is let be without mentally engaging in anything whatsoever and self-arising conduct is freely let go without blocking anything.

4c4. The defining characteristics are seven. (1) Because of enjoying appearances as being unborn, this is the constituent of complete enjoyment. (2) Because of realizing appearance and emptiness as not being different, this is the constituent of union. (3) Because of experiencing them as not being different, this is the constituent of bliss. (4) Because of[2831] this bliss-emptiness existing in yourself from the start and arising when desired, this is the constituent of the compassion of the arising of whatever is desired. {371} (5) Because of this bliss inherently existing in yourself as something that can be directly enjoyed, this is the constituent of entity.[2832] (6) Because of this actuality being uninterrupted like a river [stream], this is the constituent of being uninterrupted. (7) Because of appearances not ceasing, this is the constituent of being unceasing. Ultimately, appearances are not stopped, but what is conceived is stopped.

4c5. Equal taste is threefold. (1) If [ordinary] experiences decrease, appearances are of equal taste as bliss. (2) If [conceptual] examination[2833] decreases, appearances are of equal taste as being unborn. (3) If analysis[2834] decreases, appearances are of equal taste as mental nonengagement.

4d. Making mahāmudrā a living experience[2835] has five parts:

1. the basic nature
2. the familiarization
3. the accomplishment
4. the conduct
5. inconceivability

4d1. The basic nature has three parts:

a. the basic nature in terms of reasons
b. the basic nature in terms of the view
c. the basic nature in terms of essence

4d1a. The basic nature in terms of reasons has three parts:

1. being reasonable as mahāmudrā
2. being reasonable as the result of stainlessness
3. being reasonable as being free from creating and blocking [or affirmation and negation]

4d1a1. Being reasonable as mahāmudrā has two parts:

a. mudrā
b. being great

4d1a1a. Mudrā refers to a seal in the sense of not going beyond it. This is threefold because of not going beyond the unity of abiding, the unity of [all-]pervasiveness, and the unity of being.

4d1a1b. Being great means that [mahāmudrā] is great because it is more supreme than all the [other] three [mudrās].

4d1a2. Being reasonable as the result of stainlessness has two parts: {372} being free from the stains of the three moments and the three ecstasies. In the former one, "three" refers to being free from the stains of the three [moments] of variety, maturation, and consummation. The second one refers to being free from the stains of ecstasy, supreme ecstasy, and cessational ecstasy.

4d1a3. [Mahāmudrā] is reasonable as being free from affirmation and negation because one's own view is not affirmed and the views of others are not negated.

4d1b. The basic nature in terms of the view has three parts:

1. cutting through[2836] three [kinds of] hopes
2. being endowed with five features
3. the four kāyas being naturally perfect

4d1b1. Cutting through three [kinds of] hopes refers to any hope for remedies, any hope for true reality, and any hope for a fruition.

4d1b2. The five features are being unborn, not having any nature of its own, being all-pervasive, being omnitemporal, and being changeless,

4d1b3. As for the four kāyas being naturally perfect, the dharmakāya consists of the cognition that isn't anything whatsoever and is devoid of superimposition and denial, the sambhoga[kāya] of the experience of true reality, the nirmāṇakāya of true reality appearing as diversity, and the svābhāvikakāya of these three being inseparable.

4d1c. The basic nature in terms of essence has three parts:

1. the time of effortlessness
2. the time of inconceivability
3. the time of unity[2837]

4d1c1. The time of effortlessness refers to finding confidence in what is present primordially, thus being free from hope and fear.

4d1c2. The time of[2838] inconceivability refers to the following: by having made this very effortlessness a living experience, the continua of both meditative equipoise and subsequent attainment fuse,[2839] and thus there is no need for meditation—that is, wisdom is free of any extremes of distraction.[2840] {373}

4d1c3. The time of unity refers to the one when the two form kāyas are just about to dawn at the time of appearances dissolving within the mind.

4d2. The familiarization has two parts:

a. initial analysis
b. making this a living experience

4d2a. Analysis is threefold: the analysis that all thoughts are born in dependence on other conditions, the analysis that this being born from conditions is being unborn, and the analysis that this being unborn isn't anything whatsoever.

4d2b. Making this a living experience[2841] is threefold: first, free of any effort and accomplishing, body and mind should be relaxed within; in the middle, free of doubt, mind should let be in an uncontrived manner; in the end, all upcoming sensations should be understood as being unborn.

4d3. The accomplishment has two parts:

a. accomplishment
b. its signs[2842]

4d3a. Accomplishment has two parts:

1. accomplishment
2. the special features of accomplishment

4d3a1. Accomplishment is threefold. (a) Since all thoughts, whichever may be born, are nothing but the unborn being born, cognition is unblocked. (b) Since inseparable bliss-emptiness is experienced, [mind] is let be [without] any thinking about afflictions and their remedies and without any hope for a fruition. (c) Since whatever may appear is mahāmudrā, this is uninterrupted meditation, like a river [stream].

4d3a2. The distinctive features of accomplishment are threefold: (a) [the special feature of lacking ignorance] by virtue of [all] thoughts[2843] of indifference being cut through by the experience of inseparable bliss-emptiness, (b) the special feature of lacking ignorance by virtue of the existence of the guru's instructions on top of scriptures and reasonings, and (c) the special feature of lacking ignorance by virtue of the result (wisdom and so on) inherently existing at the time of the cause (being ordinary). {374}

4d3b. The signs are three. (1) The sign of experiencing appearances as empty is like seeing ice. (2) Then, the sign of experiencing bliss and emptiness as inseparable is like ice being present as water. (3) The sign of appearances dissolving within the mind is their being of a single taste as great bliss, just like ice melting into water.[2844]

4d4. The conduct is fivefold: (a) Not being crooked[2845] is like a great highway. (b) Being steadfast[2846] without any bias is like the ground of the earth. (c) Being without virtue and wrongdoing is like a mad elephant. (d) Being without hope and fear is like a lion. (e) Being pervasive but without clinging is like the sun.

4d5. Inconceivability is twofold:

a. the inconceivability of experience
b. the inconceivability of the cognition of experience

That is threefold: effortless, unidentifiable, and fearless.[2847] This is the actuality of inconceivability. "Actuality" means that the cause cannot be conceived, the means is inconceivable, and the result is not conceived and self-arising.[2848]

The inconceivability of experience consists of the twenty examples of realization likened to examples. "What [are these]?" They are as follows:

(1) As in the example of the two of brass and gold becoming inseparable if everything becomes the golden ground, when everything is

realized as great bliss-emptiness, it is not divided into the seeming and the ultimate [anymore].[2849]

(2) Just as twisted knots become free if they are loosened up, the mind of yogīs becomes free if it loosens up.[2850]

(3) Just as prisoners who have escaped from a dungeon go wherever they please, {375} the mind of yogīs is let go wherever it pleases.[2851]

(4) Just like a crow flying up from a ship, the mind that becomes scattered toward objects is not summoned back.[2852]

(5) Just as a mad elephant can be made enjoyable[2853] by handling its trunk with an iron hook, all kinds of objects[2854] are handled with the iron hook of being unborn, and so the sense pleasures are enjoyed.

(6) Just as the mind of a mad elephant that has been trained[2855] is happy and at ease, the mind of yogīs is let be happily and at ease.[2856]

(7) Just as fire spreads in tinder, appearances blaze as being unborn.

(8) Just like the bliss of a young woman, experience cannot be spoken of.[2857]

(9) Just as salt dissolves in water,[2858] all thoughts, whichever may arise, are dissolved in being unborn.[2859]

(10) Just as a lamp is self-luminous by itself, great bliss is self-luminous by itself.[2860]

(11) Just as a *sakuna*[2861] bird does not hold on to any support whatsoever, mahāmudrā does not hold on to any support whatsoever.

(12) Just as a *patara* animal[2862] is without anything to adopt or to reject, yogīs should also be without anything to adopt or to reject.

(13) Just as with the medicine *bhadari*, the result exists inherently at the time of the cause.[2863]

(14) Just as with the whirling blade of a householder, [yogīs] do not have any dualistic clinging to experience.

(15) Just as with an uninterrupted river [stream], [yogīs] familiarize with their experience in an uninterrupted manner.

(16) Just like a container with food that is a pleasure for the senses, [yogīs] should not have any clinging to the sense pleasures.

(17) Just like Vulture Flock Mountain,[2864] cognition is let be without any arising and operating.[2865]

(18) Just as with the center of empty space, [yogīs] should not have any desire for philosophical systems. {376}

(19) Just as the great ocean is immovable, [yogīs] should not move the actuality that is vast and profound.[2866]

(20) Just as with a reflection in water, yogīs should realize [everything] to be like a reflection.[2867]

5. The way in which certainty about the instructions arises has four parts:

a. the essence of the four mudrās
b. understanding their purpose through causes
c. understanding these [four mudrās] as symbols
d. oneself relying on texts[2868]

5c. That [these four mudrās] should be understood as symbols has four parts:

1. the karmamudrā is explained as being like the bodhi tree
2. the dharmamudrā is explained as being like a golden wheel
3. mahāmudrā is explained as being like a nyagrodha tree
4. the samayamudrā is explained as being like the essence of a myrobalan[2869]

5c1. You may wonder: "What is the connection between the bodhi tree and the karmamudrā?" [There is a connection] because this is found in the **Bhadraherukatantra*:[2870]

As for a fully qualified and youthful awareness consort,
who has the character of being filled with the bodhicitta,
the trunk, the branches, and the leaves of the bodhi tree
are so very soft and supple, being filled with its milk

It will grow as the three fivefold sets of white ones[2871]
The two black sides are blazing as a single white one
The ten sets of ten and the five are present as the fruit
The latter[2872] black one is descending as the single bindu
Those who drink it thereby will overcome all diseases

Through those who possess realization relying upon
such a karmamudrā and being mindful of the connate,
it is the karmamudrā who will arise as the great bliss

The ripening of the fruition of those abiding in abstinence,[2873] {377}
by virtue of the Heruka who is endowed with realization,
is the experiential sphere of those yogīs who are experts
in symbols, and therefore the bodhi tree should be seized

5c2. "What is the connection between a wheel and the dharmamudrā?" [There is a connection] because Master Kamala says this:

The four ecstasies' thoughts sever thoughts of perceiver-
perceived
The rim-like realization is made a living experience
The thoughts that are [like] spokes[2874] are of equal taste
Its characteristic is similar to the nature of gold
The equilibrium of nondual bliss-emptiness's cognition
is like a wheel's two sides being equal in circumference

5c3. "What is the connection between mahāmudrā and a nyagrodha tree?" The **Mañjuśrīvyākaraṇa*[2875] [declares this]:

The trunks and the branches of a nyagrodha tree
with its lofty crown are devoid of any blemishes
To imbibe its resin is purging both heat and cold
Its fine roots are thick, adorned[2876] by many branches

It dispels the area's poisons, being always new
Its diameter grows without summer or winter[2877]
It grows with scent pervading the surroundings
From its fruits and flowers, cool water descends
From a single branch, three buds grow evenly
Greatly flourishing, it bears flowers and fruits

The tree it grows together with turns into a dead one
and that dead [tree] is then not able to grow anymore
This is the natural collection of causes and conditions—
not accomplished by water not mixed with scriptures[2878]

"What are those two [delusion and nondelusion]?" {378} This is to be taught:

> **If the realization of delusion's and nondelusion's nonduality, which isn't anything whatsoever,[2879] is effortless, it is bliss. Since there is no need to examine this, do not think of actions and things to do! If all is let go of, this is mahāmudrā.**

"**Delusion**" refers to the afflictions, which are not to be relinquished. "**Nondelusion**" refers to wisdom, which is not to be relied on.[2880] The experience of their **nonduality** is that there is nothing to mentally engage. "**The realization, which isn't anything whatsoever**"[2881] is the fruition—that is, being free from any hope. All of this **is** by virtue of **effortless bliss**. **There is no need to examine this** mahāmudrā of the pith instructions as anything whatsoever. Its distinctive feature is to be free of the causes that consist of virtuous actions and evil **actions**, as well as their [karmic] maturations. The means [to attain this] consists of being free from **things to do—do not think** [of anything]**! If all** clinging to any fruition and [all] dualistic imputations[2882] **are let go of, this is mahāmudrā**—the fourteenth bhūmi.

[Objection:] "[But] then what is [stated] in the *Tattvadaśaka* and so on would be meaningless." This is not so. The time of accomplishing what is to be accomplished is without blocking [anything]—it is explained that [everything] serves as the path. At the time of what is to be accomplished having been accomplished, since [then any accomplishing of anything] is a stain, there is no deliberate accomplishing because everything is included in true reality.[2883] This is to be taught:

> **Furthermore:**
>
> **There exist no deities, no mantras, no austerities, and no fire offerings**
> **The maṇḍala is not established and the maṇḍala inhabitants are just so**[2884]

{379} This is simply what has already been explained above—it has the meaning of [everything] being associated [with mahāmudrā].

> **This mahāmudrā constitutes deities, mantras, and austerities**
> **Fire offerings, maṇḍalas, and maṇḍala inhabitants too are this**
> **Its character is their inclusion in equal nonduality, just as it is**
> **Those realizing it will be free—Vajradhara stated it is freedom**[2885]

This is to be ascertained by way of other words from the tantras. The words of the Buddha declare this:

> The inseparable four kāyas are mahāmudrā
> The dharmakāya constitutes the connate

Furthermore:

> The prajñā that is endowed with means
> and EVAM, the mantra of āli and kāli

In addition:

> It is the union of all buddhas that
> is based in the syllables EVAṂ[2886]

Moreover:

> By eliciting great bliss in the mind,
> saṃsāra is immediately incinerated

Furthermore:

> Mental nonengagement in the heart of
> nondual bliss-emptiness procures that

In addition:

Endowed with the center of nonduality,
practitioners have[2887] threefold equal taste

Moreover:

Waters have the taste of salt in the ocean
Phenomena are the equality of great bliss

Furthermore:

Just like two [bodies of] water being inseparable,
from its very get-go, saṃsāra is perfect buddhahood

In addition:

The continuous flow of the river of bodhicitta,
just as it is, is not interrupted by anything else

Moreover:

Karma, dharma, and samaya are included in the
experience of gaining the fourth empowerment {380}
The ones who are realizing the character of that
will be free from the past and free from duality
It was Vajradhara, the Heruka who is supreme,
who has proclaimed the definitive king of tantras

Therefore, since this is clear, it should be realized.

To clarify the beginning of the [above-cited] final passage [of the text],[2888] as great bliss, all phenomena are of a single taste, **equal**, and **nondual**. "**Just as it is**" refers to bodhicitta. "**Its character is their inclusion**" refers to the dharmamudrā. It is "**mahāmudrā**" because it includes the three wisdoms at the time of the fourth empowerment. This is the [concluding] summary of the samayamudrā.[2889]

The samayamudrā as the result produced by persons consists of [the result] that has been produced by persons before, includes the result of persons at a future time, and is [the result] produced by persons that arises through the force of training. "Result" refers to the welfare of others. "**The instruction**" means the undeceiving connection of cause and result.[2890] It **is the fourth one** because it is contingent on the third one.

Taking hold of the seal of the awakening that is supreme and
the refuge of earth-touching and supreme-generosity samādhis—
if you are proceeding by way of accomplishing the activities
that are in harmony with others, this is deemed to be supreme

NRERO E HRĪḤ SAMADOKA EVĀṂ[2891] BHRABHUHA

Those [passages] are the explanation of the samayamudrā.

Thus these distinctions of the four mudrās are to be matched with the four moments, the four ecstasies, and the four empowerments. Each of the three [mudrās] that are not mahāmudrā should be understood as [involving] the four ecstasies. {381} They are not causes and results in terms of their producing [the following,] but should be understood as causes and results in terms of their depending [on the previous]. This is the very condensed meaning of the four mudrās.

Having thus explained the meaning of the text, the explanation of the meaning of applying its name is as follows. As for "**HAṂ the *Caturmudrānvaya* in six**,"[2892] "HAṂ" refers to possessing the power of the connate: abiding in the center of the mahāsukhacakra at the tip of the avadhūtī, the entire body is included in it and does not go beyond its power. Likewise, the five kinds of tantra classes are included in the gem-like four mudrās and do not go beyond them.[2893] The gist of this is that these [mudrās] are supreme and to be held in the highest esteem.

As for the actuality that nobody but supreme Nāgārjuna has,[2894]
who has been greatly prophesied in the words of the Buddha,
and that has come down from Saraha and the supreme victor,
oh supreme venerable ones, please bear with any flaws in this!

Having realized this from the father and mother tantras
and composed this topic with prajñā and compassion,
may this commentary here that is called "Jewel Heart"
be victorious by making the disheartened rest at ease!

Through the merit of having written this dharma,
may the beings who keep wandering in this place
that makes up saṃsāra train in this path and then
come to abide on the bhūmi that is the fourteenth!

This concludes "A Commentary on the Four Mudrās, Called 'Jewel Heart'" composed by the Indian upādhyāya and guru Bhitakarma, renowned as erudite. It was translated on his own by the yogī Prajñāśrījñānakīrti who lives on alms. {382}

*This Indian upādhyāya, venerable Bhitakarma, renowned as erudite, was known as *Kāropa in the context of engaging in philosophy.*[2895] *In the context of engaging in yoga, he was known as *Ḍākakauṇapa.*[2896] *In the context of engaging in conduct, he was known as Digambara.*[2897] {383}

(45) A Critical Commentary on "Instructions on Empowerment"

In the language of India: *Sekanirdeśapañjikā*[2898]
In the language of Tibet: *Dbang bskur ba nges par btsan pa'i dka' 'grel*

I pay homage to Lokanātha[2899]

To the protector with the dharmadhātu's character,
who constitutes the domain of bodhisattvas alone[2900]
and keeps promoting the welfare of sentient beings,
the unsurpassed guru, I pay homage with devotion[2901]

You good people, I don't have any skill
in working out a commentary on a text
I jotted down a commentary by the force
of the guru's command, so bear with me![2902]

Despite that, not for other's sake,
but just for my own recollection
and also for other seekers like me,
I shall put something in writing[2903]

Here, this mahāpaṇḍita and avadhūta,[2904] the glorious protector Maitreya, who is the unsurpassed guru of the kriyā-, caryā-, yoga-, yogottara-, and yoganiruttaratantras[2905] and wished to compose *Instructions on Empowerment*, which follows *The Succession of the Four Mudrās* composed by noble Nāgārjuna, {384} first, to begin with, introducing its subject matter, pays homage to the syllables EVAṂ, which represent the beginning of the descriptions of the settings of the Buddha's words or of their condensed meaning and have the very nature of prajñā and means.[2906] [He does so in the stanza] that begins "I pay homage . . . "

> **I pay homage to the syllables EVAṂ,**
> **being the causes of the four moments**
> **in which the ecstasies arise distinctly,**
> **for the sake of realizing awakening**[2907] [1]

I pay homage to the syllable E and the syllable **VAṂ**, the two sonic phonemes that have the nature of the dharmamudrā—that is, I bow to them with body, speech, and mind. Why? **For the sake of realizing awakening**—that is, in order to attain completely perfect buddhahood; thus [the line "I pay homage to the syllables EVAṂ"] is connected [syntactically] to the later [compound "for the sake of realizing awakening"]. These syllables EVAṂ have great meaning and great benefit. The Bhagavān stated this in the *Devendraparipṛcchā[tantra]*:[2908]

> Please hear, oh you lord of the gods,
> for what purpose the All-Seeing One
> has spoken "EVAṂ"[2909] at the beginning,
> [as I explain it] properly[2910] in due order[2911]
>
> Of the eighty-four-thousand items
> within the collections of dharma,
> the two syllables, thus uttered, are
> the basis of all, father and mother[2912]
>
> The syllable E represents the mother
> The syllable VA[2913] is known as the father
> The bindu there constitutes their union
> This union is supremely wonderful
>
> The syllable E is said to be the lotus
> The syllable VA is simply the vajra

The bindu there represents the seed
From it, the three worlds come forth

The syllable E constitutes prajñā {385}
The syllable VA is the lord of bliss
The bindu is indestructible reality
From it, the other[2914] syllables arise

The knowers of true reality who know
those two syllables, the dharmamudrā,
will become those who turn the wheel
of dharma for sentient beings' entirety

The people who always recite the two
syllables without understanding this
will be outside of the buddhadharmas,
like rich persons deprived of enjoying[2915]

The two syllables EVAṂ are illusion[2916]
The omniscient one is established there[2917]
For that reason, they are recited at the
beginning of the true dharma's teachings[2918]

Therefore, if the lord of the gods,
Śakra, wishes for the eternal state,
he should honor the true dharma
Recall the two illusory syllables![2919]

[Then Maitrīpa] qualifies the pertinent subject matter as being caused by that [pair of syllables, saying] "**being the causes of the four moments**," which refers to them being the causes (the makers)[2920] of the four moments that are called "variety," "maturation," "consummation," and "lack of characteristics." For the syllables EVAṂ have the nature of the dharmamudrā, and the dharmamudrā, when being cultivated, removes the afflictions, including their latent tendencies. The distinction of the moments is connected to the distinction [of the phases] of removing the [afflictions, including their latent tendencies]. Hence the syllables EVAṂ are the causes of the moments.[2921]

Again, [Maitrīpa] qualifies [the subject matter] in the same way,[2922] saying "**in which the ecstasies arise distinctly**." {386} It is only by virtue of the existence of these [syllables], which have the character of prajñā and means and represent the wisdom of the path, that the ecstasies called "ecstasy," "supreme [ecstasy]," "cessational [ecstasy]," and "connate [ecstasy]" arise distinctly (not mixed up) by virtue of the distinction of the moments. Hence the entire meaning [of this stanza] is as follows: "For the sake of realizing awakening, I pay homage to the syllables EVAṂ, which are the causes of the four moments, and by virtue of whose existence alone the ecstasies arise distinctly." [Thus] the sonic phonemes [EVAṂ] have been explained.[2923]

Now [EVAṂ] in its written form is explained. **I pay homage to the syllables EVAṂ** that have the shape of the written letters of the syllables EVAṂ: by virtue of the guru's pith instructions, they [thus] have the nature of the dharmodayā.[2924] Alternatively, I pay homage to the syllables EVAṂ (*evaṃkāram*), which, due to the elision of the prefix [*ā* in *ākāram*, should actually be understood as being equivalent to] "having the form of EVAṂ" (*evaṃākāram*),[2925] that is, the jewel casket of the buddhas, the dharmodayāmudrā. The Bhagavān himself has declared that the dharmodayā has the shape of EVAṂ:

> The divine syllable E, which is
> adorned with VAṂ at its center,
> represents all bliss's repository,
> the jewel casket of buddhahood[2926]

[Objection:] "But what is the point of this homage [to EVAṂ as the dharmodayā]?" Therefore [Maitrīpa] says: "**being the causes of the four moments**," which means that [EVAṂ] is the cause (maker) of the four moments that are variety, maturation, consummation, {387} and lack of characteristics. It is the cause of variety as well because [variety] extends up to friction.[2927] I will explain [later] that there are extensive statements by the Buddha about that.[2928] [Thus] homage is paid to the cause by having faith [or trust] in the result. The following is declared:[2929]

Just as the true reality of the cause is seen,
exactly so is the true reality of the result[2930]

[Maitrīpa] states a further reason for paying homage [to EVAṂ as the dharmodayā, saying]: "**in which the ecstasies arise distinctly**"—that is, in which the ecstasies called "ecstasy," "supreme [ecstasy]," "cessational [ecstasy]," and "connate [ecstasy]" arise distinctly (not mutually mixed up). Though the fifth [case (ablative)] would [normally] obtain ([given the statement] "[The ablative is also used for] the substantial cause of the agent of arising"),[2931] [Maitrīpa] specifically uses the seventh [case (locative)] "in which." Therefore he intends to express that [EVAṂ as the dharmodayā] is the receptacle [of the ecstasies rather than their substantial cause]. [Thus the ecstasies] arise from that in which they are based.[2932] As it is said:

Due to knowing the moments, the wisdom
that is bliss is based in the syllables EVAṂ[2933]

Likewise:

It is the union of all buddhas that
is based in the syllables EVAṂ[2934]

Likewise:

OṂ lotus, receptacle of bliss,
great passion, bestower of bliss,
the four ecstasies' partaker, the world's diversity,
HUṂ HŪṂ HŪṂ, accomplish what I need to do![2935]

[Also,] to pay homage to a receptacle [is justified] due to the Buddha's words:

Where the tathāgatas have stood,
have wandered around, have sat,
and have slept their lion-like sleep, {388}
to those locations, I pay homage[2936]

Why do I pay homage? "**For the sake of realizing awakening**"—that is, for the accomplishment of full knowledge in accordance with reality, which means as much as saying "for completely perfect buddhahood." [Furthermore,] the reason for paying homage has been stated in the phrase "being the causes of the four moments."[2937]

In that regard, what are these four moments, and what is their order like?[2938] Therefore [Maitrīpa] says: "That there is variety . . ."

> **That there is variety, then maturation,**
> **thirdly, the lack of any characteristics,**
> **and then consummation is to be known**
> **because of rejecting the forceful yoga** [2]

[Objection:] "Violating the sequence taught in the tantra, why is it held [here] that the lack of characteristics is in the third [place]?" Therefore, [to answer this objection, Maitrīpa] says: "**because of rejecting the forceful yoga**." Here, the forceful yoga is as follows: **variety** is of various kinds, which is due to the existence of perceiver and perceived in embracing and so on. **Maturation** is the opposite of that—not variegated—because something perceived does not exist; it is the blissful experience of wisdom[2939] during friction. **Consummation** is the bliss that is the nonconceptual perception pervading the jewel up to its tip. **The lack of characteristics** is something other: it is free of passion because there is no strong bliss, and it is free of dispassion because it lacks the dispassion at the [time after] emission, which is due to [merely] recollecting the experience of bliss.[2940] {389} This is stated:

> Variety is known as various kinds:
> embracing and kissing and so forth
> Maturation constitutes its opposite:
> the blissful experience of wisdom[2941]
>
> Consummation is proclaimed to be the
> consideration "I have partaken of bliss"[2942]
> Characteristics' lack is other than the three,
> being free from passion and dispassion[2943]

According to the assertion of the Nonaspectarians, this [ecstasy in the moment of the lack of characteristics that is] experienced in the jewel remains as sheer blissful awareness, which is like the stainless stretch of the midday sky in autumn and homogeneous because the pollution of the entire range of all aspects such as blue has disappeared.[2944] However, the means of proof (such as being devoid of singularity and multiplicity) that refute such aspects are not set out [here] for fear of [too many] details.[2945] This is declared [by Dharmakīrti]:

> Hence there exists no coarse appearance
> in referents or in cognition; as what has
> that nature was refuted in a single one,
> it is not possible in any multitude either
>
> This determination is internal; the part
> that presents itself as if external differs
> For the appearance of a differentiation
> of undifferentiated cognition is confusion[2946]

Exactly this [undifferentiated cognition] is the dharmakāya. The cognition subsequent to this, which has the form of the maṇḍala circle and so on, is the sambhoga[kāya]. The forms such as Śākyamuni, which are the elements and elemental derivatives, are the nirmāṇa[kāya]. The fact that these have a single nature is the svābhāvikakāya. {390} Likewise, consummation is the dharma[kāya], maturation the sambhoga[kāya], variety the nirmāṇa[kāya], and the lack of characteristics the svābhāvikakāya. This is stated:

> and the latter two are the two form kāyas[2947]

Because it has been stated "he should meditate until he gives rise to the state of nonreferentiality,"[2948] when precisely this [lack of characteristics], which is indicated[2949] through its example, is familiarized with in an attentive and uninterrupted manner for a long time, the form of the maṇḍala circle and so on will be perfected. That is, through the power of [the practitioner's] previous aspiration prayers [to benefit all sentient beings], the pair of the sambhoga[kāya] and the nirmāṇakāya [will arise]. Alternatively, this bliss that is experienced will become clearly manifest on its own through such familiarization that is attentive and so on.[2950] [Dharmakīrti] declares this:

> Hence whatever is intensely meditated on,
> no matter whether it may be real or unreal,
> once the power of meditation is perfected,
> results in a clear mind free from thoughts[2951]

Here as well, the two form kāyas [arise] through the power of penetrating the previous aspiration prayers, and precisely that is the means of entering. The following is stated:[2952]

> By the means such as maṇḍala circles
> and through the stages of self-blessing[2953]

It is exactly this that is proclaimed as the meaning of the middle:

> Since self-awareness is not extinguished, {391}
> since blue and so forth do not appear,
> and since characteristics do not arise,
> it is asserted as being the middle path[2954]

[In this stanza] here, the nonarising of characteristics is intended to refer to the lack of clinging. Therefore, by virtue of lacking any clinging to [entities as] being real, unreal, and so on, [this awareness] is free from the four extremes. In it, there is also the fourth one, because it is stated that "the fourth is again like that."[2955] "That" refers to the awareness without aspects experienced in the prajñā-jñāna [empowerment]. "Again"—that is, when the stains of the entire range of aspects such as blue have disappeared, [this awareness] should be realized "likewise"—that is, as in the case of [the awareness during] the prajñā-jñāna [empowerment]. However, the Aspectarians say that a cognition without aspects is not even experienced in dreams.[2956] They declare the following:

Discarding the entire range of aspects, there is no operation of the mind
To refute such, victory's glory lies in the powerful approach of the middle
If this irreproachable mind that is nondual yet diverse were not existent,
what opportunity would there be for the assertion of it lacking any forms?[2957]

One should not think like this: "Because of the absence of the clear appearing of aspects, it is all the more the case[2958] that aspects do not exist." For even though there is no determining of that [clear appearing of aspects], what does exist is the awareness of [aspects] such as blue, which cannot be denied, is experienced, and is determined subsequently through left impressions.[2959] {392} [Dharmakīrti] says this:

How a given cognition appears,
it is experienced in just that way
Therefore the diverse aspects in
the mind have indeed one nature[2960]

Therefore there rather exists only diverse yet nondual awareness. But with regard to this too, out of fear of textual prolixity, I have not made any considerations [here] of the epistemic means to prove or refute this. [The Aspectarians] also join this same [view] with the meaning of the middle that is [this diverse yet nondual awareness] free of the four extremes.[2961] As it is said:

It is not nonexistent due to its lucid nature,[2962] nor existent due to those other than it
It is neither both because of its being one, nor is it neither because of its being both
Given that the world is free from these four extreme positions[2963] [as stated] in this way,
what would the difference between the commentator's assertion and the middle be?[2964]

Because of a difference caused by exclusion, consummation, though not [really] distinct from the sambhoga[kāya], is the dharma[kāya], maturation is the sambhoga[kāya], variety the nirmāṇa[kāya], and the lack of characteristics the svābhāvikakāya.[2965] The prajñā-jñāna that illustrates [the connate], repeatedly practiced in just that way (as expressed [above] by the word "again"), is the fourth one—that is, the goal that is endowed with the seven constituents.[2966] Here, the seven constituents consist of (1) enjoyment because of experience, (2) union because of coming together [in sexual union],[2967] (3) great bliss because of having the nature of pleasure, (4) lack of nature because of being free of anything imagined, (5) filled with compassion {393} because of promoting the welfare of sentient beings through the power of penetrating the previous aspiration prayers by means of the sambhoga[kāya] and so on, (6) uninterrupted because of lacking any gap within it, and (7) unceasing because the continuous flow [of nondual awareness] is not cut off.[2968] This is stated as follows:

> Here, what I hold to be endowed with the seven constituents
> of complete enjoyment, union, great bliss, the lack of nature,
> being filled with compassion, uninterrupted, and unceasing
> is the goal praised by those whose minds valid cognition
> penetrated[2969]

Or rather, what is the use of this practice endowed with the seven constituents? There is indeed no [fixed] rule about this. For [just] the circle of Nairātmyāyoginī, when familiarized with, [also] represents a cause of buddhahood. And in that case, the practice is not endowed with the seven constituents, because union [the second constituent] is absent.[2970] This is stated as follows:

The goal is endowed with seven constituents
If the exact same as this goes for the practice,
is it then the case that Nairātmyāyoginī's circle
is not asserted [to be a means] for awakening?[2971]

Or the assertion may be thus that in such a case [meditating on Nairātmyāyoginī not in union with Hevajra] there is also union with the means [in the form of] the khaṭvāṅga.[2972] This is stated as follows:

The goddess is in union with the khaṭvāṅga
and fully endowed with enjoyment and such
Oh, is it not the case that Nairātmyāyoginī
represents a practice means for awakening?[2973]

[However, to understand] this [in such a way] is not nice either. {394} For there would be the [absurd] consequence that, just as in the mantra approach, the goal endowed with the seven constituents is accomplished in the pāramitā approach too because there is the possibility of union in the bodhicitta that has the character of prajñā and means, even though there is no directly visible union as intended [here].[2974] This is stated as follows:

If [union] is conceived of in some other way,
excluding the special union [of the tantras],
the same would follow for the other approach
due to emptiness and the other being united[2975]

Or [it may be held] here that the state of being endowed with the seven constituents does exist in this practice, for the following is declared:[2976]

> Removing the breasts, there is to be the bola,
> well placed within the middle of the kakkola
> It is the two shores that are to become the bell,
> and the filament should turn into the bolaka[2977]

This too is not beautiful.[2978] For this entire [description in the *Hevajratantra*] refers to the stage of accomplishment and not to the stage of practice. Hence it is difficult to avoid the [absurd] consequence that the goal endowed with the seven constituents would be accomplished in the pāramitā approach too, even though there is no practice of such a type.[2979]

First, union's lack should be cultivated
At its completion, this [union] will arise
This is [the goal] that is asserted by us
Nevertheless, the practice is otherwise[2980]

Others [Mādhyamikas of illusion-like nonduality] describe this same [goal] as illusion-like nonduality. {395} The awareness of sexual pleasure with a passionate woman experienced in a dream, being experienced by another dream awareness arising subsequent to it, is not unreal, due to being completely extinguished because it is experienced. Nor is it real, because there is no confirmation, as in the case of a thing observed during the waking state, which performs functions and can be experienced by [both] oneself and others.[2981] This is stated as follows:

When there is a dream after a dream,
then the diversity of the mind is falsity
It is not real, as it perceives the unreal,
nor is it extinct, because it is lucidity[2982]

In just the same way, because it is experienced, the world's diversity too is not delusive, due to being completely extinguished. Nor is it ultimately real, since what is unborn due to ultimately being without any arising at all and is determined as having originated in dependence by means of [reasonings] such as "since it is not reasonable for something existent or nonexistent to arise" is not reasonable to have any reality.[2983] As it is declared:

That which has arisen in dependence
has not arisen through its own nature
What has not arisen by its own nature,
how could that be designated "arisen?"[2984]

Here too, determining its being the fourth one,[2985] being connected with the dharmakāya, and so on should be understood just as before. {396}

[Objection:] "Clearly, 'forceful empowerment,' which is performed by force, is as much as to say that it has no logical support.[2986] How is it that it lacks logical support?" It is said [that this is so] because it contradicts scripture. In order to show this [contradiction to scripture], [Maitrīpa] says: "If consideration . . ."

> **If consideration is consummation,**
> **how could it be held to be the third?**
> **For there, there is no consideration—**
> **awareness is to be characteristics' lack** [3]

> Seeing what is to be marked in the middle
> of the supreme and cessational, stabilize it![2987]

[In these lines] here, it is the middle of the two [supreme ecstasy and cessational ecstasy] that is intended. In your assertion, this does not exist.

[Objection:] "This is not so, because the meaning [of these lines] is another one. It is in fact as follows: this sixth [case in the above compound] is used in a partitive sense.[2988] Therefore the meaning is this: among (*madhye*) those two, the best one should be taken here, and the best is exactly cessational [ecstasy]. So this is just fine."[2989]

Then [the following lines:]

> The beginning of the cessational, beyond the supreme,
> being emptier than being empty, represents the Heruka[2990]

are not suitable. For in this [statement] the beginning of cessational [ecstasy] is held to be beyond supreme [ecstasy].[2991]

[Objection:] "This too is not so. For here too the meaning is another one. 'The beginning of cessational [ecstasy]' refers to what is both cessational [ecstasy] and the beginning,[2992] and being the beginning is meant in relation to connate [ecstasy]. Hence this too is just fine."[2993]

Then how about [the *Hevajratantra* also saying this:]

> It is to be marked at the cessational one's
> beginning, free from the three ecstasies?[2994] {397}

"Here too this should be interpreted[2995] as 'what is both connate [ecstasy] and the beginning,' just as above."

Then how about [the *Hevajratantra* also saying this]:

> Consummation is proclaimed to be the
> consideration "I have partaken of bliss"?[2996]

[This is stated] because here it is clearly understood that the states[2997] of **consummation** and so on have the nature of thought. Now, if [consummation] were in any way stated here to be thought-free, then that too would be canceled out, just because it is invalidated by common worldly consensus. It is as follows: the world thinks that *vimarda* ("consummation") refers to "disagreement" and "crushing,"[2998] [while] "**consideration**" means thinking about such and such tasks and so on.[2999] Furthermore [the *Hevajratantra* says this]:

> During variety, there is the first ecstasy;
> during maturation, it is supreme ecstasy;
> during consummation, cessational ecstasy;
> during characteristics' lack, connate ecstasy[3000]

Here, it is ascertained that cessational [ecstasy occurs] during [the moment of] consummation. Furthermore [the *Hevajratantra* states this]:

> The first ecstasy has a worldly nature
> Likewise, supreme ecstasy is worldly
> Cessational ecstasy is worldly as well
> The connate is not found in these three[3001]

Thus it is declared that consummation, by virtue of its having a worldly nature, has the nature of saṃsāra. In this way, by virtue of the statement "saṃsāra is nothing but thought,"[3002] it shall be taught that it [consummation] is thought, {398} while being thought-free is asserted as referring to connate [ecstasy]; so this too does not tally [with the above objections].[3003] Likewise [this statement in the *Hevajratantra*]:

I have the nature[3004] of connate ecstasy,
at supreme's end and cessation's start[3005]

does not tally[3006] [with the above objections] either. In the same way,

This is the goal in the yoginītantra—
the great bliss called "the connate"
It is to be marked with effort[3007] at the
supreme's end and cessation's start[3008]

and similar [statements] also do not match [the above objections]. Likewise [this is taught]:

First is the vase empowerment,
second the supreme secret one,
third indeed is the prajñā-jñāna,
and the fourth is again like that[3009]

But since the prajñā-jñāna empowerment is [also known as] the empowerment of connate ecstasy, this [teaching] too [—if interpreted as evidence for "consummation" as the third moment—] is negated.[3010] Hence consummation with its nature of thoughts should not **be held to be** in **the third** [position] because that would contradict the scriptures by virtue of passages such as those [quoted above] not matching. **For there** [in the third moment of the lack of characteristics], nothing but thought-free **awareness** exists.[3011]

[Maitrīpa] sums up this very [point] with additional words [in the stanza] that begins "Therefore, look!"[3012]

Therefore, look! It is proper to understand
the lack of characteristics as the third one
This is established through self-awareness,
and the scriptures' meaning also agrees [4]

This is easy to understand. [Objection:] "But since invalidation by common worldly consensus is not [really] a means of invalidation, how would it be that [Maitrīpa] has demonstrated [proper] invalidation [in stanza 3] beginning with 'If consideration were consummation'?"[3013] {399} This too is the result of your not fully understanding our intention here. For since consummation has a worldly nature [and thus is in the fourth position] according to [the above-cited line] "cessational ecstasy is worldly as well,"[3014] [if it were third], all scriptures as adduced [above] would not match because they would invalidate the topic at hand here [the lack of characteristics—connate ecstasy—being the third one and being thought-free]. And the passage beginning with "[If] consideration" would not match either.[3015] Therefore, with [stanza 3] beginning with "[If] consideration," [Maitrīpa] has demonstrated the invalidation [of the assertion that consummation is third]. For the same reason, noble Nāgārjunapāda too has demonstrated [such] an invalidation in the *Caturmudrānvaya*:

> Seeing what is to be marked in the middle
> of the supreme and cessational, stabilize it![3016]

[Objection:] "Then in your position, how [about this stanza in the *Hevajratantra*]:

> "By virtue of ecstasy, there is slight bliss
> Supreme ecstasy is more intense than it
> With the cessational, there is dispassion
> Connate ecstasy [exists] as the remainder?"[3017]

That too is to be understood as follows. [The expressions] ecstasy, supreme [ecstasy], and cessational [ecstasy] pertain to slight bliss, more intense [bliss] than that, and dispassion. Hence "as the remainder"—[that is to say,] as a consequence—connate ecstasy should be understood as being other than the three [preceding ecstasies]. Alternatively, they are stated in this way by the force of the [alphabetical] order of ecstasy, supreme, cessational, and connate.[3018] However, {400} it should be **understood** that connate [ecstasy] is definitely **the third** one.[3019]

[Objection:] "If this is so, why didn't the Bhagavān solely teach the excellent empowerment? Why did he teach the sequence 'ecstasy, supreme [ecstasy], cessational [ecstasy], and connate [ecstasy],' which is a locus of doubt in terms of the forceful empowerment that is full of hardships?" This is not so. For that sequence was just taught in order to remove [the reliance on] being learned in books and to [show the necessity of having to] depend on a spiritual friend.[3020] This is declared:

> For awakening is[3021] dependent on a spiritual friend.[3022]

The same [is said] elsewhere:

> It is obtained through the guru who has been pleased[3023]

Furthermore, when [the Bhagavān mentions and then] refutes the forceful empowerment and the poor empowerment because of their contradicting **the scriptures**, he [thereby] does not at all refute the differentiation of Nonaspectarianism and so on, because it is only the application of that [differentiation of Nonaspectarianism and so on] that is contradicted.[3024] Therefore this entire differentiation should be understood as only pertaining to [the context of] the tenet of the excellent empowerment that has the nature of the Vajradhara relief. [Thus the differentiation of Nonaspectarianism and so on] has been taught here for the sake of [clarifying that] the proponents of the forceful and the poor empowerments too describe this in the same way in their own tenets.[3025] {401}

After this, [Maitrīpa] discusses the poor empowerment [in the stanza] that begins "For whom . . ."[3026]

> **For whom variety is in kissing and embracing,**
> **what is called "maturation" lies within friction,**
> **and the lack of characteristics is in the jewel—**
> **they indeed know the poor empowerment well** [5]

Variety consists of [all] the external activity beginning with looking up to friction. **Maturation** consists of the **friction** beginning with the union of bola and kakkola up to the moon arriving in the jewel. **The lack of characteristics is** [blocking bodhicitta] **in the jewel** up to [it moving to] the place where it becomes spoiled, which will be discussed [below].[3027]

They who proclaim[3028] thus "**indeed know the poor empowerment well.**" With the word "well," [Maitrīpa] laughs at them.[3029]

In order to refute them, [Maitrīpa] states [the stanza] that begins "But if it were . . ."[3030]

But if it were the case that this very awareness
that is on the jewel's inside were true reality,
it would be the Śaivist and Vedic true reality
However, this is not asserted by the Buddhists [6]

"**Śaivist**" means "of Śiva" and "**Vedic**" means "of the Veda."

[Objection:] "Is this really [the true reality] of the Śaiva [teachings] and other [non-Buddhist traditions]?" Therefore [Maitrīpa] utters [the stanza] that begins "It is this very jewel city . . ."[3031]

Thus, in the *Devīparipṛcchāśivanirnādatantra*, [this is said]:

It is this very jewel city, oh you goddess,
that turns into water within the filament
Rudra in the pair is Śiva, the excellent one
This is Śakti, more supreme than supreme[3032] [7]

"**Jewel**" means "gem." What has as its place—"**city**"—that very [jewel], held to have the nature of bliss, that is the "jewel city." "**Within the filament**" means [when it has] fallen [into the lotus]. "**Turns into water**" means [it assumes] a state without pith.[3033] "**Rudra**" refers to the Bhagavān, "**in the pair**" to union, and "**Śiva**" to the one who brings benefit.[3034] Precisely for this reason, he is "**the excellent one**." "**This**"—true reality—is **Śakti**, the nature of mind. {402} What is **more supreme than supreme** (more excellent than excellent) is [also] that very [true reality].[3035]

[Maitrīpa now] states its own nature [in the stanza] that begins "Free of . . ."

Free of characteristic and characterized,
and devoid of any utterances of speech,[3036]
thanks to the union of Śiva with Śakti,
the bliss that is marvelous springs forth [8]

This is easy to understand.

Teaching that only this supreme [true reality], the nature of the world's diversity, exists, [Maitrīpa] adduces [the stanza] that begins "Entities do not exist . . ."

Entities do not exist in true reality
They are manifested in Śakti's form
But Śakti is the view of emptiness,
the destroyer of all superimpositions [9]

Entities (external forms and so on) **do not exist in true reality** (in ultimate reality). "Then how is there the appearance of blue and so on?" Therefore [Maitrīpa] says: "**They are manifested in Śakti's form**." That is, they come to have the nature of mind's power, which means they have the character of mind. "Then just that [power of the mind] should be ultimately existent." Therefore, in order to refute this [idea], [Maitrīpa] says: "**But Śakti** . . ." This is easy to understand.[3037]

This very [true reality] is devoid of the four extremes. This has been stated in the Śakti-related tantra *Bhargaśikhā*:

It is not existent, not nonexistent, not existent
and nonexistent [both], and not devoid of both
For this state that is indeed difficult to cognize
is indescribable and incomparably supreme[3038]

[Maitrīpa now] states the very same also in another way [in the stanza] that begins "The true bliss . . ."

In the *Ucchuṣmatantra* too, [the following is declared]:[3039]

The true bliss, supremely nondual,
thanks to Śiva's and Śakti's union,
being neither Śiva, nor being Śakti,
abides in the interior of the jewel [10]

"**Abides in the interior**[3040] **of the jewel**" means abiding in the middle of the gem.

[In the stanza] that begins "For yogīs satiated . . . ," [Maitrīpa] speaks about [this true reality also being] the highest goal of the yogīs who have become aware of this wisdom.[3041] {403}

In the *Yogādhyāya* as well, [this is taught]:[3042]

For yogīs satiated with wisdom's nectar
who have done what needs to be done,
there isn't anything that should be done
If there is, they don't know true reality [11]

This is easy to understand.

Now [you may think] the proponents of Vedānta might perhaps describe [their true reality], which has come down to them through the sequence of the sacred traditions that will be mentioned [below], in this [same] way. Therefore [Maitrīpa] states the first half [of the next stanza] that begins "Bhāskara . . ." in order to easily discard this by [first properly] understanding it.[3043]

Also, the proponents of Vedānta state this:

Bhāskara asserts that wisdom is beyond
the sense faculties and without awareness
Those who follow the Bhagavān assert
that awareness consists of sheer ecstasy [12]

For this has been said:

They proclaim that the faculties are supreme
The *manas* is more supreme than the faculties
But *buddhi* is more supreme than the *manas*
Yet the one more supreme than *buddhi* is He[3044]

The rest is easy to understand.

[Maitrīpa] says in [the stanza] that begins "The bliss . . ." that in the Vedānta of the *Bhagavatsiddhānta* too there is the [same] above-mentioned [target] marked by the example.[3045]

The bliss that is the true reality of the Brahman
due to being excited in the union with the Śakti,
which is at the end of the passion for the Śakti,
that bliss is proclaimed to be your very own one[3046] [13]

[Here] "**Śakti**" means woman. **The union** with her is sexual intercourse. **Being excited** by that refers to moving **due to** that.[3047] "**Which is at the end of the passion for the Śakti**" means at the end of the passion (strong passion, further and further increasing desire) for the Śakti (for the woman)—that is, [the bliss] that arises at the consummation of that. As for **the bliss that is the true reality of the Brahman** (the true reality of wisdom), **that bliss is proclaimed to be your very own one** (your own).[3048] This signifies that [this bliss] is equivalent to [the moments of bliss] that are located within the bola, in its tip, midway between [bola and kakkola], and in the kapāla [the kakkola]. {404} For this is declared:

At the time when all the sexual pleasure
that originates from a woman disappears,
there isn't any other awareness that arises
For that long, the Kaulāgama springs forth[3049]

In order to teach the nature of that [bliss], [Maitrīpa] utters [the stanza] that begins "There exists no . . ."[3050]

There exists no coming of suffering
There, bliss is a continuous stream
Ecstasy is the nature of the Brahman
This becomes manifest in liberation[3051] [14]

This is easy to understand.

[In the stanza] that begins "No matter what . . . ," [Maitrīpa] says that [according to nondual Kaula Śaivism] the world has the single nature [that is identical] with this very [bliss that is the nature of the Brahman].[3052]

No matter what it is that may be seen,
it is to be conceived as "the Brahman"

Hence the mind does not go elsewhere
It remains within the Brahman alone[3053] [15]

This is easy to understand.

Next, [in the stanza] that begins "The beloved woman . . . ," [Maitrīpa] utters the praise of the woman who is the cause of this wisdom.[3054]

The beloved woman alone is the only sight
What is the point of different other sights?
[The sight] by which nirvāṇa is attained
is even with a mind that is full of passion[3055] [16]

"**The beloved woman alone is the sight**" is taken [to mean] that the desired liberation is seen through her. The rest is easy to understand. This amounts to saying that, through rejecting other [ways of] explanation, those [followers of the Vedānta of the *Bhagavatsiddhānta*—that is, of Kaula Śaivism] also truly desire just such women for the sake of showing the example.[3056]

For those who have entered [this path] in such a way, [Maitrīpa] now speaks about the relinquishment of all attachment [in the stanza] that begins "Abandon . . ."[3057]

Abandon dharma as well as nondharma
Abandon both, the truth as well as fiction
Having abandoned both, truth and fiction,
abandon that by which you abandon them[3058] [17]

This is easy to understand.

[In the stanza] that begins "There's no . . . ," [Maitrīpa] says that [the awareness of the followers of the *Bhagavatsiddhānta*] is free of the four extremes.[3059]

In the *Bhagavadgītā* too, [this is proclaimed]:

There's no nonexistent's being,
nor any nonbeing of an existent

The end of both of these is seen
by those who see the true reality[3060] [18]

This is easy to understand.[3061]

Having declared that [the approach of the proponents of the poor empowerment] is similar to the scriptures of others, [Maitrīpa now] says [in the stanza] that begins "Moreover" that [the approach of said proponents] contradicts our own scriptures.[3062] {405}

Moreover, if this were said to be Akṣobhya—
the mind, empty of the perceived and so on—
this is invalidated through our own scriptures,
because it would lack the seal of Vajrasattva [19]

For here [in the Mahāyāna], the matter [the nature of true reality] that is examined in the Madhyamaka and other [systems] is revealed in the mantra approach as the fruition through deity yoga.[3063] Therefore, given that whatever is sealed with something comes to have the nature of that something,[3064] in order to eliminate [the notion] that the perceived, which has the nature of the set of the [first] four skandhas beginning with form, has the state of something perceived [that is separate from the perceiver], the four of Vairocana and so on are taught to be the perceivers whose nature is the dependent [nature]. [However,] **if**, in order to seal those [four], [true reality] **were said to be Akṣobhya**, whose nature is the perfect [nature] **empty of the perceiver and** the perceived, then **the seal of Vajrasattva** taught in the **scriptures** would be contradicted because Akṣobhya, whose nature is the perfect [nature], would truly exist in the bodhicitta located inside the jewel and so on. [However,] there is no Buddhist doctrine without the seal of Vajrasattva, so how would [the forceful and poor empowerments] not be similar to outsider tenets?[3065] Thus Kambalāmbarapāda [says this]:

When analyzed with the powerful intelligence
of keenest insight, the doctrine is all the same,
if the one thing—emptiness—that distinguishes
Buddhists and outsiders were not indicated here[3066]

> "Let there not be any abiding in cognizance"—[3067]
> because he was afraid of exactly that, the Sage
> has differentiated the dharma of his teachings, {406}
> repeatedly stating it has emptiness's character[3068]

The Buddha's words also [say this]:

> Between all the Vedas and tenets,
> composed by Īśvara and so forth,
> and Buddhist tantras and mantras,
> the difference is about emptiness[3069]

The difference between the statements on emptiness as imagined by others and the statements on emptiness by the Tathāgata, which is caused by [their different] intentions, is clear and will thus not be expanded on [here].[3070]

[Objection:] "In that case, then for what reason is this [experience of connate ecstasy as the third one during the prajñā-jñāna empowerment] taught?" Therefore [Maitrīpa] utters [the stanza] that begins "What then is the reason . . ."

> **What then is the reason that this is**
> **invariably taught by the teachers?**
> **This is illuminated first by way of**
> **having the tathāgata relief in mind** [20]

"**The tathāgata relief**" is the relief of the tathāgata,[3071] and "tathāgata" refers to Vairocana. [But] since he has the meaning of a synecdoche, Ratnasambhava and so on [may also be] included. Therefore Ratnasambhava, Amitābha, and Amoghasiddhi are included [here]. Their relief is that they are turned into consciousness once they are sealed with Akṣobhya. "**By way of having** that **in mind**" means "by way of intending that."[3072] {407}

Now, [in the stanza] that begins "Being inside . . . ," [Maitrīpa] teaches [what] which proponents [experience] in which location.

Being inside the bola is to be with aspect
Being at its tip means to be without aspect
Some claim this as being the very middle
The guru's view is that this is not the case [21]

Being inside the bola is to be with aspect and **being at its tip means to be without aspect**. Alternatively, being at its tip means to be with aspect and being inside it is to be without aspect. The **claim** of **the very middle** in this way here **is not** the **view of** our **guru**.[3073]

Why? [Maitrīpa] utters [the stanza] that begins "Neither inside . . ."[3074]

Neither inside the vajra, nor at its tip,
nor as having dropped into the kapāla,
nor in between is true reality asserted
As per the guru's mouth, it's in awareness [22]

Because it **is not asserted**. Why is it not asserted? [Maitrīpa] says: "Because, by virtue of Akṣobhya, who has the nature of bliss, existing **inside the vajra** and **at its tip**, the seal of Vajrasattva is absent [there]. [Nor is true reality] **in between** or **in the kapāla**, for the following reason: letting alone for the moment the absence of the seal of Vajrasattva, since the experience of bliss that is [consciously] ascertained exists [there], there exists something perceived and so on, and by virtue of that even the seal of Akṣobhya is not present. One obtains this [understanding] by way of the above-mentioned [line 19d] 'because it would lack the seal of Vajrasattva' continuing to bear on this." Then where should true reality be perceived? [Maitrīpa says:] "**As per the guru's mouth, true reality is in awareness**," which is the traditional teaching on the whereabouts of the location of the Bhagavān who is the holder of sixteen bindus twice halved.[3075] {408} This is stated:

Two have fallen while two are even
Falling from the vajra, they touch the lotus

Falling from the vajra is Akṣobhya
Touching the lotus is Vajra[sattva]

> The cause is sealed with the result—
> this represents the king of great bliss[3076]

One should understand that these two—the nature of vajra and the nature of sattva—are designated as Vajrasattva: emptiness and compassion, prajñā and means, nirvāṇa and saṃsāric existence, and so on. This same meaning, in the context of the creation process,[3077] was shown here and there by the Bhagavān in the form of the two bindus located in the middle of a moon and a sun, [respectively] situated below and above,[3078] in the [phase known as] attaining dissolution by virtue of great passion.[3079] On the other hand, the perfection [process] consists of the purport of the empowerment as it has been discussed [here]. The full-perfection [process] in its turn refers to the Bhagavān, arisen from the melted state, located on a sun disk having the nature of the bola,[3080] and having the character of prajñā and means, the essence of emptiness and compassion, and the nature of the dharmadhātu. His touching the [sun disk that is his] seat with [only] the toe of one foot, though, is in order to indicate the fact that he is not driven toward the time that is the phase of emission.[3081]

[Objection:] "But in that case, how about [the *Hevajratantra* saying]

> "They are to again contemplate the true reality of HŪṂ
> standing in the middle of the central part of the vajra[3082]

"For here the meaning of 'standing in the middle of the central part of the vajra' does not match up." Not so, because this has another meaning. {409} For it is as follows: what is intended [here] is that what should be contemplated is "the true reality of HŪṂ" standing in the middle between the vajra and the pericarp of the lotus—that is, between the best parts of prajñā and means—with "HA" meaning empty of causes, "Ū" meaning free from deliberation,[3083] and "AṂ" meaning utter nonabiding.[3084]

[Objection:] "But then how about 'within the jewel'"?[3085] To answer, here too, that same other meaning [applies]. For it is like this: "between[3086] the two jewels—[the jewels] of the lotus and the kuliśa." Thus this too is fine.[3087]

[Objection:] "But how is it known that in both places it is this meaning that is intended?" It is because of the following scriptural statement in the *Paramādya[tantra]*:[3088]

> In the lotus's space, at the place of
> jewel and pericarp pressed together,
> from the vajra seat, seeing the mind,
> which has arrived within the jewel,
> the wisdom that arises, this wisdom
> is of such a nature—that is enough![3089]

Here the meaning is this. "In the lotus's space" means "in the empty spot in the middle of the lotus, at the place where the jewel and the pericarp, of the lotus and the kuliśa,[3090] are pressed together (that is, at the place of close friction)."[3091] What is intended by "from the vajra seat" (*vajra-paryaṅkataḥ*) in the fifth [case (ablative)], meaning "all around—*pari*—of the vajra's lap—*aṅkataḥ*," is outside of the vajra and just touching it. {410} For those who see the mind between the two jewels, the consciousness that arises is consciousness's very own nature. This is the meaning.[3092] Likewise, in the *Vajrāmṛta[tantra*, this is said]:[3093]

> Oh goddess, it is located within the navel,
> in the hidden sphere of the lotus's pericarp
> It flows in the form of semen and is [then]
> located in between the bhaga and the liṅga[3094]

It is stated in the *Hevajra[tantra]*:

> The *a*-series is the moon, the *ka*-series the sun
> and the seed is located in the middle [of them][3095]

Likewise:

> For as long as the fluid that bears cool rays[3096] and consists of luminosity does not descend

into the petals of the lotus of the goddess, being of equal taste with the victors' assemblies,
bursting forth from the vajra peak's tip, not separated from compassion, being the world's cause,
for that long, you should know the connate that is the nature of the sovereign, Śrī Karuṇābala[3097]

For as long as, with the three vajras burned, the moon, dropping from the vajra's jewel through the vāyu,
remains in the enclosure of the lotus, longing to melt into the hall that is the excellent hollow space,
we know clearly, through reasonings and scripture, that this very mind that arises in this moment,
free from any thoughts of self, other, and so forth, and without any activity, is the connate[3098]

When the remainder is present after supreme ecstasy in the union of the prajñā's lotus and the vajra,
it is held that as long as the one marked by an antelope—the pure bindu dripped from its abode—is motionless,
for that long the mind is not moving to and fro, the flow of the stirring winds comes to an end,
the ears do not hear anything, and the eyes do not move—this is asserted to be "mahāmudrā"[3099]

[Objection]: "In that case, {411} how about the following statement [in the *Hevajratantra*]:

"The connate is not uttered by anyone else,
and it is not obtained anywhere either
It is realized by yourself thanks to merit
and by attending to the guru's observances[3100]

"Here 'the guru's observance' means the observance of the vajra, because [otherwise] it could not be connected with the meaning of 'the time of attending,' and therefore there would be no attending [at all]."[3101]

No. The word *upa*,[3102] by virtue of expressing proximity, [here] conveys that the attending is outside of yet near to the vajra.[3103]

[Objection:] "Then how about [the following lines from the *Hevajratantra*]:

> "The bola's bliss is mahāmudrā
> and the vajrāyatana is the means[3104]

"Here too, that which is the bliss of the bola is mahāmudrā. The vajra itself is the āyatana[3105]—that is, the place, because [otherwise] it would not fit with the meaning of 'means.'" No. It is taught that the bliss of the bola that is both mahāmudrā and located in the vajrāyatana is supreme ecstasy, and that is the means.[3106]

Furthermore, according to our assertion, [the famous scriptural passage] that begins

> Now, then, I will discuss the secret,
> doing so in brief but not in detail:
> In the supreme secret . . .[3107]

is fine.[3108]

This is as follows. "In the secret" (*rahasye*) is connected with "I will discuss the secret." In [the word] *rahasye*, the two [syllables] *ra* and *ha* refer to the vajra and the lotus, respectively, and [*sye*] means "in the space between those two," with "*sa*" meaning in all aspects (*sarvākārena*), "*ya*" in accordance with reality (*yathātathyam*), {412} "*a*" nondual (*advaya*), and "*i*" being beyond thisness (*idantātīta*).[3109] As it is said:

> The *ra* is proclaimed to be "the vajra"
> The syllable *ha* is said to be "the lotus"[3110]

Now, in order to properly establish [the moment of] "variety," [Maitrīpa] utters [the stanza] that begins "'How then could "variety" . . .'"

> **"How then could 'variety is known**
> **as various kinds' and so forth and**

> **'within the jewel' and so on be fine?"**
> **Based on a true guru, it's fully coherent**[3111] [23]

"**A true guru** . . ." means that what is shown [or taught] by a true guru here refers to the pith instructions to be taught by a true guru.[3112] For [a text like the *Hevajratantra*] makes [only] a brief statement:[3113]

> Variety is known as various kinds:
> embracing and kissing and so forth[3114]

For here, by using [the phrase] "and so forth," [everything] up to friction is intended as variety.[3115]

[Objection:] "But how should one know that it is [everything] up to friction [that is intended as variety]?" Because of the following teaching [in the *Hevajratantra*]:

> Embracing a sixteen-year-old
> prajñā with your pair of arms,
> due to bell's and vajra's union,
> the master empowerment is held[3116]

Here "bell's and vajra's union" is intended as the touching of lotus and vajra.

[Objection:] "But this is the master empowerment—from where should one know that the master [empowerment] at the beginning refers to variety?" Because of the detailed explanation [in the *Hevajratantra* that begins]:[3117]

> the ecstasies are to be perceived in due order
> as per the number of the four empowerments[3118]

Here the four such as ecstasy should be known in sequence as [corresponding to the four empowerments as enumerated in the *Hevajratantra*]:

> The master's, the secret, the prajñā, {413}
> and the fourth is again like that—[3119]

Given that ecstasy constitutes the very moment that is variety, variety is [everything] up to friction.

> Maturation constitutes its opposite:
> the blissful experience of wisdom[3120]

Because of this brief teaching, [what follows] up to [bodhicitta moving to] the tip of the jewel is supreme [ecstasy], since supreme [ecstasy] has the nature of bliss.[3121]

[Objection:] "But why is that?" Because of the following instruction [in the *Hevajratantra*]:[3122]

> When the supreme ecstasy is attained
> in the moment that is free of diversity,
> the teacher[3123] should say: "Oh mahāsattva,
> you should hold the bliss that is great![3124]

For only here [in our view] is the meaning of "in the moment that is free of diversity" and so on really possible.[3125] So everything is fine. The meaning of [the passage] beginning with "within the jewel" has already been understood [above].[3126]

[Objection:] "If [everything] up to friction is ecstasy and this is also the master [empowerment], and [what follows] before [bodhicitta reaching] the jewel[3127] is supreme [ecstasy] and this is also the secret [empowerment], then how about [the *Hevajratantra* saying this]:

> "The master's is by the purity of smiling
> The secret is just so in terms of looking
> The prajñā is with regard to embracing
> Then that again for the pair in its union"[3128]

This should be interpreted according to the outer creation [process].

[Objection:] "Then how about the water empowerment and so on {414} being taught as the master [empowerment]?" This too should be understood according to the outer creation [process]. With regard to the ecstasy that is the tathāgata relief, the fact of its being the master [empowerment should be understood] according to the profound creation [process]. With regard to the ecstasy that is the Vajradhara relief, [the fact of its being the master empowerment should be understood] according to the perfection [process]. In the context of the four mudrās, it is the karmamudrā that should be understood as the master [empowerment] according to the full-perfection [process].[3129]

[Objection:] "But the six [lower empowerments] are also taught to be the vase empowerment, because in all [of them] vases are used. How about this [being the vase empowerment,] then?"[3130] Since the word "vase" is a synecdoche for breast and because breasts are employed [here], this here [the six lower empowerments being the vase empowerment] is also fitting.[3131]

[Maitrīpa] teaches all of this [by way of the following stanza] that begins "The master . . ."

The master [empowerment] and such are held
by virtue of the purity of smiling and so forth
This is to be established according to creation
and not according to the nature of perfection [24]

The meaning [of this] has already been understood [through the comments on the above stanzas from the *Hevajratantra*].[3132]

Now [Maitrīpa] teaches the differentiation of the four ecstasies [with the stanza] that begins "Due to being variegated . . ."

Due to being variegated, variety is up to friction
Due to being bliss, maturation is before the jewel
True reality needs to be understood from the guru
Due to consummation, cessation is in dispassion[3133] [25]

Due to being variegated—because of the existence of perceiver and perceived—**variety** (ecstasy) **is up to friction** (ends with friction). Friction is the tactile sensation of bodhicitta up to its being near the jewel.[3134] This [understanding] is arrived at because it is said "before the jewel is supreme [ecstasy]." **Due to being bliss**—{415} because of the existence of intense bliss—**maturation** (supreme [ecstasy]) **is before the jewel** (up to the tip of the gem). The meaning of "**True reality** [needs to be understood] **from the guru**" has already been understood. **Cessation** (ceasing) **is in dispassion**" (when bodhicitta falls), **due to** its being **consummation** because of the consideration "I have partaken of bliss."[3135] This cessation is that [which is described] as "the fourth is again like that."[3136] [Here] "that" is the prajñā-jñāna, which has the nature of the basic ground (*prakṛti*). "Again" refers to having the character of dependent origination, which has the nature of being a modulation (*vikāra*) [of that basic ground].[3137] "Like" refers to reality being perceived in exactly the same way as before, which becomes the fourth one. These are the four ecstasies in relation to a karmamudrā who is an external woman. [However,] when the four mudrās are differentiated, [the four ecstasies] are a single ecstasy, which is [then simply] called "karmamudrā" because it is based on her [a karmamudrā who is an external woman].[3138] Here the differentiation of being without aspects and so on should be understood in the way it was discussed in the context of the forceful empowerment.[3139]

Now [Maitrīpa] teaches the differentiation of cause and result [with the stanza] that begins "Once you obtained . . ."[3140]

> **Once you obtained the karmamudrā,**
> **you should cultivate the dharmamudrā**
> **What is higher than this is mahāmudrā,**
> **from which the samayamudrā arises**[3141] [26]

The karmamudrā, inasmuch as it has the nature of the connate, refers to the seal (stamp or mark) of action (the activities of body, speech, and mind). It is exactly a woman who is expressed [by this term] because [it is used] with a synechdochic meaning due to metaphorical usage based on her being the [physical] support of that [prajñā-jñāna]. {416} **Once the karmamudrā** has been g**ained**, the prajñā-jñāna, which was described as having the nature of the basic ground and in reality only has the nature of a modulation [of that ground], is called "the connate" because it mimics it in being [merely] a resemblance of the [actual] connate,[3142] thus being called "the result of concordant outflow." Thus, in this concordant outflow there is only the ecstasy that is called "variety."[3143]

From that[3144] [arises] the [mudrā] of dharmas such as blue or yellow, which, by means of fivefold awakening, have first been purified through the deity as being free from being anything perceived and so on—this is **the dharmamudrā** that constitutes the sole beautiful means for supreme ecstasy and has the nature of the dharmadhātu and the essence of the utter nonabiding that comes from analysis. This [dharmamudrā] is the result of maturation because it is the special ripening inasmuch as it is the path by virtue of being the proximate cause of mahāmudrā. In this moment of maturation, there is supreme ecstasy.[3145]

From that [arises] **mahāmudrā**. It is great because it seals the three [other] mudrās. And it is a seal: it is directly perceived through attentively and uninterruptedly training in the wisdom of the path that has the nature of the utter nonabiding that does not come from analysis,[3146] lacks any nature of its own, is free from the cognitive obscurations and so forth, serves as the foundation of all accomplishment, {417} is saṃsāric existence's and nirvāṇa's single own nature, and has the single essence of great bliss that embodies nonreferential great compassion.[3147] This is the result of stainlessness because all obscurations disappear [in it]. In this moment of the lack of characteristics, there is connate ecstasy.[3148]

And **from that** in turn [arises] the samaya (symbol).[3149] **The samayamudrā** is Vajradhara's ability to assume various shapes in the forms of Heruka or other [tantric deities] that have the nature of the sambhoga- and nirmāṇa[kāyas] for the welfare of sentient beings. This is the result produced by persons. There, in [the moment of] consummation, there is cessational ecstasy.[3150]

Here, when regarded as being a respectively preceding one, the mudrās are a cause, and when regarded as being a respectively following one, a result.[3151]

Now, [with the stanza] that begins "The ecstasies . . . ," [Maitrīpa] states that each one of the [four] mudrās has the nature of [all] four ecstasies.[3152]

> **The ecstasies are related to each mudrā,**
> **with the exception of mahāmudrā, though,**
> **thanks to the scriptures, self-awareness,**
> **and the pith instructions of the true guru** [27]

Related to each of the **mudrās**, except for **mahāmudrā, the** four **ecstasies** should be known. Exactly therefore, [Maitrīpa] states three reasons by [saying] "**thanks to the scriptures** . . ." As the scriptures state:

> During variety, there is the first ecstasy;
> during maturation, it is supreme ecstasy;
> during consummation, cessational ecstasy;
> during characteristics' lack, connate ecstasy[3153]

{418} Through [passages] such as these, in the *Hevajra[tantra]* and so on, it is declared that variety and so on are ecstasy and so on. Therefore, wherever variety and so on arise, there is the differentiation of ecstasy and so on. They [variety and so on] arise only in the [first] three mudrās but not in mahāmudrā. That this matter has the nature of **self-awareness** is absolutely clear. **The pith instructions of the true guru** [as a further source of knowing this] is what will be taught [in the following stanza] that begins "Variety . . ."

[Among the four mudrās,] the karmamudrā, which has the nature of the four ecstasies and is related to the body, has already been discussed. [Now, Maitrīpa] teaches the dharmamudrā, which is related to speech and [also] has the nature of the four ecstasies, [with the stanza] that begins "Variety . . ."[3154]

> **Variety, [arising] from the karmamudrā,**
> **and maturation are the world's own being**[3155]
> **Characteristics' lack is the stability in that**
> **Consummation is the looking at the world** [28]

Variety is the world's own being, [arises] **from** the cause that is **the karmamudrā**, and is known orally through the pith instructions of the true guru because it leaves variegated impressions. **Maturation** is the very same [the world's own being] by virtue of the disappearance of these variegated impressions through meditation facing penetrating insight.[3156] **Characteristics' lack is the stability** of the absence of impressions **in that**—that is, in the world's own being—by virtue of the intensity of meditation. {419} Even within such stability—within the world's own being that is called "the emptiness endowed with all supreme aspects"—**consummation is the looking at** (observing) **the world** by the meditator, the yogī, who is still acting conventionally in exactly the same way [as before but] with the firm conviction that [everything] is utterly nonabiding. The four ecstasies should be matched in their due order with these [moments of] variety and so on. Here too, the fourth one is as before, [in accordance with the line] "the fourth is again like that."[3157] When everything has the nature of the connate—since it is declared "just this single ecstasy of sexual bliss is differentiated into four in number"[3158]—then the dharmamudrā, the very single nature of the four ecstasies, is supreme ecstasy.[3159]

Having discussed the dharmamudrā, [in the stanza] that begins "Utter nonabiding . . .," [Maitrīpa now] speaks about mahāmudrā, which is the sole nature of connate ecstasy and is related to the mind.[3160]

> **Utter nonabiding in anything at all**
> **is proclaimed to be "mahāmudrā"**
> **Since self-awareness is stainless,**
> **variety and so forth do not arise** [29]

"**In anything at all**" means "in the dependently originating skandhas, dhātus, āyatanas, and so on." **Utter nonabiding** refers to mental nonengagement—that is, being without any superimpositions. This is stated in the Buddha's words:

> The dharmas of mental nonengagement are proper
> The dharmas of mental engagement are not proper[3161]

Likewise:

> To you who are without any imaginary thinking, {420}
> whose mind is in the state of utter nonabiding,
> who lack any minding and mental engagement,
> and who are without focus, let there be homage![3162]

Here one should not think that, similar to the instructions on [using] the jewel ornament on the crown of the head of [the nāga king] Takṣaka as [a remedy to] remove fever,[3163] this is [a teaching on something that] cannot [actually] be put into practice. For **mahāmudrā**, characterized by being endowed with all supreme aspects, can certainly be directly perceived through the kindness of the venerable true guru.

[Objection:] "But how can [this mahāmudrā] here not have the nature of [all] four moments?" To answer, **since self-awareness is stainless** (by virtue of it being without stains), the three stained moments of **variety and so forth** do not arise here [in mahāmudrā]. Therefore the three [other] ecstasies do not arise.[3164]

[Objection:] "Utter nonabiding means being inconceivable. This [being inconceivable], when being conceived, is nothing but a stain because it is an obscuration." In order to remove that concern, [Maitrīpa] utters [the stanza] that begins "Effortless . . ."[3165]

> **Effortless indeed is that which**
> **is called inconceivable wisdom**
> **But what is inconceivable, once**
> **conceived, is not inconceivable** [30]

That utter nonabiding **is** the **inconceivable wisdom** that does not come from analysis. How is it then? It is **effortless** and occurs in its own natural flow. Why? Because **what is inconceivable, once conceived** (reflected [about]), becomes **not inconceivable**. This is declared in the *Jñānasiddhi*: {421}

> The wisdom of a buddha is without effort
> Therefore it is stated to be nonconceptual
> But once it is conceived, since it lacks a
> cause, it does not become nonconception[3166]

Now, in order to refute the suspicion that [this position] is [identical with] the doctrine of consciousness[3167] and, once that has been dispelled, also the suspicion of extinction, [Maitrīpa] utters [the stanza] that begins "Those who . . ."[3168]

> **Those who set their eyes on suchness**
> **in line with the very middle's actuality**
> **are the fortunate realizing true reality**
> **If directly known, it is by awareness** [31]

Those who set their eyes on (directly perceive) **suchness** (the true end) **in line with the very middle's actuality** (being free from the four extremes) **are the fortunate realizing true reality**. Is this [true reality] then [realized] through extinction? Not at all—[it is realized] **by awareness** (wakefulness)[3169] if that true reality is **directly known** (experienced) because [then] all impressions are removed without remainder. This [true reality] that is like that[3170]—having the character of the two realities, being free from both extremes, inseparable emptiness and compassion, prajñā's and means's own nature—should be known by virtue of the awareness [that dawns] thanks to the kindness of the venerable true guru.[3171]

[Then Maitrīpa] says the same thing with additional words [in the stanza] that begins "No matter . . ."[3172]

> **No matter how many they may be, in all regards,**
> **superimpositions in their entirety are not there**
> **The middle's actuality is superimposition's lack—**
> **where could there be removal or accomplishing?** [32]

For **there**, in **the middle's actuality, no matter however many they may be, superimpositions** (fixed determinations)[3173] **in their entirety are not** existent. [Objection:] "This kind of absence of superimpositions {422} is also asserted in the approach of consciousness." Therefore [Maitrīpa] says "**in all regards**." For there [in the approach of consciousness], consciousness is indeed the locus of superimposing it as a really existent entity. Hence, there, superimpositions are not absent in all regards.

Through this, the tenet of illusion-like [nonduality] too has been denied. Why? Leave aside here for the moment all thinking, since [all] fixed determinations are the objects to be removed, as well as the lack of superimposition, since a [certain] lack of superimposition is possible in the doctrine of consciousness too. Therefore **the middle's actuality is**

superimposition's lack (the lack of discursiveness). But there is the following difference. In the doctrine of consciousness, even when there is a thought-free state [in meditation], there is still the very strong power of ignorance [taking] consciousness to be really existent.[3174] Therefore, even when there is no forceful impression [of external objects] in the mind, at that very time [of thought-free meditation, there is still] grasping at [it as] self-awareness. Hence, it is absolutely clear that subsequent [to such thought-free meditation] there is grasping at awareness.

[Objection:] "But this is the same for you as well, since [for you too,] subsequent [to thought-free meditation,] all thinking exists [again]." No, because [the practitioner] acts in a conventional manner [only] to oblige the wishes of sentient beings who are not to be fixated on [as being really existent], since [everything] is utterly nonabiding. Therefore, **where could there be removal** (denial) **or accomplishing** (prescription)**?**[3175] This means they do not [occur] at all.[3176] {423}

"Then how should the entities that are cognized be known?" Therefore [Maitrīpa] utters [the stanza] that begins "In that . . ."[3177]

> **In that [state] in which there are no superimpositions**
> **of cognition and cognizable, thinking is not otherwise**
> **Everything is just the same way as it had been before,**
> **[but] the mind is certainly not the same as it had been** [33]

For **in that** [state]—in the world that is empty of any **superimposition of cognition and cognizable** and whose character consists of true reality—**thinking is not otherwise** than being conceptual and being nonconceptual. How is it then? Exactly **as it had been before**—when true reality was not known—**everything is** also **just the same way** when true reality is known. The following is declared:

> There is nothing to be removed from this
> and not the slightest that is to be added
> Actual reality is to be seen as it really is—
> whoever sees actual reality is liberated[3178]

Likewise, elsewhere too this is stated:

> Full knowledge of saṃsāric existence
> itself is what is designated as "nirvāṇa"[3179]

Alternatively, "**everything is just the same way as it had been before**" means that just as the entire world had the nature of the connate and the nature of suchness when there was no realization, it should also be known to be just the same way when there is awakening. This is said:

> Just as it is before, so it is thereafter:
> you have the realization of suchness[3180]

Elsewhere [it is stated]:

> Indeed, all phenomena have the connate as their way; they do not go beyond this way.[3181]

Likewise:

> Even if buddhas do not arise, dharmatā remains in exactly the same way.[3182] {424}

Extensive [parallel statements are also found] in other [works]. But there is the following difference: just **as the mind** with its fixed determinations of perceiver, perceived, and so on **had been** before, it **is not** existent [anymore] in **the same** way later. This is stated:

> These phenomena, however, constitute nirvāṇa
> Due to nescience, they assume saṃsāric forms[3183]

Here "nescience" refers to clinging to perceiver, perceived, and so on. The same is declared elsewhere too:

> This is what Saraha pronounces:
> being thought-free is just as it is—
> it is not the way it is conceived[3184]

[In the stanza] that begins "As for those . . . ," [Maitrīpa] teaches what the world is like for those who have experienced this kind of wisdom.[3185]

> **As for those who realize the world as unborn,**
> **their mind is simply pure by this realization**
> **For those insightful ones, in an effortless way,**
> **the world is the native state, which is reality** [34]

As for those who, by means of [arguments] such as "since it is not reasonable for something existent or nonexistent to arise," **realize** (know through direct perception) **the world as unborn, their mind**, which is dependently originated, **is simply pure by this realization** (by this penetrating insight). Therefore, **for those insightful ones, in an effortless way** (completely without any effort), **the world is the native state** (the connate), which is **reality** (not delusive).[3186]

Now, [in the stanza] that begins "The thought . . . ," [Maitrīpa] teaches that even thoughts are nirvāṇa.[3187]

> **The thought whose connection has not**
> **yet been perceived arises dependently**
> **That is, exactly this represents nirvāṇa,**
> **so do not create any delusion, oh mind!** [35]

The thought whose connection has not yet been perceived (whose connection has not yet been known) has originated **dependently**. {425} **That is** (therefore), **exactly this represents** [what is called] "**nirvāṇa**." Hence, **oh mind, do not** produce confusion! This is stated:

> Exactly what is dependent origination
> is what you assert as being emptiness[3188]

[Here] "emptiness" means "nirvāṇa."[3189]

[In the stanza] that begins "Those who . . . ," [Maitrīpa] teaches how mahāmudrā is attained by realizing the wisdom that has not [yet] been born.[3190]

Those who do not abide in the remedies,
who even lack attachment to true reality,
and who have no desire for the fruition,
it is they who will discover mahāmudrā[3191] [36]

"**Those who do not abide in the remedies**"—that is, in the attachment to the conceptions that analyze the remedies, which have the character of generosity, discipline, patience, vigor, dhyāna, and prajñā, by way of analyzing their nature, qualities, and essence—[do not abide in these conceptions] by virtue of abandoning them by not mentally engaging in them. By [speaking of] relinquishing the attachment to the conceptions that analyze the remedies, one should consider that this also refers to relinquishing the attachment to the conceptions that analyze their antagonistic factors, which have the character of the five contaminated appropriating skandhas, such as form, and further [sets, such as the dhātus and āyatanas]. For when that [first] one does not exist, this [second] one does necessarily not exist [either]. Those "**who even lack attachment to true reality**" even lack attachment (are not attached) to the conceptions that analyze true reality, which has the character of emptiness, suchness, and so on, by way of analyzing its nature and so on. {426} Those "**who have no desire for the fruition**" do not have any desire (hankering) for any fruitions, which has the nature of being attached to the conceptions that analyze attainments (beginning with the first bhūmi and ending with the knowledge of all aspects). **It is they who will discover** (attain) **mahāmudrā**. Through this, [Maitrīpa] introduces mahāmudrā as being free of all attachment due to the disappearance of any attachment to antagonistic factors, remedies, true reality, and the fruition by virtue of [all of them] having the world's own being, whose nature is utter nonabiding and the lack of superimposition.[3192]

[Objection:] "Is there then a total absence of the pāramitās of generosity and so on in mahāmudrā?" No, because this very [mahāmudrā] has the nature of the two accumulations of merit and wisdom, whose character consists of all pāramitās and so on. This is declared in the *Viśeṣacintibrahmaparipṛcchāmahāyānasūtra:*[3193]

> Abandoning all afflictions is generosity. Being free from mental application[3194] is discipline. Being free of characteristics is

patience. Careful discrimination[3195] is vigor. Utter nonabiding {427} is dhyāna. Nondiscursiveness is prajñā.[3196]

Through this, it is established that "prajñāpāramitā" consists of the very nature of utter nonabiding and nondiscursiveness. This has been stated in the *Saptaśatikā [Prajñāpāramitā]*:

> The Bhagavān said: "At the time when you, Mañjuśrī, cultivate prajñāpāramitā, abiding where do you cultivate prajñāpāramitā?" Mañjuśrī replied: "Bhagavān, at the time when I cultivate prajñāpāramitā, at that time I cultivate prajñāpāramitā [while] utterly not abiding [anywhere]." The Bhagavān said: "When you are utterly not abiding, Mañjuśrī, what is your cultivation of prajñāpāramitā?" Mañjuśrī replied: "Exactly this, Bhagavān, is the cultivation of prajñāpāramitā—utterly not abiding anywhere at all." The Bhagavān said: "At the time when you, Mañjuśrī, cultivate prajñāpāramitā, which of the two is the case at that time: will roots of virtue increase or decrease for you?" Mañjuśrī replied: "Bhagavān, at that time no roots of virtue at all will increase or decrease for me. Those, Bhagavān, {428} for whom there is any increase or decrease of any dharma whatsoever do not cultivate prajñāpāramitā. Bhagavān, that which aids in any increase or decrease[3197] of any dharma whatsoever should not be understood as the cultivation of prajñāpāramitā. That, Bhagavān, is the cultivation of prajñāpāramitā, which neither abandons the dharmas of ordinary people nor appropriates the dharmas of a buddha . . ."[3198]

Having discussed mahāmudrā, [in the stanza] that begins "Just as . . . ," [Maitrīpa] speaks about the samayamudrā, which is the four ecstasies' own nature and omnipresent.[3199]

> **Just as ecstasy and such are arrayed**
> **distinctly within the karmamudrā,**
> **it is the same in the samayamudrā**
> **due to the vajra master's kindness** [37]

"**Due to the vajra master's kindness**" means "thanks to the pith instructions of the true guru." With regard to this, the pith instructions are as follows. When the Bhagavān with his prajñā [consort] has arisen in the form of a sambhoga[kāya] from mahāmudrā, having the nature of its result produced by persons, **ecstasy** is until friction; before the jewel is supreme [ecstasy]; and after arriving at melting due to great passion, the state that has the form of two bindus—as the form of the two bindus above and below, located in the middle of and touching the union of moon and sun whose natures are prajñā and means—is connate [ecstasy].[3200] This is stated: {429}

> There is no beginning, end, or middle,
> neither saṃsāric existence nor nirvāṇa
> This constitutes the supreme great bliss
> There exists neither any other nor self[3201]

This [stanza] has a twofold meaning, according to its being [understood as] expedient or definitive. Of these, the definitive meaning is as follows. "There" means "in [the moment of] the lack of characteristics that is of such a kind [as described]," which refers to thought-free awareness. The expedient meaning is as follows. "There is no beginning" means no first bindu, and "no end" means no last [bindu]. "Middle there" means that there is no middle there, since a middle is absent due to lacking any in-between. "Neither saṃsāric existence" means there is no [bindu] whose nature is saṃsāric existence: the bindu that touches the sun of means is saṃsāric existence, [but] that is not true reality. "Nor nirvāṇa" means there is no [bindu] whose nature is nirvāṇa—the one that touches the moon of prajñā. What is there then? To reply, just "this" whose nature is the single taste of both—supreme great bliss. In this, there is no awareness of other or of self. With regard to this [connate ecstasy of the samayamudrā], it should be understood that the above-mentioned designations such as Vajrasattva [apply] just as they are established for connate [ecstasy] related to **the karmamudrā**.[3202]

Then, {430} when the Bhagavān has arisen in the form of a sambhoga[kāya], as if awakened from sleep right upon having been urged by the songs of the four goddesses such as Pukkasī,[3203] the seeing by manifesting pure worldly thinking[3204] for the welfare of sentient beings is cessational [ecstasy]. Here too, the [line] "The fourth is again like that"[3205] refers to being the fourth one. [In this context,] "that" means the perception of connate [ecstasy], "again" means in all aspects, and "like" means understanding that it should be realized to be like the connate. By virtue of the Buddha's statement that "just this single ecstasy of sexual bliss is differentiated into four in number,"[3206] if everything has the nature of the connate, then the samayamudrā has the nature of the four ecstasies, [but] cessational ecstasy is just a single one.[3207]

[Objection:] "But here, by virtue of [the Bhagavān] having the nature of bindu, awareness without aspects has been taught absolutely clearly." No, because [awareness] without aspects is rejected, since at that time too it manifests all the aspects of the world as having the nature of inexpressible bliss.

[Objection:] "Then what is the purpose of arising in the form of [two] bindus, since, just like the bliss perceived with a karmamudrā, here too nothing but having the character of prajñā and means, which have the forms of arms, faces, and so on, is suitable?" To reply, {431} this is in order to show [awareness] with aspects, inasmuch as it has the form of the bindus of bliss, through the change of state that resembles the [arising] of the form of a vase from the form of clay. This is stated: "The Bhagavān remained in the form of bindu."[3208]

Or the following may be said: "[The *Hevajratantra* says this]:

> "The covered one has the look of kunda
> The uncovered has the nature of bliss[3209]

"What is perceived with a karmamudrā is conventional, not ultimate. 'Uncovered' means not obscured—that is, nirvāṇa. Thus bliss is distinguished [as two kinds]." This too is not so. For since [the *Hevajratantra*] says: "Without bliss, this would not exist,"[3210] there is no bliss that is distinct [from semen] because bindu and bliss have an identical nature. This should be understood by virtue of the following statement:

> Hence, bliss is not declared to be true reality
> because bliss consists of the great elements[3211]

Or one might think thus: "Since variety takes on the form of bindus, this is simply [awareness] without aspects." This is also not coherent. If it were stated like this while having "being without aspects" in mind, then bindu—the cause of doubt about realizing what is without aspects—would have been left out and only bliss would have been mentioned instead. What would be the use of this bindu that involves a lot of trouble of the kind mentioned? Therefore there is no [awareness] without aspects at all.[3212] {432}

[Now, with the stanza] that begins with "Variety . . . ," [Maitrīpa] clarifies that each single mudrā represents one single [corresponding] ecstasy, as discussed just above.

Variety constitutes the karmamudrā
The dharmamudrā arises in maturation
Lack of characteristics is mahāmudrā
Consummation is the samaya[mudrā] [38]

The meaning [of this stanza] has already been understood.

[Objection:] "But [as you yourself said,] this text follows the *Caturmudrānvaya*, and that [work] conforms to the yoginītantras, while not conforming to the yogatantras." This is not so. We say the following:[3213]

What was stated by noble Nāgārjuna
in accord with the *Śrī[guhya]samāja*
by means of the five stages, just that
is declared in *The [Succession of the] Four Mudrās* [too]

[There,] in due order, in two [separate] stages,
there are mantra embodiment and mind focus[3214]
Here these two are expressed by a single mudrā
because the mind resides in mantra embodiment

Because the bliss of the dharmamudrā
represents the seeing of seeming reality,[3215]
the fact that this reality is the true end[3216]
is said to be the actuality of mahāmudrā

The fruition of the samayamudrā
is awareness of the two's nonduality[3217]
The divine combination of the stages
bestows the fruition of buddhahood[3218]

Thus it has been stated by the venerable master Candrakīrti in his *Pradīpoddyotanaṣaṭkoṭivyākhyā*:

> At first, there should be the creation process,
> which accomplishes the mantra embodiment
> What is then proclaimed to be the second
> stage is nothing but the focus on the mind {433}
>
> The third stage, which is delightful,
> makes up seeming reality's seeing
> The fourth stage is proclaimed as
> being the purity of seeming reality
>
> The fifth [stage] is called "unity,"
> being the union of the two realities
> This is the choicest part of sādhana,
> the synopsis of all tantras' meaning
>
> Those who comprehensively know
> the many distinctions of these stages,
> including the combination of them,
> are those who indeed know the tantra[3219]

Likewise, the venerable Āryadeva too, in his *Sūtakamelāpaka*, has briefly taught the five stages with the names "the true reality of mantra," "the true reality of mudrā," "the true reality of self," "the true reality of dharma," and "the true reality of the deity."[3220] Among them, "the true reality of mantra" refers to the forms of Hevajra and other [deities] arisen from mantras such as the syllable HŪṂ. "The true reality of mudrā," in terms of the expedient meaning, according to the numerical sequence, refers to nothing but the mind focus.[3221] But in terms of the definitive meaning, ["the true reality of mudrā" is used] for the karmamudrā. "The true reality of self" is the lack of nature of mind's diversity of the world. "The true reality of dharma" is the nonarising of phenomena. "The true reality of the deity" refers to making the true reality of self and the true reality of dharma {434} identical, which amounts to saying that they are not different.

It is through the gurus' pith instructions
that these five [kinds of] true realities
are to be matched with the four mudrās,
just as with the five stages, in due order[3222]

[Objection:] "But the following is declared in the tantras:

"The process that consists of creation
as well as the process of perfection—
the vajra holder's dharma instruction
is based upon these two processes"[3223]

"So how could that refer to five stages?" To reply, the condensed stage (*piṇḍīkrama*) and vajra recitation, which are alternatively named "the outer creation process" and "the profound creation process," respectively, are [included] in the creation process. The stages of self-blessing, full awakening, and unity, which are alternatively named "the perfection process," "the full-perfection process," and "the essence process," respectively, are [included] in the perfection process.[3224]

[Furthermore,] you should know that the real existence and nature of these four mudrās is discussed in the *Sarvarahasyatantra*. The following is said there:

Mahāmudrā is related to the mind,
while samayamudrā is omnipresent,
dharmamudrā is related to speech,
and karmamudrā is related to body[3225]

Now, in order to refute those who are satisfied after knowing nothing but the tathāgata relief or the Vajradhara relief in relation to a karmamudrā, {435} [Maitrīpa] utters [the stanza] that begins "Those yogīs . . ."[3226]

Those yogīs who do not know mahāmudrā,
with the karmamudrā as their single device,
fall away from sacred tradition's true reality
and will then take their journey to Raurava [39]

As for those who are hostile to the **true reality** [that comes down] through the **sacred tradition** (through the lineage of gurus), it is because of their rejecting the dharma of the unsurpassable and perfect Buddha—saying "**The karmamudrā** alone is true reality, not the dharmamudrā and the others"—that these [self-styled] **yogīs will then take their journey to Raurava**. Since the word "Raurava" [here] is a synecdoche, other hells such as Avīci should be included too. Going to hells such as Raurava, which definitely happens through rejecting the true dharma, is clear in sūtras such as the noble *Aṣṭasahasrikā [Prajñāpāramitā]* and elsewhere, so it is not expanded on [here].[3227]

[Objection:] "But why is this karmamudrā alone not true reality?"[3228] This is because of statements in the tantras such as this:

The karmamudrā is devious, fierce,
wicked, and extremely frightening—
you should stay far away from her[3229]

Likewise:

The human prajñā is transitory
Bliss from her is transitory [too][3230]

And since this too is declared:

Those who have not seen the supreme ecstasy
think much of the bliss [coming] from women

And because noble Nāgārjunapāda states[3231] the following and more in his *Caturmudrānvaya*:

> A reflection of a face contingent on a mirror is similar [to that face but] not the [actual] face—it was neither established before, nor is it established at present; this [mirror] produces a face's reflection that is a mere likeness. Accordingly, {436} by being deluded, [thinking] they have seen their own face [rather than merely its reflection], worldly people are satisfied. Similarly, having accomplished the wisdom [that is based on a] prajñā, masters of weak intelligence, thinking they have experienced the [actual] connate, give rise to satisfaction. Being satisfied [by that], they do not even understand a basic account of the dharmamudrā.[3232]

And because this is declared in the *Jñānasiddhi*:

> Some wretched people say the pleasure
> born from the two organs is true reality
> However, the greatly excellent victors
> do not proclaim that that is great bliss[3233]

[Objection:] "But by thus rejecting the karmamudrā, who is discussed in many tantras, you too will go to hell, arrive [there], and become immersed in it." No—because of what is stated in the scriptures, it is only her primarily having the nature of true reality that is found fault with. But by showing with [stanza 26], beginning with "Once you obtained the karmamudrā," that she has the nature of the cause [for realizing true reality], [Maitrīpa] has made it clear that she is useful. So why would we reject her? Enough of prolixity. The rest is easy to understand.[3234]

Demonstrating the power of his own chosen deity for realizing the [four] mudrās, [Maitrīpa] utters [the stanza] that begins "For as long as the dust . . ."[3235]

> **For as long as the dust on the feet**
> **of Śabareśa has not been touched,**
> **For that long the four mudrās and**
> **the four moments are not known** [40]

"**Of Śabareṣa**" means {437} "of the siddha, venerable Śrī Śabara."[3236] The rest is easy to understand.[3237]

Now, concluding the text with the dedication of merit, [Maitrīpa] utters [the stanza] that begins "Having laid out . . ."[3238]

> **Having laid out the correct empowerment,**
> **devoid of forceful and poor empowerments,**
> **through the merit that I have accomplished,**
> **may the world come to experience bliss!** [41]

This is easy to understand.

He, to whom the Bhagavān Śrī Śabareśvara extended his kindness in a direct way,
if foolish people despise him out of their ignorance, what could we possibly do?
Ha! Even words of people like myself that are uttered to praise him out of affection
are drowning in him, this great deep ocean of the nectar of unsurpassable dharmatā[3239]

The excellent empowerment [versus] the poor empowerment's sequence and the forceful's succession, which deviate,[3240]
have been taught in this way by the protector[3241]—but alas! such is not an object of those of little intelligence
Therefore I composed a commentary on this [*Sekanirdeśa*], my work having been made possible by his commands,[3242]
after, to the best of my abilities, concentrating my mind with Buddha words[3243] through recollection[3244]

Through the merit that I accumulated
by writing this clear commentary on
the profound ocean of the *Sekanirṇaya*,
may all people be victors in an instant![3245]

It was Śrī Rāmapāla[3246] who composed
this *Sekanirdeśapañjikā* here, which

destroys ignorance, doubt, and trouble
regarding the stage that is the fourth[3247]

This concludes "A Critical Commentary on 'Instructions on Empowerment'" composed by the venerable master Rāmapāla. It was translated, edited, and finalized by the Indian upādhyāya Maṇibhadra and the Tibetan lotsāwa bhikṣu {438} Tsültrim Gyalwa. Subsequently, it was edited slightly by Vajrapāṇi and lotsāwa Tsültrim Gyalwa. Thereafter, it was revised by the Indian upādhyāya Samantabhadra, and later [again] by the Indian upādhyāya Sugataśrī and the Tibetan lotsāwa Batsab Nyima Tra[3248] *by only slightly editing it in the light of an amended manuscript so as to make it a translation that is easier [to read].*[3249]

Appendix 1:
A Compendium of Beginner Activity

In Indian language: *Saṃkṣiptādikarmikaprakriyā*[3250]
In Tibetan language: *Las dang po pa'i bya ba mdor bsdus pa*

I pay homage to Śrī Vajrasattva

Although you fully know that all entities are just like space,
out of compassion, you teach all kinds of deeds for beings
Having bowed to you who are like Indra's weapon in space,[3251]
I shall describe a compendium of the activities of beginners[3252]

Since many people have drunk not just a little bit of the honey taste of the pith instructions that arose from the pith of the guru's lotus feet, their minds have become moistened and they have gathered an abundance of the accumulations of merit and wisdom. Therefore, since they are very familiar with the approach of yoga, they have engaged well in the approach[3253] of their tutelary deity and the accomplishment of the excellent welfare of themselves and others. [However,] since [some of] them are not wise beings yet, they may indeed not depend on the teachings and not greatly cherish the texts compiled by the [teachers].[3254] But those who are other than such [people]—those people who have [properly] entered the approach of mantra—have respect for the teachings of others who realize they are beginners, and thus wish that their entire conduct of body, speech, and mind during the major times of day and night turns into the cause of the siddhis, think: "No matter what kind it may be, I shall not let even a little bit of my conduct be meaningless." Put very concisely, the activities of these mahāsattvas are twofold—that is, the two in relation to the siddhis: (1) the activities that are supreme because they serve as the [actual] causes of the siddhis and (2) the activities that are not so supreme.

1. The supreme activities are five: (a) focusing on the mind, (b) focusing on the body, (c) focusing on mantra, (d) focusing on emanating and withdrawing, and (e) focusing on bindus and the subtle.[3255] Now, their own natures shall be explained a bit.

(a) What is mobile and immobile, [the world's] diversity, and oneself are obscured heaps of illusions, water-moons, echoes, and mirages, and the prajñā of the definitive view overcomes all the poisons of [real] entities without exception.[3256] This contemplation is called "focusing on the mind."

(b) By meditating on oneself as such a kāya at whose major and minor marks one cannot stop looking and that is adorned with all kinds of ornaments, is associated with a maṇḍala or alone, is blessed by the vajras of body, speech, and mind and the jñānasattvas, and is sealed with the lord of its family, the continuity of beginningless clinging and any ordinary thoughts about caste, eyes, and so on are completely put to an end, and those who are endowed with effort will turn into a buddhakāya in this very lifetime. This is focusing on the body.

(c) While focusing on just a seed syllable placed within one's own heart, focusing on recited syllables, or focusing on a circle of syllables, and so on, outer and inner recitations are performed, which dispels inner flaws and gives strength to speech. This is focusing on mantra.

(d) Through light rays emanating from one's own heart, the welfare of sentient beings is promoted. Through withdrawing them again, they enter one's pores and render awakened body, speech, and mind powerful, thus completely overcoming mind's flaws and dispelling the suffering of all sentient beings without exception. This is focusing on emanating and withdrawing.

(e) Through yogīs focusing on a bindu located in the heart or the navel, focusing on a subtle bindu or mark located at the nose tip, and imagining the blazing nāḍī called "caṇḍālī" and so on,[3257] mind becomes very peaceful. Thus [mind] rests and is rendered ecstatic by virtue of the descent of bodhicitta, mind becoming workable and the body supple. This is focusing on the bindus and the subtle.

These five activities are supreme. Since they are nothing but the causes of the siddhis, those who are able to contemplate them [in such ways] with their efforts and let the mind rest [in them] should perform them exclusively by day and night and not engage in any other activities. Since they serve as the causes of the siddhis, they are the supreme activities.

2. Those who do not have the fortune for making efforts in these kinds of activities or who are only able to stay with them for a little time but not for long should rely on the activities that are not so supreme. In brief, the activities that are not so supreme are of nine kinds: (a) the activity that has seven branches, (b) the activity of reading volumes, (c) the activity of consuming food, (d) the activity of oblations, (e) the activity of maṇḍalas, (f) the activity of fire offerings, (g) the activity of stamped clay images, (h) the activity of circumambulation, and (i) the activity of sustaining what one has taken upon oneself.

(a) Being endowed with the yoga of one's own tutelary deity, to perform the seven aspects of paying homage and so on in the manner in which they are explained in *The Aspiration Prayer of Conduct* of the bodhisattva mahāsattva Samantabhadra[3258] is the activity that has seven branches.

(b) Being endowed with the yoga of one's own tutelary deity, to read volumes such as the prajñāpāramitā [sūtras] with the wish that those who hear them thereby become Vajradhara is the activity of reading volumes.

(c) Thinking that what is consumed as food and drink has the character of nectar, one satisfies one's own tutelary deity, offers the first rice ball to Hārītī by [saying] the mantra OṂ HĀRĪTĪ MAHĀYAKṢIṆĪ SINDHUPUTRĪ GṚHAṆA PIṆḌA SVĀHĀ over it, and offers the leftover rice ball by [saying] "OṂ UTSṚṢṬA GṚHAṆA PIṆḌA SVĀHĀ"[3259] over the last rice ball. This is the activity of consuming food.

(d) To bless the leftovers of what yogīs have eaten, as well as any other food and drink that they have obtained in any way, and then offer it to the hosts of the bhūtas is the activity of oblations.

(e) To plaster a maṇḍala with cow dung and pure water and to offer this maṇḍala by saying "OṂ VAJRAREKHE ĀḤ HŪṂ" is the activity of maṇḍalas.

(f) To make fire offerings according to the pith instructions in order to pacify, enrich, subjugate, and for the sake of the secret is the activity of fire offerings.

(g) Being endowed with the yoga of one's own deity, over a lump of sand or a lump of clay, one recites "NAMO BHAGAVATE VAIROCANAPRABHARĀJĀYA TATHĀGATĀYĀRHATEBHYAḤ SAMYAKSAṂBUDDHĀYA / TADYATHĀ OṂ SŪKṢME SŪKṢME ŚĀNTE ŚĀNTE SAMĀROPE ANĀVARAṆE TARAMBE YAŚOVATI MAHĀTEJE NIRĀKULE SARVATATHĀGATAHṚDĀDHIṢṬHITE SVĀHĀ"[3260] twenty-one times and crafts a stamped clay image. Thereafter, one makes it sacred [by saying] "OṂ YE DHARMĀ HETUPRABHAVĀ HETUṂ TEṢĀṂ TATHĀGATO HY AVADAT TEṢĀṂ CA YO NIRODHA EVAṂVĀDĪ MAHĀŚRAMAṆAḤ"[3261] seven times over flowers and tossing them [onto the finished image], thus consecrating it. This is the activity of stamped clay images.

(h) Having built a caitya, a cast image, a buddha shrine, a storied house, and so on, one imagines that one's own tutelary deity and guru, as well as hosts of buddhas and bodhisattvas, reside in its middle. Being endowed with the yoga of one's tutelary deity, one should say "NAMO BHAGAVATE RATNAŚIKHINI TATHĀGATĀYĀRHATE SAMYAKSAMBUDDHĀYA TADYATHĀ OṂ RATNE RATNE MAHĀRATNE RATNAGIRAU RATNAPRATIMANTRITA ŚARIRE SVĀHĀ"[3262] and circumambulate them. This is the activity of circumambulation.

(i) In front of the guru, the venerable buddhas, and so on, yogīs take upon themselves as many genuine actions of body, speech, and mind that serve as the causes of accomplishing the welfare of themselves and others as possible. With the pride of having the physical appearance of their own deity and without any laziness, they engage in all the many activities such as listening, reflecting, writing, reciting, resolving discussions, protecting others, pinning down with a stake,[3263] sprinkling water, and piercing with a spear in order to establish all sentient beings in the state of mahāmudrā. This is called "the activity of sustaining what one has taken upon oneself."

By means of making efforts toward all the
bodily actions and such of beginner yogīs,
the activities that function as the causes
of the siddhis of mahāmudrā and so forth,

I compiled this compendium of activities
Through the virtue that I thus generated,
may the entire conduct of sentient beings
become their engagement in[3264] mahāmudrā!

This concludes "A Compendium of Beginner Activity" composed by master Śrīmat Advayavajra.

Appendix 2: *Taking the Pith Instructions of the Philosophical Systems as the Path*

This text, which is only found in NP[3265] and whose colophon explicitly attributes it to Maitrīpa/Advayavajra, seems to be completely unknown among both Tibetan and other scholars. It is clearly based on Maitrīpa's *Tattvaratnāvalī* (text 34) and *Dohānidhināmatattvopadeśa* (text 22), following their template of the three yānas, four positions,[3266] and nine approaches. It also shows some similarities with TRVC. According to the colophon, these instructions on the three yānas, four positions, and nine approaches came from both Śavaripa and Maitrīpa, and then Maitrīpa's student Vajrapāṇi passed them on to the Newar master *Ajamahāsukha (a.k.a. Balpo Asu).

Different from the *Tattvaratnāvalī* and the *Dohānidhināmatattvopadeśa*, though, the work does not present much philosophical discussion of the four positions and their nine approaches but mainly focuses on the actual meditation instructions of each of these approaches. It clearly blends the style of direct pith instructions on meditation as they are familiar from a Mahāmudrā context with more formal sūtra-based teachings on analytical meditation. Thus the text presents Śavaripa's and Maitrīpa's version of the progressive stages of meditation on emptiness (or the two kinds of identitylessness) as performed in the increasingly subtle and profound approaches of śrāvakas, pratyekabuddhas, Sautrāntikas, Yogācāras, and Mādhyamikas.[3267]

Taking the Pith Instructions of the Philosophical Systems as the Path

In this *Taking the Pith Instructions of the Philosophical Systems as the Path*, there are the three yānas, the four positions, and the nine approaches. Among them, the paths and fruitions of the three yānas teach the gates through which the persons who are the psychophysical supports enter. The four positions teach the basic nature. The nine approaches teach the practice of yogīs. They are taught to put an end to any clinging to entities. Here, the three yānas are the Śrāvakayāna, the Pratyekabuddhayāna, and the Mahāyāna. The four positions are the position of the śrāvakas, the position of the pratyekabuddhas, the position of the Yogācāras, and the position of the Mādhyamikas. The nine approaches consist of śrāvakas of lower faculties, śrāvakas of medium faculties, śrāvakas of highest faculties, pratyekabuddhas, Sautrāntikas, Aspectarian Yogācāras, Nonaspectarian Yogācāras, and Mādhyamikas of illusion-like [nonduality] and utter nonabiding.

Here, the three yānas engage in the four positions, and the four positions in the nine approaches. As for the nine approaches teaching the practice of yogīs, the one of the lower śrāvakas is taught in order to show how to put an end to clinging to the ordinary body as an entity. That is, the one of the lower śrāvakas is taught in order to put an end to thoughts about it and to relinquish the clinging to that entity's cleanness.[3268] The one of the medium śrāvakas is taught in order to relinquish clinging to feelings as being entities. The one of the highest śrāvakas is taught in order to relinquish clinging to phenomena as being entities. The one of the pratyekabuddhas[3269] is taught in order to relinquish clinging to mind[3270] as being an entity.

1. The view of the lower śrāvakas is twofold. (a) Through counting, the clinging to your own body as being clean is put to an end.[3271] The guru discussed this as the gauge of the teachings. It purifies the stains of clinging to purity and cleanness. (b) Contemplating means gradually visualizing yourself and the entire world as skeletons.

Meditating on emanating and withdrawing [light] in that way,
when eating food, putting on clothes, and sitting down again,

you should cultivate the meditation on nothing but skeletons
This is what relinquishes the stains of solidity and cleanness[3272]

2. The assertion of the medium[3273] śrāvakas is to cultivate prāṇāyāma. The cause of being born in saṃsāra consists of thinking. This is the meditation in order to relinquish pleasure.

Just like a weak person sitting on a horse,
once vāyu-thinking has mounted the mind,
all kinds of thinking keep proliferating
As thinking seized by vāyus does not proliferate,
therefore they are controlled by prāṇayāma

This is to be understood as sixfold:
it is held to be the six of counting,
following, suspending, examining,
transforming, and complete purity[3274]

3. The assertion of the highest śrāvakas is that the root of saṃsāra is the clinging to a self. Emptiness is like an extinguished lamp. They first meditate on the lack of a self by scrutinizing all the parts of the body as to whether such a self exists anywhere. Then, they examine the mind: past and future minds cannot be the self, and since the present mind is impermanent and fluctuating, it is not established as a personal self either. Their stains of dhyāna are due to superimposing peacefulness onto emptiness.

4. In addition to realizing the lack of a self, the pratyekabuddhas also put an end to the root of being born in saṃsāra, which consists of outer objects. What puts an end to such objects is the yoga of the faculties reversing on their own. Their contemplation of self-arising wisdom is as follows. Once they are born in a place and time where there is no buddha, they see skeletons in charnel grounds and examine them, seeing that they come from death and so on all the way back to ignorance. With this ignorance, they familiarize as actually being self-arising wisdom. Similar to lucid nonconceptual cognition in the moment of

waking up in the morning, those who realize the lack of a personal self are free from afflictive obscurations. Similar to lucid nonconceptual cognition in the evening, not thinking about outer objects is being free from cognitive obscurations. The self-arising wisdom of realizing this is also called "superior insight." The calm abiding of meditative equipoise is to straighten out the triad of body, speech, and mind. The calm abiding of subsequent attainment is to control body, speech, and mind with dhyāna, thus avoiding the nonvirtues of body, speech, and mind and engaging in the ten virtues instead. Their stains are intoxication and states without mind.

5. The Sautrāntikas (the lower followers of the Mahāyāna) are taught as belonging to the Mahāyāna because, through the Mahāyāna instructions, they take the great desire that is free from desire to be compassion. These Mahāyāna Sautrāntikas have the faculties of pratyekabuddhas: though they have turned away from the village of perceptible objects, they still have doubts about hidden referents. To overcome that, those in whom thoughts are not predominant meditate by directing their mind's movements to the tip of their nose. Thoughts may become scattered toward things, but they become unobservable thereafter. Then, mind is seized as they please, and without thinking about it either, they rest in a thought-free state. Those in whom thoughts are predominant meditate by directing their mind to whichever objects may appear. When cognition becomes scattered toward mind-like objects in between, they seize mind by directing their attention toward it, and cognition remains thought-free without engagement. Having perfected this meditation, they should engage in other virtues of making efforts in the six pāramitās. Their stains are as above.[3275]

6. In order to refute the Mahāyāna Sautrāntikas' assertion that all phenomena are aspects of cognition cast by hidden external referents, the Aspectarian Yogācāras assert that what casts these aspects is not different from the mind, similar to the sun and its light. It is held to be the lucid nonconceptual self-awareness that is nondual diversity.[3276] As for the meditation, in the moment when cognition arises, it arises as lucid nonconceptual cognition, and the subsequent moments are familiarized with in the same manner. Thus they familiarize with lucid yet nonconceptual cognition.

7. According to the Nonaspectarian Yogācāras, cognition is free from aspects, held to be like water, gold, and space without any stains. Thus familiarize with self-awareness without appearances and thoughts. Letting cognition be fresh and relaxed, generate whichever among the five afflictions in your mind is strongest. When something like desire arises, without thinking of the object of clinging, let self-aware experience be. Just as not rejecting some superficial film on gold, but asserting it to be gold, without rejecting the object of desire, familiarize with self-awareness as lucid experience. In accordance with the dynamic energy[3277] of hatred, rest right within the native state.[3278] Therefore let itself be just itself!

8. The Mādhyamikas of illusion-like nonduality put an end to the assertion that self-aware mind is the ultimate. When inner and outer entities[3279] are analyzed with reasonings, they actually do not exist, being empty of being such entities. The yoga of a face's reflection involves calm abiding and superior insight: calm abiding is the seeming appearance of that reflection and superior insight is the mind in which the clinging to it has ended. Visualizing the oath deity[3280] in front, gather the accumulations through the seven branches. Then, looking at your face in a mirror in front, the flesh and blood of that face are empty of being entities. The reflection looks hither and the actual face looks thither. Since they are discordant in terms of thinking, [the reflection] is actually empty of the entity of the face. While putting an end to clinging, the appearance of the reflection is your own mind, so meditate on the color of "the empty mind." When something like desire comes up, meditate on the mind as being like a reflection. What appears as the body is also your own mind. If people do not accept that body and mind are like reflections, by again looking at a reflection in a mirror, they eventually become free from clinging. Familiarize with the mind free of clinging, without thinking of it as anything whatsoever; thus the guru said. The stain of their dhyāna is the notion that the mind that is free from clinging does not exist either.

9. The dhyāna of utter nonabiding of the Mādhyamikas of utter nonabiding consists of putting an end to delusive clinging, which consists of calm abiding and superior insight. Calm abiding refers to the methods for doing meditation. By focusing on some support in front, gaze directly at it. Similar to putting an end to clinging to a reflection, through

examining the very mind of having put an end to clinging to that entity in terms of whether this mind is one or many, it does not even abide as a mere illusion free from clinging but appears as a mere imputation: rest in empty unceasing appearance. Familiarize with lucid experience as being empty. Thus, looking nakedly at the mind that appears as what is immobile and your own body, familiarize with this as above. Having become familiar with the mind and having trained with other appearances in this way, familiarize with any appearing object just as before. If mind is able to look at that, train with the mind that appears as afflictions such as desire. Having looked at mind like that, again, by mind nakedly looking at space, familiarize as before. By thus realizing that all appearances are empty, this is superior insight. To focus in accordance with the emptiness of emptiness is to gaze directly, and thus all entities are destroyed. The meaning of this is utterly nonabiding emptiness. You may wonder at the need for this view of emptiness with regard to all phenomena being illusions. It is the means to subdue and be free from clinging to their being illusion-like. The realization of the actuality of utter nonabiding moisturizes the mind stream. Within the mind streams of the persons who have such an experience, the experience of equality arises.

10. Finally, the fruitional yāna of secret mantra is discussed very briefly as (a) the outer creation process (based on the vase empowerment, visualizing oneself as a deity couple in union through the fivefold ritual), (b) the perfection process with characteristics (visualizing an upside-down OṂ in the mahāsukhacakra at the crown of the head and a standing HUṂ in the dharmacakra in the heart, meditating on them as having the essence of the four bindus), (c) the perfection process of complete purity (meditating that the outer world and your abode are a palace and all inner sentient beings are male and female deities, enjoying the five nectars in a kapāla and meditating within the natural state of nondual great equanimity), and (d) the perfection process of essence, which consists of this:

All phenomena that are experiences of cognizance
are declared to be your own mind without minding[3281]
The mind comes down to not being identifiable
Emptiness is familiarized with as being like space

*This "Taking the Pith Instructions of the Philosophical Systems as the Path"—these philosophical systems of the three yānas, four positions, and nine approaches, as well as the fruitional secret mantra—[came] from the awakened mind streams of Śrīmat Śabara and Advayavajra, and venerable Vajra[pāṇi] gave it to *Ajamahāsukha. This concludes "The Progressive Stages of Taking These Mahāmudrā Pith Instructions of the Philosophical Systems as the Path" that was composed by venerable Maitrīpa.*

Appendix 3: Tipi Bumlabar's Outline of Divākaracandra's *An Illumination of Prajñā Wisdom*

According to Tipi Bumlabar, the outline of *An Illumination of Prajñā Wisdom* (text 16) is as follows:[3282]

1. introduction
1a. expression of auspiciousness
1b. mainly subduing pride[3283] and requesting forbearance
1c. demonstrating the qualities of greatness by way of possessing a lineage
2. meaning of the text
2a. prajñā wisdom's own essence
2a1. brief introduction
2a1a. the essence of prajñā wisdom (what is pointed out)
2a1b. the essence of empowerment (the means to point out)[3284]
2a1c. rebutting the flaws in disputes about empowerment
2a1c1. objection
2a1c2. its answer
2a1c2a. the lack of necessity for those of low intelligence
2a1c2b. the presence of necessity for those of highest intelligence
2a1c2b1. the actual [necessity]
2a1c2b2. its concluding summary
2a1c2b3. proving through scriptures that not being bound [by passion] is tenable

2a2. detailed explanation of prajñā wisdom's own essence
2a2a. instantiation of prajñā wisdom
2a2b. definition of prajñā wisdom
2a2c. definition of wisdom
2a2d. by summarizing four, teaching that they are not different
2a2e. establishing the instantiation
2a2f. the instruction on true reality depending on the seeming [reality] that is karmamudrā
2b. the succession of the four mudrās
2b1. the differences of the four mudrās
2b1a. teaching that the karmamudrā is contrived
2b1b. the meaning of the dharmamudrā being uncontrived
2b1c. mahāmudrā not[3285] arising from a contrived cause
2b2. causes and results in terms of the four mudrās
2b3. presenting the four ecstasies in each mudrā except for mahāmudrā
2c. the difference between Mantra[yāna] and Pāramitā[yāna]
2c1. objection by those in the Pāramitā[yāna]
2c1a. untenability of what is endowed with the seven constituents in the Mantra[yāna] and its tenability in the Pāramitā[yāna]
2c1b. untenability of buddhahood in a single lifetime
2c1c. buddhahood from right now not being reasonable
2c1d. [the Pāramitāyāna] being equally endowed with the four distinctive features [of the Mantrayāna]
2c1e. the Pāramitā[yāna] being the definitive meaning and the Mantra[yāna] being the expedient meaning
2c1f. [the Pāramitāyāna and Mantrayāna] being equal in enjoying the five sense pleasures[3286]
2c2. teaching the answer given by those in the Mantra[yāna]
2c2a. brief introduction
2c2b. detailed explanation
2c2b1. great bliss being accomplished through the Mantra[yāna]
2c2b1a. untenability of mahāmudrā if there is no karmamudrā at all
2c2b1b. great bliss being free from the two extremes
2c2b1c. concluding summary of the distinctive features of the [Mantrayāna]

2c2b2. untenability of what is endowed with the seven constituents in the Pāramitā[yāna]
2c2b2a. it not being accomplished through [just] equanimity and true bliss being accomplished through the nonduality of prajñā and means
2c2b2b. it not being accomplished through mere nonthought and being accomplished through bliss without fear
2c2b3. being the deity from right now being established as the essence
2c2b4. [the Pāramitāyāna] not being equally endowed with the four distinctive features [of the Mantrayāna]
2c2b4a. general instruction
2c2b4b. lacking ignorance
2c2b4c. abundance of means
2c2b4d. lack of difficulty
2c2b4e. sharp faculties
2c2b5. [the Pāramitāyāna and the Mantrayāna] not being equal in enjoying the sense pleasures[3287]
2c2b6. the reasonings of the Pāramitā[yāna] being untenable as the definitive meaning
2c2b7. the Mantra[yāna] free from thoughts about happiness and suffering being tenable in the scriptures
2c2b8. the secret mantra not being the expedient meaning
2c2b9. teaching that the existence of the means to accomplish [buddhahood] in a single birth cannot be invalidated
2c2c. concluding summary of the [answer]
2d. brief teaching on the five stages
2d1. matching the five stages with both the creation and the perfection [processes]
2d2. special engagement in the five stages within the perfection process
2d2a. the outer creation process that is not different from mahāmudrā
2d2b. the profound [creation process] being taught as the karmamudrā
2d2c. the perfection process being taught as the dharmamudrā
2d2d. the full-perfection [process] being taught as the samayamudrā
2d2e. the essence process being taught as mahāmudrā
2d2e1. the actual [mahāmudrā]
2d2e2. all that is associated with realizing that [mahāmudrā] becomes the path

2d2e3. it not being an object of hearing, reflecting, and so on
2d2e4. it being realized thanks to the guru
3. conclusion

May these notes written by Bumlabar
be of benefit to some who are vessels

Appendix 4: Tipi Bumlabar's Outline of Sahajavajra's *A Synopsis of Positions*

According to Tipi Bumlabar, the outline of *A Synopsis of Positions* (text 17) is as follows:[3288]

1. expression of homage and commitment [to explain]
2. meaning of the text
2a. Pāramitāyāna
2a1. the position of the Vaibhāṣikas
2a1a. Śrāvaka[yāna]
2a1b. Pratyekabuddhayāna
2a2. [the position of] the Sautrāntikas
2a2a. own approach
2a2b. refuting the approaches of others
2a2b1. refuting that function lies in anything other than entities
2a2b2. refuting a cause of perishing apart from[3289] the one that causes arising
2a2b3. refuting a part-possesser's substance
2a2c. accomplishing omniscience is contingent on conditions
2a2d. by virtue of gradually training in profound actuality, all are presented as the Mahāyāna
2a3. the position of the Vijñaptimātra[vādins][3290]
2a3a. Nonaspectarians
2a3a1. refuting the approaches of others
2a3a1a. [refuting] outer referents

2a3a1a1. [refuting] the actual [assertion]
2a3a1a1a. refuting coarse [referents]
2a3a1a1b. refuting infinitesimal particles
2a3a1a1c. concluding summary of the two
2a3a1a2. refuting the assertion of an infinitesimal particle
2a3a1a3. concluding summary of the two
2a3a1b. [refuting] aspects
2a3a1c. concluding summary of the two
2a3a2. own approach
2a3a2a. meditation
2a3a2b. the stages of training
2a3a2c. incorporating the four realities into the three natures
2a3b. Aspectarians
2a3b1. conduct
2a3b2. meditation
2a3b3. fruition
2a3b4. establishing being free from the four extremes as the middle
2a4. the justification for the tīrthikas not being included
2a5. the position of the Mādhyamikas
2a5a. paying homage and commitment to explain
2a5b. [explaining] the text
2a5b1. refuting the approaches of others
2a5b1a. formulating the reasoning
2a5b1a1. the actual [reasoning]
2a5b1a2. removing flaws of not being established
2a5b1b. what is to be refuted
2a5b1b1. a nature of entities
2a5b1b2. a nature of delusiveness
2a5b2. own approach
2a5b2a. thesis
2a5b2b. mind is entirely free
2a5b2c. there is nothing to be seized[3291] by natural mind
2a5b2d. the inexpressible freedom from extremes
2a5b2e. the characteristic of unity
2a5b2f. synonyms of true reality
2a5b2g. the means to make this a living experience

2a5c. giving a summarizing statement
2b. the differences between the Mantra[yāna] and the Pāramitāyāna
2b1–2b2. the possession of the four distinctive features not existing and existing, respectively, in [the path of] inference and the path of direct perception even at the time of ordinary beings[3292]
2b2a. brief introduction
2b2b. fivefold detailed explanation in terms of the same goal, lacking ignorance, abundance of means, lack of difficulty, and sharp faculties
2c. the distinguished Secret Mantrayāna[3293]
2c1. paying homage and commitment to explain
2c2. meaning of the text (the eight firm natural paths)[3294]
2c2a. the pointing-out empowerment of karmamudrā
2c2b. the fourth empowerment of mahāmudrā
2c2c. making essential bliss a living experience by relying on physical bliss
2c2c1. seizing physical bliss
2c2c1a. brief introduction
2c2c1b. explanation
2c2c1c. detailed explanation
2c2c1d. very detailed explanation
2c2c1e. concluding summary
2c2c2. the aspect of the essence
2c2c3. concluding summary of these two
2c2d. its result, the level of equal taste (dharmin)
2c2d1. the actual [equal taste]
2c2d2. the example of being equal taste
2c2d3. presenting the example of irreversibility
2c2d4. concluding summary of these two
2c2e. other means of equal taste
2c2e1. giving rise to bliss through the means
2c2e2. holding bliss through the means
2c2e3. since the cause of bliss is bodhicitta, not relinquishing it but holding it
2c2f. the distinctive features of the connate
2c2g. concluding summary of the above [points]
2c2h. means of practice [according to] the distinctions of faculties

2c2h1. the actual [means]
2c2h1a. the lower ones [cultivate] the samaya [maṇḍala]
2c2h1a1. the very lowest ones complete the ritual
2c2h1a2. the medium ones lack the accumulation of merit
2c2h1a3. the highest ones [cultivate] the deities in an instant[3295]
2c2h1b. the medium ones [cultivate] the dharma[mudrā]
2c2h1b1. lowest ones
2c2h1b2. medium ones
2c2h1b3. highest ones
2c2h1c. the highest ones cultivate mahāmudrā
2c2h1c1. [the lowest ones] cultivate it by taking the aspects of the maṇḍala circle of means as the means
2c2h1c2. the medium ones cultivate it by taking the bliss of an outer mudrā[3296] as the means
2c2h1c3. the highest ones cultivate all that appears and is experienced as dharmamudrā and mahāmudrā, without being dependent on anything at all
2c2h2. the purpose of the distinctions
3. concluding points

Having relied upon many gurus,
with devotion, vigor, and prajñā,
Bumlabar wrote the *Sthitisamāsa*'s
precis as per the guru's command

Appendix 5: Outline of *A Commentary on The Four Mudrās*

[Introduction]
The common meaning
(1) subject matter
(2) essence
(3) defining characteristics
(4) the pertinent word
The dharmamudrā
(1) subject matter
(2) pertinent word
(3) essence
(4) defining characteristics
(5) benefit
[Actual comments on the *Caturmudrānvaya*]
[Insertion: The four mudrās]
(1) subject matter
(2) the pertinent word
(3) essence
(4) defining characteristics
(5) benefit
The ascertainment of the karmamudrā
1. the reason to posit [the karmamudrā] as the dharmodaya
2. this very [karmamudrā] being suitable as the exemplifying wisdom
3. while excluding the two inferior and forceful [empowerments], the

wisdom of the correct [empowerment] is suitable as the exemplifying wisdom

4. making [connate ecstasy] a living experience by way of connecting with what boosts it

The ascertainment of mahāmudrā

1. the persons who are the [psychophysical] supports
2. the instructions for them
2a. the symbol for all phenomena being born
2b. the symbol for their being unborn
2c. the symbol for experiencing being born and being unborn as nondual

[Main part:] the pith instructions on bringing these [four mudrās] onto the path

1. the pith instructions on the reasons [for positing four mudrās]
2. the pith instructions on pursuing true reality
2a. the pith instructions on pursuing the true reality of the karmamudrā
2a1. action
2a2. with which mudrā there is sealing
2a3. through what is it accomplished
2a4. what is accomplished
2a5. through what is it ascertained
2a6. what it is named
2a7. which result is attained
2b. the pith instructions on pursuing the true reality of the dharmamudrā
2b1. dharma
2b2. sealing with which mudrā
2b2a. sealing the means with emptiness
2b2a1. appearances to be encountered
2b2a2. diversity to be made equivalent
2b2a3. many to be made of a single taste
2b2b. sealing emptiness with the means
2b2b1. familiarizing with all phenomena as the connate
2b2b2. letting go of clinging to the experience of that
2b2b3. embracing upcoming sensations with mindfulness
2b2b4. the signs of being familiar

2b2b4a. the common signs
2b2b4b. the uncommon sign
2b2b4c. the special sign
2b2c. sealing difference with nonduality
2b3. through what is it accomplished
2b3a. in terms of what is to be explained
2b3b. in terms of the instructions' own essence
2b3c. in terms of time
2b4. what is accomplished
2b5. through what is it ascertained
2b6. what it is named
2b7. what is its result
2b7a. maturation of the past
2b7b. maturation of the present
2b7c. maturation of the future
2c. the pith instructions on pursuing the true reality of mahāmudrā
2c1. mudrā
2c1a. not going beyond the actual unity
2c1b. not going beyond the exemplifying unity
2c1c. not going beyond the unity of abiding
2c1d. not going beyond the unity of being
2c2. being great
2c3. through what is it accomplished
2c3a. freshness through examination
2c3b. freshness in meditation
2c4. what is accomplished
2c5. through what is it ascertained
2c6. what is it named
2c6a. cutting through three [kinds of] hopes
2c6b. being endowed with five features
2c6b1. not being born through any essence
2c6b2. not having any nature of its own
2c6b3. being all-pervasive
2c6b4. being changeless
2c6b5. being omnitemporal
2c6c. the four kāyas being naturally perfect

2c7. which result is accomplished
2d. the pith instructions on pursuing the true reality of the samayamudrā
2d1. samaya
2d2. mudrā
2d3. through what is it accomplished
2d4. what is accomplished
2d5. through what is it ascertained
2d6. what is it named
2d7. which result is attained
2d7a. the result that has been produced by persons
2d7b. the result of persons
2d7c. the result produced by persons
3. the pith instructions on the special means
3a. the four moments in order to ascertain the time
3b. the four ecstasies in order to ascertain the wisdom
3c. the four locations in order to ascertain the realization
3d. the four dharmas in order to ascertain the defining characteristics
4. the pith instructions on making [these mudrās] a living experience
4a. the samayamudrā that appears as cause
4b. the karmamudrā that is the example
4b1. what is to be realized
4b2. self-blessing
4b3. training in bliss
4b4. the yoga of the syllables
4b4a. the conditions for emission
4b4b. the means for guarding it
4b4c. the means for abiding
4b5. the bliss that is to be made to abide
4c. the dharmamudrā that is the path
4c1. what is to be realized
4c2. the familiarization
4c3. the aids
4c3a. if water is predominant, it is [made] of equal taste with wind
4c3b. if wind is predominant, it is [made] of equal taste with earth
4c3c. if earth is predominant, it is [made] of equal taste with fire

4c3d. if fire is predominant, it is [made] of equal taste with space
4c4. the defining characteristics
4c5. equal taste
4d. the mahāmudrā that is the result
4d1. the basic nature
4d1a. the basic nature in terms of reasons
4d1a1. being reasonable as mahāmudrā
4d1a1a. mudrā
4d1a1b. being great
4d1a2. being reasonable as the result of stainlessness
4d1a3. being reasonable as being free from affirmation and negation
4d1b. the basic nature in terms of the view
4d1b1. cutting through three [kinds of] hopes
4d1b2. being endowed with five features
4d1b3. the four kāyas being naturally perfect
4d1c. the basic nature in terms of essence
4d1c1. the time of effortlessness
4d1c2. the time of inconceivability
4d1c3. the time of unity
4d2. familiarization
4d2a. initial analysis
4d2b. making this a living experience
4d3. accomplishment
4d3a. accomplishment
4d3a1. accomplishment
4d3a2. the special features of accomplishment
4d3b. its signs
4d4. conduct
4d5. inconceivability
4d5a. the inconceivability of experience
4d5b. the inconceivability of the cognition of experience
4e. the samayamudrā that is the welfare of others
5. the pith instructions on certainty about the instructions arising
5a. the essence of the four mudrās
5b. understanding their purpose through causes
5c. understanding these [four mudrās] as symbols

5c1. the karmamudrā is explained as being like the bodhi tree
5c2. the dharmamudrā is explained as being like a golden wheel
5c3. mahāmudrā is explained as being like a nyagrodha tree
5c4. the samayamudrā is explained as being like the essence of a myrobalan
5d. oneself relying on texts

Appendix 6: Tipi Bumlabar's Outline of Rāmapāla's *A Critical Commentary on "Instructions on Empowerment"*

In BKC, Tipi Bumlabar presents a very detailed outline that is said to be an outline of Maitrīpa's *Instructions on Empowerment* (text 42).[3297] However, this outline's highly specific phrasing and order of topics, most of them lifted directly from Rāmapāla's *Critical Commentary on "Instructions on Empowerment"* (text 45), leave no doubt that it is actually an outline of that commentary.

1. [Rāmapāla's] homage
2. the reason for composing the treatise
3. eliminating excessive pride[3298] about composing it
4. commenting on the root text
4a. [Maitrīpa's] homage
4a1. summary
4a2. purpose [stanza 1]
4a3. meaning of the branches
4a3a. paying homage to the dharmamudrā that consists of the sonic phonemes EVAṂ
4a3a1. the essence of [the object of] paying homage, including its purpose
4a3a2. the reason[3299] for paying homage to the syllables EVAṂ
4a3a2a. an extensive scriptural passage about EVAṂ
4a3a2b. explaining the meaning of the word [EVAṂ]

4a3a3. conclusion

4a3b. paying homage to the karmamudrā that consists of the written shape of the word EVAṂ

4a3b1. essence of the object [of homage]

4a3b2. the reason for paying homage

4a3b3. the purpose

4b. the [actual] text

4b1. the path of the messenger, karmamudrā, which is the means of pointing out

4b1a. the definite sequence of the four moments through one's own body [stanza 2]

4b1b. teaching the refutation of other approaches

4b1b1. the forceful empowerment

4b1b1a. teaching its way in which the four moments arise

4b1b1b. the way in which the three views are asserted as what is to be pointed out by empowerments

4b1b1b1. the assertion of having no aspect

4b1b1b2. the assertion of having an aspect

4b1b1b3. the assertion of aspects as illusions[3300]

each one of these three points has four subpoints: (1) the view pointed out by empowerments, (2) presenting the four kāyas in order to posit the fruition as the path, (3) the meaning of the middle path free from the four extremes, and (4) the pith instructions on practicing this (the fourth subpoint of "having an aspect" is twofold: (a) possessing the [seven] constituents and (b) refuting [wrong views about] that)

4b1b1c. the justification for refuting their approach

4b1b1c1. it contradicts the scriptures [stanza 3]

4b1b1c2. consummation[3301] is not justified as belonging to the sphere of nonthought

4b1b1c3. taking consummation as the third [moment] contradicts what is to be accomplished by the mother tantras

4b1b1c4. by taking consummation as thought, it is not justified to be asserted as the third [moment] [stanza 4]

4b1b1c5. to say it is nonthought is not justified, because that is only a seeming invalidation [of our position]

4b1b1c6. the answer to saying that [consummation as the fourth moment] contradicts the scriptures
4b1b1d. the purpose of mixing up [the sequence of the third and fourth moments in] the tantras
4b1b1e. the purpose of the three views being posited as what is to be pointed out by empowerments
4b1b2. the poor empowerment
4b1b2a. presenting their approach [stanza 5]
4b1b2b. the justification for refuting them
4b1b2b1. brief introduction by way of formulating reasonings [stanza 6]
4b1b2b2. detailed explanation by way of nescience not being established
4b1b2b2a. [the poor empowerment's] accordance with the approaches of others
4b1b2b2a1. accordance with the Śaivas
4b1b2b2a1a. accordance with the wrathful [Śiva] [stanza 7]
4b1b2b2a1b. accordance with [bliss's] own essence [arising from Śiva's and Śakti's union] [stanza 8]
4b1b2b2a1c. accordance with being free from extremes [stanzas 9–11]
4b1b2b2a2. accordance with followers of the Vedas
4b1b2b2a2a. accordance with Bhāskara, [for whom] wisdom [arises] by suppressing [mental activity] [stanza 12]
4b1b2b2a2b. accordance with the followers of the *Bhagavat[siddhānta]*
4b1b2b2a2b1. brief introduction
4b1b2b2a2b2. detailed explanation
4b1b2b2a2b2a. becoming a particularly blissful union [lines 13ab]
4b1b2b2a2b2b. the true reality of the Brahman [lines 13cd]
4b1b2b2a2b2c. the essence of wisdom [stanza 14]
4b1b2b2a2b2d. [the Brahman] being the single essence of the world [stanza 15]
4b1b2b2a2b2e. praising women as the cause[3302] of wisdom [stanza 16]
4b1b2b2a2b2f. relinquishing clinging [stanza 17]
4b1b2b2a2b2g. being free from extremes [stanza 18]
4b1b2b2b. [the poor empowerment] contradicting our own scriptures
4b1b2b2b1. the seal of the tathāgatas [stanza 19]
4b1b2b2b2. the seal of Akṣobhya

4b1b2b2b3. if the seal of Akṣobhya is temporarily established, this does not [text: no negative] contradict the seal of Vajrasattva [stanza 20]
4b1b2b2b4. the seal of Akṣobhya is the extinction of the tathāgata relief[3303]
4b1b2b2b5. refuting that wisdom arises [with bodhicitta] in many locations [stanzas 21–22]
4b1c. detailed explanation of our own approach
4b1c1. the connate
4b1c1a. brief introduction
4b1c1b. detailed explanation
4b1c1c. very detailed explanation through the meanings of nine scriptural passages
4b1c2. the four moments
4b1c2a. variety
4b1c2a1. brief introduction [stanza 23]
4b1c2a2. detailed explanation
4b1c2a3. very detailed explanation
4b1c2b. maturation
4b1c2b1. brief introduction
4b1c2b2. detailed explanation
4b1c2c. the answer to saying this contradicts the tantras [stanza 24]
4b1c3. the four ecstasies [stanza 25]
4b1c4. positing the four[3304] as ecstasies through the progression of karmamudrā
4b2. presenting the four mudrās as causes and results [stanza 26]
4b2a. karmamudrā as the result of concordant outflow
4b2b. dharmamudrā as the result of maturation
4b2c. mahāmudrā as the result of stainlessness
4b2d. through those, [samaya]mudrā as the result produced by persons
4b2e. a summary of their being results [of the respectively preceding ones]
4b3. presenting the four mudrās, except mahāmudrā, as four ecstasies each
4b3a. brief introduction [stanza 27]
4b3b. detailed explanation
4b3b1. since karmamudrā has already been explained, it is not explained now

4b3b2. the four ecstasies of the dharmamudrā [stanza 28]
4b3b3. the justification for not presenting the four ecstasies in mahāmudrā
4b3b3a. teaching [mahāmudrā] as mental nonengagement [lines 29ab]
4b3b3b. the justification for the [first] three moments not arising [in mahāmudrā] [lines 29cd]
4b3b3c. being free from the extreme of characteristics [stanza 30]
4b3b3d. being free from the extreme of extinction [stanza 31]
4b3b3e. teaching the distinctive feature of realization [stanza 32]
4b3b3f. thought and nonthought have the same essence [stanza 33]
4b3b3g. demonstrating one's own realization to others [stanza 34]
4b3b3h. dependent origination is nirvāṇa [stanza 35]
4b3b3i. the realization of [dependent origination] being unborn is the realization of mahāmudrā [stanza 36]
4b3b4. the four ecstasies of the samayamudrā
4b3b4a. the four ecstasies [stanza 37]
4b3b4b. the connate of the four ecstasies
4b3b4b1. positing the bindu as the connate
4b3b4b2. the scriptural passage for this being justified
4b3b4b3. commenting on the meaning of this passage
4b3b4b3a. its definitive meaning
4b3b4b3b. its expedient meaning
4b3b4c. relinquishing the flaws of disputes about bindu
4b3c. one [among the four] moments being included in [the corresponding] one [among the four] mudrās [in due order] [stanza 38]
4b4. the yogas[3305] of the four mudrās being a synopsis of [both] the father tantras and the mother tantras
4b5. eliminating wrong ideas about karmamudrā[3306] as the [sole] practice [stanza 39]
4b6. demonstrating the power of the oath deity [stanza 40]
4c. concluding dedication [stanza 41]
5. conclusion

Appendix 7: The Fivefold Classification of the Creation and Completion Processes in the Texts of Maitrīpa and His Students

As a unique template in a number of texts by Maitrīpa and his disciples, the creation process is typically divided into "the outer creation process" and "the profound (inner) creation process," and the completion process into "the perfection process," "the full-perfection process," and "the essence process."[3307] Ultimately, this fivefold classification may go back to two stanzas in Saraha's *Kāyakoṣāmṛtavajragītā*:

> Hey! Outer, inner, profound, nonprofound creation processes,
> full perfection, essence, as well as the reliefs,
> sealing, karma[mudrā], and dharmamudrā
> are the stages of completely perfecting yoga
>
> Mahāmudrā is the process of the essence
> Samayamudrā is the process of perfection,
> the seal of the imaginary with the perfect
> Karmamudrā is empowerment's essence,
> the nature of means with the four ecstasies
> Dharmamudrā is appearances' diversity:
> as it shows the four ecstasies' connate,
> it is the connate with the four ecstasies[3308]

In more detail, this fivefold classification is found in Maitrīpa's *Nairātmyāprakāśa* and *Caturmudropadeśa* (text 92), Divākaracandra's *Prajñājñānaprakāśa* (text 16), the *Caturmudrāṭīkā* (text 44), Rāmapāla's *Sekanirdeśapañjikā* (text 45), and Vajrapāṇi's *Guruparamparākramopadeśa* (text 213). However, these six texts have various ways of describing the five processes and matching them with the creation and perfection processes.

Maitrīpa's *Nairātmyāprakāśa* (a sādhana of Hevajra's consort Nairātmyā) describes the outer creation process as the typical successive visualization of Nairātmyā's maṇḍala, including the fifteen yoginīs who surround her, the seven-branch prayer, merging the jñānasattvas with the samayasattvas, and so on. This also includes an explanation of some of the symbolism of Nairātmyā's physical appearance and attire. Then the text says this:

> Possessing the pride of being Nairātmyā, you should be identical with Nairātmyā. Here, in order to engage in the six-branch yoga, in due order, you should meditate on her in the colors black, red, yellow, green, blue, and white. Through the progressive intensity [or vividness] of meditation, she first appears like the full moon obscured by clouds. Then, thanks to [meditation] becoming more intense, she appears like an illusion. Then, thanks to it becoming [even] more intense, she manifests as lucidly as in a dream. Immediately after that, thanks to the [full] maturation of [meditation's] intensity, mahāmudrā yogīs who have attained [a state] in which dreams and the waking state are not different gain accomplishment [in this practice]. This is the creation process.[3309]

The profound (inner) creation process involves sexual union, giving rise to the bodhicitta of great bliss that is found in the middle of supreme and cessational ecstasy:

> In another manner, by virtue of the union of the bola and the kakkola, the bodhicitta that has the nature of great bliss and is located in the middle of supreme [ecstasy] and cessational

> [ecstasy] arises. Having the character of fifteen digits, it should be instantly seen as having the nature of the fifteen yoginīs with the previously mentioned colors, [hand-held] symbols, and forms, because it has the nature of the five skandhas, the four elements, the six objects, and body, speech, and mind. This is the profound creation process.[3310]

The perfection process means to view the maṇḍala circle that has the character of the fifteen yoginīs in an instant. The full-perfection process consists of visualizing thirty-two nāḍīs (having the character of the fifteen yoginīs) within the vajra body (the circle of Nairātmyā). The essence process consists of the detailed related practices of caṇḍālī and karmamudrā as "the process of making the bodhicitta that is the flow of effortless nondual unity directly perceptible."[3311]

In a more general manner, Maitrīpa's *Caturmudropadeśa*[3312] first says that the Mantrayāna consists of the outer creation process, the profound creation process, the perfection process, the full-perfection process, and the essence process. Then, it matches these five with the four mudrās: the outer creation process with the samayamudrā, both the profound creation process and the perfection process with the karmamudrā, the full-perfection process with the dharmamudrā, and the essence process with mahāmudrā.

Divākaracandra's *Illumination of Prajñā Wisdom*[3313] first typically divides the creation process into the outer creation process and the profound creation process, and the perfection process into the perfection process, the full-perfection process, and the essence process. For the description of the outer and profound creation processes as subdivisions of the creation process, Divākaracandra merely refers to the above two passages in Maitrīpa's *Nairātmyāprakāśa*. However, within the overall category of the perfection process, he speaks again of all five processes, including the outer and profound creation processes. That is, for Divākaracandra, the outer creation process within the perfection process appears to consist of the preliminaries of karmamudrā and the tathāgata relief, while he matches the profound creation process, the perfection process, the full-perfection process, and the essence process, respectively, with the karmamudrā (and the Vajradhara relief), the dharmamudrā, the samayamudrā (both in relation to the four ecstasies), and mahāmudrā.[3314]

The *Caturmudrāṭīkā*[3315] first includes all five processes in the perfection process alone, saying that the outer creation process, the inner creation process, the perfection process, the full-perfection process, and the essence process are to be understood as illusory body, mind focus (another name of "mind isolation"), vajra recitation, luminosity, and unity, respectively. Thus he matches these five with the five stages of perfection-process practices in the *Guhyasamājatantra* according to the Ārya tradition, but the first three are in reverse order.[3316] Later,[3317] the *Caturmudrāṭīkā* explicitly speaks of only four among these five (omitting "the perfection process"), covering both the creation process and the perfection process: the outer creation process (the actual creation process), the profound creation process (familiarizing with nāḍīs and vāyus), the full-perfection process (realizing all that appears and resounds to be emptiness), and the essence perfection process (which refers to being effortless without being contingent on causes and conditions).

Rāmapāla's *Sekanirdeśapañjikā*[3318] similarly matches the five with a slightly different version of the five stages of the Ārya tradition, but classifies the first two as belonging to the creation process. In that context, he says, the outer creation process and the profound creation process are just different names of the condensed stage (*piṇḍīkrama*) and vajra recitation, respectively. Within the perfection process, the perfection process, the full-perfection process, and the essence process are simply equivalents of the stages of self-blessing, full awakening, and unity.[3319] Elsewhere,[3320] Rāmapāla also says that the water empowerment and so on being taught as the master empowerment should be understood according to the outer creation process. The ecstasy of the tathāgata relief being the master empowerment should be understood according to the profound creation process. The ecstasy of the Vajradhara relief being the master empowerment should be understood according to the perfection process. Among the four mudrās, it is the karmamudrā that should be understood as the master empowerment according to the full-perfection process.

Vajrapāṇi's *Guruparamparākramopadeśa*[3321] matches the five processes with persons of higher and lower faculties and the four mudrās. The outer creation process (the samayamudrā)—the master empowerment and the creation process (deity yoga)—pertains to those with lower faculties. Pertaining to those with medium faculties, the karmamudrā is twofold: the tathāgata relief and the Vajradhara relief. The secret empowerment and the tathāgata relief constitute the profound inner creation process, while the prajñā-jñāna empowerment and the Vajradhara relief represent the perfection process.[3322] The full-perfection process (the dharmamudrā) pertains to those with highest faculties, and the essence process (mahāmudrā) to the highest among those with highest faculties.

Later,[3323] Vajrapāṇi provides yet another presentation of the five processes in relation to the four mudrās for those with highest faculties. The karmamudrā consists of the outer creation process (not seized by ordinary notions, familiarizing with having the deity's essence, and blessing space and the secret place) and the profound inner creation process (the experience of self-aware connate wisdom through the union of vajra and lotus). The dharmamudrā is the perfection process (the path). Mahāmudrā is the full-perfection process (the fruition). The samayamudrā is the essence process (meditative equipoise and subsequent attainment as well as the dharmakāya and the form kāyas are a nondual unity—the welfare of others).[3324]

BKC[3325] matches Maitrīpa's twofold creation process and three among the four mudrās with the five stages of the Ārya tradition, referring to Maitrīpa's *Sekanirdeśa* for details. According to BKC, vajra recitation is the inner creation process, mind isolation and illusory body are the dharmamudrā, luminosity is mahāmudrā, unity is the great fruitional samayamudrā, and the outer creation process is the causal samayamudrā (the gate that accords with the previous one).

In sum, Maitrīpa's *Nairātmyāprakāśa* simply relates the five processes to different parts of the meditation process in a concrete sādhana. Divākaracandra follows this as far as the first two processes—the outer and profound creation processes—go, but then further matches all five processes with the four mudrās of the perfection process. Maitrīpa's *Caturmudropadeśa* and Vajrapāṇi's *Guruparamparākramopadeśa* likewise match these five with the four mudrās, but their identical way of doing so differs from Divākaracandra's way (Vajrapāṇi additionally matches the five with four types of persons with different faculties). The only thing that all three agree on is that the essence process corresponds to mahāmudrā. Both *Karopa and Rāmapāla match the five processes with the five stages of the Ārya tradition of *Guhyasamājatantra*, but they differ with regard to both the names and the orders of this school's stages.

Overview

Maitrīpa's *Nairātmyāprakāśa*

outer creation process: progressive maṇḍala visualization
profound creation process: karmamudrā
perfection process: instantaneous viewing of the maṇḍala
full-perfection process: visualizing the nāḍīs
essence process: caṇḍālī and karmamudrā as means to realize mahāmudrā

Maitrīpa's *Caturmudropadeśa* and Vajrapāṇi's *Guruparamparākramopadeśa*

outer creation process: samayamudrā
profound creation process and perfection process: karmamudrā
full-perfection process: dharmamudrā
essence process: mahāmudrā

Vajrapāṇi's *Guruparamparākramopadeśa*
Additional presentation for those of highest faculties:
outer creation process and profound inner creation process: karmamudrā
perfection process: dharmamudrā
full-perfection process: mahāmudrā
essence process: samayamudrā

Divākaracandra's *Prajñājñānaprakāśa*

creation process
outer creation process and profound creation process: as in Maitrīpa's *Nairātmyāprakāśa*

perfection process
outer creation process: karmamudrā preliminaries and tathāgata relief
profound creation process: karmamudrā and Vajradhara relief
perfection process: dharmamudrā
full-perfection process: samayamudrā
essence process: mahāmudrā

Caturmudrāṭīkā

(A) *perfection process*
outer creation process: illusory body
profound creation process: mind focus
perfection process: vajra recitation
full-perfection process: luminosity
essence process: unity

(B) *creation process*
outer creation process
perfection process
profound creation process (nāḍīs and vāyus)
full-perfection process (realizing all to be emptiness)
essence perfection process (effortless and not contingent on causes and conditions)

Rāmapāla's *Sekanirdeśapañjikā*

creation process
outer creation process: condensed stage
profound creation process: vajra recitation

perfection process
perfection process: self-blessing
full-perfection process: full awakening
essence process: unity

BKC

vajra recitation: inner creation process
mind isolation and illusory body: dharmamudrā
luminosity: mahāmudrā
unity: great fruitional samayamudrā
[outer] creation process: causal samayamudrā

Notes

1. The most widely accepted hermeneutical etymology of "ḍākinī" says that it derives from the root *ḍī* or *ḍai* ("to fly"), as explained in Kaṅha's *Yogaratnamālā* (a commentary on the *Hevajratantra*), Jayabhadra's *Cakrasaṃvarapañjikā*, and other texts. Earlier Indian and Buddhist literature represents ḍākinīs (*mkha' 'gro ma*) as malevolent devourers of humans. This aspect still survives as the class of ḍākinīs known as "flesh eaters." In popular North Indian belief to this day, as one of the "shadows" of the traditional Hinduist view of women, the understanding of ḍākinīs (Hindi *ḍāin*) is close to the Western notion of human and nonhuman witches. In tantric Buddhism, there is a division into "mundane ḍākinīs" (Skt. *lokaḍākinī*), usually representing a negative force inimical to Buddhism that needs to be subdued and converted, and supramundane "wisdom ḍākinīs" (Skt. *jñānaḍākinī*), who embody the wisdom as well as the inner impetus that leads to buddhahood. They may appear in human or nonhuman forms, offering guidance to tantric practitioners and serving as the guardians of secret teachings.
2. Excerpted from *Do ha skor gsum gyi Ti ka 'bring po sems kyi rnam thar ston pa'i me long* by Karma Trinleypa (1456–1539); translation by Dzogchen Ponlop Rinpoche. The text preceding the quotation, as well as the paragraph that immediately follows it, also closely follows Karma Trinleypa's text.
3. Tib. *Nges don phyag rgya chen po'i rgya gzhung*. In the blockprints of Palpung Monastery (GZ1), this collection consists of three large volumes, while the modern Tibetan book edition (GZ3) has six volumes.
4. Tib. Chos grags rgya mtsho (1456–1539).
5. The Tengyur consists of the canonical texts of Tibetan Buddhism by Indian and some Tibetan authors other than the Buddha.
6. As Roger Jackson (2009, 3–4 and 12–13) says, the *Anāvilatantra* was probably included in GZ and other mahāmudrā collections as the only tantra because it was included in the old list of "the ten dharmas of mahāmudrā" (Tib. *phyag rgya chen po'i chos bcu*) that is mentioned in BA (865) as going back to Maitrīpa and as having been transmitted by his student Vajrapāṇi.
7. Tib. Karma bkra shis chos 'phel blo gros rgya mtsho'i sgra dbyangs (born nineteenth century). This catalogue also includes a description of the general background of the collection and the diverse lineages through which its texts were transmitted.

8. Tib. 'Jam mgon kong sprul blo gros mtha' yas (1813–99).
9. Tib. *Grub pa sde bdun* (different sources have varying lists of seven or eight "siddhi texts").
10. Thematically, and as indicated by their names, these two texts as well as Kerali's *Tattvasiddhi* at the beginning of volume 2 are also considered as belonging to the corpus of "siddhi texts."
11. Tib. *Snying po skor drug*; again, different sources have varying lists of the texts in this cycle.
12. Except for Saraha's *Dohakoṣa* and Sahajavajra's *Sthitisamāsa* (a doxography), the remaining texts of this cycle discuss the perfection process. I translate *utpattikrama* (Tib. *bskyed rim*) and *utpannakrama* (or *niṣpannakrama*; Tib. *rdzogs rim*) as "creation process" and "perfection process," respectively, rather than more familiar but somewhat misleading terms such as "creation stage" (or "generation stage") and "completion stage" (the term **saṃpannakrama*, which is still very common in contemporary secondary literature, is not attested in any known Indic text and appears to be nothing but a wrong back-translation of Tib. *rdzogs rim*). As for the reasons, Skt. *utpatti* means "arising" and "production," while *utpanna* means "arisen," "produced," and "ready" (*niṣpanna* means "arisen," "brought about," "completed," and "ready"). Skt. *krama* means "an uninterrupted or regular progress, order, series, or succession," "progressive stages," "way," "course," "system," and "method." Merriam-Webster defines "process" as "a series of actions or operations conducing to an end," which is exactly what *utpattikrama* and *utpannakrama* are: increasingly refined progressive sequences (and not just one stage) of visualization, recitation, and meditation that have clearly defined goals. The process of the *utpannakrama* is based on the readily available fruition of having sufficiently cultivated the *utpattikrama* (in that sense, more literally, the *utpannakrama* means further meditative training based on "what has been created" before, during the *utpattikrama*).
13. Both the names and the numbers (ranging from twenty-four to twenty-six) of the texts in "The Cycle of Twenty-Five Dharmas of Mental Nonengagement" (Tib. *Yid la mi byed pa'i chos skor nyi shu rtsa lnga*) vary in different sources. The classification of Indic mahāmudrā texts into "The Seven Siddhi Texts," "The Sixfold Pith Cycle," and "The Cycle of Twenty-Five Dharmas of Mental Nonengagement" existed at least since the time of Butön Rinchen Drub (Tib. Bu ston rin chen grub; 1290–1364). For more details, see Jackson 2008 and Mathes 2011.
14. In addition, Saraha's "Queen Dohā" and another commentary on his "People Dohā" by Advaya Avadhūtīpa are found in appendices.
15. Alias Ajitamitragupta and Mitrayogī (twelfth century); though he is hardly known in the later Tibetan tradition, he also taught extensively in Tibet and was undoubtedly one of the most realized masters to ever visit there.
16. Maitrīpa's main works (many under his aliases Advayavajra and Avadhūta/Avadhūtipa) included here add up to about thirty-five (plus eight by his direct students), while more than twenty are attributed to Saraha. In addition, further songs attributed to these two masters are found in some of the anthologies of dohās and vajra songs in volumes 4 and 5.
17. For more details, see Robinson 1979 and Dowman 1985.

18. These people are said to have originated from the union of a brahman (the highest of the four castes) woman and a śūdra (the lowest caste) man.
19. I am fully aware that other contemporary authors choose a different approach, providing detailed explanations of virtually every practice that the Indo-Tibetan tradition used to keep confidential.
20. Maitrīpa's four closest Indian disciples were Vajrapāṇi, Sahajavajra, Divākaracandra, and Rāmapāla, and *Kāropa (a.k.a. Bhitakarma) was another one of his significant students.
21. As Mathes 2015 (4n20) says, this title of Maitrīpa's collection is not found in any of the available Sanskrit manuscripts and is probably an invention by Śāstrī (its first editor).
22. For details, see the introduction to text 14 below.
23. As with virtually all Indian Buddhist figures, Maitrīpa's dates are difficult to assess. BA (842–43) says that he was born in a sheep year or a dog year (identified as 1007 and 1010, respectively, by the translator Roerich) and passed away at seventy-eight (however, Tibetans count the time in the womb as one year, so Maitrīpa only lived seventy-seven years according to Western counting). The research in Tatz 1987 leads to the similar dating c. 1007–c. 1085, which has been generally repeated. However, based on the biographies of Maitrīpa's disciples, Roberts (2011, 11) suggests that he died before 1066 when Vajrapāṇi went to Nepal and proposes the dates 986–1063. Maitrīpa thus would have been born in the dog year that is two twelve-year cycles earlier than the dog year 1010. Still, following BA, the sheep year 983–1060 would also be possible. For the implications of these dates for Maitrīpa's having met Atiśa and Marpa Lotsāwa Chökyi Lodrö, see the discussion of Atiśa's relationship to Maitrīpa in the introduction to volume 1. For detailed biographical information about Maitrīpa, see Tatz 1987 and 1988, as well as Brunnhölzl 2007, 125–31. For a detailed analysis of the difficult-to-ascertain dates of Maitrīpa and Marpa, see Ducher 2017, 169–71 and 180–83.
24. Among the thirty-four texts here, all but five are available in Sanskrit or Apabhraṃśa (in the case of Saraha's "People Dohā"; text 13). Since the various Tibetan versions of these works in GZ and CDNP typically show a wealth of considerable variations and corruptions, my primary translations of these works are always from the Sanskrit, with Tibetan variants in the notes. I chose this approach in order to prioritize the Sanskrit of these Indic works while still taking the Tibetan transmission into account (the sole exception is Saraha's "People Dohā," which I translated only from the Tibetan because there are already numerous renderings of several Apabhraṃśa versions). This approach resulted in a rather bulky volume.
25. The short and long lineages of "The Seven Siddhi Texts" in NG (62–63) list a Keraḍipa between Svayambhūyoginī Cinto (author of text 8) and Maitrīpa. In all likelihood, Keraḍipa is just a variant spelling of Keralipa. Due to their similar names, Padma Karpo (Padma dkar po 2005, 7, 27) even counts Keralipa's *Śrītattvasiddhi* together with Sahajayoginī Cinto's *Vyaktabhāvānugatatattvasiddhi* (text 8) as one of "The Seven Siddhi Texts." Thus the association of text 12 with "The Seven Siddhi Texts" is probably not just by virtue of its title but also by virtue of the transmission of these texts (karmamudrā as the main topic of text

12 is of course also related to some parts of these texts but is equally found in many other texts). Note also that, besides texts 3–12 in GZ, there are fifty-five further texts in the tantric section of Tg with "siddhi" in their titles, including *Samayavajra's *Sahajasiddhi*, Divākaracandra's *Śrītattvajñānasiddhi*, Śāntarakṣita's *Tattvasiddhi* (text 210), Jālandhara's *Śrīcakrasaṃvaragarbhatattvasiddhi*, Advayavajra's *Tilakasiddhi*, Dhokari's *Prakṛtisiddhi*, and Atiśa's *Ratnālaṃkārasiddhi*, as well as sixteen texts with *amṛtasiddhi* in their titles.

26. Padma dkar po 2005, 28.
27. Note that, contrary to common popular usage, *vāyu* and not *prāṇa* is the general term for Tib. *rlung*. *Prāṇa(vāyu)* (Tib. *srog rlung*; "life-force vāyu") is the primary one of the five main vāyus, and not their general category. The other four main vāyus are the pervading vāyu (Skt. *vyāna*, Tib. *khyab byed kyi rlung*), the upward-moving vāyu (Skt. *udāna*, Tib. *gyen rgyu'i rlung*), the (fire-) accompanying vāyu (Skt. *samāna*, Tib. *me mnyam gyi rlung* or *mnyam gnas kyi rlung*), and the downward-moving or downward-expelling vāyu (Skt. *apāna*, Tib. *thur sel gyi rlung*). Note also that in Indian Buddhist tantric texts, the term *bindu* is often replaced by its equivalent *tilaka*.
28. As the four ecstasies refer to levels of intense sexual pleasure in the context of the practice of karmamudrā, the common English rendering "joy" is indeed quite an understatement. For more details, see the introduction to Nāgārjuna's *Caturmudrānvaya* (text 14) and Maitrīpa's *Sekanirdeśa* (text 42).
29. This exactly matches Butön's *Record of Teachings Received* (Bu ston rin chen grub 1971, 115–16; slightly different order). Curiously, BA (857) mentions the term *grub snying* as an abbreviation of "The Seven Siddhi Texts" and "The Sixfold Pith Cycle" several times but does not provide an actual list of "The Sixfold Pith Cycle." Instead, BA assigns four of this cycle's texts to two other cycles: three "Pith" texts (consisting of Saraha's "People Dohā," "King Dohā," and "Queen Dohā") and "The Cycle of Minor Texts" (Tib. *phra mo skor*), which, among others, includes the *Caturmudrānvaya*, *Prajñājñānaprakāśa*, and *Sthitisamāsa* (the English of BA here does not properly render the Tibetan ['Gos lo tsā ba gzhon nu dpal 2003a, 1001]). The *Cittāvaraṇaviśodhananāmaprakaraṇa* and *Acintyādvayakramopadeśa* are not mentioned. Padma Karpo's list (Padma dkar po 2005, 28–36) replaces the *Prajñājñānaprakāśa* and *Sthitisamāsa* with Saraha's *Tattvopadeśaśikharadohagīti* (text 62) and *Svādhiṣṭhānakramaprabheda* (text 81), instead including the *Sthitisamāsa* in "The Cycle of Twenty-Five Dharmas of Mental Nonengagement." In addition, Padma Karpo (28–29) identifies Saraha's "King Dohā," "Queen Dohā," lesser dohā treasures, "Alphabet Dohā" with its autocommentary (texts 60–61), and *Twelve Stanzas of Pith Instructions* (text 82), as well as Nāgārjuna's *Bodhicittavivaraṇa* (text 206), *Cittavajrastava* (text 212), and so on as being associated with "The Sixfold Pith Cycle." Similarly but more specifically, according to the introduction to a collection of Tibetan commentaries on Saraha's three main dohās (Grub thob gling ras, Par phu ba blo gros seng ge, Karma pa rang byung rdo rje 2011, xii), it is said that Saraha's "King Dohā," "Queen Dohā," lesser dohā treasures, and "Alphabet Dohā" with its autocommentary follow the "People Dohā," while the *Bodhicittavivaraṇa*, *Cittavajrastava*, and so on follow *The Succession of the Four Mudrās* (a rather strange association, since there is no trace of any of the four mudrās in either the *Bodhi-*

cittavivaraṇa or the *Cittavajrastava*, unless one holds that these two texts discuss mahāmudrā; said introduction was written by a Tsering Sharpa [Tib. Tshe ring shar pa], said to be a monk from Shar sba khang don grub sdings—Don grub sdings being the hermitage established by the Drugpa Kagyü master Barawa Gyaltsen Balsang [Tib. 'Ba' ra ba rgyal mtshan dpal bzang; 1310–91], a disciple of the Third Karmapa and Butön). The list of the texts in this cycle in BKC (vol. *ka*, fol. 4a.4–5) agrees with those in NG and *Butön's Record of Teachings Received* except for replacing the *Prajñājñānaprakāśa* with Maitrīpa's *Sekanirdeśa* (text 42). Among the actual texts that appear in BKC, the *Prajñājñānaprakāśa* is still missing in this cycle (it appears at the end of vol. *kha* after Maitrīpa's "Cycle of Twenty-Five Dharmas of Mental Nonengagement" under commentaries by his disciples, between Sahajavajra's *Tattvadaśakaṭīkā* and Rāmapāla's *Sekanirdeśapañjikā*). The *Sekanirdeśa*, however, is found under Maitrīpa's "Cycle of Twenty-Five Dharmas of Mental Nonengagement." Furthermore, similar to Padma Karpo, Saraha's *Tattvopadeśaśikharadohagīti* and *Svādhiṣṭhānakramaprabheda* are added to "The Pith Cycle." Jackson 2011 (162–63) and Mathes 2011 (94–95) and 2015 (3–4) also refer to the list of six "pith texts" as found in NG and Butön.

30. BKC, vol. *ka*, fol. 4a.4–5.
31. BKC reads *snying rje don* ("the actuality of compassion"), but given the cycle glossed here (*snying po skor drug*) and the often-used term *snying po'i don* that is obviously referred to here, I emended *snying rje don* accordingly.
32. The reason why the "People Dohā" is included in volume 2 of GZ and not with the bulk of Saraha's other works in volume 3 is that it is considered as belonging to "The Sixfold Pith Cycle." The four canonical commentaries on this dohā in Tg are found in volume 3 (texts 66 and 67, as well as appendix 4) and volume 4 (text 70). For details on the Tibetan controversy over whether the "King Dohā" and "Queen Dohā" are authentic works by Saraha and the probable reason why neither of them is found in GZ, see the introductions to text 65 and appendix 3 in volume 3 (English translations of "King Dohā" and "Queen Dohā," respectively).
33. Dowman 1985, 66–68. Another account of Saraha's life, traceable to Balpo Asu, says that he was a South Indian brahman for whom a bodhisattva manifested as a female arrow-smith in order to teach him how to make arrows and show him the symbolic tantric meaning of this process and the arrow's various parts (see the foreword and the introduction to volume 1). Thanks to this, realization dawned in Saraha and he lived with the fletcheress in a charnel ground, holding tantric gatherings and singing dohās. Requested by the people, the king tried to stop Saraha's conduct that violated his status as a brahman and bring him back into the brahman fold. As a response, Saraha taught 160 stanzas to the common people ("People Dohā"), 80 to the queens ("Queen Dohā"), and 40 to the king himself ("King Dohā"). According to Karma Trinlépa's commentaries on these three dohās (Karma phrin las pa phyogs las rnam rgyal 2009, 118, 194, 230), the "King Dohā" is a song on the realization of the dharmakāya (the unborn fundamental way of being of the mind), the "Queen Dohā" a song on the realization of the sambhogakāya (mind's own radiance), and the "People Dohā" a song on the realization of the nirmāṇakāya (what can appear

as anything whatsoever from the diversity of mind's own dynamic energy). Note that the stories about Saraha's life vary greatly, and he has been variously dated between the third and twelfth century, having flourished in either east, north, or south India. The themes of being instructed by and living with the female arrow-smith or a "radish girl" (Dowman 1985) are found in distinct hagiographies but also blended in others. Mathes 2021 (311–12n7), referring to Szántó, says that at least the "People Dohā" must have been composed before the middle of the tenth century (because it is cited in Bhavabhaṭṭa's *Catuṣpīṭhanibandha*) and also suggests that its earliest date was "when the *Hevajratantra* (which some take to be around 900 CE) was composed because the *Hevajratantra* shines through different parts of Saraha's *Dohākoṣa*. Saraha thus uses, for example, the tantric code word *kunduru* exactly as in the *Hevajratantra* (where it had for the first time the meaning of 'sexual union')." For more details on Saraha's life, see the introduction to volume 1 and Schaeffer 2005.

34. Karma phrin las pa phyogs las rnam rgyal 2009, 5 (Karma Trinlépa sides with the first version). The most well-known life story of Śavaripa is the one included among those of the eighty-four mahāsiddhas. Śavaripa competed in shooting deer with Avalokiteśvara, who appeared in the garb of another hunter. Wanting to learn how to shoot with a bow like Avalokiteśvara, Śavaripa and his wife were first instructed by Avalokiteśvara to become vegetarians and then were shown a vision of how they would burn in hell due to killing many animals. Scared, Śavaripa learned the basic Buddhist instructions and eventually, meditating on nonreferential compassion in a thought-free state for twelve years, attained mahāmudrā (see Dowman 1985, 60–65). Pawo Tsugla Trengwa's *History of Dharma* (Dpa' bo gtsug lag phreng ba 2003, 772) presents a very different story. Śavaripa, who originally was a traveling dancer and singer named "the one who has three sisters," met Nāgārjuna when he begged for food at Nālandā. Nāgārjuna, who did not entertain any discriminating thoughts about low-caste people, invited him in and gave him excellent food. Then Nāgārjuna sang some dohās by Saraha and asked him: "Do you understand the meaning?" Śavaripa answered that he did not but wished to. Seeing that he had the proper fortune, Nāgārjuna bestowed empowerments and blessings upon him, which caused instantaneous realization to arise in him, and he had a vision of the bodhisattva Ratnamati (Saraha's guru in the distant lineage of Mahāmudrā: a bodhisattva considered as an emanation of either Vajradhara or Mañjuśrī who, together with the bodhisattva Sukhanātha, is regarded as the one responsible for bringing the mahāmudrā teachings into the human realm; the close or short Mahāmudrā lineage begins with Tilopa receiving mahāmudrā directly from Vajradhara and then passing it on to Nāropa and Marpa Lotsāwa). Nāgārjuna then told Śavaripa to promote the welfare of sentient beings in the garb of a hunter around Mount Śrī Parvata (a mountain range to the northwest of Dhānyakataka—modern-day Amaravati—in Andhra Pradesh, whose tribal inhabitants are called Śabara). Mathes 2006a (273) reports another version (found by van der Kuijp in the Langthang valley north of Kathmandu) of the latter story that indirectly links it to the first one. Śavaripa, a Bengali dancer and singer, was visited by Nāgārjuna in his

house. Realizing that Śavaripa was an emanation of the South Indian Śavaripa, Nāgārjuna bestowed empowerment upon him, during which Saraha and Ratnamati appeared. Ratnamati taught Saraha a stanza on essential reality, and Saraha passed it on to Śavaripa. Ratnamati asked him whether he had understood it, and then blessed him with an explanation of it. Seeing that Śavaripa had some realization from previous lifetimes, Ratnamati gave him further instructions and revealed to him that he was an emanation of the South Indian Śavaripa; therefore he should go to the south and wear his hunter garb. Together with his two sisters, Śavaripa went south and lived there by killing the roosters of desire, the snakes of hatred, and the boars of ignorance (the three main mental poisons) with the bow and arrow of means and prajñā. In the sphere beyond duality, he and his sisters ate the flesh of the killed animals and enjoyed the taste of great bliss and changeless wisdom. IaS (433n6) says this on Śavaripa: "In fact, the name Śavaripā is an ethnonym which refers to a tribal group of South India, the Śabara or Śavara, who have been identified with the modern Saora tribe of Orissa, Chattisgarh and Madhya Pradesh. The Śabaras and other outcaste groups are frequently found in Buddhist tantric literature, where they embody an idealized state of freedom and spontaneity. Such rhetoric of spontaneity, which may sound like an Indian version of the 'good savage', does not necessarily imply that the Buddhist establishment effectively allowed individuals belonging to tribal groups to be part of the Buddhist community. It is highly implausible that those siddhas who called themselves Śabara did actually belong to tribal groups; it is more plausible, indeed, that those siddhas appropriated the customs, rituals, symbols or lifestyles of the tribal people in order to pursue their own specific religious purposes. For a discussion of the role of tribal and outcaste people in Indian Vajrayāna Buddhism see Davidson (2002[b], 224–234)." As Davidson 2002b (228–29) points out, there seem to have been at least three siddhas with the name Śabara/Śavaripa: (1) the well-known guru of Maitrīpa, (2) a Śabara of the brahman caste who taught the Tibetan Kyungpo Naljor (Tib. Khyung po rnal 'byor tshul khrims mgon po; tenth–eleventh century), and (3) an eleventh-century Śabareśvara who taught the *Cittaguhyagambhīrārthagīti* (D2448) to Patampa Sangyé (Tib. Pha dam pa sangs rgyas). In addition, according to BA (727, 796), there was also a later Śavaripa, who is said to have transmitted the six-branch yoga (Skt. *ṣaḍaṅgayoga*) of the *Kālacakratantra* (!) to Vibhūticandra, a *Kālacakratantra* master of the late twelfth/mid-thirteenth century.

35. Tib. Bcom ldan rig pa'i ral gri (1227–1305).
36. Schaeffer 2005, 129. According to the introduction in Grub thob gling ras, Par phu ba blo gros seng ge, Karma pa rang byung rdo rje 2011 (xii), Saraha's "King Dohā" (text 65), "Queen Dohā" (appendix 3 in volume 3), "Alphabet Dohā" (text 60), lesser dohās, and so on all follow the "People Dohā" (this probably includes his tetrad of dohās on body, speech, and mind; texts 53–56).
37. Padma dkar po 2005, 32.
38. Text 66 is its paraphrased Tibetan translation (for details, see the introduction to this text in volume 3).
39. All of these are critically edited in Mathes and Szántó forthcoming 2023, which also includes Sanskrit and Tibetan editions of DKPS and Mokṣākaragupta's

Dohakoṣapañjikā (text 67), as well as translations of all these texts. For English translations of Saraha's *Dohakoṣa* based on the Apabhraṃśa editions by Śāstrī, Shahidullah, and Bagchi, see Guenther 1952, 1969, and 1993, Snellgrove 1954, and Jackson 2004 (Shahidullah's translation of 1928 is in French). Bhāyāṇī's English translation (1997) is primarily based on Sāṃkṛtyāyana's edition.

40. Shahidullah's edition has 114 stanzas.
41. Among these, the Sakya manuscript contains 164 stanzas (though Nara 1966 counts 170; there is neither a Tibetan translation nor any Indic or Tibetan commentary), while the above-mentioned fragment from Nepal has only a few stanzas.
42. Like Saraha's "People Dohā," many dohā texts are difficult to break down into regular stanzas, especially in their Tibetan translations. Thus, according to Sāṃkṛtyāyana, this version has 134 stanzas, Jackson 2004 counts 138 (as do I), Guenther 1993 lists 145, and the traditional Tibetan count is 160.
43. Besides some variants here and there in certain lines, text 13 and the canonical Tibetan version share almost all their stanzas (except six that are very different), but text 13 also has fourteen additional lines.
44. Schaeffer 2005 (106) counts only 769 lines.
45. Saraha 1999; rendered into English in Kongtrul Lodrö Tayé 2022.
46. Rin chen rnam rgyal 1976, 123–36. According to Schaeffer 2005 (104, 106), the Sakya manuscript edited by Sāṃkṛtyāyana has 81 stanzas that are completely unique to it, DKPA has only a single stanza, the canonical Tibetan version 13 stanzas, and text 68 has 205 lines. The canonical Tibetan version shares forty-eight stanzas not found elsewhere with DKPA and five such stanzas with the Sakya manuscript. Schaeffer 2005 (129–73) also contains an English translation of the version found in Rigpé Raltri's commentary.
47. Translation by Bagchi 1935a, 8.
48. The first two sentences of the colophon are in Apa., while its remainder is in Sanskrit. The colophon continues by mentioning two further persons, saying: "This is the book of the supreme upāsaka Śrī Rāmavarman, [inhabitant] of Śrī Nugal [*nogvalake*]. It was copied as seen by the Buddhist monk, the elder Pathamagupta." My rendering of the colophon agrees with Szántó's (2018, 5), who criticizes Schaeffer's (2005, 103–4) assumptions about the editorial history of this text based on Schaeffer's misreading Apa. *paratthakāmeṇa* as "according to the stages of the ultimate concern" instead of "out of the desire to benefit others." Szántó (2012, 1:99, 102, 411–12, and 2018, 6) also mentions that the earliest (unattributed) quotation of Saraha's *Dohakoṣa* (Apa., stanza 96; text 13, stanza 91) is found in Bhavabaṭṭa's *Catuṣpīṭhanibandha* (middle of tenth century).
49. See also the remarks under "A Note on Dohā, Vajragīti, and Caryāgīti" below.
50. There are some phrases or lines in text 13 that were not translated in accordance with DKPA but in accordance with how text 66 (or DKPS) glosses its version of these stanzas (the same phenomenon also appears in the translated Apa. songs that are embedded in text 90). In general, most Tibetan translators knew Sanskrit very well but were only insufficiently or not at all familiar with the various Prakrit languages current at their times in India. However, virtually all dohās, caryāgītis, and vajragītis were composed in one of these vernaculars,

especially Eastern Apabhraṃśa. Thus it seems that the translators sometimes used commentarial glosses in the stanzas themselves either because they did not understand the Apa. or because the glosses seemed to make more sense. It could also be that the translator(s) received additional instructions from other Indian paṇḍitas (as explicitly mentioned in the colophon of text 90), so the translator(s) (or even the paṇḍitas) decided to adapt certain words of the songs closer to the commentary. Furthermore, as Kapstein 2015 (292) says, "Some parts of the Indian Buddhist *caryāgīti* and *dohā* verses translated into Tibetan are not textual translations at all. They are, rather, the products of continuing improvisation in Tibet; they are, as some have designated works of this type, 'gray texts'" (see also Davidson 2002c).

51. The same goes for the potential existence of an independent Apa. manuscript that exactly corresponded to the canonical Tibetan translation. An additional question is why the Seventh Karmapa's compilation of Indian mahāmudrā texts includes the version in text 13, which exists nowhere else but in text 67 and in Rigpé Raltri's commentary, and not the canonical translation that is more or less followed by all other Tibetan commentaries.
52. For details of Vajrapāṇi's life and accomplishments, see the introduction to volume 1 and the introduction to text 213 in volume 6.
53. Tib. Rma ban chos 'bar (ca. 1044–89).
54. Tib. 'Brog mi jo sras ye shes rdo rje (one of Drogmi Lotsāwa's sons).
55. Tib. Nag tsho lo tsā ba tshul khrims rgyal ba (1011–64).
56. Schaeffer 2005, 75.
57. Tib. Grags pa rdo rje dpal bzang po (fifteenth century).
58. Tib. Bal po a su.
59. Tib. Gnyal steng pa lo tsā ba tshul khrims 'byung gnas (1107–90).
60. See Schaeffer 2005, 172.
61. Karma phrin las pa phyogs las rnam rgyal 2009, 118, 194, 230.
62. Tib. 'Jam dbyangs bzhad pa'i rdo rje (1648–1721/22).
63. 'Jam dbyangs bzhad pa'i rdo rje 1997 (665) and Rin chen rnam rgyal 1976 (136). The commentaries by Lingjé Repa, Barpuwa, the Third Karmapa, and Ju Mipham do not mention any translator.
64. I primarily focus on the Tibetan versions of text 13 because there already exist the above-mentioned numerous translations of its Apa. versions.
65. For an exhaustive analysis and comparison of the available Apa. versions, see Mathes and Szántó forthcoming.
66. Saraha's *Vākkoṣarucirasvaravajragītā*, *Cittakoṣājavajragītā*, and *Kāyavākcittāmanasikāra* (texts 54–56) also contain critiques of Buddhist and non-Buddhist approaches, but in a way of being more scattered throughout these texts.
67. NG *phyag rgya bzhi rjes su bstan pa* Tg AIBS Skt. *Caturmudrāniścaya* Tib. *phyag rgya bzhi gtan la dbab pa*.
68. The Tibetan tradition usually considers the author of this text (as well as all works attributed to Nāgārjuna in Tg) to be the same Nāgārjuna (second century) who was the founder of the Madhyamaka school, whereas most contemporary scholars distinguish at least two Nāgārjunas, the later one being a master of the *Guhyasamājatantra* (mahāsiddha no. 16). IaS (95) says the following on the name of this text: "This text has itself been published in the

Advayavajrasangraha under the title *Caturmudrā*, and was also re-edited by the Japanese team of Taishō University, under the title *Caturmudrāniścaya*, i.e. Determination of [the correct view concerning] the Four Seals. But neither of these titles is to be preferred; and Advayavajra is certainly not to be reckoned as the author of this work. The title *Caturmudrāniścaya* preferred by the Japanese editors is that which is given as Sanskrit title within the Tibetan translation; it is well-known that such titles have no authority, having been commonly re-translated from the Tibetan title without any access to a Sanskrit original. *Caturmudrānvaya*, on the other hand, is the title that is given by the only manuscript consulted by the editors that gave any title at all; and furthermore, it is the name by which this small but important and indeed controversial work was normally referred to by Indian authors, including students of Maitreyanātha such as Rāmapāla and *Sahajavajra." IaS continues (95n10): "The same title is given also in Dhyāyīpāda's *Paramagambhiropadeśo Vajrayoginyāḥ Karaṅkatoraṇakramaḥ Svādhiṣṭhānam* (= *Guhyasamayasādhanamālā* 34), fol. 115r4–5." Note here that besides "succession," Skt. *anvaya* can also mean "(logical) connection," "relation," "concordance," "purport," and "the logical connection of cause and result."

69. IaS, 95–96, Mathes 2015, 3–4, 13; Almogi 2022b, 415–22.
70. Abhayākaragupta's text (*Śrīsampuṭatantrarājaṭīkāmnāyamañjarī*; D1198, fol. 67a.3–4) is very dismissive of the author of *The Succession of the Four Mudrās*, saying it "was surely composed by an ordinary person who does not understand the instructions (Skt. *āmnāya*); the noble ones do not put together what is mutually exclusive."
71. IaS (95n7) identifies two main reasons for misattributing the *Caturmudrānvaya* to Maitrīpa instead (throughout referring to him by his other name, Maitreyanātha): "Firstly, the *Caturmudrānvaya* may have been included in some manuscripts of Maitreyanātha's works initially for another reason, i.e. because of its importance for our author, especially in his *Sekanirdeṣa*; subsequently—the true author and the original reason for its inclusion forgotten—it would have been natural to assume that it was by the same author as the other works with which it was transmitted. Secondly, there may have been also some confusion due to the fact that Maitreyanātha did himself write a work with a similar title (which unfortunately has not been preserved in Sanskrit), viz. the **Caturmudropadesa* . . . Perhaps it should also be borne in mind that in a few sources (notably the Sanskrit verse prophecy text—see especially vss. 10–14, but also some Tibetan sources, such as that by Padma dkar po quoted in Schaeffer 2005, 26) Maitreyanātha himself is identified with or presented as an incarnation of Nāgārjuna, to whom the *Caturmudrānvaya* was commonly attributed (see below). Might this have been a further factor which facilitated the attribution of the *Caturmudrānvaya* to Maitreyanātha?" As for Raviśrījñāna's and Vibhūticandra's commentaries on the *Kālacakratantra* disputing Nāgārjuna's authorship, IaS (96) says this: "Here the issue at stake is, to put it simply, the sequence of the Four Blisses (*ānanda*), concerning which the position of the *Amṛtakaṇikā* (and of the other Kālacakra texts) is different from that of the *Caturmudrānvaya* (and of Maitreyanātha, who as we have just remarked follows that work, as well as of, e.g., Ratnākaraśānti; see our discussion of this topic on

p. 97f. below). So for the author of the *Amṛtakaṇikā* it is important to deny that the Ārya Nāgārjuna is the author of the *Caturmudrānvaya*, and to claim that instead it is written by an ordinary person, without spiritual attainments and hence without authority. Were it written by Ārya Nāgārjuna, as Rāmapāla says (and as his master Maitreyanātha no doubt also believed), it would be considerably harder to maintain that the sequence of the Blisses as taught in it is to be rejected." Tipi Bumlabar's outline (BKC, vol. *kha*, fols. 84a.6–85a.1) also includes the *Caturmudrānvaya* under Maitrīpa's "twenty texts on mental nonengagement."

72. Such authors include Butön (referring to Abhayākaragupta and unnamed others), Rigpé Raltri, and Üpa Losel (Tib. Dbus pa blo gsal; ~1270–1355) in their catalogues of Tg, while other catalogues, such as two associated with the Third Karmapa, unreservedly attribute the text to Nāgārjuna.
73. BKC, vol. *kha*, fols. 84a.6–85a.1.
74. According to BKC (vol. *ka*, fol. 217a.1–2), *Instructions on Empowerment* is even a commentary on the meaning of *The Succession of the Four Mudrās*. Indeed, Maitrīpa's *Sekanirdeśa* (text 42), *Commentary on Half a Stanza on True Reality Teaching That All Phenomena Are Utterly Nonabiding* (text 73), and *Caturmudropadeśa* (text 92), Divākaracandra's *Prajñājñānaprakāśa* (text 16), Sahajavajra's *Sthitisamāsa* (text 17), the *Caturmudrāṭīkā* (text 44), Rāmapāla's *Sekanirdeśapañjikā* (text 45), and Vajrapāṇi's *Guruparamparākramopadeśa* (text 213) show close connections with *The Succession of the Four Mudrās* and with one another. TOK (2:688–89) also says that Maitrīpa and his followers rely on the *Caturmudrānvaya*: "Taking this to be the intended meaning of the *Hevajratantra*, Nāgārjuna composed the text *Caturmudrānvaya*. Those who follow it are the mighty adept Maitrīpa and his followers, whose assertion is as follows. The karmamudrā is twofold: an actual mudrā (the primary one) and a mentally cultivated jñānamudrā (the auxiliary one). The dharmamudrā consists of the yogas of vāyus, bindus, and caṇḍālī and of the indestructible [yoga of] those of highest faculties focusing on nothing but mind's bliss. This is as it is explained in the *Sthitisamāsa* composed by Sahajavajra:

    "for the cultivation of the dharmamudrā,
    the lower do so with bindus and letter series,
    the medium ones with caṇḍālī's specificities,
    and the highest ones as what is indestructible,
    asserted to be the awareness that consists of
    the yogas of the subtle bindus and so forth [V.25cd–26]

"Mahāmudrā is the native nature—the wisdom that is free from all discursiveness. The samayamudrā is the body of the deity that appears without being imagined. As its cause, the enhancement and the sealing of the creation process are held to be partially concordant [with it]." As for the interrelations between the above texts by Sahajavajra, Rāmapāla, and Vajrapāṇi, it cannot be said with any certainty which rely on which or whether they all represent common instructions that those students of Maitrīpa received from him. Things are different, though, with the *Caturmudrāṭīkā* (text 44): since it was obviously composed in Tibetan, it seems clear that its author relied on the above works and not the other way round (for the interrelation of texts 44 and 45, see also IaS, 88–89). In any case, a detailed comparison of all these texts is certainly beyond the scope of the present work.

75. Text 92, 21. There is strong evidence that text 92 is indeed by Maitrīpa, because it employs his unique template of the three yānas and the four Buddhist philosophical systems with their nine subdivisions (for details, see the introduction to text 34), and is also otherwise closely related to his *Tattvaratnāvalī* (text 34) and *Sekanirdeśa* (text 42), as well as Rāmapāla's *Sekanirdeśapañjikā* (text 45).
76. Text 16, 57.
77. Bu ston rin chen grub 1971, 116. As mentioned before, the introduction to a collection of Tibetan commentaries on Saraha's three main dohās (Grub thob gling ras, Par phu ba blo gros seng ge, Karma pa rang byung rdo rje 2011, xii) says that Nāgārjuna's *Bodhicittavivaraṇa*, *Cittavajrastava*, and so on also follow *The Succession of the Four Mudrās* (a rather strange association, since there is no trace of any of the four mudrās in either the *Bodhicittavivaraṇa* or the *Cittavajrastava*, unless one holds that these two texts discuss mahāmudrā). Mathes 2015 (4, 13) furthermore says that the text "may not be by Maitrīpa, but its combination of tantric *mahāmudrā* with the *amanasikāra* practice of the *sūtras* provides the *amanasikāra* cycle with a perfect doctrinal basis," and "whether taught by the tantric Nāgārjuna or not, the *Caturmudrānvaya* is of crucial importance to Maitrīpa's *amanasikāra* cycle, inasmuch as it combines the tantric *mahāmudrā* system of the four seals with the non-tantric teachings of the *Jñānālokālaṃkāra* and the *Abhisamayālaṃkāra* (or *Ratnagotravibhāga*), and thus with the Maitreya works." In particular, Mathes says (x), in its blend of Mahāmudrā and Madhyamaka, Maitrīpa's *Sekanirdeśa* is directly based on the *Caturmudrānvaya* (also stated in the introduction of Rāmapāla's *Sekanirdeśapañjikā*). According to the *Caturmudrāṭīkā* (text 44, 277), the *Caturmudrānvaya* was "composed by following the father tantra *Guhyasamāja*, the mother tantra *Cakrasaṃvara*, and the [*Hevajratantra* in] Thirty-Two Chapters." The *Caturmudrānvaya* is certainly in agreement with the *Hevajratantra* and cites four (maybe five) stanzas from it, with one of them also found in the Cakrasaṃvara-related *Saṃvarodayatantra*, while there is no quotation or discernible influence from the *Guhyasamājatantra*.
78. The sequence of these four that appears to be predominantly accepted in Indic Buddhist tantras and treatises (called "position B" in IaS, 97–98) consists of ecstasy (Skt. *ānanda*, Tib. *dga' ba*), supreme ecstasy (Skt. *paramānanda*, Tib. *mchog dga'*), cessational ecstasy (Skt. *viramānanda*, Tib. *dga' bral*, *dga' bral gyi dga' ba*, or *khyad par gyi dga' ba*), and connate ecstasy (Skt. *sahajānanda*, Tib. *lhan cig skyes dga'*). In due order, these four ecstasies are matched with the four moments of variety (Skt. *vicitra*, Tib. *rnam par sna tshogs*), maturation (Skt. *vipāka*, Tib. *rnam par smin pa*), consummation (Skt. *vimarda*, Tib. *rnam par nyed pa*), and lack of characteristics (Skt. *vilakṣaṇa*, Tib. *mtshan nyid dang bral ba*). *Hevajratantra* I.1.29 lists the four ecstasies in this order, and II.3.7–9 explains them as well as the four moments, as follows:

> Variety is known as various kinds:
> embracing and kissing and so forth

> Maturation constitutes its opposite:
> the blissful experience of wisdom
> Consummation is proclaimed to be the
> consideration "I have partaken of bliss"
> Characteristics' lack is other than the three,
> being free from passion and dispassion
> During variety, there is the first ecstasy;
> during maturation, it is supreme ecstasy;
> during consummation, cessational ecstasy;
> during characteristics' lack, connate ecstasy

This same sequence is also found in *Hevajratantra* I.8.22b, I.8.30–32, I.10.13, and I.10.15 (note that I follow the numbering of the stanzas of the *Hevajratantra* as given in Farrow and Menon 1992, and Mathes 2015), as well as in the *Kālacakratantra* and its commentarial literature. It appears to be followed by Indian masters such as Padmavajra (in his *Guhyasiddhi*), Nāropa, Abhayākaragupta, Mahāsukhavajra (in his *Padmāvatī* commentary on the *Caṇḍamahāroṣaṇatantra*), Kamalanātha, Raviśrījñāna, Vibhūticandra, all other *Kālacakratantra* commentators, Keralipa (text 12), and Munidatta (as his predominant stance in text 90). The alternative sequence of these two sets of four ecstasies and four moments (called "position A" by IaS) switches the order of the last two ecstasies (as well as the last two moments). It is found in *Hevajratantra* I.10.16cd, II.2.40ab, and (depending on how they are read) II.5.65b and II.5.69ef, and is generally followed by Ratnākaraśānti, Nāgārjuna's *Caturmudrānvaya*, Maitrīpa, Sahajavajra (text 17), Vajrapāṇi (texts 47 and 213), *Kāropa (text 44), Rāmapāla (text 45), Saraha's "People Doha" (Apa., stanza 96; text 13, stanza 119), and apparently Saraha's autocommentary on his "Alphabet Dohā" (text 61 on stanza 6), as well as Kumāracandra (text 2), Sujayaśrīgupta's *Abhiṣekanirukti*, sometimes Munidatta (such as in his comments on songs 12 and 27 in text 90), apparently Tilopa's *Dohakoṣa* verse 31 (at least in its Tibetan version), the commentary on Tilopa's *Dohakoṣa* verse 28, and (indirectly) the Tibetan of Kṛṣṇa's *Dohakoṣa* verse 24. Maitrīpa argues in his *Caturmudropadeśa* (text 92, 19–20) that texts that list connate ecstasy as the fourth one do so by deliberately obscuring the correct sequence in order to confuse outsiders who do not rely on a proper guru. Davidson 2002a (62) says the following on this point: "The *Hevajra Tantra* is the earliest work known to me to unify three forms of ecstasy with the ideology of a natural ecstasy, although the problems encountered by its authors are obvious enough when the text is examined in detail. Accordingly, we will peruse the core statements to see if textual criticism can lend support to the proposal that *sahaja* was not fundamental to an arrangement of varieties of sexual bliss. Most important will be two points: first, that the *Hevajra* exhibits three different series of a threefold *ānanda*, and, second, that since each *ānanda* series evolved separately, the precise placement or relationship of *sahaja* to these groupings became a contentious issue." As IaS (97n17, n18, and 100) points out, the crucial point that distinguishes these two sequences is that the terms *virama* and *viramānanda* (or sometimes *ānanda/virāmānanda*) are understood in different ways. In the first sequence, they are obviously not read most naturally as "cessation" and "cessational ecstasy," respectively, but interpreted as "[the state] free of ecstasy," "ecstasy free of ecstasy," or even "special ecstasy" (the usual Tibetan renderings *dga' bral* ["free of ecstasy"], *dga' bral gyi dga' ba* ["ecstasy free of ecstasy"], and *khyad dga'* ["special ecstasy"] obviously reflect such interpretations). Thus IaS proposes that the difference between these positions A and B may have arisen from those different understandings of what *virama* means. That is, some ("position B") understood the prefix *vi-* in *virama* as either an intensifier (*viśiṣṭo ramo viramaḥ*, as explicitly analyzed in Vibhūticandra's *Amṛtakaṇikoddyotanibandha*) or expressing diversity (*vividharamaṇam*, as in *Sekoddeśa* 81). From this perspective, the sequence of the four ecstasies is one of increasing intensification, with any return to a lower state being located entirely outside of this sequence and thus not even worth being called "ecstasy." However, others ("position A") understood *virama* as "cessation" in the sense of a postclimactic experience of re-entering the lower state of conceptual thought. With such an understanding, the crucial climactic point to be identified and with which to practice here—connate ecstasy—must precede *virama*. An example of "position A" is Ratnākaraśānti's *Muktāvalī* commentary on *Hevajratantra* I.8.33, saying that since ecstasy arises during the various acts of foreplay, it is said to entail variety (*vicitra*) and amounts to the desire for actual intercourse. Supreme ecstasy arises thereafter as a consequence or maturation (*vipāka*) of ecstasy. It is the still-conceptual enjoyment of intercourse with the anticipation of connate ecstasy. During orgasm, a glimpse of connate ecstasy is experienced. However, since the actual connate ecstasy is the space-like nonconceptual wisdom that lacks all defiling appearances, it is said to not be characterized by appearances (*vilakṣaṇa*). Subsequent to the experience of connate ecstasy, cessational ecstasy comes last, being characterized by exhaustion or consummation (*vimarda*), and by reflecting on the experience of connate ecstasy as one's own. However, since cessational ecstasy is characterized by the annihilation of the most excellent bliss, thinking, "I have partaken of true bliss!," it is mistaken because it has the nature of a thought remembering past bliss. Thus only connate ecstasy is the ultimate one, whereas the other three ecstasies are delusive in that they all involve some degree of appearance and thinking. Similarly, Mahāsukhavajra's *Padmāvatī* commentary on the first chapter of the *Caṇḍamahāroṣaṇatantra* (see Grimes and Szántó 2018) says that ecstasy represents the bliss that is experienced during foreplay up to the moment of penetration. Supreme ecstasy is the increased bliss experienced during actual intercourse up to the moment of seminal fluid reaching the root of the glans penis. Connate ecstasy is the supreme nonconceptual bliss devoid of any thoughts of subject and object that occurs during the time the seminal fluid travels from the root of the glans into the vagina. Cessational ecstasy is again conceptual, experienced after ejaculation, when the yogī, after a few moments of stillness, realizes "I have partaken of bliss" (a short ancillary pith instruction on the various points yogīs should direct their attention to during these moments is found in the commentary on the third chapter). Note, though, that these are not the only interpretations of the four ecstasies according to "position A." BKC (vol. *ka*, fols. 149a.6–150a.3) says that the assertions of connate ecstasy being the third or the fourth one refer to different intentions of the tantras. For those who assert that cessational ecstasy is the third one, it refers to fainting into unconsciousness once thoughts have ceased by virtue of the bliss in the middle of the jewel. If it is taken as the fourth one, it refers to the moment of bliss fading once bodhicitta is emitted outside. Given that both assert connate ecstasy to be perceived at the tip of the jewel, they are not deluded about the triad of location, essence, and path. However, by virtue of merely being free of perceiver and perceived, connate ecstasy is coarse, which accords with Mere Mentalism. To perceive the subtle special feature of this ecstasy at the tip is in accord with the Madhyamaka of utter nonabiding (for details, see the note on this in the translation). In conclusion, it should be pointed out that which ecstasy is identified as the fourth one can be determined in two ways. First, both sequences of the four ecstasies agree on connate ecstasy being the highest one in terms of realization. Second, in terms of the time when this highest ecstasy occurs, it is taken as the third one when it is held to arise in the middle between supreme ecstasy (the second one) and cessational ecstasy (as the fourth one) ("position A"). In the other sequence ("position B"), connate ecstasy is regarded as the fourth one that occurs after cessational ecstasy (the third one). Thus, in terms of ranking, connate ecstasy is always the fourth one, but in terms of timing and in terms of how *virama* in *viramānanda* is understood, it can be numbered either third or fourth. For more details on these two sequences, see Mathes 2009, IaS (96–100), Callahan 2014 (357–59 and 613–14), and Stenzel 2015.

79. For details on the five yogas, see the translation.
80. Skt. *prakaraṇa* can also mean "explanation," "treatment," and "monograph."
81. As Patel 1949 (xiii) remarks, the Sanskrit manuscript itself has no title, but its final stanza speaks twice about "taking up the purification of the mind" (*cittaviśuddhim ādāya*), and the *Subhāṣitasaṃgraha*, which quotes some of its stanzas, gives its title as *Cittaviśuddhiprakaraṇa*. Thus, it has become the generally accepted title of this work. Patel (xii) says this on the state of the manuscript: "The original MS. of the work is of palm leaves in old Newari script. As it is very defective, its transcription and the printed text based on it are not free from mistakes. In the original MS. the first leaf is missing, the obverse side of the seventh leaf is totally illegible and many padas, phrases or words are too much defaced to be deciphered with any certainty." All three currently available editions appear to be in need of improvement (Wedemeyer 1999 is critical of both Śāstrī's and Patel's editions, and Szántó 2015a, 756, says that Varghese's edition, which is based on both Śāstrī's and Patel's, and Varghese's study of 2008 are "greatly in need of revision"). The Tibetan version in GZ (no translators indicated) by and large corresponds to the canonical versions in Tg (D1804, P2669, N1468; translated by Jñānākāra and Nagtso Lotsāwa Tsültrim Gyalwa), all titled *Cittāvaraṇaviśodhananāmaprakaraṇa* (Tib. *Sems kyi sgrib pa rnam par sbyong ba zhes bya ba'i rab tu byed pa, A Treatise Called "The Purification of Mind's Obscurations"*). The third Tibetan version (P5028, N3811), attributed to Indrabhūti in its colophon and translated by Atiśa Dīpaṃkaraśrījñāna and Kudön Ngödrub (Tib. Khu ston dngos grub), is titled *Cittaratnaviśodhana* (Tib. *Sems rin po che sbyong bar byed pa, The Purification of the Jewel of the Mind*).
82. For details on the issue of different Āryadevas, see Patel 1949 (xv–xvii) and

Wedemeyer 1999 (27–150, 202–3, 219–20) and 2007 (9–14, 56–57). Somehow not accounting for the most famous Āryadeva who wrote the *Catuḥśataka*, Szántó 2010 says: "For the time being I distinguish three Āryadevas: i) the author of the CMP [*Caryāmelāpakapradīpa*] and perhaps the CVP [*Cittaviśuddhiprakaraṇa*]; ii) the *Catuṣpīṭha* Āryadeva with several works; iii) the present, post-Hevajra Āryadeva" (referring to the alleged author of the *Pratipattisāraśataka*; text 207). According to some Tibetan sources primarily related to the Chö tradition of Machig Labdrön (Tib. Ma gcig lab sgron; 1055–1149), there was also a brahman Āryadeva (a South Indian from Vikramaśīla), said to be a maternal uncle of Padampa Sangyé and the author of *The Great Stanzas on Prajñāpāramitā* (P5871), and thus one of the forefathers of the Chö tradition (it is unclear, however, whether he was the third Āryadeva mentioned by Szántó above). For example, a modern Tibetan history of the Chö lineage (Ngag dbang bstan 'dzin nor bu 1972, 10–11) explicitly identifies three Āryadevas in India: the king Āryadeva who left his throne and attained siddhis, the master Āryadeva who was a disciple of Nāgārjuna, and the brahman Āryadeva who summarized the essence of the tantric instructions and had six characteristics: being undefeatable by opponents in debate by virtue of being learned in linguistics, not being held in contempt by the erudite by virtue of having studied many treatises, being immortal by virtue of having attained the vajrakāya, being unassailable by harm through the outer elements by virtue of his vāyus being workable, being unassailable by humans and nonhumans by virtue of having seen the face of his oath deity, and not being ignorant about the meaning of secret mantra by virtue of having mastered the four empowerments. As for the *Cittaviśuddhiprakaraṇa* in particular, Jadusingh 2017 (15–20), despite noting the text's pervasive Yogācāra stance, holds that its attribution to the Mādhyamika Āryadeva is "fairly unproblematic" because it contains much rationalization of Vajrayāna principles characteristic of the polemical style of the *Catuḥśataka*, draws on many nontantric sources, and features the *Guhyasamājatantra*'s six-branch yoga (though not as a systematic exposition), thus linking it doctrinally to Nāgārjuna's *Pañcakrama*. Varghese 2008 (23) contends that the text "contains enough evidence to show that it has authorial allegiance to Āryadeva, the Mādhyamika." However, apart from many general remarks, he fails to substantiate this claim in any concrete manner. Nevertheless, he says (xvi) that the main purpose of his book "is to understand and interpret the philosophical content of the text and put it in perspective with the philosophical position of the early Mādhyamikas." In that vein, he claims (6) that the text "follows the philosophical tradition of early Mādhyamikas . . . [and] also employs a systematic way of discussing the philosophical position of the Mādhyamika. It proves the *dharma-nairātmya* of the experienced objects and the *pudgala-nairātmya* of the knowing self, which is a very important feature of this text," and (34) that "the *Cittaviśuddhi-prakaraṇa* is a continuation of a certain philosophical discussion initiated by Āryadeva in the *Catuḥśataka*." However, like many other passages in Varghese's book, and in his translation, phrases such as "the *dharma-nairātmya* of the experienced objects and the *pudgala-nairātmya* of the knowing self" or "*Pudgala-nairātmya* (essencelessness of the self) as the manifestation of God" show that he lacks a proper grasp of even basic Buddhist concepts (*dharma-*

nairātmya pertains not only to objects but to subjects as well, and something like a "knowing self" is not asserted by Buddhists). Varghese's own admission that his translation "is deficient in many respects" (xvi) can only be underlined, since many of his renderings are completely untenable and he also adds his own comments to the translation without clearly identifying them as such. As for Varghese's claim that the text is a Madhyamaka work, it in fact contains no specific Madhyamaka themes or phraseologies at all. The word "empty" is only mentioned once, in a very generic sense, together with impermanence and suffering, in relation to the body (this triad represents three among the four "marks of existence," the fourth being "lack of a self," which are, for example, listed in the *Yogācārabhūmi*). The term *nairātmya* (identitylessness) is only mentioned three times and only once divided into personal identitylessness (*pudgalanairātmya*) and phenomenal identitylessness (*dharmanairātmya*). But there this twofold identitylessness is explicitly equated with the notion of *cittamātra*, which no Mādhyamika would even dream of doing. In addition, stanza 5 speaks of "Yogācāra," which, given what is said in stanzas 7 and 8 about *cittamātra* and in stanza 10 about the preeminence of the mind, makes it very clear that this term refers to the Yogācāra school (and not just "yogic practice" in general), which is said to be what should be practiced. Moreover, several stanzas speak about the natural purity of the jewel of the mind being purified from its temporary obscurations. Further stanzas contain a number of other metaphors well known from the teachings on mind's natural purity or buddha nature unaffected by adventitious stains, such as butter extracted from milk, the sun freed from clouds, and a lamp within a vase shining forth once the vase is broken. All this shows beyond question that Varghese's claim of this text being "a systematic way of discussing the philosophical position of the Mādhyamika" (and a continuation of the *Catuḥśataka*)—the central theme of his thesis—is completely off the mark.

83. The five stages of perfection-process practices in the *Guhyasamājatantra* according to Nāgārjuna's *Pañcakrama* and Āryadeva's *Caryāmelāpakapradīpa* ("Ārya commentarial tradition" of this tantra) are (1) speech isolation (or "vajra recitation"), (2) mind isolation (or "mind focus" or "universal purity"), (3) self-blessing (or "the illusory body of seeming reality"), (4) the luminosity of ultimate reality (or "the full awakening [of supremely secret bliss]"), and (5) the unity of the two realities, prajñā and means, and the emptiness endowed with all supreme aspects and immutable great bliss, or the unity of (3) illusory body and (4) luminosity (or simply an equivalent of nondual buddha wisdom). According to BGTC (2462), "unity" stands for the unity of the emptiness endowed with all supreme aspects (object) and immutable great bliss (subject), the unity of connate bliss (means) and the emptiness of luminosity (prajñā), or the unity of emptiness (prajñā) and great compassion (means). In addition, Āryadeva often uses the terms "mind isolation" (Skt. *cittaviveka*) and "mind purification" (Skt. *cittaviśuddhi*) interchangeably. As for "body isolation" (Skt. *kāyaviveka*, Tib. *lus dben*), it can either be included in the creation process or in the stage of speech isolation as its preliminary. Or, if body isolation is counted separately, there are six stages. According to Candrakīrti's *Pradīpoddyotana*, vajra recitation is just a preliminary for mind isolation as the

true causal perfection process. Thus the five stages consist of the creation process and the above four stages (2)–(5) of the perfection process. Alternatively, the five stages are sometimes also presented as body isolation, speech isolation, mind isolation, luminosity, and unity. Finally, another way of classifying these stages begins with the propaedeutic *piṇḍīkrama* (instructions on the creation process of the thirty-two-deity maṇḍala of Guhyasamāja) while omitting the above second stage ("universal purity"). For a detailed discussion of all the different names and meanings of these five stages, see Wedemeyer 2007 and Kongtrul Lodrö Tayé 2008 (138–47).

84. BKC *dgos* em. *dgongs*.
85. Vol. *ka*, fols. 149b.6–150a.4. There is obviously some corruption here in BKC, because the passage up through "as the earlier gurus did" is found twice, separated by a stanza that clearly belongs to BKC's preceding comments on the *Caturmudrānvaya*, and there is no life story of Āryadeva in BKC. Note also that since this passage mentions Butön and Jé Rinpoche (= Tsongkhapa), it is definitely not written by Tipi Bumlabar.
86. As IaS (109 and n40) points out, though this work is more commonly known in modern scholarship as *Caryāmelāpakapradīpa*, this "title has yet to be found attested in any Sanskrit source. Cf. Wedemeyer 2007: 55 n. 113. On the other hand, *Sūtakamelāpaka* is found not only in Wedemever's MS C of the work itself (with support from the Tibetan translation of the work, as Wedemeyer points out in the same note; in our opinion MS C's reading should have indeed been preferred) but also, for instance, here in Rāmapālas quotation in the *Sekanirdeśapañikā* and in Jagaddarpana's quotation from Āryadeva's work in his *Ācāryakriyāsamuccaya* (Moriguchi [1998: 74] prints *sūtrakamelāpake*, but as he reports in his critical apparatus, one of the five manuscripts he consulted reads *sutakamelāpake* and three *sūtakamelāpake*). *Sūtakamelāpaka* could perhaps be translated as *Bringing together the Sū[trāntas], Ta[ntras] and Ka[lpas]*; at the same time there may well be an alchemical pun intended, as *sūtaka*—an abbreviated form of the title which is often used by other authors in referring to Āryadeva's work (cf. e.g. Nāropā's *Sekoddesaṭīkā*, p. 19817)—in Sanskrit normally means mercury. See also the excellent discussion of the title of Āryadeva's work and of its significance in Tomabechi 2006: 15 (where however the possibility of an intended pun is not mentioned)." The title *Sūtakamelāpaka* with the meaning as explained above is also clearly supported by the Tibetan of the *Sekanirdeśapañjikā* (GZ CDNP *mdo rgyud rtog bsre*). Nevertheless, for the sake of common reference, I use the title *Caryāmelāpakapradīpa* throughout.
87. "S[K]P" refers to Āryadeva's *Svādiṣṭhāna[krama]prabedha*.
88. Wedemeyer 2007, 57.
89. Wedemeyer 1999, 220. By contrast, Tillemans 1990 (1:6) considers the *Cittaviśuddhiprakaraṇa* as a text based on Nāgārjuna's *Pañcakrama* on the *Guhyasamājatantra*.
90. Padma dkar po 2005, 34.
91. Apa., stanza 41; text 13, stanza 44.
92. According to Szántó 2015a (756), the text "is a defense of antinomian practice and an attempt to show that in spite of all appearances, such a path is in perfect harmony with Mahāyāna philosophy."

93. The Yogācāra influence of the text has already been noted in Joshi 1967, 352, and Jadusingh 2017, 16–17.
94. Note also that the text shares twelve stanzas with (or silently quotes from) other works (*Prajñopāyaviniścayasiddhi* 4, *Advayasiddhi* 3, and one each from the *Hevajratantra*, *Caṇḍamahāroṣaṇatantra*, *Pañcakrama*, *Bodhicaryāvatāra*, and *Dhammapada*), and that two stanzas refer to episodes in the Vinaya.
95. The name Padmanarteśvara most commonly refers to a red form of Avalokiteśvara (for details, see the note in text 15).
96. Note that the explanation of "mere mind" (*cittamātra*) as phenomenal and personal identitylessness is not at all as unusual as it may sound. For the beginning of Sthiramati's *Triṃśikābhāṣya* declares that one of the main objectives of the *Triṃśikā* is to help those who, owing to their attachment to the real existence of persons and phenomena, do not correctly understand *cittamātra* to fully realize personal and phenomenal identitylessness in order to accomplish the true fruition of the teaching of *cittamātra*. To demonstrate that phenomena do not exist permanently (that is, do not have an intrinsic nature of their own) means to avoid the extreme of superimposition, while to say that they are *vijñaptimātra* (mere cognizance) avoids the extreme of denial. Similarly, Vasubandhu's *Viṃśatikāvṛtti* on stanza 10 (Sanskrit in Anacker 1986, 416) says this about "mere cognizance" (Skt. *vijñaptimātra* as an equivalent of *cittamātra*): "How does the teaching on mere cognizance serve as the entrance to phenomenal identitylessness? It is to be understood that mere cognizance makes the appearances of form and so on arise, but that there is no phenomenon whatsoever that has the characteristic of form and so on. 'But if there is no phenomenon in any respect at all, then also mere cognizance does not exist, so how can it be presented as such?' Entering into phenomenal identitylessness does not mean that there is no phenomenon in any respect at all. . . . It refers to the identitylessness in the sense of an imaginary identity, that is, a nature of phenomena as imagined by childish beings, which is the imaginary [nature, consisting of fictional identities,] such as perceiver and perceived. But it is not [meant] in the sense of [the nonexistence of] the inexpressible identity that is the object of the buddhas. Likewise, one enters into the identitylessness of this very mere cognizance as well, in the sense of [it lacking] any identity imagined by yet another cognizance. It is for this reason that, through the presentation of mere cognizance, one enters into the identitylessness of all phenomena, but not through the complete denial of their [relative] existence. Also, otherwise, [mere] cognizance would be the referent of another cognizance, and thus [a state of] mere cognizance would not be established, since it [still] has a referent." For more details, see Brunnhölzl 2009 (17–27), and *Mahāyānasaṃgraha* III.8–9 and III.11–12 with its commentaries (Brunnhölzl 2018, 203–5, 327–28, 332–34, 700–705, and appendices 5 and 18).
97. This text is only available in two Tibetan translations. Divākaracandra is also referred to as Devacandra, Devākaracandra, Śūnyatāsamādhivajra, Śunyatavajra, and Samādhivajra (the last three are three versions of his secret name). IaS (83n105) elaborates that Devākaracandra (like Devacandra, only appearing in Tibetan as De ba ā ka ra tsandra) "as a Sanskrit name, seems not to make good sense . . . the name should be rather Divākaracandra, which not only

appears intrinsically more plausible as a name, but is also attested in numerous, though principally unpublished, Sanskrit sources."

98. BA, 392–94.
99. Tib. Yam 'gal (Lo Bue 1997, 637: "the townlet which eventually grew into the southern sector of Kathmandu").
100. According to Davidson (2002b, 135), "Bhāro, was a new political name title given to important members of the merchant (*vaiśya*, *urāya* or similar) castes and marked in the bearer as a minor aristocrat with a title attested primarily from the eleventh century onward. These Newar nobles had a particular involvement with Buddhism."
101. Better known among Tibetans as "White Hamu" (Tib. Ha mu dkar po), but also named Varendraruci.
102. This lineage runs from Vajradhara to Vajravārāhī, Princess Lakṣmīṃkarā, Virūpa, Avadhūtīpa (Maitrīpa), Divākaracandra (Śūnyatāsamādhivajra), Jinadatta, Buddhadatta, Hamu Karpo (Varendraruci), Chel Lotsāwa Kunga Dorjé (Tib. Dpyal lo tsā ba kun dga' rdo rje), and so on. "The Six Texts of Vajravārāhī" consists of a longer and shorter text on her form Dvimukhā: Śūnyatāsamādhi's *Śrītattvajñānasiddhi* (D1551) and *Jñānāveśa* (D1553); a longer and shorter text on her severed-headed form Chinnamuṇḍā: Śrīmatī's *Chinnamuṇḍavajravārāhīsādhana* (D1554) and Virūpa's *Chinnamuṇḍāsādhana* (D1555); and a longer and shorter text on her form Sarvārthasiddhā: Avadhūtipā's *Sarvārthasiddhāsādhana* (D1552) and Advayavajra's *Śrīvajravārāhīkalpasarvārthasādhasādhana* (D1578). As a supplement, there is also Buddhadatta's *Śrīvajrayoginīhomavidhi* (D1556) (see English 2002, 94–103, 384n4). According to Tāranātha's supplementary historical anecdotes on this lineage (Kongtrul Lodrö Tayé 2020, 190–91; Tāranātha strangely says that Śūnyatāsamādhivajra was an alias of Śavaripā), Śūnyatāsamādhivajra composed an excellent poetic work on Vajravārāhī, becoming wealthy and renowned for his learning. Proud about his poetics, he composed the *Śrītattvajñānasiddhi* and another work, but these were not approved by Vajravārāhī and thus his resources faded. After three years of practicing confession, Vajravārāhī appeared in front of him and said: "If you, rather than writing these texts, had meditated and attained the rainbow body, such obstacles could have been averted. But from now on I bless your two sādhanas so they will benefit many beings and your activities will be accomplished unimpededly." Thereafter, Śūnyatāsamādhivajra's merits increased greatly, he became the teacher of the kings of Nepal and Magadha, and his sādhanas spread widely throughout India and Nepal.
103. IaS (83n105) adds that it "seems plausible that this is the same Divākaracandra who is said by the famous Sa skya master Nor chen Kun dga' bzaṅ po (1382–1456 CE, TBRC P1132) to have written a commentary (which seems not now to be extant, either in Sanskrit or Tibetan) on Ratnākaraśānti's sādhana of the *utpattikrama* in the Hevajra-system, the *Bhramahara*, and who according to the Tibetan master was a direct disciple (*dṅos slob*) of Ratnākaraśānti (see *gNad kyi zla zer* fol. 4r4 5; cf. Sobisch 2008: 40–41). At least it would not be too surprising if several students of Ratnākaraśānti, probably the most famous and one of the most widely sought out teachers of his time, should have also become students of the slightly younger Maitreyanātha." It could also be that Divākaracandra

was a student of Nāropa (see Guenther 1963, 99, referring to a Devākara), though this may have been another person. Besides his *Illumination of Prajñā Wisdom*, Tg contains twelve practice-oriented tantric texts attributed to his aliases Śūnyatāsamādhivajra (7), Samādhivajra (2), Śūnyatāvajra (1), Devākaracandra (1), and Divākaracandra (1; some of these works are preserved in Sanskrit), and at least one translation (Ratnākaraśānti's *Khasamanāmaṭīkā*, D1424). For details, see IaS (83–84n105), which ventures that the name *Divākaravajra—the author of four works in Tg (IaS lists only three)—may be another alias of Divākaracandra. For further details on Divākaracandra, see BA (392–94), and Lo Bue 1997 (635–38), who says that Divākaracandra is "perhaps the most noteworthy Newar author" (Lo Bue discusses the usually unacknowledged or underestimated role of Newar Buddhist masters from the area today known as the Kathmandu valley in the transmission of Indian Buddhism to Tibet).

104. For Tipi Bumlabar's detailed outline, see appendix 3.

105. According to Maitrīpa's *Sekatātparyasaṃgraha* (text 37, 203), prajñā-jñāna has the following two meanings: "[The compound] 'prajñā-jñāna' admits two etymological derivations here: 'the wisdom of prajñā' and 'the wisdom that is prajñā itself.' Now, the former etymological derivation is as follows. Prajñā refers to the mental state that [still] bears the [two] aspects of perceiver and perceived and is the nature of a well-shaped woman consisting of the four elements, the five skandhas, and the six objects such as forms. The bodhicitta that has this [form of prajñā] as its cause is wisdom. The latter etymological derivation is that wisdom refers to this very [prajñā] in its being empty of said two aspects [of perceiver and perceived]."

106. Text 217, 457.

107. "The seven constituents of union" (Skt. *sampuṭasaptāṅga*, Tib. *kha sbyor yan lag bdun*) are said to characterize the fruitional state of Vajradhara, the state of unity (*yuganaddha*), the wisdom of the fourth empowerment, and the supreme siddhi of mahāmudrā. These seven consist of (1) complete enjoyment, (2) union, (3) great bliss, (4) the lack of nature, (5) compassion, (6) uninterrupted, and (7) unceasing (for details, see Divākaracandra's text).

108. The corresponding Sanskrit terms *utpattikrama*, *gambhīrotpattikrama*, *utpannakrama* (lit. "process of the arisen," mostly used as an equivalent of the not-so-frequent *niṣpannakrama*), *pariniṣpannakrama*, and *svābhāvikakrama* are found in Rāmapāla's *Sekanirdeśapañjikā*. While these five names appear to ultimately go back to Saraha's *Kāyakoṣāmṛtavajragītā* 90–91 ("the essence process" is also mentioned in Saraha's *Vākkoṣarucirasvaravajragītā* 8), they are explained in detail as a set of five in Maitrīpa's *Nairātmyāprakāśa* and *Caturmudropadeśa*, Divākaracandra's *Prajñājñānaprakāśa*, the *Caturmudrāṭīkā*, Rāmapāla's *Sekanirdeśapañjikā*, and Vajrapāṇi's *Guruparamparākramopadeśa*. Nevertheless, the ways in which these six texts describe those five stages and match them with the creation and perfection processes vary. There is also a handful of other tantric commentaries that mention the names of one up to three of these five stages, but they often have a different meaning, and "the essence process" is not mentioned in any of them (for details on all this, see appendix 7).

109. For details on "the tathāgata relief" and "the Vajradhara relief," see this section of Divākaracandra's *Illumination of Prajñā Wisdom*. As for the citations in his

text, the most frequently quoted work is the *Hevajratantra* (thirteen times), followed by Maitrīpa's *Sekanirdeśa* (six) and *Mahāyānaviṃśikā* (three), as well as the *Guhyasamājatantra* and *Laṅkāvatārasūtra* (two each). Further quotes come from other works by Maitrīpa (*Pañcatathāgatamudrāvivaraṇa* and *Apratiṣṭhānaprakāśa*), several among "The Seven Siddhi Texts" and related works (*Guhyasiddhi, Jñānasiddhi, Prajñopāyaviniścayasiddhi*, and Keralipa's *Śrītattvasiddhi*), and a considerable number of other sūtras and tantras. As mentioned before, Divākaracandra's text, Maitrīpa's *Sekanirdeśa* (text 42), *Commentary on Half a Stanza on True Reality Teaching That All Phenomena Are Utterly Nonabiding* (text 73), and *Caturmudropadeśa* (text 92), Sahajavajra's *Sthitisamāsa* (text 17), the *Caturmudrāṭīkā* (text 44), Rāmapāla's *Sekanirdeśapañjikā* (text 45), and Vajrapāṇi's *Guruparamparākramopadeśa* (text 213) share a lot of common themes and quotations. In particular, they are all based on Nāgārjuna's *Caturmudrānvaya* (texts 16, 44, and 45 declare this explicitly) and adhere to the specific sequence of the four ecstasies that is found in both the *Caturmudrānvaya* and Maitrīpa's works.

110. Skt. *sthiti* ("position") here means "philosophical position" and equals the broader term *siddhānta* ("philosophical system"). A note in BKC (vol. *ka*, 329; copied in Grub thob gling ras, Par phu ba blo gros seng ge, Karma pa rang byung rdo rje 2011, xi–xii) says that there seem to be two traditions of including the *Sthitisamāsa* in either "The Cycle of Twenty-Five Dharmas of Mental Nonengagement" or "The Sixfold Pith Cycle," but there seems to be no difference as to the actual intention (*don gyi dgongs pa*), just two different ways of enumerating these two sets of texts. To my knowledge, the only author who includes the *Sthitisamāsa* in "The Dharmas of Mental Nonengagement" is Padma Karpo (Padma dkar po 2005, 38).

111. BA, 842.

112. See Mathes 2021, 25–26. Otherwise, nothing is known about Sahajavajra's life. His two preserved works are the *Synopsis* and his commentary on Maitrīpa's *Tattvadaśaka* (text 46). There is another text in Tg called *Cūḍāmaṇi* (D4324) that is wrongly ascribed to him in BDRC, but its colophon has no author and only says that it was translated by the East Indian master Śrī Sahaja and Urgyenpa Rinchen Bal (Tib. U rgyan pa rin chen dpal; 1229/30–1309). Given the dates of Urgyenpa, this Śrī Sahaja cannot be the Sahajavajra who was Maitrīpa's student.

113. The ms. in Newari script (perhaps thirteenth century) was originally catalogued by the National Archives in Kathmandu (NAK MS 5-139) and subsequently by the Nepal-German Manuscript Preservation Project (reel nos. B 24/4 and B 25/15). Among its original nineteen folios, five are missing (folios 3, 9, 13, 15, and 19). Mathes 2019 (157n86) comments as follows: "There is only one Sanskrit palm-leaf manuscript which has been photographed. Confusingly, the microfilm of the manuscript (B 24/4) and the photos (B 25/5) were catalogued separately. Further, both texts (the original and the photographed text) were provisionally catalogued under the title *Kośakārikā* by the National Archives in Kathmandu and consequently also by the NGMPP. The text was identified by Matsuda (1995: 848–843 (= 205–210) as *Sahajavajra's '*Sthitisamuccaya*' (SS). I thank Alexis Sanderson, who pointed out that the correct title of the work should be **Sthitisamāsa*." That this should be the title is clearly suggested by the fact that each of its sections (except those of the Vaibhāṣikas

and the Mantra tradition) concludes with the term *sthitisamāsa*. Unfortunately, I had no access to the ms. itself, but Péter-Dániel Szántó kindly provided me with his unpublished preliminary transcription of its available folios, including his partial emendations and conjectures (Szántó n.d.). Szántó's transcription also mentions another possible manuscript (NAK 5/143 = NGMPP B 25/15), but in a more recent email communication (February 2022), he said he was unable to find a second one. I also had access to those portions of the text that have been edited in Iwata 1997, 1999, 2011, 2013, and 2014, Matsuda 1995, Onians 2002, Matsumoto 2016 and 2020, and Mathes 2006b and 2019. These publications include the complete Vaibhāṣika section (I.1–8), twelve stanzas in the Sautrāntika section (II.1–7ab and II.18cd–23; II.7cd–18ab are on the missing folio 3), the complete Nonaspectarian Yogācāra section (III.1–15), the complete Aspectarian Yogācāra section (IV.1–8), nine-and-a-half stanzas in the Mādhyamika section (V.1–6ab, V.10, V.36–38), and thirteen-and-a-half stanzas in the mantra section (VI.1–13, V.18ab). In addition, the Madhyamaka section silently includes thirteen stanzas from the *Laṅkāvatārasūtra*, and the mantra section cites twenty-seven-and-a-half stanzas from the *Sekkodeśa* (on folios 13–15) and also quotes or incorporates about fifty-four lines from the *Śrīmahāsaṃvarodayatantra*, the *Hevajratantra*, and some of Maitrīpa's works (fols. 16–18) that are preserved in Sanskrit elsewhere. In sum, from among the c. 177 stanzas in the *Sthitisamāsa* (including its citations), about forty-nine are on the missing folios 3, 9, 13, 15, and 19: II.7c–18b (fol. 3), V.22d–V.32c (fol. 9), VI.19d up through the quote of *Sekoddeśa* 102a (fol. 13), the quote of *Sekoddeśa* 122cd up through the stanza that ends in "they rest by persevering in wisdom" (fol. 15), and everything from the line "that is accordingly declared to be 'wisdom'" onward, including the colophon (fol. 19). However, since twenty-nine among these missing forty-nine stanzas are found in the above other sources, only twenty stanzas of the *Sthitisamāsa* are solely preserved in Tibetan. This is fortunate because, as Onians 2002 (139–40) remarks, "the Tibetan translation seems to be even more obscure than the Sanskrit original and does not assist much in deciphering the meaning. Both textual transmissions are very problematic (and in many places discrepant)." In sum, it is of course not ideal to translate from a Sanskrit ms. that has been edited only in parts and otherwise just transcribed, but that is the best I could do under the circumstances. I hope that a future complete Sanskrit edition will improve on my current work. Needless to say, all mistakes contained herein are my own.

114. Texts 22, 34, and appendix 2, respectively.

115. For details, compare the descriptions of the four philosophical systems and the mantra approach in those texts by Maitrīpa and Vajrapāṇi's *Guruparamparākramopadeśa* (text 213). According to Mathes 2021 (35–36), the *Guruparamparākramopadeśa* combines extensive commentaries on Maitrīpa's *Tattvaratnāvalī*, *Sekatātparyasaṃgraha*, and *Sekanirdeśa*. However, this is only true for the *Tattvaratnāvalī*; while Vajrapāṇi's text shares some passages with the *Sekatātparyasaṃgraha* and is in general agreement with the *Sekanirdeśa*—as it is with Nāgārjuna's *Caturmudrānvaya* (text 14), Maitrīpa's *Saṃkṣiptasekaprakriyā* (text 38), *Commentary on Half a Stanza on True Reality Teaching That All Phenomena Are Utterly Nonabiding* (text 73), and *Caturmudropadeśa* (text 92), and the

works of Maitrīpa's other main students—it is certainly an overstatement to consider the *Guruparamparākramopadeśa* as an actual commentary on the *Sekatātparyasaṃgraha* and *Sekanirdeśa*.

116. In Indian philosophy in general, the distinction between "Aspectarians" (*sākāravādin*) and "Nonaspectarians" (*nirākāravādin*) is a very common one. Somewhat simplified, the former assert that mind apprehends an object via, or simply as nothing but, a mental "aspect" or image that appears to consciousness, thus being mind's actual cognitive content, while Nonaspectarians deny such an aspect altogether, or at least its real existence. Among Buddhist schools, the Sautrāntikas and certain Yogācāras are usually said to be Aspectarians, while the Vaibhāṣikas and certain other Yogācāras are held to be Nonaspectarians (or False Aspectarians). With regard to the Yogācāras, however, the situation is rather complex and there are various (later) interpretations of what exactly the terms "Aspectarian" and "Nonaspectarian" refer to. Often, Yogācāras such as Dignāga and Dharmapāla are classified as Aspectarians, while Asaṅga, Vasubandhu, Sthiramati, Kambala, and others are said to be Nonaspectarians. However, there is no mention of either such names or the corresponding positions in their own writings, and it is highly questionable whether the standard descriptions of these terms adequately represent their view (for example, Asaṅga, Vasubandhu, and others say that, in being the imaginary nature, both the apprehended and apprehending aspects are equally unreal, while not asserting any ultimately real or independent kind of consciousness). Most of the explicit references to the controversy between Aspectarians and False Aspectarians are only encountered from the eighth century onward, the most detailed discussion taking place between Ratnākaraśānti and Jñānaśrīmitra in the eleventh century. Earlier Indian Mādhyamikas such as Jñānagarbha, Śāntarakṣita, Kamalaśīla, and Haribhadra refer to the notion of a really existent consciousness or self-awareness in both the Aspectarian and Nonaspectarian versions and unanimously refute both (without, however, mentioning specific persons). It is mainly in a number of late Indian works dating from the eleventh and twelfth centuries—usually written as or containing doxographies from a Mādhyamika point of view—that the explicit distinction between Aspectarians and Nonaspectarians with regard to the Yogācāras is found (though by no means is it always described in the same way). Besides Maitrīpa's *Tattvadaśaka*, such texts also include his *Tattvaratnāvalī* (text 34) and *Pañcatathāgatamudrāvivaraṇa* (text 36), Rāmapāla's *Sekanirdeśapañjikā* (text 45), Sahajavajra's *Sthitisamāsa* and *Tattvadaśakaṭīkā* (text 46), Vajrapāṇi's *Guruparamparākramopadeśa* (text 213), Jitāri's *Sugatamatavibhāgabhāṣya* (D3900, fol. 46a.8ff), Bodhibhadra's *Jñānasārasamuccayanibandhana* (D3852, fol. 43b.2–5), Ratnākaraśānti's *Prajñāpāramitopadeśa* (P5579, fol. 168a.4f.), and Mokṣākaragupta's *Tarkabhāṣā* (P5762; Iyengar 1952, 69.11–19: though not mentioning the terms "Aspectarian" and "Nonaspectarian," the text distinguishes them in almost literally the same way as Jitāri's *Sugatamatavibhāgabhāṣya* and also includes parts of Jñānaśrīmitra's *Sākarasiddhi*, followed by a Madhyamaka refutation). Besides Sahajavajra's *Tattvadaśakaṭīkā*, Ratnākaraśānti's *Prajñāpāramitopadeśa* also applies the distinction between Aspectarians and Nonaspectarians not only to the Yogācāras but even to the Mādhyamikas. For more details on this distinction, see for example Brunnhölzl

2004, 864n161, and 2007, 517–20nn492–93. See also Sahajavajra's specific discussion in his *Tattvadaśakaṭīkā* (text 46) on *Tattvadaśaka* 2.

117. "Nondual diversity" renders Skt. *citrādvaita*. This is one of the very few cases in which this term, which later in Tibet was claimed to be the name of one of three "subschools" of Aspectarian Mere Mentalists (Tib. *sems tsam rnam bcas pa*), appears in an Indic text. However, just as Maitrīpa's *Pañcatathāgatamudrāvivaraṇa* (text 36, 192) and *Taking the Pith Instructions of the Philosophical Systems as the Path* (appendix 2, section 6), with this term Sahajavajra refers to Aspectarian Yogācāra in general, not to one of its "subschools." The *Pañcatathāgatamudrāvivaraṇa* defines "nondual diversity" as "the nondual [consciousness] with its diversity, which is empty of perceiver and perceived" (in other words, the diversity of seemingly outer objects appears but is not in any way different from the mind, which, on its own, is the nonduality of perceiver and perceived). For more details, see Brunnhölzl 2018, 1510–16.

118. In the sūtra system, the meaning of the crucial term "the emptiness endowed with all supreme aspects" is that genuine emptiness is not just some blank state of nothingness but entails many supreme qualities. "All aspects" is usually explained as the six pāramitās and further pure qualities that represent the means on the path and reach their "supreme" culmination on the level of buddhahood. This is described in detail in the *Ratnacūḍaparipṛcchāsūtra* (D45.47, fols. 220b.2–221b.7), and in a more succinct way in *Uttaratantra* I.88–92 and its *Ratnagotravibhāgavyākhyā*. Kamalaśīla's second and third *Bhavanākrama* (quoting the *Ratnacūḍaparipṛcchāsūtra*) emphasize the need for cultivating this emptiness in meditation. For, unlike a bare emptiness without compassion and all virtues such as generosity (the aspect of skill in means), this is the only path that leads to buddhahood. Sahajavajra's commentary on Maitrīpa's *Tattvadaśaka* 6 (text 46) uses the term "the emptiness endowed with all supreme aspects" in its explanation of the union of calm abiding and superior insight in Maitrīpa's pāramitā-based mahāmudrā approach. In that vein, Karma Trinlépa's commentary on lines VI.24–27 of the Third Karmapa's *Profound Inner Principles* (Karma phrin las pa phyogs las rnam rgyal 2006, 329) reports the Seventh Karmapa's position: "Since the emptiness endowed with all supreme aspects and the sugata heart are equivalent, 'being endowed with all supreme aspects' refers to the sugata heart's being actually endowed with the sixty-four qualities of freedom and maturation, and the meaning of 'emptiness' is that this is not established as anything identifiable or as any characteristics. Therefore he asserts that making it a living experience—cultivating this lucid yet thought-free [state]—is mahāmudrā meditation." In the Vajrayāna teachings and in accordance with the four empowerments, the term "the emptiness endowed with all supreme aspects" is explained as indicating the inseparability of appearance and emptiness, luminosity and emptiness, bliss and emptiness, and awareness and emptiness. In particular, the union of the emptiness endowed with all supreme aspects and great bliss is explained as representing the secret caṇḍālī and the meaning of EVAṂ. With regard to the *Kālacakratantra*, the term *Śrīkālacakra* is explained as follows: *kāla* (time) refers to changeless great bliss; *cakra* (wheel) to the emptiness endowed with all supreme aspects; and *śrī* (glorious) to this bliss and emptiness being nondual. This "wheel of

time" appears as "the outer" (worldly realms), "the inner" (the vajra body), and "the other" (the phenomena of the maṇḍala circle). In the Mahāmudrā tradition, we find a similar use of the term. For example, a short mahāmudrā text by Mipham Rinpoche on stillness, movement, and awareness (Brunnhölzl 2007, 451–52) says: "Through directly looking at the nature of that mind that is still or moves, you will realize that it is empty in that any possible essence of whatever appears in whatever ways is not established. You will further realize that this 'being empty' is not being empty in the sense of extinction, as in [empty] space, but that it is the emptiness endowed with all supreme aspects: while its aspect of luminosity that knows everything and is aware of everything is unimpeded, it is not established as any nature whatsoever. When you realize this secret pith of the mind, despite there being no looker that is different from something to be looked at, the fundamental state of naturally luminous mind as such is experienced. This is called 'recognizing awareness.'" According to TOK (3:379–80), in the context of tantra mahāmudrā, *mudrā* ("seal") refers to the notion of "union." Since the nature of this union pervades all phenomena, it is "great" (*mahā*)—that is, there are no phenomena that go beyond it. Such union is threefold. All outer appearances are the union of appearance and emptiness, while all forms of inner awareness that perceive these appearances are the union of awareness and emptiness. These two kinds of union are called "the emptiness endowed with all supreme aspects." All feelings of those appearances and awareness meeting are the union of bliss and emptiness, which is called "utterly changeless great bliss." Through taking the emptiness endowed with all supreme aspects as the object that is to be perceived and through taking the realization of the entirety of this emptiness as being changeless great bliss as the perceiving subject, subject and object fuse as one. The empty forms that appear while practicing in that way are merely signs on the path of means, whereas the actual ultimate object to be realized is that just these ordinary present appearances are empty forms in every respect. For more details, see Brunnhölzl 2014, appendix 4.

119. Lines 9abc.

120. For an explanation of Maitrīpa's understanding of the notion of "utter nonabiding," see the introduction to Maitrīpa's works below. Sahajavajra's *Tattvadaśakaṭīkā* (46, 13–17) does not mention the positions of illusion-like nonduality and utter nonabiding either but makes a distinction between Aspectarian Mādhyamikas (Śāntarakṣita) and Nonaspectarian Mādhyamikas (Kambala). The "true Madhyamaka" is identified as the one of Nāgārjuna, Āryadeva, and Candrakīrti. However, even that is middling Madhyamaka without the guru's pith instructions. Madhyamaka with the guru's instructions is "the Madhyamaka of unity," since "what is to be realized as true reality is the very unity of arising and nonarising and not just nonarising" (20). Among Indian texts, the distinction between proponents of illusion-like nonduality and proponents of utter nonabiding within Madhyamaka is found in Maitrīpa's *Tattvaratnāvalī* (text 34), *Pañcatathāgatamudrāvivaraṇa* (text 36), *Caturmudropadeśa* (text 92), *Taking the Pith Instructions of the Philosophical Systems as the Path* (appendix 2), **Dohānidhināmatattvopadeśa* (text 22; "illusion-like nonduality" is implied), *Madhyamakaṣaṭka* (text 26; "utter nonabiding"

is implied), *Amanasikārādhāra* (text 27; "utter nonabiding" is implied), and *A Commentary on Half a Stanza on True Reality Teaching That All Phenomena Are Utterly Nonabiding* (text 73; "illusion-like nonduality" is implied), the *Caturmudrāṭīkā* (text 44; implied by Maitrīpa's "nine approaches"), Rāmapāla's *Sekanirdeśapañjikā* (text 45), Vajrapāṇi's *Guruparamparākramopadeśa* (text 213), Jñānavajra's (late eleventh–early twelfth century) *Cittamarārgaśodha* (text 211) and **Tattvadarśanamārga* (D3715; the Sanskrit title **Tattvadarśanamārga* is clearly suggested by its Tibetan title *de nyid mthong ba'i lam*, as well as throughout the text, but the Sanskrit title in Tg and AIBS is given as **Tattvamārgadarśana*; for details, see the introduction to text 211 in volume 6 and Almogi 2010, 146–52), Candrahari's (eleventh century) **Ratnamālā* (D3901), and the **Paramārthabodhicittabhāvanākrama* (D3912/4518) ascribed to an Aśvaghoṣa/Śūra. In addition, a Tibetan work ascribed to Atiśa (*Bka' gdams bu chos*), but very probably written by some of his direct Tibetan disciples, distinguishes between Mādhyamikas of mere appearance and utter nonabiding. The former are said to establish the delusiveness of delusive appearances by way of the eight examples of illusion (dreams and so on). Thus "mere appearance" is obviously used here as a synonym of "illusion-like" (see Almogi 2010, 161–63). On the Indic sources in which the division into illusion-like nonduality and utter nonabiding appears, Almogi (2010, 140 and 182) says that "tellingly, all authors cited seem to be Apratisthānavādins, inasmuch as in all cases the Apratisthānavāda position is presented as doxographically higher, whereas the Māyopamavāda position is vehemently criticized," and "since all Indian sources cited above present the matter from the Apratiṣṭhānavādin viewpoint, one wonders whether there was anyone at all who considered himself a Māyopamavādin—that is, in the sense portrayed by their Apratiṣṭhānavādin 'opponents'—or whether the entire 'controversy' and 'debate' took place, at least initially, within Apratiṣṭhānavāda circles alone with (more or less) imaginary opponents. Whatever the case, this subclassification of Madhyamaka is certainly a late one, and apparently confined to a small circle of primarily Tantric Indian masters. This scheme therefore seems—possibly because institutionalised Buddhism on the Indian subcontinent was virtually coming to an end—to have never had the chance to undergo proper systematisation in India or to be systematically subjected to refutation by its opponents. Tibetans therefore inherited this doxographical scheme in a very rudimentary form." Note, though, that there is at least one Indic text—the **Tattvadarśanamārga* (D3715)—whose author explicitly defends the view of "establishing illusion through reasoning" (considered by Tibetans as an equivalent of the Madhyamaka of illusion-like nonduality) with regard to ultimate awareness (see appendix 4 in volume 6). Elsewhere in Indic texts, the term "illusion-like nondual wisdom" as an equivalent of prajñāpāramitā and the dharmakāya appears in Haribhadra's *Abhisamayālaṃkārāloka* (D3791, fols. 127a.6–7, 127b.2, and 128a.2) and Dharmakīrtiśrī's *Durbodhāloka* on the *Abhisamayālaṃkāra* (D3794, fols. 225b.1 and 246a.5), but it is not clear (though not unlikely) that it is authors such as these who are considered Mādhyamikas of illusion-like nonduality in the above-mentioned texts. Almogi (2010, 163) also summarizes the different positions of Tibetan masters on this division as follows: "The nature of this division was heatedly debated between those who dismissed it and those who accepted it, particularly as regards whether it was made on the basis of a view concerning the ultimate level, and—related to this—as regards the methods employed by these two branches to establish the ultimate level. Even those who accepted this division held different positions as to its relation to the more familiar division of Madhyamaka—whether Apratiṣṭhānavāda is to be equated with Prāsaṅgika-Madhyamaka and Māyopamavāda with Svātantrika-Madhyamaka, or whether both should be subsumed under Svātantrika-Madhyamaka." For more details on those two Madhyamaka approaches in India and Tibet, see the above-mentioned works by Maitrīpa and his students, Ruegg 2000 (34–35), Tauscher 2003 (209–11), Brunnhölzl 2004 (335–37), Kongtrul Lodrö Tayé 2007a (199–200), and Almogi 2010. Note also that those two Madhyamaka approaches are mentioned in Tangut sources (see Solonin 2015, 445).

121. V.10 says that "as mind is unborn, by nature, it is without nature," and V.30 says that "the characteristic of being unborn eliminates all views."

122. A common Buddhist definition of the often-misunderstood notion of "self-awareness" is "a nonconceptual, nonmistaken awareness that experiences itself." "Self-awareness" is sometimes understood slightly differently in the Pramāṇa, Yogācāra, Vajrayāna, and Mahāmudrā traditions. In the texts in this collection, it usually refers to the nonconceptual and nondual wisdom that is aware of its own nature—that is, mind's ultimate nature being cognizant or aware of itself. This is in line with Dharmakīrti's "*saṃvedana* argument" in his *Pramāṇaviniścaya* (slightly elaborated paraphrase): "'Awareness' is simply appearing as such (or in a certain way) because it has that nature. This awareness is not of anything else, just like the awareness of awareness itself is not of anything else. For this reason, too, it is not reasonable for awareness to apply to any referent other than awareness itself" (1.42, 3–6: *saṃvedanam ity api tasya tādātmyāt tathāprathanam, na tad anyasya kasyacid ātmasaṃvedanavat. tato 'pi na tad arthāntare yuktam*). That is, by its very nature, cognition cannot be of some external entity. Thus awareness of any object is fundamentally not different from cognition's reflexive awareness of itself, because by its own nature cognition is just an intransitive "appearing in a certain way," as opposed to a transitive apprehending of something else. It is important to acknowledge that "to appear" (*prathate*) is an intransitive verb of occurrence, as opposed to transitive activities such as someone cutting down a tree with an axe. The treatment of cognition by Dharmakīrti's opponents (such as different Hindu schools and Sarvāstivāda Buddhists) in a transitive sense appears to be in line with ordinary language, but it is not correct when analyzed. When people such as Dharmakīrti or the mahāsiddhas use expressions like "cognition cognizes itself" (*dhīr ātmavedinī*) or "self-awareness," this is only in terms of speaking in a conventional or metaphorical sense. Actually, cognition simply arises with an intrinsic awareness of its own nature, similar to light having luminosity as its nature. Therefore, unlike someone shining a flashlight on something else or on themselves, it is not that cognition actively illuminates itself or others within the framework of an agent, an object, and their interaction. Consequently, the well-known Madhyamaka arguments against self-awareness, such as a sword

being unable to cut itself or a finger being unable to touch itself, entirely miss the point for two reasons. (1) Self-awareness does not operate within the triad of agent, object, and action (this point is, for example, explicitly made in Śāntarakṣita's *Madhyamakālaṃkāra* 17 and *Tattvasaṃgraha* 2000–2002, with *Tattvasaṃgraha* 2000–2001 also being cited in an opponent's statement to the same effect in Prajñākaramati's *Bodhicaryāvatārapañjika* on IX.19; a similar stanza is also found in the *Tattvasiddhi*, text 210, 83). (2) Self-awareness is unlike anything material that has any physical dimensions in terms of space, shape, color, weight, density, resistance, and so on. Indeed, it seems that Sahajavajra does not take these arguments as refutations of self-aware mind but limits their validity to reified notions of self-awareness in the above sense. Thus the mind *is* aware of itself, but the way in which this happens is *unlike* a sword not cutting itself and a fingertip not touching itself, in the sense that self-awareness is not an agent that acts on itself as an object that is distinct from itself. For Sahajavajra emphasizes that mind is unborn, free of the three spheres and the four extremes, without any aspect, and equivalent to emptiness and so on—all a far cry from dualistic material examples (points (1)–(2) are also explained at length in Mipham Rinpoche's commentary on *Madhyamakālaṃkāra* 17–18ab; see Padmakara Translation Group 2005, 202–3). For a detailed discussion of how *Laṅkāvatārasūtra* X.568 is usually interpreted by Mādhyamikas as a wholesale rejection of self-awareness, while Ratnākaraśānti and others argue that this is not what this stanza means, see the note on *Synopsis* V.21.

123. In this regard, Maitrīpa's **Dohānidhināmatattvopadeśa* 10 speaks of self-awareness free of the four extremes as characterizing the proponents of illusion-like nonduality, and his *Madhyamakaṣaṭka* 3 says that "the lucidity free of the four extremes and characterized by being delusive constitutes illusion-like nonduality." *Madhyamakaṣaṭka* 4–6 speaks of "awareness empty of being an entity, without aspect, unborn, and unsullied" as representing utter nonabiding, and also links this to the Mantrayāna by saying that "lucidity free of the four extremes possesses the character of the deity, has the nature of nondual bliss, and is sheer dependent origination." Similar statements on unborn ultimate (self-)awareness or nondual self-aware wisdom are found in Maitrīpa's *Apratiṣṭhānaprakāśa* (text 24), *Amanasikārādhāra* (text 27), *Pañcatathāgatamudrāvivaraṇa* (text 36), *Mahāyānaviṃśikā* (text 40), *Sekanirdeśa* (text 42), and *A Pith Instruction on Letting Cognizance Be without Projecting and Withdrawing* (text 43; see also the introductions to these texts below). In the same vein, Sahajavajra's *Tattvadaśakaṭīkā* (text 46, 24–25) says this: "Since this is the type [of teaching] of the seal of the tathāgatas when teaching in the manner of the secret mantra, and through the power of the awareness that becomes lucid, it is cognized that the character of the skandhas, dhātus, and āyatanas is nothing but consciousness. Therefore, mostly in terms of [mind] having aspects and a little bit in terms of not having any aspect, this will become the experience of the samādhi of emptiness. Since that wisdom originates in a dependent manner, and since it is very lucid, it is not nonexistent. Since ultimately the essence of entities is to be unborn, it is not existent [either] . . . Thus, in the manner of needing to be taken as valid cognition, through these [statements], the existence of the self-aware wisdom of all aspects is established, while impurity refers to [all] that

is not the lack of a nature because it is clear through unborn awareness that wisdom exists." As for "the seal of the tathāgatas," as explained in a number of Maitrīpa's works, in a Vajrayāna context, the five skandhas are sealed with the five tathāgatas (indicating that they are not truly existent entities but mere appearances), the tathāgatas are in turn sealed with Akṣobhya (indicating their being mere mind), and Akṣobhya must be further sealed with Vajrasattva (indicating that mind has no nature of its own).

124. This ultimate unity of the two realities is also discussed at length in Sahajavajra's *Tattvadaśakaṭīkā* on 2cd, such as saying: "Therefore, just as people with blurred vision see [floating hairs and such], to see all phenomena is [nothing but] ignorance. [However,] simply not seeing anything at all in any respect, just as when [the problem of] blurred vision has been removed [and one looks into empty space], does not constitute being a victor. Furthermore, in not seeing anything in any respect, there is no occurrence of seeming reality. Thus, since that is lacking, how could this be the unity [of the two realities]? Just as with being produced and being impermanent, the character of both [realities] is that neither occurs without the other one . . . The seeming and the ultimate exist in the same way. Therefore, at the time of revealing the expanse of the dharmakāya, in the Bhagavatī, there is not even any ceasing on the level of seeming [reality]" (text 46, 20–21).

125. According to Mathes 2015 (8–9), the approach in Maitrīpa's *Tattvaratnāvalī* of the four Paramitāyāna-based Buddhist schools being immediately followed by a brief Mantrayāna presentation that refers to the *Sekanirdeśa* for details "is interesting since it builds a bridge between the non-tantric method of perfections and the *Sekanirdesa*'s explanation of the four seals (*karma-*, *dharma-*, *mahā-*, and *samaya-mudra*), skipping the six vase empowerments and implicitly any creation stage practice. It should be noticed that in his **Sthitisamāsa*, *Sahajavajra follows the lead of his master's *Tattvaratnāvalī* and presents the four seals and thus completion stage practice immediately after the four tenets. In his **Guruparamparākramopadesa*, Vajrapāṇi includes between the four tenets and the four-seal-based empowerments the six vase empowerments, though." Note, however, that the *Tattvaratnāvalī*, besides its mere reference to the *Sekanirdeśa*, does not explicitly advocate an approach that skips the vase empowerments and thus any creation-stage practice. Furthermore, Maitrīpa's own *Compendium of the Purport of Empowerment* (text 37) and *Compendium of the Procedures of Empowerment* (text 38) do discuss the entire sequence of the six vase empowerments (implying the practice of the creation process) as well as the remaining three main empowerments of the *niruttarayoga* tantras (secret empowerment, prajñā-jñāna empowerment, and fourth empowerment). Note here also that the back-translation **anuttarayogatantra* of Tib. *rnal 'byor bla na med pa'i rgyud* for the highest tantra class that is still commonly used is not attested in Indian texts and is thus obsolete; attested are instead *niruttarayogatantra*, *yoganiruttaratantra*, and *yogānuttaratantra*. Furthermore, as Dalton 2005 has shown, the common fourfold classification of kriyātantra, caryātantra, yogatantra, *anuttarayogatantra (= niruttarayogatantra) in Tibetan texts and modern scholarship is "a late (maybe twelfth century) and uniquely Tibetan innovation."

126. Though the *Synopsis* does not explicitly teach the samayamudrā, stanzas

VI.39–40 and the three cited stanzas that precede them can be regarded as touching on the explanation of the samayamudrā in *The Succession of the Four Mudrās* (as being the sambhogakāya and nirmāṇakāya for the welfare of all beings). As for matching the four mudrās with practitioners of lower, medium, and highest faculties, compare Maitrīpa's *Tattvaviṃśikā*, which says that those of lower faculties rely on the karmamudrā and samayamudrā, those of medium faculties on the jñānamudrā, and those of highest faculties on mahāmudrā. According to Vajrapāṇi's *Guruparamparākramopadeśa* (text 213, 198), the samayamudrā pertains to those with lower faculties, the karmamudrā to those with medium faculties, the dharmamudrā to those with highest faculties, and mahāmudrā to the highest among those with highest faculties. Likewise, the *Caturmudrāṭīkā* (text 44, 347 and 364) says that those with the very highest, highest, medium, and lower fortunes accomplish mahāmudrā, dharmamudrā, karmamudrā, and samayamudrā, respectively. That is, those of inferior fortune aspire for the creation process; those of medium fortune aspire for the nāḍīs, vāyus, and bindus; those of highest fortune give rise to certainty about the guru's pith instructions; and those of very highest fortune are able to make the basic nature a living experience. Thus, in due order, they have the ability to make the four mudrās a living experience.

127. This is also found verbatim in *A Pith Instruction on Letting Cognizance Be without Projecting and Withdrawing* (text 43), ascribed to Maitrīpa.

128. In addition, the mantra section speaks of "self-blessing" and "unity" in conjunction. As mentioned before, these are the third and fifth of the five stages of perfection-process practices in the *Guhyasamājatantra* according to Nāgārjuna's *Pañcakrama* and Āryadeva's *Caryāmelāpakapradīpa* (some of Maitrīpa's works also mention some of these stages). For Tipi Bumlabar's detailed outline of the *Synopsis*, see appendix 4. Note that the vast majority of quoted and silently incorporated passages in the *Sthitisamāsa* are found in the mantra section: the *Sekoddeśa* (29 stanzas; 22 in full, 7 in half), *Srīmahāsaṃvarodayatantra* (46 lines), *Hevajratantra* (5 lines), *Sarvarahasyatantra* (1 stanza), *Nayatrayapradīpa* (1 stanza), *Mañjuśrīnāmasaṃgīti* (1 line), Maitrīpa's *Saṃkṣiptasekaprakriyā* (about 5 stanzas), *Pith Instruction on Letting Cognizance Be without Projecting and Withdrawing* (4 lines; 3 more are very similar to 3 lines from the *Srīmahāsaṃvarodayatantra*), *Mahāyānaviṃśikā* (2 lines), and *Tattvaprakāśa* (1 line), and further unidentified quotes make up fifty-two (two-thirds) of the eighty stanzas of the mantra section. Among the other sections, in the Vaibhāṣika section, three lines are also found in the *Sugatamatavibhaṅga* (two of these also in the *Jñāsārasamuccaya*). In the Nonaspectarian Yogācāra section, the first stanza is very similar to two stanzas of Vasubandhu's *Viṃśatikākārikā*, several other lines echo lines in Śāntarakṣita's *Madhyamakālaṃkāra*, two stanzas echo passages in Maitrīpa's *Tattvaratnāvalī*, and four stanzas are cited or silently incorporated from the *Laṅkāvatārasūtra*. In the Madhyamaka section, thirteen stanzas are from the *Laṅkāvatārasūtra*, and two stanzas echo *Madhyāntavibhāga* I.14 and two lines of a stanza in the *Madhyamakālaṃkāra*. Note also that Sahajavajra, just as in his *Tattvadaśakaṭīkā* (text 46), often rearranges lines and stanzas in his citations and intersperses them with lines and stanzas from other works.

129. IaS (83n104) says that "the **Sthitisamāsa* also differs from Maitreyanātha's

works in one perhaps very significant way. This is that it shows strong influence from the early Kālacakra school, an influence which, as far as we can tell, cannot be detected in Maitreyanātha's writings. This influence manifests itself primarily in the quotation of numerous verses from the *Sekoddeśa*, the teaching on initiation which, though transmitted independently and the object of commentaries in its own right, is regarded, in the Kālacakra tradition, as a section of the Kālacakra root tantra, the *Ādibuddha*. See especially fol. 14*r*–14*v*, on which the following verses of the *Sekoddeśa* are quoted (sometimes with minor variants compared with the text as given in the edition of the *Sekoddeśaṭīkā*): 102ab, 103ab, 108, 110ab, 106ab, 117, 118ab, 119, 146–147, 98, 120 and 122" (note that Isaacson and Sferra here do not mention the stanzas from the *Sekoddeśa* on the missing ms. folios 13 [stanzas 80–82, 135, 139, 140ab, 141ab, 142–43, and 101] and 15 [123–25, 127–28, and 134]). Mathes 2019 (159 and 161–62) says: "*Sahajavajra surprisingly explains empowerment in line with the *Sekoddeśa* . . . There is no refutation or critical assessment of this relatively long quotation. In other words, with his tacit acceptance of these verses, *Sahajavajra not only contradicts his own initial statement but also stands against his teacher in one of the most controversial debates in eleventh-century India. On the other hand, it could also be argued that Maitrīpa himself had already given an explanation of this contradiction: in treatises such as the *Hevajratantra*, the correct sequence was not made explicit in order to protect the instructions from those who do not rely on a *guru* . . . To summarise, there is a strong *Kālacakra* influence in *Sahajavajra's **Sthitisamāsa*, which is missing in Maitrīpa's own works. Given these differences, one could be inclined to doubt whether the author of the **Tattvadaśakaṭīkā* is the same person who composed the **Sthitisamāsa*. Of course there are other possible explanations, such as that *Sahajavajra may have adopted his doctrine in an environment of growing Kālacakra influence. But if this was the case, he could have also abandoned his idea of Pāramitānaya-based *mahāmudrā*." Note here that the *Caturmudrāṭīkā* and Vajrapāṇi's *Guruparamparākramopadeśa* contain citations of two lines ("The cause is sealed with the result and the result is also sealed with the cause") that correspond to *Sekoddeśa* 146cd, and Rāmapāla's *Sekanirdeśapañjikā* also cites the first of these lines. However, in these three texts, those lines are embedded in a number of other cited lines that are not found anywhere else, and all of them are in Apabhraṃśa in the *Sekanirdeśapañjikā*. Furthermore, said two lines are also found as *Guhyasamājatantra* XVIII.79ab. Thus, one can certainly not speak of any Kālacakra influence on *Kāropa, Vajrapāṇi, and Rāmapāla.

130. Text 92, 19–20.

131. Maitrīpa's *Sekanirdeśa* and other texts distinguish between "forceful empowerment" (Skt. *haṭhaseka*), "poor empowerment" (Skt. *duḥseka*), and "excellent empowerment" (Skt. *suśeka*). For details, see Maitrīpa's *Sekanirdeśa* (text 42, stanzas 2–18), *Commentary on Half a Stanza on True Reality Teaching That All Phenomena Are Utterly Nonabiding* (text 73, 188ff.), and *Caturmudropadeśa* (text 92, 19–21), Sahajavajra's *Sthitisamāsa* (text 17, VI.14–19), the *Caturmudrāṭīkā* (text 44, 263–64, 280–303, 342–44), Rāmapāla's *Sekanirdeśapañjikā* (text 45, 388–415), and Vajrapāṇi's *Guruparamparākramopadeśa* (text 213, 209–21). Birch 2011 (532–33) refers to the esoteric definition of the term *haṭha* ("forceful")

as being the union of *ha* and *ṭha*, standing for sun and moon, or prāna and apāna, and speaks of some circumstantial evidence for the possibility that this definition was behind the name Haṭhayoga. Though the Buddhist tantras do not clearly define Haṭhayoga, Birch (535–37) adduces the earliest definition of Haṭhayoga in the Kālacakra system in Puṇḍarīka's *Vimlalaprabhā* commentary, pointing out that the same definition is repeated verbatim in Anupamarakṣita's *Ṣaḍaṅgayoga*, Nāropa's *Sekoddeśaṭīkā*, and Raviśrījñāna's *Amṛtakaṇika* (for the exact references, see Birch, 536n66). This definition is as follows (my translation): "Here, when the unchanging moment does not arise because the prāṇa is uncontrolled [despite] the image being seen by means of withdrawal and so on, then [yogīs], after having forcefully made the prāṇa flow in the madhyamā through the repeated training in sound, may come to realize the unchanging moment through motionlessness by virtue of arresting the bindu of bodhicitta in the kuliśa gem placed in the lotus of the prajñā. This is the haṭhayoga" (Skt. *kuliśa* is another word for Indra's vajra). Birch adds that there are three features of this definition that identify it with the Haṭhayoga of later texts: (1) making prāṇa flow in the central nāḍī madhyamā (the term used in Haṭha texts for *suṣumnānāḍī*), (2) the practice of sound (*nāda*), and (3) the expression "arresting the bindu of bodhicitta" (*bodhicittabindunirodha*), paralleling the term "retaining bindu" (*bindudhāraṇā*) in Haṭha texts. Furthermore, the connection between the practice of sound and the retention of bindu in the *Vimalaprabhā* parallels the combined use of these two expressions sometimes found in Haṭha texts. In these texts, the adverbial use of the word *haṭha* or its equivalent *bala* most frequently means to forcefully move the kuṇḍalinī, the apānavāyu, or the bindu upward. Thus, "force" in Haṭhayoga means forcing what normally moves down (apāna, bindu) or is usually dormant (kuṇḍalinī) to move upward. Birch (538–40) also says here that the number of instances of the term *haṭhayoga* in Buddhist tantras is sharply contrasted by its scarcity in Śaiva tantras, despite the Śaiva origins of Haṭhayoga being affirmed by several Haṭha texts and early Śaiva tantras containing passages on yoga that resemble the Haṭha texts in style and terminology. Though the earliest known references to *haṭhayoga* are in the Buddhist tantras, its role in them is a secondary one because it was only recommended when other techniques had failed (this may suggest that the tantric Buddhists appropriated this name and practice from an earlier source). Finally, Birch (548) concludes: "Rather than the metaphysical explanation of uniting the sun (*ha*) and moon (*ṭha*), it is more likely that the name Haṭhayoga was inspired by the meaning 'force'. The descriptions of forcefully moving *kuṇḍalinī, apāna*, or *bindu* upwards through the central channel suggest that the 'force' of Haṭhayoga qualifies the effects of its techniques, rather than the effort required to perform them."

132. A thorough comparison of Sahajavajra's discussions of Aspectarian Yogācāra, Nonaspectarian Yogācāra, Madhyamaka, and the mantra approach in his *Sthitisamāsa* and *Tattvadaśakaṭīka* (text 46) is far beyond the scope of the present work. Interested readers are encouraged to compare the corresponding sections in these two texts.

133. For details of the Sanskrit manuscripts, see Samdhong and Dvivedī 1987 (8; the edition is pp. 195–208). As mentioned before, on its own, Skt. *krama* can

mean "an uninterrupted or regular progress, order, series, or succession," "progressive stages," "way," "course," "system," and "method." In the same vein, our text also uses *kramāgata*, which means "legacy" or "tradition" (lit. "having come down in a progressive manner" or "a come-down system"; compare also the same expression in Rāmapāla's *Sekanirdeśapañjikā*; text 45, 403). Thus, though *krama* often does mean "progressive stages" (such as in Kamalaśīla's famous *Bhāvanākrama*), given the use of *krama* and *kramāgata* in our text here, *acintyādvayakrama* in its title does not mean "progressive stages of inconceivable nonduality." For one, not only does it seem ironic to speak of the progressive stages of something like nonduality, which is moreover said to be altogether inconceivable, but the gist of the text is clearly the immediate recognition and realization of this inconceivable nonduality in a nongradual manner. More importantly, none of the Tibetan authors who discuss this text speaks of "stages of the inconceivable" or "stages of nonduality" (for details, see below). Given that nonduality is the all-pervasive theme of the text (the term appears seventy-one times, while "inconceivable" appears fourteen times), it is also remarkable that the word "nonduality" is left out in the Sanskrit and Tibetan titles in GZ CDNP, as well as in the alternative translation by Ratnavajra and Drogmi Lotsāwa Śākya Yeshe (Tib. 'Brog mi lo tsā ba shākya ye shes; 992/993–1072?). The often very different version by Ratnavajra and Drogmi Lotsāwa is found in the Sakya volumes of the *Gdams ngag rin po che'i mdzod* (Kuddālapāda 1999) and the *Lam 'bras slob bshad* (11:347–62; plus an anonymous commentary, 11:362–87; for details, see Davidson 2005, 194–204). In the *Gdams ngag rin po che'i mdzod*, the text is followed by a brief lineage history and a meditation manual based on it, both authored by the early Sakya hierarch Tragpa Gyaltsen (1147–1216; Grags pa rgyal mtshan 1999a and 1999b), as well as an instruction manual by Jamgön Kongtrul (Kong sprul blo gros mtha' yas 1999; the reader is referred to English translations of all these texts in *The Treasury of Precious Instructions* series published by Snow Lion Publications and Tsadra Foundation). In the Sakya tradition, Kuddālapāda's text is one of the eight ancillary cycles of practice of "The Path and the Result" (nine cycles together with Virūpa's *Vajrapāda; lam skor dgu*), said to be authored by eight mahāsiddhas. According to Jamgön Kongtrul (Kong sprul blo gros mtha' yas 1999, 232), six of these eight texts are related to the perfection processes of Cakrasaṃvara, Hevajra, and Guhyasamāja, while those of Kuddālapāda and Indrabhūti represent the perfection process of the *niruttarayoga* tantras in general. For a more detailed list of the same texts (though sometimes linked with different tantras and varying titles), see TOK (1:520–21; Kongtrul Lodrö Tayé 2010, 337, and 2007b, 113), Stearns 2006 (132–36), and Sobisch 2008 (24–28). Note, though, that various sources show considerable divergences in identifying those eight cycles. In any case, among these eight, only the *Bodhicittavivaraṇa* and the *Acintyakramopadeśa* by Kuddālapāda more or less match the corresponding works as found in Tg (as mentioned above, both translation and translators of the *Acintyakramopadeśa* are different). As for the others, as Davidson (2005, 195) says, "Most are as 'gray' as they can be, for while these instructions claim to be from an Indian author, they often were composed by later Tibetans around very short teachings attributed to Indians" (see also

Davidson 2002c, 215–17). Note also that the numbers of stanzas in Sanskrit (124) and in the above-mentioned two Tibetan translations all vary.

134. Vol *ka*, fols. 156b.5–158b.6.

135. Tib. *tshogs drug dag na* could also be read as "within the six collections."

136. With minor variations, this stanza is the second of two attributed to the mahāsiddha Koṭalipa (no. 44) in text 177 (44), as well as stanza 3 in text 179 and stanza I.38 in text 183. According to the commentary on it in text 177, different from other contexts, "ordinary mind" (Tib. *tha mal gyi shes pa*) here refers to mistaken states of mind—that is, the consciousnesses of childish ordinary beings who do not realize mahāmudrā. This ordinary mind first awakens in the middle of the heart. This is understood as the heart of all entities—the basic nature that is the heart of all phenomena, mahāmudrā—that is called "the nature of essential reality" and "the middle free of all extremes." That ordinary mind wakes up in the center of the heart means that ordinary thoughts become exhausted and cease within the natural state of mahāmudrā that is the nature of essential reality. With such thoughts having become exhausted, all thoughts of the six collections of consciousness are naturally pure. Since all hosts of thoughts of the six collections arise within the perspective of mahāmudrā, this is the great bliss that abides as "the uninterrupted dhyāna." If there are any imaginings in this natural state, all discursive awareness of mind and mental factors is meaningless, serving as the cause of suffering. For those with realization, exactly this will dawn as the guru. "Taking this as the guru, is there then something to meditate?" No, if it is meditation, there is nothing to meditate. "But if there is nothing to meditate, do you then not meditate?" "Let be in the native state" means "let be in the natural state of that without any contrivance." However, both the Eighth Karmapa, Mikyö Dorje, and Padma Karpo understand "ordinary mind" in this stanza in its mahāmudrā sense (the ultimate nature of the mind), which seems a more natural reading. In his commentary on *The Single Intention* (Mi bskyod rdo rje 2004c, 893), Mikyö Dorje says: "As for the buddha heart, great bliss, '*prākṛta*' was also translated as 'nature,' 'native [state],' 'uncontrived,' 'connate,' and 'ordinary.' Therefore Kuddāla said: 'Ordinary mind wakes up in the center of the heart.'" Padma Karpo (Padma dkar po 1974a, 485–86) agrees, saying: "These days many people without understanding take 'ordinary mind' as something bad and unpleasant. This is the major flaw of not having arrived at even a partial linguistic understanding of terms such as this. Since *prākṛta* means 'nature' or 'ordinary,' it means 'natural mind.' You may think this term has no authoritative scriptural source, but Kuddālapa said: 'Ordinary mind wakes up in the center of the heart. If the six collections are pure, bliss is uninterrupted.' Given that, there are limitless names for this ordinary mind, such as some calling it 'natural luminosity' and some 'ground mahāmudrā.' In the mantra texts, it is known as 'the natural connate.' Though this is explained as emptiness (the object) and natural luminosity (the subject) being connate, in experiential language, it is just this suddenly arising awareness that is sheer, lucid, and unimpeded cognition. Its nonrecognition is saṃsāra; its recognition is nirvāṇa." The term "ordinary mind," which later became a hallmark of Tibetan Kagyü Mahāmudrā, is clearly used as an equivalent of mahāmudrā or mind's native state in a number of Indic works as well.

It occurs most frequently in text 70 (55 times) but also in several other works in Tg, such as texts 44, 49, 56, 58, 182 (VIII.27 and IX.16), and 183 (I.38), as well as Siddharājñī's *'Phags pa 'jig rten dbang phyug gsang ba'i sgrub thabs* (D2140, fol. 208b.7), and Niguma's *Mahāmudrā* (N3422, fol. 138a.6 and N3435, fol. 155a.3). However, besides the commentary here, there are also other cases in Indic works where this term is not used as an equivalent of mahāmudrā but is used in its more literal sense, referring to discursive states of mind of ordinary beings, such as the *Vajrasattvamāyājālaguhyasarvādarśanāmatantra* (H797, fol. 276a.2), texts 56, 182 (II.3–4), the **Mañjuśrīnāmasaṃgītilakṣabhāsya* (D2538, fol. 93b.5), and the **Ratnavādacakra* (D4354, fol. 225b.3). Since the meanings of Skt. *prākṛta* include "original," "natural," and "unfabricated," as well as "normal," "ordinary," "low," and "vulgar" (as in designating any provincial or vernacular dialect cognate with Sanskrit), it is not too surprising that **prākṛtajñāna* was used in these two different ways. That is, while **prākṛtajñāna* thus can also be easily understood as "original mind" or "natural mind," Tib. *tha mal* clearly and exclusively means "common" or "ordinary" (though the latter is taken to have both of the above two meanings).

137. Commenting on these two stanzas, Padma Karpo (Padma dkar po 2005, 36–37) mentions that some others say that master Paramāśvajina received his name ("Victor Supreme Horse") because he filled Uḍḍiyāna with the sound of neighing when he attained the siddhi of Hayagrīva. However, in our own tradition, this is his secret name, while his actual one is Mañjuśrīmitra. The Indrabhūti here is the middling Indrabhūti, and his daughter is Lakṣmīṃkarā. Or, it is explained that there were two Vilāsavajras (greater and lesser), but the one here is the greater one. Guḍhira or Gundhiri was so named because he sustained himself by eating the corpses of small birds called *ghundhiri* (thus this seems to be the mahāsiddha Godhuri [no. 55]; note that Guḍari and Gudhari are also aliases of Kuddālapāda). He is the Sūryasiṃha who later became known as Śrī Siṃha (the names Mañjuśrīmitra and Śrī Siṃha are of course well known in the Dzogchen tradition, which is probably what Padma Karpo refers to, but the connection to this lineage here is really unclear). Padmācārya refers to master Padmavajra, and "compassion" to the source of ambrosial ecstasy. The Dharmapāda here is not the same person as the great Kukkuripa's disciple (though two different mahāsiddhas by the name Dharmapāda are found in the stories of the eighty-four mahāsiddhas, neither of them was Kukkuripa's disciple); he was a direct disciple of Vajrapāṇi, and his student here is Bhadrapa. There are also two Kuddālapādas, the one here being the great master from Uḍḍiyāna. The other one is a disciple of Śāntipa among the eighty [*brgya* em. *brgyad bcu*] mahāsiddhas (obviously mahāsiddha no. 44). According to Tragpa Gyaltsen (Grags pa rgyal mtshan 1999a, 95–96), while Paramāśva was living in a charnel ground, he was repeatedly attacked by the retinue of the precious king of Uḍḍiyāna, Indrabhūti. Paramāśva filled the whole land with horses that destroyed all the fields of rice, withdrawing these emanations in the end. After thus taming the king, Paramāśva placed him in the Vajrayāna. Gundhiri's meals consisted of a satiating stew made with countless small birds called *ghundhiri*. When he opened his mouth, the birds flew out. With such displays of killing and reviving, he guided many beings. According to Jamgön Kong-

trul (Kong sprul blo gros mtha' yas 1999, 233; obviously derived from Grags pa rgyal mtshan 1999a and 1999b), Vajradhara taught this text to the wisdom ḍākinī nirmāṇakāya, who passed it on to Paramāśva in the land of Oḍiviśa. Then, in due order, it was bestowed upon the further Uḍḍiyāna mahāsiddhas Vīṇāpa, Indrabhūti, Lakṣmīṃkarā, Lalitavajrā, Gundhiri, Padmavajra the lesser, Dharmasena, Bhadrapāda, and Kuddālipa (note that Jamgön Kongtrul here explicitly equates Oḍiviśa = Orissa with Uḍḍiyāna [Tib. O rgyan], because he explicitly speaks of "the ten masters from Uḍḍiyāna"). It is said that his lineage continued further through Bhusanapa, Karṇapa, and Vīravajra to Drogmi Lotsāwa, Sedön Künrig (Tib. Se ston kun rig), Gönpa Chöbar (Tib. Ggon pa chos 'bar), and Sachen Kunga Nyingpo (Tib. Sa chen kun dga' snying po) into the Sakya lineage.

138. According to Tāranātha 1980 (262), "The great master, greater Kaudālika/Koṭali, the author of the text on inconceivability" (Tib. *slob dpon chen po tog rtse ba che ba bsam mi khyab kyi gzhung gi mdzad pa po*) lived during the reign of king Gopāla (c. 750s–770s CE). The appellation "greater Koṭali" may suggest that Tāranātha speaks here of the mahāsiddha with that name (who would the lesser Koṭali be?). The related note 30 by the translators explicitly says that the *Acintyakramopadeśa*, *Ātmayoga*, *Sarvadevatāniṣpannakramamārga*, and *Cittatattvopadeśa* in Tg are attributed to the Kaudālika (Kuddālipāda, Koṭali, Kotali, Kuddali, *alias* Gudhari, Guḍarī, Ghadhari) who was the mahāsiddha taught by Śāntipa.

139. According to Dowman 1985 (162), Bhadrapāda was a student of Kāṇhapa (no. 17) and probably the guru of the mahāsiddha Vīṇāpa (no. 11). For this reason and because mahāsiddha no. 11 is said to have been from Bengal, it is rather unlikely that the Vīṇāpa in our text here was this mahāsiddha. Dowman further mentions here that "Śavaripa also had a disciple named Bhadrapa, and there is record of a Bhāvabhadrapa of Vikramaśīla who wrote a commentary on the *Hevajra-tantra* (the *tantra* of our legend's Bhadrapa) during King Dharmapāla's reign." Finally, Bhadrapa is a very common name (in itself or as an abbreviation of longer names containing this word); obviously, the same goes for Dharmapa (for details on the mahāsiddhas by those names, see Dowman 1985, 159–62, 207–9, 256–59). Furthermore, given the close relation of Kuddālapāda's text to at least some of the authors of "The Seven Siddhi Texts," one may indeed wonder about it being classified as one of "The Sixfold Pith Cycle" and be tempted to rather group it with "The Siddhi Texts." Indeed, as mentioned before, the Sanskrit edition of the latter texts (Samdhong and Dvivedī 1987) includes Kuddālapāda's *Acintyakramopadeśa*, thus speaking of and containing eight instead of seven "Siddhi Texts." The two reasons why this text was included in this collection are probably as Krug 2018 (n488) says: "Though Kuddālapāda's *Acintyādvayakramopadeśa* is not counted among *The Seven Siddhi Texts* but is included in its companion corpus, *The Sixfold Corpus on the Essence* (*Snying po skor drug*) in the Tibetan tradition, Kuddālapāda himself counts several authors of *The Seven Siddhi Texts* as part of the lineage of his *Acintyādvayakramopadeśa* and this text often appears alongside works from *The Seven Siddhi Texts* in the Sanskrit multiple-text manuscript witnesses to these works."

140. Padma dkar po 2005, 37.
141. Krug 2018 (335) opines that "the fact that the mahāsiddha Bhadrapāda is remembered by the tradition to have been a pure brahmin prior to taking a Vajrayāna guru may account for the heavily inclusivist trend throughout Kuddālapāda's text." However, as was shown above, the Bhadrapāda who was Kuddālapāda's guru is not the better-known master with the same name (mahāsiddha no. 24) among the eighty-four mahāsiddhas. Given the inclusivist tendencies in Kuddālapāda's text and the specific term *krama* that is found in the title and throughout, one may also wonder whether he was influenced by the tantric Śaiva Krama tradition (closely related to the Trika and Kaula systems and discussed extensively in the works of Abhinavagupta; c. 950–1020), one of the four main schools of Śaivism in Kashmir that requires the offering of substances considered impure from a brahmanic perspective. However, given the location of that tradition, its main focus of worshipping the goddess Kālasaṃkarṣiṇī (a manifestation of pure consciousness), and the explicit lineage in Kuddālapāda's work, this seems rather unlikely.
142. According to Davidson 2005 (195–96), "The Sakyapas rounded out the text by providing a commentary and a short discussion of selected sections of the work, as well as a traditional chronicle of its principals. The chronicle, in fact, is derived from a direct statement in the body of the text itself and is amplified in both the two translations, which have somewhat disparate readings of the lineage. Ngorchen, writing in 1405, maintained that the text was composed based on the *Sampuṭa-tilaka-tantra*, but at most the connection seems to be only indirect . . . The text has no obvious structure, but an anonymous commentary included in the modern printing of the *Yellow Book* divides it according to a triple continuity strategy. The 'causal' material is devoted to perspective, in which twelve instructions are included: instructions on the psychophysical continuum, on concentration, on the indivisibility of appearance and emptiness, and on the three epistemes that define the path. The path material covers seven goals: grasping the mind, establishing it in reality, cultivating the practices, overcoming obstacles, identifying eight specific activities of benefit, comprehending experiences, and relying on a consort. The result of the path are the forms of gnosis and the bodies of the Buddha. This breakdown, we should emphasize, is not at all evident in the received text and should be considered the product of an emerging exegesis."
143. Padma dkar po 2005, 35–36.
144. Tib. *bsre skor*.
145. Tib. *lam rdzogs*. According to Kongtrul Lodrö Tayé 2008 (162–63), the expression "fusion and transference" (Tib. *bsre 'pho*) refers to the perfection-process practices of the *Hevajratantra* as taught by Nāropa to Marpa Lotsāwa. He says that "fusion" comprises instructions for both the creation process and the perfection process. Those on the creation process consist of training with regard to forms, training with the bindus, and training in the union of the creation and perfection processes. The instructions on the perfection process consist of caṇḍālī (including karmamudrā), illusory body (the illusory body of the waking state, of dreams, and of the intermediate state), and luminosity. Transference consists of the transference of consciousness at the time of death and

letting consciousness enter the body of a deceased as an auxiliary practice (see below for these practices; for details on them as per Tāranātha's *Instruction Manual on the Hevajratantra in Marpa's Tradition*, see Kongtrul Lodrö Tayé 2008, 343–50nn48–56). According to Kemp 2015, "fusion and transference" refers to the scriptural collections of Nāropa's Six Dharmas as transmitted to Marpa and popularized later by the Drikung Kagyü master Jigten Sumgön (Tib. 'Jig rten gsum mgon; 1143–1217) and the Drugpa Kagyü master Padma Karpo (Tib. Pad ma dkar po; 1527–92)." By contrast, Ducher 2017 (95–97) and 2020 (148–49) holds that "fusion and transference" is the special name given to Nāropa's Six Dharmas, related to the *Hevajratantra* in the Ngog tradition, originating with Ngog Chöku Dorje (Tib. Rngog chos sku rdo rje; dates according to Ducher, 1023–90), one of Marpa Lotsāwa's four main students. At the time of Marpa and Ngog, Ducher says, it was customary to use a diversity of tantras, depending on the student's aspirations. As Milarepa focused particularly on the *Cakrasaṃvaratantra* and its related practices, the Kagyü subschools derived from him also relied on this tantra, and thus the Six Dharmas of Nāropa in these schools are likewise related to the *Cakrasaṃvaratantra*. In the Ngog school, however, there was no emphasis on this tantra, but on three others (the *Hevajratantra*, the *Catuṣpīṭhatantra*, and the *Mahāmāyātantra*), and thus the perfection-process practices in this lineage are related to these three. Marpa received various sets of pith instructions on the perfection process that can all be referred to as "fusion and transference," and many of Marpa's distant disciples in various Kagyü subschools used these terms in various syntheses. However, the tantra particularly favored by Marpa and Ngog was the *Hevajratantra*. It was therefore the practice of "fusion and transference," as related to this tantra, that became representative of Marpa's tradition as it was continued by the Ngog lineage. The practice system of this school made clear distinctions between the instructions coming from Nāropa and those coming from Maitrīpa, thus sometimes being called the "Six Dharmas of Ngog." Beyond that, the term "fusion and transference" was also used in other lineages (for example, in the Drugpa Kagyü, covering a meaning larger than that in the Ngog tradition).

146. As mentioned before, Padma Karpo does not refer to these five as "stages" (Tib. *rim pa*), nor does he comment on this term in the text's title. His five points of inconceivability appear to be based on a text by Gampopa called *The Progressive Stages of Familiarizing with Inconceivable Mahāmudrā* (Tib. *phyag rgya chen po bsam gyis mi khyab pa'i sgom rim*; see Kragh 2015, 441–43), which consists of instructions transmitted from the bodhisattva Vajrapāṇi to Dharmapāda (obviously unaware of the Sanskrit of Kuddālapāda's *Acintyādvayakramopadeśa*, Kragh renders Tib. *chos kyi ba* as *Dhārmika), Bhadrapāda, Kuddālapāda, Kambala, Tilopa, Nāropa, Marpa, and Milarepa, closely intertwined with quotations from the *Acintyādvayakramopadeśa*. Gampopa's text is structured around the same five points that Padma Karpo lists, but in slightly different order. (1) The inconceivability of the nature of all inner and outer phenomena is discussed by way of its essence, its classification, and its appearance as the special support. Its essence is said to be bliss, lucidity, emptiness, and their inseparability. Its classification consists of the impure creation and completion processes. Appearing as the special support means that this nature abides in

mahāmudrā, signifying what is unborn, unceasing, and unchanging. (2) The inconceivability of the means consists of the means for the five poisons becoming of equal taste, the means for appearances becoming aids, the means for sealing appearances with being unborn at the time of engaging in the dynamic energy of cognition, and the means for effortlessly perfecting the five kāyas. (3) The inconceivability of the conduct consists of a series of meditative techniques aimed at realizing equal taste. (4) The inconceivability of the manner of subsuming all phenomena consists of nonattachment to appearances, nonconceptuality in meditation, and mental nonengagement in bliss within the realization of the emptiness of the multiplicity of appearances. (5) The inconceivability of the succession of the bhūmis, including the paths and the fruition, is presented by way of the four empowerments matched with the fourteen bodhisattvabhūmis and the five paths. The first explanation of these five points represents the one that Vajrapāṇi gave to Dharmapāda. It is followed by explanations of the same five points and their subpoints as they were realized by Dharmapāda, Bhadrapāda, Kuddālapāda, Kambala, Tilopa, Nāropa, Marpa, and Milarepa, respectively, covering topics such as the four mudrās, the nāḍīs, caṇḍālī, luminosity, death, the intermediate state, and the kāyas.

147. Kong sprul blo gros mtha' yas 1999, 233.

148. Tib. *dbang bskur bsam gyi mi khyab pa lnga'i gdams pa*.

149. Kong sprul blo gros mtha' yas 1999, 234–36.

150. The term *tīrthika* (as well as the related terms *tairthika*, *tīrthya*, and *tīrthaṅkara*; lit. "forder" or "ford-maker") has a wide range of meanings. It can generally refer to any adherent of an Indian spiritual path whose goal it is to create a fordable passage across the stream or ocean of saṃsāra. Buddhists and Jainas use it as a designation for followers of spiritual traditions other than their own, especially those of brahmanical origin. Specifically, in Jainism, the twenty-four tīrthaṅkaras of this age are persons who have crossed saṃsāra on their own and created a path for others to follow, with Mahāvīra (sixth century BCE) being the twenty-fourth tīrthaṅkara. In Śaivism, a certain group of siddhas during the tenth and eleventh centuries was known as "tīrthika siddhas." They were famous for the public display of their extraordinary knowledge and their fondness of debate (one of them is said to have challenged Atiśa).

151. Jamgön Kongtrul's presentation is obviously based on a section in a meditation manual based on Kuddālapāda's text by Tragpa Gyaltsen (Grags pa rgyal mtshan 1999b, 99–100; the italicized parenthetical passages are interlinear notes): "As for the triad of body, speech, and mind, since one being supported by the other (*the natures of body and speech are supported by the mind, and the state of the mind is supported by body and speech; for as long as body and mind are not separated, it is asserted that they are of one essence*) is the state of their being one, both body and speech are ascertained implicitly by ascertaining the mind alone (*for everything is of a single type as the single experiential awareness of the mind and there are no phenomena not included* [*de las ma rtogs pa* em. *de la ma gtogs pa*] *in that*). When the mind is ascertained (*for those not realizing the essence, the eight groups of conceptions of the six realms of saṃsāra are subsumed by the eight consciousnesses*), (*from the perspective of isolates*) inconceivability is fivefold. (1) The inconceivability of the characteristic (*not being mixed with different thoughts* [*rnam rtog gi mi 'dra*

ba em. *rnam rtog gis mi 'dre ba*]) refers to its being unmixed and fully complete (*by way of different ways of realizing this essence, there appear the paths of outsiders and Buddhists, as well as all kinds of philosophical systems*). (2) The inconceivability of qualities resembles the examples of a precious wish-fulfilling jewel or the orb of the sun (*a single one appears in all kinds of different modes of arising*). (3) The inconceivability of power (*due to its single essence encountering the conditions of means, all the siddhis arise*) refers to being neither bound (*'not bound' means that the mind's power to generate virtue is its essential state*) nor free, as in the example of a nutmeg flower and oil (*if sesame does not meet the conditions of a stick and so on, [oil] will not come forth, but if it meets them, it will come forth; thus, if [the inconceivable] does not meet the conditions of means, it will not come forth and hence is said not to be free*). Since these three are not conceivable (*the single mind appearing as the entirety of cause, path, and result*), they are inconceivable, which represents the means. (4) The inconceivability of nature (*since all three [above inconceivabilities] are ultimately empty of the triad of cause, own essence, and result*) corresponds to the example of space: it is not found (*as any cause, result, and so on*) by thinking, which represents prajñā. (5) The inconceivability of essence (*since two seemingly contradictory phenomena abide within a single phenomenon without contradiction*) refers to not being disassociated and not being possessed (*not being found if examined*). Since it is not asserted as conceivable, it is inconceivable, which represents inconceivable unity (*[Unity] is neither like blending both existence and nonexistence, nor like dividing one into two, nor like one side existing and the other side not existing [or existing on one hand and not existing on the other hand], nor like combining two into one. In brief, if one searches by thinking in terms of means, there is total existence. If one searches by thinking in terms of prajñā, there is total nonexistence. In short, the mere assertion that it cannot be made dual* [I follow Kong sprul blo gros mtha' yas 1999, 236, *gnyis su byar med pa tsam*, against the nonsensical *gnyis su bu ram 'dod pa tsam*] *is called 'unity as nonduality,' which is said to be beyond any object of all cognitions and expressions. This is labeled with names such as 'suchness,' just as above*)."

152. According to Dpa' bo gtsug lag phreng ba 2003 (772), Maitrīpa was the name he received when he was ordained by Ratnākaraśānti. "Maitrīgupta" is found in his life story in BKC (vol. *kha*, fols. 173b.6–178a.4), which otherwise sometimes also speaks of Maitreyanātha. In his *Sekanirdeśapañjikā*, Rāmapāla calls his teacher "Maitreyanātha," which is also the name used for Maitrīpa in Kyotön Mönlam Tsültrim's (Tib. Skyo ston smon lam tshul khrims; 1219–99) *Instructions on the "Mahāyānottaratantra"* (see Brunnhölzl 2014, 777–88). IaS throughout also refers to Maitrīpa as Maitreyanātha and notes the following on Maitrīpa's several names (59n2): "In some cases, at least, it appears to be true that 'the siddhas bear different names at stages of their lives' (Tatz 1987: 696). According to the Sanskrit hagiography of Maitreyanātha, this master was known by four names—that is, as Dāmodara, in his youth, and as Martabodha (on this name see below n. 14), Maitrīgupta and Advayavajra in the course of different phases of his religious life (see below Appendix 7; cf. also Lévi 1931: 423–424 and the summarizing table in Tatz 1987: 699). As far as we are able to see, our author at no place in his works, at least those extant in Sanskrit, refers to himself by any name. The colophons of the manuscripts transmitting his works usually give his

name as Advayavajra, or, to be more precise, use expressions such as *kṛtir iyam paṇḍitāvadhūtādvayavajrapādānām* (or *mahāpaṇḍitāvadhūtādvayavajrapādānām*); but it is well-known that such authorship-statements in manuscript colophons as a rule do not go back to the author himself. In Tibetan sources he is sometimes referred to also as Maitrīpāda and Avadhūtipāda (often adopting the abbreviated forms, i.e. Maitrīpā/Maitrīpa/Maitripa and Avadhūtipā/Avadhūtipa respectively; cf., e.g., *Deb ther sṅon po*, book ṄA, fol. 11*r*5; vol. JA, fol. 17*v*5). In this volume we have generally preferred the name Maitreyanātha, principally because it is the only appellation that can with certainty be traced back to the master's own circle, this being the name by which Rāmapāla, his direct student, refers to him in the *Sekanirdeśapañjikā* in the prose after the *maṅgalaśloka*s (cf. also *nāthena* in the second of the final stanzas, and perhaps even, with a double sense, *nātham* in the first opening verse). Given this fact, and the strong association of our author with some of the works of the so-called Maitreya corpus, and particularly his alleged rediscovery of, within that corpus, the *Ratnagotravibhāga* (cf. Kano 2006: 27–31), it seems conceivable that the preference for the name Maitreyanātha might have originated with the master himself, though equally it is possible that the students might have placed more importance on making such an association, also through their preferred name for their master, than he did." In Indian texts, Maitrīpa is mostly referred to by his secret tantric name Advayavajra or with the epithet Avadhūta. In general, the appellations Advayavajra and Avadhūta (in Tibetan texts Avadhūtipa or Avadhūtīpa) are rather common. Tg contains fifty-three texts attributed to Advayavajra (some of which are definitely not the same person) and fifteen to Avadhūtipa (including three Avadhūtīpa Advayavajra and one Advaya Avadhūtīpa). In addition, there are four texts attributed to an Advayagupta, two to an Avadhūtavajra, and one to an Avadhūta Kumāracandra. AIBS attributes about seventy texts to "Jñānavajra/Advayajñānavajra" (said to be from Kashmir in BDRC), but those texts are by at least three different Jñānavajras, while the name Advayajñānavajra does not appear anywhere in Tg. Note here that the Sanskrit words *avadhūta* (male) and *avadhūtikā* (female) from the root "to shake (off)" are commonly used in Indian Buddhist and non-Buddhist traditions alike, referring to persons who have reached a level on their spiritual path where they have shaken off or are beyond any ego-based consciousness, duality, common worldly concerns, and standard social norms. Thus the terms *avadhūta* or *avadhūtikā* are rather common epithets and, on their own, have nothing to do with the avadhūtī (the central nāḍī), though some persons may have reached the level of an avadhūta through avadhūtī-related practices.

153. The twenty-four texts in the **Advayavajrasaṃgraha* are the *Kudṛṣṭinirghātana*, *Kudṛṣṭinirghātavākyaṭippinikā*, *Mūlāpattaya*, *Sthūlāpattaya*, *Tattvaratnāvalī*, *Pañcatathāgatamudrāvivaraṇa*, *Sekanirdeśa*, *Caturmudrānvaya*, *Sekatātparyasaṃgraha*, *[Vajrasattva]pañcākāra*, *Māyānirukti*, *Svapnanirukti*, *Tattvaprakāśa*, *Apratiṣṭhānaprakāśa*, *Yuganaddhaprakāśa*, *Mahāsukhaprakāśa*, *Tattvaviṃśikā*, *Mahāyānaviṃśikā*, *Nirvedhapañcaka*, *Madhyamaṣaṭka*, *Premapañcaka*, *Tattvadaśaka*, *Amanasikārādhāra*, and *Sahajaṣaṭka*.

154. Text 43 is considered anonymous in both GZ and Tg. What may support Maitrīpa's authorship is that four of its lines are incorporated (not cited) in

Sahajavajra's *Sthitisamāsa* (VI.36), and that three more of its lines also appear in similar form as *Sthitisamāsa* VI.37abc (these three furthermore correspond to *Śrīmahāsaṃvarodayatantra* III.14cd–15a). It could of course also be that this overlap of lines is due to Sahajavajra being the author of text 43. NG's sentence "[All these texts] were composed by Maitrīpa" that immediately precedes its listing of text 43 shows that NG also does not explicitly include it in the collection of texts authored by Maitrīpa. At the same time, before listing texts 19–43, NG speaks of "Twenty-Five Dharmas of Mental Nonengagement." Hence, in terms of these numbers, NG seems to include text 43 implicitly, which fits with this text's position in Tg and GZ, suggesting it is at least related to, if not authored by, Maitrīpa. For an overview of the different lists of Maitrīpa's texts on mental nonengagement in the **Advayavajrasaṃgraha*, *Butön's Record of Teachings Received*, and GZ, see Mathes 2015, 5.

155. Bu ston rin chen grub 1971, 116–17. Note that Butön adds "the four ordered dharmas" (Tib. *bkas bskul gyi chos bzhi*)—Rāmapāla's *Sekanirdeśapañjikā* (text 45), Sahajavajra's *Tattvadaśakaṭīkā* (text 46), and Vajrapāṇi's **Kudṛṣṭinirghātacintā* (Tib. *lta ba ngan sel gyi dran pa*; just an alternative (Tibetan) name of Maitrīpa's *Kudṛṣṭinirghātavākyaṭippinikā*; text 20) and *Vajrapada*—to his list of twenty-two texts by Maitrīpa himself (see below), and thus explicitly counts twenty-six works on mental nonengagement.
156. BKC, vol. *ka*, fols. 178a.4–220a.5, and vol. *kha*, fols. 1a.1–79b.1.
157. Padma dkar po 2005, 37–38.
158. Note though that, despite his unquestionable significance, Maitrīpa is not found in any known list of the famous eighty-four Indian mahāsiddhas. The only list of mahāsiddhas in which his name appears as one of eighty-eight mahāsiddhas is in Chandra 1986 (no. 1182).
159. According to the Eighth Karmapa Mikyö Dorje (Mi bskyod rdo rje 1996, 7 and 9), Maitrīpa realized that the meaning of the Madhyamaka of the elder Saraha, the younger Saraha (Śavaripa), Nāgārjuna, and Candrakīrti was the same, and thus taught it to others. The dharma cycle of Madhyamaka of this system is well known as "The Dharma Cycle of Mental Nonengagement." In Tibet there are three distinct ways of fulfilling the intended meaning of Maitrīpa's Madhyamaka of mental nonengagement: (1) the practice that emphasizes the profound and luminous Madhyamaka of mantra, (2) the practice that emphasizes the profound Madhyamaka of the sūtras, and (3) the practice that emphasizes the Madhyamaka of False Aspectarian Mere Mentalism. The latter practice explains that the actual meaning of the dohās of the siddhas lies in the ultimately established, self-aware, and self-luminous cognition that is empty of perceiver and perceived. This view has been represented by many in India and Tibet, such as Vajrapāṇi, Balpo Asu, and Kor Nirūpa. Among these three approaches, Marpa and Milarepa transmitted and accomplished the entirety of the first two, while Gampopa specifically emphasized the second one and propagated it widely. Moevus 2019 (66–67) says this about Maitrīpa's blend of Madhyamaka and tantric terminology: "In the texts that I have deemed nontantric . . . Maitrīpa was describing reality in accordance with *Madhyamaka*, particularly with his view of *apratiṣṭhāna* . . . In those texts, Maitrīpa's description of reality emphasizes the union of emptiness and dependently arisen

phenomena. In tantric texts where he writes about *yuganaddha*, especially the *Mahāsukhaprakāśa*, Maitrīpa uses more tantric terms to emphasize this union when describing reality, such as bliss, insight, means and so on. As such, there seems to be two ways to speak of reality as the union of the apparent nature of phenomena and their lack of own existence. While tantric descriptions describing the nature of reality as being the union of means and insight are not surprising, Maitrīpa's decision to emphasize this union while using a terminology which accords with the *Apratiṣṭhānavāda* seems to support his efforts to equate the teachings of the Tantra with the teachings of the Common Mahayana. As such, his non-tantric description of reality, *yuganaddha-apratiṣṭhāna*, can be understood as an effort to take an important characteristic of the Tantras, the emphasis on the union of means and insight, and to translate it into terms and philosophical [ideas] which were more commonly accepted by Buddhists of the times. Translating this important characteristic of the tantric view into a non-tantric view could also be understood as Maitrīpa laying down the philosophical foundation for practices where the union of emptiness and compassion is trained simultaneously outside of the Tantras." Mathes (e.g., Mathes 2015) usually speaks of Maitrīpa's approach as "a fine blend of Mahāmudrā and Madhyamaka," and specifies this as a "system that combines the profound Madhyamaka view of 'nonabiding' or non-foundationalism (*apratiṣṭhāna*) with mainly *Hevajra Tantra*-based Mahāmudrā . . . Another refreshing point of his teachings is an element Maitrīpa inherited from Saraha's spontaneous songs of realization (*dohā*), namely, the immediate access to the true nature of mind. The possibility of such an instantaneous approach occasionally shines through the works of Maitrīpa and his circle" (Mathes 2021, xi–xii). Mathes's statement that Maitrīpa's Mahāmudrā is mainly based on the *Hevajratantra* seems to be based on Gö Lotsāwa's statement that Maitrīpa's Mahāmudrā is "pāramitā, while the way in which its conduct is performed, which accords with secret mantra, is similar to explanations in the *Hevajra[tantra]*" ('Gos lo tsā ba gzhon nu dpal 2003a, 1133) and Maitrīpa's approach to the four mudrās. However, as explained below, note that Maitrīpa also uses terminologies typical for the *Guhyasamāja* literature and other tantric materials.

160. Mikyö Dorje (Mi bskyod rdo rje 1996, 9) says that many, such as the logician Trolungpa, objected to this tradition of "mental nonengagement" being explained as Madhyamaka, saying that systems such as mental nonengagement (*amanasikāra*) were not in accord with Madhyamaka. Only based on these words, Sakya Paṇchen and certain Kadampas developed a hostile attitude toward Maitrīpa's pure dharma, the entire cycle of mental nonengagement. Subsequently, there appeared more people who denigrated the great brahman Saraha's mental nonengagement (the meaning of his *Dohakoṣagīti*), as well as Maitrīpa and the elder and younger Sarahas. Later, Mikyö Dorje (12) adds that the "Pacification of Suffering" by Patampa Sangyé, the mahāmudrā transmissions to Tropu Lotsāwa by many Indian paṇḍitas and siddhas (such as Mitrayogī and Śākyaśrībhadra), as well as the mahāmudrā teachings transmitted later to the great translators Jamba Lingba (Tib. 'Jam ba gling pa), Gö Lotsāwa Shönnu Bal, Trimkang Lotsāwa Sönam Gyatso (Tib. Khrims khang lo tsā ba bsod nams rgya mtsho; 1424–82), and others when the great

Bengali paṇḍita Vanaratna (1385–1468) visited Tibet three times (several years between 1433 and 1454) also belong to Maitrīpa's type of Mahāmudrā system. Similarly, in answer to the question of whether both noble ones and ordinary beings practice the view and meditation of profound emptiness by way of his approach of mental nonengagement, Mikyö Dorje's commentary on *The Single Intention* (Mi bskyod rdo rje 2004a, 98–99) says that mind's nature is directly introduced by realized masters to suitable disciples. Though this direct mahāmudrā approach is not presented as the mahāmudrā of the perfection process of the unsurpassed Mantrayāna, this direct approach of view and meditation is an unrivalled practice that is common to sūtras and tantras because it consists of the excellent instructions by the great lord Maitrīpa, who emphasized "mental nonengagement," "being unborn," and "being beyond mind" in his "Dharma Cycle of Amanasikāra." The instructions of this approach are that all phenomena are mere appearances imputed by thoughts, and the aspects of appearances as they are imputed are not established as any substance other than the imputing cognition. Its true nature (*dharmatā*)—profound emptiness—does not exist as anything other than this very imputing cognition (*dharmin*). To primarily take the domain where the nature of these two (cognition and its empty nature) is like water poured into water as the view and meditation is what is called "sustaining ordinary mind." This occurred to a great extent in the traditions of all those who maintained the transmission renowned as Mahāmudrā in Tibet, such as the explanations of the dohās transmitted via the Indian Vajrapāṇi, the Tropu Kagyü transmitted via lord Mitrayogī, and the Tagpo Kagyü. In his commentary on *Introducing the Three Kāyas* (Mi bskyod rdo rje 2004b, 22:362), Mikyö Dorje adds that the teachings on mental nonengagement had been preserved in the Mahāmudrā traditions of earlier and later commentators on Saraha's dohās who taught the fourfold progression of minding, nonminding, being unborn, and beyond mind.

161. Note, though, that the debate with Ratnākaraśānti is absent from Maitrīpa's Sanskrit biography and one of the Tibetan ones. Also, as the following will show, Maitrīpa does follow his teacher Ratnākaraśānti in asserting the sequence of the four ecstasies as ecstasy, supreme ecstasy, connate ecstasy, and cessational ecstasy, versus many others who switch the positions of connate ecstasy and cessational ecstasy, and also frequently employs a number of typical Yogācāra notions, such as "(self-)awareness," "nonduality," and "luminosity."

162. According to Pawo Tsugla Trengwa's *History of Dharma* (Dpa' bo gtsug lag phreng ba 2003, 774), it was in the hermitage of Mount Blazing Fire that Maitrīpa composed his cycle of works on mental nonengagement. However, as will be seen below, BKC provides several stories about the different backgrounds of composing certain texts in that cycle. For details on Maitrīpa's life, see Tatz 1987 and 1988, Brunnhölzl 2007 (125–31), IaS (59–85, 421–28), Passavanti (431–42), and Mathes 2015 (24–40; a translation of BKC, vol. *kha*, fols. 173b.6–178a.4) and 2021. BKC (vol. *ca*, fols. 26 b.1'og ma [!]–38a.1) also contains another longer life story in the first volume of the collected works of Marpa Lotsāwa Chökyi Lodrö (Tib. Mar pa lo tsā ba chos kyi blo gros; eleventh century; as Ducher 2017, 302, points out, there are three traditions of asserting Marpa's dates in Tibetan

sources: 1000–1081, 1012–97, and 1024–1107). According to BA (842–43), Maitrīpa had "four great disciples" (Divākaracandra, Vajrapāṇi, Sahajavajra, and Rāmapāla), "seven medium disciples" (such as Dhiriśrījñāna), and "ten lesser disciples" (such as Tipupa). As is well known, Maitrīpa's foremost Tibetan disciple was the great translator Marpa Chökyi Lodrö. According to some, Maitrīpa's "four spiritual sons" were *Kāropa, Vajrapāṇi, Marpa Lotsāwa, and the Newar Śīlabharo. In addition, as IaS (85) points out, Maitrīpa had at least one prominent female disciple. The final verse of Maitrīpa's (unpublished) *Śrīhevajraviśuddhinidhisādhana* says that it was composed for the sake of Ratnadevī (this agrees with Rin chen lha mo as the name of the yoginī who is mentioned as Rāmapāla's consort in Tibetan sources), which means that Maitrīpa had at least one female student significant enough to compose a work specifically for her. According to Tāranātha, Ratnadevī was indeed so powerful that her realization equaled that of Maitrīpa himself (see the introduction to Rāmapāla's *Sekanirdeśapañjikā*, text 45). Furthermore, Padampa Sangyé is reported to have received direct instructions on mahāmudrā from Maitrīpa, which strongly influenced his own "Pacification of Suffering" teachings, and, indirectly, Machig Labdrön's "Cutting Through." BA ('Gos lo tsā ba gzhon nu dpal 2003a, 1133) says the following on this: "The dharmas of the later lineage [of 'Pacification of Suffering'] were given the name 'The Cycle of Making the Drop of Stainless Mahāmudrā a Living Experience.' 'Mahāmudrā' refers to the very Mahāmudrā of Maitrīpa because Dampa Sangyé was a direct disciple of Maitrīpa. 'Stainless' refers to genuine statements. 'Making a living experience' is said to mean that there is a back alley of practice that is slightly different from other teachings. This has been called 'pāramitā in essence and in accord with secret mantra' [text 46, 1]. In [Sahajavajra's] commentary on Maitrīpa's *Tattvadaśaka*, this system is also found [and said] to be pāramitā, while the way in which its conduct is performed, which accords with secret mantra, is similar to explanations in the *Hevajra[tantra]*. It appears to be in accord with [Sahajavajra's] statement that this is not the secret mantra because it is not based on deity yoga and does not follow [the sequence of] the four mudrās [text 46, 46]." Thus, BA applies the same three criteria of a path that is pāramitā in essence, has the name "Mahāmudrā," and accords with the Mantrayāna to the teachings of Maitrīpa, Sahajavajra, and Padampa Sangyé. As for the term "back alley" (Tib. *srang* or *srang lam*), in a Mahāmudrā context this is often explained as a small alley or hidden path in a city that not many people know, and is thus less traveled, allowing one to reach one's goal more swiftly than on the crowded main streets. Gö Lotsāwa's commentary on the *Uttaratantra* also makes the same points about both Sahajavajra ('Gos lo tsā ba gzhon nu dpal 2003b, 17.7–9, 137.15–23) and Padampa Sangyé (5.18–9, 53.2–4): "Maitrīpa's direct disciple, Dampa Sangyé, having given the name 'Pacification of Suffering' to the dharma of mahāmudrā that is pāramitā in essence and accords with secret mantra, taught it extensively to countless disciples in Tibet," and "The instructions called 'Pacification of Suffering' from the mouth of the great mighty siddha Dampa Sangyé, which are said to be the path of prajñāpāramitā in essence, have the name 'mahāmudrā,' and accord with secret mantra, were taught to many fortunate ones in this land of Tibet."

163. Tib. *yid la mi byed pa.*
164. Tib. *rab tu mi gnas pa.* Given that *pratiṣṭhāṇa* means "foundation," "ground," "basis," and "firm-standing place," *apratiṣṭhāṇa* could be rendered more literally—and more radically—as "foundationlessness" (or "nonfoundation"), "groundlessness," and "baselessness." This means that all phenomena are primordially without any foundation, ground, or basis through which they could be reified in any way. Or, in other words, there is no phenomenon that can be pinpointed as abiding as anything anywhere, in any way, and at any time. In this vein, Mathes 2015 (15) says the following: "Maitrīpa chose the term *apratiṣṭhāna* as a label for his strongly anti-foundationalist Madhyamaka, in which the true reality of all phenomena not only 'lacks any foundation,' but also, for this reason, cannot be grasped conceptually. However well-refined one's model of reality may be, the model inevitably distorts true reality by introducing wrong superimpositions or denials." On a number of interpretations of this term see also Higgins and Draszczyk 2016 (1:33–34), Isaacson and Sferra 2014 (321), Mathes 2007 (555), and Almogi 2009 (208–9).
165. Tib. *zung 'jug.*
166. In sūtra-based texts, the term "mental nonengagement" is, for example, discussed in Kamalaśīla's *Bhāvanākrama* and *Avikalpapraveśaṭīkā* as being the final fruition of the practice of superior insight based on Madhyamaka reasoning. Among Saraha's works, the term rarely occurs in his famous trilogy of dohās for the people, the queen, and the king, but it is a central theme in his vajragīti quartet, consisting of the *Kāyakośāmṛtavajragīti*, *Vākkośaruciras-varajagīti*, *Cittakośājavajragīti*, and *Kāyavāccittāmanasikāra* (texts 53–56), as well as in his *Mahāmudropadeśa* (text 58) and *Bhāvanādṛṣṭicaryāphaladohagītikā* (text 107). As for Tilopa, the term occurs in his *Dohakoṣa* (text 72), *Mahāmudropadeśa* (text 79), and *Acintyamahāmudrā* (D2305–D2312). It also appears in Virūpa's *Dohakoṣa* (text 71), Nāropa's *Ratnaprabhā* (text 49) and **Mahāmudrāsamāsa* (text 80), Maitrīpa's *Mahāmudrākanakamālā* (text 183), Sahajavajra's *Tattvadaśakaṭīkā* (text 46), the *Caturmudrāṭīkā* (text 44), Rāmapāḷa's *Sekanirdeśapañjikā* (text 45), Jñānakīrti's *Tattvāvatāra* (text 214), *Ajamahāsukha's commentaries on Saraha's "People Dohā" and "King Dohā" (appendices 4 and 5 in volume 3), and the *Sarvayogatattvālokānāmasakalasiddhavajragīti* (text 182).
167. Thus, the mention in text 36 is not Maitrīpa's own words, and if text 43 is not counted among his "Cycle of Twenty-Five Dharmas of Mental Nonengagement," as all above-mentioned sources (except, by implication, NG and GZ) do, the term is actually only used in a single text in this cycle.
168. The list of forty-three letters and their order (beginning with *a*) in the *Prajñāpāramitā Sūtra in Twenty-Five Thousand Lines* and other sources corresponds to the early Arapacana alphabet of the Karoṣṭhi language of the northwestern Indian region of Gāndhāra, which was later widely used as a mnemonic device to symbolize Buddhist key terms (with each letter representing the first letter of a certain Sanskrit word). These letters and the terms they stand for were often taken as the bases for contemplating their meanings. For example, the first letter *a* of the Arapacana alphabet symbolizes that all phenomena are unborn (*anutpannatva*), or emptiness.
169. That Maitrīpa explains the first letter *a* in *amanasikāra* as referring to luminosity

is supported by Moksākaragupta's *Dohakoṣapañjikā* (text 67, 340–41), which also quotes *Hevajratantra* II.4.43cd–44ab as well as other similar stanzas and makes an even stronger statement on this by saying that in the tantras the letter *a* does *not* teach "being unborn," because that is just a common expression in Buddhist Mahāyāna texts and would be pointless in the specific context of the Vajrayāna. Rather, in the tantras, *a* stands for "fundamental luminosity." The same also appears to be implied in Amṛtavajra's commentary on Kṛṣṇa's *Dohakoṣa* (text 64, 213). "Self-blessing" is glossed by the *Pañcakrama* as "the true seeing of the seeming" (*saṃvṛteḥ satyadarśanam*). According to Sahajavajra's *Tattvadaśakaṭīkā* (text 46, 51), "adorned with their self-blessing" means that the yogīs' mind stream, whose character is the suchness of the true reality that is the native nature, is blessed by itself as having the character of that suchness. Thus it is naturally adorned by what radiates from this nature of suchness.

170. TOK, 3:375. It seems that the distinction between "sūtra mahāmudrā," "mantra mahāmudrā," and "essence mahāmudrā" originated with Jamgön Kongtrul Lodrö Tayé (1813–99); it is not attested earlier. TOK (3:381) defines sūtra mahāmudrā as follows: "The first of these three traditions is the sūtra tradition, or this [tradition] that later came to be held as the mahāmudrā of blending the realizations of sūtra and mantra. It corresponds to what the *Tattvadaśakaṭīkā*, composed by master Sahajavajra, clearly explains as the wisdom that realizes suchness and has the three features of its essence being pāramitā, being in accord with mantra, and its name being 'mahāmudrā'" (see text 46, 1, 41, and 47). The last sentence is found in almost literal form in the Tibetan of Gö Lotsāwa's BA ('Gos lo tsā ba gzhon nu dpal 2003a, 2:847–48), which is followed by: "Therefore, the prajñāpāramitā mahāmudrā of lord Gampopa was explained by lord Götsangpa as being the position of the mighty lord Maitrīpa". However, in the English translation of this text (BA, 725), this sentence is misrepresented (and followed by several contemporary authors) as being a direct quote from the *Tattvadaśakaṭīka*. Gö Lotsāwa's commentary on the *Uttaratantra* also repeats this sentence several times, relating it to both Sahajavajra ('Gos lo tsā ba gzhon nu dpal 2003b, 17.7–9, 137.15–23) and Padampa Sangyé's "Pacification of Suffering" (5.18–9; 53.2–4). As for tantra mahāmudrā ("the mahāmudrā of great bliss"), TOK (3:388–89) says that it comes from the *niruttarayoga* tantras, being based on the path of means, such as the highest empowerment, self-blessing, and the stages of mudrā. Thus, tantra mahāmudrā is realized through practicing methods such as the Six Dharmas of Nāropa. As for essence mahāmudrā, TOK (3:389–90) explains that the path of realizing the profound essence with sudden force is more profound than both sūtra and tantra mahāmudrā. Merely through the descending of the blessings of the vajra wisdom empowerment conferred by gurus with realization upon fortunate students of the very sharpest faculties, ordinary mind is awakened in the middle of their hearts and thus realization and liberation become simultaneous. Therefore, since this path does not depend on elaborate means and efforts in training, it is nothing but the direct appearance of the liberating life examples of the siddhas of the Kagyü lineage's reaching infinitely great levels of realization in an immediate manner. TOK (3:380–81) also states that the ultimate view and realization in the *Uttaratantra* (there is

nothing to be removed from and nothing to be added to the tathāgata heart), the Vajrayāna (familiarizing with the mahāmudrā of the inseparability of appearance and emptiness), and the view of Madhyamaka are said to be the same. For more details on "sūtra mahāmudrā," "mantra mahāmudrā," and "essence mahāmudrā," see Brunnhölzl 2014, 151–65. Mathes (2019, 138) says that "**sūtra-mahāmudrā* does not mean that *mahāmudrā* becomes 'Sūtric,' but that sūtra passages that support pith instructions become Tantric. This 'upgrade' of sūtra passages must also be seen in the wider context of integrating the new mahāmudrā teachings into mainstream Buddhism by showing that they are in line with the view, conduct, and practice of traditional Mahāyāna. In the process, Tantric terms were explained in a broader Mahāyāna context with the purpose of demonstrating that their meaning was already latent in more traditional forms of Buddhism. By showing that mahāmudrā is compatible with more traditional presentations of view and meditation, such as *apratiṣṭhāna* and *amanasikāra* . . . it must have been easier for Maitrīpa to propagate the teachings of his guru Śavaripa among the communities of the big monastic universities in Northern India. Once the bridge between *mahāmudrā* and *amanasikāra* had been built, it was possible to traverse it in both directions." Mathes adds: "To what extent this was in fact intended by Maitrīpa is another question." However, this is exactly what Maitrīpa's biographies explicitly say. For Śavaripa had ordered him to return to the monastic universities in North India as his representative in order to "teach the ācāryas how things really are." Following Śavaripa's command, Maitrīpa taught that the view is "utter nonabiding" and meditation is "nonminding and mental nonengagement." His special way of blending mainstream sūtra teachings with tantric elements and the oral instructions of the mahāsiddhas had certainly raised some controversies at that time. However, by combining his realization of mahāmudrā with his prior scholarly training, he is said to have been able to utter the undefeatable lion's roar of these teachings in his former world of the Buddhist monastic and scholarly establishment (see Brunnhölzl 2007, 130, and Mathes 2021, 25–27). For more details on "sūtra mahāmudrā," see the introduction to Sahajavajra's *Tattvadaśakaṭīkā* (text 46) in volume 3 and the excellent explanations of the Eighth Karmapa, Mikyö Dorje on the different transmissions of Mahāmudrā and the relationship between "sūtra mahāmudrā" and the *Tattvadaśakaṭīkā* (Brunnhölzl 2014, 206–11). In modern academia, the position that Maitrīpa, as well as his students, indeed taught a mahāmudrā path that could be called "sūtra mahāmudrā" and that lies outside of the classical tantric approach to mahāmudrā is advocated repeatedly by Mathes (2006b, 2008, 2009, 2015, 2016, and 2021). While Kragh (2015) does not dispute that Maitrīpa taught an immediate approach to buddhahood that is nontantric, he is skeptical about this approach of Maitrīpa's and Gampopa's mahāmudrā being equivalent. IaS (411–20) rejects Mathes's position rather vehemently. Jackson 2019 (61–62) says that "Maitrīpa's own writings leave it open to question whether he saw mahāmudrā as (a) a doctrine and practice inseparable from the tantras, (b) a tantra-based doctrine and practice that also is found independently in the sūtra tradition, or (c) a doctrine and practice that both combines and transcends the Perfection and Mantra Vehicles. Maitrīpa's disciple Sahajavajra certainly seems to have allowed for the second or third possibilities . . . it is not clear whether Sahajavajra is describing a mahāmudrā that is strictly Mantra Vehicle, strictly Perfection Vehicle, or a great seal that combines and transcends both approaches, but at the very least he establishes a consonance between the tantric realization of mahāmudrā and the sūtra tradition's realization of emptiness." Moevus 2019 provides a thorough overview of all the arguments of Mathes versus IaS and suggests the following approach (15–16): "My analysis will show that Isaacson and Sferra ignored at least one major argument of Mathes, and that they only succeeded in showing that Mathes' interpretation is dependent on commentaries from direct students of Maitrīpa. As such, Mathes' argumentation succeeds in showing that there most likely was an Indian non-tantric practice where emptiness and compassion were trained simultaneously, at least in the writings of the students of Maitrīpa. Mathes fails, however, to show that this practice finds direct support in Maitrīpa's writings, or even to show that this practice was indeed called *mahāmudrā* by his students . . . Maitrīpa has two ways to describe reality while emphasizing its nature as being the union of two different natures, one tantric, where reality is described as the union of insight and means, and one non-tantric, where reality is described as the union of emptiness and dependent-arising. I will also argue that those two descriptions also correspond to two different practices that he outlines in various texts. Thus, Maitrīpa will be presented as having offered the possibility for *amanasikāra* to be practiced outside of the Mantrayāna, through a particular understanding of emptiness called *yuganaddha-apratiṣṭhāna* . . . I will show that Maitrīpa can be read as offering a unique access to *mahāmudrā*, where one first needs to perceive reality by practicing *amanasikāra* on the basis of non-tantric *yuganaddha-apratiṣṭhāna* pith instructions. Afterwards, one can simply enter the practice of *mahāmudrā*, without the need for any real or visualized consort. I will then compare this path to other Indian thinkers, particularly Saraha, to demonstrate that my reading of Maitrīpa shares similarities with current understandings of Saraha's teachings. Finally, I will compare my interpretation of Maitrīpa with the path taught by Gampopa, to show that Sapaṇ's criticism of Gampopa's teachings as being from Chinese sources was too harsh. Maitrīpa certainly set the necessary pre-requisites for Gampopa to teach a non-tantric practice simultaneously training compassion and emptiness, and also to teach a direct entry into *mahāmudrā*, but there are two important differences that can't be ignored. Maitrīpa never called a practice outside of tantra *mahāmudrā*, and Gampopa divided his *mahāmudrā* practices in various subdivisions, such as the four yogas, which are not found in Maitrīpa's texts." Indeed, Maitrīpa's works do not use the term "mahāmudrā" in nontantric contexts (though some of his students do), but he does speak about a nontantric path of directly realizing mind's true nature, which in its essence comes down to how tantric mahāmudrā is taught and practiced. In this vein, Moevus (51–52) concludes: "Instead of asking whether or not Maitrīpa taught a non-tantric *mahāmudrā*, one should ask whether or not Maitrīpa taught a non-tantric practice that shares the same principle as *mahāmudrā*, i.e., trains compassion and insight simultaneously while working directly with one's own mind."

171. Sahajavajra's *Tattvadaśakaṭīkā* on 7cd (text 46, 41–43) explains that mental nonengagement does not refer to a complete absence of mental engagement, such as closing one's eyes and then not seeing anything at all. Rather, be it through analysis or the guru's pith instructions, mental nonengagement refers to the very nonobservation of any entity. Therefore mental nonengagement with regard to characteristics means nothing but fully penetrating the very lack of characteristics. Yet the realization that states of mind of thinking "there is no mind" and "there is no thought" lack any nature of their own is not nonexistent. Padma Karpo (Padma dkar po 2005, 38–42) gives three meanings of *amanasikāra*. (1) The letter *i* in that term represents a locative case (referring to a place or a basis), with a location or basis being what is negated by the first letter *a*. Thus the term refers to there being no location, basis, or support on which to focus. Hence to hold one's mind firmly on its focal object through the mode of apprehension of the mental factor of mental engagement is necessary during the practice of ordinary forms of calm abiding, but here this is to be stopped. (2) Without considering the locative *i*, what is negated through the first letter *a* is mental engagement—that is, mental activity. This refers to eagerly engaging in the mode of apprehension of the mental factor intention (Skt. *cetanā*), which is the mental activity of mental formation—mind's engaging in virtue, nonvirtue, and what is neutral. The eight applications are needed in order to remove the five flaws in ordinary calm abiding, but mahāmudrā meditation is free from doing and does not arise from accumulating. All mental activities are presented here as entailing reference points or focal objects, so what is taught by this is the utter peace of all reference points or focal objects. Therefore it is said in *Jñānālokālaṃkārasūtra* VI.12 [2004, 146.1–2]:

> To you who are without any imaginary thinking,
> whose mind is in the state of utter nonabiding,
> who lack any minding and mental engagement,
> and who are without focus, let there be homage

(3) The initial *a* in *amanasikāra* stands for prajñāpāramitā and all expressions for nonduality, such as nonarising (Skt. *anutpanna*) and nonceasing (Skt. *anirodha*). Thus the term means to mentally engage in a proper manner in this meaning of the letter *a*. In terms of the Vajrayāna, nonduality refers to the union of prajñā and means, which has the nature of great bliss, since this bliss arises from that union. In terms of the Pāramitāyāna, duality refers to perceiver and perceived, me and what is mine, or cognition and what is to be cognized, which will always be dual for as long as there is mental flux. The identitylessness of all phenomena that is free from all flux and without any reference points arises as the kāya whose character is the nature of phenomena, which is nondual in essence. Since this arising of nonduality is specified by the aspect of nonarising, it is called "the dharma of nonarising" (for a complete translation and explanation of this section by Padma Karpo, see Higgins 2016, 453–63). The translation of the *Amanasikārādhāra* in BKC (vol. *ka*, fols. 202b.5–203a.4) is followed by Tipi Bumlabar's supplementary explanation of what "mental nonengagement" means. According to him, *manasikāra* refers to mind as such appearing as the diversity of all phenomena, while *a* means

being unborn. Thus *amanasikāra* refers to these two—diverse appearances and being unborn—being of the same nature. Its synonyms are utter nonabiding, nonconceptuality, and inconceivability. However, mental nonengagement does not refer to the utter nonexistence of any object, the complete lack of any cognition, fainting, the stopping of any discriminating notions, weak cognitive faculties, analysis through discriminating prajñā, or just thinking "there is no mental engagement." Rather, mental nonengagement means genuine realization through experiencing the heart of the matter. Dpa' bo gtsug lag phreng ba (n.d., 325) explains mental nonengagement as follows: "Its meaning is to rest one-pointedly on the focal object [of meditation], without being distracted by other thoughts. If this [one-pointed resting] were stopped, all samādhis would stop. Therefore, in general, 'mental nonengagement' has the meaning of not mentally engaging in any object other than the very focus of the [respective] samādhi. In particular, when focusing on the ultimate, [mental nonengagement] has the meaning of letting [the mind] be without even apprehending this 'ultimate.' However, this should not be understood as being similar to having fallen asleep." In his *Ri chos kyi rnal 'byor bzhi pa phyag rgya chen po snying po'i don gyi gter mdzod* (Rgyal ba yang dgon pa 1984, 1:247–48), the early Drugpa Kagyü master Gyalwa Yanggönpa (1213–58) interprets mental nonengagement as an absence of mental engagement in the sense of not dwelling in mentation (*yid*), being liberated from mentation, or transcending mentation. More specifically, he explains the term through its component "mentation," which he, following classical Yogācāra teachings, presents as twofold: being afflicted and being what triggers the other six active consciousnesses. He says that with thoughts and imagination functioning as the cognizing subjects of bases of mistakenness, "mental nonengagement" means that these engagers do not engage in such a way. With this understanding of the term, even when there is mental nonengagement in this sense, there is still engagement in one's own mind. This means that however the ālaya-consciousness and the five sense consciousnesses may arise, their being self-lucid in a nonconceptual state is mahāmudrā's very own basic ground. When the afflicted mind (*nyon yid*) looks inward at the ālaya-consciousness, it takes it to be a self. When the mental consciousness (*yid shes*) looks outward through the five sense gates, it breaks up the ālaya-consciousness into distinct objects. Thus all the subjects and objects of this twofold mentation (*yid*) are the phenomena of saṃsāra, and all clinging to good and bad are just this mentation. To go beyond this and not dwell in it is mahāmudrā in the sense of mental nonengagement. In other words, he says that "mental nonengagement" does not imply a complete stop of all mental activity but only of the dualistic mental engagements that appear as dealing with our assumed self and its separate objects. The same author's *Ri chos yon tan kun 'byung gi lhan thabs chen mo* (2:76) adds that if the term "mental nonengagement" had been translated as "not dwelling in mentation," it would have been straightforward, but since it was translated as it is (lit. "not doing [anything] in mentation"), some people went a bit wrong. When they speak of "mental nonengagement in the past, present, and future," they take "mentation" as the subject and the three times as the objects, and then say that not engaging in them is "mental nonengagement." However, the past, the future, the present, existence, nonexistence, saṃsāra, and nirvāṇa are all nothing but superimpositions by mentation anyway. Here, the point of mental nonengagement in the context of mahāmudrā—be it understood as "not engaging in mentation" or "not dwelling in mentation"—is, in brief, not to dwell in either existence, nonexistence, past, future, saṃsāra, or nirvana. Thus the terms "beyond mind" (*blo 'das*), "free from discursiveness," "unity," and "mahāmudrā" are all equivalent. Compare also the sections "Maitrīpa's Mahāmudrā of 'Mental Nonengagement'" and "Gö Lotsāwa's Unique Mahāmudrā Interpretation of the *Uttaratantra*" in Brunnhölzl 2014 (167–76 and 243–78), as well as Brunnhölzl 2004 (52–57 and 310–20) for the significance and scope of the often-misinterpreted term "mental nonengagement" and its relation to mahāmudrā. For a history and further analysis of this term, see Mathes 2015, 248–58. For an overview of the main strands of understanding the term "mental nonengagement" in Indo-Tibetan Buddhism, see Higgins 2006 and 2016, 436–52.

172. Among Maitrīpa's works outside of his cycle of mental nonengagement, only his *Commentary on Half a Stanza on True Reality Teaching That All Phenomena Are Utterly Nonabiding* (text 73, 188) mentions the term "mental nonengagement" once, saying that "since in actuality all phenomena are unarisen, there is nothing to engage in mentally and nothing whatsoever to aspire for. That is what is called 'this approach of mine.'" Among his students' works, besides the above-mentioned explanation of mental nonengagement in Sahajavajra's *Tattvadaśakaṭīkā* on 7cd (text 46, 41–43), the *Caturmudrāṭīkā* (text 44, 274, 279–80), attributed to *Kāropa but in all probability written by Kor Nirūpa, says that the meaning of mudrā ("seal") in mahāmudrā refers to experience being sealed with mental nonengagement and gauging the view through mental nonengagement. Furthermore (379), mahāmudrā is procured by mental nonengagement in the heart of nondual bliss-emptiness. About realizing the connate, the *Caturmudrāṭīkā* (316) states this: "First, there is becoming familiar with the connate, resting in a way of this not being different from thoughts, thoughts dissolving within experience, and letting be without anything to engage mentally. Once realization has arisen from that, letting be occurs in a way of not being different from the previous mental nonengagement." Elsewhere (324), great bliss is said to "constitute the kāya of not mentally engaging in the freedom from superimposition and denial." In the comments on the dharmas of mental nonengagement and mental engagement being virtuous and nonvirtuous, respectively, *amanasikāra* is explained as *a* referring to being unborn, *mana* to thoughts, and *si[kāra]* as engagement in them. Since thoughts and engagement obstruct *a*, they are negated as being true reality, and hence this is mental nonengagement. Since nonengagement refers to being without engagement and engagement is not engaged in, this is virtuous. The antagonistic factor of that consists of engagement in thoughts. As for letting go of clinging to the experience of the connate, the text (355–56 and 369–70) says that all phenomena dissolve into and are experienced as the connate, but grasping at that experience should be let go—that is, nothing is to be engaged mentally. As for embracing upcoming sensations with mindfulness, adventitious thoughts may arise again from within the natural state of such mental nonengagement. In that case, these two—the previous mental nonengagement and the adventitious thoughts—are let be as not being different. Later (361),

it is said that "the wisdom that isn't anything whatsoever is the mahāmudrā of mental nonengagement." Equal taste is described as threefold (371): if ordinary experiences decrease, appearances are of equal taste as bliss; if examination decreases, appearances are of equal taste as being unborn; and if analysis decreases, appearances are of equal taste as mental nonengagement. Furthermore (378), the experience of the nonduality of delusion (the afflictions, not to be relinquished) and nondelusion (wisdom, not to be relied on) is that there is nothing to mentally engage.

173. BKC, vol. *kha*, fols. 60b.4–61b.1.

174. *Yuktiṣaṣṭikā* 19.

175. *A Commentary on the Five Seals of the Tathāgatas* (text 36), 193.

176. *A Critical Commentary on "Instructions on Empowerment"* (text 45), 419–20.

177. Later (text 45, 427), Rāmapāla also says that prajñāpāramitā consists of the very nature of utter nonabiding and nondiscursiveness. Statements like these are obviously the basis for the later Kagyü stance of referring to Maitrīpa's mahāmudrā system as "the mahāmudrā of utter nonabiding." For example, as Draszczyk 2019 (205–6, 208–11) says, the Fourth Shamarpa Chötra Yeshé (Tib. Chos grags ye shes; 1453–1524) states in his *Sixty Stanzas on Mahāmudrā* and elsewhere that the pith instructions transmitted in the Tagpo Kagyü lineage that illuminate the path to awakening are to be seen against the background of the most supreme Madhyamaka of utter nonabiding unity (nonabiding in any extremes of superimposition or denial in terms of phenomena, mind, and its nature). This Madhyamaka of utter nonabiding unity is said to come from Saraha and his followers, Maitrīpa, and Sahajavajra. This kind of Madhyamaka, which is superior to all other forms of Madhyamaka, provides the ideal philosophical basis to realize the mahāmudrā of nonconceptual yogic perception that is beyond any particular view. However, the explicit synthesis of Tagpo Kagyü Mahāmudrā and the Madhyamaka of utter nonabiding unity seems to appear in the writings of this lineage only from the fifteenth century onward: besides the works of the Fourth Shamarpa, it also appears in those of Karma Trinlépa Choglé Namgyal (1456–1539), the First Sangyé Nyenpa, Dashi Baljor (Tib. Sangs rgyas mnyan pa bkra shis dpal 'byor; 1457–1525), and the Eighth Karmapa Mikyö Dorje (Tib. Mi bskyod rdo rje; 1507–54). Obviously, they all relate back to Maitrīpa's approach of connecting the originally tantric term "mahāmudrā" with the sūtric Madhyamaka of utter nonabiding and the notion of "mental nonengagement."

178. Similar statements on unborn ultimate (self-)awareness or nondual self-aware wisdom are also found in *In Support of Mental Nonengagement* (text 27), *Twenty Stanzas on the Mahāyāna* (text 40), *Instructions on Empowerment* (text 42), and *A Pith Instruction on Letting Cognizance Be without Projecting and Withdrawing, "The True Secret"* (text 43; see also the introductions to these texts below). Note also that Maitrīpa's *Pith Instructions on the Four Mudrās* (text 92, 17–18) says that the yāna of secret mantra can be practiced through the Mahāyāna approaches of Aspectarian and Nonaspectarian Yogācāra and the Madhyamaka of illusion-like nonduality and utter nonabiding, adding that "the texts of the master himself match [this yāna of secret mantra] with the [view of the Madh-

yamaka of] utter nonabiding." Since the text otherwise says it relies on the *Caturmudrānvaya*, "the master" here is probably Nāgārjuna.

179. Mathes 2015 (183n490) comments as follows: "According to Kuladatta's *Kriyāsaṃgrahapañjikā* . . . the term is listed as the last of four *cakras*: *vajracakraṃ ratnacakraṃ padmacakraṃ viśvacakraṃ*."
180. See appendix 2, section 9 of this volume.
181. Padma Karpo's *Gate for Entering the Prajñāpāramitā Scriptures* (Padma dkar po 1974b, fols. 38b.6–39a.5) contains an interesting similar passage on the relationship between illusion-like Madhyamaka and the Madhyamaka of utter nonabiding: "Within the generation of a buddha's bodhicitta, the entire Mahāyāna is contained, all sentient beings have the buddha heart, there is a single yāna, and the wheels of dharma are of a single meaning, but [appear to be] many by virtue of [different] ways of understanding [this meaning]. Since explaining and listening, cultivating the path, and the fruition to be manifested appear in an illusion-like manner, they are determined in this way [as being illusory]. Therefore, this manner of explanation is called 'the illusion-like hidden meaning.' It is in terms of this [understanding] that former masters, such as Asaṅga, Āryavimuktisena, and Haribhadra, have guided [beings] in the illusion-like Madhyamaka—they are the masters of vast activity. The Madhyamaka of utter nonabiding is to determine the ultimate through not taking the illusion-like appearances during subsequent attainment as primary, but regarding the very prajñā during meditative equipoise as primary. Therefore, master Nāgārjuna and his followers guide [beings] as the masters who teach the profound view. [However,] the actuality [of this] must be made a living experience as the unity of [said profound] view and [vast] activity." "The lineages of profound view and vast activity" represents one of the standard Tibetan subdivisions of the entire sūtra teachings of the Mahāyāna—the former starting with Mañjuśrī (continued by Nāgārjuna and his followers), and the latter starting with Maitreya (continued by Asaṅga and his followers). In India and in Western scholarship, these are simply known as the traditions of Madhyamaka and Yogācāra, respectively.
182. The author's name is given as Avadhūtapa, and in this case there is little doubt about it indeed being one of Maitrīpa's aliases because the text argues for the specific sequence of the four ecstasies that is typical for Maitrīpa and explicitly refers to his guru Śavaripa as the source of its teachings. In addition, the two lines of verse that are commented on by this text are explicitly quoted as Maitrīpa's words in one of his Tibetan biographies (see Mathes 2015, 40).
183. Text 73, 214.
184. Text 73, 217.
185. Text 73, 186–87 (H130, fols. 271b.4–272a.7).
186. Text 73, 187–88.
187. Text 73, 191.
188. Text 73, 200. In general, in Maitrīpa's text, the elephant stands for views and practices to be superseded by the more advanced ones, while the lion is the correct approach of the ultimate reality that is utter nonabiding. On the level of the Sūtrayāna, this refers to the elephant-like Yogācāra approach being defeated by the lion-like Madhyamaka scriptures and reasonings of utter

nonabiding. On the level of the Vajrayāna, the elephant stands for the conditional connate ecstasy or wisdom that is accomplished by virtue of a karmamudrā as its cause. The lion represents mahāmudrā free from any causes or conditions: ultimate bodhicitta, the inseparability of the emptiness endowed with all supreme aspects and nonreferential great compassion, which is omnitemporal, formless, all-pervasive, immutable, and utters the roar of no-self.

189. "Threefold valid cognition" consists of valid direct perceptions, valid inferential cognitions, and understanding based on scriptures that have been established to be valid.

190. Text 73, 208.

191. Text 73, 212–13.

192. In the *Avikalpapraveśadhāraṇī*, these four conceptions are referred to as the conceptions in terms of (1) nature (perceiver and perceived or the five skandhas), (2) remedies (the six pāramitās), (3) true reality (emptiness and its equivalents), and (4) attainment (the ten bhūmis of bodhisattvas and buddhahood with all their qualities). These four characteristics are relinquished in a gradual manner by means of analyzing their nature, their qualities, and their essence, and finally by not mentally engaging in them at all (for the section on relinquishing these characteristics, see Brunnhölzl 2012, 330–31). Maitreya's *Dharmadharmatāvibhāga* (lines 164–72) likewise speaks about relinquishing these four characteristics in order to attain nonconceptual wisdom (Brunnhölzl 2012, 167, 187, 260–61, 308–19). These four are explained in detail in Kamalaśīla's commentary on the *Avikalpapraveśadhāraṇī*, as well as in the Third Karmapa's and Gö Lotsāwa's commentaries on the *Dharmadharmatāvibhāga* (for details, in particular Gö Lotsāwa's distinction between Kamalaśīla's and Maitrīpa's approaches to these four, see Brunnhölzl 2012, 260–61, 308–19, and 330–31).

193. Text 73, 213. Note that the relinquishment of the last three among these four conceptions is a theme that is mentioned in several other works by Maitrīpa and his students: the beginnings of the *Kudṛṣṭinirghātana* (text 19) and *Nirvedhapañcaka* (text 28), *Tattvaprakāśa* 13b (text 35), *Sekanirdeśa* 36ac (text 42), Rāmapāla's *Sekanirdeśapañjikā* (text 45), the *Caturmudrāṭīkā* (text 44, 320), Sahajavajra's *Sthitisamāsa* VI.32cd (text 17) and *Tattvadaśakaṭīkā* on stanza 7 (text 46), and Vajrapāṇi's *Guruparamparākramopadeśa* (text 213, 226–27). For details, see these texts.

194. Besides Rāmapāla's above-mentioned comments on "utter nonabiding" as mental nonengagement and lack of superimposition in Maitrīpa's *Instructions on Empowerment* 29, Rāmapāla's commentary (text 45, 416–17, 420, 426–27) furthermore says that the dharmamudrā has the nature of the utter nonabiding that comes from analysis, while mahāmudrā is the utter nonabiding that consists of the effortless, inconceivable wisdom that does not come from analysis. Mahāmudrā's nature is utter nonabiding and lack of superimposition, and prajñāpāramitā similarly has the nature of utter nonabiding and nondiscursiveness. Furthermore, mahāmudrā is free from all obscurations, serves as the foundation of all accomplishment, is saṃsāra's and nirvāṇa's single nature, and has the single essence of great bliss that embodies nonreferential great compassion. Sahajavajra's *Tattvadaśakaṭīkā* (text 46, 35) presents an unidentified quotation attributed to the Buddha, saying that foolish people

proclaim that awakening is attained through the single approach of emptiness. In answer, he says this: "Through realizing the nature of [both] means and prajñā of this [sūtra passage], the utterly nonabiding middle devoid of superimposition and denial is realized. For prajñā relinquishes superimposition and the means relinquish denial." In Vajrapāṇi's *Guruparamparākramopadeśa* (text 213), "utter nonabiding" is only mentioned as a part of the name of the supreme Madhyamaka school of the utter nonabiding of all phenomena, but the text also uses expressions such as "not abiding in anything whatsoever," "the lack of nature refers to not abiding as any essence of existence, nonexistence, both, or neither," "not abiding in any superimposition and denial is the realization of true reality," and "not even emptiness, unity, and nonduality abide." The *Caturmudrāṭīkā* (text 44, 258) speaks of the nonabiding unity of having relinquished abiding in saṃsāra by virtue of prajñā and having relinquished abiding in nirvāṇa by virtue of compassion (means). In its comments on the superiority of the Mantrayāna compared to the Pāramitāyāna (265), the text says their goal is the same, because the basic nature of the Madhyamaka of utter nonabiding and the basic nature of mahāmudrā are free from creating and blocking (or affirmation and negation), but there is a difference with regard to the path of persons accomplishing that goal. Elsewhere (325, 327), mahāmudrā is said to be "the inconceivable wisdom that is nonabiding and free from effort," and "the utter nonabiding in bliss or emptiness and sleepless passion constitute the kāya of great bliss, which is the view." The text also quotes three sets of stanzas that are identified as stemming from or belonging to "utter nonabiding" (340, 344, 345).

195. See BGTC, 2462.

196. In this vein, a brief commentary on the *Illumination of Unity* in BKC (vol. *kha*, fol. 34b.6) says that one needs to know the two ways in which unity appears: either connected or not connected to empowerment. According to Moevus 2019, the distinction between Maitrīpa's tantric and nontantric notions of unity is that the tantric one is the unity of prajñā and means, while the nontantric one is the unity of emptiness and dependent origination (or, as a practice, the unity of emptiness and compassion). However, the inseparability of prajñā and means is not a specifically tantric idea but the very common description of the nature of the path of bodhisattvas in general (and also often as the nature of the path in Madhyamaka specifically). Furthermore, as the following will show, the distinction between tantric and nontantric unity in Maitrīpa's texts is not as simple and clear-cut as Moevus says because Maitrīpa speaks of "the unity of emptiness and dependent origination" and "the unity of emptiness and compassion" in tantric contexts too, and in both tantric and nontantric contexts adds further elements to describe unity, such as being the unity of the two realities, free from the four extremes, endowed with all supreme aspects, great bliss, and nondual awareness. Thus it seems very difficult to make a clear and exclusive distinction between a strictly tantric and a strictly nontantric notion of unity in Maitrīpa's texts (and the same goes for those of his students). The only thing that is clear is that Maitrīpa freely employs the notion of "unity" in both tantric and nontantric contexts.

197. In other words, to take phenomena to be truly existent would mean to reify

dependent origination, which is nothing but their arising from many causes and conditions, each of which is not truly existent; hence there is no true arising and ceasing of anything. On the other hand, to take phenomena's ultimate nonarising as nonexistence would mean to mistake their emptiness or lack of any nature as being nothing whatsoever. Rather, phenomena's true nature is the dynamic inseparability of dependent origination (functioning appearances) and emptiness (nonreification of these appearances).

198. Skt. *timira/taimira*, Tib. *rab rib*. There is usually a wide range of translations of this term (such as "cataract" or "ophthalmia"). Judging by the symptoms of this visual impairment that are described in Tibetan texts, it must primarily refer to what—in Western terms—is called "floaters." These are congealed proteins in the gel of the vitreous body of the eye that appear as floating, out-of-focus threads in the visual field. They are set into motion through eye movements, and when the eyes are kept still, they pass through one's visual field or sink down slowly, which can give the impression of slowly sinking hairs or a hairnet (Skt. *keśa/keśoṇḍuka*, Tib. *skra shad*). Sometimes they also appear as little dark dots, or as hazy spots in the visual field, etc. They usually increase with age and can be seen best against bright backgrounds. Floaters are not really considered a disease in the West (unless they severely disturb one's vision), since—to a varying degree—the same process happens in everybody's eyes. Some Tibetan texts also mention double vision—such as seeing two moons—which can be a symptom of cataracts (degeneration of the eye lens). Double vision, though, does not appear due to the above changes in the vitreous body, and patients with cataracts do not report "floating hairs" or the like. However, the mention in Tibetan texts of a scalpel removing a membrane, which is often found in connection with this eye condition, would point to turbidities in the cornea or to cataracts (the changes within the vitreous body became operable only in recent times). Thus one could describe *rab rib* as a general term for "blurred vision" due to turbidities in the eyes, be it in the vitreous body, the lens, or the cornea.

199. BKC (vol. *kha*, fol. 32a.3–32b.4) also identifies *An Illumination of True Reality* as a Madhyamaka work, saying that its purpose is to differentiate the subtle difference in terms of what is negated in the Madhyamaka approaches of illusion-like nonduality and utter nonabiding.

200. Text 37, 203–4.

201. Text 27, 160.

202. Text 36, 193.

203. Text 19, 124.

204. Text 92, 21–22.

205. Tipi Bumlabar (BKC, vol. *kha*, fol. 85b.4) confirms that this text first instructs on unity based on worldly conventions and then describes its greatness by way of marvelous realization.

206. This corresponds to Maitrīpa's *Mahāyānaviṃśikā* 5cd.

207. The only exception is the text's opening stanza, which speaks of "the luminosity of unity that has the character of emptiness."

208. *Bhagavatīprajñāpāramitāhṛdayaṭīkārthapradīpa* (D3820, fols. 288b.6–291b.3); for details, see appendix 7 in volume 3.

209. This appears to refer to the desire realm, form realm, and formless realm within saṃsāra, and the nirvāṇas of śrāvaka arhats, pratyekabuddha arhats, and buddhas.
210. Appendix 4 in volume 3, 1130. As Almogi 2010 (172–73, 176–79) points out, a few Nyingma works present the nonabiding of emptiness, the nonabiding of discontinuation, the nonabiding of equanimity, and the nonabiding of unity as hierarchical subdivisions of the Madhyamaka proponents of utter nonabiding, considering the nonabiding of unity as the supreme.
211. Appendix 5 in volume 3, 1068. The *Caturmudrāṭīkā* (text 44) speaks of both "the unity of prajñā and means" (258) and "the unity of bliss and emptiness" (299, 323), elsewhere glossing unity as "that in which there isn't any notion of duality" (326). The text (358–59) further describes mahāmudrā as the actual unity of luminosity and emptiness, the exemplifying unity that illustrates inseparable bliss-emptiness, the unity of abiding (connate wisdom), and the unity of being (the great bliss of the entirety of saṃsāra and nirvāṇa being nondual). In addition, it mentions "the unity of all-pervasiveness" (371).
212. Stanza 4.
213. The words "bliss" or "great bliss" are found sixty-five times in Maitrīpa's cycle of mental nonengagement (seventeen times in texts 73 and 92).
214. "True reality" occurs about sixty times in Maitrīpa's cycle of mental nonengagement (twelve times in texts 73 and 92), being equated with "nonabiding," "great bliss," "nonduality," and "being unborn," and said to be free from the four extremes of existence and so on, as well as permanence and extinction.
215. Though some instances of the terms "awareness" (twenty-six times) and "self-awareness" (fifteen times) occur in Maitrīpa's presentations of Aspectarian and Nonaspectarian Yogācāra, his understanding of ultimate "(self-) awareness" in the Madhyamaka of utter nonabiding and the Vajrayāna is that it is luminous and blissful, yet unborn and free from all extremes. This has already been outlined in detail above in the discussions of mental nonengagement," "nonabiding," and "unity" (in texts 73 and 92, "(self-)awareness" occurs nine times).
216. This expression is found about twenty times in Maitrīpa's cycle of mental nonengagement (two times in texts 73 and 92).
217. Note that there is a range of meanings for Skt. *prakāśa* in Maitrīpa's works, such as "lucidity," "illumination" (also in the sense of "elucidation"), and "display" or "manifestation." In four of his texts, *prakāśa* is included in the title (*Yuganaddhaprakāśa*, *Apratiṣṭhānaprakāśa*, *Mahāsukhaprakāśa*, *Tattvaprakāśa*), and beyond these titles (and the appearance of these titles within these texts and their colophons), the word appears nineteen times with different meanings in "The Cycle of Twenty-Five Dharmas of Mental Nonengagement": *Tattvaratnāvalī* (8 times, meaning "illumination," "lucidity," and "elucidation"), *Madhyamaṣaṭka* (4, "lucidity"), *Mahasukhaprakāśa* (2, "[delusive] display"), *Svapnanirukti* (2, "lucidity"), *Tattvaprakāśa* (1, "display"), *Yuganaddhaprakāśa* (1, "lucidity"), and *Sthūlapattaya* (1, "elucidate"). The Tibetan renderings of the four texts with *prakāśa* in their titles help to distinguish the meanings: in the *Yuganaddhaprakāśa*, *Apratiṣṭhānaprakāśa*, and *Tattvaprakāśa*, the Tibetan for *prakāśa* is *gsal bar ston pa* or *rab tu bstan pa* ("clearly teaching" or "elucidation"),

while the Tibetan of the *Mahasukhaprakāśa* says *gsal ba* ("illumination" or "lucidity"). Though I render *prakāśa* as "illumination" in all these titles, in the *Yuganaddhaprakāśa*, *Apratiṣṭhānaprakāśa*, and *Tattvaprakāśa* this has the sense of "elucidation," while in the *Mahasukhaprakāśa* it refers to the actual luminous manifestation of great bliss in one's experience. Since texts 73 and 92 are only available in Tibetan, the frequency of possible occurrences of *prakāśa* cannot be determined, but possibly equivalent terms, such as Tib. *gsal ba*, do appear.

218. Note, however, that only four texts in Maitrīpa's cycle of mental nonengagement as listed in NG mention the term "mahāmudrā" (twelve times): *A Compendium of the Procedures of Empowerment* (text 38; two times), *Twenty Stanzas on True Reality* (text 41; two times), *Instructions on Empowerment* (text 42; six times), and (the anonymous) *Pith Instruction on Letting Cognizance Be without Projecting and Withdrawing* (text 43; two times). Furthermore, in Maitrīpa's *Pith Instructions on the Four Mudrās* (text 92), the term occurs four times, and in his *Commentary on Half a Stanza on True Reality* (text 73), five times (not surprising, given that its topic is the four mudrās).

219. Apart from frequent mentions of "connate ecstasy" and "the connate" appearing in quotes, when Maitrīpa explains "the connate" as such (ten instances) in his own words in this cycle of mental nonengagement, he glosses it as great bliss, the inseparability of prajñā and means, and being without contrivance and attachment. In text 73, outside of "connate ecstasy," "the connate" appears four times. Note also that, among the three natures (imaginary, dependent, and perfect nature), Maitrīpa uses the term "imaginary (nature)" (*parikalpita*) six times in this cycle and another two times in text 92, while "dependent (nature)" (*paratantra*) and "perfect nature" (*parinispanna*) are only found in text 92 (three times each).

220. In this vein, as Higgins and Draszczyk 2016 (1:160–61, 166–67) have pointed out, Karma Trinlépa says in several of his texts that, according to the previous Kagyü masters, "the Great Madhyamaka of utter nonabiding unity" consists of the five dharmas of Maitreya, Nāgārjuna's works such as the *Bodhicittavivaraṇa* and the *Dharmadhātustava*, Saraha's three main dohās, the ultimate view of the mahāsiddhas Dignāga (480–540) and Dharmakīrti (seventh century), and everything connected with those. This Madhyamaka of utter nonabiding is not different from mahāmudrā and superior to the Madhyamaka propounded by the Prāsaṅgikas and Svātantrikas, because it does not abide in any superimposition or denial. In equating the Great Madhyamaka of utter nonabiding with mahāmudrā, Karma Trinlépa follows one of his teachers, the Fourth Shamarpa, whose *Sixty Stanzas on Mahāmudrā* (stanzas 4–5) says that those who comment on the true reality of Madhyamaka by holding on to it as being with aspects or without aspects have not understood the supreme Madhyamaka of utter nonabiding unity. The wise ones of this lineage maintained that the mahāmudrā ornamented with the guru's pith instructions shows the essential points of the last turning of the Pāramitāyāna that is in accordance with mantra (see also Draszczyk 2019, 209–10). This is followed by citing Maitrīpa's *Tattvadaśaka* 2, so the Shamarpa's remarks here are obviously a commentary on this stanza, explicitly equating the Madhyamaka of utter nonabiding unity with mahāmudrā, as well as on Sahajavajra's stance on this in his *Tattvadaśakaṭīkā*, which

says at its beginning that the *Tattvadaśaka* consists of Maitrīpa's pith instructions on prajñāpāramitā (utter nonabiding) that accord with the approach of secret mantra. Finally, it should be mentioned that parts of the Tibetan tradition credit Maitrīpa with rediscovering the then-lost *Uttaratantra* and *Dharmadharmatāvibhāga* attributed to Maitreya. However, all that Maitrīpa quotes from these two texts in his own works is a single line from the *Uttaratantra* (II.61b in his *Pañcatathāgatamudrāvivaraṇa*; plus what corresponds to *Uttaratantra* I.154 in the *Caturmudrānvaya*), and there seems to be no significant discussion of this text either by him or in the available works of his students. The single notable exception consists of Vajrapāṇi's extensive comments on what corresponds to *Uttaratantra* I.154 in his *Guruparamparākramopadeśa* (for details, see text 213, and Brunnhölzl 2014, 177–84).

221. These include texts 26, 31, 32, 35, and 36.

222. Note also that Maitrīpa has a tendency to "recycle" some of his stanzas in others of his texts: his *Eradicating Bad Views, Twenty Stanzas on the Mahāyāna, A Jewel Garland of True Reality, A Commentary on the Five Seals of the Tathāgatas, Instructions on Empowerment, An Illumination of True Reality,* and *Five Stanzas on Penetrating Insight* share certain stanzas. For a detailed account of the numbers and types of Buddhist and non-Buddhist textual sources that Maitrīpa quotes or refers to in his works (foremost among them the *Hevajratantra*), see IaS (76–82).

223. Bu ston rin chen grub 1971, 116.

224. Padma dkar po 2005, 37–38.

225. The colophon of the *Amanasikārādhāra* has **Nairātmyāprakāśa* (Tib. *bdag med pa gsal ba*) as an additional part of the name of this text, and it is sometimes referred to under both names. However, as mentioned before, there is an actual separate text called *Nairātmyāprakāśa* by Advayavajra (D1308; a sādhana of Nairātmyā).

226. Jackson (2008, 166) takes *ma rtogs pa rtogs par byed pa rnams te* before the following texts to refer to Advayavajra's *Abodhabodhaka* (text 76). Given the inclusion of this text in the same position in BKC (though it is glossed differently there), one may be tempted to follow that. However, grammatically, the plural *rnams*, the particle *te*, and the next three texts, followed by the number three (and not "four"), make it clear that this means "those [texts] that make the unrealized realized . . ." Furthermore, if *ma rtogs pa rtogs par byed pa* referred to text 76, this sentence would simply consist of a list of four texts without saying what they teach.

227. BKC (vol. *kha*, fol. 79b.1–6) agrees with most of this verbatim except for the following variants. *Eradicating Bad Views*, its commentary, and *A Compendium of Beginner Activity* were composed in order to teach that there exists conventional conduct. *Six Stanzas on the Middle* and *Six Stanzas on the Connate* were taught to elucidate the distinctive features of viewing unity, *Twenty Stanzas on the Mahāyāna* and *Twenty Stanzas on True Reality* to explain the unity that involves that view in detail, and *The Illumination of Great Bliss* and *An Illumination of Unity* to show that this is the utter nonabiding of dependent origination. *Ten Stanzas on True Reality* and *An Illumination of True Reality* give a synopsis of profound actuality in a few words. *An Illumination of Utter Nonabiding* and

The Means to Realize the Unrealized (text 76) identify the subtle distinctive features of the profound. *A Commentary on Half a Stanza on True Reality* (text 73) presents the way in which Maitrīpa's own approach is especially excellent. By contrast, a summary and topical outline of "twenty dharmas of mental nonengagement" by Tipi Bumlabar in BKC (vol. *kha*, fols. 80a.5–89a.2) includes the following twenty texts: *Instructions on Empowerment, A Synopsis of Positions* (text 17; by Maitrīpa's student Sahajavajra), *A Jewel Garland of True Reality, The Succession of the Four Mudrās* (text 14), *A Commentary on the Five Seals of the Tathāgatas, A Discourse on Illusion, A Discourse on Dream, Five Stanzas on the Love between Means and Prajñā, An Illumination of Utter Nonabiding, Five Stanzas on Penetrating Insight, Six Stanzas on the Connate, Twenty Stanzas on the Mahāyāna, Twenty Stanzas on True Reality, An Illumination of True Reality, The Illumination of Great Bliss, An Illumination of Unity, Ten Stanzas on True Reality, Vajra Words* (text 47; by Maitrīpa's student Vajrapāṇi), *In Support of Mental Nonengagement*, and *An Illumination of Prajñā Wisdom* (text 16; by Maitrīpa's student Divākaracandra). According to Atiśa's extensive Tibetan biography (Eimer 1979, 2:139–40), Maitrīpa wrote his *Eradicating Bad Views, A Discourse on Dream*, and *A Discourse on Illusion* in order to atone for acting as he liked and accumulating unwholesome deeds, which led Ratnākaraśānti to accuse him of flaws with regard to view, conduct, and fruition. For further summaries and details of the texts in Maitrīpa's cycle, see Mathes 2015 and 2021.

228. Padma dkar po 2005, 37; BKC, vol. *kha*, fol. 79b.1.
229. Tib. Zhi ba bya las zlog pa.
230. Following the name Gaganagarbha in the concluding stanzas in the Sanskrit of text 19, Tib. *nam mkha'i snying rje* is emended to *nam mkha'i snying po*.
231. Tib. *dri med dpal*. Based on one of Atiśa's biographies (see below), this probably should read Vikramaśīla (one of the most famous Buddhist centers of learning, where, according to some Maitrīpa biographies, he resided for a while).
232. As mentioned before, Tib. *Lta ba ngan sel gyi dran pa* (*A Recollection of "Eradicating Bad Views"*) is just an alternative (Tibetan) name of Maitrīpa's *Kudṛṣṭinirghātavākyaṭippinikā* (text 20); Tg *Kudṛṣṭinirghātaṭīkā* AIBS *Kudṛṣṭinirghātacintā* GZ NP colophon *A Commentary on the Difficult Points—or A Recollection—of "Eradicating Bad Views" composed by Śrīmat Advayavajra* BKC *A Commentary on the Difficult Points of Recollecting "Eradicating Bad Views" or A Recollection*. NG lists a separate work with the title **Kudṛṣṭinirghātacintā* attributed to Vajrapāṇi as the third text in vol. AḤ, but no such text appears in this volume (nor does such a text exist in Tg). Rather, all these names refer to one and the same text—the *Kudṛṣṭinirghātavākyaṭippinikā*.
233. Vol. *ka*, fol. 203b.1–4. This is a more detailed version of the concluding stanzas in text 19. The preface in Śāstrī's edition (Maitrīpa 1927, vii) renders the bulk of these stanzas in a different way (see the note in the translation below) and adds: "The work gives the duties of one initiated in Buddhism. It is of the nature of a work on *Āhnika* of the Hindus." Note that *A Compendium of Beginner Activity* (translated in appendix 1) is neither found in the **Advayavajrasaṃgraha* nor in Tg but only in BKC. The text is obviously related to *Eradicating Bad Views* but written specifically from the perspective of Vajrayāna practitioners (for BKC's description of the difference between those two works, see the final note

on text 19). Similar Buddhist works on beginner conduct or initial activity in Tg include *Tribhuvanaviśuddhavajra's **Ādikarmikasambhārakriyākramasaṃgraha* (D3765), Jitāri's *Ādikarmikabhūmipariṣkāra* (D3945, D4494), and Atiśa's *Bodhisattvādikarmikamārgāvatāradeśanā* (D3952, D4477) and *Caryāsaṃgrahapradīpa* (D3960, D4466), as well as Anupamarakṣita's extracanonical *Ādikarmapradīpa* (Sanskrit edition and French translation in La Vallée Poussin 1898, 162–232). According to Bajracharya 2014 (273–81), such works are still the basis of many daily activities and rituals in Newar Buddhist vihāras and communities in the Kathmandu valley. Gellner 1991 also shows that the most basic and widely known Newar ritual of "guru maṇḍala" appears under the same name, with minor variations in order and only slightly less elaborated, in Jagaddarpaṇa's *Vajrācāryakriyāsamuccaya* (D3305). Both texts also share some material with *Eradicating Bad Views* (see especially Gellner 1991, 191n30, 193nn70, 72, 79).

234. Mathes 2015, 46–47.
235. Wallis 2003, 208–9.
236. Wallis 2003, 203.
237. Wallis 2003 (206) comments on the way in which Maitrīpa uses the term "initial activity" as follows: "The term employed by Advayavajra to denote the initial phase of practice is *ādikarma*. Normatively, this has the sense of a beginning (*ādi*) act or endeavor (*karma*). More technically, it refers to an initial or a preliminary practice that precedes more advanced ones. While Advayavajra certainly employs this usage, he adds a dimension to it that plays somewhat on the term. The initial endeavor remains first, primary, chief (*ādi*), even after the initial stage of practice (*karma*). The *ādikarma*, for Advayavajra, thus stands perpetually at the beginning, in the sense of 'ground.'" Mathes 2015 (7) says: "The *Kudṛṣṭinirghātana* situates Maitrīpa's blend of mahāmudrā and Madhyamaka within the more general Mahāyāna context of the six perfections (*pāramitā*) . . . With these many details, Maitrīpa shows the necessity of conventional Dharma practice. The quintessence of the *Kudṛṣṭinirghātana* is that even though the first five perfections of generosity, discipline, patience, diligence, and meditation (i.e., 'initial activity') are performed automatically by those who are realized, they need to be intentionally performed by those who are still learning. In other words, if initial activity does not unfold without effort, one is obviously still in need of learning on the path of accumulating merit and wisdom. The sixth perfection, i.e., the perfection of insight (*prajñāpāramitā*), is inseparably linked with the first five perfections. This union results in an advanced practice of initial activity, such as being generous (*dāna*) by even offering one's body. This is how Maitrīpa defines the tantric concept of 'mad conduct' (*unmattavrata*)—that is, conduct in which the adept appears to be mad in order to test his own freedom from worldly concerns." Mathes continues (47): "Moreover, the initial activity of the first five perfections is nothing more than the burden of a golden chain when it is performed without the realization of the perfection of insight (*prajñāpāramitā*). The combination of the first five perfections with *prajñāpāramitā* is thus taken as the optimal form of initial activity."
238. Vol. *kha*, fols. 33a.1–34a.1.
239. As mentioned before, as a technical term, "unity" refers to the fifth of the five stages of perfection-process practices in the *Guhyasamājatantra* according

to Nāgārjuna's *Pañcakrama* and Āryadeva's *Caryāmelāpakapradīpa*. The term "unity" is also often used as a synonym of mahāmudrā. Compare also Sahajavajra's terms "the middle of unity" and "the suchness of unity" and his discussions of these in his *Tattvadaśakaṭīkā* (text 46), which follow his guru Maitrīpa's treatment of unity in *An Illumination of Unity*.

240. Vol. *kha*, fol. 34b.6.

241. For details, see the introduction to text 34.

242. Vol. *kha*, fol. 25a.2–4. Following this text, BKC (fol. 25b.2) says that it explains the manner of union through the yāna of ground, path, and fruition. As Mathes 2015 (5–6) points out, the compilers of Tg (as well as GZ) obviously did not realize that the *Prajñopāyadayāpañcaka* and the *Prīṇapañcaka* (D2237 (b); text 29) are two variant translations of the same text, the *Prajñopāyapremapañcaka*.

243. Vol. *kha*, fols. 60b.4–61b.1.

244. Yakṣas are a class of normally benevolent and helpful but somewhat fickle spirits who live on the earth (often in forests), in the air, and in the lower divine realms. Exceptions to their benevolence are that they may cause epidemics or possess humans, and some of them even eat human flesh.

245. In the tantric context, the term *vīra* indicates the medium one of three types of practitioners with lesser, medium, and highest faculties: (1) cattle (Skt. *paśū*), (2) hero (Skt. *vīra*), and (3) divine (Skt. *divya*). The main difference in practical ritual behavior between "cattle" and "hero" is that the former takes the five practices whose names begin with *m* (Skt. *pañcamakāra*)—*madya* (liquor), *māṃsa* (meat), *matsya* (fish), *mudrā* (probably some aphrodisiac grain), and *maithuna* (sexual intercourse)—to be metaphorical, whereas the latter take them as literal (a.k.a. "right-hand" and "left-hand" practices, respectively). The divine practitioner is far beyond both the substitutional, "safe-and-sane" approach of the cattle and the fearless, "bring-it-all-on" approach of the hero. As this episode of Maitrīpa and many others in the life stories of the mahāsiddhas show, a crucial element of achieving the mindset of a hero is a transformative encounter with ḍākinīs or yoginīṣ, during which the male yogī faces and overcomes fear, shame, disgust, and any other limiting concepts and emotions.

246. BKC *khang sar pa ni*. Khasarpaṇa (in Tibetan texts often spelled Khasarpāṇi, Khasarpaṇi, Karsapāṇi, Karṣapaṇi, Kharsapāṇi, or Kharṣapāṇi) is a form of Avalokiteśvara. It is said that he received this name after he provided money and resources (*paṇa*) to an upāsaka named Śāntivarman. Later, when these resources had become exhausted, Avalokiteśvara flew through the sky (*khasar*) to meet Śāntivarman. The name is also explained as "exhaustion of the paṇas." It is often used generically for any form of Avalokiteśvara with one face and two hands, with the right hand in the mudrā of supreme generosity and the left in the mudrā of teaching the dharma and holding a lotus with a long stem blooming at the level of his left ear. With his right leg pendant, the right foot rests on a separate smaller lotus. Thus, this form of Avalokiteśvara represents a male version of the typical appearance of Green Tārā, and is consequently often confused with her depictions. More specifically, the term is applied to Khasarpaṇa Amoghapāśa ("The Fruitful Noose"), Lokeśvara "Resting in the Nature of the Mind" (both kriyātantra), and Lokeśvara in the *Sarvadurgatipariśodhanatantra* (a yogatantra).

247. Skt. *viśva* can also mean "world" or "universe." In his texts, Maitrīpa often uses this word in the sense of the diversity of the world's appearances, which he does not regard as outer matter but as manifestations of the mind.
248. Vol. *kha*, fol. 28a.4.
249. Vol. *kha*, fol. 26b.2–4.
250. Vol. *ka*, fol. 200b.5–6.
251. Vol. *kha*, fol. 25b.2–4.
252. Vol. *kha*, fol. 36a.2–6.
253. The second stanza contains a number of phrases that can be understood in more than one way. "Beyond misery" is a literal rendering of Tib. *mya ngan 'das*, which usually means "(passed into) nirvāṇa." Given the story and the matching of its elements with Buddhist teachings, "amazed" appears to be meant in the sense that those with the mahāyāna disposition (and thus with an understanding of emptiness) are amazed at people who cling to illusory appearances, but it could also mean "those with the mahāyāna disposition are amazing." "Hollow jewels" (Tib. *rin chen khong*) could also be understood as "what is inside the jewels" (that appear precious but are empty) or, less likely given the story, "precious mind." See also BKC's concluding comments on *A Discourse on Illusion* in the final note on the translation.
254. Ratnākaraśānti (eleventh century; mahāsiddha no. 12) was the famous southern gatekeeper of the Buddhist university of Vikramaśīla and one of Maitrīpa's teachers.
255. Vol. *kha*, fols. 34b.6–35b.1
256. Tib. *mthong* ("see") em. *thong*.
257. Ibid., fol. 37a.5–37b.5.
258. Skt. *cakravāka* ("cakra bird"; *Anas casarca* or *Tadorna ferruginea*; a.k.a. "brahmany duck"). These birds are known for their steadfast love as couples, and some Buddhists regard them as sacred. According to the *Mahāprajñāpāramitāśāstra* (chapter XXVII), if sensual desires, passion, and ignorance were predominant in a person, a common rebirth would be as a cakra bird with fine and smooth plumage, a big and wide beak, and an inability to distinguish touch and taste. These birds are also said to exhibit diverse amorous dalliance gestures with brows and other limbs, conjured up by Kāma (the god of love) in an attempt to charm Śiva (according to Śivapurāṇa 2.2.9).
259. These are linguistics, epistemology, arts and crafts, medicine, and the Buddhist teachings.
260. For details, see the introduction to Sahajavajra's *Tattvadaśakaṭīkā* (text 46) in volume 3.
261. Vol. *kha*, fol. 31a.3–31b.2.
262. In BKC, this text immediately precedes *The Illumination of Great Bliss*.
263. The reasons for my generally translating *satya* (Tib. *bden pa*) as "reality" and not as "truth"—as in the pervasive and unquestioned, but nonsensical, renderings "the two truths" or "the four noble truths" in modern Buddhist literature (both popular and academic)—are as follows. The *Viniścayasaṃgrahaṇī* (D4038, fol. 68b.1–3) says, "What is the meaning of reality [here]? The meaning of reality is the actuality that has the characteristic of not being in discord with the teachings and the actuality that, when seen, serves as the cause for purity. What is

the meaning of the reality of suffering? It is the actuality of the formations that arise from the afflictions. What is the meaning of the reality of the origin [of suffering]? It is the actuality that produces the reality of suffering. What is the meaning of the reality of cessation? It is the actuality of both of the [former two] being at peace. What is the meaning of the reality of the path? It is the actuality of accomplishing the three aims." The *Śrāvakabhūmi* (D4036, fol. 94b.3–5) explains: "In the sense of suffering being suffering up through the path being the path, they accord with what is real (*yathābhūta*), accord with what is unerring, are unmistaken, and are unimpaired. Therefore, they are called 'realities.' They are also called 'realities' because they are undeceiving by virtue of their own specific characteristics and [because] unmistaken mental states arise when they are seen. You may wonder, 'Why are they the realities of the noble ones alone?' They are called 'the realities of the noble ones' because the noble ones, by virtue of these realities being real in that they precisely accord with true reality, realize and see them in accordance with what is real, whereas childish beings do not realize or see them in accordance with what is real. By virtue of the nature of phenomena, these [realities] are indeed real for childish beings too, but not by virtue of their being realized by them. For noble persons, however, they are realities by virtue of both [being realities and being fully realized as such]." Tsongkhapa (Tsong kha pa 1985, vol. *tsa*, fol. 118a.2–3) elaborates that the four realities are real for the noble ones in terms of both the facts and their minds. Though they are real in terms of the facts for childish beings too, since these beings do not realize these realities, they are not presented as the realities of these beings. The *Abhidharmakośabhāṣya* on VI.2 (D4090, vol. *khu*, fols. 2b.6–3a.2) agrees: "What is the meaning of 'the four realities of the noble ones' that are found in the sūtras? Since they are real for noble persons, they are explained as 'the realities of the noble ones' in the sūtras. 'Does this mean that they are delusive for others?' Not being mistaken, they are real for everyone, but the noble ones see them exactly as they are, [that is, in their sixteen aspects], while others do not. Therefore, these [realities] are called 'the realities of the noble ones.' But they are not those of nonnoble ones because they see in mistaken ways." As a stanza [in Saṃyutta Nikāya IV.127] says:

What the noble ones speak of as happiness
is perceived as suffering by others
What others speak of as happiness
is perceived as suffering by the noble ones.

The Eighth Karmapa's commentary on the *Abhisamayālaṃkāra* (Mi bskyod rdo rje 2003, 104) explains the meaning of the four realities as follows: "The reality of suffering is what arises as the nature of suffering in accordance with the noble ones seeing that the entirety of all-pervasive conditioned existence is suffering. The reality of the origin of suffering is what is present and established in accordance with the noble ones seeing that all sufferings in the three realms originate from karma and afflictions. The reality of the path is the actuality of identitylessness being seen as the reality of the path by the noble ones and its actually being just as it is seen by them. The reality of cessation is the ultimate's own essence being seen as the actuality of nonorigination, since this is how it is seen by the noble ones." The same explanations are also found in TOK, 3:481, BGTC, 1371 and 1777, and Samtani 2002, 107. Thus, the translation "the four noble truths" is obviously misleading in at least two ways. In general, the Sanskrit word *satya* can indeed mean both "truth" and "reality," but in the context of the two or four realities, this term does not signify any abstract or semantic truth (such as "one and one equals two," "all apples are fruits," or "everything is suffering"). As the above descriptions of the four realities as perceivable entities that perform specific functions (such as the five skandhas and afflictions, which can hardly be said to be abstract truths) make clear, "reality" is understood here in the sense of the individually experienced reality of life of certain persons. As Broido 1988 (54) rightly says, "Truth is a property of sentences (relativized to contexts) or, philosophically, a property of propositions, but in any case not a property of cognitions or cognitive states or appearances or experiences or 'things.' It is only with a very great sense of strain that an English-speaker can say of a visual object or experience that it is true or false . . . Given this strain and the resulting confusion it is not surprising that many Western accounts of the satyas are unintelligible." It is an often-overlooked fact that, in general, Buddhism does not speak about abstract or philosophical statements or "truths," but its main thrust is soteriological in nature—identifying the deluded and undeluded ways in which we experience ourselves and the world and how we may arrive at the latter from the former. Thus, the Buddha did not say that we suffer because suffering is some kind of universal truth or law, but because suffering constitutes our basic experienced reality. Likewise, suffering is not caused by just another "truth" (its origin—karma and afflictions), but by very tangible physical, verbal, and mental actions and emotions. As for the reality of the cessation of suffering, a mere truth does not constitute the cessation of anything, let alone all of our problems and pain, but it has to be a radical transformation of our entire outlook on and experience of our world. The path that leads there is not just a "truth" either, because the noticeable changes in one's body, speech, and mind that come about through practicing the methods of the Buddhist path do not represent a "truth." In sum, the point of the four realities is neither some mere truth nor something that is noble in itself—specifically, one wonders what should be noble about suffering or its origin as such (note that, according to the *Mahāvibhāṣā* [Taishō 1545, 27.401c27], the last two realities can be said to be good, whereas the first two contain good, bad, and neutral elements. Likewise, the last two realities are uncontaminated, but the first two are contaminated). Therefore, what we deal with here are the fundamental facts of suffering, its origin, its cessation, and the path as these are directly seen or experienced from the perspective of the noble ones. "Noble" are all those on the path of seeing and onward who realize these four facts in a direct and immediate manner. In other words, these four realities, or the knowledge about them, represent the deeply internalized reality of these noble ones. On the other hand, from the perspective of ordinary ignorant beings, these four are neither taken to be true nor are they the reality that they experience (with the possible exception of the first two of the three kinds of suffering—that is, manifest suffering and the suffering of change). Even if ordinary beings on the Buddhist path accept these four facts as true and attain more or less thorough insights into them, they still do not represent the experiential reality of their everyday lives, just as someone may understand the laws of aerodynamics but still cannot actually fly. That is, ordinary beings never experience or realize the full extent of these four fundamental facts as long as they have not attained the path of seeing.

264. For the background and details of the Buddhist deity Heruka and his Śaivaite counterpart Bhairava, see Davidson 1991 and 2002b (211ff.), and Gray 2001 (473–505), 2016, and 2019 (39–54). Furthermore, the word Heruka is used to indicate the wrathful forms of the five principal buddhas of the five buddha families (such as Buddha Heruka, Vajra Heruka, and so on). It is also found generically as an epithet of many *niruttarayoga* tantra deities, especially wrathful ones, such as Cakrasaṃvara, Yamāntaka, and Hevajra. Finally, Heruka can also signify a male realized tantric practitioner. The etymologies of Heruka vary greatly in different texts, but the term is generally understood as signifying the embodiment of inseparable bliss and emptiness or inseparable expanse and wisdom. The Tibetan rendering *khrag 'thung* ("blood drinker") refers to drinking the blood of ego-clinging, doubt, and dualistic delusion. Having drunk that blood, Heruka experiences great bliss and all other awakened qualities of the mind.

265. The *Tattvaratnāvalī* does not explicitly speak of "nine approaches," but the other texts that use this template (except for the **Dohānidhināmatattvopadeśa*; see the following paragraph), all only preserved in Tibetan, speak of them as *sbyor ba dgu*. Since Tib. *sbyor ba* renders a wide range of Sanskrit words, the Sanskrit term could be *yoga*, *prayoga*, *anuyoga*, *upayoga*, *yukti*, *yojana*, or other derivatives. However, TRVC (370) explains the term as "yoga of meditation," being that by which these nine are divided.

266. Maitrīpa's *Caturmudropadeśa* (text 92, 16) explains that among the four topics through which the nine approaches are discussed, "analysis" refers to their specific discriminating prajñās that are based on study and reflection. "Dhyāna" refers to their specific prajñās of meditation. "The stains of dhyāna" refers to the factors that are directly antagonistic to those prajñās. "The view" refers to the distinctive features of their specific prajñās embracing their specific conducts, as well as mentally taking their specific fruitions as objects. According to TRVC (370–73), "analysis" is in terms of what is to be validated (perceived), what validates it (perceiver), and true reality. "Dhyāna" refers to the specific meditations. "The stains of dhyāna" teaches the points of going astray in order to stop going astray into anything else that is not meditation—that is, what is not conducive to engage in meditation. "The view" refers to the branches of renunciation, the branches of means, and the branches of the prajñā of realization being complete.

267. As mentioned before, Mathes 2015 (8–9) says that this "is interesting since it builds a bridge between the non-tantric method of perfections and the *Sekanirdeśa*'s explanation of the four seals (*karma-*, *dharma-*, *mahā-*, and *samaya-mudra*), skipping the six vase empowerments and implicitly any creation-stage practice. It should be noticed that in his **Sthitisamāsa*, *Sahajavajra follows the lead of his master's *Tattvaratnāvalī* and presents the four seals and thus completion-stage practice immediately after the four tenets. In his **Guruparamparākramopadesa*,

Vajrapāṇi includes between the four tenets and the four-seal-based empowerments the six vase empowerments, though." Note that, by contrast, Maitrīpa's own *Compendium of the Purport of Empowerment* (text 37) and *Compendium of the Procedures of Empowerment* (text 38) discuss the entire sequence of the six vase empowerments (implying the practice of the creation process) as well as the remaining three main empowerments of the *niruttarayoga* tantras (secret empowerment, prajñā-jñāna empowerment, and fourth empowerment).

268. The *Caturmudrāṭīkā* (text 44, 365) briefly refers to just "the nine approaches." As a summary of the *Tattvaratnāvalī*, the **Dohānidhināmatattvopadeśa* discusses all nine approaches but does not explicitly mention the two subdivisions each of Yogācāra and Madhyamaka. Also, only some of its stanzas explicitly refer to one or more elements of the four subtopics of each approach: (1) dhyāna, (2) stains, (3) view, and (4) examination (the latter seems only implied). The *Caturmudropadeśa* lists the four subtopics as (1) the approach of analysis, (2) dhyāna, (3) the stains of dhyāna, and (4) the view; the *Guruparamparākramopadeśa* has (1) discernment, (2) meditation, (3) the stains of meditation, and (4) the view; and the *Dohakoṣahṛdayārthagītāṭīkā*'s comments on stanzas 10–12 speak of (1) view, (2) analysis, (3) meditation, and (4) stains of dhyāna. *Taking the Pith Instructions of the Philosophical Systems as the Path* uses only three of these terms ("dhyāna," "view," and "stains"), but "view," "dhyāna," and (most frequently) "assertion" all refer to the actual meditation instructions, while the stains are listed for only some of the nine approaches. Note that the first 60 percent of Jñānavajra's **Tattvadarśanamārga* also discusses the same nine approaches with similar four subtopics: (1) conduct, (2) view, (3) meditation, and (4) flaws, often (though not consistently) described similarly to the *Tattvaratnāvalī*, including some of the same or similar quotations. The author refers twice to Śabarapāda (Tib. Ri khrod zhabs) as his guru (once in reference to him bestowing the higher empowerments up through the fourth one), which may be considered as support for attributing the text to Maitrīpa or someone close to him. However, the text also includes many passages featuring Tibetan-style outlines with headings and subheadings, seems not very well organized, and, according to its colophon, was translated (rather unclearly in parts) by Jñānavajra himself (according to BDRC and a number of teaching records of Tibetan masters said to be from Kashmir) and Ngog (Tib. Rngog) Buddhapāla (late eleventh century; a student of Jñānavajra). However, Maitrīpa was not from Kashmir and only a single translation in collaboration with a Tibetan translator (D1180; possibly two more suggested in Almogi 2022a, 376–82) is ascribed to Maitrīpa, while Ngog Buddhapāla is not associated with any other text in Tg. Nevertheless, it is striking that the **Tattvadarśanamārga* uses this template, since it seems not to appear in any texts other than those mentioned above (for more details on the **Tattvadarśanamārga*, see appendices 4 and 5 in volume 6 and Almogi 2010, 146–52). Note also that Candrahari's *Ratnamālā* (D3901, fol. 68b.4) says that "the Buddhists are of seven kinds: Vaibhāṣikas, Sautrāntikas, pratyekabuddhas, Aspectarians, Nonaspectarians, illusion[-like Mādhyamikas], and [Mādhyamikas of] utter nonabiding," but the text lacks the other features of Maitrīpa's ninefold template with four subtopics.

269. If the author of the **Tattvadarśanamārga* was indeed, like Maitrīpa, a student

of Śavaripa, it would lend further support to said template originating with Śavaripa. Jñānavajra's several mentions of śrāvakas and pratyekabuddhas together in contrast to the Mahāyāna schools may even echo the original presentation of the four positions as śrāvakas, pratyekabuddhas, Yogācāras, and Mādhyamikas in *Taking the Pith Instructions of the Philosophical Systems as the Path* instead of the standard set in the *Tattvaratnāvalī* and so on.

270. Thus, these four texts are clearly interrelated in terms of this template. Vajrapāṇi's *Guruparamparākramopadeśa* (text 213) is an extensive commentary on Maitrīpa's *Tattvaratnāvalī* and also parallels his *Sekatātparyasaṃgraha* (text 37), *Saṃkṣiptasekaprakriyā* (text 38), *Sekanirdeśa* (text 42), *Commentary on Half a Stanza on True Reality Teaching That All Phenomena Are Utterly Nonabiding* (text 73), and *Caturmudropadeśa* (text 92), as well as Nāgārjuna's *Caturmudrānvaya* (text 14) and the texts by Maitrīpa's other main disciples, such as Divākaracandra's *Prajñājñānaprakāśa* (text 16), Sahajavajra's *Sthitisamāsa* (text 17), Rāmapāla's *Sekanirdeśapañjikā* (text 45), and the *Caturmudrāṭīkā* (text 44). Vajrapāṇi fleshes out the details of the four empowerments of the *niruttarayoga* tantras and the related practices in terms of Maitrīpa's typical fivefold division of the creation and perfection processes (outer creation process, inner creation process, perfection process, full-perfection process, and essence process) that are not spelled out in Maitrīpa's *Tattvaratnāvalī*, **Dohānidhināmatattvopadeśa*, and *Taking the Pith Instructions of the Philosophical Systems as the Path* (the *Caturmudropadeśa*'s brief discussion of the four mudrās pertains only to the practices related to the last three among the four empowerments). Two other works by Maitrīpa (texts 37 and 38) speak about the meanings, purposes, and performances of the four empowerments but not about the related practices, while text 42 is limited to elucidating the proper way of performing and receiving the third empowerment—the prajñā-jñāna empowerment—and a brief discussion of the four mudrās. In works by Maitrīpa's students, in Sahajavajra's *Sthitisamāsa*, similar to the *Caturmudropadeśa*, the Sūtrayāna approaches are immediately followed by a discussion of the four mudrās (skipping the creation process related to the first empowerment). The same author's *Tattvadaśakaṭīkā* (text 46) speaks about Yogācāra and Madhyamaka but gives no systematic presentation of Vajrayāna topics. Divākaracandra's *Prajñājñānaprakāśa* mentions the Pāramitāyāna without differentiating it and only briefly discusses Maitrīpa's fivefold creation and perfection processes in the Vajrayāna. Similarly, the *Caturmudrāṭīkā* and Rāmapāla's *Sekanirdeśapañjikā* briefly refer to this fivefold division but otherwise focus almost entirely on the perfection process. In sum, Vajrapāṇi's work not only can be considered as his efforts to fill in all the blanks of the extremely brief Vajrayāna section in the *Tattvaratnāvalī* but also represents the most systematic and complete presentation of Maitrīpa's views of both the Pāramitāyāna and the Vajrayāna. When read in conjunction with the other works mentioned above, the full picture of the Vajrayāna in particular, as it is presented by Maitrīpa and his disciples, appears clearly.

271. Vol. *kha*, fol. 32a.3–32b.4.

272. Interestingly, a commentary on this text, probably by Tipi Bumlabar, explicitly and in detail identifies the main opponents of Maitrīpa's view as Jñānaśrīmitra, who is called an "Aspectarian of Nondual Diversity," Ratnākaraśānti, who is

said to be a "Nonaspectarian with Stains" (in some of Maitrīpa's biographies, it is said that both Jñānaśrīmitra and Ratnākaraśānti had been his teachers, but also that at least Ratnākaraśānti was later defeated by Maitrīpa in debate), and Śāntarakṣita, who is identified as a proponent of illusion-like nonduality.

273. The same topic is also discussed in Maitrīpa's *Sekanirdeśa* (text 42) and its commentary by Rāmapāla (text 45), Maitrīpa's *Caturmudropadeśa* (text 92, 18), and extensively in Vajrapāṇi's *Guruparamparākramopadeśa* (text 213). For details, see this section in text 36.

274. Vol. *ka*, fols. 216b.6–217a.2.

275. Tib. *dgongs pa mdor bsdus* (GZ CDNP *dgos pa mdor bsdus*).

276. Tib. *dbang rnam nges = Sekanirṇaya*, the alternative name of the *Sekanirdeśa*.

277. In BKC, the text of *Instructions on Empowerment* precedes *A Compendium of the Purport of Empowerment*, while none of the other three texts are included.

278. As mentioned before, Padma Karpo also mentions *The Purity of Empowerment*.

279. In general, the term "prajñā-jñāna" refers to the wisdom that arises based on a prajñā, which is another word for a karmamudrā (a consort in the practice of the same name); see, for example, Vaidyapāda's *Yogasapta* 26cd (D1875, fol. 70b.6: "Wisdom [arises] through the actions of prajñā—this is empowerment because what has not been realized is realized"). In Maitrīpa's *Sekatātparyasaṃgraha* (text 37, 203), "prajñā-jñāna" is explained in two ways. First, in "the wisdom of prajñā," "prajñā" refers to the mental state of the duality of perceiver and perceived that is the nature of a well-shaped woman consisting of the four elements, the five skandhas, and the six objects, while "wisdom" means the bodhicitta that has this prajñā as its cause. "The wisdom that is prajñā itself" means that wisdom refers to this very prajñā in its being empty of the duality of perceiver and perceived.

280. For further details on the four empowerments, see also Vajrapāṇi's *Guruparamparākramopadeśa* (text 213).

281. Within the text's fourteen pages on the vase empowerment, the water and master empowerments take up thirteen pages, and the remaining four empowerments one page. The secret empowerment is discussed on less than one page, the prajñā-jñāna empowerment on three, and the fourth empowerment on six (however, most of the latter consists of quotes from the *Hevajratantra*, the *Guhyasamājatantra*, and Saraha).

282. There are more than thirty texts of this genre in Tg, such as Advayavajra's *Trayodaśātmakaśrīcakrasaṃvarasya abhiṣekavidhi* (D1486), Vanaratna's *Trayodaśātmakaśrīcakrasaṃvaramaṇḍalopāyikā* (D1489), Jayasena's **Śrīḍākārṇavatantrābhiṣekavidhi* (D1521), Bhairavadeva's **Mārgābhiṣekaprakaraṇa* (D1534), Rāhulaśrīmitra's *Yuganaddhaprakāśanāmasekaprakriyā* (D1818), and *Nandivajra's *Sekaprakiyā* (D1881). All these texts seem to be based, at least in part, on certain passages in the *Sarvamaṇḍalasāmānyavidhiguhyatantra* (H762).

283. BKC (vol. *kha*, fols. 27b.4–28a.4) contains a brief obscure background story of this text, which is attributed to Rāmapāla (Tib. Ra ma pha la). However, as IaS (86) already pointed out, "It seems to us clear that this must be a Tibetan composition."

284. The colophons of the Sanskrit manuscripts are divided between calling this text either *Sekanirdeśa* or *Sekanirṇaya*, Maitrīpa's own *Tattvaratnāvalī* refers to it

as *Sekanirṇaya*, and Rāmapāla's *Sekanirdeśapañjikā* uses both names. In recent secondary literature, however, there seems to be a preference for *Sekanirdeśa*.

285. According to BKC (vol. *ka*, fol. 217a.1–2), *Instructions on Empowerment* is even a commentary on the meaning of *The Succession of the Four Mudrās*. *Instructions on Empowerment* and its commentary by Rāmapāla (text 45) show close relationships with the *Caturmudrānvaya* and with Maitrīpa's *Commentary on Half a Stanza on True Reality Teaching That All Phenomena Are Utterly Nonabiding* (text 73) and *Caturmudropadeśa* (text 92), Divākaracandra's *Prajñājñānaprakāśa* (text 16), Sahajavajra's *Sthitisamāsa* (text 17), the *Caturmudrāṭīkā* (text 44), and Vajrapāṇi's *Guruparamparākramopadeśa* (text 213).

286. Note that this is not a sequence in terms of hierarchy of realization—only mahāmudrā is the supreme realization—but in terms of cause and result (see the following note).

287. That is, the moment of variety is related to the karmamudrā, the moment of maturation to the dharmamudrā, the moment of freedom from characteristics to mahāmudrā, and the moment of consummation to the samayamudrā. Based on the *Sekanirdeśapañjikā*, Mathes 2015 (11) comments on stanza 38 as follows: "The four joys are first enjoyed physically with a karmamudrā (a technical term standing for a consort). This proceeds to the phase of dharmamudrā wherein the practitioner again realizes the four joys, but this time on the basis of teachings such that the sights and sounds of the manifold world are one's own mind. This leads to the realization of mahāmudrā. The four joys of the samayamudrā are experienced when the yogin manifests as a Heruka in union with his consort for the sake of benefiting others."

288. Whether and to what extent this approach can skip at least a certain degree of initial "mental engagement" (that is, conceptual examination) and the progression through the practices related to the first three mudrās was and is controversial. However, in *Tattvaviṃśikā* 7–11, for example, Maitrīpa distinguishes a progressive approach of more ordinary practitioners within the Vajrayāna from a more direct mahāmudrā approach of those of keenest faculties, and Sahajavajra's *Tattvadaśakaṭīkā* outlines a mahāmudrā practice that functions outside the usual tantric framework of the creation and perfection processes.

289. Rāmapāla's commentary (text 45, 419–20) explains that "utter nonabiding" means being without any superimpositions and mental nonengagement. "In anything at all" refers to the dependently arisen skandhas, dhātus, āyatanas, and so on. Since mahāmudrā—self-awareness—is stainless, the stained three moments of variety and so on, and thus the first three among the four ecstasies, do not arise in it. This utter nonabiding is inconceivable wisdom, which does not arise from analysis.

290. Note that this can be seen as a basis of Gampopa's famous statement that the nature of thoughts is the dharmakāya.

291. For a detailed overview of the *Sekanirdeśa* and its commentary by Rāmapāla, see IaS (94–111). As IaS points out, stanzas 7–10 and 12–17 of the *Sekanirdeśa* are found in Bodhibhadra's **Jñānasārasamuccayanibandhana*, stanzas 26, 36, 37a, and 38–39 in the **Prajñājñānaprakāśa* (text 16, actually also citing stanza 25), and stanzas 31–32 (with attribution to scripture) in Muniśrībhadra's *Yogimanoharā* (*Pañcakramatippaṇī*). Furthermore, stanzas 7–17, 19, 21–22, and 33–35 are

embedded in the *Yogāmbaramahātantra* (see Szántó 2012, 94–95). For a more detailed list of parallels and citations of the *Sekanirdeśa*, see IaS, 361–63.

292. As mentioned before, text 43 is not included in the Sanskrit **Advayavajrasaṃgraha* and is considered anonymous in both GZ and Tg. Its long title is found only in NG *Shes pa spro bsdu med par 'jog pa'i man ngag gsang ba dam pa* Tg *u pa de sha pa ra ma pa ya / gsang ba dam pa* (no translator) AIBS *Upadeśaparama / gsang ba dam pa* (no translator) GZ3 (2:253–54), author unclear (*mi gsal*), *Shes pa spro bsdu mi byed par 'jog pa'i man ngag*, colophon *u pa de sha pa ra mo pa ya / gsang ba dam pa* (no translator). Obviously, the transliterated and probably reconstructed Sanskrit title(s) and the short Tibetan title do not match. Going by the Sanskrit *Upadeśaparama* (or *u pa de sha pa ra ma pa ya / u pa de sha pa ra mo pa ya*), Tib. *man ngag* and *dam pa* would belong together ("The True Pith Instruction"), but there is no equivalent of Tib. *gsang ba*, and the meanings of *-paya/-upaya* (*gopāyana*? *upāya*?) in the longer transliterated title are unclear. On the other hand, that *gsang ba dam pa* ("The True Secret") alone is given as the Tibetan title in Tg and GZ suggests that it is either the original title (if there was one at all) or the ornamental title of "A Pith Instruction on . . ." (as also rendered in Mathes 2015). It is equally uncertain whether *Letting Cognizance Be without Projecting and Withdrawing* was a part of an original title, but what is clear is that it is based on the last three stanzas of the text:

> Don't grasp cognizance, let it be in its own pellucidity!
> Within the state of unborn mind as such,
> what is withdrawn and what projected?

What is furthermore conspicuous is that, similar to the main theme of Kuddālapāda's *Acintyādvayakramopadeśa* (text 18), this short text often uses the terms "inconceivable" (5 times) and "nonduality" (3 times), both together and separately; another frequent term is "unborn" (6 times).

293. IaS refers to this as **Caturmudrānvayaṭīkā*.

294. As per the colophon of text 44, Bhitakarma was known as *Kāropa in the context of engaging in philosophy, as *Ḍākakauṇapa ("Corpse-Eating Ḍāka") in the context of engaging in yoga, and as Digambara ("The Sky-Clad One") in the context of engaging in conduct. BA (843) says that, according to some, *Kāropa was one of Maitrīpa's "four spiritual sons" (as mentioned before, the other three were Vajrapāṇi, Marpa Lotsāwa, and the Newar Śīlabharo). The only other known work ascribed to *Kāropa is the brief versified *Yogacāryasamādhi* (text 88 in vol. 4; not found in Tg) about the prerequisites, view, meditation, conduct, and samaya of mahāmudrā.

295. BA, 847–49 and 853–55.

296. In Indo-Tibetan sources, the elusive land of Sahor (Tib. Za hor) is said to have played a significant role in the formation of the Vajrayāna. However, its location is presented in several different ways. The majority of these sources suggest that Sahor was a kingdom to the east of Bodhgayā, on the border with or within Bengal or Orissa. For example, Atiśa's earliest biography says that he was born in a large city (said to be Vikramapura, supposedly a part of present-day Dhaka) in the country of Sahor in Bengal, and similar statements about Sahor's location are found in the Third Karmapa's biography of Tilopa and in

Mandarava's life story revealed by Samten Lingpa (Tib. Bsam gtan gling pa; born 1655). Gendün Chöpel (Tib. Dge 'dun chos 'phel; 1903–51) says that the kings of the Pāla dynasty (750–1199) made Sahor their capital and suggests that its ruins are either on the banks of the Brahmaputra in Bengal or on the southern banks of the Ganges near Bihar. According to Torricelli 2018 (128–30), Sahor probably included most of the present-day administrative division of Chittagong in Bangladesh, as well as the southern part of the Dhaka division, and some parts of the Indian state Tripura. However, other sources say that Sahor was in close vicinity to Oḍḍiyāna in the northwest of India, or even conflate the two (especially since both countries are said to have been ruled by a King Indrabhūti). Among Tibetans, it is thus often the area of Mandi and Rewalsar (known as Tso Pema) that is identified as the location of Sahor. For the complexity of the location of Sahor, see also van der Kuijp 2013.

297. As for the term *vidyādhara* ("knowledge-holder"), in its non-Buddhist use, it signifies someone who has special forms of knowledge relating to metallurgy, distillation, machinery, and magic (it is in this sense that the word is found in the *Vetāla Tales*). In early Indic mythology, vidyādharas and vidyādharīs were very beautiful semidivine beings attending Śiva and wielding special powers, such as flying, invisibility, shape-shifting, and extraordinary skill in music. Living in their own splendid kingdoms in the Himalayas, both males and females were also believed to bewitch and seduce travelers. In its general Buddhist use, a vidyādhara (often translated as "awareness-holder") is a highly realized master of the tantric path, possessing the wisdom of deity, mantra, and great bliss. In the Mahāyoga system, four levels of vidyādharas are distinguished: vidyādhara of maturation (Tib. *rnam par smin pa'i rig 'dzin;* paths of accumulation and preparation), vidyādhara of mastery over life (Tib. *tshe la dbang ba'i rig 'dzin;* path of seeing), vidyādhara of mahāmudrā (path of familiarization), and vidyādhara of innate presence (Tib. *lhun grub rig 'dzin;* path of nonlearning).

298. Depending on different calculations, this ancient Indian measure of distance has a range of about seven to fifteen kilometers, most commonly about thirteen.

299. As mentioned before, Natekara was the original name of Sahajavajra, who received this name when he became a student of Maitrīpa.

300. The name of this charnel ground is given as Tib. Kem ri; maybe Karaṅkin (Tib. *keng rus can*), one of the eight charnel grounds in the *Saṃvarodayatantra.*

301. Tib. Skor ni rū pa, 1062–1102. Based on BA, Schaeffer 2005 (66–67) suggests that Prajñāśrījñānakīrti is an alias of Kor Nirūpa (see right below). That the names Prajñāśrījñāna(kīrti) and Kor Nirūpa refer to the same person also seems to be corroborated by Tāranātha 2008 (204), but he says that Kor Nirūpa is the alias of a Prajñāśrījñāna who was a paṇḍita from Copper Island (according to BGTC, 2448, some say that "Copper Island" (Tib. *gzangs gling*) refers to Java, while others say it is Śrī Laṅkā).

302. Note that texts 44 (128 pages) and 70 (172 pages) are the two longest works in all of GZ. Under the assumption that Kor Nirūpa is their author, their total of 300 pages represents the largest body of material by any single author in GZ:

more than one-tenth of the entire collection and more than all the works by Saraha or Maitrīpa in it.

303. BA, 849–55.
304. Tib. Dam pa kor.
305. Tib. *sems tsam rnam rdzun gyi dbu ma* (Skt. **alīkākāra-cittamātra-madhyamaka*).
306. Mi bskyod rdo rje 1996, 9. The account in TOK (1:502) of the spread of mahāmudrā teachings and the dohās in Tibet says that Kor Nirūpa was a part of their early transmission, preceding Vajrapāṇi and giving extensive explanations on essential reality. Note that according to Solonin (2015, 435), a Xixia mahāmudrā lineage contains a Prajñākīrti as a disciple of Maitrīpa (while Zhang 2019, 187, 195 has a Jñānakīrti). Xixia (known as Minyag to Tibetans), was a Tangut Buddhist imperial dynasty from 1038 to 1227 (covering the modern-day Chinese provinces of Ningxia, Gansu, eastern Qinghai, northern Shaanxi, northeastern Xinjiang, as well as southwest Inner Mongolia and southernmost Outer Mongolia).
307. In particular, Schaeffer (2005, 66–67 and 105–15) makes a detailed and convincing case that at least parts of the stanzas in texts 68 and 70 were deliberately and significantly rewritten in Tibetan based on the already existing Tibetan canonical translation, or simply written newly, and that text 70 comments on these rewritings in a specific and systematic manner. In addition to what Schaeffer says, it is obvious that the comments of text 70 always follow the word order of the Tibetan translation of the stanzas and not the Apabhraṃśa of Saraha's *Dohākoṣa*. Also, many (though not all) passages of text 70 do not read like the usual "Sanskrit-Tibetan translationese" but more like natural Tibetan. Furthermore, several of the commentary's interpretations and at least some of its hermeneutical etymologies can only be based on readings unique to the Tibetan translation (being impossible or hard to conceive in either Apabhraṃśa or Sanskrit). Finally, at least some phrases and lines in the stanzas in text 70 appear to be taken from or inspired by the commentary's extensive quotations from otherwise unknown sūtras and tantras (or vice versa).
308. See Jackson 2004 (7–8), Schaeffer 2005 (102–5), and Mathes and Szántó forthcoming.
309. Schaeffer 2005, 67.
310. For more details on text 70, see its introduction in volume 4.
311. This is so despite texts 44 and 70 also having significant differences: commenting on *The Succession of the Four Mudrās* as a formal tantric treatise that systematically discusses all four mudrās versus commenting on Saraha's informal and unsystematic "People Dohā" (primarily dealing with mahāmudrā and just a little bit of karmamudrā, while not mentioning samayamudrā and dharmamudrā at all).
312. Maybe *Kāropa had a hand in some parts of the text or some or all of it was composed based on his instructions. One may even consider the possibility that *Kāropa himself composed the text in Tibetan (given that he had traveled to Tibet). However, not only is there no evidence for that, but it would make the colophon's mention of Prajñāśrījñānakīrti as its translator obsolete, and it is also clearly refuted by the evidence for Prajñāśrījñānakīrti/Kor Nirūpa as the text's actual author presented below. Given that evidence, I refrain from identifying

*Kāropa as the text's author (except in the general introduction). Though it is attributed to *Kāropa/Bhitakarma in its colophon, in NG, BA, AIBS, and by all contemporary scholars (including Mathes, Isaacson, and Sferra), it is well known that the colophons of translations from Sanskrit were usually added later in Tibetan and are not reliable (NG and AIBS just follow those colophons). Though especially the above-mentioned among contemporary scholars have dealt with the *Caturmudrāṭīkā* in some detail, no one seems to have looked at it thoroughly enough or compared it with text 70 to notice the many issues that I mention. This is surprising, since even a cursory glance quickly reveals that the quoted text of *The Succession of the Four Mudrās* is a unique Tibetan version that contains many additional passages, and that the comments on it are always based on the words and their order in this Tibetan version and not the Sanskrit.

313. For the larger issues of pseudepigrapha, "gray" texts, and so on in Tg, see Wedemeyer 2009 and Kapstein 2015. That Tibetans were not unaware of this issue is attested by Tāranātha 2008 (204), who interestingly says that in the case of many dohās, it is not certain that they are definitely translations (or translations in their entirety), as there are also dohās (or parts of them) that seem to have arisen in someone's awakened mind. However, in Tāranātha's view, this just means that the life stories of the siddhas are not determinate one way or another (that is, instructions that siddhas have not uttered before can appear in the minds of others even at times when these siddhas are not present or alive anymore, which is also well known as the notion of "mind treasures [*termas*]" in the Nyingma tradition).

314. In the same vein, most identifiable quotations from the scriptures usually follow their (sometimes greatly variant or mistaken) Tibetan translations. In such cases, I usually follow the Sanskrit (if available) and document the differences in GZ CDNP of this commentary in the notes.

315. As Mathes 2009 (91) said, this insertion is missing in the version of the text in BKC, but is found in GZ (GZ3, 339–77; GZ2, fols. 296a.6–314b.6) and P, though he does not mention that it is likewise contained in CDN.

316. Tib. *shes pa rnal ma* (text 70 also has *sems rnal ma* a few times).

317. Tib. *snang grags kyi chos*. Though this is also found once in Maitrīpa's *Caturmudropadeśa* (text 92), it appears sixteen times in text 70 and five times in text 44.

318. Tib. *ci yang ma yin pa'i*.

319. In addition, there is the expression "thoughts about distinctions" (*tha dad kyi rtog pa/tha dad du brtags pa*; eleven times in text 70 and two times in text 44), though this also appears one time each in D1490, D1920, D2090, and D4421.

320. Given all this, the phrase "translated on his own" (Tib. *rang 'gyur*) in the translator's colophon in texts 44 and 70 could also be taken as "altered on his own," though this is of course not what it is meant to say. Furthermore, as mentioned before, text 44 shows close parallels with passages in other works by Maitrīpa and his students—Maitrīpa's *Sekatātparyasaṃgraha* (text 37), *Saṃkṣiptasekaprakriyā* (text 38), *Sekanirdeśa* (text 42), *Commentary on Half a Stanza on True Reality Teaching That All Phenomena Are Utterly Nonabiding* (text 73), and *Caturmudropadeśa* (text 92), Divākaracandra's *Prajñājñānaprakāśa* (text 16), Sahajavajra's *Sthitisamāsa* (text 17), Rāmapāla's *Sekanirdeśapañjikā* (text 45), and Vajrapāṇi's *Guruparamparākramopadeśa* (text 213). In particular, the many parallels with the

Guruparamparākramopadeśa are striking, such as the classification of five tantra classes (kriyātantra, caryātantra, yogatantra, yogottaratantra, and yoganiruttaratantra), the presentation of the sixfold master empowerment, the majority of the discussion of the three approaches to karmamudrā (forceful, poor, and correct), the five features of mahāmudrā, passages on the samayamudrā and dharmamudrā, and the passages on the two bindus between the vajra and the lotus. Since text 44 was obviously written in Tibetan and, in all probability, later than the above texts, it seems clear that it borrowed from those texts and not the other way around. However, since the *Guruparamparākramopadeśa* also seems to have been composed in Tibetan, the textual relationship between it and the *Caturmudrāṭīkā* is not entirely beyond doubt as to who copied whom, but there is enough parallel material in those among the above texts that are preserved in Sanskrit to determine the general direction of borrowing.

321. Different from the elaborate Tibetan-style outlines with many subdivisions as in the insertion mentioned below, simple enumerations of a given topic's points without subdivisions are also found in other Indian commentaries.

322. According to text 44 (277), *The Succession of the Four Mudrās* was "composed by following the father tantra *Guhyasamāja*, the mother tantra *Cakrasaṃvara*, and the [*Hevajratantra* in] Thirty-Two Chapters." *The Succession of the Four Mudrās* is certainly in agreement with the *Hevajratantra* and cites four (maybe five) stanzas from it, with one of them also found in the Cakrasaṃvara-related *Saṃvarodayatantra*, while there is no quotation or discernible influence from the *Guhyasamājatantra*. In text 44, the *Hevajratantra* is cited copiously (42 stanzas), the *Guhyasamājatantra* appears with 6 stanzas, but the *Cakrasaṃvaratantra* is not cited (there are only a few lines that, besides other tantras, also appear in the Cakrasaṃvara-related *Saṃvarodayatantra*, *Śrīvajraḍākatantra*, *Vajraḍākanāmottaratantra*, and *Śrīḍākārṇavamahāyoginītantra*). Further citations in text 44 include the *Devendraparipṛcchātantra* (5 stanzas), the *Sekanirdeśa* (5 or 6:2–4, 21–22, in all probability 26, 29c), the "People Dohā" (10 lines), the *Pañcakrama* (2), and an abundance of unidentified quotes. Furthermore, among the twenty examples of mahāmudrā (374–76), fourteen are also found in Saraha's "People Dohā" (texts 13 and 70), *Body Treasure* (text 53), *Speech Treasure* (text 54), and "King Dohā" (text 65).

323. For example, in the initial introduction of the four mudrās in general, the subject matter is said to consist of empowerment and the essence of means and prajñā, while the introduction in the insertion says that the subject matter is the general aspect of bliss-emptiness and the essence is the object generality of bliss-emptiness.

324. Some of these outlines also contain headings that are not mentioned again in the following explanations.

325. Monier-Williams defines a *pañjikā* as "a perpetual commentary which explains and analyzes every word." Similarly, in stanza 4 of Nāropa's *Sekoddeśaṭīkā*, *pañjikā* is explained as *padabhañjikā* ("[a commentary] that examines the words"), while stanza 5 glosses *ṭīkā* as *sarvārthasūcikā* ("[a commentary] that points out all meanings"; I am indebted to Klaus-Dieter Mathes for providing this reference). BGTC (50) defines the Tibetan *dka' 'grel* ("commentary on what is difficult") for *pañjikā* as "a text that does not explain the meanings of the words

of a scripture one after another but provides explanations by highlighting the difficult points." The *Sekanirdeśapañjikā* often comments on every word in a stanza, but there are also several other stanzas that it does not explain at all.

326. BA, 729, 842, 857.

327. No other texts are attributed to Rāmapāla in Tg, so the *Sekanirdeśapañjikā* was probably his only work.

328. Tib. Khyung po rnal 'byor tshul khrims mgon po. The only thing that seems to be certain about his dates is that he was born in a tiger year (without providing evidence, Roerich's translation of BA, 728, identifies this as 1086). Most traditional hagiographies give his birth year as 978 or 990, obviously due to the fact that he supposedly lived for 150 years and in all probability died in the early or late 1130s (according to Kapstein 2005). Based on traditional hagiographies, other sources (such as BDRC and https://treasuryoflives.org/biographies/view/Khyungpo-Naljor/6285) provide the year of death as 1127. However, even BA (733) says that Kyungpo Naljor's statement that he lived for 150 years was made with an underlying intention (Tibetan. *dgongs pa can*), such as when Patampa Sangyé answered a question about his age by saying "My age is 99990 years." Furthermore, as Kapstein shows, most of Kyungpo Naljor's identifiable Indian and Tibetan teachers lived in the mid-to-late eleventh century. Some Tibetan biographies of Rechungpa say that Rāmapāla was one of his Indian teachers, especially for the transmission of Vajravārāhī, and that Rāmapāla also taught the Nepalese Mahākāruṇa (see Roberts 2007, 116, 151, 164, and 168).

329. I follow the Tibetan of Tāranātha's text (Tāranātha 1970, 18, and 2011, 450; also reproduced in IaS, 89n122); the English translation of it in Templeman 1983 (13–14) contains numerous mistakes.

330. Tib. Dpal yon can.

331. However, other sources, such as BA (384 and 857–59), BKC (vol. *kha*, fol. 93b.6), and an anonymous and untitled thirteenth-century lineage history of Saraha's dohās (edited in Passavanti 2008, who calls it *Bla ma brgyud pa'i rim pa*; fols. 13a.8–9 and 14a.2) explicitly say that Vajrapāṇi was a siddha with many common siddhis and the highest siddhi of mahāmudrā.

332. The last sentence here is remarkable, since it spells out the profound realization of Ratnadevī in particular. The Tibetan of its first clause is unambiguous that it is Ratnadevī (and not Rāmapāla), who has the same realization as Maitrīpa himself (Tib. *mnga' bdag nyid*), while the second clause seems to imply Rāmapāla's realization; however, since that clause has no grammatical subject, it is possible for it to also apply to Ratnadevī (though that is quite unlikely, since it would imply that Maitrīpa's consort Gaṅgādhara had twice the realization of Maitrīpa). Note that Pawo Tsugla Trengwa's *History of the Dharma* (Dpa' bo gtsug lag phreng ba 2003, 774) refers to Rāmapāla as a king, maybe identifying him with the homonymous king of the Pāla dynasty (reigned c. 1075–1128 CE). However, this is quite implausible and was not put forth by any other Tibetan historiographers, such as Gö Lotsāwa and Tāranātha (the latter discusses King Rāmapāla without any identification with Maitrīpa's disciple; see Tāranātha 1980, 313–15), while BKC (vol. *kha*, fol. 93a.1) says that Vajrapāṇi was originally a scribe of the dharma king Rāmapāla in Bengal.

333. Rāmapāla's commentary states twice that Maitrīpa's *Instructions on Empowerment* follows Nāgārjuna's *Succession of the Four Mudrās* (text 14). Though Rāmapāla adduces only a single explicit quote from Nāgārjuna's work, there are four more passages in Rāmapāla's comments on stanza 26 that show clear parallels with the *Succession of the Four Mudrās*, and the two quotes in his comments on stanza 29 are likewise cited in that text. As mentioned before, Rāmapāla's commentary is furthermore closely related to Maitrīpa's *Commentary on Half a Stanza on True Reality Teaching That All Phenomena Are Utterly Nonabiding* (text 73) and *Caturmudropadeśa* (text 92), Divākaracandra's *Prajñājñānaprakāśa* (text 16), Sahajavajra's *Sthitisamāsa* (text 17), the *Caturmudrāṭīkā* (text 44), and Vajrapāṇi's *Guruparamparākramopadeśa* (text 213). Also compare Rāmapāla's section on karmamudrā with the one in the **Sarvadharmāprasahadeśakatattvārdhagāthāvṛtti* (text 73, 188ff.). Apart from this commentary by Rāmapāla, there are no known other works by him. Though BKC (vol. *kha*, fols. 27b.4–28a.4) attributes a brief background story of Maitrīpa's *Mahāyānaviṃśikā* (text 40) to him (Tib. Ra ma pha la), as IaS (86) pointed out, this must be a Tibetan composition. For a detailed overview of Rāmapāla's commentary, see IaS (94–111; 106: overview of Rāmapāla matching the four ecstasies, the four moments, the four empowerments, the four mudrās, and the four results). For an outline of the text by Tipi Bumlabar, see appendix 6. According to the brief colophon in CDNP, Rāmapāla's work was translated into Tibetan by Samantabhadra and Nagtso Lotsāwa. However, according to the extensive colophon in GZ, the translation was revised three times, with four Indians and two Tibetans (one of them Nagtso Lotsāwa) involved in the process (for details, see the colophon). As IaS (118) says, "The quality of the Tibetan translation can . . . frankly be described as poor. Evidence for this can be found on every page (and on some pages on nearly every line) of our edition. We have tried to point out and discuss at least the major (and certainly also some relatively minor) mistakes and problems of the Tibetan translation in the annotation to the English translation." For an extensive list of translation variants and problems, see IaS 116–20, and the notes in my own translation.
334. For BKC's description of the difference between these two works, see the final note on text 19.
335. For details on the crucial role of the Newar master *Ajamahāsukha (better known as Balpo Asu in Tibetan) in the transmission of the dohā tradition and Maitrīpa's texts, see the introduction in volume 1 and the introduction to appendix 5 in volume 3.
336. As mentioned before, the text's introduction contains simple outlines of two of its topics, and the lengthy insertion found in the section on the samayamudrā shows a detailed Tibetan-style outline with headings and multiple subheadings, while the remainder of the text does not include any outline.
337. Karma phrin las pa phyogs las rnam rgyal 2009, 8–10.
338. In this context, the term "conduct" (*caryā*) is either used in a general way or for the specific form of practice that is reserved for highly advanced practitioners and consists of all kinds of antinomian behaviors as an enhancement to induce the nonconceptual nondual wisdom that is free of all reference points (on the latter, see Wedemeyer 2011 and 2013). Thus whenever we encounter the word

"conduct" in our text, we need to keep in mind that, depending on the context, this term may refer either to mainstream Mahāyāna and Vajrayāna conduct or to the transgressive yogic practices that aim at going beyond all reference points, including the precepts of the classical Mahāyāna and Vajrayāna (these latter practices are sometimes also called "the conduct of a lunatic," "crazy wisdom," and so on).

339. This has led many to render *caryāgīti* as "performance song." However, this appears to confuse the contents of these songs (yogic conduct) with how they became used later (as songs performed with accompanying music and dance).
340. Jackson 2004, 10.
341. D2268, fol. 66a.4–5.
342. Schaeffer 2005, 97–98.
343. PDMT, 24:555–60 (A) and 26:1007–12 (B). Note that with texts whose title is given in both Sanskrit and Tibetan, the English title always corresponds to the Sanskrit. The Tibetan title may sometimes vary, thus sometimes also varying in the colophon. Numbers in { } refer to the page numbers of GZ3, vol. 2.
344. GZ *ci 'dod bsten pa* CDNP (AB) *ji ltar 'dod pa bsten* ("how to rely on sense pleasures").
345. GZ CD (B) *mkhas pas dag par sngon 'gro spyad* CDNP (A) NP (B) *mkhas pa dag pas sngon 'gro spyad* ("the pure wise ones who are blessed by mantra engage in the preliminary"). However, though *sngon 'gro* clearly means "preliminary" in Tibetan, it renders a number of Sanskrit terms such as *pūrvaka* ("previous," "former," "first," "forefather," "pioneer"), *puroga* ("leader," "principal," "preceding"), *agraga* ("leader," "preceding"), *agresara* ("best, "preceding"), and *agrya* ("proficient," "best," "foremost," "principal"). Thus this phrase could also be read as "the wise ones act as the foremost/are proficient in purity" or "the pure wise ones act as the foremost/are proficient," respectively.
346. This appears to refer to the "Milk Ocean" (Skt. *kṣīrasāgara*) in Hindu mythology, which the gods churned in order to obtain the nectar of immortality.
347. I follow GZ *nus mod* against CDNP (AB) *nus med* ("are not able").
348. In virtually all its other occurrences in Tg, the phrase "the state of the five" refers to the five skandhas. Thus this probably refers back to buddha awakening in the sense that it is the true nature of the five skandhas and thus can be extracted from them.
349. The examples of using poison as a remedy for poison and fire as a remedy for fire (representing passion) are also found in *Hevajratantra* II.2.46 and 49.
350. I follow CDNP (AB) *'dam gyi padma* against GZ *padma'i 'dab ma* ("the petals of a lotus"), since the latter does not fit well with the following line.
351. I follow GZ CDNP (A) NP (B) *smyung ba* against CD (B) *gdung ba* ("tormented").
352. GZ *dngos grub* CDNP (AB) *byang chub* ("awakening").
353. This stanza is quite similar to one in the *Śrīvajraḍākatantra* (H386, fol. 332a.7–332b.1).
354. GZ *gnyer bas* CD (A) CDNP (B) *gnyer na* ("if you seek") NP (A) *mnyen na* ("if supple").
355. I follow CDNP (AB) *'dam las skyes* (lit. "born from mud") against GZ *'doms las skyes* ("born from the genitalia/instructions").
356. Note that Skt. *cakra* is a polyvalent term in texts like this: it can refer to the

cakras in the body, the entire maṇḍala, the whole world or universe, a certain sphere or realm (such as the cakra of the three kāyas or the dharmadhātu-cakra), or several of these. In the term *Kālacakra*, *cakra* is specifically explained to refer to the emptiness endowed with all supreme aspects.

357. GZ CDNP (A) *rab tu dgod* CDNP (B) *rab tu rgod* ("excited").
358. GZ *ki li ki li phaṭ* CDNP (AB) *ki li ki li phreng* ("strings of KILI KILI").
359. I follow GZ CD (B) *sngangs* against CDNP (A) NP (B) *sngags* ("mantra").
360. GZ *sos gcod* CDNP (A) CD (B) *sa bskyod* ("shaking the earth") NP (B) *sa bskyong* ("protecting the earth").
361. GZ *brgyal bar rab tu ngu ba ldog* CDNP (A) *brgyal ba rab zhi ngu bas rtogs* CDNP (A) *brgyal ba rab zhi du bas* ["through smoke"; typo for *ngu bas*] *rtogs* (difficult to make sense of; something like "fainting, being at peace, and realizing through crying"). "Reversing" seems to better fit with "cause descent" in stanza 16 in this context of the practice of karmamudrā.
362. On some of the many meanings of EVAṂ, see Amṛtavajra's commentary on Kṛṣṇapāda's *Dohākoṣa* (text 64) and its notes (especially the final note on the comments on stanza 21).
363. Stanzas 21–22ab correspond to *Hevajratantra* II.3.4–5ab.
364. Since GZ CDNP (AB) *rab tu gsal* in line 25a (somewhat unusually) renders Skt. *prabhāsvara*, I follow this here too. In texts such as Nāgārjuna's *Pañcakrama* and other literature related to the *Guhyasamājatantra* according to the Ārya school, the four kinds of empty—empty (Skt. *śūnya*, Tib. *stong pa*), very empty (Skt. *atiśūnya*, Tib. *shin tu stong pa*), greatly empty (Skt. *mahāśūnya*, Tib. *stong pa chen po*), and all-empty (Skt. *sarvaśūnya*, Tib. *thams cad stong pa*)—correspond to the tetrad of illumination (Skt. *ālokā*, Tib. *snang ba*), increase of illumination (Skt. *ālokābhāsa*, Tib. *snang ba mched pa*), culmination of illumination (Skt. *ālokopalabdhi*, Tib. *snang ba thob pa*), and luminosity (Skt. *prabhāsvara*, Tib. *'od gsal*), respectively. They are furthermore matched with the four ecstasies, the four moments, and sometimes the four empowerments. In due order, the first three kinds of illumination are also related to the ceasing of the thirty-three obscuring thoughts of hatred, the forty obscuring thoughts of desire, and the seven obscuring thoughts of ignorance. For details, see Dasgupta 1946 (51ff.), Kongtrul Lodrö Tayé 2005 (251–72) and 2008 (109 and 128), Wedemeyer 2007, and Tsongkhapa 2013.
365. My rendering of lines 23c–25b follows the Sanskrit as quoted in the *Subhāṣitasaṃgraha* (Bendall 1903–4, 25). GZ CDNP (AB) read as follows:

> Through true reality manifesting, purity—
> the supreme state—will clearly manifest
>
> Hence [CDNP (AB) *de phyir* GZ *de gsal*, "its clear manifestation"], it is to be perceived by yogīs
> who possess a motionless subtle mind
>
> . . .
>
> If lucid manifestation is attained,
> it will arise in the form it likes [CDNP (AB) *rang dga'i gzugs* GZ *rab dga'i gzugs* "in supreme ecstasy's form"].

366. CDNP (AB) read line 27d in the exact same way as line 28b and omit line 28d. Stanzas 27–28 are similar to *Hevajratantra* II.3.7–8. Given the repetition of "I am experiencing bliss" and the readings of CDNP, unless these two stanzas here were deliberately changed, it seems they are somewhat corrupt compared with those in the *Hevajratantra*:

> Variety is known as various kinds:
> embracing and kissing and so forth
> Maturation constitutes its opposite:
> the blissful experience of wisdom
>
> Consummation is proclaimed to be the
> consideration "I have partaken of bliss"
> Characteristics' lack is other than the three,
> being free from passion and dispassion.

367. GZ *dga' ba dang ni mchog dga' dang / dga' bral las mchog lhan cig skyes* CDNP (AB) *dga' ba dang po mchog dga' dang / dga' bral la sogs lhan cig skyes* ("the first ecstasy, supreme ecstasy, cessational ecstasy and so on, the connate").
368. GZ *cung zad tsam* CDNP (AB) *cung zad bde* ("a slight bliss").
369. In Sanskrit linguistics, a *mātrā* indicates the time it takes to pronounce a short syllable ("mora" in modern linguistics), while "half a mātrā" is half of that time. The text here seems to use these terms to speak about the increasing time of experiencing bliss in the sequence of the first three ecstasies.
370. GZ *rnal ma'i ror/ dbye ba* CDNP (AB) *rnam par rol/ dbye bas* ("differentiating the play").
371. I follow GZ *mnyam pa* against CDNP (AB) *rnam pa* ("aspect").
372. GZ *de bzhin nyid* CDNP (B) CD (A) *de nyid nyid* ("this very true reality") NP *de nyid*.
373. GZ *de las phyi rol ci zhig bsam* CDNP (AB) *de la phyi rol ci zhig bsam* ("what could outsiders think of it?").
374. GZ *'phrul pa* CDNP (AB) *'khrul pa* ("deluded").
375. With reference to the *Sādhanamālā*, Edgerton 1953 (1:106 and 181) explains āli as "*a-series* (i.e., a plus āli), name for a series of syllables (chiefly vowels and combinations of a or ā with semivowels)," and kāli as "(ka plus āli), *ka-series*, name for a series of syllables beginning with ka (consonants plus a or ā)." As Miller 1966 (138) points out, these two terms are unknown in conventional Sanskrit grammatical and lexical sources as well as the *Mahāvyutpatti*. The *Sādhanamālā* has at least twelve citations of the two terms as "vowel" and "consonant," but their main use in Vajrayāna texts is to indicate the following two series of syllables: a ā / i ī / u ū / ṛ ṝ / ḷ ḹ / e ai / o au / aṃ aḥ / and k kh g gh ṅ / c ch j jh ñ / ṭ ṭh ḍ ḍh ṇ / t th d dh n / p ph b bh m / y r l v ś ṣ s h kṣ / ka kā / ki kī / ku kū / ke kai / ko kau / kaṃ kaḥ /. As for the most probable etymology of the two terms, Miller (1966, 146–47) suggests *a* + *ādi* ("beginning with a") and *ka* + *ādi* ("beginning with ka"), given that later Buddhist Hybrid Sanskrit at times resulted in replacing intervocalic *-l-* for *-ḍ-* as well as *-d-*. In a tantric context, āli usually stands for the lalanā (the moon), while kāli stands for the rasanā (the sun).

376. This could also be read as "it is achieved by seeing wisdom."
377. GZ *der 'dod pas ni* CDNP (AB) *der ni 'dod pa;* GZ could also be read as "those who desire that remain," but *der* probably refers back to "the jewel" in line 40a.
378. This could be understood in two ways: the yogīs themselves appearing to be ordinary, or these yogīs practicing mahāmudrā with and within ordinary appearances.
379. Lines 42ab correspond to *Sekoddeśa* 146cd and *Guhyasamājatantra* XVIII.79ab. As *Sekoddeśa* 146cd, they are also cited in the mantra section of the *Sthitisamāsa* (text 17, 103); according to *Sekoddeśa* 146ab, the cause is the emptiness that bears reflections and the result is compassion bearing the immutable.
380. GZ *lhan cig min par* CDNP (AB) *lan cig min par* ("not just once").
381. I follow GZ CDNP (B) CD (A) *mtshan min* against NP (B) *mtshan nyid* ("characteristic").
382. DCNP (AB) omit the last sentence, and NP (A) add *maṇgā laṃ.*
383. PDMT, 26:193–210. My translation of this version of Saraha's dohā is indebted to all the previous and contemporary scholars who edited and translated its many Apabhraṃśa and Tibetan versions. As mentioned before, the division of the stanzas of text 13 that it shares with DKPA—as edited by Bagchi, Jackson, and Mathes and Szántó—follows those editions. However, since both text 13 and the canonical Tibetan version show variations and also include additional lines and stanzas when compared with the available Apa. manuscripts, my overall numbering of the stanzas of text 13 as per GZ differs from both the Apa. versions and the canonical Tibetan translation. In the notes, I indicate significant differences between text 13 and the canonical Tibetan translation. In addition, I consulted the following canonical and Tibetan commentaries: texts 66, 67, and 70, the *Dohakoṣahṛdayārthagītāṭīkā* (appendix 4 in volume 3), and the commentaries by Rigpé Raltri, Lingjé Repa, Barpuwa, the Third Karmapa Karma Trinlépa, Jamyang Shéba, and Ju Mipham.
384. According to KTP (10–11), following a command of the king, Tibetan translators prefaced their translations by certain formulas of paying homage in order to indicate which one among the three piṭakas a given text belongs to. At the beginning of texts belonging to the Vinaya, the formula is "I pay homage to the omniscient one." At the beginning of texts belonging to the sūtras, the formula is "I pay homage to all buddhas and bodhisattvas." At the beginning of texts belonging to the Abhidharma, the formula is "I pay homage to youthful Mañjuśrī." Since this text here also teaches the training in superior prajñā, in order to indicate its belonging to the piṭaka of the Abhidharma and to pacify obstacles, the translators respectfully pay homage with body, speech, and mind to Mañjuśrī, who is endowed with the glory (*śrī*) of gentle (*mañju*) and pleasing speech and possesses youthful qualities by virtue of dwelling on a pure bhūmi. In terms of the definitive meaning, this means paying homage to the mind that is connate wisdom. It is gentle or smooth because it lacks the edges of thoughts, is the glory of both saṃsāra and nirvāṇa, and is youthful in the sense of being fresh.
385. With texts 67 and 70, I follow GZ *'go ba* against CDNP *dgod pa* ("laugh," "establish," "formulate").
386. I follow GZ NP *rig byed bzhi* against CD *rigs byed gzhi* ("ground of Vedas"). As

Samuel 2008 (154) points out, at the time of the Buddha, there was a variety of brahmans: traditional village-dwelling brahmans, urban brahmans (perhaps spiritual teachers of new ritual practices for householders), semirenunciate brahmans in settlements outside of towns and villages, and fully fledged brahmanic renunciates who had abandoned their householder lifestyle and internalized their sacred fires. The latter brahmans were part of a common pan-Indic spiritual environment with many teachings and practices that were at least partly shared between different brahmanical and nonbrahmanical approaches.

387. "One with a single staff" (Skt. *ekadaṇḍin*) is the generic name for a class of Sannyāsins, divided into four orders: Kuṭīcaka, Bahūdaka, Haṃsa, and Parahaṃsa. More specifically, it indicates followers of Śaṅkarācārya's Advaita Vedanta school (Daśanāmi Saṃpradāya) and the Uttara-Mīmāṃsakas. "One with three staffs" (Skt. *tridaṇḍin*) refers to another type of Sannyāsin who holds three long bamboo staves tied together as one (symbolizing their command over body, speech, and mind). More specifically, this expression refers to the followers of Bhaṭṭabhāskara's Bhedābheda Vedānta, Rāmānuja's Viśiṣṭādvaita Vedānta, or the Pūrva-Mīmāṃsakas. Thus, though *tridaṇḍin* is interpreted as "one with a trident" by some Tibetan commentaries and translated that way by some contemporary authors, the term does not refer to the well-known ascetic followers of Śiva or Viṣṇu who carry a trident (*triśūla* or *triśikha*).

388. GZ CDNP *legs ldan gzugs* ("the form of the Bhagavān"; "Bhagavān" here being an epithet of the god Śiva/Maheśvara) is a somewhat unusual Tibetan rendering of DKPA *bhaavaṃvesem*, probably to avoid any conflation with the term "Bhagavān" as an epithet of Buddha Śākaymuni.

389. I follow DKPA *viṇuā hoiai haṃsauesem* against the entirely corrupt GZ CDNP *tha dad pa dang dad pas bsten* [CDNP *bstan*] *pa* ("being different and serving/teaching with faith"; probably mistaking *viṇuā* for Skt. *vinu* or *vinunna* and confusing Tib. *ngang pa* and *bstan pa* with the similar-looking *dad pa* and *bsten pa*, respectively). Besides its plain literal meaning "goose," Skt. *haṃsa* is also used as a metaphorical term for the soul or the spirit, which is considered similar to a goose in that it is of pure white color and migratory. The term *haṃsa* is sometimes also understood as the "Universal Soul" or "Supreme Spirit," variously identified with Virāj, Nārāyaṇa, Viṣṇu, Śiva, Kāma, and the sun. In this sense, *haṃsa* can be seen as incorporating or representing the Upaniṣads' famous statement of the individual soul or self (Skt. *ātman*) being fundamentally identical with the cosmic spirit (Skt. *brahman*): "I am that" (Skt. *so 'ham* or *ahaṃ saḥ*), which is thus called "the haṃsa mantra" (*so* and *haṃ* are mentally recited during inhalation and exhalation, respectively). In addition, *haṃsa* can refer to one of the vāyus or the movement of the vāyus in the central nāḍī, as well as a certain kind of ascetic. Note here that the Sanskrit term *haṃsa* is often translated into English as "swan," mostly because it sounds more poetic than "goose" to Western ears. However, the Sanskrit term clearly refers to a special type of white wild goose that is common in India (swans are not indigenous to India, though a few species of swans are listed in ornithological checklists as vagrant birds in a small number of places in India).

390. I follow GZ *mi shes par mnyam* against CDNP *shes par mi mnyam* ("not alike in knowing").
391. DKPA *airiehim* (understood by most modern authors as Skt. *ācārya* or maybe *ārya*) *uddūlia cchāreṃ* is rendered as GZ CD *e ra'i thal ba* . . . NP *i ri thal ba*, as if *airiehiṃ* and *cchāreṃ* belong together, thus meaning some kind of ashes. The Sanskrit of Advayavajra's *Dohakoṣapañjikā* first quotes *airiehiṃ* and then refers to it as "*ayiri*" but does not explain it, while its Tibetan version (text 66) appears to gloss *airiehiṃ* as *slob dpon gyis* ("master"). However, following the Tibetan, the *Dohakoṣahṛdayārthagītāṭīkā* glosses "*eri* ashes" as the ashes of cow dung or human bones. Text 70 and Rigpé Raltri (https://library.bdrc.io/show/bdr:UT3JT13307_008_0000; the electronic text does not show any page numbers, so this link will not be repeated in the following references to Rigpé Raltri's text) say that this refers to the ashes of having cremated a brahman's corpse ('Ju mi pham rgya mtsho 1984, 763: "the ashes of having cremated a corpse and so on"). According to Lingjé Repa, Barpuwa, the Third Karmapa (Grub thob gling ras, Par phu ba blo gros seng ge, Karma pa rang byung rdo rje 2011, 34, 212, 373), and KTP (13–14), it is a mix of the ashes of having burned cow dung that has not fallen to the ground and the ashes of human bones, which, when smeared onto the body, give it a light blue color.
392. GZ *bsgos* CDNP *byugs*.
393. GZ *sbar* CDNP *gtang*.
394. GZ CDNP *khyo med* generally means "a woman without a husband or bridegroom," but DKPA *raṇḍī* clearly means "widow." CDNP *skra med* literally means "without hair, bald" and does not indicate the sex, but DKPA *muṇḍī* clearly refers to a woman with a shaved head (usually a nun).
395. GZ CDNP *nam mkha'i yid can* (the same term occurs in stanza 10); DKPA *khavana* (Skt. *kṣapaṇaka*; obviously misread as *khamana* in GZ CDNP) means "one who fasts," "one who is abstinent," "one who chastises the body," and thus "religious mendicant," especially a Jaina mendicant who wears no garments. According to KTP and other Tibetan commentaries, here the term refers to the Jainas, whereas in stanza 10 it refers to tīrthikas in general. Guenther 1993 (160n7) remarks that the derisive term *nam mkha'i yid can* refers to the Jainas' belief that the self is as encompassing as space.
396. CDNP omit this line.
397. While DKPA *niambaha* refers to a woman shaving off the hair of her private parts, which is a custom of low-caste women in India, the Tibetan phrasing is rather vague and neutral.
398. DKPA here says *tā kariha turaṅgaha* ("then [also] elephants and horses [would be free]"), glossed by the equivalents *hastyaśvāṇāṃ* in Advayavajra's *Dohakoṣapañjikā*. Obviously, the use of Tib. *g.yag* in text 13 here (as well as in the corresponding stanza 13 of text 70) is a classical Tibetanism. Though this animal (bos grunniens; called *camaraha* in Sanskrit) was also known and domesticated in the mountains of northern India in ancient times (as it is in smaller numbers today) and its tail was used as a fly whisk by royalty, the elephant and horse are classical Indian stock examples of animals. Differing from the Sanskrit of Advayavajra's *Dohakoṣapañjikā*, its Tibetan version (text 66) and the *Dohanidhikoṣaparipūrṇagītināmanijatattvaprakāśaṭīkā* (text 70) also read "peacocks and

yaks," while Mokṣākaragupta's *Dohakoṣapañjikā* (text 67) and the *Dohakoṣahṛdayārthagītāṭīkā* neither cite nor comment on the stanza that contains this line.

399. Śrāmaṇeras are Buddhist male novices, bhikṣus are fully ordained monks, and sthaviras ("elders") are those who have upheld the bhikṣu vows for ten or more years.

400. I follow GZ *'dug* against CDNP *'jug* ("enter").

401. CDNP omit this line, but it is obviously just a slight reformulation of the preceding one.

402. DKPA *dhāvai/dhāviu* CDNP *rgyug byed* GZ *rgyur byed* (this is probably an abbreviation of *rgyu bar byed*; literally "taking as the cause").

403. I follow GZ *gzhan dag stong nyid lta bar byed pa ste* against CDNP *gzhan yang stong nyid ldan par byed pa de* ("others are endowed with emptiness").

404. GZ CDNP *cig shos* ("the other one" in a pair) is a rather misleading rendering of DKPA *ekka* ("one," "single"; text 66: *gcig kyang*).

405. GZ *de la ci bya gsang sngags bsten pa gang zhig gis* NP *de la ci bya gsang sngags brten pa gang zhig gis* CD *de la ci bya gsang sngags bstan pa ci zhig dgos* ("What's the point of that? What's the need for the teachings of secret mantra?").

406. GZ *rdzun pas log pa* CDNP *rdzun zhing log pa* ("lies and falsities").

407. Following DKPA *satthapurāṇeṃ*, the obvious typo GZ CDNP *snying* ("heart") is emended to *rnying* (= *purāṇa*). This minor typo, which must have occurred early on in the Tibetan transmission, results in a completely different meaning of this line ("explaining the treatises in the heart is it too") that is retained in all presently known Tibetan versions as well as in all Tibetan commentaries, which explain this line accordingly. "Purāṇa" (lit. "ancient") refers to a vast genre of Indian literature, found in both Hinduism and Jainism, about a wide range of topics, primarily myths, legends, and other traditional lore, but also cosmogony, cosmology, genealogies of divine beings, demigods, kings, heroes, and sages, as well as materials on theology, philosophy, pilgrimage, temples, medicine, astronomy, grammar, mineralogy, and even humor and love stories. The Hindu Purāṇas are anonymous and difficult to date, while most Jaina Purāṇas can be dated and their authors identified. Traditionally, in Hinduism, there are eighteen Purāṇas ("the Mahāpurāṇas"). In addition, there are also the eighteen "Minor Purāṇas" as well as a large number of "local Purāṇas" or "magnifications" that glorify temples or sacred places and are recited during the services at those locations.

408. According to Maitrīpa's biographies, with occasional variations, lines 21ab (preceded by stanza 42 and followed by Saraha's *Dohakoṣanāmamahāmudropadeśa* 35cd) are incorporated in what Śavaripa sang when he granted empowerment to Maitrīpa.

409. GZ *bus pas* CDNP *byis pas*.

410. I follow CDNP *'khrul pas byis pa (b)slus* against GZ *'khrul pa bus pas bslus* ("delusion is deceived by childish beings").

411. I follow GZ *nga* against CDNP *da* ("now").

412. Following text 66, text 70, and most Tibetan commentaries, GZ CDNP *shes pa yin* ("you do know") is emended to *shes pa min*.

413. With DKPA *gahaṇa guhira*, I follow CDNP *gsang mthon po* against GZ *gsong mthon po* ("loud and clear").

414. NP omit *med* ("no").

415. I follow GZ CD *rang yid* against NP *rang nyid* ("yourself").
416. The third and fourth lines in GZ (*rang bzhin dag pa'i sems nyid la / bsam gtan dag gis mi bslad de /*) are a single line in CDNP (*rang bzhin dag pa'i sems la bsam gtan dag gis mi bslad de /*).
417. With DKPA *suha acchanta*, GZ *bdag nyid de la gnas* CDNP *bdag gi de nyid bde la gnas* are emended to *bdag nyid bde la gnas*.
418. I follow GZ *gnyis sprod kyis* against CD *gnyid sprod kyis* ("by uniting with sleep") NP *gnyis sprod kyi*.
419. I follow GZ *mgo bor rdog pas mnan nas song* against CDNP *mgon por rdog pas mnan nas song* ("I went trampling on the protector").
420. Following DKPA *jahi . . . tahi* ("where . . . there"), GZ CDNP *gang du* is rendered "where" and not the grammatically possible "when" (GZ of text 66 reads *gang tshe* "when," which is followed by some Tibetan commentaries).
421. DKPA *pavaṇa* (Skt. *pavana*), GZ CDNP *rlung*. Skt. *pavana* can mean both "breath" and "vital air" in its technical sense that is otherwise denoted by "vāyu." Tib. *rlung* typically renders "vāyu," but can also mean "breath." Nevertheless, since Apa. *pavaṇa* is a different word from *vāyu*, throughout this text, I render *rlung* as "breath" (even in those stanzas that have no Apa. equivalent).
422. In accordance with the imperative *visāma karu* in DKPA, the imperative *gyis* in text 66, and CDNP *mi shes pa dag gnas de dbugs phyung zhig* [CD *cig*] ("fools, let that state find relief!"), GZ *mi shes pa dag gnas der sems ni dbugs dbyung zhing* ("fools let their minds find relief within that state and") is emended to . . . *zhig*.
423. I follow DKPA *ekku karu* and CDNP *gcig tu bya ba ste* (supported by text 67, text 70, and the *Dohakoṣahṛdayārthagītāṭīkā*) against GZ *gcig tu'ang mi bya ste* ("nor make it single"; also found in text 66).
424. GZ *kha dog 'gyur* CDNP *kha dog sgyur cig dang* ("dye them the color of this . . .").
425. I follow GZ *srid min mya ngan 'das pa min* against CDNP *ji srid mya ngan 'das pa min* ("as long as it is not nirvāṇa").
426. This stanza is very similar to *Hevajratantra* II.5.67, which is in Apabhraṃśa.
427. GZ *de ring da ltar 'khrul pa chad* CD *de ring nyid du mgon po da ltar 'khrul pa chad* ("Today, the protector now has cut through delusion") NP *de ring nyid du mgon pos de ltar 'khrul pa chad* ("Today, the protector has thus cut through delusion"). GZ of text 67 has *nga ltar* ("someone like me") instead of *da ltar*, as do almost all Tibetan commentaries.
428. I follow GZ NP *dris* against CD *bris* ("write," "draw").
429. GZ *dbang gang du nub gyur tsa na* CDNP *dbang po gang du nub gyur cing* ("Where the sense faculties vanish and").
430. GZ *de ni lhan cig skyes* CDNP *de ni lhan cig skyed pa'i lus* ("this constitutes the body of the connate").
431. Lines 32cd–33a are similar to lines I.10abd in text 183.
432. Lines 33ab have some resemblance with lines 7ab of Tilopa's *Dohakoṣa* (text 72).
433. In general, Tib. *mtshams*, here rendered as "borderline," renders a long list of Sanskrit words, each one of which in turn can mean a lot of different things, including "gap," "pause," "junction," "connection," "union," "critical juncture," "opportune moment," "interval," "twilight," "boundary (line)," and "retreat." Text 67 comments as follows: "The illumination of buddhahood is power, but since it has not been attained at present, the borderline between the

two [illuminations of ignorance and buddhahood] by way of the progression of the faculties refers to the [progressive] cultivation of luminosity by yogīs. [In other words,] 'borderline' refers to the full realization of the [ultimate] ground that has the character of luminosity." The *Dohakoṣahṛdayārthagītāṭīkā* (appendix 4 in volume 3) says: "The ultimate bindu is realized as the borderline between minding and nonminding." The terms "minding" and "nonminding" are the first two in Saraha's famous tetrad of minding (Tib. *dran pa*), nonminding (Tib. *dran med*), unborn (Tib. *skye med*), and beyond mind (Tib. *blo 'das*). The literal rendering and common meaning of *dran pa* would be "mindfulness," "recollection," or "memory." However, in a mahāmudrā context, especially in Saraha's dohās and some of their commentaries, as well as a number of stanzas in text 182 and others, this term often has the connotation of the dualistic mind's natural tendency to think, opine (it is also used with those two meanings in colloquial Tibetan), project, grasp, and cling. Thus I chose the rendering "minding," with its counterpart being "nonminding" (*dran med*). A literal rendering of *dran med* would be "lacking mindfulness" or even "being unconscious." However, in a mahāmudrā context, especially in Saraha's dohās and so on, this term has the positive connotation of mind completely letting go of its tendency to think, opine, project, grasp, and cling, similar to Maitrīpa's key term "mental nonengagement" (Skt. *amanasikāra*, Tib. *yid la mi byed pa*). Thus I chose the rendering "nonminding" (for details on minding, nonminding, unborn, and beyond mind, see the introduction to Saraha's tetralogy of vajra songs on body, speech, and mind—texts 53–56—in volume 3). Rigpé Raltri explains "borderline" in line 33c as follows: those who do not understand nonduality are fools in that regard and thus should fully realize it as the borderline of saṃsāra. According to Lingjé Repa (Grub thob gling ras, Par phu ba blo gros seng ge, Karma pa rang byung rdo rje 2011, 75), the present body is either realized or not realized by relying on this, thus being the borderline between saṃsāra and nirvāṇa. Barpuwa (ibid., 246) explains that the sky-like mind that is without any birth and death is to be known and realized as this very present mind that is the borderline between the past and the future. KTP (38), following the Third Karmapa, comments that when realization dawns through having bound the vital points of the elements, mind and the vāyus fade like clouds in the sky (not having gone anywhere whatsoever). This essential point is to be fully realized as the borderline between ignorance (foolishness) and nirvāṇa.

434. I follow CDNP *gti mug rgya mtsho 'chad pa gang shes pa* against GZ *gti mug rgya chad gang shes pa*, which can be understood as a brief form of CDNP, but on its own reads as "those who realize the fragmentation [or limitation] of nescience."
435. GZ CD *gtod* NP *sdod* ("remain," "dwell").
436. This line corresponds to line 91ab, as well as line 28b of text 58. It is also similar to line 22a of Saraha's *Body Treasure* (text 53).
437. I follow GZ *bla ma dam pa'i bka' yis bden par yid ches na* against CD *bla ma dam pa'i bka' yis bde bar yid ches par* ("trusting in bliss through the true guru's words") NP *bka' yi bde bar yid ches par* ("trusting in the bliss of the true guru's words").
438. These two lines are similar to lines 20ab of text 58.
439. GZ *gnyug ma'i yid la skyon gyis bus pa* CDNP *gnyug ma nyid la skyon gyis byis pa* (". . . about the native state . . .").

440. GZ *mtshon ma yin* CDNP *mtshon du med* ("cannot be perceived").
441. GZ *sems kyi rtsa bar rang bzhin mi mtshon te* CD *sems kyi rtsa ba min mtshon te* ("perceiving that it is not mind's root") NP *sems kyi rtsa ba mi mtshon te* ("not perceiving the root of mind").
442. According to text 67, the three aspects are perceiver, perceived, and perception, or what is to be expressed, means of expression, and their connection. The *Dohakoṣahṛdayārthagītā* identifies the three aspects of the connate as the connate of appearances, the connate of emptiness, and the connate of being unborn. KTP (43) says that the three aspects of the connate consist of the body as connate appearance-emptiness, speech as connate sound-emptiness, and mind as connate awareness-emptiness, or of appearances and emptiness being connate, emptiness and being unborn being connate, and being unborn and being beyond mind being connate.
443. GZ *thob* CDNP *mthong* ("see").
444. CDNP omit *tse ne* ("calmly").
445. I follow GZ NP *'khor ba* against CD *khro ba* ("anger").
446. GZ *sngags dang rgyud rnams kyis kyang ngas ma mthong* CDNP *sngags dang rgyud rnams gcig kyang ma mthong ngo* ("I do not even see a single mantra or tantra"). Compare stanza 31 of Saraha's "Queen Dohā." As mentioned before, according to Maitrīpa's biographies, with occasional variations, "People Dohā" 42 (followed by lines 21ab and Saraha's *Dohakoṣanāmamahāmudropadeśa* 35cd) is incorporated in what Śavaripa sang when he granted empowerment to Maitrīpa.
447. I follow GZ CD *las las* against NP *la las* ("some").
448. GZ *yid* CDNP *rgyud* ("mind stream").
449. I follow DKPA *mukkeṃ mukkei ṇātthi sandehā* and text 66 *grol bas grol ba the tshom med* against GZ CDNP *de nyid grol na the tshom med* ("if it becomes free, there is no doubt").
450. This stanza is very similar to stanza 53.
451. GZ *chos rnams kun kyang nam mkha mnyam par blta* CDNP *nam mkha'i rang bzhin nyid du sems bzung bya* ("Mind is to be grasped as having the very nature of space"). Lines 46ab and 47ab bear some resemblance with stanza 5 of Tilopa's *Dohakoṣa* (text 72).
452. GZ *sems de bsam gyis mi khyab bsam bya na* CDNP *yid de yid ma yin par byed 'gyur na* ("If this mind is rendered what is not mind"; this has its parallel in line 95d).
453. I follow GZ NP *mkha' 'drar* against CD *mkhas 'drar* ("erudite-like").
454. "The great mighty one" is an epithet of earth.
455. This stanza is almost identical with stanza 96.
456. I follow text 67, text 70, and *Dohakoṣahṛdayārthagītāṭīkā bsam yas ye shes bla med pa'o* against GZ CDNP *bsam pas ye shes bla med pa'o* ("wisdom is not surpassed by thinking").
457. I follow GZ CD *don rnams* against NP *don dam* ("ultimate").
458. I follow GZ NP *bya ba mi byed* against CDNP *bya ba min byed* ("doing what is not to be done").
459. GZ *mi 'ching mi gtong ngo* CDNP *'ching dang grol ba med* ("there's no bondage or freedom").
460. GZ *yi ge med par 'chad par yod 'jug par* CDNP *yi ge med las 'chad par yod 'dod pa* ("It is letterless, yet claiming it to be explainable").

461. These two lines are very similar to lines 105cd of Saraha's *Body Treasure* (text 53).
462. GZ *rtsol* CDNP *rtsom*.
463. I follow GZ *btang bar gyur na* against CD *mthong bar gyur na* ("If it is seen") NP *thongs sar gyur na*.
464. I follow GZ *de ltar rang la 'tshol te ltos* against CD *rang la cher te ltos* NP *rang la char te ltos* (some Tibetan commentaries read *cher te* as *gcer te* "nakedly").
465. GZ *dbang pos* (confirmed by text 67 and the comments in most Tibetan commentaries) CDNP *dbang po* (at least the *Dohakoṣahṛdayārthagītāṭīkā* takes this to mean "at the sense faculties").
466. I follow GZ *rtogs* against CDNP *gtogs* ("included").
467. I follow CDNP *zin* against GZ *byin* ("given").
468. As used in line 55d, CDNP *sems thag chod* usually means "resolve one's mind," "determine," "come to a firm decision," and "make up one's mind" (Tib. *thag chod pa* also renders Skt. *chinna* "cut (off)," "cut through," "interrupt," as well as *vighāta* "break off" or "in pieces," "destroy," "remove," "interrupt"). Text 66 does not mention this stanza. Text 67 glosses *sems thag gcod pa* as GZ *rtogs pa thag gcod pa* ("resolving realization") CDNP *rtog pa thag gcod pa* ("resolving thoughts" or "cutting through thoughts"). In line with GZ's gloss, text 70 (lines 73cd) says, "emphatically resolve your mind of realization before true reality!" On the other hand, the *Dohakoṣahṛdayārthagītāṭīkā*, in its comments on stanzas 54–55, first speaks about being bound by the rope of the mind and thus roaming saṃsāra, and then cutting the rope of the mind and thus ending such roaming. All Tibetan commentaries understand this expression as "resolve your mind," but most do not gloss it. However, those who do seem to attempt to incorporate both meanings. Rigpé Raltri says: "Before yourself—a person done with their deeds (who has cut through thoughts)—you need to resolve your thinking mind!" KTP (55) states: "Cut through all doubts in your mind until you have resolved your mind!" Mipham ('Ju mi pham rgya mtsho 1984, 775) says: "Seeing that there is nothing whatsoever to be done, before a person done with their deeds—self-arising cognizance—you need to resolve your mind by cutting though the entire web of your wishful thinking!"
469. I follow GZ NP *kye* against CD *skye* ("arise").
470. DKPA *kaṭṭhajoi ṇasāgga ma vaṃdaha* ("Wooden yogī, do not focus on the tip of your nose!") GZ CDNP *shing gi rnal 'byor sna rtser ma 'dug cig*. Though DKPA *joi* clearly means "yogī" and *rnal 'byor* could also be understood that way, text 66 (in both Sanskrit *kaṣṭena yogena* and the corresponding Tibetan) takes it to mean "yoga" (saying that "wooden yogas" means "Do not be attached to yogas that have the character of thinking!"), and this is also found in all other commentaries. According to text 67, *shing gi rnal 'byor* means that binding the vāyus is meaningless and "tip of the nose" refers to conceptual yogas, which are not the proper means. Rigpé Raltri does not explicitly mention *shing gi rnal 'byor* but speaks of "making the mind rigid." By contrast, Lingjé Repa, the Third Karmapa, and KTP all use the example of forcefully bending a tree (or a piece of wood), though in slightly different senses. Lingjé Repa (Grub thob gling ras, Par phu ba blo gros seng ge, Karma pa rang byung rdo rje 2011, 56–57) says that a tree, even when forcefully bent, goes back to being as it was

before. Likewise, even if the mind dwells on the nose tip of its focus when binding the vāyus, if true reality is lacking, mind's thoughts and so on will proliferate just as before (*shing* can mean "wood," "piece of wood," or "tree," but going back to being as it was before, and proliferate seems not to work for a piece of dry wood, unless it refers to a fresh branch). Similarly, KTP (56) says this is like forcefully bending a tree: "Yogīs who wish to rest in the connate, do not try to dwell in it by making binding the mind on the nose tips of the cakras the main thing! If you lack this means, thoughts will proliferate just as before." The Third Karmapa (Grub thob gling ras, Par phu ba blo gros seng ge, Karma pa rang byung rdo rje 2011, 407–8) says that even if the mind is settled in the dhyāna of the bliss that is based on the nāḍīs and vāyus on the paths of maturation or liberation, this is like forcefully bending a tree (or a piece of wood)—it will not (naturally) rest in the connate. Mipham ('Ju mi pham rgya mtsho 1984, 775) says not to dwell on the tip of your nose through the approach of yogas whose character is to be as immovable as a piece of wood—what's the point of meditating on subtle bindus and such on the nose tip? Text 70 has a completely different interpretation: "'Wood' refers to the nature of uncontaminated native wisdom: its arising and growing ripens the fruition. This is not the sphere of beginners, so don't think of the equality of the wisdom of this yoga by directing your thoughts at your nose's tip and so on!" As some of these comments show, often in tantric texts, instead of the more obvious meaning of phrases such as "meditating on the tip of the nose" and "resting the mind on the tip of the nose," they refer to the mind being focused on the cakras along the avadhūtī, on the lower part or end of the avadhūtī, or on the secret space of a visualized deity couple (the nonduality of prajñā and means), employing techniques of working with vāyus and bindus (such as caṇḍālī). In particular, the explanatory tradition of the *Guhyasamājatantra* speaks of the upper nose tip of the face, the middle nose tip of the heart cakra, and the lower nose tip of the secret place (which is obviously what the commentary here refers to); for details, see Thurman 2010 (63, 167, 173–74, 187–88, 223–24, 231–32, 278–80, 283–84, 287–89, 293, 298, 309, 328, 389), and Kittay and Jamspal 2020 (67–69).

471. GZ *ma yengs* CDNP *ma yin* ("that's not it").

472. GZ *'di ni yid dang rlung ni g.yo phyir phyar / shin tu mi srun pa yi rta 'dra thong / lhan cig skyes pa'i rang bzhin rtogs gyur na / de yis yid ni brtan par 'gyur ba yin* CD *'di ni yid 'dus pa la rlung gi rlabs / g.yo zhing phyar la shin tu mi srun 'gyur / lhan cig skyes pa'i rang bzhin rtogs gyur na / de yis bdag nyid brten par 'gyur ba yin* [NP . . . *de yi bdag nyid brtan par gyur pa yin*]:

> This is the collected mind where the vāyus' flow
> is moving and surging, becoming very unruly
> If the nature of the connate has been realized,
> its character will thereby be relied upon (NP "its character has
> become unwavering").

473. GZ *gang la lhan cig skyes pa ro mnyam pa / de la rmongs* [em. *dman*] *rigs dang ni bram ze med* / CDNP *gang tshe lhan cig . . . / de tshe dman pa'i rigs dang . . . /* ("When there is . . . then there are neither . . ."). In descending order of hierarchy, the four Indian Castes (Skt. *varṇa*, lit. "color," "class") consist of Brahmans

(priests), Kṣatriyas (also called rājanyas; rulers, administrators, and warriors), Vaiśyas (artisans, merchants, tradesmen, and farmers), and Śūdras (laboring classes). The *varṇa* system came to implicitly have a fifth category, consisting of those people who are considered to be outside of its scope (Skt. *avarṇa*), such as tribal people and the so-called untouchables.

474. In the second and third lines of this stanza, I follow DKPA *jamuṇa etthu se gaṅgāsāaru / etthu paāga vaṇārasi* against the largely corrupt GZ *'di la yang na ganggā'i rgya mtsho dang / wā rā ṇā sī sra ya ga ya ti* / CDNP *'di ni* [NP *na*] *ganggā'i rgya mtsho nyid dang ni / bā rā* [NP *ba ra*] *ṇa sī sra ya gha ya ti* (based on the corruption at the end that has no equivalent at all in DKPA, some Tibetan commentators mention an additional location: "Ghayati"). "The Ocean of the Moon" seems to refer to the mythical Moon Lake (Skt. Candrasaras), a sacred place mentioned in the *Nīlamatapurāṇa*. The *Pañcatantra* (III.1) and the *Kathāsaritsāgara* (112.29), collections of Indian legends, fairy tales, and folk tales, also speak about a Moon Lake. According to KTP (58), "The Ocean of the Moon" is a lake in the west of Jambudvīpa, which has its name because its water and the light of the full moon fuse, so that the color of the water becomes like that of the moon (possibly Candra Tal [Moon Lake] in Spiti, Himachal Pradesh (32.47518°N 77.61706°E); text 70 provides a rather different description). The Yamunā is the main tributary of the Ganges, and these two rivers sacred to all Hindus are said to be the homes of the goddesses Yamunā and Gaṅgā, respectively. Bathing in either river is believed to purify bad karma. "The Ganges Ocean" refers to the estuary of the Ganges entering the Bay of Bengal, which is also considered an important pilgrimage site in Hinduism. Vārānasī and Prayāga are the two most important land-based pilgrimage sites in the Yamunā-Ganges river system. Prayāga (now Allāhābād) is the place where the Yamunā joins the Ganges (as well as the mythical underground Sarasvatī river); as another major pilgrimage site, it is one of the four places where every twelve years one of India's largest religious festivals, a kumbhamelā, occurs. "Illuminator" (DKPA *divāaru*, Skt. *divākara*, Tib. *gsal byed*) is an epithet of the sun.

475. GZ *lus dang dran pa'i mu na gnas pa'i mtsho*, which is also found in text 67. CDNP *lus dang 'dra ba'i mu gnas gzhan na med* ("a pilgrimage site like the body exists nowhere else"), which all Tibetan commentaries follow, is closer to DKPA *dehasarisaa titha maiṃ suha aṇṇa ṇa dīṭhṭhao* ("I have not seen any other pilgrimage site as blissful as the body").

476. With the *Dohakoṣahṛdayārthagītāṭīkā* and text 70, I follow CDNP *dge ba nga yis yang dag* against GZ *dge ba nga yis gang dag* ("any virtues that I see . . .").

477. CDNP omit the last two lines. For comments on these two lines, see text 70 on the identical two final lines of its stanza 81.

478. I follow GZ *snal ma* against CDNP *rnal ma* ("natural(ness)") because it fits better with the analogy of a lotus and its parts. This is supported by texts 66 (though there is no comment on *snal ma*) and 70, while the *Dohakoṣahṛdayārthagītāṭīkā* has CD *rnal ma* NP *snal ma*, and text 67 does not mention either word. Most Tibetan commentaries read *rnal ma* and comment accordingly. The long DKPA compound *saṇḍapuaṇidalakamalagandhakesaravaraṇālem* only roughly corresponds to the first two lines here and shows no equivalent for "in

the middle" and "filament" (unless its possible equivalent *kesara* ("anthers") is rendered twice, since Tib. *ge sar* is already an unambiguous rendering).

479. In line with DKPA *chaḍḍahu veṇima ṇa karahu . . . vaḍha*, I follow GZ *bye brag bor cig rmongs pa . . . gdung bas* against CDNP *bye brag 'ongs shing rmongs pa . . . gdung ba'i* [commented on as *gdung bas* in all Tibetan commentaries] ("distinctions come and fools are tormented by such misery; do not let that annihilate the fruition!").

480. Trilocana ("the one with three eyes") is an epithet of the god Śiva.

481. GZ *gang du tshangs pa khyab 'jug mig gsum dang / 'jig rten ma lus thams cad gzhir gyur pa /* CDNP *gang tshe tshangs pa . . .* NP *gang tshe tshangs pa khyab 'jug mig gsum / 'jig rten ma lus gzhir gyur pa /* ("when . . ."). Here, *gang du* has no equivalent in DKPA and *gzhir gyur pa* appears to be a misrendering of DKPA *ṇilīṇao* ("Brahmā, Viṣṇu, Trilocana, and the entire world disappear"), which corresponds to *zhir gyur pa* in texts 66 and 70. However, the *Dohakoṣahṛdayārthagītāṭīkā* and all Tibetan commentaries also read *gzhir gyur pa* and comment accordingly.

482. It seems that the last two lines in GZ CDNP *rigs med* [NP *mig med*] *de la mchod na las yi yang / mtha' yi tshogs ni yang dag zad par 'gyur /* are very corrupt forms of DKPA *kāma tattha* [Shahidullah 1928 *kāma manta sattha*] *khaya jāi pucchaha jagu kulahīṇao* (the first line of the corresponding stanza 50 in DKPA): *kāma* ("desire") appears to have been misread as Skt. *karma (las)*, *pucchaha* ("ask") as some form of Skt. *pūj* ("revere," "offer"), and *hīṇao*, which can mean "inferior," "deficient," "bad," or "without," as the latter. In any case, I here follow GZ CD *rigs med* ("no family") against NP *mig med* ("without eyes"). KTP (61) comments that, in terms of the literal meaning, the tīrthikas assert that Brahmā, Viṣṇu, and Trilocana serve as the foundation of the entire world because they have created it. In terms of the hidden meaning, in the context of ascertaining the basic nature, Brahmā refers to ignorance, Viṣṇu to hatred, and Trilocana to desire. These three mental poisons serve as the foundation of the entire world because we are bound in saṃsāra by accumulating various karmas through those three. Some tīrthikas claim that one attains liberation if one worships those three gods without any bias as being inseparable. Here, however, the intention behind this is to cut off saṃsāra at its root through the path of the native state. Thus "the one who has no family" refers to Vajradhara, who resides as the ground that is of one taste as dharmatā (suchness) and has no different "families" or types (*rigs*) of the three poisons. If the worship of true reality, in which what is worshipped and the worshipper are nondual, is offered to him during both meditative equipoise and subsequent attainment, the host of actions' outcomes that has been accumulated since beginningless lifetimes fully vanishes in the very instant of realization.

483. GZ *rtsod pa'i ro ni dga' bar yang dag gnas shes pa* CDNP *rtsod pa'i ro ni dag par yang dag gnas shes pa* ("knowing that the taste of debate truly abides in purity").

484. GZ has the second line as two lines, but I follow the format of CDNP. This is a rather cryptic stanza that is entirely different from DKPA and thus does not appear as such in texts 66 and 67. Text 70 has yet another variant version, while the *Dohakoṣahṛdayārthagītāṭīkā* is the only commentary in Tg that has this stanza as it appears here. It can certainly be read in more than one way, as also

attested by the different explanations in Tibetan commentaries. My rendering follows KTP's comments.

485. CDNP *de nyid sna tshogs kyis / ro 'di bstan par nus pa ma yin te /* ("through the diversity of true reality, this taste is not anything that could be taught") GZ *de nyid sna tshogs kyis / ro 'di bstan par bzod pa ma yin te* ("through the diversity of true reality, this taste isn't anything that bears/endures to be taught"). The beginning of the Tibetan is a rather literal but ambiguous rendering of DKPA *tatto vicittarasa* ("the wonderful taste of true reality"; *vicitra* also has a lot of other meanings, such as "diverse," "variegated," "manifold," "colorful," "surprising," "lovely," and "charming," but also "strange"); my rendering of this follows DKPA. More correctly but still ambiguously, texts 66 and 70 as well as the *Dohakoṣahṛdayārthagītāṭīkā* read *de nyid sna tshogs kyi / ro* (text 67 does not mention these two lines). Accordingly, text 70 and the *Dohakoṣahṛdayārthagītāṭīkā*, as well as all Tibetan commentaries, comment by treating *sna tshogs* as an attribute of *de nyid* ("the diversity of true reality") instead of *ro*.

486. This rather cryptic line is a misrendering of DKPA *varajagu uajjai tatthu* ("the best of worlds arises there"), linking *vara* with "state of bliss" and obviously misunderstanding *tatthu* ("there") as Skt. *tathā* ("like"). Thus this line is commented on in all kinds of creative ways by different Tibetan commentaries. Surprisingly, text 67 also has this line as it stands, commenting that uncontaminated bliss is born similar to a child being born from his or her mother.

487. GZ *rab zhi ba* CDNP *pham gyur pa* ("has been defeated").

488. GZ *rab zhi na* CDNP *rang bzhin na* ("has a nature just like space").

489. GZ *gdod nas skye med rang bzhin yin pa la / de ring dpal ldan bla ma mgon pos bstan pa yi / dbye ba rnam spangs de la gnas par byos* / CDNP *gdod nas skye med rang bzhin yin pa la / de ring dpal ldan bla ma bstan pas rtogs /* ("Within what is the nature of being originally unborn, this is realized today through the teachings of the glorious guru!").

490. GZ *zas skom 'chams* CDNP *za snom 'khyam* ("eating, smelling, wandering . . .").

491. GZ *sems so zhe na* [em. *zhes ni*] *rnam pa gcig las mi spyod* CDNP *sems so zhe na rnam pa gcig la* [NP *las*] *mi bskyod* ("do not waver from the single trait . . .").

492. Interestingly, the exact same version of stanza 68 as it is found here in GZ CDNP (which is more elaborate than DKPA) is quoted in the *Samādhisambhārapaṭala* (D3924, fol. 83a.1) by Bodhibhadra (one of Atiśa's teachers). This text also cites lines 79cd, curiously attributing both to a *don dam pa'i rigs pa* (**Paramārthayukti*). Obviously referring to his teacher's attribution, Atiśa likewise cites stanza 68 (with slight variations) in his *Bodhimārgapradīpapañjikā* (D3948, fol. 274a.4–5) under the same title, adding Saraha as its author. In addition, stanza 68 is echoed in Atiśa's *Saṃsāramanoniryāṇīkāranāmasaṃgīti* (D2313, fol. 254a.7–254b.1).

493. I follow NP *bstan pa* against GZ CD *bsten pa* ("rely on"). This stanza resembles stanza 10 of Tilopa's *Dohakoṣa* (text 72). As Schaeffer (2005, 203n11) points out, this stanza is also found in the oldest available manuscript of a fragmentary dohā text attributed to Saraha (not included in Tg). Szántó reports (email communication) that, with some variants, Tilopa's *Dohakoṣa* 10 is also found as stanza 77 of an alternative version of Saraha's *Dohakoṣa* edited in Sāṃkṛtyāyana 1957 (18), as well as twice in Bagchi 1935a (7, 28), likewise attributed to Saraha.

Furthermore, the beginning of this stanza here is cited in the *Caryāgītikoṣavṛtti* (text 90, 398) and ascribed to Saraha.

494. I follow CD *tshad mar 'dzin pa'i dbang gis su* NP *gang gis tshad mar 'dzin pa'i dbang gis su* against GZ *gal te tshad mar 'dzin pa'i dbang gis su* ("If, under the sway of clinging . . .").

495. In translations from Indic materials, Tib. *lhun gyis grub pa* usually renders Skt. *anabhoga* ("effortless"; such as in effortless buddha activity), and it could definitely be understood in that way here. However, when regarded on its own from a Tibetan perspective, BGTC (512 and 3107) explains *lhun* to mean "natural state," "power," or "nature" (*ngang ngam shugs sam rang bzhin*), while *'grub pa* (intransitive verb; past tense *grub pa*) means "to be well finished, completed, or accomplished," "to exist," "to abide," "to be established," or "to occur" (*legs par tshar ba dang / chags pa and yod pa dang / gnas pa'am 'byung ba*). Thus *lhun gyis grub pa* is explained as "accomplished/established/existing effortlessly by nature" (*'bad med rang bzhin gyis grub pa*). The most commonly used English translation of this term is clearly "spontaneous presence" (especially in a Dzogchen context). However, "spontaneous" for *lhun gyis* is somewhat problematic because its English definitions either refer to (1) being performed or occurring as a result of a sudden inner impulse or inclination and without premeditation or external stimulus (thus often involuntarily), or (2) involving some form of arising, growing, or being produced. In its technical use in Tibetan Buddhist texts, this term obviously does not refer to spontaneous, unplanned, or involuntary actions due to sudden impulses, nor does it refer to any kind of arising, growing, or being produced. Rather, the point is usually that mind's true nature (including its innate qualities of luminosity and so on) is naturally and intrinsically complete and perfect without any need for increasing or improving anything through any kind of method or effort. This also seems to be what is meant here, since Lingjé Repa, the Third Karmapa (Grub thob gling ras, Par phu ba blo gros seng ge, Karma pa rang byung rdo rje 2011, 67, 416), and KTP (66) all gloss *lhun grub* as "not produced by any causes and conditions." Lingjé Repa says that the native nature of mind itself abides in an immovable manner, since it is not stirred up by any flaws. Since it does not adopt, reject, accomplish, or stop anything with regard to saṃsāra and nirvāṇa, it abides in an equanimous manner. Since it is not produced by any causes and conditions, it abides in an innately present manner. KTP considers these three features as the three ways or qualities that characterize resting in the natural state of the native true reality of one's own mind. Thus, though "not produced by any causes and conditions" certainly also entails being effortless, the main point is clearly not being produced or created, and thus being "innately present." Similarly, Barpuwa (Grub thob gling ras, Par phu ba blo gros seng ge, Karma pa rang byung rdo rje 2011, 278) says that to rest in native uncontrived mind as such means that through letting naturally immovable dharmatā be as the equanimity that consists of the dhyāna of nothing to adopt and nothing to reject, mahāmudrā is innately present (thus this is resting in innately present mahāmudrā). Since stanza 72 is only found in the Tibetan version of Saraha's text, I follow the above interpretation.

496. CDNP omit *gus* "respect."

497. CDNP switch "letters" and "qualities."
498. Tib. *dbang phyug dam pa* renders DKPA *paramesaru* (Skt. *parameśvara*), a decidedly Hinduist term meaning "supreme lord," "supreme being," or "supreme god." In that sense, the term is an epithet of Śiva, Viṣṇu, and Indra. It can also refer to any eminent royalty or illustrious person. Obviously, Saraha uses this theistic term not in the sense of an external god or person but as a deliberate and provocative (to both Buddhists and Hindus) epithet of the connate.
499. GZ *gang / der* CDNP *dang / der*.
500. GZ *gang tshe yid ni mi g.yo rab gnas brtan par bya* CD . . . *mi g.yo rang gnas brtan pa ste* NP . . . *brtan pa de* ("When mind is motionless, resting in itself, and steady").
501. GZ *gang tshe bdag gzhan yongs su shes med na / de tshe bla med lus su grub pa nyid* / CDNP *gang tshe bdag gzhan yongs su shes med ni / de tshe bla med lus ni thob par 'gyur* / (". . . will the unsurpassable body be attained?"). DKPA *jāva ṇa appahiṃ para pariāṇasi* is tricky because *para* can mean "other" as well as "highest" or "supreme." The Sanskrit *yāvan nātmānaṃ paramutkṛṣṭaṃ tattvarūpaṃ parijānāsi* of text 66 clearly glosses this line in the latter sense: "As long as you do not realize yourself as the supreme consummate nature of true reality . . ." (text 66: *ji srid bdag gis phul du bung ba de kho na nyid ma rtogs pa*, "As long as you yourself do not realize consummate true reality . . ."). However, all other commentaries interpret *bdag gzhan* as "self and other," often explicitly inserting "and" between them. Text 67, text 70, and Rigpé Raltri say that thoughts about self and other have been relinquished, are not perceived, and are absent, respectively. The *Dohakoṣahṛdayārthagītāṭīkā* says that it is due to mind and mental factors that a self and what is mine seem to exist, but no such two entities are actually established. Ultimately, buddhahood is not established as any referent that is a self. Therefore, when self and other are perceived no more, the vanishing of minding is the attainment of the body of the unsurpassable nirmāṇakāya. According to Lingjé Repa (Grub thob gling ras, Par phu ba blo gros seng ge, Karma pa rang byung rdo rje 2011, 68), this refers to being free of the thoughts of perceiver and perceived. Barpuwa (ibid., 281) states that mahāmudrā, the native state, is not perceived as self or other. The Third Karmapa (ibid., 418) says that since oneself (the striving for peace) and what is other (saṃsāra) do not exist as being different, saṃsāric existence and peace are realized to not exist as two, and there is no more clinging. KTP (68) combines the above: perceiving oneself (having become a buddha) and others (those afflicted in saṃsāra) as not being different, by being free of thoughts of perceiver and perceived, saṃsāric existence and peace are realized to not exist as two. According to 'Ju mi pham rgya mtsho 1984, 780, not perceiving self and other means to see them as equal.
502. CDNP omit "I."
503. GZ *rang gis rang la legs par bstan te shes par byos* CDNP *rang gis rang la legs par shes par byas nas ni* ("realizing it well by yourself within yourself").
504. GZ *yod* CDNP *gnas* ("dwells").
505. This line resembles line 11b of text 58.
506. GZ *gal te bla mas bstan zhing bden par thams cad shes byas kyang / bdag gis yongs su brtags pas ma rtogs thar pa rnyed dam ci* / CDNP *gang tshe bla mas bstan cing thams cad shes byas kyang / bdag gis yongs su brtags pas thar pa thob bam ci* / ("Even if

. . . you understand all of it, do you attain liberation by your own thoughts, or what?").

507. GZ *utpal blangs kyang chu yis mi reg* CDNP *utpal 'dab ma chu yis* [NP *yi*] *ma reg* ("the petals of an utpala not being touched by water"). According to Gyatso 2010 (578), Skt. *utpala* can refer to Meconopsis, of four varieties, white, blue, yellow, and red (Clark, Pasang): blue lotus, Nelumbo nucifera (Clark); species of Nymphaea, including white *kumuda*, Nymphaea lotus; blue *nilopala*, Nymphaea stellata; and red *raktopala*, Nymphaea rubra (Dutt). Here, since this refers to a flower in water, it must be either the blue lotus or one of the Nymphaea (Clark, Dutt, and Pasang are referenced by Gyatso).

508. GZ *gang yang 'di ltar rtsa ba skyabs su song* CDNP *gang ltar rtsa ba rnal 'byor skyabs su 'gro* ("The yogīs take their refuge in . . .").

509. GZ *bdag nyid 'ching 'gyur de yis ci zhig bya* CDNP *bdag nyid de yis* [NP *yi*] *'ching 'gyur ci zhig bya*.

510. GZ *'dir goms ma gtogs ma lus brgal ma yin* CDNP *gnyug ma'i rang bzhin ma rtogs* [NP *gtogs*] *ma lus rgal mi nus* ("not realizing the nature of the native state, you are not able to traverse it").

511. GZ *sems ni 'gags pa na* CDNP *sems kyang mi 'gog dang* ("The eyes . . . and the mind has not stopped") NP *sems 'gog dang* ("The eyes . . . and the mind has stopped").

512. GZ NP *rgyu* CD *rgyud*.

513. GZ *'chi ba* CDNP *'ching ba* ("being bound").

514. GZ *las ngan* CDNP *las med* ("nonkarma" or "inaction") both render DKPA *akammo* (Skt. *akarma*), which can have either of these meanings. Given the preceding line, it seems very clear that the former is meant here (as supported by Shahidullah's translation (1928) and Jackson's note (2004, 92). However, all Tibetan commentaries read *las med*, and most relate this to the preceding *rang nyid* ("there is nothing other than . . . itself"). The exceptions ignoring the negative in *las med* are Rigpé Raltri ("various bad karmas are performed through the vāyus") and the Third Karmapa ("For as long as there is clinging, innumerable karmas produce the result that is saṃsāra"; Grub thob gling ras, Par phu ba blo gros seng ge, Karma pa rang byung rdo rje 2011, 423).

515. GZ *da lta ci byed gar 'gro soms dang kye* CD *da ltar ci byed sam dang kye* NP *da lta ci byed soms dang kye* ("Think about what you are doing now, hey!").

516. GZ *glang chen lobs nas sems tshags tshud pa ltar* CD *glang chen . . . tshud pas na* ("Since mind . . .") NP *glang chen lam nas sems tshags chud pas na* ("Since mind is placid via the path of the elephant"). Text 66 does not mention this line, while text 67 comments on it as follows: "If a Śabara who makes his livelihood with elephants has trained an elephant, the trainer's mind is happy. Likewise, if mind's thoughts are let go, mind is placid because mind does not move." The *Dohakoṣahṛdayārthagītāṭīkā* also speaks of the placid mind of a person whose elephant has been trained, while text 70, the Third Karmapa, and KTP speak of the placid mind of a person who has managed to sell his elephant. Lingjé Repa (Grub thob gling ras, Par phu ba blo gros seng ge, Karma pa rang byung rdo rje 2011, 77) says that one's mind is naturally happy and relaxed once one has trained an elephant, since then there is no more need to dispel one's previous suffering due to lacking the wealth of such an elephant and no more

need to earn one's livelihood. According to Barpuwa (Grub thob gling ras, Par phu ba blo gros seng ge, Karma pa rang byung rdo rje 2011, 289–90), once the unruly elephant of thoughts has been trained within the state of thought-free samādhi, space-like unborn mind is placid. Thus it is clear in all these commentaries that "placid mind" does not refer to the elephant's mind. The only exception is Mipham's commentary ('Ju mi pham rgya mtsho 1984, 782), which says that the elephant's own mind is placid once it has been trained.

517. I follow GZ *de ni 'gro 'ong bcad nas dal ba ste* against CDNP *der ni 'gro 'ong chad nas* [NP *dang*] *ngal ba ste* ("having stopped coming and going there, it is tired"). Lines 84cd are very similar to lines 106cd in Saraha's *Body Treasure* (text 53).

518. GZ *de ltar ngo tsha med smra mkhas pa nga* CDNP *mkhas pa ngo tsha med pas de ma rtogs* ("Since the erudite are shameless, they do not realize this").

519. With texts 66 and 67, I follow GZ *bsten bya min* against CDNP *bstan bya min* ("isn't anything to be taught").

520. The last two lines of this stanza are very similar to lines 21ab of text 58 and line 106a of Saraha's *Body Treasure* (text 53).

521. I follow GZ *blta bar bya* against CDNP *bya bar byos* ("you must do as . . .").

522. GZ *de bzhin* CDNP *de srid* ("for that long").

523. This line corresponds to line 26d of text 58 and 1d of text 107. It is also echoed in lines 69bc of Saraha's *Body Treasure* (text 53).

524. I follow GZ *srid zhi mnyam nyid nam mkha'i rang bzhin no* against CDNP *srid dang mnyam zhing nam mkha'i rang bzhin no* ("This is existence, being equal, and the nature of space"). Texts 67 and 70, the *Dohakoṣahṛdayārthagītāṭīkā*, and all Tibetan commentaries read *srid dang nmyam nyid nam mkha'i rang zhin no* ("Existence and equality have the nature of space").

525. I follow DKPA *kāsu kahijjai ko suṇai* (*kāsu kahijjai* has its parallel in DKPA 58c; text 13, 74d). Read on its own, GZ *gang zhig bstan de gang thos pa* CDNP *gang zhig bstan te gang thos pa* could mean a number of things, such as "Who hears that which is taught?" "What is heard by what being taught?" "Who teaches? Who hears?" "What is taught? What is heard?" and "Who is taught? Who hears?" Different commentaries thus interpret *gang zhig* as referring to the one who teaches, the one who is taught, or what is taught, and *gang* to mean what is heard, by whom it is heard, or even where it is heard.

526. GZ *skyol ba ni* CDNP *skyol ba na* ("when the ultimate . . .").

527. GZ and CDNP all have more or less corrupt versions of DKPA *duṭṭha suruṅgādhūli jima* ("like dust in a damaged/collapsed tunnel"). Here, I follow GZ *gdug pa'i skungs sa sa yi rdul zhin brlag* (text 67: *gdug pa'i skungs sa rdul zhin brlag*) against CD *nyi zer lkugs pa sa yi rdul bzhin brlag* ("it is annihilated like dust motes when sun rays are blocked") and NP *nyi zer skugs sa rdul bzhin brlag* ("it is annihilated like dust [in] a gambling place" or "a gambling place is annihilated like dust"). Rigpé Raltri's commentary refers to luminous mind as "the gambling place (*skugs sa*) or hideout (*skungs sa*) of the afflictions." Though *lkugs pa* usually means "mute" or "stupid," Barpuwa (Grub thob gling ras, Par phu ba blo gros seng ge, Karma pa rang byung rdo rje 2011, 295–96) and KTP (79), all following CD, obviously understand it as "to block" (maybe in analogy to muting sound), saying that dust motes become invisible when the sun rays coming through a window are blocked.

528. Lines 91ab correspond to line 35f, as well as line 28b of text 58. They are also similar to lines 22ab of Saraha's *Body Treasure* (text 53).

529. GZ *mtshon ma gyur* CDNP *mthong mi 'gyur* ("not seen").

530. GZ *me 'bar* CDNP *me lce* ("flame").

531. GZ CD *sems kyi rtsa ba* NP *khyod kyi rtsa ba* ("your root").

532. GZ *gal te yid du 'ong ngam mnyam pa'i sems / snying la bab pa gces spras bya ba yi*. Line 93b in text 70 reads *gal te yid du 'ong ba mnyam pa'i sems* / ("Given this mind that is so equal in its pleasure") and comments: "Given . . . that [certain] yogīs are endowed with this mind that is equal in that its essence of lucidity, nonthought, bliss, and pleasure isn't anything whatsoever, those who realize this have the supreme mind of yogīs." Piecing the cited phrases in text 67 (which is usually followed by text 13) together, line 93b there reads *gal te yid du 'ong ba la mnyam pa'i sems* / ("Given this mind that is equal toward what is pleasurable"), and the text comments: "'Pleasurable' refers to entities that agree with the mind. As for 'this mind that is equal,' if the state of mind of [those pleasant entities] being of equal taste with emptiness does not arise, suffering is produced by clinging to them as being [real] entities." CDNP (followed by virtually all Tibetan commentaries) read *gal te yid du 'ong ngam snyam pa'i sems / snying la gces par byas na ni* ("If this mind that thinks, 'Is this pleasurable?' is cherished within your heart"; Rigpé Raltri, who usually also follows text 67, does not mention either *mnyam* or *snyam*). Barpuwa (Grub thob gling ras, Par phu ba blo gros seng ge, Karma pa rang byung rdo rje 2011, 298) and KTP (81–82) explain that if a mind that thinks "My own view and tenet is justified because it is pleasurable" is cherished by clinging within your heart, even a pain due to merely a sesame husk's worth of clinging always causes nothing but suffering. In his inner explanation, KTP also applies this to letting go of any clinging to meditative experiences such as bliss, lucidity, and nonthought. In his secret explanation, he says that this stanza is about realizing all phenomena from form up through omniscience without any clinging whatsoever. Should clinging arise, through the pith instructions on minding, don't grasp at any object by thinking it is pleasurable, unpleasurable, or neutral. Through the pith instructions on nonminding, determine the mind that grasps at that object to be empty as well. Through the pith instructions on being unborn, sustain what is held deep within your heart as real cognitions without the duality of perceiver and perceived to be the unborn that is real as the unity of appearance and emptiness. Through the pith instructions on being beyond mind, make this a living experience in the manner of fully resolving it while not even cherishing the mahāmudrā that is the basic nature.

533. GZ *de ltar yin no de ni ma yin no* CDNP *de ltar yin te de ltar ma yin no* (CDNP switch the first and second lines). That this line is far from clear is evidenced by different commentaries providing very different explanations. Without referring to pigs and elephants (the first line is not in DKPA), the Sanskrit of text 66 says: "Though [the connate] may be perceived as aspects of blue, yellow, red, and so on, or the essence of experiencing [them], it does not constitute such, because the two [kinds of] thoughts that have a focal object and do not have a focal object, and those that involve mind and are without mind, have the nature of all contaminated seeds lacking any basis." According to text 67, though pigs

and elephants are partially similar, pigs are not elephants. Likewise, though they are similar in being empty, the kinds of being empty that are conceived by other yānas are not the path. Rigpé Raltri follows this and adds that the awareness of this emptiness, in which all flaws dissolve within the empty mind itself, overcomes all delusion. Text 70 comments that the conduct of yogīs that is concordant with the dharma is similar to the behavior of pigs and so on, but it does not constitute full concordance with that, because it is meant to stop adverse factors. Just as pigs are free of thoughts, for yogīs, there is nothing clean or dirty about food and they are free of thoughts about such. Just as the minds of elephants cannot be changed and are firm, the minds of yogīs cannot be impaired by māras, tīrthikas, opponents, or inner and outer distractions and are firm. Barpuwa (Grub thob gling ras, Par phu ba blo gros seng ge, Karma pa rang byung rdo rje 2011, 299) says that pigs and elephants are similar in shape but not similar in qualities. Likewise, though spiritual friends who teach the native state of the connate and evil friends who teach the dharma of clinging to entities are similar in many respects, such as gathering retinues and giving explanations, there is a big difference between the dharma that teaches the path to liberation and the instructions of bad friends. Therefore you should abandon evil friends and rely on spiritual friends. The Third Karmapa (ibid., 430) explains that, ultimately, the nature of phenomena and the phenomena that bear this nature are inseparable, but experience and realization are not alike, just like the difference between pigs and elephants cannot be inferred just from some partial features. KTP (82–83) provides outer, inner, and secret comments about the difference between experience and realization. As for the outer explanation, though it is the case that subject and object are inseparable, the kind of appearance in which they appear as two is not the basic nature. Look at the difference between pigs and elephants, which is not pointed out just by some partial features! As for the inner explanation, the experiences of bliss, lucidity, and nonthought that arise in such ways have the nature of unstable seeming experiences, while the immutable view of realizing the basic nature is not like that. Though these experiences and realization are similar in being the mere reverse of the triad of suffering, dullness, and thoughts, there are very big differences between them in terms of overcoming versus not overcoming the seeds of the obscurations and so on. For example, look at the difference between pigs and elephants: though they are partially similar in their form, they are very different in their qualities and so on. No matter how much a pig may be fed, it is impossible for it to become an elephant. Likewise, it is impossible to become a buddha by practicing while clinging to experiences as being the awakened mind of a buddha. No matter how much an elephant may deteriorate and be flawed, it is impossible for it to become a pig. Likewise, once realization has dawned, it is impossible to circle in saṃsāra under the sway of karma and afflictions. As for the secret explanation, being similar refers to minding, but nonminding is not like that, and it is not being unborn. There is no difficulty by joining with being beyond mind. Mipham ('Ju mi pham rgya mtsho 1984, 784) says that "if you think, 'You should act like this but not act like that,' look at pigs and crazy elephants, for whom there is nothing clean or filthy, and let your focusing on reference points collapse!"

534. I follow CDNP *zhig pa* (supported by all Tibetan commentaries and the *Dohakoṣahṛdayārthagītāṭīkā*) against GZ *gzhig pa* ("is scrutinized"), which is also found in texts 66, 67 (GZ), and 70. By contrast, DKPA *ṇāsia* and text 67 (CDNP) *bshig pa* are causative ("the erudite who have destroyed delusion").

535. With DKPA *saasamvitti mahāsuha vāsia*, I follow GZ CD *rang la rang rig* against NP *rang la rang gis* ("in itself, by itself"). This line in DKPA can be read in more than one way, as its greatly differing translations by various authors show. In particular, *vāsia* can have many potential meanings: either Skt. *vāsita* ("dressed," "caused to dwell in," "scented," "influenced by," "infused," "steeped," "affected with," and "knowledge") or *vāśita* ("bellowed" or "desired"). However, the Sanskrit of text 66 seems to gloss it as *bhāśitam* ("said"). I would say something like: "Self-awareness is steeped in great bliss." GZ CD *rang la rang rig bde ba chen po'i bag chags gzugs* is even more cryptic (*vāsia* has obviously been misunderstood as Skt. *vāsanā*, while *gzugs* has no equivalent in DKPA). Thus the explanations of this line in different commentaries vary greatly, especially in interpreting *bag chags gzugs* as the propensities for great bliss itself (as the Tibetan suggests) versus the propensities for dualistic appearances. Text 66 reads *rang rig bde ba chen po'i bag chags kyis*, saying that great bliss is characterized by self-awareness, while not commenting on *bag chags kyis*. Text 67 (*rang rig bde ba chen po'i bag chags gzugs*) says that this line refers to the cause of great bliss. Or, if that bliss is not pure, it manifests as propensities, which are called "ignorance." If it is pure, it becomes form—that is, empty form. Text 70 comments: "[True reality] is not something that is attained from anywhere else: it is the great bliss that is aware by itself due to itself. This [bliss] appears in the form of propensities [manifesting] in the manner of appearances and mind." The *Dohakoṣahṛdayārthagītāṭīkā* says: "What is present within yourself should realize itself by itself: mind's luminous nature untainted by the stains of adventitious minding abides within the natural state of great bliss beyond mind that consists of the propensities for the uninterrupted dhyāna." Rigpé Raltri says that the propensities of the great bliss that is self-aware of itself exist like form. According to Lingjé Repa (Grub thob gling ras, Par phu ba blo gros seng ge, Karma pa rang byung rdo rje 2011, 80), through our own mind being aware of itself by itself, primordially present great bliss is seen; hence it is "the form of propensities." Barpuwa (ibid., 300) explains that since personally experienced wisdom is self-aware of itself, the nondual great bliss free of the pain of thoughts is experienced, and thus delusion—the form of propensities—collapses. The Third Karmapa (ibid., 430) says that there is freedom from clinging to a self by virtue of the great bliss that is self-aware of itself becoming manifest on the path of seeing. But on the path of familiarization with the form of the propensities for aspiration prayers, all phenomena are rendered equal to space. (Karma phrin las pa phyogs las rnam rgyal 2009, 83) synthesizes the last three explanations: "By attaining the path of seeing that consists of the primordially present wisdom of great bliss—our own mind being aware of itself by itself—becoming free in a personally experienced manner, the forms of propensities that appear as perceiver and perceived are purified. Since all phenomena are realized to be equal to space at that point, this represents one's own welfare. Since those to be guided are established in

realizations that are equal to space, this represents the welfare of others. In that way, both welfares are effortlessly promoted." Mipham ('Ju mi pham rgya mtsho 1984, 784) says: "This principle of great bliss, which is self-aware of itself and not realized from anywhere else, appears as all kinds of appearances in the form of propensities for appearances and mind, but if its nature is realized, at that point, all will be bliss equal to space."

536. GZ *smos su mi rung* CDNP *smos su ci rung* ("how could it be appropriate to speak about . . . ?"). The Sanskrit term *kālakūṭa* can refer to the name of a mountain in the Himālayas (the *Kathāsaritsāgara* mentions it as the home of the Vidyādhara King Madanavega), the name of a people, poison in general, a specific poison contained in a bulbous root, and the utterly deadly poison that was produced by the gods when churning the great ocean of milk. A traditional explanation of the latter meaning is that *kāla* ("time" or "black") refers to Yama (the lord of death) and *kūṭa* ("summit," "deceit," "trick," or "iron mallet") means "to destroy"; thus this poison is so toxic that it "even destroys Yama." Here, the term is a symbol for mind's true nature as understood in the dohās, which cannot and should not be expressed by any words. Just as a fun fact, in Swahili, "kalakuta" means "rascal." There is also the famous "Kalakuta Republic," the communal compound that housed the Nigerian musician and political activist Fela Kuti's family, his band members, a recording studio, and a free health clinic ("Kalakuta" was a parody on "The Black Hole of Calcutta," an infamous prison in Calcutta in which Fela had spent some time). In 1970, Fela declared this compound independent from the state of Nigeria ruled by a military junta. In 1977, however, the compound burned to the ground following an assault by one thousand armed soldiers.

537. GZ CDNP *rang bzhin lhan cig skyes pa* renders DKPA *sahajasahāveṃ* but switches the order of the two words of the compound. Both Tib. and DKPA can be understood as "the nature of the connate" or "the connate nature," while the Tibetan could also be read as "the natural connate" (as in some of the commentaries in the following note). Given the many parallel phrases "the nature of the connate" or "the nature that is the connate" elsewhere, this is the most likely meaning.

538. Compare stanza 31 of Saraha's "Queen Dohā." According to Rigpé Raltri, just as whoever consumes the poison kālakūṭa dies, in whomever the connate dawns, all their afflictions and thoughts are killed. Therefore the connate is spoken of by a name that represents a discordant example. That it is not appropriate to speak of it with words means that it is not understood thereby; rather, it is perceived by the mind that realizes its nature to be equal to space. Through that, all flawed states of mind become nonexistent, whereby the connate is beautiful and brave. Lingjé Repa (Grub thob gling ras, Par phu ba blo gros seng ge, Karma pa rang byung rdo rje 2011, 71) explains that when fresh experiences and realization arise, if one practices with them in secret, all that is needed and wished for will arise. But if something is not kept secret, it may become the cause of suffering, such as being punished by a king. Likewise, if one practices with experiences and realizations in secret, all siddhis will arise. But if these are not kept secret, they will turn into the causes of obstacles, such as being punished by the ḍākinīs. Or, if this actuality is not expressed in

words, realization will dawn from within. But if it is voiced, with the mind pursuing conventional expressions, realization will not dawn. Therefore it is not appropriate to speak about it. The nature of the mind that is equal to space is seized and made a living experience by native mind. "If the mind becomes rendered what is not mind" means "if the mind that seizes mind's nature as being like space vanishes in the expanse and thus becomes nonexistent." "The connate nature is extraordinarily beautiful" means that nothing but this is the connate. Barpuwa (ibid., 300–301) says that though kālakūṭa refers to a poison, here it refers to mahāmudrā. It is not appropriate to speak about mahāmudrā by means of words and conventional expressions. If one were to speak about it, when it is expressed as "the mahāmudrā without any middle or extremes that is like space," this means the nature of all phenomena is equal to space, but by pursuing these words, the mind clings to it and makes it into a mental object. Therefore it will not become free. "So how will it become free?" If the mind that takes dharmatā as a mental object becomes what is not mind and thus becomes free within the natural state of dharmatā, the basic nature of native mind as such and the basic nature of native dharmatā are revealed and are stainless as the natural connate. Therefore this is extraordinarily beautiful. The Third Karmapa (ibid., 431) says that just as it is not appropriate to speak about the poison kālakūṭa, it is not appropriate to think about dharmatā, because it is free of any thinking. Kālakūṭa and all flaws arise from the mind's clinging; if it is free of clinging, the body of the natural connate is attained. Therefore those who do not see the reality of dharmatā should not promote the partial welfare of beings in a manner that involves effort. According to KTP (84), as metaphorically indicated by it not being appropriate to speak about the poison kālakūṭa, it is not appropriate to speak about the actuality of the basic nature by means of words and conventional expressions. For if one were to speak about it, with the mind pursuing these conventional expressions, realization will not arise. Therefore, since the nature of the mind that is equal to space is seized and experienced by native mind, it rests in meditative equipoise within the natural state of being free of any duality of perceiver and perceived (such as what is to be expressed and the means of expression). Hence the mind that seizes dharmatā as being like space also vanishes within the expanse. Being free of any identification, if it becomes rendered what is not mind, it is the revealing of the actuality of the natural connate, and thereby its beauty is more extraordinary than any of ordinary beings, which refers to dwelling on the bhūmis of the noble ones. Mipham ('Ju mi pham rgya mtsho 1984, 784–85) explains that what is to be familiarized with is the native connate that is beyond being an object of mind. "Kālakūṭa" is a symbolic expression for poison or for an inexpressible experience. Therefore, how could it be appropriate to speak about it? If one were to speak about it, since one would be seized by the poison of thoughts, there is nothing to think and say. The uncontrived nature is seized through sheer mindfulness by the mind that is equal to space, but how could it be possible to explain that? Mind is the pain of imagination; when it, in the manner of subsiding without any effort, becomes rendered what is not mind, the natural connate will be extraordinarily beautiful and luminous.

539. I follow GZ *brjod pa* against CDNP *brjod min* ("is not proclaimed").
540. I follow GZ *khyer ba mda' bsnun smra* against CDNP *khur ba(r) mda' bsnun 'dra* ("sentient beings carrying their mental burden are like Saraha").
541. GZ *kye ma rnal 'byor bsgom pa dris / mgo snying lte gsang rkang lag spangs de ngas mthong ba'o / bsam pas yul ni mtshon par byed / gzhan dag bsam pas rlung 'gag 'gyur /*. Among the commentaries, this stanza is only found in text 67 (of the first line, only "AHO" is mentioned, but the rest is implied by *la sogs pa*), which comments as follows: "You may wonder, 'If beings do not see this emptiness, how do yogīs see it?' Saraha says: 'AHO! . . .' 'Rid of head, heart, navel, secret, legs, and arms, I see it' means 'I see the form that is without any form.' *Mañjuśrīnāmasaṃgīti* VIII.3ab says:

> Formless, of beautiful form, supreme,
> multiform, and consisting of mind

'Through which method will this emptiness be seen?' Saraha says, 'By means of contemplation, objects . . .' Contemplation refers to familiarizing with nonthought, through which 'objects are perceived.' What appears as objects is perceived (will be seen) as empty forms. 'How will these empty forms be seen through the power of nonthought?' Saraha says, 'By contemplating what's other, the vāyus will cease.' 'What's other' refers to nonthought. 'Contemplating' means settling the mind within bliss. 'The vāyus will cease' means that the vāyus will enter the madhyamā. This teaches the following. Since the vāyus are the root of saṃsāra, once they have been purified by having entered the madhyamā, the bondage of perceiver and perceived is cut through and empty forms will be seen." GZ's first two lines (with others interspersed) are also found almost verbatim in text 70, while the remaining lines in this text differ from both GZ and CDNP. CDNP have an entirely different stanza: *bde gsang yan lag yongs su spangs pa na / bsgom dang mi sgom dbyer med bdag gis mthong / yul gyis mtshon pas gzhan dag bsam par byed / de nyid bsam pas ma rtogs rang gzhan 'gags par 'gyur /* [NP . . . *ma gtogs rang bzhin 'gags par 'gyur*]:

> When the branches of secret bliss are fully relinquished,
> I see the inseparability of meditation and nonmeditation
> Others contemplate by this being pointed out by objects
> By contemplating true reality, nonrealization, oneself, and others
> will cease
> [NP: Except by contemplating true reality, this will cease naturally].

The *Dohakoṣahṛdayārthagītāṭīkā* follows the first three lines of CDNP, but reads the last line as *de nyid bsam pas rnam rtog rang bzhin 'gags par 'gyur* ("By contemplating true reality, thoughts will cease naturally"). The Tibetan commentaries also seem to basically follow CDNP, but comment in different ways. Also, all except Mipham read the last line in a number of ways that vary from both CD and NP. Rigpé Raltri does not explicitly quote this stanza, but seems to comment on a hybrid version of GZ and CD, beginning with "AHO! Ask the familiarization that is the yoga of the connate! I see the relinquishment of all forms such as the secret place," followed by quoting *Mañjuśrīnāmasaṃgīti* VIII.3ab. He continues that other yogīs, by contemplating this during subsequent attainment, perceive and know it to be dream-like. Through their contemplation, all vāyus (the causes of saṃsāra) will cease. Lingjé Repa (Grub thob gling ras, Par phu ba blo gros seng ge, Karma pa rang byung rdo rje 2011, 72) explains that the first two lines teach the bliss with and without focal object. The mind is held on the four or six cakras of the body, including their branches (the petals of the nāḍīs) and so on. When this focus is fully relinquished, I see the inseparability of meditation and nonmeditation (I see the actuality of not being separate from the native state). The following lines (as well as stanzas 98–99) teach that objects serve as pointers if they are understood as means. As for "Others contemplate by this being pointed out by objects," in the approach of others who prioritize focal objects, the mind is held on objects. By contemplating that, thoughts will cease naturally—that is, by holding the mind through that, thoughts stop. Barpuwa (ibid., 302–4) also comments on the same reading as the *Dohakoṣahṛdayārthagītāṭīkā*, saying that in the wisdom of thoughts being free, meditation and nonmeditation do not exist as two. Bliss means to be free of the pain of thoughts. Since it is difficult to realize, it is there like a secret. Thus, by realizing secret bliss (mahāmudrā, the connate), the branches of saṃsāric existence are fully relinquished. The branches of saṃsāric existence consist of thoughts, and their relinquishment consists of thoughts becoming free—that is, thoughts dawning as luminosity. Therefore, through realizing great bliss (the connate) and thoughts dawning as luminosity, meditation and nonmeditation are inseparable. There is nothing good that has to emerge by having meditated, nor anything bad where one has to go by not having meditated. If thinking, thinking and luminosity are inseparable; if not thinking, not thinking and luminosity are inseparable. Hence there is not the slightest difference. Those with the approach of the paṇḍita who cut through doubts from the outside ascertain with reasonings such as being free of one and many that objects are without any nature of their own. When they thereby hold the focusing mind in a wrong way, they wish to realize the true reality of nonduality. On the other hand, kusulu yogīs who cut through doubts from within cut through the root of the very mind that ascertains outer objects. By not observing that very mind, thoughts that appear as objects cease naturally. Therefore, what is the need for refuting objects? Thus others who cut through doubts from the outside contemplate true reality by it being pointed out by objects, but we kusulus cut through doubts from within. By contemplating the very mind that ascertains outer objects, we do not find anything to contemplate: thoughts that appear as objects and mind will cease naturally. The Third Karmapa (ibid., 432) comments that having relinquished the efforts of the branches of the means to realize the great bliss that is present in a self-secret manner, by realizing that there is neither meditation nor nonmeditation, dharmatā is seen. Objects such as forms and other objects pointed out by the messengers dawn as empty bliss. By realizing their inseparability, there is freedom from something to meditate on and a meditator. KTP (85–86) first quotes the last line as *de nyid bsam pas ma rtogs rang bzhin 'gags par 'gyur* ("By contemplating true reality, nonrealization will cease naturally"), but declares that *ma rtogs* ("nonrealization") in some translations is explained to be equivalent to *rnam rtog* ("thoughts"). Thus he comments on this stanza as per the reading of the *Dohakoṣahṛdayārthagītāṭīkā*, doing so in five different ways, with his outer and inner explanations questioning the comments on the first two lines by Barpuwa and Lingjé Repa, respectively. KTP's outer comments on these two lines say that they discuss settling without any focal object. True reality is bliss because it lacks the pain of thoughts. It is secret (emptiness) because it is difficult to realize. Since it is the inseparable actuality of the unity of these two, the clinging to the branches of secret bliss as being distinct and the clinging to these two being linked together is fully relinquished. Thus, by relaxing and settling within the inseparability of meditation and nonmeditation in the natural state of the blissful empty connate, without being tainted by any identification and characteristics, I will see the actuality of the basic nature. The next two lines explain settling with a focal object. Others who prioritize focal objects hold the mind on an object of focus and, pointed out by way of that, contemplate the basic nature. Through contemplating by holding the mind on that, thoughts will cease naturally. Mipham ('Ju mi pham rgya mtsho 1984, 485) says that through fully relinquishing the distinctions of the branches of the yogas of the vāyus that rely on the nāḍīcakras of the navel [reading *lte* instead of *bde* ("bliss")], the secret place and so on—that is, through them being empty, I see that meditation and nonmeditation are inseparable as the great equality of the single sole bindu. Others contemplate true reality by this being pointed out by objects. By contemplating mind as such's own true reality, nonrealization and the clinging to oneself and others will cease.

542. I follow GZ *rlung dang yid ni* (supported by text 67) against CDNP *rnam rtog dang ni* ("thoughts and . . . ?"). In his comments, Rigpé Raltri only mentions "vāyus," while most Tibetan commentaries have *rnam rtog dang yid* ("thoughts and mentation"), except Mipham reading *rnam rtog dag ni* ("thoughts").

543. This example is also used in line 107e of Saraha's *Body Treasure* (text 53) and line 32a of Kṛṣṇa's *Dohakoṣa* (text 63), though with slightly different meanings.

544. DKPA *ekku deva vahu āgama dīsai* / corresponds to text 66 *lha cig lung ni mang po'i nang nas mthong* ("The single deity is seen in many scriptures"). In text 67, GZ NP twice read *lha cig*, while CD twice have *lhan cig*. In the *Dohakoṣahṛdayārthagītāṭīkā*, NP read *lha cig*, while CD have *lhan cig*, but the text clearly comments according to *lha cig* (text 70 has *rtags gcig* "single emblem"). Following DKPA and the predominant reading in those commentaries, GZ *lhan cig la ni lung rnams mang por mthong* is emended to *lha gcig* . . . CDNP read *lhan cig la ni lung rnams ma lus mthong*. *Lhan cig*, which means "together" or "simultaneous," is interpreted by almost all Tibetan commentaries as a shorthand of *lhan cig skyes pa* ("the connate"), but its usual shorthand is otherwise always *lhan skyes*. Of course, to read *lhan cig* as such as shorthand is tempting in terms of the context and also because CDNP's line as it stands makes no sense (Rigpé Raltri has *lta gcig* "single view"). Given the interpretation by those commentaries, the line in CDNP would read: "In the connate, all scriptures without exception are seen." However, in their comments, the Tibetan commentaries (except Mipham's) then follow the reading *lhan cig la ni lung rnams mang por mthong* ("The connate is seen as many scriptures").

545. GZ *gzhan kun tshim* CDNP *thams cad (')tshig* ("all are burned/consumed").

546. I follow CDNP *'ongs kyang* against GZ *'on kyang* ("however").

547. An appendix to text 209 with the mahāpaṇḍita Vanaratna's pith instructions glosses "waveless" as not being an object of thoughts of perceiver and perceived. Text 70 (138) says that "waves" refers to contrived states of mind or thoughts.
548. GZ *sems* CDNP *gzugs* ("form").
549. GZ *de ni* CDNP *de ltar* ("thus").
550. Compare stanza 31 of Saraha's "Queen Dohā."
551. GZ *khyim bdag dang ni khyim bdag mo longs spyod* CDNP *khyim bdag zos nas khyim bdag mo longs spyod* ("Devouring the husband, the mistress has fun") DKPA *gharavai khajjai ghariṇiehi* ("The mistress devours the husband").
552. According to KTP (93–107), in due order, stanzas 105cd–108, 109–10, 111–19, 120, and 121 discuss the dharmakāya, sambhogakāya, svābhāvikakāya, mahāsukhakāya, and nirmāṇakāya.
553. Texts 66, 67, and 70, as well as Rigpé Raltri, do not mention this line. Lingjé Repa quotes it, but then, just as do Barpuwa, the Third Karmapa, and KTP, explains it by using *a ma gzhan nas bu de skye mi 'gyur* ("the child is not born from any other mother"). The only commentary that follows GZ CDNP *a ma ghzag nas bu de skye mi 'gyur* is Mipham's ('Ju mi pham rgya mtsho 1984, 787), explaining, "Leaving behind the mother who gives rise to everything (the native state), no excellent children of experience and realization are born."
554. I follow text 67 NP *gzhan ni yod ma yin* against GZ *ghzan na yod ma yin* ("It does not exist anywhere else") and text 67 GZ *gzhan na ni yod pa ma yin* CD *gzhan na ni yod ma yin* (hypermetrical; can be read as in GZ or even as "If it were other, it would not exist," since the gloss in text 67, see next note, may indicate that *gzhan na ni* is a hypothetical position). If GZ or text 67 CD were correct, the next line would be a question that is already answered by this line that precedes it, and thus the next line would become redundant. Also, Rigpé Raltri's comments clearly read *gzhan ni yod ma yin* (see next note). Thus text 67 NP appears to make the most sense.
555. CDNP omit the third and fourth lines of this stanza and have the second line after the third line of stanza 108. The only two commentaries that mention the third and fourth lines at all and include the second line in stanza 106 versus 108 are text 67 and Rigpé Raltri's commentary. Text 67 explains that in the wise, fire (wisdom) burns its very fuel (thoughts). Having thus taught binding the mind, now Saraha teaches that if bodhicitta is not bound, there is no immutable bliss. Without that, buddhahood does not arise. Therefore, in order to accomplish immutable bliss, bodhicitta is bound. "It does not exist anywhere else" means "Is it something else or itself?" "Well, is it then present elsewhere, or what?" means "Does it exist anywhere else or does it exist always?" In answer, Saraha says: "The conduct of yoga is free of any example." It is free of reference points, such as "not existent" and "not nonexistent." Rigpé Raltri says that, being thought-free, true reality is realized by nothing but itself alone, just like a fire burning its fuel. As for fire burning its fuel, in the wise, the fire of wisdom burns its fuel of thoughts. "AHO" signifies a weary mind: there is no other means for freedom that is existent, just as, apart from that, there is nothing anywhere else that gives rise to trust or the body.
556. CDNP begin this line with *des ni* ("Thereby").

557. GZ *chags pa'i yul gyis* CDNP *chags pa'i spyod des* ("with the conduct of desire").
558. I follow DKPA *kijjai rāa virāa, Dohakoṣahṛdayārthagītāṭīkā chags dang chags bral spangs nas gnyug mar zhugs,* text 70 *chags dang chags bral med pas gnyug mar zhugs,* and all Tibetan commentaries *spangs nas* (except Rigpé Raltri). GZ as well as texts 66 and 67 (despite DKPA *kijjai rāa virāa* "destroyed desire and desire's lack") reads *chags dang chags bral byas nas gnyug mar zhugs* ("having produced desire and desire's lack, entered naturalness"), while CDNP say *chags dang chags bral spangs nas dbu mar zhugs* ("rid of desire and desire's lack, entered the madhyamā").
559. With DKPA *joiṇi mahu paḍihāa,* I follow GZ *rnal 'byor ma ngas mthong* against CDNP *rnal 'byor ngas ma mthong* ("I do not see yoga").
560. GZ *grogs dag 'di na sems la gang snang ba / phyi rol par sems sdug bsngal dag gis 'dzin* CDNP *grogs mo 'di ni sems la gang snang ba / phyi rol sems la mtshon med bdag gis 'dzin* ("My lady friend, I grasp that that which appears in the mind cannot be perceived in the mind as external").
561. With DKPA *joiṇi,* I follow GZ *rnal 'byor ma ni* against CDNP *rnal 'byor pa ni* ("yogī").
562. CDNP omit the first two lines of this stanza. The only two commentaries that mention these two lines are text 67 and Rigpé Raltri's commentary. Text 67 explains that "Thinking of activities as being merely this" means that the activities of appearances should be treated as being mere illusions. "The mind made inseparable from any effort" means that since there is nothing to make any effort for, mind gives up exertion, relaxes, and lets be. Rigpé Raltri says that since yogīs who realize what is outside as being like an illusion are free of any saṃsāric examples, they should think of it as being merely this. The mind that takes the efforts of the three gates to be inseparable from dreams and illusions will be stainless on the three planes (body, speech, and mind).
563. CDNP have this as a four-line stanza, whose first two lines are *sa gsum du yang dri med mi gnas mi 'byung ste / me ni spra ba nyid la rkyen gyis 'bar /*:

> What is stainless even on the three planes neither abides nor arises
> Fire burns its very fuel by way of conditions.

564. GZ *yi ge ba yi 'gro ba* CDNP *yi ge 'gro ba.*
565. CDNP omit this line. Text 67 says that "letter" in "the letterless" refers to the letters that are symbols, and if there are no such symbols, the letter is "A," which is understood as empty form. Or, in "for that long letters are understood," "letter" is *akṣara,* which refers to knowing unchanging bliss. "What is a letter?" Saraha says: "This represents the letterless letter." "Letterless" refers to letters—thoughts—being absent. "This represents the letter" refers to thought-free bliss. In order to put an end to clinging to the letters of the outsiders, Saraha says: "Through reciting Vedas without effort, you are ruined." Through that, the recitation of the ultimate "OṂ" is ruined, so you will suffer in saṃsāra. Note that Skt. *akṣara* means "letter" or "syllable," as well as "immutable" and "imperishable." In the latter sense, *akṣara* is an epithet of Śiva and Viṣṇu. The term is also applied to the syllable OṂ, associated by the Śaivas with Śiva in his form of *nādatanu* ("he whose body is sound"). As Mokṣākaragupta's mention of "clinging to the letters of the outsiders" and

"the ultimate OṂ" (connate bliss) shows, all of this seems to be at play here. Rigpé Raltri explains that it is good to translate "By wiping out letters, the ink vanishes" (a variant of the following line) as "This is the letterless letter." In Indian language, "letter" is *akṣara*, which in Tibetan is "unchanging" and explained as "being without many enumerations." Since connate wisdom does not change from sentient beings to buddhas, it is called "the supreme unchanging." There is not even a single sentient being who lacks the pair of ultimate and conventional letters. When the conventional expressions of clinging to characteristics fade, the ultimate letter of the connate will become clear, just as paper becomes clear when the ink vanishes by wiping out letters. Or, this is to be explained as the ultimate letter being the lack of the letters of the conventional expressions of clinging to characteristics.

566. GZ *rtsol med rig byed 'don pas nyams*. I follow CDNP *rig byed don med 'don pas nyams* ("Through reciting meaningless Vedas, you are ruined").

567. GZ *dam pas soms dang* CDNP *dam pa sems dang* text 67 *dam pa soms dang*. Tib. *dam pa* here renders any one of the Sanskrit terms *śreṣṭha, śiṣṭa, ārya, sādhu, sajjana,* or *sujana*, meaning "noble," "well-born," "distinguished," or "good or virtuous person" (*sādhu* is also well-known as "saint," but it seems very unlikely that Saraha would address his audience in that sense). While this stanza does not appear in DKPA and text 66, most commentaries are not explicit as to whether *dam pa* is an appellation in the above sense and *soms/sems* an imperative ("think!"), while all (except Mipham) agree that *cig shos* is an equivalent of the ultimate or the connate. The only two commentaries that are explicit about *dam pa* and *soms* in this regard are those by KTP and Rigpé Raltri. Text 70 clearly takes *dam pa* to mean "ultimate" and *sems* "mind" (glossing them as equivalents: "the ultimate intention of all buddhas—the mind (ordinary mind)"), while *cig shos* ("the other one") is glossed as "the true reality that has the nature of great bliss." By contrast, Mipham ('Ju mi pham rgya mtsho 1984, 788) glosses *dam pa yi sems* ("the ultimate mind") as "the native state" and *cig shos* as "what has the nature of imagination."

568. The *Daśabhūmikasūtra* lists thirteen bhūmis: the well-known ten bodhisattva bhūmis followed by the buddhabhūmi, consisting of the three bhūmis called "Incomparable" (Skt. *anupamā*, Tib. *dpe med*), "Endowed with Wisdom" (Skt. *jñānavatī*, Tib. *ye shes ldan*), and "All-Illumination" (Skt. *samantaprabhā*, Tib. *kun tu 'od*). Later Sūtrayāna texts also speak of thirteen bhūmis (such as the beginner bhūmi, the bhūmi of engagement through aspiration, the ten bodhisattva bhūmis, and the buddhabhūmi) or even fourteen bhūmis (such as the bhūmi of engagement through aspiration, the ten bodhisattva bhūmis, Incomparable, Endowed with Wisdom, and All-Illumination). In Vajrayāna presentations, one finds further names and enumerations of bhūmis, such as the fourteen bhūmis that consist of the ten bodhisattva bhūmis, Incomparable, Endowed with Wisdom, All-Illumination, and the Vajrabhūmi (Tib. *rdo rje'i sa*). Another way of arriving at fourteen is to count the two paths of accumulation and preparation, the ten bhūmis, and All-Illumination as the thirteen bhūmis of the Sūtrayāna, while in the Vajrayāna, buddhas are said to reside even beyond these thirteen, which is thus referred to as "the fourteenth bhūmi." According to Rigpé Raltri, the first thirteen bhūmis consist of the two paths of accumulation and

preparation, the ten bodhisattvabhūmis, and All-Illumination. Since the inner buddhahood of secret mantra exists even above those, it is the fourteenth. According to Lingjé Repa (Grub thob gling ras, Par phu ba blo gros seng ge, Karma pa rang byung rdo rje 2011, 87), beyond the well-known ten bhūmis, the eleventh is called "The Bhūmi of All-Illumination" because true reality is stable without meditative equipoise and subsequent attainment. The twelfth is called "The Bhūmi of the Attachment-Free Lotus" (Skt. **asaṅgapadminī* [or *-padmāvatī-*]*bhūmi*, Tib. *ma chags padma can gyi sa*) because despite promoting the welfare of beings, it is not tainted by saṃsāra's flaws. The thirteenth is called "The Bhūmi of the Great Assembly of the Wheel of Letters" (Skt. **akṣaracakramahāgaṇabhūmi*, Tib. *yi ge 'khor lo'i tshogs chen gyi sa*) because the qualities of the three kāyas unfold in a complete manner just as they are. The fourteenth is called "The Bhūmi of Great Bliss" (Skt. *mahāsukhabhūmi*, Tib. *bde ba chen po'i sa*) because the essence of all of those is not different and not tainted by any mire. KTP (99) lists the same four bhūmis as Lingjé Repa, adding that they are presented in the Mahāmudrā tradition. The Third Karmapa (Grub thob gling ras, Par phu ba blo gros seng ge, Karma pa rang byung rdo rje 2011, 441) lists the first three among these bhūmis by name, explaining the first two in the same way as Lingjé Repa. The thirteenth is said to be "The Great Assembly of the Wheel of Letters" because all phenomena are realized to be symbols. Since all of these are not different and are thus a single state of nongrasping, they are beyond what is to be traveled and a traveler in terms of the paths and bhūmis. Nevertheless, it is by way of having relinquished the aspect of abiding in them that there is a constant abiding on the fourteenth bhūmi. Barpuwa (ibid., 314) says that the fourteenth bhūmi is the one of a vajra holder's own essence. Very differently, text 67 identifies the fourteen bhūmis here as the six cakras, the six spaces in between, the ratnacakra, and the bhūmi of thought-free vartaka ("existing" or "abiding").

569. I follow GZ CD *lus med lus la sbas pa ste* against NP *lus med lus la sbas pa med* ("the bodiless is not hidden in the body").

570. GZ *nga yis grub yig dang po bton* CDNP *grub yig bzhi las dang po bdag gis ston* ("I teach the first among the four syllables of accomplishment"). According to the outer explanation by KTP (100–101), in Hinduist texts, the four syllables *siddhi hūhū* in the sentence *Oṃ atha siddhi hūhū* (obviously a variant of DKPA *siddhir atthu*, Skt. *siddhir astu* "May it be accomplished!") represent the four syllables of accomplishing the four Vedas. In terms of the inner explanation, the four syllables of accomplishment are EVAM MAYĀ because they are the main body or setting of all sūtras and tantras. In terms of the secret explanation, the means to accomplish the supreme siddhi symbolized by four syllables are four: minding, nonminding, being unborn, and being beyond mind. As for the words EVAṂ MAYĀ ("Thus I [have heard]"), besides being the opening words of all sūtras and many tantras, there are many different extensive explanations on these four syllables in numerous commentaries from both sūtric and tantric perspectives. For example, see text 67 and the beginning of appendix 7 in volume 3.

571. GZ *nags khrod gsum na yi ge gcig / yi ge gsum gyi dbus na lha / gang zhig gsum las 'babs pa ni / gdol pa'i rig byed bzhi yang ngo /*. This stanza is only mentioned in

text 67 and Rigpé Raltri's commentary. Text 67 says that the three groves are body, speech, and mind. The single letter is "A," which is invincible. "In the middle of the three letters, there is the deity." That is, through the threefold retraction and immobilization of the vāyus, in the middle of the vanquishers that consist of the three syllables OṂ ĀḤ HŪṂ, there is the deity—that is, what consists of empty form. The three in "that which keeps descending from those three" are body, speech, and mind. The passion that arises from the triad of body, speech, and mind, through the kindness of being empty, constitutes "the Vedas of an outcaste"—that is, it dawns as the four thought-free ecstasies. Rigpé Raltri explains that the three groves are body, speech, and mind. The single letter is the connate. In the middle of the three letters of this being ground, path, and fruition, there is the deity of luminosity. As for that which keeps descending from those three and stays there, like an outcaste of bad family shying away from the path, the four ecstasies (the four Vedas that involve passion) shy away from the path of the connate. CDNP read very differently *rkyen bral gsum ni yi ge gcig / zag med gsum gyi dbus na lha / gang zhig gsum po zag pa ni / gdol pa rig byed de bzhin no /*:

> What is free of the three conditions is the single letter
> In the middle of threefold noncontamination is the deity
> The ones in whom all three involve contamination
> bear a resemblance to the Vedas of an outcaste

KTP (102–3) says that if realized to be free of the three conditions of the body (illusion), speech (expression), and mind (realization), the true actuality of the single ultimate letter *a* (being unborn) is known. The noncontamination of the body is being empty, the noncontamination of speech is being free of expression, and the noncontamination of mind is being unborn. In the middle of the inseparability of these three, the dharmadhātu beyond thought and expression, which resides as natural luminosity, is the ultimate deity (the dharmakāya). Therefore, if the true actuality of the basic nature is realized, the paths and bhūmis are complete in itself. Those who proclaim to have realized the basic nature while the triad of their body, speech, and mind is still contaminated with regard to objects do not realize the basic nature, just like an outcaste never becomes a brahman even if teaching the Vedas by pretending to be a brahman.

572. GZ *mi shes gang* CDNP *mi shes pas*.
573. Ordinarily, Skt. *kunduru* refers to *Boswellia thurifera* as well as its resin, known as frankincense. In tantric texts, the term is often used as a synonym for *kunda* ("white jasmine"), one of the many epithets of semen. As applies in this case here, it is also glossed as "the union of the two organs (male and female sex organs)" (Skt. *dvīndriyasamāpatti*)—that is, sexual intercourse. According to Davidson 2002b (268), the term is probably derived from the Dravidian root √*kund* (to pierce, to prick, to prod).
574. I follow GZ *ji ltar skom pas smig rgyu snyegs pa bzhin* against CDNP *ji ltar sgom pas smig rgyu'i chu snyegs bzhin* ("similar to chasing after a mirage's water through meditation").
575. GZ *rdo rje padma gnyis kyi bar gnas pa / bde ba gang gi rnam par bskyed pa ni / ci*

ste de bstan nus pa med pas na / sa gsum gang du rdzogs su re ba lags /. As it stands, this stanza is only commented on in text 67 and Rigpé Raltri's commentary. Connecting back to stanza 116, text 67 asks: "Why do they not find it?" The line "that is present in the midst of the vajra and lotus pair" refers to the bliss that is present in the midst of the pair of the vajra and the lotus. "What is generated by means of the bliss" means "though those two [this bliss versus great bliss] accord in terms of the aspect of bliss." "Since it is powerless to demonstrate what this is like"—that is, since it does not have the power to demonstrate how uncontaminated bliss is, "where's hope for fulfillment on the three planes?" That is, how could the triad of body, speech, and mind be purified? Or, if the bliss of vajra and lotus did not exist, how could uncontaminated bliss arise? It would not arise. Rigpé Raltri says that stanza 117 states the reason for what is said in stanza 116. As the bliss that arises from the union of the two does not have the power to rely on and give rise to the connate, where would the relinquishments and realizations of the three planes (the three gates) be fulfilled? They are not fulfilled. CDNP differ as follows: *rdo rje padma gnyis kyi bar gnas pa / bde ba gang gis rnam par rol pa ni* [CD *yin*] */ ci ste de bden nus pa med pas na / sa gsum re ba gang gis rdzogs par 'gyur /*. Thus NP read as follows:

> Since the play by means of the bliss present
> in the midst of the pair of the vajra and lotus
> doesn't have the power of what reality is like,
> by what could it fulfill the three planes' hopes?

CD say this:

> This is the play by means of the bliss present
> in the midst of the pair of the vajra and lotus
> Since it doesn't . . .

According to KTP (104), not having realized the native actuality that is the basic nature, it is not appropriate to wish to realize this basic nature solely through that method or to cling to the play and the experiences by means of experiencing this bliss, which arises from the conventional body and is present in the midst of the pair of the vajra of means and the lotus of prajñā, as being this basic nature. What is the reason for this? Since conventional bliss is not the reality of dharmatā, this contaminated bliss does not possess the power of realizing the basic nature. Therefore, by virtue of not realizing the dharmakāya for one's own welfare, there is no power to appear as the form kāyas for the welfare of others. Hence, by what could it fulfill the hopes of all beings on the three planes? It will not do so.

576. DKPA of this stanza is very corrupt. Also, there is no equivalent of GZ CDNP *de nyid* ("exactly that") in the second line, but Shahidullah 1928 and Jackson 2004 insert *tatta*, obviously based on DKPS *tattvaṃ*. Thus, especially the first two lines are explained in several ways in different commentaries and rendered differently in contemporary translations. Text 66 comments: "[Saraha speaks of] 'momentary' because this refers to the distinctions of the moments of the four ecstasies. Or, alternatively, it refers to perceiving true reality at the time of not being two. Since that [not being two] is the case in the middle

of supreme [ecstasy] and cessational [ecstasy], being different refers to the beginning moments—that is, the time of [bliss] arising in [the moments of] variety [and so on]. Not being different refers to the nature of the connate." The *Dohakoṣahṛdayārthagītāṭīkā* explains: "Since the bliss in the moment of the lack of characteristics constitutes the third empowerment, it is pointed out by the wisdom that is an example. But since you also need to be mindful of the ultimate jñānamudrā, it only serves as a means [to an end]. Therefore it is either the momentary bliss of the means or it exists as mere minding but does not exist in mere nonminding. Hence [Saraha speaks of] alternatively exactly that in its being two." Text 70 says: "It is either the uncontaminated bliss by relying on the momentary bliss of connate wisdom as the means to identify [the actual] connate wisdom or, alternatively, at a later time, the inseparability of emptiness and bliss due to uncontaminated bliss and inconceivable great emptiness not being two by virtue of not clinging to exactly those two." Lingjé Repa (Grub thob gling ras, Par phu ba blo gros seng ge, Karma pa rang byung rdo rje 2011, 90) says: "'It is either the momentary bliss of the means' because the bliss that arises from the means of union is only experienced momentarily, 'or, alternatively, exactly that in its being two' because it exists at the time of relying on that, but does not arise when not relying on it. The taste of contaminated bliss entails perishing." Barpuwa (317) comments that since it is the momentary bliss of the means, it is not the path. Or, alternatively, exactly that bliss is twofold in terms of its example and the actual one: through relying on a karmamudrā (the example), mahāmudrā (the actual one) is pointed out. The Third Karmapa (444–45) says that in the fourth moment of the third empowerment, thought-free bliss-emptiness arises in a momentary manner. Having understood that it arises from the collection of its causes and conditions, being free of clinging, it is possible for this actuality to be realized because it did not go anywhere whatsoever. KTP (105) comments on this stanza by combining the explanations of Barpuwa and the Karmapa, saying that the bliss that arises from the means of union in the context of the third empowerment dawns as momentary and thought-free bliss-emptiness. Realizing that this arises from a specific collection of its causes and conditions, realization is possible by being free of clinging to that bliss. Or, alternatively, exactly that bliss is twofold in terms of its example and the actual one: through relying on a karmamudrā (the example), mahāmudrā (the actual one) is realized by it being pointed out in that way. That is, the connate bliss of melting in the context of the third empowerment is enhanced as the nature of the context of the fourth empowerment—the connate itself. Therefore, thanks to the kindness of the blessings and the instructions of the true guru, yet again, by relying on this means, just a few persons with sharp faculties among hundreds and hundreds will realize this actuality of the basic nature. "Yet again" means that after it has been said above [in stanza 117] that this is not realized through the third empowerment alone, it is possible to realize it if that path is yet again backed up by being unborn.

577. GZ *nyams su myong bas shes* CDNP *nyams su myong bar shes* ("is known as experience").

578. GZ *skad cig* CDNP *skad cig gcig* ("single instant").

579. GZ *sdig pa ma lus pham byed pa'o* CDNP *bsam pa'i sdig pa ma lus phan par byed pa'o* ("all wrongdoing of thinking will be benefited").
580. Almost all Tibetan commentaries as well as the *Dohakoṣahṛdayārthagītāṭīkā* gloss "the lord of the stars" (GZ CDNP *skar ma'i bdag po*) as "the moon." Text 67 glosses this as "nonconceptual wisdom," while DKPA *sukka* (Skt. *śukra*; here meaning "Venus") is rendered correctly as its equivalent *pa va sangs* in text 66. Text 70 and Rigpé Raltri read *sgrol ba'i bdag po* ("lord of liberation").
581. GZ *rmongs pa'i sems kyis sems la rtogs pa ni / lta ba ngan pa thams cad las ni grol 'gyur te* CDNP *rmongs pa'i sems kyis sems la brtags na ni / lta ba ngan pa thams cad las rang grol 'gyur* ("If the mind of a fool examines the mind, it will become free from all bad views on its own"). In the first line, except Barpuwa and Mipham (*brtags na ni*), all commentaries read *rtogs na(s)*. In the second line, except Lingjé Repa, Barpuwa, and Mipham (*rang grol 'gyur*), all read *grol 'gyur*.
582. This line is similar to line 64d of text 56.
583. I follow GZ *de ni bdag nyid la dris shig* against CDNP *de ni bdag nyid dris la gcig* ("Let it question itself—it's one!").
584. This line corresponds to the second line of DKPA *ettha viappa ṇa puccha*. CDNP omit it, but it appears in NP of text 66, text 67, and Rigpé Raltri's commentary. Text 67 glosses it as "At that time, you should not mentally engage in characteristics," and Rigpé Raltri says, "Let it be without any thoughts!"
585. The Tibetan of the first line of this stanza (GZ *yul gyi glang po dbang po'i lag pas blangs* CDNP *yul gyi glang po'i dbang po lag pas blangs*) renders DKPA *visaagaendeṃ kareṃ gahia* in a very literal way. However, DKPA/Skt. *kara* can mean "hand" as well as "(elephant) trunk," so the most straightforward meaning of this line would be "seized by the trunk of the mighty elephant of objects." This is also how it is unambiguously rendered in Tibetan in text 66 (*sna* instead of *lag pa*). On the other hand, Tib. *lag pa* only means "hand," not "trunk." In DKPA, it is very clear that *gaendeṃ* (Skt. *gajendrena*; "by the mighty elephant") is a single word (as is *gaenda* in line 123a; though *inda* has no Tibetan equivalent there), that it is in the instrumental case, and that *kareṃ* in the same case is related to it. Thus, if text 67 is really a translation from a Sanskrit text (and its comments here certainly make one wonder), its interpretation of this line is certainly very creative in separating *glang po dbang po'i lag pas* by glossing *dbang po'i lag pas* as "the king's hand" and taking *glang po* ("elephant") as the object instead of the grammatical subject. Similarly, the *Dohakoṣahṛdayārthagītāṭīkā* and all Tibetan commentaries take *lag pa* to mean "hand," and the *Dohakoṣahṛdayārthagītāṭīkā*, Lingjé Repa, and KTP also understand *dbang po* as someone who masters elephants, thus taking the second line to mean that such a person even has the power to kill the elephant with his iron hook. By contrast, text 70, Barpuwa, and Mipham read *dbang po* as "sense faculties." In the fourth line, "precisely that" from which mind's well-trained elephant returns is interpreted in a number of ways (text 66 does not speak to that). Text 67 glosses this as "[mind] returning on its own." The *Dohakoṣahṛdayārthagītāṭīkā* says that apart from true reality, there is no place for mind to go. According to text 70, "that" refers to appearances. Lingjé Repa (Grub thob gling ras, Par phu ba blo gros seng ge, Karma pa rang byung rdo rje 2011, 94) says that though thoughts proliferate toward objects, since there is no place to go, they return to their

natural state: this is the dharma of sustaining true reality. Similarly, KTP (109) says that though thoughts proliferate toward objects, since there is no place to go, they return from the very recognition of that. The Third Karmapa (Grub thob gling ras, Par phu ba blo gros seng ge, Karma pa rang byung rdo rje 2011, 448) speaks of yogīs realizing the dharmatā of objects and being free of any objects toward which thoughts proliferate. Barpuwa (ibid., 322) explains that by virtue of yogīs letting the mind move freely, if bad thoughts arise, by controlling them with the iron hook of self-recognition, mind will return from these thoughts. Uniquely, Rigpé Raltri glosses this stanza as follows: "As in the example of a king killing a mighty elephant of his country (*yul*) by seizing it with his hand that holds an iron hook, by gaining power over mind's elephant, yogīs, like elephant herders, will kill the discursive mind in the manner of it coming to an end on its own."

586. GZ *yul gyi dbye bas gzhan du sems par ma byed cig* CDNP *dbye ba gzhan du sems pa* [NP *dpa'*] *ma yin te* ("not thinking of them as other distinctions").
587. I follow GZ NP *gi* against CD *gis* ("by").
588. I follow GZ *dmigs med stong pa nyid yin no* against CDNP *dmigs pa stong pa nyid yin la* ("the referent is emptiness").
589. GZ *bsgom bya* CDNP *sgom pa* ("familiarization").
590. Some commentaries comment on "timely" and "means" as two separate things. Text 70 says: "It is known by experiencing the guru's lessons and having familiarized with that over time, thus relying on it at all times through perpetual mindfulness (the means)." Similarly, Mipham ('Ju mi pham rgya mtsho 1984, 791–92) explains: "What is experienced at the time of the pith instructions of the guru—that which is supremely unsurpassable and self-arising on its own—is known by relying on perpetual mindfulness (the means)." KTP (110) comments that mahāmudrā—the unsurpassable self-arising wisdom that is more supreme than other qualities—is realized through the blessings of the guru if one has the notion that the guru is a buddha. The fortunate who rely on the timing of the guru's blessing, the special skillful means taught by the guru, and the profound essential points of the instructions will know mahāmudrā in an unmistaken manner.
591. GZ *ma 'dug cig* CDNP *ma 'dug par* ("neither going . . . nor remaining at home").
592. GZ *gang yang de ru yid kyis yongs shes na* CDNP . . . *nas* is a somewhat corrupt rendering of DKPA *jahi tahi maṇa pariāṇa* ("Wherever it/you may be, realize the mind!"). Text 66 has this as: "Wherever you may be, look at the mind!" Text 67 glosses *gang yang de ru* as "whether in the forest or at home, it is the same." The *Dohakoṣahṛdayārthagītāṭīkā* explains this phrase differently: "By virtue of knowing that any minds and mental factors of thought lack a nature of their own, no clinging to that is entertained. Therefore, if the mind knows to relinquish anything as that (*gang gang de ru*)—that is, if [this lack of nature] is known, [minds and mental factors] are not to be viewed as sentient beings." Lingjé Repa (Grub thob gling ras, Par phu ba blo gros seng ge, Karma pa rang byung rdo rje 2011, 96) says: "if all these appearances, such as places and friends, are realized as true reality (*de nyid du*) . . ." Barpuwa (ibid., 325) says: "if minding is not forgotten—that is, if there is no distraction . . . at whichever (*gang gang de ru*) place one may be . . ." The Third Karmapa (ibid., 450) says: "if

any (*gang gang*) phenomena of saṃsāra and nirvāṇa are fully realized as (*du*) equality . . ." KTP (111) combines both of those two kinds of explanation: "No matter at which (*gang du*) place you may be, with an undistracted mind, fully realize any (*gang gang*) phenomena as that (*de ru*) native actuality!" Mipham ('Ju mi pham rgya mtsho 1984, 792) says: "no matter which place you may come across or in which you may be, once your own mind fully realizes native actuality there . . ."

593. In line with DKPA *vohiṭhia*, I follow NP *byang chub rtogs par gnas* against GZ *byang chub rtogs pas gnas* ("is present by realizing") CD *rtag par gnas* ("is always present").

594. GZ *yid ni dri med lhan cig skyes pa'i gnas skabs so / de tshe 'gro ba'i rigs la 'jug pa med / de tsam zhig la nges par gnas pa ni / de ni rgyal ba yin te bye brag med /*. Only parts of this stanza are mentioned in text 67 and Rigpé Raltri's commentary (nowhere else). Text 67 only mentions and comments on the second line, saying that it refers to nonthought, because it does not enter the classes of thoughts. Rigpé Raltri combines his comments on stanzas 129 with those on 130. Line 129a refers to having arrived at the connate mind that is without any thoughts of clinging to the duality of saṃsāra and nirvāṇa. Then, thoughts—the enemies of nonthought—are not entered. By resting in nonthought, this is the victory over thoughts, without any distinctions or differences as to whether realization is present in the forest or at home. By understanding this, you must rely on being thought-free! By contrast, CDNP read *yid kyi dri ma dag la* [NP *na*] *lhan cig skyes pa ste / de tshe mi mthun phyogs kyis* [NP *kyi*] *'jug pa med / ji ltar rgya mtsho dang bar gyur pa la / chu bur chu nyid yin te de nyid thim par 'gyur /*:

> Mind's stains are pure—this is the connate [NP "If mind's stains
> are pure, this is the connate"]
> Then, it is not entered by any adversities
> Just like upon the ocean that is so clear,
> bubbles are just water and dissolve into it

KTP (111–12) comments that if the stains (perceiver and perceived) of the mind that strives for objects are pure, this is the manifestation of connate wisdom. Then, when all is of the nature of the connate, it is not even entered by a speck of any adversities (the factors to be relinquished), just as you do not find anything that is not gold on an island of gold. For example, if bubbles arise upon the clear water of the ocean, they are just water, do not go beyond water, and dissolve again into that water. Just like that, if the bubbles of thoughts stir on the clear ocean of naturally pure mind, these thoughts are that very mind: thoughts and luminosity are not different. Even when these thoughts dissolve, they dissolve into mind's pure nature. Therefore thoughts do not harm in the slightest those with realization.

595. GZ *rtogs pa* CDNP *byang chub* are just different renderings of DKPA *vohi* (Skt. *bodhi*).

596. I follow GZ NP *dbye ba* against CD *byed pa* ("doing").

597. GZ *bsten par byos* CDNP *(b)rten par 'os* ("is suitable to be relied on").

598. GZ *de nyid bdag yin gzhan yang de nyid yin* CDNP *de ni bdag yin gzhan yang de bzhin* [NP *yin*] *no* ("this is the self and likewise the other too").

599. CDNP omit this line. It only appears in text 67 and Rigpé Raltri's commentary, which both combine it with the second line. Text 67 asks what the appearance of differences is like. Since all appearances are mind, once mind is deluded, it roams saṃsāra (or the intermediate state). "Just as in the case of reflections in the ocean" means that this resembles mistaking a reflection of one's face that appears in clear water for a nāga and thus fainting. "Do not create delusion about a self and others!" means being deluded, thinking what is single is two. Rigpé Raltri asks the same question and provides the first line as the answer, adding that just as all kinds of reflections appear in a clear lake yet do not exist, do not create the delusion of the appearance of all kinds of a self and others!

600. GZ *thams cad snga na gnas pa'i sangs rgyas* CDNP *ma lus rgyun du gnas pa'i sangs rgyas* ("all without exception are perpetually present buddhas").

601. CD switch the last two lines. The last four lines of this stanza are virtually identical with Tilopa's *Dohakoṣa* 13 (Apa.). Lines 132bc also echo Tilopa's *Dohakoṣa* 16a (text 72).

602. GZ *sa gsum* CDNP *khams gsum* ("three realms").

603. GZ *gzhan don* CDNP *gzhan phan* ("others' benefit").

604. GZ *de la ming ni gzhan la phan pa'o* CD *ming ni mchog tu gzhan la phan pa'o* ("Its name is 'the supreme benefit of others'") NP *ming ni mchog tu gnas la phan pa'o* ("Its name is 'the supreme benefit of the abode'"). This stanza is virtually identical with Tilopa's *Dohakoṣa* 12 (Apa.).

605. As virtually all commentaries clarify, Tib. *lhun grub* here means "effortlessness." In this sense, it corresponds to Skt. *anābhoga* (in itself, however, a misreading of DKPA *aṇṇa bhoa* "the enjoyment of others"). On its own in Tibetan, *lhun grub* can also mean "innate presence" or "naturally established," which would also make sense here.

606. I follow NP *stong pa'i sdong po dam pa snying rje min* (DKPA *suṇṇa taruvara ṇikkaruṇa*) against GZ CD *stong pa'i sdong po dam pa'i snying rje min* ("the tree of emptiness is not supreme compassion" or "it is not the compassion of the supreme tree of emptiness").

607. GZ *'chag par 'gyur* CDNP *med par 'gyur* ("will turn to nothing").

608. As for stanzas 137–38, CDNP are overall closer to DKPA than GZ is, especially in the third and fourth lines: CDNP *gang zhig 'dod pa can gyi skye bo 'ongs pa'i tshe / de ni re ba med na gal te 'gro ba ni / phyi sgor bor ba'i kham phor blangs nas su / de bas khyim thab bor nas bsdad pa rung / gzhan la phan pa'i don ni mi byed pa / 'dod pa po la sbyin pa mi ster ba / 'di ni 'khor ba'i 'bras bu gang yin lo / bdag nyid bor bar byas na rung /*. The translation of the second line follows the *Dohakoṣahṛdayārthagītāṭīkā* and all Tibetan commentaries (except Rigpé Raltri's), reading *de ni re ba med nas gal te 'gro na ni/* (text 66 has the similar *de ni red ba med song nas*). Text 66 comments on these two stanzas that the entire meaning taught above will be realized when there is no attachment to saṃsāric possessions. Attachment to possessions and children and grandchildren thriving and so on bring harm, like the venom of a snake. Therefore, when a beggar who has a wish arrives, those who are endowed with compassion, thinking, "Being under the sway of craving, if I don't give even a little bit, siddhis will not arise in me," should

depart from their own home, pick up a clay bowl that has been tossed outside, and not entertain any attachment to possessions. If you are not able to benefit others, what need is there for a home and possessions? If someone who has gold and so on does not practice generosity, abiding in saṃsāra, what result does this wealth have? It has none. At that point, you are better off leaving behind yourself, departing from your home, and living without any regard for your body and your life. KTP (116–17) explains these stanzas by using the following example (also found in Lingjé Repa's and the Third Karmapa's commentaries). Once someone such as a king makes a promise to give others whatever they may need, beggars who wish for daily necessities may learn about that promise and arrive to beg. If those beggars are not given anything in accordance with that promise, their hopes of receiving something are dashed, and they leave empty-handed. Thus that king acquires a bad reputation of not keeping his promise, and his own [good] qualities become ruined. Therefore, rather than being like that, you are better off picking up a clay bowl with food scraps that was tossed out the door by others, leaving behind all worldly activities, including your home, and taking up the poor life of a beggar. Likewise, from the level of an aspirant all the way to the buddhabhūmi, the entrance gate to the Mahāyāna is nothing but the benefit of others. Therefore, by mentally giving up the welfare of others and thus not promoting it, not gathering people to be guided by the four means of attracting them based on compassion and aspiration prayers, and not providing the three kinds of generosity to those wishing for the dharma and material things (such as not teaching others in accordance with one's own realization), what benefit to sentient beings who live in saṃsāra is there supposed to be? Rather, there is the danger of falling into the one-sided peace of śrāvakas and pratyekabuddhas. For that reason, you are better off leaving behind any clinging to a self and solely promote the welfare of others in saṃsāra. In brief, the example of a beggar's life being preferable to reigning over a kingdom and contradicting one's promise explicitly teaches that if you do not promote the welfare of others once you have entered the path of the Mahāyāna, you will fall into the Hīnayāna. The underlying intention behind this is that the ultimate fruition of the Mahāyāna is the enlightened activity of the welfare of others arising in a completely effortless manner. GZ's version of these two stanzas is *gang zhig 'dod pa can gyi skye bo 'ong ba'i tshe / de ni gal te 'gro na re ba med / kham phor dum bu slong ba'i mi / phyi sgor bor ba blangs nas su / gzhan gyi don ni mi byed la / 'dod pa po la mi ster ba / 'di ni 'khor ba'i 'bras bu gang yin lo / rang nyid bor bar byas na rung* /. GZ expands CDNP's third line into two lines (thus having a third line that is quite similar in meaning to the first line) while omitting the crucial last line in CDNP and DKPA about leaving your home. Thus the meaning of stanza 137 is greatly changed in GZ, and it sounds as if it is one with stanza 138:

> At the time when a person with a wish arrives,
> if they were to leave, they would have no hope
> A person begging with a shard of a clay bowl,
> having picked it up once tossed out the door,
> does not promote the welfare of any others,
> not giving anything to those who have a wish—

> what saṃsāric result is there supposed to be?
> You are better off leaving behind yourself

Only text 67 and Rigpé Raltri comment on this version. Text 67 explains that a person with the wish to be an individual who has attained the nonabiding nirvāṇa strives for that. At the time when a beggar arrives, "if there are beings, they will have no hope"—that is, they will give to any being [obviously taking DKPA *jai jāi* (Tib. *'gro na* "if . . . leave") as *jai jaga* ("if [there is] a being")] without hoping for anything in return. Now, to teach that the welfare of others is not accomplished without one's own welfare, Saraha says: " . . . a shard of a clay bowl . . ." This is just like a beggar who "does not promote the welfare of any others"—that is, who does not benefit others. "Not giving anything to those who have a wish" refers to not practicing generosity. "What saṃsāric result is there supposed to be?" means that being born in saṃsāra has been rendered meaningless. "You are better off leaving behind yourself" means that it is better to leave your striving for yourself behind—that is, you should promote the welfare of others. Or, this teaches that if you do not cling even though you promote the welfare of yourself and others, you are not tainted by the flaws of saṃsāra. "Does not promote the welfare of any others" refers to not entertaining any notion of benefiting. "Not giving anything to those who have a wish" means not having any clinging to generosity. "What saṃsāric result is there supposed to be?" means that such a person is not tainted by saṃsāra. "You are better off leaving behind yourself" means relinquishing the grasping of clinging to "me." "A shard of a clay bowl . . ." is to be regarded as in the example of not hoping for anything in return when giving to a beggar. Referring back to the last line of stanza 136, Rigpé Raltri says that stanzas 137–38 teach that a person with such realization (being free from saṃsāra as well as nirvāṇa) needs to promote the welfare of others with compassion at the time of the path as well. At the time when a person with the wish and striving for this dharma arrives, if they were not given this dharma and left, they will have no hope of buddhahood—that is, they will not attain it. For example, if a beggar begging with a shard of a clay bowl, having picked up a vessel tossed out the door as well as some food and drink, does not promote the welfare of others and does not give anything to those who have a wish, what he has picked up has been rendered meaningless. Likewise, not to explain the dharma to others when understanding it, what result of saṃsāric birth is there supposed to be? There is none. "Supposed" is a word of disapproval. Therefore you are better off leaving behind your own welfare and promoting the welfare of others. For example, this is as master Kamalaśīla's lesser *Bhavanākrama* says [the quote is in fact the concluding stanza of his *Yogabhāvanāvatāra* (D3918, fol. 70b.3–4)]:

> If nonconceptual wisdom is not accomplished,
> buddhahood cannot be accomplished by words
> Nevertheless, because beings have a wish for it,
> it is appropriate for the wise ones to explain it

Master Mokṣākaragupta explains the following (this is a somewhat creative summary of text 67). If such a person with such a wish arrives, they (the wise) will give to any being without hoping for anything in return. " . . . a shard of a clay bowl . . ." teaches that the welfare of others is not accomplished without one's own welfare: since being born in saṃsāra would otherwise become meaningless, you should promote the welfare of others by leaving behind your own welfare. Or, if you do not cling even if no welfare of others comes about, what result of saṃsāra is there supposed to be? Such a person is not tainted by saṃsāra's flaws. Finally, some commentaries (obviously referring to text 66) explain this to mean that the entire meaning taught above will be realized when there is no attachment to saṃsāric possessions, just as in the case of a beggar. Therefore you are better off leaving behind yourself: you should depart from your home, not have any regard for your body and your life, and live without any attachment toward all enemies and friends. In text 70, the first two lines also correspond to GZ's version here (except replacing "person" with "someone"), being explained as follows: "'Someone' refers to some fortunate son of noble family. At the time when [such a person] with the excellent mindset of wishing for the special actuality of nonduality arrives, if yogīs did not benefit them and were to leave, they would kill the mind of that other [person] and thus [that person] would have no hope of [attaining] perfect buddhahood. Therefore [yogīs] should not even engage in the subtlest undertaking that displeases others" (for the comments on the following lines, which differ from the above, see text 70, 168–70).

609. CDNP add *chen po* ("great") and omit the following two sentences about the translators (P has *bkra shis* "auspiciousness" instead).
610. Interestingly, KTP (118) quotes the following alternative translator's colophon, obviously referring to a different version: "Having asked the venerable Indian Vajrapāṇi, Balpo Asu touched an Indian manuscript [of his] and translated and finalized it on his own." KTP then glosses this as follows: "Lotsāwa guru Balpo Asu or Balpo *Ajamahāsukha, who was well-trained in both languages, touched an Indian manuscript of the Indian Vajrapāṇi and translated its words on his own."
611. PDMT, 26:211–18. As Almogi 2022b (417–19) has pointed out, differing from the text's versions in CDNP, its version in the Tshal pa Tengyur is very similar to the one in GZ.
612. CDNP *phyag rgya bzhi gtan la dbab pa.*
613. GZ CDNP add *dpal* ("Śrī").
614. GZ CDNP omit this.
615. CDNP omit "first." GZ has "nature" instead of "wisdom," and "succession" is rendered as *dgod pa* ("establishment," "array").
616. GZ "Here, in order that those who roam the ocean of saṃsāric existence and suffer very much due to being deluded and their minds being ignorant about the establishment of the mudrās may easily realize the meanings of the four mudrās, the means, endowed with the supreme actuality to swiftly accomplish the siddhi of great bliss, shall be composed by following the tantras." CDNP ". . . the means to accomplish great bliss shall be established . . ."
617. Though maybe less likely in this context, the last phrase could also be read as

"imagination's own nature." Read on its own, GZ *rang gi ngo bo brtag pa* means "examining its own nature."

618. GZ CDNP read the first two lines as prose: "From that karmamudrā, the ecstasies will arise by being distinguished by the distinctions of the moments."
619. *Hevajratantra* II.3.5 (begins "It is there that . . .").
620. Skt. *lakṣya* ("what is to be marked or perceived") in the first line is rendered as "target" in IaS (275) and "goal" in Mathes 2015 (120). As IaS (275n120) points out, besides here in the *Caturmudrānvaya*, these two lines of uncertain origin are also cited in Rāmapāla's *Sekanirdeśapañjikā* (text 45, 396, 399), Sujayaśrīgupta's *Abhiṣekanirukti*, *Kuladatta's *Kriyāsaṃgrahapañjikā*, and Kumāracandra's *Ratnāvalī* (for exact references, see IaS). In addition, two very similar lines (obviously variants of the two here) are found in the *Caturmudrāṭīkā* (text 44, 284) and Vajrapāṇi's *Guruparamparākramopadeśa* (text 213, 210). IaS (98–99) comments on these two lines as follows (as mentioned before, "position A" refers to the fourfold sequence that consists of ecstasy, supreme ecstasy, connate ecstasy, and cessational ecstasy, while in "position B," the order of the last two ecstasies is reversed): "One more passage should be mentioned here which the proponents of position A quote in support of their view. It is this line of (slightly irregular) verse: *paramaviramayor madhye lakṣyaṃ vīkṣya dṛḍhīkuru*. In the *Caturmudrānvaya* (which, again, Maitreyanātha is following) this is in fact the sole passage quoted as proof of the correctness of position A. The same passage is often quoted in other texts too. We are inclined to think that it may be from a lost tantra; certainly the proponents of position A treat it as if it were scriptural, though it cannot be found in any surviving tantra, as far as we know. Proponents of position B, on the other hand, tend not to explicitly refer to this line; but note that Abhayākaragupta, in his *Āmnāyamañjarī*, quotes it and casts doubt on its scriptural status." However, as Dalton 2019 (230n93) points out, while Abhayākaragupta questions the scriptural authority of these two lines—very close to line 124b of Buddhajñāna's *Dvitīyakramatattvabhāvanānāmamukhāgama* (D1853; for the justification of the Sanskrit of this title, see Dalton, 71–72)—he also cites as scriptural—and attributes to the *Paramādyatantra*—a stanza that parallels lines 124cd of the *Dvitīyakramatattvabhāvanānāmamukhāgama*. According to IaS (98–99), said two lines may be from a lost tantra, since the sources that cite them tend to give them the reverence usually reserved for scriptures attributed to the Buddha. But as Dalton (226–30) shows, these lines are very similar to *Dvitīyakramatattvabhāvanānāmamukhāgama* 124b, which reads "an absence" (Tib. *bden gnyis* em. *dben nyid* according to Vaidyapāda's commentary *Sukusuma* and his *Yogasapta*) instead of "what is to be marked" and "cessational and ecstasy" (close Sanskrit parallel in Vāgīśvarakīrti's *Saṃkṣiptābhiṣekavidhi*: *viramānandayor madhye lakṣya vīkṣya dṛḍhīkuru*) instead of "supreme and cessational" in all other later Sanskrit sources (*paramaviramayor madhye lakṣya vīkṣya dṛḍhīkuru*). Whether the two lines cited in the *Caturmudrānvaya* are a variant of those in the *Dvitīyakramatattvabhāvanānāmamukhāgama* (and the *Saṃkṣiptābhiṣekavidhi*) or both versions are based on a different earlier source (such as a lost tantra) is unclear. Dalton suggests that *Dvitīyatattvakramabhāvanānāmamukhāgama* 124b (and the *Saṃkṣiptābhiṣekavidhi*) refers to the three ecstasies in Buddhajñānapāda's system: the two members of the compound

viramānandayor thus are *viramānanda* ("cessational ecstasy") and *ānanda* ("ecstasy"), while *madhye* ("in the middle") refers to **madhyamānanda* ("middling ecstasy"). Thus, Buddhajñānapāda's "middling ecstasy" is also identified with the "absence" to be seen and stabilized here, which is identified several lines later in the *Dvitīyakramatattvabhāvanānāmamukhāgama* with the perfection process (understood as the glimpse of suchness that is experienced directly in the context of the prajnā-jnāna empowerment). According to Dalton, Buddhajñānapāda's "middling ecstasy" corresponds to the "connate ecstasy" of later systems, since, as shown by IaS, this line is frequently cited by proponents of position A (connate ecstasy between supreme ecstasy and cessational ecstasy). This suggests that what is in the middle—be it Buddhajñānapāda's "middling ecstasy" or position A's connate ecstasy—should be understood as coming down to the same: the target to be focused on and marked by the practitioner. Later proponents of position A seem to have modified *Dvitīyakramatattvabhāvanānāmamukhāgama* 124b (and the *Saṃkṣiptābhiṣekavidhi*) to read *paramaviramayor* instead of *viramānandayor* in order to support their position in a more explicit manner. Likewise, the modification to *lakṣyam* ("what is to be marked") from whatever Sanskrit was behind *dben nyid* ("absence"; a modification also found in the *Samkṣiptābhiṣekavidhi*) may also be based on this concern. Whether the two lines cited in the *Caturmudrānvaya* are a variant of those in the *Dvitīyakramatattvabhāvanānāmamukhāgama* and *Saṃkṣiptābhiṣekavidhi* or both versions are based on a third earlier source (such as a lost tantra) is unclear. However, Dalton says, since there are no known attestations of these lines earlier than the *Dvitīyakramatattvabhāvanānāmamukhāgama*, it is worth considering the possibility that the issue of these lines' scriptural authority (as the Buddha's words) or lack thereof may be based on their being found in the *Dvitīyakramatattvabhāvanānāmamukhāgama* as a work that lies on the border of authentic scripture (90 percent being Mañjuśrī's revelatory teaching) and commentarial treatise (for more details, see Dalton 226–32, 395–96nn265–68). It should further be noted that the two lines cited in the *Caturmudrānvaya* are obviously closely related to *Hevajratantra* II.2.40ab (line b is also found in II.5.65b and II.5.69e):

> I have the nature of connate ecstasy,
> at supreme's end and cessation's start

GZ reads the two lines quoted here as follows:

> In the middle of the supreme and cessational ecstasies,
> it should be pointed out, looked at, and relied upon

CDNP:

> The middle of the supreme and the cessational ecstasies
> is to be stabilized [D "demonstrated"] by examining it as what is to be pointed out.

621. GZ CDNP *bstan pa* ("is taught").
622. Following the text of the *Caturmudrānvaya*, BKC (vol. *ka*, fols. 149a.6–150a.3) briefly discusses the controversy about whether connate ecstasy should

be understood as the third or the fourth one in the progression of the four ecstasies: "Among the four mudrās, in the context of the karmamudrā, both assertions that connate [ecstasy] is the third or the fourth one obviously refer to [different] intentions of the tantras because [both assertions] occur in the tantras and [also] are the positions of true supreme siddhas. If you think that, in this case, there is a contradiction [between these two positions], there is no such flaw. For those who assert that cessational ecstasy is the third one, it refers to fainting into unconsciousness once thoughts have ceased by virtue of the bliss [BKC *bde ba'i rtog pa* ('thoughts of bliss') em. *bde bas rtog pa*] in the middle of the jewel. If it is taken as the fourth one, it refers to the moment of bliss fading once bodhicitta is emitted outside. Given that both assert that connate [ecstasy] is perceived at the tip of the jewel, they are not deluded about the triad of location, essence, and path. You may think: 'But isn't that contradictory to the explanation that connate [ecstasy] is perceived within the jewel?' By virtue of merely being free of perceiver and perceived, connate [ecstasy] is coarse, which is stated in accord with Mere Mentalism. To perceive the subtle special feature [of this ecstasy] at the tip is in accord with the Madhyamaka of utter nonabiding. 'However, when considering cessational ecstasy as external, if the ecstasies are divided into four, internal cessational ecstasy would be included in connate ecstasy, but [BKC *lhan skyes bu 'dul* em. *lhan skyes su 'du la*] when considering an internal cessational ecstasy, an external cessational ecstasy would not be counted.' This is not contradictory either. When the four ecstasies are divided into sixteen, in the cessational ecstasy of connate ecstasy, this is [already] connate ecstasy, [but] the connate [ecstasy] of connate [ecstasy] that is more subtle than that is perceived when two are emitted and two are equal [for details on this, see Maitrīpa's *Caturmudropadeśa* (text 92, 20–21), the *Caturmudrāṭīkā* (text 44, 287 and 351–52), Rāmapāla's *Sekanirdeśapañjikā* (text 45, 408ff.), Vajrapāṇi's *Guruparamparākramopadeśa* (text 213, 217ff.), and IaS (399–409)]. The vajra recitation is the inner creation process. Mind isolation and illusory body constitute the dharmamudrā. Luminosity is mahāmudrā. Unity is the great fruitional samayamudrā. The [outer] creation process is the gate that accords with that—that is, the causal samayamudrā. In detail, this should be understood from the *Sekanirṇaya* [the alternative name of the *Sekanirdeśa* (text 42)], which is a commentary on the meaning of this. It is said that [there] Maitrīpa dispelled [flaws such as the above] . . . The following is stated:

> "Once the noble [Nāgārjuna] had composed the explanation of
> the mother tantras' four mudrās, he instructed venerable Śabara
> Then, in a gradual manner, it was disseminated in all directions
> The mighty lord Maitrīpa dispelled the intention's [BKC *dgos* em. *dgongs*] contradictions."

For more detailed matchings of Maitrīpa's five stages of the creation and perfection processes with the four mudrās and the five stages of perfection-process practices in the *Guhyasamājatantra* (according to Nāgārjuna's *Pañcakrama* and Āryadeva's *Caryāmelāpakapradīpa*) in works by Maitrīpa and his students, see the overview in appendix 7.

623. Besides "resemblance," Skt. *chāyā* can also mean "shadow," "reflection,"

"luster," "light," "play of light or color," "gracefulness," "beauty," "complexion," and "features." Given the context and the following explanations, all of these meanings are certainly implied in that the wisdom generated with the help of a karmamudrā is only a reflection or a shadow of the actual connate but nevertheless is a very vivid and colorful experience intimately related to the connate, similar to the rays of the sun being related to the sun itself.

624. GZ "The connate is called 'the connate' because it mimics it in being a shadow of the [actual] connate in all of that. Since this shadow of the connate leads to realizing . . . there is no arising of the [actual] connate from the wisdom [that is based on a] prajñā. For the nature of what is called 'the connate' refers to all phenomena's being uncontrived being called 'specific characteristic' [*ces bya ba'i bar du'o* is difficult to construe]. Therefore, by relying on a karmamudrā, the result that is a concordant outflow [of the actual connate] is produced." CDNP "All that is the connate [in essence]; mimicking it in being a shadow of the [actual] connate is called 'the connate' . . . Hence the [actual] connate does definitely not emerge from the wisdom [that is based on a] prajñā . . . the result that is a concordant outflow [of the actual connate] is caused to be attained."

625. Skt. *śālī* refers to *Nigella indica*, while *kodrava* is *Paspalum scrobiculatum*.

626. GZ "'Similar' is referred to as similar because of arising similar to the cause. The reflection of a face that arises in dependence on a mirror does not become that [actual] face, because it was neither established before, nor is it established at present. The present reflection of that face is realized to be a mere likeness [CDNP omit this sentence]. However, by being deluded . . . masters of weak intellect, saying they have experienced the [actual] connate wisdom [CDNP omit "wisdom"], bring forth joy. Since they are joyful and delighted about that, they do not understand any discourses about the dharmamudrā either. Without understanding the dharmamudrā, how could the nature of the uncontrived connate arise and emerge from nothing but the contrived [practice with a] karmamudrā? It is [only] from a cause of concordant type that a result of concordant type arises, but not from a discordant type. This is just as a sprout of rice growing from a rice seed but not from millet and ? [the meaning of GZ *hu tse* is unclear; CDNP *drug cu pa*, "sixtieth" is meaningless]. Likewise, the nature of [CDNP omit "the nature of"] the uncontrived connate arises from the nature of the uncontrived dharmamudrā. Therefore the mahāmudrā that is not separate from the dharmamudrā itself will arise." CDNP "'Concordant outflow' is referred to as concordant outflow because of arising similar to the cause. The reflection of a face that arises in dependence on a mirror and a face is not that face [CD "other"] itself . . . By being deluded about certainly seeing just a reflection of their face [CD "other"] that is a concordant outflow, worldly people will be joyful . . . Since they do not understand the dharmamudrā . . . Therefore by experiencing it in a manner of being inseparable from the cause that is the dharmamudrā, it will become the cause of mahāmudrā."

627. *Hevajratantra* II.3.4.

628. In the *sandhyābhāṣā* chapter of the *Hevajratantra* (II.3.56–61), *vola* ("gum myrrh") is glossed as *vajra* (understood as "penis") and *kakkolaka* ("perfume") as *padma* ("lotus"; understood as the female genitals). Skt. *manthamanthāna* lit. means "churning (or what is churned) and churning stick."

629. Though it is not obvious from the Tibetan *srub cing bsrubs pa* (lit. "churning and churning" or "churning and having churned") here and in other parallel cases, "the churner and the churned" (Skt. *manthaka* and *manthya*) is a common expression for the union of vajra and lotus during karmamudrā.

630. Skt. *apara* can also mean "distant"; CDNP wrongly take it to have its other meaning, "supreme."

631. GZ "'The jewel of buddhahood' mimics the shadow of buddhahood. 'Casket' means abode and basis. Therefore, from the lotus and the jewel source of the limbs of a karmamudrā, the lotus ornament of delightful ecstasy arises. Here, it will arise thanks to the conventional bodhicitta having arrived from the avadhūtī in the interior of the jewel through the union of the bola and the kakkola (the churner and the churned). This is the arising of a mere moment of the wisdom that is designated as 'the supreme connate named "the momentary [connate],"' but that is not the [actual] connate; it is only its concordant outflow. The wisdom [that is based on a] prajñā and has the nature of being a concordant outflow, the [first] three ecstasies, the four moments, empowerment, and the forceful yoga will arise as results of concordant outflow in dependence on a karmamudrā. This is the detailed instruction on karmamudrā and the result of concordant outflow, which is the first one." CDNP "For it mimics the shadow of buddhahood. 'Casket' means abode or basis. Therefore, from a well-shaped karmamudrā, delightful ecstasy arises [CDNP *kyis* em. *skye*] as the lotus and source of jewels. For as long as the conventional bodhicitta has arrived from the avadhūtī in the interior of the jewel through the union of the vajra and the lotus (the churner and the churned), this is called 'the moment of that [wisdom]': a mere moment of the wisdom that is called 'the connate' will arise, but that is not the [actual] connate; it is not the concordant outflow. Its nature is the wisdom [that is based on a] prajñā and is endowed with the [first] three ecstasies and the four moments. It is declared to be the karmamudrā's result of concordant outflow thanks to the forceful yoga. This is the instruction on the empowerment of the karmamudrā, which is the first one." The *Caturmudrānvaya* matches the four mudrās with four among the classic five results in the Abhidharma (result of concordant outflow, result of maturation, result of freedom, and result produced by persons; not considering the dominated result). Ultimately, this appears to go back to *Hevajratantra* II.4.59–61 and its commentaries (which additionally match the four mudrās and four results with the secret cakra, dharmacakra, sambhogacakra, and mahāsukhacakra). In the Abhidharma, the definition of a result of concordant outflow is "a phenomenon that is either the same as its specific cause or accords with it in its aspect of appearance." There are two types of such results: (1) results of concordant outflow that are actions (for example, the wish to engage in virtue in this life by virtue of having committed virtuous actions in former lives) and (2) results of concordant outflow that are experiences (for example, the experience of abundant wealth in later lives as a result of having performed generosity in the present life). Note that Saraha's *Kāyakoṣāmṛtavajragīti* (text 53, stanzas 38, 65, 66, 70–72, 82, 90–95) also speaks about the four mudrās and the results of concordant outflow, maturation, and stainlessness (not mentioning the result produced by persons). Saraha explicitly matches mahāmudrā with

the result of stainlessness, while the other relations are not spelled out (the samayamudrā is glossed twice as "the welfare of beings," which can be understood as the result produced by persons).

632. This seems the most natural reading of the compound *paramānandaikasundaropāyabhūtā*, but it could also be read as "constitutes the means for the unique beauty of supreme ecstasy," which is supported by the comments in the *Caturmudrāṭīkā* (text 44).

633. That is, the karmamudrā.

634. GZ CDNP ". . . is uniquely beautified by supreme ecstasy, has the essence of the means, is permanent in terms of its continuum, and not different from the connate of the prajñā whose nature is the connate arising as mahāmudrā . . . [CDNP 'and inseparable from the prajñā whose nature is the connate and from arising from the connate'] . . ."

635. Skt. *śalya* (Tib. *zug rngu*) refers to anything that torments or causes pain (such as a thorn or sting). In that vein, it can also mean "arrow," "lance," "pike," and "dart." Other meanings include "defect," "poison," and "boundary," which would make sense here as well.

636. GZ "Its characteristic is another one [as well]. Having relinquished the torments of the delusion that is mere straw and dust thanks to the guru's pith instructions that are like sunrays for those agitated by the darkness of ignorance, it is to be understood as the single nature of all three worlds bound by the power of the four elements (wrong ideas [obviously reading *mithyāsaṃkalpa* instead of *sakala*], earth, water, fire, and wind) . . ." CDNP "Furthermore, its characteristic is as follows. Like sunrays for those agitated by darkness, it is realized after having relinquished the torments of the delusion of being agitated by the darkness of ignorance, which is mere straw and dust, thanks to the guru's pith instructions. It is to be understood as the inseparability of emptiness and compassion that is the single waveless nature of all three worlds bound by the power of the four elements (earth, water, fire, and wind)."

637. *Hevajratantra* I.1.15 and *Saṃvarodayatantra* VII.21.

638. GZ "By being assiduous about this, the proximate cause that has the form of suchness should be understood as the path. Understanding this as the path, by always familiarizing with that path in a respectful and uninterrupted manner, cessation and the nature of the connate will be directly perceived." CDNP "By making efforts in such a way . . . By understanding this as the path, the path is its being uninterrupted in a respectful manner. Cessation—the nature of the connate—will be directly perceived."

639. This stanza is one of the most famous and often-cited stanzas in the literature of the Mahāyāna, best known as *Uttaratantra* I.154 and *Abhisamayālaṃkāra* V.21 (besides the many further texts listed in Brunnhölzl 2014, 1103–4n1488, it also appears in texts 44, 313–14; 45, 423; 46, 29; 66, 267; 76, 228; 90, 318; 213, 193–94; 215, 398; and 217, 472). As for its origin, Gampopa's *Ornament of Liberation* (Lha rje bsod nams rin chen 1990, 289) says that it is found in the *Gaganagañjaparipṛcchāsūtra* (D148), but I could not locate it there. Instead, except for the third line, this stanza is found in the *Śrīmahābalatantra* (D391, fol. 216b.2–4). To provide a bit more of the context of these three lines in that tantra, the lines immediately preceding and following them are as follows:

Once phenomena's identitylessness is realized,
it is the mind that will come to be realized
Everything is filled with emptiness's taste—
this is what is called "mahāsukhakāya"
This constitutes the pāramitā of prajñā—
in this, there is nothing to be removed
and not the slightest to be added on
Whoever sees true reality is liberated
Be it a single disposition, three dispositions,
five dispositions, a hundred dispositions, and such,
in this true reality, there is no difference
Once you managed to find the buffalo,
you don't search for the buffalo's tracks
Likewise, if you found mind's true reality,
you don't search for any thoughts at all

Note that the last four lines allude to a common example in the Mahāmudrā tradition for finding mind's true nature. A farmer was looking for his buffalo by pursuing the tracks of all kinds of other buffalos, but not finding his own anywhere. Returning completely exhausted, he found that his buffalo had been in its stable all along. Compare also stanzas 8 and 56 of text 84, stanzas 18 and 38 of text 178, and stanza 36 of text 181.

640. GZ ". . . By aspiring to realize this, it will be realized [thanks to] engaging in a one-pointed mind comprehending the entire actuality of the connate's nature and thanks to the pith instructions of a true guru. The dharmamudrā serves as the cause that is inseparable from mahāmudrā." CDNP ". . . By aspiring for this, it will be realized [through] a mind that is one-pointed with regard to the entire state of the actuality of the connate's nature and through the pith instructions of a true guru . . ."

641. In the Abhidharma, the definition of a result of maturation is "a nonobscured and neutral phenomenon arisen from its specific causes that consist of contaminated virtuous or nonvirtuous actions."

642. GZ ". . . is the single nature beyond the extremes of saṃsāric existence and nirvāṇa, embodies nonreferentiality, embodies great compassion . . ." CDNP ". . . is the single nature beyond the extremes of saṃsāric existence and nirvāṇa, embodies nonreferential compassion . . ."

643. Note that Skt. *kuśala* can also mean "skillful," "clever," "happy," "good," "suitable," "right," and "virtuous" (all Tibetan versions of these recurrent two lines have *dge ba*, "virtuous"). The same two lines as well as the following stanza are explicitly attributed to the *Jñānālokālaṃkārasūtra* in Maitrīpa's *Amanasikārādhāra* (text 27, 156–57) and also cited (without attribution) in Rāmapāla's *Sekanirdeśapañjikā* (text 45, 419–20). As they stand, these two lines are not found in the *Jñānālokālaṃkārasūtra*, which only contains the following passage: "All nonvirtuous mental engagement is the cause of afflictive phenomena. All virtuous mental engagement is the cause of purified phenomena" (*Jñānālokālaṃkāra* 2004, 94.14–15). Certain commentaries on the *Abhisamayālaṃkāra* say that statements to the effect of mental nonengagement being virtue and mental

engagement being nonvirtue are found in the prajñāpāramitā sūtras (see Brunnhölzl 2011, 35, 147, 271). The first two mentions in those commentaries distinguish virtue and nonvirtue in the context of the four correct efforts on the path of accumulation. The last mention in the context of the six recollections of Buddha, dharma, saṃgha, and so on obviously refers to the statements that each of these recollections consists of nonrecollection and mental nonengagement (for example, *Pañcaviṃśatisāhasrikāprajñāpāramitāsūtra* H10, vol. *ga*, fols. 260a.6ff.). Beyond that, I could only find the statement that when bodhisattvas do not mentally engage in all phenomena from form up through completely perfect awakening, their roots of virtue will increase, and thus they will perfect the six pāramitās and attain omniscience (for example, *Śatasāhasrikāprajñāpāramitāsūtra* H9, vol. *da*, fols. 6b.1–8a.7). By implication, by mentally engaging in form and so on, virtue will not increase or even decrease.

644. *Jñānālokālaṃkārasūtra* IV.12 (*Jñānālokālaṃkāra* 2004, 146.1–2), *Saṃvarodayatantra* VIII.36′ (Tsuda 1974, 101), and *Pañcakrama* IV.10. Explicitly attributed to the *Jñānālokālaṃkārasūtra*, this stanza is also found in the *Amanasikārādhāra* (text 27, 157). Without attribution, it appears in the *Pañcatathāgatamudrāvivaraṇa* (text 36, 194) and the *Sekanirdeśapañjikā* (text 45, 419–20). Note that "lacks minding" (Skt. *asmṛti*), instead of the other possible meaning "lacks mindfulness" (or even "being unconscious"), is understood in the sense of "nonminding," as the second one in Saraha's famous tetrad of minding, nonminding, being unborn, and being beyond mind; see the notes on stanzas 33, 93, and 94 of Saraha's *Dohakoṣa* (text 13).

645. Mathes 2015 (12–30) comments here as follows: "A closer look at the definition of *mahāmudrā* (built around the quote from the *Jṇānālokālaṃkāra* ending in *iti*), reveals a problem in the form of the feminine relative pronoun (*yā*) and correlative (*sā*) construction. To go by the Tibetan translation, the quotation should be taken up by something like *iti yad uktaṃ tad* . . . . If the passage containing the quotations starting with *tathā ca* was removed, however, *yā sā* perfectly falls into place with the feminine attributes of *mahāmudrā* at the beginning. I thus suggest that after the insertion of the *Jṇānālokālaṃkāra* quotes the author or compiler failed to adjust the *yā sā*. Moreover, the original definition of mahāmudrā without the passage from the *Jṇānālokālaṃkāra* has exactly the same structure as the preceding one concerning the dharmamudrā. Whether an insertion or not, the *Jṇānālokālaṃkāra* passage links mahāmudrā with the view of non-abiding and with the practice of *amanasikāra*. As we have seen above, this blend of Sūtras and Tantras is fully elaborated in the *Sekanirdeśa* and the commentary on it by Rāmapāla." What Mathes says is definitely worth considering, but, as he says, it does not prove that these quotations were inserted later. That is, the feminine relative pronouns *yā sā* are not too far removed to still be understood as referring back to the list of mahāmudrā's feminine attributes that immediately precede the two short quotes attributed to the *Jṇānālokālaṃkārasūtra*. The *Caturmudrāṭīkā* (text 44) comments on both quotes, obviously considering them as parts of the *Caturmudrānvaya*, but due to the fact that the *Caturmudrāṭīkā* was composed in Tibetan and contains numerous redactions and additions, this is not conclusive one way or the other either.

646. GZ CDNP "This should be understood as being mahāmudrā. Therefore, from

the inconceivable nature of mahāmudrā, the supreme result that is called [CDNP omit "called"] 'samayamudrā' will arise."

647. Compare this description of mahāmudrā with stanzas 70–72 and 92 in Saraha's *Kāyakośāmṛtavajragīti* (text 53), which also describes mahāmudrā as the result of stainlessness, and Maitrīpa's *Caturmudropadeśa* (text 92, 22): "Mahāmudrā is the unity that is the essence of all phenomena, being unborn, free of thoughts of perceiver and perceived, devoid of the obscurations that are afflictive, cognitive, and so on, and experiencing its own specific characteristic just as it is. This is expressed as the result that is stainlessness. Its essence is that it does not have the form of any phenomena of extremes or a middle, is all-pervading, immutable, and [present] at all times. Therefore mahāmudrā refers to fully perfect buddhahood in a single instant, which lacks any division into the four moments or the four ecstasies." Like the *Caturmudrānvaya*, a number of tantric texts, such as those two and Rāmapāla's *Sekanirdeśapañjikā* (text 45), speak of "the result of stainlessness" (ultimately going back to *Hevajratantra* II.4.59–61 and its commentaries), which obviously is an equivalent of the result of freedom, since it is explained in those texts as the consummate state of mind that is free from all afflictive and cognitive obscurations, including their latent tendencies (sometimes also explained as great bliss). In the Abhidharma, the definition of the result of freedom is "the exhaustion or relinquishment of the specific factors to be relinquished through the force of the remedy that is prajñā" (this specifically refers to the relinquishment of afflictive and, in the Mahāyāna, cognitive obscurations through the paths of seeing, familiarization, and nonlearning).

648. According to the *Caturmudrāṭīkā*, this refers to purifying the body through the vase empowerment, specifically the vajra master empowerment.

649. Given GZ *cho ga rnam pa lngar* (CDNP *ye shes lnga'i cho ga*) and *Caturmudrāṭīkā cho ga lngar*, the second Skt. *pañcavidhaṃ* in *pañcavidhaṃ jñānaṃ pañcavidhaṃ* would be **pañcavidhavidhiṃ/pañcavidhiṃ* or **pañcavidhavidhinā/pañcavidhinā* (understood as *pañcavidhinā* in the sense of "by way of the five-fold ritual" in Mathes 2015, 125). The *Caturmudrāṭīkā* glosses *cho ga lngar btags pa* (**pañcavidhiparikalpa*) by *mngon par byang chub pa lnga* ("fivefold full awakening"), which refers to a specific five-step technique of creating the visualization of a deity (for details, see text 44, 264 and 334). According to Mathes (ibid., 125n331), "The fivefold ritual performance is identified in the *Bod rgya tshig mdzod chen mo* (s.v.) as: 'chanting the ritual melodies, visualizing during the mantra recitation, assuming different hand gestures, playing the drum, dancing.'" However, BGTC has no entry *cho ga lnga*; rather, Mathes's quoted explanation is found verbatim under the entry *cho ga lnga* at https://dictionary.christian-steinert.de, attributed to James Valby.

650. The samādhi of the initial yoga (Skt. *ādiyogasamādhi*, Tib. *dang po sbyor ba'i ting nge 'dzin*), the samādhi of the supreme king of the maṇḍala (Skt. *maṇḍalarājāgrīsamādhi*, Tib. *dkyil 'khor rgyal mchog gi ting nge 'dzin*), and the samādhi of the supreme king of activity (Skt. *karmarājāgrīsamādhi*, Tib. *las rgyal mchog gi ting nge 'dzin*) make up the basic framework of the creation process as first established in the *Sarvatathāgatatattvasaṃgraha*, the earliest and most fundamental yogatantra. According to TOK (3:171–72), these three samādhis pertain to all

yogatantras and above in general. (1) The samādhi of the initial yoga includes everything from progressively visualizing all the parts of the maṇḍala up through visualizing the two principal male and female deities. These two deities are the primary source of emanating all the other deities of the maṇḍala. Since this samādhi is the beginning of the remaining two samādhis, it is the initial one. Since means and prajñā are united in a nondual way, it is yoga (union). (2) The samādhi of the supreme king of the maṇḍala consists of visualizing all the remaining deities of the maṇḍala emanated from the bodhicitta of the two principal male and female deities. Once they have been completed, they are arrayed in their own abodes. This is the supreme king of the maṇḍala because what needs to be arrayed in the maṇḍala has been fully completed. (3) After having fully completed the maṇḍala, the samādhi of the supreme king of activity consists of the enlightened activities of the deities of the maṇḍala, such as purifying all realms. This is the supreme king of activity because it accords with the deeds of buddhas. For more details, see Kongtrul Lodrö Tayé 2008 (68–69), Dalton 2019 (25n126, 187–207, and passim), and Kittay and Jamspal 2020 (97); BGTC (1028) reverses the order of (2) and (3). For an extensive presentation of this as pertaining to the creation process of the *Guhyasamājatantra* in the Ārya tradition, see Gyumé Khensur Lobsang Jampa 2019. The *Caturmudrāṭīkā* glosses "the initial yoga" as "yoga and anuyoga," "the supreme king of the maṇḍala" as "atiyoga," "the supreme king of activity" as "mahātiyoga," "yoga" as rendering "bliss and mind not different," "the bindu" as "the semen of bodhicitta," and "the subtle" as "the vāyus and nāḍīs."

651. According to the *Caturmudrāṭīkā*, "the samayamudrā entails all kinds of discursiveness, is the experiential object of thoughts, involves clinging, is a cause of saṃsāra, and is contrived." GZ "The 'samayamudrā,' which has the essence of being initial and the nature of the forms of the sambhoga- and nirmāṇakāyas, consists of manifestations such as Vajradhara and Heruka for the welfare of sentient beings. This is asserted as the samayamudrā. Once they have taken up this samayamudrā, to imagine the aspects of saṃsāra as the five kinds of wisdom and the fivefold ritual by means of mirror-like [wisdom], [the wisdom of] equality, discriminating [wisdom], all-accomplishing [wisdom], [the wisdom of] the pure dharmadhātu, the initial yoga, [the yoga of] the supreme king of the maṇḍala, [the yoga of] the supreme king of activity, the yoga of bindus, and the yoga of the subtle constitutes the circle of the samayamudrā. The masters who meditate on this will generate mere merit. [However,] by virtue of that [alone], they will not attain the result of the dharmamudrā. The gist of this is 'From a cause . . .'" CDNP ". . . As for 'having taken up this samayamudrā,' to imagine the ritual of the five wisdoms that has the form of a [maṇḍala] circle means that the masters who meditate on this circle of the samayamudrā by means of mirror-like [wisdom] . . . and the yoga of the subtle will generate merit . . ."

652. GZ ". . . imagined by childish beings turn into the gold of the bodhicitta that is connate . . . as the form of the [maṇḍala] circle." CDNP "Therefore, if [all] things such as the mobile and the immobile that are imagined by childish beings are penetrated by the taste of the connate, they turn into the gold of awakening. Through this, the [maṇḍala] circle of the threefold world will be contemplated well." GZ here inserts another stanza with six lines of uneven

lengths (a variant version in seven lines is found in BKC, vol. *ka*, fol. 149a.1–3) that is found neither in the **Advayavajrasaṃgraha* nor any of the canonical Tibetan versions in CDNP: "The following is taught:

"This is not the three abodes, it is the palace
These are not living creatures, they are victors
I'm the cakra lord—no humans, no objects, no faculties,
neither earth and so on, nor form and so forth
Dharmatā's very character is the maṇḍala and the maṇḍala inhabitants
If diversity is known as the maṇḍala circle, why would mind create delusion?"

The *Caturmudrāṭīkā* (text 44, 338) includes a somewhat similar version of this stanza in four lines (attributed to the Buddha) and also comments on it. Likewise, similar four-line stanzas are also cited in Devacandra's *Prajñājñānaprakāśa* (text 16, 71; attributed to Nāgārjuna), Sahajavajra's *Sthitisamāsa* (text 17, 105), Maitrīpa's *Pañcatathāgatamudrāvivaraṇa* (text 36, 196; in both attributed to Nāgārjuna), and Muniśrībhadra's *Pañcakramaṭippaṇī Yogīmanoharā* (fol. 24a.4–5; see Mathes 2015, 103n272). Curiously and maybe based on the comments on this stanza in PTMC on the *Pañcatathāgatamudrāvivaraṇa*, Mathes (ibid., 103) adds in his translation of the *Pañcatathāgatamudrāvivaraṇa* that this stanza stems from Nāgārjuna's *Caturmudrānvaya*. However, as Mathes himself says in his Tibetan edition (ibid. 401), this stanza only appears in GZ, while it is found neither in the **Advayavajrasaṃgraha* (from which Mathes translates) nor in CDNP. Furthermore, the stanza in GZ of the *Caturmudrānvaya* is clearly marked as a quote by *gang gsungs pa . . . ces bstan to*.

653. *Hevajratantra* I.10.41. The last line in GZ CDNP reads *mdor bsdus na ni sems su 'dus pa'i tshul can no* ("In brief, they have the mode of being included in the mind"), and GZ mistakenly separates this last line from the first four by inserting *zhes gsungs so*. As the preceding stanza in the tantra makes clear, "this" in the third line refers to the ultimate bodhicitta that is the unity of prajñā and means or emptiness and compassion. Kṛṣṇa's *Yogaratnamālā* (Snellgrove 1959, 2:135) glosses the last three lines as follows: "'This . . .' refers to the true reality of the samādhis, mantras, and so on of familiarizing with the connate during the perfection process, as described. This bodhicitta is communion—the merging of all phenomena into a single taste. Yogīs become of that nature. Here, precisely this refers to the fourth one, the empowerment of mahāmudrā."

654. GZ "'In brief' means that all phenomena are singular as the form of great bliss . . . 'Contained' refers to the wisdom whose mode consists of dharmamudrā and mahāmudrā, which is called 'the mode of being contained.'" CDNP "'In brief' means that all phenomena have a single form. 'What is it?' It is the nature of great bliss . . . 'The mode of being contained' refers to the wisdom through the empowerment of dharmamudrā and mahāmudrā . . ."

655. The definition of a result produced by persons is "a phenomenon that has arisen due to the force of its specific causes." Here, the expression "being produced by persons" is a case of labeling something general by one of its instances, such as a harvest that results from the specific efforts of a farmer. Thus this type of result is not limited to things being produced by people but

includes any result that comes about through its own specific causes, such as a rose flower growing from a rose seed, earth, water, and warmth.

656. As for the otherwise unattested *no pi ka* in GZ here, *sādhanopika* also appears (wrongly) for *sādhanopāyika* in the Sanskrit reconstruction of the title of Ratnākaraśānti's *Piṇḍīkṛtasādhanopāyikāvṛttiratnāvaḷī* in Tg; just like *sādhana*, *sādhanopāyikā* is simply rendered there as *sgrub thabs* in Tibetan, with *upāyikā* meaning "what serves as the means." Thus it seems that *no pi ka* here is a corrupt form of *upāyikā*. Mathes 2015 (127) renders *no pi ka* as "manual," while https://dictionary.christian-steinert.de. has "propitiatory rite," which does not make sense here.

657. CDNP "This concludes 'The Ascertainment of the Four Mudrās' composed by the great master Nāgārjunagarbha. It was translated, edited, and finalized by the venerable guru Dhirisrījāna and the Tibetan lotsāwa Mapen Chöbar" (BA, 843, has a Dhiriśrījñāna [English: Dhītiśrijñāna] as one of the seven middling disciples of Maitrīpa). According to Tipi Bumlabar (BKC, vol. *kha*, fols. 84a.6–85a.1), the outline of this text is as follows:

1. the title
2. [the text] that bears this title
2a. expression of homage and commitment to explain
2b. teaching the purpose and the connection (the branch of others engaging)
2c. meaning of the text
2c1. presenting the body [of the text] by way of a brief introduction
2c2. detailed explanation of its branches
2c2a. karmamudrā, the path of the messenger (the means of first pointing out)
2c2a1. its own essence
2c2a2. teaching the progressive manner of arising of the four moments and the four ecstasies in which locations
2c2a3. refuting wrong ideas about wisdom's own essence
2c2a4. refuting wrong ideas about the path of accomplishment
2c2a5. teaching the answer to saying this contradicts the scriptures
2c2a6. teaching the manner of arising of the four moments and the four ecstasies
2c2b. dharmamudrā, the path of yoga (what is to be pointed out)
2c2b1. its own essence
2c2b2. the difference between dharmamudrā and mahāmudrā
2c2b3. teaching the presentation of dharmamudrā and mahāmudrā being cause and result
2c2b4. teaching that making this a living experience is contingent on the pith instructions of the guru
2c2c. mahāmudrā, [the result of] stainlessness
2c2c1. its own essence
2c2c2. teaching mahāmudrā as the dharma of mental nonengagement
2c2c3. teaching that fruitional mahāmudrā is inconceivable

2c2d. samayamudrā, the result produced by persons (manifesting for the welfare of others)
2c2d1. the fruition
2c2d2. the path
2c2d3. teaching that there will be no buddhahood through samayamudrā alone
2c2d4. teaching the fruition of having made unity a living experience (the way in which the three kāyas dawn)

For further details, see Mathes 2015, x, 4, 12–13, 127–31.

658. PDMT, 18:291–305. My translation follows the Sanskrit ms. as much as possible. Complete editions are found in Śāstrī 1898 (henceforth "Śāstrī"), Patel 1949 (henceforth "Patel"), Varghese 2008 (henceforth "Varghese"), Jadusingh 2017, and partial editions in Bendall 1903–4 (henceforth "Bendall") and Dasgupta 1974 (197–217). However, as mentioned before, according to Patel (xii), "the first leaf is missing, the obverse side of the seventh leaf is totally illegible and many pādas, phrases or words are too much defaced to be deciphered with any certainty." Patel reconstructed both the missing passages from Bendall (if cited there) and the Tibetan versions in Sanskrit, but in such cases I usually follow the Tibetan, and the variant readings in the three Tibetan versions (GZ; D1804, P2669, N1468 = DNP; P5028, N3811, henceforth abbreviated CRV) are provided in the notes. In addition, I also retain the Tibetan titles and the translation colophons as they appear in these versions. I am greatly indebted to the previous translation and summary of the text, as well as the annotations, in Wedemeyer 1999 (220–22, 357–82; henceforth "Wedemeyer"), who outlines his approach as follows (231): "As Sanskrit texts are available for the *Cittaviśuddhi-prakaraṇa* and the *Svādhiṣṭhāna-[krama]prabheda*, I have relied on both the Tibetan and the Sanskrit in translating these. The translations of these texts (particularly the CVP) reflect the eclectic text which I believe should be established on the basis of these alternative testimonies. I recognize that not all scholars are comfortable with such eclectic texts, but in this I follow the editorial tradition of G. Thomas Tanselle in seeking to establish a text which (in my judgment) reflects the author's intention. I have noted the relevant passages, so that anyone interested in the 'pure' reading of either the Tibetan or the Sanskrit may note these alternative readings." Thus there is a significant number of instances where Wedemeyer choses to translate from the Tibetan rather than the Sanskrit, though this is often not warranted when the Sanskrit makes good sense.

659. CRV *tsi ta rad na bi ṣo da na ma / bod skad du / sems rin po che sbyong bar byed pa zhes bya ba* ("The Purification of the Jewel of the Mind").

660. Since the first leaf of the Sanskrit ms. is missing, these homages are only found in GZ DNP; CRV has "I pay homage to glorious Vajrasattva." Unlike the usual four-line stanzas in GZ DNP, the first five stanzas in CRV consist of two long lines of fifteen syllables (obviously following the Sanskrit prosody more closely).

661. CRV has the first line at the end of this stanza.

662. Patel's reconstruction *nirālamba* usually means "supportless, "self-supported," "independent," and "free." In its specific Buddhist use, it also means "without

object" or "without focus" (GZ *dmigs pa bral* DNP *dmigs dang bral* CRV *dmigs pa med* may suggest the latter).

663. GZ DNP *gnas pa med pa* CRV *rab tu mi gnas* (*apratiṣṭhāna*). Though Patel's reconstructions often follow CRV, here he has *anavasthitaṃ* ("without firm stand/ground"), which, according to Negi 1993 (2940, 2953–54), is not attested as being rendered as *gnas pa med pa* (or *gnas med*). I follow CRV *rab tu mi gnas*, the specific and often attested translation of *apratiṣṭhita/apratiṣṭhāna*, which is also one of the expressions rendered by *gnas pa med pa*. According to Negi (2940), other attested Sanskrit expressions rendered by *gnas pa med pa* are *anālaya* ("abodeless") and *aniketa* ("having no residence"). The same problem of manifold meanings of *gnas* with negatives arises in line 2c.

664. In the first two lines, I follow CRV *bsam med dpe dang bral ba / brjod du med cing bstan du med /*. Patel's reconstruction *adṛṣṭāntaṃ anākhyānaṃ acintyaṃ anidarśanam* agrees, but moves "inconceivable" to the third place. In GZ DNP, the first two lines read "without going, without example, inexpressible, unseeable." However, as is often the case in GZ DNP, *'gro ba med pa* appears to be an overly literal rendering of Skt. *agamya*, which means "unintelligible" (and also "unattainable" and "inaccessible"), thus being similar to "inconceivable." Both "indemonstrable" (CRV *bstan du med*) and "unseeable" (GZ DNP *bltar med pa*) are meanings of *anidarśana*. Without knowing the exact underlying Sanskrit, the Tibetan of the third line (GZ DNP *gnas pa med pa gnas med pa* CRV *gnas pa med pa gnas med pas*) on its own is ambiguous, maybe most straightforwardly "without abiding, without abode." Patel reconstructs this as *anāśrayāpratiṣṭhānaṃ* ("without support, utterly nonabiding"). Possible other attested Sanskrit expressions rendered by *gnas med pa* are *anālaya/nirālaya* ("abodeless"), *nirāśraya* ("supportless"), *aniketa* ("having no residence"), *nirāspada* ("homeless," "objectless"), and even *anāvila* ("untainted").

665. The first two lines in GZ DNP *sangs rgyas thams cad kyi ni gnas / sku ni snying rje'i rang bzhin nyid* are somewhat freely reconstructed by Patel as *sarveśām āśrayaṃ buddhaṃ karuṇāmayavigrahaṃ* ("the Buddha, the foundation of all, whose body is made of compassion"); following this, Wedemeyer renders the first line as "Buddha, the universal refuge." More literally, the last two lines in GZ DNP say "is the one to teach various means to beings of various aspirations." However, CRV has the explicit instrumental *thabs kyis* and reads as follows:

> The supreme abode of all buddhas without exception,
> the body with the nature of compassion,
> is the one who teaches sentient beings with
> various aspirations through various means.

666. This could also be read as "in the way of great passion." Patel's reconstruction *mahārāgaṃ namaskṛtya* does not have any equivalent of Tib. *tshul* ("way" or "principle"), on which all Tibetan versions agree, while Wedemeyer adds it as "[method of]."

667. DNP has this line as "I pay homage to you, Lotus Lord of Dance." The name "Lotus Lord of Dance" (Skt. Padmanarteśvara) refers to a number of different figures. First, most commonly and obviously referred to here, Padmanarteśvara is the name of a red form of Avalokiteśvara, of which there are various

forms, such as a form with one face and eighteen arms, with a double lotus in each hand, being in the "half cross-legged posture" or dancing on one leg; a form with one face and two arms in the *sūcī* mudrā with a lotus, with his consort Śakti, and surrounded by eight goddesses on an eight-petaled lotus; and a form with eight arms holding various implements. Padmanarteśvara is celebrated in the annual Mani Rimdu ritual in parts of Nepal. In the "Tibetan Book of the Dead," Padmanarteśvara also appears in the central position in the throat cakra. Second, according to Śubhākaragupta's *Abhisamayamañjarī*, Padmanarteśvara is an alternative name of Amitābha, red, standing in the warrior stance (Skt. *ālīḍha*), having three eyes, matted locks, and bearing the mudrās. Third, Padmanarteśvara is a dark-blue four-armed vīra who is the male consort of the ḍākinī Mahābalā in the kāyacakra of the *Vajraḍākatantra* and the vajracakra of the *Ḍākārṇavatantra*, as well as the consort of the ḍākinī Padmanarteśvarī in the hṛdayacakra of the *Ḍākārṇavatantra*.

668. On the last line, Wedemeyer (357n1) comments as follows: "This reading is attested by all the Tibetan versions. Patel's reconstruction reads, 'from the observation of my own mind' (*svacittapratyavekṣaṇāt*), which seems to make more sense in this context. Patel cites the testimony of '*JS*' as evidence. Though he refers to this text several times in his work, nowhere is its referent explained. I imagine this is the *Jñānasiddhi* but have not been able to find the reference." However, Skt. *pratyavekṣaṇa* corresponds to Tib. *rab tu rtog pa*, while CRV *rab tu rtogs pa* and GZ DNP *rtogs pa* rather suggest something like Skt. *prabuddha*, *prabodhana*, *avabodha*, *prativibuddha*, *prativedha*, or *suvidita*, all meaning "realize" or "awaken." Moreover, an ablative ending (such as *-āt*) is not typically translated as Tib. *bya('i) phyir* (as found in GZ DNP CRV), which rather suggests a dative ending. Thus, both as an aspiration and the commitment to compose this text, the Tibetan makes good sense. That being said, Patel's reconstruction is also possible and meaningful, since *rtog* and *rtogs* are very often conflated in Tibetan texts.

669. CRV *rnal 'byor spyod pa'i spyi lugs kyis* DNP *rnal 'byor spyod pa'i tshogs kyi ni* ("through the accumulation of Yogācāra/yogic practice") GZ *rnam par spyod pa'i tshogs kyis ni* ("through the accumulation of analysis"). In the last line in CRV, "practiced" is replaced by "presented," while GZ omits this entire line. Patel's reconstruction *yogācārasya nayataḥ sarvam eva suniścitam / tat sarvam iha vaktavyaṃ tasmād etat samācaret /* is some kind of hybrid between GZ DNP and CRV:

> Due to the approach of Yogācāra,
> everything is completely certain
> All this is to be discussed here
> Therefore this is to be practiced

However, *thams cad (nyid) du* in all Tibetan versions does not suggest *sarvam* ("everything"), but something like *sarvathā*, *sarvatra*, or *sarvataḥ*. Also, the second *sarvam* has no equivalent in Tibetan. One may wonder whether "Yogācāra" here specifically refers to the Mahāyāna school of this name or "yogic practice" in general. Given what is said in stanzas 7 and 8 about *cittamātra* and in stanza

10 about the preeminence of the mind, it seems very clear that "Yogācāra" refers to the view and practice of that school.

670. This stanza is identical to *Hevajratantra* II.2.50. Wedemeyer (358n2) comments that this raises interesting questions concerning the relationship of these two texts, especially since the author of the *Subhāṣitasaṃgraha* (Bendall, 33, 39, 93) cites this stanza from the *Cittaviśuddhiprakaraṇa* and not the *Hevajratanta*, which is usually considered as more authoritative. The stanza is also found in the *Yoginīsañcārya* (H394, fol. 341b.6–7), the *Sampuṭatantra* (H396, fols. 418b.7–419a.1), Kālapāda's *Mañjuśrīnāmasaṃgītisvānuśaṃsāvṛtti* (D1399, fol. 264b.5), Padmavajra's *Śrīḍākārṇavamahāyoginītantrarājasyaṭīkāvohitaṭīkā* (D1419, fol. 86b.2), Kṛṣṇapāda's *Kṛṣṇayamāritantrarājāprekṣaṇapathapradīpanāmaṭīkā* (D1920, fol. 253b.2–3), Cilupa's *Ratnavṛkṣanāmarahasyasamājavṛtti* (D1846, fol. 38b.2), as *Guhyasiddhi* VI.86cd–87ab, and as *Advayasiddhi* 7. It is furthermore similar to Saraha's "People Dohā" 45cd and 53cd (text 13).

671. In the ms., the first two lines are a lacuna. Patel's reconstruction of the first two lines reads *viśuddher eva sattvasya viśuddhaṃ jāyate phalam* ("A pure fruition arises only from the purity of mind/beings" [Wedemeyer says "mind" but acknowledges that *sattva* can mean either]); *jāyate* has no equivalent in Tibetan. However, all Tibetan versions agree on *sems tsam kho na* ("mere mind alone"). Wedemeyer (358n3) claims that Patel's reconstruction follows CRV reading *sems can kho na* (which in Tibetan can only mean "sentient beings alone"), but all versions of CRV in N, P, PDMT, and the *gser bris ma* Tg clearly read *sems tsam kho na*. Wedemeyer continues: "One wonders if this reading was influenced by the association of the expression *sems tsam* with the *yogācāra* (*rnal 'byor spyod pa*) mentioned two verses above and the *cittamātra* (*sems tsam*) mentioned just below. If, however, one takes *sattva* as meaning 'character,' or even 'mind,' the different readings do not present a problem and conform to the obvious intention of the verse." Given the unanimous readings of all Tibetan versions here, this is obviously a pseudo-problem, and "Yogācāra" in line 5a in DNP and CRV and the Sanskrit *cittamātra* in line 8b clearly support the Tibetan reading *sems tsam* here as well.

672. The first two lines in Śāstrī read *dharmapudgalanairātmyāt cittamātraṃ jagau muniḥ*, while Patel has *dharmapudgalanairātmyaṃ . . .* ("The Sage has proclaimed mere mind to be phenomenal and personal identitylessness"). As explained below in this note, either reading makes sense. The last line follows Śāstrī *gamakaṃ sunirākulaṃ* (which conforms to the ms. and is supported by GZ DNP *rigs pa* [GZ *rig pa*, "awareness"] *dang yang rab tu mthun*, though a more common reading of this would be "in full accordance with reasoning"). Patel emends this to *āgamātyanukūlakam* ("greatly in accordance with the scriptures"), obviously paraphrasing CRV *lung dang shin tu 'gal ba med*. GZ DNP:

> The Sage has declared that phenomenal and
> personal identitylessness [DNP "the inseparability of phenomena
> and the person"] are mere wisdom (*ye shes tsam*)
> In that manner, this kind of arising . . .

The first two lines in CRV agree with GZ, but the last two lines say:

Therefore that all this arises from it
does not at all contradict the scriptures

As mentioned in more detail in the introduction to this text, the explanation of "mere mind" (*cittamātra*) as phenomenal and personal identitylessness is not as unusual as it may sound, as evidenced by Sthiramati's *Triṃśikābhāṣya* identifying the main objective of the *Triṃśikā* as helping those not understanding *cittamātra* (due to their attachment to the real existence of persons and phenomena) to fully realize personal and phenomenal identitylessness in order to accomplish the true fruition of *cittamātra*. Similarly, Vasubandhu's *Viṃśatikāvṛtti* on stanza 10 says that the teaching on "mere cognizance" serves as the entrance to phenomenal identitylessness. Mere cognizance makes appearances arise, but there is no phenomenon that has the characteristic of form and so on. Entering into phenomenal identitylessness does not mean there is no phenomenon in any respect at all. It means identitylessness in the sense of an imaginary identity (a nature of phenomena as imagined by childish beings)—the imaginary nature, consisting of perceiver and perceived and so on. It is not meant in the sense of the nonexistence of the inexpressible identity that is the object of the buddhas. Likewise, one enters into the identitylessness of mere cognizance, in the sense of it lacking any identity imagined by yet another cognizance. Therefore it is through the presentation of mere cognizance that one enters the identitylessness of all phenomena, but not through the complete denial of their relative existence (see also Brunnhölzl 2009, 17–27, and 2018, 203–5, 327–28, 332–34, 700–705, and appendices 5 and 18). Thus, as our stanza here says, the arising of all phenomena is sufficiently explained by the notion of "mere mind" in connection with phenomenal and personal identitylessness (as the following stanzas will show, mind is regarded as the primary one among all phenomena and their source). In addition, the connection between arising (dependent origination) and identitylessness (emptiness) here is reminiscent of what Nāgārjuna says in *Mūlamadhyamakakārikā* XXIV.14 and XXIV.20:

If all of this were not empty,
nothing would arise or cease,
and it would follow that, for you,
the noble ones' four realities do not exist
For whom emptiness is feasible,
everything is feasible
For whom emptiness is not feasible,
nothing is feasible.

673. GZ DNP:

In order to realize [DNP "dispel"] the grasping by being
seized by the demon of clinging to entities,
he of compassionate character has spoken
clearly and extensively in the scriptures

CRV basically reflects the Sanskrit, except reading *gzung bas* for *gṛhitān* (misreading it as an ablative), and N having *lus* ("body") instead of P *lung* ("scripture").

674. This stanza *manaḥpūrvaṅgamā dharmā manaḥśreṣṭhāḥ manojavāḥ / manasā hi paduṣṭena bhāsati vā karoti vā //* is obviously an abbreviated form of the first two stanzas of the *Dhammapada*: *manaḥpubbaṅgamā dhammā manoseṭṭhā manomayā / manasā ce paduṭṭhena bhāsati vā karoti vā / tato naṃ dukkham anveti cakkaṃ'va vahato padaṃ // manaḥpubbaṅgamā dhammā manoseṭṭhā manomayā / manasā ce pasannena bhāsati vā karoti vā / tato naṃ sukkham anveti chāyā'va anapāyinī //*. The *Dhammapada* says that all phenomena are preceded by mind, have mind as their chief, and are made by mind. Thus, the experiences of happiness and suffering are contingent on the purity or impurity, respectively, of the mind. The problem in the stanza here lies in its third line, where Śāstrī reads *praduṣṭeṇa*, Patel *prasannena* (following CRV), and Wedemeyer *prakṛṣṭena* ("distinguished," "preeminent"; but then translates as "preceded by"). Given that the stanza makes a general statement without, as the *Dhammapada* does, differentiating between a wicked (*paduṭṭha*) mind and a pure (*pasanna*) mind, I tentatively follow Wedemeyer *prakṛṣṭena* but translate it according to its meaning ("preeminent"). Śāstrī and Patel obviously each picked one of the options "wicked" and "pure" as found in the *Dhammapada*, while GZ has "single" and DNP "two" (possibly referring to those two states of mind in the *Dhammapada*). Given all that, it may be that an additional stanza that would provide the gist of the *Dhammapada* more fully is missing. GZ DNP:

> The mind that precedes phenomena
> is foremost, the mind proceeds them [DNP "that mind is foremost,
> that mind is swift"]
> It is due to the efforts of the single [DNP "two"] mind
> that one is speaking or acting

CRV:

> The mind precedes phenomena
> It is by virtue of the clear mind
> that speaking or acting are suitable
> Mind is chief, they arise from mind.

675. I follow Patel *patanāc ca* against Śāstrī *āyuṣyaca*.
676. I follow Patel *vṛddhaḥ* against Śāstrī *ādiṣṭaḥ*.
677. D CRV *'dod* ("wish") NP *gyis* instead of *'dong*.
678. GZ *'phul bas* ("due to jostling") DNP *bskul bas* ("due to urging on").
679. This refers to an episode in the *Vinayavastu*. A bhikṣu and his old father, also ordained, arrived in Jetavana. When they heard the sound of the bell, the bhikṣu thought this was the call for the distribution of donations and urged his father to walk faster. However, the old man took a fall and died from it. When the bhikṣu confessed what he regarded as breaking his monastic vows (having killed someone), the Buddha told him it was not a negative action because of having been unintentional. "The five actions of immediate consequence" (Skt. *pañcānantaryāṇi karmāṇi*, Tib. *mtshams med lnga*) are killing one's mother, father, or an arhat, creating a schism in the saṃgha, and deliberately causing a buddha's blood to flow. These actions are often translated as "inexpiable sins" or "sins of immediate retribution," which sound rather theistic

and vengeful. Rather, the reason for the name of these actions is that when those who have committed one or more of them die, they will directly plunge into the hell realms without going through the intermediate state between two rebirths.

680. I follow Patel *suglanena* against Śāstrī *svaglanena.*
681. GZ DNP CRV *gnad g.yog(s)* ("nurse").
682. I follow Patel *madgalaṃ paripīḍaya* against Śāstrī *svagalaṃ paripīḍitaṃ.*
683. This also refers to an episode in the Vinaya. The position taken here is interesting, since the Buddhist tradition otherwise often says that one is not allowed to kill very sick or dying beings ("assisted suicide") because then the negative karma that caused the present state of the diseased or dying person will not have been exhausted and will continue into the next life. CRV:

    Seeing an arhat who is tormented
    by illness, a bhikṣu who is a nurse
    may wring his neck and he may die
    thereby—there is no flaw in that.

684. I follow Patel *anyasaṃjñayā nānyāṃ stu* against Śāstrī *anyasaṅgīni cālyaṃ stu.*
685. GZ DNP:

    Even if, by virtue of another intention,
    others die, one is not tainted by flaws [DNP "no flaws are committed"],
    as it is clearly taught in the Vinaya
    Thus a virtuous mind is without flaw

    The last two lines in CRV read as follows:

    If there is no bad mind, there is no flaw—
    this is clearly declared in the Vinaya.

686. I follow Patel *khanane* against Śāstrī *khalane;* GZ DNP *bshig* ("destroyed").
687. I follow Patel *yataḥ* against Śāstrī *mataṃ.*
688. I follow Patel *upānantaryakāraṇāt* against Śāstrī *ukhānantaryakāriṇāṃ;* CRV *mtshams med pa dang nyes byas pa* ("having committed secondary acts of immediate consequence and flaws").
689. The five acts of immediate consequence are having sex with a female arhat, killing someone who definitely has bodhicitta, killing a bhikṣu who is in training, stealing the property of the saṃgha, and destroying a stūpa.
690. GZ DNP omit "result." In the Tibetan tradition, there's a commonly told story about a man placing his boots on the head of a buddha statue in order to protect it from the falling rain. Later, another man came along and, deeming it sacrilegious to place footwear on the head of a buddha, removed the boots. As the karmic result of their outwardly opposite actions that were, however, equally rooted in their virtuous intentions, both men became kings later.
691. Patel *anyasaṃjñayā nānyāṃ stu* against Śāstrī *anyasaṅgīni cālyaṃ stu.*
692. I follow Patel *puṇya* (supported by *bsod nams* in all Tibetan versions) against Śāstrī *karma.* With GZ DNP *rnam par gnas* and CRV *gnas pa yin* as overly literal but here misleading renderings of Skt. *vyavasthitiḥ,* GZ DNP read as follows:

Therefore merit and wrongdoing
abide within the root of intention
Since it is stated thus in the scriptures,
no flaw exists in a mind that is virtuous

CRV:

Therefore intention is abiding as
the root of merit and wrongdoing
With no flaw in a virtuous mind,
this is hence stated in the scriptures.

693. I follow Patel *yogī* against Śāstrī *yogān*.
694. In a general sense, the expression "the yoga of their own supreme deity," which occurs several times in this text, could also be understood as "being united with their own supreme deity." However, in all likelihood, this expression refers to the specific practice of the creation process of one's chosen deity, which includes being united with that deity, but also entails more than that.
695. I follow Patel *lipyate* against Śāstrī *caliṣyate*. GZ DNP:

Even if yogīs enjoy [DNP add "desired"] objects by making
efforts in promoting the welfare of beings
by means of the yoga of their own deity,
they will be liberated, not tainted by flaws [DNP omit "flaws"]

CRV:

If yogīs enjoy objects by themselves
meditating on their own deity, by making
efforts in promoting beings' welfare,
they will be liberated, without any taint.

696. GZ *dpyad* ("analyzing") DNP *spyad* ("enjoying").
697. I follow Patel *muhyate* against Śāstrī *mucyate*.
698. CRV:

This is just as when those knowing poison's reality,
being familiar with the poison, consume it,
they alone are without any harm and
will become free from all sicknesses.

699. GZ omits this line. The gandharvas are the celestial musicians of Indra who sustain themselves only through smells and live in the air and the heavenly waters. It is said that some part of the lowest heavenly realms in which the gandharvas live can occasionally be seen down on Earth as a marvelous, shimmering castle floating in the sky at a distance. In ancient India, the appearance of such a mirage was usually called "the city of gandharvas."
700. I follow Patel *rajyanti*, supported by GZ DNP *chags* ("are attached to"); Śāstrī *majjanti* ("are immersed in") would also make sense here.
701. GZ DNP ". . . if knowing the essence of forms and so on . . ."

702. This stanza corresponds to *Yuktiṣaṣṭikā* 55. CRV seems at least partially corrupt:

> The entirety of childish people as well as
> those not free from desire are medium ones
> If there is such knowledge, they are liberated
> because their insight is of supreme nature.

703. GZ DNP have the second and third lines as follows:

> through the ritual of worshipping the deity,
> regard them as excellent without any doubt!

The second line in CRV agrees with GZ DNP, while the third and fourth lines say this:

> by familiarizing with them as pure, as there is no doubt,
> what is enjoined by mantra is to be consumed.

704. I follow Patel *akṣara* against Śāstrī *aṅkura*.
705. For "purify" and "illuminate," I follow Patel *ṣodhyaṃ* and *dīpyaṃ* against Śāstrī *śoṣyaṃ*.
706. GZ DNP CRV "satisfy."
707. Patel *agra* Śāstrī *vaktra*.
708. This appears to describe the "inner offering" of purifying, transforming, and increasing the five meats and the five nectars with OṂ ĀḤ HŪṂ and then offering them by flicking a small portion with the thumb and the ring finger. "The five meats" (Skt. *pañcamāṃsa*), otherwise forbidden or considered impure in the Indian tradition but used in tantric practices, consist of the flesh of cows, dogs, elephants, horses, and humans. Most Tibetan traditions consider "the five nectars" (Skt. *pañcāmṛta*) to be feces, urine, semen, menstrual blood, and marrow (Dung dkar blo bzang 'phrin las 2002, 1123, lists semen and blood as "white and red bodhicitta"). The *Guhyasamājatantra*, as probably the earliest source, never explicitly mentions the fifth one, while the *Anāvilatantra* and the *Cakrasaṃvaratantra* list "flesh" as the fifth. BGTC (1362) has feces, urine, blood, flesh, and vajra dew (*rdo rje'i zil pa*). There is also a list of feces, urine, semen, menstrual blood, and brains. As Törzsök 2020 (40) points out, in non-Buddhist tantric sources, the five nectars are not listed in a systematic way but seem to usually include the following four: semen, blood, fat/marrow (Skt. *medas*), and grease/fat (Skt. *sneha*).
709. Patel reads *gacchann antam anenaiva*, obviously following CRV *de nyid kyis ni mthar phyin pa* (however, for *mthar phyin pa* one would typically expect something like *niṣṭhāgata*, *paryavasāna*, *paryanta*, or *pāramiprāpta*, while Śāstrī has *kāyenaiva tu saṃprāptāṃ* ("but those who attained/reached it through the body"). GZ DNP *de tsam zhig tu yang dag par* (hard to make sense of) and DNP *de tsam zhig tu longs spyad pa* give very different meanings (see next note).
710. GZ DNP:

> What appears as real for childish beings, [DNP "This, which is real for childish beings,"]

that is delusive to the yogīs
As just that, in actuality, [DNP "[For] those who enjoy it as just that"]
there is neither bondage nor liberation

CRV:

What is real here for childish beings
is the opposite of that to the yogīs
Those reaching the end through this
are without bondage and liberation.

711. Here and in the following line, GZ replaces "think" by *shes* ("know," "perceive").
712. CRV:

With saṃsāra and nirvāṇa
being other, true reality is not seen
When true reality is known with a mind
of neither saṃsāra nor nirvāṇa . . .

713. I follow Patel *pātakaḥ* against Śāstrī *pāṭakaḥ*.
714. GZ DNP "harmed" CRV "killed."
715. I follow Patel *viṣeneva* against Śāstrī *viṣenaiva*.
716. I follow Patel *utkhātya* against Śāstrī *utkhālya*.
717. CRV "realize."
718. Patel *yathaiva* Śāstrī *yathaikaḥ*.
719. Here and in the last line, GZ DNP CRV replace "tinted" and "colored" by "changed"; CRV omits "colors."
720. Following GZ DNP *tha mal* and the context, ms. *prakṛta-* ("natural") is emended to *prākṛta-* ("ordinary"). As Wedemeyer (363n23) points out, the emendations by Patel (*prakṛtyā*) and Śāstrī (*prakṛte*) appear to try to avoid the prosodic flaw of having both the second and third syllables light, but the author of our text seems to be willing to occasionally flout this convention, as exemplified by *dvādaśayojana* in stanza 32.
721. "Its own nature" follows the ms. and Śāstrī *nijarūpam*, which is supported by GZ *rang gi rang bzhin* and DNP *gnyug ma'i rang bzhin*. Patel emends this to *niḥsvabhāvam* (supported by CRV *rang bzhin med*), probably also because the last two lines—with *niḥsvabhāvam* instead of *nijarūpam* as the third word—are again found verbatim as lines 34ab. While *niḥsvabhāvam* ("without nature") certainly makes sense here as well, there is some difference of context between stanza 28 and stanza 34. The stanza here speaks about the nature of the jewel of the mind being naturally pure of thoughts (which are said throughout to be adventitious, thus not having any intrinsic nature). This stance is explicitly repeated in some of the following stanzas: stanza 46 says that "the mind that is purified appears thought-free and is stainless by its very nature," stanza 90 that "the very clear and pure mind is freed from the web of thoughts," and stanza 120 that once the vase of thoughts is broken, "the lamp of wisdom, being naturally clear and stainless, is illuminating" (in a similar vein, stanza

70 says that "the body as a blend of identitylessness and impurity is stainless by its nature"). By contrast, in stanza 34 it is the true state of the world that is described as "pure from the beginning, unborn, without any nature, and taintless." GZ DNP (DNP omit the fifth line):

> If this jewel of mind is devoid
> of the colors of ordinary thoughts,
> it is pure from the beginning, unborn,
> and its own nature is stainless—
> yogīs should always familiarize with this

CRV:

> This jewel of mind that is devoid
> of the changes by natural thoughts,
> as it is pure from the beginning, is unborn,
> without nature, and free of stains—
> you should diligently render it such.

722. I follow Patel *bālaiḥ* against Śāstrī *bāla*; CRV "the world."
723. I follow Patel *kāraṇāt* against Śāstrī *kāriṇā*.
724. As the phrasing of GZ DNP ("in order to make the mind stainless through the yoga of your own deity") suggests, the last two lines could also be read in reverse order.
725. Śāstrī *saṃyuktā* ("connected with") Patel *saṃmugdhā* (corresponding to GZ DNP *rmongs pa*, "ignorant," "bewildered") CRV *gdungs* ("tortured"). CRV seems to make the most sense here, so I emend to *saṃtaptā*.
726. Patel *kāmamokṣaphala* (Śāstrī *kāmamokṣyaphala*) could of course also be read as "the result of liberation from passion," but all Tibetan versions agree on *'dod pas* ("through passion"). GZ DNP:

> Through the virtuous mind of the yogīs,
> by engaging in passion with passionate women
> bewildered by the poison of dispassion [*chags med* instead of *chags me*],
> liberation is attained through passion

CRV:

> With those tortured by the poison of passion's fire,
> through the virtuous mind of the yogīs,
> they should behave passionately for sure
> Through passion, the result of liberation arises.

727. I follow Śāstrī Bendall *gāruḍiko viṣaṃ piban*; based on his reading of Bendall's ms., Patel emends to *viṣamākṛṣya saṃpiban* ("extracting the poison, one drinks it").
728. GZ DNP:

> It is like meditating on yourself as a garuḍa
> and drinking all the poisons; through that, [CRV "summoning poisons and drinking them; . . ."]

> what is to be accomplished is to annihilate poison
> and not be overpowered by any poison.

729. GZ DNP CRV add "made of iron." As mentioned before, this ancient Indian measure of distance has a range of about seven to fifteen kilometers, most commonly about thirteen.
730. I follow Patel *samutpādya* against Śāstrī *anutpādya*.
731. GZ DNP "it becomes nonexistent."
732. Skt. *śrutiḥ* DNP *thos pa yin* (GZ *thos pa yis*) CRV *rab tu grags* ("well known"). It is not clear what this "received tradition" (*śrutiḥ*) refers to. Jadusingh 2017 (101n160) notes the similarity of lines 32ab with an account in the *Mittavindaka Jātaka* (Jātaka 369). There, Buddha Śākyamuni in one of his previous lives as a bodhisattva had been born as Indra and, on a visit to the hells, saw a man on whose head a sharp revolving wheel twelve yojanas in diameter had lodged. Having questioned the man on the events that led to this karmic fruition, the bodhisattva decides he cannot help the man and returns to his heavenly realm. Here, this story seems to be adapted to the Mahāyāna: once that man generates bodhicitta, the wheel is removed; however, a possible source for this remains untraced. Wedemeyer (364n31) suggests this "may refer to the wheel which is said to revolve over the head of kings (unlikely) [probably referring to the wheel of a cakravartin king]; or to the 'wheel of sharp weapons' of karmic retribution."
733. GZ DNP "through."
734. GZ DNP *gzung ba* "caring for."
735. CRV:

> Adopting the mind for complete awakening,
> by means of giving rise to bodhicitta and
> the intention of liberating the world/beings,
> there is thereby nothing that is not to be done.

736. GZ DNP "this is seen by thinking of the world/beings."
737. CRV has the last two lines as follows:

> Correctly view the nature of the world!
> There is no bondage and nothing to be freed.

738. I follow Patel *rajyate* against Śāstrī *rāgayet*.
739. I follow Patel *rāgabhogena* against Śāstrī *rajyatena ca*. In GZ the last two lines read as follows:

> should be passionate through the mind of passion
> Despite looking at passion, they will be liberated

DNP:

> being passionate through the mind of passion
> or engaging in passion, they will be liberated

CRV:

> by being passionate about the mind of clinging
> through passion, they should be liberated.

740. I follow Patel *kutra vai* against Śāstrī *kalayā*.
741. I follow Patel *viṣākrānto* against Śāstrī *viṣājjā[grā]to*.
742. GZ DNP read the first two lines as follows:

> If you know what to do and what to focus on,
> [DNP "You may wonder, 'What to do? What to focus on?'"]
> it is all kinds of powers of things

CRV:

> What to focus on in whatever you may do
> consists of all kinds of focusing on things
> It is like someone in the grip of poison
> eliminating that poison through poison.

743. GZ DNP [NP omit the last two lines]:

> Similar to a launderer annihilating
> the stains of clothes through stains,
> the wise are to make themselves
> stainless through their own stains

CRV:

> For example, the stains of a laundress's
> cotton are purified by means of stains
> Likewise, those whose character is wise
> remove stains through the very stains.

744. I follow Patel *doṣo* against Śāstrī *doṣāt*.
745. GZ DNP:

> Just as the stains of a mirror
> become clean through dust,
> so the wise should rely on
> flaws in order to purify flaws

CRV:

> Just as a mirror becomes clean
> by means of wiping off the dust,
> so the wise, by attending to them,
> overcome flaws through flaws.

746. GZ DNP:

> Just as even a small iron ball
> will sink to the bottom of water,
> but if it has been made a vessel,
> carries itself and others across . . .

CRV:

> If an iron ball is placed into water,
> all it does is to go to the bottom

Once it has been made a vessel,
it doesn't sink and it holds up others.

747. GZ DNP "while" CRV "if."

748. GZ DNP:

If passion is relied on with bad consciousness [Skt. *durvijñaiḥ* rendered literally but misleadingly as *rnam shes ngan pas*; DNP omit "passion"],
one will be bound through passion [DNP "passion will become bondage"]
If the same is relied on by the wise,
they accomplish liberation by passion

CRV agrees with the last two lines and has the first two lines as follows:

When fools rely on passion,
they are bound in saṃsāric existence by passion.

749. I follow Patel *sakale loke* against Śāstrī *sahasālokya*.

750. Probably due to its generally high status in Ayurvedic medicine, such as in the compendium *Basavarājīyam*, milk is also recommended as an antidote against certain poisons (though there is no scientific evidence for that). Indian lore has it that snakes drinking milk increases the amount of their poison or makes it more toxic. However, snakes only drink milk when they are dehydrated (and thus drink anything), but since they cannot digest it, they can even die from larger amounts. Nevertheless, on the traditional Hindu religious festival Nag Panchami, following common popular belief, people in India offer milk to snakes. However, those snakes are usually trapped for a whole month before the day of the festival and not given much food or water, so when they drink milk on that day, it is because of dehydration and not a miracle. GZ DNP CRV:

It is well known in all the world [GZ "how" instead of "world"]
that poison is pacified [CRV "eliminated"] by milk
If the same is drunk by snakes,
the poison will increase greatly.

751. In India, the mythological *haṃsarāja* (the king of wild geese, considered as the mount of the goddess Sārasvatī) is said to be able to filter out the milk from a mixture of milk and water (as here, it seems that this ability became ascribed to ordinary geese as well). This symbolizes Sārasvatī's ability to discriminate between what is good and bad or between what is permanent and impermanent. In that vein, enlightened Indian Hindu gurus or renunciates (*saṃnyāsa*) of great spiritual attainments are often given the honorific title "Paramahaṃsa" ("Supreme Goose").

752. GZ DNP:

Similar to a goose drinking
the milk out of the water,
so the wise will be liberated by
purifying and then enjoying poisonous objects

The first two lines in CRV correspond to the Sanskrit, while the last two match GZ DNP.

753. According to Patel (90), this is "'a kind of sweetmeat' composed of flour, milk, coconut, and sugar, and is fried in ghee"; GZ "white butter" DNP "mouthful of butter."

754. CRV "the flaw of children eating butter and molasses in secret becomes poison."

755. GZ DNP (the last two lines in DNP follow the Sanskrit):

> Thus, this very mind, once it has
> been purified by excellent reasons, [Skt. *hetu* rendered literally but misleadingly as *gtan tshigs*]
> if it is thought-free and without focus [or "unobservable"],
> appears as stainless by its very nature

CRV:

> This very mind, when the wise have
> purified it through wholesome causes,
> is thought-free, without focus [or "unobservable"],
> and greatly stainless by its very nature.

756. DNP follow the Sanskrit except reading *snang ba* ("shine," "light") for "lamp." GZ:

> It is similar to a flame, even if small,
> by being put together with butter, a wick, and so on,
> becoming stable as a stainless, unwavering
> shine, and thereby destroying the darkness

CRV:

> It is similar to a lamp close to dying ['*chir phyogs*]
> being prepared with oil, a wick, and so on,
> blazing clearly and without wavering,
> and eliminating any enduring [I follow P *brtan pa* against N *bstan pa*] dimness [*rab rib* usually means "blurred vision," the other meaning of Skt. *timira*].

757. Nonsensically choosing the other meaning of Skt. *sahakāra* ("mango tree/blossom/juice"), GZ has the second line as "that is endowed with a mango" and then adds the following three repetitive lines after this stanza:

> It is like a large tree adorned
> with roots and leaves emerging
> from a large tree's tiny seed

By contrast, instead of a full stanza, DNP only have the following three lines:

> It is like a large tree adorned
> with leaves and fruits emerging
> from a tiny stalk

CRV:

> For example, though a nyagrodha [another word for banyan tree] seed
> is small, when joined with conditions,
> it will grow into a large tree
> with roots, branches, and fruits.

758. Among its several meanings, Skt. *cūrṇa* (just like Tib. *rdo thal*) refers to both "chalk" and "quicklime," but what is meant here is the latter. Chemically speaking, chalk is almost pure calcium carbonate ($CaCO_3$), and quicklime (calcium oxide, CaO) is made through the thermal decomposition of materials, such as chalk or limestone, that contain $CaCO_3$ in a lime kiln. Quicklime is a strong alkali able to convert the benzenoid structure of turmeric with its yellow appearance into a quinonoid structure with red color (by contrast, turmeric is often adulterated with chalk, without any chemical reaction but with potential health hazards). The same example of mixing turmeric and quicklime is also found in the *Tattvadaśakaṭīkā* (text 46, 26), used in a similar way in terms of prajñā, means, and "the true reality of unity."
759. Skt. *viduḥ* is the nominative of *vidus* ("wise"; both as a noun and an adjective) and also the third-person plural perfect of the verb *vid* ("know," "realize," "observe," "perceive"). Unless this plural verb is taken in a general way, it can only refer back to "the wise" in line 42c. If *viduḥ* is taken as a nominative noun, not only would it lack a verb but the entire stanza would be without any verb; and if the last line were to mean "likewise the dharmadhātu is for the wise," one would expect the genitive *vidusaḥ*, but that would moreover be hypermetrical. The reading *mkhas pas de ltar shes* in GZ DNP includes both meanings, while CRV only has *mkhas pas*. Also, none of the Tibetan versions understands the example here. GZ DNP:

> Due to joining mustard and quicklime,
> another color will come forth
> Due to the joining of prajñā and means,
> the wise likewise perceive the dharmadhātu

CRV:

> By preparing mustard powder,
> it manifests as if of another color
> Joining prajñā and means,
> so the wise [perceive] the dharmadhātu.

760. I follow Patel *samāṃśaṃ* against Śāstrī *samaṃsaṃ*.
761. Wedemeyer (367n45) comments as follows: "This notion seems to be confirmed as a tenet of ayurvedic dietetics. Consider the testimony of a recent ayurvedic cookbook: 'equal quantities of ghee and honey are a bad combination (ghee is cooling, but honey is heating and they have different post-digestive effects),' thus creating a toxic effect. Cf. Usha and Vasant Lad, *Ayurvedic Cooking for Self Healing* (Albuquerque 1994), 46."
762. GZ DNP:

Butter and honey in equal parts
will turn into poison
The same, if enjoyed with proper
know-how, turns into the supreme elixir

CRV:

Butter and honey in equal parts,
in brief, will turn into poison
The same, if eaten with proper
know-how, is excellent elixir.

763. Patel *ghṛṣṭaṃ* (supported by CRV *byug pa*) Śāstrī *spṛṣṭaṃ* (supported by GZ DNP *reg pa*).
764. Patel *bhavet* Śāstrī *vrajet*.
765. In the last two lines, Śāstrī reads *jñānavṛddhās tathā kleśāḥ kleśāḥ-*, Bendall *jñānavidas tathā samyak klesā[ḥ]*, and Patel *jñānasuddhyā tathā kleśāḥ samyak kalyāṇakārakāḥ*. Wedemeyer follows Patel, except for switching *kleśāḥ* and *samyak* (which corresponds to CRV and, except for the position of *samyak*, to DNP). GZ DNP:

Just as, if handled with proper know-how, [DNP omit this line]
copper touched by mercury
turns into gold that is without flaw,
so, afflictions embraced by true
wisdom are rendered excellent
[DNP "so, by being purified by true wisdom,
afflictions are rendered excellent"]

CRV:

For example, copper that is rubbed with
a gold-making elixir becomes flawless gold
Likewise, if they are purified by wisdom,
the afflictions are truly made into virtue [or "made into true virtue"].

766. Skt. *abhirūḍha* GZ DNP CRV *zhon pa* literally means "mounted."
767. The second line in GZ DNP reads "think of [DNP 'create'] being bound in every moment."
768. I follow Patel *saṃgrāmajayacittas* against Śāstrī *saṃgrāmajayatuntena*.
769. GZ DNP omit "dharma."
770. I follow Patel *prajñātantudhanurbāṇa* against Śāstrī *kṛpānayadhanurbāṇa*. That *tantu* means "bowstring" here is supported by GZ DNP *rgyud* (though CRV has *rang bzhin*, "nature"). The compound *prajñātantudhanurbāṇa* could also be read as "prajñā's string, bow, and arrow," or "the string, bow, and arrow that represent prajñā," but GZ DNP *shes rab rgyud bcas* suggests that prajñā here only refers to the bowstring.
771. GZ DNP "of taking care of beings." CRV has the second and third lines as follows:

made of the endowment with great compassion,
with the bow and arrow whose nature is prajñā.

772. GZ *gnyis spangs pa* "devoid of duality" DNP *gnyid sangs nas* ("awakened from sleep").

773. GZ CRV *bsgral* ("cross," "liberate") DNP *(b)rgal* ("cross") em. *rgyal*. Without that emendation, the last phrase in this line would mean "the battle difficult to cross/be liberated from." CRV has the last two lines as follows: "they liberate themselves and others from the battle difficult to be liberated from."

774. Besides "fortunate," Skt. *dhanya* can also mean "blessed," "wealthy," virtuous," "good," "auspicious," and "happy," all of which make sense here too. The last two lines in GZ DNP CRV are hard to make sense of: GZ "if people who promote the welfare of beings are thus just a few," DNP "those who promote the welfare of beings toss those beings into the Ganges," CRV:

> Animals, who are endowed with suffering,
> are absorbed in just their own welfare as supreme
> [There are] people who lack wealth [obviously misreading *viraha*
> for *virala* and understanding *dhanya* as "wealth"],
> manifesting as promoting beings' welfare.

775. GZ:

> If even those engaging in their own welfare
> endure sufferings such as cold and wind,
> how would those who are engaged in
> the welfare of beings not endure them?

DNP:

> If sufferings such as cold and wind
> are endured even by engaging in one's own welfare,
> look at those engaged in the welfare of beings—
> how would they not endure them?

CRV:

> Sufferings such as wind and cold
> are endured for just one's own welfare
> How would those engaged in the welfare
> of beings not endure them?

776. GZ DNP CRV:

> If the compassionate endure even
> sufferings such as those of the hells,
> what need is there to mention [DNP "think of"] present [CRV
> "they should endure the sufferings that are"]
> sufferings such as cold and wind?

777. Śāstrī *aniṣṭakalpanā* ("unpleasant practices"); Patel (probably following the reading of the identical stanza *Advayasiddhi* 14) emends to *kaṣṭakalpanā*; GZ DNP *dka' thub brtag pa* ("thinking of/examining austerities") CRV *sdug bsngal*

rtog pa ("thinking of/examining suffering"). Though Skt. *kalpanā* does not mean "thought" here, but "practice," all Tibetan versions misleadingly have a form of the correlate *rtog pa*, thus arriving at a very different meaning.

778. Śāstrī *upavāsaṃ* Patel *upavāsena* ("by means of fasting").

779. GZ DNP have the first two lines as follows (GZ also mistakenly adds a negative in the last line):

> You should not entertain thoughts [or "examinations"] of austerities
> There is no fasting and there are no things to do [DNP "and fasting is not to be done either"]

CRV:

> You should not entertain thoughts of suffering—
> you should not perform any fasting
> Here, bathing, ritual cleansing,
> and village dharmas should be abandoned

"Village dharma" (Skt. *grāmadharma*) refers to the traditional religious rites and observances practiced in villages usually by uneducated people, or simply to the established cultures and customs of a village.

780. DNP "arise from the cause that is the father's semen." CRV adds "brains" to the first line and has the second as "arise from the father's semen."

781. GZ "tainted by."

782. GZ DNP render *piṇḍa* with its other meaning as *ril po* ("ball").

783. CRV *gang gi khrus kyis* ("by means of which bath").

784. GZ DNP:

> An unclean jar, even if washed with waters
> in the Ganges [DNP "again and again"], will not become purified
> Likewise, this jar as well . . .

CRV:

> Even if it is washed again and again,
> unclean pus will not become purified by water

The third line begins with *ji ltar* instead of *de ltar* or *de bzhin*, resulting in the opposite of the intended meaning: "How could this body, being filled with impurity, not become purified?"

785. Śāstrī *tasmāt* (supported by GZ DNP *de phyir*) Patel *tadvat* (CRV *de bzhin*).

786. GZ DNP:

> Even if dogs swim and float in the river
> Ganges, they will not become purified
> Hence, even if people desiring the dharma
> bathe at sacred places, this is fruitless

CRV:

> It is not suitable that ferrymen
> crossing the Ganges become pure

> Just so, for persons with virtuous minds,
> bathing at sacred places is fruitless

787. DNP "If one became pure by bathing" CRV "If one were restored by bathing" (reading *'chos* for *chos*).
788. GZ DNP omit "in the water"; CRV "And how about fish and such that operate in the water day and night?"
789. CRV "purified."
790. GZ DNP "just as."
791. I follow Patel *vṛddhi* against Śāstrī *buddhi*.
792. DNP "pride, view, and doubt."
793. GZ DNP CRV "well-known."
794. Śāstrī *janminām* Patel *janminaḥ*; *janminaḥ* could be understood as a nominative plural, a genitive singular, or an ablative singular. In the first case, *janminaḥ* would grammatically and logically connect with *ete*, meaning "these living beings are born here." In the second case *ete* would refer back to the afflictions in the preceding stanza and the meaning would be the same as with *janminām*. GZ *srog chags rnams la* suggests a genitive or dative plural and DNP *srog chags rnams las* an ablative plural. The only Tibetan version that has an equivalent of *ete* is CRV *'di dag las*, but it is an ablative plural, most probably referring back directly to the twofold grasping at me and mine, thus giving yet another meaning.
795. Patel *hetukaḥ* Śāstrī *mūlataḥ*; "its" refers to "grasping . . ." in the first line.
796. GZ DNP have the second and third lines as follows:

    > [these] arise in [CDNP "from"] living beings
    > This is due to the root of ignorance

    CRV:

    > [There is] grasping at me and mine—
    > it is from these that rebirths [*skye ba rnams*; probably for *jātayaḥ*] arise
    > Its cause consists of ignorance
    > With ignorance, delusion arises.

797. Patel *dṛṣṭau* Śāstrī *dṛṣṭe*.
798. GZ DNP "becomes nonexistent" CRV "is eradicated"; "this" (*sā*) refers to "ignorance" in the last stanza.
799. Patel *dṛṣṭa* Śāstrī *dṛṣṭe*.
800. As in DNP, Skt. *janmani* ("in this person") could also be understood as "in this birth." GZ DNP:

    > Just as [DNP "for example"] the perception of a snake in a rope
    > disappears by seeing [DNP "if it is known"] that it is a rope,
    > the arising [I follow GZ *'byung ba* against DNP *yi rab* NP *yi bar*] of a
    > perception of a snake there [DNP "from there" or "due to that"]
    > will not come about in that person [DNP "birth"]

    The first two lines in CRV follow the Sanskrit, while the last two read as follows:

    > just as with that perception of a snake,
    > there is no certainty about that in this person.

801. Śāstrī *satya* (supported by GZ DNP CRV *bden pa*); Patel *sattva* could also be understood as "sentient being," but the parallel mention of *bhāva* ("existence") in the third line and all Tibetan versions reading "reality" make that more than unlikely.

802. Patel *bhāvaḥ* Śāstrī *bhūyaḥ*; GZ DNP CRV omit "existence."

803. Śāstrī *nairātmyāśucisaṃsṛṣṭaḥ* Patel *nairātmyāśucisaṃghātaḥ* (either one supported by GZ DNP *bdag med* [DNP *nyid*] *mi gtsang 'dus pa*) Wedemeyer *nairātmyaśucisaṃsṛṣṭaḥ* (rendered as "the body created from the purity of selflessness"; obviously following CRV *bdag med gtsang sbras yang dag 'byung*).

804. Patel *kaṣṭaṃ* (= GZ *dka' ba*; CRV *sdug bsngal*) Śāstrī *kathaṃ* (no equivalent in any Tibetan version). With *kaṣṭaṃ*, the last phrase could also be read as "it is hard for childish beings to imagine the dharma." However, CRV *sdug bsngal* clearly suggests that Skt. *kaṣṭam* GZ *dka' ba* is not an adverb (DNP *dga' bar*). In other words, this means that in the midst of their body-related sufferings, beings misperceive what actually is the dharma (identitylessness) as being suffering. With *kathaṃ*, said phrase would mean "how could childish beings imagine the dharma?" GZ DNP:

> This ball [again rendering Skt. *piṇḍa* in its other meaning as *gong bu*] as a compound of identitylessness
> and impurity has the nature of flesh [DNP "earth"]
> Due to the torments of that [body], childish
> beings imagine what is the dharma as hardship
> [DNP "childish beings imagine what are the
> dharmas of that compound as being joy"]

CRV:

> The body with its ordinary nature
> arises through identitylessness and purity [or "identitylessness's purity"]
> It is its tormenting dharmas that
> childish beings conceive as suffering.

805. Skt. *apekṣya*, as well as *apekṣayā* and *apekṣā* in lines 72b and 73a, can also mean "looking at."

806. DNP:

> Dependent on the moon's waxing and waning,
> we conceive of the number of dates
> Through the waxing and waning of the sun,
> we conceive [I follow NP *rnam par brtag* against D *rtag par brtag*] of day and night

GZ omits "the number of" and says "day and night are present." CRV:

> Dependent on the shining of the moon,
> we conceive of planets and date numbers
> [In] the place of the sun rising and setting,
> day and night are present.

807. GZ misrenders Skt. *pūrva* as "first."

808. Patel *api* Śāstrī *ākyhaḥ*.

809. I follow Patel *kalpanāpekṣayā kṛtaḥ* against Śāstrī *śabdatrayavikalpanā*.

810. I follow Patel *graha* against Śāstrī *vāra* (ditto in 75a). *Graha* refers to the positions of planets in the zodiac (it can also mean "eclipse," but that is unlikely in connection with the following two terms). *Nakṣatra* is the term for the twenty-eight (or twenty-seven) constellations of the zodiac through which the moon passes, each occupying the section of the ecliptic through which the moon moves in one day. *Rāśi* is the term for the twelve signs of the zodiac (or the twelve solar signs), each occupying one-twelfth of the ecliptic (that is, the section through which the sun moves in one month). In all Tibetan versions, *gza' dang rgyu skar khyim* is probably meant as a rendering of Skt. *grahanakṣatrarāśi*, but more literally it means "the houses (positions) of planets, constellations, and stars."

811. Patel *sarvalokaiḥ* Śāstrī *sarvaloka*. CRV:

> Based on conventional terms such as
> "east," conceptions are created—
> the times of planetary and lunar positions and such
> are conceived of by worldly people

812. Patel *apekṣā* Śāstrī *apekṣaṃ*.

813. This refers to the three seasons of winter, spring, and the rainy season that are distinguished in India.

814. CRV:

> It is in the same manner that cold,
> heat, and rain are conceived of
> The experiences of our own karma and its results
> arise through seizing virtue and nonvirtue

CRV *dge dang mi dge 'dzin pas byung* in the last line is a possible way to render the Sanskrit *śubhāśubhagrahodita*: considering the connection between virtue and nonvirtue and the arising of their karmic results, "arise through seizing virtue and nonvirtue" makes sense. However, given the previous and the following stanzas and GZ DNP *bzang dang ngan pa'i* [GZ *las* em. *pa'i*] *gzar bstan*, this meaning is rather unlikely.

815. GZ DNP:

> If a wise person has washed . . .
> through what would they experience ignorance again? [DNP
> "through what would ignorance be produced?"]

CRV:

> The jewel of the mind of beings
> is tainted [P *bsgos* against N *bskos*, "entrust"] by the mud of
> ignorance
> Both the intelligent's obscurations and purity—
> which [or "whose"] ignorance would [they?] increase?

[*blo ldan bsgribs dang dag pa dag / gang gi ma rig 'phel bar byed /* is difficult to construe; *gang gi* could also be *gang gis* "by what," but that does not make the overall meaning of the last two lines clearer].

816. Patel *viharet* Śāstrī *viharan.*
817. As in the Tibetan versions, in the last line, Skt. *nirnimittam* can also mean "without characteristics" and *aśaṅkita* "without doubts." GZ DNP CRV:

   Without depending on planets, numbers of days,
   constellations, stars, locations, time, and so forth,
   you should behave without any characteristics,
   [I follow GZ CRV *mtshan (ma) med* against D *mtshams med* NP *'tshom med*]
   without any doubts, and without any thoughts.

818. This stanza is *Pañcakrama* III.36. According to Wedemeyer (371–72n67), it is slightly odd that our text quotes from this chapter of the *Pañcakrama* because its third stage of self-blessing follows after the second stage of mind purification (*cittaviśuddhi*). Wedemeyer further points out that the reading *susamahita-* is attested in all Sanskrit mss. of the *Cittaviśuddhiprakaraṇa* and the *Pañcakrama*, while all Tibetan versions suggest *asamahita-* (a reading followed by Mimaki and Tomabechi in their recent edition of the *Pañcakrama*), and that Patel *yad yad indriyamargatvaṃ yāyāt tat tat svabhavataḥ / susamāhitayogena sarvaṃ buddhamayaṃ vahet /* seems to be the most likely reading (however, Patel ends with *vadet*, while it is Śāstrī who reads *vahet*). In addition, though less likely from a grammatical point of view (since *tat tat* is the exact correlate of *yad yad*), *tat tat svabhāvataḥ* could also be read as *tat tatsvabhāvataḥ* (supported by DNP *de ni de'i ngo bo nyid*; it also seems to be how Wedemeyer translates this phrase: "that should be taken as such a reality," though he reads *tat tat svabhāvataḥ*). In that sense, given the last two lines of this stanza, "nature" would mean that everything has the nature of being a buddha. The reading *de dang de'i gno bo nyid/yis* in GZ CRV links both *tat* to *svabhāva*, thus meaning "that and that essence" or "such and such an essence," which then seems to refer to the six senses being described as having the natures of different buddhas in the following two stanzas. GZ DNP:

   Whatever serves as the [DNP "whatever in the nine"] paths of the senses
   has such and such an [DNP "that has that"] essence
   Through the yoga of nonabsorption,
   render all the nature of buddhas!

   CRV could be read in at least two ways:

   By virtue of whatever serves as the paths
   of the senses having such and such an essence,
   through the yoga of nonabsorption,
   always make all the nature of buddhas!

   Or:

> Through the yoga of not being absorbed
> in whatever serves as the paths of the senses
> as having such and such an essence . . .

819. GZ CRV *mgon* ("protector") DNP *gtso* ("chief," "lord").
820. Śāstrī *virocana.*
821. Śāstrī *vajraśūnyaka.*
822. CRV adds "protector."
823. As Wedemeyer (372n70) says, "This enumeration of the correspondences of enlightened beings to the senses and so forth is not that of the Guhyasamaja Tradition. It seems to follow the 'Mother Tantra' systems of Hevajra or Cakrasamvara. In this list Heruka corresponds to Akṣobhya, Vajrasūrya/Vajraprabhā to Ratnasambhava, Paramāśva to Amoghasiddhi, and Padmanarteśvara to Amitābha."
824. I follow Patel *sadā* against Śāstrī *yadā.*
825. In GZ DNP, the last two lines read as follows:

> Thus it is through the perfect yoga that
> those with compassion's character engage

CRV:

> Thus the perfect yogīs abide,
> engaging [with] compassion's character.

826. I follow Patel *siddhāntī* against Śāstrī *siddhāntaḥ*; all Tibetan versions read *'grub par 'gyur,* obviously taking this as a form of the verb *sidh* ("accomplish"). Usually, a *siddhāntī* is someone who follows a particular philosophical system or who establishes their conclusions with reasonings. The remainder of this stanza makes it clear that here this does not refer to just anyone like that but only to those who follow what has been taught so far. Jadusingh 2017 (108) takes this term to refer to one who has reached perfection—that is, a siddha.
827. Among the many meanings of Skt. *kalpa,* besides "resolve," "practice" is another possible one here; all Tibetan versions read *sems* ("mind").
828. I follow Patel *vyāpāraḥ* against Śāstrī *vyāhāri.*
829. GZ DNP:

> If the mind of the wise has become stable,
> they thereby accomplish being thought-free
> Through deeds in just the way they like,
> they thus consume all [I follow GZ *kun za* against DNP *kun bzang*]
> and do everything

CRV:

> Through the know-how of a stable mind,
> being free from thought is accomplished
> Just as they like, with performing actions,
> they thus consume all and do everything.

830. I follow Patel *rucita* against Śāstrī *rucira.*

831. I follow Patel *caṃkramaṇa svapaṃs tathā* against Śāstrī *caṃkramo svayaṃ tathā*. GZ DNP have six lines:

> If they do all actions and activities,
> it is by means of desired deeds
> Be it standing up, sitting down,
> and likewise walking around,
> laughing and conversing too,
> it is exactly as above [GZ *gong* DNP *gang* "it is exactly like that"]

CRV:

> With the conduct of doing all they desire,
> they act with a mind of doing as they like
> Be it standing up, sitting down,
> or likewise walking around,
> being wild, or discussing,
> or anything in any way, they do it thus.

832. I follow Patel *amaṇḍala* against Śāstrī *āmāṇḍala*.
833. CRV "uniting with the deity who has a great nature."
834. Stanzas 79cd–80 are a condensed version of two stanzas in the *Śrīsarvabuddhasamāyogaḍākinījālasaṃbaranāmottaratantra*, and stanza 81 is virtually identical to the following stanza in that tantra (H376, fol. 248a.3–5). As Szántó (2020, 366n3) already noted, the last two of these stanzas were adopted from the *Paramādyatantra* (H454, fol. 250a.6–250b.1).
835. As Patel points out, here, ms. *sauritva* is to be understood as *śauritva*, as indicated by GZ DNP *dpa' bo* (CRV *sras rnams kun dang bcas* renders something like *sarvasunutvaṃ*).
836. This stanza is very similar to stanza 85 and 86. GZ DNP:

> Through this, all the buddhas
> and the heroes in their entirety
> will attain omniscience in this very lifetime—
> there isn't any doubt about this

CRV:

> Through this, all the buddhas,
> including all their children,
> if they know true reality, doubtlessly
> attain true actuality by this life.

837. This stanza is almost identical to *Bodhicaryāvatāra* IX.3cd–4ab. GZ DNP:

> Similar to the world [DNP "samādhi"] of yogīs
> being victorious over the ordinary world,
> through their differences in higher
> and higher insights, yogīs are victorious [over others]

CRV:

> Similar to the ordinary world
> not binding the world of yogīs,
> through the differences in mind
> being bound, yogīs are higher and higher too.

838. GZ DNP:

> The great prajñā, great means,
> great compassion, and aspiration
> that are taught in the Mahāyāna
> are the sphere of great sentient beings

CRV follows the Sanskrit except for also rendering mahāsattva as "great sentient being."

839. Patel *asaṃkhyeyair* against Śāstrī *asaṃkhyāyai*.
840. Patel *nātra* Śāstrī *na ca*. GZ DNP:

> The buddhahood that is often engaged
> but not attained for incalculable eons
> [DNP "The buddhahood that is desired but not
> attained for incalculable eons by many"]
> is attained through this life . . .

CRV:

> What many wish to attain
> for a great number of eons—
> buddhahood through this birth—
> is attained, no doubt about this.

841. I follow Patel *māhātmyaṃ* against Śāstrī *māhātmyāt*.
842. I follow Patel *saṃbhṛtaṃ* against Śāstrī *saṃbhavaḥ*.
843. GZ DNP:

> The greatness of the Mahāyāna is that,
> through the accumulations of merit and wisdom,
> the delightful [GZ "hard-to-attain"] state of omniscience
> will be attained in this very lifetime

CRV has "is the gathering of merit and wisdom" as the second line, and "in the present life" in the last line.

844. In Hinduism, *Āgama* (lit. "that which has come down") is a generic name for several collections of canonical texts of the followers of Śiva (twenty-eight Āgamas), Viṣṇu (one hundred and eight Āgamas), and Devī (Shaktism; seventy-seven Āgamas). While the origin and chronology of the Āgamas is not clear, some passages in them appear to reject the authority of the Vedas, while others claim that they reveal the true spirit of the Vedas (the four Vedas are the Ṛgveda, Yajurveda, Sāmaveda, and Atharvaveda). The Āgamas cover a wide range of topics, including cosmology, epistemology, philosophical doctrines (ranging from Dvaita to Advaita), precepts on meditation and ritual practices, different kinds of yoga, mantras, temple construction, and deity worship. *Śruti*

refers to the sacred knowledge of the Vedas and so on that is orally transmitted by brahmans from generation to generation.

845. I follow Patel *na* against Śāstrī *tu*.

846. I follow Śāstrī *yānabheda* against Patel *yānābheda* ("nondistinction . . .").

847. GZ DNP:

> Statements about deviating [DNP "evenly," "equally"] from scripture
> are not appropriate in the Mahāyāna
> The distinction of the yānas is taught
> by distinctions in intention and superior intention (= *adhyāśaya* instead of *anuśaya*)

CRV:

> A mind of deviating from the Sugata's scriptures
> should not be applied in the Mahāyāna
> The distinction of the yānas is illuminated
> by distinctions in intention and latencies.

848. I follow Patel *anya evādhimokṣo* against Śāstrī *anyatra bodhi*.

849. I follow Patel *tathānyā* against Śāstrī *anyathā*.

850. GZ DNP:

> If [DNP omit "if"] aspiring for something other,
> the awakening conduct is also other
> Through another mind purification,
> another fruition is [DNP add "not"] seen here

CRV:

> In the aspiration for another aspect,
> awakening conduct for something other,
> and mind abiding in something other,
> as another fruition, it deviates from this.

851. GZ DNP omit "nearby."

852. CRV has stanza 89 as follows:

> In a nearby stainless mirror,
> reflections clearly appear to the eyes
> Just as these appearances are very clear,
> naturally pure, and stainless.

853. GZ DNP read stanza 90 as follows:

> likewise the wisdom of yogis as well
> is very clear in the mirror of stainless
> prajñā within the virtuous minds
> that are purified of the web of thoughts

CRV basically has the same four lines but switches the first two and last two, which makes it sound as if the phrase "is very clear within the virtuous minds that are purified of the web of thoughts," followed by "likewise," still belongs to the example in stanza 89.

854. Here and below GZ DNP have "fire crystal."
855. I follow Patel *kanti* against Śāstrī *kānta*.
856. Two similar stanzas are found as *Prajñopāyaviniścayasiddhi* II.30–31. CRV:

> For example, fire blazes up suddenly
> when a fire crystal that is pure
> is struck by the rays of the sun,
> enabling you to accomplish your own goals
> The mind that resembles a fire crystal
> and has accumulated imagination's web,
> when struck by the sun of prajñā,
> is blazing in the same way for yogīs.

857. GZ DNP add "forcefully."
858. I follow Patel *sarvavastuprakāśakaḥ* against Śāstrī *sa vai vastuprasādhakaḥ*.
859. GZ DNP read the last two lines as follows:

> in the same way, yogīs know
> due to uniting prajñā and means

The last four lines in CRV can be read in more than one way, such as:

> endowed with illuminating all things
> in the beginning, middle, and end,
> yogic wisdom knows the union of
> prajñā and means in the same way.

860. GZ DNP:

> This is like a single lamp spreading
> in dependence upon other wicks,
> matching your own goal [DNP add "and others"] in a setting,
> allowing you to see [DNP "illuminating"] from a high place

CRV:

> This is like a single blazing lamp
> relying on a number of other wicks,
> as it is clearly illuminating
> your own goal in your own setting.

861. Patel *adhimukta* Śāstrī *adhimukti*.
862. GZ DNP:

> By cultivating prajñā and means
> and manifesting limitless bodies,
> activities according to the diverse
> aspirations of beings are to be practiced

CRV basically follows the Sanskrit, but switches the first two and the last two lines.

863. Patel *vidhijñena* Śāstrī *viddhijño hi.*

864. Skt. *amṛta* ("ambrosia") in the second line can also mean "ghee," which is considered to have many healing qualities in Ayurvedic medicine. In that vein, *hṛdya* ("pleasant") can also mean "pleasant to the stomach." That ghee is obviously what is meant here is clearly spelled out in CRV's first two lines:

> For example, one who knows the means
> extracts the butter by churning the milk

Alternatively, this example could refer to the famous episode in the ancient Indian myth of creation when the gods and the asuras used the nāga king Vāsuki as a churning rope around the churning rod of Mount Maṃdara. Pulling Vāsuki's head and tail back and forth, the mountain rotated and thus churned the great Milk Ocean. In this way, first a lethal poison and later the ambrosia of immortality were produced.

865. I follow Patel *mahopāyād* against Śāstrī *mahopāyaṃ.*

866. Śāstrī has the last line as *sa śubhāśubhavināśakaḥ,* and Bendall has it as *sat sukhāsukhanāśakaḥ;* Patel reads it as *sa sukhāsukhavināśanaḥ,* but then has *sat sukhāsukhavināśanaḥ* in his corresponding note, adding that this is supported by DNP and CRV, with DNP taking the compound to mean *satsukhena (bde ba dam pas) asukha (sdug bsngal) vināśanaḥ.* Wedemeyer (375n79) says this: "The last two pādas of this verse appear in numerous variants throughout the extant Sanskrit MSS. I have followed the version that contains the most general import, to wit *śubhāśubha-vināśanaḥ.* Other readings imply something like pleasure and pain (*sukhāsukha* or *satsukho duḥkhanāśanaḥ*)." Obviously, all Tibetan versions follow *satsukhena* or *satsukha,* which I also adopt as the most likely reading (*sat* on its own could also be the adverb "truly"). It is of course possible to read the above versions of this line as "which destroys good and evil" (Wedemeyer), "annihilating virtue and nonvirtue," or "annihilating happiness and suffering." However, given the example in the preceding stanza that first describes the positive qualities of ghee and then says it overcomes all diseases, as well as the positive descriptions of buddhahood and so on in other stanzas, it is unlikely that our text regards the dharmadhātu as something that destroys both happiness and suffering (or good/virtue and evil/nonvirtue). Rather, in analogy to ghee being pleasant and overcoming all diseases, it makes sense to describe the dharmadhātu as the true (ultimate) bliss that overcomes all suffering. GZ DNP CRV have the third line as "the dharmadhātu that is very pure." DNP read the last line as "annihilates suffering with true bliss," while CRV has "is the supreme bliss that pacifies suffering." Note that stanzas 96–97 correspond to the common example of buddha nature (the dharmadhātu) being like butter or ghee to be extracted from milk (sentient beings), as for example found in *Dharmadhātustava* 3–4.

867. Śāstrī *yathā latāsamudbhūtaṃ phalapuṣpasamanvitam / yathaikakṣaṇasaṃbodhiḥ saṃbhāradvayasaṃyutā* / Patel *yathā latā samudbhūtā phalapuṣpasamanvitā / tathaikakṣaṇa . . .* As Grimes and Szántó 2018 (n201) point out, this stanza is also found in a very similar form in the thirteenth chapter of the *Caṇḍamahāroṣaṇatantra,* and it is quoted in Mahāsukhavajra's commentary *Padmāvatī* on its sixth chapter and in Ratnarakṣita's *Padminī.* According to Grimes and Szántó,

"The best Ms of the *Padminī* has a reading which is much closer to ours: *yathā latāsamudbhūtaṃ phalaṃ puṣpasamanvitam | tathaikalakṣeṇasambodhiḥ sambhāradvayasambhṛtā | |*. The closest match is that of the *Caṇḍamahāroṣaṇatantra* itself. In Mical's draft edition we have the same forms as here, except *ekakṣaṇāc ca sambodhiḥ* for *pāda c* . . . Supposing that the original reading was metrical, we find it much more likely that *ekakṣaṇāt* is a corruption of *ekakṣaṇātta°*, rather than *ekakṣaṇāc ca*. Of course, it is equally likely that all these are simply corruptions of *tathaikakṣaṇa°*, the reading conjectured by Patel . . . Āryadeva's text seems to be saying that a vine appears together with both fruit and flower, in which case the vine is quick awakening, and its fruit and flower are the two equipments of merit (*puṇya°*) and knowledge (*jñānasambhāraḥ*). However, the *Caṇḍamahāroṣaṇatantra* and Mahāsukhavajra seem to think that the fruit born of the vine is already endowed with a flower. Judging by Mahāsukhavajra's argumentation just before the quotation, this would seem to mean that by cultivating wisdom (*prajñā*, synonym for *jñānam*, but here punningly the consort, too), which is the cause of experiencing Great Pleasure, which in turn causes merit, one obtains the equipment of merit as well. If this is indeed his idea, it is certainly a somewhat unusual one. But the point perhaps is this: one needs to cultivate both equipments on the slower path, i.e. the pāramitānaya, but in the case of quick awakening, i.e. the mantranaya, this is not the case." According to the above-mentioned reading, Grimes and Szántó translate the stanza as follows: "Just like the fruit born of the vine is endowed with a flower, perfect awakening achieved in a single moment is complete with the two equipments." GZ and D begin with the additional line "From a seed endowed with a person . . ." GZ DNP CRV read "momentary" instead of "in a single moment" and "endowed" instead of "joined." The first two lines in CRV say this:

> Just as flowers that have grown from
> a creeper are endowed with fruits.

868. This line is missing in the ms. but can be reconstructed based on its citation in Bendall and the Tibetan (CRV has "strife" instead of "hatred"; "paralyzing" is supported by GZ D CRV *rengs* [NP *rangs*]). The ms. shows further lacunae up through stanza 111 and also in stanzas 116, 117, 119, 120, and 126, as indicated in detail below.
869. Śāstrī Patel *varṣaṇākarṣanādikam* Varghese *gharṣaṇā* . . . ("grinding," "pounding") Wedemeyer (375n81) "perhaps *dharṣaṇa* ('assault'), a possible reading noted by Bendall (p. 40), who nonetheless follows the Tibetan in reading *varṣaṇa*." If the text means to speak here about pairs of opposites, such as "mobility" and "immobility," *dharṣaṇa* could make sense as the opposite of "attracting" (*ākarṣaṇa*). However, all the items in this stanza are typical instances of yogīs performing miraculous feats or behaving in unconventional ways, as for example found in the *Hevajratantra* (such as I.8). Thus, the most straightforward reading of the compound *varṣaṇākarṣanādikam* is "summoning/attracting rain" (GZ D *char dbab dgug* [NP *dgu*] *pa* also suggest a compound, while CRV *char dbab pa dang dgug* has "and" between these two words). As a more unlikely option, with *vaśa* ("power") in its other meanings "licentiousness" or "desire," and the possible *dharṣaṇa* in its other meanings "seduction" or even "rape" (or

even *gharṣaṇa*, "grinding"), the first two lines could also be read as having an entirely different meaning, possibly related to the practice of karmamudrā: "licentiousness, aversion, moving, stopping/stiffening, seduction, attraction/ summoning . . ." However, the wording of GZ DNP CRV does not support this in any way.

870. GZ DNP "but will see." CRV has the last two lines as follows:

> from [*las*; or *la*, "in"?] yogīs delighting in wine and meat,
> those will be found close by.

871. In the ms., the second line as well as "why" constitutes a lacuna. Śāstrī Patel reconstruct *hastakaṅkaṇabimbāya kim*, but *bimbāya* ("for the image/reflection of" or "for the round form of"?) has no correspondence in any Tibetan version. In his note on the first and second lines, Patel refers to CRV *lag dub lag par mthong ba la* as being translatable into Sanskrit as *haste kiṃ kaṃkaṇe dṛṣṭe* (GZ DNP *lag pa'i gdu bu blta ba la*). Patel also quotes an almost identical Marathi proverb, *hātacyā kaṃkaṅās ārasā kasālā* ("Why do you require a mirror to see the bangles on your own hands?").

872. GZ *dngos song yang* D *de song yang* NP *de rgyas yang* CRV *de ltar*.

873. Skt. *darśana* can also mean "see" (CRV *mthong*), "look," "teach" (GZ NP *bstan*), and "know." GZ DNP have the first two lines as follows:

> To look at your arm bracelets,
> do you need a mirror, or what?

CRV:

> To see the bracelets on your arms,
> what's the point of thinking of a mirror?
> For that reason, in the Mahāyāna,
> the power of mantras is seen like that.

874. In the ms., the second and third lines are a lacuna. Patel reconstructs *tattvato' tra na kalpyate / bhagnāyodhūpavarttīva* ("is not conceived of in terms of true reality here. Like broken iron or an incense stick"). The second line in GZ DNP reads *'dir ni de nyid med par brtag(s)* ("here, it is conceived of/imputed as nonexistent" or "here, without any true reality, it is conceived/imputed" or "here, [in terms of] true reality, it is conceived as nonexistent"), while CRV has *'di dag brtags pas de nyid min* ("since these are imputations, they are not true reality"), which seems to make the most sense here. In his note on the third line of this stanza, Patel says this: "One may also read *bhagnalauhaśalākeva* or *bhagnāyaḥkhaṇḍasaṃkāśaṃ* (*lcags. kyi. reṅ. bu. bdsig. pa. ltar*) in CAV [Cittāvaraṇaviśodhanaprakaraṇa]. CRV [here Cittaratnaviśodhana] (*legs. thur. spaṅ pas. bsdus. pa. bdsin*) also seems to agree with the above," and then speculates about the meanings of *spang* as *bhaṅga* or *bhagna* and *bsdus* (*saṃghāta*) as being taken for *saṃkāśa*. However, GZ DNP *lcags kyi reng bu bshibs* [DNP *bshig*] *pa ltar* ("like well-arranged ['destroyed'] iron pellets") corresponds only vaguely to Patel's reconstructions *bhagnalauhaśalākeva* ("like splinters of broken metal") or *bhagnāyaḥkhaṇḍasaṃkāśaṃ* ("like broken fragments"). In any case, the meaning intended here appears to be that the world is just like a pile

of fragments without any intrinsic cohesion to them (CRV reads *lcags thur sbar bas bsdus pa bzhin*, "like being put/welded together with a blazing iron spoon"). Both Wedemeyer's rendering ("[One does not conceive truly here] The relationship of mother to daughter; The Transcendent Lord said beings are [Like a wisp of smoke from an iron censor]") and Jadusingh's translation ("A relationship of father, mother, and daughter is not here conceived in reality (*tattvato*). The Tathāgata said that [beings] in the world are like wisps of smoke (*dhūpavarti*) from an incense burner") seem to be eclectic mixes of Patel and the Tibetan versions. Varghese translates Patel's reconstruction as "According to the Tathāgata, there is no such relationship with one's mother, daughter, etc.; in reality, it is like broken armour or an extinguished lamp." In my own translation, I follow CRV in the second line and GZ in the third, since these make the most sense in this context. GZ DNP on their own read as follows:

> The relationship of mother [DNP "father, mother"] and daughter,
> here, in terms of true reality, is conceived as nonexistent
> Just like well-arranged [DNP "destroyed"] iron pellets,
> thus the Sugata declared that beings are

CRV:

> As for the relationships of mother and daughter,
> these are due to imputations and not true reality
> As if being put together with a blazing iron spoon,
> the Tathāgata has declared all beings to be

Note that Jadusingh 2017 (112n187) adds that lines 101ab might have an entirely different meaning—one that addresses the practice of karmamudrā—and points to the *Hevajratantra* (I.5.2), which uses "mother" and "sister" as symbolic names for prajñā (see also I.5.16). However, since the immediately following stanzas are a discussion of any notions of castes being mere conventions, it is more likely that lines 101ab speak about the conventionality of family relationships and descent.

875. I follow Patel *pañcabhūta* GZ DNP CRV *'byung ba lnga* against Śāstrī *pañcabuddha*. Given what stanzas 76–78 say, "five buddhas" would also be a possibility, but as the following stanzas show, the context here is a more conventional one.

876. As GZ DNP *gang . . . gang* shows, Skt. *ko . . . kaḥ* could also be understood as "what . . . what?," while CRV has *su zhig . . . gang*. GZ DNP have the third line as "As for this ball [DNP "As for these five balls"] that has the nature of those." The last two lines in CRV read as follows:

> For sure, the body has the nature of those,
> so who is of the brahman caste?

877. In the ms., this line and "all" constitute a lacuna.

878. GZ:

> All these bodies of bhikṣus
> . . .

> They are known to be impermanent, suffering,
> empty, unborn, and without any birth

DNP have the last two lines as follows:

> In what is impermanent, suffering, and empty [I follow NP *stong pa* against D *stob pa*],
> there is no caste, and what would having a caste be?

CRV:

> Whether it is bhikṣus or all bodies,
> they have the five skandhas' character
> They are impermanent, suffering, and empty,
> so there is no caste and none having a caste.

879. In the ms., "does belong to the caste of caṇḍālas" up through the end of stanza 108 is a lacuna (stanza 106 is found in Bendall). Caṇḍālas are a class of people in India considered to be outcastes and untouchables. According to the ancient law code of the *Manusmṛti*, the class originated from the union of a brahman woman (the highest caste) and a śūdra man (the lowest class). The term is also used in modern times for a specific caste of agriculturists, fishermen, and boatmen in Bengal, more commonly referred to as Namaśūdra.
880. GZ DNP:

> Those who are born from a fisher womb
> and someone with the birth of a caṇḍāla,
> by performing austerity, are born as brahmans
> For this reason, caste is not a cause

The first two lines in CRV follow the Sanskrit and the last two read as follows:

> by performing austerity, they become a brahman
> For this reason, there is no certainty about caste.

881. DNP CRV *bu mo* GZ *ma ma* ("nanny").
882. I follow DNP *dmangs rigs mo* CRV *rmangs rigs mo* against GZ *rmongs rigs mo*.
883. DNP CRV *cho ga shes pa(s)* GZ *de nyid shes pas* ("by knowing true reality").
884. Two similar stanzas are found as *Advayasiddhi* 5–6. As for "by manifestations" (Skt. *prabhāvanaiḥ*), Wedemeyer (377n92) says here: "Patel, following the citation of this verse in the *Subhāṣita-saṃgraha*, has restored this as *prabhāvana*, 'splendour' or 'power'; however, the Tibetan versions read *rnam bsgoms*, which would reconstruct more exactly as *vibhāvana*, which I have followed in my translation." However, the identical line *Advayasiddhi* 6d also reads *prabhāvanaiḥ*, and CRV *rab bsgoms pas* matches this in a very literal way. Moreover, unlike *prabhāva*, *prabhāvana* does not mean "splendor" or "power," but "manifesting" or "disclosing," which is also the meaning of *vibhāvana*. Note that the exhortation to honor and worship women, such as all one's female relatives and even outcaste women, is frequently found in Vajrayāna literature, such as in the *Hevajratantra* (I.5.2, I.5.16–18, II.5.59–60, and II.7.10–11), where all

women are moreover identified as embodiments of prajñā, and the *Śrīḍākārṇavamahāyoginītantra* (H390, fols. 75aff., 129b.1ff.).

885. CRV switches the last two lines.

886. The rendering of this stanza follows CRV and the according reconstruction in Patel. GZ DNP:

> see and look at the moment through display [or "through the teaching"],
> likewise engage in hearing and listening,
> experience [GZ "swift"] and enjoy bliss,
> and also [DNP "should"] utter clear speech

887. This stanza is also quoted in Bendall. GZ DNP:

> Making efforts in bathing, massaging,
> clothes and such, food, drink, and so on
> are to be regarded as your own desired deity's
> character, to be worshipped by the ritual

CRV has the last two lines as follows:

> these are to be regarded as worship by the ritual
> through uniting with the deity of great character.

888. In the ms., stanzas 110–111ab are a lacuna. The rendering of stanza 110 follows CRV and the according reconstruction in Patel. In the first line, instead of CRV *rol mo* ("music"), GZ has *gdung ba* ("torment") and DNP *brdung ba* ("beating," "drumming"). The third line in GZ DNP reads, "In this, they should not entertain any attachment."

889. Śāstrī reads the third line as *cittaṃ yathā sukhaṃ dhyāyan*, while Patel emends this to *sukhād yathā sukhaṃ dhyāyet* ("in accordance with being absorbed in bliss thanks to bliss"); *sukhād yathā sukhaṃ* accords with *ji ltar bde bas bde ba* in all Tibetan versions, but instead of *dhyāyan/dhyāyet* GZ DNP read *gzung* and CRV *zung* ("seize"). As Wedemeyer (378n101) says, it is not clear how Patel arrives at the optative *dhyāyet* (adding "perhaps it is a better reading in the MS"). However, Wedemeyer still translates it as an optative, saying: "Just as one should meditate easily because of comfort." It seems that Patel chose his optative based on the Tibetan verb forms *gzung* (either future tense or optative) and *zung* (imperative), though these are forms of Skt. *dhṛ* instead of *dhyā*. In any case, despite the agreement of all Tibetan versions on *ji ltar bde bas bde ba* and Patel's matching emendation *sukhād yathā sukhaṃ*, my translation of the third line follows Śāstrī's reading (without optative), which seems to make more sense here. In GZ DNP, the third line reads "in accordance with seizing bliss by bliss" (CRV "in accordance with needing to seize . . ."), and the fourth line begins with "here, this . . ."

890. I follow Patel *bhogais* against Śāstrī *bhogas*.

891. In GZ DNP, the first two lines are as follows:

> You should enjoy the entirety of yogas
> and make music, not fearing anything

CRV:

> You are to enjoy the entirety of beings
> and be joyful, not afraid of anything
> You are without fear of misdeeds
> The samaya is hard to transgress.

892. I follow Patel *kaṣṭaṃ* against Śāstrī *kāryaṃ*. GZ DNP:

> Though this is difficult for nescient matter,
> if wood and so on, purified with a mantra,
> will turn into the very deity,
> what need to mention the body having cognition?

CRV:

> If wood and such blessed with a mantra
> turn into something extraordinary, a deity,
> what need to mention the body having wisdom
> with regard to actions of suffering and nescience?

893. GZ DNP:

> It is ordinary pride that is cast off
> through meditative absorption
> By the procedure [DNP "union"] of prajñā and means,
> all should be engaged as being equal

CRV:

> That is to entertain natural pride [or "the nature of this is to entertain pride"],
> cast off by meditative absorption
> Knowing the procedure of prajñā and means,
> all activities are engaged in equally.

894. GZ DNP:

> Just as [DNP "for example"] a lotus is born from mud
> but is not stained by the mud's flaws,
> so the yogīs do not become stained
> by the flaws of all kinds of imprints

CRV agrees with the Sanskrit except "all kinds" for "thoughts."

895. In the ms., this stanza is a lacuna. DNP:

> For example . . .
> You will not be stained by any flaws of seeing
> what is similar to various reflections

The last two lines in CRV read as follows:

> when seeing [things] like reflections,
> you will not be stained by various flaws.

896. In the ms., "if washed" and "will be shining brightly" is a lacuna. This stanza resembles the example of an encrusted beryl in *Dharmadhātustava* 9–10. CRV:

> Your own precious mind is stained
> by beginningless imprints of mud
> By being washed with this water of
> prajñā and means, it shall shine brightly.

897. GZ DNP:

> Once the intelligents' minds have become
> stable through their own deity's yoga and
> become free from the clouds of bad views,
> the sun of the mind will be clear
> [DNP "If the intelligent's . . . yoga, they become free from . . . views and the sun . . . clear"]

CRV:

> Having become free from the clouds of bad views
> through the minds of the intelligent ones
> [engaging in] the yoga of their own deity,
> the sun of the mind shall shine forth.

898. As in Patel's reconstruction, GZ DNP *kun btubs* CRV *yang dag bcad* are probably renderings of Skt. *pariccheda*, which can also mean "discern" and "determine." However, given the relation of this line to the following "cocoon of ignorance," the image of cutting down this cocoon with prajñā seems fitting.
899. In the ms., stanzas 119–120ab are a lacuna. The rendering of stanza 119 follows CRV (in the last line, I follow P *gsal* against N *bsal*, "eliminated"). In GZ DNP, the last two lines read as follows:

> the dharmadhātu that is covered
> by ignorance's cocoon is to be seized

900. CRV "shall illuminate." The example in this stanza corresponds to the same one in *Dharmadhātustava* 5–7.
901. DNP *rab tu gsal* "very clear" (probably a typo for *rab tu grags*).
902. DNP "make them arise as something else."
903. GZ DNP switch "power" and "yoga."
904. In the ms. "mantra talk" is a lacuna, but is attested in Bendall.
905. I follow Patel *saukhyabhāva*; Śāstrī *sūkṣmadeva* ("the subtle deity") GZ *bde dang dngos grub kun* DNP *bde ba'i dngos grub* CRV *lha'i bde ba*.
906. In GZ DNP, the last two lines read as follows:

> Look at this power of mantra
> that grants all bliss and siddhis! [DNP "the siddhi of bliss"]

CRV has the last three lines thus:

> undertake mantra recitation!
> Through the power of mantra,

the deity's bliss will be achieved too.

907. Patel *triratnaṃ* Śāstrī *strīratnaṃ* ("woman-jewel" or "precious women") CRV *bud med rin chen.*
908. GZ "the same goes for unsurpassable bodhicitta."
909. I follow Patel *vadhyāḥ* against Śāstrī *hy ātmā.*
910. GZ "pure samayas."
911. CRV has the first three lines as follows:

    Women and precious bodhicitta, [or "precious women and bodhicitta"]
    and likewise the guru, are not to be abandoned
    Living beings should never be killed.

912. Patel *madhu raktaṃ* Śāstrī and *Prajñopāyaviniścayasiddhi mahāratnaṃ* GZ *dri chen* ("feces") DNP *rin chen* ("jewel") CRV *mtshal chen* ("great blood" = *mahāraktaṃ*). Thus Patel's reading is the only one that matches "five" in the last line, while all others only list four items.
913. I follow Patel *munivajrodakaṃ*, supported by all Tibetan versions, against Śāstrī *ali vajrādikaś*. Given the descriptions of the five buddhas in Maitrīpa's *Pañcākāra* (text 39, 235) being matched with the five nectars, "vajra water" refers to urine.
914. With some variations, this stanza also appears as *Prajñopāyaviniścayasiddhi* III.23 (text 4).
915. I follow Patel *samayair divyaiś* (obviously following the identical phrase in the *Prajñopāyaviniścayasiddhi* and GZ DNP *lha'i dam tshig*) against Śāstrī *samayadravya*; CRV *dam tshig bzang po* (Skt. *samayabhadra*) may be a typo for *samayadravya*.
916. Patel *cittavajrakaṃ* Śāstrī and *Prajñopāyaviniścayasiddhi cittavajriṇaṃ* (GZ CDNP of that text *thugs kyi rdo rje can*). With minor variations, this stanza also appears as *Prajñopāyaviniścayasiddhi* V.21 (text 4). GZ DNP:

    Other divine samayas
    that delight the mind,
    to still wind and fire,
    are to satisfy mind's vajra

    CRV:

    Furthermore, excellent samayas,
    in order to illuminate the mind
    and still disturbances by wind,
    should satisfy the vajra of mind.

917. GZ D *mtshams med* NP *'tshom byed* ("what makes angry").
918. GZ DNP CRV *mnyam par sbyor ba* (lit. "evenly/equally joining") is attested as Skt. *samāśleṣiṇī* ("close embrace," "join together"), while Patel reconstructs *samāyukta* ("joined," "read," "prepared," "devoted," "brought into contact").
919. In the ms., this stanza does not appear at all. I follow GZ DNP, while Patel's reconstruction *nāśucibhāva āśaṅkyo 'vikalpayogalīlayā* of the first two lines is an eclectic mix of GZ DNP and CRV, but *līlayā* corresponds to Tib. *brtsen pas* ("by

playing") rather than GZ DNP *brtson pas*. In the last line, GZ DNP *mnyam par spyad* (lit. "engage/practice/enjoy evenly/equally") is attested to render Skt. *samācaret*, which is also Patel's reconstruction. However, the first two lines in GZ DNP can also be understood in other ways. If *rnal 'byor* is understood as "yogīs," they could be read as follows:

> Through thought-free yogīs making efforts
> [even] in [actions of] immediate consequence without doubt

Or, when these lines are connected more closely with the third line, one could also read them like this:

> Through evenly/equally joining their minds [or "their minds readily embracing"] [even] with
> [actions of] immediate consequence without doubt
> by making efforts in thought-free yoga [or "by thought-free yogīs making efforts"]

CRV:

> Courageously unafraid of impurity,
> by being thought-free, undistracted,
> and having a readily embracing mind,
> mantrīs should undertake everything

In the first line, CRV *dpa' bos* usually is the instrumental case of "vīra" or "hero," but here I take it as the adverb "courageously" because there is already the logical and grammatical subject "mantrīs" in the last line. Though Patel's reconstruction otherwise clearly follows CRV, it has no equivalent of *dpa' bos*.

920. The last two lines in Patel read *aṇumātrā ghṛṇā śaṅkā mṛtyukaṣṭena saṃyutā*, while Śāstrī has *aṇumātrāṃ ghṛṇāṃ lajjāṃ dūrataḥ parivarjayet* ("even an atom of aversion and embarrassment should be kept far off"). More literally, Skt. *mṛtukaṣṭena* could also simply be taken as "the hardship of death." In GZ DNP, the last two lines read as follows:

> even a little anger [I follow NP *'tshom* against GZ D *mtshams*] and doubt
> will produce suffering in them

CRV:

> The poison that amounts to merely
> the leg of a flesh fly [*skang pa* em. *rkang pa*] makes them die
> Even the slightest fear [or doubt] of impurity
> entails being tormented by suffering.

921. I follow Patel *suyuddhaṃ vācaret* against Śāstrī *hyayuddhaṃ* (?) *vācaraṃ*.
922. I follow Patel *supalāyanaṃ* against Śāstrī *svaparāyatanaṃ*.
923. GZ DNP:

> The wise should fight well
> or make a good run for it

> Any thing that is in between
> is pointless—they will fall
> [DNP: "In a pointless thing in between, they will fall"]

CRV:

> The wise supremely fight a battle
> or they make a complete run for it
> When staying in a thing in between,
> this is pointless—they'll be defeated.

924. With regard to the shadow, Skt. *na laṅghayet* ("should not step over") is used in a literal sense; with regard to the commands and the seals, it is used in the figurative sense of transgressing.
925. GZ DNP omit "as supreme."
926. CRV "their faults should never be examined/thought of." Śāstrī reverses the order of stanzas 128 and 129.
927. CRV *lan cig gzugs* ("one-time form") is probably a typo for *lhan cig gzugs* ("simultaneous form").
928. I follow Patel *śuddha* against Śāstrī *samyak*.
929. I follow Patel *śodhakaḥ* against Śāstrī *śoṣakaḥ*.
930. DNP "purifying all turbidities."
931. I follow Patel *śraddhāmaṇi* (GZ *dad pa'i nor bu* DNP *dang ba'i nor bu*) against Śāstrī *saddharmāṇaḥ*. CRV reads this line as "The same is said for a pure gem."
932. GZ DNP omit "is said to."
933. I follow Patel *śraddhāvān* against Śāstrī *śardhāvān*.
934. I follow Patel *muhyate* against Śāstrī *pūjyate*.
935. CRV:

> Never deluded through devotion,
> one possesses the eye of prajñā
> Prajñā is brought forth from what
> is characterized by scripture and realization.

936. Skt. *vindati* can also mean "find," "seize," "obtain," "seek out," "perform," "accomplish," "attend to," "experience," and "partake of" ("discover" seems to cover most of these meanings). GZ DNP read the last line as "they should know (*shes bya*) its means of bliss" and CRV as "they entail penetrating it through [*kyi* em. *kyis*] the means of bliss" (*'bigs par bcas* renders Skt. *savedhanaṃ*, probably based on misreading *sa vindati* as *sa vindhati*).
937. I follow Patel *sukhito janaḥ* against Śāstrī *sukhino janāḥ*. GZ DNP:

> Through the virtue I have accumulated
> by composing this *Purity of the Mind*,
> having attained the mind that is pure,
> may beings thereby attain happiness

CRV has the last two lines as follows:

> possessing the mind that is pure,
> may beings thereby possess happiness.

938. Skt. "This was composed by Āryadevapāda." DNP add "It was translated by Ācārya Jñānākara and lotsāwa Tsültrim Gyalwa." CRV "This completes 'The Purification of the Jewel of the Mind' composed by King Indrabhūti. It was translated, edited, and finalized by the Indian upādhyāya Dīpaṃkaraśrījñāna and the Tibetan lotsāwa Kudön Ngödrub."
939. PDMT, 26:219–52.
940. CDNP have no plural.
941. To make more immediate sense, GZ CD *de yis* [NP *yi*] *rgyal ba'i 'gro ba* is emended to *de yi rgyal bas 'gro ba; rgyal ba'i 'gro ba* is difficult to make sense of (lit. "beings who are [actually] victors"?).
942. GZ *ji ltar dran pa tsam brjod* CDNP *ji srid dran pa(r) brjod pa* ("for as long as it is expressed as recollection").
943. Tib. *nyi ma 'char ka* ("Newly Risen Sun"). Usually, the mahāsiddha Śabara is associated with Mount Śrī Parvata, flanked by the twin mountains Manobhaṅga and Cittaviśrama.
944. CD omit "guru."
945. CDNP *rnam pa thams cad kyi mchog dang ldan pa* GZ *rnam pa thams cad mkhyen pa'i mchog dang ldan pa* ("endowed with the supreme knowledge of all aspects"); the latter is of course also possible, but given that "endowed with all supreme aspects" is such a stock phrase and "prajñā wisdom" is equated below (p. 56) with "the emptiness endowed with all supreme aspects," this phrase seems more likely here.
946. GZ inserts *bstan to* after *'dzin pas* ("taking on") and reads *bstan pa'ang* instead of CDNP *bstan yang* before "with the intention," which gives a rather different and less satisfactory meaning: "Nevertheless, it is the unity that the Bhagavān, through the power of his former aspiration prayers, taught in an effortless manner by excellently taking on kāyas that solely benefit all sentient beings. As for teaching the profound and vast yoga of great bliss . . ."
947. GZ *rim par mdzad pa* CDNP *mtshungs par mdzad pa* ("made equal/similar" or "equally provided").
948. In Ayurvedic medicine, milk is usually considered as an antidote against at least some poisons; on the other hand, as mentioned before, Indian lore has it that snakes drinking milk increases the amount of their poison or makes it more toxic (see stanza 43 of text 15). Thus, it seems that this example probably refers to the latter case (thus, people with the poison of passion, who are like poisonous snakes, when fed more passion, which is like milk, increase that poison).
949. I follow GZ *'dod chags dang bral ba* against CD *'dod chags dang chags pa* NP *'dod chags chags bral ba*.
950. Given the context and the following quote, I follow GZ *'dod chags bral ba'ang rigs mi bya* against CDNP *'dod chags bral yang reg mi bya* ("they should not touch dispassion either" or "though they are passion-free, they should not touch it").
951. *Sarvatathāgatabuddhānuttaraguhyāśvottamavīṇāsamatāmahātantra* (H803, fol. 148a.5–6).
952. GZ *'ba' zhig* CDNP *dga' zhig* em. *'ga' zhig*.
953. I could not locate this stanza, but an almost identical one is quoted and attributed to Saraha in Amṛtavajra's commentary on Kṛṣṇa's *Dohakoṣa* (text 64, 219).

954. The fourfold progression of "passion, dispassion, moderate passion, and great passion" is a typical terminology of the *Guhyasamājatantra* literature, being an equivalent of the sets of "illumination, increase of illumination, culmination of illumination, and luminosity" and "empty, very empty, greatly empty, and all-empty." The triad of "passion, dispassion, and moderate passion" also serves as a shorthand for the three sets of the eighty "tempers" (Skt. *prakṛti*)—thoughts that obscure the three stages of illumination culminating in natural luminosity: (1) the thirty-three thoughts of aversion or hatred that obscure and are indicative of illumination, (2) the forty thoughts of desire that obscure and are indicative of the increase of illumination, and (3) the seven thoughts of ignorance that obscure and are indicative of the culmination of illumination. In the final stages of the process of dying, or during the realization of luminosity via these three stages, these eighty thoughts dissolve progressively. They are listed and discussed extensively in relation to the three stages of illumination in Kongtrul Lodrö Tayé 2005 (251–72). For an overview of the eighty tempers in Nāgārjuna's *Pañcakrama* and Āryadeva's *Caryāmelāpakapradīpa*, see Wedemeyer 2007, appendix IV.

955. *Hevajratantra* II.2.46.

956. I could not locate this stanza in the *Jñānasiddhi*, but an almost identical one is found as *Cittaviśuddhiprakaraṇa* 51 (text 15).

957. I follow GZ *mi 'jig pa* against CD *mi 'dzin pa* NP *mi 'jigs pa*.

958. With minor variants, this stanza is found in the *Anavataptanāgarājaparipṛcchāsūtra* (D156, fol. 230b.2–3), where its two middle lines read as follows:

> It does not possess any being born by nature
> What depends on conditions is said to be empty

In this form, the stanza is also quoted in Maitrīpa's *Pañcatathāgatamudrāvivaraṇa* (text 36, 194), but attributed to the *Candrapradīpasūtra* (it is not found there nor in the *Samādhirājasūtra*). The *Caturmudrāṭīkā* (text 44, 259) follows this attribution. Szántó 2016 (323) likewise considers this stanza as "ultimately from the *Candrapradīpasūtra*," but points out that it is also found as stanza 26 of the *Yogāmbaramahātantra*. By contrast, Vajrapāṇi's *Guruparamparākramopadeśa* (text 213, 190), Kamalaśīla's *Madhyamakāloka* (D3887, 150a.7–150b.1), Avalokitavrata's *Prajñāpradīpaṭīkā* (fols. 131b.4, 214b.2–3, 241a.1), and Abhayākaragupta's *Munimatālaṃkāra* (D3903, fol. 145a.7) explicitly identify this stanza as coming from the *Anavataptanāgarājaparipṛcchāsūtra*. As IaS (78n77) points out, Candrakīrti quotes this stanza four times in his *Prasannapadā*, once explicitly attributing it to an *Anavataptahradāpasaṅkramaṇasūtra*, and once (unattributed) in his *Catuḥśatakaṭīkā*.

959. I could not locate this stanza in the *Tattvāvatāra* (text 214) or anywhere else in Kg or Tg.

960. Given what the text's opening paragraph says, GZ *snying po chen po zhes bya ba dang / ming gzhan pa can gyi shes rab ye shes* CDNP *snying rje chen po zhes bya ba ming gzhan pa can gyi ye shes* are emended to *snying rje chen po zhes bya ba ming gzhan pa can gyi shes rab ye shes*.

961. *Mahāyānaviṃśikā* 13. GZ CDNP:

> If the wise have relinquished imagination,
> all aspects are not the true reality of bliss
> Emptiness is not the true reality of bliss
> It is neither inconceivable, nor is it bliss.

962. I could not locate this stanza in Maitrīpa's works or elsewhere.

963. *Hevajratantra* I.10.38cd. GZ CDNP:

> The bliss arising from the great elements,
> that bliss does not constitute true reality.

964. *Hevajratantra* II.2.31–32. GZ CDNP only cite a variant version of three of these lines:

> Bliss is white, bliss is black
> Recollect the bliss arising from kunduru
> Bliss is being, bliss is nonbeing

Kṛṣṇa's *Yogaratnamālā* (Snellgrove 1959, 2:138–39) says here: "What is attained in the prajñā-jñāna empowerment is the sheer bliss that is characterized by nondiscursiveness. So how could the maṇḍala circle that is endowed with all supreme aspects arise from that?" Usually, it is appropriate for like to arise from like. Here, however, that is not the case, because that is just a worldly convention. Similar to those who speak of the ālaya-consciousness as the substratum that contains the seeds of the world, in the Mantramahāyāna, it is the great bliss attained in the prajñā-jñāna empowerment that is described as "the emptiness of all phenomena" because it is the substratum of all buddha qualities. Specifically, "kunduru" refers to the union of prajñā and means, "being" to the nature of the five buddhas, and "nonbeing" to their nondiscursiveness. Given the nature of bliss of the maṇḍala of Hevajra by virtue of its nature of prajñā and method, what is the nature of bliss of the maṇḍala of Nairātmyā? "Vajrasattva is known as bliss"—that is, "vajra" is the symbol arising from the seed born from the union of the moon and the sun, which have the nature of prajñā and method, respectively. "Sattva" refers to the seed that is the essence of this vajra. Therefore Vajrasattva is the being with the vajra, also known as bliss. According to Jamgön Kongtrul's commentary (Kong sprul blo gros mtha' yas 2005, 514–15), through the three higher empowerments that establish the realization of mahāmudrā in the mindstream, the deities and their colors in the creation process become wisdom deities, having the nature of the maṇḍala of great bliss. Thus, colors and shapes appear as the play of great bliss as their source. Black refers to Akṣobhya, yellow to Ratnasambhava, red to Amitābha, white to Vairocana, green to Amoghasiddhi, and blue to Vajradhara. Great bliss being mobile refers to the assembly of deities or sentient beings, and its being immobile to their palaces or the ordinary world. This bliss is also prajñā (female or ultimate reality), method (male or seeming reality), kunduru (the melting bliss without emission that arises in sexual union), being (perceiver and perceived or the illusory body), and nonbeing (emptiness and luminous wisdom). In brief, Vajrasattva—the all-pervading sovereign who is inseparable from all of these—is also said to be the play of connate great bliss. Hence, great bliss is the all-pervading sovereign of all phenomena.

965. I follow GZ *las kyi* against CD *lam gyi* ("of the path").

966. I follow GZ *shes rab pha rol phyin bsten bya'o* against CD *shes rab pha rol phyin pa'o* NP *shes rab pha rol phyin bya'o.*

967. *Hevajratantra* II.3.4.

968. I follow GZ *dog pa* CD *dogs pa* against CDNP *dgos pa* ("need," "purpose").

969. I follow GZ NP *rjes su gnang ba* against CD *rjes su gnas pa.* "Permission" in the context of empowerment refers to being permitted to visualize the form of the related deity (or deities) and recite their mantra.

970. I follow GZ *bsten par bya'o* against CDNP *brtan par bya'o* ("should stabilize").

971. As mentioned before, "a prajñā" is another word for a karmamudrā (a consort in the practice of the same name).

972. The first line is found in the *Śrīvajramālābhidhānamahāyogatantrasarvatantrahṛdayarahasyavibhaṅga* (H417, fol. 81b.1), and the last two lines (following the reading in other texts, GZ CDNP *yid kyis bral ba* are emended to *'di dang bral ba*) resemble the last two lines in the above-cited stanza from the *Sarvatathāgatabuddhānuttaraguhyāśvottamavīṇāsamatāmahātantra* (H803, fol. 148a.5–6). Together, this and the following stanza are found as a stock quotation in the context of the third empowerment in a number of texts related to different tantras in Tg, but the source of these stanzas is never identified; the first two lines are also quoted in text 90 (333).

973. The first line corresponds to Padmavajra's *Guhyasiddhi* III.34a, also found in Narendrakīrti's *Pradarśanānumatoddeśaparīkṣā* (N3400, fol. 36a.6–7) and the *Śrīmadvimalaprabhātantrāvatāraṇivādahṛdayāloka* (D1349, fols. 33b.7–34a.1); see NG, 12. The first and third lines are also cited in Maitrīpa's *Commentary on Half a Stanza on True Reality Teaching That All Phenomena Are Utterly Nonabiding* (text 73, 191), and all three lines (without "cunning") are in Rāmapāla's *Sekanirdeśapañjikā* (text 45, 435). IaS (330n461) says this: "This quotation seems to be three *pādas*, a, b (hypermetrical), and d, of a verse, the source of which we have not been able to identify . . . *Pāda* d is a stock phrase which can be found in many texts, non-Buddhist as well as Buddhist; see, e.g., *Dharmasamuccaya* 10.25d (991d), *Manusmṛti* 4.73d, *Kubjikāmatatantra* 25.114b."

974. GZ *bu mo* CDNP *bud med* ("women").

975. Given the very similar lines cited in the *Sekanirdeśapañjikā*, GZ CDNP *'jigs tshul can* is emended to *'jig tshul can.*

976. I could not locate these two lines in the *Vajrārallitantra*, the *Rigyarallitantra*, or any other text in Kg or Tg. Two very similar lines, equally sandwiched between the three preceding lines and the following stanza from the *Jñānasiddhi*, are found as a quotation in the *Sekanirdeśapañjikā* (text 45, 435). As Szántó 2017 points out, Rigī (also spelled Rigi and explained as "ḍākinī" in the *Rigyarallitantra*) and Aralli (also spelled Āralli, Arali, and Ārali) are the names of the two central deities in the *Rigyarallitantra*. In the *Vajrārallitantra* (most likely earlier than the *Rigyarallitantra*), the male deity, more often called Heruka and only thrice Ārali, appears without consort and there is no mention of the four ecstasies. Sanderson 2009 (148n340) remarks: "The origin of the Herukas Rigi-ārali and Vajra-ārali of the Tantras of those names are also, it seems, the

apparently unmeaning syllables of Mantras: OṂ ĀRALI RIGI PHEṂ PHEṂ PHEṂ BHYO SVĀHĀ (*Ri gi ā ra li'i rgyud* f. 187v2) and OṂ VAJRA ĀRALI PHAṬ . . . PHEṂ PHEṂ SVĀHĀ (*Ri gi ā ra li'i rgyud* f. 187v7)."

977. VII.11. As IaS (331n469) says: "Verses with a similar first half, and with the same general idea, can be found also in the *Vimalaprabhā* (vol. 2, p. 215: the first half runs *sukhaṃ dvīndriyajaṃ tattvaṃ buddhatvaphaladāyakam*) and the *Sekoddesaṭīka* (p. 172: the first half runs *sukhaṃ dvīndriyajaṃ tattvaṃ devānāṃ rāgiṇāṃ smṛtam*)."

978. CD add *phyir*.

979. See Nāgārjuna's *Caturmudrānvaya* (text 14, 27–29).

980. As mentioned before, Skt. *āmnāya* also means "tantra," "received doctrine," "sacred texts handed down by repetition," "advice," and "that which is to be remembered, studied, or learned by heart."

981. *Sekanirdeśa* 39. In Buddhism, Raurava ("The Dreadful One") is the name of one of the eight hot hells, explicitly confirmed by Rāmapāla's *Sekanirdeśapañjikā*, which adds other hells, such as the worst hell, Avīci. Coincidentally, however, Raurava is also the name of one of the twenty-eight *Siddhāntāgamas*, which are a subclassification of the Śaiva division of the Śaivāgamas (representing the wisdom come down from Śiva, received by Pārvatī, and accepted by Viṣṇu). The Śaivāgamas are divided into four groups: Śaiva, Pāśupata, Soma, and Lākula, with Śaiva being further divided into Dakṣiṇa, Vāma, and Siddhānta (tantric Śaivism, with Raurava being a part of it). Given that Maitrīpa's text rejects the theory and practice of karmamudrā in Śaivism, one wonders whether the use of the term "Raurava" here is maybe also a side blow against the doctrines of Śaivism, possibly even equating their outcome with the hells (Raurava as a hell is also known in Śaivism). GZ CDNP:

> Without knowing mahāmudrā,
> they practice karmamudrā alone
> Falling from tradition's true reality,
> these yogīs therefore go to Raurava.

982. GZ CDNP *legs bsgrubs* ("well practiced").

983. *Sekanirdeśa* 26.

984. CDNP omit "like."

985. Nāgārjuna's *Caturmudrānvaya* explains the karmamudrā as the result of concordant outflow, the dharmamudrā as the result of maturation, mahāmudrā as the result of stainlessness, and the samayamudrā as the result produced by persons. The same is said in the *Caturmudrāṭīkā* and Rāmapāla's *Sekanirdeśapañjikā*.

986. *Sekanirdeśa* 38.

987. *Sekanirdeśa* 25. GZ CDNP:

> Due to being variegated, variety refers to the throat
> Due to being bliss, maturation is at the jewel's tip
> True reality needs to be known through the guru
> Consummation constitutes the cessational ecstasy.

988. *Hevajratantra* II.3.7–8ab.

989. *Yuktiṣaṣṭikā* 19.

990. CDNP "What need is there to elaborate with a multitude of words on procedures?"

991. This is the first half of the second stanza of Vāgīśvarakīrti's *Saptānga* (D1888, fol. 190a.4–5; adding "meaningful" related to "the goal"). The initial part of this text in Tibetan consists of four stanzas (commented on in the remainder of the text), and thus IaS (271n102) identifies these four lines as the third stanza of the *Saptānga*. However, immediately after these stanzas, the text explicitly refers to all these stanzas as "two stanzas," and the same remark is repeated in the colophon. These same four lines are also cited in Rāmapāla's *Sekanirdeśapañjikā* (text 45, 393) and Śraddhākaravarman's **Yoganiruttaratantrārthāvatārasaṃgraha* (D3713, fol. 109a.4–5; wrongly attributed to Vāgiśvarakīrti's *Tattvaratnāvaloka*, in which it is not found).

992. Here, GZ CD *yan lag med par* could also be understood as referring to the absence of the seven constituents, but NP *yan lag ma med par* makes it very clear that this refers to a woman who is a karmamudrā.

993. CDNP "It is completely enjoyed in such a way: thanks to dependent origination, experience appears as all aspects."

994. As mentioned before, the seven constituents of union (Skt. *sampuṭasaptāṅga*, Tib. *kha sbyor yan lag bdun*) are usually said to characterize the fruitional state of Vajradhara, the state of unity (*yuganaddha*), the wisdom of the fourth or word empowerment, and the supreme siddhi of mahāmudrā. The primary source for this template in relation to the fourth empowerment is Vāgīśvarakīrti's *Saptāṅga* (for a brief outline of the entire work, see Tiso 1994, 886–87). According to the second chapter of the *Saptāṅga* (D1888, fols. 190b.7–198a.4), (1) complete enjoyment consists of the thirty-two major and eighty minor marks of the sambhogakāya. (2) Union refers to the sexual union with the female deity. The sambhogakāya mentioned in the Pāramitāyāna is the mere sambhogakāya that lacks the union of two consorts. Therefore the constituent "union" in this sense is adduced here. The Buddha taught sexual union in order to take care of the sentient beings of the desire realm who experience excessive passion, and the goal here refers to the buddhahood that manifests by way of extensively enjoying the pure great bliss of passion through sexual union. (3) Though there is a visible union when an illusory man and woman created by an illusionist have intercourse, this union does not become great bliss. Rather, the great bliss here is the special bliss that is very vast, uncontaminated, and sublime, and remains for as long as saṃsāra lasts. (4) The lack of nature refers to the buddhahood that has the nature of mahāmudrā. "Lack of nature" refers to nothing but the emptiness that is endowed with all supreme aspects, whose synonyms include suchness, dharmatā, equality, unsurpassable awakening, and nondual wisdom. The emptiness that is endowed with all supreme aspects is not some kind of emptiness in the sense of sky flowers, horns of a rabbit, and so on. However, if it is reified as some essence, it becomes an inferior view. (5) Compassion means the great compassion that accomplishes the welfare of all sentient beings. (6) Uninterrupted refers to the nonabiding nirvāṇa by virtue of the continuity of the above-mentioned qualities of the sambhogakāya manifesting in all kinds of ways for the benefit of beings. (7) Unceasing refers to remaining in such a manner for as long as saṃsāra lasts. Compare also the

differing brief explanations in the *Caturmudrāṭīkā* (text 44, 306) and Rāmapāla's *Sekanirdeśapañjikā* (text 45, 392–93). TOK (2:678) says the following: "The word empowerment is conferred in order to introduce the actual connate wisdom—mahāmudrā endowed with the seven constituents . . . the wisdom of the fourth empowerment is explained as Vajradhara endowed with the seven constituents," and explains the seven constituents as follows (3:658): (1) complete enjoyment refers to the utter completeness of the major and minor marks, (2) union means being unified with the self-appearing awareness consort, (3) great bliss is to dwell in the essence of natural connate bliss, (4) lacking a nature is the emptiness of being free of all discursiveness, (5) being filled with compassion means always being endowed with nonreferential compassion for all beings, (6) being uninterrupted means that both kāyas and wisdoms are permanent in terms of their continua, and (7) being unceasing means that both awakened mind's engagement in the cessation without appearances and each form kāya are ceaseless in that they are not discontinued. TOK adds that the wisdom at the time of empowerment also possesses these seven constituents, and when one has familiarized with it in that way during both the creation process and the perfection process at the time of the path, the buddhakāyas (as the fruition) are also attained in such a manner that they are endowed with these seven constituents. According to Dung dkar blo bzang 'phrin las 2002 (291), (1) complete enjoyment refers to being completely adorned with the major and minor marks; (2) union means being unified with the self-appearing awareness consort; (3) great bliss is the experience of physical bliss and the great bliss of the mind in dependence on having made the vāyus enter, abide, and dissolve in the central nāḍī; (4) lacking a nature is the realization of emptiness within mind abiding as the essence of uncontaminated bliss; (5) being filled with compassion means to remain in saṃsāra for as long as it lasts without passing into nirvāṇa; (6) being uninterrupted means not being indolent about promoting the welfare of sentient beings thanks to great nonreferential compassion; and (7) being unceasing means that enlightened activity always lacks any condition for it stopping. According to the *Rdo rje 'chang rnam thar* by the thirteenth-century Drugpa Kagyü master Gyaltangpa Dechen Dorje (Tib. Rgyal thang pa bde chen rdo rje), (1) complete enjoyment consists of the thirty-two major and eighty minor marks of the sambhogakāya as well as wisdom, (2) union refers to the union of wisdom and compassion, (3) great bliss consists of the four ecstasies, (4) the lack of nature refers to the lack of nature of a self and phenomena, (5) compassion means being endowed with conventional and ultimate bodhicitta, (6) uninterrupted refers to the continuity of compassion always being unbroken, and (7) unceasing refers to never passing into nirvāṇa for good (for details, see Tiso 1994, 885).

995. CDNP omit "great."
996. GZ *khrel bgad byed* CDNP *smod par byed* ("disparage").
997. GZ *shing 'thun pa dag* NP *shing thun dag* CD *shin tu blun po dag* ("utter fools").
998. GZ *grags pa* CDNP *smras pa* ("said to be").
999. CDNP *sngags la khyad par ma mthong* GZ *bsngags pa khyad par can ma mthong* ("we do not see this to be especially praised [or 'praiseworthy']").

1000. Given the available Sanskrit versions (see next note), I follow CDNP *sngags kyi bstan bcos* against GZ *sngags kyi theg pa* ("Mantrayāna").

1001. This often-cited stanza is from the *Nayatrayapradīpa* (D3707, fol. 16b.3–4; text 217, 457). Skt. *artha*, here rendered as "goal," also has many other meanings, such as "meaning," "purport," "purpose," "motive," and "cause." The *Nayatrayapradīpa* itself comments on this term that there is no difference between the Mantrayāna and Pāramitāyāna in terms of the fruition that consists of nondual omniscience, but the Mantrayāna is more distinguished by virtue of the following four points in this stanza. On the other hand, the *Caturmudrāṭīkā* (text 44, 265) glosses *artha* as the basic nature of the Madhyamaka of utter nonabiding and the basic nature of mahāmudrā, both of which are free from blocking and creating (or negation and affirmation), and Vajrapāṇi's *Guruparamparākramopadeśa* (text 213, 196) glosses *artha* as "true reality." As for Skt. *adhikāra*, besides "prerogative," it can also mean "subject," "topic," "property," "privilege," "right," and "interest." In the available Sanskrit quotations of this stanza, the last line is found as *mantraśāstraṃ viśiṣyate* (corresponding to the version here), *mantranītir viśiṣyate*, and *mantranītiḥ praśasyate* ("it is the mantra approach that is praised"). In the expression *mantraśastra*, *śāstra* can also mean "body of teaching," "scripture," "treatise," "manual," "precept," "direction," "discipline," "science," and "art." Besides the extensive comments on that stanza in this text here, a detailed (sometimes quite different) explanation of it is found in the *Nayatrayapradīpa* itself, while some shorter comments are contained in Sahajavajra's *Sthitisamāsa* VI.6–13, the *Caturmudrāṭīkā* (text 44, 265–66), Vajrapāṇi's *Guruparamparākramopadeśa* (text 213, 196), and Tipi Bumlabar's commentary on the *Tattvaratnāvalī* (TRVC, 394; see the note on this stanza in text 34, 184). In what follows, first, an opponent accepts that (1) the Pāramitāyāna and the Vajrayāna have the same goal, but objects to the four reasons for the superiority of the Mantrayāna (2)–(5) in this stanza. In answer, after (1) a general explanation of the Pāramitāyāna and the Vajrayāna having the same goal but being taught separately, the objections to those four reasons (2)–(5) are rebutted in detail.

1002. *Saṃpūṭanāmamahātantra* (H396, fol. 402a.6).

1003. Statements like this are found in the prajñāpāramitā sūtras.

1004. CDNP "form is Vairocana, and that has the nature of being sealed with consciousness bearing the name Akṣobhya." For this process of threefold sealing, see texts 36, 39, 42, 45, 92, and 213 (204–7; see the concluding note on *Pañcatathāgatamudrāvivaraṇa* 10 below).

1005. CDNP omit "what is stated."

1006. I follow GZ CD *chog gi* against NP *mchog gis*.

1007. This stanza is very cryptic (and likely corrupt), and the variant readings in GZ and CDNP do not make it any better. The first two lines could also be read as something like: "Has the protector expressed this? Who taught what is called 'support'?" (*rgyab*, "support," can also mean "back," but that does not yield more clarity). The first two lines in CDNP read as something like this:

> Who taught the protector did not
> express this here or was support?

In the fourth line, CD read *bkyigs* ("being tied") instead of *kyog* ("crooked").

1008. CDNP omit "is the [ultimate] reality."

1009. GZ CDNP *phung po . . . rang bzhin can gyi shes rab kyis sbyang bar bya'o* ("it needs to be purified through the prajñā that has the nature of the skandhas, dhātus, and āyatanas") em. *phung po . . . rang bzhin can ni shes rab kyis sbyang bar bya'o.*

1010. This appears to be a somewhat "sanitized" version of *Guhyasamājatantra* XV.18:

> Through the samayas of feces, urine, and such
> and through the joining of the two organs,
> unsurpassable true reality—the peaceful
> state of buddha awakening—is achieved.

1011. The bodhisattva Dharmodgata appears in the prajñāpāramitā sūtras (for example, in chapters 28–29 of the *Aṣṭasāhasrikāprajñāpāramitāsūtra*) as the teacher of the bodhisattva Sadāparudita. Living in a magnificent palace in the city of Gandhavatī, he partook of all sense pleasures in the company of 68,000 women and taught prajñāpāramitā three times a day.

1012. I follow GZ NP *bred par byed pa* against CD *bde ba byed pa* ("are happy about").

1013. GZ *mnyam pa* CDNP *nyams pa* ("perish," "decay").

1014. GZ omits "what."

1015. Here GZ repeats the phrase "we have neither fears nor likes" and links it to what follows, but that seems redundant.

1016. CDNP "for the sake of guiding those who are passionate."

1017. CDNP "the Pāramitā[yāna] is to be taken as the meaning of this very yāna."

1018. CDNP switch the fifth and sixth lines with the third and fourth.

1019. Several commentaries in the *Guhyasamāja* literature cite *Pañcakrama* II.4 (D1802, fol. 48a.5–6), which specifically identifies the fourfold set of "empty, very empty, greatly empty, and all-empty" as "the specifics of causes and their results." Later, *Pañcakrama* III.13–14ab (ibid., fol. 52b.1–2) says that luminosity (the result) is attained through the stage of self-blessing (the cause), which also represents the two realities (seeming and ultimate, respectively). According to Bhavyakīrti's *Pradīpoddyotanābhisaṃdhiprakāśikānāmavyākhyāṭīkā* (D1793, fols. 42b.5–43a.1, 88a.6–7, 111a.5–6), in the unity of one taste, the mentally imputed specifics of causes and their results do not exist ultimately. Thus, for yogīs who attained omniscient wisdom, all entities that abide as the specifics of causes and their results are of a single essence and do not appear as such specifics. Later, the text twice cites *Pañcakrama* II.4, once adding the triad of illumination, increase of illumination, and culmination of illumination. Similarly, Vīryabhadra's *Pañcakramapañjikārthaprabhāsa* (D1830, fol. 165b.4–6) says that the fourth one—all-empty (luminosity)—should be realized through the specifics of these causes and their results. In that vein, other commentaries declare that the divisions of emptiness and so on are the specifics of the causes, and that luminosity represents the specifics of the result.

1020. Except for the third line differing here, this is a stanza in the *Tattvāvatāra* (text

214, 299). CDNP read the fourth line as "It is in this way that the true guru abides."

1021. GZ *de kho na nyid bstan pa de ji ltar 'chad pa yin no* ("How is this teaching on true reality explained?") CDNP *de kho na dam pa zhes bshad do / chad pa ma yin nam* ("This is explained as genuine true reality. Is this not extinction?") are emended to *de kho na nyid bstan pa de ji ltar chad pa ma yin.*

1022. Nāgārjuna's *Acintyastava* 40.

1023. Almost identical passages (omitting "kāya" and, except for the *Śālistambasūtra,* reading "Tathāgata" instead of "buddha") are found in the *Śālistambasūtra* (H21, fol. 180b.5–6), *Bodhisattvapiṭakasūtra* (H56, fol. 123a.6), *Vikurvāṇarājaparipṛcchāsūtra* (H168, fol. 307a.2–3), and *Pratītyasamutpādasūtra* (H213, fol. 195b.6–7).

1024. H161, fols. 57b.5–6.

1025. *Prajñopāyaviniścayasiddhi* I.27ab.

1026. Maitrīpa's *Pañcatathāgatamudrāvivaraṇa* 13 (GZ CDNP omit "by virtue of" and have "flower" instead of "lotus").

1027. I follow NP *rgyun* against GZ CD *rgyu* ("cause").

1028. Maitrīpa's *Apratiṣṭhānaprakāśa* 10.

1029. GZ *'bras bu'i rgyu mtshan rtogs pa las ji ltar* CD *'bras bu'i rgyu mtshan rtogs pa ji ltar* NP *'bras bu'i rtog pa ji ltar* em.*'bras bu'i rgyu mtshan rtog pa las ji ltar.*

1030. GZ *'dod;* CDNP *srid* seems to be a typo for *sred.*

1031. *Sekanirdeśa* 36. The *Avikalpapraveśadhāraṇī* describes how bodhisattvas enter the expanse of nonconceptuality by relinquishing all coarse and subtle characteristics of conceptions in terms of (1) nature (perceiver and perceived or the five skandhas), (2) remedies (the six pāramitās), (3) true reality (emptiness and its equivalents), and (4) attainment (the ten bhūmis of bodhisattvas and buddhahood with all their qualities). These four characteristics are relinquished in a gradual manner by means of analyzing their nature, their qualities, and their essence, and finally by not mentally engaging in them at all (for the section on relinquishing these characteristics, see Brunnhölzl 2012, 330–31). Maitreya's *Dharmadharmatāvibhāga* (lines 164–72) likewise speaks about relinquishing these four characteristics in order to attain nonconceptual wisdom (Brunnhölzl 2012, 167, 187, 260–61, 308–19). The last three of these four characteristics are also mentioned at the beginning of Maitrīpa's *Kudṛṣṭinirghātana* (text 19) and *Nirvedhapañcaka* (text 28), in his *Tattvaprakāśa* 13 (text 35), and Rāmapāla's *Sekanirdeśapañjikā* on it (text 45), and discussed extensively in Sahajavajra's *Tattvadaśakaṭīkā* on stanza 7 (text 46, 40–44). The *Avikalpapraveśadhāraṇī*'s general notion of relinquishing conceptual characteristics is likewise quoted in Maitrīpa's *Amanasikārādhāra* (text 27).

1032. GZ *des na* CDNP *de nas* ("then").

1033. *Mahāyānaviṃśikā* 8. GZ CDNP:

> Awakening is not other than afflictions,
> nor do afflictions arise from awakening
> . . .
> yet delusion's nature is without stain.

1034. This is in line with *Bodhicaryāvatāra* IX.3cd:

Here, the world of common people
is invalidated by the world of yogīs.

1035. CDNP only have *yid bzhin du* ("as they like" or "wish-fulfilling").
1036. CDNP omit *nam yang* ("ever").
1037. I follow GZ *mos pa'ang gal che ste* against CDNP *mos kyang* ("though aspiring").
1038. GZ CD *rkyen rtog* NP *skyon rtogs* em. *rkyen rtogs*.
1039. CDNP omit "being treated with great."
1040. CDNP "the nature of [your] face."
1041. The first phrase of this sentence in GZ is not in meter, while the second one could be. In CDNP, both phrases seem to be in meter, but the first line reads *blang zhing dor ba cung zad ma yin te*, thus missing at least *yod pa* before *ma yin* as in GZ. Obviously, this echoes *Uttaratantra* I.154 (also cited in Nāgārjuna's *Caturmudrānvaya* in the context of the dharmamudrā):

There is nothing to be removed from this
and not the slightest that is to be added
Actual reality is to be seen as it really is—
whoever sees actual reality is liberated.

1042. Though less likely, this could also be read as "through being the maṇḍala circle that has the character of diverse deities."
1043. Somewhat similar versions of this stanza are also cited in Sahajavajra's *Sthitisamāsa* (text 17, 105), Maitrīpa's *Pañcatathāgatamudrāvivaraṇa* (text 36, 196; attributed to Nāgārjuna), the *Caturmudrāṭīkā* (text 44, 338; attributed to the Buddha), Muniśrībhadra's *Pañcakramaṭippaṇī Yogīmanoharā* (fol. 24a.4–5; see Mathes 2015, 103n272), and the versions of the *Caturmudrānvaya* in GZ (text 14, 32–33) and BKC (vol. *ka*, 149a.1–2).
1044. *Hevajratantra* I.10.41. The last line in GZ CDNP reads *mdor bsdus na ni sems su 'dus pa'i tshul can no* ("In brief, they have the mode of being contained in mind"). As the preceding stanza in the *Hevajratantra* makes clear, "this" in the third line refers to the ultimate bodhicitta that is the unity of prajñā and means or emptiness and compassion. Kṛṣṇa's *Yogaratnamālā* (Snellgrove 1959, 2:135) glosses the last three lines as follows: "'This . . .' refers to the true reality of the samādhis, mantras, and so on of familiarizing with the connate during the perfection process, as described. This bodhicitta is communion—the merging of all phenomena into a single taste. Yogīs become of that nature. Here, precisely this refers to the fourth one, the empowerment of mahāmudrā."
1045. This stanza is from the *Guhyendutilakatantra* (D477, fol. 251b.5; since that name is well attested in the extant Sanskrit literature, the reconstruction *Śrīcandraguhyatilakatantra* in its Tibetan versions in Tg is mistaken). It is found in Sanskrit in Indrabhūti's *Jñānasiddhi* (D2219, fol. 55a.2), explicitly attributed to the *Guhyendutilakatantra* and the seventh chapter of the *Caryāmelāpakapradīpa*. With some variants, it is also found in a number of other tantric commentaries. In the second line, Skt. *kalpanākalpa* is ambiguous: the Tibetan of the tantra has *rtog dang mi rtog* ("thought and nonthought"), while all other versions have *rtog dang rnam rtog* ("thoughts and thinking") or *rtog dang brtags (bya)*

("thoughts and what is thought"). In the third line, Skt. *mātrābindu* (rendered here as "minute portions and bindus") is difficult to interpret, as amply attested by its three very different Tibetan renderings. The Tibetan of the tantra itself says *'dren dang tshig* ("guiding/pulling/inducing? and words"), GZ CDNP have *cha dang thig le* ("digits and bindus"), while the Tibetan translations of the *Caryāmelāpakapradīpa*, the *Jñānasiddhi*, our text here, and P5049 read *gug skyed*. Following the latter, Wedemeyer 2007 (260n44) says: "I believe it is referring to the visualized dissolution process, in which the practitioner, having dissolved their body into a graphic syllable (often *hūṃ*), then dissolves this from the bottom up, into the brilliance/void. Thus, the last two visible elements of the syllable-body are the upper line of the *ha* and the *anusvāra*-drop above. Thus, this verse suggests that the ultimate reality/brilliance (the subject of this chapter) is the supreme maṇḍala, which one experiences after the dissolution of the head (*mātrā*) and the drop (*bindu*). TIB roughly supports this interpretation, reading *gug skyed thig le*. According to the *Tshig-mdzod Chen-mo*, *gug kyed* refers to the vowels of the Tibetan syllabary, *gug* being *i* and *u*, *kyed* being *e* and *o* (*gug kyed: gug ni gi gu dang zhabs kyu gnyis dang / kved ni 'breg bu dang na no gnyis /*); cf. *Tshig-mdzog Chen mo*, vol. I, p. 357. While this does not exactly correspond to my interpretation of the Sanskrit—the usual Tibetan term for *mātrā*, in this sense, being *mgo* ('head'), it indicates that the Tibetans understood *mātrā-bindu* to refer to lexical signs; and from there, my interpretation follows." While this is a possible interpretation, *mātrā* has an abundance of meanings, with the possible ones here being "the upper horizontal limb of Devanāgarī characters," "particle," "minute portion," "measure of anything," "moment," and "unit of time." Since the Tibetan of Amṛtavajra's *Dohākoṣaṭīkā* (text 64, 233), where this stanza is also cited, reads *cha* (a common rendering of Skt. *kalā*, "digit") *dang thig le* and the *Dohākoṣaṭīkā* speaks about "digit" and "bindu" in its comments that precede this quote, *mātrā* could mean "unit of time" here. In any case, my rendering "minute portions and bindus" allows for either interpretation.

1046. Given the preceding quote, one is tempted to emend GZ CDNP *langs pa* to (or at least understand as) *'das pa* ("transcend").

1047. *Prajñopāyaviniścayasiddhi* IV.12.

1048. *Laṅkāvatārasūtra* II.178.

1049. *Śrīguhyasamājatantra* II.3. The Skt. *abhāve bhāvanābhāvo bhāvanā naiva bhāvanā / iti bhāvo na bhāvaḥ syād bhāvanā nopalabhyate /* is (probably deliberately) enigmatic and obviously a multilayered wordplay on the Sanskrit root *bhū*, with *bhāva* meaning "being," "existence," and "entity," and *bhāvanā* meaning "meditation" or "creation." In addition, quotations of these lines in other Sanskrit texts as well as their various Tibetan renderings show sometimes significant variants (GZ CDNP *bsgom du med pa sgom pa dngos* [CD *des*]/ *bsgom pa nyid ni bsgom pa min / de ltar dngos po med bsgom pas* [CDNP *de ltar dngos po dngos med pas*] / *sgom pa dmigs su med pa'o /*). My translation follows the above Sanskrit. In Nāgārjuna's *Piṇḍīkramasādhana*, this stanza is found immediately before the visualization of the maṇḍala and the deity, bracketed by the text's lines 15cd "You meditate that ultimately the three realms lack any nature of their own" and stanza 17: "Having meditated with this stanza that the character of what is mobile and what is immobile is empty, through this ritual method, they [what is mobile and what is immobile] are blessed as the ground of wisdom." Candrakīrti's *Pradīpoddyotana* (D1785, fol. 24a.2–24b.4) explains this stanza through the four principles (Tib. *tshul bzhi*). That is, (1) in terms of the literal meaning, if there is "no being" of all mobile and immobile phenomena, "there's no meditation" because there is nothing to meditate on. "Meditation" on being "is not meditation" either—because it does not exist, due to lacking anything to meditate on. "Given that," anything that involves assertions of nonbeing or "being" "is not being," because it contradicts both possibilities. Hence, something to meditate, a meditator, and "meditation are not observable." (2) In terms of the general meaning, "there's no meditation" on all conditioned and unconditioned phenomena as being empty after having eliminated all phenomena because that is the view of clinging to emptiness. "Meditation indeed is not meditation" is said in order to put an end to signs: if you meditate by clinging to the aspects of cause and result, this is not suitable, because cause and result do not exist as two. "Given that being . . ." is said in order to put an end to wishes: there is no wished-for result that has any external form, because wishing prayers are not observable [here, Candrakīrti obviously refers to the three doors to liberation: emptiness, signlessness, and wishlessness]. Therefore, a "meditation" on something like external entities "is not observable" and nonexistent, because they have the nature of mind. (3) In terms of the hidden meaning, "no being" refers to the skandhas and so on: anything to be meditated on, which is mere mind, has no being because it is impure and always nonexistent. "Meditation indeed is not meditation" is said in order to put an end to seeming reality: meditating on the illusory form of a deity, which has the character of seeming reality, is not suitable either, because it is pure by virtue of luminosity. Therefore, the "being" of mere seeming reality "is not being," because the two realities are inseparable. Therefore, any "meditation," such as meditating on the two realities, "is not observable," because they are unobservable. (4) In terms of the ultimate meaning, "with no being, there's no meditation" on ultimate reality, because it is primordially pure. "Meditation" on what has the character of seeming reality is not what is to be cultivated either, because seeming reality is not real. Thus, any being that has the character of the two realities is not what is to be meditated on, because liberation will occur by merely seeing that the two realities do not exist as two. Hence, any clinging to something to meditate, to a meditator, and to meditation "is not observable" in those who realize the progression of engaging through unity. This is what the bhagavān Vajradhara declared. Ratnākaraśānti's *Piṇḍīkṛtasādhanopāyikāvṛttiratnāvaḷī* (D1826, fols. 3b.4–5 and 25b.1–26b.7) on Nāgārjuna's *Piṇḍīkramasādhana* first identifies our stanza as indicating meditation on emptiness, then reproduces Candrakīrti's above comments almost verbatim, and finally provides an additional set of six comments by way of the alternative hermeneutical template of literal, nonliteral, intentional, nonintentional, expedient, and definitive meanings. In terms of the nonliteral meaning, Ratnākaraśānti refers to the three natures of Yogācāra, saying that since all phenomena do not exist ("with no being"), "there's no meditation" that is characterized by clinging to phenomena (empty). The "meditation" that is the imaginary "indeed is not meditation" (very empty). Hence, "being"—the dependent characteristic—"is not being": it is of no substance (greatly empty). "Meditation is not observable" means that the meditation that is the perfect is not imaginary (all-empty). In terms of the nonintentional meaning, Ratnākaraśānti concludes that "meditation"—mahāmudrā meditation—"is not observable": the thoughts of the other three mudrās are not observable in it. In terms of the definitive meaning, he says that since mere cognizance does not exist ("with no being"), "there's no meditation": there is no meditation that is the path that makes one attain it. "Meditation indeed is not meditation" means that meditation on emptiness is not suitable either, because it depends on eighteen [probably referring to the eighteen emptinesses] and is just the side of extinction. Hence, "being is not being": what has the character of creation-process meditation is not the ultimate, because it is imaginary. Thus, perfection-process "meditation is not observable," because it is without discursiveness and is established by its very essence. See also Bentor 2009 and Yiannopoulos 2014.

1050. GZ CDNP *ro* renders Skt. *rasa*, which can also mean "nectar," "elixir," "essence," "finest part of anything," and "fluid," as well as "desire," "delight," and "disposition of the mind."

1051. GZ *'tshol ba* CD *tshor ba* ("sensed") NP *tshul ba*.

1052. CDNP "dhyāna."

1053. GZ *bstan pa med pa zhig* CD *gtan med pa zhig* ("does not exist at all") NP *bsam gtan zhig* ("a dhyāna").

1054. In accordance with the initial quote from the *Nayatrayapradīpa*, I here follow CDNP *don gcig yin na yang* against GZ *don gcig pa yod pa ma yin na'ang* ("though there is not the same goal").

1055. GZ *don dam pa ma yin* CDNP *don ma yin* ("not actual" or "not tending toward the facts").

1056. GZ *med kyang* CDNP *med pas* ("because there is no").

1057. GZ *blos zer* CDNP *blo bzod*.

1058. CDNP omit "five."

1059. As mentioned before, this line is from the *Śrīvajramālābhidhānamahāyogatantrasarvatantrahṛdayarahasyavibhaṅga* (H417, fol. 81b.1).

1060. I follow CDNP *dbang bkur* against GZ *dbang phyug* ("mighty").

1061. Tg contains one text with *gsang ba mdzod kyi mdo* in its title (*De bzhin gshegs pa thams cad kyi gsang mdzod chen po mi zad pa gter gyi sgron ma brtul zhugs chen po bsgrub pa'i rgyud ye shes rngam pa glog gi 'khor lo zhes theg pa chen po'i mdo*; a Nyingma tantra), and there is also the *'Phags pa spyan ras gzigs dbang phyug mdzod thogs pa med pa'i yid bzhin gyi 'khor lo'i snying po zhes gzungs*. However, this quote is not found in either text, or anywhere else in Kg or Tg.

1062. *Śrīsarvabuddhasamayogaḍākinījālasaṃbaranāmottaratantra* (H376, fol. 247a.6).

1063. CDNP "the sambhogakāya of enjoying the taste of wisdom is not tenable."

1064. I follow GZ *la goms pa* against CDNP *la sogs pa* ("and so on").

1065. CDNP "through the true reality of lacking [this kind] of familiarity, the state of Vajrasattva that has the character of great bliss . . ."

1066. *Abhisamayālaṃkāra* VIII.12.

1067. GZ *ci ste mi sto* CDNP *ci ste sto.*
1068. CDNP omit "in their entirety."
1069. With the *Samādhirājasūtra,* I follow NP *sangs rgyas 'gyur* against GZ CD *sangs rgyas rgyu* ("the causes of buddhas").
1070. *Samādhirājasūtra* X.27cd (H129, fol. 53a.7–53b.1).
1071. CDNP *rtsed mo tsam du* GZ *rtsed mo tsam las* ("by virtue of mere play").
1072. I follow CD *de dag la sngags kyi tshul gyis* against GZ *de dag las sngags kyi tshul gyis* NP *de dag las kyi tshul gyi.*
1073. A number of utras say that at the end of the tenth bhūmi, bodhisattvas receive the empowerment of great light rays from all buddhas, which enables them to become fully complete buddhas (see, for example, the *Dhāraṇīśvararājasūtra;* D147, fol. 157a.7–157b.3). As in our case here, several commentators take this as an indication that complete buddhahood can only be attained by means of the Vajrayāna. For a more detailed discussion, see Dudjom Rinpoche 1991, 142–43 and 912–13.
1074. GZ *ji bzhin pa'i man ngag gis* CDNP *ji bzhin pa'i man ngag can* ("those with the pith instructions . . ."); "pith instructions on how things are" could also be understood as "concordant pith instructions."
1075. CDNP omit "or."
1076. *Hevajratantra* II.2.13–14ab.
1077. The first line is indeed found in this tantra, but the rest of the stanza continues in a very different way (H402, fol. 53a.6).
1078. I take GZ CDNP *dngos po* here as a rendering of Skt. *svabhāva.*
1079. This passage is not found in the *Vajrārallitantra* or elsewhere.
1080. It is somewhat difficult to tell whether the passage that includes the two "quotes" from the *Vajrārallitantra* and this concluding sentence is a part of Divākaracandra's rebuttal or already the beginning of the following objection, since this passage seems to make a point of the common ground of the Pāramitāyāna and the Mantrayāna. The preceding quote from the *Hevajratantra,* however, is surely not part of the objection, since its context in that tantra is the introduction to practicing with a karmamudrā.
1081. The most common explanation of "irreversibility" refers to bodhisattvas on the eighth bhūmi and above, meaning that at that point it is impossible for them not to attain buddhahood and impossible to regress on the bodhisattva path or into lower yānas. Another explanation is that "irreversible bodhisattvas" (as well as "the level of irreversibility") are those on the path of seeing (the first bhūmi) and above. In more detail, according to the eighth point ("the signs of irreversible learners") of the fourth topic ("the complete training in all aspects") of the *Abhisamayālaṃkāra* (IV.38–59), "irreversible bodhisattvas" consist of those bodhisattvas on the paths of preparation, seeing, and familiarization who exhibit specific signs of irreversibility according to their faculties (those who show signs of irreversibility already on their path of preparation are of highest faculties, those who show such signs on the path of seeing are of medium faculties, and those who show these signs on the eighth bhūmi are of lowest faculties).
1082. CD *theg pa chen po pa* ("Mahāyānists") NP *theg pa chen pos de la spyod pa* ("Pāramitāmahāyāna not accomplish engaging in that?").

1083. GZ *phyir de dang de dag gis* CDNP *phyir/ dang de dag gis* (thus taking the two clauses beginning with "because" to be two different reasons).
1084. I follow GZ *de ltar* against CDNP *de ltal na yang* ("though this is the case").
1085. GZ CD *bzhugs pa* NP *zhugs pa* ("entered").
1086. CDNP "cakra."
1087. With several variants, two similar stanzas are quoted in a number of tantric commentaries; among them, Jinadatta's *Śrīguhyasamājatantrapañjikā* (D1847, fol. 146.4) and Ānandagarbha's *Māyājalamahātantrarājaṭīkā* (D2513, fol. 197b.7) attribute them to the *Vajraśikharatantra*, but they are not found there (or elsewhere).
1088. GZ *brten nas* CDNP *brtul nas* ("disciplining with").
1089. This stanza is almost identical to one in the *Śrīvajraḍākatantra* (H386, fol. 332a.7–332b.1) and is also very similar to Keralipa's *Śrītattvasiddhi* 11.
1090. The first two lines resemble *Guhyasamājatantra* VII.3ab (H416a, fol. 447a.2–3). A very similar stanza in Kṛṣṇapāda's *Kṛṣṇayamāritantrarājaprekṣaṇapathapradīpanāmaṭīkā* (D1920, fol. 176a.5–6) is also attributed to the *Guhyasamājatantra*.
1091. These are the first two lines of the fifth opening stanza of Ratnākaraśānti's *Prajñāpāramitopadeśa* (D4079, fol. 134a.3).
1092. CDNP omit "of the deity."
1093. CDNP "doubts will be reversed."
1094. CDNP omit *bar du* and *gyi sa* ("the bhūmi of").
1095. CDNP *yin nam* GZ *min nam* ("Is it not so?").
1096. GZ *spre'u bun dza'i* CD *spre'u na dza yi* NP *dpe'u 'gu 'dzi'i*; it is unclear what *bun dza*, *na dza*, or *'gu 'dzi* refers to (maybe *guñjā*; *Abrus precatorius*, rosary pea, which is poisonous).
1097. I follow GZ *myos pa* against CD *bsnyems pa* ("haughty") N *snyom pa* P *snyoms pa* ("even").
1098. CDNP omit "five."
1099. CDNP omit "definitive."
1100. *Mahāyānaviṃśikā* 15cd. GZ CDNP:

> The essence of all entities
> is difficult to discriminate.

1101. GZ *rang rig pas grub pa la* CDNP *rang rig pa grub pa la* ("in self-awareness being accomplished").
1102. GZ *sdug bsngal gyis* [em. *gyi*] *lam bde bar rtogs pa yod pa ma yin* CDNP *sdug bsngal lam bde bar rtogs pa ma yin*.
1103. *Hevajratantra* I.10.15. The first two lines are also found in *Hevajratantra* I.8.33ab, the *Pañcakrama* (II.64ab), the *Saṃpuṭatantra* (H396, fol. 367b.6), the *Śrīvajramaṇḍālaṃkāratantra* (H459, fol. 82b.6), the *Śrīvajraḍākatantra* (H386, fol. 328a.3–4), the *Vajraḍākanāmottaratantra* (H387, fol. 519a.4–5), and the *Śrīḍākārṇavamahāyoginītantra* (H390, fol. 75b.7).
1104. I follow GZ NP *rang gi rig (pa)* against CD *rang gi*.
1105. GZ can also be read as "self-awareness is not established/accomplished through dependent origination" and NP as "dependently originating self-awareness is not established/accomplished."

1106. These two stanzas are not found in any of Saraha's preserved works. With some variants, the second stanza also appears (unattributed) in Vanaratna's *Trayodaśātmakaśrīcakrasaṃvaramaṇḍalopāyikā* (D1489, fol. 183b.5–6). CDNP:

> By thoughts being at peace, the mind also is at peace—
> . . .
> So why would this not be more superior than the sky?
> This mind in which all thoughts are cured . . .

1107. I follow GZ *gdungs pa* against CDNP *'dul ba* ("guided").

1108. GZ *'dod chags can / 'dod chags zhi bar bya ba'i phyir* / CD *'dod can 'dod pa zhi ba'i phyir* / NP *'dod chags 'dod pa zhi bya'i phyir* / em. *'dod can 'dod pa zhi bya'i phyir /*.

1109. Given that the first stanza has a prose parallel above and that the second is only followed by *zhes pa'o* but not by *zhes gsungs so* or the like (which Divākaracandra otherwise uses after each of his citations), these appear to be two stanzas by the author himself (they are not found anywhere else in Kg or Tg).

1110. This stanza is found in the *Saddharmapuṇḍarīkasūtra* (H116, fol. 32b.7–33a.1). GZ CDNP have some variant readings and switch the first two lines with the last two.

1111. *Laṅkāvatārasūtra* II.204.

1112. GZ *song nas mthong ba ldog* CDNP *mthong nas song ba ldog* ("saw . . . went, and returned").

1113. GZ omits "on the [maṇḍala] circle of Nairātmyā as it is described [there]."

1114. As mentioned before, the *Nairātmyāprakāśa* is a sādhana of Hevajra's consort Nairātmyā by Advayavajra, which describes her outer and profound creation processes (D1308, fols. 218b.7–221b.4). The practice begins with the typical successive visualization of Nairātmyā's maṇḍala with the surrounding fifteen yoginīs, the seven-branch prayer, and merging the jñānasattvas with the samayasattvas (including an explanation of some of the symbolism of Nairātmyā's form and attire). Then the text says this (excerpt from Isaacson's unpublished Sanskrit edition in IaS, 374n34; D1308, fol. 221a.7–221b.4): "Possessing the pride of being Nairātmyā, you should be identical with Nairātmyā. Here, in order to engage in the six-branch yoga, in due order, you should meditate on her in the colors black, red, yellow, green, blue, and white. Through the progressive intensity [or vividness] of meditation, she first appears like the full moon obscured by clouds. Then, thanks to [meditation] becoming more intense, she appears like an illusion. Then, thanks to it becoming [even] more intense, she manifests as lucidly as in a dream. Immediately after that, thanks to the [full] maturation of [meditation's] intensity, mahāmudrā yogīs who have attained [a state] in which dreams and the waking state are not different gain accomplishment [in this practice]. This is the creation stage. In another manner, by virtue of the union of the bola and the kakkola, the bodhicitta that has the nature of great bliss and is located in the middle of supreme [ecstasy] and cessational [ecstasy] arises. Having the character of fifteen digits, it should be instantly seen as having the nature of the fifteen yoginīs with the previously mentioned colors, [hand-held] symbols, and forms because it has the nature of the five skandhas, the four elements, the six objects, and body, speech, and mind. This is the profound creation stage."

1115. I follow CDNP *'dod pa na spyod pa* against GZ *'dod pa na skyod pa.*

1116. *Hevajratantra* II.3.11. I follow the Sanskrit without noting the minor variants in GZ CDNP.

1117. CDNP omit "creation."

1118. CDNP have only "consisting of the Vajradhara relief." In the texts of Maitrīpa and his disciples, in due order, the five skandhas are said to be sealed with the five tathāgatas Vairocana, Ratnasambhava, Amitābha, Amoghasiddhi, and Akṣobhya. These tathāgatas are in turn to be sealed with Akṣobhya (indicating their being nothing but mind), which is also called "the tathāgata relief." Akṣobhya is then to be sealed with Vajrasattva (indicating the unity of emptiness and compassion), which is also called "the Vajradhara relief" or "the Vajrasattva relief." As for the term "relief" here, the Sanskrit equivalent *āśvāsa* (Tib. *dbugs dbyung ba*) can also mean "consolation," "solace," "encouragement," "reassurance," "refreshment," and "revival." All of these meanings apply here as well because sealing the skandhas with the tathāgatas, the tathāgatas with Akṣobhya (being nothing but mind), Akṣobhya with Vajradhara (emptiness and compassion), and Vajradhara with great bliss represents a progression of being reassured of the true nature of the skandhas, mind, emptiness, and great bliss, a progressive revival of that nature, a progressive consolation that nothing is as solid as it may seem, and a progressive encouragement to realize this. Experientially, this progression manifests as an increasing sense of relief from reification and the ensuing afflictions and sufferings. This sense of relief or resting at ease is clearly explained in Vajrapāṇi's *Guruparamparākramopadeśa* (text 213, 204–7; see the concluding note on *Pañcatathāgatamudrāvivaraṇa* 10 below and also texts 36 and 45). Note, however, that the kinds of relief mentioned here are explained in many different ways in different tantric texts. For example, the tathāgata relief is also explained as saṃsāra, being referential, becoming a suitable vessel through the accumulation of merit, or the profound inner creation process. The Vajradhara relief is described as nirvāṇa, being nonreferential, the attainment of buddhahood through the accumulation of wisdom, or the perfection process.

1119. NP omit "the cognition of."

1120. *Sekanirdeśa* 38a.

1121. Though not immediately recognizable, GZ CDNP *las kyi phyag rgya nyid bzhin du zhes bya ba la sogs pa* (lit. "Just like the karmamudrā . . .") must refer to *Sekanirdeśa* 37, since this stanza exactly fits the context here:

> Just as ecstasy and such are arrayed
> distinctly within the karmamudrā,
> it is the same in the samayamudrā
> due to the vajra master's kindness.

1122. CDNP omit "accumulations of."

1123. GZ *gsum pa lhan cig skyes pa brjod du med* CDNP *lhan cig skyes pa brjod du med*. There is a possibility that this line is a conflation of *Hevajratantra* I.10.11d ("The fourth is expressed as the connate") and I.10.13d ("The connate is not found in these three").

1124. GZ CDNP *brtag tu med pa* usually renders Skt. *atarka*, but could also be understood as "not conceivable" or "not examinable."
1125. CDNP *lung bstan par sla ba* GZ *lung bstan par bla ba* (*bla ba* is an old expression for "speak").
1126. GZ *bral ba min* CDNP *blangs pa ni* ("assumes").
1127. Without omitting the genitive at the end of the third line, GZ *stong nyid snying rje dbyer med pa'i / bla ma dam pa bsten pa las /* would mean "This is by virtue of relying on the true guru of emptiness and compassion inseparable." However, given the first two lines and CDNP, this is less likely. CDNP:

   The awakening in which emptiness and compassion
   are inseparable is by virtue of relying upon the guru.

1128. I follow GZ CD *'bad* against NP *'bab.*
1129. GZ *thob pa* CDNP *thos pa* ("hearing").
1130. NP "self-awareness."
1131. This and the following four lines have more and irregular numbers of syllables (thirteen, fifteen, eleven, thirteen, and thirteen) than the preceding and following stanzas. Given that the last line of the preceding stanza ends in *gang yin pa*, it could be that it is an apposition of the first line here.
1132. The last two lines could also be read as "in order that all sentient beings attain the genuine path for the sake of their benefit."
1133. I follow CDNP *de ba tsandra* against GZ *de ba tsandra ka ti.*
1134. For an outline of text 16 by Tipi Bumlabar, see appendix 3.
1135. PDMT, 26:253–72.
1136. GZ CDNP "I pay homage to the [CDNP add "glorious"] Bhagavān Mañjuvajra." In the following, "Matsuda" refers to Matsuda 1995 (in the sections of Vaibhāṣikas and Sautrāntikas), "Iwata" to Iwata 1997, 1999, 2011, and 2013 (in the section of Nonaspectarian Yogācāra), and Iwata 2014 (in the section of Aspectarian Yogācāra), "Onians" to Onians 2002 (who says that her "textual apparatus is largely as given to me in the first instance by Harunaga Isaacson"), "Mathes" to Mathes 2019 (both in the mantra section), and "Szántó" to Szántó n.d. (throughout).
1137. Note that, true to its name, the *Sthitisamāsa* here refers to the positions of the four Buddhist schools rather than to the names of their proponents; "the very middle" renders Skt. *madhyamā* (rather than *madhyamaka*; *madhyamā* is also found at the end of the Madhyamaka section). GZ CDNP switch the first two and the last two lines and link the genitive *gsal ba yi* (instead of the Skt. adverb *sphuṭam*, "clearly") with "phenomenal and personal identitylessness":

   Having bowed to the phenomenal and personal
   identitylessness that is clear as per the sequence
   of Sūtrānta [CD "vajra"], Vaibhāṣika, Vijñapti[vāda],
   and Madhyamaka, it shall be explained.

1138. These two lines correspond to *Jñāsārasamuccaya* 21ab and *Sugatamatavibhaṅga* 1ab; in addition, line I.2a corresponds to *Sugatamatavibhaṅga* 1c. Together, these three lines plus the fourth line "empty of a self and without agent" are cited as a stanza in several tantric and nontantric commentaries, which in some of them is attributed to the Buddha himself. As for "the two cessations," "analytical cessation" refers to the cessation by virtue of having terminated the factors to be relinquished through insight into the nature of phenomena by having applied the remedies of the Buddhist path, and "nonanalytical cessation" is the termination of all factors to be relinquished through the termination of all their causes (that is, absence of any new results due to the complete lack of their causes). These two kinds of cessation refer to attaining nirvāṇa while the skandhas still remain during one's lifetime and the final nirvāṇa without any remainder of the skandhas at death, respectively. Note that this original Vaibhāṣika distinction between these two kinds of cessation differs from how they are often presented in Tibetan doxographies: analytical cessation is simply equated with nirvāṇa, while nonanalytical cessation is considered as the fact of a given result not arising due to its specific causes and conditions being incomplete temporarily (such as a certain flower not arising at present due to the current lack of a seed, earth, water, and so on).

1139. GZ CDNP switch the first two and the last two lines.
1140. GZ CDNP have the last two lines as follows:

> Being the reality of suffering of existence [CDNP "existence is the reality of suffering"],
> they are to be understood as the result.

1141. GZ CDNP "The cause is the reality of the origination [of suffering]."
1142. Matsuda *sāśravaṃ* Szántó *āśravaṃ*.
1143. Skt. *atyanta* can also mean "perfect," "absolute," and "complete."
1144. Ms. *sākṣātkāyaḥ* Matsuda *sākṣātkāraḥ* Szántó *sākṣātkāryaḥ* ("to be directly realized").
1145. GZ CDNP:

> Having terminated afflictions and karma,
> this will be the utter cessation, and hence [CDNP "then"]
> the wise's liberation is the directly realized goal [or "actuality"]
> It is peace, the termination of suffering.

1146. I follow Szántó *tasyāryāṣṭāṅgiko mārgo*; Matsuda ms. *taś yāryāṣṭāṅgiko mārgo* em. *sa cāryāṣṭāṅgiko mārgo*, corresponding to GZ CDNP *'phags lam yan lag brgyad de ni*. What was said in the introduction about "noble" in the expression "the four realities of the noble ones" (instead of "the four noble truths" or the like) applies here as well. Thus, according to the classic explanations, it is not the path or its eight branches that are noble (though that is not wrong factually), but rather "the eightfold path of the noble ones" specifically designates the path that can only be practiced by the noble ones (in general, those from the path of seeing onward, but in this case only those on the path of familiarization).
1147. GZ CDNP "by cultivating the eightfold . . . , it is deliverance's best means."
1148. I follow ms. *saṃyagdṛṣṭ-* and GZ *yang dag lta ba* ("correct view") against CDNP *yang dag bstan pa* ("correct teaching"). Except for *saṃyagdṛṣṭ-*, the remainder of the last two lines is missing in the ms.

1149. GZ CDNP have the last two lines as follows:

> independent of teaching any scriptures, [GZ CDNP *lung ston pa* usually means "prophecy" or "teaching the definition of words," but none of these seem to make sense here]
> but by their own former aspiration prayers.

1150. Skt. *parinirvāti* has the double meaning of "be completely liberated" (or "attain absolute rest") and "become extinguished."

1151. GZ CDNP show some variants and switch lines I.7cd and I.8ab:

> Having directly manifested their goal,
> by the nirvāṇa with the body as remainder,
> in all regards, those magnificent ones [or "that magnificent state"]
> have the ability for their own and others' welfare
>
> Having demonstrated this as they wish, [I follow *'dod pas bstan nas su* against GZ CD *'dod pa bsten nas su,* "having relied on their own wish"]
> they pass into parinirvāṇa like a lamp
> This is middling buddhahood . . .

1152. Unlike with the corresponding concluding sentences of each of the following sections, the section on the Vaibhāṣikas simply ends with stanza I.8. For the sake of consistency I insert an additional concluding sentence here (though it is more or less a repetition of line I.8d).

1153. I follow Matsuda's and Szántó's emendation *skandhāyatanadhātavaḥ* of ms. *sandhāyannadhātava.*

1154. I follow Matsuda's emendation *nirātmānaś ca te* (which is very close to GZ CDNP *de dag bdag med pa ru ni*) of ms. *nirātmānaś ya te;* Szántó *nirātma naśyate* ("perishes [as] the absence of a self").

1155. I follow Szántó *matam;* Matsuda *satam* em. *satām* ("of the wise"), which may be influenced by GZ CDNP *dam pa'i shes pa* (which, however, here simply renders *samyagjñānaṃ*).

1156. GZ CDNP:

> The modes of the two genuine cognitions
> consist of direct perception and inference
> The specifically characterized phenomena
> of objects are directly manifest and hidden.

1157. I follow Szántó *kāladeśasamānatvāt* against Matsuda *kāladeśāsamānatvāt;* GZ CDNP *nyi tshe bar* "trifling."

1158. Matsuda *arthakriyāsumaktatvāt* em. *arthakriyāsamaktatvāt;* Szántó *arthakriyāsu maktatvāt* em. *arthakriyāsu śaktatvāt,* both corresponding to GZ CDNP *don gyi bya ba nus pa'i phyir.*

1159. GZ CDNP "ultimate entities."

1160. I follow Matsuda's emendation *ākāśādivyudāsena* of ms. *ākāśādivyudāśena;* Szántó leaves ms. as is.

1161. I emend ms. and Szántó *parīkṣāte* to *parīkṣate;* Matsuda em. *parīkṣyate.*

1162. GZ CDNP:

> Forget about space and so forth, but
> those wishing for functions to be performed
> scrutinize those here by taking them
> as the objects of valid cognition.

1163. In GZ CDNP, the last two lines read as follows:

> they function as their own entities
> in those individual moments.

1164. I follow Matsuda's emendation *tat karoti* of ms. *naṃt karoti;* Szántó *naṃttharoti.*

1165. Skt. *kṛtasya karaṇāyogād* "not linking the execution of that which has been executed" could also be read as "the cause of what has been executed" or "the cause of the result." What this stanza seems to say is that function (as a continuity or process) is not performed by a single moment of an entity; rather, the process of functioning in a certain way is performed by a series of moments that, however, nevertheless remain distinct moments and essentially unconnected. GZ CDNP:

> Having executed a single function to be performed,
> it is not that this is the execution [of function]
> Not linking execution with execution [*byed pa byed par mi sbyor te*
> could be understood in many ways],
> if executed, this turns into another.

1166. GZ CDNP render Skt. *rūpa* as "nature."

1167. Matsuda reads *kṣanānta(re/)* as the end of folio 2b, which is very close to GZ CDNP *skad cig gzhan gyi;* Szántó *kṣanān ta.* Since folio 3 of the ms. is missing, the Sanskrit of stanzas II.7cd–18ab is not available.

1168. Usually, the technical terms "positive determination" (Skt. *pariccheda,* Tib. *yongs gcod*) and "negative determination" (Skt. *viccheda,* Tib. *rnam bcad*) refer to the two complementary aspects of the process of ascertaining something that remains after the exclusion of certain mistaken features of this something, such as first eliminating the wrong notion that a tree in the dark is a robber and thus positively determining that the tree is indeed just a tree. Here these terms seem to refer to the direct perception of momentary entities in the present while excluding any superimpositions, such as lasting during the three times, onto them.

1169. I follow GZ *rgyu gzhan dgos pa ma yin* against CDNP *rgyud gzhan dgod pa ma yin* ("other continua are not established").

1170. I follow GZ *'jig pa* against CDNP *'jigs pa* ("are afraid").

1171. I follow GZ *rang gi rgyu yis* against CDNP *rang rig rgyu yis* ("through the cause of self-awareness").

1172. I follow CDNP *rgyu ni dbang po dang mnyam 'gyur ba* against GZ *rgyu ni dbang po nyams 'gyur ba* ("the cause is the decline of the sense faculties").

1173. Given the parallel phrases in III.3b and III.4a, GZ CD *phyed dang mi (ma) phyed* NP *phye dang ma phye* (could also mean "visible and invisible") seems to render Skt. *bhedābheda.*

1174. I follow GZ CD *bems min* against NP *sems min* ("nonmind").

1175. GZ *sngon par byed pa* CDNP *mngon par byed pa* render Skt. *āmukhīkaraṇam* and *sammukhībhāva* or *sākṣātkaraṇam*, respectively. Since *āmukhīkaraṇam* and *sākṣātkaraṇam* ("make visible," "put before the eyes, "perceive directly") do not make any sense here, it seems that *sammukhībhāva* in its sense of "be opposed to" (rather than "standing face to face or opposite") is what is meant here.

1176. I follow Matsuda's emendation *anyathā tan mahāyānaṃ* of ms. *anyathā tana mahāyānaṃ*; Szántó *anyathātanamahāyānaṃ*.

1177. GZ CDNP:

> By cultivation through the Mahāyāna's progressive stages,
> why would this not become perfect awakening?
> Otherwise, how could the insight of the realization
> of the Sautrāntikas [NP "sutrānta"] be the Mahāyāna?

1178. Skt. *madhyamā* usually means "middle finger," "womb," "midnight," and so on, but here appears to be the noun of the adjective *madhyama*, among whose many meanings "impartial" (here in the sense of impartial compassion toward all sentient beings) seems to be the one that makes the most sense, given the context of compassion being what distinguishes the Hīnayāna and the Mahāyāna. Another possibility (less likely though, given the context of compassion) would be that *madhyamā* means "the very middle" as an epitome of the Mahāyāna path. The same goes for the occurrence of *madhyamā* in II.21b.

1179. I follow Matsuda's and Szántó's emendation *buddhatā* of ms. *buddhatāṃ*.

1180. Matsuda *niścayaḥ* Szántó *niśvayaḥ* em. *niścayaḥ*. GZ CDNP read the last two lines as follows:

> because there is no certainty about the yānas
> merely through the distinctions of the positions.

1181. Ms. *kevalaprakṣayārhatvaṃ* Matsuda em. *kevalaprajñārhatvaṃ* Szántó em. *kevalaṃ prajñayārhatvaṃ*.

1182. As it stands, ms. *madhyamāyām ca dṛśyate* is difficult to construe. One may be tempted to read *madhyamāyāṃ* here as *madhyameṣu* ("in those who are middling"); this is not only unmetrical, but also unlikely in terms of its meaning, given that the parallel occurrence of *madhyamā* in II.20a cannot mean "middling" and that "middling" in II.22d and elsewhere in the text is phrased as *madhya*. GZ CDNP *dgra bcom dang / dbu ma pas kyang mthong ba'o* is of no help. Therefore, given that the issue here is the superiority of the Mahāyāna by virtue of its impartial compassion, I emend the second line to *madhyamāyāṃ na dṛśyate*.

1183. Matsuda *mahāyānakṛpāyogāt mārgo* Szántó *mahāyānakṛpāyogān mārge* are emended to *mahāyānakṛpāyogān mārgo*.

1184. GZ CDNP:

> Arhathood by virtue of nothing but prajñā
> is something seen by Mādhyamikas too

By joining it with the Mahāyāna's compassion,
the path of generosity and such will be superior

In the first line, *dgra bcom dang* is replaced by *dgra bcom nyid;* otherwise, the first two lines would read thus:

Nothing but prajñā is also seen
by arhats and Mādhyamikas.

1185. CDNP:

The realities such as suffering
become other distinctions of the positions.

1186. Matsuda *yāne sthitau* Szántó *yānaisthitau*.
1187. In GZ CDNP, the last four lines read as follows:

If examined by making distinctions
in terms of lesser, middling, and so on,
then each one becomes ninefold
This distinguishes the yānas through the positions [CDNP ". . . as the positions"].

1188. Ms. *sūtrānta;* GZ CDNP *mdo sde pa* ("Sautrāntikas") is a closer parallel to the concluding lines of the following sections.
1189. I follow Iwata's and Szántó's emendation *paramāṇor niraṃśatvān* of ms. *paramāṇo niraṃtvān*.
1190. I follow Iwata *saṃbandhe;* Szántó *sattvatve*.
1191. GZ CDNP read the last two lines as follows:

As all have the character of being unconnected [or "as they have the character of being entirely unconnected"],
there exists not even the slightest that is coarse

Note that stanza III.1 is very similar to Vasubandhu's *Viṃśatikākārikā* 12–13:

By virtue of six being joined together,
a minutest particle would have six parts
If the six occupied a single location,
their aggregation would only be one particle

If minutest particles are not connected,
what would exist in their aggregation?
Because they have no parts, it is not
accomplished through their connection

Stanza III.1 also echoes *Madhyamakālaṃkāra* 12–13.
1192. Ms. and Szántó *atīndriyasvatantrāṇāṃ;* Iwata em. *atīndriyāsvatantrāṇāṃ;* CDNP *dbang po las 'das rang rgyud pas* confirms ms. (except for the final instrumental instead of a genitive, but that does not significantly change the meaning here), while GZ reads *dbang po las 'das rab brgyud pa*. In any case, neither ms. nor any of the Tibetan versions have a privative connected with *svatantra*, as suggested by Iwata's *atīndriya + asvatantrāṇāṃ*. It is not clear to me why Iwata

thus would say "non-independent ones beyond the senses," since this phrase still seems to refer to the independent (= partless) infinitesimal particles that are below the threshold of sense perception, as in III.1.

1193. Iwata *dṛśaḥ* em. *tādṛśaḥ*; Szántó *tādṛśaḥ*.

1194. The last two lines in GZ CDNP (*gal te rags pa'i chos kyi don / shes pa ji ltar dngos med 'gyur /*) do not make much, if any, sense because the words of the corresponding Sanskrit are all jumbled up (something like "If referents that are coarse phenomena, how could cognition become a nonentity?")

1195. Szántó emends ms. dittography *cācāsāv* to *cāsāv*.

1196. GZ reads the last two lines as follows:

> If [CDNP omit "if"] distinctions [or "partitions"] of the subtle are made,
> how could that substance be coarse?

1197. Iwata *bhāvābhāvavirodhataḥ* Szántó *bhāvābhāvau virodhataḥ*.

1198. I follow Iwata *kampākampādidūṣaṇāt*; Szántó *kamyāmakyādidūṣaṇāt* (Skt. *dūṣaṇa* can also mean "refutation," "objection," and "adverse argument"). The last two lines echo *Madhyamakālaṃkāra* 47cd (if a part-possessor were single, then all parts would move if one part were to move) and also parallel 51cd. GZ CDNP:

> Because being and nonbeing are contradictory,
> partition and nonpartition are not a single one
> Due to flaws of motion, nonmotion, and such,
> there exist no parts in a single one either.

1199. GZ CDNP:

> Due to distinctions of locations, aspects, [GZ CDNP *snam* ("blanket") em. *rnam*] and such,
> there is no certainty about established entities
> because these referents constitute nonentities,
> being similar to dreams, reflections, and so on.

1200. I follow Iwata's emendation *nārtho* of ms. *nātho*; Szántó leaves ms. as is.

1201. Skt. *bādhaka* can also mean "opposing," "hindering," "annulling," and "suspending."

1202. I follow Iwata's emendation *ekaṃ tāvan na* (GZ CDNP *gcig pa min*) of ms. *ekaṃ tāvan*; Szántó leaves ms. as is.

1203. Lines III.6cd echo *Madhyamakālaṃkāra* 23ab and 43. GZ CDNP:

> Since there are no entities such as blue,
> a consciousness [of them] is not tenable
> Because of appearing as diverse aspects,
> for that long, blue, and such are not one.

1204. These two lines echo parts of *Madhyamakālaṃkāra* 19, 20, and 57.

1205. GZ CDNP:

> As they are mutually untenable,
> consciousness is not a diversity

> For it is split as if it were a perceiver
> and perceived by latent tendencies' power.

1206. I follow Iwata's emendation *sad bhrāntyā* of ms. *sadgrānta;* Szántó *saṃgran (?) na.*

1207. Lines 7cd–8ab echo *Madhyamakālaṃkāra* 44 and 52cd. Compare also the *Madhyamakālaṃkāravṛtti* (D3885, fol. 66b.5–6) on 52: "Ultimately, this consciousness is like a pure crystal. Given that it does not constitute distinct appearances such as blue, such [appearances] appear to it as aspects through the power of the ripening of mistaken latent tendencies of time without beginning, just as a lump of clay and such appears as horses, elephants, and so on to those whose eyesight is tampered with through mantras and so on."

1208. Iwata *vijñaṃpti* em. *vijñapti;* Szántó *vijñapti.* The last two lines obviously refer to the famous sentence "Oh sons of the victor! This [saṃsāra] with its three realms is mere mind," which is found in the *Daśabhūmikasūtra*, the *Laṅkāvatārasūtra*, and others (for details, see the quote of this sentence in the Nonaspectarian Yogācāra section of Maitrīpa's *Tattvaratnāvalī;* text 34). GZ CDNP have the first two lines as follows:

> Distinct appearances, blue and so forth,
> are unreal—due to delusion, aspects do not exist.

1209. Iwata *bāhye* em. *bāhyo;* Szántó leaves ms. as is.

1210. NP omit "external referents do not exist."

1211. Iwata *cintam* em. *cittam;* Szántó *cittam.*

1212. Iwata *arthābhāṣaṃ* em. *arthābhāsaṃ;* Szántó *arthābhāsaṃ.* This stanza is identical to *Laṅkāvatārasūtra* X.154cd–155ab, which is also found as a quote in the section of Nonaspectarian Yogācāra in Maitrīpa's *Tattvaratnāvalī* (text 34, 180).

1213. Given GZ CDNP *'khor gsum* (Skt. *trimaṇḍala*) for "threefold," this—as well as "the triad"—must refer to the triad of agent, action, and object. Thus, also in light of the following stanza, what this stanza seems to say is that said triad is ultimately unobservable due to aspiring for consciousness's true state of being without any aspects by means of practicing the sixth pāramitā of prajñā (in hearing, reflection, and meditation). While cultivating this insight, on the level of the conventional practice of the first four outer pāramitās (generosity, discipline, patience, and vigor), these are to be cultivated as seemingly entailing the three aspects of agent, action, and object (such as a giver, the act of giving, and a recipient). With said threefold prajñā having arisen, the realization of aspect-free mind needs to be cultivated and deepened through the fifth pāramitā of dhyāna. This is in line with Maitrīpa's *Tattvaratnāvalī* (text 34, 179) saying this about the Sautrāntikas' view (which in that text means "practice"): "By way of the nature of the pāramitā of prajñā (not observing the triad [of agent, action, and object]), their conduct of the [first] five pāramitās is to bring the welfare of sentient beings to its maturation while turning away their face from the fruition." Later, the *Tattvaratnāvalī* says that the view of both Aspectarian and Nonaspectarian Yogācāras is the same as this (182) and that "the dhyāna of the Nonaspectarians is to directly perceive mind without appearances, which is nondual inconceivable bliss free from discursiveness" (180). Alternatively, "threefold" could also be understood as referring to generosity, discipline, patience, and vigor each being of three types (the threefold generosity of material things, protection, and the dharma, and so on). GZ CDNP:

By aspiring for the nonexistence of aspects,
the triad will not be observable anymore
The three spheres of generosity, discipline,
patience, and vigor are each to be made one-pointed

Note here that Kamalaśīla's *Bhāvanākrama* defines calm abiding as mind's one-pointedness and superior insight as discerning actual reality (*śāmathaś cittaikāgratāś vipaśyanā bhūtpratyavekṣā*).

1214. Iwata's *samarthena vipaśyanāṃ* em. *śamatham ca vipaśyanāṃ* (GZ CDNP *zhi gnas dang ni lhag mthong ngo*); Szántó *śamathena vipaśyanāṃ* is also viable, meaning "through the calm abiding that is the yoga of dhyāna, you should rely on superior insight." GZ CDNP:

The prajñā that arises from hearing and
reflection and is born from meditation
is the calm abiding and superior insight
through the yoga that is based on [GZ *la brten* CDNP *las skyes*, "arisen from"] dhyāna.

1215. I follow Iwata's and Szántó's emendation *samāruhya bāhyam* of ms. *samāruhyam*.
1216. I follow Iwata's and Szántó's emendation *tathatālambane . . . cittamātram* of ms. *tathatārambaṇṭhe* (Iwata *tathatārambaṇ{b}e*) . . . *citramātram*.
1217. CD *sems can las kyang 'brang bar bya*.
1218. I follow Iwata's and Szántó's emendation *cittamātram* of ms. *cintamātram*.
1219. I follow Iwata's and Szántó's emendation *mahāyānaṃ* of ms. *mahāyāna*.
1220. Iwata *anābhogā gatiḥ śāntā praṇidhānai vvisodhitā* em. . . . *praṇidhānair viśodhitā*; Szántó *anābhogagatiḥ śāntā praṇidhānair viśodhitā*.
1221. I follow Iwata's emendation of ms. *jñānaṃ nirā(t?)makāṃ śreṣṭam . . . pasyati / / iti* to *jñānaṃ nirātmakaṃ śreṣṭhaṃ . . . paśyati // iti*; Szántó *jñānanirātmakāṃ śreṣṭhaṃ . . . paśyatīti*.
1222. *Laṅkāvatārasūtra* X.256–58. GZ CDNP have the first two lines of the last stanza as follows:

Engagement is effortless as well as peaceful
once aspiration prayers have become pure

In the last line, CDNP read *snang ba med pa mthong ba yin* ("beholds appearances' lack").

1223. I follow Iwata's emendation *paratantrarūpam* of ms. *paramantrarūpaṃ*; Szántó leaves ms. as is.
1224. Iwata *nivṛr{t}tir* em. *nirvṛtir*; Szántó *nivṛttir*. Besides "liberation," the meanings of both *nivṛtti* and *nirvṛti* include "cessation," "extinction," "escape," "disappearance," and "destruction," but also "pleasure," "bliss," "satisfaction," and "final beatitude."
1225. Iwata *anākṛtivittimātram* (GZ CDNP *rnam med rnam par rig pa tsam*); Szántó *anākṛti vittamātraṃ* em. . . . *cittamātraṃ* ("mere mind"). This stanza matches

the four realities of the noble ones with the three natures: the reality of suffering consists of the imaginary nature (the diversity of the appearances of perceiver and perceived), the reality of the origination of suffering consists of the dependent nature (the arising of latent tendencies from the ālaya-consciousness), and the two realities of the path and cessation consist of the perfect nature (aspect-free mere cognizance). GZ CDNP:

> Since [CDNP omit "since"] these diverse appearances are imaginary, they are suffering
> The latent tendencies of origination constitute the dependent nature
> The full completion of the path of generosity and so on is cessation—
> the completely perfect mere cognizance that is without any aspects.

1226. I follow Iwata's and Szántó's emendation of ms. *samāsa* to *samāsaḥ*.
1227. CDNP "This is the synopsis of the Nonaspectarian position of the Yogācāra path." GZ "This is the synopsis of the Nonaspectarian position within/due to analysis" (*rnam par dpyod pa las* instead of *rnal 'byor spyod pa las*).
1228. I follow Iwata's emendation *taj jñānam* of ms. *tajñānam*; Szántó *tat jñānam*; GZ CDNP "is very clear in the mind."
1229. GZ CDNP "mind."
1230. Compare an almost identical passage in the *Jñānaśrīmitranibandhāvalī* (Thakur 1987, 358.11): "Whatever may appear that is consciousness, just like what is seen in a dream" (*yat yat prakāśate tat tad vijñānam svapnadṛṣṭavat*). As Iwata 2014 (25n2) points out, the first two lines are also very similar to two lines in Anantavīrya's *Siddhiviniścayaṭīkā* and Prabhācandra's *Nyāyakumudacandra*.
1231. Iwata *pratibhāsacasājñāna* em. *pratibhāsanam ajñānavyavasthāyāṃ*; Szántó *pratibhāsa camā jñāna(?) vyavasthāyāṃ*.
1232. I follow Iwata's emendation of ms. *vijñānatvaṃ* to *vijñānatve*; Szántó leaves ms. as is.
1233. Ms. *nīlāde jñānatvaṃ*; Iwata em. *nīlāder jñātatvaṃ*; Szántó *nīlāder jñānatvaṃ*. GZ CDNP:

> How does the mind of appearances
> abide within [CDNP *la* GZ *las*] latent tendencies?
> How could consciousness without referents
> be perceived by virtue of anything other?

1234. Iwata *ato bratīt* em. *ato 'bravīt*; Szántó *ato 'bravīt*.
1235. Skt. *nirābhāsa* often has the sense of being without any fallacious appearances.
1236. I follow Iwata's and Szántó's emendation *grāhyagrāhakaśūnyaṃ* of ms. *grāhyagrāhaśūnyaṇ*. GZ CDNP:

> The Sage stated that outer appearances
> of referents are similar to rhinoceroses [it seems that GZ CDNP misread *bahirmukhatayādhyāsam* for *bahirmukhatavārdhrāṇasam*]
> He asserted the absence of appearances,
> being empty of perceiver and perceived.

1237. I follow Iwata's and Szántó's emendation *nīlādikaṃ* of ms. *nīdikaṃ*; Iwata also emends ms. *vijñānaṃpratibhāsanāt* to *vijñānapratibhāsanāt* (or *vijñāne pratibhāsanāt*); Szántó *vijñānaṃ pratibhāsanāt*.

1238. Iwata *savākāram . . . nivvikalpo* em. *sarvākāram . . . nirvikalpo*; Szántó *sarvākāram . . . nirvikalpo*.

1239. Skt. *samudaya* can also mean "coming together," "collection," "multitude," and "battle," but GZ CDNP read *kun 'byung*.

1240. Iwata *samasnute* em. *samaśnute*; Szántó *samaśnute*.

1241. GZ CDNP:

> What is taught [or "displays"] as the latent tendencies of origination
> is relinquished by the path [CDNP "the latent tendencies"] of generosity and so on
> It is the cessation of all sufferings
> that is attained [CDNP "seen"] as [CD "by"] nondual diversity

As mentioned before, "nondual diversity" renders Skt. *citrādvaita*. This is one of the very few cases in which this term, which later in Tibet was claimed to refer to one of three "subschools" of Aspectarian Mere Mentalists (Tib. *sems tsam rnam bcas pa*), appears in an Indic text. However, just as in Maitrīpa's *Pañcatathāgatamudrāvivaraṇa* (text 36, 192) and *Taking the Pith Instructions of the Philosophical Systems as the Path* (appendix 2, section 6), with this term Sahajavajra refers to Aspectarian Yogācāra in general, not to one of its "subschools." The *Pañcatathāgatamudrāvivaraṇa* defines "nondual diversity" as "the nondual [consciousness] with its diversity, which is empty of perceiver and perceived" (in other words, the diversity of seemingly outer objects appears but is not in any way different from the mind, which, on its own, is the nonduality of perceiver and perceived). For more details, see Brunnhölzl 2018, 1510–16.

1242. Iwata *savvākāra* em. *sarvākāra*; Szántó *sarvākāra*. For the significance of the expression "the emptiness endowed with all supreme aspects," see the final note in the introduction to Maitrīpa's *Yuganaddhaprakāśa* (text 21).

1243. I follow Iwata's emendation *saṃbhoganirmitī spharet* (GZ CDNP *longs spyod rdzogs* and *sprul pa 'phro*) of ms. *saṃbhogonimmatī spharet*; Szántó *saṃbhogo nimmatīspharet*. Skt. *spharet* literally means "quiver," "throb," "vibrate," or "penetrate." GZ CDNP:

> From the dharmakāya, which manifests
> the emptiness of perceiver and perceived
> endowed with all the supreme aspects,
> the sambhoga[kāya] and emanations radiate [or "proliferate"].

1244. Given that this stanza speaks about the four extremes of existence, nonexistence, both, and neither, I follow Iwata's emendation *pratibhāsavaśān nāsan na sad grāhyādibhāvataḥ* of *pratibhāsavasānnāsata na sad . . .*; Szántó *pratibhāsavaśān nāsat na saṃgrāhyādibhāvataḥ*.

1245. This stanza is difficult due to the many meanings of *bhāvataḥ* and *antara* ("absence" as well as "other" and so on). Thus GZ CDNP read very differently:

The true state without the perceived and such
lacks the latent tendencies of appearances
It is likewise not both,
nor is it conceived as other than form.

1246. I follow Iwata's emendation *catuṣkoṭi* of ms. *catuḥkoṭi*; Szántó leaves ms. as is.

1247. Iwata *nivvikalpaṃ* em. *nirvikalpaṃ*; Szántó *nirvikalpaṃ*.

1248. "Self-experienced within itself" renders Skt. *svasmin svavedana*, which could also be rendered as "self-aware/perceived in itself." In any case, though common parlance would rather render it "self-experienced within oneself," "self-experienced" here does not mean that nonconceptual wisdom is experienced by "oneself" (as someone or something different from that wisdom itself), since the whole point of that experience is that there is no "(one)self." In other words, nonconceptual wisdom can only be experienced by itself or within its own state, but not by anything else. GZ CDNP:

This true state that is free of the
four extremes is not nonexistent
The nature of being thought-free
is the experience of wisdom's self-awareness

For the contents of stanzas IV.7–8 describing the Aspectarian Yogācāra position, compare Maitrīpa's *Madhyamaṣaṭka* 1 and *Tattvaprakāśa* 10. Note also that, according to *Tattvaprakāśa* 9, what makes Madhyamaka superior to Yogācāra is not the relinquishment of the four extremes, because these four are relinquished in Yogācāra as well. Thus it seems that the description of the ultimate fruition in IV.6–8 here is meant to apply to both Nonaspectarian and Aspectarian Yogācāra: while the section on Nonaspectarian Yogācāra refers only briefly to the reality of cessation as aspect-free mere cognizance, the description at the end of Aspectarian Yogācāra appears to be an apt portray of buddhahood in both systems. This has a clear parallel in what Maitrīpa's **Dohānidhināmatattvopadeśa* 9abc says on buddhahood at the end of its stanzas on Yogācāra that do not explicitly differentiate between Aspectarians and Nonaspectarians:

The nonduality that is equal to space, inconceivable, and pure,
has compassion's nature and has no aspect, is perfect buddhahood
The two kāyas with form are those that issue forth from this root

Note also that Maitrīpa's *Tattvaratnāvalī*, *Madhyamaṣaṭka* 3, and **Dohānidhināmatattvopadeśa* 10 speak about self-awareness free from the four extremes as the position of the Mādhyamikas of illusion-like nonduality, and *Madhyamaṣaṭka* 6 describes the Madhyamaka of utter nonabiding by combining awareness or lucidity free of the four extremes with the Vajrayāna notions of "having the character of the deity" and "great bliss."

1249. CDNP "This is the synopsis of the Aspectarian position within Yogācāra." GZ "This is the synopsis of the Aspectarian position within/due to analysis" (*rnam par dpyod pa las* instead of *rnal 'byor spyod pa las*).

1250. Skt. *khaṇḍana* can also mean "reduce to pieces" and "dismiss."

1251. "The three Buddhist tīrthikas" here are obviously the Vaibhāṣikas, Sautrāntikas, and Yogācāras. Compare the *Yogaratnamālā*'s explanation of "Buddhist tīrthikas" in *Hevajratantra* II.2.51 (Snellgrove 1959, 2:141), which says that they are the śrāvakas and so on. They are Buddhists because they accept the Buddha as their teacher. But they are tīrthikas because they hate the Vajrayāna, which is the quintessence of the Buddha's teachings. Through the cultivation of the maṇḍala circle, the siddhi of mahāmudrā is accomplished.

1252. Skt. *pāmara* can also mean "wicked," "low," and "foolish." Szántó *trīrthikair boddhair* em. *tīrthikair bauddhair* Matsumoto *tīrthikair bauddhais*; Matsumoto *tribhinnāstitvakhaṇḍanaṃ* em. *tribhir nāstitvakhaṇḍanaṃ*; Szántó *tribhir nāstitvakhaṇḍanaṃ*.

1253. Skt. *sādhu* can also mean "right," "proper," "virtuous," "honorable," "successful," "skillful," and "efficient."

1254. Skt. *agha* can also mean "impure," "suffering," "dangerous," and "mishap." CDNP are completely corrupt:

> The tīrthikas are not included in the Buddhists
> Because the three do not assert nonexistence,
> the true dharma that is excellent and beautiful,
> then, is the misdeed of abiding in nonexistence.

Based on the Tibetan, Tipi Bumlabar's outline (see appendix 4) says that this stanza represents the justification for the tīrthikas not being included.

1255. Szántó *madhyamāpratipannatvaṃ* Matsumoto *madhyamāpratipattattvaṃ* (both *pratipatta* and *pratipanna* have similar sematic ranges, also including "understood," "obtained," "undertaken," "familiar with," and "arrived").

1256. GZ CDNP:

> Having bowed down to great Madhyamaka's
> nature, the one to relinquish all the positions,
> this very means that terminates the positions
> is to be discussed by scripture and reasoning.

1257. This stanza echoes *Madhyamakālaṃkāra* 1:

> In true reality, these entities that we and others
> speak about are without a nature of their own
> As they are devoid of any nature of singularity
> and multiplicity, they are similar to reflections.

GZ CDNP:

> What is established by virtue of the dhātus
> arises from conditions and is momentary
> As it is free of being one and being many,
> it is just that which constitutes a nonentity.

1258. GZ CDNP:

> By virtue of the body being partitioned
> into feet, hands, head, back, and so on,

not even a single hand and so on exists
They arise by way of distinct partitions.

1259. GZ CDNP:

As long as minutest particles are analyzed
by way of dividing them into their parts,
by virtue of discussing this body, support,
what is supported, and so on are understood.

1260. Skt. *ekasaṃdoharūpatvād* (read thus by Szántó and Matsumoto) in the first line must mean "by a single one having the nature of a multitude" because its alternative meaning "by having the nature of a single totality/mass" is the opposite of what is at stake here. However, given that GZ CDNP read *gcig gi dngos po bkag pas na*, the Sanskrit could also be *ekasaṃdohārūpatvād* ("by not having the nature of a single totality/mass") or even *ekasaṃdoharūpaṇād* ("by having examined one as many"). Especially with *-rūpaṇād*, the first two lines echo *Madhyamakālaṃkāra* 61:

Whichever entities you analyze,
there is nothing singular in them
Where there is nothing singular,
there is nothing multiple either.

1261. GZ CDNP:

As a single entity has been refuted,
a multitude does not exist either
Being present equal to a dream,
this is not due to prior refutation.

1262. Given the many meanings of Skt. *hetu*, *rūpa*, and *nyāsa*, Szántó *heto rūpanyāso* can be read in several ways, among which GZ CDNP *gtan tshigs kyis brjod pa* is one (though it does not have any equivalent of *rūpa*). However, *rūpa* can also mean "word," "nature," "character," "mode," "feature," and so on, while the meaning of *nyāsa* includes "introduce," "mention," "entrust," "write down," and "direct." GZ CDNP:

As the nature of cognition does not exist,
this is not in contradiction to reasoning [given Skt. *yujyate*, GZ CDNP *rig pa* em. *rigs pa*; but "awareness" would also make sense]
For expressing such by means of general
arguments is the approach of the wise [GZ CD *dam pa'i tshul* NP *dam pa'i chos*, "true dharma"].

1263. GZ CDNP:

The seeming—this diversity that is able
to perform functions—is without nature
It is the duality [GZ *gnyis* CDNP *nyid*] of cognition and cognized—
what is it that we could examine [in this]?

1264. GZ CDNP:

> As for [GZ CD *ni* NP *la*] these very appearances of forms
> and so forth constituting nothing but consciousness,
> this is to be viewed as [GZ *blta bya ste* NP *lta byas te* CD *lta bu ste*, "like"] being the expedient—
> for the intelligent, there is nothing not to be established by reasoning [given Skt. *yujyate*, I follow CD *rigs pas* against GZ NP *rig pas*, "by awareness"].

1265. Lines V.10ab are almost identical to lines V.36cd; Skt. *saṃvṛtyā* ("as the seeming") could also be read more literally as "through the seeming," but GZ CDNP *kun rdzob tu* suggest the former (in line V.36 though, GZ CDNP render *saṃvṛtyā* literally as *kun rdzob kyis*).

1266. GZ CDNP:

> Just that which is born as the seeming
> constitutes the actuality that is unborn
> For that reason, the mind that is unborn
> is of the nature of not having any nature
> [I follow GZ *rang bzhin med pa'i rang bzhin* against CDNP *rang bzhin med pa'i phyir bzhin*].

1267. In the first two lines, I follow Szántó's emendation *janma siddhatvād asato 'pi* of ms. *jarma siddha dvatvādaśato pi*; in the fourth line, I emend ms. *svābhāve* to *svabhāve* (GZ CDNP seem to read *svabhāvataḥ*).The last three lines (*asato 'pi svato na hi / kāraṇābhāvato nāpi svabhāve parato janiḥ //*) could be read in a number of other ways, but this seems to make the most sense, given the classical Madhyamaka arguments of this type, such as in *Mūlamadhyamakakārikā* XXI.12–13 and *Madhyamakāvatāra* VI.8–97 (especially VI.21–22), though at least one negative is then only implied. To wit, *sataḥ* and *asasataḥ* can be not only genitives but also ablative forms, thus meaning "from something existent" and "from something nonexistent" (see, for example, *Mūlamadhyamakakārikā* XXI.12), since Mādhyamikas make both the argument that results (or existents) arise neither *as* something existent (since an existent already exists and its [re]arising thus would be pointless and endless) nor *as* something nonexistent, and the argument that results (or existents) arise neither *from* something existent nor *from* something nonexistent. Since *svataḥ* and *parataḥ* clearly mean "from itself" and "from something other" here, all four words would align as four possibilities of causes of arising that are denied. Now, *kāraṇābhāvataḥ* can also be understood in two ways: as yet another possibility of arising—"from the absence of any cause"—to be denied or as the reason "because causes do not exist" (corresponding to GZ CDNP *rgyu yi dngos po med pas na*) for what is said in the fourth line. In my rendering, it seems that five possibilities of arising are refuted (including the two pairs of "existent" and "nonexistent" and "itself" and "other"), with the last two lines being related: since not arising without any cause seems to imply the necessity of causes, which are other than their results, as far as causes that have a nature of their own are concerned, that possibility is also refuted. Thus, just speaking from a conventional point of view on the level of mere appearances, arising from something other is acceptable for Mādhyamikas, as long as neither cause nor result are reified in any way. Given the above considerations, another reading of the last three lines would be as follows:

> nor of a nonexistent [that is born] from itself
> Since there are no causes, as far as a nature goes,
> there exists no birth from anything other either

GZ CDNP:

> There exists no establishment of any arising
> As existents don't exist, nonexistents don't either
> [I follow GZ *skye ba grub pa yod ma yin / yod pa med pas* against CDNP *skye ba grub pas yod pa yin / yod pa yin pas*, "Arising exists due to being established. Since it is existent . . ."]
> Since there are no entities that are causes,
> arising is not from any other nature either.

1268. GZ CDNP:

> Being like the occurrence of reflections,
> forms are not real, nor are they delusive
> [CDNP *bden min brdzun pa ma yin* GZ *bden min brdzun min ma yin*, "not unreal or nondelusive"]
> Exactly this is what all phenomena are,
> the way of those who know their nature.

1269. GZ CDNP:

> Due to being collections, aggregations of castles,
> bodies [GZ *lus* CDNP *gos*, "garments"], and so forth are entities of the seeming
> As these have the nature of being unborn,
> [GZ *ma skyes rang bzhin pas* CDNP *rang bzhin ma skyes pas*; could also be read as "are naturally unborn"]
> these very collections are also just like that.

1270. Of course, the prajñāpāramitā sūtras abound with statements about all phenomena being mere names, but such statements are also found in the *Buddhāvataṃsakasūtra*, the *Laṅkāvatārasūtra*, the *Ghanavyūhasūtra*, the *Niṣṭhāgatabhagavajjñānavaipulyasūtra*, and many other sūtras and tantras.

1271. GZ CDNP:

> Therefore, it was the Bhagavān himself
> who said these universes are mere names
> The entirety of the statements by others
> I have expressed in an excellent manner.

1272. "Thesis uttered first" refers to an opponent's opening statement in a debate that is then to be refuted.

1273. GZ CDNP correspond rather literally to the Sanskrit; in the second line, GZ

CD *rnam par gsal* is emended to *rnam par bsal* (NP omit this line altogether), and in the third line, I follow CDNP *de yi blo gros bsal* against GZ *blo de rnam par gsal*.

1274. I follow Szántó's insertion *bhāveṣu*.

1275. GZ CDNP:

> Similar to a reflection within a mirror
> being devoid of oneness and otherness,
> likewise, the nature of entities does not
> exist anywhere else than in appearances

[CDNP *snang las gzhan na yod min te* GZ *nang las gzhan du yod min te*, "not existing anywhere but within"].

1276. GZ CDNP "since it always appears without a cause."

1277. The first two lines in GZ CDNP read as follows:

> Since entities do not exist in it,
> it is to be realized as mere mind.

1278. Remarkably, stanza V.18 and many that follow are a defense of self-aware mind, as long as it is qualified as being unborn, nondual without any aspects, and equivalent to emptiness, suchness, the dharmadhātu, and prajñāpāramitā. In this vein, V.10 says that "unborn mind is by nature without any nature" and V.30 that "the characteristic of being unborn eliminates all views." As mentioned in the introduction to this text, this stance appears to be in agreement with Maitrīpa's notion of unborn luminous awareness in his Madhyamaka of utter nonabiding.

1279. GZ CDNP "these worldly minds."

1280. GZ CDNP:

> If the body, possessions, and faculties
> arise in a way that is similar to dreams,
> it is the mind that turns into duality
> but mind's characteristic does not exist as duality (or "is nonduality").

1281. Unfortunately, the last word on folio 8b is *cittaṃ* ("mind") and the following phrase is GZ *rang snang ngo* CDNP *rang snang ba'o*. Since everything in this stanza up through *cittaṃ* corresponds exactly to the Sanskrit of *Laṅkāvatārasūtra* X.568 (which ends in *cittaṃ svadarśane*), it is reasonable to assume that *rang snang*—though rather unusual—indeed renders *svadarśane* (unless it is deliberately meant to have another meaning here, such as "self-illuminating" or "self-appearing," as suggested by the Tibetan on its own). Note that the Tibetan of the *Laṅkāvatārasūtra* (*sems kyis rang lta la'o*) corresponds well to *cittaṃ svadarśane*, but some Tibetan quotations of this stanza read *sems kyis rang mi mthong* ("mind does not see itself"). GZ CDNP:

> For, just like the blade of a sword
> and just like your own [I follow CDNP *rang gi* against GZ *gang gi*] thumb's tip

not cutting and not touching [itself],
mind as such [CDNP *sems nyid* GZ *sems ni*] is illuminating itself [or
"self-appearing"]

As for *rang snang*, in Sthiramati's *Madhyāntavibhāgaṭīkā* (Pandeya 1999, 111.14), for example, the corresponding Sanskrit is *svanirbhāsa* (in the sense of consciousness "self-appearing" as seeming outer referents); other corresponding words and phrases include *svanirbhāsana, svapratibhāsa* (as in Jñānaśrīmitra's *Jñānaśrīmitranibandhāvali*), and *svayam prakāśate* (as in *Pramānaviniścaya* 1:38: *buddhi . . . svayaṃ saiva prakāśate*, and in the works of Ratnākaraśānti and Jñānaśrīmitra). The notion of mind's "self-illumination" is of course familiar from Yogācāra texts, being especially advocated by Jñānaśrīmitra and Ratnākaraśānti. For example, Ratnākaraśānti's *Prajñāpāramitopadeśa* says things such as *jñānaṃ prakāśarūpatvāt svayam eva prakāśate* ("Since cognition has the nature of lucidity/illumination, it illuminates itself"), and both speak of *prakāśamātra* ("mere lucidity/illumination") as the ultimate nature of the mind. Furthermore, the notion of mind's "self-illumination" also appears in other texts. For example, the *Mahābherīsūtra* (H223, fol. 182a.6–182b.1) clearly uses *rang snang* in the sense of "self-illumination" being the characteristic of a lamp in a vase whose light benefits sentient beings once the vase is broken; likewise, buddha nature (the tathāgata heart) is cocooned in the afflictions and benefits beings once the afflictions cease. The same image appears in the opening stanzas of Nāropa's *Ratnaprabhā* (text 49) about lucid awareness, which is said to be self-illuminating like the sun. Similarly, stanza 3 of Saraha's *Kāyakoṣāmṛtavajragītā* (text 53) speaks of self-awareness being self-illuminating like a lamp. A stanza in the *Sarvayogatattvālokanāmasakalasiddhavajragīti* (D2453, fol. 112a.6–7; a collection of songs by ḍākinīs) says this:

This actuality of mental nonengagement
lacks arising, ceasing, coming, and going
What is self-illuminating [or "self-appearing"] is your own mind
It is not conceived of as being different
If free of dualistic clinging, it is mahāmudrā

Furthermore, Tipi Bumlabar's commentary on Maitrīpa's *Pañcatathāgatamudrāvivaraṇa* (PTMC) also speaks repeatedly about self-illuminating self-awareness (see the notes to text 36). As mentioned before, mind's "self-illumination" or "self-appearing" is in line with Dharmakīrti's "*saṃvedana* argument" in his *Pramāṇaviniścaya* (slightly elaborated paraphrase): "'Awareness' is simply appearing as such (or in a certain way) because it has that nature. This awareness is not of anything else, just like the awareness of awareness itself is not of anything else. For this reason, too, it is not reasonable for awareness to apply to any referent other than awareness itself" (1.42, 3–6: *saṃvedanam ity api tasya tādātmyāt tathāprathanam, na tad anyasya kasyacid ātmasaṃvedanavat. tato 'pi na tad arthāntare yuktam*). That is, by its very nature, cognition cannot be of some external entity. Thus, awareness of any object is fundamentally not different from cognition's reflexive awareness of itself, because by its own nature cognition is just an intransitive "appearing in a certain way," as opposed to a transitive apprehending of something else. It is important to acknowledge that "to appear" (*prathate*) is an intransitive verb of occurrence, as opposed to transitive activities such as someone cutting down a tree with an axe. The treatment of cognition by Dharmakīrti's opponents (such as different Hindu schools and Sarvāstivāda Buddhists) in a transitive sense appears to be in line with ordinary language, but it is not correct when analyzed. When people such as Dharmakīrti or the mahāsiddhas use expressions like "cognition cognizes itself" (*dhīr ātmavedinī*) or "self-awareness," this is only in terms of speaking in a conventional or metaphorical sense. Actually, cognition simply arises with an intrinsic awareness of its own nature, similar to light having luminosity as its nature. Therefore, unlike someone shining a flashlight on something else or themselves, it is not that cognition actively illuminates itself or others within the framework of an agent, an object, and their interaction. Consequently, the well-known arguments against self-awareness, such as a sword being unable to cut itself or a fingertip not being able to touch itself, entirely miss the point for two reasons. (1) Self-awareness does not operate within the triad of agent, object, and action (this point is, for example, explicitly made in Śāntarakṣita's *Madhyamakālaṃkāra* 17 and *Tattvasaṃgraha* 2000–2002, with *Tattvasaṃgraha* 2000–2001 also being cited in an opponent's statement to the same effect in Prajñākaramati's *Bodhicaryāvatārapañjika* on IX.19). (2) Self-awareness is not something material that has any physical dimensions in terms of space, shape, color, weight, density, resistance, and so on. Now, given all that, *Laṅkāvatārasūtra* X.568 should not be understood as a wholesale rejection of self-awareness (though similar passages in Madhyamaka works take it to indicate precisely that), because its scope and validity is limited to reified notions of self-awareness in the above sense. Thus, given the many other passages in the *Laṅkāvatārasūtra* that clearly accord with Yogācāra (such as *cittamātra* and the ālaya-consciousness), and the *Sthitisamāsa*'s qualified endorsement of *cittamātra* ("mere mind") and self-awareness even within a Madhyamaka context, stanza V.21 can only mean that self-aware mind is *unlike* the examples of a sword not cutting itself and a fingertip not touching itself, because it is not an agent that acts upon itself as an object that is distinct from itself. In other words, mind *does* see itself, but the way in which this happens is not comparable to said examples. This is exactly the point that Ratnākaraśānti makes in his *Prajñāpāramitopadeśa* in response to an opponent using the above two examples and quoting *Laṅkāvatārasūtra* X.568:

> This stanza [in the *Laṅkāvatārasutra* just] refutes the entities of apprehender and apprehended of self-aware mind, because those result from difference, just as in the cases of cutting and touching. [However,] it does not refute the nature of experience, because it has the nature of lucidity. For this lucidity is self-awareness, within which difference is contradictory. Since it is definite by virtue of lacking difference, it is not suitable to be refuted. Therefore what is [implied as] a supplement in the [last line of this stanza]

("so it is for mind in terms of seeing itself") is that [said lucidity] does not cling to [itself as] "me."

As the *Āryasaṃdhinirmocanasūtra* says: "[Maitreya asked:] 'Bhagavan, if the image that is the experiential object of samādhi is not different from the mind [that perceives] form, how does mind itself examine that very mind?' [The Bhagavān] said: 'Maitreya, though there is indeed no examining of any phenomenon by any phenomenon here, nevertheless, what appears in that way is mind itself arising in that way.'" Furthermore, mere cognizance's most fundamental own nature is that it arises as having the character of self-awareness. Through the valid cognition of directly perceiving it as just that [self-awareness], it is unmistakenness, but it is also mistakenness, if experiencing superimpositions' own nature. Therefore, the perfect realization of the ultimate is to experience, through gradually relinquishing all the characteristics of mistakenness, the manifestation of the lucidity of all phenomena that is empty of duality, just as space completely without stains and without end. However, the cessation of mind and mental factors is not reasonable [as such a realization].

In this vein, it makes sense to understand the last line of *Laṅkāvatārasūtra* X.568 and thus V.21 (*tathā cittaṃ svadarśane*) as "so it is with mind in [its] seeing itself" or "so it is when mind sees itself," which is thus not a complete denial of self-awareness: it rather points out that self-awareness exists but does not function like those examples. The very same point is also made in the fifth chapter of Jñānaśrīmitra's *Sākārasiddhiśāstra*, including a quote of Śāntarakṣita's definition of self-awareness in his *Tattvasaṃgraha* (lines 1999cd–2000ab). For more details on Ratnākaraśānti's defense of self-awareness, see Tomlinson 2019 (184–89). Now, as for the *Sthitisamāsa*'s qualified endorsement of "mere mind" and self-awareness, Sahajavajra already said above that mind is unborn, lacks the duality of perceiver and perceived, and is free of the three spheres and the four extremes; and he will add in the following discussion that it is without any aspects and is equivalent to emptiness, suchness, the dharmadhātu, prajñāpāramitā, and so on—all a far cry from these material and dualistic examples. Moreover, the first two stanzas of the Mantranīti section summarize that in the pāramitā approach, true reality, which is free of the four extremes, is without arising, abiding, ceasing, or characteristics, and yet consists of dependent origination, is to be experienced through self-awareness. In brief, there is no doubt that Sahajavajra's Madhyamaka section, similar to Maitrīpa's Madhyamaka of utter nonabiding, supports an ultimate self-aware mind that is free of all reference points. It is also interesting that Sahajavajra explicitly identifies *Laṅkāvatārasūtra* X.256–58 in the Aspectarian Yogācāra section as a quotation from the Buddha, while he silently incorporates this and the many following stanzas from that sūtra.

1282. Since folio 9 of the ms. is missing, the Sanskrit of stanzas V.22–32ab is not available. However, since all these stanzas are from the *Laṅkāvatārasūtra*, I follow its Sanskrit. Stanza V.22. is *Laṅkāvatārasūtra* X.708. GZ CDNP:

The mind that appears like a reflection,
by a mind familiar with it from before,
is seen in just the manner it originates
It has an object's form but there is no object.

1283. In the Sāṃkhya school, among the twenty-five factors that make up the universe, the original distinction is between the *prakṛti* or *pradhāna* (the infinite, single, and unconscious primal substance) and the *puruṣa* (the person, self, or ātman), which is infinite consciousness. Except for the *puruṣa*, all other manifold appearances of the world are said to manifest out of the primal substance.

1284. This is *Laṅkāvatārasūtra* II.139 and X.133. GZ CDNP read *rgyu* ("cause") instead of *rgyun* ("continuum"), and the last line in CDNP says *sems tsam po la rnam par brtags* ("are conceived in mere mind").

1285. This stanza is no doubt *Laṅkāvatārasūtra* X.153cd–154ab, though the second and third lines in GZ CDNP differ somewhat: ". . . it is mind as such without other referents. By examining mind with reasonings . . ."

1286. This is *Laṅkāvatārasūtra* II.175. GZ CDNP begin with "If examined . . . ," and read the third line as "Because of being inexpressible."

1287. This is *Laṅkāvatārasūtra* II.198 and X.374. GZ CDNP:

If the mind is examined through insight,
if [GZ omits "if"] there is no dependent and no imaginary,
and if there is no entity that is the perfect . . .
how [I follow CDNP *ji ltar* against GZ *ji bzhin*, "just like"] could
they be it analyzed by insight?

1288. This is *Laṅkāvatārasūtra* III.48 and X.91. GZ CDNP:

There is no nature and no Veda,
neither any entity nor real thing [GZ CDNP *gzhi* could also mean
"basis" or "ground"]
As power is similar to a corpse,
bad dialecticians discern these.

1289. This is *Laṅkāvatārasūtra* III.53 and X.94c–f. In the third line, GZ CDNP read *lus* ("body") instead of *sras* ("children").

1290. Vasubandhu's *Madhyāntavibhāgabhāṣya* on I.14 explains "the true end" (Skt. *bhūtakoṭi*) to mean the absence of imagining what is unreal to be real (or the absence of mistakenness; Skt. *aviparyāsa*) because imagining what is unreal to be real is insubstantial (or unreal).

1291. This is *Laṅkāvatārasūtra* X.576. GZ CDNP read the third line as "phenomena that are unborn." This stanza also echoes *Madhyāntavibhāga* I.14, which lists suchness, the true end, signlessness, the ultimate, and the dharmadhātu as the synonyms of emptiness. A very similar list of synonyms for emptiness—replacing "dharmadhātu" with "supreme bodhicitta" and adding "true reality"—is found in Nāgārjuna's *Bodhicittavivaraṇa* 71. A more extended list that also includes the five synonyms here is found below in V.37cd–38.

1292. This is *Laṅkāvatārasūtra* III.99abef and X.595abef. GZ CDNP read the first two lines as follows:

> Outer being constitutes nonbeing,
> which is ungraspable by the mind.

1293. This is *Laṅkāvatārasūtra* III.101 and X.597. The first two lines in GZ CDNP read as follows:

> For if a collection's conditions exist,
> it will be arising and come to an end.

1294. This is *Laṅkāvatārasūtra* III.103 and X.599: last two lines *anyātra hi kalāpo 'yam pravartati nivartate;* Szántó last one-and-a-half lines *lāpān na pravarttati nivarttate /* (beginning of ms. folio 10a); corresponding to GZ *gang phyir gzhan du 'dus pa las / 'jug pa dang ni ldog pa min /;* CDNP *gang phyir las gzhan 'dus pa las / . . .* If one, as per the *Laṅkāvatārasūtra,* assumes the beginning of the third *pāda* in ms. to be *anyātra hi ka*º, the meaning appears to come down to the same. In GZ CDNP (and probably ms.), the last three lines read as follows:

> Mind is not existent nor nonexistent
> For, apart from a collection,
> there is no arising or ceasing.

1295. This is *Laṅkāvatārasūtra* III.110 and X.606. As Edgerton 1953 (1:545) points out, the Buddhist Hybrid Sanskrit term *saṃkalā* (in classical Sanskrit meaning "slaughtering" or "killing") is connected with Skt. *śṛṅkhalā* ("chain," "fetter"). In the *Laṅkāvatārasūtra,* the term is used in the sense of the chain or concatenation of mutual dependence (*saṃketamātram . . . anyonāpekṣasaṃkalāt* and *janyam arthaṃ na caivāsti pṛthak pratyayasaṃkalāt*). The last line in GZ CDNP reads *de tshe sems la mnyam par gnas* (with *mnyam par gnas* being an unusual rendering of Skt. *samādhyate*); without knowing the Sanskrit, this would rather mean something like "abides in the mind in an equal way."

1296. Ms. *yasya notpadyate kiṃcin na rudhyate* / Szántó "eyeskip: *yasya kiṃcin na rudhyate*? for b"; Szántó seems to be supported by GZ CDNP *gang la cung zad skye med pas / dgag pa cung zad yod ma yin /.*

1297. A virtually identical stanza is found in the "Chapter of the Essence of the Buddha's Speech" in the *Laṅkāvatārasūtra* (H111, fol. 393b.4–5). GZ CDNP:

> Where there is not the slightest birth
> and therefore not the slightest ceasing,
> that is neither existent nor nonexistent—
> this world is regarded as inexpressible.

1298. GZ CDNP "if."

1299. I follow Szántó's emendation *yuganaddha*° of ms. *yuganadha*°. As the following stanzas make clear, "unity" refers to the unity of the two realities (seeming and ultimate), emptiness and appearance (dependent origination), and prajñā and compassion. This is exactly what Sahajavajra's *Tattvadaśakaṭīkā* (text 46) teaches as the supreme "Madhyamaka of unity."

1300. As mentioned before, lines V.36cd are almost identical to lines V.10ab. GZ CDNP:

> For if it were outside of the seeming,
> true reality would thus not exist at all.

1301. I follow Szántó's emendation *tattvaṃ pratītyotpādalakṣaṇaṃ* of ms. *tattvapratītyotpādalakṣaṇaṃ*.

1302. GZ CDNP read the first two lines as follows:

> This constitutes the characteristic of unity,
> the characteristic of birth from conditions.

1303. Emptiness, signlessness, wishlessness, and nonformation are known as "the four doors to liberation." The door to liberation that is emptiness means that all phenomena are empty of an essence of their own. The door to liberation that is signlessness means that all causes are empty. The door to liberation that is wishlessness means that all results are empty. The door to liberation that is nonformation means the lack of any deliberate or contrived states of mind based on superimposition or denial with regard to the true nature of all phenomena.

1304. I follow Szántó's emendation *sādhita* of ms. *sādhitā*.

1305. GZ *rnal ma rnams* ("those who are genuine").

1306. GZ *nges don mdo sde mdor bsdus pa'o* ("—the precis of the sūtra collection of definitive meaning") CDNP *nges don mdo sder bsdus pa yi* ("of what is included in the sūtra collection of definitive meaning").

1307. I follow Szántó's emendation *°puraḥsaraṃ* of ms. *°puraḥsvaraṃ*. GZ CDNP:

> By thus making effort in reviewing and listening
> to the sūtra collection, it is to be contemplated
> Giving rise to compassion for sentient beings,
> every effort is made in [cultivating] bodhicitta.

1308. I follow Szántó's emendation *bhāvayen niḥsvabhāvatāṃ* (corresponding to GZ CDNP *rang bzhin med pa bsgom par bya*) of ms. *bhāvayoḥ svabhāvatāṃ*.

1309. GZ CDNP "Abiding by awakening's vows, with great vigor . . . strive for generosity, discipline, and so on."

1310. Given GZ CDNP *ji ltar de nyid don de chad pa lta bur ni*, Szántó *tattvena dūcchedanibhaṃ yathārthaṃ* is tentatively emended to *tattvenocchedanibhaṃ yathārthaṃ*.

1311. Szántó *°bhājāṃ* em. *bhājāḥ*; Skt. *bhāj* (GZ CDNP *snod*, "vessel," obviously renders *bhājana*) can also mean "participate in," "enjoy," "perceive," "devoted to," "intent upon," "dwell or live in," and "joined with."

1312. I follow Szántó's emendation *arthato* of ms. *athato*.

1313. GZ CDNP:

> For, through [CDNP *'dis* GZ *'di*] this nonduality of the two realities,
> the wise ones,
> with true reality's actuality, as it is, being similar to extinction,
> are the vessels of perceptually determined arising and ceasing
> If referents were to arise, the flaw of annihilation would accrue.

1314. I follow Szántó's conjecture *dṛṣṭaṃ yathā mukuramadhyagataṃ hi bimbaṃ yuktyā vicārabalato 'pi na tan na draṣṭā* / of ms. *dṛṣṭayathāmuktaramadhyagatāṃ hi viyujyāvicārabalato 'pi na taṃ na dṛṣṭaṃ* /.

1315. GZ CDNP:

> For, in the manner in which a reflection is seen within a mirror,
> by the power of examining with reasoning, it does not exist and there is no seeing it
> Outer referents do not exist, and this mind of diversity does not exist either
> Still, to examine [CDNP omit "to examine"] dependence [GZ CDNP *rten 'brel* obviously reading *pratītyavicara*º instead of *pratītir avicara*º] with reasoning is not contradictory.

1316. Skt. *madhyamā* GZ CDNP *dbu ma* (as mentioned before, the text here again refers to the actual position of Madhyamaka, not its more common school name or that of its proponents).

1317. I follow Szántó's emendation of *pāramitānayo* to *pāramitānaye;* Onians *pāramitānaye*.

1318. I follow Onians's and Szántó's emendation *apratiṣṭham anutpādam* of ms. *apratiṣṭhanutpādam*.

1319. Similar to Skt. *svavedana* in IV.8, "to be self-experienced" here and in VI.3a renders Skt. *svasaṃvedya*, which could also be rendered "is to be self-aware [of itself]." As mentioned before, against common parlance, "self-experienced" here does not mean that true reality is to be experienced by "oneself" (as someone or something different from true reality itself), since the whole point of that experience is that there is no "(one)self." In other words, mind's own true reality can only be experienced by itself but not by anyone or anything else.

1320. I follow Onians's and Szántó's emendation *mantranītiṃ* of ms. *mantranīta*.

1321. I follow Onians's and Szántó's emendation *viśiṣṭānubhavād guroḥ* of their reading ms. as *viśiṣṭānubhavād aguroṃ* and *viśiṣṭānubhavāda guroṃ*, respectively.

1322. I follow Onians's and Szántó's emendation *iva* of ms. *īva*.

1323. Given the context and GZ CDNP *byang chub sems*, I follow Onians's and Szántó's emendation *bodhicittaṃ* of ms. *bodhisatvaṃ*.

1324. GZ CDNP:

> When having thus taught, by examining it,
> that which is free from the four extremes—
> neither abiding, nor arising, nor ceasing,
> nor endowed with characteristics,
> self-aware, and arising from conditions—
> this constitutes the pāramitā approach
> With the body [CDNP "scripture"], which has the four mudrās' nature, relying on the mantra approach,
> due to the special experience thanks to the guru,
> this is without analysis and without doubt
> This is the self-awareness of emptiness—[CDNP "emptiness is self-awareness—"]

the great bliss of prajñā and means
There is no debate about any other abiding in the fruition [CDNP "There is no debate about this being like abiding in the fruition"]
It is this bodhicitta that is cultivated.

1325. I follow Onians's and Szántó's emendation *mantranītijñair* of ms. *mantranītajñair*.
1326. GZ "Mantrayāna."
1327. I follow Onians's and Szántó's emendation *mantranītiviśeṣaṇaṃ* of ms. *mantranītetiviśeṣaṇaṃ*.
1328. I follow Onians's and Szántó's emendation *bahūpāyād aduṣkarāt* of ms. *bahūpād aduskarāt*.
1329. As mentioned before, this often-cited stanza is from the *Nayatrayapradīpa* (D3707, fol. 16b.3–4; text 217, 457). Besides the comments on this stanza in VI.5–12 here, detailed (and sometimes quite different) explanations of it are found in the *Nayatrayapradīpa* itself and Divākaracandra's *Prajñājñānaprakāśa* (text 16, 62ff.), while some shorter comments are contained in the *Caturmudrāṭīkā* (text 44, 265–66), Vajrapāṇi's *Guruparamparākramopadeśa* (text 213, 196), and Tipi Bumlabar's commentary on the *Tattvaratnāvalī* (TRVC, 394; see the note on this stanza in text 34, 184).
1330. I follow Onians's and Szántó's emendation *skandhas . . . veti suniścayaḥ* of ms. *skandhas . . . veti hi svaniścayaḥ* (Szántó reads *svaniśvayaḥ*). "The certainty that the skandhas are momentary, have the nature of cognition (Skt. *jñānarūpa*), or are empty" obviously refers to the views of Vaibhāṣikas and Sautrāntikas, Yogācāras, and Mādhyamikas, respectively. Though GZ CDNP render Skt. *jñānarūpa* as "the nature of wisdom," *jñāna* here is simply an equivalent of mind. GZ CDNP are completely corrupt:

    For the awareness as [or "of"] being empty
    has the momentary nature of wisdom
    For this is certain to be Vajrasattva
    The skandhas are realized as tathāgatas.

1331. Skt. *saṅgatiḥ* can also mean "going to" or "resorting to."
1332. Onians *vicārabalanirṇītanirācāroyārthasaṅgatiḥ* Szántó *vicārabalanirṇītanirācāro yārthasadgatiḥ*; with both, I also follow Isaacson's conjecture *vicārabalanirṇītā nirvicārā 'rthasaṅgatiḥ*; GZ CDNP *rigs pa'i stobs kyis bzhag pa gang / ma brtags pa ru sbyar ba'i [sbyor ba] don*.
1333. I follow Onians's and Szántó's emendation of ms. *parāmarthaṃ* ("ultimate") to *parāmarśaṃ*.
1334. This stanza could also be read as follows:

    The realization of the goal, free of analysis,
    is determined through the power of analysis
    Given it is without deliberation, how could
    it be [realized] without the mantra approach?

GZ CDNP:

    What is presented through reasoning's power
    is the actuality joined with nonexamination

> Why would it be free from discrimination
> if it were free from the approach of mantra?

1335. I follow Onians's and Szántó's emendation *sarvākāraniraupamyaṃ nirāsravamahāsukhaṃ* of ms. *sarvākāraniraupamyanirāsravamahāsukha.*

1336. I follow Onians's and Szántó's emendation *devatāhaṃkṛtipraudhaṃ śūnyatānubhavāt* of ms. *devatāṃhaṃkārapraudhaṃ śūnyatānubhava* (*prauḍha* can also mean "full of," "confident," "strong," "mighty," and "uplifted"). GZ CDNP:

> If it is without example in all respects,
> how could uncontaminated great bliss
> be the experience of emptiness through
> having stabilized [CDNP "looked at"] the pride of the deity?

1337. I follow Szántó's emendation *karmamudrāṃ samāsādya* of ms. *karmaṃ mudrāṃ samāsādyaṃ*; Onians *karmamudrāṃ samāsādyaṃ* em. same; GZ CDNP add "well."

1338. I follow Onians's and Szántó's emendation *parasparanirākāṅkṣaṃ samayākhyaphalaṅ kathaṃ* (*metri causa* for *samayamudrākhyaphalam*) of ms. *parasparanirākākṣaṃ samayāc ca phalaṅ kathaṃ* (except *ākhya*, the second half of this *pāda* matches GZ CDNP *dam tshig 'bras bu ji ltar yin*). The samayamudrā as the fruition of the nirmāṇakāyas, arising from the sequence of karmamudrā, dharmamudrā, and mahāmudrā, is found in the *Caturmudrānvaya*, which Sahajavajra identified as his authority at the beginning, as well as in his guru Maitrīpa's *Sekanirdeśa* 26 (text 42) and Rāmapāla's *Sekanirdeśapañjikā* (text 45). However, it is not clear why VI.8 omits mahāmudrā among the four mudrās. In any case, according to the *Caturmudrānvaya*, the karmamudrā is the wisdom that is based on a prajñā and associated with the first three ecstasies and the four moments. The dharmamudrā has the dharmadhātu's own nature, is free from discursiveness, is nonconceptual, uncontrived, and without arising, is the inseparability of emptiness and compassion, and is the means of supreme ecstasy (being the cause of mahāmudrā). Mahāmudrā lacks any nature of its own, is free from the cognitive obscurations and so forth, has the appearance of the stainless midday sky in autumn, serves as the foundation of everything perfect, is saṃsāric existence's and nirvāṇa's single own nature, embodies nonreferential compassion, and has the single form of great bliss (being the cause of the samayamudrā). The samayamudrā is Vajradhara's manifestation in the form of Heruka, having the nature of the forms of the sambhogakāya and nirmāṇakāya and being of clear appearance, for the welfare of sentient beings. Nevertheless, since the order of the four mudrās varies in different texts and "mahāmudrā" is not mentioned in VI.8, it cannot be ruled out that what the ms. says—"how could the fruition thanks to the samaya[mudrā] be?"—is correct, implying the sequence karmamudrā, dharmamudrā, samayamudrā, and mahāmudrā, with mahāmudrā being the final fruition. GZ CDNP read the last two lines as follows:

> if there were no mutual dependence [CDNP "hope"], how
> could the fruition of the samaya[mudrā] be?

1339. I follow Onians's and Szántó's emendation °*bāhulyaṃ* of ms. °*bāhulaṃ*.

1340. Szántó suggests the conjecture *viśeṣo 'nubhavasya* or *viśiṣṭānubhavas tathā* of ms. *viśiṣṭānubhavasya vā* (". . . abundance of means and the specialness of experiences" or ". . . abundance of means and likewise [of] special experiences"). While that is possible and also makes sense, it seems that the second line is meant as a gloss of the first one, by referring back to the special experiences of emptiness in the form of the great bliss of prajñā and means thanks to the guru mentioned in VI.2. Thus Sahajavajra appears to gloss the Vajrayāna's means as consisting of these kinds of experiences and the abundance of such means as the specifities of karmamudrā, dharmamudrā, and mahāmudrā (this is also how Onians 2002, 144, understands this stanza). As also indicated in VI.11, the Vajrayāna often says that the means consists of great bliss.

1341. GZ CDNP:

> The specialness of experiences
> by virtue of the abundant means
> and the divisions of karma-, dharma-,
> and mahāmudrā—how could they be through anything else
> [CDNP "how could they be otherwise"]?
> [or "and karma-, dharma-, and mahāmudrā—
> how could they be through/as any other distinctions"]?

1342. I follow Onians's and Szántó's emendation *atitīkṣṇendriyatvena* of ms. *atītīukṣṇendriyatvena*.

1343. Here, as well as in VI.12c and the cited stanza on page 107 that consists of *Śrīmahāsaṃvarodayatantra* III.19c and III.16ab, "awakening to great bliss" could also be read as "awakening through great bliss." In the Vajrayāna, the fruition of awakening is certainly characterized by great bliss. Still, given what is said in stanzas VI.2–3 and VI.11, great bliss is also understood as the means to accomplish awakening (as is standard in the Vajrayāna).

1344. GZ CDNP have the first three lines as follows:

> Due to having extremely sharp faculties,
> also the experience of emptiness or
> the full awakening to great bliss . . .

1345. I follow Onians's and Szántó's emendation *'duṣkaraṃ* of ms. *'duṣkara*. GZ CDNP:

> By way of the utter pleasure there
> thus being the entity of the means,
> due to cultivation at the initial [GZ CD *dang po* NP *dbang po*] time,
> how could it lack difficulty otherwise?

1346. I follow GZ Onians's and Szántó's emendation *pūryāḥ sarvāḥ* of ms. *pūryā sarvā*.

1347. Onians and Szántó *kva ca* em. *kva na*. Onians says that this emendation is "based on the presence of the negative particle in the Tibetan translation" (GZ CDNP *cis mi*), and thus renders this line "how [could the practitioner] not be clever?" That is certainly one way to look at it, but one must consider that the negative in GZ CDNP appears in the context of an overall different syntax and meaning of this stanza. Onians (145–46) offers the following alternative translation of the unamended Sanskrit: "[Of the two positions:] 'I must fulfill all the perfections through mental cultivation' or '[I] must experience the enlightenment of bliss', which is the clever [option]?" and comments further that "such a translation employs the optional sense of *kva* (lit. where) to 'imply "great difference" or "incongruity" between phrases' (ĀPTE s.v.), but, technically, that requires it to be 'repeated in co-ordinate sentences' (ibid.). There are other problems with this alternative translation, not least of which is the implication that in Tantric Buddhism one does not fulfil the perfections meditatively. After all, that was precisely Tripitaka's admittedly erroneous claim, that the rest of the Mahāyāna had failed to comprehend the mental mode of practice. However, perhaps the text is indeed better left unamended, if the point is that the Mantranaya practitioner has no business with the whole strenuous perfection path of progress (*sarvāḥ pāramitāḥ*), since he can easily realize enlightenment through and as bliss." To me, neither of these options seems satisfactory. Rather, without emending *kva ca*, I take it to indicate a rhetorical question, meaning it is obvious that the sharpest faculties are only present in those who are able to complete all the pāramitās merely (or at least mostly) through meditation (and not just through physical and verbal enactment, as in the Pāramitāyāna) and attain buddhahood through the special means of great bliss. GZ CDNP:

> When the power of cultivating the character
> of all the pāramitās has been completed,
> [or "When the power of cultivation that has the character
> of all the pāramitās has been completed,"]
> how could the accomplishment of perfect
> awakening not be accomplished by [those of] sharp faculties?

In brief, though the exact boundary lines of Sahajavajra's comments on the stanza from the *Nayatrayapradīpa* (VI.4) are not absolutely clear and sometimes also seem to overlap, the phrase "lacks ignorance" seems to be explained by VI.5–8, "abundant in means" by VI.9, "lacks difficulty" by VI.11, and "sharp faculties" by VI.10 and VI.12.

1348. With GZ CDNP *sngags kyi theg pa*, I follow Szántó's emendation *mantrayāne* of ms. *mantrapālaṃ*. GZ CDNP:

> Having paid homage to EVAṂ,
> the realizer [GZ *rtogs pa po* CDNP *rtogs pa'o*, "realize" plus period]
> of connate ecstasy,
> I shall elucidate the Mantrayāna,
> a synopsis of the mudrās' nature.

1349. I follow Szántó's emendation *nirmāṇarūpiṇī* of ms. *nirmāṇaṃ rūpiṇī*, which can also be read as "embodying/assuming/having the nature of an emanation."

1350. I follow Szántó's emendation *karmapradhānā jñānasādhanī* of ms. *karmapradhānajñānasādhanī*. GZ CDNP read the last two lines as follows:

The karmas of body, speech, and mind
have the nature of wisdom that is prime.

1351. I follow Szántó's emendation *yaj* of ms. *ya*.

1352. Ms. *madhye 'ntargatavijñānaṃ; antargata* can also mean "concealed" or hidden." Szántó tentatively presents *maṇyantargatavijñānaṃ* ("the consciousness that entered into the jewel") as an alternative, which is of course generally viable. However, given that VI.17 presents connate ecstasy as the third in the progression of the four ecstasies (following the sequence of the four ecstasies in Nāgārjuna's *Caturmudrānvaya* and Maitrīpa's works), "entered into the middle" here means that connate ecstasy is between—or in the middle of—supreme ecstasy and cessational ecstasy, as stated that way in a number of sources, including the *Caturmudrānvaya* (text 14, 27), which the *Sthitisamāsa* explicitly follows (see VI.2), *Hevajratantra* II.2.40ab, II.5.65b, and II.5.69e, Maitrīpa's *Caturmudropadeśa* (text 92, 19–20), Saraha's *Kakhasya dohaṭippaṇa* 120 (text 61, 177), and Advayavajra's *Dohakoṣapañjikā* (text 66, 290, 316–17). Note, however, that in the first stanzas of the extensive quote from the *Sekoddeśa* following VI.19, the order of the last two ecstasies is reversed. For more details, see the note on the distinction of the proper sequence of the four ecstasies versus the one in the forceful yoga in the *Caturmudrānvaya*'s section on karmamudrā.

1353. GZ CDNP:

For the cognition that [arises] thanks to her,
which is the consciousness in the middle,
arising as the progression of ecstasy and such,
is that which is expressed as "prajñā-jñāna."

1354. I follow Szántó's emendation *vā* of ms. *cā*.

1355. I follow Szántó's emendation *yathādhimokṣato jñānam* of ms. *yathādhigamokṣato jñānaṃm*. GZ CDNP:

This is the aspectarian, the nonaspectarian,
and likewise the realization [GZ CDNP *rtog pa'o* em. *rtogs pa'o*] of
  the middle
The wisdom of the according aspiration
will be attained by the pith instructions

As for "aspectarian," "nonaspectarian," and "the middle path" (in the sense of "Madhyamaka"), compare BKC (vol. *ka*, fol. 149b.3) on this: "By virtue of merely being free of perceiver and perceived, connate [ecstasy] is coarse, which is stated in accord with Mere Mentalism. To perceive the subtle special feature [of this ecstasy] at the tip is in accord with the Madhyamaka of utter nonabiding."

1356. I follow Szántó's emendation *vidyāt seke tu* of *vidyāseke*; Mathes *vidyāt / seke tu* and *turiyaṃ* em. *turīyaṃ*.

1357. Szántó *samīrakaraṇaṃ nyāsā nyāsato 'kṣarayogataḥ*; Isaacson's conjecture *samīrakaraṇān nāsānyāsato* . . . Tomabechi's (2006) conjecture *samīrakaraṇābhyāsān* . . . . ("due to the repeated practice of the working of wind"). As mentioned before, often in tantric texts, instead of the more obvious meaning of expressions such as "resting the mind on the tip of the nose," they refer to the mind being focused on the cakras along the avadhūtī, the lower part or end of the avadhūtī, or the secret space of a visualized deity couple (as the nonduality of prajñā and means), employing techniques of working with vāyus and bindus (such as caṇḍālī). Thus, given the context and GZ CDNP, I here follow Isaacson. GZ CDNP:

The connate should be realized as the third
It is the fourth of [GZ CDNP *gis* em. *gi*] the forceful empowerment
This is due to the yoga of changelessness
by placing the wind at the tip of the nose

[CDNP *rlung gi bkod pas sna rtse la / mi 'gyur ba yi sbyor ay is* / GZ *rlung gi bkod pa sna rtse las / . . .*, ". . . the yoga of the placement of the wind not changing from the tip of the nose"].

1358. I follow Szántó's emendation *sukhajñānam* of ms. *sukhajñāna*.

1359. I follow Szántó's emendation *nivṛtyo* of ms. *nivṛttyā* or *nivṛttau*. The last word of the last line on folio 12b is *sahajaṃ*, so Szántó adds *param* (accords with GZ CDNP *mchog*). GZ CDNP:

In just the ways that blissful wisdom
is accomplished [I follow CDNP *rab tu bsgrub pa yin* against GZ *rab tu bsgyur ba yin*, "altered"] through the means,
it is realized in those same ways—
this realization [I follow GZ *rtogs pa* against CDNP *rtog pa*, "thought"] is the supreme connate.

1360. Since folio 13 of the ms. is missing, stanza VI.19 and the first nine quoted stanzas from the *Sekoddeśa* are missing in Sanskrit. However, VI.19 has been restored by Isaacson (Szántó n.d.) as follows: **yan niṣyandaphalaṃ seke haṭhe sahajam iṣyate* / (or **phalena sadṛśaṃ seke haṭhe yat sahajaṃ matam* /) **akṛtrimam ataś cakraṃ dīrghakālaṃ suniṣphalam* //. Compare the discussion of karmamudrā in the *Caturmudrānvaya* (text 14, 27–29): "That the lack of characteristics [connate ecstasy] is placed in the middle [between supreme ecstasy and cessational ecstasy] is to be understood within [the context of] empowerment. It should be understood, however, that in the forceful yoga, the pair of connate [ecstasy] and the lack of characteristics is positioned at the end . . . It is called 'the connate' because it mimics it in being a reflection of the [actual] connate. This reflection of the connate leads to realizing the wisdom that is similar to the connate. Thus, [in this limited sense,] the connate [here] refers to the wisdom [that is based on a] prajñā. Hence there is no arising of the [actual] connate in the wisdom [that is based on a] prajñā. [However,] inasmuch as what is called 'the connate' is all phenomena's own nature, whose very own characteristic is to be uncontrived, therefore, by having obtained a karmamudrā, the result that is a concordant outflow (*niṣyandaphala*) [of the actual connate] arises . . . having accomplished the wisdom [that is based on a] prajñā, masters of weak intelligence, thinking they have experienced the [actual] connate, give rise to satisfaction . . . Solely through the contrived [practice with a] karmamudrā, how could what is called 'the connate that is uncontrived' arise in those who do not understand the dharmamudrā? . . . When the conventional bodhicitta has entered from the avadhūtī into the jewel . . . the wisdom that is designated as 'the lower connate'—[also] called 'the momentary [connate]'—arises. [However,] this is not the [actual] connate; it is only its concordant outflow. By its own nature, it is the wisdom [that is based on a] prajñā and associated with the [first] three ecstasies and the set of the four moments. In [the context of] empowerment and the forceful yoga, it is called 'the karmamudrā's result of concordant outflow.'" GZ CDNP:

> For the forceful empowerment that is like
> the result is asserted to be the connate
> To remain not separated for a long period
> constitutes the uncontrived accumulation.

1361. For the following stanzas cited from the *Sekoddeśa*, I follow the Sanskrit in Sferra and Merzagora 2006. As IaS (83n104) has already pointed out, the available Sanskrit of *Sekoddeśa* stanzas on folio 14 of the *Sthitisamāsa* shows only minor variants. Thus it seems safe to assume that the same is the case for the *Sekoddeśa* stanzas quoted on folio 13 (variations in GZ CDNP are found in the notes). As mentioned in the introduction, Mathes, Sferra, and Isaacson discuss the apparent contradiction between the sequence of the four ecstasies as stated in VI.17 versus these stanzas from the *Sekoddeśa* (the positions of connate ecstasy and cessational ecstasy being switched). However, to me, there is no actual contradiction, since the *Sekoddeśa* here simply serves as a scriptural example of the forceful empowerment, cited immediately after Sahajavajra's critique of that kind of empowerment and its practice. Thus I see neither any conflict within the *Sthitisamāsa*, nor with Nāgārjuna's *Caturmudrānvaya*, nor with Sahajavajra's guru Maitrīpa.

1362. GZ *gtsug gtor smin phrag padma'i tshul* CDNP *gtsug gtor smin phrag padma'i tshal* NP *gtsug gtor smin phyag padma'i tshad*. The ūrṇā hair is one of the thirty-two major marks of a buddha, located at the place between the eyebrows, and consists of thirty-two white, soft, and very fine hairs that radiate light more intense than that of the sun and the moon. Other sources say that it is a single coil of hair between the eyebrows that extends for many miles when uncoiled.

1363. As mentioned before, in a Kālacakra context, the meaning of *viramānanda* (GZ CDNP *dga' bral*) would rather be understood as "special ecstasy" and, as stated in this and the next stanza, is considered as the third in the sequence of the four ecstasies, while connate ecstasy is the fourth (which is the reverse of what Sahajavajra says in VI.17).

1364. GZ CDNP:

> With all kinds of love play, for as long as it has
> arrived at the secret place's lotus from the navel,
> for that long it remains in the secret's jewel
> Until it is emitted [GZ NP *'phos* CD *'phros*], it is connate [ecstasy].

1365. The last three stanzas correspond to *Sekoddeśa* 80–82. The last three lines in GZ CDNP read as follows:

the all-encompassing sovereign of [GZ "due to"] great passion
The unemitted bliss represents dispassion—
it is the one of abiding in nirvāṇa.

1366. This stanza corresponds to *Sekoddeśa* 135. In the second line, GZ CDNP have "supreme bliss," and the last two lines read as follows:

Therefore you should aspire to always abide
[in] the mind of immutable bliss with certainty [GZ NP *nges* CD *der*, "in the"].

1367. This stanza corresponds to *Sekoddeśa* 139.

1368. These four lines consist of *Sekoddeśa* 140ab and 141ab, arranged as if a single stanza. *Sekoddeśa* 140cd and 141cd read as follows:

Thus, due to the arising of dispassion,
sentient beings' existence is never other
. . .
by which yogīs go from bondage
within saṃsāra to immutable bliss

GZ CDNP have the following four variant lines here:

Due to death, they emerge elsewhere [or "as something else"],
bound and born in saṃsāric existence
Therefore, with all your efforts,
you should avoid rejecting passion.

1369. Skt. *kāmaśāstra* is not only the name of the well-known book but also refers to teachings on erotics in general.

1370. This stanza corresponds to *Sekoddeśa* 142. GZ CDNP:

Without passion, you are not desirous
If not wishing for means to apply [or "join with"] passion,
why should yogīs produce suffering
even in the tantra that I have taught?

1371. GZ CDNP "immutable [GZ *mi 'byung*, 'unarisen'] bliss."

1372. This stanza corresponds to *Sekoddeśa* 143. The last two lines in GZ CDNP read as follows:

By virtue of having lost the support,
the supported is [also] dispassionate.

1373. This stanza corresponds to *Sekoddeśa* 101. GZ CDNP:

The bindu flourishing in the head's crown
will melt through the passion of prajñā
It is the state of abiding in fullness
that constitutes the ultimate bondage [more literally "the actuality of being tightly/truly bound"]

1374. Skt. *udita* can also mean "visible," "grown," "increased," and "being above."

1375. These four lines correspond to *Sekoddeśa* 102ab and 103ab. In the last two lines, I follow Sferra and Merzagora 2006 (180) *tathoditaṃ kramāj jñānaṃ bhūmibhir yāti pūrṇatāṃ*; Szántó *tathoditaṃ kramāc cittaṃ kalā* [*kalābhir*? *kalayā*?] *yāti pūrṇatāṃ*. As here, in the following stanzas from the *Sekoddeśa* on folio 14 of ms., I notice significant variants only between said two sources (which mostly agree). GZ CDNP:

> Just as the stages of the risen moon
> become complete by increasing time,
> in the same way, the stages of the mind [CDNP *sems bskyed*, "generating the mind [of bodhicitta]"]
> become complete by increasing time.

1376. This stanza corresponds to *Sekoddeśa* 108. The last two lines in GZ CDNP read as follows:

> If free of passion, the nature is ruined
> It will flourish in the tip of the vajra.

1377. Sferra and Merzagora 2006 (182) *gīyate*; Szántó ms. *kathyate*.
1378. These four lines correspond to *Sekoddeśa* 110ab and 106ab. GZ CDNP:

> This nature of great bliss is taught
> by means of the sound of fullness
> Completeness has become motionless—
> fully complete awakening in a single instant.

1379. I follow Sferra and Merzagora 2006 (184) *viṣṭhaṃ* against Szántó's *viṣvaṃ*.
1380. Skt. *akṣara* could also be understood as "imperishable," but GZ CDNP read *mi 'gyur*.
1381. This stanza corresponds to *Sekoddeśa* 117. In the third line, Sferra and Merzagora 2006 (184) read *paramākṣaratāṃ yāti*; Szántó *paramākṣaratvamāyā* (with GZ CDNP *mi 'gyur mchog gi bdag nyid kyis*, this would be emended to *paramākṣarātmanā*). GZ CDNP:

> Just as all kinds of waters of the rivers [I follow NP *chu bo'i* against GZ CD *chu yi*, "of water"]
> become of equal taste in the great ocean,
> likewise all kinds of entities as well
> become equal [I follow GZ *mnyam pa* against CDNP *nyams pa* "ruined"] within that immutable.

1382. The last six lines correspond to *Sekoddeśa* 118ab and 119. In the last two lines, Sferra and Merzagora 2006 (184) read . . . *ayamakṣare tatsamo 'kṣaraḥ*; Szántó *ayam akṣaratatsamo bhavet*. GZ CDNP:

> Just like the collection of elements
> having been pierced by mercury, [obviously misunderstanding Skt. *rasa* as having one of its other meanings]
> all these kinds of entities as well
> are consumed by the supreme immutable
> The supreme immutable's character
> seizes the nature of all aspects.

1383. Sferra and Merzagora 2006 (197) *bimbaṃ*; Szántó *viṣvaṃ* ("diversity"); GZ CDNP *dngos po* ("entities").
1384. CDNP "with the resultant bliss."
1385. These two lines are also found as *Śrītattvasiddhi* 42cd (text 12).
1386. The last two lines in GZ CDNP read as follows:

> Since emptiness bears entities, it is the cause
> Since the immutable bears compassion, it is the result.

1387. GZ CDNP "If bodhicitta has not been emitted [GZ CD *'phos* NP *'phros*]."
1388. The last eight lines correspond to *Sekoddeśa* 146–47 (*Sekoddeśa* 146cd also corresponds to *Guhyasamājatantra* XVIII.79ab).
1389. The last four lines correspond to *Sekoddeśa* 98. The first two lines in GZ CDNP read as follows:

> As they do not arise by virtue of an essence,
> the elements will not become exhausted.

1390. The last four lines correspond to *Sekoddeśa* 120. Nāropa's *Sekoddeśaṭīkā* clarifies that once the venom from a snakebite has spread throughout the body, the one who has been bitten does not feel any pain at the location of the bite, nor anywhere else, nor do they notice any objects such as forms via their sense faculties. Likewise, stanza 121 says that yogīs do not sense true bliss in the vajra jewel, nor anywhere else, nor do they notice any objects with their senses, once their mind has arrived at the skill of pervading everywhere. GZ CDNP reverse the order of the first two and the last two lines of *Sekoddeśa* 120 and show further variants:

> Through the objects and sense gates,
> mind has the nature of completeness
> Otherwise, the feeling of suffering of
> being eaten by a snake is not perceived.

1391. The last four lines correspond to *Sekoddeśa* 122. Since folio 15 of the ms. is missing, the Sanskrit of what corresponds to *Sekoddeśa* 122cd up through the stanza that ends in "they rest by persevering in wisdom" is missing. GZ CDNP:

> For this is just as if a gold-making elixir
> sitting on a single part of a piece of iron
> is burned by a blazing fire—
> the entire [piece] will turn into gold.

1392. The last four lines correspond to *Sekoddeśa* 123. The *Sekoddeśaṭīkā* glosses "placed within just a single area . . . once it has been heated with passion's fire" as "made stable in the vajra jewel by virtue of blazing caṇḍālī through the yoga of karmamudrā and so on." GZ CDNP:

> Just so, if the immutable bliss that has been
> well placed in just a single area of the mind
> is burned by the fire of passion,
> the entire [mind] will turn into bliss.

1393. The last four lines correspond to *Sekoddeśa* 124. GZ CDNP:

> Just as if pieces of iron become gold,
> they will never ever turn black at all,
> likewise the realization of mind as such
> will never turn into latent tendencies at all.

1394. The last four lines correspond to *Sekoddeśa* 125. The first two lines in GZ CDNP read as follows:

> For gold purified through fire
> will not turn into a piece of iron.

1395. The last four lines correspond to *Sekoddeśa* 127. The last two lines in GZ CDNP read as follows:

> The nature of the elixir that
> transforms iron is inconceivable.

1396. The last four lines correspond to *Sekoddeśa* 128. GZ CDNP:

> If examined in terms of the ultimate,
> when the mind that is blemished by
> adventitious stains has been realized,
> what need to mention wisdom's nature?

1397. The last four lines correspond to *Sekoddeśa* 134. GZ CDNP:

> Just as iron transformed by elixir
> does not conform to iron,
> likewise the mind transformed by bliss
> does not turn into the state of suffering.

1398. This stanza and some of the following stanza are phrased very similarly in Maitrīpa's *Saṃkṣiptasekaprakriyā* (text 38, 226). A stanza corresponding exactly to Maitrīpa's text is also found in the *Trayodaśātmakaśrīcakrasaṃvarasya abhiṣekavidhi* by an Advayavajra (D1486, fol. 153a.1–2):

> It is the nāḍī of Vajradhātvīśvarī that
> resides on the left side of the females
> It is to be stimulated a bit with a finger,
> to be known from the guru's pith instructions.

1399. Kṛṣṇapāda's *Kṛṣṇayamāritantrarājāprekṣaṇapathapradīpanāmaṭīkā* (D1920, fol. 225a.7) contains a very similar stanza attributed to the *Vajramālātantra* (not found there, though that tantra, as well as other tantric works, also speak about the nāḍī of Vajradhātvīśvarī):

> Having stimulated it a bit with a finger,
> by stimulating [*bskams pa* "to dry" em. *bskyod pa*] it with outer and inner tongue,
> this nāḍī will flourish, and through that
> the bodhicitta will descend.

1400. This is *Sarvarahasyatantra* 56 (H449, fol. 5b.6–7). GZ CDNP:

The ten pāramitās are perfected
Powers and masteries are owned
Gone beyond the ten bhūmis,
no change in the marks thereby

The last line of this rendering of GZ CDNP *de la* [NP *de las*] *rtags su gyur pa med* attempts to reflect the last line in the tantra. A more literal rendering of GZ CDNP would be "in it [NP "apart from it"], there is nothing that serves as a mark."

1401. These six lines are found in a very similar way in Maitrīpa's *Saṃkṣiptaseka-prakriyā* (text 38, 227). With more or fewer variants, they also occur in a number of other tantric commentaries (in some attributed to unnamed tantras), either on their own or together with the following two stanzas quoted by Sahajavajra.

1402. I follow Szántó's emendation *na kurute* of ms. *na kure.*

1403. I follow Szántó's emendation *aninditeti* of *anendriteti.*

1404. These two stanzas (except for the second line of the second one) are found in a very similar way in Maitrīpa's *Saṃkṣiptasekaprakriyā* (text 38, 226–27) and in a number of other tantric commentaries. The first three lines of the second stanza here in GZ CDNP read as follows:

If that bodhicitta has descended,
as it is the treasury of all siddhis,
once consciousness's skandha fainted . . .

1405. As the third and fourth lines of this stanza suggest, "the fourth one" here refers to mahāmudrā as the fourth of the four mudrās (not to connate ecstasy as the fourth of the four ecstasies).

1406. GZ CDNP:

Within the context of the karma- and
dharmamudrā, the connate is realized
Both dharmamudrā and mahāmudrā
constitute the connate that is supreme.

1407. GZ CDNP add "secret" before "Mantrayāna."

1408. GZ CDNP:

By virtue of obtaining the prajñā-jñāna,
the karmamudrā constitutes the connate
By being classed as lower, medium, and such,
its nature is to be meditated on as a maṇḍala.

1409. Szántó "*karmamudrāsamāpattyā samatmamaṇḍala* | % **dhyāyāt samaya-maṇḍalaṃ*? through some strange metathesis?"

1410. Szántó *dhyāyā jhaṭityutpannaṃ maṇḍalaṃ* em. *dhyāyāj jhaṭityutpannamaṇḍalaṃ*; given that lines VI.22cd, VI.23c, and VI.24ab are very similar to *Śrīmahāsaṃ-varodayatantra* III.3 (six *pādas*), I further emend to *jhaṭitotpannamaṇḍalaṃ*. *Śrīmahāsaṃvarodayatantra* III.3 adds that the maṇḍala cultivated by the superior yogīs is an instantaneous manifestation as mere mind (Skt. *jhaṭitākāraṃ maṇḍalaṃ cittamātrataḥ*). Tsuda 1974 (244n1) adds that *jhaṭitākāra* also occurs in the *Abhidhānottaratantra* and that a stanza identical to *Śrīmahāsaṃvarodayatantra* III.3 is also found in chapter 12 of the *Yoginīsañcāratantra*.

1411. I here follow GZ CDNP "dharmamudrā" against Szántó *dharmacakra*. For the *Synopsis* says in VI.2 that it follows *The Succession of the Four Mudrās*, announces "the succession of the mudrās" in VI.13, and speaks of "dharmamudrā" in VI.20 and VI.22. Furthermore, Tipi Bumlabar's outline (appendix 4) considers what follows VI.13 to be a discussion of karmamudrā, dharmamudrā, and mahāmudrā in terms of those of lower, medium, and higher faculties, and specifically says that VI.24cd–25 refer to the lowest, medium, and highest among the persons with medium faculties (= dharmamudrā).

1412. Given GZ CDNP *yi ge* for Skt. *varṇa*, among the many meanings of the latter, "syllable" seems to be the pertinent one here, which also fits the context.

1413. Szántó *caṇḍālīṃ bhedato madhyottum asvanā* [||] (???); given GZ CDNP *gtum mo'i bye brag 'bring gis so / mi shigs pa ni rab kyis te /*, I tentatively conjecture something like *madhyaḥ uttamo 'nāhataṃ*. Skt. *anāhata* ("unstruck" but also "intact") is often rendered as Tib. *mi shigs pa* (or also as *gzhom du med pa*, "invincible"). The most common use of *anāhata* is in the expression "unstruck sound," usually glossed as "the sound of emptiness" (see text 90 on songs 11, 16, 17, and 31). Elsewhere, however, text 90 also speaks of unstruck or indestructible luminosity, wisdom, and compassion. Similarly, Kuddālapāda's *Acintādvayakramopadeśa* 119d says "unstruck or indestructible Parameśvara," and Rāmapāla's *Sekanirdeśapañjikā* (text 45, 385) has "indestructible true reality." The term reoccurs in VI.34 below: "It is indestructible, since it is not obliterated," with "it" referring to the great bliss that is the unity of emptiness and compassion.

1414. Szántó *bindusūkṣmadi yogīnām* conjectures as *bindusūkṣmādi yoginām*, which matches GZ CDNP *thig le phra sogs rnal 'byor pas*. GZ CDNP read the last two lines as follows:

> It is asserted that the yogīs realize [or "the yogīs wish to realize"]
> subtle bindus and so on in a global way.

1415. I follow Szántó's emendation *adhimātramṛdur dhyāyāt kūṭāgāraṃ* of *addhimātramṛrduddhyāyāt kūṭāraṃ*. Lines VI.26bcd correspond to *Śrīmahāsaṃvarodayatantra* III.4abd. Just as with the stanzas from the *Laṅkāvatārasūtra* silently incorporated in the Madhyamaka section, it is interesting that Sahajavajra explicitly identifies his above-cited stanzas from the *Sekoddeśa*, the stanzas that follow, and the lines from the *Hevajratantra* and so on following VI.38ab as quotations, while this is not so obvious for the many lines and stanzas from the *Śrīmahāsaṃvarodayatantra* and other texts in VI.22–24 and VI.26–37. The cited stanza that immediately follows VI.26 ("This is the mansion . . .") has its own closing quotation mark *iti* (GZ CDNP *ces bstan to*; see the following note). The next explicit indication of beginning a quote consists of lines VI.38ab ("The Bhagavān declared this clearly in the tantras, such as Śrī Hevajra"), which is followed by the text's final closing quotation mark *ces pa dang /* (only available in Tibetan) after the line "Within the native state, all are not different." Thus the most straightforward way to identify the quotations between here and that line would be that the stanza beginning with "This is the mansion . . ." is one citation and the stanzas following VI.38ab up through

"Within the native state, all are not different" make up the second one. However, as will be shown below, most of the lines of stanzas VI.27–37 can be traced back to the *Śrīmahāsaṃvarodayatantra* and other works; given that, it is also possible that everything from VI.27 up through "Within the native state, all are not different" is considered a quotation. In any case, I treat the following stanzas in accordance with the explicit opening and closing quotation markers mentioned above.

1416. Szántó:

> *kūṭāgāraṃ idaṃ na tu tribhuvanaṃ |*
> *na prāṇino 'mī jināś cakreśo 'smin amānuṣo*
> *na viṣayā nākṣāṇi na ndryādayaḥ |*
> *rūpādyā na ca dharmatātmakatayā te*
> *maṇḍayā ime viśvaṃ maṇḍacakram ākalaya*
> *tam etaḥ kim udbhrāmyasīti*

This is emended according to the virtually identical stanza cited in Maitrīpa's *Pañcatathāgatamudrāvivaraṇa* (text 36, 196; attributed to Nāgārjuna, and probably Sahajavajra's source for this stanza):

> *kūṭāgāram idaṃ na tu tribhuvanam na prāṇino 'mī jināḥ*
> *cakreso 'smi na mānuṣo na visayā nāksāni na kṣmādayaḥ /*
> *rūpādyā na ca dharmatātmakatayā te māṇḍaleyā ime*
> *viśvam maṇḍalacakram ākalayataś cetaḥ kim udbhrāmyasi //*

As mentioned before, besides the *Pañcatathāgatamudrāvivaraṇa*, somewhat similar versions of this stanza are also cited in Devacandra's *Prajñājñānaprakāśa* (text 16, 71; also attributed to Nāgārjuna), the *Caturmudrāṭīkā* (text 44, 338; attributed to the Buddha), Muniśrībhadra's *Pañcakramaṭippaṇī Yogīmanoharā* (fol. 24a.4–5; see Mathes 2015, 103n272), and the versions of the *Caturmudrānvaya* in GZ (text 14, 32–33) and BKC (vol. *ka*, 149a.1–2). GZ CDNP:

> This is not the three realms [CDNP "three abodes"]—this is the palace
> These are not living beings—these are victors
> I am the lord of the cakra, not some faculties
> They are not earth and so on, nor form and such
> As they have dharmatā's character, they are the maṇḍala inhabitants
> If diversity is known as the maṇḍala circle, oh mind [CDNP omit "oh mind"], how can you be deluded?
> Thus it is taught.

1417. I follow Szántó's emendation *dhātavaḥ* of ms. *dhācanaḥ*.

1418. With *Śrīmahāsaṃvarodayatantra* III.7a, ms. *devyo jñānaṃ* is emended to *devyā jñānaṃ*.

1419. I follow Szántó's conjecture of ms. *antamaḥ madhyamāḥ* as *uttamamadhyamāḥ* (corresponding to GZ CDNP *rab kyi bring pos*). Lines VI.27ac are obviously cobbled together from *Śrīmahāsaṃvarodayatantra* III.7ac and III.8ab (III.8b adds "and likewise emptiness"). GZ CDNP:

> The four elements as well as the skandhas
> are the suchness that is sealed as the cakra
> by the goddess's wisdom and the Heruka [or "by the goddess and the wisdom Heruka"]—
> the medium of the highest are to contemplate this

According to Tipi Bumlabar's outline, this means taking the bliss of an outer mudrā as the means.

1420. Skt. *viśva* can also mean "the entire world," "the universe," "universal," "all-pervasive," and "all-encompassing." It is furthermore an epithet of Śiva and Viṣṇu.

1421. Except for *sārasaṃgrahāt* instead of *sāram uttamam* at the end of the last line, this stanza corresponds to *Śrīmahāsaṃvarodayatantra* III.8cd–9ab. Szántó remarks that *maṇḍalaṃ sārasaṃgrahāt* is an "allusion to the nirukti 'maṇḍaṃ sāraṃ lāti dadāti'" (that is, a maṇḍala is that which "bestows or provides the pith or essence"). GZ CDNP read the second line as "through the power of means and prajñā."

1422. I follow *cintāvikalpayoge 'pi* in the edition of *Śrīmahāsaṃvarodayatantra* III.9c in Tsuda 1970 (though one ms. reads *cittāvikalpa*º) against Szántó *cittāvikalpayoge 'pi*. Except for the instrumental *sbyor bas* in GZ CDNP, *cittāvikalpayoge 'pi* is closer to GZ CDNP *sems ni rtog med sbyor bas kyang*, but given the context, it does not make good sense ("though it is linked to the nonthinking mind"), and moreover breaks the clearly intended symmetry between *cintāvikalpa*º in the first line and *acintyam akalpakam* in the second. Tsuda (245n2) also remarks that Ratnarakṣita's commentary "gives only the first word of this *pāda*, i.e. *'sems'*; this suggests that it reads *citta-avikalpayoge 'pi*=MSS BID. *cintā-* and *citta-* are paleographically indistinguishable."

1423. Lines VI.29ab are *Śrīmahāsaṃvarodayatantra* III.9cd.

1424. GZ CDNP:

> Through the yoga of the thought-free mind,
> that very mind itself should not be examined
> It is the supreme of everything in all regards,
> without aspect, and beyond any sense object.

1425. As they stand, lines VI.29cd–30ab are identical to *Śrīmahāsaṃvarodayatantra* XXXIII.13. Note, though, that *Śrīmahāsaṃvarodayatantra* III.10 is identical, except for "the faculty for bliss" (*sukhendriyam*) instead of "utterly beyond the senses" (*atīndriyam*) and "yet always made to arise as being" (*bhāvaṃ kṛtvā nityoditam*) instead of "yet is devoid of any being and nonbeing" (*bhāvābhāvavivarjitam*).

1426. GZ CDNP "free of."

1427. Lines VI.30cd are Maitrīpa's *Mahāyānaviṃśikā* 5cd.

1428. Skt. *nānāropa* could also be understood as "superimpositions of diversity"; GZ CDNP "all kinds of superimpositions [or 'superimpositions of diversity'] do not remain."

1429. As they stand, lines VI.31ab are *Śrīmahāsaṃvarodayatantra* XXXIII.12cd, though *anāropaṃ* and *anāsaṅgaṃ* are shared with *Śrīmahāsaṃvarodayatan-*

tra III.11ab. In sum, it could be that the passage from the *Śrīmahāsaṃvarodayatantra* here was originally XXXIII.9cd–12, since III.11cd–12 follow after the next two lines. However, given the text as it stands and Sahajavajra's propensity for rearranging citations, it seems more likely that he indeed inserts XXXIII.13 and XXXIII.12cd instead of III.10–11ab. Ratnarakṣita's commentary on the *Śrīmahāsaṃvarodayatantra* (D1420, fol. 99b.7) glosses XXXIII.12c as "it neither involves superimpositions nor is it free of superimpositions."

1430. Given that the phrase "the fruition, true reality, and remedies" corresponds to Maitrīpa's *Tattvaprakāśa* 13b (*phalatattvavipakṣeṣu*), I follow Szántó's conjecture *phalatattvavipakṣāṇāṃ* of ms. *phalatattvavipakoṇāṃ*, as well as his emendation of ms. *nirūpaṇaṃ m-arūpaṇaṃ* to *nirūpaṇam arūpaṇaṃ*. As in the same quote in the *Tattvadaśakaṭīkā*, lines VI.31cd refer to the last three among the four conceptions in the *Avikalpapraveśadhāraṇī* (about remedies, true reality, and attainment) that are progressively relinquished through not mentally engaging in them. Those three conceptions are also mentioned at the beginnings of Maitrīpa's *Kudṛṣṭinirghātana* (text 19) and *Nirvedhapañcaka* (text 28), *Sekanirdeśa* 36ac (text 42), and Rāmapāla's *Sekanirdeśapañjikā* on it (text 45). For details about those conceptions, see these texts.

1431. Lines VI.32ab are *Śrīmahāsaṃvarodayatantra* III.11cd; GZ CDNP:

> What is born by being attained by conditions [or "What is born by
> being attained with it as the condition"]
> is the very nature of being unborn.

1432. Lines VI.32cd–33ab are *Śrīmahāsaṃvarodayatantra* III.12. As for line VI.32d, Ratnakīrti's commentary says that it is not something to be seen, because it is not approachable by the eye-sense faculty and so on. In line VI.33a, *kūṭastha*, here rendered as "uniform" (in both its meanings of "unchanging" and "always the same"), can also mean "changeless," "immovable," "keeping the highest position," "soul," "highest spirit," and "supreme being." In the latter sense, the term is also an epithet of Śiva and Durgā. Thus, the text obviously not only plays on all these meanings but clearly distances the Buddhist ultimate reality of the mind (or great bliss) from any Hinduist notions of a soul or supreme god. GZ CDNP:

> It is not matter, but self-awareness,
> since it is not known and not seen
> By examining, space is a nonentity—
> it is without change and stable.

1433. With Tsuda 1970 *na cābhāvo 'py* and GZ *dngos med min*, Szántó *na cāvāpy* is emended accordingly.

1434. Note that the exact same sequence of the lines that correspond to *Sthitisamāsa* VI.29–33ab is likewise found in Sahajavajra's *Tattvadaśakaṭīkā* (text 46, 43), but there these lines are identified as citations.

1435. Lines VI.33cd–34ab are *Śrīmahāsaṃvarodayatantra* III.13. In GZ CDNP, VI.33 consists of five lines, with the fourth one (*skye ba med pas rang bzhin nyid*) looking like an erroneous repetition of VI.32b (*skye ba med pa'i rang bzhin nyid*). Read on their own, the fourth and fifth lines read as follows:

Since it does not arise, it is the very nature
It is the true state of arising from the seeming [or "It is the entity that arises from the seeming"].

1436. Lines VI.34cd are *Śrīmahāsaṃvarodayatantra* III.14ab. The first three lines in GZ CDNP read as follows:

All phenomena are the connate,
the very nature of native ecstasy
Since it is self-blessing, it is self-arising.

1437. Given GZ CDNP *gnyis med,* I emend Szántó *dharmamudrā mahāmudrā dvaitādhigamavādināṃ* to *dharmamudrāmahāmudrādvaitādhigamavādināṃ*. Further meanings of Skt. *adhigama* (GZ CDNP *mos pa* obviously reading *adhimukta*) include "mastery" and "attainment," but also "copulation," "marriage," and "meeting." Thus the compound *dharmamudrāmahāmudrādvaitādhigama* could also be understood as "the mastery or attainment of dharmamudrā and mahāmudrā" or "the union that is the nonduality of dharmamudrā and mahāmudrā."

1438. GZ CDNP switch the first two and last two lines, rendering the latter as follows:

They possess dharmamudrā and mahāmudrā
through having faith in their being nondual

In brief, what Sahajavajra says in VI.22–35 about those of lower, medium, and highest faculties is that the samaya maṇḍala is contemplated through the union with a karmamudrā, with those of lower faculties practicing the creation process, the medium ones practicing without all the details of that process, and the highest ones contemplating the manifestation of the maṇḍala that is instantaneous in that it is mere mind. Furthermore, the dharmamudrā is cultivated by the lower ones with nāḍīs and syllable rows, by the medium ones with caṇḍālī, and by the highest ones as what is indestructible, realizing subtle bindus and so on in a global manner (according to Tipi Bumlabar's outline, this refers to the lowest, medium, and highest among the persons with medium faculties). Then, those of highest faculties are further subdivided into three. Among these, the lowest ones meditate on the three realms as the maṇḍala palace, sentient beings as its inhabitants, and themselves as the lord of the maṇḍala. The medium ones contemplate this as the nature of the elements and skandhas, the wisdom of the male and female deities, and the space-like maṇḍala circle sealed with suchness. The highest ones contemplate the effortless unity of the lack of self (suchness) and compassion (means), which is the maṇḍala that incorporates the essence, the connate that is thought-free great bliss, and the supreme of all aspects free from the four extremes, attachment, and superimpositions. This is to be self-experienced, without being a knower or seer. These highest ones among the highest yogīs realize the nonduality of dharmamudrā and mahāmudrā. Compare this with what is said about those of lower, medium, and highest faculties in Maitrīpa's *Tattvaviṃśikā* 7–19: those of lower faculties rely on karmamudrā and samayamudrā, those of medium faculties on jñānamudrā, and those of highest faculties on mahāmudrā. The latter realize that all appearances are merely mind, yet mind is said to be "no-mind," and this "no-mind" is the self-awareness that is recognized thanks to the guru. Such yogīs embody mahāmudrā and the three kāyas: having accomplished everything and being free of all attachment, they are always buddhas, no matter what they do.

1439. Following NP *dran dang dran pa nyams pa med*, I conjecture Szántó *na smṛtim meṣo* (?) *vā yathābhutā na bhūtitaḥ* as *na smṛtir asmṛtir vā yathābhutānubhūtitaḥ*; CD *dran dang dran pa nyams pa nyid* GZ *dran pas bzung dang ma bzung med* (exact parallel line 3d in text 43). Lines VI.36ab are identical to lines 4ab of Maitrīpa's *Pith Instruction on Letting Cognizance Be without Projecting and Withdrawing* (text 43), and with said emendation, lines VI.36cd are very similar to that text's lines 3cd. GZ of VI.36 corresponds verbatim to lines 4ab and 3cd of text 43 (except for switching "experience" and "arise" in the third line). GZ CDNP:

> Because cause and result are inseparable,
> . . .
> Because it is experienced just as it arises,
> there's nothing for mindfulness to grasp or not grasp.

1440. Szántó and certain mss. of the *Śrīmahāsaṃvarodayatantra* ºvedhād; Tsuda 1970 ºvedād.

1441. I follow *Śrīmahāsaṃvarodayatantra tathāvidhā* against Szántó *tathyavidhā*.

1442. I follow *Śrīmahāsaṃvarodayatantra bhaved* against Szántó *bhāved*.

1443. This stanza corresponds to *Śrīmahāsaṃvarodayatantra* III.14cd–15ab. Lines VI.37abc are also similar to lines 4cd–5a of Maitrīpa's *Pith Instruction on Letting Cognizance Be without Projecting and Withdrawing* (GZ CDNP of those lines are almost identical). GZ CDNP:

> By tasting the taste of being unborn,
> meditation too is likewise realization [I follow CDNP *rtogs pa*
> against GZ *rtog pa*, "thought"]
> For it's by means of cultivating prajñā
> that emptiness becomes discriminated [I follow CDNP *stong nyid*
> against GZ *rtogs nyid*, "realization"].

1444. As mentioned before, unlike the many preceding lines from the *Śrīmahāsaṃvarodayatantra* and so on, the two following lines and all stanzas up through "Within the native state, all are not different" are explicitly identified as quotations by ending with *ces pa dang* /. Therefore I do not number them as the *Sthitisamāsa*'s own stanzas.

1445. These two lines correspond not only to *Hevajratantra* I.8.42cd but also to *Śrīmahāsaṃvarodayatantra* III.15cd. The first two lines of *Hevajratantra* I.8.42 say this:

> The world's entirety is meditated on
> in a way of mind not meditating on it

Most Indic and Tibetan commentaries on the *Hevajratantra* say that this stanza starts the discussion of the yoga of mahāmudrā and emphasize its character of being free from all imagining or thoughts. Ratnākaraśānti's commentary *Muktāvalī* (Tripathi and Negi 2001, 95) says that the first line just speaks about meditating on the entire world, but the question is through what the ascertainment of this (the siddhi of Mahāmudrā) comes about. Ascertainment is gained because yogīs do not imagine anything (with regard to the world) through the mind—that is, the conceptual consciousness. In other words, those who do not imagine do not meditate. Such full knowledge (nonconceptual direct insight) of phenomena is what is meant by "meditation" here. "Not meditation" refers to "not imagining," since all imaginations are mistaken by their very nature. Kṛṣṇa's *Yogaratnamālā* (Snellgrove 1959, 2:128) basically says the same, glossing that the full knowledge in terms of the connate nature (Skt. *sahajarūpatayā*) is not this kind of meditation (through imagination). Most Tibetan commentaries take the Tibetan of line 44c (*thams cad chos ni yongs shes na*) to mean "When the dharma[tā of] all [phenomena] is fully known." Accordingly, Jamgön Kongtrul's commentary (Kong sprul blo gros mtha' yas 2005, 427) says that this stanza describes the essence of what mahāmudrā meditation is and continues, "The other mudrās, such as karmamudrā and dharmamudrā, are mental imputations. Therefore, since connate mahāmudrā is beyond the sphere of anybody's mind, without contemplating by way of the characteristics and imaginations of a mind that is [involved in] rejecting and accomplishing, one should contemplate the entire world—the outer container and the inner contents, such as sentient beings—as being connate wisdom free of discursiveness. Once the dharmatā of all phenomena—the mode of being of the lack of a nature—is fully known in this way, such meditation, which is contrived through the conceptual mind, is not the meditation of true reality. Therefore, [the latter] means to meditate on nonarising and such in the manner of a meditator and so on not being observable, free from the extremes of reference points." Vajrapāṇi's *Guruparamparākramopadeśa* (text 213, 234–35) also quotes *Hevajratantra* I.8.42 in its discussion of uncontrived mahāmudrā meditation. Though not in a specifically tantric context, but in essence, brought about by virtue of the pith instructions of a qualified guru, this is also what "the samādhi of reality as it is" in Maitrīpa's *Tattvadaśaka* 6b and its comments in Sahajavajra's *Tattvadaśakaṭīkā* (text 46, 37–39), which also cite *Hevajratantra* I.8.42cd, refer to. Note also that *Hevajratantra* I.8.42ab is quoted in Maitrīpa's *Amanasikārādhāra* (text 27, 157) as a scriptural support for the term "mental nonengagement." In that regard, Mathes 2015 (243n650) says: "Reading *amanasikāra* into the *Hevajratantra* thus prepares the way for extending its semantic range from a pure negation of mental activity and objective support to include direct realization of phenomena, which in the *Tattvadaśaka* are said to be luminous by nature."

1446. The first line of this stanza is *Śrīmahāsaṃvarodayatantra* III.19c and the last two lines are *Śrīmahāsaṃvarodayatantra* III.16ab. In GZ CDNP, the first two lines read as follows:

> For, due of the stage of self-blessing,
> the stage of unity too is just like that

Śrīmahāsaṃvarodayatantra III.19cd says this:

> It is indeed this stage of self-blessing
> that is clear thanks to the guru's skill

As mentioned before, "self-blessing" and "unity" are the third and fifth of the five stages of perfection-process practices in the *Guhyasamājatantra* according to Nāgārjuna's *Pañcakrama* and Āryadeva's *Caryāmelāpakapradīpa*.

1447. According to Monier-Williams, Skt. *kṛtaśrama* means "painstaking," "laborious," and "one who has made great exertions." Thus, this line would mean "do not [have to] make a lot of effort," which makes sense. However, given GZ CDNP *ngal ba* for *kṛtaśrama*, the meaning seems to be that those who realize true reality do not become tired or weary no matter what or how much they do.

1448. The last two lines are *Śrīmahāsaṃvarodayatantra* III.16cd. Ratnarakṣita's commentary on the *Śrīmahāsaṃvarodayatantra* (D1420, fol. 16a.5) glosses these lines as "for the sake of realizing it gradually; in terms of the essence, there are definitely no distinctions." GZ CDNP:

> By being aware of phenomena's true reality, [or "Those who are aware of phenomena's true reality"]
> there will not come about any weariness
> So that phenomena's true reality is entered,
> the distinctions have been taught by that [or "by them"].

1449. The first two lines are *Śrīmahāsaṃvarodayatantra* III.17ab.

1450. With GZ CDNP *gzhan gyis*, I follow Szántó's emendation *anyena* of ms. *syavā* (?).

1451. GZ CDNP read the last two lines as follows:

> Here, it is not that the meaning is realized
> by virtue of that which is taught by others.

1452. This line is *Hevajratantra* I.8.47a. The term *dharmodaya* ("dharma source"; also *dharmodayā* and *dharmodayamudrā*) refers to the primordial space from which all phenomena arise (a.k.a. dharmadhātu), representing the female principle or divine cosmic vagina from which everything arises and ceases. It is usually depicted as a triangle with its tip pointing down, a hexagram (two overlapping triangles similar to the Star of David), or one or two three-dimensional triangles (triangular upside-down pyramids). The term can also refer to the female genitals. In the Vajrayāna, the dharmodaya in the form of a hexagram is specifically associated with Vajrayoginī, with the two triangles symbolizing the union of bliss and emptiness. For matching dharmodaya with the syllables EVAṂ, see the *Caturmudrāṭīkā* (text 44, 263–64, 342) and Rāmapāla's *Sekanirdeśapañjikā* (text 45) on stanza 1.

1453. The last words on folio 18b of ms. are *dharmodayo jñānaṃ jñānam ity ā . . .*; the remainder of the text (folio 19) is missing. GZ CDNP read this line as *ji bzhin 'di las* [CDNP *la*] *rtogs par gsungs* ("is said to be realized accordingly thanks to this").

1454. I follow CDNP *bzung ba dngos nyid ma yin* against GZ *bzung dang dngos nyid ma yin*.

1455. I follow GZ *bzhi po* against CDNP *bzhi pa'o* ("fourth").

1456. The last line is *Śrīmahāsaṃvarodayatantra* III.19d (GZ CDNP *thabs* here rendering Skt. *kauśala*, "skill"); I could not locate the other three lines.

1457. CDNP *bde ba ro mnyam bde ba nyid* GZ *bde ba ro mnyam pa nyid de* ("the bliss of equal taste").

1458. This line could also be read as "constitutes the connate dharmakāya."

1459. In both the first and third lines, GZ CDNP *de nyid* (rendered as "true reality") could also be understood as "just that/they."

1460. The renderings of the last three stanzas are partly tentative. On the last two stanzas, compare *Ajamahāsukha's commentary on lines 3cd of Saraha's "King Dohā" (appendix 5 in volume 3): "The connate of appearance is the nirmāṇakāya, the connate of emptiness the sambhogakāya, and the connate of being unborn the dharmakāya. These three kinds of kāyas pervade the entirety of saṃsāra and nirvāṇa. Therefore, [Saraha says]: 'In a similar way, though the connate pervades all.' Having never been separated from these three kāyas, they are with you at all times, accompanying you, as in the example of honey and the taste of honey [being inseparable]. Yet you do not realize that, with minding itself being sealed with nonminding, [the connate] is very close by. Therefore, [Saraha says]: 'For fools, it's very far away despite being close by.'" Compare also the comments on the opening stanza of Saraha's "People Dohā" in text 70: "'The connate' refers to the dharmakāya: connate appearance and connate mind as such. Therefore it is not adventitious: from the very outset, it is the splendorous realization of the essence of the dharmakāya. It is the nature of great bliss—that is, [of all] contaminated bliss and uncontaminated bliss. It arises from the body and the mind: it lacking any imaginary delusion is its being empty. Thus inseparable bliss-emptiness is the dharmakāya: the immutable essence of ordinary mind that is true reality is supreme." Similarly, the concluding stanza of text 70, in order to "dedicate the meaning of me having differentiated and elucidated the awakened intention of the venerable Śrī Śabara," says this:

> Connate mind as such is the cause of the dharmakāya
> Connate appearance is the light of the dharmakāya
> Appearance and emptiness inseparable is the connate
> This is the dharmakāya's awakened mind, the very dharmakaya

The first three lines correspond almost verbatim to a stanza that is famous in the Kagyü Mahāmudrā tradition. According to Tagpo Dashi Namgyal (Dakpo Tashi Namgyal 2019, 286), TOK (3:383), and Dpal ldan rang byung phrin las kun khyab bstan pa'i rgyal mtshan n.d. (19), this stanza comes from an **Acintyasahajatantra* (not known in Kg or otherwise; possibly identical or related to the **Acintyatantra* that is so often cited in text 70):

> Connate mind as such represents the dharmakāya
> Connate thought is the display of the dharmakāya
> Connate appearance is the light of the dharmakāya
> Appearance and mind inseparable is the connate

More or less literal versions or lines of this stanza are found in a number of works by Gampopa and others. For example, in the *Chos rje dvags po lha rje'i gsung snying po don gyi gdams pa phyag rgya chen po'i 'bum tig*, in Sgam po pa bsod nams rin chen 1982 (vol. *ka*, 212), the stanza reads:

> Connate mind represents the actual dharmakāya
> Connate appearances are the light of the dharmakāya
> Connate thoughts are the waves of the dharmakāya
> Connate inseparability is what the dharmakāya is all about

For yet another version of this stanza, see its extensive explanation by Padma Karpo in Brunnhölzl 2014, 214–15. For a detailed commentary on connate mind, thoughts, and appearances, see Dakpo Tashi Namgyal 2019, 272–88. Note also that the beginning of a Tibetan compilation of mahāmudrā-style pith instructions ascribed to Atiśa, called "The Concise Quintessence of Instructions on Connate Union" (Tib. *Lhan cig skyes sbyor gyi gdam ngag mdor bsdus snying po*), says: "Connate mind as such is the dharmakāya and connate appearance is the light of the dharmakāya. These two abide like the sun and sun rays or sandalwood and the scent of sandalwood" (Apple 2017, 32). As mentioned before, GZ CDNP have *ces pa dang /* as a closing quotation mark after the line "Within the native state, all are not different."

1461. This line is *Mañjuśrīnāmasaṃgīti* VI.18a and is also found in Kālapāda's *Śrīkālacakrasahajasādhana* (D1361, fol. 166b.6). In general, there are several different lists of five kāyas in tantric literature in particular. As for the five kāyas in the *Mañjuśrīnāmasaṃgīti* in particular, different commentaries on it provide varying lists, such as dharmakāya, sambhogakāya, nirmāṇakāya, svābhāvikakāya, and mahāsukhakāya; dharmakāya, sambhogakāya, nirmāṇakāya, vajra-like kāya, and abisaṃbodhikāya; svābhāvikakāya, sambhogakāya, nirmāṇakāya, dharmakāya, and jñānakāya; svābhāvikakāya, sambhogakāya, nirmāṇakāya, vipākakāya, and dharmakāya; and the five kāyas of Vairocana, Akṣobhya, Ratnasambhava, Amitābha, and Amoghasiddhi. The *Sthitisamāsa* does not name its five kāyas but says in VI.40 that the fifth kāya is nothing but the inseparability of the other four kāyas as sheer true reality. Thus its first four kāyas probably consist of the svābhāvikakāya, dharmakāya, sambhogakāya, and nirmāṇakāya.

1462. GZ CD *rnam lnga pa'o* NP *rnam lnga'o*.

1463. As mentioned before, though the *Synopsis* does not explicitly teach the samayamudrā among the four mudrās, stanzas VI.39–40 and the three cited stanzas that precede them can be regarded as touching upon the *Caturmudrānvaya*'s explanation of the samayamudrā as being the sambhogakāya and nirmāṇakāya for the welfare of all beings.

1464. Parallel to the same phrase in V.22d, I take GZ CDNP *ji ltar 'byung ba* (lit. "in just the way it arises") as a rendering of Skt. *yathābhūta*.

1465. Szántó: "I suppose the Bar ston mentioned here [nb: in the colophon] could possibly be Bar ston Rdo rje rgyal mtshan (just because he is the only Bar ston I am aware of)." However, this figure flourished in the thirteenth century, which precludes his being a contemporary of Tsur Lotsāwa (eleventh century), Dhiriśrījñāna, and Vajrapāṇi ("the Indian guru" could refer to either one, but probably to the latter). I am not aware of another Bar ston.

1466. CDNP omit "who is endowed with respect." N adds *maṅgā laṃ* at the end. For an outline of this text by Tipi Bumlabar, see appendix 4.

1467. PDMT, 26:273–87. Unless noted otherwise, I follow the Sanskrit edition in Samdhong and Dvivedī 1987, 193–208 (see for all the variant readings in the four available manuscripts). The variations in GZ CDNP are found in the notes below. Given the frequent omissions, additions, and transpositions of lines or stanzas in GZ CDNP compared with the Sanskrit, if the Tibetan stanzas are broken down and numbered on their own, the result is naturally very different. However, for the sake of easy comparison, as much as possible, I break down the Tibetan lines according to the Sanskrit.

1468. Skt. *vibhu* (also meaning "almighty," "omnipotent," "unlimited," "pervading," "eminent," "capable," and "self-controlled") is a very popular epithet of Hinduist gods (such as Brahmā, Śiva, Viṣṇu, and Kṛṣṇa) and also of the ātman. As mentioned before, this is only the first among a significant number of Hinduist terminologies and concepts in Kuddālapāda's text. GZ CDNP, however, omit this term.

1469. GZ CDNP:

> Having paid homage to primordial nondual purity [CDNP "what abides as primordial nonduality"]
> that is born from the womb of supreme prajñā,
> I shall write down [here] what has come down
> in a perfect succession from Bhadra's mouth.

1470. GZ CDNP switch the last two lines and read "the wisdom that arises from itself."

1471. GZ CDNP:

> The source of the bliss that is natural
> is self-arising, supreme nonduality
> To familiarize with it by regarding it
> as any nature of being is unobservable
> Since there is no entity, none is seen
> by bodhisattvas who are vajra-bearers [or "Vajra-bearers do not see bodhicitta, since it is not an entity"].

1472. GZ CDNP:

> Distinctions of permanence and extinction,
> ultimately, are seen as nonduality
> Entities and emptiness are familiarized with
> as being equal in that they are unobservable.

1473. GZ CDNP:

> Because neither of these are existent,
> all aspects constitute nonduality [or "they are nonduality in all respects"]
> If the entirety of duality is analyzed,
> nondual wisdom will come to blaze.

1474. In GZ CDNP, the last two lines read as follows:

> Supreme nonduality is not to be cultivated
> through the yoga of thinking and what is thought.

1475. "Creation" (Skt. *utpatti*) here seems to refer to the creation process; "noncreation" could refer to the perfection process or to a deliberate (and frustrating) attempt to not create any thoughts. In GZ CDNP, the first two lines read as follows:

> The vajra of bliss that is thought-free
> will be attained by the inconceivable.

1476. GZ CDNP:

> Being devoid of the aspects of these two,
> free of impression and impression-owner,
> the wisdom that is devoid of impressions
> came down from Bhadrapāda's tradition.

1477. GZ CDNP:

> What is self-arising and waveless
> is devoid of the entirety of thought
> Due to being's and nonbeing's nature,
> duality is the bondage of impressions [CDNP "the impressions of duality are bondage"].

1478. GZ CDNP:

> Due to the nature of nonthought,
> it is sundered by the inconceivable [I follow GZ NP *gcod* against CD *dpyod* ("analyzes")]
> It is the web of thoughts' stains
> that tarnishes [I follow GZ CD *dri* against NP *drin* ("kind")] the precious mind.

1479. In GZ CDNP, the first two lines read as follows (in the fourth line, "character" is replaced by "nature"):

> Because the wisdom that is nondual
> is stainless, it is actual buddhahood.

1480. In GZ CDNP, the last two lines read as follows:

> its nature is to be unarisen
> and there is no perishing.

1481. GZ CDNP have only two lines:

> This wisdom is not nonduality,
> being devoid of all thinking.

1482. Usually, it may seem to make more sense that "glorious" goes with "bearers," but the text speaks repeatedly of "glorious bliss."

1483. GZ CDNP omit "character" and add two lines that resemble lines 13cd:

> The buddhas, such as Vajradhara,
> explain [CDNP "teach"] thoughts as external.

1484. GZ CDNP "and wisdom arises from itself."

1485. In GZ CDNP, the first two lines read as follows:

> By thinking of unperishable bliss,
> this is inconceivable nonduality's state.

1486. Skt. *zaṅka* can also mean "doubt."

1487. Skt. *śiva* can also mean "fortunate," "gracious," "kind," "benevolent," "happy," and "dear." As a euphemistic appellation, the terrifying and destructive Vedic god Rudra came to be called Śiva ("The Auspicious One"), thus also assigning the activity of creation and reproduction to him. Given the often inclusivist nature of our text and its use of Hinduist terminology, it is more than likely that this term here is also a pun on nonduality being as exalted as the supreme god Śiva. GZ CDNP:

> With the arrow of compassion's lotus [CDNP "waking up"],
> the target of great bliss is pierced
> Being free from any and all thoughts,
> it is nondual and supremely peaceful.

1488. "The protector of glorious great bliss" (or "the glorious protector of great bliss") here appears to be another epithet of inconceivable nonduality. In addition, in the distant Mahāmudrā lineage, the bodhisattvas Ratnamati and (Mahā)sukhanātha are considered to have brought these teachings to the human realm. As mentioned before, it may seem to make more sense that "glorious" goes with "protector," particularly if this is a name, but the text speaks repeatedly of "glorious bliss." For details of different commentaries explaining the parallel phrase "the bodhisattva Protector of Bliss" in the first stanza of Saraha's "Queen Dohā" as the bodhisattva (Mahā)sukhanātha or the nondual state of mahāmudrā, see appendix 3 in volume 3.

1489. Two mss. read *bāhyā* and two *vānyā* ("are other than"). GZ CDNP have "outside."

1490. GZ CDNP have stanzas 19–21 as follows:

> The tradition coming from Dharma's mouth
> that has been discussed by Bhadrapāda
> is that the glorious Protector Great Bliss
> is due to [CDNP "in"] nonduality with aspects' distinctions
>
> From the nature that is a single one,
> living beings are becoming manifest
> Those who are deceived by false talk
> by speaking of observing emptiness,

by being bound by the dullness of thoughts,
do not realize this very [I follow GZ *nyid* against CDNP *gnyis*
("two")] genuine bliss
What is thought by bad thinking is outside
of the purity of prajñā and means.

1491. In GZ CDNP, the first line reads "The great yoga of nondual wisdom" and the fourth says "entities abides as nonduality's aspects."

1492. GZ CDNP:

They are pure by nature and peaceful
In nonduality, stainless like space,
designations are applied out of pride,
yet those designations do not exist.

1493. GZ CDNP:

Free of feeling, feeler, and perceived,
nonduality indeed represents great bliss
As it has the nature of inconceivability,
buddhahood is not the sphere of mind.

1494. GZ CDNP "Wisdom alone is nonduality."

1495. In GZ and CDNP, between the first and second lines of this stanza, the following additional lines are inserted:

The wisdom that is nondual is supreme [CDNP link this line with
the first one: "The supreme nondual wisdom in which even a
middle is not observable"]
Because everything seeming is different, [CDNP omit this line]
there are thoughts of nonduality and duality

The great yoga of means and prajñā
is declared to be nondual one taste
Free from passion and dispassion,
any middle will not be observed

The bliss that is self-awareness
is what is expressed as nonduality,
free of characterized and characteristics
and devoid of knower and known

By discriminating the lack of self,
precious mind should be realized
Since there is no nature of being,
nonbeing will not be seen either

As it is not [CDNP omit the negative] realized by sense cognitions . . .

1496. In GZ CDNP, the last two lines read as follows:

Prajñā, means, and great compassion
are one, the equality [CDNP "manifestation"] of one taste.

1497. GZ CDNP read "nondual" as an attribute of "great bliss."
1498. In GZ CDNP, the first two lines read as follows:

> The pure [CDNP "virtuous"] nature of the dharmadhātu—
> the supreme wisdom that is nondual—.

1499. CDNP *dogs pa* ("doubt," "fear").
1500. In GZ CDNP, the first two lines read as follows:

> Naturally pure and untainted,
> nonduality is the ultimate.

1501. GZ CDNP:

> Supreme nondual wisdom
> here [CDNP "this"] is mahāmudrā
> Qualities as well as flaws
> are said to be mind's aspects.

1502. GZ CDNP:

> The supreme wisdom focusing on this
> has the nature of being waveless
> This wisdom will arise from itself
> There isn't the slightest to meditate.

1503. In GZ CDNP, the first two lines read as follows:

> For this dharmatā that is inconceivable
> is nonduality, the state of the buddhas.

1504. A straightforward reading of the first two lines in GZ CDNP would be this:

> The entirety of the sources of glorious bliss
> will certainly be seen by virtue of there being no thoughts.

1505. In GZ CDNP, the second and third lines read as follows:

> the host of the maṇḍalas of yoginīs,
> the entirety of the wrathful kings.

1506. GZ CDNP:

> the stainless aspects that appear
> in the excellent maṇḍala circle,
> likewise, the sūtra-collection piṭaka,
> and furthermore the pāramitā stages.

1507. In GZ CDNP, the first two lines read as follows:

> mantras, mudrās, awareness consorts,
> likewise what is roused in the heart.

1508. GZ CDNP "arise all on their own from nonduality."
1509. The Sauras were followers of an Indian spiritual tradition that worshipped the sun (Skt. *sūrya*) as a deity. "Arhantas" here refers specifically to those who gained realization in the Jaina tradition, not to the better-known usage

of the similar term *arhat* (translated differently into Tibetan as *dgra bcom pa*) for those who have attained the fruitions of the Buddhist Śrāvakayāna and Pratyekabuddhayāna.

1510. Given the context here of providing a list of common siddhis, I take Skt. *saṃghaṭa* to mean "perfect vase" rather than its usual meanings "piled up" or "assembled" (though these literal meanings could also apply, given the following explanation). This is supported by GZ CDNP reading *bum pa* ("vase") and *bhadraghaṭa* ("excellent vase") as one of the common siddhis listed in certain sources. Thus *saṃghaṭa* here appears to refer to the vase that inexhaustibly provides whatever one wishes (see the fifth siddhi in Lopez's list in the following note).

1511. In Buddhism, a general distinction is made between the common siddhis and the uncommon or supreme siddhi of mahāmudrā (attaining perfect buddhahood). In different sources, there are varying lists of either five or eight common siddhis. The set of five consists of the ability to (1) create copies of one's own body, (2) walk through solid objects, (3) walk on water, (4) fly in the lotus posture, and (5) touch the sun and the moon. As for the set of eight common siddhis, there are several different lists and also different interpretations of what each one of these siddhis consists of. One version simply adds three more siddhis to the above five: the ability to become invisible, sink into and move below the earth, and ascend to the divine realms of Brahmā. An often-quoted list from the *Ḍākinīvajrapañjaratantra* includes the eight siddhis of (1) the eye lotion that enables one to see the entirety of the three realms of saṃsāra (or things, such as treasures, beneath the earth), (2) fleet-footedness through applying a lotion to the feet (or wearing blessed boots), (3) the sword that enables one to fly (or to overcome a hostile army), (4) seeing underground in order to discover treasures (or traveling beneath the earth), (5) the pill that enables one to assume any form one wishes (or to become invisible), (6) traveling to and dwelling in celestial realms, (7) invisibility through applying a substance to the forehead, and (8) extracting the essence in order to extend one's life and rejuvenate the body through elixirs (or extracting nourishment from inanimate things such as stones and even space). According to Lopez 2019 (4), another list of eight common siddhis consists of (1) flying to celestial realms, (2) the sword that defeats all enemies, (3) producing magical pills that make one invisible, (4) walking with great speed over long distances by putting a magical substance on one's feet, (5) making a vessel whose contents are inexhaustible, (6) making yakṣas into one's servants, (7) concocting an elixir that bestows longevity, and (8) seeing treasures beneath the surface of the earth. Referring to both Hindu and Buddhist sources, White 2003 (199) lists (1) magical sword (*khaḍga*), (2) invisibility lotion (*añjana*), (3) foot paint (*pādalepa*), (4) disappearance (*antardhāna*), (5) elixir of immortality (*rasa-rasāyana*), (6) flight (*khecara*), (7) telekinesis (*bhūcara*), and (8) ability to see into the netherworlds (*pātāla*). However, the list in Kuddālapāda's text here appears to consist of nine siddhis.

1512. GZ CDNP:

> The deity who is called Samantabhadra
> arises just like a wish-fulfilling jewel

> . . .
> the wooden shoes, the vase, the yakṣiṇī,
>
> alchemy, and the excellent eye medicine
> are accomplished on their own, not otherwise
> Mantrīs should not meditate on being,
> nor should they meditate on nonbeing
> By virtue of having faith . . .

1513. As seen above, GZ CDNP insert the first two lines of this stanza in slightly variant form after the first two lines of stanza 43, saying: "Mantrīs should not meditate on being, nor should they meditate on nonbeing." As such, this statement seems perfectly fine and parallels others in this text that deny both being and nonbeing as well as familiarizing with either one. However, all the Sanskrit mss. agree on *bhāva* ("being") and *svabhāva* ("own-being") instead of *bhāva* and *abhāva* ("nonbeing"). If these two lines refer to the theistic brahmanic traditions mentioned in stanzas 40–41 and the immediately following two lines about Śiva and Viṣṇu, the notion of *abhāva* ("nonbeing") is indeed not asserted in relation to any of those gods, while *bhāva* and *svabhāva* are. Therefore Krug 2018 (334–45) comments as follows: "The verse is somewhat problematic, and the editors of the Sarnath edition appear to have amended *svabhāvaṃ* to *abhāvaṃ* here based on the Tibetan translation, which does in fact read the verse as a refutation of both the extreme of existence (*dngos po*) and non-existence (*dngos med*). The Sanskrit manuscript sources, however, consistently read *bhāvaṃ* and *svabhāvaṃ* here, and the fact that both terms are intended to be referents for theistic brahmanical traditions related to Śiva and Viṣṇu, neither of which argue that God is fundamentally non-existent (*abhāvaṃ*), indicates that the Tibetan and the Sarnath edition have introduced an error to the text."
1514. Samdhong and Dvivedī 1987 *viṣṇurarhataḥ* em. *viṣṇurahitaḥ*. In GZ CDNP, the last two lines read as follows:

> If even buddhahood becomes accomplished,
> what is there to say about Śiva and Viṣṇu?

1515. Skt. *varṇa* can also mean "caste" and "type."
1516. GZ CDNP:

> In it, there are no conventional terms,
> nor forms, colors, or characteristics [or "nor characteristics of form and color" or "nor forms, colors, and characteristics"]
> The excellent female holder of illusory
> aspects is the original stainless nature.

1517. Skt. *jāla* can also mean "web" and "deception" (GZ CDNP obviously read *jvāla*). GZ CDNP:

> Natural luminosity is completely pure,
> always the source of the bliss of ecstasy
> Being free from body, speech, and mind,
> it resembles a mirror and a blazing flame.

1518. As here, when not understood as the second among the four ecstasies during the perfection process, Skt. *paramānanda* has a distinctly Hinduist connotation, indicating the supreme transcendental bliss of being one with the Brahman, the universal soul, or as a characteristic of gods such as Śiva and Viṣṇu.

1519. GZ CDNP:

> It is the manifestation of supreme ecstasy's bliss:
> great bliss springs forth in a perpetual manner
> Through uniting the expressions of syllables
> and names, it is taught in the form of words.

1520. Skt. *naya* can also mean "method," "conduct," "proper," and "right."

1521. GZ CDNP:

> Moreover, as it is beyond speech's path,
> there is no way this could be uttered
> Through enjoying [or "playing in"] that which is desired
> by [GZ *yi* CDNP *yin* em. *yis*] engaging in the way of activity,
>
> at the time of the supreme worship,
> it was demonstrated by Bhadra's mouth
> The prajñā that consists of nonduality
> is by the nature of the one's manifestation [in CDNP, except replacing "wisdom" by "prajñā," the last two lines match the Sanskrit].

1522. As mentioned before, Skt. *varṇa* can also mean "color" and "caste."

1523. GZ CDNP:

> By latent tendencies being terminated,
> buddhahood is attained with certainty
> through the power of various kinds
> due to the yogas of various views.

1524. GZ CDNP "accumulating."

1525. In general, Skt. *caitanya* means "consciousness," "vitality," and "sensation," but (particularly in Vedānta) also "soul," "spirit," and "pure awareness" in the sense of the Supreme Spirit that is considered the essence of all being and the source of all sensation, or the deity that is considered the essence of all being.

1526. GZ CDNP:

> Being free from mind and thinking, [I follow CDNP *sems pa* against GZ *sems dpa'* ("sattva")]
> it is the supreme nondual wisdom
> Bhadra's mouth spoke of what is
> called "nonduality" as buddhahood.

1527. GZ CDNP:

> Hence, thanks to realizing buddhahood,
> supreme practitioners become buddhas
> The teaching by connecting the words [CDNP "By teaching the connection of words"]

is buddhahood conceived as nonduality [CDNP "buddhahood and nonduality are conceived"].

1528. GZ CDNP:

> By way of the ultimate's lack of convention [GZ *tha snyad med* CDNP *tha dad med* ("nondifference")],
> nonduality and buddhahood are nondual
> Through the teaching's wisdom arising,
> thoughts are cast far off by realization [CD *rtogs pa'i rtog pa ring spangs te* ("thoughts of realization are cast far off") NP *rtog pas rtog pa* . . . ("what is thought by thoughts . . .")].

1529. The rendering "the entirety of thinking of entities" of Skt. *sarvabhāvāvikalpatā* corresponds to GZ CDNP *dngos po la sogs rtog pa kun*, but it could also be understood as "the thinking about all entities."

1530. In GZ NP, this line says: "through the yoga of becoming familiar with" [CD *nyams pa gso ba'i sbyor ba* ("yoga of mending degeneration")].

1531. GZ CDNP:

> In taking hold of what is named "nonduality,"
> the yogīs [with Skt. *yogibhiḥ*, GZ CD *ma 'byor ba* P *la sbyor bas* N *la 'byor bas* are emended to *rnal 'byor pas*] should have patience with me.

1532. GZ CDNP:

> Through the termination of latencies,
> this represents nondual buddhahood
> . . .
> if there aren't any sides in them,
> should be referred to as buddhas
> By its nature of naturelessness,
> it remains as the element of prajñā [CDNP "the element of prajñā remains"]
> What Bhadra's mouth teaches
> is that means is entities' creator.

1533. Two mss. read *tayorālambanād*, one *melavanānād*, one *melavaṇānād*, and Samdhong and Dvivedī 1987, obviously following the Tibetan *de dag 'dus pa*, emend to *tayor melanād* ("Due to those two meeting/joining"). GZ CDNP "Having the character of those two meeting/joining."

1534. GZ CDNP:

> Nothing of what is taught as talk,
> conception, and meditation exists
> Her with the form of supreme ecstasy,
> Bhadra has declared to be excellent
> in order that buddhahood is attained.

1535. In GZ CDNP, the last two lines read as follows:

It is devoid of illustrating entities in terms
of the eyes up to the mental consciousness.

1536. Skt. *ananta* can also mean "endless," "without extreme," "eternal," and "sky."

1537. GZ CDNP:

It is present as the manifestation that is
strictly singular, beginningless, and endless
Thanks to the kindness of the guru's mouth,
it will be known through the single supreme.

1538. Given the list of matched pairs in this stanza and GZ CDNP *gnyis med ye shes rnal 'byor che*, I follow the reading *-advayajñānaṃ* in two mss. against Samdhong and Dvivedī 1987 following the other two mss. reading *-advayajñāne* ("In mahāyoga's nondual wisdom"). The occurrence of the compound *advayajñāne* in two mss. in line 64c seems to be due to skipping to line 65c, where this compound is also found in the same place (correctly).

1539. GZ CDNP:

Yoga is explained as the person
Anuyoga is supreme awareness
Beyond duality is great atiyoga
Nondual wisdom is mahāyoga
Yogīs will become buddhas

Note that the third line that mentions atiyoga (**mahātiyoga*) has no correspondent in either the Sanskrit or the alternative translation by Drogmi Lotsāwa. It is possible that it originally was an interlinear note that eventually crept into the main text.

1540. In GZ CDNP the first line reads "When sun and moon are seized by planets," and the third reads "through the nondual wisdom of melting."

1541. In GZ CDNP the first line reads "The nature of the ultimate ecstasy," and the third reads "In a siddha's form, there is no doubt."

1542. GZ CDNP:

That which is low [CDNP *thog ma* ("beginning")] and mediocre,
such as form, is seen with the eyes
By the nature of ultimate actuality,
nonduality is to be viewed as genuine.

1543. GZ CDNP:

The [good] sounds and bad sounds
heard by the ears are distinguished
The chief wisdom beyond sound
is the supreme nondual hearing.

1544. GZ CDNP:

The best taste tasted by the tongue—
the supreme nonduality that consists

of the oneness of the six tastes of
bad tastes—is what is to be realized.

1545. GZ CDNP:

By virtue of the nature of the oneness
of smells such as musk in a deer navel
that are smelled by the nose as smells,
supreme nonduality is to be realized.

1546. Skt. *jātyajāti* could also mean "caste and noncaste."

1547. Skt. *niṣpanna* can also mean "arise."

1548. All mss. read *vibhāviyogena* (which could also mean "the yoga that causes to appear"), but Samdhong and Dvivedī 1987, saying they follow the Tibetan, emend to *prajñopāyaviyogena*. However, while *prajñopāya-* would make sense here, *viyoga* does not mean "union" but "disjunction" or "absence" (what corresponds to Tib. *sbyor ba* is *yoga*). GZ CDNP:

The natures of what is touched by the body
are distinguished as good kinds and bad kinds
Through the joining of prajñā and means,
this is the supreme nondual union [or absorption].

1549. Skt. *prabhāva* can also mean "power," "splendor," "majesty," and "beauty."

1550. GZ CDNP:

Through the rays of wisdom's light,
it is infinite and the all-pervading one
The supreme rapture that is self-arising [NP "awakening"]
is the true buddhahood that is nondual.

1551. In GZ CDNP, the last two lines read as follows:

are the kāya whose nature is the five wisdoms,
having the character of nonduality without five.

1552. GZ CDNP:

Eternally, this is Akṣobhya, Ratna,
Āmitāyus, and the Amogha lord
The unit that is the five's lord . . .

1553. GZ CDNP:

. . .
wind, space, as well as
the five elements' connate
become nondual awakening.

1554. GZ CDNP "what is imagined through the conditions of thoughts."

1555. Skt. *āśaya* can also mean "intention," "manner of thinking," "mind," and "fortune."

1556. Besides its general meaning "omniscience" and "an omniscient one," Skt. *sarvajña* is an epithet of both Śiva and the Buddha, as well as one of the eight manifestations of Kāpāla and Bhīṣaṇa (both forms of Bhairava). In addition, line 110b below has *sarvajña* as an epithet of "great bliss." Both grammatically and in terms of the meaning of the Sanskrit, it would also be possible to relate "omniscient" to "nonduality," but GZ CDNP read "Brahmā and Sarvajña." GZ CDNP:

> By the power of the thinking of sentient beings,
> the doctrines and so forth become distinguished
> Śiva and so forth, Viṣṇu, and Brahmā,
> as well as Sarvajña, are this single nonduality.

1557. GZ CDNP:

> It is beyond the sphere of all that derives
> from the eyes and such and of the mind,
> being called "the ultimate nonduality,"
> but [I follow NP *kyis* against GZ CD *kyi*] conventional verbal discursiveness
> [just] imagines [or imputes] nonduality.

1558. GZ CDNP:

> The state of the ultimate is undifferentiable
> There is no buddha apart from nonduality
> Through the union of realization [CDNP "thoughts"] and space,
> the discursiveness of speech is taught.

1559. GZ CDNP:

> Thanks to the succession of the treatises,
> it is explained by discerning it as words
> One is not capable of speaking of any
> buddhahood that is other than nonduality.

1560. With GZ CDNP *stong pa*, *śṛṇu tā* ("listen, these") and *śṛtāḥ* ("cooked food," "boiled milk") in the mss. are emended to *śunyāḥ*.
1561. GZ CD *rnam rig dag* ("the [two?] cognizances") NP *rnam rig brgyad* ("the eight cognizances").
1562. In GZ CDNP, the first two lines read as follows:

> Similar to reflections that appear
> in a mirror appearing everywhere . . .

1563. Three mss. read *advayajñāna udbhūtāḥ* and one reads *advayajñānam udbhūtāḥ*, while GZ CDNP say "arise from nondual wisdom." In line 84c, all mss. read *advayajñānād* ("from nondual wisdom"), but Samdhong and Dvivedī 1987 emend this to *advayajñāna* (probably to match it with line 85c). According to lines 85cd, "everything else originates within nondual wisdom's true state." Elsewhere, the text repeatedly says that everything is an aspect of nonduality or simply *is* nonduality (or its equivalent nondual wisdom). Thus Kuddālapāda variously states that all phenomena arise within, from, or as nondual wisdom, as its aspects, or are nothing but nondual wisdom. Ultimately, however, since phenomena and nondual wisdom are one in essence, all these statements come down to the same.

1564. GZ CDNP "Mother and father are the same as well."
1565. Two mss. read *advayajñānasadbhāve*, one reads *advayajñānasambhāve* ("in nondual wisdom's arising"), and one *advayajñānasvabhāve* ("in nondual wisdom's nature"); GZ CDNP "from nondual wisdom's nature."
1566. For stanzas 87–88ab, GZ CDNP have eight lines:

The nature of wisdom that is supreme,
the approach of the gurus' lineage succession,
has been taught from Bhadrapāda's mouth
from ear to ear and mouth to mouth

Out of the kindness of Bhadrapāda,
yogīs who cultivate the inconceivable,
by means of this yoga that is perfect,
attain buddhahood with certainty.

1567. GZ CDNP have this line as "it met with Bhadra's mouth."
1568. In this sense, Skt. *abhiprāya* corresponds to GZ CDNP *dgongs pa*, but it can also mean "goal," "purpose," "meaning," and "wish."
1569. GZ CDNP *bya ba* ("activity").
1570. Somasiddhānta is another name for nontantric or pretantric Kāpālikas (a particular tradition of Śaivism). GZ CDNP have the last line as "the individual philosophical systems."
1571. The *Manavadharmaśāstra* (a.k.a. *Manusmṛti*), attributed to the legendary first man, Manu, prescribes the sets of obligations of (usually) men from the four castes of Hindu society as they pertain to each of the four stages of life (*āśrama*): *brahmacārī* (religious student; from as early as five years of age up to twenty-four), *gṛhastha* (householder; twenty-four to forty-eight), *vanaprastha* (forest-dweller; forty-eight to seventy-two), and *saṃnyāsa* (renunciate; after age seventy-two, or any time).
1572. In GZ CDNP, the last two lines read as follows:

As they are not outside of nonduality,
gods and asuras are the lowest ones.

1573. GZ CDNP:

It will be clear that everything appears
in a distinct way from nondual wisdom,
distinguished as emptiness's distinctions
The fusion of compassion and nonduality
is the equal possession of means and prajñā

This guru with the entire nature of the buddhas
constitutes the approach from Bhadra's mouth,
being the ocean of wisdom that is genuine.

1574. In GZ CDNP, the first two lines read as follows:

Just as all the supreme will arise
from churning the ocean of milk.

1575. Skt. *rasa* can also mean "milk," "drink," "flavor," and "essence"; GZ CDNP "as well as tasting the best taste [or elixir]."

1576. Skt. *śubha* can also mean "splendid," "blissful," "virtuous," "gracious," "eminent," and "pure." As mentioned before, in the sūtra and tantra literatures, there are different presentations of the thirteen bhūmis. Here, the thirteenth bhūmi is called Vajradharī ("vajra holder"). GZ CDNP:

> Including Brahmā, asuras, and humans,
> everything has risen out of this nectar
> The virtuous bhūmi of Vajradhara
> is explained as being the thirteenth

Krug 2018 (360–61) interprets stanzas 95–97 as a parallel to the same cosmogonic myth of the gods churning the milk ocean in the *Vyaktabhāvānugatatattvasiddhi* (text 8), where the churning and the production of nectar are taken as a metaphor for the practice of karmamudrā. Given what follows from stanza 98 onward, this specific interpretation is possible, but there is also the more obvious general meaning of nonduality (of course, it is equally possible that both are intended). That is, given our text's pervasive theme of nonduality and that everything arises out of it, the phrase "the ocean of wisdom" (the guru who realizes this nonduality) in line 94d, and the phrase "arises from nonduality's ocean" in line 103d, it seems that "the ocean of milk" in these stanzas is a metaphor for nonduality as the source of everything.

1577. Skt. *mahojjvala* can also mean "great splendor," great light," "great beauty," and "great passion," but I follow GZ CDNP *cher 'bar ba*.

1578. GZ "From her, great bliss arises" CDNP "From bliss, great bliss arises."

1579. Nor brang o rgyan 2008 (2:2028–30) presents an extensive list of nine kinds of prajñā, each having multiple subdivisions, that stems from the *Sandhinirmocanasūtravyākhyāna* (D4358). However, given the tantric context here, "nine prajñās" is probably a reference to the nine female deities of the Hevajra maṇḍala (Nairātmyā in the center, Gaurī, Caurī, Vetālī, and Ghasmarī in the cardinal directions, and Pukkasī, Śavarī, Caṇḍālī, and Ḍombinī in the intermediate directions).

1580. GZ CDNP read "dripping" instead of "flowing" and replace "divine" with "excellent," linking it with "what gives rise."

1581. Two mss. read *svacchāmṛtasamaṃ pūrṇaṃ* ("filled as if with clear nectar") and the other two *susaṃpūrṇaṃ pūrṇaṃ*. GZ CDNP appear to render **svacchāmṛtasusaṃpūrṇaṃ*, which seems to make the most sense.

1582. Skt. *āhlāda* can also mean "revive" and "delight." GZ CDNP have "satisfy."

1583. Skt. *sāgarādvaya;* GZ CDNP *gnyis med rgya mtsho* ("the ocean of nonduality") matches the above parallel phrases "the ocean of wisdom" and "the ocean of milk." Thus *sāgarādvaya* could also be understood as *advayasāgara*.

1584. GZ CDNP "endowed with the wisdom of the ten powers."

1585. For reasons unclear to me, Samdhong and Dvivedī (1987) elide *-dhātugaṃ* in the initial *khadhātugaṃ;* GZ CDNP render this as *mkha' 'gro* (*khagaṃ*), which, without knowing the underlying Sanskrit, can only be misunderstood as the Tibetan rendering of "ḍākinī." All four mss. read *tiryagmārgaṃ*, but Samdhong and Dvivedī (1987), obviously because of the lotuses mentioned in what follows, emend to *padmamārgaṃ*. In line 107b, the text also speaks of "the crooked door" (Skt. *tiryagdvara*). Drogmi Lotsāwa's mss. probably also reads *tiryagmārga* here, but he mistranslates it as *byol song lam* ("animal path"; Skt. *tiryañc*, "animal"). To make matters worse, Skt. *tiryaga* means "air-goer."

1586. All mss. add *utpallaṃ* before this phrase.

1587. Parallel to the emendation of Skt. *śravantaṃ* in line 101a to *sravantaṃ* in Samdhong and Dvivedī 1987, I emend *pratiśravaṇa* ("promising," "listening," "answering," "agreeing," none of which make sense here) to *pratisravaṇa*, which is also confirmed by the parallel GZ CDNP *'dzag pa*.

1588. Stanzas 106–7 are rendered by the following six lines in GZ CDNP:

> The supreme path known for sure in the lotus
> of the ḍākinī came down as Bhadra's tradition
> In the lotuses in the heart and in the navel,
> likewise in the lotus in the throat,
>
> and in the lotus of the birthplace with a bell, [GZ CDNP *dril can* corresponds to Skt. *ghaṇṭika* (as also appearing in lines 111c and 112d)]
> by dripping [there] directly, it is abiding.

1589. Three mss. add *viśuddhaśuklasaṃcāra* at the beginning of the first line.

1590. GZ CDNP:

> Emission of feces, urine, and semen,
> supreme sights, smells, and hearings,
> as well as tastes will be perceived
> The seed, in form like a lotus filament,
> that courses through the nine doors
> is abiding below as well as above.

1591. In GZ CDNP, the first two lines read as follows:

> This is explained as "prajñā,"
> being the object of all buddhas.

1592. Skt. *śanaiḥ* can also mean "at leisure," "gradually," "quietly," and "alternately"; GZ *dal bur* means "slow," "not busy," and "gradually."

1593. GZ CDNP read *bye brag* ("distinctions").

1594. GZ CDNP "nose tip."

1595. Skt. *buddhamānas* em. *buddhyamānas* (GZ CDNP obviously read *buddhamālā*).

1596. GZ CDNP:

> Within the vajra aperture in the throat [*srol gong*],
> the buddha garland does not exist as two
> If you are completely afflicted by saṃsāra,
> resting at ease in the tip of the one with a bell . . .

1597. GZ CDNP "Prajñā is excellent, mind is sharp."

1598. Skt. *līlā* can also mean "grace," "elegance," "beauty," "ease or facility in doing something," "semblance," "disguise," and "mere appearance," all of which seem to apply here as well.

1599. GZ CDNP read "is supreme bliss, not so otherwise."

1600. GZ CDNP *haṃ gi rnam pa mi shigs pa* ("the aspect of HAṂ is indestructible"). As mentioned before, Skt. *anāhata* ("unstruck," but also "intact") is often rendered as Tib. *mi shigs pa* (or as *gzhom du med pa*, "invincible"). The most common use of *anāhata* is in the expression "unstruck sound," usually glossed as "the sound of emptiness" (see text 90 on songs 11, 16, 17, and 31). Elsewhere, however, text 90 also speaks of unstruck or indestructible luminosity, wisdom, and compassion. Similarly, a quote from the *Śrīmahāsaṃvarodayatantra* in Sahajavajra's *Sthitisamāsa* speaks of the connate as being unstruck or indestructible.

1601. Given the context and the parallel compounds *ghaṇṭikācchidramārga* and *ghaṇṭikārandhramārga* in lines 111c and 117c, *ghaṇṭikābhedamārga* is emended accordingly.

1602. "Digit" (Skt. *kalā*; Tib. *cha*) here refers to the extent or degree to which the four ecstasies and great bliss are experienced, similar to the sixteen digits of the waxing period ("white fortnight") and waning period ("black fortnight") of the moon in Indian astronomy. Internally, on the path, the white bindu descends from the crown of the head through the cakras to the tip of the vajra ("white fortnight"), producing the four ecstasies in sixteen digits. At the end of this, immutable great bliss arises. Then, the bindu again ascends up to the crown of the head ("black fortnight"), going through the sixteen digits of the four phases of outflow, maturation, human effort, and stainlessness (for details, see Sferra 2000, 31–36, and Gyatso 2004, 560–61). GZ CDNP:

> In the path of the orifice with a bell,
> there are thirty-two nāḍīs present
> The seats [the meaning of GZ CDNP *so* is not clear; it can also
> mean "teeth"] are said to be thirty-two
> Digits and no digits are nondual.

1603. GZ CDNP replace "the syllable KA" with "the aspect of HAṂ" and read the last two lines as follows:

> Sure guidance via the path of the opening
> with a bell constitutes the supreme path.

1604. GZ CDNP:

> It rests there at the door
> and the first vowel *āli*
> is to be rested at its door [CDNP omit the second and third lines]
> Luminosity in a pure form
> is called "beginningless,"
> abiding in the form of glorious bliss.

1605. Both Mahendra ("great Indra") and Parameśvara are decidedly Hinduist terms. The latter means "supreme lord," "supreme being," or "supreme god," being an epithet of Śiva, Viṣṇu, and Indra. Both terms can also refer to any eminent royalty or illustrious person. Obviously, Kuddālapāda does not use these theistic terms in the sense of an external god or person but as deliberate epithets (somewhat provocative at least for Buddhists) of the inner bindu of great bliss and inconceivable nonduality. GZ CDNP:

> Then, it is blown by the vāyu
> and Mahendra clearly manifests
> The definite path too manifests
> Parameśvara is indestructible.

1606. Skt. *siddhi* can also mean "performance," "dexterity," "efficiency," "fulfillment," "perfection," "readiness," "success," "beauty," "bliss," "fortune," and "prosperity," some of which seem to be implied here, since lines 120cd obviously refer to the appearance and activity of the form kāyas; GZ CDNP *grub pa* clearly means "accomplished" or "established."

1607. In GZ CDNP, the first two lines read as follows:

> The thirteen bhūmis are attained and
> the mighty lord of bliss is supreme.

1608. Skt. *āmnāya* also means "tantra," "received doctrine," "sacred texts handed down by repetition," "advice," and "that which is to be remembered, studied, or learned by heart."

1609. GZ CDNP:

> This is the pith instruction from Bhadra's mouth,
> representing the stages of transmitting the essence
> Having retained everything that has been heard,
> it is familiarized with by hearing and reflecting.

1610. GZ CDNP "these passages have been properly compiled."

1611. Skt. *kuśalī*. Sakya Paṇḍita (Kun dga' rgyal mtshan 1992–93, fol. 248b.2–5), who was well-versed in Sanskrit, says that the often-found term *kusulu* is incorrect and emends it to *kuśalī*, meaning "one with virtue." He adds that a paṇḍita is someone who is well-versed in the inner and outer fields of knowledge, while a kuśalī has cut through all outer discursiveness and reference points, being supremely absorbed within.

1612. GZ CDNP "May I be born again and again as a servant . . . without an exception."

1613. GZ CDNP read the last two lines as follows:

> If not, if I possibly go to hell,
> may hell itself be great bliss [CDNP "Sukhāvatī"].

1614. GZ CDNP have this paragraph as the following stanza:

> The essence of the guru's own nature, who knows the pith instructions on inconceivable
> nonduality's perfection process, is the supreme yoga of all mantra texts without exception
> [CDNP "The guru who knows the pith instructions on . . . process is the nature of the deity as well as the supreme yoga . . ."]

This yoga, which is infinite and vast, has originated from the guru,
and is stainless,
was written down by me, a fool with feeble intelligence, just in
order to remember it.

1615. Skt. "This concludes 'Pith Instructions on the Tradition of Inconceivable Nonduality.' It was composed by the mahāmudrā siddha Śrī Kuddālapāda." CDNP "This concludes 'The Inconceivable' composed by master Kuddālapāda, who had attained mahāmudrā. It was translated by *Sukhāṅkura and Gö."

1616. PDMT, 26:289–304. My translations of the works in Maitrīpa's "Cycle of Mental Nonengagement" that are contained in both the **Advayavajrasaṃgraha* and GZ (texts 19–21, 23–37, and 39–42), as well as texts 14, 22, 43, and 183, are greatly indebted to the Sanskrit editions and the English translations in Mathes 2015 (though I do not always agree with his renderings). I generally follow these editions and their titles (if the Sanskrit is available) but also retain the Tibetan titles and the translation colophons as they appear in GZ CDNP. Differences in the Tibetan versions are noted only if they are significant (for more details of the variant readings in the Sanskrit and Tibetan versions, see Mathes 2015). For text 19, Mathes provides only the Sanskrit and an English translation up through the second quote from the *Hevajratantra* (on *poṣadha*) and refers to Wallis 2003 (henceforth "Wallis") for the remainder of the text, saying that "Glenn Wallis had already published a good and reliable English translation" of it (Mathes 2015, xi). Though this is kind of Mathes to say, in fact, Wallis's translation not only omits parts of the text, such as the four concluding stanzas, the colophon, and a number of other phrases, but is also blatantly wrong at times, such as translating the uṣṇīṣas on the heads of the five tathāgatas as "wearing turbans," completely misinterpreting the section on making stamped clay images (Skt. *sāccha*), and not realizing that most of stanza 17 consists of the names of texts. Mathes later translated text 19 in its entirety (Mathes 2021, 169–84), but he sometimes still follows Wallis (sometimes verbatim, sometimes even if Wallis is wrong) or the Tibetan.

1617. This homage is not found in the Sanskrit.

1618. Skt. *vihāra* can also mean "delight" and "play."

1619. GZ CDNP:

If someone is abiding in this,
they attain the state of a victor
I shall explain the beginner's
procedure, the elimination of bad views.

1620. Headings in [ ] are inserted by me based on the contents and, if applicable, the concluding sentences of each section.

1621. "The superior intention" (Skt. *adhyāśaya*, Tib. *lhag pa'i bsam pa*) is a term for the superior altruistic attitude of true bodhisattvas that has solely the welfare of others in mind. Such bodhisattvas care about others with the same spontaneous intensity with which ordinary beings usually strive for their own well-being. This attitude is said to be the immediate prerequisite or cause for the arising of uncontrived genuine bodhicitta even in ordinary beings.

1622. "The engagement through aspiration" is another common expression for the path of preparation (or both the paths of accumulation and preparation).

1623. As text 20 says, the five powers in the state of having attained power are those over afflictions, birth, karma, means, and the state of maturing sentient beings.

1624. As mentioned before, the *Avikalpapraveśadhāraṇī* describes how bodhisattvas enter the expanse of nonconceptuality by relinquishing all coarse and subtle characteristics of conceptions in terms of (1) nature (perceiver and perceived or the five skandhas), (2) remedies (the six pāramitās), (3) true reality (emptiness and its equivalents), and (4) attainment (the ten bhūmis of bodhisattvas and buddhahood with all their qualities). These four characteristics are relinquished in a gradual manner by means of analyzing their nature, their qualities, and their essence, and finally by not mentally engaging in them at all (for the section on relinquishing these characteristics, see Brunnhölzl 2012, 330–31). Maitreya's *Dharmadharmatāvibhāga* (lines 164–72) likewise speaks about relinquishing these four characteristics in order to attain nonconceptual wisdom (Brunnhölzl 2012, 167, 187, 260–61, 308–19). The last three of these four characteristics are also mentioned in stanza 3 below, at the beginning of Maitrīpa's *Nirvedhapañcaka* (text 28), in his *Tattvaprakāśa* 13 (text 35) and *Sekanirdeśa* 36ac (text 42), Rāmapāla's *Sekanirdeśapañjikā* on it (text 45), and Divākaracandra's *Prajñājñānaprakāśa* (text 16, 69), and discussed extensively in Sahajavajra's *Tattvadaśakaṭīkā* on stanza 7 (text 46, 40–44). The *Avikalpapraveśadhāraṇī*'s general notion of relinquishing conceptual characteristics is likewise quoted in Maitrīpa's *Amanasikārādhāra* (text 27). Interestingly, those very three characteristics are also listed as three of the four samayas of mahāmudrā as given by Lama Shang (Tib. Bla ma zhang yu brag pa brston 'grus grags pa, 1122–93) and quoted in the Ninth Karmapa's *Ocean of Definitive Meaning* (Wangchuk Dorje 2001, 270): "There are four samayas of Mahāmudrā: The mental afflictions are not to be abandoned because they are your own mind. Wisdom, the remedy, does not need to be applied to the mind-stream because [wisdom] and those [mental afflictions] are not dual. Suchness is not meditated on because it is not a reference point. The result is not hoped for because it is realized to be your own mind."

1625. GZ CDNP "From the engagement through aspiration by way of the superior intention and the engagement when having entered the bhūmis, all the way up through the ultimate [engagement] thanks to the attainment of power over the five, learners, who dwell in the causal state, gather the two accumulations through the procedure of utterly pure beginner activity and then attain completely perfect awakening. Nonlearners, who have eliminated any thoughts about true reality and the fruition through remedial factors, just as in the case of [Buddha] Śākyamuni, through the powerful force of their [former] aspiration prayers, effortlessly promote the welfare of sentient beings within [NP omit 'effortlessly' and 'within'] unity—they dwell in 'the engagement in initial activity without its characteristics being interrupted.'"

1626. GZ NP *sems pa* ("thinking") CD *sems dpa'*.

1627. This is Nāgārjuna's *Niraupamyastava* 24. The last two lines in GZ CDNP read as follows:

> On your own accord, you engage
> in buddha activity in the world

As in this instance and many others below, the Sanskrit edition of the **Advayavajrasaṃgraha* by the Study Group of Sacred Tantric Texts (Mikkyō-seiten kenkyukai) (Maitrīpa 1988–91) does not identify unattributed stanzas in Maitrīpa's texts that are in fact quotes from other works not by him. Rather unusually, such stanzas are treated and numbered as if they constituted intrinsic parts of the texts by Maitrīpa in which they are quoted, even when Maitrīpa explicitly attributes these stanzas to other texts. Mathes 2015 usually identifies such quoted stanzas but still follows the same approach of numbering them as if they belonged to the text at hand. By contrast, I do not number such quoted stanzas as being parts of Maitrīpa's works but treat them as the citations that they are.

1628. This stanza also appears in Jñānakīrti's *Tattvāvatāra* (text 214, 248), where it looks like one of this author's own stanzas. With some variations and without attribution, it is also quoted in Kṛṣṇa Paṇḍitā's *Hevajratantrapañjikā* (D1187, fol. 147a.3–4), Phalavajra's *Samantabhadrasādhananāmavṛtti* (D1867, fol. 182b.2), Advayavajra's *Āryamañjuśrīnāmasaṃgītiṭīkāsārābhisamaya* (D2098, fol. 107a.7–107b.1), Munīndrabhadra's *Vajradhātumahāmaṇḍalopāyikāsarva-vajrodayanāmapiṇḍārtha* (D2529, fol. 192a.3–4), and Sahajavajra's *Tattvadaśakaṭīkā* (D2254, fol. 164a.1–2; text 46, 11). The *Caturmudrāṭīkā* (text 44, 363) quotes a stanza whose first two lines in particular are very similar to the first two of this stanza, attributing it to the *Candrapradīpasūtra* (Tib. *zla ba sgron me'i mdo*):

> The welfare of others that's consummate is taught
> to constitute the primary fruition of buddhahood
> For, relinquishing the welfare of sentient beings,
> there is nothing other that is of great significance

GZ CDNP have only three lines:

> Others' consummate welfare *is* buddhahood—
> the principal fruition—while others are not [CDNP "Others' consummate welfare is the principal fruition of buddhahood . . ."]
> Hence buddhahood is explained as the fruition.

1629. GZ CDNP have the first two lines as follows:

> Like a wish-fulfilling tree, it is not
> shaken by the storms of volition.

1630. This stanza is identical to *Tattvaratnāvalī* 11 and appears in almost the same form in Jñānakīrti's *Tattvāvatāra* (text 214, 280), where it is most likely a quote. However, supported by "like a wish-fulfilling tree" in the first line here in GZ CDNP, it is the following very similar stanza in Śāntarakṣita's *Tattvasaṃgraha* (chapter XXIII, 2049; D4266, fol. 74b.6–7) that seems to have served as the basis of the stanza in Maitrīpa's two texts and the one in the *Tattvāvatāra*:

Being similar to a wish-fulfilling tree,
though unshaken by volition's winds,
the Sage promotes the consummate
welfare of the world in its entirety.

1631. GZ CDNP:

By relinquishing adopting and rejecting
the fruition, true reality, and antagonists,
the wise ones realize [I follow CDNP *rtogs* against GZ *rdor*] complete awakening
The beginners should make efforts [CDNP "The beginners think (NP *bsam* CD *sam*) with effort"].

1632. Skt. *bhāvin* can also mean "blessed," "possessing," "capable," "illustrious," and "inevitable."

1633. GZ CDNP "'Though the procedure of learners is suitable for beginners, how could there be any exertion in beginner activity for nonlearners who have realized the lack of nature through meditation? For example, here too, this is like being fettered by a golden chain.' This is true because they are not separated from the realization of prajñāpāramitā. For the pāramitā of prajñā is the essence of the five pāramitās. Therefore 'the emptiness . . .' is taught. The Bhagavān said . . . receive the name 'pāramitā.' This is also stated in the *Āryavimalakīrtinirdeśanāmamahāyānasūtra*."

1634. In the sūtra (H177, fol. 313a.3–4), this stanza reads as follows:

Prajñā not embraced by means is bondage
Prajñā embraced by means is liberation
Means not embraced by prajñā is bondage
Means embraced by prajñā is liberation.

1635. This stanza is identical to *Mahāyānaviṃśikā* 16. GZ CDNP:

Emptiness and compassion inseparable
is what is held to be buddha wisdom
What is to be performed by all yogīs
is what is taught as the initial activity.

1636. GZ CDNP omit this phrase.

1637. Skt. *nābhi* can also mean "origin," "home," "center," and "nave."

1638. GZ CDNP:

What is taught as the five pāramitās
is designated as "the initial activity"
The essence of the pāramitā that is
prajñā is what should be analyzed [CDNP "should not be analyzed"].

1639. GZ CDNP:

If the intelligent always rely on
generosity, discipline, patience,

vigor, dhyāna, and prajñā with respect,
they will even become sugatas [CDNP "prajñā will arise easily"].

1640. GZ CDNP "Since this is taught, beginner bodhisattvas should abide by means of utter purity. In the opposite case, it would follow they are proponents of extinction [CDNP 'nonexistence']."

1641. GZ CDNP:

> For, though virtue and nonvirtue are without being,
> . . .
> Though the worldly seeming is like a water-moon,
> . . . [CDNP "from it, there is pleasure and unpleasant suffering"]

"Worldly seeming" is shorthand for "the seeming reality of the world."

1642. GZ CDNP "'In that case, how about learners who abide in the yogic discipline of a lunatic and wish to experience nonconceptuality by engaging in [the activity of] beginners?' This is to be discussed. They possess the conduct of giving away their body."

1643. This quote is *Hevajratantra* I.6.19ab.

1644. GZ CDNP "[It consists of] the generosity of giving away [one's own] body; the discipline of promoting the welfare of all sentient beings through body, speech, and mind; the patience through [even] enduring cold [NP *drag po'i*, 'fierce'], heat, being split by saws, and so on; the vigor of equality regarding harm by the eight worldly dharmas; the dhyāna that occurs effortlessly on its own accord following all entities; and the prajñā characterized by realizing the nonobservability of all phenomena."

1645. GZ CDNP (prose): "Engaging [CDNP omit *'jug pa ni*, 'engaging'] everything effortlessly by way of the natural state of single taste is the supreme of all pāramitās of those who desire single taste."

1646. GZ CDNP "Therefore those who dwell in the yogic discipline of a lunatic also engage in initial activity. It is not like the statement of those known as the ones who see only this life and are deceived about the ruin of any next world, which is just unreasonable in every respect. For, in this regard, the following is said in the *Hevajra[tantra]* about learner bodhisattvas who possess [such] yogic discipline."

1647. II.8.10ab (GZ CDNP omit "instructions").

1648. "The heart of awakening" (Skt. *bodhimaṇḍa*) usually refers to the vajra seat under the bodhi tree in Bodhgayā, where all buddhas in this world are said to find their perfect awakening. However, sometimes this expression can also refer to the very essence of buddhahood—the dharmadhātu or dharmakāya.

1649. Skt. *gāthā* usually means "song" or "stanza," but this passage is obviously neither.

1650. GZ CDNP "As for first bestowing the poṣadha, [monastics] should say the following one time [CDNP omit 'one time'], two times, or up to three times: 'Venerable one or master, please consider me! Until I reach the heart of awakening, I, the upāsaka with this name ". . . ," take refuge in the Buddha, the dharma, and the saṃgha.' [CDNP add 'Having taken refuge in those three,'] these are the words of bestowing the poṣadha: 'Venerable one, please take care of me so that I enter the upavāsa! [CDNP omit "so that I enter the upavāsa"] Master, please consider me! At every day of the full moon [CDNP omit this phrase], from this time onward until the sun rises, I, the upāsaka with this name ". . . ," shall refrain from killing living creatures, stealing the possessions of others, impure conduct, telling lies, and likewise drinking intoxicating beverages, eating food at inappropriate times, garlands, colors, songs, dances, sports, high thrones, and big bedsteads. I shall abide in the manner of an arhat with these eight qualities [GZ 'branches'].'" Skt. *poṣadha* (Tib. *gso sbyong*) is the specific term for the (originally) fortnightly ceremony of Buddhist monastics restoring their individual vows. Skt. *upavāsa, upavāsastha,* or *upoṣatha* (Pāli *uposatha; smyung gnas*) technically refers to a number of days (two to ten in different Buddhist traditions) in the lunar calendar when monastics restore and reaffirm their vows, while lay practitioners may observe a set of eight precepts. The eight precepts, which constitute the set of vows shared by monastics and lay followers during those days, consist of refraining from (1) killing, (2) stealing, (3) lying, (4) all sexual activity, (5) consuming intoxicating drinks or drugs, (6) eating at the wrong time (that is, after noon), (7) entertainment (such as dancing, singing, music, and watching shows) and personal adornments (such as jewelry, perfumes, and cosmetics), and (8) high or luxurious seats and beds. Usually, in Theravāda countries, *uposatha* is observed about once a week (on new moon, full moon, and the two quarter moons in between; in Sri Lanka, only on new moon and full moon). In Mahāyāna countries that use the Chinese calendar, the *uposatha* days are observed ten times a month (on the 1st, 8th, 14th, 15th, 18th, 23rd, 24th, and the last three days of the lunar month; alternatively, only six times: on the 8th, 14th, 15th, 23rd, and the last two days of the month). In the Tibetan tradition, *smyung gnas* is more commonly understood as a fasting ritual for laypersons consisting of two days of taking the above eight vows plus complete fasting on the first day (such sets of two days may be repeated several times in a row). Thus, though *poṣadha* is often presented as an exact equivalent of *uposatha*, this is not the case, because the restoration of monastic vows is a separate ceremony solely of monastics, and full monastics have a significantly larger number of vows than the above eight.

1651. The Vinaya distinguishes between "wrongdoings unacceptable by nature" and "wrongdoings unacceptable by proscription." The latter, such as drinking alcohol, are considered wrongdoings only when one has taken a vow not to commit them.

1652. GZ CDNP "Householder bodhisattvas, preceded by [CDNP omit this phrase] taking refuge in the Three Jewels, should refrain from these five: killing, taking what is not given, wrong sexual conduct out of desire, and telling lies (which are natural wrongdoings), as well as the proscribed [I follow NP *bcas pa'i* against GZ *bcos pas*, 'contrived' CD *bcas pas*] [wrongdoing of] drinking beer and [other] intoxicating beverages. Householder bodhisattvas, endowed with aspiration and engagement, should understand the ten nonvirtues well, also make a firm commitment not to commit them, and [instead] perform the ten virtues. When rising at the break of dawn, they should wash their face and so on and recollect the Three Jewels. With OṂ ĀḤ HŪṂ, they protect themselves, their place, and their yoga . . ."

1653. Jambhala, a.k.a. Kubera, is the god of wealth and, with his other alias Vaiśravana, one of the four principal gods of the desire realm at the northern base of Mount Meru (his epithet Jalendra means "lord of water"). There are five forms of Jambhala, in yellow, black, white, green, and red color, and he is sometimes also considered as an emanation of Avalokiteśvara.

1654. Wallis translates "should see that strings of food and water offerings, purified and filled with a *droṇa* of anise, are placed at the bottom of the door," and Mathes 2021 has "should see to it that one Magadha measure full of water and a torma is placed at the bottom of the door." While many Sanskrit words in this passage do have various meanings, GZ CDNP are very clear that *māgadha* here does not mean "anise," but something from the country Magadha (depending on the area, a *droṇa* equals about 10–12 kg), and that *pravartita* does not mean "purify," but "arise" or "become." This is supported by GZ CDNP *re rer* ("each"), which also suggests that *pūrita* does not mean "(ful)filled," but "multiplied." Skt. *sikthaka* usually means "beeswax," but here it is obviously understood as *siktha*, which also means "a lump or mouthful of boiled rice kneaded into a ball," or simply "boiled rice," and definitely fits the context better (Wallis's "strings" is unattested as a meaning of either word). Furthermore, to offer 10–12 kg of boiled rice every day was definitely unaffordable for most people in India at the time, and I doubt that Skt. *paśyet* is used in the English sense of "see to it" (which has nothing to do with seeing something). For these reasons and given that visualization is a common practice (as also the following shows), it seems to make more sense to understand *paśyet* as "should visualize" or "should see as" (this works with the instrumental *māgadhena droṇena*, which is different from the accusative *-sikthakāni* and *pravarttitāni* indicating the direct object). Lastly, it seems to be out of place to use the Tibetan term *torma* in this clearly Indian context.

1655. Piśācas are a class of malevolent demons who are descendants of Kāśyapa and Krodhavaśā and eat raw flesh.

1656. Wallis says "Leaving a triple portion in the vestibule for *pretas* and *piśācas* . . ." GZ CDNP "Thereafter, they should offer to Śrī Jambhala one hundred and eight handfuls of water over which they recited the mantra 'OṂ JAMBHALAJALENDRĀYA SVĀHĀ' one hundred and eight times. Then, they recite the oblation mantra . . . With five streams of nectar [dripping] from . . . they should imagine that the amount of a food bowl with oblation food and water for the hungry ghosts [CDNP omit 'for the hungry ghosts'] dwelling at the door arises as an *āḍhaka* [a quarter *droṇa*] of the country of Magadha for each [hungry ghost]. They should offer these to all hosts of hungry ghosts without exception, snapping their fingers three times each."

1657. Following GZ CDNP and the usual meaning, Skt. *duḥkhāduḥkhahetoḥ* (lit. "the cause of suffering and nonsuffering") is emended to *duḥkhaduḥkhahetoḥ*. Still, *duḥkhāduḥkhahetoḥ* could be understood in the sense of "the cause of suffering and [conditioned] happiness."

1658. GZ CDNP "Now, they should cultivate the love of regarding all sentient beings as if they were their only son, the attitude of compassion whose essence is the intention of pulling them out of the ocean of saṃsāra that consists of suffering and the causes of suffering, the joy that arises from the state of mind of being enthusiastic due to having taken refuge in the Three Jewels, and the equanimity that has the characteristic of completely relinquishing attachment [I follow GZ CD *chags pa* against NP *sogs pa*, 'and so on'] to what is not real."

1659. Skt. *adhiṣṭhita* means both "placed" and "blessed" (see GZ CDNP)—that is, on some part of the ground, a four-cornered "maṇḍala," which here just means a flat surface or platform as a basis for the following visualization, is crafted with cow dung and water and blessed with the mantra.

1660. Skt. *varaṭaka* ("seed of saffron") is emended to *varāṭaka* ("the seed vessel of a lotus").

1661. While Skt. *śyāma* can also mean "dark-colored," "black," and "blue," Amoghasiddhi's color is typically green.

1662. GZ CDNP "With the mindset of being enthusiastic about the welfare of all sentient beings, they pick up pure cow dung, mix it with clean water, and bless the maṇḍala [they craft with it] with OṂ ĀḤ VAJRAREKHE HŪṂ. On any suitable patch of earth, such as a rectangular one, they craft a maṇḍala as they like. They meditate that on top of that [maṇḍala], [arising] in his complete form from a blue HŪṂ on a moon [disk] and a sun disk in the middle of an eight-petaled multicolored lotus . . . Then . . . [arising] in his complete form from a white syllable OṂ, there is Vairocana, making the mudrā of perfect awakening . . ."

1663. GZ CDNP "Consecrating [I follow GZ *mngon par sngags pa* against CDNP *mngon par zhen pa'i sngags pa*] this with OM ĀḤ VAJRAPUṢPE HŪṂ and so on, they should offer the most supreme of everything desirable. These five tathāgatas wear saffron-colored robes and have uṣṇīṣas. They sit on [I follow GZ *la gnas pa* against CDNP *dang bcas pa*] sun disks . . . clearly visible in front of themselves, and in accordance with understanding the meaning of the stanzas of taking refuge in the Three [Jewels], [the practitioner] should recite them in front of these [Jewels]. Here, the stanzas [GZ *tshig* ('words')] of taking refuge in the Three [Jewels] are as follows."

1664. GZ CDNP omit this line.

1665. In the first line of this stanza, GZ CDNP take *vara* ("supreme") in *varabodhicittaṃ* (GZ CDNP *byang chub dam par sems bskyed*, "give rise to the mindset for supreme awakening") as belonging to "awakening," while in *varabodhicārikāṃ* (Tib. *byang chub spyod mchog*, "the supreme conduct for awakening") in the third line, "supreme" is matched with "conduct." However, following the explicit *bodhau cittaṃ* in the third line of the preceding stanza as the common meaning of *bodhicitta* and the parallel expression *varabodi* in both the first and third lines of this stanza, I match "supreme" with "awakening" in both lines.

1666. As GZ CDNP suggest, "noble" could also go with "poṣadha." GZ CDNP:

> I pay homage to the Buddha, the lord
> I pay homage to the protecting dharma
> . . .
> I take refuge in the Three Jewels
> . . .
> I rejoice in the world's virtues

. . .
I give rise to the mindset for supreme awakening
and invite all these sentient beings as my guests
I shall engage in the supreme pleasing conduct for awakening
May I accomplish buddhahood to benefit the world!

I shall confess all wrongdoings
I rejoice in the entirety of merit
I shall remain performing upavāsa, [CDNP "I shall do upavāsa and engage in it"]
the noble poṣadha's eight branches.

1667. GZ CDNP:

Those whose bodies are anointed with discipline's sandalwood,
who are swathed in the garments of dhyāna
and adorned by the flowering branches of awakening,
are abiding in just the ways they please.

1668. While Mañjuśrī's most well-known seed syllable is DHĪḤ (as in the mantra OṂ ARAPACANA DHĪḤ), MUḤ (in Tibetan usually rendered MUṂ) is Mañjuśrī's seed syllable related to his form Vāgīśvara ("Mighty Lord of Speech"; as in the mantra OṂ VĀGĪŚVARA MUḤ). According to Bühnemann 2000a (36), "A variant of the mantra, which consists of the syllables *arapacana* plus a seed syllable ending in a *visarga*, is transmitted as *arapacana muḥ* and appears, e.g., in a *sādhana* of Sthiracakra, a form of Mañjuśrī (cf. SM, p. 94, 15). The syllable *muḥ* is defined as Mañjughoṣa's heart syllable in NY, p. 65, 20. The syllable *muḥ/mūḥ* appears to be derived from the initial letter *m* in the name Mañjuśrī/Mañjughoṣa, and the *u* from the penultimate syllable *ju* of his name."

1669. GZ CDNP "Having said this, with 'OṂ VAJRAMAṆḌALA HŪṂ MUḤ,' they should request [Mañjuśrī] to approach. In this way . . . Mañjuśrī and so forth . . . This is the procedure of the maṇḍala."

1670. GZ CDNP:

. . .
Spreading it well represents discipline
Patience means removing tiny creatures
Vigor is to engage in the activities

Dhyāna is mind made one-pointed at that time
Prajñā is to beautify the complete colors well [CD *tshogs* ". . . the accumulations . . ." NP *mtshon cha* ". . . the weapons . . ."]
By having crafted the maṇḍala of the sages,
they will come to attain the six pāramitās

They will become free from all diseases, will have a golden hue,
be the supreme [I follow GZ *mi'i mchog* against CD *mi'i chos* NP *mis mchod*] of gods and humans, have a blazing glow like the moon,

and born into a royal family with an abundance of gold and
wealth,
having performed such bodily activities [for] the sugatas' supreme
abode.

1671. Skt. *anuśaṃsa* can also mean "praise," which would also make sense here, but GZ CDNP have *phan yon* both here and below.

1672. GZ CDNP:

Having always crafted the maṇḍala
with cow dung, water, and flowers,
offering a bit, they should respectfully
pay homage to the guru at the three times

Delighted by their mindset for others,
they make their own mind flourish too
Happy, with the immeasurables' gems [or "immeasurable gems"],
. . .
They will perfect the six pāramitās,
. . .
will complete immeasurable qualities

These and other benefits will arise in an extensive manner.

1673. The first four texts are very brief sūtras and dhāraṇīs in Tg (in due order, D323, D324, D143, and D141; the *Gāthādvitayadhāraṇī* is more commonly known as *Gāthādvayadhāraṇī*, and the *Ṣaṇmukhī* more fully as *Ṣaṇmukhīdhāraṇī*; for Sanskrit editions and Japanese translations, see Kano 2011, 60–67). The famous *Bhadracarīpraṇidhāna* (*The Aspiration Prayer of Noble Excellent Conduct*) was uttered by the great bodhisattva Samantabhadra and appears in the *Gaṇḍavyūhasūtra*. The abstract for Kano 2011 (2–3) says that, besides the *Kudṛṣṭinirghātana*, these five texts to be recited are also found in Ratnākaraśānti's *Muktāvalī*, and some are included in Sanskrit dhāraṇī collection manuscripts from the Kathmandu valley. The *Ekagāthā*, *Caturgāthā*, and *Gāthādvayadhāraṇī* have independent origins and were later included in such collections. The *Ekagāthā* is already cited in the *Mahāvibhāṣā* and the *Caturgāthā* in Bhaviveka's *Tarkajvālā*. In its shorter version, the *Gāthādvayadhāraṇī* is found in the *Mahāyānasūtrālaṃkāra* (XII.19–23), and its longer version integrates two stanzas from the *Tathāgataguhyakasūtra*. It is unknown when these scriptures were first regarded as a set, but they circulated as such by the time of Maitrīpa and Ratnākaraśānti, and were later transmitted to Nepal as parts of larger collections of texts to be recited. By contrast, in their renderings of the *Kudṛṣṭinirghātana*, neither Wallis nor Mathes realizes that these are names of texts. Wallis translates stanza 17 as follows: "through employing the single-syllable [dhāraṇī] or a dhāraṇī consisting of two verses, one verse, four verses, or that of the six-faced Bhadracaryā, [he should worship] three times of day." Mathes 2021 says virtually the same: "In one verse, four verses, as a *dhāraṇī* in two verses, or as the six-faced Bhadracaryā, three times a day." Thus both also omit that these texts should be recited three times during each of the three periods of the day (Skt. *triṣkālaṃ ca trikālataḥ*).

1674. This could simply be a general reference to reciting a lot of text while not being distracted. However, since prajñāpāramitā has been mentioned in stanza 16, this appears to more specifically refer to the whole range of prajñāpāramitā sūtras, from the *Ekākṣarīmātānāmasarvatathāgataprajñāpāramitā* (D23; its main part consists only of the Buddha saying, "Ānanda, for the sake of the benefit and happiness of sentient beings, retain this 'prajñāpāramitā in a single syllable'—that is, 'A.'") up through the ten-volume *Śatasāhasrikāprajñāpāramitā* (D8) in one hundred thousand ślokas (a śloka consists of thirty-two syllables).

1675. GZ CDNP:

> "With the maṇḍala procedure and so on,
> they should at all times worship and read
> the pāramitā of prajñā that is so perfect
> and should also realize her meaning
> . . .
> and the *Triskandhaka[sūtra]*, three times
>
> By resting within meditative equipoise
> from a single letter to a hundred thousand [I follow GZ against CDNP 'three']
> with a firm mind without any waning,
> the wise read according to what they find

[That is,] they should also worship canvas paintings, books, cast images, and so on of buddhas and bodhisattvas. This is the procedure of worshipping canvas paintings, books, statues, and so on."

1676. As the following shows, Skt. *sañcakatāḍana* (Tib. *tsha tsha* [GZ CDNP *sā tstsha*] *gdab pa*) refers to making sacred stamped clay images of buddhas, deities, maṇḍalas, stūpas, and so on, in which the clay is sometimes mixed with the ashes of revered teachers. The molds used to craft these images are traditionally made out of cast metal or wood. Thus, unlike the literal meaning "hammering a stamp mold" of the Sanskrit may suggest, this section is not about hammering metal molds but about making images by using such molds. Sometimes the images are painted and have either Sanskrit or Tibetan scripts, aspirational prayers, or dedications written on them. For a practical guide to the process of making these images, see https://www.lamayeshe.com/article/commentary-tsa-tsa-practice (accessed August 4, 2021), though some of the mantras are assigned to different activities and others mentioned here are not used. Wallis clearly did not recognize what the text discusses here, instead offering speculations on what he calls "smiting all [objects of worship]" (in the sense of sprinkling mantras with sandalwood water).

1677. Skt. *āhara* in the mantra means "offer" or "deliver" and *āgaccha* means "come!" (matched by GZ CDNP "request to approach"), while *visarjaṇa* means "give," "set free," "discard," "drive out," and "abandon." Thus this refers to calling all buddhas and bodhisattvas (or one's oath deity) and offering the finished clay image. Mathes 2021 follows Wallis "dismissal," which can only be understood as the opposite ("ordering or allowing someone to leave").

1678. This means that one asks all buddhas and bodhisattvas (or one's oath deity), to whom one has offered the clay image, for forgiveness in case one has made any mistakes in making or offering this image.

1679. GZ CDNP "OṂ VAJRĀYUḤṢE SVĀHĀ . . . OṂ ARAJE VIRAJE SVĀHĀ is the mantra for anointing it with oil. OṂ DHARMADHĀTUGARBHE SVĀHĀ is the mantra for putting it into the mold. OṂ VAJRAMUDGARĀKOṬAYA SVĀHĀ is the mantra for shaping it. OṂ DHARMARATE SVĀHĀ is the mantra for the invitation. OṂ SUPRATIṢṬHITAVAJRĀYA SVĀHĀ is the mantra for the request to remain. OṂ SARVATATHĀGATAMAṆIŚVATĀDHIPATI JVALA JVALA DHARMADHĀTUGARBHE SVĀHĀ is the mantra for the consecration. OṂ SVABHĀVAVIŚUDDHE . . . is the mantra for the request to approach. OṂ ĀKĀŚADHĀTUGARBHE SVĀHĀ is the mantra for the request for patience . . ."

1680. GZ CDNP "OṂ NAMO . . . TATHĀGATĀYA / ARHATESAMYAKSAṂBUDDHĀYA / TADYATHĀ / OṂ SŪKṢME SŪKṢME / SAMAYE / PRASAMAYE / ŚĀNTE ŚĀNTE / DĀNTE DĀNTE / SAMAROPE / ĀNĀLAMBHE / TARAMBHE / YAŚOVATI / MAHĀTEJA NIRKULE / NIRVĀṆA / SARVABUDDHĀDHIṢṬHANĀDHIṢṬHITE SVĀHĀ." In *A Compendium of Beginner Activity* (appendix 1), a very similar mantra is prescribed for making stamped clay images.

1681. Skt. *dhāraṇī* either refers to the power of total recall (remembering every word of dharma and its meaning ever heard or read), is used as a synonym for mantra, or indicates a genre of texts.

1682. GZ CDNP "If they build a caitya reciting this dhāraṇī up to twenty-one times over clay or sand, they will attain the merit of having built as many tens of millions of caityas as there are infinitesimal particles . . . That is what the bhagavān Vairocana declared. This dhāraṇī is of immeasurable benefit."

1683. This is the famous stanza (or dhāraṇī) of dependent origination (*pratītyasamutpādagāthā*):

> YE DHARMĀ HETUPRABHAVĀ HETUṂ TEṢĀṂ TATHĀGATAḤ HY AVADAT TEṢĀṂ CA YO NIRODHA EVAṂVĀDĪ MAHĀŚRAMAṆAḤ

In the *Mahavagga* section of the *Vinayapiṭaka* of the Pāli canon, it is said that it was first spoken by the arhat Aśvajit (Pāli Assaji) in answer to Śāriputra asking him about the Buddha's teachings. When hearing it, Śāriputra immediately attained the realization of a "stream-enterer." When he later conveyed this dhāraṇī to Maudgalyāyana, the latter attained the same realization. Upon that, they went to the Buddha and asked to become his disciples. As Boucher 1991 points out, many archaeological finds show that the practice of making miniature stūpas and clay images inscribed with this dhāraṇī was very common in medieval Buddhist India (c. 600–1200 CE). There is even a sūtra in Chinese, called *The Sūtra on the Merit of Building a Stūpa Spoken by the Buddha*, in which this dhāraṇī is spoken by the Buddha and said to be placed inside stūpas. The Buddha also explains its meaning as follows: "This verse signifies the *Buddha-dharmakāya*. You should write [this verse] and place it inside the *stūpa*. Why? Because all causes and *dharma*-nature of all things that are produced are empty. This is the reason that I call it the *dharmakāya*. If a living being understood the import of such causes, you should know that this person would then see the Buddha" (trans. Boucher, 9–10). No Sanskrit of this sūtra exists, but the *Pratītyasamutpādasūtra* (D212) in Tg closely parallels the Chinese. Anupamarakṣita's *Ādikarmapradīpa* also contains a passage almost identical to the one here: "Reciting this dhāraṇī twenty-one times over lumps of clay or lumps of sand, they should build a caitya [with them]. [Thereby,] as many infinitesimal particles as there are in this lump, that many tens of millions of caityas become created. Furthermore, they should consecrate it with this stanza: 'As for phenomena . . .'"

1684. In *A Compendium of Beginner Activity* (appendix 1), a very similar mantra is prescribed for circumambulating.

1685. GZ CDNP ". . . if they utter this dhāraṇī '. . . TATHĀGATĀYA ARHATE-SAMYAKSAMBUDDHĀYA . . . MAHĀRATNE RATNASAṂBHAVE [CDNP RATNABODHI] SVĀHĀ' and thus pay homage to the caitya and so on, through paying homage and so on to a single caitya, they will pay homage and so on to tens of millions of caityas. This is the procedure of building caityas out of clay and so on."

1686. GZ CDNP "They should dedicate through the great dedication that is mentioned in the prajñāpāramitā [sūtras]—that is, a special fruition will arise and come forth from dedicating all these [merits] in a distinguished manner. They should say the following: 'Just as the tathāgata arhats, the completely perfect buddhas, know exactly which types, which categories, which characteristics, and which natures the roots of virtue that they see and know through their buddha wisdom and their buddha eye are and through which dharmatā they exist, so I too rejoice in them. Just as they dedicate these roots of virtue to unsurpassable, completely perfect awakening, so I too shall dedicate them . . .'"

1687. GZ CDNP:

> By means of this virtuous action I have committed,
> may I become a buddha in the world before long,
> teach this dharma in order to benefit the world,
> and free all beings tormented by many sufferings.

1688. I follow Maitrīpa 1927 *kṣāntyarthaṃ* (*kṣantarthaṃ* in one ms.) versus *kṣutyarthaṃ* (*kṣuti* means "sneezing"). GZ CDNP:

> . . .
> the livelihood that is pure will be victorious
> . . .
> in order to dispel hunger, thirst, and so forth.

1689. Hārītī is mentioned as a powerful yakṣiṇī, rākṣasī, or bhūtamāta in a number of Buddhist texts (such as the *Saddharmapuṇḍarīkasūtra*, *Suvarṇaprabhāsottamasūtra*, *Mañjuśrīmūlakalpa*, *Mahāmāyūrītantra*, the *Mahāvastu*, and the Vinaya). As mentioned before, in Indian mythology, yakṣas are a class of normally benevolent and helpful but somewhat fickle spirits who live on the earth (often in forests), in the air, and in the lower divine realms. Exceptions to their benevolence are that they may cause epidemics or possess humans, and some of them even eat human flesh. Rākṣasas are fierce demons who are of giant size, have two fangs protruding from the upper jaw, sharp, claw-like fingernails, and eat human flesh. They usually are able to fly, vanish, change size, and assume the form of any creature. Bhūtas are mostly malevolent ghosts, often the spirits of the untimely deceased (bhūtamāta means "mother of spirits"). The story of Hārītī says that she snatched human children every day and fed them to her own five hundred children. Supplicated for help by the mourning mothers, the Buddha hid Hārītī's youngest son under his alms bowl. Having desperately looked for him for a long time, she finally asked the Buddha for help. The Buddha said he would help her if she gave up killing children, to which she agreed. He pointed out that she suffered because of having lost just a single one among her many hundreds of children, and that she should imagine the suffering of parents whose only child is eaten. She realized that such suffering must be far greater than her own and took an oath to protect all children from now on. Thus Hārītī became the protectress of children and women in childbirth, and the Buddha also granted her the ability to cure illness. In addition, to provide her and her children with food, the Buddha ordered his monks to give them enough food every day. Thus, traditionally, monastics offer a part of their food to Hārītī.

1690. GZ CDNP "Thereafter, by saying . . . over their food, however they may have obtained it, they should offer an oblation. Thereafter, by saying . . . they should give the food offering. Saying . . . they should offer two rice balls. Saying 'OṂ ĀGRAPIṆḌI ASĪBHYAḤ SVĀHĀ,' they should offer a third choice rice ball. Thereafter, they should bless the food in their own bowl by saying 'OṂ AH HŪṂ' and touch it first with their thumb and ring finger until any defects such as poison become pacified. After that . . . by saying 'OṂ UCCHIṢṬAPIṆḌĀSĪBHYAH SVĀHĀ' . . . They should discard the other leftovers without blessing them. For the following is taught."

1691. GZ CDNP:

Giving the oblation, making the food offering,
including the choice rice balls for Hārītī,
and giving the fifth, which is the leftover,
the fruition will become great enjoyment.

1692. GZ CDNP ". . . with a mind endowed with completely pure happiness and special bliss, they should say the following up to three times in order to benefit all sentient beings and make them happy."

1693. GZ CDNP:

. . .
always obtain long lives, be free
from illness, prosper, and be happy!

1694. I follow the ms. reading *vā sārdham dinam uddinam vā* against *vā sārdham dinamaddīnam vā* and *vā sārdham dinam anudinam vā*. On its own, *sārdham dinam anudinam* ("half a day every day") would make sense, but not with the double *vā* ("either . . . or"); it could also be that *sārdham dinam* is supposed to mean "every other day," in contrast to "every day." In any case, it is clear that the period in question here refers to all or part of the time after lunch until evening.

1695. The Jātaka tales are episodes from the former lives of Buddha Śakyamuni. The Nidānas present the circumstances that led to a certain teaching of the Buddha, such as someone asking him a particular question or someone having committed a certain misdeed (as in the Vinaya; the term "nidāna" also refers to the introductions of Buddhist sūtras). Avadānas are described by Richard Salomon (2018, 229) as "stories, usually narrated by the Buddha, that illustrate the workings of karma by revealing the acts of a particular individual in a previous life and the results of those actions in his or her present life."

1696. Skt. *yugakārādimantreṇa* (lit. "with the mantra of making a pair and so on") is unclear but, given the context of oblation, should be emended to *akārādimantreṇa*—that is, the mantra "OṂ AKĀRO MUKHAṂ SARVADHARMĀṆĀṂ ĀDYANUTPANNATVĀT OṂ ĀḤ HŪṂ PHAṬ SVĀHĀ" already mentioned above in a similar context. Disregarding *yug-*, Wallis 2003 and Mathes 2015 interpret this phrase as "the mantra beginning with the letter *a*," which is a hybrid of the Sanskrit and GZ CDNP *dang po'i yi ge a la sogs pas* ("with the first letter *a* and so on").

1697. GZ CDNP ". . . Later, with a very settled mind, they should spend time with common activities by relying on spiritual friends and [discussing episodes from] the Jātaka [tales], stories, Nidānas, and Avadānas during the day, at night, or at noon. Then, in the later afternoon, in accordance with their realization [GZ *rtog* em. *rtogs*; omitted in CDNP], they should perform recitations, praises, and so on with a mind lacking weariness. They should offer an oblation with the first letter *a* and so on and sleep . . ."

1698. GZ CDNP omit this sentence. In the classical fashion of Indian hermeneutical etymology, each contains as its key terms words that begin with the letter or syllable to be explained: each line (*pāda*) of the four following stanzas begins with a word that starts with the letter or syllable to be explained (stanza 20 even contains five words beginning with *u*, and stanza 20 has six words beginning with *s*). Stanza 20 shows four words beginning with *upa*: *udyukto buddhapūjāyāṃ upaśāntopaśāyakaḥ / upakārāya sattvānām upāyenānvito bhavet //* (*upaśāntopaśāyakaḥ* is a compound of *upaśānta* and *upaśāyakaḥ*). Wallis (220) comments here: "The classic definition of *upāsaka* is found at *Aṅguttaranikāya* viii.25. There, a lay follower asks the Buddha to explain the actions and virtues that constitute an *upāsaka.* The answer given by the Buddha is not fundamentally different from that provided by Advayavajra throughout the *Kudṛṣṭinirghātana*: an *upāsaka* is one who takes refuge in the Buddha, Dharma, and Saṅgha; who fulfills the five precepts (abstaining from the destruction of life, etc.); and who 'lives for the welfare of both himself and others' (i.e., he possesses particular virtues, such as faith and generosity, and assists others in gaining them, he examines the teachings and reflects on their meaning, and encourages others to do so, and so on)." Note here that the term "upāsaka" is used for nonordained lay practitioners in Śaivism and Jainism as well.

1699. Skt. *pāpānāṃ varjayed nityaṃ pāpiṣṭhaiḥ saha saṃgatim / pāpān nivārayej jantoḥ pāpaṃ sarvatra deśayet //*. Wallis 2003 and Mathes 2021 (maybe following the ambiguous Tibetan) translate the third line as "avoid evil people." Though that is not impossible, it would simply be a repetition of the second line and thus redundant. Moreover, the meanings of *nivārayet* that are constructed with an ablative (or rarely an accusative) are "hold back from," "prohibit," "hinder," "prevent," "stop," and "suppress" (in this line, *pāpān* can be taken as an accusative plural or, with the sandhi, as an ablative singular, while *jantoḥ* could be an ablative or genitive). Thus, "hold people back from their wrongdoings" seems to be a more cogent reading. Furthermore, GZ CDNP *skye bu sdig pa spong bar byed* is also more likely to have this meaning: as *sdig pa can* in the second line shows, if the third line meant "evil people" or "people with wrongdoing," it would be much more likely to read *skye bu sdig can* rather than *skye bu sdig pa* (which reads more naturally as an implied genitive *skye bu'i*). Finally, given that the other stanzas here clearly define an upāsaka in Mahāyāna terms, such as "being endowed with the methods to bring benefit to sentient beings," "completely maintaining compassion," and "performing utmost benefit," it is only logical that such an upāsaka would not just avoid wrongdoers but also prevent them from committing wrongdoing.

1700. Skt. *samāropavinirmuktaḥ samādhau susamāhitaḥ / sarvadā paramānandī saṃbodhiṃ sādhayed budhaḥ //*.

1701. Skt. *karoti sarvadā yatnaṃ karuṇāṃ paripālayet / kaṣṭenāpi na cāniṣṭaṃ karoty upakṛtim parām //* (*karoty upakṛtim parām* can also mean "extend utmost kindness"). GZ CDNP:

> *u*
> The upāsakas are always engaging
> in revering buddhas and are peaceful
> because they are fully endowed with the
> entirety of benefiting sentient beings
>
> They always abandon wrongdoings,
> abandon company with wrongdoers,
> prevent the wrongdoings of people,
> and always confess wrongdoings
> . . .
> By exerting [CDNP *'bad med*, "effortless"] themselves at all times,
> they completely maintain compassion
> Even if they suffer, it's not undesirable—
> they will perform the utmost benefit.

1702. Mathes 2021 follows the Tibetan in reading the passage from "have abandoned" as a stanza.

1703. "A person of illusion" can refer to an illusory person or, more probable here, a person (such as a magician) who is skilled in creating illusions—that is, displaying and working with them while always being aware that they are unreal fabrications. GZ CDNP "These statements [describe the term] upāsaka in terms of this word being endowed with the meanings of its four syllables. [Also, the following] is said:

"They are to abandon acts of wrongdoing [CDNP omit this line]
and perform actions that are virtuous,
gather the accumulation of merit and,
by familiarity's power, as if awake,
perform virtue even in their dreams

Seeing the entire world as being
just like a stainless reflection,
they do everything like a person
of illusion [CDNP *smra ba* ("speaking")] while not observing anything
Therefore they are irreversible."

1704. GZ CDNP "Thus, by always . . . they remain as the causes of sentient beings' benefit and happiness until [reaching] the heart of awakening."

1705. Skt. *viprajanyaḥ* is understood here as *viprajanaḥ*.

1706. As mentioned before, according to BKC (vol. *ka*, fol. 203b.1–4), stanzas 25–27ab refer to Maitrīpa composing the **Advayavajrasaṃgraha*: when Maitrīpa was accused for his approach of utter nonabiding, disregarding the aspect of means and representing the view of extinction, the brahman paṇḍita Gaganagarbha in Bodhgayā (here referred to as Vajrapīṭha), learned in Madhyamaka, requested that he compose a compendium of initial activity. The preface in Śāstrī's edition (Maitrīpa 1927, vii) renders the bulk of these stanzas in a different way: "There was a Paṇḍita named Gaganagarbha, a follower of the Mādhyamika system of Philosophy. A well-meaning man named Viprajanya coming from Vajrapīṭha requested Gaganagarbha to write a book on the duties of the initiated. He wrote a large work and at his request Advaya shortened it, appending a few notes which have made the meaning of the author clear." GZ CDNP:

The one greatly merged with the actuality
of Madhyamaka is called Gaganagarbha,
resting in equipoise in initial activity
and cultivating a committed mindset

Having arrived from Vajrāpīṭha,
of brahman caste, with a peaceful mind,
requested by him, I composed this *Initial Activity* [CD omit this line]

Through me having taught just a few words on this procedure
of the initial activity as it was requested by Gaganagarbha,
having familiarized with awakening, may the blurred vision
of the stains of the mind of afflicted wrongdoing be rid for sure!

Through whatever merit I have attained
through this procedure of initial activity,
may those who possess this initial activity
as well as [all] beings attain nonduality!

1707. Skt. "This concludes 'Eradicating Bad Views.'" CDNP ". . . Mahāpaṇḍita Advayavajra. It was translated by the Indian [NP omit "Indian"] upādhyāya

. . ." In BKC (vol. *ka*, fol. 214b.1–5), we find the following concluding remarks on this text and how it differs from *A Compendium of Beginner Activity*: "In *Eradicating Bad Views*, [Maitrīpa] presents the path and the fruition by way of the classification into learners and nonlearners and then explains how the fruition—the nonconceptual kāyas and wisdoms—promotes the welfare of sentient beings. Though the fruitional level of nonlearning may be revealed, as far as the path that accords with that (the emptiness that is endowed with all supreme aspects) is concerned, through a path in which means [the first five pāramitās] and prajñā are separated, there is bondage, but through the path that combines them, there is freedom. As for the means, conduct needs to be connected to the [appropriate] time, and the conduct of beginners consists of these [means]. In his *Compendium on [Beginner] Activity*, [Maitrīpa] briefly explains the progressive stages of how beginner persons who have entered the path of mantra perform activity during their [meditation] sessions and the periods in between. [Furthermore,] for you who wish for native connate wisdom to arise in yourselves thanks to the accumulations of merit you accomplished in this manner and [through] the blessings of the guru, it must [also] be explained that there are points of wrong training." For further comments and details, see Mathes 2015 (7, 41–49).

1708. PDMT, 26:305–8. GZ *ku dṛṣṭi ni ra ga ta ṭī kā* CD *ku dṛṣṭi nirga ta ṭī kā* NP *ku dṛṣṭi nirga ta ti ba*.

1709. There is no opening homage in the Sanskrit.

1710. The passage beginning with the first instance of "the state of promoting the welfare of sentient beings" up through "the causal state" is missing in the Sanskrit.

1711. GZ CDNP "the generation of the mindset of supreme awakening and extends up through dwelling in the heart of awakening."

1712. NP omit "all."

1713. GZ CDNP *nye ba'i dka' ba* em. *nye ba'i ka ba*.

1714. The last two sentences are missing in the Sanskrit.

1715. GZ CDNP "investigations."

1716. In GZ CDNP, this stanza is in prose, and the first two lines read: "The four of the disposition . . . and the patience of not being bothered by suffering are the four causes."

1717. GZ "These ten phrases teach the meaning of that—that is, the state of the superior intention." CDNP "This is taught through these ten phrases—that is, the state of the superior intention."

1718. The phrase "the ten pāramitās . . . engagement through aspiration and" is missing in the Sanskrit. The technical term "engagement through aspiration" usually refers to both the paths of accumulation and preparation or, as in this case, the path of preparation alone.

1719. *Madhyāntavibhāga* V.5. GZ CDNP have this stanza in prose.

1720. GZ "The excellencies of the generosity when having attained the bhūmis are the excellencies of intention, application, distinctiveness of the aids, taking care, and generosity." CDNP "The four excellencies when having attained the bhūmis are the excellencies of intention, application, taking care, and generosity."

1721. GZ CDNP omit "the state of."
1722. GZ CDNP "Those dwelling in the causal state—beginners— should perform all [of this]. Those dwelling in the fruitional state and . . . Śākyamuni, engage in this beginner [activity] without any effort."
1723. Skt. "This concludes 'A Commentary on the [Initial] Passage of "Eradicating Bad Views"' composed by Śrīmat Paṇḍita Avadhūta Advayavajrapāda." CDNP "This concludes 'A Commentary on the Difficult Points [NP add "—or A Recollection—"] of "Eradicating Bad Views"' composed by Śrīmat Advaya, who was well-trained. It was translated by Vajrapāṇi and Tsur." For further comments and details, see Mathes 2015 (7–8, 50–52).
1724. PDMT, 26:323–25. As mentioned before, "illumination" in the titles of the *Yuganaddhaprakāśa* (text 21), *Apratiṣṭhānaprakāśa* (text 24), and *Tattvaprakāśa* (text 35) is to be understood in the sense of "elucidation."
1725. There is no opening homage in the Sanskrit.
1726. GZ CDNP "from conditions."
1727. GZ "as with fire and a kindling stick" CDNP "as in fire [*mi* em. *me*] based on a kindling stick."
1728. GZ CDNP:

> Without being based on a kindling stick,
> a fireboard, and the hands of a person,
> a fire is not established previously—
> it arises in dependence on these.

1729. Mathes 2015 (175nn469–70) glosses "son" as "hatred and so forth" (probably based on oral comments) and reads *sute* as an abbreviation of the absolute locative *sute sūte* (*suta* means both "son" and "begotten," while *sūta* means "born").
1730. GZ CDNP:

> Is ignorance prior to its own [I follow NP *bdag gi* against CD *bdag gis* GZ *bdag ni*] son
> or does ignorance come from the son?
> If it is said that it is prior to the son, [I follow GZ *bu nyid las ni sngar zhe na* against CDNP *bu nyid la ni sngar zhen pa*, "clinging to the son before"]
> then it does not have any substance.

1731. GZ CDNP:

> Though nothing is to be rid or to be adopted,
> conventionally, such is still taking place
> Like illusions, these are without any being
> because conditioned origination is realized.

1732. GZ CDNP:

> Because of nonarising, there is no nature
> What arises from conditions does not cease [I follow CDNP *mi 'gag nyid* against GZ *med 'gag nyid*]

Because being and nonbeing are equal,
it is unity that will be manifesting.

1733. GZ CDNP:

. . .
is not produced by your own thoughts
Emptiness and lucidity
constitute natural unity.

1734. GZ CDNP:

Being directly aware of the profound
and native emptiness that is endowed
with all supreme aspects is the superb
application of venerating the buddhas.

1735. GZ CDNP "those with good mind."

1736. Skt. "This concludes 'An Illumination of Unity.'" CDNP "This concludes 'An Illumination of Unity' composed by master Avadhūtī. It was translated by Vajrapāṇi and Nagtso." According to Tipi Bumlabar (BKC, vol. *kha*, fol. 86b.3–6), the outline of this text is as follows:

1. the stage of ascertaining the view
a. dependent origination being nonarising
b. the justification of nonarising
c. the latent tendencies of ignorance do not exist substantially
2. the stage of making it a living experience once it has been ascertained
a. the actual samādhi
b. unity not being concocted by mind
c. veneration by way of practice
3. the stage of enhancing the conduct.

In BKC (vol. *kha*, fol. 34b.2–6), the text is followed by an anonymous brief commentary, probably also by Tipi Bumlabar: "The main topic of *An Illumination of Unity* is as follows. If it is realized that all phenomena that may appear are naturally pure from the very beginning, for the wisdom that realizes this, there is no change. Since the phenomena of seeming [reality] that arise from conditions [*skyon* em. *rkyen*] appear as unity, they are also called 'nonarising.' [On the unity of the two realities, compare Sahajavajra's *Tattvadaśakaṭīkā* (text 46, 20): 'What is to be realized as true reality is the very unity of arising and nonarising and not just nonarising.'] The establishment of nonarising through the reasoning of dependent origination is taught by 'Form is not found in form . . . phenomena lack any nature of their own' [stanzas 2–5ab]. Then, two lines [5cd] teach that such a realization is the cause of uncontaminated bliss. Next, two lines [6ab] teach that worldly conventions are not in contradiction with that. The following one and a half stanzas [6cd–7] teach that the meaning of dependent origination is unity. Then, one stanza [8] teaches that this is not some mentally fabricated emptiness. The next stanza [9] teaches that the realization of unity is the supreme veneration. Then, one stanza [10] teaches that the conduct of unity is the supreme conduct. This should be understood in detail from the ṭīkā [probably referring to a commentary on this text by Tipi Bumlabar, but BKC does not include such a commentary]. One must understand the two ways in which unity appears: either connected or not connected to empowerment." For further comments and details, see Mathes 2015 (16, 175–79).

1737. PDMT, 26:404–6.

1738. I follow GZ *gnas pa bzhir* against CDNP *gnas pa zhes* ("positions"). Though the text does not explicitly mention the two subdivisons each of Yogācāra and Madhyamaka, it presents the nine approaches as found in the *Tattvaratnāvalī*: highest, medium, and lower śrāvakas (stanzas 1–5a); pratyekabuddhas (5bd); Sautrāntikas (6); Aspectarian (7–8) and Nonaspectarian (9) Yogācāras; and Mādhyamikas of illusion-like nonduality (10) and utter nonabiding (11). In addition, text 22 discusses the Mantrayāna (12b–14). However, only some of its stanzas explicitly mention one or more elements of the four subtopics of each of those nine approaches: (1) dhyāna, (2) stains, (3) view, and (4) examination (the latter seems only implied).

1739. "Two" here refers to śrāvakas and pratyekabuddhas. Though it is quite unusual to include all śrāvakas and even the pratyekabuddhas under the Vaibhāṣika school, this is exactly what the beginning of Maitrīpa's *Tattvaratnāvalī* (text 34), upon which the **Dohānidhināmatattvopadeśa* is modeled, says.

1740. GZ *theg pa dman pa'i gtso bo bsgom pa ste* ("the main meditation of those in the lower [Śrāvaka]yāna:") CDNP *theg pa dman pa mi gtsang bam pa ste* ("those in the lower [Śrāvaka]yāna [meditate on] repulsive rottenness") are emended to *theg pa dman pa mi gtsang bsgom pa ste*.

1741. I follow GZ *yan lag brgyad* against CDNP *yan lag rgyas*.

1742. I follow GZ *mya ngan 'das pa zag med lam* against CD *mya ngan pa zag med pa* NP *mya ngan pa gang zag med la*.

1743. I follow GZ *zhi ba* against CDNP *bzhi pa* ("fourth").

1744. In general, the Abhidharma speaks of five "states without mind" (that is, states when mind temporarily ceases): (1) the meditative absorption of cessation, (2) the meditative absorption without discrimination, (3) the state of a god without discrimination, (4) deep sleep, and (5) fainting. Here, this expression refers to the first two of these. "The meditative absorption without discrimination" (Skt. *asaṃjñisamāpatti*, Tib. *'du shes med pa'i snyoms 'jug*) is the highest type of meditation within the fourth dhyāna (performed for a long time, it results in rebirth on the highest level of the gods of the form realm). During it, primary minds and mental factors with an unstable continuum (the five sense consciousnesses, the mental consciousness, and their accompanying mental factors) temporarily cease, while the afflicted mind and the ālaya-consciousness remain active. Thus the latent tendencies for the arising of the first six consciousnesses remain and appearances of delusion will occur again once one rises from this meditative absorption. In "the meditative absorption of cessation" (Skt. *nirodhasamāpatti*, Tib. *'gog pa'i snyoms 'jug*), not only all primary minds and mental factors with an unstable continuum, but also some with a stable continuum—the five sense consciousnesses, the mental consciousness, the afflicted mind, and all their accompanying mental factors—temporarily cease. However, their latent tendencies in the ālaya-consciousness are still present and will re-manifest as further instances of the other seven consciousnesses, including their objects, as soon as one rises from this meditative absorption.

1745. Again quite unusual but in line with the *Tattvaratnāvalī*, the Pāramitāyāna of the Mahāyāna is explained in terms of the tenets of the Sautrāntikas, Yogācāras, and Mādhyamikas.

1746. I follow CDNP *sems tsam* against GZ *sems can* ("sentient beings").

1747. I follow CDNP *rnal 'byor spyod pa* against GZ *rnam par spyod pa* (though this could be a typo for *rnam par dpyod pa*, "analysis," one of the four subpoints of each of the approaches presented here).

1748. This line could also read as "They are present as adverse factors in all respects."

1749. GZ *gnyis med mkha' mnyam* CDNP *gnyis su med mnyam* ("equal nonduality").

1750. GZ *gzugs kyi sku* CDNP *gzugs kyi sa* ("levels of form").

1751. CDNP "The extinction of abandoning self-awareness is their stain." This stanza represents the position of the proponents of illusion-like nonduality.

1752. I follow GZ CD *rnam pa thams cad* against NP *rnam chad*.

1753. NP omit *dpe med* ("unmatched").

1754. This stanza represents the position of the proponents of utter nonabiding.

1755. CDNP "in that primordial bliss is suchness."

1756. NP omit *rang bzhin* ("has the nature").

1757. As mentioned before, for details on this, see Maitrīpa's *Caturmudropadeśa* (text 92, 20–21), the *Caturmudrāṭīkā* (text 44, 287 and 351–52), Rāmapāla's *Sekanirdeśapañjikā* (text 45, 408ff.), Vajrapāṇi's *Guruparamparākramopadeśa* (text 213, 217ff.), and IaS (399–409).

1758. I follow GZ CD *gis bka' stsal* against NP *gi bka' gsal*.

1759. I follow CDNP *dhi ri śrī jñā na* against GZ *dhva ri śrī jñā na*. CDNP "This concludes 'Pith Instructions on True Reality Called "A Dohā Treasure."' Composed by Avadhūtipa, it was translated by venerable Dhiriśrījñāna." In BKC (vol. *ka*, fol. 200b.3–5), this text is followed by a brief conclusion: "The elements of delusion in the tenets of the Vaibhāṣikas up through the Mādhyamikas of utter nonabiding are relinquished by the respectively higher ones, while the good elements are assimilated in such a way that they are included in the higher ones. In the end, adorning the views of Mentalism and Madhyamaka with the pith instructions of the guru, the path of mantra is entered. To unite with the connate that is great bliss is the [ultimate] intention of these texts. Nevertheless, the intention of this master consists of his wish to guide [people] into the Madhyamaka of utter nonabiding. Since there exists Trawo's ṭīkā and outline [*sa bcas* em. *sa bcad*] on this, look [there]" (this seems to refer to Tipi Bumlabar's commentary on Maitrīpa's *Tattvaratnāvalī*; see the notes on text 34). For further comments and details, see Mathes 2015 (21, 263–67).

1760. PDMT, 26:402–3. As mentioned before, the *Prajñopāyadayāpañcaka* and the *Prīṇapañcaka* (text 29) are two variant translations of the same text—that is, the *Prajñopāyapremapañcaka* in the **Advayavajrasaṃgraha* (except for the opening homage and the colophon as found in text 23, my translation follows the Sanskrit). Note also that, as in this title here, Sanskrit titles that contain numerals ending in *-ka* literally mean "a [poem/song] in x [stanzas]," but for simplicity's sake and to avoid clumsy-sounding titles, I throughout render such phrases as "x stanzas."

1761. There is no opening homage in the Sanskrit.

1762. GZ CDNP *'ching 'gyur nyid* ("would be fettered").

1763. GZ CDNP *tha dad 'gyur* ("would be separated").

1764. GZ CDNP *bzhi* ("four").

1765. Skt. *udita* can also mean "appear," "display," and "be experienced."

1766. Skt. "This concludes 'Five Stanzas on the Love between Means and Prajñā'"; GZ interlinear gloss "by Maitreya" (*byams bas*); CDNP says "by master Avadhūtipa Advayavajra." According to Tipi Bumlabar (BKC, vol. *kha*, fol. 85b.4), the outline of this text is as follows:

1. instruction on unity based on worldly conventional expressions (stanzas 1–3)
2. description of its greatness by way of marvelous realization (4–5)

For further comments and details, see Mathes 2015 (19, 207–9) and Brunnhölzl 2007 (137–38).

1767. PDMT, 26:317–19.

1768. GZ CDNP "I pay homage to youthful Mañjuśrī."

1769. These two lines are very similar to *Svapnanirukti* 9ab (text 31).

1770. GZ CDNP:

For what arises from other-exclusion and affirmation
abides within permanence and extinction
Perpetually, it is nonarising and nonceasing
Arising and ceasing are the talk of cattle [GZ *byol song yin*, "are cattle"].

1771. GZ CDNP:

If self-awareness is valid cognition,
awareness is not asserted [GZ CD *'dod ma yin* NP *'dod pa yin*] as a sentient being
Since all appearances have been abandoned,
sentient beings are not real

Note that the use of Skt. *sattva* in lines 1d versus 3bd and 4ab differs ("sentient being" versus "existence"), but GZ CDNP throughout read *sems can* ("sentient being").

1772. It appears that "there" in line 3d and "subsequently" in line 4a refer to meditative equipoise and subsequent attainment, respectively (see also stanza 5). GZ CDNP:

If it is said: "Sentient beings are asserted subsequently,"
then sentient beings are not substantially existent
The meaning of propositions being cut through
and invalidated is expressed as "supposition"

[I follow NP *rjes su btags pa* against GZ CD *rjes su rtag pa* ("subsequent permanence"), which may correspond to *anuvitarkita* or is simply a gross misreading of Skt. *an-ullekkha* ("nondelineation")].

1773. The last two lines in GZ CDNP read as follows:

At first, it becomes free of thought
Due to that, it is the perceiving knower.

1774. The last three lines in GZ CDNP read as follows:

. . . are not existent,
the lord of the worlds taught the world
that they therefore are nonexistent.

1775. The first two lines in GZ CDNP read as follows:

The very arising of phenomena— [GZ "of the actuality of phenomena"]
native self-awareness—is inconceivable.

1776. GZ CDNP:

Just so, "dhyāna does not exist" can't be said
to those whose conduct is nonattachment
For dependently originating phenomena
always arise in accordance with experience.

1777. The last two lines in GZ CDNP read as follows:

Through the division into emptiness, diversity, and mind,
there are the dharma-, sambhoga-, and nirmāṇa[kāyas].

1778. GZ CDNP:

By whatever accumulated virtue [I follow GZ NP *dge ba* against CD *bde ba*, "bliss"] there is
due to having discussed nonabiding,
may beings attain all experiences
as well as nonabiding.

1779. Skt. "This concludes 'An Illumination of Utter Nonabiding.'" CDNP "This concludes 'An Illumination of Utter Nonabiding' composed by master Advayavajra. It was translated by Vajrapāṇi and Nagtso." According to Tipi Bumlabar (BKC, vol. *kha*, fols. 85b.4–86a.1), the outline of this text is as follows:

1. the text that is a discussion
a. ascertaining what is to be known
a1. being free from the extremes of characteristics
a1a. the position of nonabiding nonduality
a1b. teaching that characteristics are empty
a1c. teaching the reasoning of refuting the Mere Mentalists
a2. being free from the extreme of extinction

b. teaching that cause and result accord [*rgyu 'brang rjes su mthu par* em. *rgyu 'bras rjes su mthun par*]
c. the distinctive features of practice
d. the manner of the fruition—the three kāyas—arising
2. conclusion

Following this text, BKC (vol. *kha*, fol. 62a.2–3) concludes: "Nonabiding refers to cognition not abiding in a one-sided [or exclusively fixating] manner: it is realization free from extremes. Other proponents of tenets are steeped in the extremes of permanence and extinction. The Vijñapti[vādins] abide in [the extreme] of mere self-aware mind, while [the Mādhyamikas of] illusion-like nonduality abide in [the extreme of] illusion-like aspects." For further comments and details, see Mathes 2015 (15–16, 169–74).

1780. PDMT, 26:309–10.

1781. There is no opening homage in the Sanskrit. GZ CDNP *rdo rje 'dzin pa* (lit. "vajra holder") could also render *vajradharī* or *vajradhṛk* (an epithet of both Vajrapāṇi and Akṣobhya).

1782. CDNP omit the negative.

1783. GZ CDNP *shes phyir*, "because it is realized, its character . . ."

1784. GZ *dam pa ste* CDNP *dam pa bde*.

1785. GZ CDNP *ston* ("they display").

1786. Skt. "This concludes 'Six Stanzas on the Connate' composed by Paṇḍita Avadhūta, Śrīmat Advayavajrapāda." CDNP "This concludes 'Six Stanzas on the Connate' composed by guru Maitrīpa. It was translated by guru Vajrapāṇi and Tsur [Jñānākara]." According to Tipi Bumlabar (BKC, vol. *kha*, fol. 86a.2), the outline of this text is as follows:

1. the basic nature of knowable objects
2. the manner in which experience arises by virtue of the yoga of peace [*bzhi ba* em. *zhi ba*]
3. the yoga of realization
4. the experience of being without any needs, in which the bearers of this nature dawn as being of equal taste

It is difficult to definitively match these four points with the six stanzas (I suggest they match stanzas 1–2, 3, 4–5ab, and 5cd–6, respectively, but one could also regard 4–5 as "the yoga of realization" and 6 as the last topic; Mathes 2015 (261) translates the four differently and matches them with the stanzas in a different manner). In BKC (vol. *kha*, fol. 27b.1–4), this text is followed by a concluding statement: "[Maitrīpa] holds that, having eradicating appearances of deluded clinging as well as tenets of permanence through scripture and reasoning, by taking the uncontrived connate as the path through the means, the fruition will manifest.

"If you desire to behold the jewel island of unity
at the far end of ocean-like dharma approaches,
you need to enter the ship of this excellent text,
so please approach with analysis and its retinue."

For further comments and details, see Mathes 2015 (21, 259–61) and Brunnhölzl 2007 (139–40).

1787. PDMT, 26:303–4.
1788. There is no opening homage in the Sanskrit.
1789. GZ CDNP *shes pa skad cig ma yod de* ("momentary cognizance is existent").
1790. GZ CDNP *shes par bya* ("should understand"). This stanza teaches the view of Aspectarian Yogācāra.
1791. Skt. *abhāsanāt* GZ CDNP *rnam par snang* ("appears"; obviously reading *ābhāsana*).
1792. GZ CDNP *de ni mtshan nyid kyis ma skyes* (*kyis* appears to render an assumed Sanskrit instrumental in the sense of "as"; a literal reading would be "it does not arise through characteristics").
1793. This stanza teaches the view of Nonaspectarian Yogācāra. According to Rāmapāla's *Sekanirdeśa* (text 45, 391), the nonarising of characteristics is intended to refer to the lack of clinging. Therefore, by virtue of lacking any clinging to entities as being real, unreal, and so on, this awareness is free from the four extremes.
1794. CDNP *de ni* ("that") GZ *dpe ni* ("example").
1795. This stanza teaches the Madhyamaka view of illusion-like nonduality.
1796. GZ CDNP *gzhan dag dbu ma pa ru 'dod* ("it is what the others assert as Mādhyamika").
1797. GZ CDNP *gnyis med mchog tu bde ba'i dngos* ("it has the nature of nondual supreme bliss").
1798. The last three stanzas teach the (correct) Madhyamaka view of utter nonabiding, with the last stanza describing it by combining it with the Vajrayāna notions of "having the character of the deity" and "great bliss."
1799. Skt. "This concludes 'Six Stanzas on the Middle' composed by Mahāpaṇḍita Avadhūta, Śrīmat Advayavajrapāda." For further comments and details, see Mathes 2015 (18–19, 203–5) and Brunnhölzl 2007 (138–39).
1800. PDMT, 26:411–16.
1801. GZ CDNP "I pay homage to Śrī Vajrasattva."
1802. As IaS (76) points out, Pāṇini's rule that Maitrīpa appeals to here is found in *Aṣṭādhyāyī* 6.3.14 (Böthlingk 1998, 336), while the two examples he provides are from the *Kāśikāvṛtti* on *Aṣṭādhyāyī* 6.3.9. GZ CDNP "Most have wrong ideas about this [term] 'mental nonengagement.' Some say that [*amanasikāra*] it is a flawed term—in a compound [I follow GZ *bsdu bas* NP *bsdus pas* against CD *sdug pa'i*] [the appropriate form] should be thought of as *amanaskāra* . . ." The remainder of this paragraph in GZ CDNP is corrupt, and the differences in Sanskrit grammar pointed out here are not reflected at all.
1803. GZ CDNP " . . . 'This term is established by means of [accurate] characteristics, but it is not the words of the Buddha.' This is not the case because it is seen in many sūtras."
1804. As mentioned before, Skt. *kuśala* can also mean "skillful," "clever," "happy," "good," "suitable," "right," and "virtuous" (all Tibetan versions of these recurrent two lines have *dge ba*, "virtuous"). The same two lines as well as the following stanza are also cited (without attribution) in the *Caturmudrānvaya* (text 14, 31) and Rāmapāla's *Sekanirdeśapañjikā* (text 45, 419–20). As they

stand, these lines are not found in the *Jñānālokālaṃkārasūtra*, which only contains the following passage: "All nonvirtuous mental engagement is the cause of afflictive phenomena. All virtuous mental engagement is the cause of purified phenomena" (2004, 94.14–15). For further comments, see the note on these two lines in text 14.

1805. *Jñānālokālaṃkārasūtra* IV.12 (2004, 146.1–2), *Saṃvarodayatantra* VIII.36′ (Tsuda 1974, 101), and *Pañcakrama* IV.10. Without attribution, this stanza is also found in the *Caturmudrānvaya* (text 14, 31) the *Pañcatathāgatamudrāvivaraṇa* (text 36, 194), and the *Sekanirdeśapañjikā* (text 45, 419–20).

1806. D142, fol. 3a.6–7. For a translation of the *Avikalpapraveśadhāraṇī* and parts of Kamalaśīla's commentary, see Brunnhölzl 2012, 329–35.

1807. GZ CDNP "Out of fear of too many scriptural passages of various other sūtras, they are not written down here."

1808. GZ CDNP "This term is a term of the sūtra collections but not of the secret mantra. Why? Because it is seen [only] in the sūtra collections."

1809. I.5.1.

1810. I.8.42ab.

1811. GZ CDNP "Implicitly, it is to be understood that one should not engage mentally." As Mathes 2015 (243n650) says, "Reading *amanasikāra* into the *Hevajratantra* thus prepares the way for extending its semantic range from a pure negation of mental activity and objective support to include direct realization of phenomena, which in the *Tattvadaśaka* are said to be luminous by nature." In that vein, the second two lines of this stanza ("As all phenomena's full knowledge, meditation is indeed not meditation") are quoted in Sahajavajra's *Tattvadasakaṭīkā* (text 46, 38) in order to adduce scriptural support for the nonanalytical "samādhi of reality as it is," which is the effortless unity of calm abiding and superior insight. Most Indic and Tibetan commentaries on the *Hevajratantra* say that this stanza starts the discussion of the yoga of mahāmudrā and emphasizes its character of being free from all imagining or thoughts. Ratnākaraśānti's commentary *Muktāvalī* (Tripathi and Negi 2001, 95) says that the first line just speaks about meditating on the entire world, but the question is through what the ascertainment of this (the siddhi of Mahāmudrā) comes about. Ascertainment is gained because yogīs do not imagine anything (with regard to the world) through the mind—that is, the conceptual consciousness. In other words, those who do not imagine do not meditate. Such full knowledge (nonconceptual direct insight) of phenomena is what is meant by "meditation" here. "Not meditation" refers to "not imagining," since all imaginations are mistaken by their very nature. Kṛṣṇa's *Yogaratnamālā* (Snellgrove 1959, 2:128) basically says the same, glossing that the full knowledge in terms of the connate nature (Skt. *sahajarūpatayā*) is not this kind of meditation (through imagination). Most Tibetan commentaries take the Tibetan of line 44c (*thams cad chos ni yongs shes na*) to mean "When the dharma[tā of] all [phenomena] is fully known." Accordingly, Jamgön Kongtrul's commentary (Kong sprul blo gros mtha' yas 2005, 427) says that this stanza describes the essence of what mahāmudrā meditation is, and he continues: "The other mudrās, such as karmamudrā and dharmamudrā, are mental imputations. Therefore, since connate mahāmudrā is beyond the sphere of anybody's mind, without contemplating by way of the characteristics and imaginations of a mind that is [involved in] rejecting and accomplishing, one should contemplate the entire world—the outer container and the inner contents, such as sentient beings—as being connate wisdom free of discursiveness. Once the dharmatā of all phenomena—the mode of being of the lack of a nature—is fully known in this way, such meditation, which is contrived through the conceptual mind, is not the meditation of true reality. Therefore [the latter] means to meditate on nonarising and such in the manner of a meditator and so on not being observable, free from the extremes of reference points." Though not in a specifically tantric context, but in essence, brought about by virtue of the pith instructions of a qualified guru, this is also what is referred to as "the samādhi of reality as it is" in *Tattvadaśaka* 6b and "this kind of unity of calm abiding and superior insight" in the *Tattvadaśakaṭīkā* commentary.

1812. "Privative" is a grammatical term for a particle or affix expressing absence or negation, such as the Sanskrit prefix *a-* (or *a-* in English "atypical").

1813. One meaning of this is that the wives of the king always have to stay inside their quarters and thus do not see the sun. Another meaning is that, due to their seclusion among women, they do not see anything male, not even the sun (Skt. *sūrya* is masculine).

1814. GZ CDNP "'[The term "mental nonengagement"] exists in the tantras too, since a nonimplicative negation is a nonexistent object, it is to be expressed as a nonentity.' That is not the case. A nonimplicative negation is a negation of an existent entity. Or, a nonimplicative negation is the negation of a consequence that [should] not be a consequence (*thal ba med pa'i thal bar 'gyur bar 'gag pa'o*). This is as in 'the wives of the king do not [CD omit the negative] see the sun,' whose meaning is as follows. It is said that [their not seeing the sun] is not due to them not knowing [I follow GZ *mi shes pas min* against CDNP *mi min*] how [to see the sun]; since the wives of the king are very hidden, they do not even see the sun. The negation here [obviously] does not refer to the nonexistence of the sun. What [does it refer to]? If there were any seeing of the sun by the wives of the king, this is what is negated. In the case of mental nonengagement as well, the existence of mental engagement—perceiver, perceived, and so on—is negated, not the mind [itself]. There is no flaw here." Mathes 2015 (244n653) comments: "It is interesting that such a definition of non-affirming negation allows for a distinction between what is meant to be negated ('what is applicable') and a luminous nature or emptiness of the mind, to which the yogin directs his attention (*manasikāra*), as we shall see further below. This distinction could be well taken as a forerunner of the Tibetan *gzhan stong* ('empty of other') interpretation of emptiness. Likewise, in the case of taking *amanasikāra* as an affirming negation, only a particular aspect of the mind, namely that part of it which is engaged in the normal dualistic process of conceptualization, is negated. This does not entail the negation of all mental processes."

1815. GZ CDNP "When someone explains the following, thinking: 'The characteristics of permanence and extinction constitute mental engagement [CD "mental nonengagement"],' therefore we say: If mental engagement in permanence, extinction, and so on is not engaged mentally, this invalidates all clinging, which is by means of the term 'mental nonengagement.'"

1816. This "quote" is a brief digest of the beginning of the following passage in the *Avikalpapraveśadhāraṇī* (D142, fol. 3b.1–4), being further adapted by weaving in the term "mental nonengagement," which appears repeatedly in that text but not in this passage: "Sons of good family, for what reason is the dhātu of nonconceptuality called 'nonconceptual'? It is due to being beyond all conceptions that analyze, due to being beyond all conceptions in terms of demonstrating and illustrating, due to being beyond all conceptions in terms of sense faculties, due to being beyond all conceptions in terms of objects, due to being beyond all conceptions in terms of cognizance, and due to not being the locus of any afflictive, secondary afflictive, and cognitive obscurations. Therefore the dhātu of nonconceptuality is called 'nonconceptual.' What is nonconceptuality? Nonconceptuality is ungraspable, undemonstrable, unfounded, without appearance, noncognizance, and without base."

1817. On its own, Skt. *kaṭa* can mean a number of things, such as "straw mat," "corpse," "hearse," "plank," and "burning ground." As the text obviously speaks about a person, the term could refer to a straw-mat maker, someone who deals with corpses, or a hearse driver, and so on (all low-caste jobs). Since GZ CDNP *shing rta mkhan* means "wagoner" or "charioteer," I follow this.

1818. GZ CDNP "There is no flaw in the position that [mental nonengagement] is an implicative negation [I follow GZ NP *ma yin par dgag pa* against CD *ma yin par brtags pa*] either. It is obvious that 'Come and bring a non-brahman!' [means] 'Come and bring somebody such as a king, who is similar to a brahman,' not a low-caste person of discordant type, such as a charioteer. Here too, one should rest in the awareness of the lack of any nature. Thereby, this becomes dwelling in the proposition of illusion-like nonduality. [Thus,] from what would the view of extinction follow?"

1819. There is a lacuna in the Sanskrit from "here" up through "negating the world," which is filled in by GZ CDNP.

1820. GZ CDNP "But this is only the convention of nonexistence . . . negating the world. This is to be explained here . . . Thereby, all mental engagement represents *a*, which means being unborn." The expression "vegetable king" (Skt. *śākapārthiva*) means "a king [for whom] vegetables [are the main ingredient in his diet]." In the manner of classical Sanskrit grammar, Maitrīpa analyzes *amanasikāra* as a compound in which the main part (*pradhāna*) has been elided. As Mathes 2015 (245–46n656) says: "This is fully in line with Jayāditya's and Vāmana's *Kāśikāvṛtti* on *Aṣṭādhyāyī* 2,1,60, in which Maitrīpa's example of 'vegetable king' is analyzed as a 'king for whom vegetables are the main thing.' (see KV, vol. 2, 84: *śākapradhānaḥ pārthivaḥ śākapārthivaḥ*) When it is understood thus—that one directs one's attention (*manasikāra*) to the letter *a* as the main [focus]—'*a*' can no longer be the simple privative, but must stand for a more profound negation, such as the one implied by emptiness or nonorigination (*anutpāda*). In other words, the first analysis, in accordance with the *Kāśikāvṛtti*, implies a second analysis of *amanasikāra*, in which *a* is taken as having the nature of *anutpāda*. This suggests that a form of *manasikāra* which is aware of its true nature of non-origination or emptiness is not excluded by the term *amanasikāra*. Padma dkar po's remarks in this regard are as follows: 'The letter *a* being taken to mean non-origination, [the remaining] *manasikāra* is [then] explained as mental engagement. Thus the correct mental engagement [of realizing] the meaning of the letter *a* is "the mental engagement of *a*" (*a-manasikāra*). The middle word [of the compound] has been dropped, just as in the case of calling a king who is fond of vegetables a "vegetable king." *A* stands here for the "perfection of insight" (*prajñāpāramitā*), "not arisen" (*an-utpanna*) and "not obstructed" (*a-nirodha*).' (*Phyag chen rgyal ba'i gan mdzod* 40.18–41.6 . . .). Padma dkar po's analysis of the compound 'vegetable king' is in accord with Jāyakṛṣṇa's *Subodhinī* commentary on the *Siddhāntakaumudī* (no. 739), where we find: *śākapriyaḥ pārthivaḥ śākapārthivaḥ* (SB, p. 178). Maitrīpa's own analysis of the compound as '*manasikāra* for which the letter *a* is the main thing' shows, however, that he followed the *Kāśikāvṛtti*."

1821. GZ CDNP "'Where did the Bhagavān teach [this]?' That the word that has the meaning of being unborn is the letter *a* is as follows. In the chapter on mantras in the *Hevajra[tantra]*, it is said . . ."

1822. I.2.1. This sentence (*OṂ akāro mukhaṃ sarvadharmāṇāṃ ādyanutpannatvāt*) could also be read as "The letter *a* is the source because all phenomena are unborn from the beginning."

1823. GZ CDNP "it arises from within."

1824. V.lc–2b.

1825. II.4.22a.

1826. GZ CDNP "Due to that, since all mental engagement lacks a self, it is said to lack a nature."

1827. GZ CDNP "prajñā."

1828. *Hevajratantra* II.4.44; as the preceding and following lines make clear, "she" here refers to Nairātmyā, who is the nature of the great bliss of connate ecstasy as well as mahāmudrā.

1829. This means that, in this explanation, *amanasikāra* is taken as a *karmadhāraya* compound.

1830. GZ CDNP ". . . Since it is both *a* and *manasikāra*, it is *amanasikāra*. Due to that, the inconceivable state of amanasikāra, which has the character of luminosity and self-blessing, will arise as the awareness . . ."

1831. It is somewhat mysterious how "*An Illumination of Nairātmyā*" (*Nairātmyāprakāśa*) made its way into this colophon, since this is the title of a sādhana for Nairātmyā (the consort of Hevajra) composed by Maitrīpa (D1308).

1832. Skt. "This concludes 'In Support of Mental Nonengagement.'" CDNP ". . . great master Advayavajra. It was completed [CD *bcos pa*, "corrected"] by the Indian upādhyāya Vajrapāṇi and the Tibetan lotsāwa Nyenchung." According to Tipi Bumlabar (BKC, vol. *kha*, fol. 87b.3–4), the outline of this text has seven points:

1. teaching the elimination of the flaw of the term being ungrammatical
2. answer to the statement "it is not [*yin* em. *min*] the dharma of the Buddha"

3. answer to the statement "it belongs to the Mantra[yāna] and so on but has the flaw of being a nonimplicative negation"
4. statements by biased disputants [it is unclear what this refers to in the text because in it, point 3 is immediately followed by point 5]
5. answer to the statement "mental engagement [text: "nonengagement"] [has the characteristics of] permanence and extinction"
6. answer to the statement "it entails the flaw of being an implicative negation"
7. teaching on the letter *a* as the main component by way of a concluding summary.

In BKC (vol. *ka*, fols. 202b.5–203a.6), the text is followed by illuminating remarks on the meaning of mental nonengagement: "*Manasikāra* means mental engagement: it refers to mind as such appearing as diversity. [The letter] *a* represents being unborn. With the two having the same character, [we speak of] *amanasikāra*. Utter nonabiding, mental nonengagement, nonconceptuality, and the inconceivable are synonyms. In the ṭīkā by Drawo [Bumlabar], this is said: 'Mental nonengagement does not refer to the nonexistence of any objects, because it would follow that it is [like] the horn of a rabbit and so on. It does not refer to the nonexistence of cognition, because it would follow that it is [like] a vase and so on. It is not the stopping of any discriminating notions, because it would follow that it is the meditative absorption without discrimination and so on. It does not refer to cessation either, because it would follow that it is [like] fainting and such. It does not refer to some feeble cognition, because it would follow that it is [like] the cognition of a small child. It does not refer to thinking "there is no mental engagement," because exactly that is mental engagement. It does not refer to analysis by means of discriminating prajñā, because [such analysis] is not the path free of thoughts. Therefore mental nonengagement is a realization by virtue of experiencing the heart of the matter and is free from all thoughts. As for the ultimate path of this [mental nonengagement], the thoughts of perceiver and perceived of the mental engagement in the context of illusory body are terminated by the actual luminosity that is the fourth stage [of the five stages of body isolation, speech isolation, mind isolation, luminosity, and unity]. [During the stage of] unity of a learner, there is still [some] mental engagement by way of personally experienced wisdom, but there is no mental engagement by way of thoughts of perceiver and perceived. [Just that is then] called "mental engagement." Since the practice that corresponds to this exists in the pith instructions of this lineage, it should be understood from the mouth of the guru.

> 'Since emptiness and dependent origination are not contradictory,
> mental engagement and nonengagement are not contradictory here
> Having perfected the luminosity that is without any thoughts,
> resting on the path of the unity that is supreme takes place

Moreover, this is said:

> Rid of the extremes of permanence and annihilation
> through the view that consists of utter nonabiding,
> it is the pith instructions for entering the immense
> hosts of merit that shall be explained here.'"

Note that several of the above seven points of Tipi Bumlabar saying what mental nonengagement is *not* match the five points at the beginning of the eighth chapter of the *Mahāyānasaṃgraha*, in the *Dharmadharmatāvibhāga* (lines 216–20), the *Bodhisattvabhūmi* section of the *Viniścayasaṃgrahaṇī* (D4038, vol. zi, fol. 27a.1–7), and the *Abhidharmasamuccaya* (D4049, fol. 117a.2–5), that exclude what nonconceptual wisdom or prajñā is not (the complete lack of mental engagement, mental states beyond the levels that entail examination and analysis, the cessation of discriminations and feelings, having the nature of inanimate form, and picturing true reality (for details, see Brunnhölzl 2012, 135–36, 160, 168–69, 190–91, 270–71, 322–23, and 428–29n707, and Brunnhölzl 2018, 225, 363–64, 747–48, and 1109–11n723). For further comments and details on the *Amanasikārādhāra*, see Mathes 2015 (20, 241–58).

1833. PDMT, 26:328–30.

1834. GZ CD *nir bhe da* NP *nirbe te*; thus the Tibetan rendering *mi phyed* ("the indivisible").

1835. GZ CDNP "I pay homage to the Buddha."

1836. As the comments by Tipi Bumlabar indicate (see final note on this text), "the buddha" appears to be understood here as the "buddha within"—that is, buddha nature or mahāmudrā. GZ CDNP:

> If the buddha is realized, beings become pure
> Those with the realization of the buddha are relatives
> AHO! The buddha is pure in a primordial way.

1837. GZ CDNP "This teaches the essence: terminating the conceptions about remedies, true reality, and the fruition, possessing what is naturally inseparable." As mentioned before, the *Avikalpapraveśadhāraṇī* describes how bodhisattvas enter the expanse of nonconceptuality by relinquishing all coarse and subtle conceptions in terms of (1) nature (perceiver and perceived or the five skandhas), (2) remedies, (3) true reality, and (4) attainment. These four characteristics are relinquished in a gradual manner through analysis, and finally by not mentally engaging in them at all (see Brunnhölzl 2012, 330–31). The last three of these four characteristics are also mentioned at the beginning of Maitrīpa's *Kudṛṣṭinirghātana* (text 19), in his *Tattvaprakāśa* 13 (text 35) and *Sekanirdeśa* 36ac (text 42), in Rāmapāla's *Sekanirdeśapañjikā* on it (text 45), and are discussed extensively in Sahajavajra's *Tattvadaśakaṭīkā* on stanza 7 (text 46, 40–44). The *Avikalpapraveśadhāraṇī*'s general notion of relinquishing conceptual characteristics is likewise quoted in Maitrīpa's *Amanasikārādhāra* (text 27).

1838. GZ CDNP "free from any being and nonbeing." Note that though Maitrīpa describes wisdom here and elsewhere in a positive manner, such as having the nature of effortless compassion, this wisdom is still said to arise in dependence (just like any other phenomenon). This matches his *Pañcatathāga-*

tamudrāvivaraṇa (text 36), stating that the nonabiding awareness (GZ CDNP "self-awareness") of effortless nondual unity too arises in dependence, which marks the flawlessness and superiority of the Madhyamaka view of phenomena's utter nonabiding.

1839. GZ "This explains the own essence of the realization of being inseparable." CDNP "Here, the nature of the realization of inseparability is taught." Given that GZ CDNP render Skt. *pratirūpa* as "essence/nature," among its many meanings (including "image," "resemblance," and even "forgery"), "a model for imitation" seems to be the most appropriate one here. Note that in texts on the progressive realizations on the five paths and the ten bhūmis, "penetrating insight" (Skt. *nirvedha*) is typically associated with the nonconceptual wisdom first attained on the Mahāyāna path of seeing (the first bhūmi).

1840. GZ "of supreme bliss" CDNP "of Cakrasaṃvara."

1841. GZ "This explains the power arising from the utterly inseparable connate" CDNP "This explains the power of the utterly inseparable [I follow CD *shin tu dbyer med pa* against NP *shin tu 'jungs pas*, "due to utter avarice"] connate."

1842. The last three lines in GZ CDNP read:

> By [CDNP "If"] explaining, which people understand?
> If realized, it is changeless,
> appearing as effortlessness.

1843. GZ CDNP "teaches."

1844. GZ ". . . have faith in the words of utter nonabiding, the approach of the profound dharma, are difficult to find."

1845. As Mathes 2015 says, the last line of the Sanskrit is incomplete and restored from the Tibetan. GZ CDNP:

> This is the fruition of cutting to the vitals
> of the threads [I follow GZ *skud* against CDNP *sku*, "kāya"] of the seeds of one's own karma
> I do not inflict any harm upon others—
> AHO, even those I endure!

1846. GZ "This [says that] in order to take care of all sentient beings with minds that are fettered by the knots of the threads of their own karma, bodhisattvas consider them in their minds." CDNP "This [says that] bodhisattvas take care of all sentient beings with minds that are fettered by the knots of the threads of their own karma and consider them in their minds."

1847. Skt. "This concludes 'Five Stanzas on Penetrating Insight.'" CDNP "This concludes 'Five Stanzas on Penetrating Insight' composed by master Maitrīpa. It was translated by guru [Vajra]pāṇi and lotsāwa Mapen [Chöbar]." According to Tipi Bumlabar (BKC, vol. *kha*, fol. 86a.1), the outline of this text is as follows:

    1. the experience of realization
    2. the essence of realizing unity
    3. presentation of cause and result
    4. difficulty to find a person who is a [suitable] support
    5. promoting the welfare of others out of compassion

In BKC (vol. *kha*, fol. 26a.4–26b.2), the text is followed by a short commentary, probably also by Tipi Bumlabar: "The first stanza [teaches] the naturally pure basic element of beings (what is to be purified), the effortless means to purify it, its gradually becoming pure of the stains of thoughts, and the gradual realization of suchness. Through these primary and secondary factors, [there are] the dharma, the saṃgha, and the buddhahood that is purified through the path in such a way. From the perspective of buddhas endowed with threefold purity [natural purity, means of purification, and gradual purity of thoughts] realizing unity, this is taught as the single essence free of thought, which is the unity of the triad of ground, path, and fruition. The second stanza [teaches] the manner in which the common unity of emptiness and compassion is realized. The third stanza explains uncommon emptiness and compassion, the gathering of the vāyu mind of the five cakras within the madhyamā, and the manifestation of its power, which is the seeming illusory kāya; this is pure as luminosity, the power of the connate. As for the fourth stanza, explanations on the experience of luminosity are not something that [can] be understood, but when realized, the unchanging basic nature to be realized is effortless. Nevertheless, let alone realizing it, it is difficult to even find mere faith in it. The fifth stanza [expresses Maitrīpa's] thought: Out of loving-kindness, I cannot endure that sentient beings who are bound by their own karma are mistaken about the state of true bliss. How could I endure even thinking of this? So I shall take care of those to be guided." Note that the comments on the first stanza resemble the second model of the cause-and-effect relationship of the seven vajra points of the *Uttaratantra* as outlined in its stanzas I.23 and I.26: the basic element (vajra point 4; buddha nature) is the cause; awakening, its qualities, and its enlightened activity (vajra points 5–7) are the conditions; and the Three Jewels of Buddha, dharma, and saṃgha (vajra points 1–3) are the results (in the second model in *Uttaratantra* I.3, the first three vajra points are the conditions, while the last three are the results). For further comments and details, see Mathes 2015 (18, 199–202).

1848. PDMT, 26:326–27. As mentioned before, this text is merely a variant translation of text 23.
1849. I follow GZ CD *bde'i* against NP *de yi*.
1850. GZ *gnyug ma* CDNP *rang bzhin* ("nature").
1851. GZ interlinear glosses *kun spangs sam kun 'dar* (Tibetan renderings of *avadhūtī*).
1852. CDNP "This concludes 'Five Stanzas on Love' composed by master Maitrīpa. It was translated by guru [Vajra]pāṇi and lotsāwa Mapen [Chöbar]."
1853. PDMT, 26:314–16.
1854. GZ CDNP "I pay homage to youthful Mañjuśrī."
1855. Skt. *iha* can also mean "in this world."
1856. GZ:

> The wise realize that the world,
> like an illusion, lacks any nature
> It is known with happiness's intent
> Why is this world deluded?

CDNP:

When worlds, like illusions, are nonbeing,
this constitutes actual [CD *dngos* NP *mngon*] buddhahood
Why have the wise, with the intent
of happiness, not freed this world?

1857. GZ CDNP:

A burning house that is an illusion,
having been created by an illusionist,
may appear to be real for some
The wise, like an illusionist, know [what it is].

1858. The last two lines in GZ CDNP read as follows:

They enjoy everything as illusion
because all is realized as illusion.

1859. GZ CDNP ". . . turn into matter."
1860. The last two lines in GZ read as follows:

Because phenomena arise from emptiness,
there is no phenomenon other than being empty

CDNP:

Because [*pa'i* em. *pas*] phenomena arise from [I follow NP *las skyes* against CD *la bskyed*] emptiness,
dharmatā is not other than being empty.

1861. GZ CDNP:

For that reason, through omniscience,
there isn't any decline of buddhahood
By its power of effortlessness, everywhere,
it engages in turning the wheel of dharma.

1862. GZ CDNP:

Refraining from stretching their legs,
as well as abandoning pride and such,
properly abiding in the nonabiding abode,
yogīs [I follow CD *yis* against GZ NP *yi*] are engaging in the dharma.

1863. Skt. *khānapānarasa* could also be understood as "food, drink, and condiments," but GZ CDNP *bza' dang btung ba'i ro* clearly says "the flavor of food and drink."
1864. GZ CDNP:

The bed of the earth, the garment of the directions,
consuming the food of going for alms,
poised readiness for the dharma of nonarising,

and engaging in effortless loving-kindness [I follow NP *brtse* against GZ CD *rtse*].

1865. The last two lines in GZ CDNP read as follows:

> Look at the fruition of this in this life—
> what need to mention the unsurpassable fruition?

1866. The last two lines in GZ CDNP read as follows:

> may the world attain the state
> of nonduality beyond the world!

1867. Skt. "This concludes 'A Discourse on Illusion.'" According to Tipi Bumlabar (BKC, vol. *kha*, fol. 85a.5–85b.2), the outline of this text is as follows:

1. meaning of the text
1a. view
1a1. not being bound by virtue of realizing everything as illusion
1a2. distinctive features of realizing everything as illusion
1b. conduct
1b1. benefit of realizing everything as illusion
1b2. conduct free from extremes
1b3. such realization being one's own and others' welfare
1b4. instruction to engage in the nonengagement in conduct
1b5. rarity of person in whom this does not decline
1b6. the actual conduct
2. concluding dedication of virtue.

In BKC (vol. *kha*, fol. 37a.1–5), the text is followed by a brief commentary, probably again by Tipi Bumlabar: "The meaning of those [stanzas] is that the illusion-like basic nature of all phenomena is bound by those who cling to real existence. Just like illusionists, those who realize reality are free. For example, being free of permanence and extinction is not something made up by the mind, nor is it limited. If the emptiness endowed with all supreme aspects is realized once, this is unchanging, which is due to the power of the basic nature lacking any change. Once found, there is no forgetting it because whatever is seen during the path is seen as true reality, and because, by virtue of realizing all phenomena simultaneously at the point of the fruition, there are not even any impregnations of negative latent tendencies that produce superimpositions. Therefore, since there is no decline of the state of buddhahood, the wheel of the dharma is turned without any effort. Those who strive for such a [state], after having relinquished idleness and worldly excellencies, are instructed to practice in a one-pointed manner and so on. You who strive for this fruition, look at the ṭīkā!" (BKC does not contain any commentary on this text). For further comments and details, see Mathes 2015 (14, 155–58).

1868. PDMT, 26:311–13.
1869. GZ CDNP "I pay homage to the Buddha."
1870. GZ CDNP "the mind of diversity or mind without aspects."
1871. GZ CDNP:

> "Without being realized . . ."
> In the first case, they were known [GZ *shes pa* CDNP *shes bya*, "are to be known"] as permanent;
> In the second case, they would become extinct.

1872. The last two lines in GZ CDNP read as follows:

> The character of lucidity plus mind's diversity [GZ CDNP *sel* em. *gsal*; also, GZ CDNP obviously read *saciccitra-* instead of *sacciccitra-*]
> represents a magnificent experience.

1873. "The active ones" and "they" refer to the seven consciousnesses other than the ālaya-consciousness. GZ CDNP:

> Instantaneous perishing is the ālaya, the root [I follow NP *kun gzhi rtsa* against GZ *kun gzhi tsam*, "the mere ālaya" CD *kun gzhig rtsa*, "the root of scrutinizing all"]
> The appearance of diversity is the active ones
> Being conceived [GZ NP *rnam par brtag* CD *rnam par gnas*, "abiding"] as such and such,
> this very mind is asserted in such a way.

1874. GZ CDNP:

> If dreams are just dreams,
> then actual mind's diversity is falsity [GZ CDNP *sems dngos sna tshogs* seems to read *sacciccitrā-* instead of *syāt ciccitrā-*]
> As [CDNP omit "as"] existence and nonexistence do not operate,
> there is no extinction in lucidity.

1875. GZ CDNP "a name is simply nonabiding."
1876. CDNP *gnyis der byos* ("make into the two").
1877. GZ "four are asserted as what is to be realized" CDNP "four [DP *bzhi* CD *gzhi*, "basis"] are what is to be realized."
1878. GZ CDNP "These diversities . . ."
1879. These two lines are very similar to *Apratiṣṭhānaprakāśa* 1ab (text 24).
1880. GZ:

> The texts on nirvāṇa are to be realized—
> since they are the supreme of all buddhas,
> they are known through self-awareness,
> the guru's words, and the distinctive features of scripture.

CDNP:

> The texts on nonabiding are to be realized—
> since they are the wealth of all Buddhists . . .

1881. Skt. "This concludes 'A Discourse on Dream.'" According to Tipi Bumlabar (BKC, vol. *kha*, fol. 85b.2–4), the outline of this text is as follows:

1. teaching the purpose and the connection as the branch of introducing others
2. meaning of the text
2a. brief introduction by way of questions
2b. detailed explanation by way of answers
2b1. detailed explanation of the manner in which permanence and extinction are eliminated
2b2. detailed explanation of Aspectarians
2b3. detailed explanation of Nonaspectarians
2b4. the means to practice conduct
2b5. detailed explanation of illusion-like [nonduality]
2b6. detailed explanation of utter nonabiding.

Mathes 2015 (14–15) comments: "Maitrīpa discusses here the role the dream example plays in six different philosophical positions. Two of them (Vaibhāṣikas and Sautrāntikas) have to be abandoned, and among the remaining four (i.e., the two Yogācāra and two Madhyamaka tenets), Apratiṣṭhāna-Madhyamaka is considered to be supreme" (as explicitly stated in stanza 9). The positions of the Vaibhāṣikas and Sautrāntikas are refuted in stanza 3, the two Yogācāra tenets of Aspectarians and Nonaspectarians are presented in stanzas 4–5, and the two Madhyamaka tenets of illusion-like nonduality and phenomena's utter nonabiding in stanzas 6–7. Apart from what stanza 8 says ("among the six here, two are to be abandoned"), that the views of Vaibhāṣikas and Sautrāntikas must be abandoned is further concluded by Mathes "from Maitrīpa's statement in the *Tattvaratnāvalī* that tantra can only be practiced on the basis of Yogācāra and Madhyamaka, and thus not Vaibhāṣika and Sautrāntika" (for further comments and details, see Mathes 2015, 159–61).

1882. PDMT, 26:320–22.

1883. GZ CDNP "I pay homage to youthful Mañjuśrī."

1884. GZ *yod dang med pa'i sbyor ba spangs / spangs pa gang zhig dri med pa'i / byang chub rang bzhin rtogs pa gang / de bzhin nyid der phyag tshal 'dud /* CDNP *yod dang med pa'i sbyor bas kyang / . . . de bzhin nyid de phyag tshal 'dud /* are corrupt and difficult to make sense of on their own. GZ means something like:

I pay homage to and salute this suchness,
lacking a connection to existence and nonexistence
This lack is what represents the realization
that has the nature of stainless awakening

The third line in CDNP simply says "It represents the realization."

1885. GZ CDNP *rnam bcas ma yin rnam med min* omit the locative but repeat the negative.

1886. As mentioned before, stanzas 4–5 of the Fourth Shamarpa's *Sixty Stanzas on Mahāmudrā* (Higgins and Draszczyk 2016, 1:166–67) say that those who comment on the true reality of Madhyamaka by holding on to it as being with aspects or without aspects have not understand the supreme Madhyamaka of utter nonabiding unity. The wise ones of this lineage maintained that the mahāmudrā ornamented with the guru's pith instructions shows the essential points of the last turning of the Pāramitāyāna that is in accordance with mantra. This is followed by citing *Tattvadaśaka* 2, so the Shamarpa's remarks here are obviously a commentary on this stanza, explicitly equating the Madhyamaka of utter nonabiding unity with mahāmudrā, as well as on Sahajavajra's stance on this in his *Tattvadaśakaṭīkā* (which says at its beginning that the *Tattvadaśaka* consists of Maitrīpa's pith instructions on prajñāpāramitā [utter nonabiding] that accord with the approach of secret mantra). Furthermore, Gö Lotsāwa's explanation of *Tattvadaśaka* 2 in his commentary on the *Uttaratantra* ('Gos lo tsā ba gzhon nu dpal 2003b, 16.16–17) says that Maitrīpa and Sahajavajra assert that the emptiness taught in Candrakīrti's *Madhyamakāvatāra* is only middling Madhyamaka, while "the emptiness that is awareness" (Tib. *rig pa'i stong pa nyid*) is the approach of supreme Madhyamaka. It is not that what Gö Lotsāwa says here is explicitly stated in this way in the *Tattvadaśaka* or Sahajavajra's commentary. However, *Tattvadaśaka* 5 says—and Sahajavajra comments—that all phenomena are "of a single taste (the single taste of suchness)," "unobstructed (the nature of phenomena being without superimpositions)," and "without abiding (being unborn)," all of which are common equivalents of emptiness in Madhyamaka. Then, the stanza equates all that with phenomena being "luminosity." In his comments, Sahajavajra says that "luminosity, by virtue of being naturally free from stains, refers to self-awareness because [self-awareness] is utterly luminous." This kind of suchness/emptiness is seen through "the samādhi of reality as it is," which is "the path that entails the unity of calm abiding and superior insight." Thus the superiority of Maitrīpa's Madhyamaka lies in the direct experience of the connate unity of emptiness and luminosity. Since Sahajavajra describes this experience as self-awareness, it seems that this is what Gö Lotsāwa had in mind when using his above term "the emptiness that is awareness." Also, Sahajavajra's later disapproving comments on *Madhyamakāvatāra* VII.1, VIII.1ac, and XI.17 in his *Tattvadaśakaṭīkā* make it clear that the cessations Candrakīrti speaks about in those stanzas do not qualify as the unity of emptiness and luminosity or the two realities that Sahajavajra himself propounds.

1887. GZ CDNP *chags pa spangs pa'i rang bzhin nyid* ("It is the nature of having got rid of attachment").

1888. I follow the Sanskrit and GZ against CDNP *'khrul pa las ni chags med gyur* ("Nonattachment is what's born from delusion").

1889. GZ CDNP unusually render Skt. *rūpa* and *arūpa* as *dngos po* and *dngos med* and also omit "because." This stanza plays on Skt. *rūpa*, which indicates not only material or visible form but also any appearance or image in general, also having the sense of a dreamy or phantom shape, a reflection, or a show. It can also refer to the body, characteristics, and the nature of something (as in line 4a, supported by GZ CDNP *rang bzhin*).

1890. NP *thog ma med* ("beginningless").

1891. Skt. *prasthānacitta*, Tib. *'jug pa'i sems*. This term refers to the bodhicitta of engagement (as opposed to the bodhicitta of aspiration). According to Sahajavajra's commentary (text 46), in the context of mahāmudrā, this is the nondual cognition that has the nature of the unity of prajñā and means and engages suchness (the unity of appearance and emptiness or the two realities) as the unity of calm abiding and superior insight, being cultivated through a nonanalytical mind right from the start. In that way, thanks to the pith instructions of the guru, true reality—the ultimate bodhicitta that is the inseparability of emptiness and compassion—is directly encountered.

1892. GZ CDNP *gang phyir de yi* [CD *yang*] *gnas rig pas / de nyid rgyun mi 'chad las skyes* ("since, by being aware of its abode, it dawns from ceaseless true reality").

1893. CDNP *de ltar 'od gsal ba nyid do* GZ *gang phyir 'od gsal nyid du 'dod* ("since even the conceit . . . is asserted to be luminosity").

1894. Skt. *yena tena yathā tathā* GZ CDNP *ji lta de ltar gang de na.*

1895. GZ CDNP only have *kun tu* (probably short for *kun tu rgyu*), thus omitting "roam," saying, "are everywhere just like lions."

1896. Compare *Hevajratantra* I.6.25:

> Even if a titan similar to Indra
> comes in front of them for sure,
> they do not become frightened
> because they roam like lions

Similarly, *Guhyasamājatantra* XVIII.67cd–68 says this:

> Mantrīs should roam like lions,
> with their mind free from fear
>
> For them there is nothing they should not do
> There is also nothing that they should not eat
> Nor is there anything that they should not say,
> nor ever anything that they should not think

Likewise, *Mahāsukhaprakāśa* 16cd states: "Having made [all] entities into gurus, they roam the earth just like lions," which in effect glosses *Tattvadaśaka* 8d with *Sahajaṣaṭka* 6c. Padmavajra's *Guhyasiddhi* VI.40 similarly says this:

> Then, those who are well-grounded in
> the secret siddhi should roam like lions

This is also what Anaṅgavajra's *Prajñopāyaviniścayasiddhi* V.10 declares:

> Then, having arisen in the way they please,
> those who turned away from all clinging,
> whose character is to be joined with reality,
> should roam everywhere, similar to lions.

1897. Compare *Tattvadaśaka* 7cd–9 with *Mahāyānaviṃśikā* 7:

> Once the single taste of the world,
> luminous and unsullied, is realized,
> if you aren't afraid of any thoughts,
> you may live in any way you please

Maitrīpa's *Kudṛṣṭinirghātana* (D2229, fol. 114a.2–114b.8) clearly drives home the point that "the yogic conduct of a lunatic"—the form of conduct of advanced yogīs in which they act as if crazy in order to test their realization and freedom from any worldly concerns—is not at all just some whimsical outrageous behavior but firmly grounded in the basic practices of the Mahāyāna. Maitrīpa says that bodhisattvas must unite means (the first five pāramitās) and prajñā—or emptiness and compassion— throughout their entire training because only the two accumulations of merit and wisdom in union lead to buddhahood. Thus they must engage in all six pāramitās, not just the pāramitā of prajñā. They must abide by the basic practices in a very pure manner, or else they are just nihilists. Though both virtue and nonvirtue have no nature, they must practice virtue and not nonvirtue. In this seeming world, which is like a reflection of the moon in water, at all times happiness is wanted and suffering unwanted. Among bodhisattvas who train on the path, those with the yogic conduct of a lunatic—who aspire to nonconceptual wisdom—engage in the six pāramitās as follows. They practice generosity by giving away everything, including their own bodies; discipline by performing the welfare of all sentient beings through controlling their body, speech, and mind; patience by enduring unbearable heat in the hot hells and so on; vigor by being unaffected by the troubles of the eight worldly dharmas; dhyāna by resting in the effortless flow of the natural taste that matches the nature of all things; and prajñā by realizing that all phenomena have the characteristic of being unobservable. Within the single taste of effortlessness, they engage in all supreme pāramitās. Therefore the basic practices are definitely to be engaged in even by those who adopt the yogic conduct of a lunatic. Maitrīpa concludes that he thus does not subscribe to the position of the Cārvākas (materialistic hedonists) who deny a world beyond this one and say that all such practices are pointless. Compare also the extensive discussions of "the conduct of a lunatic" in some of the "Siddhi Texts" (such as the *Guhyasiddhi*, *Prajñopāyaviniścayasiddhi*, and *Jñānasiddhi*).

1898. Skt. "This concludes 'Ten Stanzas on True Reality.'" CDNP "This concludes 'Ten Stanzas on True Reality' composed by master Avadhūtipa Advayavajra. It was translated by guru [Vajra]pāṇi and Tsur [Jñānākara]. Later, it was [re] translated by lotsāwa Tsültrim Gyalwa." According to Tipi Bumlabar (BKC, vol. *kha*, fols. 86b.6–87a.1), the outline of this text is as follows:

1. expression of homage
2. meaning of the text
2a. a discussion that explains suchness
2b. unity's own essence
2c. removing the flaws of disputes about it
2d. application of samādhi
2e. application of enhancement
3. concluding summary.

For Sahajavajra's detailed commentary on the *Tattvadaśaka* and Tipi Bumlabar's subcommentary, see text 46 and its notes in volume 3. For further comments and details, see Mathes 2015 (19–20, 211–240).

1899. PDMT, 26:3314–34. As mentioned before and as the text will show, different from the *Yuganaddhaprakāśa*, *Apratiṣṭhānaprakāśa*, and *Tattvaprakāśa*, "illumination" in this title refers to the actual luminous manifestation of great bliss in one's experience.

1900. There is no opening homage in the Sanskrit.
1901. The last two lines in GZ CDNP read as follows:

> I shall explain great bliss, which summarizes
> the true reality of entities, as nonduality [CDNP omit "nonduality"].

1902. GZ CDNP "perfection."
1903. GZ CDNP have this line as "is what I shall describe here."
1904. With Mathes, I understand *vinyasa* as the opposite of *nyāsa* (GZ *rnam par* CDNP *de* for the Skt. prefix *vi-* are misleading here).
1905. GZ CDNP "for the sake of inner realization."
1906. GZ CDNP have the first two lines as follows:

> As for what is asserted as the essence of bliss,
> if actual [CDNP omit "actual"] bliss did not exist, awakening wouldn't [either].

1907. The last two lines in GZ CDNP read as follows:

> Therefore it is said that it is a nonentity
> Bliss is neither existent nor nonexistent.

1908. GZ CDNP:

> First of all, this constitutes nonarising,
> which is the ultimate of phenomena
> It's the delusive display of pleasure that [CDNP *bde ba brdzun par gsal ba ni* GZ *bden pa rdzun par mi gsal ba*, "reality displaying in a delusive way"]
> is to be understood as the pure seeming.

1909. GZ "This purity of the two realities is . . ." CDNP "This very reality is pure . . ."
1910. GZ "This is to be established as nonduality."
1911. CDNP "the ultimate has been cast off."
1912. GZ CDNP "have gone to that bliss."
1913. The last two lines could also be read as follows:

> Therefore it is in such a fashion that they see
> the diversity that is illusion-like and nondual

GZ:

> Then, as it is illusion-like and nondual,
> they should regard diversity as such.

1914. GZ CDNP:

> Then [GZ "there"], they enter the true end
> and will come to realize the state of unity
> Those yogīs who are dwelling in unity
> make efforts for beings' welfare alone.

1915. Mathes 2015 (183n490) says: "According to Kuladatta's *Kriyāsaṃgrahapañjikā*, chapter 6 (6.6.6.), prose after verse 14, the term is listed as the last of four *cakras*: *vajracakraṃ ratnacakraṃ padmacakraṃ viśvacakraṃ*." Another more common meaning of *viśvacakra* is a wheel made of gold that represents the entire universe, usually offered as a precious gift.

1916. GZ CDNP:

> The blissful mind involves the deity yoga [*lha yi rnal 'byor pa*, lit. "is the yogī of the deity"]
> The cakra of diversity serves as the means
> Prajñā is designated as being "emptiness"
> This is held to be what I need to accomplish.

1917. GZ:

> True reality with its character of prajñā and means
> consists of external and internal purity—
> in brief, this should be understood by mantra
> practitioners with the yoga of nonabiding bliss [or "the nonabiding yoga of bliss"]

CDNP:

> External and internal purity's true reality
> has the character of prajñā and means
> It is the yogīs of nonabiding bliss who
> should understand this in such a way.

1918. GZ has the last line as "has the nature of being without any nature." The last two lines in CDNP read:

> appearances whose nature it is to be
> without nature are the yoga of deities.

1919. The last two lines in GZ say:

> Any cognitions of duality and nonduality
> are free from any mental imprints

CDNP:

> The cognitions of duality and nonduality
> are free from the mental imprints of that [NP "are the fruitions of the mental imprints of that"].

1920. NP *he ru ka yi rnam byed pas / gnas /* ("since they assume the form of the Heruka . . . resting").
1921. GZ "those with insight abide just like lions."
1922. Mathes 2015 renders Skt. *cakre* as "made" and comments by quoting the *Hevajratantra*: "The Tibetan did not render *cakre*, probably taking it as a locative ('in the circle') and thus as a redundant modifier. For the concept, that the lord of the circle, i.e., Heruka, 'made' the world, see HT 1.8.41 . . . 'This entire world arises from me. The three parts of the world arise from me. Everything is pervaded by me; the visible world consists of nothing else.'" While the

notion that the world is a manifestation of Heruka (or any other lord of a deity maṇḍala) is of course well-known in the Vajrayāna, a common meaning of Skt. *cakra* is "world" or "realm." Thus I see no problem with *cakre* being a locative here, in the sense of "the lord of this world (*cakrādhipa*) [dwelling] within this world," which, as the first line says, is nothing but a manifestation of its own natural purity (or, in other words, of Heruka's purity). GZ CDNP:

> Thanks to its purity, this utter diversity is always inexpressible by the pure victors [CDNP "The purity of the victors, always and everywhere, appears as these diversities"]
> Primordially unarisen and unceasing, throughout millions of eons . . .
> It is certain as this entity [CDNP "Since it has the nature"] of nonduality, being the equality of existence and peace, appearing as real and delusive [NP "appearing as delusive bliss"]
> This cakra lord is the basis of the qualities of the victors, the vajraḍāka, and the mighty Sage [CDNP "This will certainly be the cakra lord, the mighty Sage of the qualities of the victors, and the vajraḍāka"].

1923. Skt. "This concludes 'The Illumination of Great Bliss.'" According to Tipi Bumlabar (BKC, vol. *kha*, fol. 86b.2–3), the outline of this text is as follows:

1. expression of homage and commitment to compose
2. meaning of the text
2a. those of lower faculties meditating on unity in terms of the deity
2b. those of medium faculties meditating on unity in terms of bliss
2c. those of highest faculties [meditating on] unity in terms of appearances
2d. the means of meditation that are indefinite
3. conclusion.

BKC (vol. *kha*, fols. 32b.1–33a.1) adds the following summary of this text: "As for the intention of *The Illumination of Great Bliss* [*bden gsal ba* em. *bde chen gsal ba*], through the twelve [links of] the dependent origination of saṃsāra with its cause that is ignorance, the vicious cycle of nothing but saṃsāric suffering arises. To see the opposite of that—the true reality of dependent origination—induces the wisdom of uncontaminated and supreme [*mchog tu med pa* em. *mchog tu*] great bliss. Hence, within the means for that—the two processes of creation and perfection—the causes and results of the path arise in a gradual manner. Since [all] this is naturally unarisen, to mistakenly cling to the bliss that arises through conditions and is created through the means of the creation and perfection [processes] serves as the cause of suffering. On the other hand, the realization that dependent origination is emptiness and the progressive samādhis of the creation and perfection processes within that state [of realization serve as] the sole causes and results of great bliss. Therefore, since [what is discussed] in this [text] applies to the emptiness that is realized through the progressive stages of dependent origination on the path of the creation [and perfection] processes, it is called '*The Illumination of Great Bliss*.' Hence, since this needs to be realized [through] the dependent origination on the path of the creation and perfection processes, 'with their character of the yoga of mantra and form' (line 10a) represents the stage of vajra recitation; 'those gifted with insight become submerged in bliss' (line 10b) refers to great bliss as the focal object of mind; 'Then, they should regard that diversity as illusion-like and nondual' (lines 10cd) represents the illusory body that is the third stage; 'Then, they enter the true end and' (line 11a) refers to the ultimate luminosity that is the fourth stage; and 'will come to realize the state of unity' (line 11b [and so on]) teaches the stage of unity in detail. Therefore this text mainly teaches the fifth stage." For further comments and details, see Mathes 2015 (16, 181–85).

1924. PDMT, 26:335–48.

1925. The Sanskrit contains only the first homage, while CDNP have only the second one.

1926. GZ CDNP:

> For those people who have fallen from
> the scriptural tradition of the lineage and
> whose eyes are occluded by blurred vision,
> I shall explain this perfect *Tattvaratnāvalī*.

The following excerpts from TRVC are for the most part slightly abbreviated paraphrases. On the two introductory stanzas, TRVC (363–66) says that there are two kinds of persons when it comes to giving rise to wisdom: gradualists (like a monkey gradually climbing through the branches of a tree to pluck its fruits) and simultaneists (like a crow simply landing right at the fruits). This text here is taught in terms of giving rise to wisdom by gradually entering the three yānas. That the feet of Vajrasattva are referred to as lotuses means that though he remains in saṃsāra, he is not tainted by its flaws. As for "Vajrasattva," "vajra" refers to emptiness because it cannot be split: it cannot be made different, does not offer any opportunities for other disputants, and cannot be realized by thoughts. As for "sattva," no matter how the entities of the three realms may appear, they are like reflections: no matter how big a reflection may appear in water, it is just water. Likewise, all appearances have the essence of mind as such, and hence are called "sattva." Since these two (emptiness and appearance) are connected by having the same identity, just like being impermanent and being produced, they are referred to as "Vajrasattva." As Maitrīpa's *Pañcatathāgatamudrāvivaraṇa* 5 says:

> Through vajra, emptiness is declared
> Through sattva, mere cognition's state
> The identity of both is established
> through the nature of Vajrasattva

As for Vajrasattva's qualities, "as bright as the spotless autumn moon" means that the moon in autumn is not tainted by any stains, such as clouds or dust, but its light is clear and pervades everywhere simultaneously. Likewise, Vajrasattva possesses the relinquishment of being absolutely free of all afflictive obscurations and their latent tendencies, as well as the wisdom of simultaneously knowing all knowable objects (seeming and ultimate), just as they are, by virtue of being free of cognitive obscurations. This treatise called *A Jewel Garland of True Reality*, which has been taught by reflecting on the individual flawless approaches and the true reality to be known in the individual assertions, is like a garland of jewels, coming from the ocean and being strung up on a string of stainless silk or the like, that delights the persons who wear it on their necks. Likewise, the jewels of the three yānas coming from the ocean of the Tathāgata's teachings and being strung up on the string of the flawless words of the master delight the learned who understand it (here, TRVC quotes *Tattvaratnāvalī* 13 in support). You may think: "Since the Bhagavān already taught all this in the sūtras, what's the point of teaching it here again?" Just as a precious jewel in front of those with blurred vision is free of flaws but its flawlessness is not visible to them, though the Buddha has given teachings, there may accrue outer flaws (lineage instructions having been cut off since) and inner flaws (most people being under the sway of self-made bad ideas and thus not realizing these teachings as they are). Therefore Maitrīpa shall explain this garland of unerring approaches to true reality based on the undeclined instructions of the lineage from the bhagavān Ratnamati up through Śavaripa and their teachings as they were handed down without any bad ideas (in the Mahāmudrā lineage, Ratnamati is identified as Saraha's guru and as the one who, together with the bodhisattva Sukhanātha, brought these teachings to the human realm).

1927. According to Jñānavajra's **Tattvadarśanamārga* (D3715, fols. 141b.1–2 and 153a.2), unlike the Vaibhāṣikas, the Sautrāntikas are able to promote the welfare of others and thus are asserted to belong to the Pāramitāyāna. Furthermore, citing an otherwise unknown *Mahāyāna Sūtra That Teaches All Philosophical Systems* (Tib. *grub pa'i mtha' ma lus par ston pa theg pa chen po'i mdo*), the Sautrāntikas are said to be Mahāyānists because of dedicating the six pāramitās to others, engaging in the Mahāyāna dharma, and saying that virtue is connected to mind. However, the Sautrāntikas are not able to promote the welfare of others in the Mantrayāna because they assert mind and objects to be distinct.

1928. GZ CDNP ". . . The positions are four because they are divided into Vaibhāṣikas, Sautrāntikas, Yogācāras, and Mādhyamikas. Here, the position of the Vaibhāṣikas consists of the Śrāvakayāna and the Pratyekabuddhayāna. The Mahāyāna is twofold: the Pāramitāyāna and the Mantrayāna. Here, the Pāramitāyāna is threefold: it is to be analyzed in terms of the positions of the Sautrāntikas, Yogācāras, and Mādhyamikas. The Mantrayāna is twofold: the positions of the Yogācāras and Mādhyamikas. The Yogācāras are twofold because they are divided into Aspectarians and Nonaspectarians. Likewise, the Mādhyamikas are twofold because they are divided into . . ." According to TRVC (366–70), the actual text has five points: (1) the yānas, (2) the positions, (3) the approaches, (4) the fruitions, and (5) all being included in a single yāna. (1) A yāna is a gateway onto a certain path due to wishing for a certain fruition. It is the combination of a path and a fruition in terms of liberation. A yāna for liberation consists of prajñā and compassion; it is called "yāna" because it allows one to travel there, just like a mount. There are three yānas because there are three fruitions to be attained, three kinds of faculties, and three kinds of dispositions. The Śrāvakayāna is characterized by unbearable compassion on account of one's own saṃsāric suffering and the realization of only personal identitylessness because it is the path of wishing to listen to the dharma from others (the teachers) and thus proclaiming the resultant knowledge to others. The Pratyekabuddhayāna is characterized by unbearable compassion on account of the saṃsāric suffering of oneself and others and the realization of one part of phenomenal identitylessness—the lack of nature of the perceived—in addition to personal identitylessness because it is the path of wishing for the awakening of oneself, being endowed with relinquishment and wisdom without having to rely on a master in order to attain this fruition. The Mahāyāna is characterized by unbearable compassion solely on account of the suffering of others and the prajñā of realizing both parts of phenomenal identitylessness. It is the great yāna because of its three greatnesses. It has a great focus because it is profound by virtue of realizing identitylessness in its entirety and vast by virtue of taking all sentient beings as its objects out of compassion. It has great conduct because it engages in the six pāramitās with immeasurable hardships over three incalculable eons. It has great fruition because it naturally accomplishes all goals. Or, it is the great yāna because it is the path of wishing for the awakening of completely perfect buddhahood. (2) The three yānas and the four positions are not the same or redundant, because "position" refers to ascertaining through prajñā what is to be known by way of the study and reflection that are connected to liberation, since one wishes to be positioned within the true state of how things are. The four positions of the Vaibhāṣikas and so on are divided in terms of different faculties. For the Vaibhāṣikas, the perceiver—the six consciousnesses—has the nature of being awareness of something other than mind, while the perceived consists of objects such as blue that are aggregations of infinitesimal particles and without aspects, being perceived directly and simultaneously with the arising of the perceiver, because forms, mind, mental factors, nonassociated formations, and unconditioned phenomena are all held to be distinct particulars. For the Sautrāntikas, the aspects cast by objects that are aggregations of infinitesimal particles but remain hidden are different from them, and thus the six consciousnesses themselves appear as blue and so on because they maintain their philosophical system based on the *Daśabhūmikasūtra* and such. For the Yogācāras, ultimately, there is mere [*btsal* em. *tsam*] cognition because theirs is a philosophical system that accords with calm abiding and superior insight. For the Mādhyamikas, neither cognition nor what is cognized is established, because they do not fall into any extremes. Among those four positions, there is no difference in their being connected to liberation, and there are no other names of Buddhist philosophical systems than those four. Since the positions are presented in dependence on what is to be known, they are divided into four in terms of appearances (the basis of disputes). Since the yānas are presented in dependence on the fruitions, they are divided into three in terms of benefiting oneself, others, and both. Thus there is no flaw. As for the yānas and the nine approaches, for the pratyekabuddhas, the perceiver is not different from how the Vaibhāṣikas see it. Though the pratyekabuddhas assert the perceived to belong to seeming reality, their way of describing it is not different from the Vaibhāṣikas, because they describe it as distinct particulars. As for the Mahāyāna, the remaining three positions are not suitable for its entirety. Therefore the Mahāyāna is first divided into two in terms of cause and fruition. The Pāramitāyāna is the causal yāna because it is practiced in the manner of causes that are dissimilar from the fruition and because the causes of buddhahood eventually introduce to the secret mantra. The Mantrayāna is the resultant yāna because it is practiced as the creation and perfection processes by mentally adopting the form kāyas and the dharmakāya as the manifestations of the fruition and because it is the path of wishing for the actual fruition that is buddhahood. The Pāramitāyāna practices the six pāramitās preceded by the generation of bodhicitta because it is the path of wishing to travel to the nirvāṇa that is on the other side of saṃsāra. The Mantrayāna is the path of the creation and perfection processes preceded by empowerments because it is secret for those who have not been matured and is the path by means of practicing the creation and perfection processes in minds with ordinary thoughts and thoughts of clinging to real entities. The Pāramitāyāna and the Mantrayāna are not different in their being the Mahāyāna. The Sautrāntikas belong to the Mahāyāna because they derive from the Mahāyāna sūtras and hold great compassion. Also, in the second chapter of his *Pramāṇavārttika*, Dharmakīrti explains the path to buddhahood based on the Sautrāntika view, and the Sautrāntikas and śrāvakas have been given different prophecies. The Mantrayāna is discussed through only two positions (Vaibhāṣikas and Sautrāntikas are excluded). For the Mantrayāna is pervaded by the creation process, and this becomes the path by way of transforming appearances. But since one is not able to transform real outer referents through consciousness, it is not suitable to place the Sautrāntikas within the Mantrayāna. By contrast, since for Yogācāras and Mādhyamikas, outer referents are nothing but cognition and delusion, these two are suitable for the Mantrayāna. Since the view that is common to the Mantrayāna and the Pāramitāyāna is to be understood through study and refection, the division into Yogācāra and Madhyamaka is made. The Aspectarians assert that the nature of the consciousness of blue and so on is established through valid cognition and is substantially established ultimately because cognition assumes aspects. For the Nonaspectarians, mere self-awareness is substantially existent ultimately, whereas blue and so on do not exist in any respect but are mind's luminosity because cognition does not have any aspects. With regard to referents not existing and cognition existing, it is not possible to speak of anything other than this cognition having or not having aspect. Therefore the Yogācāras are divided into those two. As for illusion-like nonduality, if appearances are examined with valid cognition by denying their real existence, ultimately, they are not found. However, while not being findable, delusive appearances are maintained because illusion-like appearances involve both nonexistence and appearance. The proponents of utter nonabiding do not claim any ultimate phenomena whatsoever because phenomena do not abide as anything [or anywhere]. With regard to there being no essence of entities ultimately, it is not possible to speak of anything other than this being [*min* em. *yin*] or not being mere delusion. Therefore the Mādhyamikas are divided into those two.

1929. CDNP *phyi ma* ("later," "posterior") is a completely literal but nonsensical rendering of Skt. *pāścātya*.

1930. TRVC (370) says that "approach" refers to the yogas of meditation, through which these nine are divided. The śrāvakas are divided into three by way of their faculties. If divided in terms of time, the highest are the earlier ones. If divided in terms of area, the medium and lower are those from the west of India.

1931. Here and in the following, GZ and TRVC mostly read *spyad pa* ("experience" or "engagement") instead of *dpyad pa*. As mentioned before, Maitrīpa's *Caturmudropadeśa* (text 92, 16) explains that among the four topics through which the nine approaches are discussed, "analysis" refers to their specific discriminating prajñās that are based on study and reflection. "Dhyāna" refers to their specific prajñās of meditation. "The stains of dhyāna" refers to the factors that are directly antagonistic to those prajñās. "The view" refers to the distinctive features of their specific prajñās embracing their specific conducts, as well as mentally taking their specific fruitions as objects.

1932. GZ CDNP link "blue and such" with "exist" and have the second Sanskrit line ("the world . . . for the most stupid") as the fourth, thus making the whole stanza very difficult to make sense of. This unidentified stanza is also cited in Jñānakīrti's Tattvāvatāra (text 214, 251) and the Subhāṣitasaṃgraha (Bendall 1903–1904, 388).

1933. The first quote is in Prakrit and refers to the *Bhārahārasutta* in the Pāli Saṃyutta Nikāya (III.22.22), which says that the burden consists of the five skandhas, the bearer of that burden is the person, the taking up of that burden is the craving that leads to rebirth, and the laying down of that burden is the cessation of such craving. As IaS (78n75) points out, this quote "is likely drawn from one of the canonical versions of the *Bhārasūtra* (a.k.a. *Bhārahārasūtra*). The sentence is not present in the Pāli version of the sutta in the Samyutta Nikāya (22.22, vol. 325–26), nor in the Sanskrit version of the same quoted by Yaśomitra in his *Abhidharmakośavyākhyā* (ed. p. 7063ff.) . . . It is possible that it is drawn from another canonical version of the sūtra, perhaps the one of the Sāṃmatīya. Cf. Skilling 1997: 100–106, and von Hinüber 2001: 112" (see also Eltschinger 2014). IaS (78) continues: "More significantly, just the same passage is quoted also in the *Vimalaprabhā*, a work roughly contemporary with or perhaps slightly earlier than the *Tattvaratnāvalī*. The chances are that both Puṇḍarīka (as the author of the *Vimalaprabhā* calls himself) and Maitreyanātha quoted the phrase not directly from a Middle-Indic version of an entire scripture, let alone the entire canon, but from an earlier citation of it in some Sanskrit work of the Mahāyāna." In his notes, Bhikkhu Bodhi provides the following comments (Bhikkhu Bodhi 2000, 1050–51n36: "Spk: In what sense are these 'five aggregates subject to clinging' called the burden? In the sense of having to be borne through maintenance. For their maintenance—by being lifted up, moved about, seated, laid to rest, bathed, adorned, fed and nourished, etc.—is something to be borne; thus they are called a burden in the sense of having to be borne through maintenance." Bhikkhu Bodhi, 1051n37: "The *puggalavāda* or 'personalist' schools of Buddhism appealed to this passage as proof for the existence of the person (*puggala*) as a real entity, neither identical with the five aggregates nor different from them. It is the *puggala*, they claimed, that persists through change, undergoes rebirth, and eventually attains Nibbāna. This tenet was bluntly rejected by the other Buddhist schools, who saw in it a camouflaged version of the *ātman*, the self of the non-Buddhist systems. For an overview of the arguments, see Dutt, *Buddhist Sects in India*, pp. 184–206. The mainstream Buddhist schools held that the person was a mere convention (*vohāra*) or concept (*paññatti*) derivative upon (*upādāya*) the five aggregates, not a substantial reality in its own right. For the Theravāda response, see the first part of Kvu, a lengthy refutation of the 'personalist' thesis. Spk: Thus, by the expression 'the carrier of the burden,' he shows the person to be a mere convention. For the person is called the carrier of the burden because it 'picks up' the burden of the aggregates at the moment of rebirth, maintains the burden by bathing, feeding, seating, and laying them down during the course of life, and then discards them at the moment of death, only to take up another burden of aggregates at the moment of rebirth." The second quote "The person who has desire roams [saṃsāra]" is too unspecific but obviously found in many sources.

1934. GZ CDNP ". . . Therefore, in order to relinquish desire, they need to cultivate the dhyāna of the repulsiveness [of the body]. This meditation on repulsiveness consists of analyzing the body's collection of . . . intestines, fat, lungs, heart, kidneys, spleen, stomach, and so forth."

1935. GZ CD "split them right down to the marrow."

1936. *Bodhicaryāvatāra* V.62–63.

1937. GZ *tshogs pa* ("collection") CDNP no equivalent of "desire."

1938. That is, Śāriputra and Maudgalyāyana.

1939. Mathes 2015 takes this sentence to be a line of verse in the Indravajrā meter.

1940. GZ CDNP omit "and will make myself alone enter parinirvāṇa." TRVC (371–73) says that "analysis" is in terms of what is to be validated, what validates it, and true reality, which goes for all nine approaches. Here, what is to be validated refers to aggregations of infinitesimal particles that do not touch one another, which thus are permanent and direct appearances of balance. What validates this consists of the six consciousnesses that are the perceivers and have the character of other-awareness, consisting of the direct perceptions that perceive their objects simultaneously and the inferential cognitions that are connected to them. True reality has three aspects: the true reality of what is impermanent (infinitesimal particles, nonassociated formations, minds, and mental factors), the true reality of what is permanent (the three kinds of unconditioned phenomena), and the true reality of what is neither (the inexpressible person). The person that becomes contaminated later in saṃsāra through the latent tendencies of karma is not permanent by way of not perishing, because it transits into later births. How could transition occur in something that does not perish? However, what has the nature of perishing in the previous moment and arising in the next one is not impermanent either, because the maturations of any given karmas are experienced later. In something in which earlier and later are different, the certainty of karma and its maturation is not suitable, because it would follow that someone may experience the karma of someone else. "There are outer referents . . ." is to be understood as referring to the scriptures that say actual outer referents are taught in the sūtras, since it is taught that the scriptures that say outer referents exist do so by having those of lower faculties in mind. "The bearer of the burden" refers to the scriptures that speak of the existence of the person, and the burden refers to the seeds that are accumulated through karma. "The person who has desire . . ." teaches the meditation. The intention here is the reason [*rgyun* em. *rgyu*] for specifically meditating on repulsiveness: the cause [*rgyud* em. *rgyu*] of later skandhas in saṃsāra is karma, the cause of karma consists of the afflictions, the afflictions arise from desire, and desire comes from clinging to one's own body as being attractive. Therefore, through meditating on the repulsiveness that is the direct opposite of that clinging, it will stop. Once that has stopped, desire and the following factors will also gradually stop. Hence the primary cause of nirvāṇa is to meditate on repulsiveness. This is twofold in terms of mindset and enumeration: (a) focusing the mind on a single piece of bone between one's eyebrows and then multiplying it until it covers the size of the ocean and reducing it back to its original size, which is the meditation of beginners, and (b) recollecting the repulsiveness of one's own body, which is described by "This meditation on repulsiveness . . ." "The stain of their samādhi" teaches the points of going astray in order to stop going astray into anything else that is not meditation—that is, what is not conducive to engage in meditation. The same goes for the stains of meditation of the remaining approaches. If the body is perceived as being permanent and pure, one contemplates its impurity, which is taught by "the view of the permanence of the person." The view refers to the branches of renunciation, the branches of means, and the branches of the prajñā of realization being complete. The prajñā of realization refers to realizing the lack of a personal self. As for the branches of means, out of the desire to exit from saṃsāra, until death, these śrāvakas primarily take refuge in a nirmāṇakāya buddha, the dharma that is taught, and the four pairs of noble persons [stream-enterer, once-returner, nonreturner, and arhat], and then take full ordination. They pay homage to sugatas, the dharma, and elder learners, but not to bodhisattvas in the attire of householders and those who are their juniors in training, so forget about any others. "As long as I live . . . parinirvāṇa!" represents the branches of renunciation. The text speaks of "alone" because there is no welfare of others at all. "Discipline" consists of having disciplined the sense faculties in the nirvāṇa with the remainder of the skandhas: it means being free of afflictions, while the skandhas produced by the karma of previous births still remain. "Roots of virtue" refers to those arising from generosity, discipline, and meditation. "Calm" consists of having calmed the afflictions in the nirvāṇa without remainder: since the causes of the skandhas—karma and afflictions—have been relinquished, no skandhas are appropriated anymore later.

1941. GZ CDNP "The view and analysis . . . The stain of their samādhi is the nature of states without mind through vase breathing because of becoming [like] matter." TRVC (373–74) says that the text presents what is common and what is different compared to the lower śrāvakas. Their analysis and two among the three branches of the view are without difference. The difference in their view is in terms of renunciation, which refers to promoting the plain and simple welfare of others, if they have the capacity and something happens to others, as in the case of seizing someone who is carried away by a river. As for their meditation, the root of saṃsāra consists of karma and afflictions. Their causes consist of thoughts, which operate based on the breath. Therefore, since afflictions and thoughts are put to an end when the breath calms down, the root of nirvāṇa is meditation based on the breath; as it is said: "The remedy of thoughts is meditation based on the breath." For as long as the breath of desire flows, one cycles in saṃsāra. For that reason, they meditate in the manner of counting the breath: counting exhaling and inhaling, as well as counting the resting, as described in six ways [*Abhidharmakośa* VI.12]. The stain of their samādhi is to be without mindful awareness.

1942. GZ CDNP "The highest śrāvakas assert external referents and present and analyze the lack of a self with regard to the body. By thoroughly knowing the four realities of the noble ones . . . superimpose the aspect of thoughts being at peace [CDNP "the aspect of permanent peace"] onto emptiness. Their view has the distinctive feature of performing the welfare of others."

1943. GZ CDNP ". . . Others say this:

> ". . .
> There is no one here lacking that fortune

"Hence they think: 'I should not be disheartened about accomplishing completely perfect awakening' and say that even the lower śrāvakas will become completely perfect buddhas. Those whose disposition is definite . . . will become [buddhas] by depending on some buddha. The medium [śrāvakas] will become pratyekabuddhas, and the highest [śrāvakas] will become buddhas after four incalculable eons." TRVC (374–77) says that the analysis of the highest śrāvakas is the same as the previous one in terms of what is to be validated and what validates it. As for true reality, they do not assert any person that is a third alternative beyond being permanent and impermanent, but assert five [*bzhi* em. *lnga*] bases of knowable objects that are impermanent and three unconditioned phenomena that are permanent (space and the two kinds of cessation). Among the five bases of knowable objects, the three, such as particles, represent the perceived, and mind and mental factors represent the perceiver. What cannot be destroyed physically or broken down mentally is something ultimate. As for their meditation, since the four realities of the noble ones teach the causes and results of afflicted phenomena and purified phenomena, they are specifically used because they are connected to the necessity of meditating on the lack of a self. From clinging to a self, the saṃsāra of karma and afflictions arises. If that clinging comes to an end, saṃsāra also stops. Therefore they meditate on the lack of a self. Each one of the four realities is to be understood through its name, essence, and training. "Thinking" refers to clinging to a self and saṃsāric existence. "Superior insight" refers to the relinquishment of the afflictions and a self that is a third alternative [text: *phung po gsum*; lit. "three skandhas"]. "Emptiness" refers to the mindset of the lack of a self. The stain of their dhyāna is to try to relinquish the clinging to a self without negating that self. The next "emptiness" refers to being empty of the clinging to a self. "Superimpose" means not negating the self. As for the view, in terms of renunciation, their distinctive feature is that they wish for the welfare of others. In terms of the prajñā of realization, their distinctive feature is not to make the distinction of a person that is inexpressible. In terms of the means, they accord with the other śrāvakas. As for teaching the differences of them becoming buddhas, Vasubandhu and others hold that śrāvakas who are naturally born with lower intelligence attain the awakening of śrāvakas but not perfect buddhahood. "Others" refers to Nāgārjuna and others saying, based on passages in the *Samādhirājasūtra*, that even lower śrāvakas eventually become buddhas, so that the above is not definite. Ultimately, since there is no disposition other than the dharmadhātu, there arises only a single type of mind of realizing it, which is perfect buddhahood. For, for as long as the dharmadhātu has not been realized, the path is an adventitious phenomenon and thus suitable to be changed, and it is impossible for anyone not to become a buddha. How is that? "For those whose disposition is definite . . ." refers to the meaning of the disposition not being definite as described in the *Mahāyānasūtrālaṃkāra*. As for "the medium," since their disposition is not definite, they are not separated from the desire to see true reality; when they are first born, they become śrāvakas, next they become pratyekabuddhas, and then they become buddhas by having engaged in the causes of buddhahood. The highest śrāvakas are of indefinite disposition—that is, after having been śrāvakas for one incalculable eon, they become buddhas by having engaged in the causes of buddhahood for three incalculable eons.

1944. That is, without any mental activity.

1945. Skt. *anupraveśa* can also mean "imitation."

1946. GZ CDNP "The analysis of the pratyekabuddhas is like that of the highest śrāvakas. The persons who have entered this [yāna realize] emptiness, the characteristic of the inconceivable, have no master, [and realize] self-arising wisdom, superior insight, and calm abiding. Here, superior insight consists of the cessation of [the operation of] the sense faculties and the nonobservability of a person . . . The stains of samādhi here consist of the dhyāna of the mind that is the blissful state of mind being withdrawn due to sleep [I follow NP *gnyid* against GZ CD *gnyis*, "two"] and the state of [all] mental factors having completely ceased. The former here is [the meditation] of those who follow the system of Bhāskara [*nyi ma*, lit. "the sun"; the more literal *'od byed* would be clearer]." Bhāskara or Bhaṭṭabhāskara was a proponent of Bhedābheda Vedānta (ca. 800 CE), who wrote a commentary on the *Brahmasūtra* (in order to refute the famous Advaitin Śaṅkara), and commentaries on the *Bhagavadgītā* (only fragments preserved) and the Upaniṣads (lost; Pillai 1965, 2:247, also lists a Sanskrit manuscript titled *Bhāskarīyamatam* by Bhāskara of tantric content; ms. no. T.164). Bhāskara is also referenced below as someone with a mistaken view and practice. Tatz 1990 (493) says the following about this: "Why does Advayavajra reduce some schools to the absurdity of following Bhāskara, whereas his contemporaries accuse their rivals of resembling Śaṃkara? The deficiencies that Advayavajra perceives in the system of Bhāskara could equally be imputed in that of Śaṃkara, but Bhāskara is the more unpleasant speaker to Buddhists; one might say that he represents the 'extreme right wing' of Brahmanism. Bhāskara is a critic of Śaṃkara, according to his works that come down to us. Rejecting the philosophic Illusionism (*māyāvāda*), the soteriological emphasis on understanding (*jñāna-yoga*), and the ethical appreciation of celibacy (*brahmacarya*) that label Śaṃkara a 'crypto-buddhist', Bhāskara stands for a fundamentalist Vedicism that includes the impossibility of attaining liberation before death, the importance of social status (*karma-yoga*), and the superiority of the brahman class. Furthermore, Śaṃkara's followers are characterized as 'single staff', those of Bhāskara as 'triple staff' (*tridaṇḍin*). If Advayavajra's pre-conversion training was triple staff, rather than single staff, his citation of Bhāskaran spirituality as an instance of fruitlessness could be derived from his own experience of it." IaS (77n73) says that neither this reference to Bhāskara, nor the one below (in the context of Nonaspectarians), nor the brief one in the *Sekanirdeśa* can be linked with any specific passage in his surviving works, while the second reference seems to echo a passage in Vācaspati Miśra's *Nyāyavārttikatātparyaṭīkā* (for details, see below). IaS continues: "It certainly cannot be excluded that Maitreyanātha had some direct knowledge of a work of Bhāskara which has not come down to us, and has drawn on it. But it seems also possible that the lack of agreement between his references and the works of Bhāskara presently available is due rather to the fact that he did not have precise knowledge of Bhāskara's teaching at all. We are inclined to think this a real possibility, certainly likelier, to our feeling, than the (admittedly quite tentatively put forward) suggestion of Tatz that Maitreyanātha's 'citation of Bhāskaran spirituality as an instance of fruitlessness could be derive (sic) from his own experience of it' (1990: 493). For a brief overview of references to Bhāskara in post-Bhāskaran Sanskrit texts, see Kato 2011: xxv–xxvi." For further details on Bhāskara's position, see Tatz 1990 and 1994, Ingalls 1953 and 1967, and below.

1947. As Sferra 2003 (64–65) and Mathes 2015 (63n153) point out, this is a reformulation of stanza 75 of one of the most important Śaiva tantras, the *Vijñānabhairava* (the full stanza there says: "If one reaches with the mind the state of being on the verge of sleep when external objects have disappeared, the supreme goddess shines forth"). GZ CDNP:

> One should make efforts and cultivate
> the experiential object of the mind
> when sleep has arrived—that is, [when] outer
> experiential objects have faded away.

1948. GZ CDNP "The other one is [the meditation] of those who follow the system of the Vaiśeṣikas."

1949. GZ CDNP:

I'm better off becoming a fox
in the pleasant Jetavana Grove,
but Gautama never seeks for
the liberation of the Vaiśeṣikas

This stanza is also cited as being from the sūtras in Jñānavajra's **Tattvadarśanamārga* (D3715, fol. 141b.5).

1950. CDNP omit this sentence.

1951. That is, pratyekabuddhas very rarely teach through words but typically by way of symbols, gestures, performing miracles, and so on. GZ CDNP ". . . the compassion that they give rise to [in this way] is the compassion that is focused on sentient beings. The śrāvakas teach by means of their speech, and the pratyekabuddhas teach by means of their body."

1952. *Mūlamadhyamakakārikā* XVIII.12. GZ "arises without their [physical] support" ("those" and "their" refers primarily to buddhas, but also to śrāvakas). CDNP "arises without any thought." TRVC (377–79) says that though the analysis of the pratyekabuddhas is for the most part the same as that of the highest śrāvakas, there is a slight difference in the context of meditation. Based on the rationale that mind becomes scattered toward outer objects due to clinging to a self, by virtue of karma and afflictions, one engages in saṃsāra in accordance with the links of dependent origination in their progressive order. Without a self and without engaging in outer objects, the order of these links is reversed. By being free of the clinging to a self so as to pass into nirvāṇa, they meditate while cognition does not become scattered toward outer objects. As for what is to be meditated on here, "the person being empty" means that there is not even a mere person that is inexpressible, which is their difference from the lower and medium śrāvakas. In terms of the inconceivable ultimate, outer objects as something perceived are inconceivable, due to which pratyekabuddhas also differ from the highest śrāvakas. "But if there is nothing perceived, how could a perceiver, which is dependent on it, be reasonable?" They answer that this is thanks to the latent tendencies of a perceiver in dependence on the seeming existence of something perceived. The way in which their wisdom arises is "without having a master"—the wisdom that is the specific fruition of all śrāvakas and bodhisattvas arises in dependence on a master, but theirs is not dependent in this way. "Self-arising" means it arises as they intend. As for the nature of their meditation method, "the cessation of the sense faculties" means to realize that what is perceived does not exist ultimately. "A person not being observable" means that a personal self is not seen in the body. Since their meditation differs in these two features from other people, this is their superior insight. "The control of body, speech, and mind" means that during meditative equipoise, their cognition does not become scattered toward these three; during subsequent attainment, they do not perform the ten nonvirtues, and the actions of body, speech, and mind are few. The stains of meditation consist of an experience that is like falling asleep because they then have arrived at the approach of the tīrthika Bhāskara. He explains that a state like deep sleep, being without identification and any movement of cognition, is wisdom. This is not something that Buddhists, Bhāskara, and the Vaiśeṣikas have in common, because the Buddha said that even being born as a fox is better than this kind of wisdom. The view of the pratyekabuddhas accords with that of the highest śrāvakas. Their way of becoming buddhas is like that of the highest śrāvakas. Among the three kinds of compassion, they give rise to the compassion that focuses on sentient beings: seeing their minds suffer, they wish for them to be free of suffering. The pratyekabuddhas are those who gain realization based on conditions because they realize the reverse order of the twelve links of dependent origination. Their specific way of teaching the dharma is by way of the body because this is superior to teaching by way of speech, does not harm their meditation, and does not end the respect of the disciples, since they do not have untoward thoughts about the master. The specific time of their occurrence is when there are no buddhas or śrāvakas present: by abiding in their fruition, they promote the welfare of beings because they had made aspiration prayers in that regard due to their fondness of meditation.

1953. GZ CDNP "Now, [the view] of the yogīs of the pāramitās is discussed . . . Their [understanding of an external] referent is that it has the essence of being an aggregation of infinitesimal particles, having the essence of producing a cognition that has a [mental] aspect [of that referent]. The essence of this is therefore referred to as . . ."

1954. *Pramāṇavārttika* III.247. The last two lines in GZ CDNP are full of typos/ mistranslations and read as something like this:

> For those who know awareness, it is a reason
> Cognition has the endurance to take an aspect.

1955. I here follow GZ CDNP, which is confirmed by the same phrase in *Taking the Pith Instructions of the Philosophical Systems as the Path* (appendix 2); Skt. "the village of sense faculties turning away from their objects."

1956. GZ CDNP ". . . 'This refers to the time of needing to familiarize, not the time of needing to directly perceive.' Therefore one surely needs to familiarize. Such familiarization [is described like this]."

1957. This unidentified stanza is also quoted in Munidatta's *Caryāgītikoṣavṛtti* (text 90, 373); it could be from another uncommented song in this collection. GZ CDNP:

> When familiarizing through
> mind's realization of no-mind,
> from where to where did it go?
> At that time, I don't see mind.

1958. This stanza is also cited in Jñānavajra's **Tattvadarśanamārga* (D3715, fol. 141b.1), which attributes it to a *Mahāyāna Sūtra That Teaches All Philosophical Systems*. GZ CDNP:

> Relying on moment after moment
> and assuming the vajra posture,
> directing the moving mind to the nose tip,
> even householders should meditate.

1959. That is, the stains of the pratyekabuddhas.

1960. GZ CDNP ". . . By way of not observing the three spheres [of agent, action, and object]), they engage in the [first] five pāramitās having the nature of the pāramitā of prajñā [CDNP omit "having the nature of the pāramitā of prajñā"] and mature sentient beings without any hope for the fruition. This is the view." TRVC (379–81) says that what is to be validated consists of aggregations of infinitesimal particles without interstices, but not touching, that present aspects similar to themselves. What validates this consists of the perceptions and inferential cognitions to which these aspects of referents are presented. As for true reality, momentary objects, ultimate infinitesimal particles, and ultimate momentary cognitions are specifically characterized phenomena because they are the ones that perform functions. What performs functions exists ultimately, while everything else exists as seeming reality. These are explained as specifically and generally characterized phenomena, respectively. In Dharmakīrti's quote, "at a different time" refers to the referent being earlier and the cognition later. As for the meditation, mind being scattered toward objects due to clinging to a self is the root of saṃsāra, because the latter stops if the former stops. Nonconceptual meditation means to turn away from the village of objects: since no referents are identified, mind does not become scattered toward objects. "Inconceivability" means to rest within, without any thoughts of clinging to a self. The realization of no-mind is nonconceptual meditation. "Not see mind" means that this is peaceful thanks to swiftly noticing being scattered and thus redirecting the mind to its focal object. "Moment" refers to a little bit of meditation being possible, which means even for householders, let alone monastics. The stains of meditation accord with those of the pratyekabuddhas. As for the prajñā of realization in the context of the view, "not observing" means not clinging. The means are to perform the five pāramitās. The branch of renunciation means practicing generosity without any hope for gaining possessions through generosity and dedicating it and its results to the awakening of all sentient beings.

1961. Vasubandhu's *Viṃśatikākārikā* 12ab.

1962. GZ CDNP ". . . even infinitesimal particles will not be observed; rather, all these are mere mind. Mind as such is free from any essence of the aspects of perceiver and perceived and clearly displays clarity. This is what they realize."

1963. As Schmithausen (1973, 172–76, and 2014, 615–16) points out, this famous sentence is found not only in the sixth chapter of the *Daśabhūmikasūtra* but also in a number of other sūtras. (1) In the *Daśabhūmikasūtra* (ed. by Johannes Rahder 1926, 49.10), the context in which this sentence appears is a discussion of dependent origination, in which both the preceding and the following passages clearly presuppose the realist ontology of the Hīnayāna and attack only the existence of a substantial self. Vasubandhu's commentary (D3993, fol. 199a.4–5) appears to first gloss this sentence in an "idealist" way, saying, "Thus [the Buddha] said that this [saṃsāra] with its three realms is mere mind because it is nothing but mere modulations (*pariṇāma*) of mind." However, as his comments on the immediately following sentence in the sūtra confirm, the term *cittamātra* is here (and in a number of other texts) directed only against a substantial self behind the stream of impermanent cognitions and not against the existence of a material world out there. (2) In the *Laṅkāvatārasūtra* (D107, fol. 87a.3), the sentence "This [saṃsāra] with its three realms is merely one's own mind" accords well with that sūtra's context of denying external objects. Nevertheless, that sentence is still followed by the gloss "it lacks a self and what is mine." (3) In *The Sūtra of the Buddha Ascending to the Tuṣita Heaven and Teaching the Dharma to His Mother* transmitted in two Chinese translations, the sentence appears abruptly without any preparation at the beginning of the answer to the question of how bodhisattvas comprehend that everything is like empty space—that is, in the context of Mahāyāna illusionism. (4) In the Chinese translations of the *Lokottaraparivarta* of the *Buddhāvataṃsakasūtra*, the sentence is introduced as a fact and extended to the three times, with emphasis on mind's boundlessness. In particular, Dharmarakṣa's translation presupposes a very different understanding of *cittamātra*, saying that "this bodhisattva, in an instant [as short as] producing [but one single] thought (*cittamātra*), pervades the three world-spheres, and completely comprehends the meaning (?) of the three periods of time. As for what is attained by his mind, there is, in between and far off, nothing it does not penetrate" (trans. Schmithausen 2014, 616). (5) In Bodhiruci's Chinese translation of the *Dharmasaṃgītisūtra*, a series of characterizations of phenomena is introduced by the statement that they all are **cittamātra*, that their essence is nothing but imagination (**parikalpa*), and that they are insubstantial and rootless, like illusions. Thus, in all these sources, except for the comparatively late *Laṅkāvatārasūtra*, the sentence in question appears rather abruptly and solitary, and thus looks like an already established phrase taken over from another source. According to Schmithausen, there is indeed such an earlier source, which is the *Pratyutpannabuddhasaṃmukhāvasthitasamādhisūtra* (P760, fol. 15b.1; translated into Chinese in 179 CE). In this sūtra, the sentence appears as the culmination of a long section that explains that appearances within meditative absorption, as well as all that appears normally as external objects, are nothing but appearances in and by the mind. Immediately following this sentence, the sūtra also gives a reason for it: "Because however I imagine things, that is how they appear." Thus, contrary to most of the above sūtras, this sentence occurs here in a context that very well matches the "idealistic" meaning that its words immediately suggest. Moreover, it does not appear abruptly or isolated but as the culmination of a long sequence of preparatory concordant reflections (for details, see Schmithausen 1973, 175–76, and 2014, 608–18). Schmithausen (2014, 603 and 603n2450) also remarks that the expression *cittamātra* (or *vijñaptimātra*) is one of those that became specific technical terms only in the course of time. In early sources, it may, but need not, have its typical Yogācāra meaning of indicating the nonexistence of external phenomena other than mind; other meanings of the term being as follows. (1) *Cittamātra* as excluding merely a substantial self: besides the *Daśabhūmikasūtra*, the *Śrāvakabhūmi* (Shukla ed., 490.21–23), the *Vastusaṃgrahaṇī* (D4039, fol. 163a5f.), the *Abhidharmasamuccaya* (Pradhan ed., 34.20–23), the *Abhidharmasamuccayabhāṣya* (Tatia ed., 86.11f., using *vijñaptimātra* instead of *cittamātra*), and Sthiramati's *Sūtrālaṃkāravṛttibhāṣya* (D4034, vol. *tsi*, fol. 104a.5–6); this is also how Mādhyamikas like Bhāviveka and Candrakīrti interpret *cittamātra*. (2) *Cittamātra* as excluding mental factors associated with the mind (*caitasikā dharmāḥ*) to be entities of their own apart from *citta*: the view of an opponent in the *Viniścayasaṃgrahaṇī* (D4038, vol. *zhi*, fol. 77a.1). (3) *Cittamātra* referring to purely mental feelings, based on the mind only, in contrast to such feelings as are (also) based on the physical sense faculties: *Abhidharmakośabhāṣya* (Shastri 1987, 145.3). (4) *Cittamātra* referring to karma dependent on the mind only, in contrast to physical and verbal karma: *Abhidharmakośabhāṣya* (Shastri 1987, 239.2). (5) *Cittamātra* in the sense of "as soon as they think of them" (*Suvarṇabhāsottamasūtra* III.84–85: *saha cittamātrena* [ed. J. Nobel 1937, 39f.] or "through one's mere thought" (*Mahāyānasūtrālaṃkāra* XVIII.75: *cittamātrāt samṛddhitaḥ*; *Sūtrālaṃkāravṛttibhāṣya* [D4034, vol. *tsi*, fol. 129a.6]: *sems tsam gyis = bsam pa'am smon lam btab pa tsam gyis*).

1964. This stanza is very similar to *Pramāṇavārttika* III.433:

> If the mind has the form of something blue and such,
> what is the valid cognition of an external referent then?
> If mind doesn't have the form of something blue etc.,
> how could there be an experience of that [blue etc.]?

GZ CDNP:

> If mind has the essence of something blue and such,
> what is the cause of an external referent then?
> If the mind is not something blue and such,
> what is the cause of an external referent then?

1965. I could not locate this stanza, but since our text says "elsewhere," it is clearly regarded as a citation. TRVC (382) attributes it to Prajñākaragupta's *Pramāṇavārttikālaṃkāra*. Tatz 1994 uncritically follows Lhalungpa's mistaken attribution to the *Vajrapañjaratantra*, and Mathes 2015 follows both Lhalungpa and Tatz. However, the stanza is not found in that tantra nor elsewhere in Kg or Tg. GZ CDNP:

> An essence of the sense faculties' referents
> doesn't exist as anything else than the mind
> What is appearing as form and so forth
> consists of the appearances of mind as such.

1966. GZ CDNP "examination."

1967. According to TRVC (381–82), among the three different assertions of the Aspectarians—aspects and self-awareness are distinct like a split egg, the number of cognitions is the same as the number of aspects, and variety is nondual—the last one is taught here. What is to be validated consists of the appearances of the aspects that are the portion of what is perceived. What validates this consists of self-awareness—the appearances of the portion of the perceiver (perceptions and the inferential cognitions connected to them). As for true reality, though variety manifests clearly, it is solely self-awareness free of perceiver and perceived that exists because experience is not invalidated by reasoning. If it did not exist, where would delusion come from? The variety of perceiver and perceived is seeming reality because it is invalidated by reasoning. The reasoning "By virtue of six being joined together . . ." means that these appearances are not outer referents. A particle in the center of an aggregation must have six parts—its four sides, a top, and a bottom—if it were to align with other such particles. But if they were to join having just a single part, there would be no room apart from that single side, so how would coarse things be established? Since appearances are mind, what is mind itself like? It does not appear as perceiver and perceived yet clearly displays, and this clear display is the mere clear display of blue and so on. In the *Daśabhūmikasūtra*, "sons of the victor" refers to bodhisattvas, because they hold the victors' family lineage. The sūtra speaks of "the three realms" because there is no debate that the dharmas of the noble ones are mind. "Mere" means that anything other than mind is negated and thus gauged to be mind. The quote from the *Pramāṇavārttika* means that if the appearances of referents are mind, there is no need for any referents that are something other. If these appearances are not mind, this would contradict their appearing. Prajñākaragupta's quote means that appearances are nothing other but mind. "Therefore . . ." is the summary of all this: mind's basic nature clearly displays as variety, which means there is nothing else whatsoever.

1968. GZ CDNP ". . . think that all these [appearances] are mind as such—the mind that has the nature of self-awareness without any [really existing] aspects. What is taught in the following is their examination:"

1969. *Laṅkāvatārasūtra* X.154cd–155ab.

1970. GZ CDNP:

> As long as something appears,
> it appears similar to an illusion
> True reality without appearance
> is like the infinite and pure sky.

1971. This stanza is identical to *Pañcatathāgatamudrāvivaraṇa* 3.

1972. *Jñānasārasamuccaya* 35. According to Sferra 2003 (65n17), this is *Vijñānabhairava* 116 (one of the most important Śaiva tantras), but only the first line "wherever the mind may go" is shared, while the remainder of that stanza says: "whether outside or inside, there the all-pervasive state of Śiva goes." GZ CDNP:

> If mind bonds with any
> knowables to which it moves,
> wherever it goes and moves,
> all of that is of its nature.

1973. GZ CDNP ". . . directly perceive wisdom without appearances, which is real, nondual, inconceivable, and free from discursiveness."

1974. *Ālokamālā* 53.

1975. *Triṃśikākārikā* 27. GZ CDNP:

> If anything is placed before [the mind]
> through focusing while thinking
> "All of this here is mere mind,"
> there is no dwelling in merely that.

1976. *Triṃśikākārikā* 28. GZ CDNP read the last two lines as follows:

it is resting within mere mind
Without a perceived, there is hence no perceiver of it.

1977. Skt. *bhagavataḥ saṃsthita-* appears to be a mixed-up form of *Brahmasamhitā* or its alternative name *Bhagavatsiddhānta(saṃgraha)*, which is a versified text in the *Skandapurāṇa* that consists of excerpts from a number of Upaniṣads.

1978. GZ CDNP "The stain of the samādhi of the proponents of cognition with aspects is the claim that [this cognition] is ultimately permanent. They follow the approach of the Vedas, [CDNP add "by dwelling in"] the *Bhagavat[siddhānta]*. They assert that beings have the essence of being modulations, not other than Brahman, within the essence of one's own ultimate and permanent mind."

1979. This stanza is identical to *Sekanirdeśa* 15. As IaS (288n200) remarks, though it is otherwise unidentified, the last line is identical with *Manusmṛti* 6.81d.

1980. GZ CDNP ". . . Likewise, the stain of the meditation of the Nonaspectarians is a permanent, self-aware consciousness without thoughts and appearances and free from [CDNP omit "and free from"] discursiveness. It follows they follow the texts [or approach] of Bhāskara . . . free from all names and forms, pure of all delusion of discursiveness . . ." For Bhāskara's views on *paramātman* as ultimate reality, sentient beings as "modulations" (Skt. *pariṇāma*), meditation, and his positions compared with those of Śaṃkara, see Ingalls 1953 and 1967 (63–64, 67), as well as Nakamura 1968.

1981. Given this stanza's matching with the preceding paragraph, the phrase "for me" in its second line, and a very similar stanza cited in Jñānavajra's **Tattvadarśanamārga*, it is in all probability an unidentified quote by Bhāskara. GZ CDNP:

Within the clear ocean of my thoughts,
all kinds of water bubbles are gathering
Their rising as well as their vanishing
are not conceived by means of thinking

[as the similar stanza in the **Tattvadarśanamārga* below suggests, *gsog* ("gathering") in the second line is most probably a typo for *sogs* ("and such")]

The stanza in the **Tattvadarśanamārga* is said to be from a "tīrthika *Bhāskaratantra*" (Tib. *mu stegs nyi ma'i rgyud*) or, given the immediately preceding reference to just Bhāskara, "a tantra by the tīrthika Bhāskara." Possible sources of this stanza are the above-mentioned works by Bhāskara (it is not found in the first two chapters of his *Brahmasūtrabhāṣya*; see Kato 2011, whose announced edition of the remaining two chapters has not appeared yet) or some other work entirely. In any case, in the **Tattvadarśanamārga* (D3715, fol. 143b.1–3), this stanza and its explanation read as follows:

Within the clear ocean of realization [Tib. *rtog pa*, "thoughts," but
  the comments below say *rtogs pa*]
though bubbles, waves, and such arise,
their arising as well as their vanishing
are of a single equal taste as that water

According to Jñānavajra, this stanza asserts the following. For example, though there are bubbles from below the ocean, waves, and turbidities, and other waters flow into it, they are all the same within the ocean. Likewise, if one's own mind, which is without aspect, discursiveness, and end or limit, inconceivable, and entirely permanent, is realized, no matter as which entities it may appear and which thoughts may arise, by virtue of being mind as such, these are Brahmā, dharmatā, and buddha.

1982. GZ CDNP "Their view . . ." According to TRVC (382–85), the Nonaspectarians are twofold: by virtue of the difference of whether aspects do or do not appear in buddhas during subsequent attainment, there are those who say that a buddha's mind has stains and those who say it is stainless. Here, the former position is taught. Self-awareness is both what is to be validated and what validates it. Since the appearances of aspects are invalidated in all respects by reasoning, they are merely seeming, while true reality consists of nothing but cognition. Aspects are nonexistent yet clearly appear. In the quote from the *Laṅkāvatārasūtra*, six lines teach aspects to be delusive, while one line teaches self-awareness free of any aspects [obviously, TRVC considers stanza 5 as also being from the *Laṅkāvatārasūtra*, but it is not found there; in addition, TRVC says that stanza 6 is from the *Uttaratantra*]. The dharmakāya, the ultimate, and meditative equipoise are equivalents, being free of what is thought of and aspects. The form kāyas, the seeming, and subsequent attainment are also equivalents, referring to delusive aspects. As for the meditation of the Aspectarians, while mind has aspects, they all have the nature of mind itself. By not realizing this, these aspects are taken to be all kinds of referents, through which afflictions arise, because this arises as saṃsāra. Once the former ceases, the latter also ceases. Thus they meditate on everything being mind. By meditating on everything as mind and imaginary entities not existing, mind clearly displays as diversity, since it is free of thought and its aspects are not blocked. Since it is free of perceiver and perceived, there are no dualistic appearances. While experiencing everything as mind, they meditate based on certain distinctive features. The quote from the *Jñānasārasamuccaya* [TRVC *dznya na mi dra*; thus referring to Jñānaśrīmitra] means that in the meditation of the Aspectarians, no matter how cognition may be scattered, by being recognized as cognition, its being scattered subsides. As for the meditation of the Nonaspectarians, not realizing that there is nothing apart from mind, it is taken to be all kinds of referents, because one thus cycles in saṃsāra. Out of the wish to stop this, they meditate on the mere mind that is free of all this. Since this meditation is not separated from aspects such as bliss and constitutes the branch of calm abiding, it is blissful. Since it is free of anything imaginary, the duality of perceiver and perceived does not appear. Since it is free of thinking, it is devoid of what is thought of. Since aspects do not exist ultimately, they do not appear, while there is an experience of cognition without any aspects. Thus they meditate with this special instruction. The meaning of Śāntipa's quote [TRVC seems to attribute the stanza from the *Ālokamālā* to Ratnākaraśānti] is that self-awareness is lucid, aspects have vanished in it, and it is not tainted by any thoughts. If one does not meditate, this will not be known. The quote from the *Triṃśikā* means that by understanding that there is nothing other apart from mind, mind turns away from all aspects. When not separated from the experience of aspects having ceased, perceiver and perceived do not exist. Hence this is the realization of mind being without any aspects. As for the stains of the meditation of the Aspectarians, even if endowed with the four characteristics of their meditation as discussed above, if it is preceded by clinging to cognition with aspects being permanent, this is a stain because it means straying into the *Bhagavatsiddhānta*. This text asserts that everything that appears has the nature of one's own mind and that the entirety of one's own mind is Brahman, whose essence is a permanent cognition that is all-pervasive [TRVC also attributes stanza 7 to this text]. As for the stains of the Nonaspectarians, if their meditation as discussed above is preceded by clinging to cognition without aspects being permanent, this is a stain because it means straying into the position of Bhāskara. Here, "names and forms" refers to the five skandhas, "discursiveness" to what is imaginary, "lucid" to self-awareness, "infinite" to its continuum being incessant, "uninterrupted" to there being no intermittent ceasing of its arising, and this awareness being "permanent" to it being changeless. As for the source of this ("The empty water bubbles . . ."), by realizing the ocean of the permanent self—cognition without aspects—it is pellucid. Though the diversity of aspects is without any arising and ceasing, thoughts are adventitious, and the self's own nature is without any taints. The view of the Yogācāras is like that of the Sautrāntikas.

1983. GZ CDNP "analysis."

1984. CDNP *de gnyis* ("the two") instead of GZ *de nyid*.

1985. With minor variations, this stanza is found as *Jñānasārasamuccaya* 28 (ascribed to Āryadeva), Jetāri's *Sugatamatavibhāgakārikā* 1 (D3899, fol. 7b.5), and Atiśa's *Dharmadhātudarśanagīti* 45 (text 153), and in the *Vimalaprabhā* commentary on the *Kālacakratantra* (D1347, fol. 196b.3). The first two lines are also found in the *Śālistambasūtra* (Vaidya 1961, 1:115).

1986. GZ CDNP ". . . [True reality] is not existent, because this is invalidated through proof statements. Nor does it not exist: through the power of latent tendencies, it appears as what is unreal. Because there are these two flaws in both of these [positions], it is not [both]. It is not neither of the two, because such a thought does not exist [CDNP omit this sentence]. Furthermore, without analyzing past and present, how and where could it follow that the diversity [of the world], in just the way it appears, is real in the same way as a substance? This is the examination of 'illusion-like nonduality.'"

1987. GZ CDNP "This is the dhyāna of illusion-like nonduality."

1988. CDNP "To be confident about illusion-like nonduality and to perfect the six pāramitās is their view." TRVC (385–88) says that if the Mādhyamikas are divided by way of the seeming, they are of two types: those who speak of outer referents and those who speak of internal mere mind [*sems can* em. *sems tsam*]. Here, however, if divided by way of the ultimate, they are the two Mādhyamikas of illusion-like nonduality and utter nonabiding. Though those of illusion-like nonduality are also twofold, here, they are ascertained in common. What validates consists of the perceptions and inferential cognitions that follow the conventions of the seeming. Inferences are understood through the reasons that are the means for understanding and that cut through superimpositions. To yogīs, illusion-like nonduality is manifest in a clear and direct manner. What is to be validated is the delusive ultimate, free of discursiveness. In terms of true reality, the ultimate that accords with reasoning is called "the reality [*bde* em. *bden*] that follows reasoning." The appearances of delusion, just as they are, make up seeming reality, which is called "the reality that accords with conventions." The seeming is twofold: by way of being or not being able to perform functions from the perspective of conventional states of mind, there is the correct seeming and the false seeming, such as what appears as water and a mirage taken to be water, respectively. The false seeming is also twofold: by way of being in a conceptual or nonconceptual state of mind, there is the conceptual and the nonconceptual false seeming, such as what appears as a self and a conch shell appearing to be yellow, respectively. By way of being the actual one and the imputed one, the ultimate is twofold as well: nominal and nonnominal. The nominal ultimate is again twofold: the nominal ultimate in terms of objects in which one portion of reference points has been cut through and the nominal ultimate in terms of a cognition based on reasoning that is undeceiving. The stanza beginning with "neither existent" teaches the dimension of the ultimate that is nonnominal and is free of the four extremes. What is to be expressed by this stanza is cognition. Its being nonexistent means that imputations are not to be found. "Proof statements" refers to reasoning statements, such as the four arguments [*rtag pa* em. *rtags*] of being free from one and many, the vajra slivers, negating arising from the four possibilities, and dependent origination. "Appears as what is unreal" means to appear while not being findable. Ultimately, such appearances are not findable if examined through reasoning, but while they are unfindable, they are present as the delusiveness that has the characteristic called "appearance." "Furthermore," appearances are not present as any reality that accords with the way they appear. This implicitly teaches that they are present as mere mistaken appearances: if known to be mere delusion, what is not delusion is identified. As for their meditation, by fixating on anything, even if it is the cognition of the ultimate, as being real, the afflictions arise, karma is accumulated, and one thus cycles in saṃsāra. If the clinging to real existence ceases, saṃsāra ceases [*bzo lag pa* em. *'khor ba log pa*]; hence they meditate on everything being delusive. Once the certainty that all appearances are delusive has arisen, similar to an illusionist being certain that his illusion is delusive, to again and again give rise to a conceptual state of mind of being certain that appearances are unceasing delusiveness is the meditation here. The stain of meditation is the clinging to mere delusiveness. However, it is said that if appearances are negatively determined to be mere delusiveness, this is not [TRVC no negative, but "However" requires one] a stain of meditation. In the context of the view, since the branches of prajñā and means are the distinctive features of what is sealed and what seals, they are not [TRVC no negative, but the context requires one] mentioned here, while the branch of renunciation accords with the one of the Sautrāntikas.

1989. This stanza is identical to *Mahāyānaviṃśikā* 4. GZ CDNP omit "nor without both."

1990. To my knowledge, this line (*yac cit vetti na cittatām*) contains the single but remarkable attested instance of Skt. *cittatā* in the sense of mind's true nature, in contradistinction to *citta* ("mind"). While Tibetan texts otherwise frequently use *sems nyid* in this sense (usually, however, without a Sanskrit equivalent), curiously, GZ CDNP here read *sems ni sems kyis rig ma yin* (thus using *sems* twice instead of *sems nyid* for *cittatā*). For details on the Tibetan distinction between *sems* and *sems nyid* as a hallmark in the context of Mahāmudrā, see the introduction in volume 1. GZ CDNP:

> The wise realize entities' true reality
> here as being everything's nonabiding [CDNP "since this does not abide at all"]
> Hence, by way of this kind of thinking,
> the mind does not perceive the mind.

With slight variations, the last line of this stanza as well as the following four stanzas are also found in the *Mahāmayūrīvidyārājñīsūtraśatasahasraṭīkā* (D2691, fol. 116a.4–6) by Karmavajra (maybe one of Patampa Sangyé's gurus; see BA, 869), but are attributed there to master Karmavajra himself as being stanzas on the inconceivable and inexpressible nature of *vidyā(mantra)*.

1991. Skt. *apoha* can also mean "denial" and *vidhi* "creation," "contrivance," "conduct," "application," "precept," and "rule." This stanza is identical to *Sekanirdeśa* 32. GZ CDNP:

> As long as there are all superimpositions,
> their entirety does not exist in any respect
> Thus the middle's actuality lacks superimpositions
> Hence there is neither any negation nor affirmation.

1992. This stanza is identical to *Sekanirdeśa* 30. GZ CDNP:

> That which is effortless cognition
> is expressed as being inconceivable
> Not conceiving while conceiving
> is not expressed as inconceivable.

1993. This stanza is identical to *Sekanirdeśa* 34. GZ CDNP:

> The mental state of "the world is unborn"
> is pure, and hence it is realization as such
> The native state of the world is the reality
> Due to being intelligent [or "by having that mental state"], there is no effort.

1994. GZ CDNP:

> Being free of all superimpositions
> is what I express as true reality

Designations such as emptiness [CDNP "It is designated as emptiness and so on and"]
cut through superimpositions onto it.

1995. GZ CDNP "The meaning of this examination [GZ *rtag pa* CDNP *btags pa* em. *brtags pa*] is as follows. Their dhyāna is [GZ CDNP mistakenly add "not"] to directly perceive, without any clinging, the nature of the actuality that is without any superimpositions. To view all referents as extinction or to become [like] the nature of [inanimate] matter are the stains of their samādhi. To perfect the six pāramitās that are without any superimpositions is their view."

1996. GZ CDNP ". . . [This compassion] is to be understood as arising by focusing on all dharmas that consist of [GZ adds "all"] dharmas stirred by the wind of impermanence. The one of those who are the highest [Mādhyamikas] is the compassion that is nonreferential—the direct realization by mentally engaging in phenomena that lack any nature." Thus GZ CDNP support the translation of the last sentence in this paragraph. Vajrapāṇi's commentary *Guruparamparākramopadeśa* (text 213, 195–96) says: "[Theirs] is the compassion that is without focus because they mentally engage in not observing any phenomenon as anything whatsoever." Translating Vajrapāṇi's comment slightly differently and taking that as a support for his rendering, Mathes 2015 (73) translates: "But for those with superior faculties (i.e., the Mādhyamikas), compassion, for which essencelessness is the focus, is without a focus, phenomena being understood by directing [one's] attention [towards their emptiness]." In a note (n187), Mathes adds: "This in accordance with Vajrapāṇi's commentary . . . '[Their] compassion is without a focus, since they concentrate their mind by not focusing on any phenomenon whatsoever.' (*chos thams cad cir yang mi dmigs par yid la byed pas na (B ni) mi dmigs pa'i snying rje'o* |). It would be also possible to read *amanaskāra-* instead of *manaskāra*. If the reading *adhigamo* of N and T (which is supported by the Tibetan) was followed, and *cālambanā* changed into *cānālambano* (i.e., as depending on *adhigamo*), the context would require to read *naiḥsvabhāvya-* or *niḥsvabhāvatā-* instead of *niḥsvabhāvā* in compound. According to the *Amanasikārādhāra* the concentration (*manaskāra* or *manasikāra*) on essencelessness is one possible meaning of *amanasikāra*, the privative *a* standing for *anutpāda* and thus emptiness. Such a reading would result in 'And for those with superior faculties compassion is without a focus, [their] realization of phenomena through concentrating on essencelessness being without a focus.' (*adhimātrasya cānālambano naiḥsvabhāvyamanaskāradharmādhigamo 'nālambanā karuṇā* |)."

1997. *Abhisamayālaṃkāra* VIII.33, VIII.12, and VIII.1. According to TRVC (388–93), the proponents of the utter nonabiding of all phenomena are twofold, speaking of the utter nonabiding in terms of emptiness and the utter nonabiding in terms of unity. Those who propound the utter nonabiding in terms of emptiness assert two things. (a) The buddha wisdom that involves appearances of the seeming and has the character of delusion is a cognition during subsequent attainment. (b) All cognitions belong to the seeming, everything seeming is delusion, and therefore there are no cognitions in buddhas because all delusion has been relinquished. The stains of meditation discussed below refer to those two assertions. Their approach accepts valid cognitions that validate by following conventions, but since they lack any scriptural tradition of their own assertions, they do not assert anything to be validated or what validates it in terms of ascertaining such assertions—all they do is to negate the scriptural traditions of others by demonstrating their (internal) contradictions. Since the seeming is [TRVC *min* em. *yin*] entirely in terms of worldly people, it is exactly like worldly people say. Ultimate true reality constitutes the thesis of reasonings—how things really are for the noble ones—that is, it is nothing but the mere extinction of any reference points of appearances. They also assert that the seeming and the ultimate cannot be expressed as being the same or different. Now, in the approach of the utter nonabiding in terms of unity—the philosophical system of Maitrīpa's own ultimate scriptural tradition—what validates consists of scriptures, pith instructions, and cognitions based on reasoning. What is to be validated consists of the inseparability of the two realities. As for true reality, all appearances are mind, but mind refers to merely being beyond all the reference points and discursiveness of mind. It is from the perspective of appearance that he speaks of "the seeming," while he speaks of "the ultimate" from the perspective of being free from reference points. These two have a connection of same identity, similar to what is impermanent and what is produced. In this text, which teaches this, Maitrīpa speaks of "being free from extremes" and "lacking superimpositions." The first expression refers to "diversity . . ." "Permanent" does not refer to merely not perishing but to the nature of not rejecting anything, as in the case of the natural moistness of water. The text says it "is not" permanent because nothing is established by any essence. "Extinct" does not refer to the mere discontinuation of existence but is a synonym of sheer nonexistence. "Nor is it held" refers to not relinquishing the appearances of the seeming. "The wise . . ." refers to the true reality that does not abide as any extreme, which is the experiential sphere of the cognition of those who are skilled in the three cognitions. Though "hence . . ." is stated by matching this with a valid cognition that validates, ultimately, the true state is not observable as anything whatsoever. Therefore, within mind itself, mind's nature does not abide as any extreme at all. "The sum . . ." refers to lacking superimposition and denial. According to our own position, the meaning of "middle" refers to appearances being free of superimpositions. To that, Aspectarian and Nonaspectarian Mere Mentalists object: "Since superimpositions are the imaginary nature, we also assert their nonexistence," and the proponents of illusion-like nonduality object: "Since superimpositions refer to superimpositions of real existence, we also assert their nonexistence." Therefore Maitrīpa explains the manner of lacking superimpositions by saying: "The sum of superimpositions, however many, does not exist in any respect in its entirety." Here, lacking superimpositions refers to all superimpositions without exception being extinct, lacking all aspects of apprehended and clung-to objects, and lacking all states of preparation, main part, and conclusion. Thus it is not the case that the Mere Mentalists and the proponents of illusion-like nonduality lack the superimpositions of mind and delusiveness, respectively. Hence it is not that they lack these kinds of apprehended objects and objects of clinging; though they assert that they do not superimpose these during meditative equipoise, they do assert superimposing them during its preparation and conclusion. Consequently, what is called "lacking superimpositions" here is not [TRVC has no negative, but the context requires one] possible for them. In this way, here, since appearances are not relinquished, there is nothing to deny; since there is no superimposing, there is nothing to be affirmed either. This state of mind that is free from any superimpositions is what is to be realized by the inconceivable state of mind. There are three such states: being inconceivable by not conceiving, being inconceivable by conceiving, and being inconceivable without conceiving but fully knowing true actuality. Here, Maitrīpa's statement "That which is effortless prajñā is proclaimed to be inconceivable" teaches the realization of being inconceivable without conceiving but fully knowing actuality. This is similar to knowing moistness by seeing water or the ceasing of any state of mind in terms of color and shape by looking at space. Likewise, by experiencing the nature of the mind, nonconceptuality comes on its own accord thanks to thoughts being dismantled. "But a conceived inconceivable cannot truly be inconceivable" means that it is not findable by searching for it through reasoning. Therefore, merely by thinking of nonconceptuality, the inconceivable is not realized. Merely by realizing a cognition that lacks the realization of true actuality, the inconceivable is not realized either. Rather, it abides within. "The mental state . . ." teaches that through realizing one's own mind as such, the true reality of all beings is realized. "Being free . . ." means that the characteristic of true reality is to be free from superimpositions, which the Buddha taught as emptiness and so on: this kind of lack of superimpositions is merely for the sake of putting an end to the superimpositions of entities. In general, not realizing the true reality of entities is the cause of saṃsāra. Through mistaken cognitions, the flaws of the afflictions arise. For, as stated here in particular, no matter how the mind may create superimpositions, it is there that the afflictions arise and one circles in saṃsāra. The intention behind this is to not even abide in mind, being free of any superimpositions: if one finds anything to abide in, one will be seized by the beguiling venomous snakes of the afflictions. Thus, by experiencing the nature of the mind that is free from any superimpositions, these Mādhyamikas familiarize with the lucid awareness in which mind is without thoughts and clinging and all appearances are unceasing. "The extinction of all referents . . ." refers to the stains of meditation. To meditate by wishing to be free from all appearances of the seeming and the ultimate, and thus wishing for cognition to cease altogether, represents the stain of familiarizing with being free from superimpositions. "To perfect . . ." describes the view in terms of the means not being separated [TRVC *'brel ba* em. *bral ba*] from prajñā. The branch of renunciation is like that of the Sautrāntikas. Now, the differences in compassion are taught. Though those who are lower and medium—Sautrāntikas and Vijñaptivādins—also give rise to the compassion that focuses on sentient beings, they mainly give rise to the compassion that focuses on phenomena: understanding that all phenomena are impermanent, they see that, by taking them to be permanent, sentient beings are under the sway of saṃsāric suffering and therefore they wish for them to free from suffering. Since śrāvakas and pratyekabuddhas assert permanent unconditioned phenomena, they are not presented as giving rise to this kind of compassion. As for "the compassion of those who are the highest," by seeing that, similar to reflections of the moon in moving water, beings are empty of any movement or nature, the Mādhyamikas feel compassion for these beings. Though they also give rise to the two former kinds of compassion within the scope of seeming reality, the compassion in terms of their very own approach is the compassion that is without focus (or nonreferential): having realized that all phenomena lack any essence, it is the wish that all sentient beings who do not realize this are free from suffering. As the fourth main point, the three kāyas are taught. By cultivating the nine approaches in a progressive manner and finally training in familiarizing with nonabiding, the five paths are traveled, the ten bhūmis attained, and buddhahood is reached. The first stanza here describes the nirmāṇakāya, which guides all beings and brings all kinds of benefits to them until saṃsāra is empty. The second stanza refers to the sambhogakāya, which is the rainbow-like kāya endowed with the major and minor marks that is the experiential sphere of bodhisattvas on the bhūmis because they enjoy the Mahāyāna through this kāya. The third stanza explains the dharmakāya, which is endowed with twofold purity (being the nature of buddhahood, it is also called "svābhāvikakāya"). "Uncontaminated" refers to its purity of all stains because it is free of the two obscurations that are the contaminations. "The purity of dharmas in every respect" refers to its natural purity.

1998. This often-cited stanza is from the *Nayatrayapradīpa* (D3707, fol. 16b.3–4; text 217, 457). According to Tipi Bumlabar's commentary on the *Tattvaratnāvalī* (Ti pi 'bum la 'bar 2004a, 394), the *Nayatrayapradīpa* teaches the difference between the Mantrayāna and the Pāramitāyāna through reasons [*rgyud kyis* em. *rgyus*] that excellently establish it. "It lacks ignorance" because afflictions and thoughts are realized as dharmatā. "It is abundant in means" because there are many collections of causes of the four mudrās with regard to the individual faculties. "It lacks suffering" because bliss is made into the path. "It is the prerogative of those of sharp faculties" because even ordinary beings, when relying on the creation process in the manner of taking a direct leap, accomplish not returning to any lower yānas. For detailed (and sometimes quite different) explanations of this stanza, see the *Nayatrayapradīpa* itself and Divākaracandra's *Prajñājñānaprakāśa* (text 16, 62ff.), while some shorter comments are contained in Sahajavajra's *Sthitisamāsa* VI.6–13 (text 17), the *Caturmudrāṭīkā* (text 44, 265–66), and Vajrapāṇi's *Guruparamparākramopadeśa* (text 213, 196).

1999. This is an alternate name of Maitrīpa's *Sekanirdeśa*. GZ CDNP "We do not explain the approach of secret mantra here because it is very profound, because it is an experiential object [only] for persons who have faith in this profound yāna, and because the accomplishment of the four mudrās and so on is to be taught in an extensive manner. For this is taught as follows: . . . We have taught this in the '*Sekanirdeśa*.'" According to TRVC (393–94), the reasons for Maitrīpa not explaining the Mantrayāna here are as follows. "Profound" means that since it is difficult to realize, it is not understood even if it is explained. For "not understanding" does not refer to explaining the meaning of the three yānas [those based on the sūtras], which is explained to students by way of the progressive stages of training. The training in the Mantrayāna, however, is only explained to those with great faith in the secret mantra. It is possible, though, that people become suitable vessels by training. For them, the meaning of the four mudrās is explained in treatises such as the *Caturmudrānvaya*, so there is no need to explain this here. The scriptural source of the first two justifications here [the *Nayatrayapradīpa*] teaches the difference between the Mantrayāna and the Pāramitāyāna through reasons [TRVC *rgyud kyis* em. *rgyus*] that excellently establish it. "It lacks ignorance" because afflictions and thoughts are realized as dharmatā. "It is abundant in means" because there are many collections of causes of the four mudrās with regard to the individual faculties. "It lacks suffering" because bliss is made into the path. "It is the prerogative of those of sharp faculties" because even ordinary beings, when relying on the creation process in the manner of taking a direct leap, accomplish not returning to any lower yānas. This approach of secret mantra is also explained in the *Sekanirdeśa*, in which these four differences are likewise complete in an implicit manner.

2000. Mathes's edition reads *mahāyānanirṇīta evārthaḥ paramārtho 'bhyasyaḥ* ("if this reality that is only ascertained in the Mahāyāna refers to familiarizing with the ultimate" or "if the familiarization with this reality that is the ultimate is only ascertained in the Mahāyāna"). For simplicity's sake, I follow *mahāyānanirṇīta evārthaḥ paramārtho 'sti asya/atra* in two of the other manuscripts.

2001. GZ CDNP "'If this actuality that is the ultimate is ascertained [only] in the Mahāyāna, why did the Bhagavān teach the yānas of śrāvakas and pratyekabuddhas in order to familiarize with the ultimate?' They are [for] those of lower intelligence—they were taught like the steps of a staircase in order to realize the Mahāyāna, which is what is to be attained."

2002. *Ālokamālā* 176. GZ CDNP:

> When those sentient beings who are
> beginners are introduced to the ultimate,
> the perfect buddhas have proclaimed
> these means like the steps of a staircase.

2003. In the *Saddharmapuṇḍarīkasutra* (H116, fols. 32b.7–33a.1), the first two and the second two lines are switched. Skt. *upadarśayāmi* can also simply mean "I explain" or "I show," but the context seems to make it clear that the Buddha's presentation of three yānas is not for real. GZ CDNP:

> The yāna is single, the approach is single,
> and this teaching by the chiefs is single too
> Any of the teachings of the three yānas
> are the entity of my skill in methods.

2004. *Niraupamyastava* 21.

2005. *Pramāṇavārttika* II.253cd (*Pramāṇasiddhi* chapter). GZ CDNP:

> You will be liberated by virtue of emptiness
> If this is not understood, you will be bound

The remaining meditations are for that purpose.

2006. GZ CD "For this kind of teaching on the three yānas will be examined [GZ *brtag* CDNP *rtogs*, "realized"] by the Bhagavān for the sake of sentient beings by way of the differences of general and specific thoughts." NP "For this kind of teaching on the three yānas is for the sake of realizing the meaning of thinking, 'It is empty of being conceptual and nonconceptual.'"

2007. *Niraupamyastava* 7. GZ NP read the first two lines as follows:

> Lord, in one speech of yours
> you did not speak a single word.

2008. GZ CDNP omit "shaken by imaginations."

2009. As mentioned before, this stanza is identical to *Kudṛṣṭinirghātana* 2 and appears in almost the same form in Jñānakīrti's *Tattvāvatāra* (text 214, 280), where it is most likely a quote (being in the middle of a string of other quotes). However, supported by "like a wish-fulfilling tree" in the first line in GZ CDNP of *Kudṛṣṭinirghātana* 2, there is a very similar stanza in Śāntarakṣita's *Tattvasaṃgraha* (chapter XXIII, 2049; D4266, fol. 74b.6–7) that seems to have served as the basis of the stanza in Maitrīpa's two texts and the one in the *Tattvāvatāra*:

> Being similar to a wish-fulfilling tree,
> though unshaken by volition's winds,
> the Sage promotes the consummate
> welfare of the world in its entirety.

2010. *Laṅkāvatārasūtra* X.458.

2011. GZ CDNP add "stainless" here.

2012. GZ CDNP:

> As I aspire for the quintessence,
> this is not an extensive teaching
> All you learned ones who delight
> in all the details, bear with me!

2013. GZ CDNP:

> Requested by fortunate ones, I composed this,
> which has unsurpassable meaning, with effort
> Through the merit that I have attained thereby,
> may future sentient beings attain tathāgatahood!

According to TRVC (394–97), this section of the text teaches the fifth main point: (5) in terms of the definitive meaning, all that was said so far is included in a single yāna. This has two parts. First, the intention behind teaching three yānas is explained. Though the text explicitly explains the meaning of certain sūtras, implicitly, this also matches the path of this very treatise. The meaning of the dispute here is as follows. "If the Mahāyāna exists as the definitive meaning, the ultimate that is the attainment of buddhahood, this is what is to be familiarized with, but what is the point of teaching the two yānas that are not this kind of ultimate that is to be familiarized with?" These two yānas were taught for those who are inferior so that they give rise to the experience of the Mahāyāna, progressively entering it like ascending the steps of a staircase. Here, it is to be understood that there are those who engage in a progressive manner and those who engage in a simultaneous manner. "In order to attain the Mahāyāna" means that the purpose of teaching the other two yānas is not to attain their two kinds of awakening but to give rise to the path to buddhahood in the mind stream. As for "like the steps of a staircase," it is to be understood that this is said for the sake of actually familiarizing with the progressively later stages based on the preceding ones, beginning with those of the śrāvakas, and thus finally giving rise to the familiarization with nonabiding; it is not taught as merely something to be known. It is to be understood that all of these approaches thus give rise to the path to buddhahood, and since their fruition is buddhahood alone, they constitute a single yāna. "Beginners" are those who have not trained before. "Introduced to the ultimate" refers to giving rise to the realization of nonabiding. "The means" consists of cultivating those two yānas. "The yāna is single" refers to the single path and fruition. "The approach is single" means that for us, there is no approach that is discordant with that. "Methods" means to cultivate those two yānas as the means to bring forth the cultivation of the Mahāyāna. The meaning of Nāgārjuna's *Niraupamyastava* is that since the object—dharmatā—is one, the subject is also one, which is buddhahood. Thus any other yānas are not possible. However, they were taught as a means to give rise to the Mahāyāna path in the mind stream. The *Pramāṇavārttika* says that emptiness matches nonabiding, while the remaining meditations match being illusion-like, missing parts. "For that purpose" means that the preceding meditations are cultivated for the sake of giving rise to nonabiding. Second [TRVC does not explicitly pick up its above-mentioned second part, but it seems that it consists of the following], "This illumination . . ." teaches the reasons for teaching three yānas. Though buddhas do not have any thoughts, through the power of their previous aspiration prayers, they have the ability to teach. The dharma of the buddhas is not uttered to others, it only appears for those to be guided. However, in our approach, there is not even a single dharma spoken by buddhas while being impaired by thinking; rather, buddhas teach the dharma without any thinking. Unlike in this explanation, the Buddha also said: "I made the statement 'The Bhagavān did not teach the slightest thing from the night he attained realization until he passed into parinirvāṇa' by having individual distinct dharma approaches in mind." "Imaginations" means that though there are no thoughts, the welfare of others is promoted, similar to a wish-fulfilling jewel. "A turning wheel" means that though there are no thoughts, the explanation of the dharma takes place thanks to previous accumulations of merit. For as long as the mind operates by way of thinking, since the yānas are not the fruition that is the end of the path, the dharma continues to be taught. However, once the mind has become without thought, there is no yāna (no path), nor is there any traveling higher and higher. Finally, the activities of completing the composition of this text are threefold. Stanza 17 refers to the composition of these instructions, saying: "By relying on this *Tattvaratnāvalī*, whose name was given to it based on the example of a jewel garland, persons with compassion, keep it in your minds without forgetting it!" Stanza 18 requests forbearance, saying: "As I, Maitreyanātha, delight in teaching the dharma that is compassionate, I have not taught all the dharmas that could be taught in detail but just some quintessential parts. Thus I request the learned who delight in details to bear with me." Therefore this is called "the cycle of the pith." Stanza 19 represents the dedication, saying: "Having been requested by fortunate ones, may I through the merit of having composed this treatise attain tathāgatahood at a future time!" Note that BKC (vol. *kha*, 314–53) contains yet another, anonymous commentary on the *Tattvaratnāvalī* (attributed to "king Göla's [Tib. 'Gos la] minister Bhavya" in the table of contents), which, however, seems not to contain significant additional materials.

2014. Skt. "This concludes 'A Jewel Garland of True Reality.' It was composed by the venerable Paṇḍita Avadhūta Advayavajra." CDNP ". . . composed by master Avadhūtipa Advayavajra. It was translated by Nagtso Tsültrim Gyalwa." According to Tipi Bumlabar (BKC, vol. *kha*, fols. 83b.5–84a.6), the outline of this text is as follows:

1. introduction
1a. paying homage
1b. commitment to explain
1c. teaching the purpose and the connection by way of possessing a lineage
2. meaning of the text
2a. teaching the entrance gates of the three yānas by way of their paths and fruitions
2b. teaching the different ways of making assertions about appearances as the four positions
2c. teaching which positions are included in which yānas
2d. teaching the means to practice the nine approaches
2d1. lower śrāvakas [TRVC *nyams* em. *nyan thos*]
2d2. medium śrāvakas
2d3. highest śrāvakas
all three śrāvakas are discussed under four points: 1. analysis, 2. dhyāna, 3. stains of dhyāna, and 4. view; by way of the distinctions of their dispositions, in terms of the definitive meaning, all train as people with the Mahāyāna disposition
2d4. pratyekabuddhas (same four points; stains of dhyāna: brief introduction and detailed explanation; additional teaching on the differences of their distinct compassions)
2d5. Sautrāntikas in the Mahāyāna (same four points)
2d6. Mere Mentalist Aspectarians
2d7. Mere Mentalist Nonaspectarians (both same four points; both explained, as they are well-known)
2d8. Mādhyamikas of illusion-like [nonduality] (same four points; analysis: brief introduction and detailed explanation)
2d9. Mādhyamikas of utter nonabiding

2d9a. actual explanation
2d9b. and the difference in compassion
2d9c. the way in which the fruition—the three kāyas—arises from having practiced this
2d9d. justification why the yāna of secret mantra is not discussed here
2d9e. showing the purpose of teaching three [TRVC omits "three"] yānas and so on, though the yāna is a single one in terms of the definitive meaning
3. conclusion
3a. teaching the name of the treatise
3b. concluding justification of the composition and request for forbearance
3c. dedicating the roots of virtue
For further comments and details, see Mathes 2015 (8–9, 59–94).

2015. PDMT, 26:349–51.
2016. GZ CDNP "I pay homage to youthful Mañjuśrī."
2017. GZ CDNP "what has the three buddhakāyas' essence."
2018. GZ CDNP have "I salute what has the character of prajñā and means" as the last line.
2019. GZ CDNP:

> Just as strands of hair appear in the sky
> for persons who have blurred vision,
> so the childish beings who are obscured
> by the darkness of ignorance, think of the world.

2020. GZ CDNP:

> Look with pure eyes at the strands of
> hair perceived in the sky due to delusion!
> In their pure vision, the yogīs realize
> that the entirety of existence is like that.

2021. GZ CDNP:

> "Hey, look into the sky's center,
> I see tangled-up strands of hair!"
> Those with pure eyes would say:
> "There are none, your perceptiveness is confused."

2022. GZ CDNP have the last two lines as follows:

> As removal and nonremoval [CDNP "display and nondisplay"] are empty,
> at the time of [CDNP "in"] true reality, there is no stopping or creating.

2023. GZ CDNP:

Likewise, the uncontaminated dharmas
unfold for the welfare of sentient beings
through the dependent aspiration prayers
of the sambhogakāyas [CDNP "the [sam]bhoga- and nirmāṇakāyas"].

2024. GZ CDNP read the last two lines as follows:

They are uncontrived and effortless— [CDNP "their nature is established as uncontrived"]
the distinction dispels mind's doubts.

2025. GZ CDNP *rnam rig* "Vijñapti[vādins]."
2026. GZ CDNP:

A cognition free from the four extremes,
which is real as a substance and nondual,
empty of thought, and without any duality,
is known by the Vijñaptivāda learned ones.

2027. GZ CDNP "empty of substance."
2028. GZ "is relied on."
2029. GZ CDNP include "the view of."
2030. As mentioned before, the *Avikalpapraveśadhāraṇī* describes how bodhisattvas enter the expanse of nonconceptuality by relinquishing all coarse and subtle characteristics of conceptions in terms of (1) nature (perceiver and perceived or the five skandhas), (2) remedies, (3) true reality, and (4) attainment. These four characteristics are relinquished in a gradual manner by means of analyzing their nature, their qualities, and their essence, and finally by not mentally engaging in them at all (see Brunnhölzl 2012, 330–31). The last three of these four characteristics are also mentioned at the beginnings of Maitrīpa's *Kudṛṣṭinirghātana* (text 19) and *Nirvedhapañcaka* (text 28), *Sekanirdeśa* 36ac (text 42), and Rāmapāla's *Sekanirdeśapañjikā* on it (text 45), and discussed in detail in Sahajavajra's *Tattvadaśakaṭīkā* (40–44). The *Avikalpapraveśadhāraṇī*'s general notion of relinquishing conceptual characteristics is quoted in Maitrīpa's *Amanasikārādhāra* (text 27).
2031. GZ CDNP "attained."
2032. Skt. "This concludes 'An Illumination of True Reality.'" CDNP ". . . composed by the master Advayavajra" (NP add "It was translated by Paṇḍita Vajrapāṇi and lotsāwa Mapen Chöbar."). In BKC (vol. *kha*, fol. 33b.1–5), this text is followed by addressing its underlying intention. Through the power of the contrivances of the conventional presentations of what is justified in the minds of the Mādhyamikas of illusion-like nonduality, their refutations, and the bliss-emptiness that is experienced by them, one will not arrive in the connate's innermost. Therefore, without examining and analyzing conventions and clinging to real existence, the connate is introduced by pointing it out as naturalness. The ultimate is the nonfinding of both objects [maybe perceiver and perceived or ultimate and seeming] when searching. In that, not even mere appearances are established, while appearances dawn as empty dependent

origination. This is taken as the view of our own system. Given the reason that what arises from conditions is actually unarisen, if you Mādhyamikas of illusion-like nonduality assert arising, your justification for that would correspond to Mere Mentalism, and if you assert nonarising, your justification for that would follow our system. Thus, explain to us what your own tenet would be like! "Freedom from the four extremes" and "dependent origination" are mere names—by making the true reality in which there is nothing to be removed or to be added a living experience by adorning it with the pith instructions (compare *Tattvadaśaka* 2cd), the fruition is revealed through the path of the illusory body, luminosity, and unity. Since this is what Nāgārjuna declared, this approach is the definitive one [that is, the last three of the five stages of perfection-process practices in the *Guhyasamājatantra* according to Nāgārjuna's *Pañcakrama*]. According to Tipi Bumlabar (BKC, vol. *kha*, fol. 86b.1–2), the outline of this text is as follows:

1. expression of homage
2. meaning of the text
2a. distinctive features of the three cognitions
2b. the fruition of practice—the four kāyas
2c. distinctive features of the view
2d. the means for letting the mind be
2e. this being composed by following whom
3. conclusion.

For further comments and details, see Mathes 2015 (15, 163–67).

2033. PDMT, 26:352–58.

2034. In accordance with GZ NP *kun brtags* PTMC *kun brtag* (CD *kun rtag*) and the context, I take Skt. *parikalpa* in the sense of *parikalpita*; this is further supported by the quote of this stanza in text 46 (28) reading *brtags pa* and PTMC's gloss (see below).

2035. GZ CDNP:

> . . .
> have the nature of being empty, and don't exist as entities [CDNP "since they are empty of a nature of their own, they do not exist as entities"]
> . . .
> may form and all the rest be victorious . . .

In BKC (vol. *kha*, fol. 17a.5–25a.2), this text is followed by a commentary on selected phrases (abbreviated PTMC), based on the Tibetan translation and in all probability written by Tipi Bumlabar (see the parallels with his outline of text 36 in the final note). Usually, the commentator cites only one or two words to explain, but sometimes these explanations refer to the entire phrase or sentence that begins with these words. Also, in this commentary as well as in Tipi Bumlabar's outline, "Vajradhara" is considered a synonym of "Vajrasattva" (obviously based on the fact that the seal of Vajrasattva is equivalent to "the Vajradhara relief"). The comments on the title and the first stanza say this: "After Śrī Maitreyanātha [Maitrīpa] had refuted the scriptural traditions of others, out of the wish to teach nothing but his own system of accomplishing the seal of Vajradhara, he composed *A Commentary on the Five Seals of the Tathāgatas.* [In the title,] 'the five tathāgatas' refers to examining entities from the perspective of meditating on them as being deities—that is, establishing appearances as mind. 'Seal' refers to the topic, from one point of view, being nonconceptuality [given the following explanations, *mi rtag pa* "impermanence" is emended to *mi rtog pa*]. Among the two parts of this [text], (1) the brief introduction [is as follows]. 'In dependence' refers to appearances being able to perform functions. 'They arose' means that the respectively latter ones arise from the respectively former ones. 'The imaginary' refers to having imagined that referents, which [actually] do not exist outside of the mind, do exist so. 'Are empty' means they are mere [appearances], empty of outer referents, which represents the seal of the tathāgatas. 'The nature of being empty' refers to thought-free self-awareness empty of duality—the view of Mere Mentalism—which represents the seal of Akṣobhya. The seal of Vajradhara refers to 'don't exist as entities'—that is, this thought-free [self-awareness] empty of duality is also not established as an entity. Because of being free from extremes [*mi* em. *mu*], this is the view of Madhyamaka free from discursiveness. Thus what is to be refuted by the seal of the tathāgatas is something perceived that is external, what is to be refuted by the seal of Akṣobhya is the perceiver, and what is to be refuted by the seal of Vajradhara is both perceiver and perceived. But this is 'not extinct'—that is, the seal of Vajradhara is not the view of extinction; that flaw is relinquished. 'Diversity' means 'pellucid emptiness.' 'Nature of the mind' means that mind's nature abides as the unity [*zung dag* em. *zung 'jug*] that is free from discursiveness. The Two-Chapter [*Hevajratantra* II.2.36 says]:

"Just as the scent that is based on a flower
cannot be perceived in that flower's absence, [tantra: 'does not occur . . .'] so, in the absence of form and so forth,
their emptiness cannot be demonstrated [tantra: 'bliss will not come to be perceived']

"Thus there are three sealings of the fundamental ground of what is perceived: engaging appearances as being mind represents the seal of the tathāgatas, thought-free mind empty of the duality of perceiver and perceived represents the seal of Akṣobhya, and this thought-free mind free from extremes that is the Madhyamaka view and has the aspect of bliss represents the seal of Vajradhara. If what is perceived is sealed with these three views, these three are pointed out by the three ecstasies at the time of their being pointed out through the empowerment that allows them to be perceived: ecstasy points out the seal of the tathāgatas, supreme ecstasy points out the seal of Akṣobhya, and connate ecstasy points out the seal of Vajradhara. To experience these once they have been pointed out by the empowerment that allows them to be perceived, [there are] the nondual fourth yoga and the creation process with passion as the means. As for the fourth yoga, perceiving appearances as being mind represents the seal of the tathāgatas, perceiving mind as being thought-free represents the seal of Akṣobhya, and experiencing this thought-free [mind] as the unity of bliss and emptiness represents the seal of Vajradhara. If this is matched with the creation process that is the path of passion as the means, in terms of the *Hevajra[tantra]*, the circle of the fifteen female deities represents the seal of the tathāgatas, the circle of the chief figure with a skull-cup represents the seal of Akṣobhya, and the four-finger-width piece of a skull-cup on the crown of the head represents the seal of Vajradhara. In terms of the *Cakrasaṃvara[tantra]*, the circle of bones on the crown of the head represents the seal of the tathāgatas; the half-moon at the forehead, with all vīras moving to the right and all vīrās moving to the left, [represents the seal of Akṣobhya]; and the viśvavajra on the crown of the head represents the seal of Vajradhara. In terms of the *Guhyasamāja[tantra]*, the five [buddha] families represent the seal of the tathāgatas, the chief figure being marked with Akṣobhya represents the seal of Akṣobhya, and Vajrasattva on the crown of the head represents the seal of Vajradhara. In the meditation on the aspects of a karmamudrā, the three sealings are done in reverse [*log pa* "wrongly"?]. The [proper] understanding of sealing is stated as follows: 'Whatever is sealed with something comes to have the nature of that something' [cited in Rāmapāla's *Sekanirdeśapañjikā* on stanza 19 and several times in Vajrapāṇi's *Guruparamparākramopadeśa*]. (2) The detailed explanation has three parts. (a) [The first] among these is the seal of the tathāgatas. 'Form and all the rest' refers to the five skandhas such as form. 'As the five victors' means meditating on the skandha of form as being Vairocana and so on. As for 'may . . . be victorious,' when meditating on these [skandhas] as being deities, if they are not meditated on clearly, they remain unclear; thus appearances are mind."

2036. In the following, the text repeatedly speaks of "subsequent" (GZ CDNP *rjes thob*, "subsequent attainment"), and PTMC explicitly differentiates between meditative equipoise and subsequent attainment (the periods between formal meditation sessions). Therefore Skt. *maulam* here seems to refer to the actual state of mind during the "actual meditation practice."

2037. The last two sentences have parallels in sentences in Rāmapāla's *Sekanirdeśapañjikā* (text 45, 389) and Vajrapāṇi's *Guruparamparākramopadeśa* (text 213, 188).

2038. GZ CDNP ". . . Here, since the [first] four [CDNP *gzhi* em. *bzhi*] of them are to be realized as mere cognizance [CDNP "consciousness"], they are to be sealed with Akṣobhya. Thus, since outer appearances are mere mind, there is no perceived entity and the perceiver is empty as well. This abides as a cognizance that is a supreme and ultimately existing mere experience free from perceiver and perceived. This is precisely what is accomplished by the Nonaspectarians, speaking of the actual consciousness that is like the center of a pure autumn sky." PTMC: "(2b) 'The five skandhas' refers to experiencing self-aware thought-free mind by virtue of sealing the [first] four [buddha] families with Akṣobhya. As for 'thus,' the sealing of the tathāgatas refers to knowing that appearances without any entities that are the perceived are mind. 'The perceiver' refers to realizing the awareness free from perceiver and perceived (subject and object) when that [mind] is sealed with Akṣobhya. That this is ultimately established by reasoning and not invalidated by reasoning is the view of Mere Mentalism. Vajra[dhara here] presents the approach of Nonaspectarian Mere Mentalism. Ratnākaraśānti says: 'Your sealing with the tathāgatas renders the entity of what is perceived empty. The sealing with Akṣobhya also renders the perceiver empty; this is [your] system once these have been negated, which is exactly the view of the Mere Mentalists. I do not assert any appearance of aspects but assert cognition as self-illuminating self-awareness. Therefore yours is my view.' But what are these outer aspects? [Ratnākaraśānti] says: 'They are inexpressible as being the same [as mind] or other.' Still, what are these appearances that appear and are present in this way? 'They are delusion.' So you say that if there is a connection between outer referents and cognition, this is delusion. Hence, if you say that [such a connection] exists, [it must be one of] identity or causality—there is no [connection] but those two connections. 'There is a mere superimposed connection of identity at the time of ordinary beings.' But what is that like on the fruitional buddhabhūmi? 'A mere minor delusion of being slightly deluded is endured [there by buddhas].' Thus this represents [Ratnākaraśānti's] claim that within the ultimate, self-aware, and self-illuminating dharmakāya free from adventitious stains, the two form kāyas during subsequent attainment constitute delusion [this is a remarkably accurate if very brief portrayal of Ratnākaraśānti's position; for further crucial details of his view, see Seton 2015]. As for 'exactly this,' you may wonder with which example this self-aware and self-illuminating cognition free from perceiver and perceived is correlated. It is '[the midday sky] in autumn.' 'The Nonaspectarians' [here] are the Nonaspectarians with Stains who assert that outer referents are delusion. As for 'accomplished . . . the actual consciousness,' you may wonder: 'What is the meditative equipoise of the buddhabhūmi's actual yoga being accomplished as self-aware and self-illuminating cognition?' It is said that the meditative equipoise consists of self-aware and self-illuminating cognition, while the appearances during its subsequent attainment are delusion."

2039. GZ CDNP:

> The nature of being empty of the imaginary
> is to be without appearance and without aspect
> It is the sheer bliss that is real self-awareness,
> yet [also] the confusion of the hosts of forms of subsequent
> attainment.

2040. II.61b (GZ CDNP "Later, the two form kāyas are attained"). The full stanza in the *Uttaratantra* reads:

> Here, the first one is the dharmakāya,
> and the latter two the two form kāyas
> Just as form is abiding within space,
> so the latter dwell within the first one.

2041. This stanza is identical to *Tattvaratnāvalī* 4. PTMC: "'Being empty of the imaginary' refers to the reality free from the imaginary appearances of perceiver and perceived, which is established and not invalidated by reasoning. Sheer self-aware bliss is self-illuminating self-awareness. 'What is it that appears as red?' As for the cognitions during subsequent attainment, in yogīs there is a superimposed connection between cognitions and aspects, which represents cognition's element of stains. This is what [Ratnākaraśānti] claims to be the minor delusion during the subsequent attainment on the buddhabhūmi. 'From it' means 'from the dharmakāya.' 'Form kāyas' means that the two form kāyas appear from the dharmakāya like illusions."

2042. GZ CDNP "If this . . . seal of Akṣobhya, why would the scriptural passage that says: 'Akṣobhya is sealed with Vajrasattva' make it empty of the aspects of realization?" (*rtogs pa* is mistaken for *brtags pa*, the construction of the last phrase is off, and *ji srid du* as a literal rendering of *yāvat* makes no sense here). PTMC: "'If' means that if my [Maitrīpa's] sealing with Akṣobhya is asserted to be the ultimate, as per your thinking, this is an insolent statement. Why is that? It is [exactly] the point that is relinquished [by me]. Akṣobhya refers to thought-free self-awareness free from the duality of perceiver and perceived, and that it is said in the scriptures that he 'is sealed with Vajrasattva' is the declaration that thought-free self-awareness is sealed with the seal of Vajradhara—that is, all-empty luminosity. This is stated in such words in the *Guhyasamāja[tantra]*. Therefore your self-illuminating self-awareness free from perceiver and perceived does not go beyond my seal of Akṣobhya, and hence is not the basic nature. But if you possess the seal of Vajradhara, by expelling the view of Mere Mentalism, may you come to me over here! The elimination of that [flaw] is disputed by Śāntipa: 'as far as this goes' means that he says: 'the seal of Vajradhara is [nothing but] thought-free self-awareness.'"

2043. GZ CDNP ". . . established by the first seal. Therefore the subsequent attainment is other than the seal of Akṣobhya, the self-awareness that is actual wisdom; likewise, the seal of Vajrasattva, consciousness, is the subsequent attainment, while the vajra is the actual one." PTMC: "The answer to that is 'That is not the case'—mere self-aware mind is not the seal of Vajradhara. 'The first' means that thought-free and self-illuminating self-awareness is [already] established by the seal of Akṣobhya, which is prior to the seal of Vajradhara, so any being sealed [again] by Vajradhara is meaningless. 'Therefore,' since thought-free self-awareness represents my seal of Akṣobhya, 'Akṣobhya' means that the meditative equipoise that is the seal of Akṣobhya consists of thought-free self-awareness free of perceiver and perceived, while the appearances during subsequent attainment are delusion. Hence, likewise, the meditative equipoise of the seal of Vajradhara or Vajrasattva consists of all-empty luminosity, while the subsequent attainment here is thought-free self-awareness, because what you assert as meditative equipoise has become my subsequent attainment. 'The vajra' refers to the empty actual practice or meditative equipoise of the seal of Vajradhara."

2044. GZ CDNP "being indestructible as well as without deterioration."

2045. H448, fol. 331a.3–4. PTMC: "'Having a steadfast essence' refers to emptiness pervading everything. 'Not being hollow' means that the appearances of self-awareness are not stopped. 'Being unbreakable' means that [emptiness] cannot be broken by knowing remedies. 'Indivisible' refers to emptiness and compassion being inseparable. 'Not [PTMC has a negative] marked' means not established as an entity. 'Being indestructible' [*mi shes* em. *mi shigs*] refers to being [indestructible] through remedies. 'Without deterioration' refers to being without decrease and separation. 'Emptiness' means being unborn by virtue of the essence of being free from discursiveness."

2046. GZ:

> If, by means of the seal of Akṣobhya, actual wisdom
> is cognized as form and so on in subsequent attainment,
> why would this not be asserted as the seal of the vajra,
> which becomes the sattva during subsequent attainment?

CDNP:

> If the actual wisdom through Akṣobhya's seal
> is the form and so on of subsequent attainment,
> why would this not be attained as the sattva
> of subsequent attainment through the vajra's seal?

PTMC "This stanza is a concluding summary. 'The actual' refers to self-aware and self-illuminating cognition. As for 'subsequent attainment,' aspects during meditative equipoise are not asserted, while the arising of aspects during subsequent attainment is delusion. 'This' means that the seal of Akṣobhya has become the subsequent attainment by virtue of having been sealed with Vajradhara. 'Sattva' means that Maitrīpa asserts meditative equipoise to be empty while subsequent attainment lacks any nature of its own."

2047. That is, if "vajra" (emptiness) and "sattva" (compassion) are not practiced and experienced as being inseparable, the vajra of emptiness would be some sheer nothingness that is disconnected from compassion. GZ "But if it is said that the sattva is subsequent attainment [CDNP omit this phrase], it would follow that compassion is proclaimed to be an extinction that is nonbeing. This is to be discussed as follows." PTMC: "'But' refers to an insolent dispute by Śāntipa: 'compassion . . .' refers to him saying: 'Your seal of Vajradhara stops the appearances of self-awareness, and that is the view of extinction. The answer to that begins with 'This is to be discussed as follows.' [Maitrīpa's] position is that the seeming is asserted as mere illusion, while there is no delusion in the basic nature."

2048. As IaS (81nn93–94) points out, the first two lines are *Acintyastava* 43ab, while the last two correspond to *Bodhicittavivaraṇa* 68cd.

2049. GZ CDNP:

> Vajra is expressed to be emptiness
> Sattva is this very mere wisdom
> This establishment of their character
> represents the nature of Vajrasattva
> . . .
> This is the certainty of entities not being separable,
> [in addition, GZ CDNP mistakenly insert "For it is certain that it is
> indispensable," which more or less corresponds to the Sanskrit
> of this line, after the first line of the following stanza]
> just like being produced and impermanent

Just as in [GZ "through"] teaching true reality,
the seeming is what is not extinguished, [GZ *tshad ma med pa'i kun rdzob ste* "it is the seeming without valid cognition"]
in being separated from the seeming,
true reality will not become observed

In PTMC, the comments on these stanzas and what follows were somehow shifted below, following the comments on the stanza from the *Laṅkāvatārasūtra*, but are inserted here: "'Which example establishes unity?' 'Vajra' indicates the seal of Vajradhara. 'Sattva' refers to the seal of Akṣobhya [*mi song* em. *mi bskyod*]: not being separated from the lucidity of self-awareness. 'Their' refers to the unity of the seal of Vajradhara (being empty) and the seal of Akṣobhya (the lucidity of self-awareness). 'Through Vajrasattva' refers to the wisdom of awareness. 'Nature' means that the seal of Vajradhara does not represent the view of extinction—it is [also] present as form. 'But what about explaining these as being two?' 'Emptiness' refers to the seal of Vajradhara. 'Compassion' refers to the seal of Akṣobhya (the lucidity of self-awareness). 'Difference' means being different as two. 'A lamp' means that there is no clear light without butter [or oil], and without clear light, there is no lamp. Thus 'a lamp and its light' refers to their unity [*drug pa 'jug pa* em. *zung du 'jug pa*]. Likewise, though there is no emptiness in which the means of lucidity (compassion) has been stopped, in terms of the dimension of appearance, it is the seal of Akṣobhya, and in terms of the dimension of emptiness, it is the seal of Vajradhara. 'Compassion' is the seal of Akṣobhya. 'Oneness' means one as a pair. 'A lamp' means that, similar to a lamp and its light not being different, appearance and emptiness abide as a unity. 'Entities' means there is no seal of Vajradhara (being empty) that is separated from the experience of appearance. 'Separated' means there is no experience that is separated from the seal of Vajradhara (being empty) and established as an entity. 'Not being separable' refers to the pair of appearance and emptiness being inseparable. 'This is the certainty of entities' means that these very appearances are empty. Just like being impermanent because of being produced, at the very time of appearing, they are empty. 'Just as' refers to the unity of appearance and emptiness. 'The seeming' refers to not being separated from the experience of appearance (the seal of Akṣobhya). [The second] 'seeming' refers to 'the thought-free emptiness that is not [PTMC has no negative] separated from appearance,' which is unity."

2050. As mentioned before, "nondual diversity" renders Skt. *citrādvaitavāda*. As in Sahajavajra's *Sthitisamāsa* IV.5, this is one of the very few cases in which this term, which later in Tibet was claimed to refer to one of three "subschools" of Aspectarian Mere Mentalists (Tib. *sems tsam rnam bcas pa*), appears in an Indic text. However, as the following clearly shows, Maitrīpa refers with this term to Aspectarian Yogācāra in general, not to one of its "subschools." The same goes for his *Taking the Pith Instructions of the Philosophical Systems as the Path* (appendix 2, section 6) and Sahajavajra's text. For more details, see Brunnhölzl 2018, 1510–16.

2051. GZ CDNP "'How [CDNP "Thus"] are Akṣobhya and Vajrasattva one? But then this would be the supreme of nondual diversity because form and so on are not abandoned through consciousness.'" . . .

"The entity of mere mind with its diversity that is empty
of all thought [GZ CDNP *rtogs pa* em. *rtog pa*] is held to be the
system of the Aspectarians
This is equal, similar to touching the grass when walking
People pronounce it to be the meaning of the middle"

PTMC "'Thus' represents the perfect link [to what was said before]: just like a lamp and its light being one, possessing Akṣobhya refers to appearance or the emptiness of Vajrasattva. 'One' means that appearance and emptiness are a unity. 'But' means being insolent. Master Jñānaśrīmitra says: 'Your unity is included in my Aspectarianism: this [unity] is [actually] my supreme view. It does not refute aspects: the eyes do not [PTMC omits the negative] abandon objects such as form—the diversity of appearances and cognition abide as nonduality.' 'Consciousness' refers to self-awareness. 'Form and so on are not abandoned' means not stopping appearances. 'Diversity' refers to those who speak of nondual appearances, saying: 'Since [appearances] and the mind are nondual, this is the supreme [view]. It is similar to your unity, but our view is supreme.' How do you know that this is the [supreme] view? 'Nāgārjuna and others have composed texts with our assertion. "Diversity" refers to the realization that this diversity of appearances and the mind are nondual. Cognition and aspects that are empty of thoughts of perceiving [actual external] forms [PTMC *gzugs 'dzin gyi rtog pa* could be a typo for *gzung 'dzin gyi rtog pa*, "thoughts of perceiver and perceived"] are nondual. This is similar to [here and below *ngang 'gro'o* em. *dang 'dra'o*] your seal of Vajradhara.' What example is this like? 'For example, when walking, while walking on grass, one touches this grass but does not think "I [PTMC adds a negative here] touch this grass." Similarly, self-aware cognition does not have any thoughts thinking: "I experience the diversity of appearances." Though it does not have any thoughts, it experiences [this diversity]. "Middle" means that exactly this is the view of the great Madhyamaka that is free from any corporeality. It is not different from your utterly nonabiding unity.'"

2052. In other words, the diversity of seemingly outer objects appears but is not in any way different from the mind, which, on its own, is the nonduality of perceiver and perceived. GZ CDNP "Those who propound nondual diversity say that [consciousness] is ultimate reality, but by virtue of asserting that consciousness [really] exists, this is not nice. Through sealing the consciousness [CDNP "self-awareness"] whose nature is that of Akṣobhya—the nondual [consciousness] with its diversity, which is empty of perceiver and perceived—with Vajrasattva, the reality of an entity is excluded." PTMC "As for 'diversity,' the statement 'The nonduality of appearances and mind is supreme' is also called 'ultimate reality' here, which means that self-aware and self-illuminating cognition is [said to be] established by reasoning and not invalidated by reasoning. 'By virtue of [asserting that] consciousness [really exists], this is not nice' means that your assertion of the nonduality of appearances and mind being the seal of Akṣobhya is temporarily established, but it is said in the scriptures that [the seal] of Akṣobhya is sealed [*gang* em. *gdab*] by Vajradhara, which is contradictory to that [consciousness being ultimate reality]. As for 'perceiver and perceived,' the inseparability of cognition and aspects empty of perceiver and perceived is the nature of the seal of Akṣobhya. 'Vajrasattva' means that, by sealing [this inseparability of cognition and aspects empty of perceiver and perceived] with Vajradhara, it is refuted by the assertion that the mind that consists of the inseparability of cognition and the aspect that is Madhyamaka is the ultimate."

2053. "It" in the last line refers to "mere cognizance." GZ:

> If it is said it is empty of thoughts such as forms,
> through thereby [CDNP "here"] sealing cognition—the seal
> of Akṣobhya—with the seal of Vajrasattva,
> its existence as an entity is refuted
>
> This is not to be created as Vajrasattva
> by means of mere cognizance
> As it does not abide from the start,
> everything imaginary is emptiness

CDNP:

> By sealing the wisdom empty of thoughts
> such as forms—the seal of Akṣobhya—
> with the seal of Vajrasattva here,
> . . .
> Vajrasattva should not be created . . .

PTMC "[Jñānaśrīmitra] disputes this. 'This is declared in the following' means he explains that thought-free self-awareness together with its appearances is the ultimate. However, 'form and such' means he [also] says that these very appearances [empty] of the thoughts [*rtogs pas* em. *rtog pa'i*] of perceiver and perceived (such as form) constitute the seal of Vajradhara. In answer, [Maitrīpa] speaks of 'wisdom' (the experience of self-aware thought-free mind), and 'it' means sealing it with the empty seal of Vajradhara. 'Entity' refutes the statement that self-aware and self-illuminating cognition with its appearances exists ultimately by being established through reasoning. The self-illumination empty of any thoughts about that is the seal of Vajradhara. As for 'aspects in that mind,' by means of that mere self-aware and thought-free cognition with aspects, there is no 'Vajra'—the seal of Vajradhara—here. Why is this? 'From the start' means that the seal of Vajradhara [PTMC has "Akṣobhya"] is not arrived at through that. 'Examination' means that, after having examined [thus PTMC understands *brtags pa* not as "imaginary"], that [seal of Vajradhara] is the sheer freedom from discursiveness empty of the duality of perceiver and perceived."

2054. GZ CDNP "Having thus removed the thorn [GZ "form"] of ultimate existence, to establish what has the nature of not abiding anywhere and is the continuous flow [I follow GZ NP *rgyun* against CD *rgyu*] of effortless nondual unity as being self-awareness is the most excellent Mādhyamika tenet.

This is to be realized due to the kindness of the true guru." PTMC "'Thus' means that self-illuminating self-awareness with its aspects, without any establishment by reasoning or any clinging but with [all] forms and their causes removed, is the utter nonabiding that does not abide anywhere at all, is free from all extremes, and is the unity of appearance and emptiness that is the natural unity. 'Effortless' refers to the primordially present fundamental ground of knowable objects [or "that is to be known"]. 'The continuous flow of nonduality as being self-awareness' is the seal of Vajradhara that is unity. This 'Mādhyamika tenet' is the utter nonabiding that is the most excellent freedom from all extremes. This constitutes the seal of Vajradhara. Thanks to what is the seal of Vajradhara realized? 'This' refers to this seal of Vajradhara. 'The true guru' means it is realized during the time of empowerment." The progression here of sealing the five skandhas with the five tathāgatas, the tathāgatas with Akṣobhya, and Akṣobhya with Vajrasattva (or Vajradhara) is explained most clearly in Vajrapāṇi's **Guruparamparākramopadesa* (text 213, 204–7): "The five skandhas have the essence of the five buddhas. Here it is said that the skandha of form is Vairocana. The skandha of feeling is Ratnasambhava. The skandha of discrimination is Amitābha. The skandha of karmic formation is Amoghasiddhi. The skandha of consciousness is Akṣobhya. In order to relinquish any clinging to the skandhas and so on, the five skandhas (the imaginary [nature]) are sealed with the five tathāgatas (the dependent [nature]) . . . Therefore, at the time when the five skandhas are sealed with the five tathāgatas, by becoming free from clinging to them as the five skandhas, one is made to realize them as the five tathāgatas. The five tathāgatas are not different: Vairocana is the body, Amitābha is speech, Akṣobhya is the mind, Ratnasambhava is qualities, and Amoghasiddhi is enlightened activity. In order to counteract the fixation of clinging to what is thus not different as being different in the form of the deities that are the dependent [nature] and in order to realize them as being mere cognizance, the [other] four [tathāgatas] are sealed with Akṣobhya . . . Hence, by sealing the four such as Vairocana with Akṣobhya—the skandha of consciousness that [really] is dharmadhātu wisdom—the fixation of clinging to them as the deities that are the dependent [nature] is relinquished, and thus thoughts of perceiver and perceived are relinquished. Through this perfect [nature] of being empty of the thoughts of perceiver and perceived, mind as such is realized as self-awareness, which is the tathāgata relief. Those who suffer due to being weary and exhausted by thinking of and clinging to tathāgatas such as Vairocana and Ratnasambhava, the skandhas, the dhātus, the āyatanas, and so on [as being real entities] need to realize that they are Akṣobhya—mind's essence, self-awareness. Without thoughts and the clinging to perceiver and perceived, they rest at ease or are relieved. Hence this is called 'the tathāgata relief.' [However,] though there is no thinking in terms of perceiver and perceived, there is still the fixation of clinging to mere self-awareness. Therefore there is no difference as far as the pain of thinking goes. For example, though there is a difference between a chain made of iron and a chain made of gold in terms of their material, there is no difference in terms of [both] fettering. Likewise, though clinging to something on the outside and clinging to mind as such as self-awareness on the inside are [somewhat] worse and better, respectively, there is no difference in terms of [both] being the pain of fixating thoughts. In order to relinquish such fixation, Akṣobhya (the nature of the skandha of consciousness) is sealed with Vajrasattva . . . By sealing Akṣobhya with Vajrasattva (emptiness), mind as such too is to be realized as emptiness . . . The extreme of permanence is eliminated through Vajrasattva (emptiness), while the extreme of extinction is eliminated through Akṣobhya: unity is the Vajradhara relief. The relief through rendering the clinging of thinking of mind as such as self-awareness without any nature is called 'the Vajradhara relief.'" As mentioned before, the Sanskrit equivalent *āśvāsa* (Tib. *dbugs dbyung ba*) for "relief" can also mean "consolation," "solace," "encouragement," "reassurance," "refreshment," and "revival." All of these meanings apply here as well because sealing the skandhas with the tathāgatas, the tathāgatas with Akṣobhya (being nothing but mind), Akṣobhya with Vajrasattva (emptiness and compassion), and Vajrasattva with great bliss represents a progression of being reassured of the true nature of the skandhas, mind, emptiness, and great bliss, a progressive revival of that nature, a progressive consolation that nothing is as solid as it may seem, and a progressive encouragement to realize this. Experientially, this progression manifests as an increasing sense of relief from reification and the ensuing afflictions and sufferings. This sense of relief or resting at ease is clearly explained in the above passage from Vajrapāṇi's *Guruparamparākramopadeśa*. Compare also *Ajamahāsukha's *Dohakoṣahṛdayārthagītāṭīkā* on stanza 31 of Saraha's "People Dohā," which matches the five supramundane skandhas with the five tathāgatas, sealed with the five wisdoms (appendix 4 in volume 3). Note, though, that the kinds of relief mentioned here are explained in many different ways in different tantric texts. For example, the tathāgata relief is explained as saṃsāra, being referential, becoming a suitable vessel through the accumulation of merit, or the profound inner creation process. The Vajradhara relief is described as nirvāṇa, being nonreferential, the attainment of buddhahood through the accumulation of wisdom, or the perfection process. Vajrapāṇi's *Guruparamparākramopadeśa* (text 213) explains these two kinds of relief also in the context of the karmamudrā. According to the *Jñānodayopadeśa* (D1514, fol. 372a.4–5), the relief of great bliss is bestowed by a particular type of movement of bodhicitta.

2055. GZ CDNP "You may wonder: 'If self-awareness is established here, it follows that this is the proposition of illusion-like nonduality—it is not utter nonabiding in every respect.'" PTMC: "As for refuting illusion-like [nonduality], the great master Śāntarakṣita formulates the following proposition: 'Your seal of the tathāgatas means that appearances are established as mind. The seal of Akṣobhya means that mind is established as being thought-free. Since this is present as a mere illusion, this view of mine that [all] is illusion-like is supreme.' 'If self-awareness is established here' constitutes the following dispute: 'In your establishing the seal of Vajradhara by means of the appearance of self-awareness, if this is the basic nature that is not ultimately established, as it is for the Mere Mentalists, it is "illusion-like" that makes up the seal of Vajradhara: it is not different from being illusion-like. "In every respect" means there is no seal of Vajradhara that is utter nonabiding; it is my being illusion-like.'"

2056. *Yuktiṣaṣṭikā* 19. PTMC: "'This' refers to your 'being illusion-like.' 'Is not the case' means that the seal of Vajradhara is not that illusion-like basic nature. 'Why is it not?' Just as later [causes and results] arise in dependence on previous causes and results, it originates dependently. Therefore it has no nature of its own and does not [arise] by its own nature. 'Its own nature' means that the basic nature of the seal of Vajradhara is without any being established or arising by its own nature. Hence it is not established as being illusion-like in terms of a positive determination."

2057. GZ CDNP "Experience too arises from conditions. Therefore, since experience does not abide, it constitutes the state of being unarisen."

2058. GZ CDNP "experience."

2059. PTMC: "'Experience' means that the experience of self-awareness too arises from conditions; it does not arise by its essence. 'Therefore' means 'because it arises from conditions, not by its essence.' 'Experience' is said to refer again to self-illuminating self-awareness. 'The state of being unarisen' refers to not even abiding as a mere illusion. 'Accordingly' means not arisen by virtue of any essence. As for 'entities,' to say that they exist as delusiveness or mere illusions is in itself a lie. You may wonder: 'Well, how do they abide then?' 'Vajra' means 'as the unity of Vajradhara.' 'World' refers to appearances. 'The Sage declared this very' means 'the Buddha declared it is the unity of appearance and emptiness.'"

2060. I could not locate this quotation, but some parts of it resemble passages in the *Avikalpapraveśadhāraṇī*. Note also that "the inconceivable dhātu is the very mind . . . Mind is not found in no-mind, but in mind. [The dhātu] that is without mind is mind because [through it] mind is realized in just the way it really is" certainly echoes the famous passages "The mind is no-mind. The nature of the mind is luminosity" in the *Aṣṭasāhasrikāprajñāpāramitāsūtra* (H11, fol. 4b.5) and "The mind is no-mind. In that no-mind, there is no attachment" in the *Pañcaviṃśatisāhasrikāprajñāpāramitāsūtra* (H10, fol. 266a.7). In that vein, compare also *Tattvaviṃśikā* 14. GZ CDNP "Furthermore . . . 'What is the inconceivable dhātu here?' Mañjuśrī replied: 'One should think about the mind that is the inconceivable dhātu, the mind that cannot be expressed and is without measure, is not to be fathomed by the mind, and cannot be conceived by the mind. This is called "the inconceivable dhātu." Thus, Bhagavān, mind as such is the inconceivable dhātu. Why is that? Thinking is not found in the inconceivable dhātu. For mind refers to the mind of realizing what is unthinkable in just the way it really is. Still, Bhagavān, all aspects are the inconceivable dhātu.'" PTMC: "Having thus refuted the approaches of others, now, in [Maitrīpa's] own scriptural tradition, the seal of Vajradhara [is explained by] refuting the extremes of characteristics through the meanings of six scriptural passages. 'Furthermore' means teaching his own approach after having refuted the approaches of others. 'This . . .' means refuting the extremes of characteristics through a scriptural passage by Mañjuśrī. 'What is this inconceivable . . .' asks what the nature of the unity of unborn mind is in essence. 'Dhātu' refer to the diversity of appearances. 'Inconceivable' means that this mind is not an object of consciousness. In this freedom from discursiveness, there are no antagonistic factors or great remedies. 'The mind that cannot be meditated on' [PTMC instead of 'the mind that cannot be expressed'] means it cannot be traversed by those who are involved in a path with progressive stages. 'The mind that is without measure' means that one cannot say about this freedom from discursiveness that it has a certain extent. It is not something to be validated or contrived by mind—one cannot say this freedom from discursiveness has a certain size, nor is there anything to be validated and what validates it. 'By the mind' means that there is nothing to posit but 'true reality without anything to be validated and what validates it.' 'This' refers to this emptiness free from discursiveness that is beyond being an object of examination and analysis. 'Thus . . .' refers to the luminous mahāmudrā that is not established as any essence whatsoever. 'Why is that?' means 'Why is the mind called "inconceivable"?' In the inconceivable, the unborn mind, there is no mind—it is not established as any essence such as subject and object [*yul dang yan* em. *yul dang yul can*]. 'For' means 'for there is no subject and object.' 'Mind refers to . . . what is unthinkable' means it is beyond mind, thinking, and analysis."

2061. *Jñānālokālaṃkārasūtra* IV.12 (edition by Study Group on Buddhist Sanskrit Literature 2004, 146.1–2), *Saṃvarodayatantra* VIII.36′ (Tsuda 1974, 101), and *Pañcakrama* IV.10. Explicitly attributed to the *Jñānālokālaṃkārasūtra*, this stanza is also found in the *Amanasikārādhāra* (text 27, 157). Without attribution, it appears in the *Caturmudrānvaya* (text 14, 31) and the *Sekanirdeśapañjikā* (text 45, 419–20).

2062. As mentioned before, this stanza is not found in the *Candrapradīpasūtra* (or the *Samādhirājasūtra*) but in the *Anavataptanāgarājaparipṛcchāsūtra* (D156, fol. 230b.2–3; except "heedful" for "not heedless"). Vajrapāṇi's *Guruparamparākramopadeśa* (text 213, 190), Kamalaśīla's *Madhyamakāloka* (D3887, 150a.7–150b.1), Avalokitavrata's *Prajñāpradīpaṭīkā* (fols. 131b.4, 214b.2–3, 241a.1), and Abhayākaragupta's *Munimatālaṃkāra* (D3903, fol. 145a.7) explicitly identify it as coming from this sūtra. As IaS (78n77) points out, Candrakīrti quotes this stanza four times in his *Prasannapadā*, once explicitly attributing it to an *Anavataptahradāpasaṅkramaṇasūtra*, and once (unattributed) in his *Catuḥśatakaṭīkā*. On the other hand, the *Caturmudrāṭīkā* (text 44, 259), probably following Maitrīpa here, attributes this stanza to the *Candrapradīpasūtra*. Szántó 2016 (323) likewise considers it as "ultimately from the *Candrapradīpasūtra*," but points out that it is also found as stanza 26 of the *Yogāmbaramahātantra*. Without attribution, this stanza is also cited in Divākaracandra's *Prajñājñānaprakāśa* (text 16, 55; as in GZ CDNP here). The last three lines in GZ CDNP read as follows:

> It does not possess any nature of being born
> That which depends on conditions is empty
> Those who understand emptiness are heedful

PTMC "'What . . .' means arisen from conditions but not arisen through any essence or nature. Why? 'On conditions' means when something depends on conditions, it did not arise through any essence . . . 'Emptiness . . .' means 'Make the realization of the unity of emptiness a living experience!'"

2063. II.169. GZ CDNP begin with "For . . ." PTMC "The passage from the *Laṅkāvatāra[sūtra]* also refutes the extremes of characteristics. 'For' refers to the relinquishment of thoughts of perceiver and perceived. 'Should' refers to clinging to characteristics. 'That itself' refers to delusion by clinging to extremes. 'Blurred vision' means [appearances] like entangled strands of hair in the sky."

2064. Given what was said above about "nonabiding awareness," I follow *saṃvit-* in Mathes 2015 (380) and IaS (182) in the sense of GZ CDNP *rnam rig* (usually rendering *vijñapti*) against *samvṛt-* ("convention") in Lindtner's edition of the *Ālokamālā* (Lindtner 1985), though *saṃvit-* can also mean "convention."

2065. This is Kambalāmbara's *Ālokamālā* 248. GZ CD:

> May you not dwell in cognizance!
> Therefore for those afraid, the Sage,
> teaching dharmas in different ways,
> has correctly taught it as emptiness

NP:

> Through awareness, superimpositions did not arise
> Through exactly that, the Victor has conquered
> . . .
> expressing and expressing, this is empty

PTMC "'Likewise' refers to the *Laṅkāvatāra[sūtra]*. 'Cognizance' means mind. 'May you not dwell' means that [cognizance] is not the basic nature of entities. 'But then what is the use of teaching mind and so on itself?' 'Therefore' means 'because those up through Mere Mentalism are afraid when teaching utter nonabiding.' 'Dharmas' refers to teaching the three yānas, the nine [*rgyu* em. *dgu*] approaches, and the four positions. 'Emptiness' means [the Sage] later taught utter nonabiding."

2066. II.3.36ab. PTMC: "'Nature' means 'because of not being born by any nature." 'Is neither real' means not being permanent [*brtag pa la yin* em. *rtag pa ma yin*]. 'Nor delusive' means not being extinct either, thus being free from extremes.'

2067. *Ālokamālā* 274. As Szántó 2016 (323) points out, this stanza is also found as stanza 101 of the *Yogāmbaramahātantra*. Kambalāmbara's *Ālokamālā* (fifth century) is a brilliant poetic treatise in 282 stanzas that represents an unusually early and unique approach of synthesizing Madhyamaka and Yogācāra. Combining the framework of the three natures with that of the two realities, Kambala assimilates Madhyamaka to Yogācāra, and not vice versa (as, for example, Śāntarakṣita and Kamalaśīla did much later). Similarly, his autocommentary on his *Bhagavatīprajñāpāramitānavaślokapiṇḍārtha* (better known as *Navaślokī*) exhibits typical Yogācāra features. Though both Kambala and Śāntarakṣita present their own syntheses of Madhyamaka and Yogācāra, unlike Śāntarakṣita, Kambala clearly prioritizes Yogācāra over Madhyamaka. Thus it is noteworthy that Kambala (and not a more famous and undisputed Madhyamaka authority, such as Nāgārjuna or Āryadeva) is quoted here by

Maitrīpa in support of his own highest Madhyamaka system of utter nonabiding. Interestingly, Sahajavajra's *Tattvadaśakaṭīkā* (text 46, 16) quotes the same stanza of the *Ālokamālā* (plus ten more) in support of labeling Kambala a "Nonaspectarian Mādhyamika" (Sahajavajra then explains the difference between Nonaspectarian Yogācāras and Nonaspectarian Mādhyamikas: The former claim the cognition that is the perfect nature to be true reality—the essence of self-awareness is empty of perceiver and perceived but is not nonexistent. The Nonaspectarian Mādhyamikas hold that the perfect nature does not exist either—it just represents the essence of the seeming reality of yogīs but is ultimately unborn). Similarly, Rāmapāla's *Sekanirdeśapañjikā* on stanza 19 quotes *Ālokamāla* 248 and 274 in support of the need to seal Akṣobhya (nondual mind) with the seal of Vajrasattva (emptiness and compassion) in accordance with the Madhyamaka understanding of true reality. Furthermore, Atiśa's *Madhyamakopadeśa* identifies the Madhyamaka texts by Nāgārjuna, Āryadeva, Mātṛceṭa, Candrakīrti, and Kambala as the unrivaled model texts for all Madhyamaka scriptures. Thus the positioning of Kambala by Maitrīpa, Sahajavajra, Rāmapāla, and Atiśa as a Mādhyamika is remarkable and further supports the impression that the demarcation lines of different Buddhist "schools" in India were not as hard and fast as many later authors assume. GZ CDNP:

> After having settled everything as being equality,
> the intelligent one who sees subtleties, when making
> a distinction between the tenets of Buddhists and of
> outsiders, the one [tenet] here is stated to be emptiness

PTMC "'Furthermore' means that if one looks at tīrthikas and Buddhists with an honest mind, the intelligent one who sees subtleties is Kambalāmbara. 'Tenets' refers to those of both tīrthikas and Buddhists. That one line ["making . . . outsiders"] is easy to understand. 'When . . . the one here' means that tīrthikas and Buddhists are the same in terms of mere tenets. You may wonder: 'But is there primordially no difference between those two?' 'Is stated to be emptiness' means that there is the difference of the seal of Vajradhara."

2068. GZ CDNP have this as two lines of verse, thus making it look as if the previous quotation simply continues into the following one:

> So as to eliminate that, due to these,
> emptiness constitutes extinction

PTMC "As for the explicit teaching of being free from the extreme of extinction, 'due to these' refers to [what was said] above. 'Emptiness' means that the seal of Vajradhara is not a view of extinction."

2069. GZ repeats this line as an additional third line.

2070. This stanza is identical to *Sekanirdeśa* 31. GZ CDNP:

> That which is seen is suchness [CDNP do not have this additional line]
> Those who are seeing suchness
> by following the middle's actuality
> are aware of true reality, having its fortune,

when they are directly aware [CDNP *rtogs pa*, "realize"] [of it]
[or "When directly known, it is awareness"]

PTMC "'Madhyamaka' refers to not being a view of extinction because of being free from extremes. 'Who set their eyes on' refers to appearances. 'Suchness' means being free from extremes at the time of experience. 'Those' means 'persons.' 'Suchness' refers to the unerring seal of Vajradhara. 'Realizing true reality' refers to the basic nature, the seal of Vajradhara. 'Fortunate' refers to the wealth of the noble ones, such as the ten powers. 'How is this realized?' 'If' refers to the time of [direct realization]."

2071. This stanza is not found in that tantra, nor in any other work in Kg or Tg. CDNP read *Ḍākinījālasaṃvara*, which is another name of the *Hevajratantra*. GZ CDNP:

If someone has realized the mind of
emptiness and compassion inseparable,
they are hence taught to be the Buddha,
the dharma, as well as the saṃgha

PTMC "'How is this known?' The words of the ḍākinīs [*mkhro* seems to be an abbreviation of *mkha' 'gro*] [speak of] the unity that is the seal of Vajradhara. As for 'the mind,' if it is perfected by a person, buddhahood has the essence of the three kāyas; this dharma is the ultimate dharma. This is also stated in *Hevajra[tantra* I.5.20]: 'Mudrā is the hand gesture . . .' 'The saṃgha' refers to making the path a living experience."

2072. The Sanskrit says "five aspects" (*pañcākāra*), but this sentence clearly refers to the text's overall theme as well as its opening statements.

2073. GZ CDNP "Therefore the five skandhas arise in dependence. Since they have the nature of the five tathāgatas, they are the inseparability of emptiness and compassion by nature. Hence beings abide as the inseparability of emptiness and compassion. Exactly this should be made dhyāna in an uninterrupted manner thanks to . . ." PTMC "'Therefore' means 'because appearances do not arise through their essence.' 'The five skandhas' means 'because the five skandhas primordially are the five [buddha] families and the five wisdoms.' As for 'beings,' with the dimension of appearance not arising through its essence, this is unity—the seal of Vajradhara. As for the means of making this a living experience, 'exactly this' refers to unity. 'Guru' means 'through all four.'" It is not clear what *bzhi pos* refers to here, but mahāmudrā texts speak of four kinds of gurus: the guru as a person, scriptures, appearances, and dharmatā. Given that PTMC speaks about "the actuality of the fourth [empowerment]" below, this could also be *bzhi pas*, "through the fourth."

2074. This line is missing in the Sanskrit.

2075. The first two lines of this stanza are identical to *Hevajratantra* I.8.54ab and the remaining two are somewhat similar in meaning to I.8.54cd ("always, day and night, one should remain united with true reality"). GZ CDNP switch the last two lines and read the first two lines as follows:

Like a flowing river stream's midst
and a gleaming lamp's continuum

PTMC "'How is this to be made a living experience?' 'River' means uninterrupted clear realization; this is described by 'looking at all forms,' and Saraha says: 'whatever may appear constitutes true reality' ["People Dohā" line 31b]. 'Through what is this realized?' As for 'mantra,' when the ears protect the mind, this is mantra: its appearance serves as the guru. The fruition is thus the seal of Vajradhara; since appearances do not arise through their essence, it is like that."

2076. GZ CDNP "Nāgārjunagarbha."

2077. As mentioned before, somewhat similar versions of this stanza are also cited in Devacandra's *Prajñājñānaprakāśa* (text 16, 71; attributed to Nāgārjuna), Sahajavajra's *Sthitisamāsa* (text 17, 105), the *Caturmudrāṭīkā* (text 44, 338; attributed to the Buddha [*gsung rab*]), Muniśrībhadra's *Pañcakramaṭippaṇī Yogīmanoharā* (fol. 24a.4–5; see Mathes 2015, 103n272), and GZ's version of the *Caturmudrānvaya*. Curiously, and maybe based on PTMC's comments below, Mathes adds here that this stanza is from Nāgārjuna's *Caturmudrānvaya*. However, it only appears in GZ's version of that text and is clearly marked as a quote by *gang gsungs pa . . . ces bstan to*, while it is not found in the Sanskrit of the **Advayavajrasaṃgraha* (from which Mathes translates) nor in the canonical Tibetan versions in CDNP. Furthermore, if Maitrīpa here quoted a stanza that he attributes to Nāgārjuna and it were indeed a part of the *Caturmudrānvaya*, this would be a solid argument against Maitrīpa himself being the author of the *Caturmudrānvaya* and its inclusion in the **Advayavajrasaṃgraha*. GZ CDNP:

> This is the palace, not the three realms, nor objects, nor faculties, elements, and such,
> neither form and so forth, not living creatures, and not humans—these are the victors
> The cakra lord has the character of dharmatā, so they are the maṇḍala's inhabitants
> If these three realms' diversity is known as the cakra, why, oh mind, create delusion?

PTMC "'Nāgārjuna' refers to [what he says] in the *Caturmudrā[nvaya]*. 'This' refers to making the actuality of the fourth [empowerment] a living experience. 'The palace' [*gzhal bya* em. *gzhal yas*] means this is not the outer container, but a palace. 'Nor objects' means that the six objects do not entail their own continua but are the vajra of form and so on. 'Nor faculties' means that the six faculties do not entail their own continua but that the obscurations are eliminated and so on. 'Elements' means that the four elements do not entail their own continua and are not four objects. 'Form and so forth' means that the five skandhas do not entail their own continua but are the five [buddha] families. 'Sentient beings' means that the humans who are the inner contents do not entail their own continua but are deities. 'Cakra' means that the aspects of the chief figure and their retinue also arise from unity. 'The three realms' means 'if container and contents are known as what is supported [by unity].'"

2078. It could be that this stanza is a citation, but I could not locate it. GZ CDNP (not versified): "The deities that have arisen from conditions manifest like the city of gandharvas. The diversity of discursiveness does not abide by any nature, nor is it some utter nonexistence like a sky flower." PTMC "'But then they have become phenomena that are entities.' 'From conditions' means that deities appear from unity by virtue of conditions but do not arise through their essence. They are the diversity of appearances. 'Nature' refers to unity."

2079. II.4.38ab. PTMC "'How is this known?' 'This' refers to unity. 'These phenomena' refers to the skandhas and so on. 'Nirvāṇa' means they are not arisen through their essence. 'But then all are free.' 'Nescience' means this is saṃsāra due to being obscured by the ignorance about luminosity. *sa ma ra sthi la / u pa de sha.*"

2080. Skt. "This concludes 'A Commentary on the Five Seals of the Tathāgatas.'" CDNP ". . . composed by master Advayavajra. It was translated by the Indian upādhyāya Vajrapāṇi and lotsāwa Mapen Chöbar" (NP add "Auspiciousness!"). According to Tipi Bumlabar (BKC, vol. *kha*, fol. 85a.1–5), the outline of this text is as follows:

1. brief introduction
1a. the seal of the tathāgatas
1b. the seal of Akṣobhya
1c. the seal of Vajradhara
1d. eliminating the flaw of the statement "the seal of Vajradhara represents the view of extinction"
2. detailed explanation
2a. detailed explanation of the seal of the tathāgatas
2b. detailed explanation of the seal of Akṣobhya
2c. detailed explanation of the seal of Vajradhara
2c1. refuting the assertions of others [the text says "three points" but then only mentions the following two]
2c1a. refuting Aspectarians
2c1b. refuting False Aspectarians
2c1b1. presenting their system
2c1b2. refuting their system through the essential point [*gnas kas* em. *gnad kas*] of lacking the seal [of Vajradhara]
2c1b3. eliminating flaws in [Maitrīpa's] own system
2c1c. refuting illusion-like [nonduality]
2c2. teaching [Maitrīpa's] own system
2c2a. explaining the seal [of Vajradhara] through six scriptural meanings in order to be free from the extremes of characteristics
2c2b. teaching being free from the view of extinction
2c2c. the means to practice conduct
2c2d. concluding summary by way of the fruition of practice.
For further comments and details, see Mathes 2015 (9–10, 95–106).

2081. PDMT, 26:359–66. The semantic range of Skt. *tātparya* includes "meaning," "purpose," "aim," and "devoting oneself to," while Tib. *dgos pa* means "purpose" or "necessity." Since the text explains both the meanings as well as the purposes of the six vase empowerments, the secret empowerment, the prajñā-jñāna empowerment, and the fourth empowerment, all the above meanings seem to be implied more or less clearly.

2082. GZ "I pay homage to Vajrasattva" CDNP "I pay homage to youthful Mañjuśrī."

2083. GZ CDNP:

> Since the spiritual friend's speech is hard to realize,
> as if the true reality that is not an object of words
> were to be present in the palms of one's hands, [CD *log pa'i lam du ston pa* ("were taught as the wrong path")]
> may the character of greatness be victorious!

2084. GZ CDNP:

> Through knowing the supreme [CDNP *chog shes* ("being content")] vajra master,
> I shall compose *A Compendium of the Purport of Empowerment*, in accordance with realization
> due to an abundance of texts on empowerment.

2085. Except for "empowerment" instead of "supreme" in the second line, this stanza is identical to *Guhyasamājatantra* XVIII.113cf, which is quoted in many tantric commentaries in Tg (such as the *Caturmudrāṭīkā* (text 44, 257) and is no doubt the source intended here too. The same goes for Rāmapāla's *Sekanirdeśapañikā* (text 45, 398), in which this stanza appears in the exact same form as here, and where its last line is glossed in various ways. With the additional replacement of "vase" by "master" in the first line and adding "empowerment" in the third, this stanza is also found in the *Mahāmudrātilakatantra* (H380, fol. 435b.2) and the *Jñānatilakatantra* (H382, fol. 9a.1–2). The first three lines (followed by "Just as it is, the body is the tathāgata") are also found in the *Ḍākinīvajrapañjaratantra* (H379, fol. 401a.7). Thus text 37 can be considered as a commentary on this stanza (according to the *Jñānagarbhatantra* [H381, fol. 476a.7], its last line refers to stabilizing the very prajñā-jñāna empowerment). Note that, exactly as it appears here in the *Sekatātparyasaṃgraha*, this stanza is also included in Vajrapāṇi's *Vajrapada* (text 47, line 4d), while his *Guruparamparākramopadeśa* (text 213, 210) replaces "vase" by "master" in the first line, thus being closer to the *Mahāmudrātilakatantra* and *Jñānatilakatantra*. See Isaacon 2003 on the standard four empowerments in the yoganiruttaratantras (some, such as the *Candramahāroṣatantra*, only have three), yogatantras such as the *Guhyasamājatantra* only having two or three empowerments (the prajñā-jñāna empowerment appears for the first time in the *Guhyasamājottaratantra*, later incorporated into the *Guhyasamājatantra* as its eighteenth chapter), and the debate on the existence and nature of the fourth empowerment originating with the single cryptic line *Guhyasamājatantra* XVIII.113f.

2086. The Sanskrit words *seka* and *abhiṣeka* are here glossed as derivatives of the verb *siñc*, which means "(be)sprinkle" but also "scatter," "emit," and "pour." Thus another hermeneutical etymology is that empowerment scatters or dispels obscurations and pours wisdom into one's body and mind.

2087. "Lord empowerment" (Skt. *adhipatyabhiṣeka*) is another name of "bell empowerment" (Skt. *ghaṇṭābhiṣeka*).
2088. CD omit "awareness" but CDNP add "wisdom."
2089. GZ CDNP ". . . They are called 'empowerment' because they purify and wash in order to wash away the stains of ignorance [CDNP 'Because of washing away the stains of ignorance and by virtue of this purification (*dag par bya ba* em. *dag par byed pa*), they are called "empowerment"'], just as external stains are washed away by external water. Because the activity of a vase is used in all these [empowerments], they are called the 'vase empowerment' [CDNP omit this sentence]. These six are also called 'irreversible empowerments' . . . The [first] five empowerments among these are called 'the empowerments of awareness [*rig pa* instead of *rig ma* in the next phrase]' because they are the activities of Buddhalocanā and the other awareness consorts." The last sentence has its parallel in text 38 (219).
2090. That is, both the vajra master and the disciple visualize the vajra master as Akṣobhya and the disciple as Vairocana. GZ CDNP "Here, since it washes away the stains of unawareness, it is the awareness empowerment [CDNP conform to the Sanskrit]. The vajra master, who abides as the form of Akṣobhya, should bestow the water empowerment upon the disciple, who is visualized as the form of Vairocana. Such [vajra] pride should be entertained in all [or 'all respects']."
2091. GZ CDNP "[There] is the crown empowerment that represents the seed of the essence of a buddha's uṣṇīṣa in the future."
2092. Skt. *uha* can also mean "examination," "conception," "inference," "change," and "modification"; GZ CDNP *rtog pa* ("thought," "conception").
2093. GZ NP *oṃ* CD *a*.
2094. Thus, in Sanskrit, *h* is glossed by *hetuviyuktaḥ*, *ū* by *ūhāpagataḥ*, and *aṃ* (that is, the *anusvāra*; the dot above *hū*) by *apratiṣṭitāḥ*. Compare the almost identical explanation of HŪṂ in Rāmapāla's *Sekanirdeśapañjikā* (text 45, 409) and Vajrapāṇi's *Guruparamparākramopadeśa* (text 213, 199), as well as the similar one in the *Caturmudrāṭīkā* (text 44, 328). GZ CDNP "In the round navel in the middle of a vajra that has the size of twelve finger-widths by virtue of representing the purity of the twelve links, the essence of dependent origination, there is a syllable HŪṂ, which illustrates unsurpassable dharmatā . . ."
2095. GZ CDNP read this stanza as prose: "Here, what [I follow CDNP *ni* against GZ *gi*] has the forms of the five spokes that are the sages who [CDNP omit *thub pa'i* ("the sages who")] emerge from the aperture of the lotus of existence has the forms of existence that come forth from the purity of the five skandhas."
2096. Mathes 2015 (135n356): ". . . i.e., that everything arises in dependence (Thrangu Rinpoche)." GZ CDNP "In order to make one understand that everything has the character of everything, all are quadrangular."
2097. GZ CDNP read this stanza as prose: "Thus the vajra [means that] the wise who have realized all dharmas, the ultimate five vimuktikāyas whose form has the nature of the sound of HŪṂ resounding, individually spring forth everywhere." As for the term "vimuktikāya," in the Yogācāra system in general (as exemplified by *Mahāyānasaṃgraha* I.48), the usual distinction

between the vimuktikāya and the dharmakāya is that the former designates the removal of only the afflictive obscurations as attained by śrāvaka and pratyekabuddha arhats, while the latter represents the removal of both afflictive and cognitive obscurations as well as the possession of all buddha qualities. Thus when speaking about the dharmakāya as the actual state of buddhahood in a general sense, it is understood that both types of obscurations have been relinquished in it, and it is in this sense that it can be said that the dharmakāya includes the vimuktikāya. On the other hand, *Uttaratantra* II.21–26 describes these two kāyas as the two aspects of relinquishment (purity) and realization (wisdom), respectively, of unconditioned perfect buddhahood, without relating them to any distinction between buddhas and arhats (more commonly, it is the svābhāvikakāya that is said to represent the aspect of the purity or the relinquishment of all obscurations). Most Tibetan commentaries on these stanzas agree that a bodhisattva's nonconceptual wisdom of meditative equipoise (familiarizing with the wisdom of knowing suchness) perfects the vimuktikāya (being the ultimate relinquishment), while the wisdom of its aftermath or subsequent attainment (training in the wisdom of knowing variety) purifies the stains of the dharmakāya (being the ultimate realization). Thus some commentators make it clear that, in the case of buddhas, the vimuktikāya is understood as the state of being free from both afflictive and cognitive obscurations, and this is certainly how the term is used here.

2098. GZ CDNP "In order to realize emptiness, signlessness, and wishlessness, all have three flowers each . . . 'Pointing out indivisible wisdom' is a summary."

2099. GZ "being indestructible as well as without deterioration" CDNP "being incombustible as well as unequal."

2100. *Vajraśekharatantra* (H448, fol. 331a.2–3). For comments on this stanza, see the note on it in the *Pañcatathāgatamudrāvivaraṇa* (text 36).

2101. I.1.4a.

2102. Skt. *pratipāda* can also mean "teach," "accomplish," "grant," and "cause to attain" (compare GZ CDNP *bsgrub pa*).

2103. GZ CDNP "Likewise, with the purpose of the bell being the same as above, it has the size of twelve finger-widths; since it represents a lotus, its aperture faces down. Its resounding refers to the union with the vajra in order to accomplish that all phenomena lack any nature . . . it is beautified by a pair of vajra garlands . . . In order to demonstrate it as the palace that is the nature . . . Therefore it is marked with the marks of the five tathāgatas. In order to show that it is inseparable by any division [CDNP 'activity'] of the wisdom of inseparable emptiness and compassion, the face of prajñā-jñāna [CDNP omit 'jñāna'] is displayed . . . In order to show that the character of such dharmadhātu wisdom has the essence of the five tathāgatas such as Vairocana, is the nature of the five skandhas such as form, is the nature of the five elements such as earth, and is the essence of the five dhātus [CDNP omit this clause], it is embellished by five spokes above. Here too, the purpose of [the four outer spokes] facing the middle spoke [CDNP omit 'spoke'] is as above. Therefore, since it serves as the cause that makes one realize the thus-described terms as well as unsurpassable dharmatā without exception, it is the bell [empowerment]. In order to demonstrate its preeminence and to establish it as the

[main] cause, the vajra empowerment should be given first, while the bell empowerment is set aside . . ."

2104. GZ "In order to bestow the foundation of the name of a sage's state, since the actuality of the namelessness of all phenomena will arise, setting aside one's previous name, the name empowerment that is in accordance with the disposition of the deity of one's own family is given." CDNP "In order to realize the namelessness of all phenomena and in order to obtain the name of a mighty sage arising later, setting aside . . ."

2105. In popular and even some academic books on Buddhism, *iṣṭadevatā* or *iṣṭadevaḥ* (a chosen, desired, or revered deity or divine being) is often given as the equivalent of Tib. *yi dam* (*kyi lha*). However, these Sanskrit terms are not literal equivalents of the Tibetan and are in all cases rendered as *'dod (pa'i) lha*, not *yi dam* or *yi dam gyi lha*. The use of *iṣṭadevatā* and *iṣṭadevaḥ* in Hindu tantric texts refers to an actual external god who is invited to dwell in the practitioner's heart, while the deities of tantric Buddhism are clearly understood to be nothing other than skillfully visualized aspects of the nature of the mind of the meditator.

2106. CD "characteristics."

2107. "The five lamps" (Skt. *pañcapradīpa*) is another name of "the five meats" (Skt. *pañcamāṃsa*): the flesh of cows, dogs, elephants, horses, and humans, which are otherwise forbidden or considered impure in the Indian tradition but used in tantric practices. For "the five nectars," see the final note on *Cittaviśuddhiprakaraṇa* 22 (text 15).

2108. That is, "May you have the nature of earth and so on!" Mathes 2015 (138n367): "An old Vedic mantra (oral information from Harunaga Isaacson)."

2109. GZ CDNP ". . . the mudrā samaya, the samaya of needing to be made a [suitable] vessel . . . The vajra samaya is that the following is to be realized: 'Beginning well with this conditioned body, your samaya is to realize the unconditioned dharmatā that is indivisible and a unity.' The bell samaya is that the following is to be realized: 'You should proclaim the eighty-four-thousand dharma collections.' The mudrā samaya is that the following is to be realized: 'You have the essence of your own chosen deity' [I follow CDNP *'dod pa'i lha* against GZ *lha'i 'dod pa*]. Needing to be made a [suitable] vessel consists of . . . In the domain of the perfection process, you need to familiarize with [CDNP 'ascertain'] these as being without any being . . . [the passage about prophecy is very corrupt and blends into the one on reassurance] This [mantra] *bhurbu vaḥsvaḥ* represents the reassurance about the actuality that is to be realized: 'All buddhas and bodhisattvas assert to you that you are free from all obscurations. This is from now on.'" Compare the presentation of the six vase empowerments in the *Caturmudrāṭīkā* (text 44, 269–73).

2110. GZ CDNP "The secret empowerment is that the bodhicitta of accomplishing [CDNP "of being protected by"] both means and prajñā at the same time is to be conferred in order to render . . . The dual secret of means and prajñā is to be bestowed. This is what you should understand."

2111. The available mss. all read *vijñāna*, but the context obviously requires *jñāna* (compare GZ CDNP "the ultimate consciousness").

2112. GZ CDNP "[The compound] 'prajñā-jñāna' is to be understood as twofold [CDNP *gnyis su med pa* ("nondual")] here: the wisdom of prajñā or prajñā being wisdom. [The first one] is to be understood as follows. Prajñā refers to the essence of the limbs and secondary limbs [NP "what possesses the limbs"] that, through the mental state with the thoughts of perceiver and perceived, have the character of the four elements, the five skandhas, and the six objects such as forms; what arises from that, serving as its cause, is bodhicitta. The other is to be understood as the actuality [CNP omit "actuality"] of the ultimate consciousness that is this very [prajñā]'s emptiness of said two aspects [of perceiver and perceived]."

2113. This is clearly a reference to the position held in Vāgīśvarakīrti's *Saptāṅga* (D1888). As mentioned before, "the seven constituents of union" (Skt. *sampuṭasaptāṅga*, Tib. *kha sbyor yan lag bdun*) characterize the fruitional state of Vajradhara, the state of unity (*yuganaddha*), the wisdom of the fourth or word empowerment, and the supreme siddhi of mahāmudrā. For details, see the explanations of the seven constituents in texts 16 (60–61), 44 (306), and 45 (392–93).

2114. Maitrīpa's reference to Skt. *prakṛti* and *vikāra* (the natural state and its modulations) is obviously also playing on the specific meanings of these terms familiar from the Sāṃkhya tradition, where they refer to the universal cosmic substance (*prakṛti*) and the entirety of the phenomenal manifestations as which it may appear (*vikāra*).

2115. As spelled out in the final sentence of text 27, this refers to the continuous flow of the nondual unity emptiness and compassion. Compare the description of mahāmudrā in the *Caturmudrānvaya* (text 14, 31): "It lacks any nature of its own, is free from the cognitive obscurations and so forth, has the appearance of the stainless midday sky in autumn, serves as the foundation of all accomplishment, is saṃsāric existence's and nirvāṇa's single own nature, embodies nonreferential compassion, and has the single form of great bliss."

2116. GZ CDNP "Others say . . . which is pointed out by prajñā-jñāna . . . Others say that the meaning . . . is the cognition without aspects [CDNP omit this phrase] that is like the center of the stainless autumn sky thanks to having become familiar with this very prajñā-jñāna empowerment. Yet others . . . is the nature of prajñā-jñāna, which has the form of any modulations of the natural state, has the character of dependent origination, has arisen as unity, and has an utterly pure nature. Further other positions are not mentioned [here] for fear of too many scriptural passages."

2117. GZ CDNP (it seems that in the second line, GZ CDNP mistakenly use the title of text 38):

> Through however much merit I attained from
> this compendium of the very secret [CDNP omit "secret"] empowerment's procedure,
> may all beings attain the poised readiness
> of the Sugata that is stainless and clear.

2118. Skt. "This concludes 'A Compendium of the Purport of Empowerment.' It was composed by Paṇḍita Avadhūta Advayavajrapāda." CDNP ". . . It was translated by the Indian upādhyāya, guru Vajrapāṇi, and lotsāwa Tsurdön." For further comments and details, see Mathes 2015 (13–14, 133–45).

2119. PDMT, 26:367–94. As mentioned in the introduction, with some variants, the structure of this text and many of its lines of verse to be spoken by the vajra master and the disciples are also found in several similar works on empowerments and maṇḍala arrangements in Tg, such as Advayavajra's *Trayodaśātmakaśrīcakrasaṃvarasya abhiṣekavidhi* (D1486), Vanaratna's *Trayodaśātmakaśrīcakrasaṃvaramaṇḍalopāyikā* (D1489), Jayasena's **Śrīḍākārṇavatantrābhiṣekavidhi* (D1521), Bhairavadeva's **Mārgābhiṣekaprakaraṇa* (D1534), Rāhulaśrīmitra's *Yuganaddhaprakāśanāmasekaprakriyā* (D1818), and *Nandivajra's *Sekaprakiyā* (D1881). At least in part, all these texts seem to be based on certain passages in the *Sarvamaṇḍalasāmānyavidhiguhyatantra* (H762).

2120. As mentioned before in text 14 under the dharmamudrā, the three samādhis of the creation process of the yogatantras and up in general are (1) the samādhi of the initial yoga, (2) the samādhi of the supreme king of activity, and (3) the samādhi of the supreme king of the maṇḍala.

2121. I follow CDNP *rig pa* GZ against *rigs pa.*

2122. It could be that GZ CDNP *mtshan ma bri ba* should be *mtshan bri ba* ("write the names").

2123. Given the names of these figures, this refers to the deity maṇḍala described in the first chapter of the *Guhyasamājatantra.* It consists of Vajrasattva (also called Bodhicittavajra, Vajradhara, and Samantabhadra); the five buddhas Akṣobhya, Vairocana, Ratnaketu (Ratnasambhava), Lokeśvara (Amitābha), and Amogha(siddhi); the four female consorts Locanā (Moharati), Māmakī (Dveṣarati), Pāṇḍaravāsinī (Rāgarati), and Samayatārā (Vajrarati); the four wrathful deities Yamāntaka, Aparājita (Prajñāntaka), Hayagrīva (Padmāntaka), and Amṛtakuṇḍalī (Vighnāntaka); and the six embodiments of form and such (Rūpavajrī and so on); see also below in this text. The basic maṇḍala of Vajrasattva, the five buddhas, the four female consorts, and the four wrathful deities is expanded with six more wrathful ones in the fourteenth chapter, and the secondary literature of the Ārya and Jñānapāda schools adds further bodhisattvas and female deities. "On nineteen, nine, five, or one" appears to refer to selective numbers of deities in this maṇḍala.

2124. According to BGTC (1585), this specifically refers to an eight-petaled lotus whose four petals in the cardinal directions are red, those in the southeast and northwest yellow, the one in the southwest green, and the one in the northeast black.

2125. GZ CDNP *las thams cad pa* (lit. "all-effective"); according to Negi 1993, this refers to wrathful deities. In other similar texts on empowerment in Tg, *sarvakarmika* appears in the places where this text speaks of Amṛtakuṇḍalī. Here, the term appears to refer to the four of Yamāntaka, Prajñāntaka, Padmāntaka, and Vighnāntaka.

2126. Within the five-vase maṇḍala in an empowerment, this refers to "the buddha vase."

2127. "Bodhi tree"; CD *bu ta ta ba pa* NP *bu ta ta ba la.*

2128. GZ *mu men* CD *rā dza barti* NP *ra tsa barti.* According to Monier-Williams, Skt. *rājāvarta* also refers to "a kind of diamond or other gem (of an inferior quality, said to come from the country Virāṭa, and regarded as a lucky possession, though not esteemed as an ornament)."

2129. I follow CDNP *bṛ ha ti* against GZ *bṛ ha spa ti.*
2130. GZ *hā sa de ba* CDNP *ha sa de ba*. The first four names refer to poison berry (*Solanum indicum*), betel nut (*Areca catechu*), butterfly pea (*Clitoria ternata*), and purple fleabane (*Vernonia cinerea*). *Sahadevā* (which is misspelled as *hasadeva* in other texts as well) can refer to jelly leaf (*Sida rhombifolia* or *Sida alnifolia*), black creeper (*Ichnocarpus frutescens*), or perfumed cherry (*Callicarpa macrophylla*), all used in Ayurvedic medicine. Moreover, the term is also a synonym of *daṇḍotpala.*
2131. GZ *rang rigs pa'i lha* CDNP *rang rig lhag pa'i lha.*
2132. This line is found as the beginning of the praises of the tathāgatas in Nāgārjuna's *Piṇḍīkṛtasādhana* (D1796, fol. 10a.4f.), Candrakīrti's *Vajrasattvasādhana* (D1814, fol. 204a.3f.), and *Paiṇḍapātika's *Śrīguhyasamājābhisamayanāmasādhana* (D1881, fol. 114b.2).
2133. GZ *stobs / stobs chen* CDNP *sde / stobs chen* ("greatly powerful hordes").
2134. CDNP reverse the order of HŪṂ and ĀḤ.
2135. Throughout, GZ CDNP read *spyi bo* ("crown of the head"), but usually the syllable OṂ is located at the forehead.
2136. According to James Valby (https://dictionary.christian-steinert.de/#home), GZ CDNP *ma gas pa* is *Calotropis gigantea* (Hindi *madār*). In English, this shrub is known as crown flower or giant milkweed. "Aśvattha tree" refers to the pipal tree or "bodhi tree" (*Ficus religiosa*).
2137. GZ CDNP *niṣcasya* em. *niścayasya.*
2138. CDNP *vi kalpa a pa na ya* GZ *vi ka wa a pa na ya.*
2139. Botanically speaking, Skt. *uḍumbara* refers to *Ficus glomerata*. As with all figs, its flowers are enclosed within its fruit (a fig "fruit" is a multiple fruit called "syconium," derived from an arrangement of many tiny flowers on an inverted, nearly closed receptacle). Since these small flowers are not visible unless the fig is cut open, a legend developed to explain the absence (or rather supposed rarity) of the visible uḍumbara flower. According to some Buddhist sources, this mythical flower blooms only once every three thousand years, while others say that it blossoms only if a cakravartin or buddha is born. In any case, it is a symbol for events of extremely rare occurrence. See https://en.wikipedia.org/wiki/Udumbara_(Buddhism)#cite_note-McCullough-1. In addition, in medieval Japan (and possibly elsewhere), this flower was believed to have the power to save the lives of those dying from disease.
2140. CDNP read the last two lines as follows:

    who is able to promote the unequaled welfare
    of sentient beings and not pass into nirvāṇa?

2141. NP *bde ba* ("bliss").
2142. NP omit this sentence and the following stanza.
2143. CDNP *-ā mṛ toda ka tha.*
2144. CDNP omit "brandish the vajra and."
2145. CDNP "red, white, yellow."
2146. The classic four kinds of activities in the Vajrayāna are pacifying (Skt. *śānti*, Tib. *zhi ba*), enriching (Skt. *pauṣṭika*; Tib. *rgyas pa*), subjugating (Skt. *vaśīkāra*, also meaning "making someone subject to one's will," "bewitching," "con-

trolling," "taming," "overcoming by chants and incantations," and "attracting", hence the more palatable, usual English rendering "magnetizing"; Tib. *dbang byed*), and wrathful (Skt. *raudra*, "fierce," "violent," "savage," "terrible"; Tib. *drag po*). The last one is also referred to as casting fierce spells (or black magic; Skt. *abhicār(uk)a;* Tib. *mngon spyod*). Similar activities are also found in many Hindu tantras, usually referred to as "the six activities" (or "six rites"; Skt. *ṣaṭkarmāṇi;* see Bühnemann 2000b).

2147. As mentioned before, the "ūrṇā hair" is one of the thirty-two major marks of a buddha (described as either a single coil of white hair between the eyebrows that radiates light and extends for many miles when uncoiled or a tuft of such hair).
2148. GZ NP *rang gi gnas* CD *rigs* ("families").
2149. I follow GZ *re khā* against CDNP *reg* ("touch").
2150. GZ NP *snying po* (CD *snying ga*) here probably render Skt. *maṇḍa* (as in *bodhimaṇḍa*), referring to the platform on which the maṇḍala rests.
2151. Given what the text says right below, I follow CD *rdo rje lag pa g.yas su gtad* against GZ *rdo rje sems drag chus gdab* NP *rdo rje sems grags chus btab.*
2152. CDNP omit this sentence.
2153. CDNP omit the last phrase.
2154. As mentioned before, this sentence has its parallel in text 37 (198).
2155. "Primal being" renders Skt. *ādipuruṣa* (Tib. *dang po'i skye bu*), which is also an epithet of Brahmā and Viṣṇu.
2156. CDNP *a.*
2157. GZ *sems kyis* CDNP *sems dpa'* ("sattva").
2158. P omits the second and third lines.
2159. GZ *khyud* CD *khong du chud* ("realize").
2160. *Hevajratantra* II.3.13.
2161. I follow GZ *padma'i dkyil 'khor dkyil 'khor brtan* against CDNP *padma'i dkyil 'khor zhes su brtan* ("it is stable as 'the lotus maṇḍala'") NP . . . *zhes su bstan* ("it is taught as 'the lotus maṇḍala'").
2162. CDNP omit "VAJRASATTVA."
2163. GZ omits this line.
2164. I follow GZ CD *grol ba* against NP *'go ba* ("going").
2165. GZ CDNP *byang chub* ("bodhi"), but this stanza is obviously the same as the one toward the end of the water empowerment.
2166. GZ *gtod pa dang dang lhan cig* CDNP *gtad do / lan cig* (". . . One time").
2167. GZ *khyo bzhin du* CDNP *khyud bzhin du* ("while embracing her").
2168. The last four stanzas, the two sentences in prose in between, and the concluding mantra are more or less similar to stanzas 91–95 and the mantra in Buddhajñāna's *Dvitīyakramatattvabhāvanānāmamukhāgama.* In the third line of the last stanza, I follow this text's *rang byung* against GZ CDNP *rang nyid* ("oneself"). In the mantra, following Abhayākaragupta's *Vajrāvalī, bhañja* is emended to *bhaja* (second-person imperative: "Grant HŪṂ liberation HO!"). Vaidyapāda's *Sukusuma* (D1875, fol. 106b.6) clarifies that this mantra is spoken by the disciple to the consort. I am indebted here to Dalton 2019 (313, 383–85).
2169. Some parts of the last three sentences are a bit cryptic in Tibetan (possibly

corrupt) and could also be read in other ways. However, the rendering of the last sentence follows what is discussed in virtually identical terms in other tantric commentaries and Sahajavajra's *Sthitisamāsa* (text 17, 104); GZ CDNP *yi ge hūṃ las padma dang rdo rje āḥ dang yi ge oṃ dag gi ze'u 'bru dag gi nang du yi ge phaṭ rnam par bsgom mo / rdo rje dbyings kyi dbang phyug ma'i rtsa g.yon gyi ngos na gnas pa sor mos bskyod de cung zad shes pas so / 'di'ang bla ma'i man ngag las so /.*

2170. GZ CDNP *phung po rnam shes* is taken as *rnam shes phung po* (as in this stanza's citation in text 17, 104).

2171. GZ *dman pa* CDNP *smad pa* ("disparaged").

2172. The last two lines are similar to the well-known unattributed lines cited in the *Caturmudrānvaya* (text 14, 27) and may be a variant or corrupted version of them (especially since the Tibetan of the second line is identical in both texts):

> Seeing what is to be marked in the middle
> of the supreme and cessational, stabilize it!

2173. These two lines are also found in the *Hevajratantra* (I.8.33ab and I.10.15ab), the *Pañcakrama* (II.64ab), the *Saṃpuṭatantra* (H396, fol. 367b.6), the *Śrīvajramaṇḍālaṃkāratantra* (H459, fol. 82b.6), the *Śrīvajraḍākatantra* (H386, fol. 328a.3–4), the *Vajraḍākanāmottaratantra* (H387, fol. 519a.4–5), and the *Śrīḍākārṇavamahāyoginītantra* (H390, fol. 75b.7).

2174. I follow GZ *sogs pa nyams pa* against CDNP *sogs pas 'phags pa.*

2175. The last three lines of this stanza are found in the *Śrīlaghusaṃbaratantra* (H384, fol. 80a.5–6), the *Abhidhānottaratantra* (H385, fol. 280b.1–2), and the *Saṃpuṭatantra* (H396, fol. 432b.5). In the first two texts, the first line reads "Without a mantrin seeing the maṇḍala," and in the third text, it says "Not being aware of a timely death."

2176. This stanza is well known from the *Daśadharmakasūtra* (H53, fol. 274a.3–4) and is also found in the *Jñānatilakatantra* (H382, 40b.3–4).

2177. I could not locate these lines.

2178. The first two lines are unidentified, but the second two are *Hevajratantra* II.3.10ab and are also found in the *Raktayamarītantra* (H441, fol. 489a.1). In addition, the last line also corresponds to *Guhyasamājatantra* XVIII.113f and *Sampuṭodbhavatantra* II.1.46d, and the preceding three lines in both of these texts represent a more extensive version of the second-to-last line of the stanza here. Its last line (here rendered "and the fourth is again like that") can be understood in several ways and is also commented on in a variety of ways in the commentaries on the above tantras, Rāmapāla's *Sekanirdeśapañjikā* (text 45), and Vajrapāṇi's *Guruparamparākramopadeśa* (text 213).

2179. As they stand, these two stanzas are not found in Kg or Tg. However, in one way or another, several of their lines or phrases appear in a number of tantras, such as the *Hevajratantra* (the last two lines of the first stanza correspond to I.1.29 and the first two lines of the second stanza to I.1.26 and II.3.6ab).

2180. *Hevajratantra* II.3.4.

2181. *Hevajratantra* II.3.11. In this and the following cited stanzas, I follow the Sanskrit of the *Hevajratantra* and the *Guhyasamājatantra* without noting the variants in GZ CDNP.

2182. Kṛṣṇa's *Yogaratnamālā* (Snellgrove 1959, 2:127) glosses Skt. *śeṣataḥ* ("as remainder") as *pariśeṣād* (basically same meanings as *śeṣa*). Note, however, that *śeṣataḥ* can also mean "otherwise" or "else," which is one of its two glosses in Rāmapāla's *Sekanirdeśapañjikā* (text 45, 399; *tribhyo anyatayā*, "other than the three [preceding ones]").

2183. The last two stanzas are *Hevajratantra* I.8.30–31.

2184. The last three stanzas are *Hevajratantra* II.3.9 and II.3.7–8.

2185. With slight variants in the last two lines, this stanza is found in the *Hevajratantra* (I.8.33 and I.10.15), the *Pañcakrama* (II.64ab), the *Saṃpuṭatantra* (H396, fol. 367b.6), the *Śrīvajramaṇḍālaṃkāratantra* (H459, fol. 82b.6), the *Śrīvajraḍākatantra* (H386, fol. 328a.3–4), the *Vajraḍākanāmottaratantra* (H387, fol. 519a.4–5), and the *Śrīḍākārṇavamahāyoginītantra* (H390, fol. 75b.7).

2186. These two stanzas are *Guhyasamājatantra* XVIII.176–77 (H416b, fol. 532b.5–7). In this text, the progressive set of approach (or "worship"; Skt. *sevā*), close accomplishment (*upasādhana*), accomplishment (*sādhana*), and great accomplishment (*mahāsādhana*) corresponds to the better-known set of four that consists of approach (*sevā*), close approach (*upasevā*), accomplishment (*sādhana*), and great accomplishment (*sādhana*). This fourfold template is used in the Vajrayāna in a number of different contexts, such as the creation process, the mantra recitation, and the stages of karmamudrā (thus the individual meanings of these four terms can vary greatly). "The nature, its own bliss, and peacefulness" means that the three main afflictions (ignorance, desire, and hatred) are at peace and that intense (innate) great bliss is experienced instead, which is mind's own nature inasmuch as the fruition in the form of this bliss is continuously present. For details, see Onians 2002, 216ff.

2187. I could not locate the last two stanzas.

2188. These stanzas are *Hevajratantra* II.5.67, I.8.32, and II.3.21–22ab. The first stanza is also found in almost identical form as Saraha's *Dohakoṣa* 30.

2189. I could not locate this stanza. As the following citations show, the point here is the fourth ecstasy in the sense of the wisdom of mahāmudrā.

2190. *Hevajratantra* II.5.69ef (GZ CDNP read "middle" instead of "start" and "vajra holder" instead of "Heruka"). According to Kṛṣṇa's *Yogaratnamālā* (Snellgrove 1959, 2:155), the wisdom here is empty yet nonempty because it has the nature of the single taste of the unity of prajñā and means. This very wisdom is designated with the term "Heruka" because it has the nature of the nonduality of emptiness and compassion.

2191. *Guhyasamāja Uttaratantra* (H416b, fol. 524b.1–2).

2192. *Hevajratantra* II.4.33ab. In the tantra, the bodhisattva Vajragarbha asks the Buddha: "Through which means should bodhicitta be generated?" The Buddha answers with this stanza, whose last two lines read as follows:

> one should give rise to the bodhicitta
> that has uncovered and covered forms.

2193. *Hevajratantra* I.8.49cd.

2194. *Hevajratantra* I.8.34. As for the last two lines, according to Kṛṣṇa's *Yogaratnamālā* (Snellgrove 1959, 2:127–28), connate ecstasy is observed in a direct manner, whereas someone else's pith instructions are not appropriate for something that is to be perceived directly. Therefore the tantras speak of "merit." Think like this: worldly connate ecstasy is not what is to be accomplished here, because it is stained by the contaminations of what is saṃsāric. "But can the connate—the dharmakāya of the tathāgatas that is to be personally experienced—be accomplished here?" Since there is no other approach, while being intent on this worldly connate ecstasy according to the pith instructions, the connate "is realized by yourself" through the maturation of familiarizing with it, not before. Therefore study, reflection, and familiarization are not useless here. "Attending to" refers to the path of means—that is, perfectly familiarizing with it. That familiarization has many "observances" (Skt. *parva*; Tib. *dus thabs*, "timely means"), which means many aspects. These observances to be obtained from the guru are provided by the guru to suitable disciples according to procedure, which means they are the pith instructions. According to IaS (299–300n251), "The compound *guruparva* has a complex history. In earlier sources it is simply a synonym of *guruparampara*, 'lineage of the gurus' (the earliest occurrence is perhaps the one in Kumārila's *Ślokavārttika*, Pratijñāsūtra, st. 23d). This meaning continued to be used (Abhinavagupta's *Īśvarapratyabhijñāvimarśinī* . . . and Vilāsavajra's commentary on the *Nāmasaṅgīti* . . .), but in later times others also became current. Thus in Śaiva texts *guruparva* sometimes refers to certain special days (cf., e.g., *Kularatnoddyota* 14.10), which may be either specific days of fixed months (cf., e.g., *Puraścaryārṇava*, vol. 1, p. 82), or days which are special through their connection with one's own guru, such as his birthday or the anniversary of his death (cf., e.g., *Tantrāloka* 25.11–12 . . .). In this verse of the *Hevajratantra*, too, the word has received, both in India and in Tibet, widely differing interpretations. For instance, Ratnākaraśānti's explanation, which is somewhat intricate . . . , ultimately comes down to taking it to mean 'oral instruction (of the guru) aiming at realization (*avavāda* = *avagamāya* [= *adhigamāya*] *vādah* = *upadeśaḥ*)' (cf. *Muktāvalī*, ed. p. 9212–14 [cf. also the *Yogaratnamālā*, pp. 127–128])." Thus "observance" could also be understood as "a timely opening provided as an opportunity for realization," which then also includes nonverbal pointing-out situations. IaS adds that this stanza is considered important in the Kagyü traditions in particular, and the stanzas immediately following it are regarded as crucial for the Kagyü understanding of Mahāmudrā.

2195. The second two lines are similar to *Hevajratantra* I.8.49ab: "The wisdom that is to be aware of itself . . ."
2196. I could not locate this stanza.
2197. GZ CDNP read "gradually" twice.
2198. With some variants, the first stanza is *Dohakoṣa* 69. As mentioned before, Schaeffer (2005, 203n11) points out that this stanza is also found in the oldest available ms. of a fragmentary dohā text attributed to Saraha (not included in Tg). Szántó reports (email communication) that, with some variants, Tilopa's *Dohakoṣa* 10 is also found as stanza 77 of an alternative version of Saraha's *Dohakoṣa* edited in Sāṃkṛtyāyana 1957 (18), as well as twice in Bagchi 1935a (7, 28), likewise attributed to Saraha. The second stanza here is unidentified. With some variants, it is likewise attributed to Saraha in Ratnarakṣita's *Śrīsaṃvarodayamahātantrarājasyapadminīnāmapañjikā* (D1420, fol. 6b.5–6), and its last two lines are also cited (without attribution) in Raviśrījñāna's *Nāmasaṃgītiṭippaṇī* (D1395, fol. 61a.7).

2199. I could not locate the first two stanzas. With minor variants, the second one also appears in text 90 (292), said to be from "the scriptures." The third stanza is a slight variant of Saraha's *Dohakoṣa* 32.
2200. I could not locate these two stanzas.
2201. I follow NP *'dul ba can* against GZ *'dus ba can* CD *'du ba can*.
2202. Lit. "Through the immeasurability arisen from the merit due to composing . . ."
2203. CD omit this line.
2204. CDNP "This concludes 'A Compendium of the Procedures of Empowerment.' It was composed by Śrī Advayavajra."
2205. PDMT, 26:395–401.
2206. GZ CDNP "I pay homage to Śrī Vajrasattva."
2207. GZ "The character of the five aspects is explained . . ."
2208. Skt. *-repha-*, "letter *r*."
2209. GZ CDNP "from a blue HŪṂ."
2210. "Akṣobhya" is only found in GZ CDNP (GZ also adds "blue"), while "springs" is left out.
2211. Skt. *sauṣirya*, GZ CDNP *bu ga* ("pores").
2212. GZ CDNP "dharma robes."
2213. GZ CDNP omit this sentence.
2214. GZ CD *rtag pa* "permanence" NP *brtags pa* "imaginary."
2215. GZ CDNP "Just that diversity is emanation."
2216. *Mahāyānaviṃśikā* 19.
2217. GZ *mi rigs* ("not suitable") CDNP *mi rig* ("not aware").
2218. In the Sanskrit alphabet, the consonants are organized according to where they are pronounced in the mouth: the series of the velar consonants starts with *ka*, that of the palatal consonants with *ca*, of retroflex consonants with *ṭa*, that of the dental consonants with *ta*, that of the labial consonants with *pa*, and finally there are the approximant and fricative consonants *ya*, *ra*, *la*, *va*, *śa*, *ṣa*, *sa*, and *ha*.
2219. Vajradhṛk ("Vajra Holder") is another name of Akṣobhya, primarily found in the Ārya tradition of the *Guhyasamājatantra* (as are the names in the following mantras for the remaining four buddhas).
2220. GZ "from a white HŪṂ."
2221. GZ CDNP add "sealed with emptiness."
2222. In ancient India, a cycle of day and night (delimited by sunset and sunrise) was divided into eight watches or intervals (Skt. *prahara*, Tib. *thun*). There are four watches from sunrise to sunset and four during the night, each lasting approximately three hours (the closer to the equator, the more day and night, and thus these watches are of equal length). Thus "from midnight until dawn" under Vajrasattva refers to the last two watches of the night, "the morning period" under Vairocana to the first two watches of the day, "the third and fourth watches" under Ratnasambhava to the last two watches of the day (from noon to sunset), and "the first part of the night" under Amitābha to the first two watches of the night. Lastly, Amoghasiddhi is simply related to midnight. Strangely, Akṣobhya is not included in this format at all.

2223. GZ "from a white OṂ" CDNP "from an OṂ."
2224. GZ CDNP spell out "wisdom."
2225. GZ CDNP omit "to recite."
2226. The meaning of *jinajik* (given some of the comments below and in other commentaries, maybe rather *jinajit* or even *jinadhṛk*) is not entirely clear. The term appears in the first and fifteenth chapters of the *Guhyasamājatantra* as the mantra of the buddha family of ignorance (Skt. *moha*), in the seventh chapter of the *Guhyagarbhatantra*, and in *Mañjuśrīnāmasaṃgīti* VIII.36c; the Tibetan says *rgyal bas rgyal* ("victory/victorious through the victor"), which should be *rgyal ba'i rgyal*, meaning either "victor of victors" (as glossed in *Surativajra's *Āryamañjuśrīnāmasaṃgītyarthālokakara*; D2093, fol. 54b.5: "the supreme secret mantra that is even more victorious than the victors who are śrāvakas and so on") or "king of victors" (as, for example, glossed in Vimalamitra's *Nāmasaṃgītivṛttināmārthaprakāśakaraṇadīpa*; D2092, fol. 26b.2: *rgyal ba'i yang rgyal po*). Narendrakīrti's *Mañjuśrīnāmasaṃgītivyākhyā* (D1397, fol. 167a.6) glosses the term as "holding the victor" and explains: "'victor' refers to great bliss. What is held by it is HAṂ" (Tib. *rgyal ba 'dzin pa ste / rgyal ba ni bde ba chen po'o / des gzung ba ni haṃ ngo /*).
2227. GZ "from a yellow TRĀṂ" CDNP "from a TRĀṂ."
2228. Skt. *piśuna* can also mean "malice" and "treacherous," but GZ CDNP have *phra ma* ("slander"), and malice seems already covered by "anger" under Akṣobhya. Usually, however, Ratnasambhava is associated with the affliction of pride.
2229. GZ CD "the nature of the wisdom of equality" NP "the nature of equality."
2230. GZ CD "purity" NP "nature."
2231. GZ CDNP omit "and fourth."
2232. GZ CDNP omit "to recite."
2233. GZ CDNP "from a red HRĪḤ."
2234. The meaning of *ārolik*, which appears in a number of tantras (mostly embedded in mantras), is interpreted in several different ways in the commentaries on some of these tantras. For example, this term appears in *Hevajratantra* I.5.12b and in *Vajramālātantra* 23.10, 54.56, and 54.156. Kṛṣṇa Paṇḍita's *Yogaratnamālā* on the *Hevajratantra* says, "It [the nature of nondiscursiveness] is *ārolika* because of discriminating them [the jewels of all buddhas] in every aspect" (Skt. *sa evārolikaḥ teṣām sarvākāratayā paricchedāt*; Farrow and Menon 1992, 56, render this as "Arolika, the Impartial One, is so called because of not discriminating between anything at all," but neither the Sanskrit nor the Tibetan have a negative). Curiously, the Tibetan of the *Yogaratnamālā* renders *ārolika* as "beyond saṃsāra" (Tib. *'khor 'das*; Snellgrove 1959, 1:61–62n4, renders this as "*saṃsāra-nirvāṇa*," which does not make much sense here, though it is a common meaning of this Tibetan abbreviation). Similarly, Alaṃkakalaśa's commentary *Gaṃbhīrārthadīpikā* on the *Vajramālātantra* (D1795, fol. 155a.5–6) glosses it as follows: "As for 'ārolik,' *ā* means 'in all respects,' *ro* 'from saṃsāra,' and *lik* 'go'; hence *ārolik*. This is the expedient meaning. [Or] '*aro*' refers to going to luminosity through the three wisdoms; hence *ārolik*. This is the definitive meaning" (similar hermeneutical etymologies are also found in some commentaries on the *Guhyasamājatantra*, and it is obviously

based on the expedient etymology here that Kittay and Jamspal 2020, 80 and 600n1944, renders the term as "crossing over from cyclic existence" and "transcender of cyclic life"). A number of other commentaries simply render *ārolik(a)* as "immeasurable" (Tib. *dpag med*), some explicitly equating it with the obvious Amitābha (Tib. *'od dpag med*). Yet other commentaries explain *ārolik(a)* as enjoying the relationships between all that defines and is defined (indicating the meaning of the skandha of discrimination, which is usually matched with Amitābha). However, two other commentaries on the *Hevajratantra* gloss *ārolik(a)* as *rtsod pa med pa* ("without dispute/conflict/quarrel"). Saroruha's *Hevajratantrapañjikāpadminīnāma* (D1181, fols. 134b.1–2 and 135a.3) explains this: "*Ārolika* refers to Amitābha, with *rolika* being [one who] disputes. He is Ārolika because it [dispute] does not exist in the great passion that has the nature of supreme ecstasy . . . He is Ārolika because non-discursiveness does not have the nature of dispute." Similarly, Kṛṣṇa Paṇḍita's commentary *Smṛtinipāda* (D1187, fol. 154a.4) says: "*Rola* refers to mutual dispute; since he is without that, he is Ārolika." According to Snellgrove 1959 (1:61–62n4), this must be the correct interpretation, since *rolā* (glossed as "dissension" or "discord" in the commentaries) appears in *Hevajratantra* 2.4.6d (in Prakrit), and *ārolika* is thus a *vṛddhi* form of *arola*.

2235. The Sanskrit omits this phrase.

2236. GZ CDNP "from a green KHAṂ."

2237. The Sanskrit omits the last four sentences.

2238. The Sanskrit omits "to recite."

2239. GZ CDNP "They are mere stainless appearances—the sambhogakāya. They are the svābhāvikakāya, which is the single taste of the three kāyas. They are the dharmakāya, which has the character of unconditioned suchness. They are not different from the kāya of imaginary consciousness."

2240. Here, "has the character of cause and result" refers to Akṣobhya, who was described above in that way, and "the sheer single taste of saṃsāric existence and nirvāṇa" refers to the seal of Vajrasattva—that is, "consciousness's lack of any nature and the identical nature of emptiness and compassion." Maitrīpa's *Caturmudropadeśanāma* (text 92, 18) elaborates on this as follows: "There is also the tathāgata relief and the Vajradhara relief. Furthermore, the imaginary [nature] is sealed with the dependent [nature], the dependent [nature] is sealed with the perfect [nature], the perfect [nature is sealed] by Vajrasattva, and he is sealed with great bliss . . . The seal of the dependent [nature] in the imaginary [nature] consists of the outer creation process. The seal of the perfect [nature] means that even all deities are mere cognizance. The seal of Vajrasattva consists of understanding cognizance to be emptiness. The seal of great bliss consists of rendering this very [emptiness] a living experience [through] the pith instructions." For a more detailed explanation of this, see Vajrapāṇi's *Guruparamparākramopadeśa* (text 213, 204–7).

2241. Text 36 also quotes this stanza, attributing it to the *Ḍākinīvajrapañjaratantra*, but it is not found in that tantra or in any other work in Kg or Tg.

2242. *Bodhicittavivaraṇa* 57.

2243. *Yuktiṣaṣṭikā* 6cd.

2244. GZ CDNP "from a white LAṂ."

2245. The Sanskrit omits "and mantra."
2246. GZ CDNP "the red-colored one named Pāṇḍaravāsinī."
2247. GZ CDNP "from a light-green TĀṂ."
2248. GZ CDNP "of extraordinary beauty, [well-]shaped, and youthful."
2249. CDNP *rang bzhin* ("nature").
2250. As mentioned before, Edgerton 1953 (1:106 and 181) explains āli as "*a-series* (i.e., a plus āli), name for a series of syllables (chiefly vowels and combinations of a or ā with semivowels)" and kāli as "(ka plus āli), *ka-series*, name for a series of syllables beginning with ka (consonants plus a or ā)."
2251. Instead of this sentence, GZ CDNP read: "She is the primordially established vajradhātu."
2252. In GZ CDNP, the last two stanzas are four long lines with different numbers of syllables each, which are somewhat hard to make sense of: "Summarizing a bit the effort for the virtue of composing this text, by compiling this ritual in order to make my disciples realize, since it is endowed with all victors' scriptures and reasonings for the long-term benefit of sentient beings, may [all] beings be victorious through the entirety of this virtue that I have attained!"
2253. Skt. "This concludes 'The Five Aspects.'" CDNP add "It was composed upon having been supplicated with a request by Amṛ[ta]deva." For further comments and details, see Mathes 2015 (14, 147–54).
2254. PDMT, 26:407–10.
2255. GZ CDNP *snying po'i sku* (this seems to be an alternative rendering of svābhāvikakāya instead of the standard *ngo bo nyid sku*). There is no opening homage in the Sanskrit.
2256. GZ CDNP have the four lines of this stanza in reverse order.
2257. The last two lines in GZ CDNP say this:

> By [GZ *ldan pa'i* em. *ldan pas*] possessing the seeing of it in them,
> completely perfect awakening is accomplished.

2258. GZ has the first three lines as follows:

> Diversity lacks the mode of permanence,
> and there is no thinking of it as extinct
> It is neither permanence nor extinction

In CDNP, the first and fourth lines read differently:

> Diversity has no ground of permanence [I follow NP *rtag pa* against CD *rtog pa*, "thought"]
> . . .
> Since both do not exist, it is not these two.

2259. This stanza is identical to *Tattvaratnāvalī* 6.
2260. Sahajavajra's commentary on the *Tattvadaśaka* (text 46, 41) quotes lines 5cd in its explanation of stanza 7, and he also cites them in his *Sthitisamāsa* (text 17, 105).
2261. GZ CDNP omit "without equal."
2262. GZ "inconceivable mind as such."
2263. Compare this stanza 7 with *Tattvadaśaka* 7cd–9. GZ CDNP:

If the world is realized as single taste,
it is luminous and unsullied [GZ CD *rnyog pa med* NP *rtog pa med,*
"without thought"]
If you have no fear of thoughts' attachment, [CDNP omit "attachment"]
you shall live in any way you please.

2264. The last three lines in GZ read as follows (CDNP agrees on the second and fourth lines, but the third one follows the Sanskrit):

nor do afflictions arise from awakening
Delusion and afflictions are thoughts,
yet delusion's nature is without stain.

2265. Sahajavajra's commentary on the *Tattvadaśaka* (text 46, 47) quotes line 9a in its explanation of stanza 8.

2266. GZ CDNP:

The actions of the body are the conduct,
the actions of speech are the dharma teachings,
the action of mind is holding a firm resolve— [GZ *yi dam 'dzin*
CDNP *yang dag 'dzin*]
the insightful ones are free from thoughts.

2267. The last three lines in GZ CDNP read as follows:

do not make it an illusion through illusion!
Nescience through illusion is great delusion [CDNP "Illusion,
through nescience, is great delusion"]
The way of the wise is: delusion is delusion.

2268. Note that the last line of this stanza is identical with *Prajñopāyaviniścayasiddhi* V.43d. GZ CDNP:

If the nature is known just as it is,
the buddhas and so on condense it
Experiencing all in every respect,
it is established as knowing true reality.

2269. Strange as it may seem, "annihilation" is here used as an equivalent of "emptiness." GZ CDNP:

The so-called "realization through thousands
of collections of the dharma" is emptiness
This realization is not by virtue of analysis;
it is by virtue of the guru, free from analysis

Sahajavajra's commentary on the *Tattvadaśaka* (text 46, 38) quotes this stanza in its explanation of stanza 6. Tipi Bumlabar's subcommentary (Ti pi 'bum la 'bar 2004c, 367) explains that "by virtue of analysis" here refers to the Pāramitāyāna and the last line to the Mantrayāna.

2270. GZ:

As for persons who are free of thoughts,
bliss in all aspects constitutes true reality

It is way beyond any imaginations—
emptiness is not the true reality of that bliss,
bliss is inconceivable, bliss does not exist

CDNP:

As for persons who are free of thoughts,
all aspects are the true reality of bliss
Emptiness is not the true reality of bliss,
nor is it inconceivable, nor is it bliss.

2271. Both GZ and CDNP differ and can be read in more than one way; GZ:

What is buddhahood is superimposition's lack
Ultimately speaking, it is not to be seen [or "in the ultimate, there is nothing to see"]
Not seeing it, its application [or "union"] is known,
engaging accordingly later

CDNP:

Hence buddhahood is superimposition's lack
Ultimately speaking, it is not to be seen [or "This is the unseeable ultimate"]
Engaging in it as you please, [or "how is engaging in it bliss?"]
the corresponding awareness is not seen [or "Thus awareness is not to be seen"].

2272. GZ:

The awakening that is neither dual nor
nondual [*gnyis ni* em. *gnyis med*] lacks the characteristic of purity
Great yogīs are free from any thinking,
[and yet] they comprehend all aspects

CDNP:

Being neither dual nor nondual,
awakening lacks the characteristic of purity
This freedom from hope is the great yoga,
the realization of all aspects.

2273. This stanza is identical to *Kudṛṣṭinirghātana* 4. GZ CDNP read the last two lines as follows:

As emptiness and compassion are inseparable,
this is held to be the wisdom of buddhahood.

2274. GZ *rtse ba* ("play") CDNP *snying rje* ("compassion").
2275. GZ has the first three lines as follows:

Perform the dhyāna of that yoga
of any form such as a vase
Through this . . .

CDNP:

> With regard to perceiving a vase and such,
> the dhyāna of all yogīs is to be performed
> Through this . . .

2276. Sahajavajra's commentary on the *Tattvadaśaka* (text 46, 38) quotes this stanza in its explanation of stanza 6. Tipi Bumlabar's subcommentary (Ti pi 'bum la 'bar 2004c, 367) explains that "dhyāna" here refers to the experience of calm abiding and superior insight that consists of the wisdom of the fourth empowerment. "A vase and such" refers to worldly appearances arising through conditions. "They" refers to yogīs of the fourth empowerment. "This realization is the great realization" (this is how text 46 quotes the third line of this stanza) refers to the realization that is not produced by analysis—that is, the union of calm abiding and superior insight of secret mantra. "All aspects" refers to the experience of all conditioned appearances, which is calm abiding. "Single kāya" refers to experiencing whatever appears as luminosity free of discursiveness, which is superior insight. Note here that by explicitly connecting dhyāna with the perception of objects, this stanza refers back to *Tattvadaśaka* 6ab and alludes to the Mahāmudrā approach of meditation: instead of blocking sense perceptions in samādhi, they are used for realizing and enhancing the inseparable union of appearance-emptiness, lucidity-emptiness, bliss-emptiness, and awareness-emptiness.
2277. CDNP: "The mind of variety is emanated."
2278. This stanza is quoted in the *Pañcākara*.
2279. GZ:

> Through increasing my intention of merit
> by having accumulated this and so on,
> may the entire world thereby [GZ *des* CDNP *de*]
> attain the awakening of buddhahood!

The first two lines in CDNP differ as follows:

> By the merit of the one with the merit
> attained through this in such a way . . .

2280. Skt. "This concludes 'Twenty Stanzas on the Mahāyāna.'" CDNP ". . . by master Advayavajra. *Pa ri pa ta prajñā sha ra sa ma dhya na*. It was translated and edited by the Indian upādhyāya Divākaracandra and the Tibetan lotsāwa bhikṣu Śākya Dsöndrü." Following this text, BKC (vol. *kha*, fol. 29a.4–29b.1) says that these twenty stanzas teach the meaning of unity in detail: commitment to compose the text (including purpose and connection), refuting wrong [*dog* em. *log*] extremes, identifying the systems of others, the manner of realization, the relief following realization, the great remedy there dawning as equal taste, displaying the conduct of the three gates as equal taste, dispelling illusory clinging, since delusion about the basic nature is eliminated through both meditative equipoise and subsequent attainment, the manner in which luminosity [an interlinear note on *'dol* says *gsal*; thus *'dol gyis* is emended to *'od gsal gyi*] operates, the greatness of that, realizing the unity of nonduality, the manner in which the fruition is revealed in the unity of emptiness and compassion, and concluding dedication of virtue. According to Tipi Bumlabar (BKC, vol. *kha*, fol. 86a.2–4), the outline of this text is as follows:

1. the four fruitional kāyas by way of an expression of homage
2. the four kāyas of the path by way of the commitment to explain
3. the meaning of the text
3a. the natural yoga
3b. the yoga of realization
3c. the yoga of conduct
3c1. the actual conduct
3c2. the stains of conduct
3c3. the aspects of conduct
3c4. realizing this through the guru's pith instructions
3c5. teaching the way to practice that accords with realization
3d. teaching the fourfold fruition
4. concluding dedication of roots of virtue.

For further comments and details, see Mathes 2015 (17–18, 193–97).

2281. PDMT, 26:417–20. GZ *ta ttva ma hā yā na bing sha ka raṃ si* CDNP *tā ttva ma hā yā na bingsha ti.*

2282. GZ CDNP "I pay homage to the venerable Buddha."

2283. CDNP *rnam* [NP *snang*] *med dang ni rnam nyed bral.* Note here that the order of the third and fourth moments is switched compared with Maitrīpa's usual sequence. As Mathes 2015 (187n497) points out, this may be the case for metrical reasons.

2284. GZ CDNP read the last two lines as follows:

> Through her, it is held that true reality is known, [CDNP "The true reality of this is held to be prajñā"]
> for she is the world's all-encompassing sovereign.

2285. GZ CDNP "has the character of being."

2286. Mañjuvajra is one of the many forms of Mañjuśrī, orange in color, with three faces (orange, blue, and white) and six arms. He holds a sword, an arrow, a bow, and a blue utpala flower (or a scripture), and his two forward-most hands are crossed over his chest in the mudrā symbolizing the union of prajñā and means, embracing his consort. In the Jñānapāda commentarial tradition of the *Guhyasamājatantra*, Mañjuvajra is the central deity in a nineteen-deity maṇḍala (in the Ārya Nāgārjuna tradition, the central deity in a thirty-two-deity maṇḍala is Akṣobhyavajra); for details, see Tanemura 2015.

2287. GZ CDNP "Distinct appearances are prajñā."

2288. GZ CDNP:

> She is duality yet nonduality,
> inconceivable yet conception [I follow NP *sems pa* against GZ CD *sems dpa'*],
> . . .
> being yet nonbeing, perceiver and perceived.

2289. According to Tipi Bumlabar's outline (BKC, vol. *kha*, fol. 86a.4–86b.1; for details, see the final note on this text), the first five stanzas are divided into (1) the combined presentation of both karmamudrā and dharmamudrā, (2) the presentation of the samayamudrā, and (3) the presentation of mahāmudrā. What is clear is that stanza 1 discusses karmamudrā and stanzas 4–5 mahāmudrā. Thus, if one considers stanza 1 as "the combined presentation of both karmamudrā and dharmamudrā," stanzas 2–3 would represent the presentation of the samayamudrā. Mathes 2015 (187) relates "prajñā" to karmamudrā in stanza 1, dharmamudrā in lines 2ab, samayamudrā in lines 2c–3c, and mahāmudrā in line 3d (he does not indicate whether mahāmudrā continues into the next stanzas). A difficulty with both of these outlines is not only that Maitrīpa's text never mentions the word "dharmamudrā" but that stanza 8 instead relates the jñānamudrā to Mañjuvajra (who, according to both the above outlines, would be related to the samayamudrā in his first appearance in stanza 3). Moreover, in stanzas 7–19, the practices of karmamudrā and samayamudrā are explicitly related to those of low faculties, jñānamudrā to those of medium faculties, and mahāmudrā to those of highest faculties. Thus, if Maitrīpa's brief presentation of the four mudrās in the first five stanzas matches their subsequent detailed presentation in terms of the persons with the three kinds of faculties (which seems reasonable), stanza 1 would refer to the karmamudrā, stanzas 2–3 in one way or another to the samayamudrā and the jñānamudrā (possibly one stanza each), and stanzas 4–5 to mahāmudrā.

2290. CDNP "through the dharma of secret mantra." As mentioned before, in the expression *mantraśastra*, *śāstra* can also mean "body of teaching," "scripture," "treatise," "manual," "precept," "direction," "discipline," "science," and "art."

2291. According to IaS (416), this stanza can be read in three ways: "If we take the first half to form one clause, and the second half to be a causal phrase expressing a justification for the first, then *atra* might be interpreted in two ways: either as referring to *praveśa* or to *mantraśāstra*. Taken the first way, we would have the following sense: 'And entry into this [wisdom] is, clearly, in accordance with the mantra teaching; for there are various means for this [entry into wisdom], according to [the different types of practitioner, viz. those of] weak, middling, and powerful [faculties].' The second possibility would give us the following, which seems rather more cogent: 'And entry into this [wisdom] is, clearly, in accordance with the mantra teaching; for in this [mantra teaching] there are various means [for entering into wisdom], according to [the different types of practitioner, viz. those of] weak, middling, and powerful [faculties].' But a yet slightly different interpretation may be still more preferable: one in which the first, main, clause runs not just to the end of the second verse-quarter but includes the word *nānā* at the beginning of the third. Then *yasmāt* would stand clause-initial, and the sense might be: 'And entry into this [wisdom] is, in accordance with the mantra teaching, various; for there are [different] means in this [mantra teaching] according to [the different types of practitioner, viz. those of] weak, middling, and powerful [faculties].'"

2292. GZ:

> The karma- and the samayamudrās
> look at pure true reality on the outside
> To perfectly meditate on the cakra
> is the lower ones' dhyāna of awakening

CDNP:

> The karma- and the samayamudrās
> are the perfect meditation on the cakra
> The lower ones' dhyāna of awakening
> looks at pure true reality on the outside.

2293. Skt. *nāyaka* can also mean "lord," "husband," and "lover."
2294. CDNP *rdzun gyi rnam pa min* corresponds to this, while GZ reads *rdzun min rnam pa'ang ste* ("an appearance that is not false").
2295. On their own, GZ CDNP are quite hard to make sense of but mean something like this:

> Since the comprehension of the state of
> self-blessing lacks true reality's power,
> they are taught in a correct manner
> and gradually accomplish awakening.

2296. GZ CDNP "You may wonder: 'How is the deity arranged?'"
2297. GZ CDNP:

> Again, yogīs see true reality,
> supremely merging with mahāmudrā
> Those of supreme faculties should rest
> by way of the nature of all entities.

2298. GZ CDNP "is without thought."
2299. GZ CDNP:

> Outer entities are perceived by the mind
> In [CDNP "from"] them, delusion will not appear
> The clear form of a woman [CDNP *bud med* GZ overly literal *yan lag* for Skt. *aṅganā*] in a dream
> performs functions but is merely mind [CDNP "performs the welfare of sentient beings"]

GZ CDNP here insert the line "This is the nature of all entities." CDNP *thams cad dngos po'i rang bzhin 'di* suggests that it is the beginning of stanza 14, while GZ *thams cad dngos po'i rnag bzhin no* could also be the last line of stanza 13.

2300. These three lines are of course reminiscent of the famous statement in the *Aṣṭasāhasrikāprajñāpāramitāsūtra* (H11, fol. 4b.5: "The mind is no-mind. The nature of the mind is luminosity.") and the *Pañcaviṃśatisāhasrikāprajñāpāramitāsūtra* (H10, fol. 266a.7: "The mind is no-mind. In that no-mind, there is no attachment."). In that vein, compare also the quote from an unidentified sūtra in the *Pañcatathāgatamudrāvivaraṇa* (text 36, 193–94).

2301. GZ CDNP:

> What becomes mere mind is awakening
> The ground of mind is not mind, [CDNP "mind's desire is not mind"]
> self-awareness is not mind—
> for awareness, the guru is needed [CDNP "awareness depends on the guru"].

2302. CDNP read the first two lines as follows:

> The emptiness [CD *ngo bo nyid* "essence"] of the entirety of nonbeing
> is not held to be this name.

2303. GZ ". . . to be discriminated."

2304. GZ CDNP:

> Just as when it is associated with fire [GZ *med* CDNP *de* em. *me*]
> and so on, this rice becomes porridge,
> likewise, within pure suchness,
> unawareness turns into awareness.

2305. GZ has the last two lines as follows:

> The buddhas taught the world
> that yogīs are inconceivable

CDNP:

> The buddhas taught that
> inconceivable yogīs are free.

2306. GZ CDNP:

> This is the yoga of the cakra
> because it is mahāmudrā
> It is the dharma-, sambhoga-, and nirmāṇa[kāyas]
> because it is all manifestations.

2307. As for "thriving," a more common meaning of Skt. *yukta* that applies here is "endowed with" or "associated with" (as in GZ CDNP *ldan pa*). However, in this context, the mere association with or engagement in the four ordinary ways of conduct—walking, standing, sitting, and lying down—is obviously far from sufficient to qualify someone as a buddha. As in other similar passages in Maitrīpa's texts, this rather means that yogīs who are buddhas thrive by sustaining their realization of mahāmudrā in whatever they may do. GZ CDNP:

> By having done what had to be done, they are thought-free,
> looking away from any and all doubts
> Endowed with the four ways of conduct,
> these buddhas are asserted to be buddhas.

2308. GZ CDNP:

Having made nonduality into nonduality,
through the merit that I have attained,
may the world thereby turn into
nonduality and thereby into great bliss.

2309. Skt. "This concludes 'Twenty Stanzas on True Reality.'" CDNP omit "Śrī." According to Tipi Bumlabar (BKC, vol. *kha*, fol. 86a.4–86b.1), the outline of this text is as follows:

1. presentation of the topic of the four mudrās
1a. the combined presentation of both karmamudrā and dharmamudrā
1b. the presentation of the samayamudrā
1c. the presentation of mahāmudrā
2. the ways of practicing the four mudrās by the three persons of highest, medium, and low faculties
2a. brief introduction
2b. detailed explanation
2b1. the practice of persons of low faculties
2b2. the practice of persons of medium faculties
2b3. the practice of persons of highest faculties
3. concluding dedication of virtue.

For further comments and details, see Mathes 2015 (17, 187–91).

2310. PDMT, 26:424–30. As mentioned before, this text as well as its commentary (text 45) are closely related to Maitrīpa's *Caturmudropadeśa* (text 92) and Nāgārjuna's *Caturmudrānvaya* (text 14).

2311. GZ CDNP "I pay homage to youthful Mañjuśrī."

2312. This stanza echoes *Hevajratantra* II.3.5:

It is there that the ecstasies will originate,
distinguished by the moments' distinction
Due to knowing the moments, the wisdom
that is bliss is based in the syllables EVAṂ

GZ CDNP:

To that in which all the ecstasies arise
and which is the four moments' cause,
for the sake of accomplishing awakening by distinction,
I pay homage to the syllables EVAṂ.

2313. GZ CDNP:

Through rejecting the forceful yoga,
that there is variety . . .
and then consummation is known.

2314. GZ CDNP:

If it is said: "consummation is agitation," [GZ *kun tu bskyod* CD *kun tu spyod* ("conduct") NP *kun tu dpyod* ("analysis")]
how could it be held to be the third one?

Because there is no agitation at that time, [CDNP *dpyod* ("analysis")]
there is awareness of characteristics' absence.

2315. GZ CDNP:

Hence it is known [GZ NP *rig* CD *rigs* ("proper")] as characteristics' lack
Therefore the third one is exactly this one
This self-awareness [I follow GZ NP *rang rig* against CD *rang gi* ("own")] becomes the siddhis,
and it also bears the scriptures' meaning [I follow GZ NP *lung don* against CD *lung ston* ("prophecy")].

2316. GZ CDNP:

"Kissing and embracing are variety,
the friction constitutes maturation,
and characteristics' lack is in the jewel"—
saying this, the correct empowerment is proper [CDNP "So it is said—then the correct . . . NP *rig* ". . . is known"]
This represents the bad empowerment

On this, compare Maitrīpa's *Caturmudropadeśa* (text 92, 19–20).

2317. GZ CDNP:

If it were the case that the awareness [CDNP "self-awareness"]
in the jewel's middle were true reality,
it would be Śiva's and the Veda's true reality [without knowing the Sanskrit, it is far from clear that *zhi ba* here does not have its usual meaning "peace(ful") but refers to Śiva]
This is not asserted by the Buddhists.

2318. IaS (282–83n166) says that "we are not aware of other references to a text of exactly this title. It should be remarked that *Devīparipṛcchā* as a (part of a) title sounds much more Buddhist in style than Śaiva; there are numerous Buddhist scriptures the title of which includes x-*paripṛcchā* (where *x* is a name or reference to an individual), but we cannot cite any Śaiva example. Note also that *Bodhibhadra, who quotes the same verses in his **Jñānasarasamuccayanibandhana* (*ad* st. 15; cf. ed. p. 150 and D fol. 40r7-*v*2), attributes them to *sGra bsgrags pa'i rgyud*, which might well render **Nirnādatantra*, and thus be basically a shorter form of the same title (for some further discussion of the parallel between Bodhibhadra's citations and Maitreyanātha's, see above, Introduction, p. 102). Although *Nirnāda(tantra)* is not known to us as a title of a scripture from any Śaiva source, lists of Śaiva scriptures do contain the titles *Nāda(tantra)*, *Mahānāda(tantra)*, and *Nādendu(tantra)*; cf., e.g., Dyczkowski 1988: 48, 107–108, 122." IaS (102–3) further comments on the provenance of stanzas 7–18 as follows: "Maitreyanātha next (verses 7–18) gives an intriguing series of quotations from non-Buddhist texts, ranging from Śaiva tantras to the *Mahābhārata*, and even a verse which seems to be *kāvya* rather than *sāstra* (vs. 16); evidently all intended to demonstrate how close the position of the proponents of *duḥseka* is to the teachings of the 'outsiders.' The provenance of this string of quotations is uncertain. It is striking that most of them are quoted by *Bodhibhadra in his **Jñānasārasamuccayanibandhana*, in two separate groups, the first consisting of verses 12–17 (with attribution to *rig byed*, which suggests Veda [cf. the *vedāntavādino 'pi* with which Maitreyanātha introduces verses 12 ff.]) and the second consisting of verses 7–10 (7–9 with attribution to *sGra bsgrags pa'i rgyud*, i.e., perhaps *Nirnādatantra*, and verse 10 with attribution to *sMe brtsegs źes bya ba'i rgyud*, i.e., probably *Ucchuṣmatantra*). Within these two groups the verses are in exactly the same order in which Maitreyanātha has quoted them. This similarity is most unlikely to be mere coincidence. The question therefore arises which of the two authors was influenced by the other, or whether both have borrowed from a third (as yet unidentified) source . . . To verses 7–18 Rāmapāla in his commentary adds three further quotations. Some of the citations from Śaiva tantras contain phrases which sound indeed remarkably Buddhist; but the suspicion, which might perhaps arise, that they have been simply invented by Maitreyanātha or Rāmapāla, must be set aside, for they include some which are known also from the surviving literature of the Śaivas themselves (see below p. 284 n. 179, p. 285 n. 182, p. 287 n. 191 and p. 288 n. 199). The majority of these quotations are presumably supposed to show that the non-Buddhists mistakenly believe (the bliss of) liberation to be identical with the bliss of coition. The last two, from the *Mahābhārata* (12.316.40 = 12.318.44 and 6.24.16 [*Bhagavadgītā* 2.16]), however, rather than speaking of bliss are, to put it somewhat simplistically, descriptions of the highest knowledge as devoid of duality, whether ethical or ontological." Note that in this case of quotes (stanzas 7–18) being woven into Maitrīpa's own text, I continue the consecutive numbering of all stanzas for the sake of easy reference and cross-reference.

2319. As the context and Rāmapāla's *Sekanirdeśapañjikā* shows, "jewel city" (Skt. *ratnapura*) refers to the glans penis. Thus, it is not to be conflated with the Vedic tradition's maṇipūracakra (either understood as "flood or sea of jewels" or "city of jewels") that is located in the area of the solar plexus (about four finger-widths above the navel).

2320. GZ CDNP:

> Oh you goddess, it is this very jewel city
> that will melt in the anthers of the lotus
> Rudra, joined together, is Śiva's supreme
> This is Śakti, supreme of the supreme

[Again, without knowing the Sanskrit, it is far from clear that *nus pa* here does not have its usual meaning "power" or "ability" but refers to Śakti; thus a more literal reading would be "This is the supreme of the supreme power."]

Among the many meanings of Śakti, in the sense of referring to Śiva's wife, the *Devībhāgavatapurāṇa* (fifth and ninth skandhas) says that the sound *Śa* means "welfare" or "prosperity" and *kti* means "prowess." Therefore *Śakti* means "she who is the embodiment of, or grants, prosperity and prowess." The definition of *Bhagavatī* is "she who combines in herself the affluence of knowledge, wealth, reputation, power, and the female organ." Hence the word *Śakti* may be taken to mean Bhagavatī and Pārvatī, and those called Bhagavatī, Śakti, Devī, Ambikā, Pārvatī, etc. are the manifestations of Śakti, Śiva's spouse. This Śakti exists as a fraction of all gods. In Śaivism, Śakti or Śivakāmī is Śiva's wife: the primal cosmic energy is called *puruṣa* or Śiva and the primal cosmic substance is called *prakṛti* or Śakti; thus the universe is created when Śiva and Śakti unite. Śaktism (the worship of the Supreme as the Divine Mother Śakti or Devī in her many forms, both gentle and fierce) greatly resembles Śaivism, such as both promulgating the same ultimate goal of nondual union with Śiva, which is liberation. However, Śāktas solely worship Śakti as the Supreme Being (the dynamic aspect of Divinity), responsible for the creation, expansion, and destruction of the universe, while Śiva is considered strictly transcendent and not worshipped. Thus Śiva is of secondary importance, though Śakti cannot accomplish the creation of the universe without him. Therefore, in Śaktism, Śakti is the main deity and Śiva a subordinate one (see https://www.wisdomlib.org/definition/shakti).

2321. The first two lines of this stanza (also) correspond to *Lokātītastava* 12ab. GZ CDNP:

> Free of characteristic and characterization,
> and being devoid of any attributes,
> [GZ *gang gi mtshan ma rnams* CDNP *ngag gi mtshon pa rnams,*
> "devoid of characterization of speech"]
> through the union of Śiva and Śakti,
> the bliss that is marvelous is supreme.

2322. Note that the Sanskrit does not mark the end of any of the quotations below, while GZ CDNP mark some of them, though not always in accordance with the attributions in Rāmapāla's commentary, which I follow here. GZ CDNP:

> If it has been meditated on as the form of Śakti, [CDNP "If it is to
> be meditated on as the objects of Śakti"]
> saṃsāric existence does not exist in true reality
> This constitutes the ruin of all superimpositions
> Seeing that it is empty is what represents Śakti.

2323. IaS (284n180): "As far as we are aware, no manuscript(s) of a tantra of this name survive(s). Several Śaiva tantric texts mention a *Ucchuṣmatantra* or *Ucchuṣmabhairavatantra*, though; for a collection of such references, and some discussion (not arriving at a firm conclusion), see Hatley 2007: 275–280."

2324. GZ CDNP "middle."

2325. IaS (285n182): "We are not sure what text Maitreyanātha was referring to with the label 'Yoga Chapter' (*yogādhyāya*). The verse is one which occurs in quite a few texts, sometimes with slight variants. Probably the oldest source, and perhaps the original one, in which the verse occurs in exactly the form quoted is the *Śivadharmottara*, in which . . . it is found in chapter 3 (in the published, non-critical, edition the verse is numbered 332 . . .). It is worth noting that in this printed edition the chapter colophon reads *iti śivadharmottare jñānayogo nāma tṛtīyo 'dhyāyaḥ*, which is somewhat reminiscent of *Yogādhyāya*, the source which Maitreyanātha indicates. However, the manuscript transmission of the *Śivadharmottara* does not seem to support this title, giving instead *pañcamahāyajnaguṇādhyāyaḥ* as chapter title. Already before the eleventh century, the verse had been borrowed in several other Śaiva works, some of which might also be candidates for being Maitreyanātha's source. Thus, for instance, it is identical with the last verse of chapter 15 of the Śaiva (Trika) *Tantrasadbhāva* and with *Kubjikāmatatantra* 25.171 (this entire section of the *Kubjikāmatatantra*, 25.29–171, is borrowed from the *Tantrasadbhāva*; cf. Sanderson 2001: 6); and it is very similar to *Jābāladarśanopaniṣad* 1.23 . . . and Jayadratha's *Haracaritacintāmaṇii* 30.75 . . . The verse is also cited (often without indication of source) in other texts, e.g., in Vidyāraṇya's famous *Jīvanmuktiviveka* (4.4.8, Goodding 2002: 436)."

2326. GZ CDNP:

> If yogīs who have done what needs to be done
> have become satiated with wisdom's nectar,
> there is not the slightest that should be done
> If there is, they don't know [I follow CDNP *rig* against GZ *rigs* ("suitable")] true reality.

2327. GZ CDNP add "secret" before Vedānta; I agree with the comments in IaS (286n186): "The Tibetan translation here has *rig byed kyi mtha' gsaṅ bar smra ba*, which might suggest an underlying *vedāntopaniṣadvādinaḥ*; *gsaṅ bar* is however probably simply an explanatory addition of the translators."

2328. GZ CDNP:

> It is the texts of Bhāskara that assert the wisdom
> in which the sense faculties do not sense objects
> That the entirety of sensations is just sheer bliss
> is asserted by the text of the Bhagavān's followers

Given that the *Tattvaratnāvalī* (text 34, 181–82) obliquely refers to the *Bhagavatsiddhānta(saṃgraha)* (a versified text in the *Skandapurāṇa* that consists of excerpts from a number of Upaniṣads) in a very similar context and that GZ CDNP add *gzhung* ("text" or "approach"), "those who follow the Bhagavān" probably refers to those who follow this text.

2329. Skt. *āveśa* can also mean "taking possession of" (see GZ CDNP), "being devoted to," "being absorbed in," and "entering into," which are obviously pertinent here as well.

2330. As pointed out in IaS (287n191), this stanza is *Vijñānabhairava* 69 (one of the most important Śaiva tantras). GZ CDNP:

> As for the bliss of the true reality of the Brahman,
> which is the end of having power over the Śakti
> by virtue of meeting and uniting with the Śakti,
> by means of that bliss, you will be directly free.

2331. IaS (287n191): "The first two *pāda*s are identical with *Niśvāsakārikā* 20.29cd (p. 127); we are aware of no other close parallel for this half-verse. Note also that the fourth *pāda* is close to *Niśvāsakārikā* 20.30b. For the second half of the verse there are many more parallels; for the third *pāda*, indeed, too many to easily list here. It is often quoted in a way that implies that it is from Vedic *śruti* (cf., e.g., Jayaratha in his *Tantrālokaviveka ad* 30.97), although as far as we know, no actual Vedic text contains exactly these words." GZ CDNP:

> There, bliss is a continuous stream
> There exists no arising of suffering
> Utter ecstasy is the Brahman's form
> This is expressed as "liberation."

2332. This stanza is also quoted in the *Tattvaratnāvalī*. As IaS (288n200) remarks, though it is otherwise unidentified, the last line is identical with *Manusmṛti* 6.81d. GZ CDNP:

> Whatever tiny bit that may be seen,
> it is conceived to be the Brahman
> Hence mind does not become other—
> it remains within the very Brahman.

2333. IaS (288n201): "This verse is found in the *Sūktimuktāvalī*, the great collection of *muktakas*/*subhāṣitas* compiled by Jalhaṇa in Śaka 1179, i.e. 1258 CE, at the court of the Yādava King Śrīkṛṣṇa, who ruled from Devagiri, modern Daulatabad in northern Mahārāṣṭra. In the *Sūktimuktāvalī*, the verse is the second of the section on *nāyikānāyakayor avalokanam*, the hero and heroine looking at each other. Jalhaṇa does not inform us of the name of the author of the verse . . . Another source in which the verse is found is the Jaina recension of the *Vikramacarita* (p. 77)." Furthermore, IaS attributes the position in this stanza and the following one to the followers of the Vedānta of the *Bhagavatsiddhānta* (289–90). GZ CDNP:

> That through which [I follow CDNP *gang gis* against GZ *gang phyir*]
> nirvāṇa is seen
> is the very mind of passion and dispassion [CDNP *chags pa chags pa'i sems nyid* ("a mind that is attached to passion")]
> Seen by solely seeing the beloved,
> what is the use of any others?

2334. This stanza is *Mahābhārata* 12.316.40 (= 12.318.44), which is traditionally attributed to the saint Vyāsa (also one of its main characters). Thus the text is not a part of Vedānta, though it is sometimes referred to as "the fifth Veda" (as are some other texts, such as certain Purāṇas and the *Natyaśāstra*). IaS (289n204): "The same verse is cited occasionally by other authors; it may be worth mentioning here its quotation in the *Bhagavadgītā* commentary attributed to Śaṅkara (intro, *ad* st. 3.1), in Abhinavagupta's *Parātriṃśikātattvavivaraṇa* (*ad* stt. 5–9ab, ed. p. 241) and in Vibhūticandra's *Amṛtakaṇikoddyotanibandha* (ed. p. 202), and its reuse in the *Saṃnyāsopaniṣad* (ed. p. 253.2–3)." GZ CDNP:

> Having abandoned dharma and nondharma,
> . . .
> also abandon what you have abandoned.

2335. *Bhagavadgītā* 2.16 = *Mahābhārata* 6.24.16. The *Bhagavadgītā* (1st–2nd century

CE) is the earliest text of the Bhagavata tradition, the earliest Hindu sect recorded, marking the beginning of theistic devotional worship (*bhakti*). The tradition centered around a personal godhead, variously called Viṣṇu, Vasudeva, Kṛṣṇa, Hari, or Nārāyaṇa, and its followers practiced simple rites of worship while rejecting Vedic sacrifices and austerities. Bhagavata remained prominent in Vaishnavism until at least the eleventh century CE. GZ CDNP:

> There exists no real entity,
> nor is there an unreal entity
> To see the end of both these
> is the seeing of true reality [CDNP "Those who see . . . see
> true reality"].

2336. GZ CDNP read "Moreover" as preceding this stanza, say "forms" instead of "and such," and omit "not" in the last line. The first two lines in both Sanskrit and Tibetan could also be read as "Were the mind, which is empty of the perceived . . . called 'Akṣobhya,'" but the point here is that nondual mind—whether it is called "the seal of Akṣobhya" in Buddhist texts or described as in some of the above non-Buddhist texts—is not the ultimate seal, but must in turn be sealed with Vajrasattva (the unity of emptiness and compassion). For details on the seals of Akṣobhya and Vajrasattva, as well as the tathāgata relief in the next stanza, see Maitrīpa's *Pañcatathāgatamudrāvivaraṇa*, *Pañcākara*, and *Caturmudropadeśa* (text 92, 18), as well as Rāmapāla's *Sekanirdeśapañjikā* on stanzas 19 and 20.

2337. GZ CDNP have "vajra" instead of "bola," and CDNP read the first and second lines as ". . . it arises with aspect" and ". . . it arises without aspect." The last two lines say:

> The statement "abiding in the middle"
> does not represent what my guru holds.

2338. The last two lines in GZ CDNP read as follows:

> nor as abiding in between this is asserted
> True reality is known from the guru's mouth.

2339. The first quoted phrase in this stanza is *Hevajratantra* II.3.7a and the second is, according to Rāmapāla's *Sekanirdeśapañjikā*, embedded in a passage from the *Paramādyatantra*. As IaS (297n239) says, this passage is "attributed to the *Paramādya* both here and in Abhayākaragupta's *Amnāyamañjarī* (D fol. 68r1–2). We could not locate them, however, in the two Tibetan *Paramādya* translations (Tōh. 487 and 488), nor in the translation of the *Vajramaṇḍālaṅkāratantra* (Tōh. 490), which can be regarded as an expanded version of the *Paramādya*. On the complex history and multiple versions of the *Paramādya* and closely related texts see Weinberger 2003: 110–139." Given the brevity and the generic nature of this phrase, it is naturally found in many texts, such as the *Śrīḍākārṇavamahāyoginītantra* (H390, fols. 202a.7 and 224a.5), the *Amoghapāśakalpa* (H689, fols. 272a.5 and 272b.3), and a vast number of tantric commentaries in Tg. For details, see text 45. IaS (301n259) adds that "the interpretation of this verse is not entirely straightforward, and the commentary of Rāmapāla is in the first part, which deals most directly with the verse, is obscure, due to the unfortunate coincidence of a lacuna in both Sanskrit manuscripts with an apparent problem in the Tibetan translation (see n. 260 below). We think it likely, however, that the verse contains both a question raised by an objector (*katham*) and a reply by the Siddhāntin. The Tibetan translation differs slightly . . . We wonder if here the translation of stanza 23 could have been influenced by the translation of the commentary (for a possibly similar case, see below *ad* st. 37)." GZ CDNP:

> How then could what is well established,
> such as "ecstasy is described as variety"
> and "inserted into the jewel' and so on'
> be matched with the teaching by the guru?

Without knowing the underlying Sanskrit, the last two lines would more probably be understood as "be matched with the teaching by the guru, such as 'inserted into the jewel'?"

2340. Skt. *utpanna* as an abbreviation of *utpannakrama* (lit. "process of the created"). GZ CDNP:

> What consists of the ecstasy [CDNP "purity"] of smiling and so on,
> and what is held to be the master [empowerment],
> their presentation is in terms of the creation process
> and is not the essence of the perfection [process] [CDNP "and is not the perfection process"].

2341. Since this stanza presents the sequence of the four moments and thus the four ecstasies that Maitrīpa asserts, *ramaḥ* ("pleasure") in the last line is shorthand for *viramaḥ* ("cessation"; confirmed by the *Sekanirdeśapañjikā*), referring to *viramānanda* ("cessational ecstasy"), probably for metrical reasons. The third line thus refers to the moment of the lack of characteristics and the corresponding connate ecstasy. GZ CDNP:

> Due to being variegated, variety refers to the throat
> Due to being bliss, maturation is at the jewel's tip
> True reality needs to be known through the guru
> Consummation constitutes the cessational ecstasy.

2342. GZ CDNP *brten* ("relied upon").

2343. As IaS (306–7n294) points out, this stanza is cited in the *Prajñājñānaprakāśa* (text 16, 58), an Advayavajra's **Āryamañjuśrīnāmasaṃgītiṭīkāsārābhisamaya* (D2098, fol. 106b.5), and Raviśrījñāna's *Amṛtakaṇikā* (Lal 1994, 95; attributed to the *Vairocanābhisambodhitantra* but not found there). IaS adds that this stanza may not be by Maitrīpa originally but taken (or modified) by him from some yogatantra source. Indeed, a somewhat similar but problematic stanza cited in the *Caturmudrāṭīkā* (text 44, 347) is attributed there to an unspecified tantra. Lastly, a stanza whose first two lines are very similar but whose last two are very different is found in an Indrabhūti's *Śrīcakrasaṃvaratantrarājaśambarasamuccayanāmavṛtti* (D1413, fol. 99a.2–3):

Having relied on the karmamudrā,
you should cultivate the dharmamudrā
Blissful empty true reality is mahāmudrā
What is unchanging is the samayamudrā.

2344. IaS (310) renders the first two lines *vicitraṃ karmamudrāto vipāko jagadātmatā* as "Vicitra *is the being of the nature of the world, [arising] from the Action Seal;* vipāka *is [the same],*" noting: "This interpretation may seem at first sight very unnatural, but it follows Rāmapāla's commentary" (n318). Apart from my different phrasing, what is thus clear is that "the world's own being" pertains to both "variety" and "maturation." Note that, at first sight, the first two and the last lines of this stanza seem to match the lines with the corresponding ecstasies instead of the moments in the above quoted stanza I.10.13 from the *Hevajratantra*:

The first ecstasy has a worldly nature
Likewise, supreme ecstasy is worldly
Cessational ecstasy is worldly as well
The connate is not found in these three

However, in the commentaries on the *Hevajratantra*, it is very clear that ecstasy, supreme ecstasy, and cessational ecstasy all belong to the mundane sphere—that is, seeming reality—though they are increasingly more subtle. By contrast, Rāmapāla's comments on stanza 28 in his *Sekanirdeśapañjikā* explicitly equate "the world's own being" with the emptiness endowed with all supreme aspects (that is, ultimate reality).

2345. With Skt. *sthairyaṃ*, I follow CD *brtan pa* against GZ NP *bstan pa* ("teaching," "showing").

2346. GZ CDNP *dri ma med phyir rang rig phyir* ("because of being stainless and because of self-awareness").

2347. This stanza is identical to *Tattvaratnāvalī* 8. The last two lines in GZ CDNP read as follows:

A conceived state made inconceivable [CDNP "what is made inconceivable by conceiving"]
will not become inconceivable.

2348. This stanza is identical to *Pañcatathāgatamudrāvivaraṇa* 12. GZ CDNP:

Once they set their eyes on suchness
by following the middle's actuality,
when directly knowing, they are aware
They are the fortunate realizing true reality.

2349. Skt. *apoha* can also mean "denial" and *vidhi* "creation," "contrivance," "conduct," "application," "precept," and "rule." This stanza is identical to *Tattvaratnāvalī* 7. GZ CDNP:

As long as there are all superimpositions,
everything will arise in every respect
The middle's actuality is superimposition's lack—
where could there be negation or affirmation?

2350. GZ CDNP:

> Cognition and cognizable are given names
> That thinking is not otherwise
> All is just the way it was before
> Just as the mind was, so it is not.

2351. This stanza is identical to *Tattvaratnāvalī* 10. GZ CDNP:

> The mindset of the world being unborn [this is a gracious reading of *ma skyes 'gro bar gang yin blo* so as to accord somewhat with the Sanskrit, but it could also be read in a number of very different ways]
> is pure, so the Buddha has instructed
> For the insightful ones, without effort,
> all the world has [I follow GZ *ldan* against CDNP *'dren*] the nature of that.

2352. GZ CDNP:

> This very thought arises in dependence
> [Its] connection has not been cultivated [or "This is not a meditation on connection"]
> Exactly this is what represents nirvāṇa—
> oh mind as such, do not create delusion!

2353. GZ CDNP *shes* ("know").

2354. The first three lines are very similar to Maitrīpa's *Tattvaprakāśa* 13ab (text 35) and prose passages at the beginnings of his *Kudṛṣṭinirghātana* (text 19) and *Nirvedhapañcaka* (text 28). As mentioned before, the *Avikalpapraveśadhāraṇī* describes how bodhisattvas enter the expanse of nonconceptuality by relinquishing all coarse and subtle characteristics of conceptions in terms of (1) nature, (2) remedies, (3) true reality, and (4) attainment in a gradual manner by analysis and finally by not mentally engaging in them at all (see Brunnhölzl 2012, 330–31). The last three of these four characteristics are also discussed in detail in Sahajavajra's *Tattvadaśakaṭīkā* (text 46, 40–44), and the *Avikalpapraveśadhāraṇī*'s general notion of relinquishing conceptual characteristics is quoted in Maitrīpa's *Amanasikārādhāra* (text 27).

2355. GZ CDNP:

> Just as ecstasy and such abide
> within the karmamudrā,
> so the vajra master instructs
> on this in the samayamudrā

Note that "instructs" in the third line is a case of the not unusual approach of Tibetan translators replacing a word or phrase in a stanza with its gloss in a commentary. In this case, Tib. *nye bar ston* (though not rendering the suffix *-taḥ*) corresponds to Rāmapāla's *Sekanirdeśapañjikā* glossing Skt. *prasādataḥ* with *upadeśataḥ*. As, for example, also demonstrated in some versions of text 13 and in many stanzas in text 90, it seems that Tibetan translators sometimes used commentarial glosses in the stanzas themselves either because they did not understand the words in the stanza (especially if they were in Apabhraṃśa) or because the glosses seemed to make more sense.

2356. As mentioned before, Skt. *āmnāya* also means "tantra," "received doctrine," "sacred texts handed down by repetition," "advice," and "that which is to be remembered, studied, or learned by heart."

2357. As mentioned before, in Buddhism, Raurava ("The Dreadful One") is the name of one of the eight hot hells, explicitly confirmed by Rāmapāla's *Sekanirdeśapañjikā*, which also adds other hells, such as the worst hell, Avīci. Coincidentally, however, Raurava is also the name of one of the twenty-eight *Siddhāntāgamas*, which are a subclassification of the Śaiva division of the Śaivāgamas (representing the wisdom come down from Śiva, received by Pārvatī, and accepted by Viṣṇu). The Śaivāgamas are divided into four groups: Śaiva, Pāśupata, Soma, and Lākula, with Śaiva being further divided into Dakṣiṇa, Vāma, and Siddhānta (tantric Śaivism, with Raurava being a part of it). Given that our text rejects the theory and practice of karmamudrā in Śaivism, one wonders whether the use of the term "Raurava" here is maybe also a side blow against the doctrines of Śaivism, possibly even equating their outcome with the hells (Raurava as a hell is also known in Śaivism). GZ CDNP:

> Without knowing mahāmudrā,
> they practice karmamudrā alone
> Falling from tradition's true reality,
> these yogīs therefore go to Raurava.

2358. GZ CDNP add *gtso bo* ("lord"). "Śabareśa" refers to Maitrīpa's guru Śabareśvara (Śavaripa).

2359. In GZ CD, stanza 40 is followed by an additional stanza:

> Protector, just like dharmatā,
> thus all phenomena are pure
> Just as it is stated to be found,
> it is all phenomena's essence.

This stanza is not found in Rāmapāla's *Sekanirdeśapañjikā* (text 45) either.

2360. GZ CDNP:

> The meaning of the correct empowerment's ritual
> is devoid of forceful bad empowerments
> Through the merit of what I have composed,
> may [all] beings come to be blissful!

2361. Skt. "This concludes 'Instructions on Empowerment.'" CDNP ". . . It was translated by the Indian upādhyāya Kṛṣṇa Paṇḍita and lotsāwa Tsültrim Gyalwa." Tipi Bumlabar (BKC, vol. *kha*, fols. 80a.6–82a.5) presents a very detailed outline under the title of this text. However, the specific phrasing and order of its topics, most of them lifted directly from Rāmapāla's *Sekanirdeśapañjikā*, leave no doubt that it is actually an outline of that commentary. Thus this outline is included in the final note on text 45. For further comments and details, see text 45, Mathes 2015 (10–12, 107–17), and IaS.

2362. PDMT, 26:421–23. As mentioned before, this extended title is only found in NG *Shes pa spro bsdu med par 'jog pa'i man ngag gsang ba dam pa*; GZ *Shes pa spro bsdu mi byed par 'jog pa'i man ngag* but colophon *u pa de sha pa ra mo pa ya / gsang ba dam pa*, Tg *u pa de sha pa ra ma pa ya / gsang ba dam pa*, AIBS *Upadeśaparama / gsang ba dam pa*.

2363. I follow GZ NP *snang bas* against CD *snang ba'i* ("of appearances").

2364. GZ CDNP *so sor rtog pa*, "discrimination" [Mathes 2015 has "discriminating awareness"] seems too conceptual, contrived, and weak an expression to indicate what is revealed by the guru's kindness. Thus I emend to *so sor rtogs pa*, which can render the same Sanskrit terms as *so sor rtog pa* (*pratyavekṣaṇā*, *pratisaṃkhyāna*) but also *pratibodha* ("awakening") and *pratyavagama* ("exact knowledge"), and *Sthitisamāsa* VI.37d renders Skt. *prativedhikā* ("what penetrates") in the parallel line *Śrīmahāsaṃvarodayatantra* III.15b; hence my choice "penetrating awakening."

2365. Except for switching "arise" and "experience," lines 3cd are almost identical to lines VI.36cd of Sahajavajra's *Sthitisamāsa* (text 17).

2366. I follow GZ CD *rtogs pa* against NP *rtog pa*. Lines 4ab are virtually identical to lines VI.36ab of the *Sthitisamāsa*, and lines 4cd are similar to lines VI.37ab (which correspond to *Śrīmahāsaṃvarodayatantra* III.14cd).

2367. This line is identical to GZ CDNP of *Sthitisamāsa* VI.37c, which is a variant or corruption of *Śrīmahāsaṃvarodayatantra* III.15a. Thus, it is possible that line 5b is an echo of *Śrīmahāsaṃvarodayatantra* III.16ab:

> The fully perfect awakening to great bliss
> likewise constitutes supreme mahāmudrā.

2368. Literally, lines b and d say "is in mahāmudrā."

2369. GZ NP *nas* CD *ni*.

2370. GZ *ma lus bde ba'i ye shes pas* CDNP *de las bde ba'i ye shes pas* ("those with the blissful wisdom due to that").

2371. I follow GZ NP *la* against CD *las*.

2372. I follow GZ *rigs pa med* against CDNP *rig pa med* ("there is no equipoise, aftermath, and awareness").

2373. I follow GZ NP *dngos po* against CD *dngos por*.

2374. I follow GZ NP *spyad* against CD *bcas*.

2375. GZ *rang dvangs* CD *rang thang* ("unfabricated") NP *dang thang*.

2376. GZ *u pa de sha pa ra mo pa ya* CDNP *u pa de sha pa ra ma pa ya*.

2377. P adds *sarva manggā laṃ* N adds *manggā laṃ bha vantu // shubhaṃ*. For further comments and details, see Mathes 2015 (21, 269–71).

2378. PDMT, 26:819–936; GZ CDNP *mu drā tsa tura ṭī kā ratna hṛ da ya*. As mentioned before, as a commentary on Nāgārjuna's *Caturmudrānvaya* (text 14; henceforth CMA), this text bears a close relationship with Maitrīpa's *Caturmudropadeśa* (text 92) and *Sekanirdeśa* (text 42), Rāmapāla's *Sekanirdeśapañjikā* (text 45), and some parts of Vajrapāṇi's *Guruparamparākramopadeśa* (text 213). Also compare the section on karmamudrā with the one in the **Sarvadharmāprasahadeśakatattvārdhagāthāvṛtti* (text 73, 188ff.).

2379. NP omit "mahā."
2380. GZ CDNP *mnyam par rigs* (lit. "suitable to be equal") is probably *mnyam par rig*, which could also simply be an overly literal rendering of a form of the Sanskrit verb *saṃvid* or *saṃveda(na)*, thus "This is known as having . . ."
2381. Kumuda flowers are edible white water lilies (*Nymphaea esculenta*), which are said to bloom at night, while closing their petals during the day.
2382. GZ *sbyar ba* CDNP *sbyangs pa* ("train in" or "purify").
2383. In texts on the progressive realizations on the five paths and the ten bhūmis, "penetrating insight" (Skt. *nirvedha*) is typically associated with the nonconceptual wisdom first attained on the Mahāyāna path of seeing (the first bhūmi).
2384. Assuming that this stanza is supposed to present *Kāropa as the author, "the guru" and "the venerable one" must refer to Maitrīpa and "the tantras' king" probably to the *Hevajratantra* as the text's main cited source.
2385. This fivefold classification of tantra is not very common in Indian Buddhism but is also found in Rāmapāla's *Sekanirdeśapañjikā* (text 45, 383), Vajrapāṇi's *Guruparamparākramopadeśa* (text 213, 197), Ratnākaraśānti's *Muktāvalī* and Kṛṣṇa's *Yogaratnamālā* commentaries on *Hevajratantra* II.2.10, and Advayavajra's *Gūḍhapadā* (for the detailed references of the latter three, see Sanderson 2009, 146n337). In different texts, there are various classifications of five tantra classes in Indian Buddhism, such as yogottaratantra in this classification here being replaced by mahāyogatantra and yoganiruttaratantra by yoginītantra or yogānuttaratantra. For details on the different tantra classifications, see for example Mimaki 1994 (121–22n17), English 2002 (2–6), and Dalton 2005. Later, text 44 (330) speaks of "four tantra classes." Note also that, curiously, Dunhuang manuscript PT 849 lists *Yogottaratantra*, *Yoganiruttaratantra*, and *Yoginītantra* as three texts among "the thirty-six yogatantras" (see Kapstein 2006, 20n32).
2386. *Hevajratantra* I.8.23 and *Guhyasamājatantra* XVIII.84. GZ CDNP ". . . vajra holder explained the dharma based upon . . ."
2387. The five stages of perfection-process practices according to the Ārya commentarial tradition of the *Guhyasamājatantra* are (1) speech isolation (or vajra recitation), (2) mind isolation (or "mind focus" [Skt. *cittanidhyapti*] or "universal purity"), (3) self-blessing or the illusory body of seeming reality, (4) the luminosity of ultimate reality (or "the full awakening (of supremely secret bliss)"), and (5) the unity of the two realities, prajñā and means, and the emptiness endowed with all supreme aspects and immutable great bliss, or the unity of (3) illusory body and (4) luminosity (or simply an equivalent of nondual buddha wisdom). For a detailed discussion of all the different names and meanings of these five stages, see Wedemeyer 2007 and Kongtrul Lodrö Tayé 2008 (138–47). Thus our text here matches all five steps of the creation process and the perfection process with only the perfection process of the *Guhyasamājatantra* in the Ārya tradition, with the additional peculiarity of the first three of the latter's five stages being in reverse order. Compare also the different way of matching these two sets of five in Rāmapāla's *Sekanirdeśapañjikā* (text 45, 434).
2388. This stanza is identical to *Guhyasamājatantra* XVIII.113cf. In Maitrīpa's *Sekatāt-*

paryasaṃgraha (text 37, 197) and Rāmapāla's *Sekanirdeśapañjikā* (text 45, 398), this stanza appears with "supreme" instead of "empowerment" in the second line. With the additional replacement of "vase" by "master" in the first line and adding "empowerment" in the third, this stanza is also found in the *Mahāmudrātilakatantra* (H380, fol. 435b.2) and the *Jñānatilakatantra* (H382, fol. 9a.1–2). The first three lines (followed by "Just as it is, the body is the tathāgata") are also found in the *Ḍākinīvajrapañjaratantra* (H379, fol. 401a.7). Text 37 can be considered as a commentary on this stanza (according to the *Jñānagarbhatantra* [H381, fol. 476a.7], its last line refers to stabilizing the very prajñā-jñāna empowerment). Also, Rāmapāla's *Sekanirdeśapañjikā* explains its fourth line several times in different contexts. Note that, exactly as it appears in the *Sekatātparyasaṃgraha*, this stanza is also included in Vajrapāṇi's *Vajrapada* (text 47), while his *Guruparamparākramopadeśa* (text 213) replaces "vase" by "master" in the first line, thus being closer to the *Mahāmudrātilakatantra* and *Jñānatilakatantra*.

2389. As the comments on these lines in the following note show, the term *saṃvara* (Tib. *sdom pa*) here has neither its common meanings nor the specific Buddhist meanings "restraint" or "vow" but refers to "union" (or "binding" or "weaving together"). Moreover, it indicates not only the practice but also its fruition, which is the supreme bliss of awakening. This sense of *saṃvara* is attested by its interpretive Tibetan rendering *bde mchog* ("supreme bliss"; as below for *Cakrasaṃvara*, 277). *Vara* indeed means "supreme," but the derivation of "bliss" from *sam* (or rather *śam*) represents a hermeneutical Buddhist etymology based on the Sanskrit prefix *saṃ-* (similar to the Latin prefix *con-*) suggesting "conjunction," "union," and so on. Indian commentators also acknowledge the alternate spelling of *saṃvara* as *śamvara* or *śambara*, which is attested at the beginning of the *Sarvabuddhasamāyogaḍākinījālaśaṃvaratantra* (D366, fol. 151a.6–7):

> "*Śam*" is explained to be bliss
> It is the great bliss of all buddhas
> Employing the entirety of illusions,
> this bliss is supreme and hence *śamvara*

As Sugiki 2015 (360–61) points out, texts in the Cakrasaṃvara and Hevajra traditions contain similar glosses of *saṃvara* (or *śaṃvara*) as "supreme bliss" (*sukhavaram* or *paraṃ sukham*). A second etymological explanation of *saṃvara*, in Jayabhadra's *Cakrasaṃvarapañjikā*, derives from the verb *saṃvṛ* (thus meaning "concealment" or "protection"). Thus in this context, *śaṃvara* or *saṃvara* refers to the "union," "enclosure," or "assembly" in which supreme or genuine bliss-emptiness is experienced. In this sense, *saṃvara* is also an abbreviation of Cakrasaṃvara: the beginning of the first chapter of the *Cakrasaṃvaratantra* describes Cakrasaṃvara as "a being made of all ḍākinīs, Vajrasattva, highest pleasure, the self-existing Bhagavān and vīra, and the supreme bliss of the web of ḍākinīs." Thus Cakrasaṃvara is rendered in Tibetan as either 'Khor lo sdom pa or 'Khor lo bde mchog. Literally, Cakrasaṃvara means "the union (or binding) of the wheels," usually referring to the main Cakrasaṃvara maṇḍala circles that pervade the universe. Note though that, as Gray 2019

(13) and Sugiki 2015 (360) point out, in Indic Buddhist texts the appellations *Saṃvara* or *Śaṃvara* (sometimes followed by *-tantra*) are typically shorthand designations for the *Sarvabuddhasamāyogaḍākinījālaśaṃvaratantra* (not belonging to the scriptural tradition beginning with the later *Cakrasaṃvaratantra*), while the *Cakrasaṃvaratantra* is typically referred to as *Laghusaṃvara* or *Cakrasaṃvara*.

2390. These lines are *Hevajratantra* II.3.2ab and *Saṃvarodayatantra* III.17cd. *Hevajratantra* II.3.2cd continues as follows:

> The syllables EVAṂ, which are great bliss,
> are fully known by means of empowerment

Hevajratantra II.3.1 lists the means that are the foundations of the entire tantra, such as union (*saṃvara*), empowerment, intentional speech (*sandhyābhāṣā*), the four ecstasies, and the four moments. Kṛṣṇa's *Yogaratnamālā* explains these as the topics of the entire *Hevajratantra*, the means of practice to attain completely perfect awakening, with "union" referring to the wisdoms of great bliss. On II.3.2, Kṛṣṇa says that great bliss is the union of all buddhas because all buddhas lack any diverse notions in that they have the nature of great bliss. This bliss is located in the syllables EVAṂ, the dharmodayamudrā. "Empowerment" refers to the pith instructions of the guru. The following stanzas in *Hevajratantra* II.3 explain how this great bliss within EVAṂ is realized through the four ecstasies. As mentioned before, the term *dharmodaya* ("dharma source"; also *dharmodayā* and *dharmodayamudrā*) refers to the primordial space from which all phenomena arise (a.k.a. dharmadhātu), representing the female principle or divine cosmic vagina from which everything arises and ceases. It is usually depicted as a triangle with its tip pointing down, a hexagram (two overlapping triangles similar to the Star of David), or one or two three-dimensional triangles (triangular upside-down pyramids). The term can also refer to the female genitals. In the Vajrayāna, the dharmodaya in the form of a hexagram is specifically associated with Vajrayoginī, with the two triangles symbolizing the union of bliss and emptiness. For matching dharmodaya with the syllables EVAṂ, see below (263–64, 342) and Rāmapāla's *Sekanirdeśapañjikā* (text 45) on stanza 1.

2391. *Hevajratantra* II.2.40.

2392. Here these two refer to the seal of Akṣobhya and the seal of Vajradhara (or Vajrasattva). As mentioned before, the first four skandhas (whose nature consists of Vairocana, Ratnasambhava, Amitābha, and Amoghasiddhi) are sealed with Akṣobhya to make it clear that they are nothing but mind. In this way, the seal of Akṣobhya represents the realization of Yogācāra emptiness: awareness without any duality of perceiver and perceived. The seal of Vajrasattva—the true realization of emptiness as awareness's ultimate nature—refers to seeing that this awareness also lacks any pinpointable nature of its own.

2393. Tg does not contain a *Mañjuśrīmāyājālatantra*, but a text of this name is mentioned in Dunhuang manuscript PT 849 as one among "the thirty-six yogatantras," together with the *Māyājālatantra* (D466), *Vairocanamāyājālatantra*, *Avalokiteśvaramāyājālatantra*, *Vajrasattvamāyājālatantra* (D833), and *Devīmāyā-*

jālatantra (see Kapstein 2006, 19n32). According to certain Tibetan traditions, the *Mañjuśrīnāmasaṃgīti* is a part of the *Mañjuśrīmāyājālatantra* in sixty million stanzas. The first three lines of the stanza here are also quoted in Mañjuśrīkīrti's *Vajrayānamūlāpattiṭīkā* (D2488, fol. 201a.3), attributed to a *gzhung 'bum pa* (the fourth line reads "the welfare of beings is performed without thinking"). The first two lines are also cited without attribution in Lakṣmī's **Pañcakramaṭīkā* (D1842, fol. 274a.1–2).

2394. I follow GZ *snang ba gsum stong par rab tu gyur* against CD *snang ba gsum rab tu gyur* NP *snang stong gsung rab tu gyur*. Tib. *rab tu gyur* renders Skt. *prakṛṣṭa*, *prakarṣa*, and *utkarśa* ("eminent," "superior"), which is supported by Tib. *lhag pa* in the following quotation (*rab tu gyur* also renders Skt. *parāvṛtti* and *nivṛtta*, "revert to," "change into"). Here, "the three appearances" (Tib. *snang ba gsum*) probably refers to what I otherwise render as "the three illuminations" (Skt. *ālokā*, Tib. *snang ba*) in the literature related to the *Guhyasamājatantra* according to the Ārya school. There, the four kinds of being empty—empty, very empty, greatly empty, and all-empty—correspond to the tetrad of illumination, increase of illumination, culmination of illumination, and luminosity, respectively. They are furthermore matched with the four ecstasies, the four moments, and sometimes the four empowerments. In due order, the first three kinds of illumination are also related to the ceasing of the thirty-three obscuring thoughts of hatred, the forty obscuring thoughts of desire, and the seven obscuring thoughts of ignorance. For details, see Dasgupta 1946 (51ff.), Kongtrul Lodrö Tayé 2005 (251–72) and 2008 (109 and 128), Wedemeyer 2007, and Tsongkhapa 2013. Another meaning of "the three appearances" (also rendered as "the three visions") consists of impure appearances, appearances of yogic experience, and pure appearances, referring to a preliminary practice of the Sakya "Path and Fruition" (Tib. *lam 'bras*) tradition.

2395. "The weightiest one" (GZ CDNP *bla mar gyur pa*; Skt. *gurubhāva*) plays on the literal meaning of guru (being "weighty"—that is, full of qualities).

2396. I follow GZ NP *btsal mi bya* against CD *btsa' mi ba*.

2397. I follow GZ *ston* against CDNP *don*.

2398. I follow GZ NP *stong pa stong par* against CD *snang ba stong par* ("appearance as emptiness").

2399. As mentioned before, this stanza is not found in the *Candrapradīpasūtra* (nor the *Samādhirājasūtra*) but (with some variants) in the *Anavataptanāgarājaparipṛcchāsūtra* (D156, fol. 230b.2–3). Vajrapāṇi's *Guruparamparākramopadeśa* (text 213, 190), Kamalaśīla's *Madhyamakāloka* (D3887, 150a.7–150b.1), Avalokitavrata's *Prajñāpradīpaṭīkā* (fols. 131b.4, 214b.2–3, 241a.1), and Abhayākaragupta's *Munimatālaṃkāra* (D3903, fol. 145a.7) explicitly identify it as coming from this sūtra. As IaS (78n77) points out, Candrakīrti quotes this stanza four times in his *Prasannapadā*, once explicitly attributing it to an *Anavataptahradāpasaṅkramaṇasūtra*, and once (unattributed) in his *Catuḥśatakaṭīkā*. On the other hand, Maitrīpa's *Pañcatathāgatamudrāvivaraṇa* (text 36, 194) attributes this stanza to the *Candrapradīpasūtra*, and our text appears to follow him here. Szántó 2016 (323) likewise considers this stanza as "ultimately from the *Candrapradīpasūtra*" but points out that it is also found as stanza 26 of the

Yogāmbaramahātantra. Without attribution, this stanza is also cited in Divākaracandra's *Prajñājñānaprakāśa* (text 16, 55).

2400. GZ CDNP *las* makes it sound as if Avalokitavrata is the name of a text.

2401. These two lines are not found in this author's *Prajñāpradīpaṭīkā*, which is his only text in Tg.

2402. Kg contains a *Vajraśṛṅkhalātantrakalpa* (D758). Vajraśṛṅkhalā ("Vajra Chain") is one of the emanations of Amoghasiddhi, mentioned in the *Sādhanamālā*, there being green in color, with three faces, and holding a chain marked with a vajra in one of her eight hands (another such chain-bearing deity is Vajrasphoṭā). In certain representations of Hevajra, Vajraśṛṅkhalā is one of his consorts. In the body maṇḍala of Kālacakra, black Vajraśṛṅkhalā is the consort of Mahabala. In the *Mañjuśrīmūlakalpa*, Vajraśṛṅkhalā is the name of dūtīs (messengers of Vajrapāṇi) mentioned as attending the teachings. In addition, *vajraśṛṅkhalā* is the name of a particular hand gesture (mudrā). However, it is not clear what "the inexhaustible vajra-chain casket" refers to (GZ CDNP *dag*—usually a dual/plural—here seems to be one of the many cases in this text and others when *dag* is not a dual/plural).

2403. The meaning of a word derives only from correctly and uninterruptedly pronouncing and mentally connecting a row of letters or syllables, thus conceptually joining them to form a meaningful whole. However, though the intended object of expression and the means to express it appear to be mutually dependent, their nature is entirely different: the object one wishes to express is a specifically characterized phenomenon of direct sense perception, while what is held to be the means to express this object is a generally characterized phenomenon—a conceptual term or image in the thinking mind (which may or may not be verbalized subsequently). Since a conceptual image can never really capture the uniqueness of a concrete, specific, and momentary object, nothing is ever really expressible. In more detail, we usually think that a word expresses a certain object, such as pointing at a wooden construction with four legs and a board on top in front of us and saying, "This is a table." Thus we think that one specifically characterized phenomenon (the sound "table") actually expresses another specifically characterized phenomenon (the wooden construction we see in front of us). However, what really happens is that the sound "table" triggers a conceptual mental image in English speakers (a "term generality"; Skt. *śabdasāmānya*, Tib. *sgra spyi*), while the seeing of the wooden construction in front also triggers a conceptual image (an "object generality"; Skt. *arthasāmānya*, Tib. *don spyi*). When these two conceptual images match, we understand what was said. Hence babies do not understand words such as "table"—though they hear the sound "table" and see what we call a "table," that sound does not (yet) trigger a term generality "table" in them, nor does their seeing a table trigger an object generality "table." In other words, when we try to express something, we simply match one conceptual object with another, while conflating our term generality "table" with the sound "table" that we hear, and the object generality "table" with what we see in front of us. This is the basis of all verbal communication.

2404. GZ NP *gzhi* CD *bzhi* ("four").

2405. GZ CDNP *snyoms par zhugs* [CNP *bzhugs*] could also mean "resting in meditative equipoise," but the paragraphs that precede and follow these lines suggest otherwise.

2406. These four lines are *Sarvarahasyatantra* 30 (H449, fol. 4a.5–6), though the tantra has them in a different order (c, d, b, a); compare the literal quote in the *Sekanirdeśapañjikā* (text 45, 434). In the same order as here, these lines are again cited below (340) and in the *Guruparamparākramopadeśa* (text 213, 209).

2407. GZ CDNP all agree on this rather strange plural.

2408. As it stands, this phrase in GZ CDNP reads "find [them] in both the fruition and the karmamudrā," but the context suggests that "the dharmamudrā" has been elided.

2409. I follow GZ CD *gang zhig lung* against NP *de don lus.*

2410. This is a variant version of the opening stanza of the third chapter of Jñānakīrti's *Tattvāvatāra* (text 214, 247; the Sanskrit differs).

2411. GZ CDNP *de nyid* could also mean "those very [phenomena]."

2412. Just as in the Tibetan of the *Sekanirdeśapañjikā* (text 45, 384), GZ CDNP here mistakenly render this sentence as "In *[The Tantra of] Devendra Questioning the Bhagavān*, this is stated."

2413. IaS (166) points out that this stanza from an (unidentified) *Devendraparipṛcchātantra* is also quoted in Candrakīrti's *Pradīpoddyotana* and Raviśrījñāna's *Amṛtakaṇikāṭippaṇī* (see IaS for the exact references).

2414. GZ CDNP *baṃ.*

2415. This and the following stanza are also cited and attributed to the *Devendraparipṛchātantra* in the *Subhāṣitasaṃgraha* (Bendall 1903–1904, 32–33).

2416. GZ CDNP *las* ("from") em. *la.*

2417. I follow GZ CD *gang zag* against NP *gang.*

2418. Here and in the following instance, GZ CD *rigs* NP *rig* ("known").

2419. NP *rtsi ba* ("counted").

2420. As is clear from the *Sekanirdeśapañjikā*, this is another stanza from the *Devendraparipṛcchātantra.*

2421. *Hevajratantra* II.3.4; GZ CDNP only cite the first two lines.

2422. In all instances in this paragraph, GZ CDNP *rtog pa* ("thought") is emended to *rtogs pa.*

2423. For an explanation of this, see below, 286ff. and 343–44.

2424. About the syllables E and VAṂ being symbols for the lotus and the vajra, respectively, IaS (260n34) explains the following: "Since the form of the written letter E resembles a downward pointing triangle in all northern scripts, to a greater or lesser extent (in Gupta script it is often an almost perfectly equilateral one), it was in a way natural that this phoneme (whether written or pronounced) came to be regarded as an equivalent of the Dharmodaya. And since the form of the written letter Va more or less resembles an upwards pointing (in Gupta script) or (later more commonly) a sideways pointing triangle, a shape which lends itself to being interpreted as a symbolic representation of the male organ, the Vajra (and thus also Means), it became possible to understand Evaṃ, from the point of view of the written forms of the phonemes, as the combination or union of Lotus = Dharmodayā and Vajra. The locus classicus for this in Buddhist tantric literature appears to be *Hevajratantra* 2.3.4."

2425. It is not clear what "the three kinds of training" here refers to (Tib. *sbyor ba* could also mean "preparation"; thus maybe the three preliminaries—offering oblations, visualizing a protection circle, and gathering the two accumulations of merit and wisdom—as described in Kongtrul Lodrö Tayé 2008, 89–92). "The modes of the four [ways of] being born" are birth in a womb, birth in an egg, birth through warmth and moisture, and miraculous birth. "The four kinds of yoga" probably refers to the four ways of visualizing the deity—"the fivefold full awakening," "the fourfold vajra," "the threefold ritual," and "the completion through mere recollection"—that respectively counteract the four ways of birth and are suitable for practitioners from modest to highest faculties. However, "the four kinds of yoga" is followed by "and" and only three among these four yogas. If "the four kinds of yoga" indeed refers to said four visualization techniques, it would be the general category of the three items that follow (thus requiring eliding "and"), with "the four vajra steps" missing. In any case, the steps in the three gradual ways of visualization here are presented in different ways in different tantras. According to Kongtrul Lodrö Tayé 2008 (94–95), "the fivefold full awakening" consists of progressively visualizing, on top of a lotus seat, (1) a moon disk arising from the *a*-series, (2) a sun disk arising from the *ka*-series, (3) between sun and moon, the deity's hand-held implement marked with the seed syllable, radiating and reabsorbing light, (4) all these merging, and (5) the deity's complete form arising from that. As for this being "the fivefold full awakening," according to *Hevajratantra* I.8.6–7, the moon represents mirror-like wisdom, the sun the wisdom of equality, the seed syllable transforming into the implement discriminating wisdom, their merging all-accomplishing wisdom, and the manifestation of the complete deity dharmadhātu wisdom. "The fourfold vajra" consists of (1) meditating on emptiness and then progressively visualizing, on a seat that consists of a lotus, sun, and so on, (2) a moon, a sun, and the seed syllable, radiating and reabsorbing light, (3) their being transformed into the deity's complete form, and (4) placing the three syllables (OṂ, ĀḤ, and HŪṂ) at the three locations (forehead, throat, and heart). "The threefold ritual" consists of progressively visualizing, on a seat that consists of a lotus, sun, and so on, (1) the seed syllable, (2) the seed syllable transforming into the hand-held implement marked with the seed syllable, and (3) the hand-held implement transforming into the deity's complete form. Note, though, that according to the *Caturmudrāṭīkā* below (334), "the fivefold full awakening" consists of (1) sun and moon adorned with the *a*-series and the *ka*-series, respectively, (2) the globe of their being of equal taste, (3) the mind syllable, (4) the five-pronged vajra, and (5) the fully complete physical form.

2426. Given that the source of this stanza is the *Nayatrayapradīpa* (D3707, fol. 16b.3–4; text 217, 457), GZ CDNP *sgron ma gsal ba'i rgyud* (**Pradīpoddyotanatantra*) is emended to *tshul gsum sgron ma* (there is no known **Pradīpoddyotanatantra* or the like, and the stanza is also not from any other among the texts in Tg whose title includes Tib. *sgron ma gsal ba*, such as Candrakīrti's *Pradīpoddyotana*). In the available Sanskrit quotations of this stanza, the last line is found as *mantraśāstraṃ viśiṣyate* ("it is the mantra teaching that is more distinguished"), *mantranītir viśiṣyate* ("it is the mantra teaching that is more distinguished"), and *mantranītiḥ praśasyate* ("it is the mantra approach that is praised"), but GZ of Divākaracandra's *Prajñājñānaprakāśa* and Vajrapāṇi's *Guruparamparākramopadeśa* also read "Mantrayāna" (as do the comments in TRVC). Besides the comments on this stanza here, detailed (and sometimes quite different) explanations of it are found in the *Nayatrayapradīpa* itself and the *Prajñājñānaprakāśa* (text 16, 62ff.), while some shorter comments are contained in Sahajavajra's *Sthitisamāsa* VI.6–13, Vajrapāṇi's *Guruparamparākramopadeśa* (text 213, 196), and Tipi Bumlabar's commentary on the *Tattvaratnāvalī* (TRVC, 394; see the note on this stanza in text 34, 184).

2427. Tib. *dgag sgrub* can mean creating and blocking, stopping and accomplishing, or affirmation and negation. In one of its discussions of mahāmudrā below (372), our text glosses this as "one's own view is not affirmed and the views of others are not negated." In another explanation of mahāmudrā (360), it is said that view, meditation, and conduct are neither created nor blocked. Naturally, with regard to mahāmudrā, *dgag sgrub* includes all these meanings. One could say that being free from affirmation and negation refers more to the view of mahāmudrā in terms of lacking any conceptual ascertainment one way or another, while being free from creating and blocking (or accomplishing and stopping) refers more to mahāmudrā meditation in terms of not manipulating experience or awareness but letting it be in an uncontrived manner.

2428. I follow GZ *bsten pa* against CDNP *bstan pa*.

2429. I follow GZ D *gzhi* against CNP *bzhi* ("four").

2430. GZ D omit "of others."

2431. As mentioned in the introduction, the passages in text 44 that are cited from CMA frequently vary from that text's Sanskrit and often also from its canonical Tibetan translation, though they are generally closer to the latter. Moreover, some passages are cited in a different order than in CMA, and there is a significant number of additional passages not found in either the Sanskrit or the canonical translation of CMA. The comments generally follow the word order of the Tibetan version of CMA that is embedded in text 44, including comments on words that are found only in the canonical translation or only in text 44. In the same vein, most identifiable quotations from the scriptures usually follow their (sometimes greatly variant or mistaken) Tibetan translations. In such cases, I usually follow the Sanskrit (if available) and document the differences in GZ CDNP of text 44 in the notes.

2432. GZ D *de la* CNP *de las* ("from it").

2433. I follow GZ *de yang rdo rje* [CNP *rjes*] *ni* against D *yang na rdo rje sems dpa' ni*.

2434. This stanza is from the *Vajraśekharatantra* (H448, fol. 331a.3–4). The first line in GZ CDNP here reads: "Being hard, firm, and solid." For comments on this stanza, see PTMC on Maitrīpa's *Pañcatathāgatamudrāvivaraṇa* (text 36, 191).

2435. *Pañcakrama* II.2. The last two lines in GZ CDNP read as follows:

> The realization of this by the wisdom
> of self-aware mind is the homage here.

2436. "Approach and accomplishment" refers to the progressive set of four that consists of approach (or "worship"; Skt. *sevā*), close approach (*upasevā*; or "close accomplishment," *upasādhana*), accomplishment (*sādhana*), and great accomplishment (*sādhana*). This fourfold template is used in the Vajrayāna in a number of different contexts, such as the creation process, mantra recitation, and the stages of karmamudrā (thus the individual meanings of these four terms can vary greatly).

2437. As mentioned before, "lord empowerment" (Skt. *adhipatyabhiṣeka*) is another name of "bell empowerment" (Skt. *ghaṇṭābhiṣeka*).
2438. I follow GZ NP *rig pa* against CD *rigs pa*.
2439. Maitrīpa's *Sekatātparyasaṃgraha* (text 37, 199) elaborates that "HA" refers to being free of causes, "Ū" to being without thinking, and "AṂ" to all phenomena being utterly nonabiding; that is, in Sanskrit, *h* is glossed by *hetuviyuktaḥ*, *ū* by *ūhāpagataḥ*, and *aṃ* (that is, the *anusvāra* dot above *hū*) by *apratiṣṭitāḥ*.
2440. I follow GZ NP *sgro ma b(r)tags* against CD *sgron ma brtags* ("not affixing a lamp").
2441. As in the *Sekatātparyasaṃgraha*, GZ CDNP here read *snod du bya ba* ("the need to be made into a [suitable] vessel"), which renders Skt. *bhavyatā*.
2442. GZ CDNP read "the maṇḍala and the means of accomplishment," but I follow the parallel phrase in Maitrīpa's *Sekatātparyasaṃgraha* (text 37, 202).
2443. With the Sanskrit, I follow GZ NP *rgyur* against CD *gyur*.
2444. *Hevajratantra* II.3.12. The Sanskrit word *seka* is here glossed by the verbs *siñc* ("(be)sprinkle" but also "scatter," "emit," and "pour") and *snā* ("bathe," "wash"). Thus, with reference to the first verb, another hermeneutical etymology is that empowerment scatters or dispels obscurations and pours wisdom into one's body and mind.
2445. GZ CDNP *dbang bskur ba'i las de dag la nus pa khyad par can 'byin par byed na* ("given that the special power in those activities of empowerment is brought out") em. *dbang bskur bas las . . .*
2446. This stanza is found in the *Vajraśekharatantra* (H448, fol. 436b.7–437a.1), the *Sarvadurgatipariśodhanakalpa* (H458, fol. 427b.4), and the *Guhyamaṇitilakanāmasūtra* (H461, fol. 133a.1). The first two lines in GZ CDNP read as follows:

    By means of all of the buddhas,
    it rests in the hand of Vajrapāṇi

    In the last line, one is tempted to emend *brtan* ("firm") to *brten* ("rely on"; as here in CD), but all versions of this stanza in Kg and as cited many times in Tg (except one) read *brtan*.
2447. I follow GZ *'khor ba la zhen pa* against CD *'khor ba las zhen pa* NP *'khor ba la gzhan pa*.
2448. GZ *nges don du 'gyur bar bya* CDNP *des don du 'gyur bar bya* ("should be made useful through that").
2449. GZ CDNP *de dag gi rgyud* ("the continuum of those") is tentatively emended to *de'i rgyu*, since the beginning of the discussion of the vase empowerment spoke of "the samayamudrā that represents its cause." CDNP omit "is called."
2450. For further details on the processes of preparing for and actually bestowing the sixfold vase empowerment, see Maitrīpa's *Sekatātparyasaṃgraha* (text 37) and *Saṃkṣiptasekaprakriyā* (text 38), and Kongtrul Lodrö Tayé 2005 (217–30).

2451. I follow GZ *bdag nyid go bya'i don du* against CDNP *bdag nyid go cha'i don du* ("for the sake of my own armor").

2452. The commentary here appears to gloss *don* in GZ CDNP *don du* ("for the sake of"), which on its own can mean "meaning." This is one of the cases where the commentary is clearly based on the Tibetan translation of CMA and not its Sanskrit (which does not contain the equivalent *artha*).

2453. These otherwise-unattested lines are probably three concluding lines by the author.

2454. I follow GZ NP *bde stong* against CD *sde stong*.

2455. This unlocated stanza is probably another one by the author.

2456. With both the Sanskrit and Tibetan (*bde lag tu*) of CMA, GZ CDNP *bde bar* would rather be understood as "easily," but the comments below clearly suggest "as bliss."

2457. As explained in the beginning, the poor empowerment is not deluded about the succession of the four moments, but still deluded about the realization.

2458. I follow GZ CD *don spyi'i rnam par* against NP *don ci'i rnam pa*.

2459. P omits this sentence.

2460. I follow GZ CD *dgos pa* against NP *dgongs pa* ("intention").

2461. I follow GZ CD *bcud kyis sbyang byas nas* against NP *bcud kyi spyad byas nas* ("having experienced the elixir").

2462. This unlocated stanza is probably another one by the author.

2463. The Tibetan colophon of the currently available *Hevajratantra* and a number of its commentaries say that its two chapters were extracted from an original *Hevajratantra* in 500,000 ślokas in thirty-two chapters. Furthermore, *Hevajratantra* I.11.11 refers to a version in twelve chapters. The Chinese translation also speaks about a version in thirty-two chapters, while Butön refers to one in 100,000 ślokas. As mentioned before, the terms "father tantra" and "mother tantra" were unknown in India and only appear in Tibetan literature, which is another clear sign of this text not being a straight translation of a Sanskrit original.

2464. This appears to be a variant version of *Mūlamadhyamakakārikā* XV.2cd:

> For a nature is not contrived,
> nor dependent on anything else.

2465. I follow GZ *rtog tu zad* against CD *rtogs su zad* NP *rtags su zad*.

2466. I follow GZ *'di la* against CDNP *'di ni*.

2467. This stanza's first, third, and fourth lines in Tibetan are found in the *Sandhivyākaraṇanāmatantra* (H418, fol. 118b.4–5), with the first two lines reading as follows:

> AHO—Samantabhadra's
> birth from dependent origination

The first two lines here are found in a similar but longer stanza in both the *Māyājālatantra* (H431, fol. 329a.4–5) and the *Śrīvajrahṛdayālaṃkāratantra* (H788, fol. 435b.4–5):

> AHO—Samantabhadra possesses
> the vajras of body, speech, and mind

> Phenomena are without any birth—
> without any moving and any abiding,
> being devoid of the stains of thoughts
> This should be given birth to, it is said.

2468. NP omit "clearly."
2469. For various enumerations of fourteen bhūmis, see the note on line 113b of Saraha's "People Dohā" (text 13).
2470. It is not clear what "the fifth" here refers to: possibly the fifth and highest tantra class mentioned before (yoganiruttaratantra) or the fifth and highest form of Vajrayāna conduct ("the conduct of being victorious in all directions"; see *Caturmudrāṭīkā*, 346).
2471. *Pañcakrama* IV.36.
2472. CDNP omit "which."
2473. GZ *mkhas pa dang rnyog pa med pa* CDNP *mkhas pa rnyog pa med pa* ("who has taintless skill").
2474. I follow GZ *rtogs sla bar bya ba'i phyir* against CDNP *rtog pa blta bar bya ba'i phyir* ("in order to look at thoughts").
2475. GZ *dus kyi sna rtses tshad du 'dzin pa* CDNP *dus kyi sna rtse tshad du 'dzin pa* ("gauging the crucial point in time"). "The crucial point in time" (lit. "the nose tip of time") appears to refer to the proper time in terms of the four moments, as explained below.
2476. Based on the parallel phrase *ma smin pa* right below, GZ CDNP *ma smin par bya ba* ("those who are not to be matured") is emended to *ma smin par byas pa*.
2477. *Hevajratantra* I.10.4cd–5ab; GZ CDNP omit "divine" and show a few other minor variants.
2478. *Hevajratantra* I.10.5cd–6ab; in the first line, with the Sanskrit, I follow GZ NP *yang na gang de* against CD *yang dag de ni*.
2479. GZ CDNP *ngag* (lit. "speech").
2480. *Hevajratantra* I.10.6cf.
2481. *Hevajratantra* II.4.42cf. GZ CDNP:

> The śukra is not given with the hand
> . . .
> The tongue should take the deathless
> from the pair of the lotus and vajra.

2482. *Hevajratantra* I.10.6gh.
2483. *Hevajratantra* I.10.7–8 and I.10.9c. In line I.107c, GZ CDNP read *brtul zhugs* ("yogic discipline") instead of *rdul bral* ("free from stains"); in line I.10.8b, GZ CD read *mchog tu mi g.yo ba* ("the supremely immovable one") and NP *srog tu mi spong ba* ("not abandoned as the life force").
2484. I follow NP *'dod chags las log pa* against GZ *'dod chags la sogs pa* ("passion and so on"); CD omit this phrase.
2485. Just as in GZ CDNP of CMA, this is an expanded prose version of *Hevajratantra* II.3.5ab (cited as the actual lines of verse in CMA); lines II.3.5cd are cited further below after the two sentences on the four moments and the four ecstasies.

2486. Though GZ CDNP read "four mudrās," what follows has nothing to do with the four mudrās but discusses the proper characteristics of a karmamudrā.

2487. This cited passage is not found in either the Sanskrit of CMA or its canonical Tibetan translation, nor are the two cited lines identifiable. Nevertheless, that this passage is considered as a quote from CMA by text 44 is shown by the standard introduction "this is to be taught," the closing quotation marks, and the following comments on it.

2488. This seems to be an allusion to the sixteen kinds of emptiness discussed in the prajñāpāramitā sūtras and Madhyamaka texts.

2489. This could also be read as "the support for connate wisdom becoming nondual."

2490. I follow GZ CD *dus* against NP *bdud* ("māra").

2491. GZ *yod pa gang* CD *yod pa* NP *gong la.*

2492. GZ *nyong mongs pa spang ba'i sgo nas mi 'dra ba* CD *nyong mongs pa spong ba'i sgo nas ma 'dres pa* ("not mixed by way of relinquishing afflictions") NP *nyong mongs pa'i sgo nas mi 'dra ba* ("dissimilar by way of afflictions").

2493. I follow GZ *ngos 'dzin par byed pa'i blo* against CDNP *ngos 'dzin par byed pas / blo.*

2494. This is a variant of *Hevajratantra* II.3.5cd cited in CMA.

2495. Here and elsewhere, GZ CDNP *rnam pa med pa* ("without aspect") is emended to *rnam par nyed pa.*

2496. *Sekanirdeśa* 2. GZ CDNP:

> Through rejecting the forceful yoga,
> that there is variety, then [I follow CDNP *de nas* against GZ *de las*] . . . ,
> and then consummation is known.

2497. I follow GZ *mtshon bya* against CDNP *mtshon cha* ("weapon").

2498. *Sekanirdeśa* 3ab; in the first line GZ reads *kun tu skyod pa* ("agitation") and CDNP *kun tu spyod pa* ("conduct") instead of "consideration."

2499. Parallel to the same phrase in the *Sekanirdeśapañjikā*, I follow GZ *nges par gzung ba* against CDNP *nges bar 'byung ba*. This refers to the genitive of the compound *paramaviramayoḥ* ("of the supreme and cessational") in the above quote preceding *Sekanirdeśa* 3ab.

2500. I follow GZ CD *mchog gi dga' ba dang dga' bral gyi dga' ba* against NP *chog gi dga' bral gyi dga' ba.*

2501. The sequence of objections and answers beginning with this objection parallel the beginning of the comments on *Sekanirdeśa* 3 in Rāmapāla's *Sekanirdeśapañjikā* (text 45, 396–98) and a similar passage in Vajrapāṇi's *Guruparamparākramopadeśa* (text 213, 210–13). However, in their translation of the *Sekanirdeśapañjikā*, IaS (275–77) considers most of these objections (or parts thereof) to be Rāmapāla's answers, and vice versa. Not only does this break the symmetry of the dictions in certain objections by taking them to be answers, but most of it does not match Rāmapāla's own position either. Moreover, the *Guruparamparākramopadeśa* explicitly identifies the first and some of the further objections as coming from the proponents of the forceful empowerment that is to be rejected, and (with a single minor exception in GZ of text 45) the places of the Tibetan *zhe na* markers of the objections in the *Caturmudrāṭīkā*, the *Sekanirdeśapañjikā*, and the *Guruparamparākramopadeśa* match exactly in all three texts (for more details, see the notes on the parallel passage in text 45).

2502. This is a slight variant of *Hevajratantra* II.69ef.

2503. *Hevajratantra* I.10.18cd.

2504. *Hevajratantra* II.3.8ab. GZ CDNP:

> Consummation is said to be agitation [GZ *bskyod pa* CDNP *spyod pa* ("conduct")],
> being the experience of one's own bliss.

2505. I follow GZ *rtog pa mi rtog par* against CDNP *rtogs* [NP *rtog*] *pa mi rtogs par*.

2506. Given the parallel passage in the *Sekanirdeśapañjikā*, I follow CDNP *nges par byed pa* (Skt. *niścita*) against GZ *nges par 'byed pa* ("penetrating insight," which would also make sense).

2507. *Hevajratantra* II.3.9. GZ CDNP read these four lines by reversing and equating the first and second phrases in each line, thus saying "The first ecstasy is variety" and so on.

2508. *Hevajratantra* I.10.13. GZ CDNP omit "nature" in the first line and read "observed" instead of "found" in the last line.

2509. *Hevajratantra* II.2.40ab.

2510. *Sekanirdeśa* 3cd–4. GZ CDNP:

> Because [I follow GZ *gang phyir* against CDNP *dga' phyir*, "because of ecstasy"] there is no analysis [CDNP *dpyod* GZ *spyod*, "conduct"] at that time,
> there is awareness [I follow NP *rig pa* against GZ CD *rigs pa*] of characteristics' absence
>
> Hence it is known [GZ CDNP *rigs* em. *rig*] as characteristics' lack
> The third bliss is exactly this one
> This self-awareness [I follow GZ NP *rang rig* against CD *rang gi* ("own")] becomes the siddhis,
> and it also agrees with the scriptures' meaning [I follow GZ *'tsham pa yin* against CDNP *mtshams ma yin*].

2511. Given the preceding "root text," GZ *go rim gyis mi gnas shing* ("it does not abide by way of the [correct] sequence and") CDNP *go rims kyi mi gnas kyang* ("though it does not abide by way of the [correct] sequence") em. *go rim gyis gnas kyang*.

2512. *Sekanirdeśa* 21. GZ CDNP have "vajra" instead of "bola," and the last two lines say:

> The statement "abiding in the middle"
> does not represent what my guru holds.

2513. I follow NP *mngon du zhen pa* against GZ CD *sngon du zhen pa* ("prior clinging").

2514. *Sekanirdeśa* 22. The last two lines in GZ CDNP read as follows:

> nor as abiding in between is this asserted
> True reality is known from the guru's mouth.

2515. "Holder of sixteen bindus twice halved" corresponds to *Mañjuśrīnāmasaṃgīti* X.3b. Raviśrījñāna's commentary on this line (Lal 1994, 90) explains this as follows: "Holding sixteen bindus twice halved is referred to as 'great prajñā-jñāna' by the tathāgatas . . . Half of sixteen digits are eight. Half of these are the four bindus whose characteristics are body, speech, mind and wisdom. They are the producers of the states of waking, dream, deep sleep and the fourth [state, respectively]. 'He holds them' means that he is holding the [four] bindus of sixteen twice halved. It means that he is the protector of the fourfold samaya, Vajrasattva, the one of great passion."

2516. Except for a variant reading in the first line, these two stanzas of unknown origin are also found in Vajrapāṇi's *Guruparamparākramopadeśa* (text 213, 217; also seven lines). That these are indeed two stanzas is shown by Rāmapāla's *Sekanirdeśapañjikā* (text 45, 408) citing two almost identical Apabhraṃśa stanzas with four lines of uneven length (lacking "the result is also sealed with the cause"); the Tibetan of Abhayākaragupta's *Śrīsaṃpuṭatantrarājaṭīkāmnāyamañjarī* (D1198, fol. 68a.6) has the same in six lines. An abbreviated version in four lines is found in Maitrīpa's *Caturmudropadeśa* (text 92, 21). Interestingly, the *Caturmudrāṭīkā* here cites both stanzas in full but offers no comments. By contrast, the text's quote of only the last three lines below (344) is preceded by a detailed and clear explanation and followed by a medley of other stanzas from the *Hevajratantra* and Indrabhūti's *Śrīcakrasaṃvaratantrarājaśambarasamuccayanāmavṛtti* (D1413). Later (351–52), another quote from the *Śrīcakrasaṃvaratantrarājaśambarasamuccayanāmavṛtti*, which shares the first line of the first stanza here, is preceded by a very brief reference to said detailed explanation (for details, see below). Note also that the third and fourth lines of the second stanza here correspond to *Sekoddeśa* 146cd and *Guhyasamājatantra* XVIII.79ab (also cited as *Sekoddeśa* 146cd in the mantra section of the *Sthitisamāsa*; text 17, 103). However, as mentioned before, *Sekoddeśa* 146ab explains the cause as the emptiness that bears reflections and the result as compassion bearing the immutable, while the *Caturmudrāṭīkā* below and the *Guruparamparākramopadeśa* identify the cause as Akṣobhya (experience of bliss, means) and the result as Vajrasattva (emptiness, prajñā). For more details and the different interpretations of these two stanzas, see the note on them in the *Sekanirdeśapañjikā* (text 45, 408) and their explanation in the *Guruparamparākramopadeśa* (text 213, 217–20).

2517. GZ *yang dag par* CDNP *yang dag gis* (GZ could also be read as "the correct one").

2518. I follow GZ NP *gsung pa* against CD *gsum pa* ("third").

2519. NP omit "taught."

2520. Just like GZ CDNP of CMA, GZ CDNP read *grib ma* ("shadow"). Though this is one of the meanings of Skt. *chāyā*, it is clear in CMA and the following comments below that its sense of "resemblance" is preferable here.

2521. I follow GZ *shes rab ni* against CDNP *shes rab kyi*.

2522. CDNP omit "because."

2523. According to Maitrīpa's *Sekatātparyasaṃgraha* (text 37, 203), prajñā-jñāna has the following two meanings: "[The compound] 'prajñā-jñāna' admits two etymological derivations here: 'the wisdom of prajñā' and 'the wisdom that is prajñā itself.' Now, the former etymological derivation is as follows. Prajñā refers to the mental state that [still] bears the [two] aspects of perceiver and perceived and is the nature of a well-shaped woman consisting of the four elements, the five skandhas, and the six objects such as forms. The bodhicitta that has this [form of prajñā] as its cause is wisdom. The latter etymological derivation is that wisdom refers to this very [prajñā] in its being empty of said two aspects [of perceiver and perceived]."

2524. GZ CDNP have another *zhe na* after this sentence, but the query here obviously continues with the following two sentences (ended by the second *zhe na*).

2525. CDNP "unborn freedom from discursiveness."

2526. NP omit this phrase.

2527. *Hevajratantra* I.8.34. The last two lines in GZ CDNP read as follows:

> Thanks to the merit of relying upon the
> guru's timely means, its nature is known.

2528. *Hevajratantra* II.3.4. In the first line, GZ CDNP read "The excellent attire of E" (thus the corresponding comments below).

2529. GZ *sgo gsum la* CD *sgo gsum las* ("from . . . ") NP *grub gsum la*. As mentioned before, the three doors to liberation consist of emptiness (all phenomena are empty of an essence of their own), signlessness (all causes are empty), and wishlessness (all results are empty).

2530. I could not locate these stanzas, though similar descriptions of a proper karmamudrā are found in many texts.

2531. NP omit *bde ba la*, thus reading "the repository of the maturing of the bindu of great bliss that has the character of emptiness filled with bliss."

2532. GZ CDNP *de dang* em. *de dag*.

2533. I follow GZ CD *bdag nyid la'o / de yang* against NP *gyi la ni / de dang*.

2534. *Hevajratantra* I.10.15. The first two lines are also found in *Hevajratantra* I.8.33ab, the *Pañcakrama* (II.64ab), the *Saṃpuṭatantra* (H396, fol. 367b.6), the *Śrīvajramaṇḍālaṃkāratantra* (H459, fol. 82b.6), the *Śrīvajraḍākatantra* (H386, fol. 328a.3–4), the *Vajraḍākanāmottaratantra* (H387, fol. 519a.4–5), and the *Śrīḍākārṇavamahāyoginītantra* (H390, fol. 75b.7). The first two lines in GZ CDNP read as follows:

> It is neither passion nor dispassion,
> nor is it existent in between.

2535. NP omit "jewel."

2536. CD "the precious actual [connate]."

2537. GZ CDNP *blo'i shes rab* ("the prajñā of intelligence") em. *blo ni shes rab*.

2538. GZ CDNP *slob ma la* ("for students"?) em. *slob lam*.

2539. This could also be read as "of being unborn."

2540. I follow CD *de lta bu dag dper yang mi rigs* against GZ *de lta bu dag dper yang rigs* NP *de lta bu dgra dper yang mi rigs* ("such an enemy is not even . . .").

2541. I follow CDNP *bzhin* against GZ *de bzhin nyid* ("suchness").

2542. Given that GZ also has *nges par byed pa* below in the comments, I here follow CDNP *nges par byed pa* against GZ *nges par 'byed pa* ("penetrating insight").

2543. CD omit "they have seen."

2544. I follow GZ *de rnams rmongs so* against CDNP *rnams so*.

2545. Given the context, I follow NP *bde bas mgu ba* against GZ CD *de bas mgu ba* ("Therefore happy").
2546. GZ *gtam* CDNP *rten* ("support," "foundation").
2547. I follow GZ *bcos ma ma yin pa'i phyir 'thad pa* against CD *bcos ma yin pa'i phyir 'thad pa* ("is tenable because it is contrived.") NP *bcos ma yin pa'i phyir mi 'thad pa* ("is untenable because it is uncontrived.").
2548. As in CDNP of CMA, here, GZ CDNP *drug cu pa* ("sixtieth") is meaningless. Thus I used "Kodo millet," since that is what the Sanskrit says.
2549. That is, the dharmamudrā is only said to be uncontrived because its essence is of equal taste with the actual connate wisdom, whereas this actual connate wisdom is completely uncontrived, simply being the natural state of mahāmudrā on its own, which cannot be said to be of equal taste with itself but *is* this very taste of ultimate bliss-emptiness.
2550. I follow GZ *rtogs* against CDNP *gsungs* ("say").
2551. I follow CDNP *rig pa nyid* against GZ *rim pa nyid* ("the sequence").
2552. *Hevajratantra* II.12.6: "OṂ Lotus, receptacle of bliss, you who grant the bliss of great passion, the four ecstasies' own blessings are manifold HŪṂ HŪṂ HŪṂ Please do what needs to be done for me!"; Skt. *bhaga* (here rendered as "blessings") can also mean "good fortune," "happiness," "welfare," "dignity," "majesty," "excellence," "beauty," "love," "sexual passion," and "vulva."
2553. NP omit "what is desired."
2554. I follow GZ CD *gzims pa yi* against NP *brtags pa'i.*
2555. This is the third stanza of the *Caturgāthā* (D324). GZ CDNP read "sugatas" instead of "tathāgatas" and switch "have sat" and "have stood."
2556. CD omit "the churner and."
2557. As mentioned before, though it is not obvious from the Tibetan *srub cing bsrubs pa* (lit. "churning and churning" or "churning and having churned") here and in other parallel cases, this phrase means "the churner and the churned" (Skt. *manthaka* and *manthya*), a common expression for the union of vajra and lotus during karmamudrā. In line with the Tibetan, the commentary here understands this phrase as referring to two actions.
2558. As mentioned before, Skt. *kunda* ("white jasmine") is one of the many epithets of semen.
2559. GZ *ye shes bskyed pa'i nus pa yod pas* CD *ye shes kyi nus pa yod pas* ("because it has the power of wisdom") NP *ye shes kyi nus pas* ("because of the power of wisdom").
2560. These four stanzas are found in Kṛṣṇa's *Yogaratnamālā* (Snellgrove 1959, 2:104) as a part of commenting on the opening phrase *evaṃ mayā śrutam* of the *Hevajratantra*. With two additional lines each, they are also found at the beginning of Durjayacandra's *Kaumudīnāmapañjikā* (D1185, fol. 2b.1–4). GZ CDNP omit "the syllable" in each stanza, and NP omit everything beginning with "the samayamudrā" in the last stanza.
2561. GZ CDNP literally read "the second and the third are also to be understood implicitly," but given the descriptions of the second and third ecstasies right below, it is clear that the "two ecstasies" referred to here in relation to "having arrived in the interior of the jewel" are the second and the third (supreme

ecstasy and connate ecstasy) and not the other two (ecstasy and cessational ecstasy).

2562. In translations from Sanskrit, Tib. *ngad* is only attested as "[good] scent," but on its own, it can also mean "power," which would make sense here too.

2563. Given the context, GZ NP *lhan cig skyes pa'i dga' bral* ("cessational ecstasy of the connate") CD *lhan cig skyes pas dga' bral* ("cessational ecstasy through the connate") are emended to *lhan cig skyes pa'i dga' ba dang dga' bral*.

2564. Given the explicit parallel phrase "the pith instructions on the fourth ecstasy" above (296), the recurring phrase "the pith instructions on the fourth" is rendered accordingly (though, at least in some cases, it could also be understood as "the pith instructions on the fourth empowerment").

2565. I follow CDNP *bsten* against GZ *bstan*.

2566. I follow GZ *'dra ba dag las ni* against CDN *'dra ba ste / las ni*.

2567. I follow GZ N *dgag par* against CD *dga' bar* ("as ecstasy").

2568. GZ N *ched du byas pa* (Skt. *adhikṛta*) CD *tshad du byas pa* (probably Skt. *pramāṇīkṛta*).

2569. In the passage "a mere concordant outflow in the form of bodhicitta . . . It is declared that it is by relying on a karmamudrā," P omits everything except "in the form of bodhicitta" and "It is declared that."

2570. As before, I follow CDNP *nges par byed pa* against GZ *nges par 'byed pa* ("penetrating insight").

2571. GZ adds "chunks of."

2572. GZ NP *dgug pa* CD *'jug pa* ("enter," "engage").

2573. I follow GZ *rgyu mthun pa'i ji lta ba bzhin* against CDNP *rgyu mthun pa'i lta ba bzhin*.

2574. This could also simply mean "samaya," but below (363–64 and 365) it is said that "the causal samayamudrā . . . of making a pledge for the consummate welfare of others is the first generation of [bodhi]citta . . . In terms of the secret mantra, this refers to the time of familiarizing with the dharmamudrā [up through] mahāmudrā" and "The samayamudrā that is the cause refers to cultivating the creation process."

2575. GZ CDNP *ye shes kyi phyag rgya chen po* could also be read as "the great jñānamudrā." However, given that neither CMA nor the *Caturmudrāṭīkā* use the term "jñānamudrā," this is very unlikely. Also, below (306), mahāmudrā is glossed as "nondual wisdom" (*gnyis med kyi ye shes phyag rgya chen po*).

2576. *Hevajratantra* II.4.33. GZ CDNP read the last line as "by way of what obscures and what is free of obscurations."

2577. *Hevajratantra* II.4.34ab. Skt. *saṃvṛta* also means "conventional," and *vivṛta* means "revealed" or "naked." Here, these two are opposite terms referring to seeming and ultimate reality, respectively. GZ CDNP:

> Because of resembling unobscured kunda,
> the obscuration-free has the nature of bliss [or "it has the nature of obscuration-free bliss"].

2578. *Hevajratantra* II.4.34cd. GZ CDNP:

> Through the lotus of a woman, Sukhāvatī,
> having the nature of the aspect of EVAṂ.

2579. I follow NP *bde ba srung ba nyid kyis* against GZ *bde ba'i bsrub pa nyid kyis* ("It is by virtue of the churning of bliss") CD *bde ba gsungs pa nyid kyi[s]* ("It is by virtue of speaking of bliss").
2580. *Hevajratantra* II.4.35ab.
2581. *Hevajratantra* II.4.35cd.
2582. NP omit "nirvāṇa" and "arise."
2583. *Hevajratantra* II.4.36.
2584. I follow CDNP *'khor ba mya ngan 'das par* against GZ *'khor ba dang mya ngan las 'das par*.
2585. *Hevajratantra* II.4.37–38ad. GZ CDNP read the last four lines as follows:

> These phenomena represent nirvāṇa
> Nescience is the nature of saṃsāra [I follow CDNP *te* against GZ *las*]
> Lacking ignorance is saṃsāra's purity
> Saṃsāra is experienced like nirvāṇa.

2586. *Hevajratantra* II.4.38ef. GZ CDNP:

> With its obscuration-free and obscuring
> nature, the bodhicitta represents nirvāṇa.

2587. GZ CDNP "light blue."
2588. The *sandhyābhāṣā* chapter of the *Hevajratantra* glosses *karpūraka* ("camphor") as *śūkra* ("semen") and *sihlaka* ("frankincense") as *svayaṃbhū* ("blood"); GZ CDNP "endowed with divine substance and camphor."
2589. *Hevajratantra* II.4.39–40ab.
2590. *Hevajratantra* II.40cd. GZ CDNP:

> One with yogic discipline should
> give her alcohol and drink [I follow GZ NP *btung ba* against CD *brdung ba*, "beat"] as well.

2591. I follow GZ CD *rjes chags* against NP *rjes phyag*.
2592. *Hevajratantra* II.4.41ab.
2593. *Hevajratantra* II.4.41cd–42ab. GZ CDNP read the first two lines as follows:

> Through uniting the lotus and the vajra,
> they with yogic discipline enact [or "experience"] purity.

2594. *Hevajratantra* II.4.42cf. GZ CDNP:

> From there, it is not taken with the hand
> . . .
> It is so as to give rise to strength that
> the tongue should take the deathless.

2595. Since GZ CDNP *gus pa dang bcas shing rgyun mi 'chad par bsgom* typically renders Skt. *sādaranirantarābhyāsa*, I follow the latter.
2596. This is a tentative emendation of GZ CD *he dang / i kang* / N *he dang / i gaṃ* P *he dang / i kaṃ* (Skt. *heḍam* means "passion," but also "anger"). However, this phrase may also be some sort of Prakrit (similar problems appear at the end of the section on the dharmamudrā). Compare the opening section of text

70 abounding with Tibetan transliterations of "ḍākinī language," which by definition are supposed to be unintelligible.

2597. GZ CDNP *chos kyi ye shes* is obviously meant as an equivalent of *chos kyi phyag rgya* ("dharmamudrā").
2598. I follow CDNP *gsum pa'o* against GZ *gsum mo.*
2599. *Guhyasamājatantra* II.8. In the last line, GZ NP read *bstan pas so* ("because . . . is taught") and CD *brtan pas so* ("because . . . is steadfast").
2600. Since "unborn" appears in CMA (after "uncontrived") and is commented on below after "realized to be supreme," I add it here at the end of this sentence.
2601. I follow GZ NP *sems can* against CD *sems* ("mind").
2602. I follow GZ NP *med* against CD *ste.*
2603. *Guhyasamājatantra* II.7. GZ CDNP read "essence" instead of "being," "element" (or "realm") instead of "state," and add "thus" in the fourth line.
2604. GZ CDNP *dngos po;* in other texts, this constituent is called "lack of nature" (*rang bzhin med pa*).
2605. As mentioned before, "the seven constituents of union" are usually said to characterize the fruitional state of Vajradhara, the state of unity (*yuganaddha*), the wisdom of the fourth or word empowerment, and the supreme siddhi of mahāmudrā. The primary source for this template in relation to the fourth empowerment is Vāgīśvarakīrti's *Saptāṅga* (see the final note on this topic in Divākaracandra's *Prajñājñānaprakāśa;* text 16, 61). For other explanations of the seven constituents, compare the *Prajñājñānaprakāśa* and Rāmapāla's *Sekanirdeśapañjikā* (text 45, 392–93).
2606. CDNP omit "at which time."
2607. GZ NP *de las rtogs pa* CD *de la rtog pa* ("the thoughts about that"; though less likely, given that the text speaks about object generalities in what follows, this would also make sense here).
2608. I follow NP *nus pa* against GZ CD *nus pas.*
2609. GZ CD *gsal ba* NP *bsal ba* ("dispelled").
2610. GZ *bsal bar byed pa* NP *bsal bar byas pa* CD *gsal bar byed pa* ("illuminates").
2611. NP omit "enmeshed."
2612. GZ *gyis* CDNP *du* ("as").
2613. Here and in the next instance, I follow GZ *rtog pa* against CDNP *rtogs pa* ("realization") because *rtog pa* is compared to poison and contrasted with *rtog pa dang bral ba* ("thought-free") in the next sentence.
2614. GZ NP *dngos med kyis sel na* CD *dngos po dngos med kyis sel na* ("If nonentities are eliminated through nonentities").
2615. *Hevajratantra* I.1.10cd.
2616. *Hevajratantra* I.1.11ab.
2617. I added "waveless" here because it appears in CMA and the commentary below says "the waves of fabrication do not surge."
2618. The text here separates Tib. *'jig rten* ("world"; lit. "support for destruction" or "destructible support") for Skt. *loka* into its components *'jig* and *rten.* This appears to be based on the traditional Indian hermeneutical etymology of *loka* in the **Nighaṇṭu* (Tib. *Sgra sbyor bam gnyis*) as *lujyate* "to destroy," which is explained there as "the basis of destruction for dying and impermanent

sentient beings and so on." The exact same approach is found in text 70 on line 53a, also translated/composed by Prajñāśrījñānakīrti.

2619. The last two lines of this unidentified stanza are also cited in Advayavajra's *Mañjuśrīnāmasaṃgītiṭīkāsārābhisamaya* (D2098, fol. 105a2), where they are attributed to Nāgārjuna.

2620. GZ *mi 'gyur* CDNP *mi sbyong*.

2621. With a slight variant in the third line, the first stanza is *Hevajratantra* I.1.15 and *Saṃvarodayatantra* VII.21. The second three lines are unidentified.

2622. In many Indian and Tibetan commentaries, Skt. *bhagavān* is hermeneutically interpreted as having three meanings, with *bhaga* meaning both "destroy" and "endowed" and *vān* meaning "transcend." These three are also reflected in the term's Tibetan rendering *bcom ldan 'das*. Thus a Bhagavān has destroyed the activities of the four māras of the skandhas, the afflictions, death, and devaputra (being attached to meditative experiences). Second, as for being "endowed," the first quality is "sovereignty" or "mastery": having overpowered all afflictive and cognitive obscurations and being the sole sovereign of the awakened mind. The second quality is to be "endowed with the dharmas"—that is, the dharmakāya qualities of a buddha such as the ten powers, the four fearlessnesses, and the eighteen unique qualities (corresponding to dharmadhātu wisdom). The third quality "fame" refers to the two form kāyas (corresponding to mirror-like wisdom). The fourth, fifth, and sixth qualities—"glory," "wisdom," and "effort"—refer to the wisdom of equality, discriminating wisdom, and all-accomplishing wisdom, respectively. In brief, the six qualities consist of the freedom from all obscurations and the five buddha wisdoms. Third, the syllable *vān* is interpreted as "nir*vāṇ*a," indicating the quality of transcendence, specifically referring to the nonabiding nirvāṇa.

2623. This is a gloss of Tib. *gsung rab* (Skt. *pravacana*) that is clearly based on the Tibetan, given the order of glossing *gsung* and *rab* (as opposed to the opposite order of *pra* and *vacana*).

2624. I follow NP *tshad ma dang ldan* against GZ CD *tshad ma dang mi ldan*.

2625. This could also be read as "in the scriptures and in result reasons." The Buddhist teachings on epistemology and logic (Skt. *pramāṇa*; "valid cognition") generally speak of two kinds of valid cognition: perceptual and inferential, and sometimes scriptural valid cognition is added as a third kind. In inferential valid cognition, proper logical reasons are classified as result reasons (deducing the existence of a cause from the observability of its result), nature reasons (the reason having the same nature as the predicate, such as "sound is impermanent because it is produced"), and reasons of nonobservation (deducing the nonexistence of something from its not being observable). Here, "result reasons" appears to mean that the quoted stanzas are correct because buddhahood (the result) manifests by practicing what they say (the cause). Scriptural valid cognition refers to scriptures that are considered pure by virtue of the following threefold analysis: their teachings on what is perceptible are not contradicted by perceptual valid cognition, their teachings on what is hidden are not contradicted by inferential valid cognition, and their teachings on what is very hidden do not show any contradictions between their own earlier and later words.

2626. I follow CDNP *byed pa* against GZ *'byed pa* ("differentiated").
2627. As mentioned before, Edgerton 1953 (1:106) explains āli as "*a-series* (i.e., a plus āli), name for a series of syllables (chiefly vowels and combinations of a or ā with semivowels)."
2628. As mentioned before, Edgerton 1953 (1:181) explains kāli as "(ka plus āli), *ka-series*, name for a series of syllables beginning with ka (consonants plus a or ā)."
2629. Given the context and the parallel phrase above, GZ CDNP *rgyu ba* ("moving") is emended to *gnas pa*.
2630. As mentioned before, *avadhūta* (from the root "to shake (off)") is understood in Indian Buddhist and non-Buddhist traditions as referring to persons who have reached a level on their spiritual path where they have shaken off or are beyond any ego-based consciousness, duality, common worldly concerns, and standard social norms. Though it cannot be completely excluded that the glossing of avadhūtī here is how *Kāropa explained it, it is rather clear that glossing each part ("evil" and "shaker") of the paraphrasing Tibetan rendering of avadhūtī and even its female ending *ma* is a hermeneutical etymology that is based on the Tibetan rendering *sdig spangs ma*. Curiously, the following sentence then uses the Sanskrit *avadhūtī*.
2631. Again, to gloss each part of Tib. *dbus nyid* (rather than *madhyadeśa* in the Sanskrit of *Hevajratantra* I.1.15c) is clearly a hermeneutical etymology that is based on the Tibetan.
2632. I follow GZ NP *rnam par spangs pa* against CD *rnam pa*.
2633. GZ *don dam* CDNP *don* ("the goal/actuality").
2634. GZ *gong du* CDNP *gang du* ("as what").
2635. For details on these three, see below (354–55).
2636. GZ CD *nges par bya ba'i phyir* NP *nges par bya ba ni de bas na*.
2637. GZ CDNP add "secret."
2638. *Hevajratantra* I.5.11.
2639. Given that the text repeatedly said appearances are unborn, I follow GZ *snang ba skye ba med pa dang sems skye ba med pa* against CD *snang ba skye ba dang sems skye med* ("born appearances and unborn mind") NP *snang ba skye ba dang sems skye ba* ("born appearances and born mind").
2640. Compare also the comments on *Uttaratantra* I.154 in Vajrapāṇi's *Guruparamparākramopadeśa* in the context of both the Madhyamaka of utter nonabiding and mahāmudrā (text 213, 194–95 and 225–36).
2641. I follow CDNP *rab tu 'dar ba* against GZ *rab tu bdar ba*.
2642. As mentioned before, depending on different calculations, this ancient Indian measure of distance has a range of about seven to fifteen kilometers, most commonly about thirteen.
2643. I follow GZ *rgyal po la* against CD *rgyal po'i* NP *rgyal pos*.
2644. The better-known version of this story is found in the Saṃyutta Nikāya (V.47.20; Bhikkhu Bodhi 2000, 2:1649) as an example for mindfulness of the body. In the town Sedaka, a huge crowd gathered to see the most beautiful woman of the land presenting an exquisite show of singing and dancing.

During that event, a man was given a bowl full of oil to carry without spilling anything, accompanied by another man, with sword drawn, ordered to behead him if he spilled even a drop. The man managed to safely carry the bowl with complete mindfulness, not becoming distracted for even a single moment by the show or the hustle and bustle of the large crowd.

2645. GZ *gzung* CDNP *khyer* ("carries").
2646. I follow GZ *'bo ba* CDNP *'thor ba* against NP *'khor ba* ("circling").
2647. Given the sequence here, I follow NP *rtog pa* against GZ CD *rtogs pa* ("realization").
2648. Given the context, the parallel phrase in the third line of the second stanza, and the comments below, GZ CDNP *bcos myong* ("contrived experience") is emended to *bcas myong*.
2649. Tib. *star bu* renders Skt. *amlavetasa* (*Rumex vesicarius*), which has a sour taste.
2650. I follow GZ *gnod pa* against CDNP *snang ba* ("appear").
2651. *Hevajratantra* II.4.61cd. GZ CDNP read the last line as "because a small action has a great result."
2652. GZ *ar tar ta du da e a aṃ sar* CD *a ta ra ta ngu da . . .* NP *a ta ra ta du da . . .* Maybe *artarta* is corrupt for *arthārtha* ("effective for the accomplishment of the aim in view") and *sar* for *sāra* ("essence").
2653. "Involuntarily"; GZ CDNP *a ka ma ta sa*.
2654. This refers to the story of a wrestler who used to wear a jewel on his forehead. Eventually, through his bouts, this jewel became absorbed into his skin and thus invisible. He searched for it everywhere on the outside, until someone pointed out that it was right there under his forehead's skin.
2655. I follow GZ *dug la sngags kyis btab ba* NP *dug sngags kyis btul ba* against CD *sdug bsngal kyis brtul ba* ("tamed by suffering").
2656. GZ *dam tshig gis las chen po gsum* CDNP *dam tshig dang gsum* ("the three").
2657. GZ repeats the above sentence "Since it is both great and a seal, it is the great seal" as the beginning of this quote too.
2658. CDNP GZ *rtag chad* "permanence and extinction."
2659. GZ "the single flame of being unborn from all kinds of phenomena."
2660. *Mañjuśrīnāmasaṃgīti* IX.23c.
2661. As mentioned before, the *Avikalpapraveśadhāraṇī* speaks of four conceptions in terms of (1) nature (perceiver and perceived or the five skandhas), (2) remedies (the six pāramitās), (3) true reality (emptiness and its equivalents), and (4) attainment (the ten bhūmis of bodhisattvas and buddhahood with all their qualities). These four characteristics are relinquished in a gradual manner by means of analyzing their nature, their qualities, and their essence, and finally by not mentally engaging in them at all (for the section on relinquishing these characteristics, see Brunnhölzl 2012, 330–31). Here, our text implicitly refers to the first one among these conceptions while explicitly referring to the last three, calling them "hopes."
2662. GZ *lam du slong ba* CDNP *dbang du slong ba* ("mastered").
2663. NP omit "lacks."
2664. *Hevajratantra* II.2.39–40. GZ CDNP show minor variants, the only significant one being a switch of the third and fourth lines in II.2.40 and GZ CD reading the fourth line rather nonsensically as "What is the means to know the hole

thus?" and NP reading it as "What is the son, what is the means to know thus?" (instead of "In this way, my son . . .").

2665. GZ *la gzhag* CDNP *la gnas* ("are present in").

2666. Compare the presentations of the five features of mahāmudrā and its relationship with the four kāyas below (361–62) and in Vajrapāṇi's *Guruparamparākramopadeśa* (text 213, 227–33), which appears to include the description of the three kāyas under the last of the five features.

2667. With the minor exception "is without death" (GZ CDNP *'chi med*) instead of "lacks bondage" (*'ching med* as in texts 68 and 70), these four lines are only found as lines 44cd–45ab of the unique enlarged version of Saraha's "People Dohā" in text 68 and its commentary in text 70, also translated/composed by Prajñāśrījñānakīrti. Thus, this is further clear evidence that Prajñāśrījñānakīrti is also the translator/redactor of text 44. The first two lines are quite close to the canonical version of "People Dohā" 32cd (text 13; Apa 29cd), and the third line has some resemblance with 33a (Apa 30a).

2668. These two lines are also from the "People Dohā" (Apa 70cd; text 13, 86cd; text 69, 110ef).

2669. Together, these three lines are only found as stanza 105 of the version of the "People Dohā" in texts 68 and 70. The first two lines also correspond literally to the canonical version of "People Dohā" 84cd (text 13, 84c, no correspondence in Apa, 84d, corresponding only partially to Apa 68c), while the third line has only a partial resemblance with 84e (no correspondence in Apa).

2670. As it stands, this line is only found as line 106a of the version of the "People Dohā" in texts 68 and 70; it is similar to the canonical version of "People Dohā" 84f (text 13; Apa 68d). Note that, with the significant exception of the passage that contains the quotes from the "People Dohā," our text's explanation of mahāmudrā up to this point is very similar, sometimes verbatim, to the beginning of the explanation of mahāmudrā in Vajrapāṇi's *Guruparamparākramopadeśa* (text 213, 225–27) and there are also further parallels below.

2671. GZ *de'ang ji ltar gyur* CDNP *de'ang ji ltar blta* ("How is this to be regarded?").

2672. It is not clear who that might be: maybe a reference to Maitrīpa or, given the role of Prajñāśrījñānakīrti in the history of this text, even *Kāropa.

2673. Here and below, GZ CDNP *se* is emended to *si*.

2674. CDNP omit *med* ("without"), thus saying something like "nonengagement is engaging in engagement."

2675. GZ *ma na sya* CDNP *ma na sye* are emended in accordance with the parallel *amanasi* above.

2676. I follow GZ *rtog pa byed pa* against CD *rtogs pa med pa* ("without realization") NP *rtog pa med pa* ("without thoughts"). While the glosses of *a* and *mana(s)* here in the phrase *amanasi(kāra)* are standard, to literally gloss *si*, which in itself is not even a syllable in *amanasikāra*, as "engagement" (*kāra*), rather than glossing the locative *-i* as "in," is certainly anything but grammatical. The proper connection between *manas* and *-i* is glossed somewhat clearer (disregarding the switch to *manasya* with a grammatically wrong genitive ending) in the phrase "*manasi*—that is, engagement in thoughts," but *kāra* (as the equivalent of "engagement") is again missing in the Sanskrit. It is hardly conceivable that an erudite Indian master such as *Kāropa would himself present such a truncated and questionable hermeneutical etymology of *amanasikāra*.

2677. GZ *blta ba* CDNP *brtag pa* ("conceived," "examined").
2678. GZ CDNP *dag sha ka*.
2679. Since this paragraph and the following are very close to Rāmapāla's *Sekanirdeśapañjikā* on stanzas 29–31, the awkward repeated *bka' drin* ("the kindness that is endowed with . . .") is emended to *mtshan nyid*.
2680. This corresponds to the Tibetan rendering of *Sekanirdeśa* 29c.
2681. CDNP read both the objection and the following sentence in GZ as the following single sentence: "After what is conceivable has been analyzed, at the [subsequent] time of no conception, this is described as the nonconceptuality of the effortless wisdom in which no conceiving occurs."
2682. CDNP omit "self-."
2683. Given the context of Madhyamaka and as elsewhere in the text, the classical template of being beyond the four extremes seems to be the most likely meaning here, but this phrase could also be read as "beyond permanence, extinction, duality, and nonduality" (which is maybe supported by the explanation in the following paragraph). CDNP read "beyond the nonduality of permanence and extinction."
2684. This is a variant version of *Jñānālokālaṃkārasūtra* IV.12, *Saṃvarodayatantra* VIII.36' (Tsuda 1974, 101), and *Pañcakrama* IV.10.
2685. I follow GZ *goms pa byed pa* against CDNP *goms pa med pa* ("not familiarizing").
2686. I follow GZ *ma ri sha dag bskrun* against CD *ma ri sha dag srung* NP *ma rig sha dag srun*; Skt. *māriṣa* is Amaranthus tricolor.
2687. CDNP mistakenly add *shing* ("tree").
2688. CDNP omit the negative.
2689. A nyagrodha tree (banyan tree) is a species of fig that typically begins its life as an epiphyte (a plant that grows on another plant), with its seed sprouting in a crack or crevice of a host tree or a building (usually growing in woodlands, any of its seeds that fall to the ground are unlikely to survive). When growing, banyans send aerial roots down to the ground and envelop part of the host tree, thus also being called "strangler figs."
2690. I follow GZ *grags chen gyi sa* against CDNP *grags chen gyis* ("through great renown"); "great renown" is a general epithet for bodhisattvas.
2691. GZ CDNP *a*.
2692. I follow CDNP *mtha' thams cad dang bral ba* against GZ *thabs dang bral ba* ("free from the means").
2693. Compare the similar explanations of HŪṂ in Maitrīpa's *Sekatātparyasaṃgraha* (text 37, 199) and Rāmapāla's *Sekanirdeśapañjikā* (text 45, 409).
2694. I follow GZ CD *gzhan pa* against NP *gnas pa* ("abide").
2695. I follow GZ *khas 'ches pa* against CD *las 'ches pa* NP *khas mches pa*.
2696. I follow GZ *smon pa* against CD *dgos pa* ("need") NP *smos pa* ("say").
2697. I follow GZ *gzhan gyi don spyod pa* against CDNP *gzhan gyi(s) spyod pa* ("conduct by (of) others").
2698. Given the parallel structure of the other sentences here and the double *la* in *sgrub pa po dag la . . . gnas pa dag la*, the latter is emended to *gnas pa dag gis*.
2699. *Pramāṇavārttika* III.285 and *Pramāṇaviniścaya* I.31. In the last line, I follow GZ

NP *blo 'bras* against CD *dgos pa* ("need"). GZ CDNP render Skt. *tat* as *bde* instead of *de*, thus adding "blissful" (probably in an attempt to complete the standard triad of meditation experiences: bliss, clarity, and nonthought). The same happens in the same quote in GZ of Rāmapāla's *Sekanirdeśapañjikā* (text 45, 390).

2700. I follow GZ *bsgrub bya* against CDNP *sgrub pa*.
2701. NP omit everything in this paragraph up to here.
2702. GZ *rtogs pa* CDNP *rtog pa* ("thoughts")
2703. I follow GZ CD *smon pa* against NP *snod pa* ("vessel").
2704. CDNP omit "and medium."
2705. I follow GZ *dam bcas pa* against CDNP *dang bcas pa* ("possesses").
2706. I follow GZ NP *dgon pa* against CD *mgon po* ("protectors").
2707. This is rather strange, since the supreme siddhi usually *is* the siddhi of mahāmudrā.
2708. CDNP omit "gather."
2709. CDNP omit "one should perform."
2710. I follow GZ *shes pa dvangs par* against CDNP *shes pa dang bral bar* ("to free from cognition").
2711. I follow GZ NP *bdag dag par bya ba* against CDNP *brtags par bya ba* ("to examine" or "to imagine").
2712. GZ CD *lha'i 'khor lo la lha'i 'khor lo'i rnam pa* NP *lha'i rnam pa* em. *lha'i 'khor lo la lha'i rnam pa*.
2713. According to *Hevajratantra* I.3.11ab, the *a*-series corresponds to the moon and the *ka*-series to the sun.
2714. I follow GZ CD *rtse gcig pa ste* against NP *brtsegs pa* ("stacked").
2715. *Guhyasamājatantra* XVII.50. In the last line, GZ CDNP omit "supreme" and replace "bodhisattva" with "ḍākinī."
2716. Given the context, GZ CDNP *rjes thob kyi rnal 'byor* ("the yoga of subsequent attainment") is emended to *rjes su rnal 'byor*.
2717. I follow GZ *lam gyi rtogs pa ro* against CD *lam gyi rtog pa dang ro* ("taste and the thoughts of the path"); except for "taste," NP omit this phrase.
2718. I follow GZ CD *gser* against NP *ster* ("give").
2719. GZ *'khor lo* CD *'khor lor* NP *'khor lo sgyur* ("turning the wheel").
2720. Given the comments below, I follow NP *bral ba* against GZ CD *bral bas*.
2721. I follow GZ NP *ma rig pa* against CD *rig pa*.
2722. I follow GZ CD *las kyi phyag rgya* against NP *las bya ba'i phyag rgya*.
2723. I follow GZ CD *brtags pa* against NP *rtag pa* ("permanent").
2724. I follow GZ CD *gser* against NP *gter* ("treasure").
2725. I follow GZ *lam* against CDNP *las* ("activity").
2726. I follow CDNP *rtogs pa* against GZ *ma rtogs pa* ("nonrealization").
2727. I follow GZ NP *'bras bu rnams* against CD *'bras bu'i rnam*.
2728. I follow GZ *lus* against CDNP *las* ("activity" or "karma").
2729. Given the comments below, GZ CDNP *dag ni* (dual) is emended to *bdag nyid*.
2730. As mentioned before, somewhat similar versions of this stanza are also cited in Devacandra's *Prajñājñānaprakāśa* (text 16, 71; attributed to Nāgārjuna), Sahajavajra's *Sthitisamāsa* (text 17, 105), Maitrīpa's *Pañcatathāgatamudrāvivaraṇa* (text 36, 196; attributed to Nāgārjuna), Muniśrībhadra's *Pañcakramaṭip-*

paṇī Yogīmanoharā (fol. 24a.4–5; see Mathes 2015, 103n272), and GZ's version of CMA (text 14, 32–33). The version here is the most divergent one of all, but the following comments match it exactly.

2731. GZ CDNP *gsal ba* ("to be clearly manifested") em. *bsal ba*.
2732. Against the stanza and GZ, CDNP read "all these maṇḍalas (the supports), practitioners, deities, three realms, and what appears as diversity."
2733. I follow CDNP *'khrul par byed pa* against GZ *'khrul par bya ba* ("to be made deluded").
2734. Everything that follows from here up through the end of page 377 is an insertion that does not comment on the words of CMA and uses the Tibetan outline system. The remaining comments on the samayamudrā in CMA resume thereafter.
2735. For the details of how the four ecstasies also exist in the dharmamudrā and even the samayamudrā, see the *Guruparamparākramopadeśa* (text 213, 222–24, and 236–37).
2736. GZ *gdams ngag* CDNP *ngag*.
2737. I follow GZ NP *lugs* against CD *lus* ("body").
2738. These four lines are *Sarvarahasyatantra* 30 (H449, fol. 4a.5–6), though the tantra has them in a different order (c, d, b, a); compare the literal quote in the *Sekanirdeśapañjikā* (text 45, 434).
2739. GZ CD *grags* NP *grangs* ("enumeration," "specification").
2740. Except for the additional first line, this is a variant of a stanza from the (unidentified) *Devendraparipṛcchātantra* that was already quoted above (261). It is not clear whether "utter nonabiding" (GZ CDNP *rab tu mi gnas pa*; Skt. *apratiṣṭhita* or *apratiṣṭhāna*) is (a) the name of an actual text or (b) shorthand for the Madhyamaka approach of Maitrīpa and his students. Option (a) may be suggested by the fact that Prajñāśrījñānakīrti is the translator/redactor of both text 44 and 70, that text 70 frequently quotes from an otherwise unknown *Apratiṣṭhitatantra*, and that all quotations in text 44 attributed to "utter nonabiding" appear in this insertion here, which is obviously by Prajñāśrījñānakīrti. However, option (b) seems to be more likely because here and in the two other quotations attributed to "utter nonabiding" below, at least some of the lines of these quotations are attributed to other texts elsewhere. In this vein, compare the similar use of the expression "the Madhyamaka of unity," indicating Maitrīpa's Madhyamaka approach, that precedes a series of quotes in Sahajavajra's *Tattvadaśakaṭīkā* (text 46, 43).
2741. As stated in the introduction, these five are kriyātantras, caryātantras, yogatantras, yogottaratantras, and yoganiruttaratantras.
2742. This unidentified line was already quoted above (259); CD omit "appearance."
2743. GZ *dag snang* CDNP *rags snang* ("coarse appearances"); though a passage on cessational ecstasy below (352) characterizes it as "coarse appearances" in both GZ and CDNP, the context here seems somewhat different in that this passage explicitly speaks about realization.
2744. *Hevajratantra* II.3.4.
2745. The first two lines here are virtually identical to the first two lines of a stanza attributed to the *Devendraparipṛcchātantra* in Amṛtavajra's *Dokakoṣapañjikā* (text 64, 235) and Rāmapāla's *Sekanirdeśapañjikā* (text 45, 384), while the third

and fourth lines are similar to the last two lines of the following stanza in said tantra.

2746. Given that there are two parallel sentences elsewhere in this text, GZ CDNP *nā da bas so* is emended to *yod pas so*.

2747. I follow GZ *rang rig pa* NP *rang rig* against CD *rang gi ba*.

2748. I follow GZ NP *ngan pa* against CD *nges pa* ("certain").

2749. GZ CDNP *rdo rje bum pa* (lit. "vajra vase") must render Skt. *vajragolaka* (one of the several meanings of *golaka* besides "vase" or "jar" is "glans penis").

2750. "The aperture of the lord of the family" and "the crown of the beauty's head" refer to the lower openings of the avadhūtī in the male and the female. IaS (404) comments as follows on "the crown of the beauty's head": "Left uncommented on, a reader might mistakenly think that it is a location in the head of the female that is meant. In fact, however, *mdzes ma* (*spyi bo*, we propose, means here the tip, in the sense of the [lower] end) is rather the name of a channel in the Lotus; it is attested elsewhere as a rendering of Sanskrit *lalanā*. Here in fact it should be understood to be used basically as a synonym of *kiñjalka* or of *naranāsikā*; the location in which the three principal channels are supposed to have their lower end in a female."

2751. GZ CDNP read the two sentences in this paragraph that begin with "As for two remaining . . ." as ". . . the one that remains at the aperture of the lord of the family is the bindu of Vajradhara—that is, being empty. The one that remains at the crown of the beauty's head is Akṣobhya—that is, bliss." However, an almost identical passage in Vajrapāṇi's *Guruparamparākramopadeśa* (text 213, 218) correctly matches the bindu at the aperture of the lord of the family (male) with Akṣobhya, and the bindu at the crown of the beauty's head (female) with Vajrasattva (or Vajradhara): "The one that remains at the aperture of the lord of the family is Akṣobhya—that is, the experience of self-awareness itself is the means. The one that remains at the crown of the beauty's head is Vajrasattva—that is, emptiness, the lack of any nature, is prajñā. Vajrasattva (the result) sealing Akṣobhya (the cause) eliminates the extreme of permanence, and thus experience itself is rendered lacking any nature. Akṣobhya in turn sealing Vajrasattva eliminates the extreme of extinction, and thus the very lack of any nature is rendered experience. In that way, experience and emptiness are a unity." Also, Vajrapāṇi correctly identifies Akṣobhya as the cause and Vajrasattva as the result (as opposed to GZ CDNP switching these here). In addition, the *Guruparamparākramopadeśa* later (237) says this: "The two bindus that remain in the middle of the moon and the sun represent luminosity and emptiness. The bindu that touches the moon [below] represents prajñā (emptiness). The bindu that touches the sun above represents luminosity (means). The inseparability of the two means that they seal each other, which is unity. This constitutes the moment of the lack of characteristics." Furthermore, unlike in GZ CDNP here, bliss is usually identified with the male and emptiness with the female. For all these reasons, I have switched the matching of the two bindus with Akṣobhya (bliss) and Vajrasattva (empty). Note that it is only with this significant emendation that the statement in IaS (405) about *Kāropa being "in complete agreement with Vajrapāṇi on this point" is correct.

2752. These are the last three lines of an unidentified stanza already quoted above (287); as mentioned before, the first and second lines also correspond to *Sekoddeśa* 146cd as well as *Guhyasamājatantra* XVIII.79ab.

2753. Though GZ CDNP omit the initial "I," these two lines are clearly *Hevajratantra* II.2.40ab (line b is also found in II.5.65b and II.5.69e).

2754. I follow NP *dbus su gang zhig rig 'gyur ba* against GZ *dbus su gang zhig rigs 'gyur ba* CD *'bras bu gang zhig rigs 'gyur ba* ("the result that will be suitable"). Given the context, it could very well be that this line—at least as per NP and GZ—is in fact a corrupt version of the first line (Farrow and Menon 1992 *tatra madhye 'ham vidye*, Snellgrove 1959 *vidyate*, all mss. *vidyāt*) of *Hevajratantra* II.5.7:

> It is there in the middle that I am,
> together with you, oh lovely one,
> impassioned with great passion,
> as connate ecstasy's own nature.

2755. GZ CDNP *gsang bar smra ba* (lit. "those who speak about secrets/those who speak secretly") is an unusual but attested rendering of Skt. *upaniṣadvādī.*

2756. Lines 4–6 and 8 of this quote parallel the first four lines of an unidentified stanza quoted above (287). Together, the last six lines here are found in Indrabhūti's *Śrīcakrasaṃvaratantrarājaśambarasamuccayanāmavṛtti* (D1413, fol. 98b.1–2). As they stand in Indrabhūti's text, they are not found in any other work, nor are they marked in any way as a quotation, so they are in all probability the commentator's own words. These six lines are immediately followed by the following four:

> The Yogācāra, the Madhyamaka,
> the great Madhyamaka, and so on
> are refuted by utter nonabiding—
> this is what represents great bliss

It is not clear what the assertions of Vedānta, the Upaniṣads, Kambala, and "the great Madhyamaka" in Indrabhūti's text here are. However, given that *Kāropa was a student of Maitrīpa, the references to Vedānta and the Upaniṣads here are probably the Vedānta position of Bhāskara and the Upaniṣad teachings in the *Bhagavadsiddhānta* as specified in Maitrīpa's *Tattvaratnāvalī* (text 34, 177, 181–82) and *Sekanirdeśa* 12–15, as well as in Rāmapāla's *Sekanirdeśapañjikā* on those stanzas. As for Kambala's position, if one assumes that this name refers to the Yogācāra master who wrote the *Ālokamālā*, this would not match Maitrīpa's *Pañcatathāgatamudrāvivaraṇa* (text 36, 194–95) quoting *Ālokamālā* (248) in support of his own correct Madhyamaka position of awareness not abiding as anything whatsoever and yet being the unborn continuous flow of effortless nondual unity. Similarly, Rāmapāla's *Sekanirdeśapañjikā* (text 45, 405–6) cites *Ālokamālā* (248 and 274) in support of the excellent empowerment, in which Akṣobhya must be properly sealed with Vajrasattva (or Vajradhara) so as to counteract any reification of awareness with emptiness. Thus it is not clear at all which position of Kambala is said to be refuted here. In particular, it is hard to see how Kambala would assert duality instead of nonduality (his *Ālokamālā* denies duality). Maybe the text here refers to Kambala being portrayed as a "Nonaspectarian Mādhyamika" in Sahajavajra's *Tattvadaśakaṭīkā* (text 46, 15–16), which is said there not to be the supreme Madhyamaka view. However, the stanzas cited from the *Ālokamālā* there also include stanzas 248 and 274 and otherwise explicitly deny duality. Alternatively, given that the context here is clearly tantric, one may assume that "Kambala" does not refer to the Yogācāra master but to the mahāsiddha of the same name. However, it seems very unlikely that a mahāsiddha would be refuted, let alone a mahāsiddha who supposedly asserts any kind of duality. The expression "great Madhyamaka" is defined in a number of ways in different works in Tg; for example, a commentary on the *Saṃpuṭatilakatantra* (D1197, fol. 213b.5) ascribed to (an) Indrabhūti defines it as "the sheer essence of entities."

2757. GZ *dga' bral gyi lhan cig skyes pa spyad pas dga' ba gsum pa lhan cig skyes par khyer ram 'gyur* ("by experiencing the connate [ecstasy] of cessational ecstasy, the third ecstasy is integrated or . . .") CDNP *dga' bral gyis lhan cig skyes pa spyad pas dga' ba gsum lhan cig skyes par 'gyur* [NP *'gyer*, "is abandoned"]. Given the context, I follow CD while adding GZ's *khyer ram*.

2758. See above, 305.

2759. This is the fifth and most advanced of the five forms of conduct in the Vajrayāna. According to TOK (3:543 and 551), "the conduct that is victorious in all directions" has its name because it is truly victorious over the afflictions, tames the four māras, has the power to promote the welfare of sentient beings, and also relinquishes the cognitive obscurations. Once the greater degree of the level of heat on the path of preparation is reached, one engages in "the conduct that is victorious in all directions." This entails relying on goddesses as one's consorts and invoking Vajrasattva so as to enable one to more or less immediately experience the path of seeing. This conduct is then maintained as the primary one until the attainment of full awakening. For details on all five forms of conduct, see note 2756 in volume 3.

2760. Though GZ CDNP vary considerably here, there is no doubt that this is *Hevajratantra* I.8.34 (already quoted above, 289–90). GZ CDNP:

> It is the wisdom that is connate
> that is not found by other means,
> known by yourself by relying on
> the guru's timely means or merits.

2761. GZ CDNP *de nyid* could also mean "exactly that," but the same expression is explicitly repeated in the fourfold outline of pursuing the karmamudrā, dharmamudrā, mahāmudrā, and samayamudrā below, as well as in the headings of each one of those sections. To say "exactly that" each time seems awkward and redundant, so it is more likely that *de nyid* means true reality in each case.

2762. CD omit "the pith instructions on" and NP omit the entire point 3.

2763. I follow CDNP *nyams su blang ba* against GZ *nyams su myong ba* ("experience") because when this point is discussed below, GZ also has *nyams su blang ba*.

2764. Compare the parallel passage below (364) saying that those who have the very highest, highest, medium, and lower fortunes accomplish mahāmudrā, dharmamudrā, karmamudrā, and samayamudrā, respectively.

2765. GZ CDNP have five lines, obviously very corrupt:

> The karmamudrā is to be cultivated
> On top of that, mahāmudrā
> Just this is the mudrā to be cultivated [or "True reality's mudrā is to be cultivated"; NP "samayamudrā"]
> On top of that, mahāmudrā
> Exactly that is the samayamudrā

Thus, I replaced it with *Sekanirdeśa* 26, which is the only attested stanza that is somewhat close to this stanza. As IaS (306–7n294) points out, *Sekanirdeśa* 26 is also cited in the *Prajñājñānaprakāśa* (text 16, 58), an Advayavajra's **Āryamañjuśrīnāmasaṃgītiṭīkāsārābhisamaya* (D2098, fol. 106b.5), and Raviśrījñāna's *Amṛtakaṇikā* (Banarsi Lal 1994, 95; attributed to the *Vairocanābhisambodhitantra* but not found there). IaS adds here that this stanza may not be by Maitrīpa originally, but taken (or modified) by him from some yogatantra source (maybe thus the attribution here). Lastly, a stanza whose first two lines are very similar but whose last two are very different is found in an Indrabhūti's *Śrīcakrasaṃvaratantrarājaśambarasamuccayanāmavṛtti* (D1413, fol. 99a.2–3):

> Having relied upon the karmamudrā,
> you should cultivate the dharmamudrā
> Blissful empty true reality is mahāmudrā
> What is unchanging is the samayamudrā.

2766. GZ CDNP *mi gnas* ("is not present") em. *ni gnas*.
2767. GZ *bde stong dbyer med* CDNP *bden pa dbyer med* ("inseparable reality(ies)").
2768. I follow CD *'bras bu gang thob pa'o* against GZ *'bras bu gang thob pas gang thob pa'o* NP *'bras bu gang thob pa dang*.
2769. Given the above comments, I follow GZ CD triple *rigs* against NP triple *rig*.
2770. I follow GZ *de steng zla ba'i* CD *de'i steng zla yi* against NP *de stengs mda'i*.
2771. Between the section "2a2. sealing with which mudrā" and the following section "2a3. through what it is accomplished," the text prematurely inserts the much later section "3. [The pith instructions on] the special means." Hence I shifted this latter section to its correct place after the section "2d7. which result is attained" (page 365; see also the outline in appendix 5). Despite this shift, for orientation in GZ, I retain its page numbers in { }.
2772. I follow NP *rig pa* against GZ CD *rig ma* because what follows is a comment on "awareness," while "consort" (or rather the feminine ending *ma*) is explained thereafter.
2773. I follow NP *mtshan ldan* against GZ CD *mtshan dang mtshan ldan*.
2774. I follow GZ *mi skrag pas shes so* against CD *mi skrag pas zhes so* NP *mi sred pas shes so*.
2775. It is not exactly clear how this passage matches the three causes, because the first three clauses in the first sentence are separated in GZ while CDNP read all three as one. However, it seems that the three causes consist of "She has made special aspiration prayers . . . embraced by the guru's instructions," "a beautiful face" (though that is repeated in the following list of seven causes), and "not being afraid of what is profound."
2776. For more details on "connate appearance" and "connate mind as such," see

the final note on the cited stanza that immediately precedes *Sthitisamāsa* VI.39 (text 17, 108), the comments on the opening stanza of Saraha's "People Dohā" in text 70 (10–11), and the note on the first stanza of dedication at the end of text 70 (171) in volume 4.

2777. GZ *mnyam* CDNP *myong* ("experience").
2778. This is a sentence that is found in the opening sections of many tantras, such as the *Hevajratantra*, the *Guhyasamājatantra*, the tantras of red and black Yamāri, and several Cakrasaṃvara tantras. Kṛṣṇa's *Yogaratnamālā* commentary on the *Hevajratantra* (Snellgrove 1959, 2:103) explains that "the bhagas" (vaginas) are those of the vajra ladies such as Locanā (the consort of Vairocana) because their bodies have the dharmatā of infinite uncontaminated dharmas. "The body, speech, and mind of all tathāgatas" is a distinctive feature of "the bhagas of these vajra ladies." The Bhagavān, together with his retinue, having obtained residence there, spends his time in this mansion at the top that is the most secret of secret abodes. Note though that, given the comments below, it seems our author reads the Tibetan of the cited passage here as "the body, speech, and mind of all tathāgatas are dwelling in the bhagas of the vajra ladies."
2779. Given the context, I follow CDNP *thig le byang chub sems* against GZ *thig le dang byang chub sems* ("bindu and bodhicitta").
2780. I follow GZ *rgyud* against CDNP *rgyu* ("cause").
2781. NP omit "and."
2782. GZ CDNP *yid la med par bya ba nyid* em. *yid la bya bar med pa nyid*.
2783. Or "unborn dreams."
2784. GZ *rang gnang* CDNP *rang gnas* ("are present in oneself").
2785. NP omit "un-."
2786. The last line resembles *Hevajratantra* II.3.2a and *Saṃvarodayatantra* III.17c.
2787. I follow GZ CD *skud par* against NP *skur mar*.
2788. As mentioned before, the text repeatedly says that mahāmudrā is free of *dgag sgrub*, which can mean "affirmation and negation" or "creating and blocking." Below, *dgag sgrub* in this context is explicitly glossed as "one's own view is not affirmed and the views of others are not negated," but here the meaning is clearly not "affirmation and negation."
2789. CDNP omit "because . . . are."
2790. CDNP omit "because . . . exists."
2791. CD have the last two sentences as a single shorter one: "Meditation is uncreated, because self-arising exists on its own accord" (*rab chas* em. *rang chas*).
2792. As mentioned before, these three correspond to the last three among the *Avikalpapraveśadhāraṇī*'s four conceptions in terms of (1) nature (perceiver and perceived or the five skandhas), (2) remedies (the six pāramitās), (3) true reality (emptiness and its equivalents), and (4) attainment (the ten bhūmis and buddhahood).
2793. I follow GZ CD *de nyid bral* against NP *de gnyis 'bras*.
2794. The text here omits point "2c6b5. being omnitemporal." In its comments on these five features above (321), what is said in this sentence here is the explanation of "pervading [all] times," while "being changeless" is explained as follows: "Though diversity appears from this very [mahāmudrā], it lacks

even the slightest change, just as in the examples of space never changing from being space despite clouds, rainbows, and so on appearing in it and water never changing from being water [despite] waves, silt, bubbles, ripples, and so on."

2795. GZ CDNP *ming gzhan* ("other name") em. *mi gzhan*.

2796. GZ CDNP *'bras bu dang dri ma dang bral ba'i 'bras bu* ("the result and the result of stainlessness") em. *'bras bu ni dri ma dang bral ba'i 'bras bu*.

2797. Given the parallel comments on mahāmudrā above (325; likewise closely based on the explanation of mahāmudrā in CMA; text 14, 31) and the parallel explanations in Rāmapāla's *Sekanirdeśapañjikā* on stanzas 26 and 29–30, GZ CDNP *spyad pa* ("conduct" or "experience") is emended to *dpyod pa*.

2798. CDNP "Thus it is suitable for it to be free from these eight stains."

2799. Jñānakīrti's *Tattvāvatāra* (text 214, 248) contains a stanza whose first two lines are very similar and which, with some variations and without attribution, is also quoted in Maitrīpa's *Kudṛṣṭinighātana* (text 19, 125), Sahajavajra's *Tattvadaśakaṭīkā* (text 46, 11), Kṛṣṇa Paṇḍitā's *Hevajratantrapañjikā* (D1187, fol. 147a.3–4), Phalavajra's *Samantabhadrasādhananāmavṛtti* (D1867, fol. 182b.2), Advayavajra's *Āryamañjuśrīnāmasaṃgītiṭīkāsārābhisamaya* (D2098, fol. 107a.7–107b.1), and Munīndrabhadra's *Vajradhātumahāmaṇḍalopāyikāsarvavajrodayanāmapiṇḍārtha* (D2529, fol. 192a.3–4).

2800. NP omit "maturing as."

2801. GZ CDNP *rab 'bring gsum* is a common abbreviation for "highest, medium, and lower."

2802. NP omit "highest."

2803. As mentioned before, the nine approaches in texts by Maitrīpa and his students consist of lower, medium, and highest śrāvakas, pratyekabuddhas, and the three kinds of Mahāyānists: Sautrāntikas (lower), Aspectarian and Nonaspectarian Yogācāras (medium), and Mādhyamikas of illusion-like nonduality and utter nonabiding (highest).

2804. I follow GZ NP *gnyis* against CD *bzhi* ("four").

2805. I follow GZ CD *snang nas* against NP *gnang na* ("if given").

2806. I follow GZ NP *rgyu* against CD *rgyud* ("continuum").

2807. As mentioned before, in GZ CDNP, section "3. [The pith instructions on] the special means" was prematurely inserted between the above sections "2a2. with which mudrā there is sealing" and "2a3. through what it is accomplished" (see also the outline in appendix 5). For orientation in GZ, I retain its page numbers in { }.

2808. *Hevajratantra* I.1.26 and II.3.6ab.

2809. *Hevajratantra* I.1.29. It is curious that the text here, as well as below under (4), cites the sequence of the four moments and the four ecstasies in the *Hevajratantra* that is at odds with the sequence that it defends everywhere else (that is, switching connate ecstasy and cessational ecstasy).

2810. I follow GZ *'das* against CDNP *bzlas*.

2811. As IaS (407) points out, these five lines also appear in Indrabhūti's *Śrīcakrasaṃvaratantrarājaśambarasamuccayanāmavṛtti* (D1413, fol. 98a.2; without further explanation). However, pace IaS, these lines are neither a full stanza nor, in all probability, a quotation but Indrabhūti's own words. For these five lines are preceded by another initial line, and, like many other versified passages in this commentary, they are in no way marked as a quotation, whereas certain other passages are so marked. IaS (408) comments as follows: "Of course this verse itself sounds as if it presupposes, or to put it another way, is, in part, a commentary of sorts on, our first Apabhraṃśa stanza. Nonetheless, if it is indeed a pre-*Karopa (and pre-Indrabhūti; though in any case it is not easy to precisely date this Indrabhūti at present) work, it is at least possible that it gives us a glimpse of an interpretation of that stanza that is independent of Maitreyanātha's teaching. Unfortunately the verse does not unambiguously support either the '2 + 2 interpretation' or the '1 + 1 interpretation'. We have the impression that it is likely to have been written from the standpoint of the latter; but it may still be possible to argue that 'two are equal' might mean 'two remain the same (i.e. on the side of the Vajra)', and that thus it is rather the situation which the **Caturmudropadeśa* seems to envisage that is intended here too." Nevertheless, given the clear explanation of the "1 + 1" model above (343–44), there can be no doubt that this quote here is understood in the same way.

2812. This stanza is also found in Indrabhūti's *Śrīcakrasaṃvaratantrarājaśambarasamuccayanāmavṛtti* (D1413, fol. 98a.2–3), following right after the above-quoted five lines. In addition, the last line is almost identical to *Hevajratantra* I.10.13d.
2813. Point 4e is not mentioned again below.
2814. I follow GZ P *ni* against CD *bzhi* N *na*.
2815. I follow CD *bug pa lnga 'bru tsam* against GZ NP *bug pa rnga 'bru tsam*.
2816. I follow GZ NP *lus phril gyis* against CD *phyur gyis*.
2817. NP omit this phrase.
2818. I follow GZ CD *rtog pa ci skyes* against NP *rtogs pa ni*.
2819. Given the parallel phrase just above, GZ CD *rtog cing skye ba* NP *rtogs shing skye ba* are emended to *rtog pa ci skyes pa*.
2820. There is no further mention of point 4b4c below; it seems to be conflated with the following point "4b5. the bliss that is to be made to abide."
2821. GZ NP *gi vang* CD *'gi vang* em. *pi vang*; GZ CDNP *thag pa*—as opposed to *rgyud pa*—most probably refers to the gut strings to fasten the frets of a vīṇā, not the strings that are played (though obviously either would fulfill the purpose described here).
2822. These are ginger, long pepper, and hot pepper.
2823. I follow GZ NP *bgo ba* against CD *bsgo ba* ("command," "smear").
2824. I follow GZ CD *nub mo gnyid mi dgag* against NP *nub mi dgag*.
2825. *Padmarakta* (lit. "red lotus") is found in Tibetan texts as another (corrupt) form of *padmarāga* ("ruby"). I follow GZ NP *mi'i glad* (NP *klad*) *pa padma rakta* against CD *mi glag pa padma ragta*.
2826. GZ CDNP *lnga'i* em. *lngas*.
2827. I follow NP *bdugs* against GZ *gdur* CD *gdub*.
2828. Tib. *lkug pa* can mean both "mute" and "stupid."
2829. GZ CDNP read *lnga* ("five"), but there are only four points here.
2830. NP omit *glod la* ("in a relaxed way").
2831. I follow CD *'byung bas* against GZ *'byung ste* NP *'byung*.

2832. GZ CDNP *dngos po*; as mentioned before, in other texts, this constituent is called "lack of nature" (*rang bzhin med pa*).
2833. I follow GZ *rtog pa* against CDNP *rtogs pa* ("realization"); *rtog pa* could also mean "thoughts," but in its combination with "analysis" in the following sentence, "examination" is more likely.
2834. GZ *dpyod pa* CDNP *spyod pa* ("conduct").
2835. I follow CDNP *nyams su blang ba* against GZ *nyams su myong ba* ("experience").
2836. Here and below, I follow GZ *gcad pa* against CDNP *dpyad pa* ("analyzing").
2837. In GZ CDNP the order of 2. and 3. is switched, but I here also follow the order in which they are explained below.
2838. CDNP omit "the time of."
2839. I follow GZ CD *rgyun 'dres* against NP *brgyan 'dren*.
2840. GZ CDNP here read only *ye shes pa'i mu dang bral* ("free of any extremes of wisdom"), omitting "distraction," but above (323) it is said that wisdom's inconceivability means being free of the extremes of distraction.
2841. I follow CDNP *nyams su blangs pa* against GZ *nyams su myong ba*.
2842. CD omit the last three lines.
2843. GZ *rtog pa* CDNP *rnyog pa* ("sullies").
2844. Compare the same example with its three steps being used in a very similar but more detailed way in Saraha's *Kāyakoṣa* (text 53, stanzas 101–4).
2845. GZ *'gras 'dris* CD *'gras 'grib* NP *'gras 'gris* em. *'gras 'grus*; "crooked" refers to both a crooked path and a crooked mindset.
2846. I follow GZ N *brtan pa* against CD *rten pa* P *brten pa*.
2847. GZ CDNP *nyam mi nga ba* can also mean "not weak" and "not miserable."
2848. It is not clear whether this paragraph refers to "the inconceivability of the cognition of experience" or inconceivability in general. The former option seems supported by the fact that "the inconceivability of the cognition of experience" is not discussed anywhere else below, that at least "effortless" and "fearless" point to a subjective component, and that our text shows other instances of switching the order of points in the outline in the actual explanation. The second option seems supported by this paragraph speaking about "the actuality of inconceivability" and the following explanation of that.
2849. Many of the twenty examples here are found in the works of Saraha. Example (1) is found in Saraha's *Kāyakoṣa* (text 53, stanza 145) and "King Dohā" (text 65, stanza 26).
2850. Example (2) is also found in Saraha's "People Dohā" (text 13, stanza 53) and *Kāyakoṣa* (text 53, stanza 105).
2851. I follow GZ *gar dgar* against CD *gang dgar* NP *gar dkar*.
2852. Example (4) is also found in Saraha's "People Dohā" (text 13, stanza 86), *Kāyakoṣa* (text 53, stanza 106), *Dohakoṣanāmamahāmudropadeśa* (text 58, stanza 21), and *Dohanidhikoṣaparipūrṇagītināma* (text 68, stanza 110).
2853. I follow GZ *longs spyod du btub pa* against CD *longs skyad du btub pa* NP *longs spyad du btab pa*.
2854. NP omit *yul* ("objects").
2855. I follow GZ *lobs pa* CD *lob pa* against NP *lom pa*.
2856. Examples (5) and (6) are also found in Saraha's *Kāyakoṣa* (text 53, stanza 106).
2857. Examples (7) and (8) are also found in Saraha's *Kāyakoṣa* (text 53, stanza 108).

2858. I follow GZ CDNP *lan tshva chu la thim* against CDNP *lan tshva la chu thim* ("water dissolving in salt").

2859. Example (9) is also found in Saraha's "People Dohā" (text 13, stanza 98) and *Dohanidhikoṣaparipūrṇagītināma* (text 68, stanza 124), as well as Kṛṣṇa's *Dohakoṣa* (text 63, stanza 32).

2860. Example (10) is also found in Saraha's "People Dohā" (text 13, stanza 103) and *Kāyakoṣa* (text 53, stanza 109).

2861. GZ CDNP *sa sri ko ne* (Skt. *sasri* on its own means "running rapidly," and *koṇa* [from the verb *kuṇ*, "to sound"] is attested in *kharakoṇa*, "francoline partridge"). The same example of a bird not taking any support at all is also found in Saraha's *Kāyakoṣa* (text 53, stanza 110) and *Vākkoṣa* (text 54, stanza 9; in both GZ *sar kon ne* CDNP *sar ko ne*), as well as *Ajamahāsukha's commentary on the "People Dohā" 103 (CDNP *sa ku ne*; appendix 4 in volume 3). As *sa ku ne* suggests, this must be a Prakrit or corrupt Sanskrit form of *śakuna*, which either refers to birds in general or specifically to the Indian vulture, the common kite (*Falco cheela*), or the Pondicherry eagle (*Falco ponticeriana*). While all the above birds are known to be proficient in soaring flight, when it comes to remaining in the air without touching the ground, they are nothing compared to birds such as albatrosses, which never land once during the first six or more years of their lives and thereafter only to hatch their eggs and raise their chicks (a gray-headed albatross has been recorded to have circled the entire globe in forty-six days!); swifts, which fly ten months out of the year (being on the ground only when breeding); and frigate birds, who have been proven to sleep while flying (sometimes even with both halves of their brains inactive).

2862. I follow GZ CD *pa ta ra* against NP *pa ltar*. Skt. *patara* means "flying" or "fugitive," and there are a number of similar words for "bird" in general, such as *pattra(ratha)*, *pattri*, and *patatri*. However, since the text qualifies this creature as "animal" (*srog chags*) and not as "bird" (as in the previous example), it is probably not a bird. The same example of this unidentified animal is also found in Saraha's *Kāyakoṣa* (text 53, stanza 110; there *pa ta ri*).

2863. GZ *bha da ri* CDNP *bha ta ri*; Skt. *badarī* means "jujube tree," "velvet bean," and "cotton shrub." Saraha's *Kāyakoṣa* (text 53, stanza 110) speaks of "*beta* among the most supreme medicines." BGDC (1838) describes *be ta* as "an evergreen medicinal tree with edible fruits." Other dictionaries clearly identify *be ta* and its synonyms as the coconut tree (as well as its nuts).

2864. Skt. *gṛdhrakūṭa*, Tib. *bya rgod phung po'i ri* (usually translated as "vulture peak"). Though the Sanskrit *kūṭa* can mean both "peak" and "flock" (or "heap"), it is usually explained to mean the latter (which corresponds to the Tibetan *phung po* instead of *rtse mo* or the like). According to the *Śatasāhasrikāvivaraṇa* (D3802, fols. 3b.7–4a.1), Praśāstrasena's commentary on the *Heart Sūtra* (P5220, 292.3.7–8), and other sources, the mountain received its name from the shape of its rock formations that resemble a flock of vultures huddling together. Jñānamitra's commentary on the *Heart Sūtra* (P5217, 285.5.1–2) says that the name comes from flocks of vultures gathering on its top. Ngag dbang bstan dar lha ram pa's (1759–1831) commentary on the *Heart Sūtra* (trans. in Lopez 1988, 141) lists five ways of explaining this name by referring to Sde srid sangs rgyas rgya mtsho's (1653–1705) *Bai durya g.ya' sel*: (1) the mountain being shaped like a vulture; (2) being shaped like a flock of vultures; (3) vultures protecting the mountain on which many such birds feed on corpses; (4) being a heap/flock due to the brilliance of the birds that are beings who understand emptiness; and (5) the Buddha's robe being snatched by a demon in the form of a vulture and dropped on the mountain (which is shaped like a vulture's head), where it turned to stone in four layers, which are known as "the great vulture heap."

2865. The three phases of thoughts or the vāyus are said to be arising, operating, and resting.

2866. This example is also found in Saraha's *Kāyakoṣa* (text 53, stanza 43) and Nāropa's *Ratnaprabhā* (text 49, stanza 23).

2867. This example is also found in Saraha's "People Dohā" (text 13, stanza 132).

2868. Points 5a, 5b, and 5d are not discussed below.

2869. Point 5c4 is not mentioned again below.

2870. Kg does not contain a tantra of this name.

2871. The three white ones are milk, curd, and butter.

2872. I follow GZ *phyi ma* NP *the ma* against CD *phye ma* ("powder").

2873. GZ CDNP *sbyangs la gnas pa* Skt. *dhūtavāsana* refers to those who abide by the twelve qualities of abstinence (Skt. *dvadaśadhūtaguṇa*, Tib. *sbyangs pa'i yon tan bcu gnyis*). According to the *Dharmasaṃgraha*, these twelve consist of (1) wearing the dress of a dung sweeper (that is, only clothes that other people have thrown away), (2) owning only three robes, (3) only wearing clothes made out of one kind of material, such as wool, (4) begging for alms, (5) eating only while sitting at one's eating place (that is, not getting up and returning to eat or getting more to eat), (6) not eating food after noon, (7) living in isolated places, (8) living under trees, (9) living in places without a roof, (10) living in charnel grounds, (11) sleeping in a sitting position, and (12) being content to stay anywhere (that is, without manipulating the ground in any way to make it more comfortable). In the Pāli tradition, the *Visuddhimagga* lists thirteen *dhutaṅgas*: the above (1), (2), (4)–(12) plus not omitting any house while going for alms and eating only from an alms bowl.

2874. GZ *rtsibs rnams rnam par rtog pa* CD *rtsibs rnams mnyam par rtogs pa* ("the realization of the spokes being equal").

2875. There is no text of this name in Kg and Tg.

2876. GZ *du mas brgyan* NP *du ma brgyan* CD *du ma rgyas* ("many branches extend").

2877. NP repeat the first two lines of this stanza in a slightly different form.

2878. This stanza marks the end of the inserted text. Thereafter, the actual comments on CMA's section on the samayamudrā resume.

2879. In GZ CDNP, the phrase "which isn't anything whatsoever" can be read as either qualifying "delusion's and nondelusion's duality" or "the realization," but the comments below clearly take it in the latter sense.

2880. CDNP *bsten du med pa* GZ *bstan du med pa* ("cannot be demonstrated").

2881. This could also be read as "the realization of nothing whatsoever."

2882. I follow GZ *gnyis brtags* against CD *gnyis pa rtags* NP *gnyis pa brtags*.

2883. As the opening of Sahajavajra's *Tattvadaśakaṭīkā* (text 46, 1) says: "The subject matter of this treatise [the *Tattvadaśaka*] consists of (1) what is to be accomplished, (2) the means of accomplishment, and (3) the character of true reality (the character of the dharmatā that is otherwise expressed as 'prajñāpāramitā' and has the nature of the three kāyas)."

2884. These two lines are a variant of *Hevajratantra* I.10.41ab.

2885. The first two lines are a variant of *Hevajratantra* I.10.41cd, but the last two lines are completely different from *Hevajratantra* I.10.41e.

2886. These lines are *Hevajratantra* II.3.2ab and *Saṃvarodayatantra* III.17cd. GZ CDNP has the second line as "has entered into EVAṂ."

2887. GZ NP *bcas* CD *byas*.

2888. It is odd that the text here speaks of "the beginning of the final passage (GZ CDNP *tshogs*; an unusual word choice)." For it first comments on every word in the third line of the above-cited final four lines from CMA and then explains just a single word ("mahāmudrā") from the first line.

2889. I follow CD *bsdus pa dam tshig gi phyag rgya* NP *bsdu pa dam tshig gi phyag rgya* against GZ *bsdu ba dang dam tshig gi phyag rgya*.

2890. It is clear that the text here glosses Skt. *nirdeśa*. This may be a coincidence, but one of the meanings of Skt. *anvaya* (as in the title *Caturmudrānvaya*) is "the logical connection of cause and result" (compare also the explanation of this title below).

2891. I follow GZ *e baṃ* against CDNP *e bo*.

2892. GZ CDNP *drug pa* (lit. "sixth") is unclear. Only in the version in GZ, the colophon of CMA speaks of it as "an expedient in four stages," so maybe this is what is supposed to be (mistakenly) referred to here (in any case, the text clearly does not have six sections).

2893. GZ CDNP *de nyid* could also be read as "true reality" or refer back to "the connate." This paragraph is obviously an explanation of the title *Caturmudrānvaya*, but by using the words "included" and "not go beyond," Skt. *anvaya* is not really explained in its meaning "succession" but in its other meanings "connected," "related," and "concordant."

2894. GZ *nā gārdzu na mchog las med pa* CDNP *nā gārdzu na mchog las rnyed pa* ("that was obtained from supreme Nāgārjuna").

2895. GZ CDNP *mtshan nyid* (lit. "the definitions/characteristics/descriptions [of phenomena]").

2896. GZ CDNP Da ka ro zan ("Daka corpse-eater").

2897. Obviously, Digambara ("Sky-Clad One") here is not a reference to the Jaina ascetics of the same generic name. In the second paragraph of the colophon, CD omit "this Indian upādhyāya" and "renowned as erudite."

2898. PDMT, 26:431–80. My translation of the *Sekanirdeśapañjikā* is greatly indebted to the masterful Sanskrit edition, English rendering, and notes in IaS. As mentioned before, Maitrīpa's *Sekanirdeśa* (text 42) as well as Rāmapāla's commentary bear a close relationship with Nāgārjuna's *Caturmudrānvaya* (text 14), Maitrīpa's *Commentary on Half a Stanza on True Reality Teaching That All Phenomena Are Utterly Nonabiding* (text 73) and *Caturmudropadeśa* (text 92), Divākaracandra's *Prajñājñānaprakāśa* (text 16), Sahajavajra's *Sthitisamāsa* (text 17), the *Caturmudrāṭīkā* (text 44), and Vajrapāṇi's *Guruparamparākramopadeśa* (text 213).

2899. Besides being an epithet of Brahmā, Viṣṇu, and Śiva, Lokanātha ("Protector of the World") in a Buddhist context can be a general reference to the Buddha, refer to a specific buddha of that name, or serve as an epithet of

Avalokiteśvara. Given that the immediately following stanza also uses the word "protector" and that Rāmapāla below refers to Maitrīpa as Maitreyanātha ("the protector Maitreya"), it seems quite clear that this opening line and the following stanza of homage both refer to Maitrīpa. GZ CDNP "I pay homage to youthful Mañjuśrī."

2900. GZ CDNP omit "alone."

2901. IaS (255n1) relates the three appositions to "the protector" in the first three lines to the dharmakāya, sambhogakāya, and nirmāṇakāya, respectively.

2902. GZ CDNP:

> You people, I don't have any skill in the means
> of analyzing [GZ *dpyad pa* CDNP *mchog 'dzin*, "taking to be supreme"] [how] to explain a text of the true dharma
> An explanation to be written [GZ *bri bar bya ba* CDNP *bri bar byed pa*] ordered by the
> command of the guru is worthy of forbearance.

2903. GZ CDNP read the last three lines as follows:

> but just so I recollect easily,
> I write a little bit for the sake
> of other seekers like me too.

2904. As mentioned before, the Sanskrit word *avadhūta* from the root "to shake (off)" is commonly used in Indian Buddhist and non-Buddhist traditions alike, referring to persons who have reached a level on their spiritual path where they have shaken off or are beyond any ego-based consciousness, duality, common worldly concerns, and standard social norms. Thus *avadhūta* is a quite common epithet and, on its own, has nothing to do with the avadhūtī (the central nāḍī), though some people may reach the level of an avadhūta through avadhūtī-related practices.

2905. As mentioned before, this not very common fivefold classification of tantra is also found in the *Caturmudrāṭīkā* (text 44, 256), Vajrapāṇi's *Guruparamparākramopadeśa* (text 213, 197), Ratnākaraśānti's *Muktāvalī* and Kṛṣṇa's *Yogaratnamālā* commentaries on *Hevajratantra* II.2.10, and Advayavajra's *Gūḍhapadā* (for the detailed references of the latter three, see Sanderson 2009, 146n337). In different texts, there are various classifications of five tantra classes in Indian Buddhism, such as yogottaratantra in this classification here being replaced by mahāyogatantra, and yoganiruttaratantra by yoginītantra or yogānuttaratantra; for details, see for example Mimaki 1994 (121–22n17), English 2002 (2–6), and Dalton 2005.

2906. GZ CDNP "Here, given that [CDNP "since"] this mahāpaṇḍita and fully trained one, the glorious protector Maitreya, following *The Succession of the Four Mudrās* composed by noble [CD "master" NP omit either] Nāgārjuna, the unsurpassed guru of the kriyā, caryā, yoga, yogottara, and yoganiruttara tantras, wished to compose *Instructions on Empowerment*, first, to begin with, since the time had come for him to wish to state the subject matter, pays homage by bowing down [CDNP "bows down"] to the syllables EVAṂ, which represent the initial meaning of the words of the settings . . ."

2907. Neither the Sanskrit manuscripts nor GZ CDNP cite the full stanzas of the *Sekanirdeśa*, but they are added throughout for the sake of orientation and convenience. IaS (257n11): "This translation follows Rāmapāla's main interpretation, according to which the locative *yatra* (here rendered with the words 'given [the existence of] which') is absolute. Later, however, he also gives the possibility of taking the locative as expressing the support or locus (and suggests that it would have also been possible to use an ablative conveying the sense of the material cause). In that case too, presumably, we are to interpret Evaṃ as meaning either the Lotus and the Vajra together with the dot representing their non-dual union, the seed that is the source of the three worlds, and Unsounded Reality (see verses 3–5 of the quotation from the *Devendraparipjcchā* above [sic but meaning "below"]) or the Dharmodayā (cf. *evaṃkāraṃ dharmodayāsvabhavaṃ namaskurmaḥ* below)." As mentioned before, this stanza echoes *Hevajratantra* II.3.5 (a variant version of the last two lines is cited below):

It is there that the ecstasies will originate,
distinguished by the moments' distinction
Due to knowing the moments, the wisdom
that is bliss is based in the syllables EVAṂ.

2908. GZ CDNP ". . . I pay homage to the syllables E and VAṂ, the two syllables with the nature of sound that have the essence of the dharmamudrā . . . thus this means that ["I pay homage to the syllables EVAṂ"] is connected [syntactically] to the other [compound "for the sake of realizing awakening"] . . . This is stated in *[The Tantra of] Devendra Questioning the Bhagavān*:"
2909. GZ CDNP mistranslate *evamiti* as *'di skad ces* ("thus" or "the following").
2910. GZ CDNP omit this phrase.
2911. Here I follow the comments in IaS (257n15): "The Sanskrit on the face of it means literally rather 'Hear [...] correctly, in due order'. But as we understand it, the intended sense is closer to 'Hear [...] [the matter as I explain it] correctly, in due order'. Note that the *pāda yathāvad anupūrvaśaḥ* is a widely attested formula. The adverbs can qualify a wide variety of verbs, including *bhāvayet* and *likhet*; one of the most common verbs which they modify, however, is *vakṣye* or *(pra)vakṣyāmi* (see, e.g., *Svacchandatantra* 1.53cd, 2.lab, 2.123cd, etc.)." GZ CDNP render the more literal reading.
2912. IaS (257) renders the last two lines as "the two syllables [i.e. Evaṃ] are the basis of everything, the father [and] the mother; thus they are spoken [at the beginning of all teachings of the Buddha]" and adds the following (257–58n17): "The second half could be taken in slightly different ways too, e.g. 'the two syllables [i.e. Evaṃ] are the basis of everything, the father [and] the mother; they have been taught thus [i.e. taught, by the Buddha, to be the basis of everything and the father and the mother]'; or, reading *tathā* in a weaker sense, 'the two syllables are taught to be the support of all, and/and thus (*tathā*) the father and mother'."

GZ CDNP:

Of all items of the eighty-four
. . .

> the basis, father, and mother of all,
> are thus taught as the two syllables.

2913. Here and in the following stanzas, GZ CDNP read VAṂ.
2914. GZ CDNP "two."
2915. GZ CDNP:

> The beings who always recite [GZ "who recite the true dharma"] without
> any understanding of the two syllables
> will be outside of the buddhadharmas,
> similar to a mind deprived of enjoyment
> [CDNP *sangs rgyas chos rams la / sbyor spangs phyi rol thub pa bzhin,* "will be deprived of being united with the buddhadharmas, similar to an outsider sage"].

2916. IaS (258) renders *evaṃ* as "thus" and adds (n21): "The Tibetan translation takes *evaṃ* with *dvirakṣaram;* 'the two syllables Evaṃ'. This may be possible; but the phrasing would be rather unnatural, and without parallel in the other verses (or in Rāmapāla's own words)." In my opinion, "thus" is of course possible, but the phrase "the two syllables are illusion" lacks a connection in content with any preceding stanza that would warrant a "thus." Hence I here side with the Tibetan translation.
2917. IaS (258–59n22) points out a comment on this line in Āryadeva's *Pradīpoddyotananāmaṭīkā* (D1794, fol. 186a.3–4): "The omniscient one is established there because they are the main cause for attaining omniscience."
2918. GZ CDNP read the last two lines as follows:

> For that reason, EVAṂ is proclaimed at
> the beginning of teaching the true dharma.

2919. IaS (259n24): "It might sound more natural to have vocatives, *surādhipa* and *śakra*, and we find them, indeed, in Pt. However the reading *surādhipa* woud be metrically bad. The citation in the *Pradīpoddyotana* has the metrically required *surādhipaḥ*, but follows it with the vocative *śakra.* A mixture of the two cases might be acceptable. Note though that all sources seem to point to a third person form *icchet* (or *īkṣet*) in the second *pāda*, not a second person. On the other hand, in *pāda* d all sources have a second person imperative. One could consider conjecturing a second person form in *pāda* b, which would then read *yadīccheḥ śāsvataṃ padam*, and in that case accepting *śakra* and understanding *surādhipaḥ* as nominative for vocative, metri causa. The translation might in that case read: 'Therefore, Lord of the Gods, Śakra, if you wish for the eternal state, you should honour the True Dharma: remember the two syllables of Illusion!'" GZ CDNP have the same ambiguities:

> Therefore, if Śakra, the lord of the
> gods, wishes for the eternal state,
> he should recall the two syllables
> as illusion and honor the true dharma!

Or

Therefore, Śakra, lord of the gods,
if you wish for the eternal state,
you should recall . . .

IaS (166; see there for the exact references) points out that these nine stanzas from the *Devendraparipṛcchātantra* are also quoted in Candrakīrti's *Pradīpoddyotana* (with two additional lines at the beginning), stanzas 3 and 5–7 in the *Subhāṣitasaṃgraha*, stanzas 2–6 in Raviśrījñāna's *Amṛtakaṇikāṭippaṇī*, and stanza 5 in the *Mekhalāṭīkā* on Kāṇha's *Dohākośa* (text 63), adding that "probably the passage was accessible to Rāmapāla already as a quotation." In addition, with slight variations, stanzas 3–7 are also quoted in Amṛtavajra's commentary on Kṛṣṇa's *Dohakoṣa* (text 64, 235), likewise attributed to the *Devendraparipṛcchātantra*.

2920. Skt. *kāraṇam* and its gloss *hetuḥ* both mean "cause."

2921. GZ CDNP "Since this is the subject matter at hand, therefore, it shall be explained. As for 'being the causes of the four moments,' the four are the four moments of variety, maturation, consummation, and lack of characteristics. What is the cause is the maker . . . This is the distinction of the moments that is connected [I follow GZ *dang 'brel* against CDNP *rang 'brel*] to the distinction . . . [CDNP omit 'syllables' in the last sentence].'"

2922. That is, as being caused by the syllables EVAṂ.

2923. GZ CDNP "To explain this in the same way, [Maitrīpa] says 'in which all ecstasies will arise.' Only from what has the character of prajñā and means, the wisdom of the path—ecstasy, supreme ecstasy, cessational ecstasy, and connate ecstasy—will arise distinctly and unmixed by virtue of the distinction of the moments [CDNP "the wisdom of the path will arise distinctly and unmixed by virtue of the distinction of the moments of ecstasy that are called 'ecstasy,' 'supreme ecstasy,' 'cessational ecstasy,' and 'connate ecstasy'" NP omit "distinctly" and "by virtue of"]. For, though appearing through that [GZ *gang phyir des snang yang* CDNP *de nas gang gi phyir*; all attempting to render Skt. *tato yaḥ*], the only thing that serves as the cause of the four moments and from which the distinction of the four ecstasies arises distinctly [CDNP omit "four" and "distinctly"] is the syllables EVAṂ: for the sake of accomplishing awakening, I pay homage to them. This is the summarized meaning [of this stanza], which is also the explanation of the nature of [that] sound."

2924. As mentioned before, the term *dharmodaya* or *dharmodayā* ("dharma source") refers to the primordial space from which all phenomena arise (a.k.a. dharmadhātu), representing the female principle or divine cosmic vagina from which everything arises and ceases. It is usually depicted as a triangle with its tip pointing down, a hexagram (two overlapping triangles similar to the Star of David), or one or two three-dimensional triangles (triangular upside-down pyramids). The term can also refer to the female genitals. In the Vajrayāna, the dharmodaya in the form of a hexagram is specifically associated with Vajrayoginī, with the two triangles symbolizing the union of bliss and emptiness. About this being matched with the syllables EVAṂ, IaS (260n34) explains the following: "The Dharmodayā (also Dharmodaya, masc. or neut., or Dharmodayamudrā) is a downward pointing triangle, standing for or homologized with the female organ, the Lotus (and thus also Wisdom). The name, especially when used as a feminine . . . is most naturally understood as (originating from) an ablative or locative *bahuvīhri*: *dharmāṇām udayo yasyāt/ yasyām*, 'that/She from/in which there is the arising of the *dharmas*' (where different interpretations of *dharmas* are possible, from 'phenomena' to 'the qualities of a Buddha'). Since the form of the written letter E resembles a downward pointing triangle in all northern scripts, to a greater or lesser extent (in Gupta script it is often an almost perfectly equilateral one), it was in a way natural that this phoneme (whether written or pronounced) came to be regarded as an equivalent of the Dharmodaya. And since the form of the written letter Va more or less resembles an upwards pointing (in Gupta script) or (later more commonly) a sideways pointing triangle, a shape which lends itself to being interpreted as a symbolic representation of the male organ, the Vajra (and thus also Means), it became possible to understand Evaṃ, from the point of view of the written forms of the phonemes, as the combination or union of Lotus = Dharmodayā and Vajra. The locus classicus for this in Buddhist tantric literature appears to be *Hevajratantra* 2.3.4, quoted immediately below (see also, e.g., Kölver 1992: 103–105). Note that it appears to be significant for Rāmapāla that the verses which he quoted above from the *Devendraparipṛcchā*, while making basically the same equations of E with Lotus/Female (Mother) and Va with Vajra/Male (Father), do so without explicitly referring to the shape of either. He thus takes them as support for an interpretation in which the object of obeisance is 'the sonic phonemes', while the *Hevajratantra* verse is cited in support of the interpretation in which the object of obeisance is the written form (of Evaṃ)."

2925. This grammatical explanation is completely lost in GZ CDNP *e baṃ gyi rnam pa ni e baṃ gyi rnam pa ste*.

2926. *Hevajratantra* II.3.4. GZ CDNP "By virtue of the guru's pith instructions, I pay homage to the syllables EVAṂ, which are letters, having the shape of the syllables EVAṂ and being of the essence of the dharmodayā. Alternatively, due to the elision of the prefix . . . [the linguistic explanation is completely lost in GZ CDN simply having *e baṃ gyi rnam pa* twice] . . . For the Bhagavān praised it that the dharmodayā has such a form . . ."

2927. As IaS (261n36) says, "The point is that although *vicitra* ["variety"] includes also such preliminaries as kissing and embracing, this 'moment' is counted as going up to the beginning of intercourse; so in this sense the Dharmodayā can be said to be a cause of it too."

2928. See the comments on stanza 23 below.

2929. GZ CDNP "'But what happens by paying homage to this [EVAṂ as the dharmodayā]?' [Maitrīpa] says . . . The four moments are variety, maturation, consummation, and lack of characteristics. 'Cause' refers to maker. That cause is variety—it extends up to friction. That it is like that shall be explained [later] in detail by virtue of statements by the Buddha. [Thus] homage is to be paid to the cause . . . As it is declared:"

2930. *Sarvarahasyatantra* 22cd (H449, fol. 3b.6–7; for details on the Sanskrit, its canonical Tibetan rendering, the rendering in GZ CDNP, and parallels in other sources, see IaS, 261n39). GZ CDNP "'What happens by paying homage to this?' [Maitrīpa] says . . . The four moments are variety, maturation, consummation, and lack of characteristics. 'Cause' refers to maker. That cause is variety: it extends up to the end of friction [I follow GZ NP *bskyod pa* against CD *bskyed pa*, 'arising']. Though it is like that, it shall be explained extensively [later] in the Buddha statements. One should pay homage to the cause . . ."

2931. *Aṣṭādhyāyī* 1.4.30.

2932. IaS (261n42): "Rāmapāla is of the opinion that one might either use an ablative, if one wishes to emphasize that the Dharmodayā is the *prakṛti* of the Blisses, or a locative, if one wishes to emphasize that it is their basis or locus. The Dharmodayā is both: the Blisses are based in it, and they are born from it. The Tibetan rendering suggests the possibility that the translators read *tatra* instead of *tato*, and Pt's reading *tatro* might be taken in support of such a reading. But in view of the previous remark, we have judged the ablative(-equivalent) *tato* to be more likely to be what Rāmapāla wrote." GZ CDNP "Furthermore, in order to teach a second reason for paying homage [to EVAṂ as the dharmodayā], [Maitrīpa] states: 'in which all ecstasies will arise distinctly'—that is, through the distinction of the ecstasies called 'ecstasy,' 'supreme ecstasy,' 'cessational ecstasy,' and 'connate [ecstasy].' They arise from it not mutually mixed. Though the fifth [case (ablative)] would [normally] obtain (because of '[The ablative is also used for] the nature of the agent of arising [GZ omits 'of arising']'), to teach the seventh [case (locative)] 'in which' is to teach [EVAṂ] as the support [of the ecstasies], because they are based there, from which they arise."

2933. *Hevajratantra* II.3.5cd (CDNP *skad cig ye shes bde ye shes*, "momentary wisdom, bliss wisdom").

2934. These two lines are *Hevajratantra* II.3.2ab and *Saṃvarodayatantra* III.17cd. For comments, see the note on these lines in the *Caturmudrāṭīkā* (text 44, 257).

2935. *Hevajratantra* II.12.5. In the third line, instead of *caturānandabhāg* (GZ CDNP *tsa tur ā nanda bha ga*) here, the editions of the *Hevajratantra* by Snellgrove 1959 and Farrow and Menon 1992 read *caturānandasvabhāga* ("the four ecstasies' own locus"; both Snellgrove and Farrow and Menon render this together with the following *viśva* as "many are the blessings of your four joys"). IaS (262n45): "This verse, mantrified by the *oṃ* placed before it, and with the emphatically hypermetrical three *hūṃ*s (where two would have given regular metre; such a reading is indeed found in some sources, e.g. *Bhramahara* p. 16717) in the fourth *pāda*, is *Hevajratantra* 2.12.5, standardly used, in Hevajra practice, for the empowerment (*adhiṣṭhāna*) of the Lotus of Nairātmyā (including, of course, the consort visualized as Nairātmyā)." That this stanza is used as a mantra is also evidenced by it not being translated but transliterated into Tibetan.

2936. This is the third stanza of the *Caturgāthā* (D324). GZ CDNP read "sugatas" instead of "tathāgatas" and switch "have sat" and "have stood."

2937. GZ CDNP "'Why pay homage?' 'For the sake of accomplishing awakening'—that is, for the sake of fully knowing in accordance with reality: until completely perfect buddhahood . . ."

2938. GZ CDNP "'What arises from that?' It is the four moments. 'What is their sequence like?'"

2939. Given the context and the parallel phrase in *Hevajratantra* II.3.7 cited immediately below, following IaS, I accept the conjecture *jñānabhogo* against ms. *jñānābhogo*.

2940. As for the last sentence, IaS (264n54) says: "Considerations of sense have led us to understand the syntax to be rather unnatural. The expression *sukhānubhavasmaraṇena* must refer to the moment not of *vilakṣana* but of *vimarda*; it echoes the formulation of *Hevajratantra* 2.3.8ab, *vimardam ālocanaṃ proktaṃ sukhaṃ bhuktaṃ mayeti ca*, which will be quoted directly below. Therefore we connect it syntactically with *virāga*, the first member of the compound *virāgābhāvāt*, which is then a *sāpekṣasamāsa*. This is not too much of a stretch; but it also seems to us that *pāte*, 'when there is falling [of Bodhicitta]', i.e. when emission of semen has taken place, should refer to *vimarda* too (cf. *viratau bodhicittapāte* below, in the commentary on vs. 25). This is distinctly awkward. An alternative, which however we have not preferred, might be to take *pāte* here, unlike in the commentary on vs. 25, to refer not to the completion of emission but to the instant when Bodhicitta is, as it were, not 'fallen' but falling, i.e. the *vilakṣana* moment during which, according to the teaching of Maitreyanātha and Rāmapāla, Bodhicitta is between the Vajra and the Lotus. In that case one might translate 'devoid of nonpassion, because [in the *vilakṣana* moment of Innate Bliss] when [Bodhicitta] is falling (i.e. is between Vajra and Lotus) the dispassion, [which is] accompanied/caused by the recollection of the experience of pleasure [which characterizes the *vimarda* moment of Bliss of Cessation], is non-existent.'" Particularly toward the end of this paragraph, GZ CDNP are quite corrupt: "'Rejecting the sequence taught in the tantra, how is it held here that the lack of characteristics is the third one?' . . . variety is of various kinds—embracing and so on, which have the essence of perceiver and perceived . . . not variegated, without something perceived, the arising of blissful wisdom [GZ CD; NP *gzung ba med pa'i 'dzin pa mgrin pa'i yang dag ye shes la longs spyod* is corrupt but preserves 'experience']. Consummation is the nonconceptual bliss of nonseeing, up to pervading the end of the jewel. This is the gist. What is other is the lack of characteristics: it is free of passion—the entity of definite fullness because of not [CDNP no negative] lacking passion. It is not dispassion either, because the experienced bliss is recollected, nor is it an entity of not lacking passion, which is because of emission [CDNP '. . . recollected. Nor is it the existence of passion, which is because of emission']."

2941. GZ CDNP "the experiencer of blissful wisdom."

2942. GZ:

> Consummation is said to be friction
> "I have experienced wisdom"

CDNP:

> Consummation is said to be analysis:
> "the analysis of blissful wisdom."

2943. *Hevajratantra* II.3.7–8.

2944. This sentence parallels a passage in Maitrīpa's *Pañcatathāgatamudrāvivaraṇa* (text 36, 190).

2945. GZ CDNP "As for this [ecstasy in the moment of the lack of characteristics], according to the system of the Nonaspectarians, this very [ecstasy that is] experienced in the jewel, like the center of the stainless midday sky in autumn, definitely remains as sheer self-aware bliss, being free of the pollution of the circle of all aspects such as blue. The means of proof . . . are not elaborated [here] for fear of too much text."

2946. *Pramāṇavārttika* III.211–212. IaS (265n61 and n62): "Here Dharmakīrti is showing the logical untenability of spatially gross appearances, whether in external objects or in cognitions (supposed to be) caused by/based on such external objects, on the basis of the impossibility of grossness (*tadātman* = *sthūlasvarūpa* = *sthūlatā*) existing either in the singular atoms (*paramāṇu*) or in compound wholes (*avayavin*). The details of the proofs of this are left out by Dharmakīrti at this point, just as they are left out by Rāmapāla. The arguments are those found first in Viṃśikā 11–15, and elaborated in, e.g., *Bodhicaryāvatārapañjikā* ad st. 9.87, and in *Tattvasaṅgrahapañjikā* ad stt. 1967–1998 . . . To put this in other words and trying to summarize the main point of a quite complex topic: awareness or cognition (*jñāna*) is an undivided experience, but it has two opposite aspects or parts (*bhāga*), which are ultimately unreal, although ordinary people believe they are not. The part that is called here 'determination' (*pariccheda*) (and is internal) is the aspect of perceiver (*grāhakākāra*), whereas, distinct from it, the part that appears to be external is the (aspect of) perceivable reality (*grāhya/grāhyākāra*) (cf. Manorathanandin's *vṛtti, ad loc.*) . . . For a translation of these verses . . . within their larger context, together with extensive notes, translating also substantial portions of the commentaries by Devendrabuddhi and Śākyabuddhi, see Dunne 2004: 404–406." GZ CDNP are rather corrupt:

> Hence, in the wisdom of referents,
> there is no coarse [I follow GZ *rags* against CD *rig* NP *rigs*] appearance with that character
> A single one has been refuted
> A multitude will not arise either
>
> The part that appears [GZ *snang* CDNP *gnas*, "abides"] as if it were external
> is determined as if an internal [I follow GZ *nang* against CDNP *gang*] distinction
> Any appearance by virtue of a distinction
> of undifferentiated wisdom is corruption.

2947. *Uttaratantra* II.61b.

2948. IaS (266n66): "Cf. *Hevajrasādhanopāyikā* p. 1407.8: [...] *yāvad anupalabdhikaṃ kuryāt* [...] *bhāvayet*. Without *bhāvayet*, the same expression occurs in *Sādhanamālā* 123 (an Ekajaṭāsādhana entitled *Vidyujjvālākarālī*), ed. p. 25816, a text which is probably influenced by and partly copying from Saroruha's *Hevajrasādhanopāyikā*."

2949. Skt. *lakṣita* can also mean "recognized," "known," and "evident," all of which apply here as well.

2950. GZ CDNP "Subsequent to this, the wisdom that has the form of the maṇḍala circle of activity [NP omit 'of activity'] and so on is the sambhogakāya . . . The same nature of these is the svābhāvikakāya. As it is stated in the *Mahāyānottaratantra*: [GZ omits this phrase] . . . Because it has been taught 'one should meditate until there is nonreferentiality,' illustrated by these examples, through uninterrupted respectful familiarization [CD omit 'familiarization'] and meditation for a long time, and through the power of previous aspiration prayers, the sambhoga[kāya] and the nirmāṇakāya are definitely perfected in the form of [CD omit 'in the form of'] the maṇḍala circle and so on. Alternatively, what is called 'bliss' is experienced—that is, [this bliss] itself will clearly arise thanks to familiarization that is respectful and so on."

2951. *Pramāṇavārttika* III.285 and *Pramāṇaviniścaya* I.31. In the last line, GZ renders Skt. *tat* as *bde* instead of *de*, thus adding "blissful" (probably in an attempt to complete the standard triad of meditation experiences: bliss, clarity, and nonthought).

2952. GZ CDNP "This, through the power of the distinctions of previous aspiration prayers, constitutes the two form kāyas. The means of entering these are two. As it is stated:"

2953. *Hevajratantra* II.4.33ab. As IaS (267n74) points out, Ratnākaraśānti's *Muktāvalī* explains "self-blessing" simply as "the perfection process taught in the eighth chapter [of the first part of the *Hevajratantra*]" and Kāṇha similarly glosses it as "the pith instruction on the cultivation of the perfection process." As mentioned before, in the Ārya school of the *Guhyasamājatantra*, "self-blessing" specifically refers to the third among the five stages of its perfection process, through which the illusion-like samādhi is attained.

2954. *Madhyamaṣaṭka* 2 (this stanza teaches the view of Nonaspectarian Yogācāra). GZ CDNP:

> As self-awareness's stream is uninterrupted
> . . .
> it is the entrance into the middle.

2955. As mentioned before, this line is *Hevajratantra* II.3.10b, *Guhyasamājatantra* XVIII.113f, and *Sampuṭodbhavatantra* II.1.46d, and is also found in the *Raktayamarītantra* (H441, fol. 489a.1).

2956. IaS (268n85): "At first sight one might have expected here *suṣuptau*, 'in deep sleep,' rather than *svapne*, since it is presumably obvious that dream-cognitions involve *ākāras*. But here *(na) svapne 'pi* should be understood as an idiomatic expression. Note that very similar formulations, in the same context of the position of the Sākāravādin (or at least an objection against a Nirākāra or Alīkākāra position), can be found in several works of the early eleventh century. Cf., e.g., Ratnākaraśānti's *Sāratamā* . . . Jñānaśrīmitra's *Sākārasaṅgrahasūtra* . . . Vāgīśvarakīrti's *Tattvaratnāvalokavivaraṇa* . . ." In addition, "even in dreams" is confirmed by GZ CDNP *rmi lam du'ang*. GZ CDNP "[In this stanza] here it is taught that there is no clinging, because characteristics do not arise. By virtue of lacking any clinging to existence, nonexistence, and so on, [this awareness] is free from the four extremes. The fourth one in this [is stated] by the phrase 'the fourth is again like such.' As for 'such,' the experience at the time of the prajñā-jñāna [empowerment] is a sensation without aspects. 'Again' means being free of the taints of the entire range, such as blue. 'The fourth is like' means it should be realized like [in] the prajñā-jñāna [empowerment]. The Aspectarians say: 'We assert that a cognition without aspects is not even experienced in dreams.'"

2957. This is the last stanza of Jñānaśrīmitra's *Sākārasiddhi* I. IaS (269n88): "It may be noted here that not too long, perhaps, after Jñānaśrīmitra composed this verse, the great Naiyāyika Udayana adapted it in his *Ātmatattvaviveka* (ed. p. 5292–5), changing it from a Buddhist Sākāravādin's criticism of the Nirākāra position to an orthodox criticism of a Buddhist position . . . Since elsewhere in the *Ātmatattvaviveka* (ed. p. 119,) Udayana explicitly mentions Jñānaśrī (i.e. Jñānaśrīmitra), we may be confident that it is he who adapted the Buddhist author's verse, rather than the other way around." GZ omits the negative in the first line, and the remaining three lines in GZ CDNP read as follows:

> The vast powerful approach of the middle that refutes that is glorious
> If this irreproachable nonduality that is diverse [did not exist],
> whence would a chance for asserting that mind has no aspects manifest?

2958. GZ *lngar* ("as five") CDNP *sngar* ("before").

2959. Skt. *ullekha* means "description of an object according to the different impressions caused by its appearance," "intuitive description," "cause to come forth or appear clearly," and "bring up." IaS renders *pṛṣṭhollekha* as "subsequent imprinting" and GZ CDNP read *rjes la snang ba(s)*. GZ CDNP "Apart from [GZ *las* CDNP *la*] being unable to clarify the absence of the [clear appearing of aspects], since [aspects] are certain by [CDNP omit 'by'] appearing after having been experienced, the sensation of [aspects] such as blue does exist."

2960. *Pramāṇavārttika* III.221. GZ CDNP:

> As long as there is an appearing cognition,
> it is experienced in just that way
> The mind with diverse aspects [GZ "appearing as diversity"]
> is called "being of one nature."

2961. GZ CDNP "Due to that [stanza], there thus exists the supreme sensation that is nondual from the mind . . . In that way, the meaning of the middle that is free of the four extremes will be accomplished."

2962. Skt. *vapus* can also mean "wonderful appearance," 'beauty," and "having a beautiful form or figure," which seem to be implied as a more poetic or enthusiastic description of awareness's natural lucidity.

2963. Skt. *śikharin* literally means "a peaked mountain," "hill post," or "stronghold."

2964. *Sākārasiddhi* 6 and *Advaitabinduprakaraṇa* (in Jñānaśrīmitra's *Jñānaśrīmitranibandhāvalī* 1987, 365). "Those other than it" are the diverse aspects that appear to nondual mind, and "the commentator" refers to Dharmakīrti's commentator Prajñākaragupta. GZ CDNP:

The entity of lucidity is not nonexistent, there is nothing other than it
It is neither one, nor is it two, nor is it two and not two [together]
If the world is free from these four extremes [as stated] in this way,
what is the difference between the Aspectarian system and the
middle's approach?

2965. IaS (270n97): "The connection of the paragraph beginning here with the preceding section is not made absolutely clear. As we understand it, after stating above, before the verse quoted from the *Sākārasiddhi*, that he would not consider the arguments for and against the view of variegated but non-dual awareness (*citrādvaitavedana = citrādvaitaprakāśa*), Rāmapāla is now giving a brief account of how such a view might be integrated with the tantric practice of the consecrations. Concretely, the first sentences are intended to show how a single cognition can be at the same time variegated/differentiated as four Moments corresponding to four Kāyas. Note that the correspondences themselves are the same as those taught by Rāmapāla himself above (p. 266); the difference is only that here they are viewed as an instance of variegatedness (on a lower ontological level) of what is in fact non-dual. The expression *vyāvṛttikṛtabheda*, explaining or justifying the variegatedness/differentiation of the non-dual awareness, is synonymous with *vyāvṛttibhedah*, already used by Dharmakīrti (*Pramāṇavārttikasvavṛtti* p. 5816–17). One might perhaps compare with Rāmapāla's phrase here e.g. the following, from Durvekamiśra's *Dharmottarapradīpa*: *ekasyaiva jñānasya vyāvṛttikṛtaṃ bhedam āśritya* [...] (p. 8422). The difference here, as in Durvekamiśra's phrase, is one which is created subjectively, on the level of conceptual, linguistic, thought, in which realities are identified in a particular way (as an instance of a quasi-universal) through the exclusion (*vyāvṛtti* or *apoha*) of what is other (that is to say other concepts/quasi-universals)."

2966. IaS (270–271n98): "The connection of this sentence with the preceding is not entirely clear. The *prajñājñāna* should, probably, correspond on one level to the *vilakṣana* moment; it is possible that this is one association which links the two sentences. Presumably Rāmapāla is continuing to show how the consecrations are understood in a Citrādvaita view. Here it is the relationship between the *prajñājñāna(-abhiṣeka)* and the Fourth consecration that is explained, in a manner that, as usual, reflects the wording of the *pāda* that came to be treated as the locus classicus for that relationship, *caturthaṃ tat punas tathā* (*Guhyasamāja* 18.113f = *Hevajratantra* 2.3.10b.) The essence of the matter is that the experience of the *prajñājñāna* is related to that of the Fourth as *lakṣaṇa* to *lakṣya* and as means or practice to goal; and that goal is then further said to be characterized by the seven constituents (explained immediately afterwards). We understand that by *abhyasyamānaṃ punaḥśabdavācyaṃ sat* Rāmapāla is somewhat clumsily and inaccurately expressing that the word *punaḥ* in that *pāda* implies repeated practice or cultivation." Rāmapāla's sentence here and the explanation in IaS about the relationship between the third and fourth empowerments and the experience of the fourth one (mahāmudrā) resulting from repeatedly practicing based on the bliss of prajñā-jñāna corresponds to the more detailed explanation in the third chapter of Vāgīśvarakīrti's *Saptāṅga* (a summary of it is provided in the note on the quote from this text below).

2967. IaS (271n99): "In the usage of the Yogatantras and Yoginītantras, *samāpatti* commonly means sexual union, perhaps originally as an abbreviation of *dvayendriyasamāpatti*, 'the coming together/union of the two [sexual] organs', a compound found very frequently in the *Sarvatathāgatatattvasaṅgraha* (cf., e.g., Horiuchi vol. I p. 269). *Sampuṭa* is used to refer to the same at least in the literature of the Yoginītantras (cf., e.g., *Hevajratantra* 2.6.2c). Therefore, *sampuṭaṃ samāpatteḥ* might sound to an eleventh-century reader almost like a tautology."

2968. GZ CDNP "There is a difference through the isolates of the sambhoga[kāya] and so on: consummation is the dharmakāya. Maturation is the sambhoga[kāya]. Variety is the nirmāṇa[kāya]. The lack of characteristics is the svābhāvikakāya. The prajñā-jñāna . . . is to be familiarized with in just that way—just as it is to be expressed by the word 'again.' Thus what is endowed with the seven constituents will be asserted as what is to be accomplished. Here, the seven constituents consist of the sensation of enjoyment, coming together in union, great bliss (having the nature of bliss), lacking any essence [CDNP omit 'of essence'] and thus being free of thought, filled with compassion (promoting the welfare of sentient beings through the power of previous aspiration prayers by means of the sambhoga[kāya] and so on), uninterrupted (utterly uninterrupted), and unceasing, due to which the continual flow is not cut off."

2969. This is the first half of the second stanza of Vāgīśvarakīrti's *Saptāṅga* (D1888, fol. 190a.4–5; adding "meaningful" related to "the goal"). The initial part of this text in Tibetan consists of four stanzas (commented on in the remainder of the text), and thus IaS (271n102) identifies these four lines as the third stanza of the *Saptāṅga*. However, immediately after these stanzas, the text explicitly refers to all these stanzas as "two stanzas," and the same remark is repeated in the colophon. The same four lines as here are also cited in the *Prajñājñānaprakāśa* (text 16, 60) and Śraddhākaravarman's **Yoganiruttaratantrārthāvatārasaṃgraha* (D3713, fol. 109a.4–5; wrongly attributed to Vāgiśvarakīrti's *Tattvaratnāvaloka*, in which it is not found). The last phrase (Skt. *pramāṇaparibhāvitabuddhi*°) could also be read as "whose minds penetrated valid cognition," but the *Saptāṇga* (D1888, fol. 198a.2–3) glosses it as "those who have a mind that has been perfectly cultivated [*yongs su bsgom pa* for Skt. *paribhāvita*] and is to be cultivated with valid cognition, such as states of mind of direct perception—that is, the wise." GZ CDNP likewise read the last phrase as "whose minds have been perfectly cultivated with valid cognition [I follow GZ NP *tshad ma* against CD *mtshan ma*, 'characteristics']." As mentioned before, "the seven constituents of union" (Skt. *sampuṭasaptāṅga*, Tib. *kha sbyor yan lag bdun*) are said to characterize the fruitional state of Vajradhara, the state of unity (*yuganaddha*), the wisdom of the fourth empowerment, and the supreme siddhi of mahāmudrā. According to the second chapter of the *Saptāṅga* (D1888, fols. 190b.7–198a.4): (1) Complete enjoyment consists of the thirty-two major and eighty minor marks of the sambhogakāya. (2) Union refers to sexual union with the female deity. The sambhogakāya mentioned in the Pāramitāyāna is the mere sambhogakāya that lacks the union of two consorts. Therefore the constituent "union" in this sense is adduced here. The Buddha taught sexual union in order to take care of the sentient beings of the desire realm who experience excessive passion, and the goal here refers to the buddhahood that manifests by way of extensively enjoying the pure great bliss of passion through sexual union. (3) Though there is a visible union when an illusory man and woman created by an illusionist have intercourse, this union does not become great bliss. Rather, the great bliss here is the special bliss that is very vast, uncontaminated, and sublime, and remains for as long as saṃsāra lasts. (4) The lack of a nature refers to the buddhahood that has the nature of mahāmudrā. Lack of nature refers to nothing but the emptiness that is endowed with all supreme aspects, whose synonyms include suchness, dharmatā, equality, unsurpassable awakening, and nondual wisdom. The emptiness that is endowed with all supreme aspects is not some kind of emptiness in the sense of sky flowers, rabbit horns, and so on. However, if it is reified as some essence, it becomes an inferior view. (5) Compassion means the great compassion that accomplishes the welfare of all sentient beings. (6) Uninterrupted refers to the nonabiding nirvāṇa by virtue of the continuity of the above-mentioned qualities of the sambhogakāya manifesting in all kinds of ways for the benefit of beings. (7) Unceasing refers to remaining in such a manner for as long as saṃsāra lasts. For other explanations of the seven constituents, compare Divākaracandra's *Prajñājñānaprakāśa* (text 16, 60–61) and the *Caturmudrāṭīkā* (text 44, 306). In addition, the second half of the first stanza of the *Saptāṅga* says that the seven constituents are to be differentiated as the actuality of the fourth empowerment in order to realize mahāmudrā (a little later the text says that mahāmudrā alone is the fourth empowerment). The second half of the text's second stanza asserts the fourth empowerment as being suchness by breaking down the above-discussed line "the fourth is again like that" (*Hevajratantra* II.3.10ab, *Guhyasamājatantra* XVIII.113f, *Sampuṭodbhavatantra* II.1.46d, and *Raktayamarītantra* [H441, fol. 489a.1]) into the three words "that," "again," and "like." The detailed meanings of these three words in this context here are then explained in the text's third chapter (D1888, 198a.4–198b.7) as follows. "That" refers to what illustrates—the prajñā-jñāna deity—while the goal with the seven constituents, which has three causes and is endowed with the single essence of the bliss that arises from lotus and vajra fully touching, is more distinguished than that. Therefore, there is the term "again": the goal again entails union, but this time endowed with the special bliss that is distinguished as being vast, uncontaminated, sublime, uninterrupted, and remaining for as long as saṃsāra. This bliss is impossible in the momentary bliss of prajñā-jñāna that lacks these distinctions, but it becomes possible in the state of direct perception through having (sufficiently) familiarized with the bliss of prajñā-jñāna—this is the much more distinguished bliss that is illustrated only by the prajñā-jñāna. At the time of the mere contaminated moment of bliss that arises by virtue of a karmamudrā through the tactile sensation of the vajra, this bliss still entails stains such as tightly embracing the body of the karmamudrā, thus constituting suffering but not being sublime: for since it is the cause of perishing, it only lasts for a brief moment. Also, by virtue of being present only in the jewel, it is not vast, because it does not pervade all body parts. Nor is it uninterrupted, because it does not appear that way. And it does not remain for as long as saṃsāra lasts either, because the union with a karmamudrā is impermanent. Thus the term "again" refers to what is illustrated—the actual goal with the seven constituents. The term "like" refers to the three causes: like the bliss that arises from a karmamudrā skilled in the triad of prajñā, jñāna, and samādhi, the means, and so on, what eventually arises from being endowed with such a collection of causes, prajñā, and the means is the goal here. What thus arises as the meaning of the term "like" here has the essence of true reality: therefore I assert the goal endowed with the seven constituents as being suchness. This is the correct assertion, while others lack the second constituent and so on.

2970. IaS considers only the first sentence in this paragraph as an objection and the rest as the answer. About the last sentence, IaS (272n105) says that it "should be simply an explanation of why the soteriological efficacy of the meditation on Nairātmyā (surrounded by the other yoginīs) without Hevajra is evidence that even if the result (the liberated state) may be connected with the seven constituents the cause (the meditation that leads to liberation) does not have to be." By contrast, GZ CDNP consider this entire paragraph to be an objection: "Or you may wonder: 'What is the use of a yoga practicing with the seven constituents? There is no [absolute] certainty here. For isn't familiarization with [just] the circle of Nairātmyāyoginī also the cause of buddhahood? Given that, this here does not represent a yoga that is a means of practice endowed with the seven constituents, because union is absent.'"

2971. For the reasons explained below, this otherwise untraced stanza seems not to be a quote but Rāmapāla's summary of the preceding paragraph. GZ CDNP:

> If what is to be accomplished, endowed with
> seven constituents, is the means of practice, [I follow GZ *sgrub byed* against CDNP repeating *bsgrub bya*]
> why would it then be the case that the circle of
> Nairātmyāyoginī is not asserted as realization?

Given the different meaning of the last two lines compared to the Sanskrit, one cannot help but suspect that the last line *rtogs par ci yi phyir mi 'dod* became somehow conflated with the last line of the following stanza (*rtogs par ci phyir 'grub mi byed*).

2972. GZ CDNP "You may think this: '[Meditating on the circle of Nairātmyāyoginī alone has the seven constituents] because it also has the union with the means [in the form of] the khaṭvāṅga.'"

2973. Again, this otherwise untraced stanza seems to be Rāmapāla's summary of the preceding sentence. GZ CDNP read the last two lines as follows:

> Being [GZ *yin par* CDNP *'khor lor* "as the circle of"] Nairātmyāyoginī,
> why would realization not be accomplished?

2974. GZ CDNP ". . . just as in the secret mantra approach . . . because there exists the union of bodhicitta that has the character of prajñā and means, even though there is no union as it is taught [here]."

2975. Again, this otherwise untraced stanza seems to be Rāmapāla's summary of the preceding paragraph. GZ CDNP read it as prose: "Casting off the special union [of the tantras], if [union] is conceived of in some other way, an absurd consequence would follow for the other yāna's emptiness and natural union."

2976. GZ CDNP "Therefore you may say: 'Here too, it is reasonable for the means of practice to be endowed with the seven constituents:'"

2977. *Hevajratantra* II.2.23cd–24ab. This stanza describes the transformation of the female form of Nairātmyā, as whom the practitioner has visualized himself or herself, into the male form of Hevajra by removing the breasts and them becoming (the shaft of) the penis, the two labia being transformed into the two testicles and the scrotum, and the clitoris into the glans penis. Note that most commentaries are explicit on the breasts themselves turning into the penis. As for "bell," Kṛṣṇa's *Yogaratnamālā*'s gloss *muṣka* can mean both "scrotum" and "testicle," but other commentaries gloss "bell" as "testicles." Most Indian commentaries are silent or nondescript about the meaning of "filament" (Skt. *kiñjalka*), but a few suggest understanding it as clitoris and *bolaka* as glans penis. Kṛṣṇa's *Yogaratnamālā* glosses "filament" as *naranāsā* (lit. "man-nose"; Farrow and Menon 1992, 160: "the central part of the vagina") and Ratnākaraśānti's *Muktāvalī* glosses it as "navel" and "nose," while the commentaries by Tagpo Dashi Namgyal (Dvags po bkra shis rnam rgyal 2002, 387) and Jamgön Kongtrul (Kong sprul blo gros mtha' yas 2005, 510) explicitly speak of "the filament of the bhaga" and gloss "bolaka" as "the jewel of the vajra" (on the other hand, Rāmapāla's commentary on stanza 7 clearly suggests that "filament" refers to the inside of the vagina). In any case, given that most commentaries say that the breasts turn into (the shaft of) the penis (*bola*), it makes sense to understand "filament" as the clitoris and *bolaka* as the glans. Note though that elsewhere *kiñjalka* and *naranāsikā* refer to the lower end of the avadhūtī in a woman. GZ treats the *yataḥ* preceding this stanza as a part of another initial line of verse ("For the entirety of this"; which is actually the beginning of the second sentence following this quote), and CDNP include it in the first line of this stanza; also, GZ CDNP replace "bolaka" with "vajra" and "kakkola" with "lotus."

2978. Skt. *peśala* can also mean "skillful," "clever," and "expert," but GZ CDNP read *mdzes pa* (which matches "this is not nice" above).

2979. "Such a type" refers to a practice that is endowed with all seven constituents, especially the visible union of two actual consorts. GZ CDNP "Therefore there would be the [absurd] consequence that the goal . . . in the Pāramitāyāna too [NP omit this phrase], even though there is no such practice; hence it is difficult to avoid [this consequence] for the Pāramitāyāna as well."

2980. This otherwise untraced stanza appears to be Rāmapāla's summary of this section on the goal endowed with the seven constituents. GZ has only the first two lines in verse, while CDNP have the entire stanza in prose:

> "First, since union's lack is cultivated [CDNP omit 'is cultivated'],
> when consummated, this will exist

"Though we assert such, the means of practice is other." In GZ CDNP, this is then followed by two further lines of verse (see below), concluded by *zhes brjod par byed de,* looking almost as if this entire passage were a single quote. IaS (273n112): "This verse appears to be a summary of Rāmapāla's thought on this question of the seven constituents. As such, it is likely, we think, to be his own composition, though it cannot perhaps be entirely excluded that it has been quoted from some source that is not known to us. As a summary, however, it seems still to leave some questions open. The first half is clear enough: in the case of the practice of Nairātmyā Yoginī, without her consort Hevajra, there is no (direct, sexual) Union; but when the goal is achieved there will be Union (in that the yogin then has the form of the syzygy of Hevajra and Nairātmyā, Means and Wisdom). The word *etad* in *pāda* c could be taken to refer to this statement in the first half: 'this [position of the absence of Union in the stage of practice and its presence in the stage of the goal] is accepted by us'. In that case, however, the particle *punaḥ* in *pāda* d is hard to justify. Furthermore, in the prose immediately following this verse, *etad eva* must be taken as referring to the goal; this seems to us a more or less decisive argument in favor of taking *etat* in the verse too as having the same referent. A further question to resolve is what Rāmapāla's position is regarding the seven constituents as related to the question of the difference between the Way of the Perfections and the Way of Mantras. Though it may be putting it slightly too strongly, we think, to say, as 'Bum la 'bar in his topical outline does, that Rāmapāla is refuting the idea that the fourth empowerment/the goal possesses the seven constituents (see Appendix 3, p. 381 below), he seems to us to at least be distancing himself slightly from that teaching, associated above all with Vāgīśvarakīrti (probably Maitreyanātha's senior contemporary). One of the functions of that teaching was to give a description of the tantric goal which set it in some way apart from the goal reached by the practice of the Way of Perfections, i.e. to distinguish the two branches of Mahāyāna on the level of the goal that they lead to. Rāmapāla's attitude seems to be that he is quite willing to accept that the goal of tantric practice is indeed characterized by the seven constituents, but that one has to admit that they are not all also necessarily present in the practice that leads to that goal. Therefore the principle of the correspondence of practice/cause to goal/result does not hold for the constituents; and therefore it is at least possible that the practice of the Way of Perfections too, even though it lacks at least one of the seven constituents, can lead to exactly the same goal that is attained through the practice of the Way of Mantras. This possibility is undesired at least by the proponents of the teaching of the seven constituents (Vāgīśvarakīrti and others), but may perhaps have been not unacceptable to Maitreyanātha and Rāmapāla (note e.g. the verse quoted from the **Nayatrayapradīpa* . . . below)." For these and other reasons, this whole section on the goal endowed with the seven constituents and its relationship with Vāgīśvarakīrti's *Saptāṅga* is problematic. As mentioned before, according to IaS, only the first sentence "Or rather what is the use of this practice endowed with the seven constituents?" in the first paragraph after the quote from the *Saptāṅga* is an objection and the rest of the paragraph is the answer, with the last sentence meaning that the ultimate fruition is endowed with the seven constituents, while its cause (the meditation that leads to this fruition) does not have to be endowed with all seven. By contrast, GZ CDNP consider this entire first paragraph as an objection. Another issue is whether the following stanza is also part of the objection or (a part of) the answer (the version in GZ CDNP does not serve as an answer), and the same applies to the next short paragraph (which appears to describe yet another disagreeing position) and the stanza that follows it. Given Rāmapāla's above sentence "The prajñājñāna that illustrates [the connate], repeatedly practiced in just that way . . . is the fourth one—that is, the goal that is endowed with the seven constituents," it seems clear that he defends such a practice that, through repeated cultivation, becomes equivalent to the actuality of the fourth empowerment and thus the final goal endowed with the seven constituents. Thus, to answer the question "What is the use of this practice endowed with the seven constituents?" by saying that there is no fixed rule and that other practices that do not include all seven constituents are still the cause of buddhahood seems not to be to the point of the question (or may even be seen as outrightly undermining Rāmapāla's position; see also below in this note). From that perspective, it would make sense to consider the whole first paragraph, as well as the following stanza, which sounds like a rhetorical question confirming what is said in this paragraph, as an objection. Likewise, the stanza following the next paragraph also sounds like a rhetorical question conforming the content of said paragraph (in any case, as mentioned above, I consider these two stanzas as Rāmapāla's own summaries of the paragraphs that precede them). The first unambiguous and explicit phrase that clearly starts an answer by Rāmapāla is the sentence "[However, to understand] this [in such a way] is not nice either." So it could even be that both of the preceding paragraphs and their stanzas are objections, followed by the answer that begins with "[However . . .]" and consists of an absurd consequence. But then there is the problem that this absurd consequence only applies to the immediately preceding second objection and not the first one. The same absurd consequence is then also adduced against the third (and similar) objection that adduces *Hevajratantra* II.2.23cd–24ab. In brief, the three objections here seem to be as follows. (1) It is a contradiction that there are practices that do not fully conform to the ultimate goal/fruition, because they are not endowed with (any or all of?) the seven constituents and yet are considered causes of awakening. (2)–(3) In fact, such practices are not deficient because all seven constituents are included in them in either a symbolic (or implicit) manner or by way of a sex change that is considered as "union." Rāmapāla's answers seem to be that (1) though the ultimate fruition is endowed with the seven constituents, the practices that are its cause do not have to be endowed with (any or all of?) the seven. (2)–(3) If "union" were only meant in a symbolic or abstract manner, it would follow that the goal endowed with the seven constituents is also accomplished in the Pāramitāyāna, despite its lack of a practice that involves the visible union of two actual consorts. This still leaves the question of whether there is indeed any practice at all that is endowed with the seven constituents (such as mahāmudrā as the practice of the fourth empowerment). On the one hand, Rāmapāla seems to consider the practice of the fourth empowerment as such a practice, since he says "The prajñā-jñāna that illustrates [the connate], repeatedly practiced in just that way . . . *is* the fourth one—that is, the goal that is endowed with the seven constituents," and then again speaks of "this practice endowed with the seven constituents." On the other hand, he concludes this section by saying:

First, union's lack should be cultivated
At its completion, this [union] will arise
This is [the goal] that is asserted by us
Nevertheless, the practice is otherwise.

By contrast, in the detailed explanation of the seven constituents in the *Saptāṅga* as summarized above, there is no doubt that these seven apply only to complete buddhahood (thus the question seems not to be whether some practices are closer to the goal because they also possess the seven constituents, versus others that do not). Note that Maitrīpa's *Sekatātparyasaṃgraha* (text 37, 203) also contains a reference to what is said in Vāgīśvarakīrti's *Saptāṅga*: "Some say that the meaning of the fourth [empowerment] refers to what is to be accomplished, which is characterized by prajñā-jñāna and endowed with the seven constituents." Compare also the discussion of this issue, with a somewhat different explanation of the seven constituents, in Divākaracandra's *Prajñājñānaprakāśa* (text 16, 61): "'Isn't one able to know this experience without a shapely woman who is a karmamudrā?' This [question] is not nice: an outer [karma]mudrā is said to be a result of concordant outflow, but this is [of course] not true reality. It is tenable for what is endowed with these seven constituents to be the wisdom of emptiness and compassion inseparable. (1) Since it is completely enjoyed in such a way, complete enjoyment refers to experience: thanks to dependent origination, it appears as all aspects. (2) It is union because emptiness and compassion are completely unified in an inseparable manner. (3) It is great bliss because all thoughts of existence, nonexistence, and so on have been relinquished. (4) It lacks a nature [because] it is unborn. (5) It is filled with compassion because it has the character of compassion. (6) It is uninterrupted because it is permanent in terms of its continuum. (7) It is unceasing because it is not discontinued. Those special features do not exist in the wisdom thanks to a shapely woman who is a karma[mudrā]." Still, similar to the *Saptāṅga* and the *Sekanirdeśapañjikā* here, the *Prajñājñānaprakāśa* (70 and 75) says that the buddhahood endowed with the seven constituents can only be attained through the mantra approach's four mudrās—especially the karmamudrā—but not through the Pāramitāyāna. Thus the *Saptāṅga*, the *Prajñājñānaprakāśa*, and *Sekanirdeśapañjikā* here agree that the bliss as a result of karmamudrā practice per se is not endowed with the seven constituents (it is only the bliss that illustrates the actual bliss of mahāmudrā related to the fourth empowerment). Nevertheless, the special permanent bliss of mahāmudrā needs to arise from continuously refining the momentary bliss experienced in karmamudrā practice.

2981. GZ CDNP:

"'Others than these [hold]

illusion-like nonduality'

"Thus this is expressed. How is that? [CDNP 'Just as . . .' = Skt. *yathā*, which links this dream example with *tathā* at the beginning of the paragraph after the following quote.] Another [CDNP omit 'another'] dream entity that is an imagined dream, which will be experienced right after the experience of sexual pleasure with a passionate woman experienced in a dream, is not extinguished, because it is experienced; nor is it delusive [CDNP omit 'is not . . . experienced' and continue 'Therefore it is not delusive . . .'], because it is experienced. Nor is it real, because there is no nondeception, as in the case of a substantial thing [CDNP omit 'thing'] observed during the waking state, which performs functions and is experienced [CDNP 'perceived'] by [both] oneself and others."

2982. *Svapnanirukti* 6. GZ CDNP:

> If dreams are just like dreams,
> the diversity of mind is delusive
> It is not real, as it is not aware [I follow GZ NP *rig* against CD *rigs*]
> It is not extinct [I follow GZ NP *chad pa* against CD *chags pa* 'attachment'], as it is lucidity.

2983. GZ CDNP ". . . this diversity of the world is neither extinguished nor delusive [CDNP omit "neither extinguished"], because it is experienced. Nor is it ultimately real, because it is said 'since it is not associated with any arising of something existent or nonexistent' and so on. By clinging to it as dependent origination, it is utterly unborn ultimately, because the unborn mind does not exist [CDNP 'Nor is it ultimately real; for by grasping it as dependent origination by virtue of saying "it is not associated with any arising of something existent or nonexistent" and so on, the unborn mind does not exist in what is utterly unborn ultimately']."

2984. *Yuktiṣaṣṭikā* 19.

2985. GZ *zhi ba nyid* ("being peaceful").

2986. Here and in the following instance, GZ CDNP read *rig pa* ("awareness") instead of *rigs pa*.

2987. Skt. *lakṣya* ("what is to be marked" or "what is to be perceived") in the first line is rendered as "target" in IaS (275) and "goal" in Mathes 2015 (120). As mentioned before, these two lines of uncertain origin are also cited in Nāgārjuna's *Caturmudrānvaya* (text 14, 27), Sujayaśrīgupta's *Abhiṣekanirukti*, *Kuladatta's *Kriyāsaṃgrahapañjikā*, and Kumāracandra's *Ratnāvalī* (for exact references, see IaS, 275n120). In addition, two very similar lines (obviously variants of the two here) are found in the *Caturmudrāṭīkā* (text 44, 284) and Vajrapāṇi's *Guruparamparākramopadeśa* (text 213, 210). For more details, see the note on these lines cited in the *Caturmudrānvaya* (text 14, 27).

GZ CDNP read the two lines quoted here as follows:

> In the middle of the supreme and cessational ecstasies,
> it should be pointed out, looked at, and relied upon [CD *bstan*, "shown" NP *brtan*, "stabilized"].

2988. This refers to the genitive of the compound *paramaviramayoḥ* ("of the supreme and cessational") in the immediately preceding quotation. In addition, as the following sentence indicates, the opponent understands *madhye* in this quote not as "middle" but as "among" or "of."

2989. As mentioned before, the sequence of objections and answers beginning with this objection parallel similar passages in the *Caturmudrāṭīkā* (text 44, 284–87) and Vajrapāṇi's *Guruparamparākramopadeśa* (text 213, 210–13). However, in its translation of the *Sekanirdeśapañjikā*, IaS (275–77) considers most of these objections (or parts thereof) to be Rāmapāla's answers and vice versa. Not only does this break the symmetry of the dictions in certain objections by taking them to be answers, but most of it does not match Rāmapāla's own position either. Moreover, the *Guruparamparākramopadeśa* explicitly identifies the first and some of the further objections as coming from the proponents of the forceful empowerment that is to be rejected, and (with a single minor exception in GZ of text 45) the places of the Tibetan *zhe na* markers of the objections in the *Caturmudrāṭīkā*, the *Sekanirdeśapañjikā*, and the *Guruparamparākramopadeśa* match exactly in all three texts. By contrast, IaS (275) considers only the first sentence in this objection as the objection while taking its remainder as Rāmapāla's answer: "[Reply by the opponent:] This is not true, because this [line of verse] means something else. To explain: this genitive [*paramaviramayoḥ*] is used in partitive sense . . . So nothing is out of place.'" GZ CDNP: ". . . the middle of both [supreme ecstasy and cessational ecstasy] is asserted. In your teaching, this does not exist. 'This is not so, the meaning of this is something else [GZ 'the meaning of this is this'] . . . Among these two (in the middle) [CD 'in the middle of these two'], the best one [CDNP 'the main one'] should be taken here, and the main one is exactly cessational ecstasy. So there is not the slightest thing here that is not good.'"

2990. This appears to be a variant of *Hevajratantra* II.69ef (II.5.70ef in IaS and Snellgrove 1959), which reads as follows:

> At the supreme's end and the cessational's start,
> this is empty yet nonempty, being the Heruka.

IaS (275–76n123): "This is a curious case. One would expect the quotation to be, as all the other scriptural quotations adduced by both parties in this lengthy discussion on the order of the Blisses are, from the *Hevajratantra*. The second *pāda* indeed corresponds to *Hevajratantra* 2.5.70f. Note that although the published editions of the *Hevajratantra* all print there *śūnyāśūnyaṃ* (which is supported also by the canonical Tibetan translation of the *Hevajratantra* and by, for instance, the commentary by Kamalanātha), Ratnākaraśānti appears rather to have read *śūnyāc chūnyam*, as we find here in the Sanskrit of the *Sekanirdeśapañjikā* (*Muktāvalī*, p. 215). However the *pāda* that precedes that, *Hevajratantra* 2.5.70e, has been printed either in the form *paramāntaṃ viramādhyaṃ* (sic!), as in the editions by Snellgrove and by Tripathi and Negi, or in the form *paramāntaṃ viramādyaṃ*, as in the edition by Farrow and Menon. The majority of the manuscripts of the *Hevajratantra* appear to point to readings such as *paramāntaṃ madhyaviramaṃ* (supported by Ratnākaraśānti's commentary), *paramāntaṃ madhyaviramasya*, *paramāntamadhyaviramasya*, or *paramāntaṃ madhyaṃ viramasya* (cf. also Snellgrove's n. 1 on p. 86). The only (other) direct testimony for these two *pāda*s which we have noted so far in texts available in Sanskrit is in Raviśrījñāna's *Amṛtakaṇikā* (p. 62), where we find for the first *pāda* the reading *paramāntamadhyaviramaś ca* (where ºś *ca* might well be a corruption of º*sya*). It would seem, therefore, that Rāmapāla is quoting a strikingly different version of the *pāda*, and one which we know of no other attestation for. One might however wonder whether there could be a corruption here in the transmission of the *Sekanirdeśapañjikā*. It could be regarded as slightly suspicious that in the prose immediately following the quotation, and commenting on it, we find the words *paramāt pāraḥ*, exactly identical with the words in the first *pāda*. It may be possible that in fact Rāmapāla quoted a version of the first *pāda* that was one of those we find transmitted in the *Hevajratantra* (or close to that), and that readings from (or close to) the following explanation were in error substituted in the quotation . . . The Tibetan translation of the quotation in the *Sekanirdeśapañjikā* supports, in the first *pāda*, the Sanskrit (so that if there is indeed a major corruption there in the Sanskrit manuscripts, it was shared by the manuscript(s) used by the translators). In the second *pāda* there is a somewhat odd situation, however: the canonical witnesses read *stoṅ las stoṅ min he ru ka*, where the ablative particle *las* seems at first sight to correspond to the ablative of *śūnyāt* (supported, as mentioned above, by Ratnākaraśānti's commentary, though not by the majority of the *Hevajratantra* transmission), but *stoṅ min* seems to correspond to º*aśūnyam*. dPal's variant, *stoṅ daṅ stoṅ min*, on the other hand corresponds perfectly, not to the reading we have in the Sanskrit of the *Sekanirdeśapañjikā* but to the reading *śūnyāśūnyaṃ*, and to the canonical translation of the *Hevajratantra*."

2991. GZ CDNP: "In that case, this does not match the following either:

> "At cessational ecstasy's start and supreme ecstasy's end,
> this is empty yet nonempty, representing the Heruka

"Hence the way this passage is [or 'the scriptural tradition'] is this: 'the start of cessational ecstasy [is] the end of supreme ecstasy.'" IaS takes this passage to be an objection by the opponent.

2992. This means that the opponent interprets *viramādi* ("the beginning of the cessational") in *Hevajratantra* 2.5.69e as a *karmadhāraya* compound instead of a *tatpuruṣa* compound.

2993. GZ CDNP: "[Objection:] 'But this is not so. For the meaning is another one: [the text speaks of] "the start of cessational ecstasy," since it refers to what is both cessational ecstasy and the beginning, because the beginning is in relation to connate [ecstasy] . . .'" IaS takes this objection to be an answer by Rāmapāla.

2994. I.10.18cd. Again, IaS takes this to be an objection by the opponent.

2995. GZ CDNP omit the phrase "should be interpreted."

2996. *Hevajratantra* II.3.8ab. GZ CDNP:

> Consummation is said to be agitation [CDNP "analysis"],
> the experiencer [CDNP "experience"] of one's own bliss

IaS takes this to be an objection by the opponent and only the following paragraph to be Rāmapāla's answer.

2997. As GZ CDNP *tshig rnams* shows, Skt. *pādānām* could also be understood as "words" here, given the following explanation of what "consummation" and so on mean for worldly people.

2998. Skt. *vivāda* and *kṣodana* are equivalents of two of the more common meanings among the many meanings of *vimarda*.

2999. GZ CDNP "Here it should be clearly understood that the words 'consummation' and so on have the essence of thought. For even so, here, how could this be expressed as 'thought-free?' [GZ ends this with an out-of-place *zhe na*]. Therefore it is invalidated by common worldly consensus. The world thinks: 'This is consummation, dispute, friction, analysis, and thinking about its tasks [CDNP 'purpose'] and so on.'"

3000. II.3.9. GZ CDNP read these four lines by reversing and equating the first and second phrases in each line, thus saying "The first ecstasy is variety" and so on; the same goes for the following prose sentence.

3001. I.10.13. GZ CDNP omit "nature" in the first line and read "observed" instead of "found" in the last line.

3002. As IaS (277n132) points out, this line is *Saṃvarodayatantra* X.46c and *Netratantra* XIX.148a (an authoritative tantra of nondual Kashmiri Śaivism). Compare also Nāgārjuna's *Cittavajrastava* 5bcd (text 212):

> saṃsāra, habituation by thought,
> is indeed nothing but thought—
> the lack of thought is liberation

and Mokṣākaragupta's *Dohakoṣapañjikā* (text 67, 338): "saṃsāra's nature merely consists of the thoughts of mind as such." As here, we sometimes find the statement in Mahāyāna texts that "saṃsāra is nothing but thought (or conception or imagination)." Obviously, it would not make sense to say such when "thought" is understood in the ordinary sense of that word because that would exclude all nonconceptual experiences, feelings, and perceptions, such as those of the senses. Likewise, liberation is not simply the sheer absence of thought; otherwise, deep sleep, a coma, or being completely drunk would be liberation. Rather, "thought," conception," or "imagination" encompass the entire—fundamentally deluded and dualistic—constructive activity of the mind that can imagine or project all kinds of appearances and experiences, both conceptual and nonconceptual. In other words, mind continually imagines or constructs its own world and becomes immediately trapped in its own creation.

3003. GZ CDNP: "Here, it is taught to be mere saṃsāric conception; it will be taught that [consummation] is conceptual. But since connate [ecstasy] is asserted to be nonconceptual, this too will not be established for you [CDNP 'But the assertion of the nonconceptuality of connate [ecstasy] will not be established']."

3004. GZ CDNP *ngo bo gang* ("what has the essence . . .").

3005. II.2.40ab (line b is also found in II.5.65b and II.5.69e).

3006. Here and after the following quote, GZ CDNP read "is not tenable."

3007. GZ *ldan pas* ("with endowment").

3008. According to IaS (277n136), this unlocated stanza is also quoted in the *Abhiṣekanirukti*; in CDNP this stanza is prose.

3009. Except for "empowerment" instead of "supreme" in the second line, this stanza is identical to *Guhyasamājatantra* XVIII.113cf, which is quoted in many tantric commentaries in Tg (as it stands, this stanza is also found at the beginning of Maitrīpa's *Sekatātparyasaṃgraha*, but just as here, the reference must be the *Guhyasamājatantra*). With the additional replacement of "vase" by "master" in the first line and adding "empowerment" in the third, this stanza is also found in the *Mahāmudrātilakatantra* (H380, fol. 435b.2) and the *Jñānatilakatantra* (H382, fol. 9a.1–2). The first three lines (followed by "Just as it is, the body is the tathāgata") are also found in the *Ḍākinīvajrapañjaratantra* (H379, fol. 401a.7). Note that, exactly as it appears here, this stanza is also included in Vajrapāṇi's *Vajrapada* (text 47, stanza 4), while his *Guruparamparākramopadeśa* (text 213, 197) replaces "vase" by "master" in the first line, thus being closer to the *Mahāmudrātilakatantra* and *Jñānatilakatantra*.

3010. IaS (278n138): "Rāmapāla can hardly mean that the sequence of the consecrations as taught in the *Guhyasamāja*, the *Hevajratantra*, and other sources is wrong. What is possible instead, and what fits in the context of the passage, is that the verse is being discussed from the point of view of what evidence it provides for the sequence of the Moments. And the problem must be that the *prajñājñājnābhiṣeka* may be homologized with Bliss of Cessation, the Fourth consecration being homologized with the Innate Bliss. Since, then, the *prajñājñājnābhiṣeka* is third within the set of consecrations, this might suggest that the corresponding moment, *vimarda*, is likewise the third of the four Moments. It is this possibility that is contradicted; the sequence of consecrations does not imply a sequence of Moments/Blisses with *vimarda*/Cessation the third. And the justification given for the lack of precise numerical correspondence is that the third consecration, the *prajñājñājnābhiṣeka*, also is known as the consecration of the Innate Bliss. So in some way it too corresponds to the Innate Bliss, as the Fourth consecration also does. It is in this sense that the Fourth is 'that (i.e. the experience of the *prajñājñājnābhiṣeka*) again'. However it is not so much this correspondence of the *prajñājñājnābhiṣeka* with the Innate Bliss (which is, again, actually not its main or normal correspondence for Maitreyanātha) that is here being emphasized, but rather simply the negative point that the sequence of the consecrations must not be understood as implying the 'wrong' sequence of the Moments and Blisses."

3011. GZ CDNP "Hence the statement 'the prajñā-jñāna empowerment is the empowerment of connate ecstasy' is thereby also invalidated. Therefore, since [I follow NP *'gal bas* against GZ *'gal bas so* / CD *'gal ba'i*] the primary text/passage would be invalidated and the scriptures would also be contradicted, consummation is conceptual and therefore should not be asserted as being the third. For since in that [third moment] a nonconceptual sensation exists, this very connate including its accompanying factors is summed up." GZ CDNP omit the following sentence that introduces stanza 4 but take its phrase "sum up" as the end of the last phrase in this paragraph here.

3012. IaS (278n140): "The *upaskāra* ('enhancement', 'modification', or 'addition of words to a sentence', cf. *Aṣṭādhyāyī* 6.1.139) seems to consist in the second half of the verse, in which additional arguments are briefly given."

3013. IaS (279n143): "Here we have emended the reading of both the manuscripts, *ālocanaṃ vimardaś ced ityādibādhā darśitā*, to *ālocanaṃ vimardaś ced ityādinā bādhā darśitā*. The Tibetan translation as transmitted seems to agree with the Sanskrit manuscripts . . . The sentence below *ālocanam ityādinā* (Ca, supported by Tib.; only Pt reads again *ityādi*º) *bādhā darśitā* gives further support to the conjectures both in the Sanskrit and in the Tibetan."

3014. *Hevajratantra* I.10.13c.

3015. IaS (279n145): "We are not certain what 'the passage beginning with "Seeing"' (*ālocanam ityādigranthaḥ*) refers to. It seems hardly possible that it should be an allusion to verse 3 of the *Sekanirdeśa*, to which the immediately following '[the verse] beginning with "[If] seeing"' (*ālocanam ityādinā*) refers. That would be virtually nonsensical; and in general 'not fitting' (*vighaṭana* . . . and so on) should, we assume, refer to scriptural passages, rather than statements of Maitreyanātha or other masters. However there is no scriptural passage quoted above that begins with the word 'Seeing' (*ālocanam*). It seems that it might make sense to have a reference here to *Hevajratantra* 2.3.8, which was quoted twice above . . . However it seems likewise hardly possible that Rāmapāla should refer to that verse as 'the passage beginning with "Seeing"', instead of 'the passage beginning with "[And] *vimarda* is [taught to be] seeing"' (*vimardam ālocanam ityādigranthaḥ*) or simply 'the passage beginning with "*Vimarda*"' (*vimardam ityādigranthaḥ*). Again, it might be wondered whether this is a reference to yet another scriptural passage; but if it has not been quoted already in the preceding discussions (in which there is none that begins with the word 'Seeing') it seems very strange that Rāmapāla should not quote it here in full. It may therefore be significant that this sentence has no correspondent in the Tibetan translation. Both syntactically and as regards the argument presented the passage would read perfectly well without it. One should therefore at least consider the possibility that it has been interpolated and should be excised. This solution is attractive to us, but nonetheless at the same time we are hesitant about it because it is not easy to imagine what prompted the secondary addition, whereas the absence of a reflex in the Tibetan translation can, if the passage is after all original, be explained more easily, in more than one way . . ."

3016. As mentioned before, this is a quote of uncertain origin that is also found in the *Caturmudrānvaya* (text 14, 27) and other texts. GZ CDNP: "'Therefore it is proper for the lack of characteristics . . .' is easy to understand. [Objection:] 'But since it is not [really] an invalidation [if done] by common worldly consensus, how would it be that [CDNP omit this phrase] [Maitrīpa] has demonstrated invalidation beginning with "Thus it is expressed as consummation"?' . . . For all scriptures as taught [above], being invalidations of the topic at hand here—that is, consummation having a worldly nature by way of [the line] 'cessational ecstasy is worldly as well'—would not be established. With [the stanza] beginning with 'Consummation is said to be friction [CDNP 'analysis'],' [Maitrīpa] has demonstrated the invalidation . . .

"In the middle of the supreme and cessational ecstasies,
it should be pointed out, looked at, and relied upon [CD *bstan*,
'shown' NP *brtan*, 'stabilized']

"And this does not exist in your approach" (GZ CDNP consider this last sentence as part of this passage instead of the beginning of the following objection).

3017. I.8.30. Kṛṣṇa's *Yogaratnamālā* (Snellgrove 1959, 2:127) glosses Skt. *śeṣataḥ* ("as remainder") as *pariśeṣād* (basically same meanings as *śeṣa*). Note, however, that *śeṣataḥ* can also mean "otherwise" or "else," which is one of its two glosses by Rāmapāla below (*tribhyo anyatayā*, "other than the three [preceding ecstasies]").

3018. That is, the order of the initial letters of *ānanda*, *parama*, *virama*, and *sahaja* in the Sanskrit alphabet.

3019. GZ CDNP: ". . . ecstasy, supreme ecstasy, and cessational ecstasy pertain to slight bliss, more intense [bliss] than that, and dispassion [the rather nonsensical GZ *de bas lhag pa dang / chags 'dzin dang bral ba'i phyir ro* and CDNP *de bas na lhag pa'i 'dod chags 'dzin pa'i phyir* are emended to *de bas lhag pa dang / 'chags pa dang bral bar'dzin pa'i phyir*]. Hence the remainder, since it is the utter remainder, should be understood to be connate ecstasy, which is other than the three [preceding ecstasies]. Alternatively, 'ecstasy,' 'supreme ecstasy,' 'cessational ecstasy,' and 'connate ecstasy' are presented by the force of their [alphabetical] order. However, what should be understood is that connate [ecstasy] is the third one."

3020. This sentence clearly echoes a passage in Maitrīpa's *Caturmudropadeśa* (text 92, 19–20): "Such is explained by mixing up [the order of the ecstasies] for the sake of persons who fail to rely on a guru and become learned [just] through tomes of scriptures. In such [scriptures], [connate ecstasy] is the fourth in number, but in terms of the meaning it corresponds to the third [moment]. Therefore, [the followers of] the forceful yoga here lack expertise in terms of both the sequence and the meaning." GZ CDNP: "'Due to what didn't the Bhagavān [solely] teach the excellent empowerment in such words? Why did he teach the forceful empowerment through the sequence 'ecstasy, supreme ecstasy, cessational ecstasy, and connate [ecstasy]' with words of necessity/purpose for those with many afflictions?' . . . As for teaching that sequence like this, he taught that sequence in such a way in order to refute [the reliance on] being learned through books and not depending on a spiritual friend."

3021. GZ adds "is known to be".

3022. Compare the *Gaṇḍavyūhasūtra* (Suzuki and Idzumi 1949, 28116): *kalyāṇamitrādhīnā sarvajñatā* ("All-knowledge is dependent . . .").

3023. This is *Saṃvarodayatantra* XXVI.52d and *Pañcakrama* III.45d. I follow GZ NP *mnyes pa las thob par* against CD *mnyes par sa thob par*.

3024. IaS (281n159): "The opponent had asked two (related) questions: why the Bhagavān did not simply only teach the easy (and correct) consecration (without mentioning the wrong and forceful consecrations), and why did he in some places teach the Blisses in the sequence with the Innate Bliss as fourth, which might cause some to think that he supports the forceful initiation, which is associated with that sequence? Rāmapāla seems to have answered the second of these questions first. The second part of this paragraph (from 'Furthermore, [...]') must be related to the first question, but rather than clearly answering it, Rāmapāla seems to say that the differentiation (or separate establishing, *vyavasthā*) of the *nirākāra* and the other positions, shown in the context of the forceful and wrong consecration, is itself not intended to be refuted. It is only the wrong application (in the forceful and bad initiation) of that differentiation that is refuted. This does not seem, logically, a reason why the Bhagavān should have had to mention those wrong understandings of the consecrations, for it would have been possible for him to simply teach the excellent consecration and the differentiation of the *nirākāra* and the other positions, together with the correct application thereof. It seems that the logic, if there is one, of the answer is, then: in fact the Bhagavān has referred to the forceful and wrong consecrations, refuting them, and in the context thereof has mentioned the differentiation of the *nirākāra* and so on. If that reference and refutation were simply left out, the differentiation of the *nirākāra* would not be mentioned at all. But it should be mentioned, as it itself is not intended to be refuted."

3025. GZ CDNP "Here, the forceful empowerment and the poor empowerment are refuted because they slightly contradict scripture, but the presentation of consummation and so on is not refuted, which is because of the mere contradiction with the application of those. Therefore [CDNP 'then'] this was taught here for the sake of those who state that [NP omit this phrase] the entire presentation of the tenet of the excellent empowerment should be understood [I follow CDNP *rig pa* against GZ *rigs pa*] as the essence of the Vajradhara relief. Since the proponents of the forceful empowerment state this in such a way in their own tenet, this has been taught in such a way for their sake."

3026. GZ CDNP: "Right after this [Maitrīpa] utters [the stanza] beginning with 'For whom . . .' in order to teach the poor empowerment."

3027. IaS (282n163): "The transmission of the text is problematic here, and we have hesitated long about the best solution. The manuscripts read respectively *ratna dūṣya* (Ca) and *ratne duṣpa* (Pt). The word *dūṣya* seems semantically inappropriate, and the *lyap* for *ktvā* (the correct form would be *dūṣayitvā*) would be, as far as we can say, untypical for Rāmapāla's Sanskrit. We also considered the conjecture *ratnaṃ vyāpya*, 'pervading the jewel'. But in the end we felt that *ratne* was probably right, corresponding to *manau* in the verse, and supported by the Tibetan (*rin po cher*). The Tibetan rendering *bkag pa nas*, 'having blocked/obstructed', suggested the possibility of the conjecture *ruddhvā*, and in the end we decided that this seemed to give the most appropriate sense. For the apparently odd *vakṣyamānasthānaṃ yāvat* not directly linked with the absolutive *ruddhvā* cf., perhaps, *manyagraṃ yāvat* (with no verbal form present in the sentence at all) in the commentary on verse 23 below. It should perhaps be noted that a little later in the Tibetan translation of the same sentence, D has a phrase *su naṅ byuṅ bar* (dPal enlarges this by adding *bya ba'i*), which is lacking in P, G and N, and corresponds to nothing at that place in the Sanskrit: could it be a fragment of a revised/alternative translation of this problematic expression?" Note here that CD (according to PDMT) do not read, as IaS says, *su nang byung bar* but *sun dbyung bar*, and GZ similarly says *sun dbyung bar bya ba'i*, corresponding to Skt. *duṣyati* and *dūṣayitavyaḥ*, *dūṣaṇīyatvam*, or *dūṣyaḥ*, respectively. Thus, it seems that GZ CDNP *bkag pa nas* is a clarifying addition, while the original Sanskrit appears to have been something like *ratne dūṣyavakṣyamānasthānaṃ*, which would also resolve the above-mentioned problem with "the apparently odd *vakṣyamānasthānaṃ yāvat* not directly linked with the absolutive *ruddhvā*." The expression "becoming spoiled"—obviously in the sense of "being emitted"—certainly fits the context of the criticized poor empowerment.

3028. Skt. *āmananti* can also mean "hand down in sacred texts," "quote," "allege," "commit to memory," and "celebrate," all of which make sense here too.

3029. GZ CDNP "Variety consists of all [NP omit 'all'] the external activity beginning with looking, for as long as they last. Maturation consists of the friction beginning with engaging [obviously reading *pravṛtti* instead of *prabhṛti*] through the union of vajra and lotus up to the moon emerging at just the upper part of the jewel. The lack of characteristics is blocking [bodhicitta] in the jewel up to [bodhicitta moving through] the jewel [CDNP omit 'jewel'] [to] the place where it becomes spoiled [NP omit 'where it becomes spoiled'], which will be explained [below]. They who think thus are hence [CDNP 'those'] said to 'indeed know the poor empowerment well.' 'Know well' means that [Maitrīpa] laughs [at them]."

3030. GZ *rin chen phreng ba* instead of CDNP *rin chen*.

3031. GZ CDNP "Because this is Śiva, it is Śiva. Because this is the Veda, it is the Veda. [Objection:] 'Does such a [statement] exist in the [teachings of] Śiva and so on?' Therefore [Maitrīpa] utters [the stanza] beginning 'It is this very jewel city, oh you goddess [NP omit the last phrase] . . .'"

3032. For the many meanings of Śakti, see the note on this stanza in text 42.

3033. Skt. *niḥsāra* can also mean "worthless," "unsubstantial," and "issuing out."

3034. Skt. *kalyāṇa* can also mean "well-being," "virtue," "auspiciousness," "excellence," "prosperity," "good fortune," "happiness," and "goodness," which of course all apply to Śiva.

3035. GZ CDNP "Its 'city' (that which is [its] place), held to have the nature of bliss, is the 'jewel city.' Having fallen 'within the filament' means it has melted and thus become without pith. 'Rudra' refers to the Bhagavān Rudra. 'Joined together' refers to union. 'Śiva' refers to the one who makes virtue arise . . . 'This' refers to the essence. Śakti is the nature of mind. 'Supreme' (primary) refers to true reality."

3036. As mentioned before, the first two lines of this stanza (also) correspond to *Lokātītastava* 12ab.

3037. IaS (284n177): "Not everyone may agree that the intended meaning of the second half of the verse is easy to grasp. The overall idea in the passage seems to be that Śakti, in the sense of the power of consciousness, and identified with the highest Reality (cf. the commentary on verse 7 above), that because of which and as which things appear, should not be taken to be 'absolutely real' in an ontological sense. Rather it is beyond the four extremes of existence etc., as Rāmapāla is about to go on to say. But how, and how well, this can be rhymed with the very Buddhist sounding statement that this same

Śakti is the view/seeing of Emptiness, destroying all superimpositions, is to us less than clear."

3038. GZ CDP "'Saṃsāric existence' refers to external forms and so on. They do not exist [NP omit 'do not exist'] 'in true reality' (ultimately). 'In that case, how about what appears as blue and so on?' Therefore [Maitrīpa] says: 'If it has been meditated on as the form of Śakti.' . . . have the essence of mind. 'In that case, just that [power of the mind] should be truly existent.' . . . [Maitrīpa] says: 'Seeing that it is empty is what represents Śakti . . .' . . . In order to teach that such a [true reality] is the middle free of the four extremes, this is taught in the Śakti-tantra 'The Branches of the Peak of Berga':

"It is not real, not delusive, not real
and delusive, and not devoid of both
The state of this is difficult to realize—
what else more supreme than it exists?"

3039. As mentioned before, IaS (284n180) says: "As far as we are aware, no manuscript(s) of a tantra of this name survive(s). Several Śaiva tantric texts mention a *Ucchuṣmatantra* or *Ucchuṣmabhairavatantra*, though; for a collection of such references, and some discussion (not arriving at a firm conclusion), see Hatley 2007: 275–280."
3040. GZ CDNP "middle."
3041. GZ CDNP "The teaching [that this true reality] is the culmination of yogīs thus realizing [NP omit 'realizing'] the wisdom of awareness consists of [the stanza] . . ."
3042. As mentioned before, IaS (285n182) says that Maitrīpa's label "Yoga Chapter" (*yogādhyāya*) is unclear. Probably the oldest source in which the following stanza occurs is the *Śivadharmottara* (*jñānayogo nāma tṛtīyo 'dhyāyaḥ* in the chapter colophon is somewhat reminiscent of *Yogādhyāya*). However, several other Śaiva works that borrowed the stanza could also be Maitrīpa's source.
3043. GZ CDNP "Now, given that Vedānta is discussed through the come-down sequence of the scriptural traditions that will be explained [below], therefore [Maitrīpa] states the first half . . . in order to easily understand this through those and in order to discard this."
3044. *Bhagavadgītā* 3.42 = *Mahābhārata* 6.25.42. Here, given the technicality of the terms *manas* and *buddhi*, as found in the *Mahābhārata* and the developed Sāṃkhya system, I left them untranslated. In Sāṃkhya, the eleven faculties consist of the five sense faculties, the five physical faculties (speech, arms, legs, anus, genitalia), and the mental faculty or thinking (*manas*). *Buddhi* ("cognition") or *mahat* ("the great one") splits off from its original unity with the *prakṛti* (primal substance). This cognition (itself being matter) is like a two-sided mirror in which outside objects and the person (*puruṣa*) on the inside meet like reflections. Thus the *puruṣa* can experience the manifestations only through this cognition, which renders the senses cognizant. The objects experienced by the person trigger his or her experiences of pleasure or pain. Cognition also produces identification (*ahaṃkāra*), the basic mistaken tendency of the *puruṣa* to identify itself with the manifestations of the *prakṛti*, become entangled in them, and thus suffer. From this mistaken identifica-

tion, the remaining manifestations in the Sāṃkhya system evolve. "He" in the last line of this stanza refers to the supreme godhead, variously called Viṣṇu, Vasudeva, Kṛṣṇa, Hari, or Nārāyaṇa in the *Bhagavadgītā*. The first line in GZ accords with the Sanskrit, while CDNP have it as "The proponents of something else being more supreme than the faculties [say]." The last three lines read as follows in GZ CDNP:

The *manas* [I follow NP *yid* against GZ CD *yin*] is beyond the faculties
What is beyond the *manas* is the *buddhi*
That which is beyond the *buddhi* is that.

3045. GZ CDNP "In order to teach in detail what has been taught before, so as to illustrate the *Bhagavatsiddhānta* through the Vedānta's example, [Maitrīpa] utters [the stanza] . . ."
3046. As pointed out in IaS (287n191), this is *Vijñānabhairava* 69 (one of the most important Śaiva tantras).
3047. This indicates that *saṅkṣobhāt* ("excited") in the stanza is in the ablative.
3048. Skt. *svākyaṃ* is glossed by its equivalent *svakīyaṃ*.
3049. IaS (287n198): "Untraced. Kaulāgama here appears to be a term referring to non-dual, liberated, awareness; called Kaulāgama perhaps in the sense of 'the coming of Kaula [bliss/ awareness]', perhaps partly because the Kaula scriptures embody (and teach) it or arise from it." GZ CDNP: "[Here] 'Śakti' means the lalanā [GZ CDNP *rkyang ma* renders Skt. *lalanā* as the name of the left nāḍī, while it is clear that *lalanā* here simply means 'woman']. Meeting her is union. Moving refers to the incited moving of those two [GZ *de dag gnyis* CDNP *de nas* 'then']. In 'which is at the end of having power [here and in the following sentence, I follow GZ *dbang du gyur pa* against CDNP *dbang bskur* 'bestowing empowerment'] over the Śakti,' Śakti means 'endowed with branches' [CDNP 'endowed with Śakti's branches']. 'Having power' means strong passion, further and further increasing desire. 'The end of' that means the bliss at the end of that. 'The true reality of the Brahman' is the true reality of the wisdom of empowerment [or power; NP omit *dbang gi*]. 'That bliss' is proclaimed to be your very own one (your own). In that way, [this bliss] is equivalent to those [moments of bliss] that are located in the middle of the vajra, in its tip, in between, and in the skull. The gist of this is that the awareness that arises at the time of the unbearable ecstasy of utter ecstasy originating from the lalanā is the Veda—for that long, the scriptural system arising from the Veda springs forth [CDNP '. . . at the time of the ecstasy of utter ecstasy originating from the lalanā's entirety not becoming exhausted, for that long, it arises from the scriptural system arising from the Veda']."
3050. GZ CDNP ". . . beginning with 'By virtue of no arising of suffering.'"
3051. IaS (287n191): "The first two *pāda*s are identical with *Niśvāsakārikā* 20.29cd (p. 127); we are aware of no other close parallel for this half-verse. Note also that the fourth *pāda* is close to *Niśvāsakārikā* 20.30b. For the second half of the verse there are many more parallels; for the third *pāda*, indeed, too many to easily list here. It is often quoted in a way that implies that it is from Vedic *śruti* (cf., e.g., Jayaratha in his *Tantrālokaviveka ad* 30.97), although as far as we know, no actual Vedic text contains exactly these words."

3052. GZ CDNP "In order to teach that the world's essence is the same by virtue of these, [Maitrīpa] utters [the stanza] that begins 'Whatever tiny bit that may be seen.'"

3053. This stanza is also quoted in the *Tattvaratnāvalī*. As IaS (288n200) remarks, though it is otherwise unidentified, the last line is identical with *Manusmṛti* 6.81d.

3054. GZ CDNP: "Next, in order to praise the lalanā that is the distinctive feature [GZ CD *khyad par* NP *byed pa*, 'agent/function'] of wisdom, [Maitrīpa] utters [the stanza] that begins 'The beloved woman . . .'"

3055. IaS (288n201): "This verse is found in the *Sūktimuktāvalī*, the great collection of *muktakas*/*subhāṣitas* compiled by Jalhaṇa in Śaka 1179, i.e. 1258 CE, at the court of the Yādava King Śrīkṛṣṇa, who ruled from Devagiri, modern Daulatabad in northern Mahārāṣṭra. In the *Sūktimuktāvalī*, the verse is the second of the section on *nāyikānāyakayor avalokanam*, the hero and heroine looking at each other. Jalhaṇa does not inform us of the name of the author of the verse . . . Another source in which the verse is found is the Jaina recension of the *Vikramacarita* (p. 77)." Furthermore, IaS (289–90) attributes the position in this stanza and the following one to the followers of the Vedānta of the *Bhagavatsiddhānta*.

3056. GZ CDNP "'Seeing the beloved' refers to seeing because her and the desired liberation are viewed [CDNP omit 'are viewed'] . . . Through these, it is taught that, by rejecting explanations other than that, in order to show the example of the lalanā, the actuality of [CD omit 'the actuality of'] definite seeing is desired."

3057. GZ CDNP "In order that all attachment due to having entered [this path] in such a way is now [GZ *da ni* CDNP *de ni* 'that'] relinquished, [Maitrīpa] utters [the stanza] beginning with 'Abandon dharma as well as nondharma.'"

3058. This stanza is *Mahābhārata* 12.316.40 (= 12.318.44), traditionally attributed to the saint Vyāsa (also one of its main characters). Thus the text is not a part of the Vedānta, though it is sometimes referred to as "the fifth Veda" (as are some other texts, such as certain Purāṇas and the *Natyaśāstra*). IaS (289n204): "The same verse is cited occasionally by other authors; it may be worth mentioning here its quotation in the *Bhagavadgītā* commentary attributed to Śaṅkara (intro, *ad* st. 3.1), in Abhinavagupta's *Parātriṃśikātattvavivaraṇa* (*ad* stt. 5–9ab, ed. p. 241) and in Vibhūticandra's *Amṛtakaṇikoddyotanibandha* (ed. p. 202), and its reuse in the *Saṃnyāsopaniṣad* (ed. p. 253.2–3)."

3059. GZ CDNP "In order to teach that . . . is free of the four extremes, [Maitrīpa] utters [the stanza] that begins 'There is no nonexistent's being.'"

3060. *Bhagavadgītā* 2.16 = *Mahābhārata* 6.24.16.

3061. As mentioned before, for further brief and detailed discussions of the differences between the forceful, poor, and excellent empowerments, see Maitrīpa's *Caturmudropadeśa* (text 92, 19–21) and *Commentary on Half a Stanza on True Reality Teaching That All Phenomena Are Utterly Nonabiding* (text 73, 188ff.), Sahajavajra's *Sthitisamāsa* (text 17, VI.18–20), and the *Caturmudrāṭīkā* (text 44, 263, 286–87, and 341–44). As IaS (101n27) points out, this topic is also treated similarly, though without reference to the distinction of forceful, poor, and excellent, in Puṇḍarīka's *Paramākṣarajñānasiddhi*.

3062. GZ CDNP "Having thus declared that [the approach of the proponents of the poor empowerment] is similar to the scriptures of others, in order to teach that [the approach of said proponents] contradicts our own scriptures, [Maitrīpa] utters [the stanza] that begins 'Moreover, . . .'"

3063. Given that the Mantrayāna is called "the fruitional yāna" (versus the general Mahāyāna as "the causal yāna"), in both Sanskrit and English, the phrase "revealed . . . as the fruition through deity yoga" (*phalena devatāyogena khyāpyate*) can be understood as "by means of deity yoga, true reality is revealed as the fruition" or, less likely, "by means of deity yoga, which [in itself represents] the fruition, true reality is revealed." GZ *sngags kyi tshul gyis ni 'bras bu lha'i rnal byor* appears to consider "fruition(al)" as an apposition to "deity yoga," while omitting the instrumental in both cases, whereas CDNP *sngags kyi tshul gyi 'bras bu lha'i rnal byor gyis* links "fruition" with "mantra approach."

3064. As IaS (291n211) points out, GZ CDNP phrase this sentence as two lines of verse, but the Sanskrit is clearly not metrical. The exact same sentence is also found several times in Vajrapāṇi's *Guruparamparākramopadeśa* (text 213, 205–6), likewise phrased in GZ CDNP as two lines of verse. Given the Sanskrit, I have rendered this sentence as prose throughout.

3065. That is, the non-Buddhist sources such as Vedānta and nondual Śaivism discussed above. GZ CDNP "Here, the matter . . . is to be taught by the secret mantra approach through deity yoga, the fruition [CDNP "Here, as for the matter . . . the fruition of the secret mantra approach is to be taught through deity yoga"]. Thus [CDNP "Therefore"] this is said:

> "Whatever is sealed with something thereby [GZ *des ni de yi* CDNP *de dang de yi* 'of that and that']
> will come to have that something's nature

"Hence, in order to relinquish [the notion] of something perceived that has the nature of the four skandhas, such as form, to be perceived, the four perceivers, such as Vairocana, are taught to have the essence of the dependent [nature]. In order to seal those [*de dag gis*, 'by those' em. *de dag gi*; GZ 'the meaning of the seal of those'], the essence of the perfect [nature] empty of the perceiver and the perceived is said to be 'Akṣobhya.' In that case, the seal of Vajrasattva taught in the scriptures would be contradicted because the bodhicitta located in the middle of the jewel would be the essence of Akṣobhya, whose essence is the perfect [nature]. Since the seal of Vajrasattva is lacking in that, this would not be a tenet created by the Buddha himself. 'How so?' Because it is similar to outsider tenets."

3066. *Ālokamālā* 274. As Szántó 2016 (323) points out, this stanza is also found as stanza 101 of the *Yogāmbaramahātantra*. GZ CDNP:

> If the Buddhists and outsiders are distinguished
> by having analyzed everything as being the same
> and finished [that] with subtly looking intelligence,
> not even a single thing is observable—it is said all that [CDNP "and hence"] is empty.

3067. I follow *saṃvit-* in Mathes 2015 (380) and IaS (182) in the sense of GZ CDNP *rnam rig* (usually rendering *vijñapti*) against *samvṛt-* ("convention") in Lindtner's edition of the *Ālokamālā* (Lindtner 1985), though *saṃvit-* can also mean "convention."

3068. *Ālokamālā* 248. Given that the *Ālokamālā* represents an early unique approach of assimilating Madhyamaka to Yogācāra and not vice versa (as, for example, Śāntarakṣita and Kamalaśīla did much later), it is noteworthy that Kambala (and not a more famous and undisputed Madhyamaka authority such as Nāgārjuna or Āryadeva) is quoted here by Rāmapāla in support of the need to seal Akṣobhya (nondual mind) with the seal of Vajrasattva (emptiness and compassion) in accordance with the Madhyamaka understanding of true reality. However, as mentioned before, Maitrīpa's *Pañcatathāgatamudrāvivaraṇa* (text 36, 194–95) also cites the same two stanzas in support of his own highest Madhyamaka system of utter nonabiding. Similarly, Sahajavajra's *Tattvadaśakaṭīkā* (text 46, 16) quotes these two stanzas in support of labeling Kambala as a "Nonaspectarian Mādhyamika." Furthermore, Atiśa's *Madhyamakopadeśa* identifies the Madhyamaka texts by Nāgārjuna, Āryadeva, Mātṛceṭa, Candrakīrti, and Kambala as the unrivaled model texts for all Madhyamaka scriptures. Thus the positioning of Kambala by Maitrīpa, Sahajavajra, Rāmapāla, and Atiśa as a Mādhyamika is remarkable and further supports the impression that the demarcation lines of different Buddhist "schools" in India were not as hard and fast as many later authors assume. GZ CDNP:

> "You will not dwell in cognizance"
> Therefore, for those afraid, the Sage,
> [I follow GZ NP *'jigs la thub pa* against CD *'jig la thug pa* 'encountering perishing']
> teaching dharmas in different ways,
> fully taught dharmas that are empty.

3069. IaS (292n216): "We have preferred Ca's metrically superior reading °*vedasiddhānāṃ*, in which *siddha* must be understood as an abbreviation (m.c.) of *siddhānta*, over Pt's °*vedasiddhāntānāṃ*. Pt's reading is supported by T2 . . . With the variant *vedasiddhāntayogānāṃ* instead of *samastavedasiddhānāṃn* in *pāda* a, this stanza occurs also in the first *pariccheda* (st. 59) of the *Ṣaṭsāhasrikā* (= *Hevajratantrapiṇḍārthaṭīkā*) by Vajragarbha (ed. in Sferra 2009), within a quotation from the *Pañcalakṣahevajra*, a work of which only quotations survive and which, if it indeed ever existed as such, is most likely a late composition, and that some authors (Vajragarbha in primis, but also others, such as Sādhuputra Śrīdharānanda and Kelikuliśa) held to be the root-tantra of the *Hevajratantra*. For [a] more detailed discussion of the *Pañcalakṣahevajra* see Sferra 2011: 269–73." GZ CDNP:

> Among all the Vedas, the tenets,
> compositions by Īśvara and so on,
> and the emptiness of the buddhas'
> mantra tantras, there is a difference.

3070. GZ CDNP "The difference between what is stated as emptiness imagined by others and the emptiness taught by the Tathāgata, which is by virtue of being produced by [their different] indirect intentions, is not clearly discussed [here]." IaS (103–4) comments on the context of stanza 19 as follows: "Maitreyanātha gives a further argument against the *duḥseka* position. It is one that is somewhat subtle, being related to the concept of the 'sealing' by (and of) the five Tathāgatas. Some additional light is shed on it by passages in other works of Maitreyanātha, in particular the *Pancatathāgatamudrāvivaraṇa* and the **Caturmudropadeśa* (though the latter refers to the *Sekanirdeśa* for clarification of the point). Drawing on all these texts, as well as on Rāmapāla's *Pañjikā*, the essential point may be summarized as follows. First of all, there is an assumption, made partly explicit by Rāmapāla, and almost certainly held implicitly by Maitreyanātha, that the nature of Reality as established by the philosophical arguments of Yogācāra and, ultimately, Madhyamaka already in nontantric Mahāyāna, must in the tantric Mahāyāna, the Mantranaya, be revealed, that is to say directly experienced, in deity-yoga, the principal tantric practice, as being the nature of the fruit, i.e. of awakened consciousness, and before that should be at least hinted at or experienced in a partial way in consecration as well. Now in deity-yoga, it is common for the deities to be 'sealed' by a Tathāgata; this is visually marked by the appearance of the sealing Tathāgata in small form on the head of the deity sealed. This visualized 'sealing' represents the realization of the entity sealed as being or becoming of the nature of the sealing Tathāgata. In taking, then, the non-dual experience in the sexual union of the *prajñājñānābhiṣeka* as the true Innate Bliss, and equating it with Reality and the Dharmakāya, the proponents of *duḥseka* are, according to Maitreyanātha, sealing the other deities with Akṣobhya (i.e. realizing that underlying all phenomenal plurality there lies a single reality in which there is neither object nor subject), but they are failing to seal Akṣobhya in turn with Vajrasattva, in other words to realize that non-dual mind itself, rather than having independent existence, is of the nature of emptiness and compassion. To put it another way, to equate blissful and non-dual mind with the highest Reality is to go no further than one can go with the Yogācāra view, which for Maitreyanātha is not the ultimate one. It is necessary to go further and realize the emptiness (not, however, a sterile or inactive emptiness but a dynamic one because it is inseparable from compassion) of even mind (as *parinispanna*, devoid of object and subject duality). Of course Yogācāras are acknowledged by Maitreyanātha as Buddhists, and though their position is not regarded as the final one, it is not criticized in the way that the *duḥseka* is. It is clear enough, though, what the reason for this is: the error of the *duḥseka* proponents is not just that they claim (or at least imply) the ultimate reality of non-dual mind, but that they claim that that reality is directly experienced in sexual union. Such a position, amounting to the reification of sexual bliss as an absolute, is not only philosophically inadequate (in a manner parallel to the Yogācāra position) but is highly dangerous, entailing as it does that sexual intercourse is all that is necessary to experience (at least temporarily) true Awakening, and is also dangerously similar to the views of the Śaiva Kaula tradition, at least as understood by Maitreyanātha and Rāmapāla."

3071. That is, Rāmapāla unravels the compound *tathāgatāśvāsa* as a genitive *tatpuruṣa* compound.

3072. Rāmapāla glosses *taddhiyā* as the equivalent *tadbuddhyā*. GZ CDNP "This is the tathāgata relief, and . . . Their relief is to be understood as [GZ CDNP lit. 'by'] consciousness through being sealed with Akṣobhya; it should be known in this way. As it appears in the *Laṅkāvatāra[sūtra]*:

> "When having relied on mere mind,
> outer objects are not to be imagined
> When resting in suchness's support,
> mere mind should be transcended
>
> "When having transcended mere mind,
> nonappearance should be transcended
> The yogīs who rest in nonappearance
> will come to behold the Mahāyāna [NP omit these stanzas]."

On these two stanzas being a secondary addition (probably in the Tibetan, but maybe in another Sanskrit version), IaS (292n218) says that this "is further suggested . . . by the fact that the quotation is concluded with *źes 'byuṅ ṅo*, a quote-marking phrase which does not occur elsewhere in the Tibetan translation of the *Sekanirdeśapañjikā* . . ."

3073. With IaS, I take Skt. *gurūṇāṃ* (genitive plural) to be an honorific plural for Maitrīpa's guru Śabareśvara (as explicitly referenced in stanza 40). GZ CDNP: "The praise 'That which is like this is the very middle' is not the view of our guru."

3074. CDNP omit these two sentences.

3075. As mentioned before, "holder of sixteen bindus twice halved" corresponds to *Mañjuśrīnāmasaṃgīti* X.3b. GZ CDNP "'Why?' Because it is not asserted. 'What is this that is not asserted?' [instead of these three short sentences, CDNP only have 'Why is what not asserted?'] [Maitrīpa] says: 'Neither inside the vajra, nor at its tip . . .' Because the very essence of such bliss [CDNP 'Because such'] always exists as the form of Akṣobhya and because [CDNP omit 'and because'] the seal of Vajrasattva is absent 'inside the vajra.' In between and in the kapāla, letting alone for the moment the lack of the seal of Vajrasattva, the desired genuine bliss does not exist either. Since something perceived and so on exists, even the seal of Akṣobhya is lacking. By this, one obtains this [understanding] implicitly through the above-mentioned [line 19d] . . . 'In that case, from where should true reality be known?' [Maitrīpa says:] 'As per the guru's mouth, it's in awareness.' Here, this is the pith instruction on the location of this Bhagavatī who is the holder of sixteen bindus twice halved."

3076. These two stanzas consist of four lines of uneven length in Apabhraṃśa (broken down into six lines here for the sake of easy comparison with their Tibetan versions in different texts). GZ CDNP have an additional line and read as follows:

> Once two have passed, two are even
> . . .

The cause is sealed with the result and
the result is also sealed with the cause—
this represents the king of great bliss

With variations, some or all of the lines of these two stanzas are also found (without attribution) in the *Caturmudrāṭīkā* (text 44, 287; seven lines, last three lines also quoted on 344), Vajrapāṇi's *Guruparamparākramopadeśa* (text 213, 217; seven lines), and Abhayākaragupta's *Śrīsaṃpuṭatantrarājaṭīkāmnāyamañjarī* (D1198, fol. 68a.6; same six lines as the *Sekanirdeśapañjikā*). A similar abbreviated version in a single stanza is found in Maitrīpa's *Caturmudropadeśa* (text 92, 21), where it is attributed to the *Sarvarahasyatantra* (as IaS, 400, points out, as Gö Kugpa Lhédsé's *Gsang 'dus stong thun* also attributes both stanzas to this tantra, it is possible that he knew them from the *Caturmudropadeśa*). However, as IaS (396n242) says, neither of the stanzas is contained in the Tibetan version of the *Sarvarahasyatantra* (D481), nor are they commented on in Ratnākaraśānti's commentary *Sarvarahasyanibandha* (D2623). IaS (401) also refers to Padma Karpo's *Rten 'brel kho bo lugs kyi khrid chos thams cad kyi snying po len pa* attributing these stanzas to a **Yuganaddhaprakāśa*, but they are not found in the work of that name by Maitrīpa (text 21). While the *Sekanirdeśapañjikā* is the only work in which these stanzas are preserved in Apabhraṃśa, the additional Tibetan line "the result is also sealed with the cause" is also found in the *Caturmudrāṭīkā* and the *Guruparamparākramopadeśa*, but it is absent in the *Caturmudropadeśa* and the *Śrīsaṃpuṭatantrarājaṭīkāmnāyamañjarī* (IaS, 402, adds: "We feel that the addition of the extra words is not possible without some violence to the rhythm. Their addition (perhaps not entirely independently) in the Tibetan translations of three Indian works may rather be secondary, prompted by the fact that the principle of mutual sealing (as stated in e.g. *Guhyasamājatantra* 18.79ab . . .) is no doubt intended here, even if it may not have been originally expressed in full"). As Passavanti, in IaS (438), points out, in an early Tibetan biography of Maitrīpa, these two stanzas are presented as an oral pith instruction uttered by Śabaresvara for Maitrīpa and his fellow-student Sāgara, apparently intended to highlight their central importance for Maitrīpa (as well as his students). In addition, as IaS (401) has already stated, there seems to be a reference to these stanzas (though they are not explicitly quoted) in *Viravajra's commentary on the *Cakrasaṃvaratantra*, attributing this description of the moment of connate ecstasy to the "tradition of the brahman Saraha" (D1412, fol. 406b.7); at least according to some traditions, Śabaresvara was a disciple of Saraha. Finally, IaS (406n16) mention this: "*Narendrakīrti, a commentator, following the Kālacakra tradition, on the *Nāmasaṅgīti*, shows awareness, in his commentary on this *pāda*, of the 'two fall, two are equal' teaching (cf. comm. on st. 8.9d . . . D 160v2 and comm. on st. 10.3b . . . D fol. 177v5), though much more than that he knows this as a way to characterize the Innate Bliss cannot be determined. This is however of some interest already, since we have noticed no reference to this teaching in at least the early Kālacakra works . . . in the first of these passages . . . *Narendrakīrti calls *gñis 'das nas ni gñis mñam pa* a defining characteristic (*mtshan ñid*) of the Innate [Bliss] (*lhan cig skyes pa'i*) . . ." As IaS remarks, the translation and interpretation of these stanzas is not easy. In any case, what is clear is that they describe what happens during the moment of connate ecstasy in the context of the excellent empowerment. However, there appear to be two slightly different models in the works of Maitrīpa and his students. In brief, Maitrīpa's *Caturmudropadeśa* (text 92, 2021), after citing *Mañjuśrīnāmasaṃgīti* X.3b, says that connate ecstasy occurs when two among the four bindus are located at the tip of the vajra and two in the anthers of the lotus. Cessational ecstasy is when all four bindus are in the lotus. By contrast, the presentations in the *Caturmudrāṭīkā* (text 44, 287, 343–44, 351–52) and the *Guruparamparākramopadeśa* (text 213, 217–18) agree that two bindus have already fallen into the lotus (representing the disappearance of ordinary passion), while the third one (the bindu of Akṣobhya: the experience of bliss, representing means and the cause) is at the lower aperture of the avadhūti of the male and the fourth one (the bindu of Vajrasattva: emptiness, representing prajñā and the result) at the lower aperture of the avadhūti of the female. Vajrasattva (the result) sealing Akṣobhya (the cause) eliminates the extreme of permanence and thus renders experience lacking any nature. Akṣobhya in turn sealing Vajrasattva eliminates the extreme of extinction and thus renders the lack of nature an experience. In that way, experience and emptiness are a unity (the nonduality of emptiness and compassion and of means and prajñā, without abiding in said two extremes). Again, cessational ecstasy occurs when all four bindus are in the lotus. IaS (404–8) calls the model in Maitrīpa's *Caturmudropadeśa* the "2 + 2 interpretation" and the model in the *Caturmudrāṭīkā* and the *Guruparamparākramopadeśa* the "1 + 1 interpretation," commenting as follows: "In our view, the latter interpretation is in some respects rather more convincing than the former. It is, for one thing, more 'elegant'; that the Innate Bliss is different from, and is experienced between, the two extremes of passion and dispassion is made clear by the (implied) symmetrical structure (*rāga*, passion, is when the drops are all on the Vajra side; *virāga*, dispassion, when they are all on the Lotus side, while the Sahaja moment is distinguished from and is between these two 'extremes'). And perhaps the interpretation of the wording of our Apabhraṃśa verses which it presupposes is more natural; the *tulle* being understood as 'equal[ly divided]', instead of, as one might have to do in order to take the verses in accordance with the '2 + 2 interpretation', 'the same', in the sense of 'on the same side', i.e. 'still in contact with the Vajra'. Finally, it seems somewhat redundant, in the first interpretation, that two drops should represent Akṣobhya and Vajrasattva (or Vajradhara), Bliss (or Mind) and Emptiness, each, instead of one. Nonetheless the sense of the passage from the **Caturmudropadeśa* seems beyond doubt. And at least one consideration might speak in favour of what we might call the '2 + 2 interpretation', namely the association, in all of the texts, of this point with the *Nāmasaṅgīti pāda ṣoḍaśārdhārdhabindudhṛk*. It is possible, then, that there is a genuine difference between Maitreyanātha and his two students on this point. Possible also might be that Maitreyanātha himself changed his teaching on this point at some time after (or before?) composing the **Caturmudropadeśa*, and that his students' writings correspond to his later (or to his earlier?) view, which is not found in his own writings.

Again, it is perhaps not entirely to be ruled out that the Tibetan translation of the **Caturmudropadeśa*, in spite of appearing clear and not suspicious, has in fact some problem here, and that Maitreyanātha's view is after all not accurately conveyed therein. Provisionally we have assumed the first of these possibilities, taking all the texts as representing accurately their authors' opinions. As for Rāmapāla, it seems to us not entirely clear which of these two possible interpretations he preferred. We wonder, however, if the association in the *Sekanirdeśapañjikā* of this teaching about the moment of the Innate Bliss with the situation in *utpattikrama* practice in which the Bhagavān (and Bhagavatī), as causal deities, melt down because of great passion, after which the Bhagavān remains in the form of two drops, one in contact with a sun-disk which corresponds to Means and the other in contact with a moon-disk which represents Wisdom, should not be taken as an indication that it is the '1 + 1 interpretation' of Vajrapāṇi and *Kāropa that he follows. That might, if true, have the implication, since he is here commenting on Maitreyanātha's work in accordance with Maitreyanātha's order, and, presumably, in accordance also with explanations received from the author, his master, that Maitreyanātha indeed at some point taught this '1 + 1 interpretation' instead of, or as an alternative to, the '2 + 2 interpretation' that the Tibetan translation of the **Caturmudropadeśa* apparently attests." IaS (406n15) adds "that among the four different renderings into Tibetan of our verses found in works preserved in the *bsTan 'gyur*, two (those in the translations of the **Caturmudropadeśa* and the **Guruparamparākramopadeśa*) apparently render *tulle* with *mñam pa'i dbus*, which might perhaps be taken as '[in] the equal middle' or even 'equally [in] the middle'. Rather than reflecting a different reading in the Apabhraṃśa, we suppose that this is an interpretative translation of *tulle*. If so, perhaps one could say that it tends to suggest—and perhaps has been deliberately chosen to do so—the '1 + 1 interpretation'; it is two drops, not four, that are divided equally (between the side of the Vajra and of the Lotus)." Note though that while this interpretation of *mnyam pa'i dbus* accords well with the explanation in the *Guruparamparākramopadeśa*, it does not fit the explicit "2 + 2" model in the *Caturmudropadeśa*. In any case, in terms of the distribution of the four bindus between the two lower apertures of the avadhūtis of the male and the female, the actual difference between the two models is 2 + 2 bindus versus 1 + 3 bindus. From that perspective, it could be that the latter model is not really different but just a more explicit or nuanced version of the first model. As for which of these two models Rāmapāla follows here, I agree with the above analysis of the *Sekanirdeśapañjikā*'s immediately following paragraph in IaS, which in my view clearly supports the "1 + 1" model. That the *Sekanirdeśapañjikā*'s association of connate ecstasy with the phase in the creation process when the Bhagavān (and Bhagavatī) melts and remains as two bindus between a sun and a moon disk should be taken as an indication for the "1 + 1" model of Vajrapāṇi and *Kāropa is clearly supported by parallel passages in both the *Guruparamparākramopadeśa* and the *Caturmudrāṭīkā*. The *Guruparamparākramopadeśa* justifies at length that Hevajra appears as the two bindus and that this is connate ecstasy (text 213, 218–20), and it confirms this in another paragraph in the context of the samayamudrā (237): "The three letters of awakened body, speech, and mind and a red HOḤ . . . dissolve into the mouth of the gandharva being inserted between the two. Thereby, the venerable male and the venerable female melt into light. The two bindus that remain in the middle of the moon and the sun represent luminosity and emptiness. The bindu that touches the moon [below] represents prajñā (emptiness). The bindu that touches the sun above represents luminosity (means). The inseparability of the two means that they seal each other, which is unity. This constitutes connate ecstasy during the moment of the lack of characteristics." Similarly, the *Caturmudrāṭīkā* (text 44, 264) says this: "As for the connate [in the context] of the samayamudrā, in the middle of the union of the sun and moon of means and prajñā, there abide the two bindus that have the essence of bliss and emptiness—though they are established as color and shape, what is to be demonstrated in the experience of the specifically characterized [connate] is prajñā-jñāna. Thereby, though it is [only] the exemplifying [wisdom of the connate] that is experienced [here], its being free from thoughts about object generalities and not being experienced [as such thoughts] is to be demonstrated as being born and being unborn not being different. If becoming familiar with exactly that, it will become the specifically characterized actual [connate]" (see also 345: "To remain as two bindus once oneself [as the deity] has also dissolved represents connate ecstasy"). In addition, compare two related passages in the *Samājaparamārthasarvakarmodayanāmatārāyoginītantrarāja* (D448, fol. 290a.6–7 and 290b.4; one of the tantras brought to Tibet in the seventeenth century by Tāranātha's guru Buddhanātha, translated by the two with Nirvāṇaśrī and revised by Pūrṇavajra) that also seem to describe the "1 + 1" model: "Furthermore, it is at the boundary of half of four parts that connate ecstasy is to be familiarized with: the mouth of the vajra should drink the bindu present in the anthers of the bhaga. Through the yogas such as circling and the yoga of the vāyus, [these bindus] should be made even . . .

> "Sixteen parts descend to the jewel:
> by two stopping due to mind's bliss,
> accomplish the mind's true reality!"

In any case, the main point at stake here should not be forgotten: as *Sekanirdeśa* 22 and its comments, as well as the *Guruparamparākramopadeśa*, make very clear, the true reality within all of this is not found in any of these bindus, no matter where they may be located, but in the nonreferential awareness (or realization) of bliss-emptiness (or, as the *Caturmudrāṭīkā* and the *Guruparamparākramopadeśa* say, the nondual unity of experience and emptiness). For more details, see IaS (399–409). Finally, as an aside, given that both bindu models are entirely written from the male perspective, an obvious question is how all this is to be understood and practically applied (in the same way or differently?) from the female perspective.

3077. Among the five stages found in Maitrīpa's Hevajra sādhanas (outer creation process, profound creation process, perfection process, full-perfection process, and essence process), only three—creation process, perfection process, and full-perfection process—are mentioned here. As IaS (295n231) says, it is unclear why Rāmapāla omits the profound creation process and why the perfection process is glossed as "the purport of the empowerment as it has been discussed." Given Maitrīpa's description of these two stages in his *Nairātmyāprakāśa* (see appendix 7), one would rather expect that this gloss refers to the profound creation process. Thus, IaS wonders: "Could *utpanna-kramaḥ* here be a transmissional error for *gambhirotpattikramaḥ*, caused by the fact that a scribe unfamiliar with the five kramas of Maitreyanātha's *sādhanas* related to the Hevajra-system expected after *utpattikramaḥ* to find *utpannakramaḥ* in the next sentence?"

3078. That the moon is below and the sun above is clearly spelled out in the above-cited passage from the *Guruparamparākramopadeśa* (text 213, 237).

3079. Ias (295n230): "The point is that the fact that the Bhagavān appears as two drops between—and touching—a moon and a sun 'shows' or 'symbolizes' that the moment of Sahaja/Reality is when the drops of Bodhicitta are outside the Vajra but in contact with it, and with the Lotus." Compare Vajrapāṇi's *Guruparamparākramopadeśa* (text 213, 218–20 and 237) on this: "Then, the three letters of awakened body, speech, and mind, and a red HOḤ, whose nature is great passion, dissolve into the mouth of the gandharva, being inserted between the two [the moon and the sun]. Thereby, the venerable male and the venerable female melt into light. The two bindus that remain in the middle of the moon and the sun represent luminosity and emptiness. The bindu that touches the moon [below] represents prajñā (emptiness). The bindu that touches the sun above represents luminosity (means). The inseparability of the two means that they seal each other, which is unity. This constitutes connate ecstasy during the moment of the lack of characteristics."

3080. IaS (295n232): "One would usually expect the sun-disk to symbolize the feminine (and a moon-disk to stand for the masculine). Rāmapāla teaches otherwise because, according to him, the figure of Hevajra, standing on a sun-disk, corresponds to or 'shows' the drop(s) of Bodhicitta outside of but still in contact with the Vajra, at the moment of experience of Sahaja."

3081. IaS (295–96n233): "The expression *skhaladavasthākālākalita* (partly restored by conjecture) occurs also in the *Vyaktabhāvānugatatattvasiddhi* (p. 1716), though as part of a much larger compound which is far from clear (and on which there are several variants in the not very good MSS of this work), and which in turn forms part of a long and difficult sentence which seems corrupt as printed. In the printed edition we read º*skhaladavasthākālānukalitā*º, but we propose that the Tibetan translation, which has for this part of the compound, *ñams pa'i gnas skabs kyi dus blaṅ bar gyur pas*, probably reflects º*skhaladavasthākālākalitā*º, with the last word being (mis)understood as not *akalita* but *ākalita*, in the sense of 'seized' . . . The fact that Hevajra is in contact with the sun-disk only by the big toe of one foot symbolizes that though this experience of Sahaja/Reality occurs when Bodhicitta has just emerged from the Vajra, it is not dependent on this brief moment. Though different, Maitreyanātha's explanation of the symbolism of this iconographic detail in the *Nairātmyāprakāśa* has a similar flavour: *sarvatrānāropaviśuddhyaikapādāṅguṣṭhāgrasūryāsanalagnatā* (fol. 77*v*) 'The fact that [Hevajra] is in contact with the sun disk that is his "seat" with [just] the toe of one foot symbolizes lack of superimposition on anything.' In other words, the fact that the deity's contact with his 'seat' or 'support' is only the absolute physical minimum symbolizes that Reality is not firmly placed on or superimposed upon anything. Hevajra stands on the sun, but in a dance posture in which he barely needs the 'ground' as support, but could equally well float off or upward." IaS renders Skt. *skhaladavasthā* here as "the state that is not steady," which is of course one of its possible meanings. However, given the context here (as also just described by IaS) and that *skhala(na)* can also mean "emission," "trickle down," "drop down," and "friction," it seems more likely that it here refers to the emission of the bindu (also supported by the above-mentioned Tibetan *nyams pa'i gnas skabs* in the *Vyaktabhāvānugatatattvasiddhi*), which would end the experience of connate ecstasy. GZ CDNP: "Hence, since these two have the essence of vajra and the essence of sattva, they are Vajrasattva—they are to be understood through names such as emptiness and compassion, prajñā and means, and nirvāṇa and saṃsāric existence . . . above and below, of the melting of great passion . . . The full-perfection [process] refers to the Bhagavān standing while touching the [sun disk that is his] seat with [only] one toe of his foot in order to indicate the essence of the time that is the phase of being aware of [the Bhagavān] (dwelling on a sun that has the form of vajra melting) as having the character of prajñā and means and the nature of the dharmadhātu whose essence is emptiness and compassion."

3082. I.3.6cd.

3083. Skt. *uha* can also mean "examination," "conception," "inference," "change," and "modification"; GZ CDNP *rnam par rtog pa* ("conception," "thinking").

3084. As IaS (296n234) points out, the opponent understands *vajravaraṭaka* in *Hevajratantra* 1.3.6d as a *tatpuruṣa* compound ("the central part of the vajra"), taking this as support for the experience of connate ecstasy occurring while bodhicitta is at the tip of the vajra. Rāmapāla, however, understands *vajravaraṭaka* as a *dvandva* compound, with *varaṭaka* having one of its other meanings—"pericarp of a lotus" (the seed vessel of a plant—that is, "the ripened and variously modified walls of a plant ovary"). Thus, he again takes this as support for connate ecstasy being experienced in the moment when bodhicitta is between the tip of the vajra and the lower aperture of the avadhūtī in the vagina. GZ CDNP: "[Objection:] 'Isn't it taught that "They should again familiarize with the true reality of HŪṂ abiding in the maṇḍala of the navel of the vajra?" [prose] How about that? [NP omit the last sentence; GZ CD have *zhe na* here as well as at the end of this objection]. Here, the meaning of "abiding in the maṇḍala of the navel of the vajra" is not established.' The meaning if this is something else . . . The true reality that abides in the vajra and the anthers [I follow NP *rdo rje dang ze'u 'bru dag* against GZ CD *rdo rje'i ze'u 'bru dag*, "the anthers of the vajra"]—that is, in the middle between the best parts of prajñā and means—is called 'HŪṂ' . . . 'Ū' free from thinking, and 'A' utter nonabiding. 'Contemplate' means 'should realize.'" Thus, in Sanskrit, *h* is glossed by *hetuṣūnyam*, *ū* by *ūhāpagatam*, and *aṃ* (that is, the *anusvāra*; the dot above *hū*) by *apratiṣṭitaṃ*. Compare the almost identical explanation of HŪṂ in Maitrīpa's *Sekatātparyasaṃgraha* (text 37, 199) and the similar one in the *Caturmudrāṭīkā* (text 44, 328).

3085. IaS (296n236): "See below the stanza attributed to the *Paramādyatantra*. We have accepted Ca's reading here, but to do so forces us to assume that Rāmapāla deliberately has his opponent quote part of a passage inaccurately, with what is in the source a compound (*maṇyantargatam*) analysed in a way that fits the opponent's view. It would certainly have been more normal to have the opponent quote the passage accurately (either with some additional remark to make his interpretation clear, or, as would not seem to us too strange in this case, with his interpretation simply being implicit), i.e. to read (conjecturally) *tarhi maṇyantargatam iti katham*."

3086. Skt. *antargata* can mean both "(gone) within" and "between."

3087. GZ CDNP: "[Objection:] 'In that case, how about "inserted into the jewel should be realized as/in the jewel"?' This is to be discussed as follows: the meaning of this is also something else. It should be realized in the best [parts of; NP omit 'the best'] the two jewels—in the best [parts; NP *bar du* 'between'] of the lotus and the vajra . . ."

3088. GZ CDNP: "[Objection:] 'How should this be known? Why should the meaning of both be expressed here?' This is to be discussed as follows. It is stated in the *Śrīparamādya[tantra]*:"

3089. IaS (297n239): "These lines are attributed to the *Paramādya* both here and in Abhayākaragupta's *Amnāyamañjarī* (D fol. 68r1–2). We could not locate them, however, in the two Tibetan *Paramādya* translations (Tōh. 487 and 488), nor in the translation of the *Vajramaṇḍālaṅkāratantra* (Tōh. 490), which can be regarded as an expanded version of the *Paramādya*." GZ CDNP:

> In the lotus's space, at the place of the jewel
> and anthers pressed through the vajra posture,
> look at the mind that is inserted into the jewel!
> [GZ CDNP *sems kyi* as per commentary em. *ni*] . . . [NP *chud par blta*
> GZ CD *chud par bya*, "is to be inserted"]
> The wisdom that arises has the form of inexpressible wisdom.

3090. IaS (297n240): "One might also consider taking *paṅkajakuliśayoḥ* as a gloss of *maṇivaraṭakayoḥ*, instead of a *vyadhikaraṇa* genitive, in which case we would have a consistent structure of three quoted expressions each followed directly by a gloss. On the other hand, it would be somewhat odd if Rāmapāla really intended Jewel and Pericarp to be understood as pars pro toto; at the moment of which he is talking the Bodhicitta should be understood as in contact with the Jewel, the glans, of the penis, and not with any other part of it. One would have also expected, in that case, *kuliśapaṅkajayoḥ*, rather than *paṅkajakuliśayoḥ*, to agree with the order of words in the compound glossed." Note, however, that GZ CDNP have exactly the alternative reading mentioned here, taking "the lotus and the kuliśa" as a gloss of "the jewel and the pericarp."

3091. IaS (27n241): "We have emended the *saṅghaṭanasthāne* of both manuscripts to *saṅghaṭṭanasthāne*, since the latter seemed a more natural gloss of *pīḍanasthāne* . . . One might however keep the transmitted reading, even though *saṅghaṭa* seems a rather weaker expression, 'coming together' rather than 'striking together,' 'collision' or 'friction'." GZ CDNP *bskyod pa* (used several times for "friction" before) supports this emendation in such a sense. Note though that *saṅghaṭṭana* can also mean "meeting," "union," and "touch."

3092. As GZ CDNP *rdo rje dkyil krung* in both the quote and its explanation shows, *vajraparyaṅka* can also mean "vajra posture" (the sitting posture with crossed legs and the backs of both feet resting on the thighs). Thus, maybe more naturally, the meaning here could rather (or also) be "thanks to [supported by GZ CDNP *gis*] the vajra posture"—that is, by virtue of the union of the male assuming the vajra posture (and the female the "lotus posture"), the glans and the lower end of the female avadhūtī are pressed together. Obviously, Rāmapāla's hermeneutical interpretation of the ablative form *vajraparyaṅkataḥ* is quite different, clearly in an attempt to again make his point. Skt. *pari* constructed with an ablative (versus a genitive in English) can indeed mean "outside of" (or "away from"), but then the phrase here should be *vajrāṅkataḥ pari* (which is obviously Rāmapāla's interpretation) and not *vajraparyaṅkataḥ*. Similarly, the phrase "outside of the vajra" is also constructed with an ablative in Sanskrit (*vajrād bahir*). As before, Rāmapāla also plays on the double meaning of Skt. *antargata* ("(gone) within" and "between"), restating his hermeneutical point about the two jewels (of vajra and lotus). Finally, it is somewhat odd that he glosses Skt. *jñāna* as *vijñāna* ("consciousness"); though *jñāna* can also mean "cognition" rather than "wisdom," the context here clearly suggests a sublime awareness beyond ordinary dualistic consciousness (as also indicated by Rāmapāla's final phrase "consciousness's very own nature"). GZ CDNP: "The meaning of this is this. 'The lotus's space' refers to the empty spot in the middle of the lotus. 'Jewel and anthers' means 'in the middle of the lotus and the vajra.' 'The places of . . . pressed' refers to the place of friction. As for 'through [*gi* em. *gis*] the vajra posture,' it means fully pervading the vajra—that is, everywhere. 'OṂ *ā* [NP *a*] *ka ta*' [is meant] as what illustrates [GZ CD *mtshon byed* NP *mtshan nyid*]. If taken as the fifth, this expresses just touching outside the vajra. When the mind inserted into the jewel is looked [I follow NP *bltas pa* against GZ CD *bstan pa*, "shown"] at, consciousness will arise—it has consciousness's very own essence . . ." Note that in the cross-legged vajra posture (*vajraparyaṅka*), the left foot rests on the right thigh and the right foot rests on top on the left thigh. The similar term *vajrāsana* has three meanings in Buddhism: a synonym of *vajraparyaṅka*, the vajra seat or vajra throne under the bodhi tree in Bodhgayā, and, by extension, an epithet of Bodhgayā. By contrast, in the Hindu yoga tradition, *vajrāsana* refers to a sitting posture in which one sits erect on the heels with the calves beneath the thighs, the feet extended, the big toes touching, and the hands resting on the thighs. In modern literature, the "vajra posture" (*vajraparyaṅka*) is often confused with the "lotus posture" (*padmāsana*), predominantly used in Hindu forms of yoga, in which the positions of the left foot and the right foot are reversed (left foot on top). In Buddhist texts, *padmāsana* refers to the lotus seat on which deities or buddhas sit or, also as *padmaparyaṅka*, to the position of a female consort in union with her male counterpart.

3093. IaS (297–98n244): "MS Ca lacks this quote and the following half-verse quoted from the *Hevajratantra*. This might be explained as an error caused by eyeskip between two instances of *tathā ca*, but on the other hand the *Vajrāmṛta* and *Hevajratantra* quotations seem much less apt here than the three verses, from an unknown source, beginning *yāvan no patati*, so that it is also possible that Ca represents an earlier state of the text, and that the version of Pt and the Tibetan translation contains an interpolation."

3094. D435, fol. 24a.1–2. Note that, just as *antargata* in the preceding passages, *antare* here is ambiguous, meaning "within," "between," or "in the middle of" (GZ CDNP *dbus na* and DHN *dkyil du* in the tantra itself support the latter). As the preceding stanza in the *Vajrāmṛtatantra* makes clear, "it" here refers to "indestructible, inexhaustible, and subtle supreme suchness." Note also that the tantra's following stanza supports Rāmapāla's above phrase "consciousness's very own nature":

> It is the life force of those with a life force,
> the ground of the skandha of consciousness
> It is buddhahood and likewise Vajradhara
> It is Brahmā, Viṣṇu, and also Maheśvara

GZ CDNP: "For this is stated in the *Vajrāmṛta[tantra]*:

> "The goddess abides in the navel's middle,
> which is the sphere covered by the anthers
> Having been emitted in the form of semen,
> it dwells in the middle of bhaga and liṅga."

3095. I.3.11ab.
3096. Skt. *śītāṃśudhāara* ("bearer of white/cool rays") is an epithet of the moon.
3097. With the major variant (or misreading?) *garjad dhīkaruṇābalasya* instead of *tāvac chrīkaruṇābalasya* in the last line, which obscures the crucial *tāvat* and *śrī*, this unlocated stanza is also quoted in Munidatta's *Caryāgītikoṣavṛtti* (text 90, 300), attributed to the *Sekoddeśa* but not found there (not yet aware of the Sanskrit of this stanza here, *garjad dhīkaruṇābalasya* unfortunately led me to translate parts of the last two lines of the stanza in text 90 differently). As IaS (298n248) points out, given that Munidatta frequently misattributes his quotations, it may be that he actually knew this stanza from the *Sekanirdeśapañjikā*, citing it from memory without checking his source. Likewise, IaS says, the stanza is also quoted in a different Tibetan translation in the **Saptasiddhānta* (N1906), attributed there to a *Kuṣalanātha/Kalyāṇanātha (Tib. Dge ba'i mgon po). GZ CDNP here have some slight variants, the only major one being the omission of "you should know" in the last line.
3098. According to IaS (299n249), this stanza is also quoted in Jagaddarpaṇa's *Kriyāsamuccaya* and in a different Tibetan translation in the **Saptasiddhānta*, there attributed to Virūpa. GZ CDNP:

> As long as, with the three vajras burning in the vajra's jewel, the moon will decline and is desired
> to melt into the vāyu's location, the hut that constitutes the hollow space of the lotus, at that time,
> it is clear by means of reasonings and scriptures that, for as long as it arises, this very mind of

inferior activities, by virtue of being free from self, other, and so forth, constitutes the connate
[I follow NP *yin zhes* against GZ CD *ye shes*, "it is clear that . . . this very mind . . . is the connate wisdom"].

3099. "The one marked by an antelope" (Skt. *mṛgāṅka*) is an epithet of the moon (what is called "the man in the moon" in the West is supposed to look like an antelope or a rabbit in India). IaS (299n250) says that a related stanza is quoted in the **Saptasiddhānta*, there attributed to the Buddha, but the Tibetan translation differs considerably from the rendering of the stanza in the *Sekanirdeśapañjikā*. Here, the first two lines of this stanza in GZ CDNP are close to the Sanskrit (except omitting "when," and the second line on its own, without knowing the Sanskrit, sounding like "the pure bindu dripped from its abode is motionless, as long as it is held to be the moon"). The second two lines say this:

at that time, the mind does not move [NP *yid mi mi g.yo* GZ CDNP *mig ni mi g.yo* ("the eyes do not move") em.
yid ni mi g.yo] and stir [*'gro ste*], the flow [GZ CD *rgyun* NP *rgyu*] of the winds ebbs off,
the ears do not hear anything, and the eyes become steady, aspiring for mahāmudrā.

3100. *Hevajratantra* I.8.34 (GZ CDNP *dus thabs*, "timely means," for Skt. *parva*, "observances"). For comments on this stanza, especially on "the guru's observances," see the note on this stanza quoted in the *Saṃkṣiptasekaprakriyā* (text 38, 231).

3101. IaS (300) takes this sentence as presenting two separate reasons: "Here the 'time of worship of the guru' means the time of worship of the Vajra, since [if guru did not here mean Vajra] it could not be connected with the sense [of *parva*] 'time of worship', [and] since there is no service [of the guru as something that allows one to directly experience the Innate]." The last phrase "[of the guru as something that allows one to directly experience the Innate]" may be inspired by Ratnākaraśānti's *Muktāvalī* explaining *guruparva* ["guru observance"] as "oral instruction (of the guru) aiming at realization," as cited in IaS, 299–300n251. IaS (300n252) then comments as follows on this sentence: "We understand that the opponent is arguing that the *Hevajratantra* verse implies that the experience of the Innate is through the service of the Vajra, and hence that it takes place when Bodhicitta is still within the Jewel. That guru here means Vajra is argued on the basis of the fact that neither *parva* nor *upasevā* could otherwise be meaningfully connected with *guru*, at least in the context of the direct experience of the Innate." While these comments make sense, I think the second reason in IaS—"[and] since there is no service [of the guru as something that allows one to directly experience the Innate]"—needs too much additional explanation ("[of the guru as something that allows one to directly experience the Innate]") in order to make sense (and it is not certain that this is indeed its sense): if the phrase "since there is no service [or attending]" on its own is taken as the second reason, I fail to see what its meaning would be. Thus, to me it seems more convincing to link the two reasons, with "there would be no attending [at all]" being what follows from "[otherwise] it could not be connected with the meaning of 'the time of attending.'" This is also supported by the phrasing in GZ CD (. . . *phyir te* / . . . *phyir ro*; NP omit the first *phyir*).

3102. This refers to *upasevā* at the end of *Hevajratantra* I.8.34d.

3103. GZ CDNP "Here 'the guru's timely means' means the timely means of the vajra. For [otherwise] it could not be connected . . . No. The term *upa*, by virtue of being a word expressing being near . . ."

3104. II.4.53ab.

3105. That is, the opponent understands *vajrāyatana* as a *karmadhāraya* compound.

3106. As for this quote, the objection, and Rāmapāla's reply, IaS (300n253) says this: "The opponent quotes this line as scriptural evidence, again, that the Innate Bliss is experienced when Bodhicitta is within the Vajra, and that the Vajra is the means of that experience. The reply will be that this line is not speaking of the Innate Bliss but of Supreme Bliss, which precedes and is in that sense the means of the Innate Bliss." GZ CDNP: ". . .

> "Due to the vajrāyatana—the means—
> the bliss of the vajra is mahāmudrā

"[GZ CDNP have *zhe na* both here and at the end of this objection] . . . The āyatana of the vajra itself is the place . . ." No. It is taught that the bliss of the bola that is mahāmudrā and exists in the place of the vajrāyatana is supreme ecstasy; that is the means."

3107. *Cakrasaṃvaratantra* I.1ab and I.2c.

3108. IaS (300n254): "Having defended, so to speak, his view against attacks which tried to find a contradiction between it and the Hevajratantra, Rāmapāla now is perhaps going on the offensive, and showing that not only is the *Hevajratantra* consistent with his view, but that his view (alone?) also allows for a good understanding/interpretation of the famous opening passage of the *Sarvabuddhasamāyoga*, which was later incorporated into the *Cakrasaṃvaratantra* (which may well be the text that Rāmapāla has in mind, rather than the by his time probably already unfashionable *Sarvabuddhasamāyoga*)."

3109. The Sanskrit letters *a* and *i* here are a hermeneutical unraveling of their forming the letter *e* according to the *sandhi* rules (when *-a* as the last letter of a word is followed by *i-* as the first letter of the following word, they merge, resulting in the letter *e*). Thus, the hermeneutical meaning of *rahasye* is explained here as "the nondual [cognition] that accords with reality in all aspects, is beyond thisness, and is [experienced when bodhicitta is] in the space between the vajra and the lotus." "Being beyond thisness" as a literal rendering of *idantātīta* means being beyond anything that could be pinpointed or identified as "this is it."

3110. As pointed out by IaS (301n257), these two lines (plus two more) are also cited without attribution in Jayabhadra's commentary on the *Cakrasaṃvaratantra* I.1 and in the Tibetan of Bhavyakīrti's **Vīramanoramā* (D1405, fol. 3a.7), another commentary on the same tantra.

3111. The first quoted phrase in this stanza is *Hevajratantra* II.3.7a, and the second is, according to Rāmapāla's *Sekanirdeśapañjikā*, embedded in a passage from the *Paramādyatantra*. Given the brevity and the generic nature of this phrase, it is naturally found in many other texts as well, such as the *Śrīḍākārṇavamahāyoginītantra* (H390, fols. 202a.7 and 224a.5), the *Amoghapāśakalpa* (H689, fols. 272a.5 and 272b.3), and a vast number of tantric commentaries in Tg. IaS (301n259): "The interpretation of this verse is not entirely straightforward, and the commentary of Rāmapāla is in the first part, which deals most directly with the verse, obscure, due to the unfortunate coincidence of a lacuna in both Sanskrit manuscripts with an apparent problem in the Tibetan translation (see n. 260 below). We think it likely, however, that the verse contains both a question raised by an objector (*katham*) and a reply by the Siddhāntin . . . We wonder if here the translation of stanza 23 could have been influenced by the translation of the commentary (for a possibly similar case, see below *ad* st. 37)."

3112. In all manuscripts, the rest of this sentence after "A true guru . . ." is a lacuna.

3113. Note that most of the comments on stanza 23 are also found in similar form in Vajrapāṇi's *Guruparamparākramopadeśa* in its explanation of the correct practice of karmamudrā (text 213, 215–17). IaS (301–2n260): "Just before the end of the passage for which we lack the testimony of both Sanskrit manuscripts, there is, unfortunately, a problem which we cannot at present solve in a satisfactory manner. The Tibetan translation reads: *bla mas* (*mas* em.] *ma* P G N D dPal) *źes bya ba la sogs pas bla ma dam pas ned bar bstan pa nid ni 'dir bla ma dam pas man nag bstan pa bya ste* [...] *źes bya ba bstan* (*bstan* P G N D] *stan* dPal) *pa yin no*, i.e., perhaps 'By "through the true teacher" and so on [what is meant is that] the true teacher should give instruction here which is precisely what has been shown by the true teacher, because of the brief statement: [...]'. One possible Sanskrit retranslation of the words preceding the quotation might be *sadguror ityādinā sadguruṇpadarśita evātra sadguruṇopadeśaḥ kathitavyaḥ*. It seems certain that the text is wrong here in some way, whether because the Sanskrit as available to the Tibetan translators was corrupt, because the translation was bad, because the translation has been poorly transmitted, or some combination of these. For as it stands, the translation is repetitious and does not really yield coherent sense . . . Apart from the details of how the Tibetan translation should read and what Sanskrit reading might underlie it, we are uncertain about the point which the commentator wishes to make here. Is it that the teaching of a true guru is essential because at some places the tantra teaches only in cryptic *uddeśa*s? This might seem plausible, but in that case why is it that when an opponent asks a further question, viz. how one knows that the *ādi* of *Hevajratantra* 2.3.7b includes everything up to friction, the answer is that it is because of *nirdeśa* in the tantra itself? This would appear to undermine the argument for the need of a true guru's instruction. In view of these doubts on various levels, we have thought it best to leave the Sanskrit preceding the verse un-retranslated, and have likewise left a lacuna in the English translation." I agree with the Sanskrit reconstruction suggested by IaS and also that the Tibetan translation is somewhat repetitious. However, I disagree that it seems certain that the Tibetan text is wrong here and also with the English rendering of the Tibetan here in IaS. Considering the following series of quotes from the *Hevajratantra* (each of which is glossed briefly by the commentary), the phrase "this is well coherent" in line 23d, and the overall meaning of stanza 24, the gist of the sentence in question here seems to me as follows: the guru's pith instructions are necessary not only to unravel but also to properly connect various statements in the tantras that are not necessarily in the correct order or even scattered throughout a chapter or text (as can be seen, the lines cited here from the *Hevajratantra* are out of order but then connected in terms of their meaning in answer to the opponent's objections). Thus, the sentence and what follows again emphasize the crucial role of the guru in receiving the experientially correct oral instructions rather than just relying on written texts alone, a theme already emphasized above in the comments on stanza 4 (highlighted by the phrase "to remove [the reliance on] being learned in books and to [show the necessity of] depending on a spiritual friend"). Another possibility would be that GZ CDNP *nye bar bstan pa* should actually be *nye bar bsten pa* (Skt. *upasevā*, "attending"), thus referring back to the previous discussion of the guru's observances. Then, the sentence here would be in perfect harmony with the above-mentioned explanation of "guru observance" as "oral instruction [*upadeśa*] (of the guru) aiming at realization" in Ratnākaraśānti's *Muktāvalī*, and the similar comment in Kṛṣṇa's *Yogaratnamālā* that the observances to be obtained from the guru are provided by the guru to suitable disciples according to procedure, which means that they are the pith instructions. In any case, replacing "what is shown" by "attending" in this sense would obviously not change the overall meaning at hand.

3114. II.3.7ab.
3115. GZ CDNP "Here, condensed by the term 'and so forth,' [everything] up to friction is expressed as variety."
3116. *Hevajratantra* II.3.13.
3117. GZ CDNP: "'Given that this is the master empowerment, from where does one know "the variety of the master [empowerment] at the beginning"?' It is taught in very great detail [in the *Hevajratantra*]:"
3118. II.3.10cd.
3119. II.3.10ab. These two lines are also found in the *Raktayamarītantra* (H441, fol. 489a.1), and the second line also corresponds to *Guhyasamājatantra* XVIII.113f and *Sampuṭodbhavatantra* II.1.46d. The preceding three lines in both of the latter texts are a more extensive version of the first line here.
3120. *Hevajratantra* II.3.7cd.
3121. GZ CDNP "Because of this, this is the brief teaching. The essence of bliss up to [bodhicitta moving to] the tip of the jewel is supreme ecstasy."
3122. GZ CDNP "How should one know that supreme ecstasy has the essence of bliss? Because of the detailed instruction . . ."
3123. GZ CDNP "guru."
3124. II.3.21.
3125. IaS (303n273) says that Rāmapāla's argument is not made fully explicit here, but "in the moment that is free of diversity" should no doubt refer to the moment in which connate ecstasy is experienced, since only that can be truly free of diversity, thoughts, and so on (see stanza 3 and its commentary). What

Rāmapāla means is that *paramānande tu samprāpte* ("when the supreme ecstasy is attained") is a locative absolute indicating a necessary prior condition, and that therefore the line implies that supreme ecstasy (and the moment of maturation) must cover everything from friction up to the experience of connate ecstasy, which, as argued above, should be at the moment when bodhicitta has just emerged from the vajra but is still in contact with it.

3126. That is, "within the jewel" was already explained in the comments on stanza 22 (409–410). GZ CDNP "Here [in our view], in accordance with how the meaning of 'in the moment . . .' and so on occurs, everything is fine. The meaning of . . . has already been explained [above]."

3127. Instead of "[what follows] before [bodhicitta reaching] the jewel," GZ CDNP read "within the jewel."

3128. II.3.11. As Kṛṣṇa's *Yogaratnamālā* (Snellgrove 1959, 2:142) makes explicitly clear, it is by virtue of or as the purities of the couple smiling at each other, looking at each other, embracing each other, and their sexual union that one speaks here of the vase empowerment, the secret empowerment, the prajñā-jñāna empowerment, and the fourth empowerment, respectively.

3129. GZ "This too should be understood as the outer creation [process]. The tathāgata relief is ecstasy, the master [empowerment], which should be understood as the profound creation process. The Vajradhara relief is ecstasy, the perfection process. In the context of the four mudrās, the full-perfection [process] is the full-perfection [process] through the master empowerment, which is to be understood as the karmamudrā." CDNP "Through the profound creation process, ecstasy is the master empowerment, which is the tathāgata relief. The ecstasy in the perfection process is the Vajradhara relief. In the context of the four mudrās, the full-perfection [process] is the master empowerment, which is to be understood thanks to the karmamudrā." IaS (304n278) adds that among the five processes in the works of Maitrīpa and his students, the "essence process" "is not mentioned here, perhaps because at that level such distinctions are no longer relevant."

3130. Spelled out in terms of the meaning at hand, this brief sentence reads as follows: "[If, as explained above, these lower empowerments are the master empowerment, and that corresponds to the first phase in the union with the consort,] then how about this [fact that the six lower empowerments are the vase empowerment]?"

3131. Skt. *payodhara* literally means "containing or carrying water" or "containing milk" but also means "a woman's breasts." Thus this is obviously a play on words in relation to "vase" and karmamudrā; in addition, a part of the classical definition of "vase" is "the ability to carry or contain water." GZ CDNP obviously completely miss this point: GZ "Since the word 'vase' indicates the expression 'carrying water,' 'vase' here too indicates that" CDNP "By virtue of the word 'vase' indicating the expression 'carrying water,' since this represents the function of carrying water, it is similar."

3132. GZ CDNP "In order to teach all of this, [Maitrīpa] utters [the stanza] beginning with 'What consists of the ecstasy of smiling and so on' . . . The meaning [of this] has already been explained."

3133. Since this stanza presents the sequence of the four moments and thus the four ecstasies that Maitrīpa asserts, *ramaḥ* (lit. "pleasure") in the last line is shorthand for *viramaḥ* ("cessation"; as confirmed by the commentary below), referring to *viramānanda* ("cessational ecstasy"), probably for metrical reasons. The third line thus refers to the moment of the lack of characteristics and the corresponding connate ecstasy.

3134. IaS (305n284): "We understand *bodhicittasya* as an objective genitive dependent on *sparśaḥ*. So it is specifically the tactile sensation of Bodhicitta, which would amount to meaning almost the same as the sensation of its movement (as the tactile sensation of it is related to one location in one instant and to other locations in the succeeding instants), up to the proximity of the Jewel, in other words up to the point where the Bodhicitta (and hence the tactile awareness of it) has reached the proximity of the Jewel, that is what 'friction' refers to."

3135. The phrase "the consideration 'I have partaken of bliss'" corresponds to *Hevajratantra* II.3.8b.

3136. As mentioned before, this line is *Hevajratantra* II.3.10b, *Guhyasamājatantra* XVIII.113f, and *Sampuṭodbhavatantra* II.1.46d, and is also found in the *Raktayamarītantra* (H441, fol. 489a.1).

3137. Though the terminology here is clearly parallel to the Sāṃkhya school, which says that all the manifold appearances of the world manifest out of the primal matter (*prakṛti*) and are nothing but its illusory manifestations or modulations (*vikāra*), this is of course not what is meant here. Rather, as the following makes clear, *prakṛti* here refers to true reality as it was explained in the comments on stanza 22.

3138. IaS (306) renders the last two sentences as follows: "And these are Four Blisses [when they are experienced] in an external woman, the Action Seal; when the Four Seals are differentiated [, however,] they are a single Bliss, [which is] called the Action Seal because it is located in that [Action Seal, i.e. the external woman]." Since the text is obviously written from a male perspective, it seems clear that the locative *bhhyāṅganāyāṃ karmamudrāyāṃ* cannot mean "[when they are experienced] in an external woman, the Action Seal"; rather, the text speaks about the four ecstasies with regard to, or based on, a woman who is a karmamudrā—that is, their being experienced within the male partner by relying on an external karmamudrā (of course, these four are also experienced by the female, but that is not the point here). Thus, likewise, Skt. *tātsthyāt* (IaS "it is located in that [Action Seal, i.e. the external woman]") is not about this single ecstasy being located in the woman but about this ecstasy arising in a man by relying on a woman. Furthermore, given that Skt. *caturmudrāvyavasthitaveka* is rendered as GZ CDNP *phyag rgya bzhi'i rnam par gzhag pa la(s)* and that IaS likewise reads it as *caturmudrā* + *vyavasthita*, I somewhat reluctantly follow this reading. However, I am not sure in what way the four mudrās being differentiated equals a single ecstasy. To me, it would make more sense to consider the four ecstasies as a single one when the four mudrās are *not* differentiated (thus reading *caturmudrā* + *avyavasthita*).

3139. This refers back to the comments on stanzas 2–3. GZ CDNP "Now, in order to present the four ecstasies, [Maitrīpa] utters [the stanza] that begins 'Due to being variegated, variety.' As for being variegated [I follow NP *sna tshogs nyid* GZ against GZ CD *sna tshogs gnyis*], the existence of perceiver and perceived is variety—that is, ecstasy. 'When churning' means churning up to the end of churning. Bodhicitta touches up to being near the jewel. Through these, one will arrive at 'the supreme ecstasy of the jewel city.' Due to being bliss, the existence of filled-up bliss is maturation. Supreme [ecstasy] is in the jewel city—up to the tip of the gem. The meaning of 'True reality [needs to be understood] through the guru' has already been explained. Cessation [I follow CDNP *dga' bral* against GZ *dga ba*, 'ecstasy'] refers to being separated. Being separated refers to bodhicitta falling. Consummation refers to the experience of bliss. This is the analysis 'I experience that bliss' [I follow GZ *bdag gis bde ba de spyod do zhes bya ba* against CDNP *bdag gi bya ni* 'my activity']. Such is cessation. As for 'the fourth is again like such,' 'such' is the nature that is the essence of prajñā-jñāna . . . 'Like' means in such a way, which is to be understood as before. That becomes the fourth one. As for these [GZ CDNP *'di dag gis ni* em. *'di dag ni*] being the four ecstasies of a karmamudrā who is an external woman [GZ CDNP *yan lag can*, lit. 'having parts'], in [NP *la* GZ CD *las*] the presentation of the four mudrās, the four ecstasies abide as a single one, which is called 'karmamudrā.' Here too this [GZ *'dir yang* CDNP *'di yang*] should be understood according to the presentation of the Nonaspectarians and [GZ CDNP *dang* NP *pa'i* 'of'] what was taught in the context of the forceful empowerment."

3140. GZ CDNP "Now, in order to teach the presentation of cause and result, [Maitrīpa] utters [the stanza] that begins 'Once you relied upon.'"

3141. As mentioned before, as IaS (306–7n294) points out, this stanza is cited in the *Prajñājñānaprakāśa* (text 16, 58), an Advayavajra's **Āryamañjuśrīnāmasaṃgītiṭīkāsārābhisamaya* (D2098, fol. 106b.5), and Raviśrījñāna's *Amṛtakaṇikā* (Banarsi Lal 1994, 95; attributed to the *Vairocanābhisambodhitantra* but not found there). IaS adds that this stanza may not be by Maitrīpa originally but taken (or modified) by him from some Yogatantra source. In addition, the *Caturmudrāṭīkā* (text 44, 347) quotes a somewhat similar but problematic stanza, attributing it to an unspecified tantra. Lastly, a stanza whose first two lines are very similar but whose last two are very different is found in an Indrabhūti's *Śrīcakrasaṃvaratantrarājaśambarasamuccayanāmavṛtti* (D1413, fol. 99a.2–3):

> Once you relied upon the karmamudrā,
> you should cultivate the dharmamudrā
> Blissful empty true reality is mahāmudrā
> What is unchanging is the samayamudrā.

3142. As mentioned before, besides "resemblance," Skt. *chāyā* can also mean "reflection" (GZ CDNP *gzugs brnyan*), "shadow," "luster," "light," "play of light or color," "gracefulness," "beauty," "complexion," and "features." All of these meanings are certainly implied in that the wisdom generated with the help of a karmamudrā is only a reflection or a shadow of the actual connate but nevertheless is a very vivid and colorful experience intimately related to the connate, similar to the rays of the sun being related to the sun itself.

3143. GZ CDNP "Action refers to the activities of body, speech, and mind that have the nature of the connate. Seal refers to what is illustrated and illustration. Thus this is the karmamudrā. By virtue of a synecdochic meaning due to designating the [physical] support of that [prajñā-jñāna], it is also to be expressed as the lalanā. Once the karmamudrā has been gained, the essence of the nature of prajñā-jñāna is praised: it has solely the essence of a substance of modulation. Since it is said to mimic it in being [merely] a reflection of the [actual] connate, it is expressed as 'the result of concordant outflow' of what is called 'the connate.' This kind of concordant outflow consists of what is called 'variety' and so on—that is, ecstasy."

3144. Skt. *tataḥ* ("from that") could also mean "then" (as also suggested by GZ CDNP *de nas*). However, as line 26d and the concluding sentence in the comments below make clear, the dharmamudrā arises from the karmamudrā, mahāmudrā from the dharmamudrā, and the samayamudrā from mahāmudrā.

3145. GZ CDNP "Then [there is] the dharmamudrā: that dharmas such as blue or yellow are free from being anything perceived and so on by virtue of fivefold awakening and the purity of the deity constitutes the sole beautiful means for supreme ecstasy and has the essence of the dharmadhātu and the essence of the utter nonabiding that comes through experience. Since this is the path by virtue of being the proximate cause that is inseparable from mahāmudrā, this especially distinguished ripening is the result of maturation. This moment of maturation is supreme ecstasy."

3146. Though IaS reads *vicārāgatāpratiṣṭhāna* just as in the immediately preceding paragraph on the dharmamudrā, I emend this to *avicārāgatāpratiṣṭhāna*. For Rāmapāla's following comments on stanza 29–30, in which mahāmudrā is equated with utter nonabiding, explicitly say that "that utter nonabiding is the inconceivable wisdom that does not come from analysis . . . It is effortless and occurs in its own natural flow." Thus, it should be clear that, in contrast to the dharmamudrā, mahāmudrā does *not* arise from training in the wisdom of utter nonabiding that comes from analysis. This is further corroborated by the *Caturmudrāṭīkā* (text 44, 325 and 362) comments on mahāmudrā saying that "mahāmudrā is nonabiding, effortless, and inconceivable wisdom: it is familiarized with in the way of not arising from analysis," and "not coming from analysis, the wisdom of suchness's own essence is unborn."

3147. In the *Caturmudrānvaya*, the long compound *anālambanamahākaruṇāśarīra-mahāsukhaikarūpā* here is split into *anālambanamahākaruṇāśārīrā mahāsukhaikarūpā* ("embodies nonreferential compassion and has the single essence of great bliss"; Mathes 2015, 398).

3148. GZ CDNP "Then, this [mahāmudrā] is great because it seals the three [other] mudrās. And it is also a seal: by being directly perceived while becoming familiar, in a respectful and uninterrupted manner, with the wisdom of the path that has the essence of the utter nonabiding that comes through experience [*spyad* instead of *dpyad*], it is free from [all] cognitive obscurations and so on that are nonentities, and thus represents the basis of all excellence, is saṃsāric existence's and nirvāṇa's single nature, embodies nonreferential great compassion, and is the kāya of the single great bliss. This is the result of stainlessness free from all obscurations. It is the moment of the lack of characteristics—connate ecstasy."

3149. Skt. *saṃketa* (GZ CDNP *brda*) can also mean "signal," "gesture," "hint," "indication," "convention" (IaS), "agreement," and "stipulation." As the following shows, *samaya* and *saṃketa* refer to Vajradhara's (or formless true reality's) symbolic altruistic appearances that have diverse forms.

3150. Note that the bulk of Rāmapāla's comments on stanza 26 is closely based on the presentation of the four mudrās in the *Caturmudrānvaya* (text 14), often verbatim; compare also the *Caturmudrāṭīkā* (text 44).

3151. IaS (309) renders this sentence as "With regard to this, [each of] the Seals is the cause with respect to the preceding, and the fruit with respect to the following," and notes (n310): "It seems that the opposite should be intended; the earlier Seals are respectively the causes of the later ones, the later ones the results of the earlier ones. We are not sure whether it is possible that Rāmapāla himself was careless in formulating the idea, or whether there is a transmissional error here." Though this rendering per IaS is certainly the more straightforward one, it makes no sense here, and both the Sanskrit and the Tibetan can also be read in the way I did. Hence, there is not really a problem. GZ CDNP "Then, in turn, the samayamudrā is the symbol of samaya, the forms of Heruka and other [tantric deities] that have the essence of the sambhoga- and nirmāṇa[kāyas] for the welfare of sentient beings, and the miraculous manifestation of Vajradhara . . . There, [the moment of] consummation is cessational ecstasy . . ."

3152. GZ CDNP "Now, in order to teach that each one of the four mudrās has the nature of [all] four ecstasies, [Maitrīpa] utters [the stanza] that begins 'The ecstasies are related to each mudrā.'"

3153. *Hevajratantra* II.3.9.

3154. GZ CDNP "Through 'related to each of the mudrās,' all four ecstasies should be known in each mudrā, but not in mahāmudrā. For the sake of these, [Maitrīpa] teaches three reasons . . . Here, what is taught by the scriptures is this:

> "The first ecstasy is variety,
> supreme ecstasy, maturation,
> cessational ecstasy, consummation
> and connate ecstasy, characteristics' lack

"Through [passages] such as these, in the *Hevajra[tantra]* and so on, this is stated in a successive manner [NP omit "in a successive manner"] by matching variety with the first of the four ecstasies [and so on] . . . This very matter that will be explained [in the following stanza] beginning with 'Variety' is clear through the essence of self-awareness and is also to be understood through the pith instructions of the true guru. [The following stanza] beginning with 'Variety' will be explained [CDNP "It is clear that this very essence that will be explained . . . beginning with 'Variety' (NP omit "this very essence . . . with 'Variety'") is the essence of self-awareness. The pith instructions of the true guru will be explained . . . beginning with 'Variety']. In order to teach the essence of the four ecstasies [NP omit this phrase], after having discussed 'the nature of the four ecstasies in the karmamudrā (physical actions),' [Maitrīpa] utters [the stanza] beginning with 'Variety' in order to teach the essence of the four ecstasies in the dharmamudrā (speech)."

3155. As mentioned before, IaS (310) renders the first two lines *vicitraṃ karmamudrāto vipāko jagadātmatā* as "Vicitra *is the being of the nature of the world, [arising] from the Action Seal;* vipāka *is [the same],*" noting "This interpretation may seem at first sight very unnatural, but it follows Rāmapāla's commentary" (n318). Apart from my different phrasing, what is thus clear is that "the world's own being" pertains to both "variety" and "maturation." Note that, at first sight, the first two and the last lines of this stanza seem to match the lines with the corresponding ecstasies instead of the moments in the above-quoted stanza I.10.13 from the *Hevajratantra*:

> The first ecstasy has a worldly nature
> Likewise, supreme ecstasy is worldly
> Cessational ecstasy is worldly as well
> The connate is not found in these three

However, in the commentaries on the *Hevajratantra*, it is very clear that ecstasy, supreme ecstasy, and cessational ecstasy all belong to the mundane sphere—that is, seeming reality—though they are increasingly more subtle. By contrast, Rāmapāla's following comments explicitly equate "the world's own being" with the emptiness endowed with all supreme aspects (that is, ultimate reality).

3156. Rāmapāla's comments on stanza 34 gloss "realization" (Skt. *bodha*) as "penetrating insight" (Skt. *nirvedha*). The first two stanzas and the accompanying prose in Maitrīpa's *Nirvedhapañcaka* (text 28) discuss the nature of penetrating insight into the connate—stainless empty wisdom with the character of effortless compassion—as belonging to those in whom the thoughts about remedies, true reality, and the fruition are terminated. In texts on the progressive realizations on the five paths and the ten bhūmis, *nirvedha* is typically associated with the nonconceptual wisdom first attained on the Mahāyāna path of seeing (the first bhūmi).

3157. As mentioned before, this line is *Hevajratantra* II.3.10b, *Guhyasamājatantra* XVIII.113f, and *Sampuṭodbhavatantra* II.1.46d, and is also found in the *Raktayamarītantra* (H441, fol. 489a.1).

3158. This unidentified quotation appears again in the comments on stanza 37.

3159. GZ CDNP "Since it appears as the world's variety's own being that is the cause of the karmamudrā and is realized through the words taught by the pith instructions of the true guru, it is variety. Maturation is the facing of penetrating insight by virtue of meditating on that—the disappearance of what appears as variety. Characteristics' lack is the highest form of meditating [I follow CDNP *bsgom pa* against GZ *sgom pa po*, "meditator"] on the world's own being—the stability [I follow NP *brtan pa* against GZ CD *brten pa*, "relying on"] in the absence of any appearance whatsoever. Thus is the world's own being that is called 'the emptiness endowed with all supreme aspects' and represents stability: the yogī, the meditator, firmly convinced about observing [everything] as utter nonabiding and abiding in convention as suchness, looks at and analyzes the world—that is consummation

[CDNP "As for relying on the world's own being that is called 'the emptiness endowed with all supreme aspects,' the yogī, the meditator, having stable conviction that [everything] is utter nonabiding and abiding in convention as suchness, looks at the world (analyzes it)—that is consummation"] . . . Why? When everything has the essence of the connate—by virtue of the gist 'the single supreme ecstasy of [NP omit 'supreme ecstasy of'] utter ecstasy is differentiated into four in number'—the dharmamudrā that represents the single essence of the four ecstasies [CDNP "all four ecstasies of the dharmamudrā being a single one"] is supreme ecstasy."

3160. GZ CDNP "Having explained the dharmamudrā, in order to teach mahāmudrā—the nature of the mind that is one as the essence of connate ecstasy—[Maitrīpa now] utters [the stanza] beginning with 'Utter nonabiding in anything at all.'"

3161. As mentioned before, Skt. *kuśala* can also mean "skillful," "clever," "happy," "good," "suitable," "right," and "virtuous" (all Tibetan versions of these recurrent two lines have *dge ba*, "virtuous"). The same two lines as well as the following stanza are explicitly attributed to the *Jñānālokālaṃkārasūtra* in Maitrīpa's *Amanasikārādhāra* (text 27, 156–57) and also cited (without attribution) in Nāgārjuna's *Caturmudrānvaya* (text 14, 31). As they stand, these two lines are not found in the *Jñānālokālaṃkārasūtra*, which only contains the following passage: "All nonvirtuous mental engagement is the cause of afflictive phenomena. All virtuous mental engagement is the cause of purified phenomena" (2004, 94.14–15). For further comments, see the note on these two lines in text 14.

3162. *Jñānālokālaṃkārasūtra* IV.12 (2004, 146.1–2), *Saṃvarodayatantra* VIII.36′ (Tsuda 1974, 101), and *Pañcakrama* IV.10. Explicitly attributed to the *Jñānālokālaṃkārasūtra*, this stanza is also found in Maitrīpa's *Amanasikārādhāra* (text 27, 157). Without attribution, it also appears in his *Pañcatathāgatamudrāvivaraṇa* (text 36, 194) and in Nāgārjuna's *Caturmudrānvaya* (text 14, 31).

3163. Skt. *jvara* can also mean "pain" (GZ CDNP *rims nad* "infectious diseases"). This is one of the classical examples of not-to-be-relied-on treatises that propose accomplishing results through impossible means.

3164. GZ CDNP "Utter nonabiding refers to being without any superimpositions due to mental nonengagement [CDNP correspond to the Sanskrit]. As it is stated in the Buddha's words . . . Here one should not think [I follow GZ *bsam pa* against CDNP *gsal ba*, 'clear'] . . . [a remedy to] remove infectious diseases . . . 'But how can [this mahāmudrā] here not have the essence of [all] four moments?' [Maitrīpa] says: 'Since it is stainless and since it is self-awareness.' Stainless means that since the three moments of variety and so forth are stained, they do not arise here. Therefore [CDNP 'Likewise'] . . ."

3165. GZ CDNP "'That which is effortless wisdom.'"

3166. On the objection immediately preceding stanza 30 ("Utter nonabiding means being inconceivable . . ."), IaS (312n335) says: "We are not entirely sure what the force of the objection is. Possibly the opponent means that if *apratiṣṭhāna* is equivalent to *acintyatā*, this would then mean that all phenomena can not be thought of, i.e. known, at least as regards their true nature, and that therefore they are obscured by *jñeyāvaraṇa*." The point of the objection rather seems to be that conceptualizing what is inconceivable—mahāmudrā—is in itself an obscuration. Given that the inconceivable is considered as the true nature of phenomena by Maitrīpa and Rāmapāla, the opponent seems to imply that it is necessary on the path, at least for ordinary beings, to conceive of this inconceivable nature as the primary object of meditation. Maitrīpa's and Rāmapāla's answer is not to worry, because anything that can be conceived is simply not the inconceivable, and therefore any conceptualizing of the inconceivable is ultimately the wrong approach to attain genuine nonconceptual wisdom. According to IaS (313n339), Rāmapāla's answer here is that the utter nonabiding—the inconceivable wisdom that does not derive from analysis—occurs only at the time of buddhahood. Yet from the perspective of the path, as discussed in the context of dharmamudrā and mahāmudrā in the comments on stanza 26, Rāmapāla speaks of "the utter nonabiding that comes from analysis." Thus there is a difference between "the utter nonabiding that does not come from analysis, is effortless, and occurs in its own natural flow" (fruition) versus "the utter nonabiding that comes from analysis" (path). However, the objection immediately preceding stanza 30 is clearly referring back to the comments on stanza 29, where Rāmapāla speaks of practice, glossing utter nonabiding as "mental nonengagement" (being without superimpositions) and saying that being without imaginary thinking, abiding, minding, mental engagement, and focus is not an instruction on something that cannot actually be put into practice—mahāmudrā can indeed be directly perceived with the help of the guru. Thus, I doubt that "utter nonabiding" and "inconceivable" in the comments on stanza 30 only refer to buddha wisdom; rather, though "utter nonabiding" needs to be analyzed up to a certain point on the path, at some point, the meditator must go beyond analysis. IaS (313n342) also says that there are some doubts regarding the reading of the stanza from the *Jñānasiddhi* (IaS follows Cambridge ms. *kāraṇābhāvāt*), continuing: "With this reading the idea might be that on the stage of the path, when phenomena are being reflected on as without fixed abiding or ground, the effortless non-conceptual cognition of a Buddha cannot (yet) arise, because the necessary causes for such cognition are not yet complete." More to the point, the cause of effortless nonconceptual wisdom is precisely not to conceptualize anything, including itself. Nonconceptual wisdom is extensively discussed in that vein in the eighth chapter of the *Mahāyānasaṃgraha*. *Mahāyānasaṃgraha* VIII.2 says that the nature of nonconceptual wisdom (as an equivalent of the prajñā of bodhisattvas and not as the ultimate fruition) is to be free from five aspects: an utter lack of mental engagement (such as deep sleep), conceptual examination and analysis, meditative absorptions in which discriminations and feelings have ceased, having the nature of matter, and picturing true reality. These same five aspects to be excluded are also found in other Yogācāra texts, such as the *Dharmadharmatāvibhāga* (lines 216–20; see Brunnhölzl 2012, 51, 168–69, 270–71, and 322–23), the *Viniścayasaṃgrahaṇī*, the *Abhidharmasamuccaya*, and other works (for details, see Brunnhölzl 2018, 2:747–49, especially notes 723 and 725). On the matrix (cause) of nonconceptual wisdom in *Mahāyānasaṃgraha* VIII.3, Asvabhāva's commentary (Brunnhölzl 2018, 2:749) says this: "Since wisdom is a mental factor, mind serves as its matrix. 'It is not acceptable for mind to be [both] this matrix and nonconceptual because the term "mind" derives from the cause that is [the expression] "having in mind." But if something without mind were this matrix, [nonconceptual wisdom] would consequently not be wisdom, just like form.' [In order to cut through] this rope of twofold difficulty, [the text] provides its answer through the [latter] half of verse: 'For it has no referents in mind yet arises from that cause.' The matrix of nonconceptual [wisdom] is not mind because unlike [ordinary states of mind] it does not have any referents in mind. Something without mind is not its matrix either because it arises from the cause that is mind. It arises from the cause that is mind in the following way: through the power of meditation, one attains the state that is called 'the matrix in which one is utterly beyond [all] conceptions about mind and no mind.'" GZ CDNP "Being effortless, it arises through its own natural state. 'How?' For at the time of analysis through what is to be conceived, when not conceiving, conceiving of it [or 'there'] does not arise. As the *Jñānasiddhi* says:

> ". . .
> Since conceiving lacks a cause [or 'since there is nothing to conceive'],
> it is not nonconception either."

3167. Skt. *vijñānavāda* (Yogācāra).
3168. GZ CDNP "Now, in order to eliminate the assertion of Vijñānavāda, and then to refute the assertion of the view of extinction, [Maitrīpa] utters [the stanza] that begins 'Those who set their eyes on suchness.'"
3169. Skt. *saṃvid* is glossed here by *saṃvedana*.
3170. IaS (31n350): "It might be worth considering the possibility, though we think it is at best a very slight one, that a second meaning may also be intended to be hinted at here: *evaṃvidha*, 'of this kind' or, as we have translated it, 'like this', could also be taken as 'of the kind of E and Vaṃ'."
3171. GZ CDNP "Suchness is the true end. 'Those who set their eyes on [it]' means 'those who directly perceive it.' 'In line with the middle's actuality' means being free from the four extremes. Those with that fortune are aware of true reality. 'Does this [true reality] then become extinction?' No—'awareness' refers to self-awareness. The complete relinquishment of all thoughts without remainder is the direct experience of true reality. This kind of manifestation—having the characteristics of the two realities, being free from the two extremes . . . the nature of prajñā and means—such a manifestation should be known thanks to experiencing and being aware of the kindness of the venerable true guru."
3172. GZ CDNP "In order to teach well that this is included in the middle, [Maitrīpa] utters [the stanza] beginning with 'All superimpositions.'"
3173. Skt. *adhyavasāya* can also mean "conclusion," "clinging" (GZ CDNP *lhag par zhen pa*), and "mental effort."
3174. Given the many meanings of Skt. *vaśa*, this could also be read as "the very strong ignorant desire/craving for the real existence of consciousness," but GZ CDNP read *dbang*.
3175. As mentioned before, Skt. *apoha* (glossed here as *niṣedha*) can also mean "denial," and *vidhi* (glossed here again as *vidhi*) "creation," "contrivance," "conduct," "application," "precept," and "rule."
3176. GZ CDNP "For referents of clinging through superimpositions, no mat-

ter however many they may be, do not exist. 'If their nonexistence in their entirety is the middle's actuality, this kind of absence of superimpositions is also asserted in [the approach of] cognizance.' Therefore [Maitrīpa] says 'in all regards . . .' There, there is superimposition and labeling of the substance of cognizance as being really existent. [But] in this [approach of ours], [such] does not exist, because it is free from all superimpositions. Through this, the tenet [I follow GZ *grub pa'i mtha'* against CDNP *mtha'*, 'extreme'] of illusion-like [nonduality] too has been taught to be a superimposition. 'How?' Leave aside for the moment clinging through all thinking—the object [GZ *yul* CNP *ngo bo ltar*, 'seeming essence'] called 'removing'—because the superimposition of real aspects [NP *rnam pa bden pa* GZ CD *rnam pa med pas*, 'by virtue of no aspects'] and the labeling of the doctrine of cognizance exist . . . For the doctrine of consciousness [says] there exists the entity of consciousness that is taught [GZ CD *bstan pa* NP *brtan pa*, 'stable'] as thought-free, but it is this kind of existence of appearances under the sway of ignorance that is thought-free mind, and exactly that is grasped as self-awareness. It is absolutely clear that subsequent [to such thought-free meditation] feelings are grasped. [Objection:] 'You too assert such—since you assert that subsequent [to thought-free meditation] all thinking exists [again], the same applies to you as well [CDNP omit 'since you assert that . . . the same applies to you as well'].' No, though [everything] is nonabiding, you assert this by virtue of the conventions of seeming [reality] from the perspective of sentient beings. Therefore, where could there be negation or affirmation [CDNP 'removal or accomplishing']? . . ."

3177. GZ CDNP "'In that case, how should what appear as [NP omit 'what appear as'] very clear entities be known?' . . 'In that [state] in which.'"

3178. *Uttaratantra* I.154; also *Abhisamayālaṃkāra* V.21 and in other works; for details, see the note on this stanza quoted in text 14 (30).

3179. *Yuktiṣaṣṭikā* 6cd.

3180. *Lokātītastava* 25cd.

3181. *Aṣṭasāhasrikā Prajñāpāramitā*, Devaparivarta (see *Abhisamayālaṃkārālokā Prajñāpāramitāvyākhyā*, ed. Wogihara 1932–35, 602), *Pañcaviṃśatisāhasrikā Prajñāpāramitā* (ed. Kimura 1986–2007, 4:102_{11}–106_{7}).

3182. As Ruegg (1969, 330–31) points out, parallel statements are found in several other sūtras with regard to impermanence (Aṅguttara Nikāya I.286), dependent origination (Saṃyutta Nikāya II.25, 60, and 124; Dīgha Nikāya I.190; and the *Śālistambasūtra* [Sanskrit reconstruction in N. Aiyasvami Sastri, *Ārya Śālistamba Sūtra* (Adyar: Theosophical Society, 1950), 47]), and suchness. As for the latter, the *Daśabhūmikasūtra* (ed. Rahder 1926, 65) says, "No matter whether buddhas have arrived in the world or not, [this] is just what abides as the true nature of phenomena," and the *Pañcaviṃśatisāhasrikā Prajñāpāramitā* (D9, vol. *ka*, fol. 313a.6–313b.1) states, "No matter whether tathāgatas have appeared or whether tathāgatas have not appeared, the true state of phenomena, the nature of phenomena, the dharmadhātu, the flawless dharma, suchness, unerring suchness, suchness that is never other, and the true end abide just as they are." Very similar statements are also found in the prajñāpāramitā sūtras in one hundred thousand and eight thousand lines, the *Laṅkāvatārasūtra* (for page references, see Ruegg 1969), the *Tathāgatagarbhasūtra* (D258, fol. 248b.6), and the *Ratnameghasūtra* (D231, fol. 69a.4).

3183. *Hevajratantra* II.4.38ab.

3184. IaS (318n378): "Untraced. The reading of the *dohā* is quite tentative. The Tibetan translation has for *ṇiviappo jaïso taïso* (with *ṇiviappo* a conjecture for the *vappa* of the St. Petersburg manuscript, which is the only one available here) *sgom pa dag*, i.e. 'pure meditation'. An alternative attempt to reconstruct the verse might perhaps be: *saraha bhaṇaï kappa jaïso taïso // jaïso bujjhaï mi hoi ṇo taïso* 11 (*saraho bhaṇati kṣālitaṃ yādṛśaṃ tādṛśam / yādṛśaṃ buddhyate 'pi bhavati na tādṛśam*)." GZ CDNP: "Here, you may think that the world has the character of being empty of any superimpositions of cognition and cognizable, but even when involving thinking, this is not other than being conceptual and being nonconceptual. 'How is it then?' Exactly as when the true reality of all appearances [NP omit 'appearances'] was not known, it is just the same way when true reality is known . . . Alternatively, 'everything is just the same way as it had been before' means that it should be known that, just as the essence of the connate is thought-free, in the same way the entire world is realized [I follow CD *rtogs pa* against GZ NP *rtog pa*] as the essence of true reality. As it is taught:

> "Just as before, so it is thereafter:
> mind is buddhahood in suchness

. . .

"All phenomena are realized to be the connate, therefore they will thereby not be rejected as saṃsāra.

. . .

> "The [NP 'all'] buddhas do remain
> in this kind of unborn dharmatā

". . . The cognition of clinging to perceiver and perceived, as it had been before, does not exist in that way later . . .

> "Saraha says pure [*dag* could also be "a dual"] meditation
> is exactly the way it is—
> it is not as it is conceived."

3185. Strangely, GZ CDNP have this sentence as a stanza, with its last line being the Tibetan version of 34a: "[Maitrīpa] says:

> "Having thus cognized the world [NP omit 'the world']
> with wisdom, to teach this to the
> world in just the way it is means
> 'The mindset of the world being unborn.'"

3186. GZ CDP "[There are arguments] such as 'since arising is not tenable for something existent or nonexistent.' For the direct cognition of the mindset of [NP omit 'directly' and 'the mindset of'] the world being unborn is the purified mind that is dependently originated. 'Mind' means penetrating insight. Therefore, they are the insightful ones. 'Without effort' means free of effort. 'The nature' means the connate. 'All the world is real' means it is not delusive."

3187. GZ CDNP "Now [GZ *de ni* "that"], in order to teach that despite being thoughts they are nirvāṇa, [Maitrīpa] utters [the stanza] that begins 'Connection . . . meditation' [this is the second line of the Tibetan version of this stanza, but the comments below read *bsgom pa med* instead of *bsgom pa min*].'

3188. *Lokātītastava* 22ab.

3189. GZ CDNP "Lacking cultivation of connection means the thought whose connection is not known. This is dependent origination. Therefore, exactly this is called 'nirvāṇa.' Hence, mind as such, do not create delusion! As it is taught . . ."

3190. The compound *ajātajñānabodhena* is certainly open to more than one interpretation. IaS (320) reads "by one in whom realization of knowledge has not arisen" and notes the following (n386): "The expression 'in whom realization of knowledge has not arisen' is not exactly transparent. A possibility which is worth considering is that Rāmapāla might mean someone who has not had the *prajñājñānābhiṣeka*. If so, and if he is with this remark being faithful to Maitreyanātha's intention, this *avataraṇikā* together with verse 36 might be the one place in the *Sekanirdeśa* and *Sekanirdeśapañjikā* which could be adduced as evidence for Maitreyanātha teaching a non-tantric Mahāmudrā practice. Note however that even if this should be the case, the way in which the absence of the *prajñājñānābhiṣeka* is referred to would be an apparently deliberately cryptic one." GZ CDNP read as follows: "In order to teach 'The wisdom of realizing that [everything] is unborn is the discovery of mahāmudrā just as it is,' [Maitrīpa] teaches that it is attained [NP omit this phrase], uttering [the stanza] that begins 'Those who do not abide.'" Thus, notwithstanding that GZ CDNP switch the positions of "wisdom" and "realizing," in line with GZ CDNP, one could certainly read *ajātajñānabodhena* as "by realizing the wisdom that [everything] is unborn," "by realizing the wisdom of being unborn," or "by realizing the wisdom that is unborn." Given Maitrīpa's and Rāmapāla's general Madhyamaka stance of all phenomena being unborn and utterly nonabiding, and the specific statement "As for those who realize the world as unborn, their mind is simply pure by this realization" in lines 34ab, which uses the exact same words *ajāta* and *bodha* (as well as the related *buddhaṃ*), such a reading of this compound is definitely possible. On the other hand, stanza 36, which is introduced here, speaks about the path of attaining the wisdom of mahāmudrā.

3191. As mentioned before, the *Avikalpapraveśadhāraṇī* describes how bodhisattvas enter the expanse of nonconceptuality by relinquishing all coarse and subtle characteristics of conceptions in terms of (1) nature, (2) remedies, (3) true reality, and (4) attainment in a gradual manner by analysis, and finally by not mentally engaging in them at all. Many of the following comments here closely resemble the corresponding passages in the *Avikalpapraveśadhāraṇī*, though that text is not explicitly cited or referred to; for details, see IaS (320n389 and 365–66) and Brunnhölzl 2012 (330–31). The last three of said four characteristics are also discussed in detail in Sahajavajra's *Tattvadaśakaṭīkā* (text 46, 40–44), and the *Avikalpapraveśadhāraṇī*'s general notion of relinquishing conceptual characteristics is quoted in Maitrīpa's *Amanasikārādhāra* (text 27).

3192. GZ CDNP "'In the remedies' refers to abandoning, by not mentally engaging in them, the host of the conceptions that analyze the remedies, which have the character of generosity, discipline, patience, vigor, dhyāna, and prajñā—that is, the analysis of their nature, qualities, and essence [I follow CDNP *snying po* against GZ *gnyen po*, 'remedies']. As for 'do not abide,' by [speaking of] relinquishing the hosts of the conceptions that analyze the remedies, one should consider that this also refers to the relinquishment of the hosts of the conceptions that analyze their antagonistic factors . . . Since that [first] one does not exist, these [second] ones do definitely not exist [either]. 'Who even lack attachment to true reality' refers to even lacking attachment (being without any attachment) to the samādhi of the hosts of conceptions that analyze true reality, which has the character of emptiness and suchness, through analyzing its essence and so on. 'Who have no desire for the fruition' refers to not having any desire (hope) at all for any fruitions, which has the essence of the hosts of the conceptions [GZ CD omit "of the conceptions"] that analyze attainments [GZ omits "attainments"] (such as the first bhūmi up to [CDNP omit "up to"] the knowledge of all aspects). 'It is they who will know mahāmudrā' refers to attaining it. Through these, the world's own being—utter nonabiding and the lack of superimposition—that is free of all attachment due to the relinquishment of any attachment to [NP omit 'any attachment to'] the hosts of antagonistic factors, remedies, true reality, and the fruition is called 'the attainment of mahāmudrā.'"

3193. This sūtra is usually known as *Brahmaviśeṣacintiparipṛcchāmahāyānasūtra*. GZ CDNP "'In that case, is there then an absence of the pāramitās of generosity and so on in mahāmudrā?' . . . As it is said . . ."

3194. Skt. *anabhisaṃskāra* can also mean "without effort," "without preparation," "without performance," and "without accomplishment."

3195. GZ CD *rnam par dpyod pa med pa* ("lack of analysis") NP *rnam par spyod pa med pa* ("lack of conduct/wandering").

3196. D160, fol. 58a.2–3.

3197. The phrase °*upacayāya vāpacayāya vā pratyupasthitā* could also be read as "what is approached for the sake of any increase or decrease."

3198. *Saptaśatikā Prajñāpāramitā* (ed. Masuda 1930, 200–202). GZ CDNP "'Thus the very essence of utter nonabiding and being free from discursiveness is prajñāpāramitā' . . . '. . . I cultivate prajñāpāramitā while not abiding [anywhere].' The Bhagavān said: 'Mañjuśrī, in this nonabiding of yours, where would the cultivation of prajñāpāramitā be?' Mañjuśrī replied: 'Bhagavān, this very utter nonabiding anywhere at all is the cultivation of prajñāpāramitā.' The Bhagavān said: 'Mañjuśrī, at the time when you cultivate prajñāpāramitā, then how many roots of virtue will increase or decrease?' Mañjuśrī replied: 'Bhagavān, not abiding anywhere at all, Bhagavān, at that time there will not even be the slightest increase or decrease of any roots of virtue. Bhagavān, this cultivation of prajñāpāramitā does not have the slightest increase or decrease of any dharma. Bhagavān, this should be understood as the cultivation of prajñāpāramitā. Bhagavān, to abide in the slightest increase or decrease of any dharma is not the cultivation of prajñāpāramitā [NP omit 'this should be understood as' and the entire following sentence except 'is not the cultivation']. It neither abandons the dharmas . . .'"

3199. GZ CDNP "Having taught mahāmudrā, in order to teach the samayamudrā, which is the four ecstasies' nature [I follow CDNP *rang bzhin* against GZ *rang bzhin med par* 'lack of nature'] and has the essence of [NP omit 'has the essence of'] being omnipresent, [Maitrīpa] utters [the stanza] that begins 'Just as ecstasy and such abide.'"

3200. GZ CDNP "As for the essence of the result produced by persons [arising] from mahāmudrā, through it rising as the essence in the form of a sambhoga[kāya] from the Bhagavān Heruka with his prajñā [consort], ecstasy is until friction [CDNP "As for mahāmudrā (NP "as mahāmudrā"), the essence of the result produced by persons, the conduct of the Bhagavān together with his prajñā [consort] rising as the essence of a sambhoga[kāya] is ecstasy"]. The city of the jewel is supreme ecstasy. Located in the middle of the union of moon and sun whose essences are prajñā and means, which have melted due to great passion, the essence of the two bindus in the form of the bindus above and below is connate [ecstasy]."

3201. *Hevajratantra* II.5.67, which is also found in almost identical form as Saraha's *Dohakoṣa* 30.

3202. GZ CDNP "The meaning of this is twofold: the expedient meaning and the definitive meaning. Here, the definitive meaning refers to thought-free self-awareness at that time, in [the moment of] the lack of characteristics that is of such a procedure [as described]. As for the expedient meaning, 'beginning' means that the earlier bindu has no beginning. 'No end' means no end. 'No middle' means that since there is no end, there is no in-between, and hence there is no middle [CDNP omit this sentence]. Because of being uninterrupted, there is no middle, so there is no middle there. 'Neither saṃsāric existence' means it is not the essence of saṃsāric existence. The bindu that is included in the sun of means is saṃsāric . . . 'Nor nirvāṇa' means it is not the essence of nirvāṇa because it is included in the moon of prajñā. 'So what is it?' This is to be expressed as follows. The essence of the single taste of both is supreme great bliss—it should not be thought of as self or other. Here too, the presentations of Vajrasattva and so on should be understood like the presentations of connate [ecstasy] for the karmamudrā taught above."

3203. Pukkasī is one of the four female deities in the intermediate directions of the Hevajra maṇḍala, the other three being Śavarī, Caṇḍālī, and Ḍombinī (the four female deities in the cardinal directions are Gaurī, Caurī, Vetālī, and Ghasmarī).

3204. "Pure mundane thinking" (Skt. *śuddhalaukikavikalpa*) is an expression for the active altruistic form of wisdom that buddhas and bodhisattvas manifest and use subsequent to the meditative equipoise of nonconceptual wisdom.

3205. As mentioned before, this line is *Hevajratantra* II.3.10b, *Guhyasamājatantra* XVIII.113f, and *Sampuṭodbhavatantra* II.1.46d, and is also found in the *Rakta-yamarītantra* (H441, fol. 489a.1).

3206. This unidentified quotation already appeared in the comments on stanza 28.

3207. GZ CDNP "Then, right after the Bhagavān has risen from his seat with the form of a sambhogakāya, as if awakened from a dream upon having been urged by the songs of the four goddesses such as Pukkasī, the engagement in that by manifesting thinking of entities from the perspective of the pure worldly for the welfare of sentient beings is cessational [ecstasy]. Here too the fourth one in the [line] 'The fourth is again like so' is just that. [Here,] 'so' means the connate [ecstasy] that is found [I follow CDNP *rnyed* against GZ *nyed*] . . . 'Like' means it should be realized to be like the connate [GZ 'should be realized as the nature of the connate']. As for the words 'for [CDNP omit 'for'] just this single ecstasy of [CDNP omit 'ecstasy of'] utter ecstasy is to be ascertained as four in number,' when everything has the essence of the connate, then the single essence of the samayamudrā is the essence of the ecstasy that is cessational ecstasy."

3208. According to IaS (326n426), the source of this quote is unidentified (it may be from a lost tantra, but it is also possible that Rāmapāla did not quote the phrase—which appears to be prose—in its entirety). However, the phrase "remained in the form of bindu" is found as a line of verse preceded by the line "Vajradhara who dwells there," both being part of a longer quote, in several tantric commentaries, such as *Śāśvatavajra's *Śrītattvaviśadānāmaśrīsaṃvaravṛitti* (D1410, fol., 257b.6), Candrakīrti's *Pradīpoddyotana* (D1785, fol. 10a.6), Āryadeva's *Pradīpoddyotana* (D1794, fol. 187b.1), and Alaṃkakalaśa's *Śrīvajramālāmahāyogatantraṭīkāgaṃbhīrārthadīpikā* (D1795, fol. 4b.6–7). Both Alaṃkakalaśa and Bhavyakīrti's *Pradīpoddyotanābhisaṃdhiprakāśikānāmavyākhyāṭīkā* (D1793, fol. 108b.7) explicitly attribute the quote in which these two lines are embedded to the *Vajramālātantra*, an explanatory tantra of the *Guhyasamājatantra*. The commentaries by Candrakīrti (D1785, fol. 10a.4) and Āryadeva (D1794, fol. 186b.5) on the *Guhyasamājatantra* also attribute it to "the explanatory tantra." In Kumāra's subcommentary *Pradīpadīpaṭippaṇīhṛdayādarśa* (D1791, fol. 179a.5) on Candrakīrti's *Pradīpoddyotana*, "remained in the form of bindu" is also found as the last line of the same longer quote (spelling out only the first and last lines). However, neither of said two lines is found in the canonical Tibetan versions of the *Vajramālātantra* (only fragments are preserved in Sanskrit). Amoghavajra's **Anukampopakramatattvayogāvatāropadeśa* (D1745, fol. 115b.3) contains the following two lines (not a quote):

> Within the dhūtī, your own mind
> remained in the form of bindu.

GZ CDNP "[Objection:] 'But here, since [the Bhagavān] has the form of bindu, this is clearly taught as awareness without aspects.' No, since thus the essence of bliss is inexpressible, when it proliferates as all the aspects of the world, [awareness] without [CDNP omit 'without'] aspects is invalidated. [Objection:] 'In that case, why arise in the form of [two] bindus as in the bliss arising [CDNP 'obtained'] from a karmamudrā? [GZ CDNP have an additional *zhe na* after this sentence]. Here too it is suitable to teach the character of prajñā and means as having the forms of arms, faces, and so on.' This is to be expressed as follows. For [GZ omits 'for'] since it exists in the form of the bindus of bliss, it is expressed as the [awareness] with aspects that is a change of state resembling the [arising] of the form of a vase from the form of clay. As it is said . . ."

3209. *Hevajratantra* II.4.34ab. As mentioned before, Skt. *kunda* ("white jasmine") is one of the many epithets of semen. The following comments show that Skt. *saṃvṛta* ("conventional," "covered") and *vivṛta* ("uncovered," "revealed," "naked") are opposite terms here in terms of seeming and ultimate reality, respectively.

3210. *Hevajratantra* II.2.42b (II.2.42a: "Without this [semen], bliss would not exist").

3211. *Hevajratantra* I.10.38cd. GZ CDNP: "'The following is to be expressed:

> 'The conventional one is similar to kunda
> The obscuration-free has the essence of bliss

'The conventional one obtained from [CDNP 'by relying on'] a karmamudrā is not ultimate. Not arising like the bliss obtained from a karmamudrā [CDNP omit this phrase], the obscuration-free is not obscured—that is, nirvāṇa. Here the two [CDNP omit 'the two'] blisses are different.' This too is not the case. For since [the *Hevajratantra*] says: 'Having relinquished bliss, this is not,' there is no bliss that is different from having the character of bliss and bindu . . .

> "Since bliss consists of the great elements,
> hence, bliss [CD *bde ba'i bde ba* 'the bliss of bliss' NP *bde bas bde ba* 'the bliss through bliss'] is not true reality."

3212. GZ CDNP "'Since mind as such arises in the form of various bindus, this is simply [awareness] without aspects.' It will not be like that either. If it were stated 'It is just like thinking without aspects' [CDNP 'It is like that due to thinking without aspects'], in that case, there would be no need for doubts due to thoughts without [NP omit 'without'] aspects—the mere bliss devoid of bindu [CDNP 'by relinquishing bindu'], which is the cause of doubt [NP omit this phrase], would have been taught. What would be the use of a lot of effort as was taught? Therefore, for the Nonaspectarians, the very bindu does not exist."

3213. GZ CDNP "In order to state 'It is clear that [there is] a [corresponding] ecstasy in each of the mudrās taught just above,' [Maitrīpa] utters [the stanza] that begins 'The karmamudrā constitutes variety.' The meaning [of this stanza] has already been explained. [Objection:] '. . . it is taught [NP omit 'taught'] as conforming to the yoginītantras, but does not conform to the yogatantras.' It is not like that. The following is to be expressed." IaS (327n438): "In the absence of any evidence to the contrary, we take it that the following verses are not quoted but are Rāmapāla's own formulation of a point which he regards as important but for which there were no statements, whether verse or prose, in the works of his master Maitreyanātha, which he could quote as an authority." It could of course also be that Rāmapāla here summarizes oral instructions that he received from Maitrīpa.

3214. As another term for the creation process, the expression "mantra embodiment" (Skt. *mantramūrti*) stems from Candrakīrti's *Pradīpoddyotana*, indicating the first of the five stages in the Ārya exegetical tradition of the

Guhyasamājatantra (by generally referring to one of the three forms a deity can manifest, *mantramūrti* can also mean "having the form/body of mantra"). As IaS (327n440) points out, the technical term "mind focus"—*cittanidhyapti* (in the *Pañcakrama* and *Pradīpoddyotana*)—is here rendered by the metrically expedient synonym *cinnidhyapti*. The *Pradīpoddyotana* describes this second among the five stages as the one when the ordinary five sense faculties and their objects have dissolved.

3215. "The seeing of seeming reality" (Skt. *saṃvṛtisatyadarśana*) is an expression for the third of the five stages (otherwise known as "self-blessing") in the *Pañcakrama* and *Pradīpoddyotana*.

3216. As IaS (328n443) points out, "the fact that this reality is the true end" (*satyasya bhūtikoṭitvam*) is an unusual expression that must correspond here to the fourth one among the five stages, which is more commonly called "purity of seeming reality" (Skt. *satyasya saṃvṛteḥ śuddhiḥ*), as in the corresponding stanza from the *Pradīpoddyotana* below.

3217. This line appears to be a paraphrase of the fifth stage "unity" (*yuganaddha*).

3218. In GZ CDNP, these four stanzas are in prose: "Here this was taught by master Nāgārjuna by following the *Guhyasamāja[tantra]*. For in [that] tantra, the four mudrās are taught as the five stages. Since these stages are mantra embodiment, in due order, the mind is definitely purified. With regard to a single mudrā taught like that, the mind resides in mantra embodiment because the bliss of the dharmamudrā shows seeming reality. Reality—the true end—is expressed as 'mahāmudrā.' The fruition—the samayamudrā—should be known as nonduality. Being combined as the five stages [I follow GZ *rim pa lnga* against CD *rigs pa rnams* NP *rig pa rnams*] is the divine substance, which bestows the fruition of buddhahood."

3219. Stanzas 2–5. GZ CDNP:

> So as to accomplish secret mantra's body,
> the creation process represents the first
> It is nothing but the focus on the mind
> that is then expressed as "the second"
>
> Teaching the seeming reality
> is the delightful third stage
> The purity of seeming reality
> is expressed as "the fourth stage"
>
> What is the union of the two realities
> is the fifth one that is called "unity"
> . . .
> The distinctions of these stages
> are many [I follow GZ NP *mang* against CD *med*] kinds of elaborated stages
> Those who know the combination/synopsis
> of their purity know the tantra

And this is stated:

Knowing the points that are condensed
into the five stages, which are mantra,
mind, body, purity, as well as unity,
you then enter the six parameters [*Pradīpoddyotana* 6]

As IaS (328n446) says, the fact that the additionally cited fifth stanza here is separated from the first four by *ces gsungs pa dang*, whereas all five stanzas are continuous in the *Pradīpoddyotana*, strengthens the probability that the fifth one is a secondary addition.

3220. See Wedemeyer 2007, 139 and 338. As Wedemeyer (139n14) remarks, "the true reality of dharma" is not found in the Sanskrit or Tāranātha's commentary, but only in the canonical Tibetan and the early apocryphal commentary attributed to Śākyamitra. Thus he suspects that this true reality was added in order to create a list of five true realities that correspond to the five stages. As mentioned before, IaS (109 and n40) points out that though this work is more commonly known in modern scholarship as *Caryāmelāpakapradīpa*, this "title has yet to be found attested in any Sanskrit source . . . On the other hand, *Sūtakamelāpaka* is found not only in Wedemeyer's MS C of the work itself (with support from the Tibetan translation . . . in our opinion MS C's reading should have indeed been preferred), but also, for instance, here in Rāmapālas quotation in the *Sekanirdeśapañikā* and in Jagaddarpana's quotation from Āryadeva's work in his *Ācāryakriyāsamuccaya* . . . *Sūtakamelāpaka* could perhaps be translated as *Bringing together the Sū[trāntas], Ta[ntras] and Ka[lpas]*; at the same time there may well be an alchemical pun intended, as *sūtaka*—an abbreviated form of the title which is often used by other authors . . .—means normally in Sanskrit mercury." The title *Sūtakamelāpaka* with the meaning as explained here in IaS is also clearly supported by GZ CDNP *mdo rgyud rtog bsre*.

3221. As IaS (328n448) says, in terms of the expedient meaning, "according to the numerical sequence" simply means that "the true reality of mudrā" as the second of the five true realities corresponds to "mind focus" as the second of the five stages.

3222. IaS (329n451): "This verse, which is not marked in any way as a quotation, and which we have not found elsewhere, is perhaps an *antaraśloka* by Rāmapāla himself." GZ CDNP "Hevajra and other [deities] arisen from the syllable HŪṂ and so on . . . refers to merely the purification of the mind of true reality . . . 'The true reality of the deity' refers to making the true reality of self and the true reality of dharma the character of that . . . These five [kinds of] true reality, due to the pith instructions of the gurus, should be matched with the four mudrās. In due order, they should be made into the five stages [CDNP 'In due order, the five stages too']."

3223. *Hevajratantra* I.8.23 and *Guhyasamājatantra* XVIII.84.

3224. Mathes 2021 (129–30) points out that the five stages of the Ārya school differ in its two subschools: the Māgadhi tradition (represented by Abhayākaragupta, Muniśrībhadra, and others) lists them as the condensed stage (*piṇḍīkrama*), vajra recitation, self-blessing, full awakening, and unity, while the Kashmiri tradition (represented by Lakṣmī and Nāgabodhi) considers them as vajra recitation, universal purity, self-blessing, the full awakening of supremely secret bliss, and unity. However, different from Mathes's statement that both systems are found in Rāmapāla's commentary, Rāmapāla here mentions only the nomenclature of the Māgadhi tradition.

3225. *Sarvarahasyatantra* 30 (H449, fol. 4a.5–6); also cited in the *Caturmudrāṭīkā* (text 44, 261 and 340), but with a different order of the lines. GZ CDNP "'. . . If [GZ *na* CDNP *no*] these are the words of tantra, how could they be taught as five stages?' This is to be expressed as follows. The condensed stage . . . 'the inner creation process' . . . are taught in the perfection process . . . This is the nature of the essence of the four correct mudrās and you should know that it is taught in the *Sarvarahasyatantra*. As it is taught . . ."

3226. GZ CDNP "Now, in order to refute those who are satisfied by knowing nothing but the tathāgata relief and the Vajradhara relief thanks to a karmamudrā . . . 'The yogīs who do not know mahāmudrā.'"

3227. GZ CDNP "Those yogīs who deprecate the dharma of the unsurpassable and completely perfect Buddha, saying 'What is taught in the true reality of the tradition transmitted from one Buddhist guru to another is that the karmamudrā is true reality [lit. 'that it is only the karmamudrā'], but not the dharmamudrā and the others,' will then take their journey to Raurava [CDNP 'Since it appears in the true reality of the textual tradition transmitted from one guru to another, the karmamudrā is true reality. Those yogīs who deprecate the dharma of the . . . Buddha, such as the dharmamudrā and the others, will then take their journey to Raurava'] . . . Going to hells such as Raurava, which is brought about through rejecting the true dharma, is taught clearly and extensively in sūtras such as the noble *Aṣṭasahasrikā [Prajñāpāramitā]* [CDNP 'Since going to hells . . . is clear in sūtras such as the noble *Aṣṭasahasrikā*, it is not taught extensively']."

3228. GZ CDNP "'But how would the karmamudrā not be true reality?'"

3229. The first line corresponds to Padmavajra's *Guhyasiddhi* III.34a and is also found in Narendrakīrti's *Pradarśanānumatoddeśaparīkṣā* (N3400, fol. 36a.6–7) and the *Śrīmadvimalaprabhātantrāvatāraṇivādahṛdayāloka* (D1349, fols. 33b.7–34a.1); see NG, 12. The first and third lines are likewise cited in Maitrīpa's *Commentary on Half a Stanza on True Reality Teaching That All Phenomena Are Utterly Nonabiding* (text 73, 191) and all three lines (adding "cunning" in the second) in Divākaracandra's *Prajñājñānaprakāśa* (text 16, 57). IaS (330n461): "This quotation seems to be three *pādas*, a, b (hypermetrical), and d, of a verse, the source of which we have not been able to identify . . . *Pāda* d is a stock phrase which can be found in many texts, non-Buddhist as well as Buddhist; see, e.g., *Dharmasamuccaya* 10.25d (991d), *Manusmṛti* 4.73d, *Kubjikāmatatantra* 25.114b."

3230. According to the *Prajñājñānaprakāśa* (text 16, 57), two very similar lines, equally sandwiched between the three preceding lines and the following stanza from the *Jñānasiddhi*, are from the *Vajrārallitantra*, but I could not locate any of them in this or any other text in Kg or Tg.

3231. GZ CDNP "Master Nāgārjuna states . . ."

3232. Text 14, 28 (GZ CDNP have some variants of this quote).

3233. *Jñānasiddhi* VII.11. IaS (331n469): "Verses with a similar first half, and with the same general idea, can be found also in the *Vimalaprabhā* (vol. 2, p. 215: the first half runs *sukhaṃ dvīndriyajaṃ tattvaṃ buddhatvaphaladāyakam*) and the *Sekoddesaṭīka* (p. 172: the first half runs *sukhaṃ dvīndriyajaṃ tattvaṃ devānāṃ rāgiṇāṃ smṛtam*)."

3234. GZ CDNP "'But by thus denigrating the karmamudrā, who is discussed in many tantras, will you not also [CDNP 'you will also'] go to hell and encounter it?' . . . it is only her being the primary essence [CDNP omit "only" and "primary"] of true reality that is refuted. As for the intention behind this, given that [Maitrīpa] has uttered [stanza 26], beginning with 'Once you relied upon the karmamudrā,' in order to teach that she has the essence of an enabling cause, how could we therefore denigrate her? There is no need to say much here . . ."

3235. GZ CDNP "Now, in order to teach the meaning of realizing the [four] mudrās [CDNP 'teach that the mudrās are to be realized'] and the power of his own chosen deity, [Maitrīpa] utters . . ."

3236. GZ CDNP "Śabareṣa means having pith—that is, venerable Śrī Śabara having attained siddhis." Apparently, GZ CDNP *snying po can* read Skt. *sāravat*, which can also mean "strong," "steadfast," "precious," "nourishing," and "sumptuous," all of which make sense here too.

3237. As mentioned before, in GZ CD of the *Sekanirdeśa*, stanza 40 is followed by an additional stanza, but there is no equivalent or comment on it in Rāmapāla's text.

3238. GZ CDNP "Now, in order to conclude by dedicating the merit, [Maitrīpa] utters [the stanza] beginning with 'Having laid out the correct empowerment.'"

3239. Skt. *jaḍa* ("foolish people") is meaninglessly rendered in GZ CDNP as one of its other meanings (*bem po*, "matter"). Skt. *ratnākara* can mean not only "ocean" but also "jewel mine" (ocean thus in the sense of a place at whose ground there are precious jewels). GZ CDNP read *rin chen bdud rtsi chen po'i 'byung gnas*, thus separating *ratna* and *ākara* by "great nectar." IaS here renders *dharmatā* as "teachings" (*dharma*). GZ CDNP:

> If the one of whom the Bhagavān [GZ omits "Bhagavān"] Śrīmat Śabareśvara took care in a direct way,
> this deep source of the great nectar of the precious unsurpassable dharmatā,
> is despised by ignorant people [lit. "ignorant matter"], what is there to do for us?
> Someone like myself composing a praise is marvelous because it [shows] affection.

3240. Since the pertinent meanings of Skt. *kuṭila* ("deviating") here all have a negative sense ("crooked," "fraudulent," "dishonest," "perverse," "deceitful"), they seem not suitable to be related to "the excellent empowerment" (*suṣeka*), as IaS does in a neutral sense ("the excellent consecration, diverging from the sequence of the wrong consecration and the sequence of the forceful [consecration]"); rather, as is made clear throughout this text, both the poor and the forceful empowerments are simply considered to be wrong and deceiving.

The facts that GZ CDNP read *dang* ("and") after "the excellent empowerment" and link *dka'* ("difficult") for *kuṭila* with *drag po'i rim pa* and the preceding *ngan pa'i rim* support the stark contrast here.

3241. IaS (333n481): "It would also be possible to take *nāthena* here as an abbreviated name (as when, to use the traditional example, Satyabhāmā is called simply Bhāmā), and to translate 'by [Maitreya]nātha.'"

3242. Skt. *sambhāvita* can also mean "honored," thus "my work being honored by his commands"; as IaS (333n483) says, the plural "commands" (Skt. *ājñābhiḥ*) suggests that Maitrīpa had repeatedly urged Rāmapāla to compose this commentary.

3243. IaS renders *pravacanaiḥ* at the end of the fourth line as "with [quotations of] scriptural passages" and positions it right after "I composed a commentary" in the third line, but adds (333n482) that "*pravacanaiḥ* could perhaps be taken, as the Tibetan translation seems to do, with (*yathāśakti*) *smṛtyāhitamatiḥ*." Either option makes sense: either Rāmapāla simply refers to the fact that his commentary contains many citations from the Buddha's sūtras and tantras, or he more specifically describes how he entered the proper mindset to compose his commentary by recollecting the words of the Buddha and (probably) other masters; though *pravacana* usually refers only to the words in the Buddha's sūtras (nine categories of teachings as defined in the *Dharmasaṃgraha*, section 62, attributed to Nāgārjuna, or the well-known "twelve branches of the Buddha's words") and tantras, here it may well include the words of other masters, especially the personal instructions that Rāmapāḷa received from Maitrīpa (IaS, 333n484: "The *smṛti* here could possibly refer to Rāmapāla's remembering Maitreyanātha's direct teachings of the text or of related matter . . . according to Tibetan tradition Rāmapāla composed this commentary after the death of Maitreyanātha"). The second option implicitly seems to include the first one, since Rāmapāla's recollection of all these instructions no doubt found its expression in the many quotations in his commentary.

3244. GZ CDNP:

> The excellent empowerment, the sequence of the poor one, and the sequence of the forceful one, [both] difficult,
> as they have been proclaimed by the protector, are not an object of those of little intelligence—marvelous!
> It is the analyses of the intention that had been bestowed by him that
> [CDNP "It is the analyses of that, through cultivating what he bestowed, that"]
> I have discussed, as I was able, by my mind recollecting Buddha words.

3245. GZ CDNP:

> Through the moments of virtue I accumulated
> by virtue of writing this clear commentary on
> the profound ocean that is the *Sekanirṇaya* [*dbang gi nges par gyur pa*],
> may all beings be victors [or "be victorious"] in an instant!

3246. IaS (n485): "The use of *śrī* might strengthen the suspicion that Rāmapāla's work actually concluded with the preceding verse of dedication of merit, and that this verse is an (early) scribal colophon which has come to be attached to the text (and is also rendered in the Tibetan translation)."

3247. IaS (333–34n486): "The St. Petersburg manuscript, which alone is available here, reads *°sandohāyāsa°*, and the Tibetan translation might be taken as supporting *sandoha* by (*dpuṅ gi*) *tshogs*. We have nonetheless conjectured *sandehāyāsa; sandeha* seems intrinsically better here, though *āyāsa* remains somewhat doubtful to us . . . The meaning of *caturthakrama* is not absolutely certain. One could take *caturtha* as referring to the Fourth Consecration. But since that was not a very central topic in this work, it might also be possible that the 'Fourth *krama*' here means the fourth of the five *kramas* taught by Maitreyanātha in his *Hevajrasādhanas*, and alluded to by Rāmapāla. In that case, the implication is that the teaching of the *Sekanirdeśa* is related primarily to the *pariniṣpannakrama*. This might be consistent with the passage on p. 304 ad st. 23 above (*caturmudrāpakse ca pariniṣpannenācāryatvena karmamudrā boddhavyā*)." In my translation of the *Sekanirdeśapañjikā* (414), the passage referred to by IaS reads "In the context of the four mudrās, it is the karmamudrā that should be understood as the master [empowerment] according to the full-perfection [process]." Though this is indeed a general reference to karmamudrā, equated with the full-perfection process, as the main topic of this text, the following passage seems more specific about the crucial point that is at stake in the correct practice of karmamudrā. It is the phase of two bindus appearing between, but touching, the vajra and the lotus (symbolized by the Bhagavān appearing between a moon and a sun) that constitutes the moment of connate ecstasy: "The full-perfection [process] in its turn refers to the Bhagavān, arisen from the melted state, located on a sun disk having the nature of the bola, and having the character of prajñā and means, the essence of emptiness and compassion, and the nature of the dharmadhātu. His touching the [sun disk that is his] seat with [only] the toe of one foot, though, is in order to indicate the fact that he is not driven toward the time that is the phase of emission" (409). Thus "the stage that is the fourth" in this stanza here seems indeed to refer to the practice of karmamudrā, and the purpose of the text is to dispel ignorance, doubt, and trouble concerning the correct form of this practice versus "the poor and the forceful empowerments." In the first line, GZ reads *dpal ldan dga' ba'i mgon pos* (rather than the usual rendering *dga' ba skyong* of Rāmapāla) and CDNP *dga' ba'i dpal ldan mgon path of seeing*. The last two lines read as follows:

> destroys the hosts of the armies of
> ignorance about the fourth stage.

3248. Among the figures mentioned in this colophon, Maṇibhadra is not known otherwise (could it be Maṇigarbha, the birth name of *Kāropa?). Tsültrim Gyalwa is Nagtso Lotsāwa Tsültrim Gyalwa (1011–64). As for Samantabhadra, BA (1045–46) and BDRC mention an Indian master of that name as a disciple of Darpaṇācārya (a siddha said to have lived for twelve hundred years, active in the transmission of Raktayamāri and others). According to

BDRC, Darpaṇācārya flourished in the eleventh and twelfth centuries (he is also listed as the translator of text 203, together with his student Lowo Lotsāwa [Tib. Glo bo lo tsā ba shes rab rin chen]; according to BDRC and other sources, however, born in the thirteenth century). "Sugataśrī" is tentative, since GZ *su kād śrī* is corrupt (IaS, 116, tentatively suggests Sukhadaśrī). BA (381) mentions a Paṇḍita Sugataśrī who had been invited by Nagtso Lotsāwa and taught prajñāpāramitā and the five texts of Maitreya in Tibet. Lotsāwa Batsab Nyima Tra (Tib. Pa tshab nyi ma grags; born 1055) is primarily known for his translation of Candrakīrti's *Madhyamakāvatāra*.

3249. Skt. no colophon. CDNP "This concludes . . . by master Rāmapāla. It was translated by Samantabhadra and Nagtso [Tsültrim Gyalwa]." IaS (116) comments on the colophon in GZ (referred to as "dPal") as follows: "If the information in the colophon from dPal is to be believed, the translation was thus revised thrice, with no less than four Indian scholars being involved in the process, as well as two Tibetans. It may be suspected, however, that what has been transmitted to us is mainly the work of Tshul khrims rgyal ba, the *lotsāba* said to have been involved both in the initial translation and in the first revision. That a certain amount of revision did indeed take place, and that Tshul khrims rgyal ba was not the only Tibetan involved therein, is borne out, on the other hand, by an examination of the transmission of the translation. For dPal in particular (though sometimes together with D) contains a considerable number of readings which when compared with the readings of the canonical witnesses (sometimes, again, with the exception of D) look as if they are best understood as conscious changes made by (a) revisor(s), in some cases probably on the basis of (re)consultation of the Sanskrit, in some cases apparently without such consultation. These may therefore plausibly be taken as traces of two separate revisions of the translation, though it must be added that there are also many changes which cannot be clearly assigned to one of these two, for instance ones which appear to be purely stylistic." In addition, as NG (73) says, the entirety of GZ1 was thoroughly edited in the late nineteenth century by Püntso Gyaltsen (Tib. Phun tshogs rgyal mtshan), the general secretary of the Sakya monastery Ngor Evaṃ Chöden (Tib. Ngor e vaṃ chos ldan). Thus it is impossible to say which edits were made when or by whom. For further comments and details, see IaS (especially the overview of the *Sekanirdeśapañjikā*, 94–111). For an outline of text 45 by Tipi Bumlabar, see appendix 6.

3250. BKC *si kī ba ta a ti karmi ka tra ya* is corrupt. Given the Tibetan title and the parallel title *Saṃkṣiptasekaprakriyā* (text 38), this seems to be the most likely reconstruction. The following is a translation of another text about beginner or initial activity besides *Eradicating Bad Views* (text 19) that is attributed to Advayavajra (Maitrīpa) in BKC (vol. *ka*, fols. 211b.4–214b.1) but not found in the **Advayavajrasaṃgraha* and Tg. While *Eradicating Bad Views* is from a more general Mahāyāna point of view, *A Compendium of Beginner Activity* is written specifically from the perspective of Vajrayāna practitioners (for BKC's description of the difference between these two works, see the final note on text 19).

3251. "Indra's weapon" is an Indian epithet of a rainbow (a.k.a. "Indra's bow").

3252. BKC *dngos po'i las can* em. *dang po'i las can*.

3253. BKC *mnyen pa* ("pliable," "supple") em. *bsnyen pa*.
3254. Given that the text here says "compiled by them," it may be that the preceding *bstan pa* ("the teachings") should be *ston pa* ("teachers").
3255. A more straightforward reading of BKC *thig le phra mo* would of course be "subtle bindu(s)." However, the *Caturmudrānvaya* (text 14, 32) speaks of two separate yogas: the yoga of bindus and the yoga of the subtle. According to the *Caturmudrāṭīkā*, the latter refers to meditating with the nāḍīs and the vāyus. This seems supported by the explanation of this activity in our text here below: "focusing on a bindu located in the heart or the navel, focusing on a subtle bindu or mark located at the nose tip, and imagining the blazing nāḍī called 'caṇḍālī' and so on."
3256. BKC *lta bu'i* and *ma las* em. *lta ba'i* and *ma lus*.
3257. As mentioned before, often in tantric texts, instead of the more obvious meaning of phrases such as "meditating on the tip of the nose" and "resting the mind on the tip of the nose," they refer to the mind being focused on the cakras along the avadhūtī, on the lower part or end of the avadhūtī, or on the secret space of a visualized deity couple (the nonduality of prajñā and means), employing techniques of working with vāyus and bindus (such as caṇḍālī).
3258. This refers to the seven branches of paying homage, offering, confessing wrongdoing, rejoicing in virtue, exhorting to turn the wheel of dharma, requesting not to pass into nirvāṇa, and dedicating all virtue to awakening. For example, these seven are found in the initial stanzas of the bodhisattva Samantabhadra's *Aspiration Prayer for Noble Excellent Conduct* in the *Gaṇḍavyūhasūtra*.
3259. In BKC, the two mantras *oṃ ha ri ti ka ma hā yikṣa na shing du pu tri ghri ha na pa ḍi sva hā* and *oṃ utsim thā ghri hna pin di sva hā* are very corrupt. Most parts of these mantras can be identified based on the similar mantras in text 19 (136–37) and others, but some parts must remain tentative.
3260. BKC *na mo bha ga wa te bai ro tsa na phra ba rā dzā ya / ta thā ga ta ya / a ra ha te bya / sam myag saṃ bu dha ya / tadya thā / oṃ sug sme sug sme / sa la se sa ma te / sa ma ro be / a na ba ra ne / ṭa raṃ be ya shes / ma hā te tse / ni ra ku le / sarba tā thā ga ta hridha ṣthi de svā hā* is also largely corrupt. However, in most parts, this mantra is identical to the first one used in text 19 for building caityas, though some diverging parts remain tentative.
3261. Like the other mantras, this one is also corrupt, but since it is so well known, there are no issues about it.
3262. BKC *na mo bha ga wa ti rad na shi khe ni / ta thā ga ta ya / a ra ha te / sam myag sam bu dha ya / ta dya thā / oṃ rad ne rad ne / a hā rad ne / rad na gi re ne / rad ṇa pra ti man ti ta sha ri re svā hā* is again corrupt. However, in most parts, this mantra is very similar to the last one used in text 19 for building caityas, though some diverging parts remain tentative.
3263. For example, tantric texts speak of mantras that stake the body, speech, and mind of all three realms and mantras that stake the hosts of obstacles.
3264. BKC *spyod pa* could here also be read as "experience of."
3265. Tib. *Grub mtha'i man ngag lam du blang ba* (N3863, fols. 116b.7–121a.3; P5081, fols. 129a.8–133b.8).

3266. Remarkably, though, the four positions are not presented here as the standard set of Vaibhāṣikas, Sautrāntikas, Yogācāras, and Mādhyamikas (as in the *Tattvaratnāvalī* and *Dohānidhināmatattvopadeśa*), but as śrāvakas, pratyekabuddhas, Yogācāras, and Mādhyamikas. Thus, this must have been Śavaripa's original template of these four, which was then adapted by Maitrīpa later. Note that though the Tibetan text throughout says *sems tsam pa* ("Mere Mentalists") instead of *rnal 'byor spyod pa*, I render this as "Yogācāra" because all of Maitrīpa's other works always speak of Yogācāra and, at least in translations of Indic texts, *sems tsam pa* is just the preferred Tibetan way of rendering Yogācāra.

3267. Except for the first two paragraphs and the colophon, the text is not translated verbatim here because it is partially illegible, corrupt, and opaque, and also rather lengthy in the sections on the śrāvakas and pratyekabuddhas. Thus the following is a summarizing paraphrase of the main points. For the classical progressive stages of meditation on emptiness, see Gyamtso 2016 and Brunnhölzl 2004, 295–310.

3268. N *btsang* em. *gtsang*; the same goes for *rtsang* below.

3269. N *ra rgyal* or *nga rgyal* em. *rang rgyal*.

3270. Throughout, N *se* is emended to *sems*.

3271. This refers to counting and contemplating on the thirty-two impure substances that make up the body—that is, the meditation on the repulsiveness of the body.

3272. The stains of the lower śrāvakas are given as N *brtan rtsa dri ma*, which is unclear. According to the *Tattvaratnāvalī*, the stain of their samādhi is desire.

3273. N *byin po* em. *'bring po*.

3274. This stanza is similar to *Abhidharmakośa* VI.12. As for their stains, N has *dri ma seng ge rnam grol te phya rgya btsan thabs gzung ba*, which is unclear. The first phrase could refer to the name of a samādhi (Skt. *siṃhavikrīdita*, Tib. *seng ge rnam rol*), while the second phrase is familiar from texts on karmamudrā (the forceful yoga with a karmamudrā) and thus seems to be out of place here. The *Tattvaratnāvalī* has "The stain of their samādhi is that [their mind] becomes motionless through vase breathing because [this technique] invites [mental] numbness."

3275. That is, the stains of the pratyekabuddhas.

3276. As mentioned before, "nondual diversity" renders Skt. *citrādvaitavāda*. As in Maitrīpa's *Pañcatathāgatamudrāvivaraṇa* (text 36, 192) and Sahajavajra's *Sthitisamāsa* IV.5, this is one of the very few cases in which this term, which later in Tibet was claimed to refer to one of three "subschools" of Aspectarian Mere Mentalists (Tib. *sems tsam rnam bcas pa*), appears in an Indic text. However, this and the other two texts clearly use this term to refer to Aspectarian Yogācāra in general, not to one of its "subschools." The *Pañcatathāgatamudrāvivaraṇa* defines "nondual diversity" as "the nondual [consciousness] with its diversity, which is empty of perceiver and perceived" (in other words, the diversity of seemingly outer objects appears but is not in any way different from the mind, which, on its own, is the nonduality of perceiver and perceived). For more details, see Brunnhölzl 2018, 1510–16.

3277. N *rtsol* em. *rtsal*.

3278. N *myug ma* em. *gnyug ma*.
3279. Here and below, N *sngos* and *rngos* are emended to *dngos*.
3280. On its own, Tib. *yi dam* renders Skt. *samādāna* or *pratijñā* ("oath," "commitment," "promise," "pledge," "vow," or "bond"; the indigenous Tibetan explanation of *yi dam* is usually "mind bond"). This term is of course better known in its related meaning as an abbreviation of Tib. *yi dam kyi lha* (there is no known Sanskrit equivalent, but it is commonly rendered into English as the hybrid expression "yidam deity"): a personal meditation deity as the focus of one's continuous daily practice due to the samaya obtained through an empowerment (thus my rendering "oath deity"). To engage in the practice of a particular such deity for the rest of one's life is exactly the oath or commitment that one makes when receiving the empowerment of that deity. In popular and even some academic books on Buddhism, the Sanskrit terms *iṣṭadevatā* or *iṣṭadevaḥ* (a chosen, desired, or revered deity or divine being) are often given as the equivalents of *yidam* (*kyi lha*). However, these Sanskrit terms are not literal equivalents of the Tibetan and are in all cases rendered as *'dod (pa'i) lha*, not *yi dam* or *yi dam gyi lha*. The use of *iṣṭadevatā* and *iṣṭadevaḥ* in Hindu tantric texts refers to an actual external god who is invited to dwell in the practitioner's heart, while the deities of tantric Buddhism are clearly understood to be nothing other than skillfully visualized aspects of the nature of the mind of the meditator. Furthermore, the term *samayadevatā* (Tib. *dam tshig gi lha*) is not a rendering of Tib. *yi dam kyi lha* either, being used in a different way (*samayadevatā* versus *jñānadevatā* in the creation process).
3281. As mentioned before, "without minding" (Tib. *dran med*) instead of the other possible meaning "lacks mindfulness" (or even "being unconscious") is understood in the sense of "nonminding" as the second one in Saraha's famous tetrad of minding, nonminding, being unborn, and being beyond mind; see the notes on stanzas 33, 93, and 94 of Saraha's *Dohakoṣa* (text 13).
3282. BKC, vol. *kha*, fols. 87b.4–89a.2.
3283. BKC *khe'u* em. *kheng*.
3284. BKC switches the order of "what is pointed out" and "the means to point out," but it is clear that empowerment is the means to point out, while prajñā wisdom is that which is pointed out by it.
3285. BKC *ming* em. *mi*.
3286. BKC *'dod lnga lnga logs spyad* em. *'dod lnga la longs spyad*.
3287. BKC *'dod don las spyad pa* em. *'dod yon la spyad pa*.
3288. BKC, vol. *kha*, fols. 82a.5–83b.4. Note that most parts of this outline are written in lines of verse, but for convenience's sake I rendered all in prose.
3289. BKC *ma rtogs* em. *ma gtogs*.
3290. BKC *rnams rig* em. *rnam rig*.
3291. BKC *gzungs* em. *gzung*.
3292. To conform to the order of these two paths in the stanzas of the text, I switched their order in this phrase in BKC.
3293. BKC says that this has three points, but then only the two that follow are mentioned.
3294. BKC *gzhung don lam rnal brtan ma brgyad*. "The eight paths" appears to refer to the following eight subpoints 2c2a–2c2h.

3295. BKC *lha rnams gcig mas so* em. *lha rnams skad gcig mas.*
3296. BKC *phyag rgya'o* em. *phyag rgya yi.*
3297. BKC, vol. *kha*, fols. 80a.6–82a.5.
3298. BKC *khe'u* em. *khengs.*
3299. BKC *mtshan* em. *rgyu mtshan.*
3300. BKC *rgyud mar* em. *sgyu mar.*
3301. Here and below, BKC *rnam(s) nyid* is emended to *rnam nyed.*
3302. BKC *byed pa* obviously renders Skt. *kāraṇa* in text 45, and *rkyang ma* (as in the Tibetan of text 45) is a misrendering of Skt. *lalanā* in the sense of the main left nāḍī.
3303. In text 45, this is phrased as "The relief of those [tathāgatas] is their being turned into consciousness once they are sealed with Akṣobhya."
3304. BKC *bhzi pa'i* em. *bzhi.*
3305. BKC *rnor* is an abbreviation of *rnal 'byor.*
3306. BKC *las* em. *las rgya.*
3307. The corresponding Sanskrit terms *utpattikrama, gambhīrotpattikrama, utpannakrama* (lit. "process of the arisen," mostly used as an equivalent of the not-so-frequent *niṣpannakrama*), *pariniṣpannakrama*, and *svābhāvikakrama* are found in Rāmapāla's *Sekanirdeśapañjikā.*
3308. These two stanzas are *Kāyakoṣāmṛtavajragītā* 90–91, which link this set of five with the four mudrās, the four ecstasies, and the two reliefs (the tathāgata relief and the Vajradhara relief). In addition, "the essence process" is also mentioned in Saraha's *Vākkoṣarucirasvaravajragītā* 8. There is only a handful of other tantric works in Tg that briefly mention one up to three among the names of these five stages, but they often have a different meaning, they usually lack any further explanation, and "the essence process" is never mentioned. For example, according to Candragomin's *Mañjuśrīnāmasaṃgītināmamahāṭīkā* (D2090, fol. 180a.4–6), the outer creation process consists of meditating on single deities (no matter whether there are many or few), the inner creation process of meditating on deities in union, the profound creation process of meditating on nāḍīs, vāyus, and bindus, and the perfection process of realizing that all those are without any nature of their own. Kālapāda's *Mañjuśrīnāmasaṃgītisvānuśaṃsāvṛitti* (D1399, fol. 243a.6–7) mentions the outer creation process and the profound inner creation process without explanation. Dharmakīrti's *Śrīhevajramahātantrarājasya pañjikānetravibhaṅganāma* (D1191, fols. 245b.6–7 and 255b.4–5) twice mentions the three-part sequence of the creation process, the perfection process, and the full-perfection process. Vajragarbha's *Hevajratantraṭīkā* (D1180, fol. 56a.5–6) relates the outer creation process to the orbs of sun and moon and the coming and going of prāṇa. Kumāra's *Pradīpadīpaṭippaṇīhṛdayādarśanāma* (D1791, fol. 177b.4–5) and Bhavyakīrti's *Pradīpoddyotanābhisaṃdhiprakāśikānāmavyākhyāṭīkā* (D1793, fol. 153a.3) say that the creation process is the process of imputation, while the perfection process is the full-perfection process. Ratnarakṣita's *Śrīsaṃvarodayamahātantrarājasyapadminīnāmapañjikā* (D1420, fol. 11a.5) says that among the four ways of being born, miraculous birth is also presented as the profound creation process and the imputed perfection process. In brief, the

complete set of these five stages is indeed unique to the six texts by Maitrīpa and his disciples that are discussed in the following.

3309. Translation based on an excerpt from Isaacson's unpublished Sanskrit edition in IaS, 374n34; D1308, fol. 221a.6–221b.2.
3310. Translation based on Isaacson's Sanskrit edition in IaS, 374n34; D1308, fol. 221b.2–4.
3311. Ibid., fols. 221b.4–222b.3. As mentioned before, Maitrīpa's typical expression "the (continuous) flow of effortless nondual unity" is found in a number of his works. As the last explanation of "mental nonengagement" in *In Support of Mental Nonengagement* (text 27, 160) says, "the continuous flow of nondual unity" refers to "the inconceivable state of luminosity and self-blessing—the awareness that is the continuous flow of the nondual unity of emptiness and compassion inseparable." *A Commentary on the Five Seals of the Tathāgatas* (text 36, 193) explicitly identifies "the continuous flow of nondual unity" as the supreme Madhyamaka of "the awareness that has the nature of not abiding anywhere at all." *A Compendium of the Purport of Empowerment* (text 37, 203–4) relates this expression to the fourth empowerment. According to Divākaracandra's *Illumination of Prajñā Wisdom* (text 16, 67), "dependent origination is the continuum of effortless nondual unity, and its diversity refers to the experience of great bliss, which is to be accomplished as the primordial lack of any nature."
3312. Text 92, 18.
3313. Text 16, 84–86.
3314. Tipi Bumlabar's outline of *Illumination of Prajñā Wisdom* accords with that, saying that the text first matches the five stages with both the creation and the perfection processes and then with the perfection process alone. Within the latter, he says, the outer creation process is not different from mahāmudrā (for details, see appendix 3, "2d. brief teaching on the five stages").
3315. Text 44, 256–57.
3316. As mentioned, the five stages of perfection-process practices in the *Guhyasamājatantra* according to Nāgārjuna's *Pañcakrama* and Āryadeva's *Caryāmelāpakapradīpa* ("Ārya commentarial tradition" of this tantra) are (1) speech isolation (or vajra recitation), (2) mind isolation (or "mind focus" or "universal purity"), (3) self-blessing or the illusory body of seeming reality, (4) the luminosity of ultimate reality (or "the full awakening [of supremely secret bliss]"), and (5) the unity of the two realities, prajñā and means, and the emptiness endowed with all supreme aspects and immutable great bliss, or the unity of (3) illusory body and (4) luminosity (or simply an equivalent of nondual buddha wisdom). In addition, Āryadeva often uses the terms "mind isolation" (Skt. *cittaviveka*) and "mind purification" (Skt. *cittaviśuddhi*) interchangeably. As for "body isolation" (Skt. *kāyaviveka*, Tib. *lus dben*), it can either be included in the creation process or in the stage of speech isolation as its preliminary. Or, if body isolation is counted separately, there are six stages. According to Candrakīrti's *Pradīpoddyotana*, vajra recitation is just a preliminary for mind isolation as the true causal perfection process. Thus the five stages consist of the creation process and the above four stages (2)–(5)

of the perfection process. Alternatively, the five stages are sometimes also presented as body isolation, speech isolation, mind isolation, luminosity, and unity. Finally, another way of classifying these stages begins with the propaedeutic "condensed stage" (Skt. *piṇḍīkrama;* instructions on the creation process of the thirty-two-deity maṇḍala of Guhyasamāja) while omitting the above second stage ("mind isolation"). For a detailed discussion of all the different names and meanings of these five stages, see Wedemeyer 2007 and Kongtrul Lodrö Tayé 2008 (138–47).

3317. Text 44, 349.

3318. Text 45, 434.

3319. As mentioned before, Mathes 2021 (129–30) points out that the five stages of the Ārya school differ in its two subschools: the Māgadhi tradition (represented by Abhayākaragupta, Muniśrībhadra, and others) lists them as the condensed stage (*piṇḍīkrama*), vajra recitation, self-blessing, full awakening, and unity, while the Kashmiri tradition (represented by Lakṣmī and Nāgabodhi) considers them to consist of vajra recitation, universal purity, self-blessing, the full awakening of supremely secret bliss, and unity. However, contra Mathes's statement that both systems are found in Rāmapāla's commentary, Rāmapāla only mentions the nomenclature of the Māgadhi tradition.

3320. Text 45, 413–14.

3321. Text 213, 198.

3322. Unlike the first two (the master empowerment and the secret empowerment) among the four empowerments, Vajrapāṇi does not explicitly mention the third one (the prajñā-jñāna empowerment) here, but since the karmamudrā is the practice that is related to the prajñā-jñāna empowerment and the karmamudrā is said to be twofold here, this seems to be the only suitable place to be matched with the third empowerment.

3323. Text 213, 208–9.

3324. The remainder of the *Guruparamparākramopadeśa* is an elaboration on these five processes via the four mudrās.

3325. Vol. *ka*, fol. 149b.5–6.

Bibliography

Indic Works

Abhisamayālaṃkārālokā Prajñāpāramitāvyākhyā (Commentary on the *Aṣṭasāhasrikā Prajñāpāramitā*) by Haribhadra. 1932–35. Sanskrit edition by Wogihara Unrai. Tōyō Bunko Publications Series D, vol. 2. Tokyo: The Tōyō Bunko.

Asaṅga. *Abhidharmasamuccaya.* (*Chos mngon pa kun las btus pa*). 1947 and 1950. Fragmentary Sanskrit edition by V. Gokhale. *Journal of the Bombay Branch of the Royal Asiatic Society* 23 (1947): 13–38. Sanskrit edition/reconstruction by P. Pradhan. Santiniketan, India: Visva-Bharati, 1950. P5550. D4049.

———. *Śrāvakabhūmi.* (*Nyan thos kyi sa*). 1973. Sanskrit edition by K. Shukla. Patna, India: K. P. Jayaswal Research Institute. P5537. D4036.

Bka' 'gyur (*dpe bsdur ma*). 2006–2009. Beijing: Krung go'i bod rig pa'i dpe skrun khang.

Bstan 'gyur (*dpe bsdur ma*). 1994–2008. Beijing: Krung go'i bod rig pa'i dpe skrun khang.

Daśabhūmikasūtra. 1926. Edited by Johannes Rahder. Leuven: J. B. Istas.

Gaṇḍavyūhasūtra. 1949. *The Gandavyuha Sutra.* Sanskrit edition by Suzuki Daisetz Teitaro and Idzumi Kokei. Tokyo: The Society for the Publication of Sacred Books of the World.

Jinaputra. *Abhidharmasamuccayabhāṣya.* (*Chos mngon pa kun las btus pa'i bshad pa*). 1976. Sanskrit edition by Nathmal Tatia. Tibetan-Sanskrit Works Series No. 17. Patna: K. P. Jayaswal Research Institute. P5554. D4053.

Jñānālokālaṃkāra. 2004. Edition by Study Group on Buddhist Sanskrit

Literature. The Institute for Comprehensive Studies of Buddhism, Taisho University. Tokyo: Taisho University Press.

Jñānaśrīmitra. *Jñānaśrīmitranibandhāvali*. 1987. Tibetan Sanskrit Series 5. Edited by Anantalal Thakur. Patna, India: K. P. Jayaswal Research Institute.

Kuddālapāda. 1999. *Bsam gyis mi khyab pa'i rim pa'i man ngag*. In *Gdams ngag rin po che'i mdzod*, 6: 81–95. Delhi: Shechen Publications.

Maitrīpa. **Advayavajrasaṃgraha*. 1927. Sanskrit edition by Haraprasad Śāstrī. Gaekwad's Oriental Series 40. Baroda: Oriental Institute. Also edited by the Study Group of Sacred Tantric Texts (Mikkyō-seiten kenkyukai), "The Results of a Joint Study on the Buddhist Tantric Texts: *Advayavajrasamgraha*—New Critical Edition with Japanese Translation," in *Annual of the Institute for Comprehensive Studies of Buddhism, Taisho University*. Tokyo: Institute for Comprehensive Studies of Buddhism Taisho University, 1988–91: 10: 234–178; 11: 259–200; 12: 316–282; 13: 291–242. Mathes, *A Fine Blend*, 323–501.

Pañcaviṃśatisāhasrikā Prajñāpāramitā. 1986–2007. Sanskrit edition, 8 vols. Edited by Kimura Takayasu. Tokyo: SANKIBO Busshorin Publishing.

Saptaśatikā Prajñāpāramitā. 1930. In "Saptaśatikā Prajñāpāramitā: Text and the Hsüan-Chwang Chinese Version with Notes," edited by Masuda Jiryo, *Journal of the Taisho University, vols. VI–VII, In Commemoration of the Sixtieth Birthday of Professor Unrai Wogihara*, 185–241.

Saraha. 1999. *Do ha mdzod*. In *Gdams ngag rin po che'i mdzod*, 7: 7–22. Delhi: Shechen Publications.

Suvarṇabhāsottamasūtra. 1937. Sanskrit edition by Johannes Nobel. Leipzig: Otto Harrassowitz.

Vasubandhu. *Abhidharmakośabhāṣya*. 1987. Sanskrit edition by S. D. Shastri. Varanasi: Bauddha Bharati Series 5–9 (reprint, orig. pub. 1970–72). P5591. D4090.

Tibetan Works

A mgon rin po che, ed. 2004. *'Bri gung bka' brgyud chos mdzod chen mo*. 151 vols. Lhasa: 'Bri gung mthil dgon.

Bcom ldan Rig pa'i ral gri. 2007. *Do ha rgyan gyi me tog*. In *Bcom ldan rig pa'i ral gri'i gsungs skor*. Kathmandu: Sa skya rgyal yongs gsung rab slob gnyer khang. https://library.bdrc.io/show/bdr:UT3JT13307_008_0000.

Bkra shis chos 'phel. 2009. *Gnas lugs phyag rgya chen po'i rgya gzhung glegs bam gsum yi ge'i 'byung gnas su ji ltar bkod pa'i dkar chag bzhugs byang mdor bsdus pa sgrub brgyud grub pa'i rna rgyan*. In *Nges don phyag chen rgya gzhung dang bod gzhung*, 1:1–98. Chengdu: Si khron mi rigs dpe skrun khang.

Bu ston rin chen grub. 1971. *Bu ston gsan yig / Bla ma dam pa rnams kyis rjes su gzung ba'i tshul bka' drin rjes su dran par byed pa*. In *Collected Works of Butön*, vol. *la*, 1–142. New Delhi: International Academy of Indian Culture.

Dpa' bo gtsug lag phreng ba. 2003. *Dam pa'i chos kyi 'khor lo bsgyur ba rnams kyi byung ba gsal bar byed pa mkhas pa'i dga' ston*. 2 vols. Sarnath: Vajra Vidya Institute Library.

———. n.d. *Byang chub sems dpa'i spyod pa la 'jug pa'i rnam bshad theg chen chos kyi rgya mtsho zab rgyas mtha' yas pa'i snying po*. Rouffignac, France: Nehsang Samten Chöling.

Dpal ldan rang byung phrin las kun khyab bstan pa'i rgyal mtshan (Sangyé Nyenpa X). n.d. *Chen po gzhan stong gi lta ba dang 'brel pa'i phyag rgya chen po'i smon lam gyi rnam bshad nges don dbyings kyi rol mo*. Dharma Downloads. www.dharmadownload.net/pages/english/mahamudra/03_mahamudra%20main/04_Kamtsang/004_mahamudra_kamtsang.htm.

Dung dkar blo bzang 'phrin las. 2002. *Dung dkar tshig mdzod chen mo*. Beijing: China Tibetology Publishing House.

Dvags po bkra shis rnam rgyal. 2002. *Dpal kye'i rdo rje zhes bya ba'i rgyud kyi rgyal po'i 'grel pa legs bshad nyi ma'i 'od zer*. Chengdu: Si khron mi rigs dpe skrun khang

'Gos lo tsā ba gzhon nu dpal. 1996 [1949]. *The Blue Annals*. Translated by G. N. Roerich. Delhi: Motilal Banarsidass.

———. 2003a. *Deb ther sngon po*. 2 vols. Sarnath: Vajra Vidya Institute Library.

———. 2003b. *Theg pa chen po'i rgyud bla ma'i bstan bcos kyi 'grel bshad de kho na nyid rab tu gsal ba'i me long*. Edited by Klaus-Dieter Mathes. Nepal Research Centre Publications 24. Stuttgart: Franz Steiner Verlag.

Grags pa rgyal mtshan. 1999a. *Slob dpon tog rtse pa'i lam bsam gyis mi khyab pa lnga'i lo rgyus*. In *Gdams ngag rin po che'i mdzod*, 6: 95–98. Delhi: Shechen Publications.

———. 1999b. *Slob dpon tog rtse pas mdzad pa'i bsam mi khyab kyi gdams ngag gsal bar byed pa*. In *Gdams ngag rin po che'i mdzod*, 6: 98–118.

Grub thob gling ras, Par phu ba blo gros seng ge, Karma pa rang byung rdo rje. 2011. *Grub chen sa ra ha'i do ha skor gsum gyi bod 'grel grags pa che ba gsum phyogs sgrig*. Sarnath, India: Vajra Vidya Institute Library.

'Jam dbyangs bzhad pa'i rdo rje. 1997. *Do ha mdzod kyi mchan 'grel*. In *Gsung 'bum. 'Jam dbyangs bzhad pa'i rdo rje*, 4: 640–65. Mundgod, India: Bla brang bkra shis 'khyil par khang.

'Ju mi pham rgya mtsho. 1984. *Dpal sa ra has mdzad pa'i do ha mdzod kyi glu'i mchan 'grel gnyug ma rdo rje'i sgra dbyangs*. In *Collected Writings of 'Jam-mgon 'Ju Mi-pham-rgya-mtsho*, 12: 759–95. Paro, Bhutan: Lama Ngodrup and Sherab Drimay.

Karma phrin las pa phyogs las rnam rgyal. 2006. *Zab mo nang don gyi rnam bshad snying po gsal bar byed pa'i nyin byed 'od kyi phreng ba*. In *Karma pa rang byung rdo rje gsung 'bum*, 14: 1–553. Zi ling, Tibet: Mtshur phu mkhan po lo yag bkra shis.

———. 2009. *Do ha skor gsum gyi tshig don gyi rnam bshad sems kyi rnam thar gsal bar ston pa'i me long / btsun mo do ha'i ṭī ka 'bring po sems kyi rnam thar ston pa'i me long / rgyal po do ha'i ṭī ka 'bring po sems kyi rnam thar ston pa'i me long*. Sarnath, India: Vajra Vidya Institute Library.

Khro ru klu sgrub rgya mtsho, ed. 2009. *Phyag rgya chen po'i rgya gzhung*. In *Nges don phyag chen rgya gzhung dang bod gzhung*, vols. 1–6. Chengdu: Si khron mi rigs dpe skrun khang.

Kong sprul blo gros mtha' yas. 1982. *Theg pa'i sgo kun las btus pa gsung rab rin po che'i mdzod bslab pa gsum legs par ston pa'i bstan bcos shes bya kun khyab*; includes its autocommentary, *Shes bya kun la khyab pa'i gzhung lugs nyung ngu'i tshig gis rnam par 'grol ba legs bshad yongs 'du shes bya mtha' yas pa'i rgya mtsho* (abbreviated as *Shes bya kun kyab mdzod*). 3 vols. Beijing: Mi rigs dpe skrun khang.

———. 1999. *Tog rtse pa'i bsam gyis mi khyab pa'i khrid yig bkra shis dvangs shel me long*. In *Gdams ngag rin po che'i mdzod*, 6: 231–54. Delhi: Shechen Publications.

———. 2005. *Brtag gnyis spyi don dang / tshig 'grel gzhom med rdo rje'i gsang ba 'byed pa* (*Rgyud kyi rgyal po dpal brtag pa gnyis pa'i spyi don legs par bshad pa gsang ba bla na med pa rdo rje drva ba'i rgyan* and *Dpal dgyes pa rdo rje'i rgyud kyi rgyal po brtag pa gnyis pa'i tshig don rnam par 'grol ba gzhom med rdo rje'i gsang ba 'byed pa*). Seattle: Nitartha *international.*

Krang dbyi sun et al. 1985. *Bod rgya tshig mdzod chen mo.* 2 vols. Beijing: Mi rigs dpe skrun khang.

Kun dga' rgyal mtshan (Sa skya paṇ ḍi ta). 1992–93. *Snyi mo sgom chen gyi dris lan.* In *Dpal ldan sa skya pa'i bka' 'bum*, vol. *na*, fols. 246a.3–249b.2. Dehra Dun: Sakya Center.

Lam 'bras slob bshad (*The Sa-skya-pa Teachings of the Path and the Fruit, according to the Tshar-pa Transmission*). 1983–95. 21 vols. Dehradun, India: Sakya Centre.

Lha rje bsod nams rin chen. 1990. *Dam chos yid bzhin nor bu thar pa rin po che'i rgyan.* Chengdu: Si khron mi rigs dpe skrun khang.

Mi bskyod rdo rje (Eighth Karmapa). 1996. *Dbu ma la 'jug pa'i rnam bshad dpal ldan dus gsum mkhyen pa'i zhal lung dvags brgyud grub pa'i shing rta.* Seattle: Nitartha *international.*

———. 2003. *Shes rab kyi pha rol tu phyin pa'i lung chos mtha' dag gi bdud rtsi'i snying por gyur pa gang la ldan pa'i gzhi rje btsun mchog tu dgyes par ngal gso'i yongs 'dus brtol gyi ljon pa rgyas pa.* 2 vols. Seattle: Nitartha *international.*

———2004a. *Dam pa'i chos dgongs pa gcig pa kar ṭīka las / drug pa rten 'brel gyi tshoms kyi ṭīka chen.* In *Dpal rgyal ba karma pa sku 'phreng brgyad pa mi bskyod rdo rje gsung 'bum*, 6: 1–364. Lhasa: Dpal brtsegs bod yig dpe rnying zhib 'jug khang.

———. 2004b. *Sku gsum ngo sprod kyi rnam par bshad pa mdo rgyud bstan pa mtha' dag gi e vam phyag rgya.* In *Dpal rgyal ba karma pa sku 'phreng brgyad pa mi bskyod rdo rje gsung 'bum*, vols. 21–22.

———. 2004c. *Dgongs gcig gi gsung bzhi bcu pa'i 'grel pa.* In *Dpal rgyal ba karma pa sku 'phreng brgyad pa mi bskyod rdo rje gsung 'bum*, 5: 728–939.

Ngag dbang bstan 'dzin nor bu. 1972. *Gcod yul nyon mongs zhi byed bka' gter bla ma brgyud pa'i rnam thar byin rlabs gter mtsho.* Gangtok: Sonam T. Kazi.

Nor brang o rgyan. 2008. *Gangs can rig brgya'i chos kyi rnam grangs mthong tshad kun las btus pa ngo mtshar 'phrul gyi lde mig chen po.* 3 vols. Beijing: Krung go'i bod rig pa dpe skrun khang.

Padma dkar po. 1974a. *Rnal 'byor bzhi'i bshad pa don dam mdzub tshugs su bstan pa*. In *Kun mkhyen padma dkar po'i gsung 'bum*, 21: 465–98. Darjeeling: Kargyu sungrab nyamso khang.

———. 1974b. *Sher phyin gyi lung la 'jug pa'i sgo*. In *Kun mkhyen padma dkar po'i gsung 'bum*, 8: 403–79.

———. 2005. *Phyag rgya chen po man ngag gi bshad sbyar rgyal ba'i gan mdzod*. Sarnath: Vajra Vidya Institute Library.

Phun tshogs rgyal mtshan, ed. n.d. *Phyag rgya chen po'i rgya gzhung*. 3 vols. Dpal spungs block print. (W3CN636).

Rgyal ba yang dgon pa. 1984. *Collected Writing (gsuṅ 'bum) of Rgyal-ba yan-dgon-pa rgyal-mtshan-dpal*. 3 vols. Thimphu: Tango Monastic Community.

Rin chen rnam rgyal, Lha btsun pa. 1976. *Bram ze chen pos mdzad pa'i dho ha bskor gsum / mdzod drug ka kha dho ha / sa spyad rnams*. In *Rare Dkar brgyud pa Texts from Himachal Pradesh*, 107–79. New Delhi: Urgyan Dorje.

Sgam po pa bsod nams rin chen. 1982. *Sgam po pa bsod nams rin chen gyi gsung 'bum*. 3 vols. Darjeeling: Kargyud Sungrab Nyamso Khang.

Tāranātha. 1970. *Two Sources for the History of Buddhist Tantrism in India: The* Bka' babs bdun ldan gyi brgyud pa'i rnam thar *and the* Gshin rje gshed skor gyi chos 'byung. Tashijong, Phalampur, India: Sungrab Nyamso Junphel Parkhang, Tibetan Craft Community.

———. 2008. *Kahna pa'i do ha thor bu rnams kyi 'grel pa ngo mtshar snang ba*. In *Jo nang rje btsun tā ra nā tha'i gsung 'bum dpe bsdur ma*, 19: 166–219. Beijing: Krung go'i bod rig pa dpe skrun khang.

———. 2011. *Bka' babs bdun ldan gyi brgyud pa'i rnam thar no mtshar rmad du byung ba rin po che'i khungs lta bu'i gtam*. In *Bod kyi lo rgyus phyogs sgrigs*, 42: 429–595. Zi ling, Tibet: Mtsho sngon mi rigs dpe skrun khang.

Ti pi 'bum la 'bar. 2004a. *Rin po che'i phreng ba'i grel pa*. In A mgon rin po che, *'Bri gung bka' brgyud chos mdzod chen mo*, 1: 363–97. Lhasa: 'Bri gung mthil dgon.

———. 2004b. *De bzhin gshegs pa phyag rgya rnam lnga'i 'grel pa*. In A mgon rin po che, *'Bri gung bka' brgyud chos mdzod chen mo*, 2: 33–49.

———. 2004c. *De nyid bcu pa'i 'grel pa*. In A mgon rin po che, *'Bri gung bka' brgyud chos mdzod chen mo*, 2: 353–71.

Tsong kha pa. 1985. *Shes rab kyi pha rol tu phyin pa'i man ngag gi bstan bcos mngon par rtogs pa'i rgyan 'grel pa dang bcas pa'i rgya cher bshad pa'i legs bshad gser phreng*. In *Collected Works*, vols. *tsa* and *tsha*. Dharamsala: Bod gzhung shes rig dpar khang.

Secondary Sources

Almogi, Orna. 2009. *Rong-zom-pa's Discourses on Buddhology: A Study of Various Conceptions of Buddhahood in Indian Sources with Special Reference to the Controversy Surrounding the Existence of Gnosis* (Jñāna: Ye shes) *as Presented by the Eleventh-Century Tibetan Scholar Rong-zom Chos-kyi-bzang-po*. Studia Philologica Buddhica Monograph Series 24. Tokyo: International Institute for Buddhist Studies.

———. 2010. "Māyopamādvayavāda versus Sarvadharmāpratiṣṭhānavāda: A Late Indian Subclassification of Madhyamaka and Its Reception in Tibet." *Journal of the International College for Postgraduate Buddhist Studies* 14: 135–212.

———. 2022a. "The Translation Endeavours of Shes rab grags Revisited: An Investigation of Translations Done by Pu rang lo chung Shes rab grags and 'Bro lo tsā ba Shes rab grags." *Revue d'Études Tibétaines* 63: 289–400.

———. 2022b. "Editors as Canon-Makers: The Formation of the Tibetan Buddhist Canon in Light of Its Editors' Predilections and Agendas." In *Evolution of Scriptures, Formation of Canons: The Buddhist Case*, edited by Orna Almogi, 351–458. Indian and Tibetan Studies 13. Hamburg: The Department of Indian and Tibetan Studies, Universität Hamburg.

Anacker, Stefan. 1986. *Seven Works of Vasubandhu*. Delhi: Motilal Banarsidass.

Apple, James. 2017. "Atiśa's Teachings on Mahāmudrā." *Indian International Journal of Buddhist Studies* 18: 1–42.

Bagchi, Prabodh Chandra. 1935a. "Dohākoṣa (with Notes and Translation)." *Journal of the Department of Letters* 28: 1–180.

———. 1935b. *Dohakoṣa With Notes and Translation*. Calcutta: Calcutta University.

———. 1938. *Dohākoṣa (Apabhraṃśa Texts of the Sahajayāna School). Part I*

(Texts and Commentaries). Calcutta Sanskrit Series No. 25c. Calcutta: Metropolitan Printing and Publishing House.

Bajracharya, Surendra Man. 2014. "Monasticism in Buddhism of Nepal-Mandala: Continuity and Changes." PhD diss., Tribhuvan University, Kathmandu.

Bendall, Cecil, ed. 1903–4. *Subhāṣita-saṃgraha. Le Muséon* 4: 375–402 and 5: 1–46, 245–74. Louvain, Belgium: J. B. Istas.

Bentor, Yael. 2009. "The Convergence of Theoretical and Practical Concerns in a Single Verse of the *Guhyasamāja Tantra*." In *Tibetan Rituals*, edited by José Ignacio Cabezón, 89–102. New York: Oxford University Press.

Bhāyāṇī, Harivallabha Cūṇīlāla, ed. 1997. *Dohā-gīti-kośa of Saraha-Pāda (A Treasury of Songs in the Dohā Metre) and Caryā-gīti-kośa (A Treasury of the Caryā Songs of Various Siddhas: Restored Text, Sanskrit Chāyā and Translation)*. Ahmedabad: Prakrit Text Society.

Bhikkhu Bodhi. 2000. *The Connected Discourses of the Buddha: A Translation of the Saṃyutta Nikāya*. 2 vols. Somerville, MA: Wisdom Publications.

Birch, Jason. 2011. "The Meaning of *haṭha* in Early Haṭhayoga." *Journal of the American Oriental Society* 131.4: 527–54.

Böthlingk, Otto. 1998. *Pāṇini's Grammatik*. Delhi: Motilal Banarsidass.

Boucher, Daniel. 1991. "The *Pratītyasamutpādagāthā* and Its Role in the Medieval Cult of the Relics." *Journal of the International Association of Buddhist Studies* 14.1: 1–27.

Broido, Michael. 1988. "Veridical and Delusive Cognition: Tsongkhapa on the Two *Satyas*." *Journal of Indian Philosophy* 16: 29–63.

Brunnhölzl, Karl. 2004. *The Center of the Sunlight Sky*. Ithaca, NY: Snow Lion.

———. 2007. *Straight from the Heart*. Ithaca, NY: Snow Lion.

———. 2009. *Luminous Heart*. Ithaca, NY: Snow Lion.

———. 2010. *Gone Beyond*, vol. 1. Ithaca, NY: Snow Lion.

———. 2011. *Gone Beyond*, vol. 2. Ithaca, NY: Snow Lion.

———. 2012. *Mining for Wisdom within Delusion*. Boston: Snow Lion.

———. 2014. *When the Clouds Part*. Boston: Snow Lion.

———. 2018. *A Compendium of the Mahāyāna. Asaṅga's* Mahāyānasaṃgraha *and Its Indian and Tibetan Commentaries*. 3 vols. Boulder, CO: Snow Lion.

Bühnemann, Gudrun. 2000a. "Buddhist Deities and Mantras in the Hindu Tantras: II The *Śrīvidyārṇavatantra* and the *Tantrasāra*." *Indo-Iranian Journal* 43: 27–48.

———. 2000b. "The Six Rites of Magic." In *Tantra in Practice*, edited by David G. White, 447–62. Princeton, NJ: Princeton University Press.

Callahan, Elizabeth, trans. 2014. *The Profound Inner Principles*. Boston: Snow Lion.

Chandra, Lokesh. 1986. *Buddhist Iconography*. [Eighty-eight mahāsiddhas, nos. 1096–1183]. Kyoto: Rinsen.

Dakpo Tashi Namgyal. 2019. *Moonbeams of Mahāmudrā. With Dispelling the Darkness of Ignorance by Wangchuk Dorje, the Ninth Karmapa*. Translated by Elizabeth Callahan. Boston: Snow Lion.

Dalton, Catherine. 2019. "Enacting Perfection: Buddhajñānapāda's Vision of a Tantric Buddhist World." PhD diss., University of California, Berkeley.

Dalton, Jacob. 2005. "A Crisis of Doxography: How Tibetans Organized Tantra During the 8th–12th Centuries." *Journal of the International Association of Buddhist Studies* 28.1: 115–81.

Dasgupta, Shashi Bhushan. 1946. *Obscure Religious Cults*. Calcutta: Calcutta University Press.

———. 1974. *An Introduction to Tantric Buddhism*. Berkeley, CA: Shambhala Publications.

Davidson, Ronald M. 1991. "Reflections on the Maheśvara Subjugation Myth: Indic Materials, Sa-skya-pa Apologetics, and the Birth of Heruka." *Journal of the International Association of Buddhist Studies* 14.2: 197–235.

———. 2002a. "Reframing *Sahaja*: Genre, Representation, Ritual and Lineage." *Journal of Indian Philosophy* 30.1: 45–83.

———. 2002b. *Indian Esoteric Buddhism: A Social History of the Tantric Movement*. New York: Columbia University Press.

———. 2002c. "*Gsar ma* Apocrypha: The Creation of Orthodoxy, Gray Texts, and the New Revelation." In *The Many Canons of Tibetan Buddhism: Proceedings of the Ninth Seminar of the International Association for Tibetan Studies, Leiden 2000*, edited by Helmut Eimer and David Germano, 203–24. Leiden: Brill.

———. 2005. *Tibetan Renaissance: Tantric Buddhism in the Rebirth of Tibetan Culture*. New York: Columbia University Press.

Davidson, Ronald M., and Christian K. Wedemeyer, eds. 2006. *Buddhist Literature and Praxis: Studies in Its Formative Period 900–1400*. Tibetan Studies: Proceedings of the Tenth Seminar of the International Association for Tibetan Studies, Oxford, 2003, vol. 4. Leiden: Brill.

Dowman, Keith. 1985. *Masters of Mahamudra: Songs and Histories of the Eighty-Four Buddhist Siddhas.* Albany: State University of New York Press.

Draszczyk, Martina. 2019. "Mahāmudrā as Revelatory of the Key-Point of the Third *Dharmacakra* according to the *Sixty Verses of Mahāmudrā* by the Fourth Zhwa dmar pa, Chos grags ye shes." In *Mahāmudrā in India and Tibet*, edited by Roger Jackson and Klaus-Dieter Mathes, 204–36. Leiden: Brill.

Ducher, Cécile. 2017. "A Lineage in Time: The Vicissitudes of the rNgog pa bka' brgyud from the 11th through 19th c." PhD diss., Université de recherche Paris Science et Lettres.

———. 2020. "A Neglected Bka' brgyud Lineage: The Rngog from Gzhung and the Rngog pa Bka' brgyud Transmission." In *Mahāmudrā in India and Tibet*, edited by Roger Jackson and Klaus-Dieter Mathes, 142–69. Leiden and Boston: Brill.

Dudjom Rinpoche, Jikdrel Yeshe Dorje. 1991. *The Nyingma School of Tibetan Buddhism*. Translated and edited by Gyurme Dorje and Matthew Kapstein. 2 vols. Boston: Wisdom Publications.

Dunne, John D. 2004. *Foundations of Dharamkīrti's Philosophy*. Boston: Wisdom Publications.

Edgerton, Franklin. 1953. *Buddhist Hybrid Sanskrit Grammar and Dictionary*. 2 vols. New Haven: Yale University Press.

Eimer, Helmut. 1979. *rNam thar rgyas pa: Materialien zu einer Biographie des Atisa (Dīpamkaraśrījñāna)*. 2 vols. Wiesbaden: Harrassowitz.

Eltschinger, Vincent. 2014. "Is There a Burden-bearer? The Sanskrit *Bhārahārasūtra* and Its Scholastic Interpretations." *Journal of the American Oriental Society* 134.3: 453–79.

English, Elizabeth. 2002. *Vajrayoginī: Her Visualizations, Rituals, and Forms. A Study of the Cult of Vajrayoginī in India*. Studies in Indian and Tibetan Buddhism. Boston: Wisdom Publications.

Farrow, George W., and Indu Menon. 1992. *The Concealed Essence of the Hevajra Tantra, with the Commentary Yogaratnamala*. Delhi: Motilal Banarsidass.

Gellner, David N. 1991. "Ritualized Devotion, Altruism, and Meditation: The Offering of the 'Guru Maṇḍala' in Newar Buddhism." *Indo-Iranian Journal* 34: 161–97.

Gray, David B. 2001. "On Supreme Bliss. A Study of the History and Interpretation of the *Cakrasaṃvara Tantra*." PhD diss., Columbia University.

———. 2009. "On the Very Idea of a Tantric Canon: Myth, Politics, and the Formation of the Bka' 'gyur." *Journal of the International Association of Tibetan Studies* 5: 1–37.

———. 2016. "The Purification of Heruka: On the Transmission of a Controversial Buddhist Tradition to Tibet." In *Tantric Tradition in Transmission and Translation*, edited by David B. Gray and Ryan Richard Overbey, 230–56. New York: Oxford University Press.

———. 2019. *The Cakrasaṃvara Tantra: (The Discourse of Śrī Heruka) Śrīherukābhidhāna. A Study and Annotated Translation by David B. Gray.* Edited by Thomas F. Yarnall. New York: The American Institute of Buddhist Studies and Wisdom Publications, in association with Columbia University Center for Buddhist Studies and Tibet House US.

Grimes, Samuel, and Péter-Dániel Szántó. 2018. "Mahāsukhavajra's *Padmāvatī* Commentary on the Sixth Chapter of the *Caṇḍamahāroṣaṇatantra*: The Sexual Practices of a Tantric Buddhist Yogī and His Consort." *Journal of Indian Philosophy* 46: https://doi.org/10.1007/s10781-018-9357-3.

Guenther, Herbert V. 1952. *Yuganaddha: The Tantric View of Life*. Banaras: The Chowkhamba Sanskrit Series Office.

———. 1963. *The Life and Teaching of Naropa*. Oxford: Oxford University Press.

———. 1969. *The Royal Song of Saraha: A Study in the History of Buddhist Thought*. Berkeley, CA: Shambhala Publications.

———. 1993. *Ecstatic Spontaneity: Saraha's Three Cycles of Doha*. Berkeley, CA: Asian Humanities Press.

Gyamtso, Tsultrim, Khenpo Rinpoche. 2016. *Progressive Stages of Meditation on Emptiness*. Translated and edited by Lama Shenphen Hookham. CreateSpace Independent Publishing Platform.

Gyatso, Desi Sangyé. 2010. *Mirror of Beryl. A Historical Introduction to Tibetan Medicine*. Translated by Gavin Kilty. Boston: Wisdom Publications.

Gyatso, Khedrup Norsang. 2004. *Ornament of Stainless Light: An Exposition of the* Kālacakra Tantra. Translated by Gavin Kilty. Boston: Wisdom Publications.

Hatley, Shaman. 2007. "The *Brahmayāmalatantra* and Early Śaiva Cult of Yoginīs." PhD diss., University of Pennsylvania.

Higgins, David. 2006. "On the Development of the Non-Mentation (*Amanasikāra*) Doctrine in Indo-Tibetan Buddhism." *Journal of the International Association of Buddhist Studies* 29.2: 255–304.

———. 2016. "Padma Dkar po's (1527–92) Defense of Bka' brgyud *Amanasikāra* Teachings." *Journal of the International Association of Buddhist Studies* 39: 429–85.

Higgins, David, and Martina Draszczyk. 2016. *Mahāmudrā and the Middle Way: Post-classical Kagyü Discourses on Mind, Emptiness and Buddha Nature*. 2 vols. Wiener Studien zur Tibetologie und Buddhismuskunde 90. Vienna: Arbeitskreis für Tibetische und Buddhistische Studien Universität Wien.

Hinüber, Oskar von. 2001. *Das ältere Mittelindisch im Überblick*, Österreichische Akademie der Wissenschaften, Philosophisch-historische Klasse, Sitzungsberichte, 467. Veröffentlichungen der Kommission für Sprachen und Kulturen Südasiens Heft 20. Vienna: Verlag der Österreichischen Akademie der Wissenschaften, Wien [2nd revised ed.; 1st ed. 1986].

Ingalls, Daniel H. H. 1953. "Śaṃkara's Arguments against the Buddhists." *Philosophy East and West* 3: 291–306.

———. 1967. "Bhāskara the Vedāntin." *Philosophy East and West* 17: 61–67.

Isaacson, Harunaga. 2003. "Tantric Buddhism in India (from c. A.D. 800 to c. A.D. 1200)." www.buddhismuskunde.uni-hamburg.de/pdf/4-publikationen/buddhismus-in-geschichte-und-gegenwart/bd2-k02isaacson.pdf.

Isaacson, Harunaga, and Francesco Sferra (with contributions by Klaus-Dieter Mathes and Marco Passavanti). 2014. *The* Sekanirdeśa *of Maitreyanātha (Advayavajra) with the* Sekanirdeśapañjikā *of Rāmapāla: Critical Edition of the Sanskrit and Tibetan Texts with English Translation and Reproductions of the MSS*. Manuscripta Buddhica 2. Jointly Published with the Asien-Afrika-Institut, Universität Hamburg, and Università degli Studi di Napoli "L'Orientale."

Iwata, Takashi. 1997. "Study and Annotated Translation of the *Sthitisamuccaya*: The Position of the Nirakārayogācāras (1)" [in Japanese]. *Bulletin of the Graduate Division of Literature of Waseda University (Waseda daigaku daigakuin bungaku kenkyūka kiyō)* 43: 3–14.

———. 1999. "Study and Annotated Translation of the *Sthitisamuccaya*: The Position of the Nirakārayogācāras (2)" [in Japanese]. *Bulletin of the Graduate Division of Literature of Waseda University (Waseda daigaku daigakuin bungaku kenkyūka kiyō)* 45: 13–26.

———. 2011. "Study and Annotated Translation of the *Sthitisamāsa*: The Position of the Nirakārayogācāras (3)" [in Japanese]. *Bulletin of the Graduate Division of Literature of Waseda University (Waseda daigaku daigakuin bungaku kenkyūka kiyō)* 56: 5–17.

———. 2013. "Study and Annotated Translation of the *Sthitisamāsa*: The Position of the Nirakārayogācāras (4)" [in Japanese]. *Thought and Religion of Asia (Tōyō no shisō to shūkyō)* 30: 13–26.

———. 2014. "Study and an Annotated Japanese Translation of the *Sthitisamāsa*: Position of the Sākārayogācāras (5)" [in Japanese]. *Thought and Religion of Asia (Tōyō no shisō to shūkyō)* 31: 22–51.

Iyengar, H. R. Rangaswamy. 1952. *Tarkabhāṣa and Vādasthāna of Mokṣākaragupta and Jitāripāda*. Mysore: The Hindustan Press.

Jackson, Roger R., trans. 2004. *Tantric Treasures: Three Collections of Mystical Verse from Buddhist India*. New York: Oxford University Press.

———. 2008. "The Indian Mahāmudrā 'Canon(s)': A Preliminary Sketch." *Indian International Journal of Buddhist Studies* 9: 151–84.

———. 2009. "Two *Bka' 'gyur* Works in Mahāmudrā Canons: The *Ārya-ātajñāna-nāma-mahāyāna-sūtra* and the *Anāvila-tantra-rāja*." *Journal of the International Association of Buddhist Studies* 5. http://www.thlib.org?tid=T5706.

———. 2011. "The Study of Mahāmudrā in the West: A Brief Historical Overview." In *Mahāmudrā and the Bka' brgyud Tradition*, edited by Roger R. Jackson and Matthew T. Kapstein, 3–54. *PIATS 2006: Tibetan Studies: Proceedings of the Eleventh Seminar of the International Association for Tibetan Studies, Königswinter 2006*. Halle (Saale): International Institute for Tibetan and Buddhist Studies GmbH.

———. 2019. *Mind Seeing Mind. Mahāmudrā and the Geluk Tradition of Tibetan Buddhism*. Boston: Wisdom Publications.

Jadusingh, Laul B. 2017. *The Perfection of Desire as the Path: Three Early Indian Vajrayana Treatises*. CreateSpace Independent Publishing Platform.

Joshi, Lalmani. 1967. *Studies in Buddhistic Culture of India*. Delhi: Motilal Banarsidass.

Kano, Kazuo. 2011. "*Ekagātha, Caturgāthā,* and *Gāthādvayadhāraṇī*: A Set of Reciting Sūtras in 11th century India." *The Mikkyō Bunka* 227: 49–88.

Kapstein, Matthew. 2005. "Chronological Conundrums in the Life of Khyung po rnal 'byor: Hagiography and Historical Time." *Journal of the International Association of Tibetan Studies* 1: 1–14.

———. 2006. "New Light on an Old Friend: PT 849 Reconsidered." In Davidson and Wedemeyer, *Buddhist Literature and Praxis*, 9–30.

———. 2015. "*Dohās* and Grey Texts: Reflections on a Song Attributed to Kāṇha." In *From Bhakti to Bon: Festschrift for Per Kvaerne*, edited by Hanna Havnevik and Charles Ramble, 291–301. Oslo, Norway: Institute for Comparative Research in Human Culture, Novus Press.

Kato, Takahiro. 2011. "The First Two Chapters of Bhāskara's *Śārīrakamīmāṃsābhāṣya*. Critically Edited with an Introduction, Notes and an Appendix." PhD diss., Martin-Luther-Universität, Halle-Wittenberg.

Kemp, Casey. 2015. "Merging Ignorance and Luminosity in Early Bka' brgyud Bsre ba Literature." *Zentralasiatische Studien* 44: 35–50.

Kittay, David, with Lozang Jamspal, trans. 2020. *The Vajra Rosary Tantra (Śrī Vajramālā Tantra) by Vajradhara: An Explanatory Tantra of the Esoteric Community Tantra, with Commentary by Alaṁkakalasha*. Treasury of the Buddhist Sciences Series. Somerville, MA: Wisdom Publications; New York: The American Institute of Buddhist Studies, Columbia University.

Kongtrul Lodrö Tayé, Jamgön. 2005. *The Treasury of Knowledge: Book Six, Part Four: Systems of Buddhist Tantra*. Translated by the Kalu Rinpoché Translation Group (Elio Guarisco and Ingrid McLeod). Ithaca, NY: Snow Lion.

———. 2007a. *The Treasury of Knowledge: Book Six, Part Three: Frameworks of Buddhist Philosophy*. Translated by the Kalu Rinpoché Translation Group (Elizabeth M. Callahan). Ithaca, NY: Snow Lion.

———. 2007b. *The Treasury of Knowledge: Book Eight, Part Four: Esoteric Instructions*. Translated by the Kalu Rinpoché Translation Group (Sarah Harding). Ithaca, NY: Snow Lion.

———. 2008. *The Treasury of Knowledge: Book Eight, Part Three: The Elements of Tantric Practice*. Translated by the Kalu Rinpoché Translation Group (Elio Guarisco and Ingrid McLeod). Ithaca, NY: Snow Lion.

———. 2010. *The Treasury of Knowledge: Books Two, Three, and Four: Buddhism's Journey to Tibet*. Translated by the Kalu Rinpoché Translation Group (Ngawang Zangpo). Ithaca, NY: Snow Lion.

———. 2020. *Jonang. The One Hundred and Eight Teaching Manuals: The Treasury of Precious Instructions: Essential Teachings of the Eight Practice Lineages of Tibet*, vol. 18. Translated by Gyurme Dorje and Sarah Harding. Boulder: Shambhala Publications.

———. 2022. *Marpa Kagyu: Methods of Liberation, Part I. The Treasury of Precious Instructions: Essential Teachings of the Eight Practice Lineages of Tibet*, vol. 7. Translated by Elizabeth Callahan. Boulder, CO: Shambhala Publications.

Kragh, Ulrich Timme. 2015. *Tibetan Yoga and Mysticism: A Textual Study of the Yogas of Nāropa and Mahāmudrā Meditation in the Medieval Tradition of Dags po*. Tokyo: International Institute for Buddhist Studies.

Krug, Adam C. 2018. "The Seven Siddhi Texts: The Oḍiyāna Mahāmudrā Lineage in Its Indic and Tibetan Contexts." PhD diss., University of California, Santa Barbara.

Kuijp, Leonard W. J. van der. 2013. "On the Edge of Myth and History: Za hor, Its Place in the History of Early Indian Buddhist Tantra, and Dalai Lama V and the Genealogy of Its Royal Family." In *Studies on Buddhist Myths: Texts, Pictures, Traditions and History*, edited by Bangwei Wang, Jinhua Chen, and Ming Chen, 114–64. Shanghai: Zhongxi Book Company.

Lal, Banarsi, ed. 1994. *Āryamañjuśrīnāmasaṃgīti with Amṛtakaṇikā-Ṭippaṇī by Bhikṣu Raviśrījñāna and Amṛtakaṇikodyota-Nibandha of Vibhūticandra*. Sarnath: Central Institute of Higher Tibetan Studies.

La Vallée Poussin, Louis de. 1898. *Bouddhisme, Études et Matériaux. Ādikarmapradīpa. Bodhicaryāvatāraṭīkā*. London: Luzac & Co.

Lindtner, Christian. 1985. "A Treatise on Buddhist Idealism: Kambala's *Ālokamālā*." In *Indiske Studier 5: Miscellanea Buddhica*, edited by Christian Lindtner, 108–221. Copenhagen: Akademisk Forlag.

Lo Bue, Erberto. 1997. "The Role of Newar Scholars in Transmitting Buddhist Heritage to Tibet (c. 750–c. 1200)." In *Les habitants du toit du monde*, edited by Samten Gyaltsen Karmay and Philippe Sagant, 629–58. Nanterre: Société d'ethnologie.

Lobsang Jampa, Gyumé Khensur. 2019. *Guhyasamāja Practice in the Ārya Nāgārjuna System: Volume One: The Generation Stage*. Translated and annotated by Artemus B. Engle. Boulder, CO: Snow Lion.

Lopez, Donald S., Jr. 1988. *The Heart Sūtra Explained*. Albany: State University of New York Press.

———. 2019. *Seeing the Sacred in Saṃsāra. An Illustrated Guide to the Eighty-Four Mahāsiddhas*. Boulder: Shambhala Publications.

Mathes, Klaus-Dieter. 2006a. Vortragsmanuskript: "Formen der Gewalt und des Gewaltverzichts in den Lebensgeschichten der Mahāsiddhas und Lamas." Buddhismus in Geschichte und Gegenwart, vol. 10 (*Gewalt und Gewaltlosigkeit*), 269–81. Hamburg: Universität Hamburg, Asien-Afrika-Institut, Abteilung für Geschichte Indiens und Tibets (Weiterbildendes Studium).

———. 2006b. "Blending the Sūtras with the Tantras: The Influence of Maitrīpa and His Circle on the Formation of Sūtra Mahāmudrā in the Kagyu Schools." In Davidson and Wedemeyer, *Buddhist Literature and Praxis*, 201–27.

———. 2007. "Can Sūtra Mahāmudrā Be Justified on the Basis of Maitrīpa's *Apratiṣṭhānavāda*?" In *Pramāṇakīrtiḥ: Papers Dedicated to Ernst Steinkellner on the Occasion of his 70th Birthday*, edited by B. Kellner, H. Krasser, H. Lasic, M.T. Much, H. Tauscher, 545–66. Wiener Studien zur Tibetologie und Buddhismuskunde 70.2. Vienna: Arbeitskreis für Tibetische und Buddhistische Studien.

———. 2008. "Maitrīpa's *Amanasikārādhāra* ("A Justification of Becoming Mentally Disengaged")." *Journal of the Nepal Research Center* 13: 3–30.

———. 2009. "The 'Succession of the Four Seals'(*Caturmudrānvaya*) Together with Selected Passages from *Kāropa's Commentary." *Tantric Studies*, vol. 1 [2008], 89–130. Hamburg: Centre for Tantric Studies, University of Hamburg.

———. 2011. "The Collection of 'Indian Mahāmudrā Works' (Tib. *phyag chen rgya gzhung*) Compiled by the Seventh Karma pa Chos grags rgya mtsho." In *Mahāmudrā and the Bka' brgyud Tradition*, edited by Roger R. Jackson and Matthew T. Kapstein, 89–127. Tibetan Studies: Proceedings of the Eleventh Seminar of the International Association for Tibetan Studies, Königswinter 2006. Halle (Saale), Germany: International Institute for Tibetan and Buddhist Studies GmbH.

———. 2015. *A Fine Blend of Mahāmudrā and Madhyamaka—Maitrīpa's Collection of Texts on Becoming Mentally Disengaged (Amanasikāra)*. Vienna: Verlag der Österreichischen Akademie der Wissenschaften, Philosophisch-historische Klasse.

———. 2016. "bKa' brgyud *Mahāmudrā*: Chinese *'rDzogs-chen'* or the Teachings of the Siddhas?" *Zentralasiatische Studien* 45: 309–40.

———. 2019. "*Sahajavajra's Integration of Tantra into Mainstream Buddhism: An Analysis of His **Tattvadaśakaṭīkā* and **Sthitisamāsa*." In *Tantric Communities in Context*, edited by Nina Mirnig, Marion Rastelli, and Vincent Eltschinger, 137–70. Vienna: Austrian Academia of Sciences Press.

———. 2021. *Maitrīpa: India's Yogi of Nondual Bliss*. Boulder, CO: Shambhala Publications.

Mathes, Klaus-Dieter, and Péter-Dániel Szántó. Forthcoming. *Saraha's Treasury of Spontaneous Songs: Volume 1, the Indic Texts: The Oldest Existent Root Text in Apabhramśa and Commentaries by Advayavajra and Mokṣākaragupta*. Somerville, MA: Wisdom Publications.

Matsuda, Kazunobu. 1995. "Sahajavajra's Manual on Buddhism (*Sthitisamuccaya*): The Discovery of Its Sanskrit Manuscripts." *Journal of International Buddhist Studies* 43.2: 848–43 (= 205–10).

Matsumoto, Tsuneji. 2016. "Madhyamaka Thought in Esoteric Buddhism—Focusing on the Example of Sahajavajra" [In Japanese]. *Annual Report of the Institute of Comprehensive Buddhism, Taisho University* 38: 217–28.

———. 2020. "The Outline of the Established Theory of the Middle Way." Japanese Translation Study (1). *Modern Esoteric Buddhism* 30: 39–60.

Migmar Tseten, Acharya Lama, and Loppon Kunga Namdrol. 2012. "*The Inconceivable Stage* by the Mahasiddha Kotalipa (from Sakya Mahamudra)." *Melody of Dharma* 9: 9–15.

Miller, Roy Andrew. 1966. "Buddhist Hybrid Sanskrit *Āli*, *Kāli* as Grammatical Terms in Tibet." *Harvard Journal of Asiatic Studies* 26: 125–47.

Mimaki, Katsumi. 1994. "Doxographie tibétaine et classifications indiennes." In *Bouddhisme et culture locales: Quelques cas de réciproques adaptations. Actes du colloque franco-japonais de septembre 1991*, edited by Fumimasa Fukui and Gérard Fussman, 115–36. Études Thématiques 2. Paris: École française d'Extrême-Orient.

Moevus, Adrien. 2019. "To Be Tantric or Not to Be: An Evaluation of the Modern Scholarly Debate on Maitrīpa's *Mahāmudrā* and a Textual Analysis of his *Amanasikāra* Cycle." Master's thesis, McGill University, Montreal.

Nakamura, Hajime. 1968. "Bhāskara, the Vedāntin, in Buddhist Literature." *Annals of the Bhandarkar Oriental Research Institute* 48–49 (Golden Jubilee Volume): 119–22.

Nara, Yasuaki. 1966. "A Study of Citta and Manas in Three Dohas of Saraha." *Bulletin of the Philological Society of Calcutta* 6: 52–65.

Negi, J. S. 1993. *Bod skad dang legs sbyar gyi tshig mdzod chen mo*. 16 vols. Sarnath, India: Central Institute of Higher Tibetan Studies.

Newman, John. 1987. "The *Paramādibuddha* (the Kālacakra *Mūlatantra*) and its Relation to the Early Kālacakra Literature." *Indo-Iranian Journal* 30: 93–102.

Onians, Isabelle. 2002. "Tantric Buddhist Apologetics or Antinomianism as a Norm." PhD diss., Oxford University.

Padmakara Translation Group, trans. 2005. *The Adornment of the Middle Way: Shantarakshita's Madhyamakalamkara with Commentary by Jamgön Mipham*. Boston: Shambhala Publications.

Pandeya, Ramchandra. 1999. *Madhyānta-vibhāga-śāstra. Containing the Kārikā-s of Maitreya, Bhāṣya of Vasubandhu and Ṭīkā by Sthiramati*. Delhi: Motilal Banarsidass.

Passavanti, Marco. 2008. "The *Bla ma brgyud pa'i rim pa*: A Thirteenth-Century Work on the *Dohā* Lineage of Saraha." In *Contributions to Tibetan Buddhist Literature: Proceedings of the Eleventh Seminar of the International Association for Tibetan Studies, Königswinter 2006*, edited by Orna Almogi, 435–88. Halle (Saale): International Institute for Tibetan and Buddhist Studies GmbH.

Patel, Prabhubhai. 1949. *Cittaviśuddhiprakaraṇam of Āryadeva: Sanskrit and Tibetan Texts*. Santiniketan, India: Visva-Bharati.

Pillai, K. Raghavan, ed. 1965. *Alphabetical Index of Sanskrit Manuscripts in the University Manuscripts Library Trivandrum*. 7 vols. Trivandrum: The Alliance Printing Works.

Roberts, Peter Alan. 2007. *The Biographies of Rechungpa: The Evolution of a Tibetan Hagiography*. Abingdon, England: Routledge.

———, trans. 2011. *Mahāmudrā and Related Instructions*. Boston: Wisdom Publications.

Robinson, James Burnell. 1979. *Buddha's Lions: The Lives of the Eighty-Four Siddhas*. Berkeley: Dharma Publishing.

Ruegg, David Seyfort. 1969. *La théorie du tathāgatagarbha et du gotra: Études sur sotériologie et la gnoséologie du bouddhisme*. Publications de l'École française d'Extrême-Orient 70. Paris: École française d'Extrême-Orient.

———. 2000. *Three Studies on the History of Indian and Tibetan Madhyamaka Philosophy. Studies in Indian and Tibetan Madhyamaka Thought Part 1*. Wiener Studien zur Tibetologie und Buddhismuskunde Heft 50. Vienna: Arbeitskreis für Tibetische und Buddhistische Studien Universität Wien.

Salomon, Richard. 2018. *The Buddhist Literature of Ancient Gandhara. An Introduction with Selected Translations*. Boston: Wisdom Publications.

Samdhong Rinpoche, and Vrajvallabh Dvivedī. 1987. *Guhyādi-Aṣṭasiddhi-Saṅgraha*. Sarnath, India: Central Institute of Higher Tibetan Studies.

Sāṃkṛtyāyana, Mahāpaṇḍita Rāhula. 1997 [1957]. *Dohā-koś(Hindī-chāyānuvād-saṃhita)*. Paṭnā, India: Bihār-raṣṭṛabhāṣā-pariạd.

Samtani, Narayan H. 2002. *Gathering the Meanings: The Arthaviniścaya Sūtra and Its Commentary Nibandhana*. Berkeley, CA: Dharma Publishing.

Samuel, Geoffrey. 2008. *The Origins of Yoga and Tantra. Indic Religions to the Thirteenth Century*. Cambridge, UK: Cambridge University Press.

Sanderson, Alexis. 2009. "The Śaiva Age: The Rise and Dominance of Śaivism during the Early Medieval Period." In *Genesis and Development of Tantrism*, edited by Shingo Einoo, 41–349. Institute of Oriental Culture Special Series 23. Tokyo: University of Tokyo, Institute of Oriental Culture.

Śāstrī, Haraprasād. 1898. "The Discovery of a Work by Āryadeva in Sanskrit." *Journal of the Asiatic Society of Bengal* 67.1: 175–84.

———, ed. 1959 [1916]. *Hājār Bacharer Purāṇa Bāṅgālā Bhāṣāy Bauddh Gān o Dohā*. Vaṅgīya Sāhitya Pariṣat Series 55. Revised with emendations by Tarapada Mukherji. Calcutta: Vaṅgīya Sāhitya Pariṣat.

Schaeffer, Kurtis Rice. 2005. *Dreaming the Great Brahmin*. New York: Oxford University Press.

Schmithausen, Lambert. 1973. "Spirituelle Praxis und Philosophische Theorie im Buddhismus." *Zeitschrift für Missionswissenschaft und Religionswissenschaft* 57.3: 161–86.

———. 2014. *The Genesis of Yogācāra-Vijñānavāda: Responses and Reflections*. Kasuga Lectures Series 1. Tokyo: International Institute for Buddhist Studies.

Seton, Gregory Max. 2015. "Defining Wisdom: Ratnākaraśānti's *Sāratamā*." PhD diss., University of Oxford.

Sferra, Francesco. 2000. *The* Ṣaḍaṅgayoga *by Anupamarakṣita, with Rāviśrījñāṇa's* Guṇabharaṇīnāmaṣaḍaṅgayogaṭippaṇī*: Text and Annotated Translation*. Serie Orientale Roma LXXXV. Rome: Istituto italiano per l'Africa et l'Oriente.

———. 2003. "Some Considerations on the Relationship between Hindu and Buddhist Tantras." In *Buddhist Asia 1: Papers from the First Conference of Buddhist Studies Held in Naples in May 2001*, edited by Giovanni Verardi and Silvio Vita, 57–84. Kyoto: Italian School of East Asian Studies.

———. 2009. "The Laud of the Chosen Deity, the First Chapter of the *Hevajrapiṇḍārthaṭīkā* by Vajragarbha." In *Genesis and Development of Tantrism*, edited by Shingo Einoo, 435–68. Institute of Oriental Culture Special Series 23. Tokyo: University of Tokyo, Institute of Oriental Culture.

———. 2011. "Constructing the Wheel of Time: Strategies for Establishing a Tradition." In *Boundaries, Dynamics and Construction of Traditions in South Asia,* edited by Federico Squarcini, 253–85. London: Anthem Press.

Sferra, Francesco, and Stefania Merzagora. 2006. *The* Sekoddeśaṭīkā *by Nāropa (Paramārthasaṃgraha)*. Serie Orientale Roma XCIX. Rome: Istituto italiano per l'Africa et l'Oriente.

Shahidullah, Mohamed. 1928. *Les chants mystiques de Kāṇha et de Saraha: Les Dohākoṣa (en apabhraṃsa, avec les versions tibétaines) et les Caryā (en vieux-bengali).* Paris: Adrien-Maisonneuve.

———. *Buddhist Mystic Songs.* 1996 [1940]. Originally published in the *Dacca University Studies* 4.2. Reprinted by the Bengali Literary Society, University of Karachi, 1960. Revised and enlarged edition. Dacca, Bangladesh: Bengali Academy, 1966.

Skilling, Peter. 1997. "From bKa' bstan bcos to bKa' 'gyur and bsTan 'gyur." In *Transmission of the Tibetan Canon: Papers Presented at a Panel of the 7th Seminar of the International Association for Tibetan Studies, Graz 1995,* edited by Helmut Eimer, 2:87–111. Vienna: Verlag der Österreichischen Akademie der Wissenschaften.

Snellgrove, David L. 1954. "The Cleansing of Thought." In *Buddhist Texts Through the Ages,* edited by Edward Conze, 221. New York: Harper & Row.

———. 1959. *The Hevajra Tantra: A Critical Study.* 2 vols. London: Oxford University Press.

Sobisch, Jan-Ulrich. 2008. *Hevajra and* Lam 'bras *Literature of India and Tibet as Seen through the Eyes of A-mes-zhabs.* Wiesbaden: Dr. Ludwig Reichert Verlag.

Solonin, Kirill. 2015. "Dīpaṃkara in the Tangut Context: An Inquiry into the Systematic Nature of Tibetan Buddhism in Xixia (Part 1)." *Acta Orientalia Academiae Scientiarum Hungaricae* 68, no. 4: 425–51.

Stearns, Cyrus, trans. 2006. *Taking the Result as the Path: Core Teachings of the Sakya Lamdré Tradition.* The Library of Tibetan Classics 4. Boston: Wisdom Publications.

Stenzel, Julia. 2015. "The Four Joys in the Teaching of Nāropa and Maitrīpa." *Indian International Journal of Buddhist Studies* 16: 193–214.

Sugiki, Tsunehiko. 2015. "Śaṃvara." In *Brill's Encyclopedia of Buddhism,* edited by Jonathan A. Silk, 1: 360–66. Leiden: E. J. Brill.

Szántó, Péter-Dániel. 2010. "A Minimalist's *Pratipattisāraśataka.*" http://tibetica.blogspot.com/2010/12/minimalists-pratipattisarasataka.html.

———. 2012. *Selected Chapters from the Catuṣpīṭhatantra.* 2 vols. *Part 1: Introductory Study with the Annotated Translation of Selected Chapters. Part 2: Appendix Volume with Critical Editions of Selected Chapters*

Accompanied by Bhavabhaṭṭa's Commentary and a Bibliography. PhD diss., Balliol College, Oxford.

———. 2015a. "Tantric Prakaraṇas." In *Brill Encyclopedia of Buddhism*, 1: 755–61. Leiden: Brill.

———. 2015b. "Two Ninth-Century Works against Buddhist Antinomian Practice." Unpublished handout for Toronto symposium in honor of Alexis Sanderson.

———. 2016. "On the Permeable Boundary between Exegesis and Scripture in Late Tantric Buddhist Literature." In *Cross-Cultural Transmission of Buddhist Texts: Theories and Practices of Translation*, edited by Dorji Wangchuk, 315–34. Hamburg: The Department of Indian and Tibetan Studies, Universität Hamburg.

———. 2017. "Minor Vajrayāna Texts IV: A Sanskrit Fragment of the *Rigyarallitantra*." In *Indian Manuscript Cultures through the Ages*, edited by Vincenzo Vergiani, Daniele Cuneo, and Camillo Alessio Formigatti, 487–504. Berlin: De Gruyter.

———. 2018. "New Sources for the Saraha Corpus." Unpublished paper read at the Seventeenth World Sanskrit Conference, Vancouver, 2018.

———. 2020. "The Road Not to Be Taken: An Introduction to Two Ninth-Century Works against Buddhist Antinomian Practice." In *Mārga: Paths to Liberation in South Asian Buddhist Traditions*, edited by Cristina Pecchia and Vincent Eltschinger, 363–79. Vienna: Verlag der Österreichischen Akademie der Wissenschaften, Philosophisch-historische Klasse.

———. n.d. Unpublished transcript of Sahajavajra's *Sthitisamāsa*.

Tanemura, Ryugen. 2015. "Guhyasamāja." In *Brill's Encyclopedia of Buddhism*, edited by Jonathan A. Silk, 1:326–36. Leiden: E. J. Brill.

Tāranātha. 1980. *History of Buddhism in India*. Translated by Lama Chimpa and Alaka Chattopadhyaya. Calcutta: Bagchi.

Tatz, Mark. 1987. "The Life of the Siddha-Philosopher Maitrīgupta." *Journal of the American Oriental Society* 107.4: 695–711.

———. 1988. "Maitrī-pa and Atiśa." In *Tibetan Studies: Proceedings of the Fourth Seminar of the International Association for Tibetan Studies, Munich 1985*, edited by Helga Uebach and Jampa Losang Panglung, 473–81. Munich: Kommission für Zentralasiatische Studien, Bayerische Akademie der Wissenschaften.

———. 1990. "*Tattva-Ratnāvalī*: The Precious Garland of Verses on Reality." In *Researches in Indian History, Archaeology, Art and Religion: Prof. Upendra Thakur Felicitation Volume*, edited by G. Kuppuram and K. Kumudamani, 2: 491–513. Delhi: Sundeep Prakashan.

———. 1994. "Philosophic Systems according to Advayavajra and Vajrapaṇi." *Journal of Buddhist and Tibetan Studies* 1: 65–120.

Tauscher, Helmut. 2003. "Phya pa chos kyi seng ge as a Svātantrika." In *The Svātantrika-Prāsaṅgika Distinction: What Difference Does a Difference Make?*, edited by Georges B. J. Dreyfus and Sara L. McClintock, 207–56. Boston: Wisdom Publications.

Templeman, David, trans. 1983. *Tāranātha's "Bka' babs bdun ldan": The Seven Instruction Lineages*. Dharamsala: Library of Tibetan Works and Archives.

Thurman, Robert A. F., trans. 2010. *Brilliant Illumination of the Lamp of the Five Stages (Rim lnga rab tu gsal ba'i sgron me): Practical Instruction in the King of Tantras, The Glorious Esoteric Community. By Tsong Khapa Losang Drakpa*. New York: The American Institute of Buddhist Studies; Columbia University Center for Buddhist Studies; Tibet House US.

Tillemans, Tom J. F. 1990. *Materials for the Study of Āryadeva, Dharmapāla, and Candrakīrti. The* Catuḥśataka *of Āryadeva, Chapters XII and XIII, with the Commentaries of Dharmapāla and Candrakīrti: Introduction, Sanskrit, Tibetan, and Chinese Texts, Notes*. 2 vols. Wiener Studien zur Tibetologie und Buddhismuskunde 24. Vienna: Arbeitskreis für Tibetische und Buddhistische Studien Universität Wien.

Tiso, Francis V. 1994. "The *Rdo rje 'chang rnam thar* in the *Bka' brgyud gser 'phreng* Genre." In *Tibetan Studies: Proceedings of the Sixth Seminar of the International Association for Tibetan Studies, Fagernes, 1992*, edited by Per Kværne, 2: 884–88. Oslo: The Institute for Comparative Research in Human Culture.

Tomabechi, Tōru. 2006. "Étude du *Pancakrama*: Introduction et traduction annotée." PhD diss., University of Lausanne.

Tomlinson, Davey K. 2019. "Buddhahood and Philosophy of Mind: Ratnākaraśānti, Jñānaśrīmitra, and the Debate over Mental Content (*ākāra*)." PhD diss., University of Chicago.

Torricelli, Fabrizio. 2018. *Tilopā: A Buddhist Yogin of the Tenth Century*. Dharamsala: Library of Tibetan Works and Archives.

Törzsök, Judith. 2020. "Why Are the Skull-Bearers (Kāpālikas) Called Soma?" In *Śaivism and the Tantric Traditions: Essays in Honour of Alexis G. J. S. Sanderson*, edited by Dominic Goodall, Shaman Hatley, Harunaga Isaacson, and Srilata Raman, 33–46. Leiden: Brill.

Tripathi, Ram Shankar, and Thakur Sain Negi, eds. 2001. *Hevajratantram with Muktāvalī Pañjikā of Mahāpaṇḍitācārya Ratnākaraśānti*. Bibliotheca Indo-Tibetica Series 18. Sarath, India: Central Institute of Higher Tibetan Studies.

Tsongkhapa. 2013. *A Lamp of Illuminating the Five Stages*. Translated by Gavin Kilty. Boston: Wisdom Publications.

Tsuda, Shinichi. 1970. "The Saṃvarodaya-tantra. Selected Chapters." PhD diss., Australian National University, Canberra.

———. 1974. *The Saṃvarodaya-tantra. Selected Chapters*. Tokyo: The Hokuseido Press.

Vaidya, Paraśurāma L., ed. 1961. *Mahāyāna-sūtra-saṅgrahaḥ*, Part 1. Darbhanga: Mithila Institute.

Varghese, Mathew. 2008. *Principles of Buddhist Tantra: A Discourse on Cittavisuddhi-prakarana of Aryadeva*. New Delhi: Munshiram Manoharlal Publishers.

Wallis, Glenn. 2003. "Advayavajra's Instructions on the *Ādikarma*." *Pacific World: Journal of the Institute of Buddhist Studies* 5: 203–30.

Wangchuk Dorje. 2001. *Mahāmudrā, the Ocean of Definitive Meaning*. Translated by Elizabeth Callahan. Seattle: Nitartha *international*.

Wedemeyer, Christian K. 1999. "Vajrayāna and Its Doubles: A Critical Historiography, Exposition, and Translation of the Tantric Works of Āryadeva." PhD diss., Columbia University.

———. 2007. *Āryadeva's Lamp That Integrates the Practices (Caryāmelāpakapradīpa): The Gradual Path of Vajrayāna Buddhism according to the Esoteric Community Noble Tradition*. Treasury of the Buddhist Sciences Series. New York: The American Institute of Buddhist Studies, Columbia University.

———. 2009. "Pseudepigrapha in the Tibetan Buddhist 'Canonical Collections': The Case of the *Caryāmelāpakapradīpa* Commentary

Attributed to Śākyamitra." *Journal of the International Association of Tibetan Studies* 5: 1–31.

———. 2011 (2012). "Locating Tantric Antinomianism: An Essay toward an Intellectual History of the 'Practices/Practice Observance' (*caryā/caryāvrata*)." *Journal of the International Association of Buddhist Studies* 34, nos. 1–2: 349–420.

———. 2013. *Making Sense of Tantric Buddhism: History, Semiology, and Transgression in the Indian Traditions*. New York: Columbia University Press.

Weinberger, Steven Neal. 2003. "The Significance of Yoga Tantra and the Compendium of Principles (*Tattvasaṃgraha Tantra*) within Tantric Buddhism in India and Tibet." PhD diss., University of Virginia.

White, David Gordon, ed. 2003. *Kiss of the Yogini: "Tantric Sex" in its South Asian Contexts*. Chicago: The University of Chicago Press.

Yiannopoulos, Alex. 2014. "Luminosity in Late Indian Yogācāra: Is Reflexive Awareness Nondual?" Unpublished paper read at the Seventeenth Congress of the International Association of Buddhist Studies, Vienna, August 18–23, 2014.

Zhang, Linghui. 2019. "History and Myth: Mahāmudrā Lineage Accounts in the 12th-Century Xixia Buddhist Literature." *Religions* 10: 187–202.

About the Translator

Karl Brunnhölzl, MD, PhD, was originally trained as a physician. He received his systematic training in Tibetan language and Buddhist philosophy and practice at the Marpa Institute for Translators, founded by Khenpo Tsultrim Gyamtso Rinpoche, as well as the Nitartha Institute, founded by Dzogchen Ponlop Rinpoche. Karl also studied Buddhism, Tibetology, and Sanskrit at Hamburg University, Germany. Since 1989 he has been a translator and interpreter from Tibetan and English. Karl is a senior teacher and translator in the Nalandabodhi community of Dzogchen Ponlop Rinpoche, as well as at Nitartha Institute. He is the author and translator of numerous texts, including *The Center of the Sunlit Sky: Madhyamaka in the Kagyü Tradition* (2004), *Straight from the Heart: Buddhist Pith Instructions* (2007), *Luminous Heart: The Third Karmapa on Consciousness, Wisdom, and Buddha Nature* (2009), *Gone Beyond: The Ornament of Clear Realization and Its Commentaries in the Tibetan Kagyü Tradition*, 2 vols. (2010–11), *When the Clouds Part* (2014), *A Lullaby to Awaken the Heart* (2018), and *Luminous Melodies: Essential Dohās of Indian Mahāmudrā* (2019). He lives in Munich, Germany.

Karl has set some of the songs of realization in this and the other volumes to contemporary melodies; recordings can be accessed at the "Doha Hub" (https://soundcloud.com/karl-brunnholzl).

What to Read Next by Karl Brunnhölzl from Wisdom Publications

Sounds of Innate Freedom
The Indian Texts of Mahāmudrā, Volume 3

Sounds of Innate Freedom
The Indian Texts of Mahāmudrā, Volume 4

Sounds of Innate Freedom
The Indian Texts of Mahāmudrā, Volume 5

A Lullaby to Awaken the Heart
The Aspiration Prayer of Samantabhadra and Its Tibetan Commentaries

"Through pointing out our originally pure nature again and again, this book will make practitioners smile. Through its detailed explanations and meticulous documentation, it will make scholars rejoice." —Andy Karr, author of *Contemplating Reality: A Practitioner's Guide to the View in Indo-Tibetan Buddhism*

Milarepa's Kungfu
Mahāmudrā in His Songs of Realization

"This book is a treasure of subtle revelation."—*Lion's Roar*

Luminous Melodies
Essential Dohās of Indian Mahāmudrā

"These beautiful songs of experience offer glimpses into the awakened minds of the Mahāmudrā masters of India. Karl Brunnhölzl's masterful translations are a joy to read for how they express what is so often inexpressible."—His Eminence the Twelfth Zurmang Gharwang Rinpoche

About Wisdom Publications

Wisdom Publications is the leading publisher of classic and contemporary Buddhist books and practical works on mindfulness. To learn more about us or to explore our other books, please visit our website at wisdomexperience.org or contact us at the address below.

Wisdom Publications
132 Perry Street
New York, NY 10014 USA

We are a 501(c)(3) organization, and donations in support of our mission are tax deductible.

Wisdom Publications is affiliated with the Foundation for the Preservation of the Mahayana Tradition (FPMT).